Sociological Perspectives on Social Psychology

EDITED BY

KAREN S. COOK
UNIVERSITY OF WASHINGTON

GARY ALAN FINE
UNIVERSITY OF GEORGIA

JAMES S. HOUSE
UNIVERSITY OF MICHIGAN

ALLYN AND BACON
Boston   London   Toronto   Sydney   Tokyo   Singapore

To the memory of Morris Rosenberg, who originally stimulated the ASA Social Psychology Section to undertake volumes like this one, took the lead role in editing the first such volume, and supported and contributed to the development of this volume until his untimely death in December 1991. We hope Manny would be pleased with the result.

Executive Editor: Karen Hanson
Vice President and Publisher, Social Sciences: Susan Badger
Editorial Assistant: Sarah Dunbar
Production Administrator: Susan McIntyre
Editorial-Production Service: Ruttle, Shaw & Wetherill, Inc.
Cover Administrator: Suzanne Harbison
Manufacturing Buyer: Louise Richardson

Copyright © 1995 by Allyn and Bacon
A Division of Simon and Schuster, Inc.
160 Gould Street
Needham Heights, MA 02194

Library of Congress Cataloging-in-Publication Data
Sociological perspectives on social psychology / edited by Karen S. Cook,
   Gary Alan Fine, James S. House.
      p.   cm.
   Includes bibliographical references and index.
   ISBN 0-205-13716-4
   1. Social psychology.   I. Cook, Karen (Karen S.)   II. Fine, Gary
Alan.   III. House, James S.
HM251.S68719 1995
302—dc20   94-1890
                                                          CIP

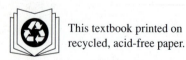

This textbook printed on
recycled, acid-free paper.

Printed in the United States of America
10 9 8 7 6 5 4 3 2 1   99 98 97 96 95 94

CONTENTS

FOREWORD

RALPH TURNER

Except for his untimely death, Morris Rosenberg would have taken the lead in preparing this Foreword. The earlier volume, *Social Psychology: Sociological Perspectives* (1981), was his idea and his project. In 1976, as Chair of the Social Psychology Section of the American Sociological Association, he secured the Section's sponsorship of a volume to set forth the approaches of sociologists to the field of social psychology. He invited me to serve as his coeditor, and with the help of a distinguished editorial board and twenty-six dedicated authors, we were able to publish the most definitive account, to that date, of the current state of sociological social psychology. Throughout the process, it was "Manny's" singleness of purpose and willingness to assume a disproportionate share of the work and responsibility that led to the project's successful completion.

For many reasons, not the least of which is the availability of an authoritative baseline, the social psychological work of sociologists has flourished in the decade since the earlier volume was published. Already in 1990, when Transaction Publishers reissued the book with a new Introduction, we were able to call attention to several notable developments in the field since initial publication. Both quantitative and qualitative research, guided by symbolic interactionist orientations, experienced explosive growth, most notably in an impressive output of insightful ethnographic studies and also in questionnaire studies of self and identity. Expectation states, or status generalization, theory produced one of social psychology's most prolific and integrated bodies of empirical research and theoretical advancement. The nascent field of emotions suddenly blossomed into a major topic of interest in sociology. To some extent this was a reaction to the widespread borrowing of rational decision models from economics and political science in explaining human behavior. Interest in social movements grew, and a renewed recognition of the importance of social psychological dynamics replaced its earlier rejection toward the end of this period. Stress and coping gained renewed attention, along with an apparently increased interest in the application of social psychological knowledge. Life course studies and conversation analysis developed into important fields of social psychological study. We overlooked, but should have mentioned, the emergence of cognitive social psychology, complementing the parallel development in cognitive psychology. Finally, we noted a growing commitment to the view of "the *human organism as agent* rather than simply as object." All of these advances, and more, are reflected in the current volume.

Elsewhere I have suggested several sources for long-term paradigmatic change in the field of sociology, some of which may help to illuminate these briefer-term changes in social psychology (Turner 1991). First, relationships with other disciplines expose scholars to new ideas and methods. Sociological social psychologists have always been responsive to trends in psychology. The recent emergence of political sociology as a major subfield in sociology has brought sociologists into close relationships with political scientists, who had already borrowed rational choice models from economics.

As a second source of paradigmatic change, critical historical events can have both immediate impacts and delayed generational effects. For example, there is renewed interest in ethnic identity and interethnic relations today in direct response to ethnic movements around the world. Of more profound significance, generational socialization has produced noteworthy delayed effects. The 1980s brought many social psychologists whose critical academic socialization took place in the 1960s to positions of leadership in the discipline. The tumultuous 1960s stimulated in students a lasting interest in social movements, an emphasis on power, and a preference for rational explanations of behavior over the irrational attributions so widely used as a tactic to discredit activists of the 1960s. The emphasis on agency—an active rather than merely receptive relationship of the individual toward social structure—certainly came out of this era.

World intellectual currents constitute a third influence on social psychological paradigms. Disillusionment with Marxist materialism and retreatist existentialism has made possible new waves of thought stressing the power of ideas and the significance of culture. These trends may have been reflected in a growing receptivity to symbolic interactionism and in renewed attention to cultural processes and effects. The rising popularity of constructivist paradigms in European thought, with

their affinity to symbolic interactionism, is also reflected in the renewed interest in social psychological aspects of social movement processes.

A fourth source of change is shifting priorities in research funding. Federal government policies favoring applied over "pure" research in the award of grants may have contributed to a noticeable increase in applications of social psychological theory and to investigation of such topics as stress and coping. Besides these four external sources of influence on the discipline, we should not overlook the working of internal disciplinary processes, including paradigm shifts.

These comments may be dismissed as idle, and certainly incomplete, speculation. But their purpose is to suggest that we look at trends in social psychology as phenomena for study in their own right, as problems for the sociology of knowledge.

If the purpose of the earlier volume was to establish a baseline from which sociologists might work, this new volume demonstrates that frequent new baselines are needed for a discipline of such vitality as sociological social psychology. It will be a measure of the success of this volume if still another volume is needed early in the twenty-first century.

REFERENCES

Rosenberg, Morris, and Ralph H. Turner. 1981. *Social Psychology: Sociological Perspectives.* New York: Basic Books. 1990. New Brunswick: Transaction Publishers.

Turner, Ralph H. 1991. The many faces of American sociology: A discipline in search of identity. Pp. 59–85 in *Divided Knowledge: Across Disciplines, Across Cultures,* ed. David Easton and Corinne S. Schelling. Newbury Park, CA: Sage.

INTRODUCTION

GARY ALAN FINE
JAMES S. HOUSE
KAREN S. COOK

Thirteen years ago a group of sociological social psychologists produced the volume that inspired this project. *Social Psychology: Sociological Perspectives,* edited by Morris Rosenberg and Ralph H. Turner, was published in 1981, and immediately became a sociological benchmark and sourcebook for the subdiscipline of social psychology. In addition, the volume became the textbook of choice for many sociologists teaching graduate courses in social psychology. The twenty-one chapters presented a broad array of the important current research and theory of the late 1970s.

Live disciplines change. By the end of the 1980s, many social psychologists felt the need for a volume that updated and expanded the previous one—not a narrow revision, but a new examination of the currently important domains of social psychology. The publications committee of the Social Psychology Section of the American Sociological Association met and eventually selected us to edit this volume. Our charter was not to produce a volume that mirrored the older one, but to create a work that, like the previous volume, would be a benchmark, sourcebook, and textbook.

The reader who compares the two volumes will recognize that several things have changed. First, this volume does, in part, reflect a change in generation in social psychology. Only five authors from the 1981 volume have contributed to this volume. (Significantly, of the twenty-six authors in 1981, only six were women; in this volume, of the forty-four authors, twenty-one are women.) Most of the scholars invited to contribute readily agreed and followed through on their commitment. Our biggest disappointment in the volume was our inability, despite prolonged efforts, to obtain a chapter on "Race, Ethnic, and Intergroup Relations." To mitigate this absence we encouraged the authors to include material on this theme where appropriate.

We felt that it was necessary to increase the number of chapters. We hoped to gain a broader perspective, even though this placed limits on the amount of material in any one chapter, and some important topics may still be included only tangentially. The vast majority of authors felt, usually quite correctly, that they could have used more space. However, aside from the pragmatics of publishing, we also felt that for a graduate textbook, chapters should not be encyclopedic but should focus on the most important themes. We hoped for teaching tools, not massive literature reviews.

This volume is divided into four parts. Part I, "The Person and Social Interaction," addresses the basic building block concepts in social psychology, particularly those that affect individual behavior. We include chapters on self and identity, attitudes and beliefs, social cognition, emotions and affect, language, social interaction, and biology. This section examines the social world from the perspective of the person. Part II, "Social Interaction and Social Structure," addresses some of the more traditional issues of experimental social psychology, particularly that of social psychology grounded in exchange theory, group dynamics, and expectation states theory. Here we include chapters on social exchange and social networks, social influence and bargaining, equity and justice, status structures and legitimacy, social dilemmas, group decision making, and gender. Part III, "Social Structure, Social Relationships and the Individual," examines the relation of macrosocial or institutional structures and processes to the functioning of individuals and small groups. We include chapters on cross-cultural and cross-national social psychology, the development and socialization of children and adolescents, adult development, stratification and mobility processes, work and organizations, deviance and law, health, and collective behavior and social movements and collective behavior.

Finally, unlike the earlier volume, in part IV, "Methodological Approach to Social Psychology," we include chapters on qualitative and observational methods, experimentation, and nonexperimental quantitative methods. These chapters are designed to teach not the how of these methods, but the why. They focus on the logic behind these methodologies that have been so influential in the development of social psychology.

Rosenberg and Turner began their Preface by noting the legitimate role of social psychology in sociology. They noted that the first sociology text devoted five chapters to social psychology; by 1908 sociologist Edward Ross wrote a social psychology text; August Comte was a father figure for both sociology and social psychology; many sociologists consider themselves social psychologists; sociological journals publish social psychology papers; sociology graduate programs require students to learn social psychology; and the American Sociological Association publishes *Social Psychology Quarterly*. In retrospect, their opening had a slightly defensive tone.

In the past decade, however, sociology has embraced its diversity, and formerly antagonistic groups or groups with few linkages have found common ground (e.g., the connection between organizational theory and the sociology of emotion, or rational choice and theories of state control).

This embracing of diversity, affects subareas as well. In an earlier age social psychology was widely perceived—even by its most loyal practitioners—as being basically separate and apart from the research traditions of other, "mainstream" sociologists. Yet, as this text indicates, sociological social psychology is now increasingly integrated into the discipline of sociology. What used to be a division is increasingly seamless.

Sociological social psychology has itself also become more whole. The chapters in this volume collectively demonstrate that diversity is characteristic of how social psychology has developed during the past fifteen years in sociology. Although there remain vigorous and healthy divergences among perspectives, there is a greatly diminished sense of social psychology being divided into "warring camps." The three faces of social psychology (House 1977) are at peace, a reality of which each chapter gives evidence through integrative substance and diverse references. This peace may be somewhat uneasy, but it is real.

The chapters and authors of this volume reflect the increasing relevance of social psychology to the mainstream of sociology, and vice versa. Social psychology and social psychologists have become central to the analysis of most major phenomena and subfields of sociology. Among those represented here are sociobiology, social interaction, language and talk, social exchange, status and power, conflict and bargaining, life course development, work and organizations, stratification and mobility, deviance and law, health, and collective behavior and social movements. Similarly, other chapters reflect how sociological perspectives have shaped and transformed topics often felt to be largely psychological in nature, including attitudes, emotions, the self, bargaining, decision making, social influence, and culture and personality.

As discussed in various places in the volume, social psychology is also integral to emerging concerns of the discipline of sociology. What has been termed the "micro-macro link" has become a central concern of sociology in the last decade. That is, how does individual human action both constitute and become constituted by larger social structures, institutions, and processes? Because of its once marginal status, social psychology has not yet been drawn on, or contributed as much, in this new debate as it can and should.

What has occurred instead is a renewed interest in what has been termed "microsociology." To the extent that they attempt a more formal, nonpsychological analysis of social relationships and interaction, a range of work—studies of the impact of numbers on social interaction from Simmel to Blau, analyses of the organization of interaction in the dramaturgical theories of Goffman, the rule-based analyses of communication by ethnomethodologists, or even the logical calculus of rational choice theory—can be and often is considered microsociological but not social psychological. Yet we believe that much social psychology is implicit, if not explicit, in almost all microsociology, as many chapters in this volume illustrate.

Similarly, social psychologists, especially in sociology but also in psychology, have become increasingly attuned to the importance of social structure and context for understanding more microsocial and psychological phenomena. How can one conceive of interaction scenes without recognizing the structural features of the settings and circumstances in which these scenes are embedded? How can social cognition be understood without reference to the historical, cultural, and economic context in which actors make choices and in which power is enacted? One should not push this demand for integration of levels too far, insisting that each social psychological study have its own structural component, but the recognition of structural components as part of any behavioral system is increasingly central to social psychological theory, as is clearly evident in parts II and III of this volume.

Some in the academy suggest that we reside in a postmodern age. To be sure, the meaning, referent, and origins of this postmodernism are uncertain, and equally surely it is a concept (or more properly a cluster of concepts) that developed and has its greatest impact outside of social psychology. However, key arguments of postmodernist theorists describing the "decentering" of meaning and the need for examining culture, social relations, texts, and even scientific theories in light of the power and authority relations that created them resonate with and were even anticipated by aspects of contemporary social psychology. These issues are most central for the writers of such chapters as those on self and identity, social cognition, emotions and affect, and gender. The decidedly distinct, refreshing, and confrontative tone raised by postmodern theorists have roots in the writings of Kenneth Gergen (1973) some two decades ago. Gergen, one of a group of "contextualists," argued against postulating the existence of universal processes, just as the postmodernists would later claim.

Likewise, the critical assessments of traditional social psychology by a group of (mostly) British social psychologists in the 1970s, as reflected in the collection *Reconstructing Social Psychology* (Armistead 1974; Parker and Shotter 1990), addresses the role of power and authority in social psychological findings.

THE NATURE OF SOCIAL PSYCHOLOGY AND THIS VOLUME

In this volume we deliberately adopt an inclusive view that recognizes that "social psychology" has become a label of convenience referring to particular types of sociology (and psychology)—a broad swath that cuts across many areas, but which still can be relatively easily recognized by practitioners and audiences. The chapters by Gecas and Burke (self and identity), Schuman (attitudes and beliefs), and Howard (social cognition) are traditionally "social psychological" in their emphasis, while those by Maynard and Whalen (talk and language) and Lofland (social interaction) and most of the authors in part II are notably microsociological. The chapters in part III address more macrosociological concerns, incorporating both microsociological and social psychological models. Yet, by design, each chapter attempts to incorporate the broadest range of social psychology. The reader will discover that even those chapters that seem at first to be most oriented to experimental methods include relevant references to nonexperimental work, and vice versa. Our intent was for each author to describe multiple methodologies and theoretical traditions in their content arena.

This eclectic stance raises the question of whether there is a core of social psychology, and whether too much now falls under its rubric to be useful. For social psychologists this is a most uncomfortable doubt. This question is, of course, not easy to answer. Ffrom our perspective—or else why publish this volume?—there is a justification for speaking of social psychology as a discipline, even if the definition is broad and the linkages to the remaining areas of sociology are emphasized.

What, then, is the commonality of social psychology? Ultimately, we believe this commonality stems from an emphasis on a few core ideas and concepts. Social psychologists begin with the physical, recognize the mental, and believe that culture makes the mental useful within a social surround—a world of actual or implicit other persons, a community of relationships or social structures. The intersections of physical and mental, persons and settings, relations and communities constitute the core of social psychology. These intersections lead to examining questions of self, identity, emotion, cognition, and perception and to exploring copresence, as in research that examines impression management, exchange, aggression, liking, and discourse. Finally, it leads us to organizational and even societal phenomena: group life, justice and legal systems, organizational dynamics, and collective action. It excludes, however, as outside its hazy boundaries, those attempts to analyze the self without consideration of an interactional field or to analyze organizations as entities governed entirely by processes or principles that transcend actors. However, most social life is to some degree social psychological.

Social psychology represents an interdiscipline lodged between the disciplines of psychology, which examines inner lives and selves, and sociology, which examines the relationships between collectivities and organizations. Social psychologists argue that it is essential to examine how self and system interpenetrate; on some level this is the theme of each chapter. In addition, social psychologists have claimed the examination of the dynamics of the ties between individuals, as exemplified in social interaction. The behavioral ballet of actors has traditionally been central to social psychology.

By setting as its primary task the knitting together of two previously distinct, disjointed approaches—self and system—social psychology has set itself up as an "honest broker," yet because of the disciplinary structure of the American university system, as expressed in those organizational units labeled departments, social psychologists tend to be housed either in psychology departments or sociology departments (some social psychologists find themselves in more applied or specialty units, such as colleges of education, medical schools, business schools, or social work programs). This bureaucratic structure of American higher education has traditionally split social psychology, leaving two "disciplinary" orientations separate and apart. This volume does not pretend to eliminate that divide; these chapters are written by those in the sociological orbit, whether affiliated with symbolic interaction, exchange theory, the sociology of emotions, sociolinguistics, or structure and personality. Still, our charge to each author was explicitly to create chapters that address the broadest range of social psychology, incorporating models from each domain and discipline. While the volume is aimed primarily at sociology graduate students enrolled in a social psychology course, the chapters should also represent a fair picture of what is happening in the domain of psychology. We hope they will also prove useful to graduate students and faculty in the psychological side of social psychology in suggesting the relevance of a broader sociological perspective to our common field.

Sociological social psychology remains, as it was at the time of the first volume, in a dynamic phase of development. This is as it should be. Little is fixed in concrete, immune to challenge, or unaccepting of revision. Rosenberg and Turner suggested that sociological social psychology was a teenager, heir to the identity crises of that life cycle. Extended, the metaphor places us in early middle age. It is perhaps too precious for this revision. Yet, we have grown as a field and become more integrated into the discipline. We hate to impose on future editors the metaphor of senescence, but perhaps there is something valuable in viewing the field as one that is on the edge of an intellectual maturity.

REFERENCES

Armistead, N., ed. 1974. *Reconstructing Social Psychology.* Harmondsworth, UK: Penguin.

Gergen, Kenneth. 1973. Social psychology as history. *Journal of Personality and Social Psychology* 26: 309–320.

House, James S. 1977. The three faces of social psychology. *Sociometry* 40: 161–177.

Parker, Ian, and John Shotter, ed. 1990. *Deconstructing Social Psychology.* London: Routledge.

ACKNOWLEDGMENTS

Ultimately, compiling an edited book involves the creation of community. In the five years that this volume has been in gestation, we have suffered each other's family losses and personal triumphs. Our contributors have become our friends, and we have suffered with them when crises made delays imperative and shared their joys at a completed chapter. It has been a long process, from which we emerge personally and intellectually altered.

Many others deserve our thanks. Each chapter was reviewed by at least two social psychologists in addition to all three editors. That is a lot of feedback—some authors surely felt, at times, too much feedback. Among those whose expertise we relied on were: Duane Alwin, Dane Archer, Howard S. Becker, Deirdre Boden, Philip Bonacich, Janet Chafetz, John Clausen, William Corsaro, Kathleen Crittenden, Doris Entwistle, William Gamson, David Gartrell, Viktor Gecas, Norvel Glenn, Lee Hamilton, Douglas Heckathorn, David Heise, Judith Howard, Theodore Kemper, Sherryl Kleinman, Edward Lawler, Robert Leik, Allan Liska, Hazel Markus, Douglas Maynard, Allen Mazur, Clark McPhail, David Mechanic, Andrew Michener, Andre Modigliani, Linda Molm, Jeylan Mortimer, G. Kent Nelson, Pam Oliver, Steven Penrod, Cecelia Ridgeway, Barbara Risman, Morris Rosenberg, Catherine Ross, Alice Rossi, Carmi Schooler, William Sewell, Roberta Simmons, Lynn Smith-Lovin, David Snow, Anne Statham, John Stolte, Ralph Turner, David Wagner, Mary Glenn Wiley, and Toshio Yamagishi. We also wish to thank the Social Psychology Section of the American Sociological Association, particularly its publication committee at the time this volume was being organized: Viktor Gecas, Edward Lawler, Joanne Miller, Jeylan Mortimer, Cecelia Ridgeway, Morris Rosenberg, Lynn Smith-Lovin, David Snow, Ralph Turner, and Mary Glenn Wiley. Jeylan Mortimer deserves special recognition for her role as Section Chair in motivating the section to undertake the sponsorship of this volume. These colleagues had the confidence that this project was possible, and their optimism infected us on the many occasions it seemed that our tunnel had no end. We have been aided throughout this process by our secretaries: Hilda Daniels, Marie Klatt, Ruth Nash, and Barbara Parrish. We also are indebted to our friends at Allyn and Bacon, particularly Karen Hanson and Susan McIntyre, who managed to tame the mess of type and transform it into a volume that people could read and hold.

PART I

The Person and Social Interaction

GARY ALAN FINE

INTRODUCTION: BUILDING BLOCKS AND THE QUADRANT OF ACTION

In any domain of knowledge, a set of core concepts provides the basis for theory and research. These ideas represent the heart of the discipline, and emphasis on these central concepts (and the jargon in which they are clothed) is sufficient to bind a community of scholars. We speak of these central concepts as building blocks in that they serve as the basis for further discourse and investigation. They are what members must recognize to participate in intellectual dialogue.

While each of the four parts of this text addresses important social psychological issues, this first part most directly confronts traditional social psychological building blocks. The seven chapters cover self and identity, beliefs and attitudes, cognition, emotion, language, interaction, and biology. In some measure the remaining parts depict how these basic concepts play themselves out in social settings and institutional arenas: in small groups, in power and authority relations, in networks of exchange, in collective action, in legal domains, cross-culturally, and so forth. One can conceive of these chapters as representing the most individual, micro, personal vision of social psychology, although each author explicitly connects the analysis with an impressive range of social spheres. Examining the past century of social psychology, one must recognize that these core constructions provide the grounds for all theoretical interpretations of social behavior.

THE QUADRANT OF ACTION

Behind these research concepts lie others that constitute epistemological bedrock. Phrased as a question, what, at the minimum, would create a social system? Four conceptual pairs seem crucial to the possibility of any theory of human action: (1) body/physicality, (2) mind/consciousness, (3) other/sociality, and (4) culture/meaning. These bedrock images constitute the *quadrant of action,* the basis on which any system of behavior must be built. The first term within these pairs refers to the locus of the concept, while the second refers to the concept as it is experienced by the individual actor. By working with these four unformed lumps of social psychological clay, we build models of social order.

Body/Physicality

Every theory of human action must properly begin with the recognition of the body. Perhaps because this is so obvious, it was not until recently taken much into account in social psychology. Yet, as Jane Piliavin and Paul LePore emphasize in chapter 1, biology affects a variety of human experiences and behaviors: intimacy, aggression, motivation, emotion, and affiliation. Chemicals, hormones, skin, and bones shape our behavior, from what Piliavin and LePore call the "inside out." Likewise, physicality is implicated from the "outside in." By this Piliavin and LePore mean that our reactions to others are based in some measure on the physical embodiment of the other. We react to the biological presence of the other. We respond to men differently than women, to the "handicapped" differently than those who are currently able-bodied, to the pretty differently than the plain, and to the tall differently than the short. Physicality affects social life in another way. As has been argued (Charmaz 1991; Olesen 1992; Ronai 1992), the reality that we inhabit a body shapes how we interpret our world. This embodiment means that we cannot escape the power of our senses. Information processing presupposes a complex sensory apparatus. We have specialized receptors through which we incorporate our five senses into the experience of our environment. The biological organization of this sensory pentad influences how the external world becomes known. The different structures of eyes and tongues causes vision to be more communal than taste. Our personal architecture channels social forces.

Mind/Consciousness

Lodged "mysteriously" within the body is the mind. Recognition of the body depends on mindedness. In the past two decades social psychology, especially in psychology but also in sociology, has embraced cognition and now increasingly recognizes that emotion is a force in its own right, influencing as well as influenced by cognition. As Judith Howard describes in chapter 4, on social cognition, humans process large amounts of information, and the modes through which we do this are impressively complex. Underlying this information processing is awareness or consciousness. Humans are reflective and self-reflexive, in their identity work (as described in chapter 2, by Gecas and Burke) and in their understanding of their social work (as described in chapter 7 by Lyn Lofland). When we cross consciousness with embodied experiences, we learn that actors experience (and express) emotions. When experiences are systematized, cognitive generalizability results. When responses occur, we speak of behavior or action. Obviously, each of these statements grossly oversimplifies how the human mind operates, but it is a feature of mind that every statement about how a mind operates is an oversimplification. A further key consequence of consciousness is a sense of self and identity. Self results from self-consciousness coupled with physicality—a recognition that I experience, therefore I am. Each chapter in part I of this book, and, indeed, in all social science depends on the reality of mind. Whether we view the mind phenomenologically or as another physical organ, capable of "scientific" interpretation, it cannot be escaped or denied.

Other/Sociality

Like Blanche DuBois in *A Streetcar Named Desire,* we depend on the kindness of strangers. Can we imagine a person surviving in isolation? Even hermits and recluses have been socialized. The literature on feral beings, raised in near isolation or in "the wild," emphasizes the tonic and necessary effects of human contact. Indeed, it is fair to assert that an infant learns about him/herself through becoming aware of others—the process that sociologist Charles Horton Cooley (1964) refers to as "the looking glass self." By this he means that our self-image is derived from the way others react to us. Our recognition of others precedes our self-realization. From our days as babes in arms, our recognition of who and what we are depends on our interaction within a social sphere. The term *inter*action, central to the symbolic interactionist approach to social psychology, recognizes that action by itself is not meaningful; what is crucial is the connection between actors.

Humans are social, as are most, if not all, members of the animal kingdom. However, as humans, we also recognize self-consciously the existence of self and others, and the divisions between selves and others. By realizing that what and who we are depends on our contrast with others and how those others react to us, we make *otherness* into a central feature of identity. As the dramaturgical theory of Erving Goffman (1959) emphasizes, we perform for these others, providing a feeling of accomplishment not from our own judgments but from the judgments of those we wish to influence or impress. Our attempts at impression management, and how impression management affects how we see ourselves, remind us that interaction and the role of the other is a bedrock of all social psychology.

Culture/Meaning

The world would be a cold, unpredictable place without knowing how actions and objects fit together. While culture may be conceptualized as created by social units, it is impossible to imagine a social organization that lacks any culture—that is, rules that make action predictable. Meaning constitutes the predictability of action, and without meaning as part of the system, how can one imagine cognition, emotion, or behavior? In this sense culture/meaning becomes as much an organizing principle of action as body, mind, or the other. To respond, a social actor must invest the world with content, and this meaning, while consensually agreed on in most instances, is ultimately a linguistically based social construction of actors, not inherent in the objects themselves.

The second face of social psychology (House 1977)—the face linked to symbolic interaction—is especially insistent that social psychologists must recognize the critical role that meaning has in social life; this is one of the emphases that differentiates a sociologically based social psychology from one grounded in psychology, though psychologists now argue that much that they felt was universal may be culturally variable (see chapters 2 and 15). A reason for this is that a focus on meaning poses a barrier for creating a scientific social psychology in that the standard methodological tools in which all cases are treated equally and melded together cannot easily understand the use of culture and the role of language. Social psychology from this perspective may seem closer to the humanities and literary arts than to the sciences, but, as this volume attests, social psychology's diverse positions are one of its strengths.

By postulating body, mind, the social, and culture as the nexus underlying human action, we avoid determining the order in which they developed. While in an evolutionary sense we might claim that "bodies" develop first, in that living cells may have coalesced, without a mind it is difficult to know how these cells were recognized as bodies. The other corners of the quadrant, while analytically distinct, are even more difficult to disentangle in their priority. Each is implicated in the creation and activation of the others.

THE TRIANGULAR CORE

Above these bedrock concepts, social psychology has set a tripod of basic elements: affect, cognition, and behavior. All that humans do represents a combination or mixture of this triad. Most social psychological constructs are second-order combinations of feeling, thinking, and acting. While the first two seem "internal," and hence psychological, social psychologists increasingly recognize that internal, "minded" processes are meaningful only because of the existence of a cultural, social, external world, mediated through the "embodied" self. Thus, emotions are directed at and expressed toward external stimuli. As Lynn Smith-Lovin demonstrates in chapter 5, the origins of emotion are a complex and not completely understood mixture of the social, the cognitive, and the biological. Likewise, as Judith Howard emphasizes in chapter 4, social cognition can never be divorced from either the external environment or emotional processes. Ordinary mental processes are not "pure," rational cognitions. Social interaction, for its part, as Lyn Lofland describes in chapter 7, is tethered to both cognitive processes (e.g., the possibility of stimuli overload) and emotion (e.g., the effects of stress). Furthermore, emotion, cognition, and behavior are affected by historical and cultural processes.

Each chapter in part I focuses on a single building block construct (or several closely related ones); each chapter deals with phenomena that are cognitive, emotional, and behavioral. Thus, attitudes are frequently defined as a melding of the three (Allport 1935): a predisposition to act, based on evaluation and recognition. Identity depends on self-worth, social evaluation, and behavioral repertoires. Likewise, language often simultaneously implicates displays of mentality, emotion, and pragmatic action. The building blocks described in the seven chapters in part I (self and identity, social cognition, attitudes, emotion, language, social interaction, and biology) interweave cognitive, affective, and behavioral processes.

THE DIVERSITIES OF SOCIAL PSYCHOLOGY

In claiming that these building block constructs are permutations of cognition, affect, and behavior, we deny any simple or singular approach implicit in these analyses. The authors are eclectic, and readers will find different approaches embedded between and within the chapters. Lyn Lofland's chapter on social interaction emphasizes the symbolic and cultural grounding of public behavior, primarily operating out of the symbolic interactionist perspective, largely based on ethnography or systematic observation. In contrast, Judith Howard's chapter on social cognition recognizes that this construct has traditionally been linked to laboratory experimentation, with theories explicating the processes of cognition more likely to be drawn from systems theory or computer modelling. Lynn Smith-Lovin's chapter on emotion and affect, more than most others, emphasizes interpretative, self-reflective methodologies, while not dismissing observation or experimentation. The chapter on language by Douglas Maynard and Marilyn Whalen discusses a variety of naturalistic approaches to discourse and conversation. The differences between chapters should not be overemphasized, as each draws on other methodologies and bodies of literature. We asked the authors to include some historical dimension in their chapters, and many address postmodern theories. The linkages between dissimilar areas should be as instructive as the focal material in the chapter.

As each chapter makes evident, contemporary social psychologists consider multiple approaches in exploring a concept. Social psychology is both science and art. So, for instance, social cognition, while it has been traditionally associated with a "scientific," positivist model derived from psychological metaphors of the brain as a rule-based "machine," has recently been examined from postmodernist, literary approaches as well. This new approach does not supplant as much as supplement the "cognitive revolution" of the 1970s and 1980s. The domain of the social self and identity as described by Viktor Gecas and Peter Burke is even broader, with scholars selecting from a diverse toolbox of methodologies, including literary analysis, participant observation, survey research, and laboratory experiments. Scholars in the area even disagree on whether the idea of "self" has a meaningful referent. The historical shibboleths and stereotypes that once constrained research are no longer seen as applicable.

No social psychology volume could ignore social cognition, and it is the rare chapter in which the author does not address those issues raised by Judith Howard. For instance, Lyn Lofland emphasizes the vitality of the strategy paradigm for understanding how individuals interact in public spaces. This model draws heavily on cognitive evaluations of social settings and the expectations of others, coupled with a desire to manage one's affective self in a way to bring credit to the actor. The discussion of affect control theory in Lynn Smith-Lovin's chapter on affect and emotion demonstrates that the cutting-edge theories in emotions research owe much to cognitive theory, whereas theories of emotional display are heavily oriented to social interaction, and still other approaches are heavily linked to biosocial understandings, as described by Jane Piliavin and Paul LePore. Similarly, language, as Douglas Maynard and Marilyn Whalen emphasize, can be understood in terms of cognitive schemas but also, as the conversational analysts have it, in terms of behavioral regularities. Attitudes, described by Howard Schuman, expressed in talk and through social interaction, do more than incorporate affect and cognition—they help to define public selves. Self and identity, representing the core of who or what the actor really is, can never be disentangled from cognition, affect, or behavior, as Viktor Gecas and Peter Burke describe.

It is increasingly clear throughout the social sciences that dividing and distinguishing disciplines and subspecialties within disciplines is no longer relevant and is even counterproductive. We do not suggest that no divisions remain. Each of these chapters provides the student with an entree into a particular intellectual community. Perhaps moving from chapter to chapter suggests that their worlds do not touch. More profitably, we can understand the chapters in this volume using the metaphor of a jar full of marbles—each marble does not touch most of the other marbles, but each has several points of contact, and several marbles have central locations in the jar.

This section begins with the "core" social psychological problem, addressed by Viktor Gecas and Peter Burke: How do individuals come to recognize themselves in a social world? How can we best conceptualize "self and identity"? As they note, self and identity have been central to a sociological social psychology for nearly a century and remain a flourishing area of research. We recognize the self as fundamentally social in character, anchored in language and social interaction. Identity, they claim, is an aspect of self, closely tied to both social structural and historical processes. The affective side of identity, self-emotions, motivations as part of an active self, defense mechanisms, and cross-cultural aspects of the self are important areas of current intellectual interest in this domain.

As classic a social psychological topic as self is the study of attitudes, beliefs, and behavior, described by Howard Schuman. Schuman emphasizes that social scientists have used the concept of attitude widely and not always precisely. After reviewing the extensive literature on attitude formation and change, Schuman demonstrates how attitudes are implicated in social structures and are historically grounded. Further, he argues that we can profitably analyze attitudes as broad orientations to life—a critical part of a person's zeitgeist.

According to most review articles, social cognition is the dominant substantive area in social psychology, although this is perhaps more true for psychologists than sociologists. Judith Howard makes connections among cognition, affect, and behavior and describes the reasons that cognition should properly be seen as a *social* phenomenon. Howard further demonstrates the relations between social cognition and traditional sociological concerns, including categorization, interaction, collective cognitions, and cross-cultural comparisons. A major contribution of social cognition has been to demonstrate that core social structural phenomena—stratification, social movements, political actions, and intergroup relations—are in part a consequence of individual thought.

The inclusion of Steven Gordon's chapter (1981) in the Rosenberg and Turner volume on "The Sociology of Sentiments and Emotion," was considered innovative or even radical. Today Lynn Smith-Lovin's chapter on affect and emotion is central to what sociological social psychology has become. In the past two decades sociologists have attempted to develop research programs and theoretical analyses about the social aspects of emotional research not necessarily focused on personality, biology, or physiological correlates. Smith-Lovin describes the broad research tradition on feeling rules and emotion work, examining emotion as a form of impression management. Closer to traditional experimental models is affect control theory, which Smith-Lovin and David Heise have been instrumental in developing. This perspective merges a cognitive information processing model with interactional expectancies to examine the production of emotional responses. Other sociological approaches emphasize structural models of emotion, which depict emotion linked to dimensions of power and status. Still others attempt to understand emotion as a phenomenological reality or a psychodynamic process grounded in a social system. Perhaps more than many topics, the social psychology of emotions is a growing and expanding area.

Language and talk should always have been part of the sociological enterprise, but until fairly recently sociolinguistic research was marginalized. In some ways like recent attention to the social psychological examination of emotions, Douglas Maynard and Marilyn Whalen, in chapter 6, demonstrate the centrality of discourse to an informed social psychology, in both experimental models and observational studies. They argue that social psychologists increasingly examine language as a form of action, rather than as a channel or conduit of information that provides a basis for action. Thus, they connect the theory of language to the study of interaction.

No concept has been more important in the distinctive tradition of sociological social psychology than social interaction. Lyn Lofland focuses on the continuities and complexities in interaction, focusing on "nonintimate sociality" such as that found in public places. The examination of public social life is to recognize in mundane behaviors social significance. For instance, the routine interactions between males and females reflects gender-based stratification; the way the homeless approach the affluent uncovers regularities of economic and political power. Although some have derided this topic as marginal, in Lofland's explication it becomes central to the understanding of the performance of attitudes, language, emotions, cognitions, power, status, and many of the other issues addressed throughout this volume.

When the Rosenberg and Turner volume was published it would have been highly unlikely to include a chapter on biology and social psychology. The chapter, by Jane Piliavin and Paul LePore, included here is in some respects equivalent to the inclusion of the chapter on emotion in the previous volume. These authors detail how biology affects social behavior from the inside out (i.e., the effects of biological and genetic processes on behavior) *and* from the outside in (how biological and genetic status affect the way one is treated). We are bodies, cells, organs, and hormones. We cannot escape our innate endowment; for this reason, biology is part of our social destiny.

Cognition, affect, and behavior are themes that will continue to resonate as long as there is a social psychology. The chapters in part I can be seen as providing building blocks on which self and identity, attitudes and beliefs, social cognition, emotion, language, social interaction, and biology depend. Each chapter reveals the diversity of substantive focuses and methodological techniques in contemporary research.

All disciplines have their cores and the specialized peripheries that are extensions of the core elements. This focus on basic concepts and issues in social psychology is the challenge of part I of the book, with the emphasis on those social components that are directly tied to individuals, spreading outward to group dynamics and organizational studies. From building blocks come the structures on which great intellectual edifices will eventually rise.

REFERENCES

Allport, Gordon W. 1935. Attitudes. Pp. 798–844 in *A Handbook of Social Psychology,* ed. C. Murchison. Worcester, MA: Clark University Press.

Charmaz, Kathy. 1991. *Good Days, Bad Days: The Self in Chronic Illness and Time.* New Brunswick: Rutgers University Press.

Cooley, Charles Horton. [1902] 1964. *Human Nature and Social Order.* New York: Scribner's.

Goffman, Erving. 1959. *Presentation of Self in Everyday Life.* New York: Anchor.

Gordon, Steven L. 1981. The sociology of sentiments and emotions. Pp. 562–592 in *Social Psychology: Sociological Perspectives,* ed. Morris Rosenberg and Ralph H. Turner. New York: Basic.

House, James S. 1977. The three faces of social psychology. *Sociometry* 40:161–177.

Olesen, Virginia. 1992. "Extraordinary Events and Mundane Ailments." Pp. 205–220 in *Investigating Subjectivity,* ed. Carolyn Ellis and Michael G. Flaherty. Newbury Park, CA: Sage.

Ronai, Carol Rambo. 1992. The reflexive self through narrative: A night in the life of an erotic dancer/researcher. Pp. 102–124 in *Investigating Subjectivity,* ed. Carolyn Ellis and Michael G. Flaherty. Newbury Park, CA: Sage.

CHAPTER 1

Biology and Social Psychology

Beyond Nature versus Nurture

JANE ALLYN PILIAVIN
PAUL C. LEPORE

". . . in the beginning there is the body."
—D. H. Wrong, 1961, 191

Dennis Wrong's phrase, "in the beginning" can have two meanings. First, there is our biological beginning in the genetic sense. At conception, we are endowed with certain genetic material. Dennis Wrong's article set out the case against the "over-socialized conception" of the human that was standard in the sociology of the 1950s, pointing out that there may well be things "built in" to humans that profoundly affect the way we turn out and that socialization may have very little influence on these tendencies.[1] The question of what are the innate endowments of humans is one focus of this chapter.

There is another meaning of "in the beginning." From the minute we emerge into the light of day, we have a physical body with a particular appearance. The first question we ask—Is it a boy or a girl?—indicates the importance of sex. The next questions are about weight and length, whether it has "all its fingers and toes"—that is, Is it "normal"?—and which side of the family it resembles. Bonding to parents can be affected by resemblance; the toys offered children, which help shape their interests, can depend on not only their sex but also their size and looks. From the time we are born, every time we meet someone, there is a new "beginning" in which we are judged by our outward appearance.

As sociological social psychologists, our major focus is on social interaction. Our first question, then, needs to be how to conceptualize the influence of "biology" on social interaction. Social interaction involves both the production and the interpretation of actions. That is, each person produces behaviors and reflects on both those behaviors and the cues provided by others. The active and sometimes spontaneous production of behavior is what is most often thought of when "genetic determination" is discussed. For example, "hyperactive" children produce behaviors that make classroom interactions difficult for others, particularly teachers. There may also be biological "givens" involved in the process of interpretation of others' and one's own actions. For example, girls and women are found in many studies to be more adept at "reading" others' emotional cues, and males with higher levels of testosterone are more sensitive to threat-related cues, more often interpreting them as requiring an aggressive response (Olweus 1980). Some global personality characteristics believed to have strong heritability, such as extraversion-introversion, may involve both the production and the interpretation of behavior.

People also bring to interactions social stimulus characteristics that affect how others relate to them. Our genetic makeup determines our sex and in large part our physical appearance—height, basic body structure, facial features, hair, skin, and eye color. Weight, although more under control than the other characteristics, also has a large genetic component. Certain skills—in the area of athletics, art, and music, for example—require physical abilities that are heavily influenced by biology. Our physical selves affect interaction by triggering expectations, attitudes, and behaviors in those with whom we interact, leading them to provide different levels of initiation of interactions and different social responses to us than to others who look different from us. No one is likely to say, "How's the weather up there?" to a man who is five-foot-eight. Very homely people are seldom swamped with exciting offers of dates. We have heard only one "brunette joke": Why are blond jokes so short? So brunettes will understand them.

Finally, the physical body affects our life chances more directly. If you are a woman you cannot be a professional football player. Whatever your sex, if you are heavy you cannot be a jockey. A career as a painter for the colorblind, as a musician for the tone-deaf, and as a dancer or athlete for the uncoordinated is not possible. That is, there are certain settings some people cannot enter; thus certain interactions simply cannot occur for individuals of some biological endowments.[2]

There is one biologically based "master status" in our society and all others that affects all aspects of social interaction: sex. Physiological differences determine our relationship to the reproductive process, expose us to different psychoactive chemicals (the sex hormones), and lead to important differences in body function. It is likely that personality, ability, and interest factors are also affected by sex. Physical sex differences trigger different patterns of social interaction from others. Finally, because of physical differences, tradition, and prejudice, access to certain statuses is extremely difficult or impossible for one sex or the other.

In sum, biology can affect us "from the inside out" by influencing the ways we choose settings, initiate and sustain interactions, and perceive the actions of others. Biology can affect us "from the outside in" because of our "stimulus value" to others, who treat us differentially as a function of our external appearance. It can also affect our life chances by preventing or facilitating access to certain statuses.

We begin this chapter with an examination of the issues having to do with biology "from the inside out"—What may be the genetic contributions to those actions that initiate and maintain social interaction? First we explore what is in "the human biogram"—the basic behavioral tendencies of the human species. In this section we briefly review the assumptions underlying the evolutionary perspective; discuss the issue of heritability, including the methodological difficulties associated with trying to assess it; and explore the nature and extent of the effects of the sex chromosomes and hormones, especially testosterone and the hormones that control the menstrual cycle. The second part of the chapter deals with biology "from the outside in"—What are the biological contributions to social stimulus values that affect social interaction? We review the literature on physical attractiveness, the impact of physical handicaps on interaction, and the issue of distinctiveness in social contexts. Finally, we present a heuristic model and discuss a topic that involves both "inside" and "outside" processes: puberty.

FROM THE INSIDE OUT

Evolutionary Theory and Social Behavior

Our first question is very broad, and clearly impossible to answer definitively at this time—What are some overall tendencies we may have *as a species* toward various forms of social behavior? The assumption of ethologists, sociobiologists, and other biologically oriented students of human behavior is that our behavior patterns as well as our morphology have been shaped by natural selection such that those behaviors that were adaptive in our early environments have been retained. It is important to stress that selection occurs in a particular environment. Traits are not universally adaptive; they are adaptive for a species in an environment.

The concept of inclusive fitness is basic to an understanding of the evolutionary approach. To Charles Darwin (1896), "survival of the fittest" referred to the individual organism; the fittest were those whose characteristics allowed them to live longer and reproduce. It is now probably the majority view (Dawkins 1976) that the gene, rather than the organism or species, is the major unit of selection. That is, a version of a gene (an allele) for a particular physical or behavioral trait that leads its bearer to be more successful in the existing environment—where "success" is defined as leaving more copies of the gene—will survive and "outcompete" other alleles of that gene. That allele of the gene, and not the organism that carries it, is then said to have greater "inclusive fitness" than other versions of the gene. It is this kind of reasoning that has made it possible to argue that a gene for altruism that leads an animal to sacrifice itself for its relatives can have high "inclusive fitness," even if the animal itself dies.

Another important concept, particularly in sociobiological theorizing, is that of reproductive strategies. There are two basic strategies, called K and r strategies by population biologists. An r strategist has a high reproductive rate and short generation time and invests little in offspring; a K strategist focuses on quality rather than quantity, having a low reproductive rate, long generations, and much parental investment (Archer 1991). Humans are said to be "the most K-selected species yet described" (Lancaster 1985).[3]

Taking these two central concepts as a starting point, we must place theories of evolution and sociobiology into a historical context. It is widely assumed that our "environment of evolutionary adaptedness" is the open savannahs and woodlands of south central Africa, and that early humans lived in relatively small bands of hunter-gatherers. The traits that facilitate survival in such a physical and social environment are those we might expect still to find in modern humans. Some critical areas of social interaction, taking an evolutionary "sur-

vival" perspective, are mating and reproduction, child care and nurturance, social organization and hierarchy (including division of labor), communication (perhaps especially of emotions), and cooperation/ competition/ethnocentrism. A variety of methods have been used to get at the contents of the human "biogram"—the set of behaviors *Homo sapiens* can be expected to display naturally, given development in a normal environment.[4]

In 1975, Wilson wrote *Sociobiology: The New Synthesis*—twenty-six chapters on other animals and one on humans. In it he claims, "if one assumes evolution from a common archaic biological origin, then, biology explains all behavior of all social animals of all times, theoretically at least" (p. 4). In attempting to deduce what lies in the human biogram he proposed a method in which comparisons are made across present-day societies that live as close to our presumed environment of evolutionary adaptedness as can be found, as well as across other primate species. Those traits that are "conservative"—those found in most societies and most primate species (e.g., dominance of males over females, prolonged maternal care)—are assumed to be "in the biogram," while those that are variable (e.g., territoriality) are probably not.

In response to critics, who decried Wilson's approach as "sociologically and psychologically naive" (Gove and Carpenter 1982) or worse, Wilson (Lumsden and Wilson, 1982) developed a theory of "gene-culture coevolution" in which he proposed a new type of evolution applicable only to the human species and any future species able to use symbols and thus develop culture:

> . . . in which the genes prescribe a set of biological processes, which we call epigenetic rules, that direct the assembly of the mind. This assembly is context dependent, with the epigenetic rules feeding on information derived from culture and physical environment. Such information is forged into cognitive schemata that are the raw materials of thought and decision. Emitted behavior is just one product of the dynamics of the mind, and culture is the translation of the epigenetic rules into mass patterns of mental activity and behavior. (p. 2)

In other words, what we inherit are biases to respond to certain situations in certain ways, and these tendencies interact in complex ways with the physical and cultural environments in which we find ourselves at any given time.

Whatever evolutionary approach we take,[5] can we say anything about what is in the human biogram? We will concentrate on four topics that are very closely tied to both survival issues and social interaction, and on which there is a good deal of research: reproductive behavior, survival as a child, ethnocentrism, and communication.

Reproductive Behavior.   In the area of sexual behavior, predictions have been made based on the assumption that men and women pursue different reproductive strategies (Trivers 1972) due to differential investment in offspring. We will discuss only the research on rape and child abuse, which have been the most controversial.[6] The feminist analysis of rape (Brownmiller 1975) states that rape is a political act that "is nothing more or less than a conscious process of intimidation by which **all men** keep **all women** in a state of fear" (p. 15). Brownmiller argues that no lower animals commit rape. However, sociologists such as Shields and Shields (1983) claim that "Mating behavior interpreted as forced copulation, stolen fertilization, or explicitly as rape has now been reported in lower invertebrates, insects, fishes, amphibians, birds, mammals, and nonhuman primates" (p. 116).[7]

In the sociobiological view, females—especially in K-selected species such as ours, in which a great deal of investment in each child is required—will be selected for caution and males for tactics to overcome such resistance, a situation that leads to inherent conflict between men and women. Buss (1989), in fact, proposes and finds that emotional responses to the use of different reproductive strategies differ between the sexes: women are more upset and angry by sexually aggressive acts, while men are more affected by sexual withholding behavior.

Relying on the sociobiological framework, Shields and Shields (1983) propose that the higher the "quality" of the female, the more vulnerable she will be to rape, and the higher the "quality" of the male the less likely he will be to need to resort to rape. They present data that show that the age distribution of rape victims matches the distribution of greatest likelihood of producing children, with the highest risk in the late teens and early twenties. Further evidence by Thornhill and Thornhill (1983) demonstrates that the age of rape victims, but *not* of female murder victims, matches the age of highest reproductive value and fertility. These authors also predict and find that males will be most likely to commit rape at the ages when competition for females is most intense (i.e., prior to the usual age of first marriage) and that men who have the most difficulty climbing the social ladder will more often be rapists than men who successfully compete. Moreover, they hypothesize that rapists will be consciously aware of their low status relative to other males. In fact, the authors report that rapists tend to have lower self-esteem and are less self-assured and less dominant than nonrapists and are in general incompetent in normal heterosexual social interactions (citing Rada 1978; Groth and Birnbaum 1979). There are clearly many alternative explanations for each of these findings taken singularly. How convincing these two articles, and others on this topic, are depends on the acceptability of the sociobiological framework to the reader.

Parenting is another aspect of reproductive behavior recently analyzed from a sociobiological perspective. Hypotheses regarding child abuse have been based mainly on the "inclusive fitness" assumption that parents should put their effort into those children who will contribute most to the survival of their genes. For example, adults should be more interested in the survival of their biological children than of children to whom they are not related, and among their own children they should invest more in those with the most reproductive potential. Stepparents did abuse more than biological parents in three studies of child abuse done from this perspective (Daly and Wilson 1981; Lenington 1981; Lightcap, Kurland, and Burgess 1982). More striking, in the Lightcap et al. study of twenty-four families in which at least one case of abuse was reported, in those families with both stepchildren and biological children it was *always* a stepchild who was abused.

Parents should also be less likely to abuse or kill "normal" children than handicapped children, because of their greater potential for carrying on the parents' genes; such results, in fact, are found in the Lightcap et al. study. Since males are physically able to pass on their genes to more children than are females and are less secure of their true biological relationship to any particular child, they should be less invested in and more likely to abuse, neglect, or kill any given child. All three studies confirmed this prediction. Lightcap et al. (1982) stress that "such findings do not represent a definitive test of sociobiological, as opposed to social science theory, because models based on psychology, sociology, or social psychology do not generate predictions that are necessarily contradictory to the evolutionary model" (pp. 65–66). However, nonevolutionary models do not predict discriminatory abuse of handicapped or stepchildren, nor do they account for the male bias among abusers.

Survival as a Child.   Infants must be adapted to survive to adulthood, and parents should be adapted to care for them. What do infants and parents do that is consistent with this assumption? Infants orient to the human face, or even a crude schematic of a human face, very early (Argyle and Cook 1976). Soon after, they smile in response to faces and differentiate between a correct schematic and one with scrambled elements (Jirari 1970). Meltzoff (1985) found that infants as young as twenty-four hours will imitate an adult's facial expressions. While toddlers are very interested in babies—with girls seeking more contact with them than boys (Dunn and Kendrick 1982)—younger children (up to age twelve) tend to prefer pictures of adults to pictures of infants. This preference shifts to infants for girls when they reach ages twelve to fourteen but for boys not until after age eighteen (Fullard and Reiling 1976). Thus there seems to be a "fit" in preference consistent with either receiving or giving care, and females tend to take on the caregiving preference earlier.

The cry is the most effective weapon in the infant's arsenal. It is a compelling stimulus that makes a response obligatory (Ostwald 1963), although the action taken can be either nurturant or abusive (Stone, Smith, and Murphy 1973). Frodi and Lamb (1978) found that children and adolescents showed physiological responses indicative of distress to a videotape of a crying infant. Bowlby (1958) suggested that the infant cry and other behaviors, such as smiling, may operate as "sign stimuli" that have the power to "release" caregiving behavior. In support of this, Murray (1979) reported data from studies of hunting-gathering people that indicate that mothers in those societies respond to infant cries on the average in six seconds. There is indirect evidence that prolactin (a hormone involved in milk production) has effects on caregiving in humans as well as in lower mammals. Breast-feeding (as compared to bottle-feeding) mothers in one study responded more quickly to an infant cry and were more likely to respond with feeding (Bernal 1972). It would appear that there is a readiness on the part of both the infant and the adult for a nurturant, caretaking relationship.

An issue raised by sociobiologists, mainly those who investigate altruism, is kin recognition. Infant survival in other animals involves recognition by the mother soon after birth, usually by smell (Kendrick, Levy, and Keverne 1992). Porter (1987), in fact, found that recognition of human infants at birth, by both looks and smell, is far better than chance. Do similar genes call to one another? There is a growing number of investigators who believe they do (Rushton 1989). If so, the interesting question, of course, is how?

Ethnocentrism.   As early as 1906, William Graham Sumner noted that people tend to like people in their own group and dislike those in competing or opposing groups; he coined the term *ethnocentrism* to describe this tendency. This bias is based on a rigid and distinct separation between an in-group and out-groups involving stereotyped negative imagery and hostility toward the out-group and stereotyped positive imagery and favorable attitudes regarding in-group members. Visible factors such as skin color, sex, and other aspects of physical appearance that make group members easily recognizable are usually most salient in determining group boundaries.

Ethnocentrism appears to be very close to a cultural universal (van der Dennen 1987). That is, most peoples around the world believe they are superior to others, have been "chosen" by their gods as something special, and are the only ones to whom the word *human* truly applies. Research shows that simply categorizing people into groups per se, without any history of association, leads to discrimination in favor of in-group members and against out-group members (Tajfel 1974). Children are afraid of strangers around six to nine months of age, with the strength and duration of this fear attributable to cultural factors such as having one or multiple caretakers (Ainsworth 1973; Eibl-Eibesfeldt 1979; Morgan and Ricciuti 1973). People with deviant beliefs or obvious physical deformities are rejected (Schachter 1951; Scherer, Abeles, and Fischer 1975). These effects are found in other social animals as well (Goodall 1971). Thus it is reasonable to think there may be some innate tendency toward in-group preference and rejection of strangers perceived as "other." That is, an "epigenetic rule" for ethnocentrism may be part of the human biogram. Who is "in" and who is "out" will, of course, be defined by the culture and may be infinitely malleable (Dunbar 1987).

Communication. Since Darwin's *The Expression of the Emotions in Man and Animals* we have recognized that the facial expressions we use to communicate the strong emotions of anger, fear, disgust, and perhaps joy are shared with our animal relatives. Extensive studies by Ekman and others (Ekman 1972; Fridlund, Ekman, and Oster 1987) have clearly shown that the "strong emotions" are expressed in the same ways by widely disparate cultures, and that these emotions are recognized cross-culturally. Children born blind or deaf display the same facial expressions, laugh, and cry as sighted and hearing infants, and on the same timetable of development. It is thus widely accepted that the patterning of the expressions of the strong emotions is universal and thus innate (see Eibl-Eibesfeldt 1989). It is much less clear that the understanding of emotions, and their categorization in languages, is the same. Russell (1991) concludes "that there is great similarity in emotion categories across different cultures and languages" (p. 444) but is unwilling to conclude that they are exactly the same.

There is also good evidence that primitive empathic responses—indicated by crying in response to another infant's cry—occur very early in life (Sagi and Hoffman 1976) and are not mediated by complex cognitive processes such as "taking the role of the other." Infants as young as twelve hours responded with more vigorous crying to a recorded cry than to stimuli matched in loudness and form. Female infants were more responsive than male infants.

It is also generally accepted, since Noam Chomsky, that humans are uniquely programmed to learn language easily, skills that are difficult or impossible for other primates and quite out of reach for other animals. But do we share other gestural communication patterns with other animals? A group of ethologists, including Blurton-Jones (1972), Hold-Cavell and Borsutzky (1986), and Smith and Lewis (1985), building on previous work with free-ranging primates, developed a fine-grained technique for the observation of preschool children based on a dictionary of gestures, postures, and facial expressions.

The early work focused on rough-and-tumble play, a common pattern (especially among males in other primate species) postulated to serve important functions in the generation of social hierarchies, social bonding, and training for adult interaction (Blurton-Jones 1967, 1972). This pattern, which includes running, chasing and fleeing, wrestling, jumping up and down, beating with an open hand or an object but not hitting, and laughing, is easily distinguished from real aggression, which consists of kicking, pushing, biting, beating with a closed hand, various vocalizations, and frowning.

Liking is significantly related to participation as rough-and-tumble play partners but not with participation in aggressive episodes (Smith and Lewis 1985). Pellegrini (1989) has also shown that the two categories are much more distinct among popular than among unpopular children, and that unpopular children are less accurate in distinguishing the two patterns. Are unpopular children unpopular because their behavior is not interpretable by others? Is their behavior "peculiar" because they have not learned the correct patterns in play groups before they begin school? Are some children constitutionally insensitive to appropriate social patterning?

These distinctions have held up in studies of German, Japanese, and African children and working-class British children (Appleton 1980), indicating relative independence from cultural influences. Thus, the specifics of the patterning of gestures of submission and dominance and of affiliative intentions among small children seem remarkably like those used by other well-studied primates. We are convinced that there is at the very least a preprogrammed readiness to employ patterns of gestures—a set of epigenetic rules—as there has been shown to be prewiring for language and facial expression. More critically, children who somehow fail to develop this repertoire very early in life are at a distinct disadvantage in social relationships and are at risk of social isolation and its sequelae.

The Heritability of Personality, Attitudes, and Interests

Horse and dog breeders have known for millennia that behavioral traits, such as abilities and temperaments, "breed true." Holden, speaking of human behavioral genetics research, claims that "Behavioral geneticists are finding that genes account for about 50% of the variance . . . in most normally distributed traits. Most of the remaining differences are attributed to environmental influences unique to individuals—ranging from individual parent-child interactions to peer influences to random events. So, although the family environment may influence personality, it does so in a nonuni-

form and therefore unpredictable way in different individuals"[8] (Holden 1987, 599). One study (Loehlin 1989) even found a negative effect of common environment on similarity between twins. Surprisingly, then, some have concluded that shared family environments contribute little or nothing to variation in most behavioral traits (Plomin and Daniels 1987).

Heritability has been investigated in three categories, arrayed from the most individual to the most social: abilities (both physical and cognitive), psychopathology, and personality and attitudes. There is very strong evidence for heritability in intelligence and other abilities.[9] With developing knowledge of chemical involvement in mental illness, there has been considerable work on heritability in that area.[10] Of most interest to social psychologists are recent investigations of personality and attitudes. Twin and adoption studies that use personality questionnaires typically yield heritability estimates in the range of 20 to 50 percent, with identical and fraternal twin correlations on the average being about .5 and .3 respectively. Evidence is strongest for heritability of activity level, emotional reactivity (neuroticism), and sociability-shyness (extraversion). Four twin studies in four countries, involving more than 30 thousand pairs of twins, yielded heritability estimates of about 50 percent for neuroticism and extraversion (Loehlin 1989), although adoption studies suggest a figure closer to 30 percent (Plomin 1990).

There is some evidence for the heritability of altruistic and aggressive tendencies (Eysenck and Eysenck 1975; Matthews et al. 1981; Rushton et al. 1986; Scarr 1966). Mednick et al. (1984) found a significant genetic component in adoption studies of crime and delinquency and cite research that indicates significant heritability of alcoholism, dominance, locus of control, sexuality, values, and vocational interests. Others have found a genetic component in vocational attitudes (Scarr and Weinberg 1978), religiosity (Waller et al. 1990), attitudes toward alcohol (Perry 1973), time spent watching television by young children (Plomin et al. 1990), and conservatism, radicalism, and tough-mindedness (Martin et al. 1986).[11]

Finally, recent work by Bailey and Pillard (1991) estimates at least 50 percent heritability of homosexuality in males, based on a sample of 161 homosexual men and their relatives. Of relatives whose orientation could be rated, 52 percent of identical twins, 22 percent of fraternal twins, 9.2 percent of brothers, and 11 percent of adoptive brothers were also homosexual. Referring to recent work by LeVay (1991) that purported to show differences in the hypothalamuses of homosexual and heterosexual men, Holden suggests that the genes involved may be those that "turn on" the prenatal androgen, arguing: "Our working hypothesis is that these genes affect the part of the brain that he [LeVay] studied" (1992, 33).

How believable are these results? There are two basic methods for estimating the heritability of traits in human populations: the twin method and the adoption method. Both rely on the fact that degree of genetic relationship is 100 percent for identical twins, 50 percent for fraternal twins, between siblings, and between parents and children, and 0 percent between unrelated individuals. Any resemblance between two individuals can be broken down into a portion attributable to genetic similarity, a portion due to environmental similarity, and an interaction term. It is assumed that twins reared together have similar environments but that identical twins have no more similar environments than do fraternal twins.[12]

There have been serious debates about the interpretation of heritability estimates. One problem is that genetic and environmental influences may be correlated not only because parents confer genes *and* provide socialization, but also because genetic makeup leads to behaviors that affect environment (Goldberger 1979; Jencks 1980). That is, one's genetic predispositions lead to seeking *and creating* social environments that are favorable to the exercise of one's traits (Lykken et al. 1990). Another problem in twin studies is partitioning shared and unshared environmental effects; however, this is now possible using structural equation modeling (Kessler et al. 1992; Loehlin 1989). Heritability coefficients are generally considered meaningful when making comparisons within one social or

ethnic group. Differences between groups cannot be analyzed in the same way because of disparities in the groups' environments.[13] Finally, there are various selection problems in twin studies (Lykken, McGue, and Tellegen 1987). Furthermore, the heritability coefficients obtained from twin studies are consistently higher than those obtained from adoption studies. Thus there is some concern about generalization from such biased samples of twins.

Is Anatomy Destiny? Sex Differences in Social Behavior

We have looked at the possible contents of the human biogram and the evidence for inheritance of socially relevant traits at a group level. We now consider one specific set of biological effects related to genetic processes: the effects of the sex chromosomes and their associated hormones. The differences between men and women we discuss here are those that can with reasonable certainty be attributable to physical differences between the sexes.

Prenatal Development and Sex and Gender Effects.   In the normal course of events, an egg with twenty-three chromosomes meets with a sperm with the same number and the fetus is endowed with the normal complement of chromosomes, ordered in pairs. With regard to sex, two X chromosomes make a girl and an X and a Y make a boy, if all goes well in fetal development. At about three months' gestation, the fetal testes in a male child start to produce androgenic hormones (testosterone and related compounds) and the external genitalia take male, rather than female, form. There is evidence that these hormones affect the developing brain as well. Having no androgens, a female fetus develops as female in outward anatomy. Some genetic males are insensitive to their own androgens or are exposed to excess female hormones and do not develop male genitalia. Some female fetuses are exposed to excess androgens, sometimes by a mother with an adrenal tumor, and are masculinized. On the basis of studies of these "accidents," some conclusions have been drawn about social impacts (Baker 1980). It is also possible to have too few or too many sex chromosomes, which can also lead to social effects. There are three well-known syndromes that result from anomalies in the sex chromosomes: XXY (Klinefelter syndrome) and XYY syndrome, both affecting males who have an extra X or an extra Y chromosome, and Turner syndrome, affecting females who lack one X chromosome and are therefore X0. If certain patterns of behavior are consistently associated with these genetic and hormonal anomalies, a strong argument can be made for genetic involvement in gender differences in social behavior.

Genetic males who were androgen-insensitive and are raised as girls have typical female patterns of interests, such as doll play, while androgenized females whose genital anomalies have been corrected and who are raised as girls have more traditionally masculine interests, such as sports (Masica, Money, and Ehrhardt 1971). Boys whose mothers were treated with female hormones (usually to prevent miscarriage) but who have normal genitals and are raised as boys are rated as less active, less interested in sports, and unassertive, compared to boys not exposed. As these children grow into adulthood, androgenized girls take longer to become interested in heterosexual dating, personal adornment, and infant care (Money and Schwartz 1977). In many cases, their relative disinterest in babies continues into adulthood. Estrogen/progesterone-treated boys are less aggressive and assertive, less athletically coordinated, and less interested in dating and marriage and show decreased physical activity and heterosexual activity (Dalton 1976; Yalom, Green, and Fisk 1973).

Turner syndrome girls are "superfeminine," being extremely interested in frilly clothes, playing with dolls, and babysitting. Bancroft, Axworthy, and Ratcliffe (1982) found that twelve XXY boys aged fifteen to seventeen were more tender-minded and sensitive, less masculine, and more insecure, but *not* less assertive or aggressive than matched controls. However, half of their mothers (as compared to only one control mother) made spontaneous comments "relating to timidity or lack of aggression " (p. 172), and the boys themselves

reported significantly more problems relating to same-sex peers.

All researchers of such children caution over-generalization based on their results, citing histories of medical treatment, parental knowledge of the child's hormone history, and non-recursive effects on later careers because of earlier effects. For example, if interest in sexual matters or parenting is delayed, lower early adult levels of the behaviors are to be expected. All authors emphasize the variability within groups, while being quite clear that between-group differences are strong. Thus the conclusion appears to be that estrogen/progesterone and testosterone indeed have "organizing effects" on the brains of developing fetuses, shaping them in the direction of masculine or feminine patterns of activity and interest. The power and extent of this shaping is, however, unknown.

In contrast to these gender role effects, there is very little evidence that the amount of testicular hormone present in the critical stage of sex differentiation or chromosomal abnormality affects gender identity—self-image as male or female—or sexual preference. Money and Ehrhardt (1972) concluded that early experience in some critical period determines these aspects of personality. However, new data challenge these conclusions. A hereditary defect has been discovered in an enzyme that prevents one form of androgen that causes the physical changes of puberty from being converted into another that causes the external genitalia to take on the male form. Babies with this defect are genetically male, have ambiguous genitalia more female than male in form, and are usually raised as girls. At puberty, however, the external genitalia grow, the voice deepens, and the "girl" becomes a "man." Imperato-McGinley et al. (1979, as cited in Sloane 1985) studied thirty-three affected men in two villages in the Dominican Republic. Of the nineteen who had been "raised unambiguously as girls," seventeen emerged from puberty with a reversed gender identity, sixteen felt and acted like men, and fifteen had lived or were living as men with women. Since such cases are widely known in these villages, it is quite possible that these "unambiguously" raised girls—with ambiguous genitals—may have had their doubts from the beginning.

There has also always been speculation regarding whether homosexuality may have a biological basis. Many male homosexuals report that they have "always" felt attraction to other males, from the first moment of awareness of sexual desire. Very recently (LeVay 1991; Swaab and Hofman 1990) it was reported that the brains of homosexual and heterosexual men differ in an area known to be involved in sexual activity and in which men and women are known to differ. This has, of course, been a highly controversial report, and far more work is needed before a genetic or prenatal hormonal determinant of sexual orientation is accepted.

Hormones and Social Behavior, I: Menstrual Cycle and Childbirth.   At about the time of the burst of interest in XYY syndrome as a potential cause of aggressive or criminal behavior, Katherina Dalton (1964), a British physician, presented a compelling argument for premenstrual syndrome (PMS) as a cause of homicide, suicide, child abuse, and a wide range of other dangerous social behaviors. It has been suggested, for example, that when "Lizzy Borden took an axe and gave her mother forty whacks" she was suffering from severe premenstrual syndrome. In Britain, PMS was successfully used as a defense in several criminal trials (Dershowitz 1975). "PMS" has since entered the common parlance, much to the dismay of many feminists who fear the reinforcement of a belief that women are unfit for highly responsible jobs because of their "instability" at "certain times of the month." What is the evidence that changing hormonal balances—over the monthly cycle and across the lifespan—affect women's social behavior?

Three important issues have been dealt with in the literature: PMS and milder mood changes of the menstrual cycle, postpartum depression, and the effects of hysterectomy and/or menopause.[14]

Menstrual Cycle Effects.   More than 150 psychological, physical, and behavioral symptoms have been associated with the menstrual cycle. The most common premenstrual mood effects are depression, irritability, tension, mood lability, and lethargy. The ovulatory phase is associated with high levels of energy, sexual interest, and positive mood. A serious difficulty with this research is that most women know when they will have their next menses, which can influence their reports about their mood states. The effect of expectations and beliefs about menstrual symptoms was demonstrated by Brooks et al. (1977) and Ruble (1977) in clever deception research. On the other hand, two studies of hysterectomized women who still had ovaries—and thus still experienced hormonal cycles but without telltale periods—found that scores for physical and psychological symptoms varied over a cycle in the same manner as did those of menstruating women (Backstrom, Boyle, and Baird 1981). Gath (1980) found that 80 percent of women who retrospectively reported experiencing PMS before hysterectomy reported similar cyclical symptoms eighteen months after hysterectomy. It seems clear that something affects moods over the cycle.

Moods need not translate into behavior, however. Sommer (1975) reviewed the evidence on cognitive and motor behavior and concluded that studies using objective performance measures, including academic examinations, reaction time measures, and quantity and quality of factory production, generally fail to demonstrate any menstrual cycle-related changes. Sexual behavior does appear to be affected by the cycle, with an increase in sexual feelings and frequency of intercourse at the ovulatory phase and around the menses (Friedman et al. 1980). D. B. Adams et al. (1978) suggest that specifically female-initiated sexual activity is most pronounced during the ovulatory phase of the menstrual cycle and propose that estrogen is the most likely hormonal influence. On the other hand, Persky and colleagues (1978) found that women's testosterone levels at their ovulatory peak related to intercourse frequency and self-ratings of sexual gratification.

Thus, for most women the mood changes that accompany hormonal cycles are not disabling and do not interfere in any way with job performance, but they do influence sexual activity. What of those who truly suffer from PMS? A major problem with studying PMS is defining it. Logue and Moos (1986) concluded that some 40 percent of women experience some mild symptoms and 2 to 10 percent experience more severe symptoms with probable functional impairment. Premenstrual syndrome appears to be most common and most severe between the ages of twenty-five and forty (Kramp 1968), and women who suffer from it are likely to have other psychopathology not linked to the menstrual cycle, including neuroses and affective illness (Halbreich and Endicott 1985). In populations of women who have committed a deviant act, including suicide attempts, nonviolent and violent crimes, disorderly conduct, and psychiatric episodes, more were in the premenstrual phase of the cycle than would have been expected by chance (Parlee 1973). It is generally concluded that many, if not most, women experience some variation in mood and physical symptoms across the menstrual cycle, but only some women interpret these symptoms as problematic, and even fewer show effects in behavior.

Postpartum Depression.   Mild mood disturbances following childbirth, including sadness, crying spells, insomnia, anxiety, and lability of mood, are very common, and can be "seen as a normal part of the birth experience" (Gitlin and Pasnau 1989). As with PMS, the cause is likely to be changes in hormonal balances in combination with a predisposition to interpret these symptoms in a negative way. A history of PMS, prior mood problems, and being a first-time mother are associated with mild postpartum depression (Handley et al. 1980; Yalom et al. 1968).

Postpartum psychosis occurs in one to two of one thousand births. A past history of psychotic illness, particularly affective disorders, is the best predictor of full-blown psychosis after childbirth. A woman with an affective disorder has a 20 to 25 percent chance of having such a reaction (Kendell, Chalmers, and Platz 1987). Other predictors are having a first baby, being unmarried, having a Cesarean delivery, and having the baby die. There was a 4 percent risk of infanticide in one analysis of

Scandinavian data (Davidson and Robertson 1985). It is clear that both social and genetic/biological factors are implicated in these reactions.

Posthysterectomy and Menopausal Depression. In the past it was widely believed that women are at risk for depression when they lose their childbearing abilities through hysterectomy or menopause. However, Gitlin and Pasnau (1989) conclude: "Based on the best, more recent studies, there is little evidence that hysterectomy is followed by a higher rate of postoperative psychopathology or depression" (p. 1418) and "most recent research has seemingly put to rest the time-honored concept of involutional melancholia (depression after menopause)" (p. 1419). Women's self-reports of depressive symptoms actually decrease as they pass through menopause (Frieze et al. 1978), and there is no good evidence for widespread "empty nest" depressions (Nolen-Hoeksema 1988). Matthews et al. (1990) recently reported a longitudinal study of more than five hundred premenopausal (forty-two to fifty years old) women and found essentially no negative psychological effects attributable to natural menopause. Since we have no reliable research on menopause in past times, we do not know whether "problem menopause" is simply a myth or whether women's responses have changed.

The possibility that women have changed in response to changing expectations is further supported by studies indicating a major effect of cultural and subcultural context on the levels of reported menopausal symptomatology (see Dan and Lewis 1992; Voda, Dinnerstein, and O'Donnell 1982). Factors that affect the level of difficulty experienced in menopause include "such cultural aspects as maternal role, social class, relational integration, and work situation" (Flint 1982, 367). The most striking examples of societal differences come from a study of Rajput women (Flint 1982) and a study comparing Mayan and Greek women (Beyene 1992). Flint reports that 10 percent of women in the United States between forty-five and sixty-four years of age have severe menopausal symptoms, a level similar to that found in Great

Britain. However, in Rajput women, she found "no classical symptoms associated with what is called 'menopausal syndrome' or any secondary symptoms, such as depressions, migraines, or incapacitations" (1982, 368). Flint attributes this striking difference to "the values and attitudes about menopause and role changes precipitated by each of these cultures when a woman reaches this reproductive landmark" (p. 368). At the onset of menopause, Rajput women gain social status: they can discard the veiled and secluded status of purdah and live in the outside world, talking with men and even drinking in public. In the United States, where youth and femininity are highly valued for women, menopause is likely to mean a loss in status.

Beyene, similarly, found not one Mayan woman who reported hot flashes or any other menopausal symptom; Greek women reported them but did not seek treatment. Mayan women, according to Beyene, expected to "be happy" and "free like a young girl again" at menopause; Greek women were ambivalent—there were some status gains, but they generally associated menopause with growing old. The changes in American society allowing women more access to power positions, especially when they reach midlife, may eventually lead to changes in attitudes toward menopause as well. But this study, and essentially all of the cross-cultural work, indicates the importance of subjective experience in defining and interpreting the meaning of physiological events.

The critical issue is that the experience of menopause is a bio*social* phenomenon. We should not ignore the physiological input, which is based on real changes in chemicals in the system, nor should we fall into the trap of total medical determinism. Koeske (1982) reviewed a number of biomedical and behavioral science models that have been used to explain the experience of menopause and concluded that we must recognize the important effects of culture and social interaction on physiology (e.g., through nutritional practices) as well as the interpretation of physiological events.

Hormones and Social Behavior, II: Testosterone Poisoning.   The current joke among feminists is

that —in parallel to the "raging hormones" arguments often leveled at women—men suffer from "testosterone poisoning." What is the evidence for effects of level of testosterone on men's (and women's) behavior?

Aggression.   Fausto-Sterling (1985), in an explicitly feminist text entitled *Myths of Gender,* unequivocally states that there is no good evidence linking aggression to levels of testosterone in human males, although she grants that there is evidence for this link in other animals. On the other hand, Dabbs and Morris (1990), Booth and Dabbs (in press), and Kemper (1990) claim that there is good evidence for the relationship of levels of circulating testosterone to aggression (as well as sexual behavior and interest) not only in males but also in females. Due to problems of definition of both sexuality and aggression and problems in assessing causation, the difference in conclusions probably boils down to a difference in interpretation. In none of the research on prison inmates (Dabbs et al. 1987, 1988) or general populations (Dabbs and Morris 1990; Udry 1989) was *actual* aggressive behavior affected by the level of testosterone, although *reports* of aggressive behavior and related "acting out" were. Similarly, studies of XXY and XYY men (Theilgaard 1984) found relationships to *reports* of physical aggression and fantasy measures, but not to *actual* behavior. Meyer-Bahlburg (1981), in a thorough review of the testosterone-behavior link literature, is cautious, stating, "it seems likely that androgens play only a limited role among many other factors in the development of aggressive behavior [and] pale in comparison to those of social factors. . . . Yet, developmental effects of androgens on aggression seem highly likely" (pp. 285–286).[15]

Sexuality.   The findings are much clearer in the area of sexual behavior. Many studies (Udry 1988) have shown that sexual interest increases after testosterone replacement. In both adult women (Bancroft et al. 1980) and adolescent boys and girls (Udry 1988) there is evidence that circulating levels of testosterone affect sexual interest and behavior. XXY men have reported much slower development of heterosexual interest, lower levels of current sexual activity, less sexual desire, and less satisfaction with their sex life than controls (Schiavi et al. 1988). XYY men report significantly more masturbation both as children and as adults and more unconventional sexual activity (sado-masochism, fetishism, exhibitionism, voyeurism, and pedophilia) than controls or XXY men. Men with high levels of testosterone are more likely to be divorced or separated, to have had extramarital sex with at least three people, and to have spent time apart from their wives because they were not getting along.

Finally, Kemper (1990) builds a theory on the relationship of dominance (status attained through the use of power) and eminence (status attained through accomplishment) with testosterone level and sexuality. He proposes that both dominance and eminence lead to a surge in testosterone (Mazur and Lamb 1980) and that these "surges" lead successful men to be more sexually motivated (and also, perhaps, more attractive to women) and more aggressive. Kemper is alert to the social prob-lematic aspects of this proposed cycle: men who are not able to attain a "testosterone surge" through legitimate means may be motivated to commit property crimes (to gain status) or overwhelm women —rape them if necessary—to experience this feeling. If these processes could be docu-mented, they might provide the individual-level mechanisms underlying the sociobiological analy-ses of rape, which have been criticized (appropri-ately) as mere metaphors based on findings from other animals.

Dabbs (1992) has also shown that men with high testosterone levels have lower-status occupa-tions. His proposed model suggests that men with high testosterone levels are more likely to be dis-tracted from school work as youths, to engage in more disruptive behavior, and thus complete their education at lower levels. The outcome is that as adults they are less able to compete in the modern postindustrial world. He concludes that, "It appears an irony . . . that testosterone, which evolved in support of a primitive kind of status, now conflicts with the achievement of occupational status" (ab-

stract). The level of testosterone is much more strongly related to deviant behaviors of all kinds among working- and lower-class men than among middle- and upper-middle-class men (Dabbs and Morris 1990). The effect of context is thus evident with regard to the impact of testosterone levels, as it is with regard to the impact of menopause.

Summary

We have examined the relationship between bio-logical makeup and the production and interpreta-tion of social interaction. We have explored what may be in the human biogram, to what extent indi-vidual differences in social orientations may be he-reditary, and how the genetic and physiological dif-ferences between men and women may affect social interaction processes. We do not propose that biology *determines* social behaviors; rather, we suggest that our choices in the instigation and inter-pretation of social encounters are importantly in-fluenced by the characteristics we bring to them by virtue of our species, sex, and individual heredity.

FROM THE OUTSIDE IN

" . . . in a very important sense there is only one complete unblushing male in America: a young, married, white, urban, northern, het-erosexual Protestant father of college educa-tion, fully employed, a good complexion, weight, and height, and a recent record in sports."
—Erving Goffman, 1963, 128.

The second way biology influences social behavior is "from the outside in." Based on how we look, sound, and act, others make judgments about us that affect how we are treated and what our selves become. There are a variety of theories as to how this occurs. Symbolic interactionists argue that so-cial interaction is a process of creating meaning or, to use George Herbert Mead's terminology, of achieving a shared definition of the situation. In this process, the individual's background charac-teristics, such as race, gender, and appearance, may be employed as part of others' construction of situated social identities. Social learning theorists see social interaction as an exchange of rewards and punishments, guided by learned expectations. Again, these expectations may in part be based on the participants' physical characteristics. Attribution theorists focus on the inductive process by which the individual's behaviors and outward characteristics provide insight into motives and personality characteristics and thus guide interaction.

Our physical capacities and appearance also limit what we can do, changing the extent to which we can even participate in interactions. The timing of our physical development influences our access to settings and others' responses to us. There are large differences across cultures, and there is social change over time regarding the availability of certain statuses to people of different physical make-ups. Expectations and stereotypes also change. In some cultures and at some times, obesity makes a woman desirable; at other times and places it makes her a social outcast. Those handicapped by physical and mental conditions were once hidden away in institutions; there are now active social movements in defense of their rights. The underlying principle, however, that our biological selves are an important factor in social chances and social interaction, remains.

Physical Appearance

Goffman states, "When a stranger comes into our presence . . . first appearances are likely to enable us to anticipate his [or her] category and attributes, his [or her] 'social identity'" (1963, 2). We tend to lean on our perceptions, transforming them into normative expectations, and typically are not aware that we have made these demands or even what they are until an active question arises as to whether or not they will be fulfilled (Goffman 1963). Basic to this inference process is the assumption that particular traits and personality characteristics are related (Asch 1946; Cantor and Mischel 1979). Cognitive theorists call these schemas implicit personality theories, suggesting that individuals believe that by knowing some information

about a person, they will gain insight into an entire constellation of related characteristics and traits. The physical appearance of the other is one immediately available salient cue and thus may be heavily weighted in initial impressions.

The "Physical Attractiveness Stereotype." Research on physical attractiveness and beliefs about the beautiful received a great deal of press in the 1970s and 1980s. Patzer states the physical attractiveness stereotype as follows: "Generally, the more physically attractive an individual is, the more positively the person is received, the more favorably the person is responded to, and the more successful is the person's personal and professional life" (1985, 1). Attractive people of both sexes are expected to be more likely to possess almost every "socially desirable" personality trait —sensitivity, kindness, sociability, sexual warmth and responsiveness, strength, poise, and modesty (Berscheid and Walster 1974)—and to fare better in life satisfaction, success, status, and achievement (Dion and Dion 1987; Kalick 1988). Physically unattractive individuals are thought to be more socially deviant (Deitz and Byrnes 1981; Unger, Hilderbrand, and Madar 1982) and, if a woman, more likely to be perceived as homosexual (Dew 1985).

Physical appearance has been shown to affect hiring preferences and salary differences (Cash and Kilcullen 1985). Frieze et al. (1991) found that more attractive men had higher starting salaries— earnings increased $2600 (in 1983) for each unit of attractiveness measured on a five-point scale—and continued to earn more over time. Attractive women gained no advantage in starting salaries but did earn more over time—$2150 more for each unit increase. The bias also appears in studies of helping behavior (Hooper et al. 1980).

Feild (1979) found that the physically attractive are treated more leniently and given more favorable punishments by juries and in the case of civil judgments are awarded more money (Patzer 1985). Alleged assailants in rape cases were given significantly longer punishments when the female victim was perceived by the jury as highly physically attractive (Thornton 1977). The stereotype appears also to apply to children (G. R. Adams 1978; Berscheid and Walster 1974)—attractive children are thought to be more self-sufficient and independent and less likely to be aggressive and antisocial, and their transgressions are dealt with more leniently.

The attractiveness stereotype is robust; effects remain even when subjects are told that physical attractiveness judgments are subjective and a matter of personal taste (Ellis, Olson, and Zanna 1983). However, the effects of appearance have been reduced or eliminated when other information, such as intelligence, is available (Solomon and Saxe 1977). As Eagly et al. (1991) argue, the effect of appearance is highly variable and depends crucially on the type of inference the perceiver is asked to make. Hence, while good looks has been shown to "induce strong inferences about social competence and weaker inferences about potency, adjustment, and intellectual competence, [appearance has] little impact on beliefs about integrity and concern for others" (1991, 124).

There is a downside to being attractive. Studies have found that the beautiful are also seen to be less faithful in marriages, more likely to engage in extramarital affairs, more likely to be divorced, self-centered, selfish, and less sympathetic to oppressed people (Hatfield and Sprecher 1986). Survey respondents generally characterized large-breasted women (one aspect of attractiveness) as immoral, selfish, and rude, as well as less competent, intelligent, and modest than women with smaller breasts (Kleinke and Staneski 1980).

Facial Appearance.   The face is the most critical dimension in physical attractiveness ratings (Rossi 1991), and the eyes and mouth are particularly relevant in our perceptions. Since the time of Aristotle, philosophers and scholars have suggested that character can be inferred from the face. For example, as Dr. Watson writes about Sherlock Holmes in Conan Doyle's first mystery, *A Study in Scarlet:* "His eyes were sharp and piercing . . . and his thin, hawk-like nose gave his whole expression an air of alertness and decision. His chin, too, had

the prominence and squareness which mark the man of determination" (Conan Doyle 1930, 20). Liggett (1974) found in surveys of university students that a large majority believed facial features provide important information about personality.

In contrast to the vast literature on the physical attractiveness stereotype, very little work has been done concerning actual "structure" of humans as stimuli. One area in which these specific structural cues have been investigated is "baby-facedness." Berry and McArthur (1986, 1988) find that people with facial features typical of human infants—large eyes, low vertical placement of features, short features, and a small, rounded chin—are perceived as warmer, weaker, more submissive, more naive, less threatening, less physically strong, dominant, intellectually astute, and/or more honest than those with more mature facial characteristics. These findings have been cross-culturally replicated (Berry and McArthur 1988; McArthur and Berry 1987).

Is there any evidence for this linkage in actual personalities? Self-ratings of facial babyishness were found to be negatively related to both males' and females' masculinity scores and self-perceived physical power measures and to females' social potency and assertiveness scores (Berry and Brownlow 1989). Although some researchers have suggested biological links between body structure and personality (e.g., Eysenck 1990), a direct link in this case is unlikely. Berry and Brownlow (1989), following McArthur and Baron's (1983) ecological model, suggest that given that it is probably adaptive to be built so as to respond to cues of immaturity, "perceivers may continue to extract information about age-related needs and capabilities when such configurations appear out of context in an adult face" (p. 266). The ecological model, therefore, predicts that individuals will perceive and attribute childlike behavioral propensities and actions to baby-faced adults (Berry and McArthur 1986). The self-fulfilling prophecy (Rosenthal 1973) would then suggest that messages sent regarding these expectations would lead baby-faced individuals to develop the expected personality characteristics.

Height.   Generally, taller persons are perceived more favorably than shorter individuals (Patzer 1985). Martel and Biller claim that "men of tall and average height were seen as significantly more mature, uninhibited, positive, secure, masculine, active, complete, successful, optimistic, dominant, capable, confident, and outgoing than men of short height" (1987, 95). Taller individuals occupy higher-status social positions (Egolf and Corder 1991) and attain higher levels of education (Teasdale, Owen, and Sørensen 1991). Taller men are more likely to be hired (Hatfield and Sprecher 1986) and receive higher starting salaries (Frieze, Olson, and Good 1990) than short men, and men with partners more physically attractive than themselves averaged 2.6 inches taller than men with less attractive partners (Patzer 1985). In fact, the taller candidate won in all of the presidential elections from 1900 to 1968 (Hatfield and Sprecher 1986).

What processes may underlie these effects? First, taller people may actually be more able (Egolf and Corder 1991). Generally, the literature has shown a positive correlation between stature and intellectual ability of about .2 (Teasdale, Owen, and Sørensen 1991). There could be a genetic basis for this relationship (for instance, some of the genes for intelligence and height may reside on the same chromosome and thus be inherited together), or the association may come about through cross-associative mating, as people possessing a greater degree of one trait (intelligence or height) are married to spouses possessing a greater degree of the other. Other factors, such as nutrition, environment, or intrauterine effects, may also account for the height-intelligence connection. Second, the relationship between height and life success might be due to differential treatment of children who differ in stature: we may expect more from taller children, who thus become more competent (Egolf and Corder 1991). Finally, taller individuals may occupy higher-status positions simply because of the stereotype that they are more competent and interpersonally dominant (Frieze, Olson, and Good 1990).

Weight.   Almost half of women and about a third of men surveyed in studies are unhappy about their weight and the parts of their bodies associated with obesity (Hatfield and Sprecher 1986). College students "describe overweight men and women as lazy, sexless, ugly, self-indulgent and sloppy and . . . deny finding them admirable, attractive, neat or sexy" (Harris, Walters, and Waschull 1991, 1561). Moreover, the physical trait most often mentioned as "disgusting" was being fat (Hatfield and Sprecher 1986).[16] Studies of children have also "found that fat boys and girls were likeliest to be seen as cheating, argumentative, being teased a lot, forgetful, unhealthy, lying, sloppy, naughty, ugly, mean, dumb, dirty" (Lerner and Gellert 1969; cited in Hatfield and Sprecher 1986, 208).

It has been demonstrated that the obese apply these stereotypes to themselves (Crandall and Biernat 1990), as being overweight leads to a tendency for social withdrawal and a lack of self-confidence (see Villimez, Eisenberg, and Carroll 1986). Whites who are currently dating are significantly thinner and more satisfied with their bodies than those not involved in a relationship (Stake and Lauer 1987). These findings do not appear to hold for African Americans (Harris, Walters, and Waschull 1991), underscoring the fact that perception of weight is strongly tied to cultural norms.

Overweight people are underrepresented in college, although no differences were found with regard to academic criteria, social class, or admissions rates between obese and nonobese high school students (Pargman 1969). They must also rely more heavily on their own funds for education than do normal-weight students. Crandall (1991) suggests that the stereotype that the overweight have little self-control and are weak-willed and lazy could lead even the students' own parents to believe they are not good candidates for higher education. Overweight men have lower starting salaries than normal-weight men, and the salary differentials increase over time (Frieze, Olson, and Good 1990). In one study of occupational status, only 9 percent of top-level executives were obese, while fully 40 percent of the middle-level managers (who had half the income of the upper group) were overweight (Half 1974).

Many people justify prejudice against the obese with the belief that the overweight—unlike the short, homely, or physically handicapped—are responsible for their condition. Even physicians and student clerks at a public outpatient medical clinic described their overweight patients as "weak-willed" and "ugly" (Maddox and Liederman 1969). Studies by DeJong (1980), in fact, showed that when plausible reasons were given for a woman's obesity (i.e., a thyroid condition) she was not derogated and was better tolerated than when she had no "excuse."

Physical Disability

Erving Goffman uses the term *stigma* "to refer to an attribute that is deeply discrediting" (1963, 3). Physical disabilities, such as blindness, spinal cord injury, amputation, and deforming scars, as well as character defects and status characteristics, such as sex, race, and religion, can all be stigmas (Havranek 1991). Studies generally find that "normal" people hold negative attitudes regarding those with physical disabilities, who are generally viewed to be "sick, dependent, bitter, sinful, incompetent, asexual, accident prone, and nonproductive" (Chubon 1982, 25; Fichten and Amsel 1986). The disabled are discriminated against with regard to housing, employment, civil rights, transportation, and recreational and cultural activities (Christman and Slaten 1991).

Interaction between the able-bodied and the physically handicapped is "strained." Able-bodied people tend to terminate interaction sooner, behave in a more inhibited and overcontrolled manner, use fewer gestures, speak faster, ask fewer questions, and show less variability in their actions and behaviors in dealing with the disabled than when interacting with able-bodied peers (Fichten 1986). Handicapped children are less likely to have their top friendship choices reciprocated (Kleck and DeJong 1983).

The disabled also terminate interaction sooner, perceive that others' behavior toward them is influenced and affected by their disability (Strenta and Kleck 1985), and engage in less eye contact and

smile less often when interacting with the able-bodied (Comer and Piliavin 1972; Fichten 1986). The mere belief that one has a stigma or physical disability (even when it is concealed) can lead to the perception that others relate to us in a negative manner (Farina et al. 1971; Strenta and Kleck 1984) and may cause us to behave differently. The disabled view themselves more negatively than the able-bodied, presumably as a result of past "strained" interactions. Two groups of disabled subjects (one group visibly disabled and the other emotionally disabled) rated able-bodied individuals more highly than wheelchair-bound or emotionally disabled persons portrayed in videotapes (Zernitsky-Shurka 1988).

The Self-Fulfilling Prophecy, the Physical Self, and Interaction

Any interaction proceeds on the basis of both individuals' attitudes and expectations about the other, developed from past experience and physical cues. Symbolic interaction theory proposes that these expectations have the power to shape not only the interaction itself but the self-images of those engaging in it, through the process of altercasting and the operation of the self-fulfilling prophecy (Rosenthal 1973).

Consistent with these expectations, the effects of physical appearance go beyond the attitudes and behaviors of others: there are *real* differences between those of lower and higher levels of physical attractiveness. More attractive females are more independent and achievement-oriented, have greater endurance, are more self-accepting and more resistant to peer influence; more attractive males are more aggressive and dominant than their less attractive peers. In general, people who rate themselves as physically attractive also consider themselves more likeable, have higher self-esteem, are more confident and outgoing, and hold themselves in higher self-regard. The attractive also enjoy greater acceptance and popularity among their peers, have more friends, are more likely to marry, marry earlier in life, and among women marry "higher income-producing husbands." The beautiful have more social skills, better nonverbal communication skills, and greater influence over others. They also elicit greater aid and helping behavior from others (Patzer 1985).

There is also a direct correlation between students' attractiveness and their school grades and scores on standardized tests (Lerner and Lerner 1977). The explanation most often offered is the self-fulfilling prophecy: "If teachers expect different behavior from students of different physical attractiveness, the students sense these messages, process the subtle cues, and develop accordingly to conform to the expectations" (Patzer 1985, 57). The most definitive demonstration of how these processes work comes from Snyder et al. (1977), who gave male students a photograph of either an attractive or an unattractive woman and told them they would interact with her over an intercom for ten minutes. The women interactants were randomly selected college students whose attractiveness was unrelated to that of the woman shown in the picture. The men treated the "attractive" women more warmly and were more enthusiastic; as a result, women talking to those men behaved in a more friendly, sociable, and likeable manner. Thus, the women's behavior confirmed the men's expectations based on the physical attractiveness stereotype.

The effects of appearance have even been shown to affect internal physiology. While results are not entirely conclusive, young women of lower physical attractiveness had significantly higher levels of blood pressure in some studies. These results may reflect the fact that the social environments of the homely and the beautiful differ; as argued by Patzer (1985), "It is a pleasant, forgiving, supportive world for the latter and the opposite for the former" (p. 116).

Distinctiveness, Appearance, and Self-Concept

Earlier we discussed the role of social context in moderating the effects of male and female hormones. Social context also affects how our outward appearance structures the behavior and attitudes of the self and other. As has been argued by Hewitt (1984), "The person is . . . a complex reality—an enduring object as well as one constituted from moment to moment . . . To introduce order into this reality we must pay attention particularly to the relationships between the situated and biographical aspects of the person" (p. 114). Two factors, relevancy and distinctiveness, determine which subset of identities we enact in a given situation, making up what is known as the situated self (Hewitt 1988). For example, when a black woman interacts with a black man she is likely to think of herself as a woman; when she interacts with a white woman she might be more likely to be aware of herself as being black (Michener, DeLamater, and Schwartz 1990). There appears to be a cultural tendency in the West to establish oneself as unique and qualitatively different from others in an interaction, and aspects of self-concept that are distinctive in a social setting are more likely to enter into the situated self (McGuire and McGuire 1982). Cota and Dion (1986) found, for instance, that subjects placed in three-person groups with two people of the other sex were more likely to list gender as an aspect of self-concept than were subjects in single-sex groups. Sixth-graders were much more likely to list age, birthplace, hair color, eye color, or weight when that feature placed them in a minority among their classmates or when they differed significantly from the class average (McGuire and Padawer-Singer 1976).

The impact of the distinctiveness of characteristics such as physical handicap, obesity, or extreme height must also be considered. What might be the consequences not only of having a particular physical characteristic, but of having it be salient most of the time to self and others? Height will not assume the centrality in self-concept for a six-foot-eight Dinka tribesman in Africa (where the average height is six feet, one inch) as it will for a man of the same ancestry in the streets of New York.

Summary

We have discussed the relationship between various aspects of physical appearance—physical attractiveness, facial appearance, disability, height, and weight—and their effects on judgments of personality, attitudes, behavior, and social interaction. Unfortunately, while we know a person's appearance has important effects on others' behaviors and attitudes, and theories such as symbolic interactionism help us understand *how* these effects come about, we are still in the dark as to *why* people make inferences based on physical appearance. As noted in the previous section, there seems to be a natural tendency for people to construct boundaries and to discriminate based on perceived group membership (see Tajfel 1982). Results of studies in which people are divided into groups on the basis of arbitrary and meaningless criteria have shown a consistent bias to favor anonymous members of one's own group over anonymous out-group members. But an evolutionary basis still needs a psychological mechanism.

Tajfel and Turner (1986) explain this bias on the basis of a need to preserve a positive self-concept. Since our individual identity is partly made up of many group identities, the more positively we evaluate our groups, the more positively we will evaluate ourselves. Applying Tajfel's social identity theory of intergroup behavior to explain bias in physical appearance, we can see why people would naturally favor physical attributes similar to their own. It is also possible that groups in power use this rather natural categorizing tendency to denigrate those they dominate, as a justification for their actions.

Unfortunately, these explanations do not help us understand why the beautiful are so positively favored. Given the fact that most of us lack the physical attributes typically found in models on the cover of *GQ* or in the *Sports Illustrated* swimsuit issue, it would seem contrary to our own sense of self-worth to hold the beautiful in such high regard. Similarly, "the beautiful people" are not, per se, in power and thus able to impose their standards on others.

Some have argued that it is merely a matter of asthetics, that is, we generally prefer what is beautiful. Studies by several researchers (see Cunningham 1986) note, in fact, that at any time in a par-

ticular culture there is a great deal of agreement among men and women about which facial and body features of the opposite sex (e.g., size of eyes, body proportions, shape of nose) are more attractive and appealing. Another explanation comes from the social exchange literature. As Sigall and Landy (1973) argue, a man seen walking with an extremely attractive woman is likely to receive more attention and prestige than a man with an unattractive woman, and vice versa. Hence, we anticipate greater rewards from associating with beautiful people. Finally, authors such as Dion et al. (1972) argue for an attractiveness stereotype— "what is beautiful is good." In this interpretation, other rewards are assumed to follow from associating with beautiful people.

A HEURISTIC MODEL FOR INTERACTION INFLUENCED BY BIOLOGICAL PROCESSES

Figure 1.1 on p. 28 summarizes the arguments presented in this chapter. We present this diagram as a heuristic device to structure thinking and research about the interplay of biological and social forces in socialization and interaction. Some important features of the diagram include, first, that this process is completely symmetrical. As the term *social interaction* suggests, this process occurs *between* individuals and is as much a product of the genetic endowment, personality, outward appearance, abilities, behaviors, expectations, norms, and stereotypes of the first participant as it is of the second. It is a dynamic process, evolving and changing over time, between contexts, and within the course of the interaction—a model that explicitly rejects a snapshot view of the interactive process.

Second, all of the aspects of self—from the physical self through abilities and personality to expectations and stereotypes—are seen to be influenced by genetic endowment, the environment of socialization, and time. The ordering (from left to right for person one, the reverse for person two) is intentional; genetic endowment has the most to do with our achieved physical selves and the least to do with the development of expectations, norms, and stereotypes. Our perceptions of the other per-

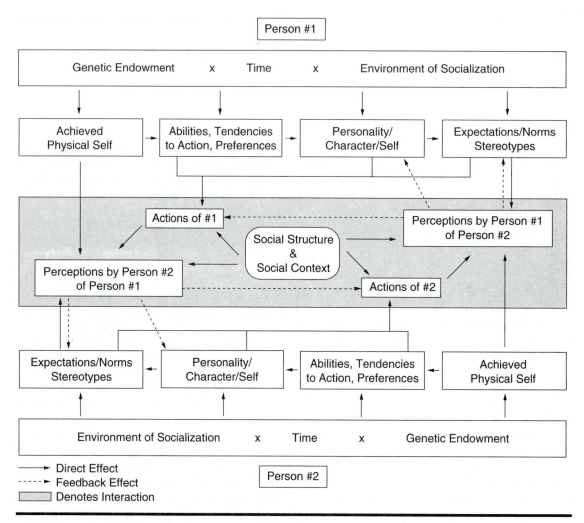

FIGURE 1.1   The interaction of biology and socialization.

son are affected by his or her observable actions and physical appearance, in interaction with our expectations and stereotypes and the social context. Those perceptions, in addition to our own personal characteristics and, again, the social context, directly affect our actions. There is, of course, feedback from the interaction to our own self-concept, expectations, stereotypes, and so on in addition to our perceptions of the other, and there are attempts to "altercast" the other as the kind of person we perceive him/her to be. (These have

been omitted from the diagram to keep it readable.) Social structure and aspects of the immediate social setting also affect the interaction and, through feedback, one's self-concept and expectations. The critical difference between this diagram of interaction and many others that could be drawn is the explicit inclusion of genetic and biological factors, both as elements of the initiation of action and as factors in the stimulus value of the other in those interactions. To illustrate the model, we briefly discuss one topic that clearly involves both biology "from the inside out" and biology "from the outside in"—puberty.

PUBERTY: THE IMPACT OF BIOLOGICAL CHANGES AND LIFESPAN TRANSITIONS

Caspi (1987) describes movement over the life course as a sequence of interactions of personality with social transitions and age-graded roles functioning within historically changing environments. These age-stratified roles constitute a basis for self-identity and the identification of others in interaction. Caspi and colleagues (see, for example, Caspi, Bem, and Elder 1989; Caspi and Moffitt 1991) developed this interactional framework to discuss the impact of personality over the life course, but we believe it can also be used to illustrate how biology affects social interaction over the life course. The process of puberty and the period of adolescence provides probably the most striking example.

Puberty is a very particular type of transition, involving major physiological and psychological changes. Along with changes in hormonal output and body size and shape as well as the development of secondary sex characteristics, the onset of puberty brings significant increases in cognitive functioning and a set of social problems and issues unique to adolescence (Tobin-Richards, Boxer, and Petersen 1983).17 Using our model, these changes have multiple effects. Changes in a child's achieved physical self and abilities affect the perceptions of others and what they expect in interactions with him/her. They also affect the child's personality, including sexual interests, self-concept, and expectations for self and how others will behave.

How the adolescent copes with these changes in many ways depends on the timing of these events, which in our model is an interaction between personal time and the social setting. Neugarten (1970) has argued that when major events are "off-time," or out of step with established societal timetables, a crisis may develop. Consequently, entry into adolescence may or may not lead to turmoil, depending on the timing and syn-

chronization of events (Tobin-Richards, Boxer, and Petersen 1983).

Personality development differs among early, medium, and late maturers, and the pattern of relationships is different for boys and girls. Early-developing boys and girls start dating earlier, perceive themselves as more popular with the opposite sex, and in some ways "act older" than their later-maturing peers (Simmons and Blyth 1987). Beyond that, early maturation is a mixed blessing for girls. The experience of menarche is frequently perceived as negative (Greif and Ulman 1982), particularly for girls with stressful childhood experiences (Caspi and Moffitt 1991) and early maturers. Girls who mature, and often date, earlier have poorer school performance and achievement test scores and rate themselves as more likely to cause school behavioral problems (Simmons and Blyth 1987). Cross-national studies have found that early-maturing girls are at greatest risk for delinquency and deviant behavior at school (Caspi et al. 1993). Early-developing girls may have greater involvement with boys, which distracts them from their school work, or late developers may compensate for a lack of popularity with boys by devoting more time and energy to their school work (Simmons and Blyth 1987). As might be expected, early-maturing girls have problems with body image (Tobin-Richards, Boxer and Petersen 1983).

Advantages of early maturing include popularity with the other sex, being allowed a greater degree of independence from parents, and parent and teacher expectations for older behavior and long-range career planning (Simmons and Blyth 1987). As adults, early-developing girls continue to perceive themselves as more popular and to date more; however, school problems, including greater deviance and less academic success, also tend to persist (Caspi et al. 1993).

In contrast, early maturation has no downside for boys (Simmons and Blyth 1987; Tobin-Richards, Boxer, and Petersen 1983). Late-maturing boys are at a competitive disadvantage in athletic activities and are treated as immature by others. This, in turn, can lead to negative self-conceptions, heightened feelings of rejection, prolonged dependent needs, and a rebellious attitude toward parents and other adults. Attitudes held by late-maturing boys can also interfere with the process of identification with parents, which may inhibit or delay the acquisition of mature attitudes and personality characteristics generally established through parental identification (Mussen, Conger, and Kagan 1979). These differences between early- and late-maturing boys tend to carry over into adulthood. Mussen and colleagues (1979; Mussen and Jones 1957) found, for example, that late-developing boys make poorer vocational choices, which consequently affect adult employment and later life chances.

Brooks-Gunn and Warren (1989) have argued that differences in behavior, emotion, and personality associated with puberty and adolescence may have a hormonal or biological foundation. The authors showed that negative affect increased during the most rapid rises in hormone levels, although hormones accounted for only 4 percent of the variance in negative affect. Social factors and the interaction between negative life events and pubertal factors explained much more of the variance in negative affect than hormonal levels.

How can our diagram help us understand these timing effects? The early-maturing boy (largely determined by genetic factors) develops a "mature" appearance and different urges (more interest in sex) before he is "ready" in chronological age. Others respond by treating him as more mature than he is: girls show sexual interest, coaches pursue him, teachers expect more of him. Being "altercast" in that role, his self-concept changes to become that more mature person, developing leadership skills, athletic abilities, and social skills with the other sex. The early-maturing girl, on the other hand, experiences more mixed messages based on her changed appearance: others treat her in terms of their expectations for adult women, which all too often involve devaluing her intellect, treating her like a sex object, and suggesting that sports are no longer appropriate. Similarly, early sexual behavior, seen as "manly" in a boy, is seen as a "problem" in a girl, so a twelve-year-old boy and a twelve-year-old girl behaving the same way are perceived very differently by others. No wonder early maturation has mixed effects for girls but positive ones for boys.

It is our hope that no one who has read this chapter ever will again use the phrases "nature versus nurture" or "heredity versus environment." These dualities that separate the physical from the mental and behavioral in Western culture no longer help us make sense of our social behavior. We are animals, with a physical and behavioral makeup that has evolved from those of our primate ancestors, in an environment of evolutionary adaptedness that is no longer ours. Perhaps most critical in that inheritance is our nature as social beings, and it is in the social arena that our genetic and cultural heritage interact to produce our social perceptions, social bonds, and self-concepts. Our genetic makeup (and our physiological state as it relates to our sex hormones) affects our selection of social settings, our social skills and abilities, and our impulses and desires, as well as our stimulus value to others, although in no sense does it *determine* them. Social interaction is thus inextricably linked to our biological natures. To deny our biology is to deny ourselves.

NOTES

We would like to thank Alice Rossi (who, although anonymous, was obviously she) and an anonymous reviewer for detailed suggestions on a ninety-nine-page version; Troy Vincent for asking perceptive questions as one of us discussed the problems of reconceptualizing the chapter; Avshalom Caspi, Anjie Emeka, Chris Fassnacht, Pam LePore, and Elliot Sober for reading and commenting on a seventy-page version; and, finally, the editors, particularly Gary Fine, for all their help.
1. For evidence that there is a growing concern with integrating biology into social psychology, note a special issue of the *Journal of Social Issues* (volume 47, 1991)

on evolutionary psychology, a special issue of the *Journal of Personality* (volume 58, 1990) on biology and personality, Kemper's *Social Structure and Testosterone* (1990), and Lancaster et al.'s *Parenting across the Life Span: Biosocial Dimensions* (1987).

2. These are issues for theorists of stratification rather than for social psychologists. Thus we will deal only with the effects of biological "givens" on interaction *per se,* avoiding discussion of access to settings and statuses.

3. In addition, males are expected to engage in more r-like behaviors than are females, since females must invest more in each child than males, from the moment of conception. These inherently differing reproductive strategies between men and women are relevant to sex differences in courtship, marriage, and childrearing behaviors.

4. There is never anything inevitable about the action of genes. No reputable biologist would ever suggest that one's genes *determine* one's outward characteristics in a one-on-one mapping.

5. There are many other approaches, as well. See, for example the work of ethologists Eibl-Eibesfeldt (1989) and Smith (1982).

6. Men are also more interested in erotica than are women (Shepher and Reisman 1985), more likely to engage in sexual deviance (Davison and Neale 1982), and, cross-culturally, more interested in having sex (Marshall 1971; Messenger 1971). Women select men more for their ability to provide support, while men select women for their reproductive potential (Buss and Barnes 1986; Cunningham 1986). Kenrick and Trost (1989) point out that some gender differences also vary by the nature of the desired relationship.

7. These authors do not claim that human rape is merely the consequence of biological factors (i.e., the relationship to inclusive fitness) but do want us to consider such factors in addition to social and psychological factors.

8. This topic has been politically sensitive as applied to humans, however (see, for example, Scarr 1987), and there is no doubt that the potential for misuse of this information by those determined to make distinctions between recognizable human groups (by race, class, gender) remains. See Plomin, DeFries, and McClearn (1990) for a thorough presentation of behavioral genetics.

9. Based on more than thirty twin studies of IQ involving more than ten thousand twin pairs, as well as adoption research, the best guess at a heritability coefficient—the proportion of variance in a trait attributable to genetic sources—for IQ is 50 percent. Hence, given possible sources of error, it can be confidently concluded that 30 to 70 percent of variation in intellectual abilities is hereditary (Bouchard and McGue 1981). The heritability of natural athletic talent, adaptability to training, and even the psychological makeup needed to compete successfully in sport has also been demonstrated (Cowart 1987).

10. Plomin (1990) states that in fourteen studies involving more than 18,000 close relatives of schizophrenics, their risk of the disease was 8 percent (eight times greater than the base rate in the population) and 30 percent for identical twins. Both simple depression and bipolar affective psychosis have strong hereditary components as well, with the former having stronger relationships than the latter.

11. It is important to point out that heritability must be assessed within populations and within environments that are more or less variable. The absolute proportion of variance attributable to genetics and environment is always in relationship to the extent to which each of those factors varies (see Plomin, Chipuer, and Loehlin 1990; Plomin and Rende 1991).

12. Although there has been argument regarding this point, Scarr and Carter-Saltzman (1980) and Morris-Yates et al. (1990) have provided compelling evidence that this assumption is essentially correct.

13. This is related to the difference between statistical analyses of mean differences as opposed to correlations. It has, for example, been shown that poor African American children adopted into middle-class white families show a large average increase in IQ (Scarr and Weinberg 1976). Across the group of adoptees, however, childrens' IQ scores are only randomly related to those of their adoptive families, while they are significantly related to the scores of their biological parents. The improved educational environment raises the average level but does not significantly reorder the children in relationship to the intelligence of their adoptive parents.

14. Gitlin and Pasnau (1989) summarized the current state of evidence regarding all of these, and in 1980 Friedman et al. reviewed menstrual cycle effects.

15. Testosterone levels have been related to personality characteristics of dominance, friendliness, masculinity-femininity, and "expansiveness." (Baucom, Besch, and Callahan 1985; Hermida, Halberg, and del Pozo 1985; Udry and Talbert 1988).

16. There also seems to be stronger parental concern for girls with regard to issue of weight and obesity than for boys, suggesting that families and society place much greater pressures on girls to remain or become thin (Villimez, Eisenberg, and Carroll 1986).

17. While some have suggested that adolescence is a period of "storm and stress," others have argued that while some adolescents may find this period stressful, the majority do not (see Simmons and Blyth 1987).

REFERENCES

Adams, D. B., A. R. Gold, and A. D. Burt. 1978. Rise in female-initiated sexual activity at ovulation and its suppression by oral contraceptives. *New England Journal of Medicine* 229:1145–1150.

Adams, G. R. 1978. Racial membership and physical attractiveness effects on preschool teachers' expectations. *Child Study Journal* 8:29–41.

Ainsworth, M. D. 1973. The development of infant-mother attachment. Pp. 1–94 in *Review of Child Development Research,* vol. 3, ed. B. M. Caldwell and H. N. Riciutti. Chicago: University of Chicago Press.

Appleton, P. L. 1980. A factor analytic study of behavior groupings in young children. *Ethology and Sociobiology* 1:93–97.

Archer, J. 1991. Human sociobiology: Basic concepts and limitations. *Journal of Social Issues* 47:11–26.

Argyle, M., and M. Cook. 1976. *Gaze and Mutual Gaze.* Cambridge: Cambridge University Press.

Asch, S. E. 1946. Forming impressions of personality. *Journal of Abnormal and Social Psychology* 41: 258–290.

Backstrom, C. T., H. Boyle, and D. T. Baird. 1981. Persistence of symptoms of premenstrual tension in hysterectomized women. *British Journal of Obstetrics and Gynaecology* 88:530–536.

Bailey, J. M., and R. C. Pillard. 1991. A genetic study of male sexual orientation. *Archives of General Psychiatry* 48:1089–1096.

Baker, S. W. 1980. Psychosexual differentiation in the human. *Biology of Reproduction* 22:61–72.

Bancroft, J., D. Axworthy, and S. Ratcliffe. 1982. The personality and psycho-sexual development of boys with 47 XXY chromosome constitution. *Journal of Child Psychology and Psychiatry* 23:169–180.

Bancroft, J., D. W. Davidson, P. Warner, and G. Tyrer. 1980. Androgens and sexual behavior in women using oral contraceptives. *Clinical Endocrinology* 12:327–340.

Baucom, D. H., P. K. Besch, and S. Callahan. 1985. Relation between testosterone concentration, sex role identity, and personality among females. *Journal of Personality and Social Psychology* 48:1218–1226.

Bernal, J. 1972. Crying during the first 10 days of life and maternal responses. *Developmental Medicine and Child Neurology* 14:362–372.

Berry, D. S., and S. Brownlow. 1989. Were the physiognomists right? Personality correlates of facial babyishness. *Personality and Social Psychology Bulletin* 15:266–279.

Berry, D. S., and L. Z. McArthur. 1986. Perceiving character in faces: The impact of age-related craniofacial changes in social perception. *Psychological Bulletin* 100:3–18.

Berry, D. S., and L. Z. McArthur. 1988. What's in a face? Facial maturity and the attribution of legal responsibility. *Personality and Social Psychology Bulletin* 14:23–33.

Berscheid, E., and E. Walster. 1974. Physical attractiveness. Pp. 158–216 in *Advances in Experimental Social Psychology,* vol. 7, ed. L. Berkowitz. New York: Academic Press.

Beyene, Y. 1992. Menopause: A biocultural event. Pp. 169–177 in *Menstrual Health in Women's Lives,* ed. A. J. Dan and L. L. Lewis Urbana: University of Illinois Press.

Blurton-Jones, N. B. 1967. An ethological study of some aspects of social behaviour of children in nursery school. Pp. 437–463 in *Primate Ethology,* ed. D. Morris. Chicago: Aldine.

Blurton-Jones, N. B. 1972. Categories of child-child interaction. Pp. 97–127 in *Ethological Studies of Child Behaviour,* ed. N. B. Blurton-Jones. London: Cambridge University Press.

Booth, A., and J. M. Dabbs, Jr. 1993. Testosterone and the quality of men's marriages. *Social Forces,* 72: 462–477.

Bouchard, T. J., and M. McGue. 1981. Familial studies of intelligence: A review. *Science* 212:1055–1059.

Bowlby, J. 1958. The nature of the child's tie to his mother. *International Journal of Psycho-Analysis* 39:350–373.

Brooks, J., D. Ruble, and A. Clark. 1977. College women's attitudes and expectations concerning menstrual-related changes. *Psychosomatic Medicine* 39:288–298.

Brooks-Gunn, J., and M. P. Warren. 1989. Biological and social contributions to negative affect in young adolescent girls. *Child Development* 60:40–55.

Brownmiller, S. 1975. *Against Our Will: Men, Women, and Rape.* New York: Bantam.

Buss, D. M. 1989. Conflict between the sexes: Strategic interference and the evocation of anger and upset. *Journal of Personality and Social Psychology* 56: 735–747.

Buss, D. M., and M. Barnes. 1986. Preferences in human mate selection. *Journal of Personality and Social Psychology* 50:559–570.

Cantor, N., and W. Mischel. 1979. Prototypes in person perception. Pp. 3–52 in *Advances in Experimental Social Psychology,* vol. 12, ed. L. Berkowitz. New York: Academic.

Cash, T. F., and R. N. Kilcullen. 1985. The aye of the beholder: Susceptibility to sexism and beautyism in the evaluation of managerial applicants. *Journal of Applied Social Psychology* 15:591–605.

Caspi, A. 1987. Personality and the life course. Special Issue: Integrating personality and social psychology. *Journal of Personality and Social Psychology* 53:1203–1213.

Caspi, A., D. J. Bem, and G. H. Elder. 1989. Continuities and consequences of interactional styles across the life course. Special issue: Long-term stability and change in personality. *Journal of Personality* 57:375–406.

Caspi, A., D. Lynam, T. E. Moffitt, and P. A. Silva. 1993. Unraveling girls' delinquency: Biological, dispositional, and contextual contributions to adolescent misbehavior. *Developmental Psychology* 29:19–30.

Caspi, A., and T. E. Moffitt. 1991. Individual differences are accentuated during periods of social change: The sample case of girls at puberty. *Journal of Personality and Social Psychology* 61:157–168.

Christman, L. A., and B. L. Slaten. 1991. Attitudes toward people with disabilities and judgements of employment potential. *Perceptual and Motor Skills* 72:467–475.

Chubon, R. A. 1982. An analysis of research dealing with the attitudes of professionals toward disability. *Journal of Rehabilitation* 48:25–29.

Comer, R. J., and J. A. Piliavin. 1972. The effects of physical deviance upon face-to-face interaction: The other side. *Journal of Personality and Social Psychology* 23:33–39.

Conan Doyle, Sir Arthur. 1930. A study in scarlet. *The Complete Sherlock Holmes.* New York: Doubleday.

Cota, A. A., and K. L. Dion. 1986. Salience of gender and sex composition of ad hoc groups: An experimental test of distinctiveness theory. *Journal of Personality and Social Psychology* 50: 770–776.

Cowart, V. 1987. How does heredity affect athletic performance? *The Physician and Sportsmedicine* 15: 134–140.

Crandall, C. S. 1991. Do heavy-weight students have more difficulty paying for college? *Personality and Social Psychology Bulletin* 17:606–611.

Crandall, C. S., and Biernat, M. 1990. The ideology of anti-fat attitudes. *Journal of Applied Social Psychology* 23:227–243.

Cunningham, M. R. 1986. Measuring the physical in physical attractiveness: Quasi-experiments on the sociobiology of female facial beauty. *Journal of Personality and Social Psychology* 50:925–935.

Dabbs, J. M., Jr. 1992. Testosterone and occupational achievement. *Social Forces* 70:813–824.

Dabbs, J. M., R. L. Frady, T. S. Carr, and N. F. Besch. 1987. Saliva testosterone and criminal violence in young adult prison inmates. *Psychosomatic Medicine* 49:174–182.

Dabbs, J. M., Jr., and Morris, R. 1990. Testosterone, social class, and antisocial behavior in a sample of 4,462 men. *Psychological Science* 1:209–211.

Dabbs, J. M., Jr., R. B. Ruback, R. L. Frady, C. H. Hopper, and D. S. Sgoutas. 1988. Saliva testosterone and criminal violence among women. *Personality and Individual Differences* 9:269–275.

Dalton, K. 1964. *The Premenstrual Syndrome.* Springfield, IL: Charles C. Thomas.

Dalton, K. 1976. Prenatal progesterone and educational attainments. *British Journal of Psychiatry* 129:438–442.

Daly, M., and M. I. Wilson. 1981. Abuse and neglect of children in an evolutionary perspective. Pp. 405–416 in *Natural Selection and Social Behavior,* ed. R. D. Alexander and D. W. Tinkle. New York: Chiron.

Dan, A. J., and L. L. Lewis, eds. 1992. *Menstrual Health in Women's Lives.* Urbana: University of Illinois Press.

Darwin, C. 1896. *The Expression of the Emotions in Man and Animals.* New York: Appleton.

Davidson, J., and E. Robertson. 1985. A followup study of postpartum illness. *Acta Psychiatrica Scandinavica* 71:451–457.

Davison, G. C., and J. M. Neale. 1982. *Abnormal Psychology,* 3rd ed. New York: Wiley.

Dawkins, R. 1976. *The selfish gene.* New York: Oxford University Press.

Deitz, S. R., and I. E. Byrnes. 1981. Attribution of responsibility for sexual assault: The influence of observer empathy and defendant occupation and attractiveness. *Journal of Psychology* 108:17–29.

DeJong, W. 1980. The stigma of obesity: The consequences of naive assumptions concerning the causes of physical deviance. *Journal of Health and Social Behavior* 21:75–87.

Dershowitz, A. M. 1975. Karyotype, predictability, and culpability. Pp. 63–71 in *Genetics and the Law,* ed. A. Milunsky and G. J. Annas. New York: Plenum.

Dew, M. A. 1985. The effect of attitudes on inferences of homosexuality and perceived physical attractiveness in women. *Sex Roles* 12:143–155.

Dion, K., E. Berscheid, and E. Walster [Hatfield]. 1972. What is beautiful is good. *Journal of Personality and Social Psychology* 24:285–290.

Dion, K. L., and K. K. Dion. 1987. Belief in a just world and physical attractiveness stereotyping. *Journal of Personality and Social Psychology* 52:775–780.

Dunbar, R. I. M. 1987. Sociobiological explanations and the evolution of ethnocentrism. Pp. 48–59 in *The Sociobiology of Ethnocentrism,* ed. V. Reynolds, V. Falger, and I. Vine. London: Croom Helm.

Dunn, J., and C. Kendrick. 1982. Siblings and their mothers: Developing relationships within the family. Pp. 39–60 in *Sibling Relationships: Their Nature and Significance Across the Lifespan,* ed. M. E. Lamb and B. Sutton-Smith. Hillsdale, NJ: Erlbaum.

Eagly, A. H., R. D. Ashmore, M. G. Makhijani, and L. C. Longo. 1991. What is beautiful is good, but . . . : A meta-analytic review of research on the physical attractiveness stereotype. *Psychological Bulletin* 110:109–128.

Egolf, D. B., and L. E. Corder. 1991. Height difference of low and high job status, female and male corporate employees. *Sex Roles* 24:365–373.

Eibl-Eibesfeldt, I. 1979. Ritual and ritualization from a biological perspective. Pp. 3–55 in *Human Ethology: Claims and Limits of a New Discipline,* ed. M.

von Cranach, K. Foppa, W. Lepenies, and D. Ploog. Cambridge: Cambridge University Press.

Eibl-Eibesfeldt, I. 1989. *Human Ethology.* New York: Aldine de Gruyter.

Ekman, P., ed. 1972. *Emotion in the Human Face,* 2nd ed. Cambridge: Cambridge University Press.

Ellis, R. J., J. M. Olson, and M. P. Zanna. 1983. Stereotypic personality inferences following objective versus subjective judgments of beauty. *Canadian Journal of Behavioural Science* 15:35–42.

Eysenck, H. J. 1990. Genetic and environmental contributions to individual differences: The three major dimensions of personality. *Journal of Personality* 58:245–261.

Eysenck, H. J., and S. B. G. Eysenck. 1975. *Manual for the Eysenck Personality Questionnaire.* San Diego: Educational and Industrial Testing Service.

Farina, A., D. Gliha, L. A. Boudreau, J. G. Allen, and M. Sherman. 1971. Mental illness and the impact of believing others know it. *Journal of Abnormal Psychology* 77:1–5.

Fausto-Sterling, A. 1985. *Myths of Gender.* New York: Basic Books.

Feild, H. S. 1979. Rape trials and jurors' decisions: A psycholegal analysis of the effects of victim, defendant, and case characteristics. *Law and Human Behavior* 3:261–284.

Fichten, C. S. 1986. Self, other and situation-referent automatic thoughts: Interaction between people who have a physical disability and those who do not. *Cognitive Therapy and Research* 10:571–587.

Fichten, C. S. and R. Amsel. 1986. Trait attributions about physically disabled college students: Circumplex analyses and methodological issues. *Journal of Applied Social Psychology* 16:410–427.

Flint, M. 1982. Male and female menopause: A cultural put-on. Pp. 362–375 in *Changing Perspectives on Menopause,* ed. A. M. Voda, M. Dinnerstein, and S. R. O'Donnell. Austin: University of Texas Press.

Fridlund, A. J., P. Ekman, and H. Oster. 1987. Facial expressions of emotion. Pp. 143–224 in *Nonverbal Behavior and Communication,* ed. A. W. Siegman, and S. Feldstein. Hillsdale, NJ: Erlbaum.

Friedman, R. C., S. W. Hurt, M. S. Arnoff, and J. Clarkin. 1980. Behavior and the menstrual cycle. *Signs: Journal of Women in Culture and Society* 5:719–738.

Frieze, I. H., J. E. Olson, and D. C. Good. 1990. Perceived and actual discrimination in the salaries of male and female managers. *Journal of Applied Social Psychology* 20:46–67.

Frieze, I. H., J. E. Olson, and J. Russell. 1991. Attractiveness and income for men and women in management. *Journal of Applied Social Psychology* 21:1039–1057.

Frieze, I. H., J. E. Parsons, P. B. Johnson, D. N. Ruble, and G. L. Zellman, eds. 1978. *Women and Sex Roles: A Social Psychological Perspective.* New York: Norton.

Frodi, A. M., and M. E. Lamb. 1978. Sex differences in responsiveness to infants: A developmental study of psychophysiological and behavioral responses. *Child Development* 49:1182–1188.

Fullard, W., and A. Reiling. 1976. An investigation of Lorenz's "babyness." *Child Development* 47:1191–1193.

Gath, D. H. 1980. Psychiatric aspects of hysterectomy. In *The Social Consequences of Psychiatric Illness,* ed. L. Robins, P. J. Clayton, and J. K. Wing. New York: Brunner/Mazel.

Gitlin, M. J., and R. O. Pasnau. 1989. Psychiatric syndromes linked to reproductive function in women: A review of current knowledge. *American Journal of Psychiatry* 146:1413–1422.

Goffman, E. 1963. *Stigma: Notes on the Management of Spoiled Identity.* Englewood Cliffs, NJ: Prentice Hall.

Goldberger, A. 1979. Heritability. *Economica* 46:327–347.

Goodall, J. 1971. Some aspects of aggressive behavior in a group of free-living chimpanzees. *International Social Science Journal* 23:89–97.

Gove, W. R., and G. R. Carpenter. 1982. *The Fundamental Connection between Nature and Nurture.* Lexington, MA: D. C. Heath.

Greif, E. B., and K. J. Ulman. 1982. The psychological impact of menarche on early adolescent females: A review of the literature. *Child Development* 53:1413–1430.

Groth, N. A., and H. J. Birnbaum. 1979. *Men Who Rape.* New York: Plenum Press.

Halbreich, U., and J. Endicott. 1985. Relationship of dysphoric premenstrual changes to depressive disorders. *Acta Psychiatrica Scandinavica* 71:331–338.

Half, R. 1974. Pay of fat executives is found leaner than checks of others. *New York Times,* January 2, 12.

Handley, S. L., T. L. Dunn, G. Waldron, and J. M. Baker. 1980. Tryptophan, cortisol and puerperal mood. *British Journal of Psychiatry* 136:498–508.

Harris, M. B., L. C. Walters, and S. Waschull. 1991. Gender and ethnic differences in obesity-related behaviors and attitudes in a college sample. *Journal of Applied Social Psychology* 21:1545–1566.

Hatfield, E., and S. Sprecher. 1986. *Mirror, Mirror: The Importance of Looks in Everyday Life.* Albany: State University of New York Press.

Havranek, J. E. 1991. The social and individual costs of negative attitudes toward persons with physical disabilities. *Journal of Applied Rehabilitation Counseling* 22:15–21.

Hermida, R. C., F. Halberg, and F. del Pozo. 1985. Chronobiologic pattern discrimination of plasma hormones, notably DHEA-S and TSH, classifies an expansive personality. *Chronobiologia* 12:105–136.

Hewitt, J. P. 1984. *Self and Society: A Symbolic Interactionist Social Psychology,* 3rd ed. Boston: Allyn and Bacon.

Hewitt, J. P. 1988. *Self and Society: A Symbolic Interactionist Social Psychology,* 4th ed. Boston: Allyn and Bacon.

Hold-Cavell B. C. L., and D. Borsutzky. 1986. Strategies to obtain high regard: Longitudinal study of a group of preschool children. *Ethology and Sociobiology* 7:39–56.

Holden, C. 1987. Research news: The genetics of personality. *Science* 237:598–601.

Holden, C. 1992. Twin study links genes to homosexuality. *Science* 255:33.

Hooper, E. M., L. M. Comstock, J. M. Goodwin, and J. S. Goodwin. 1980. Patient characteristics that influence physician behavior. Paper presented at the National Meeting of the American Federation for Clinical Research, Washington, D.C.

Imperato-McGinley, J., R. E. Terson, T. Gautier, and E. Sturla. 1979. Androgen and the evolution of male-gender identity among male pseudohermaphrodites with 5a-reductase deficiency. *New England Journal of Medicine* 300:1233–1237.

Jencks, C. 1980. Heredity, environment, and public policy reconsidered. *American Sociological Review* 45:723–736.

Jirari, C. G. 1970. Form perception, innate form preference, and visually mediated head-turning in the human neonate. Unpublished Ph.D. diss. University of Chicago. Pp. 69, 72–73 in Lumsden, C. J., and E. O. Wilson. *Genes, Mind, and Culture: The*

Coevolutionary Process. Cambridge, MA: Harvard University Press.

Kalick, S. M. 1988. Physical attractiveness as a status cue. *Journal of Experimental Social Psychology* 24:469–489.

Kemper, T. D. 1990. *Social Structure and Testosterone: Explorations of the Socio-Bio-Social Chain.* New Brunswick, NJ: Rutgers University Press.

Kendell, R. E., J. C. Chalmers, and C. Platz. 1987. Epidemiology of puerperal psychoses. *British Journal of Psychiatry* 150:662–673.

Kendrick, K. M., F. Levy, and E. B. Keverne. 1992. Changes in the sensory processing of olfactory signals induced by birth in sheep. *Science* 256:833–836.

Kenrick, D. T., and M. R. Trost. 1989. Reproductive exchange model of heterosexual relationships. Pp. 92–118 in *Review of Personality and Social Psychology,* vol. 10, C. Hendrick ed. Newbury Park, CA: Sage.

Kessler, R. C., K. S. Kendler, A. Heath, M. C. Neale, and L. J. Eaves. 1992. Social support, depressed mood, and adjustment to stress: A genetic epidemiologic investigation. *Journal of Personality and Social Psychology* 62:257–272.

Kleck, R. E., and W. DeJong. 1983. Physical disability, physical attractiveness, and social outcomes in children's small groups. *Rehabilitation Psychology* 28:79–91.

Kleinke, C. L., and R. A. Staneski. 1980. First impressions of female bust size. *The Journal of Social Psychology* 110:123–134.

Koeske, R. D. 1982. Toward a biosocial paradigm for menopause research: Lessons and contributions from the behavioral sciences. Pp. 3–23. in *Changing Perspectives on Menopause,* ed. A. M. Voda, M. Dinnerstein, and S. R. O'Donnell. Austin: University of Texas Press.

Kramp, J. L. 1968. Studies on the premenstrual syndrome in relation to psychiatry. *Acta Psychiatrica Scandinavica* 203 (suppl):261–267.

Lancaster, J. 1985. Evolutionary perspectives on sex differences in the higher primates. Pp. 3–28 in *Gender and the Life Course,* ed. A. S. Rossi. New York: Aldine.

Lancaster, J. B., J. Altmann, A. S. Rossi, and L. R. Sherrod, eds. 1987. *Parenting across the Life Span: Biosocial Dimensions.* Hawthorne, NJ: Aldine.

Lenington, S. 1981. Child abuse: The limits of sociobiology. *Ethology and Sociobiology* 2:17–29.

Lerner, R. M., and E. Gellert. 1969. Body build identification, preference, and aversion in children. *Developmental Psychology* 1:456–462.

Lerner, R. M., and J. V. Lerner. 1977. Effects of age, sex, and physical attractiveness on child-peer relations, academic performance, and elementary school adjustment. *Developmental Psychology* 13:585–590.

LeVay, S. 1991. A difference in hypothalamic structure between heterosexual and homosexual men. *Science* 253:1034–1037.

Liggett, J. C. 1974. *The Human Face.* New York: Stein & Day.

Lightcap, J. L., J. A. Kurland, and R. L. Burgess. 1982. Child abuse: A test of some predictions from evolutionary theory. *Ethology and Sociobiology* 3:61–67.

Loehlin, J. C. 1989. Partitioning environmental and genetic contributions to behavioral development. *American Psychologist* 44:1285–1292.

Logue, C. M., and R. H. Moos. 1986. Perimenstrual symptoms: Prevalence and risk factors. *Psychosomatic Medicine* 48:388–414.

Lumsden, C. J., and E. O. Wilson. 1982. *Genes, Mind, and Culture: The Coevolutionary Process.* Cambridge, MA: Harvard University Press.

Lykken, D. T., M. McGue, T. J. Bouchard, and A. Tellegen. 1990. Does contact lead to similarity or similarity to contact? *Behavior Genetics* 20:547–561.

Lykken, D. T., M. McGue, and A. Tellegen. 1987. Recruitment bias in twin research: The rule of two-thirds reconsidered. *Behavior Genetics* 17:343–362.

Maddox, G. L., and U. Leiderman. 1969. Overweight as a social disability with medical implications. *Journal of Medical Education* 44:210–220.

Marshall, D. S. 1971. Sexual behavior on Mangaia. Pp. 103–16 in *Human Sexual Behavior: Variations in the Ethnographic Spectrum,* ed. D. S. Marshall, and R. C. Suggs. New York: Basic Books.

Martel, L. F., and H. B. Biller. 1987. *Stature and Stigma: The Biopsychological Development of Short Males.* Lexington, MA: D. C. Heath.

Martin, N. G., L. J. Eaves, A. R. Heath, R. Jardine, L. M. Feingold, and H. J. Eysenck. 1986. Transmission of social attitudes. *Proceedings of the National Academy of Science* 83:4364–4368.

Masica, D., J. Money, and A. A. Ehrhardt. 1971. Fetal feminization and female gender identity in the testicular feminizing syndrome of androgen insensitivity. *Archives of Sexual Behavior* 1:131–142.

Matthews, K. A., C. D. Batson, J. Horn, and R. H. Rosenman. 1981. "Principles in his nature which interest him in the fortune of others . . .": The heritability of empathic concern for others. *Journal of Personality* 49:237–247.

Matthews, K. A., R. R. Wing, L. H. Kuller, E. N. Meilahn, S. F. Kelsey, E. J. Costello, and A. W. Caggiula. 1990. Influences of natural menopause on psychological characteristics and symptoms of middle-aged healthy women. *Journal of Consulting and Clinical Psychology* 58:345–351.

Mazur, A., and T. A. Lamb. 1980. Testosterone, status, and mood in human males. *Hormones and Behavior* 14:236–246.

McArthur, L. Z., and R. M. Baron. 1983. Toward an ecological theory of social perception. *Psychological Review* 90:215–238.

McArthur, L. Z., and D. S. Berry. 1987. Cross-cultural agreement in perceptions of babyfaced adults. *Journal of Cross-Cultural Psychology* 18: 165–192.

McGuire, W. J., and C. McGuire. 1982. Significant others in self-space: Sex differences and developmental trends in the social self. Pp. 71–76 in *Psychological Perspectives on the Self,* vol. 1, ed. J. Suls. Hillsdale, NJ: Erlbaum.

McGuire, W. J., and A. Padawer-Singer. 1976. Trait salience in the spontaneous self-concept. *Journal of Personality and Social Psychology* 33: 743–754.

Mednick, S. A., W. F. Gabrielli, and B. Hutchings. 1984. Genetic influences in criminal convictions: Evidence from an adoption cohort. Science 224: 891–894.

Meltzoff, A. N. 1985. The roots of social and cognitive development: Models of man's original nature. Pp. 1–30 in *Social Perception in Infants,* ed. T. M. Field and N. A. Fox. Norwood, NJ: Ablex.

Messenger, J. C. 1971. Sex and repression in an Irish folk community. Pp. 3–37 in *Human Sexual Behavior: Variations in the Ethnographic Spectrum,* ed. D. S. Marshall and R. C. Suggs. New York: Basic Books.

Meyer-Bahlburg, H. F. 1981. Androgens and human aggression. Pp. 109–123 in *The Biology of Aggression,* ed. P. F. Brain, and D. Benton. Rockville, MD: Sijthoff & Nordhoff.

Michener, H. A., J. D. DeLamater, and S. H. Schwartz. 1990. *Social Psychology.* Chicago: Harcourt Brace Jovanovich.

Money, J., and A. A. Ehrhardt. 1972. *Man and Woman; Boy and Girl.* Baltimore: Johns Hopkins University Press.

Money, J., and M. Schwartz. 1977. Dating, romantic and nonromantic friendships, and sexuality in 17 early-treated adrenogenital females, aged 16–25. Pp. 419–431 in *Congenital Adrenal Hyperplasia,* ed. P. A. Lee, L. P. Plotnick, A. A. Kowarski, and C. J. Migeon. Baltimore: University Park Press.

Morgan, G. A., and H. N. Ricciuti. 1973. Infants' response to strangers during the first year. Pp. 1128–1138 in *The Competent Infant: Research and Commentary,* ed. L. J. Stone, H. T. Smith, and L. B. Murphy. New York: Basic Books.

Morris-Yates, A., G. Andrews, P. Howie, and S. Henderson. 1990. Twins: A test of the equal environments assumption. *Acta Psychiatrica Scandinavica* 81:322–326.

Murray, A. D. 1979. Infant crying as an elicitor of parental behavior: An examination of two models. *Psychological Bulletin* 86:191–215.

Mussen, P. H., J. J. Conger, and J. Kagan. 1979. *Child Development and Personality.* New York: Harper & Row.

Mussen, P. H., and M. C. Jones. 1958. The behavior-inferred motivations of late- and early-maturing boys. *Child Development* 29:61–67.

Mussen, P. H., and M. C. Jones. 1957. Self-conceptions, motivations, and interpersonal attitudes of late- and early-maturing boys. *Child Development* 28: 243–256.

Neugarten, B. L. 1970. Time, age, and the life cycle. *American Journal of Psychiatry* 136:887–894.

Nolen-Hoeksema, S. 1988. Life-span views on depression. Pp. 203–241 in *Life-Span Development and Behavior,* vol. 9, ed. P. B. Baltes, D. L. Featherman and R. M. Lerner. Hillsdale, NJ: Erlbaum.

Olweus, D. 1980. Familial and temperamental determinants of aggressive behavior in adolescent boys: A causal analysis. *Developmental Psychology* 16: 644–660.

Ostwald, P. 1963. *Soundmaking: The Acoustic Communication of Emotion.* Springfield, IL: Charles C. Thomas.

Pargman, D. 1969. The incidence of obesity among college students. *Journal of School Health* 39: 621–627.

Parlee, M. B. 1973. The premenstrual syndrome. *Psychological Bulletin* 80:454–465.

Patzer, G. L. 1985. *The Physical Attractiveness Phenomena.* New York: Plenum.

Pellegrini, A. D. 1989. What is a category? The case of rough-and-tumble play. *Ethology and Sociobiology* 10:331–341.

Perry, A. 1973. The effect of heredity on attitudes toward alcohol, cigarettes, and coffee. *Journal of Applied Psychology* 58:275–277.

Persky, H., H. I. Lief, D. Strauss, W. R. Miller, and C. P. O'Brien. 1978. Plasma testosterone level and sexual behavior of couples. *Archives of Sexual Behavior* 7:157–173.

Plomin, R. 1990. The role of inheritance in behavior. *Science* 248:183–188.

Plomin, R., H. M. Chipuer, and J. C. Loehlin. 1990. Behavioral genetics and personality. Pp. 225–243 in *Handbook of Personality Theory and Research,* ed. L. A. Pervin. New York: Guilford.

Plomin, R., R. Corley, J. C. DeFries, and D. W. Fulker. 1990. Individual differences in television viewing in early childhood: Nature as well as nurture. *Psychological Science* 1:371–377.

Plomin, R., and D. Daniels. 1987. Why are children in the same family so different from one another? *Behavioral and Brain Sciences* 10:1–16.

Plomin, R., J. C. DeFries, and G. E. McClearn. 1990. *Behavioral Genetics: A Primer,* 2nd ed. New York: Freeman.

Plomin, R., and R. Rende. 1991. Human behavioral genetics. *Annual Review of Psychology* 42:161–190.

Porter, R. H. 1987. Kin recognition: Functions and mediating mechanisms. Pp. 175–204 in *Sociobiology and Psychology,* ed. C. Crawford, M. Smith, and D. Krebs. Hillsdale, NJ: Erlbaum.

Rada, R. T. 1978. *Clinical Aspects of the Rapist.* New York: Grune & Stratton.

Rosenthal, R. 1973. The pygmalion effect lives. *Psychology Today* 7:56–63.

Rossi, A. S. 1991. Research on physical attractiveness. Unpublished notes.

Ruble, D. N. 1977. Premenstrual symptoms: A reinterpretation. *Science* 197:291–292.

Rushton, J. P. 1989. Genetic similarity, human altruism, and group selection. *Behavioral and Brain Sciences* 12:503–559.

Rushton, J. P., D. W. Fulker, M. C. Neale, D. K. B. Nias, and H. J. Eysenck. 1986. Altruism and aggression: The heritability of individual differences. *Journal of Personality and Social Psychology* 50:1192–1198.

Russell, J. A. 1991. Culture and the categorization of emotions. *Psychological Bulletin* 110:426–450.

Sagi, A., and M. Hoffman. 1976. Empathic distress in the newborn. *Developmental Psychology* 12:175–176.

Scarr, S. 1966. Genetic factors in activity motivation. *Child Development* 37:663–673.

Scarr, S. 1987. Three cheers for behavior genetics: Winning the war and losing our identity. *Behavior Genetics* 17:219–228.

Scarr, S., and L. Carter-Saltzman. 1980. Twin method: Defense of a critical assumption. *Behavior Genetics* 9:527–542.

Scarr, S., and R. A. Weinberg. 1976. IQ test performance of black children adopted by white families. *American Psychologist* 31:726–739.

Scarr, S., and R. A. Weinberg. 1978. Attitudes, interests, and IQ. *Human Nature* 1:29–36.

Schachter, S. 1951. Deviance, rejection, and communication. *Journal of Abnormal and Social Psychology* 46:190–207.

Scherer, K. R., R. P. Abeles, and C. S. Fischer. 1975. *Human Aggression and Conflict: Interdisciplinary Perspectives.* Englewood Cliffs, NJ: Prentice Hall.

Schiavi, R. C., A. Theilgaard, D. R. Owen, and D. White. 1988. Sex chromosome anomalies, hormones, and sexuality. *Archives of General Psychiatry* 45:19–24.

Shepher, J., and J. Reisman. 1985. Pornography: A sociobiological attempt at understanding. *Ethology and Sociobiology* 6:103–114.

Shields, W. M., and L. M. Shields. 1983. Forcible rape: An evolutionary perspective. *Ethology and Sociobiology* 4:115–136.

Sigall, H., and D. Landy. 1973. Radiating beauty: The effects of having a physically attractive partner on person perception. *Journal of Personality and Social Psychology* 28:218–224.

Simmons, R. G., and D. A. Blyth. 1987. *Moving into Adolescence: The Impact of Pubertal Chance and School Context.* New York: Aldine De Gruyter.

Sloane, E. 1985. *Biology of Women,* 2nd ed. New York: Delmar.

Smith, P. K. 1982. Functional and evolutionary aspects of animal and human play. *Behavioral and Brain Sciences* 5:139–184.

Smith, P. K., and K. Lewis. 1985. Rough-and-tumble play, fighting, and chasing in nursery school children. *Ethology and Sociobiology* 6:175–181.

Snyder, M., E. Tanke, and E. Berscheid. 1977. Social perception and interpersonal behavior: On the self-fulfilling nature of social stereotypes. *Journal of Personality and Social Psychology* 35: 656–666.

Solomon, S., and L. Saxe. 1977. What is intelligent, as well as attractive, is good. *Personality and Social Psychology Bulletin* 3:670–673.

Sommer, B. 1975. The effect of menstruation on cognitive and perceptual motor behavior: A review. *Psychosomatic Medicine* 35:515–534.

Stake, H., and M. L. Lauer. 1987. The consequences of being overweight: A controlled study of gender differences. *Sex Roles* 17:31–47.

Stone, L., H. Smith, and L. Murphy, eds. 1973. *The Competent Infant.* New York: Basic Books.

Strenta, A. C., and R. E. Kleck. 1984. Physical disability and the perception of social interaction: It's not what you look at but how you look at it. *Personality and Social Psychology Bulletin* 10: 279–288.

Strenta, A. C., and R. E. Kleck. 1985. Physical disability and the attribution dilemma: Perceiving the causes of social behavior. *Journal of Social and Clinical Psychology* 3:129–142.

Sumner, W. G. 1906. *Folkways.* New York: Ginn.

Swaab, D. F., and M. A. Hofman. 1990. An enlarged suprachiasmatic nucleus in homosexual men. *Brain Research* 537:141–148.

Tajfel, H. 1974. Social identity and intergroup behaviour. *Social Science Information* 13:65–93.

Tajfel, H. 1982. Social psychology of intergroup relations. *Annual Review of Psychology* 33:1–39.

Tajfel, H., and J. Turner. 1986. The social identity theory of intergroup behavior. Pp. 7–24 in *Psychology of Intergroup Relations,* 2nd ed, ed. S. Worchel and W. G. Austin. Chicago: Nelson-Hall.

Teasdale, T. W., D. R. Owen, and T. I. A. Sørensen. 1991. Intelligence and educational level in adult males at extremes of stature. *Human Biology* 63: 19–30.

Theilgaard, A. 1984. A psychological study of the personalities of XYY- and XXY-men. *Acta Psychiatrica Scandinavica* 69 (suppl):1–133.

Thornhill, R., and N. W. Thornhill. 1983. Human rape: An evolutionary analysis. *Ethology and Sociobiology* 4:137–173.

Thornton, B. 1977. Effect of rape victim's attractiveness in a jury simulation. *Personality and Social Psychology Bulletin* 3:666–669.

Tobin-Richards, M. H., A. M. Boxer, and A. C. Petersen. 1983. The psychological significance of pubertal change: Sex differences in perceptions of self during adolescence. Pp. 127–154 in *Girls at Puberty,* ed. J. Brooks-Gunn and A. C. Petersen. New York: Plenum.

Trivers, R. L. 1972. Parental investment and sexual selection. Pp. 136–179 in *Sexual Selection and the Descent of Man: 1871–1971,* ed. B. Campbell. Chicago: Aldine.

Udry, J. R. 1988. Biological predispositions and social control in adolescent sexual behavior. *American Sociological Review* 53:709–722.

Udry, J. R. 1989. *Biosocial Models of Adolescent Behavior Problems.* Unpublished manuscript, University of North Carolina, Chapel Hill. In Dabbs, J. M., Jr., and R. Morris. 1990. Testosterone, social class, and antisocial behavior in a sample of 4,462 men. *Psychological Science* 1:209–211.

Udry, J. R., and L. M. Talbert. 1988. Sex hormone effects on personality at puberty. *Journal of Personality and Social Psychology* 54:291–295.

Unger, R. K., M. Hilderbrand, and T. Madar. 1982. Physical attractiveness and assumptions about social deviance: Some sex-by-sex comparisons. *Personality and Social Psychology Bulletin* 8: 293–301.

van der Dennen, J. M. G. 1987. Ethnocentrism and ingroup/out-group differentiation: A review and interpretation of the literature. Pp. 1–47 in *The Sociobiology of Ethnocentrism,* ed. V. Reynolds, V. Falger, and I. Vine. London: Croom Helm.

Villimez, C., N. Eisenberg, and J. L. Carroll. 1986. Sex differences in the relation of children's height and weight to academic performance and others' attributions of competence. *Sex Roles* 15:667–681.

Voda, A. M., M. Dinnerstein, and S. R. O'Donnell, eds. 1982. *Changing Perspectives on Menopause.* Austin: University of Texas Press.

Waller, N. G., B. A. Kojetin, T. J. Bouchard, D. T. Lykken, and A. Tellegen. 1990. Genetic and environmental influences on religious interests, attitudes, and values: A study of twins reared apart and together. *Psychological Science* 1:138–142.

Wilson, E. O. 1975. *Sociobiology: The New Synthesis.* Cambridge, MA: Harvard University Press.

Wrong, D. 1961. The oversocialized conception of man in modern sociology. *American Sociological Review* 26:183–193.

Yalom, I. D., R. Green, and N. Fisk. 1973. Prenatal exposures to female hormones: Effect on psychosexual development in boys. *Archives of General Psychiatry* 28:554–561.

Yalom, I. D., D. T. Lunde, R. H. Moos, and D. A. Hamburg. 1968. "Postpartum blues" syndrome. *Archives of General Psychiatry* 18:16–27.

Zernitsky-Shurka, E. 1988. Ingroup and outgroup evaluation by disabled individuals. *Journal of Social Psychology* 128:465–472.

CHAPTER 2

Self and Identity

VIKTOR GECAS
PETER J. BURKE

Self and identity have been central concerns of a sociological social psychology at least since the writings of G. H. Mead (1934), C. H. Cooley (1902), and the early interactionists in the 1920s and 1930s. In these writings, the self is essentially social in nature, anchored in language, communication, and social interaction. Increasingly, this focus on the social context of the self has expanded to include social structural and historical influences, particularly where "identity" is the aspect of self under consideration.

While interest in the self has remained steady in sociology over the past fifty years, it has waxed and waned in psychological social psychology.[1] Since the mid-1970s, interest in the self and self-related phenomena have become major concerns in psychological social psychology as a consequence of the "cognitive revolution" and the "crisis of confidence" precipitated by the discovery of "demand characteristics" and other self processes inadvertently operating in experimental studies (Hales 1985). As a result, many of the major psychological social psychology theories either have become self-theories or have been modified to take self-processes into account (see Gecas 1982, 1989 for reviews).

The increased interest in self phenomena in psychological social psychology and the continuing focus on the self in sociological social psychology has led to some convergences between these two traditionally separate branches of social psychology. This is particularly evident in discussions of labeling and attribution processes, impression management and identity negotiations, and self and emotions. In general, however, sociological social psychology and psychological social psychology remain largely separate and distinct in their orientations toward the study of the self. Sociologists are still much more likely to be interested in the social contexts within which selves develop and the processes by which the self is affected. Psychologists are much more likely to focus on intrapsychic processes and on the consequences of self-phenomena for behavior.[2]

The literature on the self is extensive in social psychology and extends into clinical psychology, cultural anthropology, and political science. Our emphasis in this chapter is on developments in sociological social psychology, but we will also consider some of the major trends in psychological social psychology and anthropology, particularly as they intersect with sociological concerns. We begin with some definitional and conceptual clarifications, then briefly discuss the major social psychological perspectives on self and identity. We then proceed from micro to macro considerations, specifically from discussions of various self-components and self-processes (e.g., self-esteem, identities, self-consistency) to examinations of how social structure, culture, and history affect self and identity.

DEFINITIONS AND DISTINCTIONS

To facilitate the discussion that follows, we offer definitions and distinctions between several key concepts: self, self-concept, identity, and personality. The concept of self essentially refers to the *process* of reflexivity that emanates from the interplay between the "I" and the "Me." Reflexivity or self-awareness refers to humans' ability to be both subjects and objects to themselves. Reflexivity is a special form of consciousness, a consciousness of oneself, which is frequently considered the quintessential feature of the human condition (Mead 1934; Smith 1978).

While the core of the self is the process of reflexivity, the concept of self is often used generically to encompass all of the *products* or consequences of this reflexive activity. It would be more accurate to refer to the latter as the "self-concept" or the phenomenal self (Gecas 1982). The self-concept can be thought of as the sum total of the individual's thoughts and feelings about him/herself as an object (Rosenberg 1979). It involves a sense of spatial and temporal continuity of the person (Smith 1978; R. H. Turner 1968) and a distinction of essential self from mere appearance and behavior (R. H. Turner 1976). It is composed of various identities, attitudes, beliefs, values, motives, and experiences, along with their evaluative and affective components (e.g., self-efficacy, self-esteem) in terms of which individuals define themselves.[3]

Much of the content of self-concepts can be discussed in terms of identities. *Identity* refers to who or what one is, to the various meanings attached to oneself by self and others. In sociology, the concept of identity refers both to self-characterizations individuals make in terms of the structural features of group memberships, such as various social roles, memberships, and categories (Stryker 1980), and to the various character traits an individual displays and others attribute to an actor on the basis of his/her conduct (Alexander and Wiley 1981; Goffman 1959, 1963). In a sense, identity is the most public aspect of self. As Stone (1962) observed, identity locates a person in social space by virtue of the relationships and memberships that it implies.

Last, we need to distinguish between self and personality. If personality generally refers to the various psychological traits, motivations, dispositions, and styles or patterns of thinking and feeling

(Singer and Kolligian 1987), then self is that part of personality that is aware of itself and defines itself in terms of these qualities. Even though self can be viewed as a subset of personality, the different intellectual histories and traditions associated with the two concepts (sociology versus clinical psychology) have resulted in quite different emphases and orientations: "personality theory" is still largely equated with "trait theory," emphasizing early formation and relative permanence of traits (Pervin 1985); "self theory" is more likely to emphasize the social, interactional, and changeable qualities of the self. However, there is a blurring of these historical differences as personality psychologists have increasingly turned to the study of self-processes (see Singer and Kolligian 1987) and as the "social structure and personality" area has become more prominent within sociological social psychology.

SOCIAL PSYCHOLOGICAL PERSPECTIVES ON SELF AND IDENTITY

Social psychological perspectives on self and identity can be characterized by four general orientations: (1) situational, which emphasizes the emergence and maintenance of the self in situated (typically face-to-face) interaction; (2) social structural, which focuses on the consequences of role relationships and other structural features of social groups; (3) biographical-historical, which focuses on the self as a cultural and historical construction; and (4) intrapersonal, focusing on processes within self and personality affecting behavior. The first three of these orientations are primarily sociological and build on the legacy of Mead, Cooley, James, and the early interactionists. The emphasis on meaning, its maintenance in communication and social interaction, and its relevance for the concepts of self and identity are evident in each orientation. Also evident in each is the methodological requirement to take the actor's perspective into account, and all three subscribe to some version of the interactionist proposition that self reflects society.

But there are also substantial differences in emphasis and approach between these orientations.

The *situational approach* takes as its subject matter the *process* of social interaction in naturally occurring social situations. Developed by Blumer (1969) and elaborated by Becker (1964), Strauss (1978), Stone (1962), and especially Goffman (1959, 1963, 1967) in what has come to be called the Chicago school of symbolic interactionism, the focus is on how individuals go about "defining the situations" and thereby constructing the realities in which they live. A critical aspect of these situational definitions is the establishment or construction of the relevant identities of the interactants. Identity construction is viewed as problematic, often involving considerable negotiation (Strauss 1978), bargaining (Blumstein 1973), role taking (R. H. Turner 1962), impression management (Goffman 1959), and altercasting (Weinstein and Deutschberger 1963). Goffman's (1959, 1963, 1967) influential development of this approach describes in considerable detail the "staging operations" involved in our presentations of self in everyday life, the outcomes of which are rarely certain, sometimes resulting in embarrassment and shame over "spoiled identities" and usually requiring elaborate rituals of deference and demeanor for the maintenance and protection of "face" or valued identity. Identities are social fictions created out of this symbolic milieu, but they are highly valued fictions having real consequences for the interactants and the course of the interaction. Money, power, love, esteem, or other resources may be at stake.

Research on the self based on the situational approach has favored observational or field studies, preferably participant observation. The best way to know what is going on in "natural" interaction settings, it is claimed, is to be part of the action, or at least to observe it at close range (for recent examples, see Fine 1987; Lyng 1990). While there is a preference for naturalistic methods in the situational approach to the self, occasionally experimental methods are used. Alexander's (and Knight 1971; and Wiley 1981) work on "situated identity theory" and Blumstein's (1973) work on identity bargaining are two successful attempts to bring into the laboratory some of Goffman's ideas about self-presentation and the bases of making

identity attributions. This shift to the laboratory as the setting for studying specific aspects of the situated self is particularly evident in psychological social psychology (see, especially, Snyder 1987, on self-monitoring; Tedeschi 1981, on impression management).

The situational approach to the self has contributed to our understanding of the interpersonal processes and personal strategies involved in identity formation, to our understanding of the processes involved in socialization in various subcultures ("normal" and "deviant"), and to the development of "labeling theory" in sociology. It continues to be a viable and popular approach to the self.

In contrast to the situational approach, the *structural approach* developed through two other schools of symbolic interactionism. The first, the Iowa school developed by Kuhn and his students, has advocated survey methods, objective measures, and quantitative analyses of self-concepts (Meltzer and Petras 1970). Kuhn's work emphasized structural as opposed to processual conceptions of self and society and viewed behavior not as emergent and nondeterministic in the manner of Blumer, but as determined by antecedent variables having to do with aspects of the self as well as with historical, developmental, and social conditions (Kuhn 1964). To understand the self as both cause and consequence, Kuhn and McPartland developed the Twenty Statements Test (TST) as a technique for measuring the self (Kuhn and McPartland 1954). This instrument has been widely used in studies of identities and self-structures (see Gordon 1968).

The second, growing out of the Iowa school, is the Indiana school of structural symbolic interaction as developed by Stryker and his colleagues into what has come to be called "identity theory" (Stryker 1980). While the Iowa school moved the study of self and identity into the realm of quantitative survey methods, its focus on the TST as the primary measurement instrument necessarily limited its development. The Indiana school and identity theory pushed the study of self and identity further in this direction and paid more attention to the links between self and society. By developing the concept of self as composed of a hierarchical set of identities, each of which was tied to roles within the social structure, the link between self and society was made more explicit (Stryker 1980). More recently, Burke (1991a, 1991b) has been developing a cybernetic control model of identities and procedures for measuring them, thus extending identity theory beyond its symbolic interactionist roots. The program of research generated by this approach is discussed later in the chapter.

The *biographical-historical approach* to self and identity has many similarities with the situational and structural approaches, with an emphasis on communication, meaning, and the symbolic nature of the self. But its scope is the broadest of the three: it brings in temporal considerations at the personal (as biography) and societal (as history) levels and is concerned with the larger cultural context within which selves are constructed. Insights from Mead and the interactionists are combined with those from Weber (1958) and Mills (1959) to provide the theoretical foundation for studying the intersections of culture, history, and biography. This approach to the self in sociology (e.g., Hewitt 1989; Perinbanayagam 1991; Schwalbe 1983) is also found in cultural anthropology (Geertz 1973) and parts of psychology on the fringes of the mainstream (Baumeister 1987; Gergen 1984).

A major focus of this approach is language as text or narrative, out of which self-concepts are constructed and through which they are justified and maintained. Biographies are studied as life stories that reflect the disposition, intent, and memory of the storyteller and, like history, are often rewritten. The biographical approach to the self is concerned with how individuals make sense of their lives and give continuity and coherence to their sense of self and the words they use to tell their life stories (Gergen and Gergen 1988; Shotter and Gergen 1989). The larger cultural context is viewed as the major determinant of these personal accounts, by structuring experiences of self and providing the "language" for their expression.[4]

This approach, like much of the situational approach, is antipositivistic in its orientation to

the self, particularly by practitioners who favor hermeneutics, constructivism, textual analysis, or other qualitative or interpretive methodologies. Much of this orientation is evident in cultural studies, feminist scholarship, and what has come to be called "postmodernist" literature on the self (Agger 1991).

The fourth perspective on self and identity might be termed the *intrapersonal* approach, in contrast to the prior three, which are interpersonal perspectives. Much of the current work in this approach is being done by psychological social psychologists. Indeed, studies of self-processes play a large part in the cognitive framework that has swept psychology in the last dozen years. The focus of this work is on the mechanisms and processes within the self that influence the individual's behavior (e.g., Greenwald and Pratkanis 1984). For example, Markus's (1977) notion of self-schemas characterizes the self as a cognitive structure consisting of organized elements of information about the self. The function of self-schemas is to recognize, interpret, and process self-relevant information in the situation. Some primary focal points of research in this perspective are on the self as an information processor (Kihlstrom and Cantor 1984), the self as an agent guiding actions that enhance and/or maintain self-esteem (Tesser 1986), and the self as an agent guiding behavior that serves to verify one's self-concept (Swann 1990). Within each of these focal points various theories and perspectives on the motives, motivations, and inner workings of the self have been developed, and a vast amount of empirical research has been generated based primarily on laboratory experiments.

SELF-DYNAMICS

While past writings gave much more attention to the self as a product of social influences than as a force (Rosenberg 1981), that gap is narrowing. Increasingly, the self is conceptualized and studied as a force affecting individual functioning, social interaction, and the surrounding environment (see Markus and Wurf 1987 for a review). Developments that reflect an emphasis on the active self include: (1) increased attention on the motivational aspects of the self (e.g., the self-esteem motive, self-efficacy motive, self-consistency/verification/congruence motives, and identities as sources of motivation); (2) increased emphasis on the defenses employed by the self to protect, enhance, or assert a particular self-conception, reflected in research on self-presentation, impression management, and various perceptual and cognitive distortions; and (3) increased interest in emotions and their connection with self-cognitions and behavior. In this section, we examine some of these developments dealing with the dynamic self-concept.

Identity Theories and Processes

At least since Foote's (1951) seminal article on identification as a basis for a theory of motivation, the concept of identity has provided a fertile ground for theories of self-dynamics.[5] Foote argued that individuals have multiple identities and that one's identities are active agents which influence one's behavioral choices. In this way, identities provide behavior with meaning, goals, and purpose.

Stone (1962) built on Foote's idea of identity and the process of identification by distinguishing between identification *of* (i.e., distinguishing between various persons and positions in society) and identification *with* (i.e., taking on an identity). Identification of persons and positions is accomplished largely through appearance and is a crucial, negotiated aspect of any definition of the situation. Stone also made a strong argument for separating the notion of self from identity. In his view, *identity* is not a substitute word for *self* but denotes a situatedness of the person in terms of standing in the context of a particular social relationship or group.

McCall and Simmons (1966) extended the structurally situated nature of identities. They introduced the term *role-identity,* the character and the role an individual devises *as an occupant of a particular social position,* thereby linking social structures to persons. In this way the multifaceted nature of the self (each facet being an identity) is tied to the multifaceted nature of society.

Building on McCall and Simmons's (1966) concept of role-identity, Stryker (1980, 1991) developed *identity theory,* in which the self is seen as a hierarchical ordering of identities, differentiated on the basis of salience (the probability of activating a given identity in a situation) and commitment (the number and affective strength of ties to others as a result of having a particular role-identity). Identity hierarchies have consequences for behavioral choices, variable consistency of individual action across situations, and variable resistance of individuals to change in the face of changing circumstances. Stryker's basic theory is fairly simple. The greater one's commitment premised on an identity, the greater will be the salience of the identity (Stryker 1980, 1991; Stryker and Serpe 1982). In turn, the salience of an identity directly influences the behavioral choices made among available choices in any given situation.

Burke (1980; Burke and Reitzes 1981, 1991) extended identity theory with a cybernetic control model and developed measurement procedures to capture the content and meaning of identities. In this framework, the connection between identity and behavioral choices became more explicit. Persons modify, adjust, and negotiate their behavior and its meanings to control reflected appraisals (i.e., meaningful feedback) to make them more congruent with and verify the meanings of their identities. In more recent work (Burke and Freese 1989), the control of resources, in addition to meanings, is viewed as playing an important role in understanding social behavior. In this formulation, identities become the linchpins holding together more macro social structural (resource) processes and more micro (symbolic) processes. With regard to measurement, Burke and Tully (1977) developed the use of the semantic differential to provide quantitative measurements of the meanings that comprise identities. This led to an active research program to develop and test theoretical ideas and hypotheses about the link between identities and behavior (e.g., Burke 1989; Burke and Hoelter 1988; Burke and Reitzes 1981; Serpe 1991; Stryker and Serpe 1982).

Heise (1985) framed a cybernetic theory of identity and identity processes, which he called *affect control theory*. This theory focuses on the motivational and emotional antecedents and consequences of social actions resulting from the relationship of these actions to the identity of the person, the setting, and objects of the action. In many ways similar to the work of Burke (above), an identity is conceptualized in terms of a set of meanings or affective responses. Unlike Burke's model, however, affect control theory uses only the three general dimensions of affective responses—evaluation, potency, and activity—which correspond to the social dimensions of status, power, and expressivity. An important aspect of affect control theory is that it is developed in interactional terms and thus shows the relationship between different actors and the actions in which each engages (in contrast to Stryker and Burke, above, who focus primarily on the identity-based actions of one individual at a time). By dealing with the full interactional situation, the full cybernetic control features of the model and the implications of that model for ongoing interaction are more readily apparent (see chapter 5 for a more extensive discussion).

Situated identity theory builds on the earlier work of Goffman (1959) and Stone (1962) but differs with regard to the question of how people will make choices among possible behaviors in any given situation. The theory was formulated to predict choices among normatively defined action alternatives. Alexander and Wiley (1981) suggest that perceived events and activities are processed and encoded to establish, confirm, or display identities. A long history of experimentation has shown that people are sensitive to the identity implications of most social settings and that by knowing the identities of those involved in the situation, people can predict the behaviors that will be displayed (see Alexander and Wiley 1981). In this way, situated identity theory seems to be a forerunner of affect control theory in indicating which behaviors and expectations are consistent with which identities and in showing how these change depending on others in the situation as well as past activity.

A primarily European entry to identity theorizing is *social identity theory,* developed by Tajfel (1981) and his colleagues (Abrams and Hogg 1990). This theory emphasizes group membership and belongingness and their consequences for interpersonal and intergroup relations. Social identity theory grew out of social categorization theory (J. C. Turner 1985), which deals with the propensity to perceive self and others as members of groups and social categories (e.g., "I am an American"). Groups into which we categorize others (often to their disadvantage) have relevance for our own social identity (Wilder 1986). For example, Tajfel (1982) points out that in the process of searching for a positive sense of self, persons compare their group with relevant other groups and act to create a favorable distinction between the groups, sometimes with negative consequences for intergroup relations (e.g., conflict and discrimination).

Self-Esteem

Self-esteem refers to the evaluative and affective aspects of the self-concept, to how "good" or "bad" we feel about ourselves (Gecas 1982; Rosenberg 1979). It is by far the most popular aspect of self-concept studied and for years was almost synonymous with "self-concept." For example, Wylie's (1979) monumental reviews of the self-concept literature deal almost exclusively with self-esteem. McGuire (1984) observes, and laments, that 90 percent of self-concept research is devoted to this single dimension.

The popularity of self-esteem is due largely to its perceived salutary consequences for individual functioning and to the perceived strength and pervasiveness of the self-esteem motive (i.e., the motivation to maintain or enhance one's favorable view of self). In the minds of many (scholars as well as the general public), high self-esteem has come to be associated with numerous "good" outcomes for individuals (e.g., academic achievement, popularity, personal success, health, and happiness), while low self-esteem is associated with various "bad" outcomes (e.g., delinquency, academic failure, and depression). For example, the California Task Force to Promote Self-Esteem and Personal and Social Responsibility (1990, 4) concludes: "Self-esteem is the likeliest candidate for a social vaccine, something that empowers us to live responsibly and that inoculates us against the lures of crime, violence, substance abuse, teen pregnancy, child abuse, chronic welfare dependency, and educational failure. The lack of self-esteem is central to most personal and social ills plaguing our state and nation."

Research on self-esteem gives a much more qualified and equivocal picture. While there is a tendency for self-esteem to be associated with some positive outcomes, the relationships tend to be modest, often mixed or insignificant, and specific to certain variables and conditions (Gecas 1982; Rosenberg 1981; Wells and Marwell 1976; Wylie 1979).[6] Explanations for the low associations and mixed results are common to much of the research in social psychology: problems of measurement (validity and reliability); problems of conceptualization (relating a global variable to a specific behavioral outcome); failure to control for other, confounding variables; and reliance on cross-sectional research designs (Demo 1985; Smelser 1989). Longitudinal studies are particularly valuable for understanding the relationship between self-esteem and problem behaviors, since the direction of influence can go either way. Rosenberg et al.'s (1989) analysis of the reciprocal relationships between self-esteem and three problems of youth (delinquency, poor school performance, and depression) found that low self-esteem fosters delinquency and delinquency enhances self-esteem (supporting Kaplan 1975), school performance has a greater effect on self-esteem than the reverse, and the causal relationship between self-esteem and depression is bidirectional. Even in this careful study, however, the associations, while significant, are not great.

There are reasons besides methodological shortcomings that make it difficult to determine the consequences of self-esteem. High self-esteem may be based on the individual's competence and effective performance, on reflected appraisals, or on

defensiveness and the need for social approval. These different sources of self-esteem could be expected to have different consequences for individual functioning (Franks and Marolla 1976; Gecas and Schwalbe 1983). There may also be an optimum level of self-esteem beyond which the consequences for individuals become negative (Gecas 1991; Wells and Marwell 1976, 69–73). Perhaps the greatest source of confounding effects in studies of self-esteem is the operation of the self-esteem motive, which is a major source (along with self-efficacy and congruency motives) of perceptual and cognitive bias, and the basis for many of the self's defense mechanisms.

The motivation to maintain and enhance a positive conception of oneself is a major dynamic of many contemporary self-theories (see Gecas 1982, 1991; Wells and Marwell 1976). Various self-theories suggest that people's self-conceptions are valued and protected and that a low self-evaluation (on criteria that matter) is an uncomfortable condition which people are motivated to avoid. This may occur through increased efforts at self-improvement or (more typically) through such self-serving activities as selective perception and cognition, various strategies of impression management, and restructuring the environment and/or redefining the situation to make it reflect a more favorable view of self (Greenwald 1980; Rosenberg 1979). These manipulations and distortions may indeed raise self-esteem, but sometimes at the price of self-deception (Alloy and Abramson 1979; Lewinsohn and Mischel 1980). We return to this theme in the section on defense mechanisms.

Self-Efficacy

Self-efficacy may be the most direct expression of the self-concept as a social force. Self-efficacy refers to the perception or experience of oneself as a causal agent in one's environment. There is a motivational component associated with self-efficacy, in that people typically seek to enhance their experience of self as efficacious. Much of the support for the self-efficacy motive comes from cognitive and developmental psychology, such as

Deci's (1975) theory of intrinsic motivation, and White's theory of "effectance motivation" (see Gecas 1989).

Cognitive theories of self-efficacy based on attribution and social learning theories place more emphasis on beliefs and perceptions of causality, agency, or control and less on the motivations to hold such beliefs. This is a matter of relative emphasis, however, since these beliefs have motivational implications. The self-attributions individuals make with regard to the extent of personal control over events that affect them have a wide range of behavioral consequences. Rotter's (1966) influential distinction between "internal" and "external" causal attributions spawned numerous studies of the consequences of these beliefs for individual functioning (Gecas 1989; Lefcourt 1976). Similarly, Bandura's (1977, 1986) work on self-efficacy beliefs has generated a great deal of research because of the motivational consequences of such beliefs for a wide range of individual functioning.

Ideas regarding the importance of self-efficacy can also be traced to several sociological traditions. Marx's (1844) theory of alienation emphasizes self-creation through efficacious action in the context of work activities. In the writings of Mead (1934) and the pragmatists of his day, action and its consequences are viewed as critical for the development of meaning, self, and society. The concept of "I" in Mead's reflexive self is the source of action and creativity. This emphasis on the efficacious self is also quite evident in more recent symbolic interactionist writings, such as Goffman's (1959) work on impression management as interpersonal control and Weinstein's (1969) work on interpersonal competence. R. H. Turner (1976) notes that behaviors thought to reveal the "true self" are ones whose causes are perceived as residing in the person rather than the situation, particularly when moral issues are at stake (Backman 1985).

Research on self-efficacy has consistently found it to have salutary or beneficial consequences for individual functioning and well-being. Research based on Bandura's theory has found self-efficacy to be an important factor in various health-related behaviors, such as overcoming phobias and anxieties, eating disorders, and alcohol and smoking addictions and recovery from illness or injury (see Bandura 1986; O'Leary 1985). The research of Bandura and his colleagues has increasingly turned to examining the physiological processes affected by perceived self-efficacy, which would account for its therapeutic qualities, particularly the impact of self-efficacy on the immune system (Bandura et al. 1985; Wiedenfeld et al. 1990). This exciting line of research has considerable potential for increasing our understanding of the links between mind and body.

The connection between self-efficacy and depression has also received a good deal of empirical attention, much of it inspired by Seligman's (1975) theory of "learned helplessness," which proposed that depression is likely to occur when one comes to believe that one's actions have no effect on changing one's (unfavorable) circumstances. In much of this research, self-efficacy serves a mediating or buffering role between some type of stress (e.g., economic strain, physical injury, disability) and depression (Pearlin et al. 1981). Since feelings of inefficacy are undesirable and depressing, people may engage in distortions of reality and operate under the illusion of greater personal control and efficacy than they really have (Langer 1975).

The increased prominence of self-efficacy in social psychology is understandable: not only is it in line with the increased emphasis on the active self, but it is also congruent with the western (especially American) emphasis on self-reliance, mastery, and individualism. However, self-efficacy may not be as important to physical and mental health in cultures with a more communal and less individualistic ethos, a possibility considered further in the section on cultural influences.

Consistency, Congruency, and Verification Processes

A number of self theories propose some form of congruency or consistency as a central dynamic in processing information and organizing knowledge about the self. Lecky (1945), an early advocate, argued that individuals seek to maintain a coherent view of themselves in order to function effectively in the world. Several prominent contemporary self theories, characterized by their heavily cognitive orientations, are variations on this theme (e.g., Higgins 1987; Markus 1977; Swann 1983).

The central premise of Swann's *self-verification theory* (1983, 1990; Swann et al. 1987) is that people are motivated to verify or confirm currently held views of their self-conceptions as a means of bolstering their perception that the world is predictable and controllable. What is interesting about this theory is that it suggests that people prefer self-confirming feedback even when the self-view being confirmed is not positive (Swann, Pelham, and Krull 1989). While this argument seems to conflict with self-enhancement theories, Swann et al. (1987) suggest that consistency processes operate primarily at the cognitive level of the self, whereas enhancement processes operate more on the affective level.

Similar in many ways to self-verification theory is Higgins's (1987, 1989) *self-discrepancy theory,* which deals with the consequences of the failure of self-verification. According to the theory and the research supporting it, inconsistencies or discrepancies between the *actual self* (as revealed in reflected appraisals) and the *ideal self* (those attributes one desires) or between the *actual self* and the *ought self* (those attributes one feels obliged to be or have) produce emotional responses and a strong motivation to reduce the discrepancy. The emotional responses to actual/ideal discrepancies, however, are much different from the emotional responses to actual/ought discrepancies (Higgins 1989). Actual/ought discrepancies produce social anxiety as evidenced by social avoidance, distress, and fear of negative evaluation, while actual/ideal discrepancies produce depression (Higgins, Klein, and Strauman 1985).

Backman's (1985, 1988) *interpersonal congruency theory* has strong similarities with both of the previous consistency theories but is more explicitly interpersonal. Backman suggests that congruency operates not only at the level of cognitive

organization, but also at the level of interpersonal relations; that is, people seek social relationships that are congruent with their self-conceptions. Furthermore, congruent social relationships help stabilize self-conceptions and make them even more resistant to change.

A different manifestation of consistency processes is found in theories emphasizing self-schemas. Markus (1977) suggests that the substance of one's self-concept inheres in relatively enduring self-schemas. A self-schema is a cognitive structure consisting of organized elements of information about the self that have evolved through experience and reflected appraisals (Nurius 1991). These cognitive structures or self-schemas are used to recognize and interpret self-relevant stimuli. Self-schemas determine whether information is attended to, how it is structured, how much importance is attached to it, and what happens to it subsequently (Markus 1977). In support of these ideas about self-organization, Bargh (1982) showed that individuals display a heightened sensitivity to self-relevant information; Mueller (1982) found that self-congruent stimuli are more efficiently processed; and Markus (1980) showed that self-relevant stimuli are more easily recalled and recognized. In more recent work, Markus and Nurius have elaborated the self-schema to include "possible selves," or representations of oneself in future states and circumstances (Markus and Nurius 1986; Nurius 1991).

Self-Defenses and Deceptions

An important consequence of the self as a motivational system is that persons engage in various distortions and deceptions to maintain valued self-conceptions. Increasing social psychological interest in this domain is reflected in three main areas of study: (1) self-presentation and impression management; (2) the operation of cognitive biases; and (3) self-deception.

Contemporary research on self-presentation and impression management continues to draw much of its inspiration from Goffman's (1959, 1967) insightful analysis of "facework," deference and demeanor, embarrassment, and numerous other insights into the tactics of self-presentation. Many of these tactics have subsequently been elaborated and investigated by others: self-serving accounts, in the form of excuses and justifications, for inappropriate behavior that could damage the self-image (Mehlman and Snyder 1985; Scott and Lyman 1968); disclaimers offered in anticipation of actions with possibly negative identity implications for self (Hewitt and Stokes 1975); and various other rhetorical devices used either to stage or to repair a certain self-image (Fine 1987). Individuals may even engage in self-handicapping strategies to protect self-esteem—that is, self-defeating actions (such as not studying for an exam) before a performance so they will have a ready-made excuse for failure (Rhodewalt et al. 1991). Social interaction itself is highly selective and self-serving. People tend to pick friends who like them, to choose reference groups or comparison groups that allow for more favorable comparisons, and to select areas of interaction that permit more favorable and/or consistent expressions of self (Lewicki 1983; Rosenberg 1979; Swann 1990).

Self-serving biases are also quite evident in research on cognitive processes. Perception, cognition, and retention of self-relevant information are highly selective depending on whether the information is favorable or unfavorable to one's self-conception (see Markus and Wurf 1987). For example, people are more likely to remember their successes and to distort their memories toward more favorable self-conceptions (Greenwald 1980; Ross and Conway 1986). Not only are people's conceptions of their past distorted to serve self-motives, but so are conceptions of their futures (Markus and Nurius 1986). Attribution research is replete with evidence of self-serving bias in causal attributions (Mehlman and Snyder 1985), which is quite congruent with symbolic interactionists' work on excuses, justifications, and so on.

Particularly interesting with regard to self-serving distortions is whether the self deceives *itself* in this process. The condition of self-deception (e.g., knowing something about oneself is true and at the same time believing it is not true) has been viewed as a paradoxical yet pervasive condition (Champlin 1977; Pears 1986). Sartre (1958) considered self-deception to be characteristic of life in modern society and the major obstacle to being an "authentic" self. For Freud (1938), self-deception was an unavoidable byproduct of the ego's defenses against the unconscious impulses of the id.

Gur and Sackeim (1979) provide empirical evidence to support the argument that to be self-deceived an individual must hold two contradictory beliefs simultaneously, one of which cannot be subject to awareness, and that this nonawareness is motivated. For Gur and Sackeim it is the self-esteem motive that acts to suppress one of the beliefs (the belief less favorable about self). They, along with Hilgard (1949), maintain that self-deception is a key aspect of all defense mechanisms. Swanson (1988) presents a provocative thesis that defense mechanisms are related to forms of social organization. He argues that ego defenses are a function of social interdependence and arise as a means of maintaining social solidarity in the face of threats stemming from questions about the kind of person one is. These questions arise when impulses or desires are incompatible with self-conceptions and social norms. Furthermore, different levels of social organization, having different bases of social solidarity, should be associated with reliance on different ego defenses. His findings, based on data from individuals on themselves and their family relations, generally support these expectations.

Developments in the social psychology of emotions provide another avenue for considering self-deception. Disjunctures or incongruities between thinking and feeling, attempts to generate feelings when they are not there, and the kind of "emotion labor" described by Hochschild (1983) in her study of flight attendants and R. H. Turner's (1976; Turner and Schutte 1981) work on "real" and "false" selves lead to questions of authenticity and self-deception. This, also, is a very promising line of investigation.

SELF AND SOCIETY

Proximate Processes Affecting Self and Identity

Self-conceptions are the products of various proximate processes (i.e., those that directly impinge on us) with socializing consequences, such as the learning of social roles, values, and beliefs; language acquisition; commitment to identities or adjustment to identity loss; and processes of social comparison, self-attributions, and reflected appraisals. The last three have received the most attention as sources of information used in developing a conception of self (Gecas 1982; Rosenberg 1979). Of these, the process of reflected appraisals, based on Cooley's (1902) concept of the "looking-glass self" and Mead's (1934) emphasis on role taking in the genesis of the self, is the most central to sociological perspectives on self-concept formation, and also the most problematic.

The study of reflected appraisals focuses on others' perceptions of us and their impact on our self-concept. According to interactionist theory, people come to see themselves as they think others see them. Research on the reflected appraisals process, however, has not convincingly and consistently demonstrated that peoples' self-concepts are, in fact, a reflection of the conceptions held by others, even significant others. Early correlational studies in natural settings showed little correspondence between one's self-views and the views of significant others (see Shrauger and Schoeneman 1979, for a review and critique); however, these studies were beset with methodological problems. Later, using cross-sectional data, systematic recursive causal models of the process found minimal direct effects of others' appraisals on self-appraisals but showed that others' appraisals influence one's perceptions of those appraisals, which in turn influence one's self-concept (Bachman and O'Malley 1986; Felson 1985; Schafer and Keith 1985). However, it is still possible that the relationship between self-concept and perceptions of the appraisals of others is not a one-way street.

More recent nonrecursive causal models have recognized that not only might perceptions of others' appraisals affect one's self-appraisals, but one's self-appraisals may affect one's perception of others appraisals (called the *false consensus* or social projection effect). It appears that when social projection is controlled in the nonrecursive causal analyses, much of the effect of reflected appraisals disappears (Felson 1981, 1989; Ichiyama, 1993).

Where does this leave us? It is our view that some serious rethinking about reflected appraisals is in order. The models that have been investigated, by and large, are oversimplified and fail to take account of other theoretical and empirical work on self and identity, as well as Cooley's own qualifications regarding the "looking-glass self" (see Franks and Gecas 1992, for elaboration). For example, the self is not simply a passive sponge that soaks up information from the environment; rather, it is an active agent engaged in various self-serving processes. Thus one needs to ask when one's self-appraisals depend on others' appraisals (even mediated by perception). For example, persons may be more sensitive to others' appraisals when they are feeling insecure about their self-image. Heightened sensitivity to reflected appraisals may also occur when one's motive in self-presentation is to impress others, either as a means of gaining resources or to raise one's self-esteem.

Burke (1991b) argues that any change in reflected appraisals that occurs when an identity has achieved some degree of equilibrium in a social environment will be resisted (see also Swann 1990). Action will be taken to alter others' perceptions and bring them back in line with the individual's self-appraisals. Only when the individual finds it difficult or impossible to bring about such change of others' appraisals (and distress, anxiety, or depression result) does the self-concept change, becoming more in line with others' appraisals. Thus, the reflected appraisals process does not operate all the time or under all conditions. People work hard to verify and maintain the self-concepts or identities they already hold, and do not easily change them. To test the reflected appraisals process, therefore, we need to find conditions under which the self-verification processes are minimized and, at the same time, others' appraisals are not self-verifying. In short, we need to think of reflected appraisals as Cooley did, as a variable and problematic process in self-concept formation.

Social Class, Race, and Self-Evaluation

A concern with the effects of social structure on self-conceptions distinguishes much of the sociological research on self and identity. Much of this research has focused on the consequences of social class and other major categories of social stratification and differentiation (e.g., race, gender, ethnicity) for self-evaluation, especially self-esteem.

Research that has simply looked at the global, unmediated relationship between social class and self-esteem has generally found weak and inconsistent results (see Gecas 1982; Rosenberg and Pearlin 1978). This is not surprising, since the important task in studying macrostructural effects on aspects of self-concept is to specify how the social structure affects the immediate interpersonal relations and experiences of individuals in ways that enhance, maintain, or diminish the self (Gecas and Seff 1989; Rosenberg and Simmons 1972). The current thrust of much of this research is toward greater specification—of processes, mediating variables, and the dimensions of self affected. For example, Rosenberg and Pearlin (1978) clarified much of the confusion in social class effects by showing how social class impinges on adults' self-esteem through four processes of self-concept formation (reflected appraisals, social comparisons, self-attributions, and psychological centrality) and why we would expect these processes to produce negligible social class differences for children (a pattern of relationships replicated in subsequent studies by Demo and Savin-Williams 1983 and Wiltfang and Scarbecz 1990). The significant relationships found for adults, but not for children, can be explained by the differential meanings and experiences social class has for adults and children, such as constituting a (more or less)

achieved status for adults and an ascribed status for children.

In decomposing the effects of social class on self-esteem, one fertile line of research has focused on occupations and occupational conditions (Kohn and Schooler 1973). Although self-concept was not a major focus of Kohn's research, Kohn and Schooler (1973) found that substantive complexity of work was significantly related to self-esteem. However, the class-related occupational condition that seems to be most consequential for self-esteem is work autonomy—the degree of freedom or control the worker has over his/her work. Work autonomy has a positive effect on self-esteem, based primarily on evaluations of self in terms of efficacy and competence[7] (Gecas and Seff 1989; Mortimer and Lorence 1979; Staples, Schwalbe, and Gecas 1984). The strategic importance of work autonomy for self-esteem is elaborated by Schwalbe (1985), who implicates it in the three main processes affecting self-evaluation: autonomy as freedom to act and take responsibility for success is relevant to the self-attribution process; autonomy as a status indicator in the workplace culture is used for social comparisons with others at work; autonomy as a reward given by one's boss for reliability and competent performance signifies positive reflected appraisals.

As the studies in this area have shown, individuals in more prestigious occupations (and thereby in a higher social class) are more likely to have greater work autonomy with its beneficial consequences for self-efficacy and self-esteem. However, individuals in lower-class occupations, characterized by less autonomy, less challenge, and greater supervision, are not necessarily doomed to low self-esteem: the correlations between occupational conditions and self-esteem are generally modest (in the low 0.20s). An important reason for the modest effects of occupation on self-esteem is that there are many other sources of self-esteem (e.g., family, recreation, voluntary associations); furthermore, individuals play off these different sources depending on which is most beneficial to their sense of self. Gecas and Seff (1990) argue that psychological centrality and compensation processes in the self-concept operate to mitigate the potentially negative effects of the workplace (or other contexts) on self-esteem. In a study of employed men, they found that when work is central to self-evaluations, social class and occupational conditions had a significantly stronger effect on self-esteem than when work is not central. By comparison, when family is central to self-definitions, family variables were found to have a stronger effect on self-esteem. These findings underscore the active, selective, and protective nature of the self in its relationship to various social environments.

Work autonomy and control have ramifications for workers beyond their effect on self-esteem. Loss of control over the labor process and products is, of course, a central theme of Marx's theory of alienation and the basis of his critique of capitalism. It continues to be a fertile source of ideas about the social structural bases of individual functioning and well-being (see Schwalbe 1986). An interesting and important variation on this theme of alienated labor is found in Hochschild's (1983) work on the "commodification of emotion" in the workplace and its consequences for self-estrangement. Hochschild's innovative study of flight attendants and bill collectors addressed what happens when feelings and their expression (e.g., smiling and being cheerful or being rude or threatening) become part of expected employee work behavior. Hochschild observed that employees doing "emotion work" can become alienated from their emotions, just as factory workers doing physical work become alienated from what they produce. When the private management of emotions is converted into emotional labor for wages, Hochschild observes, inauthenticity becomes an occupational hazard. Building on Hochschild's work, Erickson (1991) found similar consequences of emotion work in her study of female hospital and bank employees. This line of research is promising and important. It focuses on a phenomenon (i.e., feelings of inauthenticity and self-estrangement) that seems to be increasingly characteristic of our times (see R. H. Turner's 1976 analysis of increasing estrangement from institutional sources of authenticity).

Research on race and self-concept overlaps to some extent that on social class, since race is one important element in the American stratification system. But the research on the self-concepts of African Americans has been more controversial and puzzling than research on social class differences. Considering the history of race relations and racial discrimination in the United States, we would expect African Americans to have lower self-esteem than whites. Early work in this area, particularly the influential "doll studies" by Clark and Clark (1947), seemed to support this expectation. They found that African-American children preferred white dolls and inferred from this that African-American children viewed themselves as inferior and therefore had low self-esteem. Both the methodology and interpretations of these early studies have been subsequently criticized as seriously flawed (Greenwald and Oppenheim 1968; Simmons 1978). More recent research has found either no difference between the self-esteem levels of African Americans and whites or slightly higher self-esteem of African Americans than whites (Rosenberg and Rosenberg 1989; Taylor and Walsh 1979; Yancey, Rigsby, and McCarthy 1972). The most reasonable interpretation of this apparently counterintuitive, yet consistent, finding is that self-esteem is most affected by interpersonal relations with family, friends, and local community. These local contexts of interaction, and not society at large, provide the significant others and reference groups within which reflected appraisals and social comparison processes operate to affect African-American self-esteem (Hughes and Demo 1989; Rosenberg 1979; Rosenberg and Simmons 1972).

While African American self-esteem seems to be insulated from patterns of racial inequality, self-efficacy among African Americans is not. African Americans are found to have lower self-efficacy or sense of personal control than whites (Gurin, Gurin, and Morrison 1978; Porter and Washington 1979). This suggests that self-efficacy, unlike self-esteem, is more dependent on macrostructural systems and their consequences for power, control, and access to resources of individuals differentially located within them (Gecas and Schwalbe 1983; Hughes and Demo 1989). To the extent that racial inequality limits or hinders African Americans' access to power and resources which enable efficacious action, black self-efficacy will suffer (Hughes and Demo 1989, 1992).

Gender and Self-Conceptions

As with race and social class, gender constitutes a major basis of social differentiation in American society and can be expected to have pervasive consequences for self-concepts. But there is a good deal of confusion in research dealing with gender identities and self-conceptions, much of it a consequence of inconsistent ways of defining these concepts (Burke 1992). First, there is a distinction between feminine and masculine (gender) in a social or psychological sense and between female and male (sex) in a biological sense (Lindsey 1990). With respect to gender, there is also a distinction between the denotative social categories of male and female (usually, but not always, the same as the biological categories) and the connotative meanings of masculine and feminine that deal with degrees of masculinity and femininity. Finally, there is a question about the degree to which variations in masculinity are independent of variations in femininity.

Gender identities are the socially defined self-meanings of masculinity/femininity one has as a male or female member of society and are inherently derived from and tied to social structure. These self-meanings have both a categorical component (male-female), and a variable component (degree of masculinity or femininity). Social identity theory deals with the categorical approach to social identities, whereas identity theory has dealt more with the variability of connotative meanings of masculine and feminine. Although some researchers (e.g., Bem 1974) have measured this variability of masculine and feminine self-meanings on separate, independent dimensions, Storms (1979) has shown that most people view masculine and feminine as opposite ends of a single continuum ranging from extremely masculine to ex-

tremely feminine, along which both males and females are arrayed. *Gender roles,* in contrast to gender identities, are a dualistic mix of instrumental and expressive behaviors appropriate for persons in given statuses in the social structure (Spence and Helmreich 1978). It is important, therefore, to distinguish between the study of gender identities, which focuses on meanings, and the study of gender roles, which focuses on behavior. Dittmar (1989) examines both by studying the meanings of various personal objects for males and females. This study finds that the meanings of objects vary by sex and are partly tied to the role expectations of each. Males tend to focus on the instrumental, pragmatic, self-referential character of objects, while females are more likely to see the emotional, expressive, and interpersonal attachment character of objects.

Focusing on the impact of gender identities on behavior, Burke and Tully (1977), in a study of the gender identities of a large sample of middle school girls and boys, found that the gender identity scores for both boys and girls were normally distributed along the masculine-feminine dimension with an overlap of about 18 percent. They also found that children with cross-sex identities (boys who thought of themselves in ways similar to the way most girls thought of themselves, and vice versa) were more likely than children with "gender-appropriate" identities to have engaged in "gender-inappropriate behavior," to have been called names like "tomboy," "sissy" or "homo," and to have lower self-esteem. Among middle school children, boys and girls with a more feminine gender identity had higher marks than those with a more masculine gender identity (Burke 1989). Among college students, men and women with more feminine gender identities were more likely to inflict and sustain physical and sexual abuse in dating relationships (Burke, Stets, and Pirog-Good 1988).

Quite a different perspective on gender and self-conceptions, with paradigmatic implications, has begun to appear in the feminist literature. Here the focus is not on identities as such, but rather on some of the fundamental differences between men and women in the nature of their self-conceptions.

With respect to the differences, it is proposed that men are more likely to have a self-concept that separates or distinguishes them from others, a sense of self or "self-schema" that can be described as "individualistic," "autonomous," and "egocentric." Women, by contrast, are more likely to have a self-concept grounded in relationships and connections to others, one that has been described as "relational," "interdependent," "collectivist," and "sociocentric" (Chodorow 1978; Gilligan 1982, 1988; Lykes 1985; Markus and Oyserman 1989; Miller 1986). These gender-related conceptions of self are viewed as consequences of differential socialization associated with patterns of sexual inequality (Lykes 1985; Miller 1986).

Empirical observations of differences between men and women on various dimensions of psychological functioning become more understandable when viewed in light of gender-related self-conceptions. For example, the greater competence of girls/women in verbal abilities, field dependence, empathy, and social sensitivity is compatible with a predominantly "relational self," whereas the greater competence of boys/men in spacial and analytic skills, field independence, and abstract reasoning is more compatible with a predominantly "independent self" (see Markus and Oyserman 1989).

While these average differences between males and females have been documented, it is important to recognize the diversity among women and men with respect to their self-conceptions (see Thompson and Walker 1989). For example, Gilligan (1982, 1988) has proposed that different conceptions of self, as fundamentally relational or as fundamentally separate, give rise to different visions of moral agency: the morality of the relational self emphasizes attachment, care, and connection, while the morality of the autonomous self emphasizes equality, reciprocity, justice, and rights. At the same time, she points out that while these perspectives on morality are gender-related, they are not gender-specific, since there is much variability among both males and females. Gilligan's work on gender differences in moral reasoning, which constitutes (among other things) a critique of Kohlberg's (1964) influential theory of moral development, has launched a major controversy (Sher 1987; Walker 1986). It has also opened new and exciting lines of inquiry into the relationship between gender, self-conceptions, and morality.

Cultural and Cross-Cultural Perspectives on Selfhood

Criticisms that theories and research on the self are ethnocentric have increased in the past decade (Bond 1988; Markus and Kitayama 1991; and Marsella, DeVos, and Hsu 1985; Sampson 1988; Smith 1985). Indeed, most social psychological literature on the self can justifiably be described as the social psychology of the *Western* self. Geertz (1975, 48) describes the Western conception of the person as a bounded, self-contained, autonomous entity, comprising a unique configuration of internal attributes and acting as a consequence of these internal attributes. This view is a reflection of the Western (especially American) ethos of rugged individualism, independence, and self-reliance (Markus and Kitayama 1991). However, this is hardly a universal conception of personhood or selfhood, even within American society (see Gilligan 1988; Markus and Oyserman 1989; Sampson 1988).

A contrasting and alternative conception of selfhood is emerging, primarily from studies of Asian cultures as well as of minority groups and women in American society. This alternative view conceives of the self as essentially interdependent (rather than independent), contextual and relational (rather than autonomous), and connected and permeable (rather than bounded). Markus and Kitayama (1991) call this cultural construal of self *interdependent* and contrast it with the dominant Western view of self as independent.

Empirical support for the interdependent self is based mainly on studies of Asian cultures and populations (Chinese, Indian, and especially Japanese). The themes of interdependence, connectedness, relatedness, and social context are quite evident in descriptions of the "Japanese self" (Cousins

1989; DeVos 1985; Doi 1986; Lebra 1983). Lebra (1983), a Japanese anthropologist, identified the essence of Japanese culture as an "ethos of social relativism," by which she meant that the Japanese have a pervasive concern for belongingness, dependency, reciprocity, and occupying one's proper place. The Japanese word for self, *jibun,* refers to "one's share of the shared space" (Hamaguchi 1985). The interdependent self, with its emphasis on social context and relationships, is also evident in studies of Chinese (Hsu 1970) and Indian cultures (Bharati 1985).

These cultural comparisons are important in that they reveal fundamental differences in peoples' experiences and conceptions of self. More important, they force us to reexamine our *theories* about the self, most of which have been developed on the basis of the Western-self paradigm (Markus and Kitayama 1991). The motivation for cognitive consistency, for example, seems to be more relevant for the "Western self" than it is for the "Eastern self." Doi (1986, 240) points out that Americans are more concerned with consistency between feelings and actions than are the Japanese. In Japan there is virtue in controlling the expression of one's innermost feelings and no virtue in expressing them—the expression of one's emotions is considered a sign of immaturity. By contrast, for Americans, perceived consistency between emotions and their expression is the main criterion for feelings of authenticity (Hochschild 1983).

The self-esteem motive is also affected by these cultural self-conceptions. For independent selves, where the focus is on oneself, the self-esteem motive typically results in a pervasive self-serving bias. Numerous studies of American subjects show that they take credit for their successes and explain away their failures (Markus and Kitayama 1991). However, for interdependent selves, *other* enhancement is more desirable than self-enhancement, because the latter risks isolating the individual from the network of reciprocal relationships. Misattributions involving the self take quite different forms in these two cultural contexts: a self-enhancement bias for those with "independent selves," and a self-effacing bias for those with "interdependent selves." Markus and Kitayama (1991) maintain that the self-enhancement motive is primarily a Western phenomenon. They argue that our formulations of other self-motives (e.g., achievement motivation, self-actualization, self-verification, self-control, self-efficacy) as well as self-emotions (e.g., shame, guilt, pride) need modification when considered in the context of the interdependent self paradigm.

The cultural and societal contexts of self-conceptions are clearly important in shaping the content and processes of self-experiences, as these cross-cultural comparisons reveal. But they also oversimplify the situations *within* societies. There is considerable diversity in self-conceptions in any reasonably heterogeneous society, and certainly within American society. Hewitt (1989) persuasively argues that both cultural themes—independence and interdependence, freedom and community, individualism and communitarianism—have been present in American society from the beginning, presenting a fundamental dilemma and ambivalence in Americans' self-conceptions. He maintains that much of our academic discourse about the self in society reflects *either* one or the other of these cultural themes, resulting in either a pessimistic or an optimistic view of social change. Scholars who assume interdependence as a correlation for healthy selfhood see the decline of community and the rise of modernity, industrialization, and urbanization as undermining the self. This pessimistic view is most evident in the work of scholars in sociology and other social sciences (e.g., Bellah et al. 1985; Lasch 1984). By contrast, the optimistic view celebrates individualism. Modernity and social change are seen as liberating the self from stifling, repressive traditions and as providing new opportunities for personal growth and fulfillment. This perspective is most clearly expressed in humanistic and clinical psychology. These dominant and competing conceptions of the self in American society, Hewitt argues, provide a major axis of ambivalence for American selves as well as a major cleavage in the scholarly discourse on the self.

Historical Considerations and the "Postmodern Self"

The relationship between self and society has become increasingly problematic. Historical analyses of the "Western self" from the Middle Ages to modern times document the rise of individualism and its consequences for the self (Baumeister 1987; Logan 1987; Schooler 1990). The securities and constraints imposed by tradition have substantially receded in modern societies, presenting individuals with greater choice, freedom, and possibilities for action, as well as new threats to the self in the form of impersonal bureaucracies, depersonalizing communities, and alienating work conditions.

The pervasive themes of modernist writers on the self are fragmentation, ambivalence, and estrangement. Weigert's (1991) "ambivalent self" is a contemporary product of mixed emotions stemming from a multitude of choices, contradictory messages and expectations, and increasingly relativized values; Lasch's (1984) "minimal self" is a self under siege from the pressures of modern society; the "alienated self" of Marxist writers (Burawoy 1979; Schwalbe 1986) is a consequence of powerlessness and meaninglessness in the workplace; R. H. Turner's (1976) "impulsive self" is an emergent of the increasing delegitimation of institutional roles; and Zurcher's (1977) "mutable self" is the chameleonlike adaptation of moderns to the rapidity of social change. Perhaps the central problem of selfhood in modern societies, reflected in these various characterizations, is the problem of authenticity (Baumeister 1987; Hochschild 1983; Trilling 1972; R. H. Turner 1976; Weigert 1990). The rise of individualism associated with modernization highlights authenticity as a central concern, while at the same time the social forces associated with modernity have made authenticity increasingly problematic.

A very different view of the self is taking shape in what has come to be called "postmod-ernism." Postmodern society, with its emphasis on images and illusions and the increasing difficulty in distinguishing the "real" from the "imitation," is viewed as inimical to the maintenance of the bounded, private, centered self striving for agency and authenticity. The postmodern world is saturated with images and simulations to such an extent that the image, or what the French postmodernist Baudrillard (1981) calls "simulacra," is viewed as *replacing* reality. The implications of such a state of society for the selves that inhabit it are described as profound.

Whereas modernism heightens awareness of self and the (typically problematic) relationship between self and society, postmodernism diminishes the centrality of the self and the tension between self and society. The postmodern self is characterized as decentered, relational, contingent, illusory, and lacking any core or essence (Erickson 1991; Gergen 1991; Glassner 1989). Problems of authenticity recede as beliefs in a core or essential self to which one must remain true or committed disappear. In the postmodern world, Gergen (1991) observes, "one's identity is continuously emergent, re-formed, and re-directed as one moves through the sea of ever-changing relationships. . . . It becomes increasingly difficult to recall precisely to what core essence one must remain true. The ideal of authenticity frays about the edges; the meaning of sincerity slowly lapses into indeterminacy" (p. 15).

The postmodern emphasis on images and illusions is reflected in greater attention to self-presentation and to style over substance. For that matter, the distinction between the real and the presented self, between substance and style, disappears (Gergen 1991, 155). Fashion and personal appearance increase in importance as central means of creating the self and influencing the definition of the situation (Kaiser, Nagawawa, and Hutton 1991). The accentuated emphasis on physical fitness and body shaping is understandable when self and appearance are viewed as the same (Glassner 1989). "Self-image" has replaced "self-concept" in the postmodern discourse on the self.

These depictions of the postmodern self are reminiscent of some major lines of symbolic interactionism, particularly the situational (e.g., Blumer 1969; Fine 1987) and the dramaturgical (e.g., Goffman 1959; Stone 1962) varieties. For that matter, Goffman is considered a precursor to postmodern sociology (see Battershill 1990; Dowd 1991; Erickson 1991; Tseelon 1992), with his work on situated identities, self-presentation, impression management, and depiction of the self in a manner that evokes the deconstructionist treatment of the author (i.e., the self as a decentered reader of cultural scripts). (His work on total institutions, however, would not fit as well, since the self in *Asylums* struggles to maintain its integrity under conditions of institutional assault—a theme congruent with *modernist* writings). Stone (1962) could also be considered a precursor, with his emphasis on clothing and appearance in establishing identities. The self as depicted in this branch of interactionism is, like the postmodernist self, relational (e.g., contextual or situated), decentered (identities as elements of the social context, not the person), contingent (dependent on negotiated meanings), and a dramaturgical construction. Yet, unlike the postmodern self, it still retains some essentialist qualities (e.g., the "I" and "me" components).

There is also an affinity between the postmodern self and the relational or interdependent self in feminist writings (Gilligan 1988; Markus and Oyserman 1989) and the descriptions of self in Asian (and some American Indian) cultures (Markus and Kitayama 1991). They share the view of a decentered, relational self and contrast it with the modernist and/or predominantly Western conception of self. They differ in some important respects, however. The relational self of Asian cultures and feminist writings is grounded in relationships of greater permanence and importance and involving greater commitment than the contextual or situational self of postmodernism. Consequently, shame, guilt, and other self-emotions, as well as authenticity, are more relevant to the former relational self than to the latter.

Not too surprisingly, the postmodern self is much less compatible with that branch of symbolic interactionism most closely associated with the study of the self—the self and identity theories of Kuhn, Stryker, and Rosenberg. This branch of interactionism places much more emphasis on the phenomenal self, which is structured, relatively stable, and the source of various emotions and motivations. It also approaches the study of the self more positivistically and assumes greater determinacy than does postmodernism. This approach to the self has been the subject of much of the postmodern critique (Denzin 1988; Gergen 1984). But even Mead's (1934) view of the self has come under attack by postmodern sociologists. For example, Denzin (1988) "deconstructs" Mead's concepts of the "I" and the "me," relegating them to the status of linguistic conventions (mere pronouns) with no substantive reality beyond that, and eventually abandons the concept of self altogether. Dowd (1991) goes even further, arguing that the erosion of the self due to changes in society associated with postmodernism is the cause of the *real* crisis in social psychology. With the erosion of the self, Dowd argues, social psychology is left without its central subject of study.

We disagree with Denzin's claim that these self-constructs are merely byproducts of language and with Dowd's contention that the "demise" of the self is at the heart of the crisis in social psychology. It is premature to sound the death knell for the self. An argument can still be made for the reality of human groups and people's commitment to them, for the existence of self-reflexive beings, and for the reality of self-feelings, such as guilt, shame, and authenticity. Modernist perspectives still dominate our understanding of selves in contemporary society. However, postmodernism has presented a major challenge to our conceptions of self and society, a challenge that has yet to be adequately addressed (but see Farberman 1991 for a good start).

CONCLUDING OBSERVATIONS

These are interesting times in the social psychology of self and identity. The study of self-phenomena is flourishing in both the sociological and psychological branches of social psychology. Perennial topics of inquiry reflect new vigor and research activity: the structure and organization of self-conceptions; the internal dynamics of self-concepts; the relationship between social structure and self-conception; the interplay between identities, self-evaluations, and behavior; the consequences of self and identity for individual functioning.[8] Most of the contemporary research on these topics draws its theoretical inspiration from some version of symbolic interactionism (in sociology) or some version of cognitive and social learning theories (in psychology).

The field is also characterized by the emergence of multiple new lines of inquiry. The emergence of emotions as a major focus of social psychological interest has spilled over into studies of self and identity—previously a cognitive stronghold. Connections between emotions and self-conceptions beginning to be explored include the affective concomitants of identities; the emotional consequences of self-discrepant experiences; the significance of self-emotions, such as shame, guilt, and pride; and the consequences of "emotion work" for individual well-being. There are many interesting aspects to the interrelationships between emotions, self-conceptions, and behavior, not the least of which are questions regarding the consequences of disjunctures between these domains.

There is a renewed interest in the topic of motivation and in viewing the self-concept as a motivational system (Burke and Reitzes 1991; Gecas 1991; Swanson 1989; J. C. Turner 1987), which is part of the increasing emphasis on the active, agentive self. The proliferation of self theories emphasizing self-dynamics and self-motives is another expression of this trend. So is the renewed interest in defense mechanisms, the ways in which persons present themselves, manipulate their environments, and engage in various distortions, biases, or deceptions to protect valued self-conceptions.

Most of the developments and trends discussed here generally fall within what might be called the "dominant self-paradigm," a view of the self as bounded, centered, and the locus of motives, interests, and so on. It will be interesting to see whether the paradigmatic critiques of this view, increasingly found in cross-cultural studies of self-concept, feminist writings, and the postmodernist literature, will have an impact on subsequent studies and theories of self and identity.

NOTES

This work was supported in part by Project 0932, Department of Rural Sociology, Agricultural Research Center, Washington State University. We wish to thank David Demo, Manny Rosenberg, Michael Schwalbe, the anonymous reviewer, and the editors of this book for helpful comments and suggestions in the preparation of this chapter.

1. See Rosenberg (1989) for a discussion of the obstacles to the study of the self in psychology, psychoanalysis, and to some extent sociology due to the dominance of inhospitable scientific paradigms for much of the twentieth century.

2. Some notable exceptions to this generalization are Baumeister's (1987) historical analysis of identity, Gergen's (1984) sociohistorical approach to the self, and Sampson's (1988) call for greater sensitivity to culture and history in the study of the self.

3. In many respects the self-concept is similar to the concept of ego as used by psychologists (see Sherif 1968), although less emphasis is placed on social and reflexive qualities in discussions of ego than is found in discussions of self and self-concept.

4. An interesting variation of this orientation, found mostly in political sociology literature, focuses on ideologies and their consequences for selves and identities (Gouldner 1976; Warren 1990). Ideologies, as Warren (1990) argues, have a wide range of identity implications, such as telling individuals who they are, where they fit in the social hierarchy, and who is a member of a community and who is not and providing a moral framework for social relations and individual experience. Much of the power and persistence of ideologies derives from these identity-sustaining features for those who hold them.

5. There is also a rich tradition of work on identity in psychology, inspired largely by Erikson's (1959) conceptualization.

6. Even the scholars recruited by the Commission to review the research on self-esteem came to this assessment (Mecca, Smelser, and Vasconcellos 1989).

7. A number of scholars have distinguished between two major bases or dimensions of self-evaluation: competence and worth (Gecas 1982; Rokeach 1973; Wells and Marwell 1976). Competency or efficacy-based self-esteem is tied closely to effective or ineffective performance, whereas self-worth is grounded in norms and values concerning personal conduct (i.e., justice, reciprocity, honor; Gecas 1982; Gecas and Schwalbe 1983).

8. Our review of most of these topics has necessarily been cursory, and some topics, such as stability and change in self-conceptions (see Demo 1992 for a recent review) and measuring self and identity, were omitted altogether due to space limitations. Measurement has always been a thorny issue in studies of self-concept, and there seems to be even less agreement now than in the past regarding the best measurement strategies. The more positivistically inclined advocate the need for greater precision in measures (Burke 1980; Demo 1985; Wylie 1979). The more qualitatively inclined argue for open-ended, relatively unstructured procedures (e.g., narratives about oneself) that allow greater freedom of self-expression (Gergen and Gergen 1988; McGuire and McGuire 1988; Turner and Schutte 1981). We believe both strategies are important and should be encouraged, depending on the aspect of self or identity under study.

REFERENCES

Abrams, Dominic, and Michael A. Hogg, eds. 1990. *Social Identity Theory: Constructive and Critical Advances.* New York: Springer-Verlag.

Agger, Ben. 1991. Critical theory, post-structuralism, postmodernism: Their sociological relevance. *Annual Review of Sociology* 17:105–131.

Alexander, C. Norman, and G. Knight. 1971. Situated identities and social psychological experimentation. *Sociometry* 34:65–82.

Alexander, C. Norman, and Mary G. Wiley. 1981. Situated activity and identity formation. Pp. 269–289 in *Social Psychology: Sociological Perspectives,* ed. M. Rosenberg and R. H. Turner. New York: Basic Books.

Alloy, Lavern B., and Lynn Y. Abramson. 1979. Judgment of contingency in depressed and nondepressed students: Sadder but wiser? *Journal of Experimental Psychology* 108:441–485.

Bachman, Jerald G., and Patrick M. O'Malley. 1986. Self-concepts, self-esteem and educational experiences: The frog pond revisited (again). *Journal of Personality and Social Psychology* 50:35–46.

Backman, Carl W. 1985. Identity, self-presentation, and the resolution of moral dilemmas: Toward a social psychological theory of moral behavior. Pp. 236–259 in *The Self and Social Life,* ed. B. R. Schlenker. New York: McGraw-Hill.

Backman, Carl W. 1988. The self: A dialectical approach. *Advances in Experimental Social Psychology* 21:229–260.

Bandura, Albert. 1977. Self-efficacy: Toward a unifying theory of behavioral change. *Psychological Review* 84:191–215.

Bandura, Albert. 1986. *Social Foundations of Thought and Action: A Social Cognitive Theory.* Englewood Cliffs, NJ: Prentice-Hall.

Bandura, Albert, C. B. Taylor, S. L. Williams, I. N. Mefford, and J. D. Barchas. 1985. Catecholamine secretion as a function of perceived coping self-efficacy. *Journal of Consulting and Clinical Psychology* 53:406–414.

Bargh, John A. 1982. Attention and automaticity in the processing of self-relevant information. *Journal of Personality and Social Psychology* 43:425–436.

Battershill, Charles D. 1990. Erving Goffman as a precursor to post-modern sociology. Pp. 163–186 in *Beyond Goffman: Studies on Communication, Institution, and Social Interaction,* ed. S. H. Riggins. New York: Mouton de Gruyter.

Baudrillard, Jean. 1981. *For a Critique of the Political Economy of the Sign.* St. Louis: Telos.

Baumeister, Roy F. 1987. How the self became a problem: A psychological review of historical research. *Journal of Personality and Social Psychology* 52: 163–176.

Becker, Howard S. 1964. Personal change in adult life. *Sociometry* 27:40–53.

Bellah, Robert N., Richard Madsen, William M. Sullivan, Ann Swidler, and Steven M. Tipton. 1985. *Habitats of the Heart: Individualism and Commit-*

ment in American Life. Berkeley: University of California Press.

Bem, Sandra L. 1974. The measurement of psychological androgyny. *Journal of Consulting and Clinical Psychology* 42:155–162.

Bharati, A. 1985. The self in Hindu thought and action. Pp. 185–230 in *Culture and Self: Asian and Western Perspectives,* ed. A. J. Marsella, G. DeVos, and F. L. K. Hsu. New York: Tavistock.

Blumer, Herbert. 1969. *Symbolic Interactionism: Perspective Method.* Englewood Cliffs, NJ: Prentice Hall.

Blumstein, Philip W. 1973. Audience, machiavellianism, and tactics of identity bargaining. *Sociometry* 36:346–365.

Bond, Michael H., ed. 1988. *The Cross-Cultural Challenge to Social Psychology.* Beverly Hills: Sage.

Burawoy, Michael. 1979. *Manufacturing Consent.* Chicago: University of Chicago Press.

Burke, Peter J. 1980. The self: Measurement implications from a symbolic interactionist perspective. *Social Psychology Quarterly* 43:18–29.

Burke, Peter J. 1989. Gender identity, sex and school performance. *Social Psychology Quarterly* 52:159–69.

Burke, Peter J. 1991a. Attitudes, behavior, and the self. Pp. 189–208 in *The Self Society Interface: Cognition, Emotion and Action,* ed. J. A. Howard and P. L. Callero. New York: Cambridge University Press.

Burke, Peter J. 1991b. Identity processes and social stress. *American Sociological Review* 56:836–849.

Burke, Peter J. 1992. Femininity/masculinity (including androgyny). Pp. 689–695 in *Encyclopedia of Sociology,* ed. E. F. Borgatta and M. L. Borgatta. New York: Macmillan.

Burke, Peter J., and Lee Freese. 1989. Identity and social structure. Paper presented at the meetings of the American Sociological Association, San Francisco.

Burke, Peter J., and Jon Hoelter. 1988. Identity and sex-race differences in educational and occupational aspirations formation. *Social Science Research* 17:29–47.

Burke, Peter J., and Don C. Reitzes. 1981. The link between identity and role performance. *Social Psychology Quarterly* 44:83–92.

Burke, Peter J., and Don C. Reitzes. 1991. An identity theory approach to commitment. *Social Psychology Quarterly* 54:280–86.

Burke, Peter J., Jan E. Stets, and M. Pirog-Good. 1988. Gender identity, self-esteem, and physical and sexual abuse in dating relationships. *Social Psychology Quarterly* 51:272–285.

Burke, Peter J., and Judy Tully. 1977. The measurement of role/identity. *Social Forces* 55:880–897.

California Task Force to Promote Self-Esteem and Personal and Social Responsibility. 1990. Toward a State of Esteem: Final Report. Sacramento: California State Department of Education.

Champlin, T. S. 1977. Self-deception: A reflexive dilemma. *Philosophy* 52:281–299.

Chodorow, Nancy. 1978. *The Reproduction of Mothering: Psychoanalysis and the Sociology of Gender.* Berkeley: University of California Press.

Clark, Kenneth B., and Mary P. Clark. 1947. Racial identification and preference in Negro children. Pp. 169–178 in *Readings in Social Psychology,* ed. T. M. Newcomb and E. L. Hartley. New York: Holt.

Cooley, Charles H. 1902 (1964). *Human Nature and the Social Order.* New York: Scribner's.

Cousins, Steven D. 1989. Culture and self-perception in Japan and the United States. *Journal of Personality and Social Psychology* 56:124–131.

Deci, Edward L. 1975. *Intrinsic Motivation.* New York: Plenum.

Demo, David H. 1985. The measurement of self-esteem: Refining our methods. *Journal of Personality and Social Psychology* 48:1490–1502.

Demo, David H. 1992. The self-concept over time: Research issues and directions. *Annual Review of Sociology* 18:303–326.

Demo, David H., and Ritch C. Savin-Williams. 1983. Early adolescent self-esteem as a function of social class: Rosenberg and Pearlin revisited. *American Journal of Sociology* 88:763–774.

Denzin, Norman K. 1988. Act, language, and self in symbolic interactionist thought. *Studies in Symbolic Interaction.* 9:51–80.

DeVos, George. 1985. Dimensions of the self in Japanese culture. Pp. 141–184 in *Culture and Self: Asian and Western Perspectives,* ed. Anthony J. Marsella, G. DeVos, and F. L.K. Hsu. New York: Tavistock.

Dittmar, Helga. 1989. Gender identity-related meanings of personal possessions. *British Journal of Social Psychology* 28:159–71.

Doi, Takeo. 1986. *The Anatomy of Self: The Individual Versus Society.* Translated by Mark A. Harbison. Tokyo: Kodansha.

Dowd, James J. 1991. Social psychology in a postmodern age: A discipline without a subject. *The American Sociologist* Fall/Winter:188–209.

Erickson, Rebecca J. 1991. When emotion is the product: Self, society, and authenticity in a postmodern world. Ph.D. diss., Pullman, WA: Department of Sociology, Washington State University.

Erikson, Erik H. 1959. Identity and the life cycle. *Psychological Issues* 1:1–171.

Farberman, Harvey A. 1991. Symbolic interaction and postmodernism: Close encounter of a dubious kind. *Symbolic Interaction* 14:471–488.

Felson, Richard B. 1981. Self- and reflected appraisals among football players: A test of the median hypothesis. *Social Psychology Quarterly* 44:116–126.

Felson, Richard B. 1985. Reflected appraisal and the development of self. *Social Psychology Quarterly* 48:71–77.

Felson, Richard B. 1989. Parents and the reflected appraisal process: A longitudinal analysis. *Journal of Personality and Social Psychology* 56:965–971.

Fine, Gary A. 1987. *With the Boys: Little League Baseball and Preadolescent Culture.* Chicago: University of Chicago Press.

Foote, Nelson N. 1951. Identification as the basis for a theory of motivation. *American Sociological Review* 26:14–21.

Franks, David D., and Viktor Gecas. 1992. Autonomy and conformity in Cooley's self-theory: The looking-glass self and beyond. *Symbolic Interaction* 15:49–68.

Franks, David D., and Joseph Marolla. 1976. Efficacious action and social approval as interacting dimensions of self-esteem: A tentative formulation through construct validation. *Sociometry* 39:324–341.

Freud, Sigmund. 1938. *The Basic Writings of Sigmund Freud.* A. A. Brill, ed. and trans. New York: Random House.

Gecas, Viktor. 1982. The self-concept. *Annual Review of Sociology* 8:1–33.

Gecas, Viktor. 1989. The social psychology of self-efficacy. *Annual Review of Sociology* 15:291–316.

Gecas, Viktor. 1991. The self-concept as a basis for a theory of motivation. Pp. 171–188 in *The Self-Society Dynamic: Cognition, Emotion and Action,* ed. J. A. Howard and P. L. Callero. Cambridge: Cambridge University Press.

Gecas, Viktor, and Michael L. Schwalbe. 1983. Beyond the looking-glass self: Social structure and efficacy-based self-esteem. *Social Psychology Quarterly* 46:77–88.

Gecas, Viktor, and Monica A. Seff. 1989. Social class, occupational conditions and self-esteem. *Sociological Perspectives* 32:353–364.

Gecas, Viktor, and Monica A. Seff. 1990. Social class and self-esteem: Psychological centrality, compensation, and the relative effects of work and home. *Social Psychology Quarterly* 53:165–173.

Geertz, Clifford. 1973. *The Interpretation of Cultures.* New York: Basic Books.

Geertz, Clifford. 1975. On the nature of anthropological understanding. *American Scientist* 63:47–53.

Gergen, Kenneth J. 1984. Theory of the self: Impasse and evolution. *Advances in Experimental Social Psychology* 17:49–117.

Gergen, Kenneth J. 1991. *The Saturated Self: Dilemmas of Identity in Contemporary Life.* New York: Basic Books.

Gergen, Kenneth J., and Mary M. Gergen. 1988. Narrative and the self as relationship. Pp. 17–56 in *Advances in Experimental Social Psychology,* vol. 21, ed. L. Berkowitz. San Diego: Academic.

Gilligan, Carol. 1982. *In a Different Voice: Psychological Theory and Women's Development.* Cambridge, MA: Harvard University Press.

Gilligan, Carol. 1988. Remapping the moral domain: New images of self in relationship. In *Mapping the Moral Domain: A Contribution of Women's Thinking to Psychological Theory and Education,* ed. Carol Gilligan, J. V. Ward, J. M. Taylor, and B. Bardige. Cambridge, MA: Center for the Study of Gender, Education and Human Development.

Glassner, Barry. 1989. Fitness and the postmodern self. *Journal of Health and Social Behavior* 30:180–191.

Goffman, Erving. 1959. *The Presentation of Self in Everyday Life.* New York: Doubleday.

Goffman, Erving. 1963. *Stigma.* Englewood Cliffs, NJ: Prentice Hall.

Goffman, Erving. 1967. *Interaction Ritual.* New York: Doubleday.

Gordon, Chad. 1968. Self-conceptions: Configurations of content. In *The Self in Social Interaction,* ed. C. Gordon and K. J. Gergen. New York: Wiley.

Gouldner, Alvin. 1976. *The Dialectic of Ideology and Technology.* New York: Oxford University Press.

Greenwald, Anthony G. 1980. The totalitarian ego: Fabrication and revision of personal history. *American Psychologist* 35:603–618.

Greenwald, Anthony G., and Anthony R. Pratkanis. 1984. The self. Pp. 129–179 in *Handbook of Social Cognition,* vol. 3, ed. R. W. Wyer, Jr., and T. K. Srull. Hillsdale, NJ: Erlbaum.

Greenwald, Harold J., and D. B. Oppenheim. 1968. Reported magnitude of self-misidentification among Negro children: An artifact? *Journal of Personality and Social Psychology* 8:49–52.

Gur, Rubin C., and Harold A. Sackeim. 1979. Self-deception: A concept in search of a phenomenon. *Journal of Personality and Social Psychology* 37:147–169.

Gurin, Patricia, G. Gurin, and B. M. Morrison. 1978. Personal and ideological aspects of internal and external control. *Social Psychology* 41:275–296.

Hales, Susan. 1985. The inadvertent rediscovery of self in social psychology. *Journal for the Theory of Social Behavior* 15:237–282.

Hamaguchi, Esyun. 1985. A contextual model of the Japanese: Toward a methodological innovation in Japan studies. *Journal of Japanese Studies* 11:289–321.

Heise, David R. 1985. Affect control theory: Respecification, estimation and tests of the formal model. *Journal of Mathematical Sociology* 11:191–222.

Hewitt, John P. 1989. *Dilemmas of the American Self.* Philadelphia: Temple University Press.

Hewitt, John P., and Randall Stokes. 1975. Disclaimers. *American Sociological Review* 40:1–11.

Higgins, E. Tony. 1987. Self-discrepancy: A theory relating self and affect. *Psychological Review* 94:319–340.

Higgins, E. Tony. 1989. Self-discrepancy theory: What patterns of self-beliefs cause people to suffer? *Advances in Experimental Social Psychology* 22:93–136.

Higgins, E. Tony, R. Klein, and T. Strauman. 1985. Self-concept discrepancy theory: A psychological model for distinguishing among different aspects of depression and anxiety. *Social Cognition* 3:51–76.

Hilgard, Ernest R. 1949. Human motives and the concept of the self. *The American Psychologist* 4:374–382.

Hochschild, Arlie R. 1983. *The Managed Heart: Commercialization of Human Feeling.* Berkeley: University of California Press. Pp. 185–198.

Hsu, Francis L. K. 1970. *Americans and Chinese: Purpose and Fulfillment in Great Civilizations.* Garden City, NY: Doubleday.

Hughes, Michael, and D. H. Demo. 1989. Self-perceptions of black Americans: Self-esteem and personal efficacy. *American Journal of Sociology* 95:139–159.

Hughes, Michael, and David H. Demo. 1992. Racial inequality and personal efficacy. Paper presented at the Southern Sociological Society Meetings, New Orleans.

Ichiyama, Michael A. 1993. A longitudinal analysis of the reflected appraisal process in small group interaction. *Social Psychology Quarterly.* 56:87–99.

Kaiser, Susan B., R. H. Nagawawa, and S. S. Hutton. 1991. Fashion, postmodernity and personal appearance: A symbolic interactionist formulation. *Symbolic Interaction* 14:165–185.

Kaplan, Harold B. 1975. *Self-attitudes and Deviant Behavior.* Pacific Palisades, CA: Goodyear.

Kihlstrom, John F., and Nancy Cantor. 1984. Mental representations of the self. Pp. 1–47 in *Advances in Experimental Social Psychology,* ed. Leonard Berkowtiz. San Diego, CA: Academic.

Kohlberg, Lawrence. 1964. Development of moral character and moral ideology. Pp. 137–214, in *Review of Child Development Research,* ed. Martin Hoffman and L. W. Hoffman. New York: Russell Sage Foundation.

Kohn, Melvin L., and Carmi Schooler. 1973. Occupational experience and psychological functioning: An assessment of reciprocal effects. *American Sociological Review* 38:97–118.

Kuhn, Manfurd H. 1964. Major trends in symbolic interaction theory in the past twenty-five years. *The Sociological Quarterly* 5:61–84.

Kuhn, Manfurd H., and Thomas S. McPartland. 1954. An empirical investigation of self-attitudes. *American Sociological Review* 19:68–76.

Langer, Ellen J. 1975. The illusion of control. *Journal of Personality and Social Psychology* 32:311–328.

Lasch, Christopher. 1984. *The Minimal Self: Psychic Survival in Troubled Times.* New York: W. W. Norton.

Lebra, Takie S. 1983. Shame and guilt: A psychocultural view of the Japanese self. *Ethos* 11:192–209.

Lecky, Prescott. 1945. *Self-Consistency: A Theory of Personality.* New York: Island Press.

Lefcourt, Herbert M. 1976. *Locus of Control.* Hillsdale, NJ: Erlbaum.

Lewicki, P. 1983. Self-image bias in person perception. *Journal of Personality and Social Psychology* 45:384–393.

Lewinsohn, Peter M., and Walter Mischel. 1980. Social competence and depression: The role of illusory self-perceptions. *Journal of Abnormal Psychology* 89:203–212.

Lindsey, Linda L. 1990. *Gender Roles: A Sociological Perspective.* Englewood Cliffs, NJ: Prentice-Hall.

Logan, Richard D. 1987. Historical changes in prevailing sense of self. Pp. 13–26 in *Self and Identity: Psychological Perspectives,* ed. Krysia Yarkley and Terry Honess. New York: Wiley.

Lykes, M. Brinton. 1985. Gender and individualistic vs. collectivist bases for notions about the self. *Journal of Personality* 53:356–383.

Lyng, Stephen. 1990. Edgework: A social psychological analysis of voluntary risk taking. *American Journal of Sociology* 95:851–886.

Markus, Hazel. 1977. Self-schemata and processing of information about the self. *Journal of Personality and Social Psychology* 35:63–78.

Markus, Hazel. The self in thought and memory. Pp. 102–130 in *The Self in Social Psychology,* ed. D. M. Wegner and R. R. Vallacher. New York: Oxford University Press.

Markus, Hazel R., and S. Kitayama. 1991. Culture and the self: Implications for cognition, emotion, and motivation. *Psychological Review* 98:224–253.

Markus, Hazel, and Paula Nurius. 1986. Possible selves: The interface between motivation and the self-concept. Pp. 213–232 in *Self and Identity: Psychosocial Perspectives,* ed. K. Yardley and T. Honess. New York: Wiley.

Markus, Hazel R., and Daphna Oyserman. 1989. Gender and thought: The role of the self-concept. Pp. 100–127 in *Gender and Thought,* ed. M. Crawford and M. Hamilton. New York: Springer-Verlag.

Markus, Hazel, and Elissa Wurf. 1987. The dynamic self-concept: A social psychological perspective. *Annual Review of Psychology* 38:299–337.

Marsella, Anthony J., G. DeVos and F. L.K. Hsu. 1985. *Culture and Self: Asian and Western Perspectives.* New York: Tavistock.

Marx, Karl. (1844) 1963. *Early Writings.* T. B. Bottomore, ed. and trans. New York: McGraw-Hill.

McCall, George J., and J. L. Simmons. 1966. *Identities and Interactions,* rev. ed. New York: Free Press.

McGuire, William J. 1984. Search for the self: Going beyond self-esteem and the reactive self. Pp. 73–120 in *Personality and the Prediction of Behavior,* ed. R. A. Zucker, J. Aronoff, and A. I. Rabin. New York: Academic.

McGuire, William J., and C. V. McGuire. 1988. Content and process in the experience of self. *Advances in Experimental Social Psychology* 21:97–144.

Mead, George H. 1934. *Mind, Self, and Society.* Chicago: University of Chicago Press.

Mecca, Andrea M., Neil J. Smelser, and John Vasconcellos, eds. 1989. *The Social Importance of Self-Esteem.* Berkeley: University of California Press.

Mehlman, Rick C., and C. R. Snyder. 1985. Excuse theory: A test of the self-protective role of attributions. *Journal of Personality and Social Psychology* 49: 994–1001.

Meltzer, Bernard N., and J. W. Petras. 1970. The Chicago and Iowa schools of symbolic interactionism. Pp. 3–17 in *Human Nature and Collective Behavior: Papers in Honor of Herbert Blumer,* ed. Tomatsu Shibutani. Englewood Cliffs, NJ: Prentice-Hall.

Miller, Jean B. 1986. *Toward a New Psychology of Women.* Boston: Beacon.

Mills, C. Wright. 1959. *The Sociological Imagination.* New York: Grove.

Mortimer, Jeylon T., and Jon Lorence. 1979. Occupational experience and the self-concept: A longitudinal study. *Social Psychology Quarterly* 42:307–323.

Mueller, John H. 1982. Self-awareness and access to material rated as self-descriptive or nondescriptive. *Bulletin of the Psychonomic Society* 19:323–326.

Nurius, Paula. 1991. Possible selves and social support: Social cognitive resources for coping and striving. Pp. 239–258 in *The Self Society Interface: Cognition, Emotion and Action,* ed. Judy A. Howard and Peter L. Callero. New York: Cambridge University Press.

O'Leary, Ann. 1985. Self-efficacy and health. *Behavioral Research Therapy* 23:437–451.

Pearlin, Leonard I., M. A. Leiberman, E. G. Menaghan, and J. T. Jullan. 1981. The stress process. *Journal of Health and Social Behavior* 22:337–356.

Pears, D. 1986. The goals and strategies of self-deception. Pp. 59–77 in *The Multiple Self: Studies in Rationality and Social Change,* ed. J. Elster. Cambridge: Cambridge University Press.

Perinbanayagam, Robert S. 1991. *Discursive Acts.* New York: Aldine de Gruyter.

Pervin, Lawrence A. 1985. Personality: Current controversies, issues, and directions. *Annual Review of Psychology* 36:83–114.

Porter, Judith R., and Robert E. Washington. 1979. Black identity and self-esteem. *Annual Review of Sociology* 5:53–74.

Rhodewalt, Frederick, C. Morf, S. Hazlett, and M. Fairfield. 1991. Self-handicapping: The role of discounting and augmentation in the preservation of self-esteem. *Journal of Personality and Social Psychology* 61:122–131.

Rokeach, Milton. 1973. *The Nature of Human Values.* New York: Free Press.

Rosenberg, Morris. 1979. *Conceiving the Self.* New York: Basic Books.

Rosenberg, Morris. 1981. The self-concept: Social product and social force. Pp. 593–624 in *Social Psychology: Sociological Perspectives,* ed. M. Rosenberg and R. Turner. New York: Basic Books.

Rosenberg, Morris. 1989. Self-concept research: A historical overview. *Social Forces* 68:34–44.

Rosenberg, Morris., and L. I. Pearlin. 1978. Social class and self-esteem among children and adults. *American Journal of Sociology* 84:53–77.

Rosenberg, Morris, and Florence R. Rosenberg. 1989. Old myths die hard: The case of black self-esteem. *Revue Internationale de Psychologie Sociale* 2:355–365.

Rosenberg, Morris, Carmi Schooler, and Carrie Schoenbach. 1989. Self-esteem and adolescent problems: Modeling reciprocal effects. *American Sociological Review* 54:1004–1018.

Rosenberg, Morris, and Robert G. Simmons. 1972. *Black and White Self-Esteem: The Urban School Child.* Washington, DC: American Sociological Association.

Ross, Michael, and Michael Conway. 1986. Remembering one's own past: The construction of personal histories. In *Handbook of Motivation and Cognition: Foundations of Social Behavior,* ed. Richard M. Sorrentino and E. T. Higgins. New York: Guilford.

Rotter, Julian B. 1966. Generalized expectancies for internal versus external control of reinforcement. *Psychological Monographs* 80:1–28.

Sampson, Edward E. 1988. The debate on individualism: Indigenous psychologies of the individual and their role in personal and societal functioning. *American Psychologist* 43:15–22.

Sartre, Jean P. 1958. *Being and Nothingness: An Essay on Phenomenological Ontology.* H. Barnes, trans. London: Methuen.

Schafer, Robert B., and Patricia M. Keith. 1985. A causal model approach to the symbolic interactionist view of the self-concept. *Journal of Personality and Social Psychology* 49:963–969.

Schooler, Carmi. 1990. Individualism and the historical and social-structural determinants of people's concerns over self-directedness and efficacy. Pp. 19–49 in *Self-Directedness: Cause and Effects Throughout the Life Course,* ed. Judith Rodin, C. Schooler, and K. W. Schaie. Hillsdale, NJ: Erlbaum.

Schwalbe, Michael L. 1983. Language and the self: An expanded view from a symbolic interactionist perspective. *Symbolic Interaction* 6:291–306.

Schwalbe, Michael L. 1985. Autonomy in work and self-esteem. *The Sociological Quarterly* 26:519–535.

Schwalbe, Michael L. 1986. *The Psychological Consequences of Natural and Alienated Labor.* Albany, NY: State University of New York Press.

Scott, Marvin B., and Stanford W. Lyman. 1968. Accounts. *American Sociological Review* 33:46–62.

Seligman, Martin E. P. 1975. *Helplessness: On Depression, Development, and Death.* San Francisco: Freeman.

Serpe, Richard T. 1991. The cerebral self: Thinking and planning about identity-relevant activity. Pp. 55–73 in *The Self Society Interface: Cognition, Emotion and Action,* ed. Judith A. Howard and Peter L. Callero. New York: Cambridge University Press.

Sher, Gordon. 1987. Other voices, other rooms? Women's psychology and moral theory. Pp. 114–132 in *Women and Moral Theory,* ed. E. F. Kittay and D. T. Meyers. Totowa, NJ: Rowman & Littlefield.

Sherif, Mizzafer. 1968. Self-concept. In *International Encyclopedia of the Social Sciences,* vol. 14, ed. David K. Sills. New York: Macmillan.

Shotter, John, and Kenneth J. Gergen. 1989. *Texts of Identity.* Newbury Park, CA: Sage.

Shrauger, J. Sidney, and Thomas J. Schoeneman. 1979. Symbolic interactionist view of self-concept: Through the looking glass darkly. *Psychological Bulletin* 86:549–573.

Simmons, Roberta G. 1978. Blacks and high self-esteem: A puzzle. *Social Psychology* 41:54–57.

Singer, Jerome L., and John Kolligian, Jr. 1987. Personality: Developments in the study of private experience. *Annual Review of Psychology* 38:533–574.

Smelser, Neil J. 1989. Self-esteem and social problems: An introduction. Pp. 1–23 in *The Social Importance of Self-Esteem,* ed. Andrew M. Mecca, Neil J. Smelser and John Vasconcellos. Berkeley: University of California Press.

Smith, M. Brewster. 1978. Perspectives on selfhood. *American Psychologist* 33:1053–1063.

Smith, M. Brewster. 1985. The metaphorical basis of selfhood. Pp. 56–88 in *Culture and Self: Asian and Western Perspectives,* ed. Anthony J. Marsella, George DeVos, and Francis L. K. Hsu. New York: Tavistock.

Snyder, Mark. 1987. *Public Appearances, Private Realities.* New York: Freeman.

Spence, Janet T., and Robert L. Helmreich. 1978. *Masculinity and Femininity: Their Psychological Dimensions, Correlates, and Antecedents.* Austin: University of Texas Press.

Staples, Clifford L., M. L. Schwalbe, and V. Gecas. 1984. Social class, occupational conditions, and efficacy-based self-esteem. *Sociological Perspectives* 27:85–109.

Stone, Gregory P. 1962. Appearance and the self. In *Human Behavior and Social Processes,* ed. Arnold M. Rose. Boston: Houghton Mifflin.

Storms, Michael D. 1979. Sex role identity and its relationship to sex role attitudes and sex role stereotypes. *Journal of Personality and Social Psychology* 37:1779–1789.

Strauss, Anselm L. 1978. *Negotiations: Varieties, Contexts, Processes, and Social Order.* San Francisco: Jossey-Bass.

Stryker, Sheldon. 1980. *Symbolic Interactionism: A Social Structural Version.* Menlo Park: Benjamin Cummings.

Stryker, Sheldon. 1991. Exploring the relevance of social cognition for the relationship of self and society: Linking the cognitive perspective and identity theory. Pp. 19–41 in *The Self-Society Dynamic: Cognition, Emotion, and Action,* ed. Judith A. Howard and Peter L. Callero. Cambridge: Cambridge University Press.

Stryker, Sheldon, and Richard T. Serpe. 1982. Commitment, identity salience, and role behavior. Pp. 199–218 in *Personality, Roles and Social Behavior,* ed. William Ickes and Eric Knowles. New York: Springer-Verlag.

Swann, William B., Jr. 1983. Self-verification: Bringing social reality into harmony with the self. Pp. 33–66 in *Psychological Perspectives on the Self,* ed. J. Suls and A. G. Greenwald. Hillsdale, NJ: Erlbaum.

Swann, William B., Jr. 1990. To be adored or to be known? The interplay of self-enhancement and self-verification. Pp. 408–450 in *Handbook of Motivation and Cognition,* vol. 2., ed. E. T. Higgins and R. M. Sorrentino. New York: Guilford.

Swann, William B., Jr., J. J. Griffin, S. C. Predmore, and B. Gaines. 1987. The cognitive-affective crossfire: When self-consistency confronts self-enhancement. *Journal of Personality and Social Psychology* 52:881–889.

Swann, William B., Jr., B. W. Pelham, and D. S. Krull. 1989. Agreeable fancy or disagreeable truth? Reconciling self-enhancement and self-verification. *Journal of Personality and Social Psychology* 57: 782–791.

Swanson, Guy E. 1988. *Ego Defenses and the Legitimation of Behavior.* ASA Rose Monograph Series. New York: Cambridge University Press.

Swanson, Guy E. 1989. On the motives and motivation of selves. Pp. 3–32 in *The Sociology of Emotions: Original Essays and Research Papers,* ed. D. D. Franks and E. D. McCarthy. Greenwich, CT: JAI Press.

Tajfel, Henri. 1981. *Human Groups and Social Categories: Studies in Social Psychology.* Cambridge: Cambridge University Press.

Tajfel, Henri. 1982. *Social Identity and Intergroup Relations.* Cambridge: Cambridge University Press.

Taylor, Marylee C., and Edward J. Walsh. 1979. Explanations of black self-esteem: Some empirical tests. *Social Psychology Quarterly* 42:242–253.

Tedeschi, James T. 1981. *Impression Management Theory and Social Psychological Research.* New York: Academic Press.

Tesser, Abraham. 1986. Some effects of self-evaluation maintenance on cognition and action. Pp. 435–464 in *Handbook of Motivation and Cognition,* ed. Richard M. Sorrentino and E. T. Higgins. New York: Guilford.

Thomspon, Linda, and Alexis J. Walker. 1989. Gender in families: Women and men in marriage, work and parenthood. *Journal of Marriage and the Family* 51:845–871.

Trilling, Lionel. 1972. *Sincerity and Authenticity.* New York: Harcourt.

Tseelon, Efrat. 1992. Is the presented self sincere? Goffman, impression management and the postmodern self. *Theory, Culture and Society* 9:115–128.

Turner, John C. 1985. Social categorization and the self-concept: A social cognitive theory of group behavior. Pp. 77–121 in *Advances in Group Processes: Theory and Research,* vol. 2, ed. E. J. Lawler. Greenwich, CT: JAI Press.

Turner, Jonathan H. 1987. Toward a sociological theory of motivation. *American Sociological Review* 18: 83–101.

Turner, Ralph H. 1962. Role-taking: Process versus conformity. Pp. 20–41 in *Human Behavior and Social Processes,* ed. A. M. Rose. Boston: Houghton Mifflin.

Turner, Ralph H. 1968. The self-conception in social interaction. Pp. 93–106 in *The Self in Social Interaction,* ed. Chad Gordon and Kenneth J. Gergen. New York: Wiley.

Turner, Ralph H. 1976. The real self: From institution to impulse. *American Journal of Sociology* 81: 980–1016.

Turner, Ralph H. and Jerald Schutte. 1981. The true self method for studying the self-conception. *Symbolic Interaction* 4:1–20.

Walker, Lawrence. 1986. Sex differences in the development of moral reasoning: A critical review. *Child Development* 55:677–691.

Warren, Mark. 1990. Ideology and the self. *Theory and Society* 19:599–634.

Weber, Max. 1958. *The Protestant Ethic and The Spirit of Capitalism.* New York: Charles Scribners Sons.

Weigert, Andrew J. 1990. To be or not: Self and authenticity, identity and ambivalence. Pp. 263–281 in *Self, Ego, and Identity,* ed. D. Lapsley and C. Power. New York: Springer-Verlag.

Weigert, Andrew J. 1991. *Mixed Emotions: Certain Steps Toward Understanding Ambivalence.* Albany: State University of New York Press.

Weinstein, Eugene A. 1969. The development of interpersonal competence. Pp. 753–775 in *Handbook of Socialization Theory and Research,* ed. D. A. Goslin. Chicago: Rand McNally.

Weinstein, Eugene A., and P. Deutschberger. 1963. Some dimensions of altercasting. *Sociometry* 26:454–466.

Wells, L. Edward, and Gerald Marwell. 1976. *Self-Esteem: Its Conceptualization and Measurement.* Beverly Hills: Sage.

Wiedenfeld, S. A., A. Bandura, S. Levine, A. O'Leary, S. Brown, and K. Raska. 1990. Impact of perceived self-efficacy in coping with stressors on components of the immune system. *Journal of Personality and Social Psychology* 59:1082–1094.

Wilder, David A. 1986. Social categorization: Implications for creation and reduction of intergroup bias. *Advances in Experimental Social Psychology* 19: 293–355.

Wiltfang, Gregory L., and Mark Scarbecz. 1990. Social class and adolescents' self-esteem: Another look. *Social Psychology Quarterly* 53:174–183.

Wylie, Ruth C. 1979. *The Self-Concept.* Lincoln: University of Nebraska Press.

Yancey, William L., L. Rigsby, and J. D. McCarthy. 1972. Social position and self-evaluation: The relative importance of race. *The American Journal of Sociology* 78:338–359.

Zurcher, Louis A., Jr. 1977. *The Mutable Self.* Beverly Hills: Sage.

CHAPTER 3

Attitudes, Beliefs, and Behavior

HOWARD SCHUMAN

The term *attitude* is typically defined by social psychologists as a favorable or unfavorable evaluation of an object (Eagly and Chaiken 1993) or as affect for or against an object (Thurstone 1931).[1] Whether we speak of likes or dislikes, love or hate, admiration or scorn, we are speaking of attitudes, since all of these involve positive or negative affect toward or evaluation of some object. Moreover, the object can be anything at all—a person, group, institution, belief, or a concept such as attitude itself. The idea is thus inescapable: even sociologists who dislike the notion of attitudes as too subjective or too individualistic are, by definition, themselves expressing an attitude.

In much of social science, and in much of ordinary language, *attitude* is employed more loosely than by the definition just given, covers ideas that are usually distinguished in theoretical writing by social psychologists. Thus the historian Ashworth (1987, 821) refers to attitudes where the word *belief* might well have been used, perhaps because he intends an accompanying negative connotation as well:

> *Aristotle believed that to be a wage-laborer was to be virtually a slave, and this attitude seems to have been prevalent in Europe . . . for two thousand years after him.*

In addition, although we normally think of the objects of attitudes as delimited, sometimes the object is almost completely general, representing life itself:

> *Life had no meaning. I planned to end the agony by closing myself in the kitchen and turning on the gas*

> *. . . Just then the phone rang. It was from an old friend who said he . . . wanted to drop by and visit. Suddenly my attitude changed. I was excited at the prospect of seeing him again and flattered that he had thought about me. (Letter to Ann Landers, June 24, 1986)*

The attitude in this instance might also seem to be toward the person herself. It is certainly possible to have attitudes such as self-esteem or self-doubt (Rosenberg 1979) in such cases the self as object is treated as existing separately from the self as evaluator.

At times the word *attitude* loses its clear positive/negative evaluative aspect and is used to suggest a very broad worldview:

> *The mentalities and sensibilities of medieval men were dominated by a sense of insecurity which determined the basis of their attitudes. (Le Goff 325, 1988)*

In a similar vein, Geertz (1973, 110) notes that *attitude* might be employed interchangeably with *perspective, stance,* or *frame of reference.* In this most general sense, an attitude can be thought of simply as an *orientation* with regard to anything. Indeed, in its earliest usage in English—about 1700—*attitude* referred to the orientation of a body in space, as in a painting. The gradual shift in meaning to the orientations of individuals toward the world or objects in it can be traced in the evolution of the word (Fleming 1967).

In this chapter, we first examine the standard social psychological conception—attitudes as evaluations of or affect toward objects—on which most social psychological theory and experimental research is based, and later the broader usage of the term that is often appropriate to social science thinking more generally. This twofold goal distinguishes this chapter from the many excellent treatments of the concept of attitude already available, especially in psychological social psychology.[2]

There are other differences in their concept of attitude between sociologists and psychologists.[3] First, most sociologists are primarily interested in the social content of the attitudes they study, rather than seeing them mainly as convenient ways of investigating theoretical issues about mental structure and process. Whether the focus is on a social fact such as war (Mueller 1973) or long-lasting structures of race and class (Della Fave 1986), a primary goal is to understand the world "out there," even though the approach is from the standpoint of individual attitudes. Sociologists also place considerable emphasis on the locations of attitude holders in the social structure—such as age, education, and gender—although such variables are virtually impossible to manipulate experimentally and therefore seldom allow rigorous causal inference. Debates in the sociological literature often concern the causal interpretations of associations between such complex social background factors and particular attitudes. The correlation of education with liberal attitudes, for example, has different political meanings for different investigators (e.g., for civil liberties, Bobo and Licari 1989; Stouffer 1955; Sullivan, Pierson, and Marcus 1979).

As a consequence of these concerns, most sociological social psychologists prefer to work with probability samples of substantively important populations, since such samples allow systematic studies of the social locations of, and social change in, attitudes. For sociologically inclined social psychologists, it is the connection between social attitudes, social objects, and the social sources of attitude formation and change that holds center stage. In addition, there may be a phenomenological concern with how respondents explain and interpret their pro/con evaluations, on the assumption that these explanations are part of the essential meaning of social attitudes as orientations toward the world (Schuman 1972).

Psychologists, on the other hand, often have less interest in the content of attitudes, being concerned primarily with their formal theoretical nature, sources, and consequences. For experimental purposes, one type of attitude object may be as good as another (e.g., the attitude object frequently used by Petty and Cacioppo 1986 is tuition increases, not because of its intrinsic interest but because it is convenient for experiments with college students). This and other differences are increasingly evident as we discuss

- attitudes as conceived classically by social psychologists, especially those from a psychological background;
- the attitude-behavior problem, which is of equal interest to psychologists and sociologists;
- properties of attitudes in addition to favorable and unfavorable direction;
- the distinction between attitudes as measured for research purposes and attitudes as expressed in ordinary life;
- attitude change, as conceived differently by psychologists and sociologists;
- the relation between attitudes and other terms that appear frequently in the social psychological literature: values, norms, schemas, scripts, and opinions, plus a further comment on the distinction between affect and evaluation; and
- broader meanings of *attitude.*

ATTITUDES IN SOCIAL PSYCHOLOGICAL RESEARCH

The standard conception of attitudes emphasized by psychologists and accepted by many sociologists, despite later clarifications (e.g., Zanna and Rempel 1988), remains much as developed in Thurstone's (1928, 1931) incisive writings more than six decades ago. Thurstone acknowledged that "an attitude is a complex affair which cannot be wholly described by any single numerical index" but argued that for purposes of measurement and empirical research one can abstract the degree of favorableness/unfavorableness of an attitude toward an object, just as one can measure the height of a table without claiming to capture in such a measure all of the complex features of the table. It is this abstract dimension of favorableness/unfavorableness that constitutes most attitude measures and that most social psychologists have in mind when they discuss attitudes.

The dominant version of Thurstone's approach today is exemplified by the work of Fishbein and Ajzen (1975; Ajzen 1988). Adapting the ideas of these influential authors to our present purposes, the favorable/unfavorable dimension can be measured in several different ways. At a simple level, subjects may be asked to evaluate an object directly, using a measure such as the semantic differential to place the object on a scale between two extremes such as "good" and "bad." Indirect questioning may also be used, asking subjects for a set of beliefs about the object, with the beliefs coded as implying positive or negative evaluations.[4] Or a large set of nonverbal behaviors may be observed and their evaluative implication with regard to the object assessed. All of these approaches should point in the same direction, since the attitude itself is assumed to be an underlying disposition (or hypothetical construct) that is manifested in specific behaviors, whether direct or indirect, verbal or nonverbal (Fishbein and Ajzen 1975, 357, 362).

The model presented by Fishbein and Ajzen is more complex than the summary just provided, but only a single type of variable needs to be added to complete the basic outline. The attitudinal parts of the model can be stated as follows:

Beliefs about object X → Attitude toward X
→ Intention toward X → Behavior toward X

Thus, a person's total set of beliefs about an object leads to their overall tendency toward a positive or negative evaluation; their overall evaluative attitude shapes their intentions to behave in positive or negative ways toward the object; and, finally, these intentions—unless checked—ordinarily lead

to behaviors that are, on the whole, positive or negative toward the object. For example, if Ann holds beliefs that Armenians are smart, hardworking, and honest, she will very likely choose a positive point on a good/bad attitude scale for Armenians, will indicate intentions to behave generally in positive ways toward Armenians, and will, in fact, usually behave in such ways. No inconsistency in this system is expected, because although the term *attitude* appears as only one link in the chain, each of the variables is really a particular manifestation of attitude in the underlying "for or against" sense —an important point that some readers of Fishbein and Ajzen have failed to grasp.[5]

In the original theory, the only variable seen to inhibit the translation of belief into behavior is "subjective norm," an internal representation of how important referents *expect* one to behave, which therefore constrains the expression of attitudes in the form of intention and behavior. Thus, if Ann believes persons important to her think she should avoid Armenians, she may not express her own positive attitude through behavior, nor would she intend to do so. Indeed, without such constraints, much socially unacceptable behavior would occur every day as people simply expressed their inner attitudinal tendencies in unrestrained actions. The diagram presented above thus requires additions showing beliefs about what important referents expect and the resulting subjective norm, with an arrow from the norm to intention, since the assumption is that the norm has its effect on behavior through restraints on or changes in intentions.

Because beliefs or "reasons" are seen as leading to attitudes, and attitudes together with norms lead, via intentions, to behavior, the model is called the theory of reasoned action. The "assumption [is] that human beings usually behave in a sensible manner; that they take account of available information and implicitly or explicitly consider the implications of their actions" (Ajzen 1988, 117).

Ajzen (1988) summarized a number of studies using behavioral intention as the dependent variable. He showed interesting and intuitively meaningful differences between intentions that are mainly predicted by the attitude side of the equation (e.g., vote preference) and those that are mainly predicted by the subjective norm side (e.g., decision to have or not have an abortion). The one important limitation of his review is its dependence on the assumption of a close connection between behavioral intention and behavior, since the primary interest of most social psychologists is in the latter, not the former. We focus soon on this important connection.

The theory of reasoned action applies to intentions and behavior that are under volitional control. Recently, Ajzen (1985) added the variable of "perceived behavioral control" to the theory, to address this limitation. For example, a man may not try to lose weight because of a belief that he cannot maintain a diet, even though both his attitude and his subjective norm point in that direction. With the addition of this new variable, Ajzen employs the new name "theory of planned behavior." Numerous attempts have also been made by others to add to or amend the theory of reasoned action (see Eagly and Chaiken 1993 for a detailed discussion).

Even with the addition of perceived behavioral control, the Ajzen and Fishbein approach assumes a rational actor who develops beliefs about an object and whose attitudes flow from these beliefs. Although the beliefs themselves need not have a rational origin (e.g., they may conceivably be quite inaccurate propositions learned by rote), the whole emphasis of the theory, despite some disclaimers, is that beliefs precede attitudes and attitudes follow logically from beliefs. However, over the past decade Fazio (1986, 1990) has developed an approach that takes attitudes as the starting point not only in relation to behavior but also to an important degree in relation to beliefs. Fazio's work is also significant in connecting attitude research to recent developments in the conceptualization of cognitive accessibility and its measurement by means of response latency (the speed with which a person can make a judgment about an object when presented with it).

In Fazio's model, our attitudes can influence our *initial* perception of an object, shaping our interpretation of exactly what it is. An attitude, according to Fazio, is simply "an association in memory between a given object and one's evaluation of that object" (Fazio 1990, 81), and the stronger the association the more likely the attitude will be activated from memory when a relevant object is encountered. The strength of association is assumed to be measured by response latency, and Fazio also shows that increased frequency of expressing an attitude, as manipulated by an experimenter, increases the likelihood of activation (e.g., Powell and Fazio 1984).

Houston and Fazio (1989) used these assumptions and findings in an experiment demonstrating that subjects biased their evaluations of the cogency of arguments about the death penalty in the direction of their own attitudes for or against the death penalty. Furthermore, the bias was significantly greater for those subjects who previously revealed more rapid access to their attitude on this issue. In a second experiment the researchers went beyond this correlational finding: they stimulated an increase in the frequency of expression of a relevant attitude for some subjects and demonstrated that this also increased bias.

The Fazio research complements the Fishbein and Ajzen model, addressing situations where people do not deliberate carefully but instead proceed spontaneously, allowing their previously formed attitudes to affect their perceptions of their environment and therefore, presumably, their behavior. The basic difference between the two models is in causal direction: the extent to which beliefs determine attitudes or attitudes determine beliefs. Fazio's theoretical emphasis is not new: Allport long ago ([1935] 1985, 36) wrote that "attitudes determine for each individual what he will see and hear, what he will think and what he will do." Fazio does not go this far: he assumes that a good deal about the object is objective, since otherwise we could not speak of the appropriate attitude being activated by the object. His change of emphasis from the Fishbein and Ajzen rational model is limited to showing that the *evaluation* of the object is biased by the subject's personal values. However,

his research provides potential connections between experimental studies of cognitive accessibility and the broader view of attitudes represented by
Le Goff and Geertz, views that we return to at the
end of the chapter.

THE ATTITUDE-BEHAVIOR PROBLEM

Thus far, one of the most important issues encountered by anyone interested in attitudes has been
hardly mentioned—the "attitude-behavior problem." We can measure attitudes, chart their trends
over time, discover their relations to age, education, response latency, and a host of other social
and psychological variables, but do attitudes as
assessed by questionnaires and interviews relate to
behavior outside the assessment situation? If not,
the study of attitudes may serve to separate us from
the rest of life, rather than illuminating it. Thurstone (1967) acknowledged this, claimed there was
usually no serious attitude-behavior gap, and went
on to describe attitudes not only in terms of affect
for or against an object, but also as *potential action* toward the object with regard . . . to the question whether the potential action will be favorable
or unfavorable to the object" (p. 20). Other definitions also imply a natural link between attitudes
and behavior, as in Allport's (1985, 36) description
of an attitude as a "neuropsychic state of readiness
for mental and physical activity."

It was exactly this presumed linkage that
LaPiere, as an early symbolic interactionist, challenged in his classic 1934 essay. The challenge is
often misread today as having been primarily an
empirical attack: endless retellings focus on La-
Piere's account of his travels around America with
a Chinese couple, their positive treatment by hotel
and restaurant personnel, and the negative answers
he received later from these same hotels and restaurants when he inquired by letter about the possibility of their accepting Chinese visitors. However,
this empirical study—flawed in many ways, as critics have pointed out—is not really the main point
of LaPiere's essay. More important is his theoretical argument that responses to a symbol—by
which he meant a word describing an object—ordi-

narily do not allow valid inferences about responses to the concrete object.

The point is made best by LaPiere not in his
report on his travels with the Chinese couple, but in
a purely imaginary paragraph that opens his argument:

> *Thus from a hundred or a thousand responses to
> the question "Would you get up to give an Arme-
> nian woman your seat in a street car?" the investi-
> gator derives the "attitude" of non-Armenian
> males toward Armenian females . . . yet all that is
> obtained is a symbolic response to a symbolic situ-
> ation. The words "Armenian woman" do not con-
> stitute an Armenian woman of flesh and blood, who
> might be tall or squat, fat or thin, old or young, well
> or poorly dressed . . . And the questionnaire re-
> sponse . . . is but a verbal reaction and this does
> not involve rising from the seat or stolidly avoiding
> the hurt eyes of the hypothetical woman and the
> derogatory stares of other street-car occupants.*
> *(LaPiere 1934, 230)*

Much subsequent research on the attitude-behavior
problem has been directed toward measuring some
aspect of the contextual variables that LaPiere was
suggesting (see Schuman and Johnson 1976 for a
number of examples), though from his perspective
most of this research remains content to assess
words, not concrete situations.

LaPiere's thesis is not that verbal responses
never predict later actions, for he freely admits
that at the time of his writing (the early 1930s)
responses by southern whites probably would
have predicted their behavior toward blacks. In
that case, the symbol and its normative force were
so powerful that they overrode individual differences among blacks and whites and across situations. However, in much of life, LaPiere argues, a
verbal symbol is too abstract and too lacking in
context to allow us to know from responses to it
how a person will act when encountering real-life
instances of the category the symbol supposedly
represents (see Saenger and Gilbert 1950 for an
interesting example).

Fishbein and Ajzen (1975; Ajzen 1988) provided two different attempts to address the basic
issue of attitudes versus actions, though neither

attempt completely confronts LaPiere's theoretical argument. One of their answers essentially acknowledges the difficulties of abstract measures and claims that predictions from verbal response to actual behavior are greatly strengthened by making the question calling for the attitude response as specific as possible. Thus one attempts to measure the attitude not toward an object, but toward a particular behavior toward the object, and to specify as clearly as possible the time and other contextual factors likely to influence the behavior. For example, to predict individual voting behavior in an election, the investigator asks, as close to the election as practical: Who [target object] will you vote for [action] on November 3 [time given and place more or less implicit]? Indeed, aggregate predictions of election results based on polls are among the most successful of all such efforts in social science (Kelly and Mirer 1974).

Thus Fishbein and Ajzen emphasize that if we wish to predict a *particular* behavior, then the attitude toward the behavior itself, not simply the attitude toward the object, must be assessed. This is an important correction to much early research, which assumed that, for example, a negative attitude toward blacks on the part of whites implied the *specific* type of negative action that the investigator happened to measure—a naive assumption once its implications are thought through. However, specifying time, place, and other contextual factors leads to such circumscribed predictions that most social scientists are not very interested in making them. In addition, the success of most such predictions may be due in part to the introduction of an implicit control—the symbolic nature of both the attitude and the behavioral measure. In the case of voting, the objects are verbal symbols, not real people, in *both* cases, as indeed the electorate has sometimes learned once the candidate of their choice wins office and begins to act with more than words.

The second, and more valuable, approach by Fishbein and Ajzen (1974) is to retain a focus on attitudes toward objects (e.g., Armenians), since that is often our main concern in both social science and ordinary life, and to recognize that although such an attitude does not imply any particular behavior, the net valence of behaviors toward the object should be consistent with the overall valence of the attitude. Thus, if A has a positive attitude toward B, it is incorrect to assume that A will give B a particular gift, or indeed a gift at all; but it *is* sensible to assume that the total set of A's behaviors toward B will tend to be positive in character. Likewise, a negative attitude on the part of A toward B hardly implies that A will hit B or openly insult B, but rather that A's overall actions toward B will tend to be negative in character. The basic point is to recognize that only by generalizing across acts to reach their overall positive/negative tendency can one arrive at some constancy to correlate with a measure of attitude toward the object. It is equally important to realize that this requirement is not peculiar to the problem of relating attitudes to behavior. The same is true for relating one attitude response to another, which is why indexes or scales are built from a number of items, and it is also true for relating one behavior to another, since, like single attitude items, single instances of behavior in the same domain may show only small relations to each other (Hartshorne and May 1928), yet when aggregated will usually provide increased reliability and validity.

Following this line of thinking, Weigel and Newman (1976) performed a valuable field study showing that a measure of proenvironmental attitudes correlated well with a multiitem measure of proenvironmental behaviors (e.g., participation in a roadside litter pickup program). The attitude measure correlated, on average, only 0.29 with individual environmental behaviors, but the association rose to 0.62 with an aggregated index of fourteen observed behaviors. This type of study needs replication, especially to test further the relation of symbolic (verbal) attitude measures to nonsymbolic behavior—the issue LaPiere raised so long ago.

One early finding of Fazio's research bears directly on the strength of the attitude-action connection: when an attitude "is grounded in and based on prior behavior, the attitude-to-later-behavior relation is stronger than when the attitude is based on indirect experience" (1986, 219). For example, attitudes toward volunteering for a psychological experiment were more predictive of actual volunteering if the subjects had participated in previous experiments than if they had not (Fazio and Zanna 1981). Fazio sees direct experience as strengthening the attitude-object bond, much as this is accomplished in the laboratory by eliciting repeated expressions of the attitude through experimental manipulation. We might plausibly rephrase this in terms of LaPiere's original argument that nonsymbolic behavior is learned best in concrete (nonsymbolic) situations that people experience themselves, which then give meaning to the symbol.

In everyday life it may be impossible to go in any simple way from a verbal symbol of a complex person, group, or institution to an actualized instance of the person, group, or institution. This should be particularly true when the symbol represents something little known to those asked to judge it, as was probably the case for the hotel and restaurant owners who encountered LaPiere's Chinese companions. Faced with a questionnaire about Chinese visitors, they may well have pictured people in coolie hats and pigtails, jabbering in an impenetrable language, whereas LaPiere's friends were dressed in American clothes, spoke English well, and probably seemed foreign only in pleasantly exotic ways. Even where a symbol represents a well-known group, as in the case of "blacks," there is such variation in skin color and features, in accent and tone, in dress and manner, that the word "black" cannot capture a real person who may suddenly appear before a respondent. The symbolic versus nonsymbolic distinction remains an important issue for social psychological research.

PROPERTIES OF ATTITUDES

We have thus far considered attitudes almost entirely in terms of direction: favorable or unfavorable evaluations of an object. However, there are two other basic properties implied by *attitude* even in its narrower technical sense. The first is usually recognized explicitly by terms like intensity, centrality, importance, and extremity (Krosnick and Abelson 1992). Here we use *attitude strength* as the generic term, although unfortunately *strength* is also employed specifically to describe degrees of intensity. Another property to consider is conceptualization of the object of an attitude.

Attitude Strength

There are various approaches to measuring attitude strength, each assessed slightly differently. For example, responses can be obtained along scales such as the following: *extremity*—extremely unfavorable, somewhat unfavorable, neutral, somewhat favorable, extremely favorable; *intensity*—very strong, fairly strong, not strong at all; *importance*—very important, somewhat important, unimportant.

The extremity scale shows direction as well as strength, whereas the intensity and importance scales are asked often as follow-up questions to simple favor-oppose choices and then combined with them to give the full continuum.

A reasonable assumption and a general finding is that all of these measures are correlated. For example, intense attitudes are usually extreme, whether in a positive or negative direction (Suchman 1950). However, Krosnick and Abelson (1992) summarize literature that they consider to show a fair amount of independence among different measures of attitude strength—the correlations, even when corrected for unreliability, are far from perfect—and Krosnick et al. (1993) reach this same conclusion based on a set of studies in which eleven different measures of attitude strength were administered. The latter includes some measures that are better considered effects or correlates of attitude strength, however, and the strength measures were administered in sequence, which invites effects due to order.

A simpler approach is to use a split-sample design to study the effects of different strength measures. When this was done for intensity and importance in a series of experiments, the different wordings produced different univariate distributions that are intuitively meaningful: more people are willing to say they feel very strongly about an issue than are willing to say it is one of the *most* important issues they would consider when voting for a candidate (Schuman and Presser 1981). How-ever, this finding need not mean that intensity and importance must be different constructs, for it is also consistent with the assumption of a single underlying dimension of attitude strength that is "cut" at different points depending on the wording of the particular strength measure employed.

Moreover, in line with the latter assumption, on the issue of legalized abortion the two meas-ures—intensity and importance—produced similar anti/pro ratios: antiabortion respondents felt more strongly *and* were likely to say the issue was more important to them. In addition, each measure showed much the same positive association with a further question about whether respondents had given money or written letters to support their side of the issue, which was treated as an effect of strength rather than an indicator of it (Schuman and Presser 1981). The issue remains open, but for now it seems more parsimonious to treat most, if not all, of the differ-ent words used to measure attitude strength as tap-ping the same underlying dimensions.

The strength dimension itself can contribute to substantive understanding, even though such meas-ures are often included only to increase response variation and thus reliability. In the case of the abortion issue, the differences in strength between pro- and antilegalization camps provide insight into the relative success of the two sides. Those supporting wider definitions of legalized abortion are in the majority in the United States, but those opposing legalization indicate considerably more intensity in their position and give more impor-tance to the issue itself. This helps explain the te-nacity of antiabortion forces in the United States, especially since the same difference was found in reports of committed action (e.g., donating money to one's own side).

Subjective attitude strength and committed be-havior do not always function in the same way, however, and the discrepancy can be illuminating. On the issue of registering guns with the police, those opposed are in the minority in surveys yet have often prevailed in preventing registration laws from passing. A plausible explanation for this apparent inconsistency would be differential atti-tude strength, as was the case with abortion, but

several investigations failed to uncover much dif-ference in attitude strength between pro- and an-tiregistration respondents. Opponents of gun con-trol, however, did report themselves considerably more likely to have written letters and given money in support of their side of the issue (Schuman and Presser 1981). This suggests that some other factor may be operating to translate attitude strength into action more for opponents than for proponents. One possibility is the efficiency of the pro-gun lobbying organization (the National Rifle Associa-tion) in soliciting letters and contributions. If so, we must consider the strength of organizational and institutional sources of action, along with psy-chological strength dimensions. This is an impor-tant possibility, especially for sociologists inter-ested in political mobilization, and merits further investigation. (See Liska 1984 for a somewhat re-lated point about the importance of social structure as a source of behavior.)

Nonattitudes

The sharpest debate about attitude strength has fo-cused not on the high strength end, but on the low strength end—on attitudes so weak as to be termed *nonattitudes* by the preeminent writer in this area (Converse 1964, 1970). Converse conceptualizes the strength continuum as "one of centrality of the attitude object to the subject" (1970, 181), with objects of nonattitudes lying at the extreme of low centrality in terms of both motivation and cogni-tion. He focuses particularly on cognitive central-ity, defined as "the proportion of 'mental time' which is occupied by attention to the attitude-object over substantial periods" (1970, 182). This definition obviously does not lend itself to ready measurement, but Converse goes on to suggest that it implies little attention to the object, little infor-mation about it, and little connection of the object to other cognized objects. In particular, level of information can be regarded as one indicator of centrality.

Converse further notes that many issues that engage political elites are of no great interest (cen-trality) to the general public and therefore may be ones on which much of the public lacks attitudes altogether. If survey respondents simply admitted this, there would be no problem, other than a very high proportion of "don't know" answers. However, Converse believes most people do not like to admit the complete absence of an attitude on what sounds like an important issue. Given the possibility of choosing between offered alternatives, such as favor or oppose, they essentially flip a mental coin and select one alternative on a chance basis. Because of this coin-flipping tendency, many attitude measures show relatively little reliability, little intercorrelation ("low constraint"), and little ideological organization (Converse 1964). However, in cases where one might expect the public to have more central attitudes, such as on issues like race where no esoteric knowledge is needed to form an attitude, there is more evidence of high reliability over time (Converse and Markus 1979).

Converse's nonattitude thesis has been subject to a continuing barrage of criticisms. Some regard it as an elitist view that assumes the average citizen is without attitudes simply because they are not organized and expressed in the same way as by intellectuals (Lane 1962). Other criticisms claim that estimates based on answers to single items of low reliability are inadequate for evaluating the stability and coherence of political thinking (e.g., Achen 1975). For a recent summary of the terms and outcome of the debate, see Kinder and Sears (1985).

Interesting new support for the existence and meaning of nonattitudes comes from Bassili and Fletcher's (1991) use of response latency measures in a survey. Those who easily switched their positions on an affirmative action item when a counterargument was introduced took longer to respond than those who did not switch, which the authors interpret to mean that the former needed to construct their answers "on-line," rather than retrieving well worked-out value positions from memory. This fits evidence from responses to questions about quasi-fictional objects that suggests that people do not so much flip mental coins as attempt to make sense of a survey question even if they are ignorant of much of its content (Schuman and Presser 1981).

Whatever the eventual outcome of the debate about nonattitudes—and I believe there to be considerable truth to Converse's argument—the concept has contributed to clearer recognition of the average citizen's limited amount of knowledge and interest in many of the issues that capture the attention of political elites and intellectuals.

General versus Specific Attitude Objects

The object of an attitude is often assumed as a given—"Jews," "the Republican Party," "legalized abortion" are the kinds of objects presented in questionnaires. Yet, as noted in the discussions of LaPiere's critique and Fazio's research, objects themselves should be treated as problematic in evaluative meaning. In addition, many objects must be regarded as problematic in that they are composed of several attributes, each of which can be the object of a distinct attitude (e.g., one might like some aspects or policies of the Republican Party but dislike others). Newcomb et al. (1965) discuss this complexity of objects, using the term *inclusiveness,* and Eagly and Chaiken (1993) summarize theories that deal with the integration of attitudinal components.

A more subtle way in which objects themselves can vary in meaning depends on the knowledge respondents bring to them. Consider a question that was posed as follows:

Do you agree or disagree?—The Arab leaders are trying to work for a real peace with Israel.

People who are knowledgeable about the Middle East and the Arab-Israeli conflict may answer this question within that well informed-framework. But those who know little or nothing about the Middle East, yet wish to answer the question, may draw on their attitudes about political leaders more generally in order to provide a response, on the assumption that one political leader (or one foreign political leader) is much like another. Thus the question may be answered at different levels of generality, no one of which is necessarily invalid.

Indeed, we probably all do this if asked a question that taps a general attitude toward a specific object about which we do not know a great deal. Many people may answer the question "Do you favor or oppose the operation of (a particular) nuclear plant in (a particular) location?" on the basis of whether or not they favor nuclear plants in general, while others who know the situation in more detail may take account of the particularities of the situation. Similarly, "Do you like or dislike golden retrievers?" will be answered by some in terms of their general attitude toward dogs (or even toward pets more generally) but by others in terms of knowledge and specific attitudes that involve distinctions between golden retrievers and other breeds of dogs.

Thus a plausible hypothesis can be proposed that general attitudes are called forth when people are not aware of particularities and distinctions that the question makes relevant and yet wish to express an attitude anyway (Schuman and Presser 1981, 129–134). The classic research by Hartley (1946) that showed that substantial majorities of college students expressed attitudes toward fictitious nationalities (Danireans, Pireneans, and Wallonians) can be interpreted in just this way: in the absence of specific attitudes toward a particular group, general positive/negative attitudes toward foreign-sounding nationalities came into play. Rather than seeing this as simply a willingness to "make up" attitudes out of whole cloth, it is better to recognize that each of us has attitudes at different levels of generality and that we vary in the level at which we understand and respond to an object. There is a rich area here for study as we try to make empirical research fit what actually happens in ordinary life.

ATTITUDES AS MEASURED AND ATTITUDES AS LIVED

It is one thing to assume that people have attitudes and another to try to measure these attitudes by means of questionnaires or interviews. The main issue is that people may not bring to the questionnaire a set of preformed attitudes that are nicely cut to fit the questions as posed. For example, in the United States today it is probably reasonable to

assume that most people know what "legalized abortion" is and have genuine attitudes toward it. Yet this does not mean that when we ask the following question, we simply elicit a well-formed attitude brought into the interview:

Do you think it should be possible for a pregnant woman to obtain a legal abortion if she is married and does not want any more children?

This question, which has been a regular part of the National Opinion Research Center's General Social Survey (GSS), omits some conditions that may be important to respondents, such as the reason for the pregnancy and the reason for wanting an abortion, the month of pregnancy, the women's age, and available alternatives to abortion. It also fails to allow for the ambivalence that many people have toward abortion: seeing it as a form of killing, yet also believing a woman has a right to make her own decision. Perhaps because of both lack of specificity in the wording and ambivalence on the part of respondents, answers to this question show a well-documented context effect, with the percentage of agreement about 11 percent higher when the question appears alone than when it follows a question about legalized abortion in the case of a defective fetus (Schuman 1992).

More generally, responses to attitude questions have been shown repeatedly to be sensitive to what at first appear to be minor changes in form, wording, or context, though what is "minor" and what is "major" is exceedingly difficult to establish except by experiments that test for this sensitivity—a quite unsatisfactory circular approach (Schuman and Presser 1981). It is clear that respondents often bring to an attitude question what Zaller (1992) calls "considerations," an unsystematic mixture of beliefs and attitudinal leanings. The question elicits a set of considerations, affected and perhaps further shaped by preceding questions, preceding responses (e.g., priming), characteristics of the interviewer (e.g., race or gender), or interview situation and perhaps by a news broadcast heard while driving to work or during dinner the night before. The combination of prior considerations and immediate reactions must then be quickly adapted to fit the alternatives offered in the case of a "closed" question, which may not include what occurs most spontaneously to the respondent (e.g., "don't know," "some of both," "let me rephrase that"). Even survey questions that seem merely to repeat what is already socially formulated, such as which of two candidates for high office one prefers, appear to be susceptible at times to changes in the way they are asked (e.g., Crespi and Morris 1984).

At the extreme, some might argue it is best to think of what happens in the attitude survey as only an immediate judgment based on the immediate situation and carrying little implication for long-standing or long-lasting attitudes beyond that situation (Wilson and Hodges 1992). This can clearly become too extreme a position, however, since most context and wording effects are limited to a relatively small part of the population (e.g., the abortion context effect leaves nearly 90 percent of the sample unaffected). In addition, there are many changes in wording and context that do *not* seem to affect responses (Schuman and Presser 1981).

Equally important, even where there are significant effects due to form, wording, or context, their impact is primarily on univariate results or "marginals," and conclusions based on associations between attitude responses and other variables (other attitude responses or demographic characteristics) usually remain unchanged. For example, despite the context effect regularly obtained on the GSS abortion item, its relation to other variables (including change over time) is much the same regardless of which context is employed. The same is true for most—though not all—effects due to form, wording, and context. This "axiom" of survey analysis, labeled somewhat awkwardly as "form-resistant correlations" by Schuman and Presser (1981), allows attitude survey analysts to proceed without too much worry, provided they avoid giving undue emphasis to univariate results *and* keep context and wording constant when comparing between two or more sets of responses.

There is a related but deeper dilemma for all approaches to measuring attitudes via questionnaires and interviews, not often recognized by survey practitioners. When surveys deal with sensitive issues such as abortion or race, at what "level of candor" do we wish respondents to answer? If, as is often alleged, the survey situation succeeds in emphasizing confidentiality and the willingness to reveal one's more private attitudes, then we may achieve that goal at the cost of failing to predict how these same people will express their attitudes when they are *not* in such a confidential and private situation. From this standpoint, it may be better not to emphasize confidentiality, and instead to encourage people to treat the survey as a more or less public forum, speaking much as they would to casual acquaintances. Yet that in turn would simply highlight what is often the standard challenge to attitude survey researchers: are people expressing their "true" attitudes? The dilemma is real and perhaps ineluctable.

Probably even more important for many issues is the need for attitude investigators to recognize the fundamental complexity of many issues and the ambivalence felt by real people. For example, many white Americans are both "liberal" and "conservative" in their beliefs and attitudes toward African Americans (Gaertner and Dovidio 1986; I. Katz, Wackenhut, and Hass 1986), and African Americans also can have considerable ambivalence toward their white counterparts. The goal of reducing racial attitudes to a single dimension of "prejudice" or "racism" probably misses the most important dynamics of race in the United States. The same is true for many other highly charged attitude objects. Although the importance of ambivalence has been recognized for many years (e.g., Newcomb, Turner, and Converse 1965), only recently have there been systematic attempts to measure it directly (e.g., Thompson, Zanna, and Griffin, forthcoming).

Ambivalence, nonattitudes and its variants, and concerns about confidentiality on sensitive topics account for many of the problems in interpreting attitude data. The same phenomena occur in ordinary life but are made more salient because we too often expect a surface clarity that does not exist with attitudes. It is up to analysts of attitude data to take these and other problems into account as they seek interpretations that both provide meaning *and* make sense.

THE STUDY OF ATTITUDE CHANGE

The different interests of psychologists and sociologists emerge with special clarity when we consider attitude change, for even the term itself shifts in meaning for the two disciplines. For psychologists, attitude change refers first and foremost to the study of the effects of various forms of persuasion in creating new attitudes or altering preexisting attitudes. The typical study brings subjects, most often college students, into a laboratory or other controlled setting, divides them into experimental and control conditions, and tests hypotheses about the short-term or occasionally longer-term consequences of a deliberate attempt to form or change a particular attitude. The focus is on the success of various manipulations of the source, content, or setting of the influence effort and the psychological processes through which subjects accept, modify, or resist such attempts. Least attention is given to the content of the attitudes themselves. Indeed, as Eagly and Chaiken (1993, 219) remark, "much of the research ordinarily thought to consider attitude change has used attitudes that Converse . . . would probably label as nonattitudes."

Sociologists who study attitude change ordinarily start from an interest in a socially important attitude that has shifted (or sometimes not shifted) over a substantial period of time. Because the attitude itself is the major focus of concern, the starting point is likely to be a careful description of the amount and shape of the change in a natural population (e.g., American adults), with the unit of time often being years, though occasionally a dramatic societal event (e.g., the U.S. attack on Iraq in 1991) allows a briefer time span. Efforts at explaining change focus on parts of the population classified in terms of social background variables and frequently by point of entry into the population (as cohorts). The sample survey, repeated over time on comparable probability samples or sometimes on the same sample, is the primary method of study, since for both descriptive and explanatory purposes it is essential to be able to think in terms of a population either that is constant or in which the alteration in composition can be investigated. Causal determination can rarely be as definitive in these sociological studies as in psychological research, but the intrinsic importance of the attitude content leads sociologists to tolerate greater uncertainty in explanation.[6]

Attitude Change for Psychologists

Due to space limitations only certain important directions of psychological research on this major topic are noted. Interested readers are referred to the Eagly and Chaiken (1993) volume, which devotes most of its 700 pages to the subject. Much of the early psychological research on attitude change sprang from experimental studies by Hovland et al. (1949) of persuasion effects on soldiers during World War II, which led to a program of research at Yale University dealing with the characteristics of communicators, of the setting in which the communication takes place, and of the way the message is received by respondents (e.g., Hovland, Janis, and Kelley 1953). For example, the more credible the communicator, both as an expert on the relevant issue and as an advisor without a personal interest (or, even better, one offering advice that goes against his/her own interests), the more effective he/she will be in changing subjects' attitudes. Continuities exist between these early experiments and recent research that stresses assumptions ("heuristics") most of us make when we are the object of influence attempts, for example, the belief that "experts can be trusted" (Chaiken 1987).

The Yale studies and much subsequent research have recently been synthesized in Petty and Cacioppo's (1986) distinction between "central" and "peripheral" routes for persuasion. The central route involves presenting information to people and having them consider it thoughtfully, though not necessarily in an unbiased way. The peripheral route occurs when people do not consider carefully the content of a persuasive message but are influenced by other cues, such as the attractiveness of the source of the message. Experiments by Petty and

Cacioppo indicate that the peripheral route is more apt to be used when subjects are distracted or see the argument as less personally relevant, but that it is also less effective in creating long-term attitude change, probably because the individual fails to elaborate arguments in support of the new attitude.

Attitude Change for Sociologists

The quite different concern with attitude change for sociologists is illustrated using evidence on changes in white racial attitudes in America over five decades. The first useful survey measures of racial attitudes were administered in 1942, with infrequent subsequent measurement through the 1950s and more regular replications up until today. As Figure 3.1 indicates, the change on several basic principles has been approximately linear over time, massive in amount, and still continuing: white Americans have moved from positions of majority endorsement of discrimination and segregation and nearly unanimous opposition to racial intermarriage to positions of rejection (at least verbally) of both discrimination and segregation and of increasing tolerance for intermarriage. (For the wording of the three questions, see Schuman, Steeh, and Bobo 1985, Table 3.1.)

These basic descriptive findings pose a series of further fundamental questions:

What initiated the change in the 1940s, or perhaps earlier, since we do not know the trajectory before 1946 when a second time point was obtained on the "equal jobs" question?

How, if at all, was the change affected by particular events, such as the 1954 Supreme Court decision declaring segregation in the public schools unconstitutional?

How widespread is the change in terms of other racial issues, including issues such as affirmative action that arose only in the last few years and that are likely to have garnered much less support in the white population?

How pervasive is the change across social categories? For example, is there a regional difference due to the fact that segregation was legal in southern states prior to the 1960s, whereas it was not in northern states? Are there differences by educational level, important in themselves and also perhaps predictive of the future course of change?

How much does the overall population change involve changes in the attitudes of individuals and how much the replacement of older cohorts by new cohorts with different attitudes?

How can the survey data on attitude change in Figure 3.1 be reconciled with other sociological evidence, such as census data showing persistent patterns of very substantial residential segregation?

How "deep" is the change in the sense of both "true attitude shifts" and "actual behavior," as against verbal agreement with new norms?

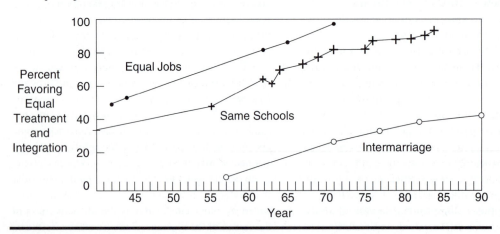

FIGURE 3.1   Trends in White Racial Attitudes.

The last question points to the difficulty of separating attitude change from normative change. Since both attitudes and nonlegal norms are located in some sense within individuals, it is difficult to see how new norms can be effective without some more or less parallel attitude change; yet we also know that people frequently give lipservice to principles in public that they do not adhere to in private. Beyond this observation, readers interested in attempts to answer these complex questions about the nature and meaning of changes in white racial attitudes are referred to other writings (Gaertner and Dovidio 1986; Jackman and Muha 1984; I. Katz, Wackenhut, and Hass 1986; Kinder 1986; Kleugel and Smith 1986; Schuman and Bobo 1988; Schuman, Steeh, and Bobo, 1985; Sears 1988; Sniderman, Brody, and Tetlock 1991). Here we simply note that many sociologists' concern with attitude change is first of all descriptive and that the description in turn then raises many issues different from those addressed by psychologists starting from a primary interest in persuasion.

ATTITUDES AND THEIR CONCEPTUAL COUSINS

Although attitude is by far the most frequent mental construct drawn on by social psychologists, other terms are often introduced in addition to or instead of attitude. We consider briefly the most common, and especially how they relate to our primary interest in attitudes.

We begin with *values,* which Rokeach (1973, 5) defined as "an enduring belief that a specific mode of conduct or end-state of existence is personally or socially preferable" to its opposite. He argued that values are more important than beliefs, among other reasons because they occupy a more central position than attitudes in one's personality and are therefore determinants of attitudes as well as of behavior. He also claimed that values are less widely drawn on than attitudes only because attitude measurement has been more advanced, but proposed to change this by creating his own value survey in which respondents rank eighteen "instrumental" and eighteen "terminal" values. (See Schwartz 1992 for a more recent attempt at systematic measurement of values across cultures.)

The dedicated attitude researcher can readily assimilate Rokeach's stress on values by regarding them as simply a special type of attitude object. For example, according to Bem (1970, 16), "a value is a primitive preference for or a positive attitude toward certain end-states of existence (like equality, salvation, self-fulfillment, or freedom) or certain broad modes of conduct (like courage, honesty, friendship, or chastity)." Once this assimilation is accomplished, how basic these attitude objects are relative to other attitude objects becomes an empirical issue. Even more important as a practical concern is whether values are best measured by simply presenting people with lists of values and obtaining rankings (Rokeach) or ratings (Schwartz), or by inferring them from more specific attitudinal responses that can be classified by investigators to imply one value or another. I do not know of any research that begins to settle either of these crucial issues.

Earlier we considered *norms* as a key concept in Fishbein and Ajzen's more general theory. They state that norms, along with attitudes, determine behavioral intentions and therefore behaviors. However, a more radical introduction of norms into attitude theory is possible by distinguishing attitudes themselves as either primarily normative in origin or primarily a matter of personal preference. For example, what to order from a restaurant menu can be considered largely a matter of attitudes in the sense of personal preferences, whereas white attitudes toward nondiscrimination by race or gender might be considered more a product of powerful normative forces. One advantage of this way of thinking about attitudes is that it reduces the need to argue over "sincerity," since the acceptance of norms can be quite genuine even when it occurs because of external reinforcement. A serious treatment of attitudes as normative in origin should thus take account of both external and internal forces. For recent research that makes interesting use of the distinction between activation of norms by means of social reminders and activation through a focus on internal (personal) standards, see Cialdini et al. (1991).

Schema has gained considerable popularity in social psychology, though as Hastie (1991) notes it is difficult to find a clear definition of the concept. It seems to imply a more organized and complex mental construct than an attitude, and one that need not have a specific object in the evaluative sense (Taylor and Crocker 1981). Thus extraversion-introversion is a schema involving conceptions about people, used in perceiving the social scene and "filling out" incoming sensory data. Schemas seem to have many of the characteristics that Allport (1985) attributed to general attitudes, but the term emphasizes beliefs and belief systems (e.g., a schema held by non-Armenians about Armenians), though in this case beliefs or belief system might do as well. It is also possible to think of schemas as the belief part of an attitude (Pratkanis 1989) or of attitudes as a special kind of schema that includes an evaluative component. In any case, since orientations toward objects remain central to social psychology, it is doubtful that "schema" can replace "attitude" as a basic concept for social psychologists. Perhaps disagreements over the meaning of schema can be reduced and its uncertain relation to attitudes clarified to the benefit of both concepts.

Scripts are sometimes treated as a type of schema, but they seem basically different in nature and certainly easier to describe. As the word suggests, a script can be thought of as a prescribed sequence of behaviors that occurs in a particular setting, the classic example being the more or less standard behaviors that a person enacts in a restaurant. As Abelson (1982) notes, the nondiscriminatory way restaurant employees treated the Chinese couple who accompanied LaPiere (1934) may be seen as a result of the script they normally follow with all customers, and this might account for the discrepancy with their answers to a letter of inquiry. Whatever the validity of this speculation and of its implications for understanding attitude-behavior discrepancies more generally, scripts are clearly quite different from attitudes in the sense of affect or evaluation toward an object.

Opinion is sometimes used interchangeably with *attitude,* especially in popular writing. However, there are three useful distinctions between the two terms. First, opinions are normally thought to be identical with their specific expression, whereas attitudes are thought to be underlying dispositions inferred from opinions and other expressions but not necessarily identical with any single one. Second, *opinion* connotes a more purely cognitive, though not necessarily well thought out, view, whereas attitudes can be treated as emotionally based as well (e.g., "I hate that person"). Finally, and probably most important, opinion is useful as part of the larger term *public opinion,* and the extent to which public opinion is simply an aggregate of individual attitudes presents an important theoretical issue that it is better not to settle by using the two terms interchangeably. See Blumer (1948) for a strong view of public opinion as a structure of influence that is quite different from an aggregate of individual attitudes.

We now return to *affect* and *evaluation.* Since each signifies favorable or unfavorable orientations toward objects, each fits comfortably under the general concept of attitude, and it is difficult to restrict the concept to one or the other. However, there have been recent efforts to make a fundamental distinction between emotional reactions to objects and evaluations of a cognitive nature (Zajonc 1980) and continuing attempts to study instances where affect and cognition appear to conflict (e.g., Millar and Tesser 1992). For now the issue remains open; it is too early to conclude that affect and evaluation need to be distinguished more generally or that *attitude* should be reserved for one or the other concept. Furthermore, it is possible that the need to make such a distinction points to the fact that in following the advice of Thurstone (1967) to abstract the positive-negative dimension from the range of orientations people have to objects, we preclude from investigation not just one important distinction—affect versus cognition—but the full range of ways humans react to objects. Every word that represents an orientation toward an object—love, like, contempt, admire, hate, worship, scorn, and so on—carries a distinctive meaning, and for *some* purposes it may be a mistake to ignore this rich array of meanings in favor of either one dimension, as Thurstone (1967) urged, or even of two. At the same time, this broader concern with how people orient themselves to their general life situation leads to ideas and research involving larger issues of interest to social psychologists and sociologists.

BROADER APPROACHES TO THE ATTITUDE CONCEPT

A focus on single attitudes or even single attitude domains may miss the richness of attitudes as orientations to life itself. Luker (1984), in an investigation of activists on each side of the abortion issue, shows that their attitudes toward abortion are part of their larger orientation toward sex, marriage, and the role of women. Probably this is less true for nonactivists on the abortion issue, but the placing of attitudes toward an object within broader orientations toward the world should be an important concern for sociological social psychologists.

There are several different ways of pursuing attitudes as general orientations. One is to conceptualize specific attitudes as reflections of underlying personality, with an emphasis on motives, needs, or dispositions. The classic research in this area was *The Authoritarian Personality* (Adorno et al. 1950), still alive, if not entirely vigorous, more than four decades after its considerable impact in the post-World War II flowering of social psychology. The attitudes investigated were primarily those toward minorities—Jews, African Americans, and others—and personality was conceptualized in largely psychoanalytic terms. (For a judicious account of the theory and resulting research, see Brown 1965; for a recent review that focuses on measurement issues, see Christie 1991.)

Adorno et al. (1950) also attempted to connect personality and social structure, using Marxist assumptions about the location of profascist tendencies, but this foundered when it was discovered that "authoritarian personalities" were located disproportionately in the working class, rather than in the lower middle class or elsewhere more compatible with Marxist assumptions. Indeed, Lipset (1981) turned the theory against its political origins by conceptualizing the main location as "working class authoritarianism." Equally or more important

was an early critique of the original research by Hyman and Sheatsley (1954) that pointed to low education as an artifactual source of scores on the F scale, the main measure of authoritarianism, and therefore cast doubt on the validity of both the measure and the theory behind it. Looking at it another way, with emphasis on acquiescence response set, Campbell et al. (1960) suggested that authoritarian measures might be valid when used in well-educated populations but that their use with the less educated was apt to yield mostly artifact. Many of the same criticisms can be applied to later attempts to improve or broaden the F scale, such as Rokeach's (1960) dogmatism measure, though some have tried to overcome problems of response set by balancing items in terms of direction (e.g., Altmeyer 1988).

More theoretical attempts at broadening the attitude concept psychologically have also been pursued. One such early effort was Smith's et al.'s (1956) attempt to show how attitudes serve important functions in individual lives: object appraisal, social adjustment, and externalization. (See also D. Katz 1960 and Pratkanis, Breckler, and Greenwald 1989 for additional discussions of attitude functions.) Such distinctions of functions are usually related to psychological studies of attitude change, since the type of persuasion needed is hypothesized to depend on the function the attitude serves. Along related lines, Sears and Funk (1991) and Abelson (1982) write about "symbolic attitudes" that are expressed when a manifest issue stands in for a deeper, real issue; the connection here to the original authoritarian personality research seems clear, though that book is seldom referred to.

A more phenomenological way to broaden the attitude concept is to try to identify the reasons people give for an expressed positive or negative attitude, because "it leads us to see something the [person] saw, or thought he saw, in his action" (Davidson 1980). For example, near the close of the Vietnam war Schuman (1972) asked samples of people who had said the war was a mistake *why* they felt that way. Social science college students tended to give ideological reasons (e.g., U.S. motives were seen as morally questionable), whereas the general adult population much more frequently gave purely pragmatic reasons (e.g., we are not winning). The different reasons people gave for opposing the war provided greater understanding of the attitude itself and also allowed better prediction to how such people would react to a future war (e.g., one with an "easy victory," as in the war against Iraq in 1990). Often it is most informative to discover that individuals at the same point on an attitude scale intend totally different meanings by their responses, so that they can be said to have the same attitude only in a quite superficial and misleading sense.

A still different approach to broadening the attitude concept is to connect its meaning directly to social structure. Thus Weber (1978) introduces a German version of the concept of attitude in discussing the necessary conditions for legitimate authority: "Naturally, the legitimacy of a system of authority may be treated sociologically only as the probability that to a relevant degree the appropriate attitudes will exist, and the corresponding practical conduct ensue" (vol. 1, 214).[7] Here attitudes refer to beliefs that support the system of authority, beliefs that are attitudinal in the sense of predisposing people to obedience, so that they make "the content of the command the maxim of their conduct for its very own sake" (vol. 2, 946). Implicitly, the absence of such attitudes would encourage actions challenging authority, as for example occurred in urban riots in the United States during the 1960s through 1990s. Weber's conceptual approach invites direct measurement of attitudinal support for authority and research on its causes and consequences.

Developing his ideas also at a societal level, Elias (1978) connects the attitude concept to fundamental cultural change. He writes about shifts between the thirteenth and sixteenth centuries in human attitudes toward bodily functions and personal habits—an "expanding threshold of aversion" (p. 83):

> People who ate together in the way customary in the Middle Ages, taking meat with their fingers from the same dish, wine from the same goblet, soup from the same pot or the same plate . . . such people stood in a different relationship to one another than we do . . . What was lacking in this courtois *world . . . was the invisible wall of affects which seems now to rise between one human body and another, repelling and separating . . . often perceptible today at the mere approach of something that has been in contact with the mouth or hands of someone else, and which manifests itself as embarrassment at the mere sight of many bodily functions of others, and often at their mere mention, or as a feeling of shame when one's own functions are exposed to the gaze of others, and by no means only then." (pp. 69–70)*

Elias's many instances from daily life in the Middle Ages, with sets of examples entitled "On Blowing One's Nose," "Changes in Attitude Toward the Natural Functions," "On Spitting," and so on point "to *attitudes* that we have lost, that some among us would perhaps call 'barbaric' or 'uncivilized'" (p. 55). Although the pro/con sense of the attitude concept can still be abstracted from Elias's book, much would be lost if such a total reduction took place. It is the content of attitudes and the transformation of this content that are important.

Still another broad use of the concept of attitude appears in the conclusion to Fleming's (1967) valuable history of the development of the concept itself. The word became popular, according to Fleming, as part of the incorporation into the polity of categories of humans previously excluded: women, nonwhites, and the working class. With their inclusion it was necessary for those previously ruling to find a term, and a concept, that recognized "wants" as legitimate yet did not bestow on them the essential cognitive character that had been accorded to upper-class white males. In this sense, Fleming returns us to attitudes as affect toward objects (Thurstone 1967) not in terms of the individual differences that Thurstone emphasized but in terms of differences across history as societies are transformed.[8]

A challenge for the sociologist as social psychologist is to combine the conceptual breadth and depth implied by these usages of Weber, Elias, and Fleming with the quantitative empirical research that is the hallmark of the simpler pro/con meaning of *attitude* that is dominant today. It is a formidable challenge.

NOTES

1. Zanna and Rempel (1988) argue that evaluation should be the primary definition and that affect (along with beliefs and past behavior) should be seen as possible sources of attitudes. However, it is difficult to imagine an evaluation of interest to sociologists that is totally devoid of affect, and thus the restriction to evaluation is not emphasized here.

2. Readers wishing a review of the attitude literature mainly from the standpoint of psychologists are referred to the recent volume by Eagly and Chaiken (1993) as well as the frequent reviews of the technical attitude literature in the *Annual Review of Psychology* (e.g., Olson and Zanna, 1993). Other valuable sources are Oskamp (1991), McGuire (1985), and Eagly (1992). A more sociological review is Kiecolt (1988).

3. These distinctions refer to modal tendencies. There are many exceptions—psychologists motivated by an interest in a particular type of socially important attitude, sociologists concerned with generic issues of attitude theory—but for the purposes of this chapter it is useful to stress the differences. Also note that *sociologist* is used in a broad sense: some of the "sociological" studies referred to were done by other types of social scientists, such as anthropologists, historians, and political scientists.

4. Fishbein and Ajzen recognize that beliefs do not always have clear positive or negative meaning. Sometimes they are simply factual and without evaluative implication (e.g., the president has brown hair), and sometimes the content is evaluated differently depending on the speaker's attitude (e.g., the president is a liberal). Both kinds of beliefs would tend to be dropped in an item analysis used to construct a scale. See Fishbein (1967) for a useful discussion of the nature of beliefs and their use in attitude measurement.

5. Beliefs, affect, and behavior (or behavioral intention) have sometimes been seen as three coequal components of an attitude—usually phrased as cognitive, affective, and conative (Milton Rosenberg and Hovland 1960)—and efforts have been made to demonstrate that the components are empirically distinguishable (Breckler 1984). These efforts have not always been successful, especially since it is difficult to separate differences due to measurement method from distinctions expected on the basis of theory. The approach taken by Fishbein and Ajzen is clearer conceptually, though we return later to the issue of affect versus cognition.

6. Another way of looking at this difference in focus between psychologists and sociologists is to note that psychologists are primarily interested in the independent variable, the causes of change no matter its content, while sociologists are primarily interested in the dependent variable—what it is that has changed—even if the reasons are not so readily or completely known. However, it is also possible within the basic survey method to include experimentation using randomized split-sample designs to test theoretical hypotheses more rigorously than correlational methods allow (Schuman and Bobo 1988; Sniderman, Brody, and Tetlock 1991).

7. The original German does not contain the word *attitude* or a close equivalent, but a bilingual translator considered the use of the English term an appropriate way to convey the meaning of the original.

8. Moreover, our attitudes are shaped by our culture not only in content but in existence. Some years ago, Lerner (1958) salvaged a large set of survey data gathered in the Middle East by making most of the analysis turn on differences between those respondents who held political attitudes at all and those who didn't. Indeed, it is no surprise that the development of the attitude concept itself occurred in Western societies, where individualism is stressed and where individuals are expected to hold attitudes toward a wide range of objects, including even distant governing bodies in their national capital.

REFERENCES

Abelson, Robert P. 1982. Three modes of attitude-behavior consistency. Pp. 131–145 in *Consistency in Social Behavior: The Ontario Symposium,* ed. M. Zanna, E. T. Higgins, and C. P. Herman. Hillsdale, NJ: Erlbaum.

Achen, Christopher H. 1975. Mass political attitudes and the survey response. *American Political Science Review* 69:1218–1231.

Adorno, T. W., Else Frenkel-Brunswik, Daniel J. Levinson, and R. Nevitt Sanford. 1950. *The Authoritarian Personality.* New York: Harper.

Ajzen, Icek. 1985. From intentions to actions: A theory of planned behavior. Pp. 11–39 in *Action Control: From Cognition to Behavior,* ed. J. Kulh and J. Beckman. Heidelberg: Springer.

———. 1988. *Attitudes, Personality and Behavior.* Chicago: Dorsey.

Ajzen, Icek, R. Darroch, Martin Fishbein, and J. Hornick. 1970. Looking backward revisited: A reply to Deutscher. *American Sociologist* 5:267–273.

Allport, Gordon W. 1935. Attitudes. Pp. 798–844 in *Handbook of Social Psychology,* ed. C. M. Murchison. Worcester, MA: Clark University Press.

———. 1985. The historical background of social psychology. Pp. 1–46 in *The Handbook of Social Psychology,* 3rd ed., vol. 1, ed. G. Lindzey and E. Aronson. New York: Random House.

Altmeyer, Bob. 1988. *Enemies of Freedom: Understanding Right-Wing Authoritarianism.* San Francisco: Jossey-Bass.

Ashworth, John. 1987. The relationship between capitalism and humanitarianism. *American Historical Review* 92:813–828.

Bassili, John N., and Joseph F. Fletcher. 1991. Response-time measurement in survey research: A method for CATI and a new look at nonattitudes. *Public Opinion Quarterly* 55:331–346.

Bem, Daryl. 1970. *Beliefs, Attitudes and Human Affairs.* Monterey, CA: Brooks/Cole.

Blumer, Herbert. 1948. Public opinion and public opinion polling. *American Sociological Review* 13:542–549.

Bobo, Lawrence, and Frederick C. Licari. 1989. Education and political tolerance: Testing the effects of cognitive sophistication and target group affect. *Public Opinion Quarterly* 53:285–308.

Breckler, Steven J. 1984. Empirical validation of affect, behavior, and cognition as distinct components of attitude. *Journal of Personality and Social Psychology* 47:1191–1205.

Brown, Roger. 1965. *Social Psychology.* New York: Free Press.

Campbell, Angus, Philip E. Converse, Warren E. Miller, and Donald E. Stokes. 1960. *The American Voter.* New York: Wiley.

Chaiken, Shelly. 1987. The heuristic model of persuasion. Pp. 3–39 in *Social Influence: The Ontario Symposium,* ed. M. P. Zanna, J. M. Olson, and C. P. Herman. Hillsdale, NJ: Erlbaum.

Christie, Richard. 1991. Authoritarianism and related constructs. Pp. 501–571 in *Measures of Personality and Psychological Attitudes,* ed. J. Robinson, P. Shaver, and L. Wrightsman. San Diego: Academic.

Cialdini, Robert B., Carl A. Kallgren, and Raymond R. Reno. 1991. A focus theory of normative conduct: A theoretical refinement and reevaluation of the role of norms in human behavior. *Advances in Experimental Social Psychology* 24:201–234, ed. M. P. Zanna. San Diego: Academic Press.

Converse, Philip E. 1964. The nature of belief systems in mass publics. Pp. 206–261 in *Ideology and Discontent,* ed. D. Apter. New York: Free Press.

———. 1970. Attitudes and nonattitudes: Continuation of a dialogue. Pp. 168–189 in *Quantitative Analysis of Social Problems,* ed. E. Tufte. Reading, MA: Addison-Wesley.

Converse, Philip E., and Gregory B. Markus. 1979. Plus ça change . . . : The New CPS Election Study Panel. *American Political Science Review* 73:32–49.

Crespi, Irving, and Dwight Morris. 1984. Question order effects on voting preferences in 1982. *Public Opinion Quarterly* 48:578–591.

Davidson, Donald. 1980. *Essays on Actions and Events.* New York: Oxford University Press.

Della Fave, L. Richard. 1986. Toward an explication of the legitimation process. *Social Forces* 65:476–500.

Eagly, Alice. 1992. Uneven progress: Social psychology and the study of attitudes. *Journal of Personality and Social Psychology* 63:693–710.

Eagly, Alice, and Shelly Chaiken. 1993. *The Psychology of Attitudes.* New York: Harcourt Brace.

Elias, Norbert. 1978. *The Civilizing Process.* New York: Urizen Books.

Fazio, Russell H. 1986. How do attitudes guide behavior? Pp. 204–243 in *The Handbook of Motivation and Cognition: Foundations of Social Behavior,* ed. R. M. Sorrentino and E. T. Higgins. New York: Guilford.

———. 1990. Multiple processes by which attitudes guide behavior: The mode model as an integrative framework. Pp. 75–109 in *Advances in Experimental Social Psychology,* vol. 23, ed. M. P. Zanna. San Diego: Academic.

Fazio, Russell H., and Mark P. Zanna. 1981. Direct experience and attitude-behavior consistency. Pp. 161–202 in *Advances in Experimental Social Psychology,* vol. 14, ed. L. Berkowitz. New York: Academic.

Fishbein, Martin. 1967. A consideration of beliefs and their role in attitude measurement. Pp. 257–266 in *Readings in Attitude Theory and Measurement,* ed. M. Fishbein. New York: Wiley.

Fishbein, Martin, and Icek Ajzen. 1974. Attitudes towards objects as predictors of single and multiple behavioral criteria. *Psychological Review* 81:59–74.

————. 1975. *Belief, Attitude, Intention, and Behavior: An Introduction to Theory and Research.* Reading, MA: Addison-Wesley.

Fleming, Donald. 1967. Attitude: The history of a concept. Pp. 287–365 in *Perspectives in American History,* vol. 1, ed. D. Fleming and B. Bailyn. Cambridge, MA: Charles Warren Center in American History, Harvard University.

Gaertner, Samuel L., and John F. Dovidio. 1986. The aversive form of racism. Pp. 61–89 in *Prejudice, Discrimination and Racism,* ed. S. Gaertner and J. Dovidio. Orlando: Academic.

Geertz, Clifford. 1973. *The Interpretation of Cultures.* New York: Basic Books.

Hartley, Eugene. 1946. *Problems in Prejudice.* New York: Kings Crown Press.

Hartshorne, H., and M. A. May. 1928. *Studies in the Nature of Character: Studies in Deceit.* New York: Macmillan.

Hastie, Reid. 1981. Schematic principles in human memory. Pp. 39–88 in *Social Cognition,* ed. E. T. Higgins, P. Herman, and M. Zanna. Hillsdale, NJ: Erlbaum.

Hastorf, A. H., and Hadley Cantril. 1954. They saw a game: A case study. *Journal of Abnormal and Social Psychology* 49:129–134.

Houston, David A., and Russell H. Fazio. 1989. Biased processing as a function of attitude accessibility: Making objective judgments subjectively. *Social Cognition* 7:51–66.

Hovland, C. I., I. L Janis, and H. H. Kelley. 1953. *Communication and Persuasion.* New Haven: Yale University Press.

Hovland, C. I., A. A. Lumsdaine, and F. D. Sheffield. 1949. *Experiments in Mass Communication.* Princeton: Princeton University Press.

Hyman, Herbert H., and Paul B. Sheatsley. 1954. The authoritarian personality: A methodological critique. Pp. 50–122 in *Studies in the Scope and Method of "The Authoritarian Personality",* ed. R. Christie and M. Jahoda. Glencoe, IL: Free Press.

Jackman, Mary R., and Michael J. Muha. 1984. Education and intergroup attitudes: Moral enlightenment, superficial democratic commitment, or ideological refinement? *American Sociological Review* 49: 751–769.

Katz, Daniel. 1960. The functional approach to the study of attitudes. *Public Opinion Quarterly* 6:248–268.

Katz, Irwin, Joyce Wackenhut, and R. Glen Hass. 1986. Racial ambivalence, value duality and behavior.

Pp. 35–59 in *Prejudice, Discrimination and Racism,* ed. S. Gaertner and J. Dovidio. Orlando: Academic.

Kelly, S., and T. W. Mirer. 1974. The simple act of voting. *American Political Science Review* 68: 572–591.

Kiecolt, K. Jill. 1988. Recent developments in attitudes and social structure. Pp. 381–403 in *Annual Review of Sociology,* vol. 14, ed. W. R. Scott and J. Blake. Palo Alto, CA: Annual Reviews.

Kinder, Donald R. 1986. The continuing American dilemma: White resistance to racial change forty years after Myrdal. Journal of Social Issues 42: 151–171.

Kinder, Donald R., and David O. Sears. 1985. Public opinion and political action. Pp. 659–713 in *The Handbook of Social Psychology,* 3rd ed., vol. 2, ed. G. Lindzey and E. Aronson. New York: Random House.

Kluegel, James R., and Eliot R. Smith. 1986. *Beliefs about Inequality: Americans' Views of What Is and What Ought to Be.* New York: de Gruyter.

Krosnick, Jon A., and Robert P. Abelson. 1992. The case for measuring attitude strength in surveys. Pp. 177–203 in *Questions about Questions: Inquiries into the Cognitive Bases of Surveys,* ed. J. Tanur. New York: Russell Sage Foundation.

Krosnick, Jon A., David S. Boninger, Yao C. Chuang, and Catherine G. Carnot. 1993. Attitude strength: One construct or many related constructs? J*ournal of Personality and Social Psychology* 65: 1132–1151.

Lane, R. E. 1962. *Political Ideology.* New York: Free Press.

LaPiere, Richard. 1934. Attitudes versus actions. *Social Forces* 13:230–237.

Le Goff, Jacques. 1988. *Medieval Civilization 400–1500.* Oxford: Blackwell.

Lerner, Daniel. 1958. *The Passing of Traditional Society: Modernizing the Middle East.* New York: Free Press.

Letter to Ann Landers, *Detroit Free Press,* p. 28, July 24, 1986.

Lipset, Seymour Martin. 1981. *Political Man.* New York: Doubleday.

Liska, Allen E. 1984. A critical examination of the causal structure of the Fishbein/Ajzen attitude-behavior model. *Social Psychology Quarterly* 47:61–74.

Luker, Kristin. 1984. *Abortion and the Politics of Motherhood.* Berkeley: University of California Press.

McGuire, William J. 1985. Attitudes and attitude change. Pp. 233–346 in *The Handbook of Social Psychology,* 3rd ed., vol. 2, ed. G. Lindzey and E. Aronson. New York: Random House.

Millar, Murray G., and Abraham Tesser. 1992. Pp. 277–300 in *The Construction of Social Judgment,* ed. L. Martin and A. Tesser. Hillsdale, NJ: Erlbaum.

Mueller, John E. 1973. *War, Presidents, and Public Opinion.* New York: Wiley.

Newcomb, Theodore M., Ralph H. Turner, and Philip E. Converse. 1965. *Social Psychology.* New York: Holt, Rinehart & Winston.

Olson, James M., and Mark P. Zanna. 1993. Attitudes and attitude change. Pp. 117–154 in *Annual Review of Psychology,* vol. 44, ed. L. W. Porter and M. R. Rosenzweig. Palo Alto, CA: Annual Reviews.

Oskamp, Stuart. 1991. *Attitudes and Opinions.* Englewood Cliffs, NJ: Prentice Hall.

Petty, Richard, and John T. Cacioppo. 1986. *Communication and Persuasion: Central and Peripheral Routes to Attitude Change.* New York: Springer-Verlag.

Powell, Martha C., and Russell H. Fazio. 1984. Attitude accessibility as a function of repeated attitudinal expression. *Personality and Social Psychology Bulletin* 10:139–148.

Pratkanis, Anthony R. 1989. The cognitive representation of attitudes. Pp. 71–98 in *Attitude Structure and Function,* ed. A. Pratkanis, S. Breckler, and A. Greenwald. Hillsdale, NJ: Erlbaum.

Pratkanis, Anthony R., Steven J. Breckler, and Anthony G. Greenwald. 1989. *Attitude Structure and Function.* Hillsdale, NJ: Erlbaum.

Rokeach, Milton. 1960. *The Open and Closed Mind.* New York: Basic Books.

———. 1973. *The Nature of Human Values.* New York: Free Press.

Rosenberg, Milton J., and Carl I. Hovland. 1960. Cognitive, affective, and behavioral components of attitudes. Pp. 1–14 in *Attitude Organization and Change,* ed. C. I. Hovland and M. J. Rosenberg. New Haven: Yale University Press.

Rosenberg, Morris. 1979. *Conceiving the Self.* New York: Basic Books.

Saenger, Gerhart, and Emily Gilbert. 1950. Customer reactions to the integration of Negro personnel. *International Journal of Opinion and Attitude Research* 4:57–76.

Schuman, Howard. 1972. Two sources of anti-war sentiment in America. *American Journal of Sociology* 78:513–536.

———. 1992. Context effects: State of the art/state of the past. Pp. 5–20 in C*ontext Effects in Social and Psychological Research,* ed. N. Schwarz and S. Sudman. New York: Springer-Verlag.

Schuman, Howard, and Lawrence Bobo. 1988. Survey-based experiments on white racial attitudes toward residential integration. *American Journal of Sociology* 94:273–299.

Schuman, Howard, and Michael P. Johnson. 1976. Attitudes and behavior. Pp. 161–207 in *Annual Review of Sociology,* vol. 2, ed. A. Inkeles, J. Coleman, and N. Smelser. Palo Alto, CA: Annual Reviews.

Schuman, Howard, and Stanley Presser. 1981. *Questions and Answers in Attitude Surveys: Experiments on Question Form, Wording and Context.* New York: Academic.

Schuman, Howard, Charlotte Steeh, and Lawrence Bobo. 1985. *Racial Attitudes in America: Trends and Interpretations.* Cambridge, MA: Harvard University Press.

Schwartz, Shalom H. 1992. Universals in the content and structure of values: Theoretical advances and empirical tests in 20 countries. Pp. 1–65 in *Advances in Experimental Social Psychology,* vol. 25, ed. M. P. Zanna. San Diego: Academic.

Sears, David O. 1988. Symbolic racism. Pp. 53–84 in *Eliminating Racism: Profiles in Controversy,* ed. P. Katz. New York: Plenum.

Sears, David O., and C. L. Funk. 1991. The role of self-interest in social and political attitudes. Pp. 2–91 in *Advances in Experimental Social Psychology,* ed. M. Zanna. San Diego: Academic.

Smith, M. Brewster, Jerome S. Bruner, and Robert W. White. 1956. *Opinions and Personality.* New York: Wiley.

Sniderman, Paul M., Richard A. Brody, and Philip E. Tetlock. 1991. *Reasoning and Choice: Explorations in Political Psychology.* New York: Cambridge University Press.

Stouffer, Samuel A. 1955. *Communism, Conformity, and Civil Liberties.* New York: Wiley.

Suchman, E. A. 1950. The intensity component in attitude and opinion research. In *Measurement and Prediction,* ed. S. A. Stouffer. Princeton: Princeton University Press.

Sullivan, John, James Pierson, and George E. Marcus. 1979. An alternative conceptualization of political tolerance: Illusory increases, 1950s–1970s. *American Political Science Review* 73:781–794.

Taylor, Shelley E., and Jennifer Crocker. 1981. Schematic bases of social information processing. Pp.

89–133 in *Social Cognition,* ed. E. T. Higgins, P. Herman, and M. Zanna. Hillsdale, NJ: Erlbaum.

Thompson, Megan M., Mark P. Zanna, and Dale W. Griffin. Forthcoming. In *Attitude Strength: Antecedents and Consequences,* ed. R. Petty and J. Krosnick. Hillsdale, NJ: Erlbaum.

Thurstone, L. L. 1928. Attitudes can be measured. *American Journal of Sociology* 33:529–554.

———. [1931] 1967. The measurement of social attitudes. Pp. 14–25 in *Readings in Attitude Theory and Measurement,* ed. Martin Fishbein. New York: Wiley.

Weber, Max. 1978. *Economy and Society,* ed. Guenther Roth and Claus Wittich. Berkeley: University of California Press.

Weigel, Russell, and L. Newman. 1976. Increasing attitude-behavior correspondence by broadening the scope of the behavioral measure. *Journal of Personality and Social Psychology* 30:793–802.

Wilson, Timothy D., and Sara D. Hodges. 1992. Attitudes as temporary constructions. Pp. 37–65 in *The Construction of Social Judgment,* ed. L. Martin and A. Tesser. Hillsdale, NJ: Erlbaum.

Zajonc, Robert B. 1980. Feeling and thinking: Preferences need no inferences. *American Psychologist* 35:151–175.

Zaller, John R. 1992. *The Nature and Origins of Mass Opinion.* Cambridge, England: Cambridge University Press.

Zanna, Mark P., and John K. Rempel. 1988. Attitudes: A new look at an old concept. Pp. 315–334 in *The Social Psychology of Knowledge,* ed. D. Bar-Tal and A. Kruglanski. New York: Cambridge University Press.

CHAPTER 4

Social Cognition

JUDITH A. HOWARD

On Monday, October 7, 1991, news headlines announced that a professor at the University of Oklahoma Law School, Anita Hill, had accused Clarence Thomas, a U.S. Supreme Court nominee, of sexual harassment. Public reaction was overwhelming; the number of phone calls received on Capitol Hill was called "stunning by any standard." Headlines varied from "Hill, a woman of great credibility" to "Thomas will look America in the eye." Seven female members of the House of Representatives marched to the 98 percent male Senate to demand attention to the charges.

This scenario portrays dramatically the social significance of cognition. At issue was the definition of behaviors as (un)acceptable, the attribution of responsibility for (in)appropriate behavior to a highly visible public official, the attribution of (il)legitimacy to a former female employee of this official, as well as concerns about whether racial stereotypes had influenced past or current treatment of the situation. This is social cognition.

According to most recent review articles, social cognition is the dominant substantive area in social psychology. This claim is made typically by psychologists (Markus and Zajonc 1985; Sherman, Judd, and Park 1989). Social cognition has not had an equally distinguished position among sociological social psychologists. Categorizations of social psychology cast social cognition in the psychological camp (e.g., House 1977), and correctly so. While there is a sociological tradition pertinent to social cognition, the lion's share of theory, empirical work, and application in social cognition, more than any other topic in this volume, has been produced by psychologists. It is against this over-

whelmingly psychological background that sociologists who work in this area are preoccupied with demonstrating the sociological significance of social cognition, the goal of this chapter.

In some respects, the early roots of social cognition stressed sociological themes. These discussions of the social nature of the mind gave way, however, to alternative metaphors of the human mind, metaphors that were more individualized, guided by a sense of the human as rational, scientific. Only recently have there begun to be signs of a renewed recognition of the sociohistorical and contextual shaping of human thought. In this chapter I mine the traditional literature for signs of this shift and point to productive future directions. The first part of the chapter defines key terms, reviews the basic structures and processes of social cognition, and suggests how cognition relates to behavior and affect. Throughout, the relevance of this primarily laboratory-based research to sociological concerns is stressed, and therefore some otherwise significant topics receive short shrift. Although this section may seem more relevant to psychological social psychologists, it may be useful for those in sociology as well. Arguing a similar point, David Wagner (1991, 793) writes: "Had we a clearer conception of the cognitive and motivational processes that mediate many of our structural arguments, mistaken assumptions [in sociological work] might occur less frequently." The second part of the chapter discusses critical issues in contemporary social cognition—questions about the accuracy of cognition, the degree of consciousness of cognition, the need to focus on dynamic, motivational aspects of cognition, and postmodern critiques of cognition.

The final section considers the sociological dimensions of social cognition, both interactive and structural.

DEFINING SOCIAL COGNITION

Definitions of social cognition are varied. Fiske and Taylor (1991) define social cognition as "the study of how people make sense of other people and themselves" (p. 1). Forgas (1981) stresses the social aspects of cognition more explicitly, arguing that cognition is more than information processing, that cognition is socially structured and socially transmitted, shaped by social values, motivations, and norms. I use *social cognition* to refer to structures of knowledge, the processes of knowledge creation, dissemination, and affirmation, the actual content of that knowledge, and how social forces shape each of these aspects of cognition.

It is also important to distinguish cognition from what it is not. Cognition is thought; it is not emotion and it is not behavior, although it is related to each of these constructs. Over the twentieth century, social psychology has tended variously to emphasize one or the other of these three aspects of the human actor, sometimes to the virtual exclusion of the other two. The 1980s were the realm of the cognitive, but as the decade drew to a close the field began to shift toward increasing attention to affective dimensions and the relationship between thinking and feeling.

Historical Perspective

Much of the research in social psychology during the twentieth century could be labeled social cognition. During the 1970s and 1980s, however, social psychology experienced a cognitive revolution (Schneider 1991), as is evident in the establishment of the "Attitudes and Social Cognition" section in *Journal of Personality and Social Psychology* and of the journal *Social Cognition*. This growth of social cognition was a reaction to the earlier dominance of behaviorism, a model that is too narrow to apply to a wide range of social behavior. Contem-

porary social psychology now takes for granted the idea that unobservable internal representations mediate between environmental stimuli and behavioral consequences.

Sociological Roots

At least three distinct lines of sociological theory, the nineteenth century work of Durkheim and of Weber, phenomenology, and symbolic interaction are intellectual ancestors of social cognition. Durkheim (1898) was critical of individual psychology but developed an important theory of collective psychology, proposing the notion of collective representations of social life, a predecessor of Moscovici's (1981) concept of social representations. Weber's (1968) sociology is based on a theory of individual behavior. Weber conceived of meaningful action as social through the subjective meaning attached by the actor. Macrosocial phenomena are ultimately derived from the actions of individuals and those meanings attached to them. And Weber's "ideal types" are a predecessor of the notion of prototypes.

The relevance of the phenomenological tradition is exemplified in the work of Alfred Schutz (1970), who elaborated those individual everyday activities that underlie macro-level social actions. According to Schutz, humans live in a subjectively perceived and interpreted "life-world." Our actions are rational and pragmatic within the terms of this understanding. Schutz's subjective understandings are remarkably similar to contemporary cognitive structures. Moreover, he anticipated contemporary emphases in social cognition in proposing that these schemas are created through everyday social interaction; they are culturally negotiated, communicated, and shared.

Charles Horton Cooley, W. I. Thomas, George Herbert Mead, and Herbert Blumer all in some way dealt with issues of perception, the construction of knowledge, and the creation of symbolic meaning, particularly as they pertain to the construction of self. Mead (1934), the most cognitive of these early sociological thinkers, held that significant symbols are created through conversations of gestures. These symbols allow us to take the role of the other, anticipating both our own and others' behaviors and thus to shape our own behavior accordingly. Minds and selves are created through these fundamentally social, as well as fundamentally cognitive, processes. Blumer (1969) presented a more contextualized, mutable picture of symbolic interaction than Mead, but his emphases on the significance of sensitizing concepts, the ongoing nature of interpretation as a basis for constructing the actions of participants, and the importance of social context in shaping those interpretations also place cognition in a central role in symbolic interaction. Each of these early sociologists contributed to a sociological tradition that is at least receptive to and sometimes fertile ground for the further development and application of cognitive concepts.

COMPONENTS OF SOCIAL COGNITION: STRUCTURES AND PROCESSES

Cognitive Structures

Knowledge must be represented in some form. Although representations can be iconic, sensory, or neural, as well as verbal, social cognition emphasizes verbal representations. Cognitive structures are these organized representations of knowledge, the elements of cognition.

Early Forms of Cognitive Structures.   Just as the substance of social cognition predates its contemporary form, so earlier social psychology offers analogs to the contemporary conception of cognitive structures. Beliefs, attitudes, and values are representations of information. Attitudes, a central concept in social psychology for most of its history (chapter 3), are cognitive evaluations about a particular target. Some prefer to define attitudes more broadly as incorporating affective, cognitive, and behavioral components, but this definition assumes a degree of consistency among these three elements, which is not always the case empirically. Cognition has played a major role in virtually every

theory of attitudes. Most of the early work focused on the measurement of attitudes and on attitude formation and change, guided by the principle of cognitive consistency. The major contribution of contemporary social cognition has been the development of models of the mediating processes involved in attitude formation and change.

Values are a remarkably understudied, but equally significant, cognitive structure. Defined as preferences for particular end states of existence (e.g., equality, freedom) or particular broad modes of conduct (e.g., honesty, courage; Rokeach 1973), values are the criteria people use to select and justify actions and to evaluate social events. Values are thought to be central in individuals' belief systems and thus to underly a variety of possible attitudes. Perhaps because values are more difficult than attitudes to manipulate, there has been relatively little application of values to social psychological problems outside of Rokeach's research. In one of the few contemporary exceptions, Schwartz (1992) has developed a model of the structure of human values, drawing on data from collaborators in over more than twenty countries. This research group also considers how social experiences affect value priorities and value change, thus paying explicit attention to the social nature of this cognitive structure.

Contemporary Cognitive Structures.   Contemporary conceptions of cognitive structures reflect the cognitive miser view of the human actor. Implicit in any model of information processing is the recognition that humans have cognitive limits. Because it is impossible to process all incoming information in a given situation, we develop systems of categorization that facilitate this process. Cognitive structures are categories into which we sort incoming information. These structures are created through multiple experiences with instances of the concepts they represent, and they function as interpretive frameworks for new information.

Prototypes are the central tendency of the characteristics associated with members of a category (Cantor and Mischel 1979). A middle-aged white man wearing a tweed jacket and brown slacks might be considered the prototype of the category "professor." Although the boundaries of categories are "fuzzy," Cantor and Mischel have found substantial agreement across raters on the typicality of category features. Consensus about category features points to the social dimensions of knowledge dissemination and affirmation, dimensions unexplored in this literature.

Schemas are abstract cognitive structures that represent organized knowledge about a given concept or type of stimulus. Schemas act as theories that shape how people view and use information. Schemas can be distinguished according to their functions or, more sociologically relevant, their content. We develop person, role, and event schemas, as well as content-free schemas, such as processing rules. *Person schemas* are organized knowledge about specific people or types of people. Most research on person schemas has focused on traits or personality categories. One particularly significant type of person schema is a self-schema, organized knowledge about one's self. A person might be self-schematic for one trait, say political activism, but aschematic—lacking a schema—for a trait such as religiosity. To be aschematic implies no organized knowledge about self on a particular trait.

Role schemas are organized knowledge about the expected behaviors of occupants of particular social positions. These can refer to instrumental social roles, such as parent or teacher, as well as to social groups, such as ethnic or age-based social groups. Role schemas are the basis for stereotyping and intergroup prejudice and discrimination, and as such have obvious sociological significance. *Event schemas* describe expected sequences of events in familiar situations, such as dining at a restaurant or grocery shopping. Event schemas are directly analogous to a script for a play that explicitly designates the actors, what they do and when, where they stand, and with what props. Like other forms of event schemas, scripts tend to be organized into major scenes or subsets of actions. These action units are identified with particular goals and are thus keys to understanding action. For example, "Why did you speak to the waiter?" could be an-swered by reference to a relevant subset of action: "I was ordering."

Different types of schemas can overlap substantially. For example, in practice person schemas often are differentiated by situation as well as by person. For example, Professor X is opinionated in the classroom, but these expectations about her do not generalize to other situations. Role schemas shape person schemas, in that group stereotypes are used as a basis for attributions about specific members of those groups. Self-schemas, as well as other person schemas, incorporate information about social roles. Thus social categories are prominent among responses to the Twenty Statements Test question "Who am I?" The correlation between person and role schemas varies depending in part on the salience of the role information. McGuire et al. (1978) report that only 1 percent of white students in a predominantly Anglo school system spontaneously mentioned their ethnic group membership in describing themselves, whereas 17 percent of African Americans and 14 percent of Hispanics did so. Thus social context shapes social cognition.

European scholars have identified other more fully social cognitive structures. Serge Moscovici's (1981) concept of *social representations* is one example. Moscovici (1981, 181) defines social representations as "a set of concepts, statements, and explanations originating in daily life in the course of inter-individual communication. They are the equivalent . . . of the myths and belief systems in traditional societies . . . the contemporary version of common sense." Although social representations are structural elements in the cognitive systems of individuals, the generation and communication of social representations are collective processes.

Derived from Durkheim's concept of collective representations, social representations are more dynamic, being created and recreated through social interaction. This construct blurs the conventional (and perhaps outdated) distinction between structure and process; representations are structures in the sense of being organized knowledge, but they are structures in process, continually transforming some forms of information into others.

Through social representations we make sense of the social world and communicate that sense to others. Social representations are created through the processes of anchoring and objectifying. Anchoring entails anchoring new ideas into preexisting systems; objectifying entails making the abstract concrete, through personifying certain aspects and creating visual representations. To use Moscovici's illustration, Freud is the objectification of psychoanalysis: many people don't know the intricacies of the theory, but they know the name Freud and a few representative aspects of his work. Moscovici's theory has been criticized (Potter and Litton 1985), but its scope and relentless insistence on the significance of social interaction for the creation and transmission of cultural concepts are a major contribution to a sociological understanding of cognition.

Cognitive Processes

As the theory of social representations illustrates, cognitive processes go hand in hand with cognitive structures. A concern with process is one of the distinguishing features of contemporary social cognition. Methodological advances have been instrumental in facilitating this research. Ingenious process manipulations are used to interfere with, augment, or interrupt various stages in cognitive processing and thereby reveal their workings. Computer simulations are also used to model hypothesized cognitive processes (Fiske and Taylor 1984, chap. 10). Three central cognitive processes are attention, memory, and social inference.

Attention. Of necessity, the first step in processing information is making some stimulus the focus of attention. Once a stimulus comes into focal attention it is identified and categorized, and thereby given semantic meaning. Attention also can be directed to the current contents of the mind, rather than to environmental stimuli. Attention involves both direction—the selection of some stimuli and not others—and intensity. The selectivity of attention is a direct reflection of the need for cognitive efficiency. In some circumstances we may consciously decide what to attend to, but in most circumstances encoding and attention occur outside fully conscious awareness. The crucial question is how we select what to attend to and what to ignore.

Several contextual variables affect the direction of attention. The salience of stimuli—the degree to which they stand out relative to other stimuli in the environment—is a primary influence. Some factors that enhance the salience of a stimulus are purely visual: someone seated at the center as opposed to the side of an observer's visual field, an object that is brighter than its surroundings, or an object that is moving in an otherwise stationary setting will be salient in their respective environments. Most influences on salience, however, have some degree of social meaning. Salience is created through the contrast of group memberships, for example, or the violation of social norms: being the sole woman in a sea of men or the only African American in an organization of whites makes a person salient. When a behavior is unusual for the particular actor, for the actor's social category, or even for people in general, it will be salient and attract attention. Thus person schemas, self-schemas, and role schemas each form a cognitive backdrop against which ongoing behaviors are evaluated, presumably preconsciously, and either attended to or not.

Increased salience and in turn attention have significant social consequences. In one illustrative study (McArthur and Solomon 1978), an "aggressor" and a "victim" were shown on videotape having a heated exchange about a bridge hand; in one version of the tape the victim wore a leg brace and in another she did not. More of the aggressor's behavior was attributed to the victim's characteristics when the victim was wearing the brace. The subjects thus appeared to discount the aggressor's obviously rude behavior by attributing it to the victim when the victim was salient. The implications of this study are profound: if the results can be generalized, victims who deviate from the norm on social attributes will be held more accountable for the negative situations in which they find themselves than those who are "normal."

The cognitive accessibility of stimuli also affects attention. Recently and frequently activated ideas come to conscious attention more easily than ideas that have not been recently activated. Through priming, the activation of knowledge about stimuli that are currently the focus of attention, socially significant categories such as ethnicity and gender influence social inferences. Racial categories primed in a presumably unconscious manner (e.g., exposure to words associated with stereotypes of African Americans) led white subjects to respond more quickly to stereotypic words and to make more negative evaluations of African Americans (Dovidio, Evans, and Tyler 1986). Similarly, men primed through viewing a pornographic film responded more stereotypically and in a sexual manner to a woman with whom they were not acquainted (McKenzie-Mohr and Zanna 1990). These effects are all the more striking when one considers that priming has sustained consequences.

Memory.   Once information has been encoded, it is potentially available to be retrieved and used for future cognitive inferences. Memory retrieval involves activating information stored in long-term memory and bringing it into short-term memory, the part of memory that is the conscious focus of attention. Short-term memory is much more limited in scope than long-term memory, consistent with the cognitive miser model. There are several models of the organization of information in long-term memory. The best developed of these posits the formation of associative networks—networks of links between nodes or elements of information. Information that is used more often is stronger and likely to be drawn on even more often with use. The procedural knowledge approach represents knowledge as condition-action pairs. When the condition element is activated, the action follows automatically. The exemplar model suggests that we store collections of instances on the basis of which we then infer category knowledge.

One major preoccupation among memory researchers is assessing the relative accuracy of memory. Recall of information improves the more

engaging and less superficial the purpose for which one encodes and retrieves information, the more one empathizes with another, and the more one anticipates future interaction with another. Interestingly, this latter effect is stronger when one has chosen one's interaction partner. The greater accuracy produced by an empathic goal orientation and by the anticipation of future interaction point both to the importance of affect for understanding memory and to social influences on memory.

Memory for appearances is much more accurate than memory for behavior or traits. At least in experimental contexts, the ability to remember and recognize faces is close to 100 percent accurate (Bower 1977). There is one striking qualification: memory for faces of out-group members is much worse than for faces of in-group members. Cross-race accuracy, for example, is poorer than own-race accuracy. Studies of the organization of information in memory provide other reminders of the social basis of memory. People often organize information by the social group to which actors belong, rather than by the actors themselves. In fact, one model assumes that memory retrieval actually starts by searching for social category information. People tend to recall more information about in-group than out-group members. And, reflecting the affective nature of prejudice, people tend to recall negative information about disliked out-groups, and they remember differences more accurately than similarities between out-groups and in-groups (Howard and Rothbart 1980). Memory for both in-group and out-group members tends to support preexisting social hierarchies and the schemas through which they are inscribed in thought.

These studies demonstrate both the significance of social context in shaping human memory and the effect of cognitive structures on this process. Numerous studies underscore the effects of social schemas on memory. In one frequently cited study by Cohen (1981), for example, subjects observed a fifteen-minute videotape of a woman having a birthday dinner with her husband. (The actors were actually married, lending greater than usual believability to the scenario.) When asked later to answer questions about the tape, subjects who thought the woman was a waitress remembered details such as her drinking beer, owning a television, having a hamburger and chocolate cake for dinner, and liking to bowl. When they thought she was a librarian they remembered details such as her wearing glasses, owning classical records, having roast beef, wine, and angel food cake for dinner, and having traveled in Europe. In both cases memory was supplemented by role schemas; some of these details were not shown in the videotape but were generated instead by what has been called reconstructive memory. Absent information is perceived and then remembered on the basis of the existing schema.

Extant models of memory focus on intraindividual storage of information. Noting that researchers themselves are prone to store information in locations such as computers, date books, and file cabinets, Wegner (1986) turns our attention to external storage capacities. In a model of special significance to sociological social psychologists, Wegner suggests that members of social groups divide cognitive labor much as family units divide physical labor. His model of transactive memory, a system whereby memory for different categories of information is divided among members of a social group, is a major contribution to understanding the cognitive capacities of both individuals and the social groups of which they are members. This intriguing formulation suggests important questions about other cognitive processes: do we allocate attention differentially among members of a social group, for example?

Cognitive Inferences. Information retrieved from memory typically is used to form a cognitive inference. The process of social inference involves combining information according to some set of rules to form one of several types of judgment: decisions, probability, cognitive evaluations, and attributions of causality and other attributes linked to social actors.

The first step in any inference is *gathering relevant information.* Presumably we should gather all relevant information, but research (and life) would suggest that we do not. Rather, we are guided by preexisting expectations and theories to select a subset of potentially relevant information, a strategy consistent with the demands of cognitive efficiency. We are particularly likely to rely on theories as opposed to data when we hold those theories with confidence, the theory is salient, and the data are ambiguous. Preconceptions about social groups and social processes, as part of the cultural legacies virtually all of us carry, thus influence what information we gather.

In most situations we cannot use all of the relevant information, so we select a sample. We are generally inattentive to sample size, overestimating the reliability of small samples. Similarly, we tend to be inattentive to biases in samples. One familiar example is the common tendency to infer general principles on the basis of one's own friends, hardly a representative sample of the culture at large. We also tend to underuse base rate information. In one socially relevant study, subjects read an account of a woman who was living on welfare with numerous children, while maintaining an affluent lifestyle. This case was presented along with base rate statistics either indicative of welfare abuse or suggesting that the average welfare recipient receives payments for only a short time. Subjects' judgments were influenced more by the case study than by the base rate information (Hamill, Wilson, and Nisbett 1980). Taken together, these effects demonstrate a general failure to understand the nature of randomness. These patterns of information selection reflect and maintain prevailing societal patterns, as the welfare study illustrates.

Once we have gathered what we perceive to be adequate information, we combine it to make social inferences. Some models of *information integration,* most notably the early theories of attribution, assume the individual is capable of relatively sophisticated and rational strategies in information processing. Others focus on a host of biases in these presumably rational processes. Still others describe a series of cognitive shortcuts developed in the service of cognitive efficiency. I will take up these judgmental heuristics first, turn to some of the errors to which individuals are prone, and conclude by discussing theories and research on attribution, a body of research particularly illustrative of the sociological significance of cognition.

Heuristics are cognitive shortcuts that reduce complex problem solving to simpler mental operations; they allow us to process information most efficiently. A groundbreaking paper by Tversky and Kahneman (1974) identified several prominent heuristics: representativeness, availability, and anchoring and adjustment. Representativeness guides judgments of probability; we judge the probability of an event on the basis of its similarity to its parent population. Representativeness involves identifying people or objects as members of categories, a tendency fundamental to social cognition. A description of a person as quiet, shy, and orderly would dispose us to guess that he/she is a librarian, because these attributes are judged as similar to those of the population of librarians. Reliance on this heuristic may make us insensitive to other equally significant information, however, such as prior probabilities. If this person lives in a town in which 75 percent of the occupants are farmers, reliance on this heuristic will lead to poor judgments. Representativeness can also undermine our understanding of chance. The opening scene of Tom Stoppard's play *Rosenkrantz and Guildenstern Are Dead,* a scene in which Rosenkrantz (or was it Guildenstern?) keeps flipping a coin that keeps coming up tails, is notable precisely because it defies common-sense notions of chance, though it does not defy chance itself.

According to the availability heuristic, we estimate frequency or probability by the ease with which instances are brought to mind. The more readily one can think of instances of a given event, the more of them may have occurred; thus availability can be a reliable strategy. However, biasing factors also affect this heuristic. Availability activates cognitive schemas, and thus attention to details that may be inappropriate. Thus availability, like other cognitive processes, can serve the goals of stereotyping. Moreover, social processes affect availability; events that are prominent in the cultural media are more available than those that receive little attention (Heimer 1988).

Anchoring and adjustment are paired heuristics. We reduce the ambiguity of judgment by starting the process from a beginning reference point, or anchor, and then adjusting it to reach a final judgment. We tend to use our own experience as an anchor, a reasonable strategy in some, but not all, circumstances. Problems also occur in the adjustment process; we do not adjust adequately for differences between our own and others' behavior in formulating assessments of probability. Generalizing to the group level, it follows that we would tend to use in-group experience as an anchor, which could lead to errors about judgments of members of other groups.

Heuristics are inferential strategies that assume the need to reduce information. As such, their vulnerability to biasing influences is a necessary evil. Other models assume a more normative, rational basis for information integration. Because the key principles necessary for accurate information integration are so often violated, much energy has gone into detecting the patterns, viewed from this perspective as errors, that plague this cognitive process. One of the key requirements for an accurate judgment is the capacity to assess covariation. Necessary or not, humans do not assess covariation very accurately (Nisbett and Ross 1980). Each of the four cells of a two-by-two table contains information necessary to assess covariation. Perceivers tend to focus on the present-present cell, however, and ignore the others, particularly the absent-absent cell. Moreover, we tend to be more accurate if the number of cases is small, since it is easier to combine all the information simultaneously. As should be no surprise, we are also more accurate when we do not have a preexisting expectation about the relationship between the two variables. In fact, with no expectation whatsoever, we sometimes err in the other direction, failing to see a real relationship.

When a relationship between two variables is expected, people tend to overestimate the strength of that relationship, at times even creating an illusory correlation. This cognitive phenomenon is one of the bases of stereotyping. Hamilton and Gifford (1976) demonstrated that illusory correlations based on paired distinctiveness shape negative stereotypes of minority group members. This effect is highly generalizable. When majority group members form a negative impression of a group in one domain, they tend to generalize to other domains as well. This tendency is especially significant because judgments of covariation often underly other cognitive inferences. Note that this pattern demonstrates again the conservative, cognitively efficient tendency of people to process information so as to confirm prior expectations. Although these inferential strategies can be successful, they can lead also to errors, as well as provide firm cognitive foundations for social prejudices.

Attribution.   The cognitive inference that has received the most sustained theoretical attention is the process of attribution. Attribution refers to the formation of a causal inference—a judgment about what factors may have produced a particular outcome—or a trait inference—the assignment of a trait to a particular individual. (Although trait inferences are treated typically as a subset of causal inferences, they are conceptually distinct.) Fritz Heider (1958) first articulated the principles of attribution in *The Psychology of Interpersonal Relations,* which remains a relatively undiscovered gold mine. His discursive discussion is the basis for the more formal models proposed by Harold Kelley and E. E. Jones. Each of these models begins with the assumption that the causes of behavior can be categorized as internal, factors associated with an individual actor, or external, factors in the situation or environment in which behavior occurs. These theories also assume an oppositional relationship between internal and external, individual and social factors.

Kelley (1967, 1973) addresses the question of when people attribute causality to the environment or to the actor. In his full information model attributions are based on profiles of covariation between behavior and three types of information: consensus—information about the behavior of other people, distinctiveness—information about

how the actor behaves toward related stimuli, and consistency—information about the actor's past behavior. Attributions to the actor follow from high-consistency, low-distinctiveness, and low-consensus profiles; attributions to the environmental stimulus follow from high-consistency, high-distinctiveness, and high-consensus profiles. Kelley (1973) suggests that in informationally impoverished situations, we make attributions by applying various causal schemas, conceptions people have about how causes interact to produce specific effects.

Jones and Davis (1965) and later Jones and McGillis (1976) address a different and narrower question: under what circumstances does an actor's behavior lead to attributions of particular traits to the actor? Trait attributions are based on an analysis of the effects that follow from this behavior and from other behavioral alternatives and prior expectancies for behavior. Target-based expectancies derive from knowledge of prior behavior of the actor; category-based expectancies derive from knowledge of relevant social group memberships and social norms. Jones and McGillis assert that high prior expectancies mitigate against dispositional inference, which contradicts Kelley's predictions for distinctiveness and consistency, the parallel information in his model. These contradictory predictions reflect different assumptions about what principles underlie dispositional inference: Jones stresses information gain, whereas Kelley stresses action-attribute correspondence.

In recent years principles from social cognition have guided the development of several alternative attribution models. These emphasize the role of cognitive structures in defining potential causes; they maintain that people bring their own world knowledge to bear in making attributions. Hewstone and Jaspars (1987) outline a natural logic model in which people use the covariation information proposed by Kelley to identify necessary and sufficient conditions for the occurrence of an effect. Others have questioned whether covariation is the major principle by which we make attributions. Hilton and Slugoski (1986) suggest that we use contrastive criteria, asking not why an event occurred, but rather why this event, rather than the normal case, occurred. These contrastive cases can be constructed only with the use of real world knowledge that defines what the situation ought to have been. The theory also differentiates between scripted and nonscripted events. It is only in response to scripted events that deviant outcomes generate causal search and attribution. Attributions may not be made about nonscripted events.

Heider emphasized the phenomenological, subjective aspects of attribution. The subsequent models of attribution generated by Kelley and Jones, however, assume that the human attributor approximates scientific models of logic. These theories have become normative criteria; determining the extent to which laypeople deviate from them has become a popular obsession. Primary among these errors of attribution is the "fundamental attribution error," a preference for attributing causality to people rather than to the environment (L. Ross 1977). Allison and Messick (1985) apply this pattern at the group level, demonstrating a systematic tendency to attribute opinions implied in group decisions to the individual members of the group, even when the group decision was not made collectively. Other deviations include the actor-observer bias, the preference for actors to attribute causality to the environment but for observers of the same behavior to attribute causality to the actor; a tendency to underuse consensus information and, when we do use it, to use the self as the basis for defining consensus; and a variety of self-serving attributions, including casting oneself in a positive light as well as self-denigrating attributions that may serve positive ends for the actor (Nisbett and Ross 1980, L. Ross 1977). All of the problems associated with assessing covariation also shape attributions, because attributions rely on perceived patterns of covariation.

Attribution was the most popular focus of empirical social psychological research during the 1970s and 1980s. Despite this popularity, there has been remarkably little critical attention to this field. Among the more serious limitations, certainly for sociological social psychologists, is the failure to conceptualize fully the social elements of attribution. Despite Heider's early recognition of the role

of categorization and its social implications, the only reference to social phenomena in the major theories is Kelley's consensus information and Jones and McGillis's analogous variable, category-based expectancies. Kelley's hypothesis that low consensus leads to a person attribution (Jones and Davis's hypothesis is similar) implicitly asserts that internally motivated behavior is individualistic and idiosyncratic. Normative behavior is assumed not to provide information about the actor. Intentional collective action thus has no conceptual place in these models. Kelley's formulation also fails to specify who those others are on whose behavior we form judgments of consensus, a limitation Jones and McGillis begin to correct.

The distinction between target- and category-based expectancies, between individual and society, also merits debate. If people internalize their group memberships, which a substantial literature suggests we do, much individual behavior is guided by social norms for the relevant reference group. The distinction between internal and external has been questioned, but only in the most limited way, and generally in terms of methodological issues. Furthermore, most attribution research has been conducted in asocial contexts, referring to unsituated behavior.

The picture is not as bleak in essays and research by non-North American social psychologists. Oakes (1987), for example, makes the important point that the validity of a distinction between person and situation rests on the typical conceptualization of persons as traits. Persons have been treated as causal forces only by dint of their individual personalities. Because individuals have social as well as personal identities, however, it is important to consider what conditions produce attributions to people as social category members. Behavior can be explained in terms of people's shared, collective, social properties, in addition to their idiosyncratic characteristics, a possibility empirically supported by Oakes (1987) .

Oakes's research is an implicit critique of Jones and Davis's assumption that personality is revealed only in antinormative behavior. Deschamps's (1983) critique is more explicit; he argues that the adaptation of a social role can be individualized without being deviant or antinormative. Jones and Davis's prediction that only behavior that contradicts social norms provides individualized information about the actor is consistent with their backgrounds as psychologists. This view contrasts strikingly with a sociological view of deviance, for example, as a product of subgroups whose internal norms guide behavior defined as deviant only by a culture at large. The attributional vocabulary lacks a term to describe adequately individual behavior that reflects the individual's group memberships and values.

I have argued elsewhere that a comprehensive theory of attribution must and can account for the social accounts that social actors provide for socially significant behavior (Howard 1990). A sociological perspective on attribution, supported by disparate lines of research, emphasizes that: (1) at the micro level, the process of attribution relies on the social categorization of actors and perceivers; (2) at the meso level, behavior itself is fundamentally social, occurring in socially meaningful and interactive contexts; and (3) at the macro level, attributions are shaped by the historical, economic, and political contexts of intergroup relations.

There is substantial empirical evidence of the effects of social categorization on attribution. Duncan (1976) demonstrates the influence of racial stereotypes on attributions about violence: white college students were much more likely to describe ambiguous behaviors of African Americans (75 percent) than whites (17 percent) as violent. Similar patterns have been found in non-Western societies. Taylor and Jaggi (1974) found that Hindus made internal attributions to other Hindus performing desirable acts and external attributions for undesirable acts, but these patterns reversed when the actor was Muslim. Social categorizations thus strongly shape the process of attribution.

Differential evaluation appears always to accompany the process of categorization; social power relations are thus fundamental to attribution. The positive in-group bias can be overturned by the culturally prevalent negative image of dominated groups; members of socially subordinate groups in some (but not all) circumstances make self-deni-

grating rather than self-serving attributions, echoing the attributions of those in power. Guimond and Simard (1979) found that English and French Canadians in Quebec explained the patterns of dominance and subordination between their groups in strikingly different terms. This implies that attributions must be elicited from members of both majority and minority groups whenever intergroup dynamics are relevant to the behavior in question. Taken together, these studies suggest that existing patterns of power, as well as consciousness of group power (Gurin, Miller, and Gurin 1980), strongly shape attributions by members of those groups and must be included in an adequate explanation of those attributions.

COGNITION, AFFECT, AND BEHAVIOR

Cognition and Affect

Throughout its history, social psychology has variously privileged cognition, affect, or behavior. The recent emphasis on cognition emerged in response to the once dominant behavioristic conception of human behavior. In recent years increasing dissatisfaction with an overly cognitive view of human nature has led to a growing literature on sentiment, affect, and emotion. Chapter 5 addresses the sociology of affect and emotion; here I address briefly the relationship between cognition and affect.

Affective Foundations of Cognition.   The influence of affect on cognition has received limited treatment. Yet, as Markus and Zajonc (1985) observe, almost all cognition is in some sense evaluative. When the targets of cognition are social objects, evaluation dominates cognitive activity, as in stereotyping or self-deception. Most theoretical models of social cognition give little attention to affective influences. Higgins et al. (1981) present an admittedly speculative outline, proposing that affectively significant stimuli may receive more effort in the attention and encoding stages and/or may produce more cognitive activity and thus bias retrieval processes.

Empirical studies have addressed relatively unintense and minor affective states, most often moods (perhaps because moods are one of the few forms of affect that can be manipulated with relative ease). Variations in mood do affect cognitive processes such as memory, inference, and decision making. People more easily remember information whose valence fits their current mood. Good moods lead people to rate almost anything more positively, to make judgments more quickly, and to make categorizations more inclusively (Isen 1987). Mood also appears to affect the potential for cognitive change; positive moods lead people to be more susceptible to persuasion. Although mood does influence cognitive activity, effects of more intense or sustained, and therefore sociologically meaningful, affect remain to be demonstrated.

Cognitive Foundations of Affect. Substantially more attention has been directed to the influence of cognition on affect. Cognition provides the major theoretical link in moving from undifferentiated arousal to differentiated emotions. The earliest statement of this relationship is Schachter's two-component theory of emotional lability (Schachter and Singer 1962), according to which diffuse physiological arousal triggers cognitive interpretation, resulting in the labeling of an emotion.

Other theoretical approaches suggest that cognitive structures may create affect. Particular schemas carry affective meaning and therefore when activated produce affective responses; if an existing schema is emotionally intense, application of that schema in a new situation will trigger emotion. Cognitive inferences also create affect. Weiner et al. (1978) proposed that an attribution's standing on three dimensions—locus, stability, and controllability—has affective consequences (which, in turn, affect behavior). So, for example, pride follows from internal and controllable attributions about a positive event. Weiner et al. (1978) demonstrated the interactionist flavor of this relationship: people attempt to provide particular attributions for their behaviors that will elicit desired emotions and deter undesired emotions from others. Cognitive simulations can also elicit affect. Past events that

are more easily undone through cognitive simulation, that is, events whose causes are abnormal, produce more intense emotional reactions (Kahneman and Tversky 1982), a finding that suggests a hint of sociological relevance.

The ways social factors create emotion is at best implicit in these approaches. Averill (1990) presents a more explicit theory of the cultural and social construction of emotion through cognitive mechanisms. Averill (1990) views emotions as organized systems of responses prescribed by cultural scripts. Emotions are transitory but are also social roles represented cognitively by those who share a culture. Because emotions are social roles, identification with particular roles is necessary to experience the scripted feelings. There are other social constructivist approaches to emotion, but Averill's is one of the few that emphasizes the cognitive structures involved in storing rules for emotion.

Summary. Although it has become fashionable for cognitive social psychologists to attest to the need for more attention to the relationship between cognition and affect, these discussions give primacy to cognition. A debate has raged within attribution theory, for example, about whether attributional biases reflect motivational or "pure" information-processing influences (see Fiske and Taylor 1991). The tone of this debate suggests that such biases should be considered nonmotivational unless evidence of motivational forces is clear-cut. It might be useful to reverse this assumption and consider whether affective factors could be sufficient to account for some aspects of social cognition. Indeed, Zajonc (1980) argues not only that affective and cognitive processes are separate, but also that affective responses are more basic. While the primacy of affect is debatable, Zajonc is right to underscore the significance of affect and its relationship to cognition.

Cognition and Behavior

For some, the relationship between cognition and behavior is the single most important aspect of social cognition, indeed, its underlying rationale. Mead (1934) went so far as to argue that cognition is nothing but a guide to behavior. Thus a few illustrations of the effects of cognitions on sociologically meaningful behavior may be useful. In a series of studies on marital violence, Frieze (1979) shows that battered women who attribute blame for the violence to stable factors are somewhat more likely to attempt to leave the relationship. Cognitions about the self also exert important effects on behavior. The self-schemas of those attempting to recover from addiction, for example, affect the possibility of recovery (Markus and Nurius 1986). The literature on "learned helplessness" demonstrates that expectancies about the effects of their own behavior can lead people to engage in self-defeating behaviors that in turn prevent the disconfirmation of those expectancies. Cognitive variables have been used to shape behavior in many applied areas, including (but not limited to) health behavior, the law, interpersonal relationships, intellectual achievement, and political behavior.

The most influential theoretical statement of the relationship between cognition and behavior has been Ajzen's (1988) model of planned behavior, an updated version of Ajzen and Fishbein's (1977) model of reasoned action. According to this model, beliefs about the probable consequences of the specific act determine the attitude toward that act. The attitude, together with subjective norms—perception of the behavioral expectations of relevant reference groups or individuals—and perceived behavioral control, affects behavioral intentions, which in turn predict behavior.

Vallacher and Wegner's (1987) action identification theory may prove to be equally influential. Analogous to Stryker's (1980) identity theory, action identification theory holds that different ways of thinking about a particular action—act identities—form an organized cognitive representation—the action identity structure. Low levels in this hierarchical structure identify the specifics of action, whereas high levels identify more abstract understanding of action. We use act identities as frames of reference for executing an action, monitoring it cognitively, and reflecting on whether or not to continue the action. Behaviors enacted at a higher level of action identification tend to be more stable than those enacted at lower levels, and thus show higher correlations with relevant attitudes.

These theoretical perspectives aside, research on this topic tends to be pragmatic, attempting to account for variability in the relationship between cognitions and behavior. The great proportion of this research concerns attitudes and focuses on measurement issues (see chapter 3). Other influences on the A-B relationship implicate cognitive processes more directly. Attitudes formed from direct experience are better predictors of behavior, for example, presumably because such experience provides more information and makes the attitude more accessible in memory (Fazio and Zanna 1981). An intriguing formulation by Millar and Tesser (1986) shows that the motivation for behavior affects the A-B relationship. The cognitive component of attitudes is highly correlated with instrumental, goal-oriented, behaviors, whereas the affective component of attitudes is highly correlated with consummatory behaviors. This is a rare demonstration of the simultaneous connections among affect, cognition, and behavior.

The cognition-behavior relationship is reciprocal. Bem's (1972) theory of self-perception posits that people infer their attitudes, and presumably other cognitions as well, from observations of their own behavior. Attitudes and other cognitions may also influence behavior more interactively. People's expectancies and attitudes lead them to use behavioral strategies interactively to elicit information about others that confirms their initial expectancies and beliefs. Snyder demonstrated this process of confirmatory hypothesis testing in situations ranging from mock job interviews to questioning courtroom witnesses. The influence of behavior becomes even more apparent in the interactive consequences of this process; the target person may alter his/her behavior so as to confirm the expectations behaviorally, creating a self-fulfilling prophecy. (See Snyder 1984 for a review.) A final example illustrates that cognition can affect behavior even at the group level. In her work on the effects of minorities on majorities, Nemeth (1986) demonstrates that the expression of minority views, whether accurate or not, whether acceded to or not, fosters the attention and cognitive effort necessary to raise the quality of group decision making. Thus the relationship between cognitions and behavior, whether intrapersonal or interpersonal, is reciprocally causal.

ISSUES IN SOCIAL COGNITION

A variety of significant issues pertinent to the scope and nature of social cognition merit discussion. Five topics are considered here. The first four speak to the concerns of both psychological and sociological social psychologists: (1) What are the goals of human thought, and how do we evaluate this process? Are accuracy, utility, or rationality appropriate or compatible standards? (2) How much do we actively engage in thought? How much of human thought is conscious? Is consciousness necessary for action? (3) What are the dynamics of cognition? When and how do cognitions change? (4) What are the implications for social cognition of the postmodernist critique of science? The fifth issue concerns the relationship between social cognition and sociology: (5) What is the significance of social categorization? What are the interactive, social structural, and cultural dimensions of social cognition? This discussion is guided by House's (1977) division of social psychology.

Evaluating Social Cognitions

The literature on social cognition portrays a rather schizophrenic thinker. On the one hand, humans are viewed as capable of quasi-scientific, rational thought. On the other, we are hopelessly flawed information processors. Both seem to be true. The key question is by what standards to assess human cognition. The early models of attribution assume a quasi-scientific, logical information processor. From this perspective, the logic and accuracy of judgments are reasonable standards. In some instances and for some types of judgments, objective standards do exist. In most social situations, how-

ever, objective standards do not exist. Moreover, accuracy and logic are not appropriate standards for attributions, if attribution is defined as a subjective judgment reflecting the perceiver's phenomenal understanding of causality. We can assess instead whether these types of judgments are adaptive or pragmatic. These judgments are important because we use them in social situations.

Despite the inappropriateness of using logic as a standard, researchers have focused substantial attention on errors (incorrect predictions or deviations from known facts) and biases (systematic distortions of otherwise appropriate inferences) and found substantial evidence of both. It may be useful to cast a sociological eye at the supporting research, however. Most of this research does not begin to approximate the real world situations in which people make social judgments. Schwarz et al. (1991) make the astute observation that in most studies of heuristics the researchers violate widespread principles of social discourse, presenting information that is neither informative nor relevant in a communicative context that suggests otherwise. Subjects' judgmental biases may reflect simply the misapplication of the rules of everyday social discourse to the experimental situation. Indeed, many cognitive "errors" are misapplications of strategies that are often appropriate for making judgments. That errors and biases occur does not mean we are so faulty in everyday life, when the consequences are much more costly.

Several compelling motives guide how we process information. Efficiency is primary. It would be not just inefficient but even paralyzing to develop and test all possible hypotheses based on all available data. Heuristics and biases allow the perceiver to limit and thus facilitate the inferential process. But social motives are also compelling. If the social or personal costs of errors are high, we are more fully attentive, search memory more carefully, and use more information in making inferences. Indeed, social motives may even lead us to adopt heuristics consciously for interpersonal ends; Heimer (1988) suggests that heuristics are used actively as a rhetorical strategy to shape public opinions about the importance of particular social problems. In short, the implications for a given inference dictate how we process information. Inferences may be vulnerable to errors and biases, but these limitations are not random. Thus the human as information processor might be characterized best as what Fiske and Taylor (1991) call a "motivated tactician."

When Do We Actively Think?

A fundamental assumption of social cognition is that we actively engage in thought. As the nature of the motivated tactician has become more evident, compelling questions arise: Just how much do humans actively think? Can thought occur automatically, or without full consciousness? To the minimal extent that the unconscious has been addressed within social cognition, it has been conceived narrowly as unactivated cognitions in long-term memory or unattended perceptual processes. The narrowness of the cognitive conception of the unconscious is evident in a special issue of *Personality and Social Psychology Bulletin* (1987, vol. 13, no. 3).

Considerably more attention has been directed toward automatic thinking. We encode a great deal of information through automatic processes, described variously as unintentional, involuntary, effortless, autonomous, and outside awareness. Automaticity depends on practice. With repetition, judgments become proceduralized so that exposure to a stimulus automatically leads to a given inference. In an intriguing line of research, Ellen Langer (1989) has analyzed most fully the characteristics of less than fully conscious cognition, or what she calls "mindlessness." Enabled through habitual repetition of actions, and modified by situational characteristics such as the novelty of the situation and the costs of behavior, mindlessness reduces attention and sensitivity to contextual details. To the extent that social dimensions such as age and ethnicity are frequently encountered stimuli, proceduralization may cause perceivers automatically to emphasize these dimensions in making social judgments.

Clearly there are circumstances in which humans do not actively process information. What circumstances, then, provoke active thought? Varied lines of research triangulate on the same answers. In novel situations, in which we do not have preexisting theories or schemas, in high-effort situations, in which reliance on habit or routine might prove costly, and in situations in which the outcomes are unexpected, especially when they are negative, people will actively and consciously think (Langer 1989; Wong and Weiner 1981). Unfortunately, this profile suggests that in many socially meaningful situations we will be less than fully aware. Stereotyping and other socially consequential cognitive processes occur semiautomatically; the situations that provoke such reactions are those that encourage mindlessness. It takes real creativity to encourage mindfulness instead.

Dynamics and Change in Cognition

The fundamental assumption that cognitive elements intervene between environmental stimuli and responses virtually requires a commitment to understanding cognitive dynamics and change. The stages of cognitive processing—attention, memory, and inference—represent the dynamics of cognition. What they do not address is how people use temporal dimensions and expectations about change in their thinking. We engage in mental simulations, for example, constructing hypothetical scenarios about the future to predict outcomes in a given situation, and presumably adjusting our own behavior accordingly (Kahneman and Tversky 1982). Counterfactual simulations of the past —imagining how events might have gone otherwise—influence subsequent judgments as well as affective responses to events.

The simulation heuristic illustrates how temporal comparisons are used in social inference. Albert (1977) recasts Festinger's (1954) social comparison theory into a general model of how intrapersonal temporal comparisons are used to define the self. Markus and Nurius (1986) delineate possible selves, a construct consistent with Albert's model. Possible selves include ideas of what we may have been in the past or would like to become (or fear becoming) in the future. They are specific representations of the self in alternative states, and as such they serve as significant motivational forces. One factor in sustaining the discipline necessary to stay on a strict diet, for example, might be an imagined past or future self as a social misfit.

Cognitive structures are vulnerable to change, but as implied in the concept of structure, change occurs slowly. New information is assimilated into existing structures whenever possible. When new information is strongly discrepant, however, cognitive structures may accommodate, changing either the content of represented knowledge (bookkeeping) or the organization of the information (subtyping). The type of change depends on the pattern of information and the existence of social differentiation. The bookkeeping model applies when incongruent information is dispersed across multiple out-group members; the subtyping model applies when incongruent information is concentrated in a few out-group members (Fiske and Taylor 1991). Morgan and Schwalbe (1990) emphasize the sociological aspects of cognitive change, arguing that neither initial learning nor cognitive change can be understood fully in the decontextualized terms typical of social cognition research.

The most sustained research on long-term enduring change in cognitive structures focuses on the self-concept (see chapter 2). The contemporary view is that the self possesses a stable core but also a phenomenal or working self that is responsive to shifts in the environment and situational contingencies. As Markus and Nurius's (1986) work on possible selves reveals, imagining and explaining hypothetical events about the self can change self-perceptions. The salient characteristics of an audience or interactive group can alter the salience of self-relevant characteristics and hence their accessibility. Chronic shifts in the accessibility of certain information may lead to deeper, more enduring changes in self-concept. Hormuth (1990) attributes significant self-change to changes in the ecological system, drawing on an empirical study of the effects of physical relocation on the self-concept. Taking an opposite tack, Michael Ross (1989), in his work on the social construction of autobiography, articulates how cognitive processes bolster the primacy of the current self. From this vantage point, our current sense of self guides reinterpretation of the past. Ross's perspective is consistent

with Mead's view that past and present, time itself, emerges through present realities.

The Postmodern Perspective on Social Cognition

The challenges to social cognition discussed above pale in comparison to those raised by a cluster of theories originating in the humanities and spreading slowly to the more skeptical and, not coincidentally, more positivist social sciences. Poststructuralism (a theory of knowledge and language) and postmodernism (a theory of society, culture, and history) address an increasing emphasis on the significance of language, symbols, and images in this postmodern era. The growth of information technology, the undermining of individual autonomy, and the penetration of modern culture by the mass media are hallmarks of postmodernism. Most important for social scientists, poststructuralism and postmodernism are critiques of positivism (Agger 1991).

One of the key tenets of poststructuralism is the belief that there is no longer a one-to-one relationship between a signifier—a material object—and a signified—the meaning of that object. Signifiers have become images without the substantiality of a material referent. This notion is applied with special force to the concept of the text and the determination of meaning. Texts conceal conflicts between multiple authorial voices; meaning is indeterminate. Deconstruction, the method of poststructuralism, entails searching not for a single true meaning but rather for oppositions and contradictions within the text (Parker and Shotter 1990). Deconstruction turns traditional experimental methodology on its head. From the traditional social psychological perspective, the existence of a reality that can be represented through empirical research is not in doubt. Poststructuralism thus poses fundamental challenges to the basic methodological and conceptual underpinnings of social psychology. (See Parker 1989, chapter 4, for a deconstruction of attribution theory.)

Although deconstruction would seem to oppose mainstream social psychology, it could be a powerful tool in the service of social cognition. From the postmodernist perspective, knowledge is grounded in everyday experience and ordinary language and is specific to particular subject positions, whether of class, race, gender, or other group affiliations. The method of deconstruction can be used to analyze the multiplicity of meaning and to assess the relative power of various interpretations (Parker 1989), thereby encouraging the growth of a more fully social cognition. Social science becomes an "accounting of social experience from these multiple perspectives of discourse/practice" (Agger 1991, 117). This conception of social science echos the original goals of Heider, among others, albeit in a different sociocultural context.

Postmodernism has other, more specific, implications for contemporary social cognition. The voluminous literature on the self assumes the reality of the experienced, phenomenal self. From Heider's conception of an active perceiver through contemporary perspectives on self as cognitive miser, motivated tactician, or interpersonal negotiator, the thinker in social cognition has a considerable degree of autonomy and agency. From the postmodern perspective, however, an autonomous, agentic self no longer exists (Gergen 1991). Social cognition thus must be uneasy with the postmodern self. Valuable contributions can be gleaned from this view of self, however, if the deeper implications are set aside. Poststructuralism adds a specifically sociological dimension to the construction of identity, theorizing how social systems ascribe a subject position to some individuals and an object position to others. This perspective reminds that social power has direct implications for social identity (Deschamps 1983), even as it casts these constraints, like all social phenomena, as relative.

It seems safe to say that descriptions of the postmodernist era ring at least partially true. To date, however, most social psychologists and social cognitivists alike have ignored this challenge. Some have responded more constructively, either developing new theories or reclaiming existing conceptions of the self more consistent with postmodernism. Goffman's dramaturgical perspective, for example, with its emphasis on the significance of appearances and deemphasis on the notion of enduring personalities, has a postmodern flavor (Young 1990). Wood and Zurcher (1988) articulate what they explicitly name the "postmodern self," emphasizing impulse, process, and change. Although this conception of self is specific to a particular historical context, in its continued assertion of the possibility of an authentic experienced self it is not fully postmodern. It will take considerable creativity to construct a social cognition that speaks to a postmodern age. The rapidity and global scope of recent social change argue that such efforts are necessary to the viability of this discipline.

SOCIOLOGY AND SOCIAL COGNITION

This section presents a more explicit discussion of the sociological aspects of cognition and suggests what social cognition can offer to sociologists. In House's (1977) first face, psychological social psychology, the social elements concern the content of social knowledge and how that knowledge is used. Social categorization is the fundamental process that constructs the social knowledge stored in particular cognitive structures, such as stereotypes or role schemas. Through categorization this social knowledge shapes social phenomena such as prejudice and discrimination. In House's second face, symbolic interaction, cognitions underlie interpersonal dynamics. Cognitions are expressed through and shaped by social interaction. At this level I consider the symbolic, interactive, and communicative aspects of social cognition, stressing the relevance of language. In House's third face, the individual and social structure, cognitions underlie intergroup relations and social structures. Moreover, cognitions are created and processed collectively as well as individually. At this level I consider collective cognitions and cross-cultural patterns of cognition.

Psychological Social Psychology: Social Categorization

Social categorization—categorization on the basis of social descriptors—is virtually ubiquitous (Wilder 1986). A series of studies by Tajfel et al. (1971)

demonstrates that people create social groups on the basis of variables as trivial as the tendency to over- or underestimate the number of dots on a dot counting test. Categorizations based on the simplest variables have led subjects to allocate money differentially to members of an in-group, evaluate more positively members of an in-group, and gather information about similarity more for in-group members and about dissimilarity more for out-group members. Through such selective information gathering we develop more complex schemas about in-group members and less differentiated views about members of out-groups; these variations, in turn, affect the extremity of cognitive evaluations. Greater schema complexity results in less extreme evaluations, a pattern whose social significance is illustrated in a study in which white subjects' evaluations of law school applications by black applicants were polarized relative to their evaluations of applications by whites (Linville and Jones 1980).

Although Tajfel's work shows that we can and do categorize on the basis of almost any characteristic, some variables are more likely to trigger categorization. We tend to categorize on visually prominent features of stimuli, for example. Characteristics that differ across groups and are visually evident are likely to stimulate categorization. Gender, for example, is typically visually evident. As if we were afraid it were not, we have developed norms of dress, hair style, stance, and so forth that make gender and its assumed sex analogue more visually prominent than it might otherwise be. The significance of visual cues reflects the principle of cognitive efficiency. It is easier to categorize on the basis of visually evident characteristics than on the basis of characteristics that must be inferred. Thus characteristics that have no inherent social meaning have taken on social import; they are used to define groups of people and are in turn attributed to members of those social groups. Ridgeway's (1991) intriguing synthesis of Blau's (1977) structural theory and expectation states theory is an important elaboration of those macro level conditions and micro level processes that intervene between social categorization and the acquisition of

status value. Membership in particular groups thus has become weighted with social import across human history, a prime example of the sociological significance of social cognition.

Social categorizations are distinct from categorizations of nonsocial objects. Social categories have a greater variety of structures, are less likely to be organized hierarchically, and exhibit greater stability within than between persons. Moreover, individuals' self-concepts generally are intertwined with one or more social categories, a link that underlies Tajfel's social identity theory, a cognitive-motivational theory of intergroup behavior. Social identity is that part of an individual's self-concept that derives from knowledge of his/her membership in a social group. The construction of social identities is thus one function of social categorization.

Turner (1987) has articulated further the components of self-categorization. The relative salience of what he calls social and personal identities depends on the accessibility of a category and the fit between the input in a given situation and stored category specifications. Structural fit reflects the degree to which observed behavioral differences and similarities among people are perceived as correlated with preexisting social categories. Normative fit reflects the ideologies prevalent in the relevant social groups. Tajfel's (1981) research suggests that cultural boundaries separating majority and minority groups are crucial to the salience of category memberships. Tajfel's emphasis on culture, together with the content-based criteria of both structural and normative fit, underscore that the social content of categorization is crucial for understanding the salience of social categories and thus their effects.

Social categorizations are not simply systems of cognitive organization; they also reflect power. Social power has direct implications for social identity. Deschamps (1983) suggested that those in positions of domination, those who are members of a category with the discursive power to define, locate, and order others, conceive of themselves as outside any particular category. They have the freedom to define themselves as specific, unique individuals. Members of dominated groups are viewed by those who dominate as undifferentiated representatives of their categories. In the terms of social identity theory, personal identities are likely to be more salient than social identities among those in dominant positions, whereas social identities are likely to be more salient than personal identities for those who are dominated, not only in interactions with members of the dominant group but also within their own self-concepts. Social power is thus a major influence on social and self categorization.

Cognitive categories also have substantial significance for broader sociological phenomena. Della Fave (1980) applies attribution and self-evaluation theories as bases for a theory of the process through which stratified social orders are legitimated. One key point is that legitimations of stratification become part of the consciousness of individual citizens. Social institutions maintain legitimacy through their effects on the self; these effects, in turn, serve to maintain the social order. The model also implies that delegitimation comes about in part through changes in the self-concept. The significance of social categorizations is implicit throughout his discussion of status attribution, cognitive consistency, and the definition of equity. (Expectation states theory also addresses the maintenance of structured inequality. See chapter 12 for elaboration of this theory and its sociological contribution.)

Gurin's research on group consciousness is explicit about the importance of social categories. Comparing superordinate and subordinate strata, Gurin et al. (1980) report that only along the racial dimension is group identification stronger in the subordinate stratum, but that power discontent and collectivist orientation are stronger among both those who identify as African Americans (versus whites) and as working-class (versus middle-class). Overall, consciousness was strongest among African Americans, weakest among women, and moderate among those with working-class occupations and older people. The role of attributions in consciousness is striking. Gurin et al. report that those women and African

Americans who hold the social structure rather than their own group members responsible for gender and race disparities most strongly endorse collective strategies to overcome those disparities. Research on social movements shows substantial empirical support for a parallel pattern: a strong sense of personal control coupled with attributions of blame to the social system is more likely than other cognitive patterns to provoke participation in social movements (Howard 1991; Zurcher and Snow 1981).

This research suggests that both self- and social categorizations shape sociological behaviors. Numerous studies of sociological phenomena, however, implicate but do not explicitly measure or recognize the importance of social categorizations. For example, Fendrich and Lovoy (1988) report high levels of consistency in the political activism of distinctive intragenerational groups: those who were radical student activists in 1971 were the most politically active as adults seventeen years later and those who were uninvolved in college were the least active as adults. The authors describe but do not attempt to explain this temporal consistency. McAdam's (1988) rich study of the Freedom Summer activists and Snow et al.'s (1986) emphasis on the alignment of individual and organizational interpretive frames both explicitly attempt to explain the processual aspects of identity-related action, but the underlying cognitive mechanisms could be developed much more fully.

Cognition and Social Interaction

Cognitions are embedded in interactive contexts, which have been underemphasized by psychological social psychologists. Interactions involve a minimum of two individuals. The typical cognitive paradigm casts one as actor and the other as a passive target. Yet others are rarely passive; generally they respond by reinforcing, disagreeing, or posing alternatives. In negotiations about meaning and interpretation, actors draw on a rich cultural repertoire of representations. The products of social cognition, then, are messages communicated among people.

Disparate lines of research indicate the significance of interaction, albeit indirectly. Explanations of the risky shift phenomenon, which refers to attitude change in groups, point to the generation of persuasive arguments in a group that any one individual member might not have thought of. Social comparisons of one's own opinions with those of other group members can also generate attitude change. Both of these explanations assume some degree of communication in producing cognitive change. Wegner's (1986) intriguing research on group memory suggests that groups rely on the differential allocation to group members of remembering chunks of information. The subsequent retrieval task requires communication of cognitions. Snow et al. (1986) stress the importance of the diffusion and communication of interpretive frames in explaining social movement participation.

Stryker and Gottlieb (1981), in their discussion of potential links between attributions and symbolic interactionism, direct explicit attention to the interactive aspects of cognition. Both perspectives agree on the importance of comprehending subjective experience. Both see individuals as rational problem solvers, but neither assumes total rationality. Both emphasize everyday life and everyday experience. On the other hand, attribution theories, like models of other aspects of cognition, view cognition as an intrapersonal process. Symbolic interactionism casts cognition and symbolization as interpersonal and interactive. Attributions are viewed as responsive to external, objectively recognizable stimuli, whereas symbolic interaction views reality itself as socially defined and therefore indeterminate. Attributions are generated to explain particular events, whereas symbolic interaction addresses the communication of meaning in social interaction.

Stryker and Gottlieb (1981) argue persuasively that a full appreciation of attribution requires increased attention to interaction. Crittenden (1983) illustrates this same message drawing on research in labeling theory, accounts, and impression management. In an empirical evaluation of the relationship between attribution and labeling,

Howard and Levinson (1985) suggest that labeling can explain socially significant but anomalous attributional patterns: labels may be applied to actors in the absence of internal attributions of cause for behavior, pointing to reconsideration of the traditional dichotomy between internal and external attributions.

Impression management also plays an important role in attribution. Bradley (1978) suggests that self-serving biases in attribution are motivated by the desire to maximize public esteem. Causal claims in interpersonal encounters may serve a communicative function and provide a way to control observers' attributional conclusions about an actor. Babcock (1989) takes the emphasis on impression management one step further, presenting a Goffmanesque dramaturgic analysis of attribution. The dramaturgic goal of attribution is to obtain enough information about the other to maintain a smooth and coherent interaction. From this perspective, patterns such as the fundamental attribution error demonstrate the desire to give good performances, rather than a basic deviation from logic.

Focus on the communicative aspects of attribution leads also to increased attention to language (see chapter 6). Language is both a mechanism whereby the individual can engage in the self-interaction we conceptualize as thought and a medium of exchange between individuals. The conversational framework emphasizes the links between everyday communication and everyday explanation (Hilton 1990). Hilton explicitly asserts the "truly social" nature of this model in that causal explanations are hypothesized to occur through communication. Hilton characterizes explanations as primarily contrastive, being sought and offered only when there is a gap between expectations and occurrences, a logic that also underlies Jones and McGillis's (1976) model of correspondent inference. Antaki and Naji (1987), in contrast, suggest that an important goal of conversation is to underscore the sensibility of things, stating facts that need bolstering by supporting evidence. This approach contradicts Hilton's model but is consistent with Kelley's action-attribute congruence model of attribution. Undoubtedly, explanations are offered and sought when unexpected things occur; they can also serve to bolster preexisting expectations. Taken together, these studies show that ordinary language is fundamentally pragmatic.

One direct implication of this expanded view of attribution is methodological: naturally occurring conversations are an important source of information for studying causal attribution. Hewstone (1983) points to other methodological concerns that follow from recognition of the significance of language. The language used to present events often carries with it implicit attributions; the way in which a phenomenon is described affects the way in which it is explained. In one well-known example, McArthur (1972) reported that the type of verb category with which actions are described affects attributions about those actions. Person attributions were found more often for accomplishment and action verbs; stimulus attributions were more likely for emotion and opinion verbs. It is not a great inferential leap to presume that as social actors we deliberately choose our words to manipulate others' inferences.

Language also can be used as a marker to communicate information about social categories. Using court transcripts, Lind et al. (1978) found that complainants using a "powerful" linguistic style were awarded higher damages. The gender of both lawyers and witnesses interacted with linguistic style in shaping the size of this effect, suggesting that social status is communicated through language. These studies also demonstrate that language plays a key role in social categorization. Individuals may be perceived in intergroup terms because of the language they speak (Tajfel and Turner 1986). Indeed, Potter and Wetherell (1987) assert that categorization is a linguistic accomplishment. Language, then, is the basis for both cognition and communication.

The more general point is that cognition is communication. The products of social cognition are interindividual communications; these communications become part of the knowledge structures of interacting individuals and part of the cultural repertoires of their societies. Despite the chal-lenges posed by a fully interactive conception of social cognition, these connections must be more thoroughly articulated.

Individual and Social Structure

Collective Cognitions.   Cognition is social in yet another, more macro-level respect: thoughts are processed collectively as well as individually. Social cognition refers also to this collective nature of the processes that underlie comprehension of the social world. Such collective processes have a significant history in sociology. Durkheim (1898) posited that social facts are independent of individual consciousness. Although they emerge from the association of individuals, the collective representations of society are distinct from individual representations. Moscovici's (1981) theory of social representations has turned attention again to the collective construction of meaning. Social representations, described earlier, are fully societal knowledge structures in that they are shared conceptions of reality created by collective communication. Like other cognitive structures social representations identify categories that influence the perception of social information, but unlike other structures they focus on the social communicative processes by which specialized knowledge is transformed into common sense (Hewstone 1989).

Social representations provide a critical sociocognitive background, stimulating other cognitive inferences. Moscovici (1981) suggests, for example, that social representations determine when we seek explanations. They also provide a vocabulary for attributions and other cognitive inferences. Research on this construct has barely begun. Sperber (1985) distinguishes between representations that are widely distributed and slowly transmitted over generations—representations we think of as culture—and representations that spread rapidly throughout a population but have a short life span, akin to the fashions of contemporary culture.

The concept of collective cognitions has been extended to the notion of "attributing societies" (Hewstone 1989). This conception may seem to revive outdated notions of national character or group mind, yet it is persuasive. More than sixty years ago Fauconnet pointed to the societal functions of attributions as ways of punishing certain behaviors and thereby preventing their reoccurrence. Hewstone applies a similar analysis to the treatment of witchcraft in medieval Europe, of Jews throughout history, and other conspiracy analyses. Such attributional patterns and beliefs are apparently societywide analyses endorsed not only by marginal people but also by those of high status. These collective attributions serve collective societal functions.

Explanations of social problems also illustrate collective cognition. Research has focused on explanations of unemployment, poverty, and racial inequality. Interestingly, unemployment tends to be attributed to societal factors, at least in Western countries. In apparent contradiction to prevailing explanations of unemployment, Feagin (1972) reports that a full half of the respondents in a study of U.S. citizens gave individualistic explanations for poverty. The degree of individualism varies substantially by country: Pandey et al. (1982) report that poverty in India is attributed more to system than to personal causes. These studies reflect the cultural specificity of collective cognitions, the concluding topic.

Cross-Cultural Perspectives.   Social psychology has been largely a North American phenomenon. Attention to the generality of social psychological research has come only belatedly. The "crisis" years of self-examination of the discipline provided an impetus for considering the cultural specificity of social psychological patterns. Gergen and Gergen (1984) suggested that social psychological findings are unique historical events reflecting specific conditions, not universal truths. Others argued that the assumptions underlying mainstream social psychology reflect ideological biases prevalent in the United States (Sampson 1977). Both arguments have sparked research that explicitly tests the cross-cultural validity of key social psychological phenomena.

Perhaps the exemplar of recent cultural expansions of social cognition is a comparative study by Joan Miller of attributions made by subjects in the United States and India. The amount of attention this study has received in and of itself attests to the timeliness of consideration of cross-cultural patterns in social cognition. Miller (1984) compared developmental theories of cognitive capacities, the effects of modernization, and cultural explanations that focused on cross-cultural variations in conceptions of the person. Miller found that as they age, U.S. citizens use increasingly more dispositional attributions than do Hindus, who use predominantly contextual attributions. This study makes clear the cultural limitations of the heretofore fundamental attribution error, the tendency to attribute cause to persons, as opposed to situations.

Other attribution biases are also vulnerable to cultural critiques: labeling attributional tendencies as self-serving requires a full understanding of the nature of the self being served, an understanding that appears to be culturally specific. According to Shweder and Bourne (1982), non-Western adults do not distinguish the person as sharply from social roles and social relationships as do Western adults. Conceptions of the person in many Asian cultures, for example, emphasize relatedness rather than independence (Markus and Kitayama 1991). Fletcher and Ward (1988) suggest that external roles and norms may have a greater impact on individual behavior in collectivist cultures, thus these patterns reflect a material reality. An alternate view is that external roles and norms have a significant influence on individual behavior in all cultures, but Western ideologies discourage recognition of this influence.

Miller's research does more than qualify attribution biases; taken to its logical conclusion, this study points to the cultural boundedness of the key theories of attribution, each of which assumes the concept of a person distinct from his/her environment and other actors. Naturally occurring explanations for interpersonal behavior are probably sought and offered in all cultures, but the individualistic emphasis on personality and individual capacities is not universal. Cha and Nam (1985) have tested Kelley's covariational model in a Korean context, replicating McArthur's (1972) original test. Consistent with Miller's findings, Korean subjects used more external attributions. Nonetheless, the results were remarkably similar to McArthur's, supporting Kelley's theoretical model. Similarly, in their review of cross-cultural attribution research, Fletcher and Ward (1988) assert that Kelley's model has some generality across cultures. While this may prove to be so, caution is advisable.

Bond (1983) identifies other fundamental questions that must be addressed cross-culturally: How frequently do people engage in attributional activity? What causal categories are used? Are attributions an internal cognitive activity, or do they serve interpersonal purposes? How does culture exert its impact? Most attributional research shows only that people can make attributions when asked; these studies reveal neither the prevalence of cognitive inferences in everyday interaction nor the purpose of such inferences and how they are used in interaction. Cognitive models developed in a Western context must also be supplemented by indigenous theories from non-Western cultures. Yang and Ho's (1988) Heiderian analysis of Yuan attributions, attributions for relationship outcomes in Chinese society, is a rare example.

Almost all of the cross-cultural work in social cognition focuses on the process of attribution. It is more than time for extension to other aspects of cognition. Regardless of the breadth of this work, however, cross-cultural research cannot help but enrich the sociological utility of social cognition. In some ways the most significant outcome of cross-cultural research in attribution, social cognition, or social psychology more generally is that it forces researchers to think about their own and other cultures, to conceptualize as fully as possible what *culture* means. An understanding of culture has not been necessary to study what are assumed to be cross-cultural similarities. Cross-cultural difference, however, can be understood only through a thorough understanding of the respective cultures at hand. At a time when the very concept and causal force of culture is being reconceptualized in sociology, the relevance of cross-cultural work in social cognition is all the greater.

CONCLUSION

Social cognition has become a technically and theoretically sophisticated specialty in psychological social psychology. Whether social cognition will engender enduring links between psychological and sociological social psychology is difficult to predict. Numerous recent trends point toward a degree of convergence. European theoretical developments in intergroup relations as well as in the social underpinnings of self and identity, increasing recognition of the reliance of cognition on language and of the complex, perhaps inextricable, relationship between cognition and communication, an expanded conception of cognitive structures as collective, not just individual, phenomena, and cross-cultural evaluations of social psychological processes each bring the psychological and sociological faces closer together.

Conceptual attention to the key constructs of social psychology, self and society, will be necessary for systematic development of such interchange. Not surprisingly, substantially more attention has been directed toward theorizing self and identity than society. Society has been viewed variously as recurring patterns of interaction, a system of beliefs and norms, a system of positions and identities, and, simply, as situated (Callero 1991). To view society as expressed in patterns of interaction is to promote a dynamic, nondeterminist social psychology. To view society as a system of beliefs and norms would seem more static and perhaps deterministic, but recognition of the collective, shared, and always constructed nature of those beliefs and norms avoids this potential determinism. To view society as a system of positions and identities recognizes explicitly the influence of social structure on self, a recognition often missing in more dynamic views of both self and society. Finally, to view society as situated is to recognize the crucial processual aspects of both identity and society.

The major contribution of social cognition has been to demonstrate that central sociological behaviors, phenomena such as stratification, social movements, political actions, and intergroup relations, are in part the product of individual thought. Failure to account for ways in which society shapes the content and communication of thought, however, has limited the potential two-way interchange between psychological and sociological social psychologies, as well as between social cognition and sociology. As suggested in the final sections of this chapter, a rich and much more sociologically aware approach has been developing since the 1980s. At least two factors suggest that this development will continue to transform social cognition and social psychology. Yang (1988) speculates that societal modernization will eventually eliminate cross-cultural psychological differences. While the jury is out on whether an effect this dramatic will occur, modernization and the increased reciprocal cross-cultural attention among not only laypeople but also scholars have generated substantially more intellectual interchange across disciplines, cultures, and nations. Moreover, today's graduate students, those just beginning their careers, seem more open, both theoretically and methodologically. Perhaps the strongest hope for disciplinary growth lies, as it should, with the next generation of social psychologists.

REFERENCES

Agger, Ben. 1991. Critical theory, poststructuralism, postmodernism: Their sociological relevance. *Annual Review of Sociology* 17:105–31.

Ajzen, Izek. 1988. *Attitudes, Personality, and Behavior.* Chicago: Dorsey.

Ajzen, Izek, and Martin Fishbein. 1977. Attitude-behavior relations: A theoretical analysis and review of empirical research. *Psychological Bulletin* 84:888–918.

Albert, Stuart. 1977. Temporal comparison theory. *Psychological Review* 84:485–503.

Allison, Scott T., and David M. Messick. 1985. The group attribution error. *Journal of Experimental Social Psychology* 21:563–579.

Antaki, C., and S. Naji. 1987. Events explained in conversational "because" statements. *British Journal of Social Psychology* 26:119–126.

Averill, James R. 1990. Emotions as episodic dispositions, cognitive schemas, and transitory social roles: Steps toward an integrated theory of emotion. Pp. 137–165 in *Perspectives in Personality: Vol. 3a. Self and Emotion,* ed. E. J. Ozer, J. M. Healy, Jr., and A. J. Stewart. Greenwich, CT: JAI Press.

Babcock, Mary K. 1989. The dramaturgic perspective: Implications for the study of person perception. *European Journal of Social Psychology* 19:297–309.

Bem, Daryl J. 1972. Self-perception theory. Pp. 1–62 in *Advances in Experimental Social Psychology,* vol. 6, ed. L. Berkowitz. New York: Academic.

Blau, Peter M. 1977. *Inequality and Heterogeneity: A Primitive Theory of Social Structure.* New York: Free Press.

Blumer, Herbert, 1969. *Symbolic Interactionism: Perspective and Method.* Englewood Cliffs, NJ: Prentice Hall.

Bond, Michael H. 1983. A proposal for cross-cultural studies of attribution. Pp. 144–157 in *Attribution Theory: Social and Functional Extensions,* ed. M. Hewstone. Oxford, UK: Blackwell.

Bower, Gordon H. 1977. *Human Memory.* New York: Academic.

Bradley, Gifford Weary. 1978. Self-serving biases in the attribution process: A reexamination of the fact or fiction question. *Journal of Personality and Social Psychology* 36:56–71.

Callero, Peter L. 1991. Conclusion. Pp. 323–331 in *The Self-Society Dynamic: Cognition, Emotion, and Action,* ed. J. A. Howard and P. L. Callero. New York: Cambridge University Press.

Cantor, Nancy, and Walter Mischel. 1979. Prototypes in person perception. Pp. 3–52 in *Advances in Experimental Social Psychology,* vol. 12, ed. L. Berkowitz. New York: Academic.

Cha, J. H., and K. D. Nam. 1985. A test of Kelley's cube theory of attribution: A cross-cultural replication of McArthur's study. *Korean Social Science Journal* 12:151–180.

Cohen, Claudia E. 1981. Person categories and social perception: Testing some boundaries of the processing effects of prior knowledge. *Journal of Personality and Social Psychology* 40:441–452.

Crittenden, Kathleen S. 1983. Sociological aspects of attribution. *Annual Review of Sociology* 9:425–446.

Della Fave, L. Richard. 1980. The meek shall not inherit the earth: Self-evaluation and the legitimacy of stratification. *American Sociological Review* 45:955–971.

Deschamps, Jean-Claude. 1983. Social attribution. Pp. 223–40 in *Attribution Theory and Research: Conceptual, Developmental and Social Dimensions,* ed. J. Jaspars, F. D. Fincham, and M. Hewstone. New York: Academic.

Dovidio, John F., N. Evans, and R. B. Tyler. 1986. Racial stereotypes: The contents of their cognitive representations. *Journal of Experimental Social Psychology* 22:22–37.

Duncan, B. L. 1976. Differential social perception and attribution of intergroup violence: Testing the lower limits of stereotyping of blacks. *Journal of Personality and Social Psychology* 34:590–598.

Durkheim, Emile. 1898. Representations individuelles et representations collectives. *Revue de Metaphysique et de Morale* 6:273–302.

Fazio, Russell H., and Mark P. Zanna. 1981. Direct experience and attitude-behavior consistency. Pp. 398–408 in *Advances in Experimental Social Psychology,* vol. 14, ed. L. Berkowitz. New York: Academic.

Feagin, Joe. 1972. Poverty: We still believe that God helps them who help themselves. *Psychology Today* 6:101–129.

Fendrich, James Max, and Kenneth L. Lovoy. 1988. Back to the future: Adult political behavior of former student activists. *American Sociological Review* 53:780–784.

Festinger, Leon. 1954. A theory of social comparison processes. *Human Relations* 7:117–140.

Fiske, Susan T., and Shelley E. Taylor. 1991. *Social Cognition,* 2nd ed. New York: McGraw-Hill.

Fletcher, Garth J. O., and Colleen Ward. 1988. Attribution theory and processes: A cross-cultural perspective. Pp. 230–244 in *The Cross-Cultural Challenge to Social Psychology,* ed. M. H. Bond. Newbury Park, CA: Sage.

Forgas, Joseph P. 1981. What is social about social cognition? Pp. 1–26 in *Social Cognition: Perspectives on Everyday Understanding,* ed. J. P. Forgas. London: Academic.

Frieze, Irene H. 1979. Perceptions of battered wives. Pp. 79–108 in *New Approaches to Social Problems,* ed.

I. H Frieze, D. Bar-Tal, and J. S. Carroll. San Francisco: Jossey-Bass.

Gergen, Kenneth J. 1991. *The Saturated Self: Dilemmas of Identity in Contemporary Life,* New York: Basic Books.

Gergen, Kenneth J., and Mary M. Gergen, eds. 1984. *Historical Social Psychology.* Hillsdale, NJ: Erlbaum.

Guimond, S., and M. Simard. 1979. Perception et interpretation des inegalités economiques entre Francophones et Anglophones au Quebec. Paper presented at the 40th Congress of the Canadian Psychological Society, Quebec.

Gurin, Patricia, Arthur H. Miller, and Gerald Gurin. 1980. Stratum identification and consciousness. *Social Psychology Quarterly* 43:30–47.

Hamill, R., Timothy D. Wilson, and Richard E. Nisbett. 1980. Insensititivity to sample bias: Generalizing from atypical cases. *Journal of Personality and Social Psychology* 39:578–589.

Hamilton, David L., and R. K. Gifford. 1976. Illusory correlation in interpersonal perception: A cognitive basis of stereotypic judgments. *Journal of Experimental Social Psychology* 12:392–407.

Heider, Fritz. 1958. *The Psychology of Interpersonal Relations.* New York: Wiley.

Heimer, Carol. A. 1988. Social structure, psychology, and the estimation of risk. *Annual Review of Sociology* 14:491–519.

Hewstone, Miles. 1983. The role of language in attribution processes. Pp. 241–259 in *Attribution Theory and Research: Conceptual, Developmental, and Social Dimensions,* ed. J. Jaspars, F. D. Fincham, and M. Hewstone. London: Academic.

———. 1989. *Causal Attribution: From Cognitive Processes to Collective Beliefs.* Oxford, UK: Blackwell.

Hewstone, Miles, and Jos Jaspars. 1987. Covariation and causal attribution: A logical model of the intuitive analysis of variance. *Journal of Personality and Social Psychology* 53:663–672.

Higgins, E. Tory, Nicholas A. Kuiper, and James M. Olson. 1981. Social cognition: A need to get personal. Pp. 395–420 in *Social Cognition: The Ontario Symposium,* vol. 1, ed. E. T. Higgins, C. P. Herman, and M. P. Zanna. Hillsdale, NJ: Erlbaum.

Hilton, Denis J. 1990. Conversational processes and causal explanation. *Psychological Bulletin* 107:65–81.

Hilton, Denis J., and Ben R. Slugoski. 1986. Knowledge-based causal attribution: The abnormal conditions focus model. *Psychological Review* 93:75–77.

Hormuth, Stefan E. 1990. *The Ecology of the Self: Relocation and Self-Concept Change.* Cambridge, UK: Cambridge University Press.

House, James S. 1977. The three faces of social psychology. *Sociometry* 40:161–77.

Howard, Judith A. 1990. A sociological framework of cognition. *Advances in Group Processes* 7:75–103.

———. 1991. From changing selves toward changing society. Pp. 209–237 in *The Self-Society Dynamic: Cognition, Emotion, and Action,* ed. J. A. Howard and P. L. Callero. New York: Cambridge University Press.

Howard, Judith A., and Randy Levinson. 1985. The overdue courtship of attribution and labeling. *Social Psychology Quarterly* 48:191–202.

Howard, J. W., and M. Rothbart. 1980. Social categorization and memory for ingroup and outgroup behavior. *Journal of Personality and Social Psychology* 38:301–310.

Isen, Alice M. 1987. Positive affect, cognitive processes, and social behavior. Pp. 203–253 in *Advances in Experimental Social Psychology,* vol. 20, ed. L. Berkowitz. New York: Academic.

Jones, Edward E., and Keith E. Davis. 1965. From acts to dispositions: The attribution process in person perception. Pp. 220–266 in *Advances in Experimental Social Psychology,* vol. 2, ed. L. Berkowitz. New York: Academic.

Jones, Edward E., and Dan McGillis. 1976. Correspondent inferences and the attribution cube: A comparative reappraisal. Pp. 389–420 in *New Directions in Attribution Research,* vol. 1, ed. J. H. Harvey, W. Ickes, and R. F. Kidd. Hillsdale, NJ: Erlbaum.

Kahneman, Daniel, and Amos Tversky. 1982. The simulation heuristic. Pp. 201–208 in *Judgment Under Uncertainty: Heuristics and Biases,* ed. D. Kahneman, P. Slovic, and A. Tversky. New York: Cambridge University Press.

Kelley, Harold H. 1967. Attribution theory in social psychology. Pp. 192–240 in *Nebraska Symposium on Motivation,* vol. 15, ed. D. Levine. Lincoln: University of Nebraska Press.

———. 1973. The processes of causal attribution. *American Psychologist* 28:107–128.

Langer, Ellen J. 1989. *Mindfulness.* Reading, MA: Addison-Wesley.

Lind, E. A., B. E. Erickson, J. Conley, and W. M. O'Barr. 1978. Social attributions and conversational style in trial testimony. *Journal of Personality and Social Psychology* 36:1558–1567.

Linville, Patricia, and E. E. Jones. 1980. Polarized appraisals of outgroup members. *Journal of Personality and Social Psychology* 38:689–703.

Markus, Hazel, and Shinobu Kitayama. 1991. Culture and the self: Implications for cognition, emotion, and motivation. *Psychological Review* 98:224–253.

Markus, Hazel, and Paula Nurius. 1986. Possible selves. *American Psychologist* 41:954–969.

Markus, Hazel, and Robert B. Zajonc. 1985. The cognitive perspective in social psychology. Pp. 137–230 in *The Handbook of Social Psychology,* 3rd ed., ed. G. Lindzey and E. Aronson. Hillsdale, NJ: Erlbaum.

McAdam, Doug. 1988. *Freedom Summer.* New York: Oxford University Press.

McArthur, Leslie Zebrowitz. 1972. The how and what of why: Some determinants and consequences of causal attributions. *Journal of Personality and Social Psychology* 22:171–193.

McArthur, Leslie Z. and L. K. Solomon. 1978. Perceptions of an aggressive encounter as a function of the victim's salience and the perceiver's arousal. *Journal of Personality and Social Psychology* 36:1278–1290.

McGuire, William J., C. McGuire, P. Child, and T. Fujioka. 1978. Salience of ethnicity in the spontaneous self-concept as a function of one's ethnic distinctiveness in the social environment. *Journal of Personality and Social Psychology* 36:511–520.

McKenzie-Mohr, D., and Mark P. Zanna. 1990. Treating women as sexual objects: Look to the (gender schematic) male who has viewed pornography. *Personality and Social Psychology Bulletin* 16:296–308.

Mead, George Herbert. 1934. *Mind, Self, and Society.* Chicago: University of Chicago Press.

Millar, M. G., and Abraham Tesser. 1986. Effects of attitude and cognitive focus on the attitude-behavior relation. *Journal of Personality and Social Psychology* 51:270–276.

Miller, Joan G. 1984. Culture and the development of everyday explanation. *Journal of Personality and Social Psychology* 46:961–978.

Morgan, David L., and Michael L. Schwalbe. 1990. Mind and self in society: Linking social structure and social cognition. *Social Psychology Quarterly* 53:148–64.

Moscovici, Serge. 1981. On social representations. Pp. 181–209 in *Social Cognition: Perspectives on*

Everyday Understanding, ed. J. P. Forgas. London: Academic.

Nemeth, Charlan. 1986. Differential contributions of majority vs. minority influence. *Psychological Review* 93:23–32.

Nisbett, Richard E., and Lee Ross. 1980. *Human Inference: Strategies and Shortcomings of Social Judgment.* Englewood Cliffs, NJ: Prentice Hall.

Oakes, Penelope. 1987. The salience of social categories. Pp. 117–141 in *Rediscovering the Social Group: A Self-Categorization Theory,* ed. J. C. Turner. Oxford, UK: Blackwell.

Pandey, J., Y. Sinha, A. Prekash, and R. C. Triupathi. 1982. Right-left political ideologies and attributions of the causes of poverty. *European Journal of Social Psychology* 12:327–331.

Parker, Ian. 1989. *The Crisis in Modern Social Psychology—And How to End It.* London: Routledge.

Parker, Ian, and John Shotter. 1990. *Deconstructing Social Psychology.* London: Routledge.

Potter, Jonathan, and Ian Litton. 1985. Some problems underlying the theory of social representations. *British Journal of Social Psychology* 24:81–90.

Potter, Jonathan, and Margaret Wetherell. 1987. *Discourse and Social Psychology: Beyond Attitudes and Behaviour.* London: Sage.

Ridgeway, Cecilia. 1991. The social construction of status value: Gender and other nominal characteristics. *Social Forces* 70:367–386.

Rokeach, Milton. 1973. *The Nature of Human Values.* New York: Free Press.

Ross, Lee. 1977. The intuitive psychologist and his shortcomings: Distortions in the attribution process. Pp. 174–221 in *Advances in Experimental Social Psychology,* vol. 10, ed. L. Berkowitz. New York: Academic.

Ross, Michael. 1989. Relation of implicit theories to the construction of personal histories. *Psychological Review* 96:341–357.

Sampson, E. E. 1977. Psychology and the American ideal. *Journal of Personality and Social Psychology* 35:767–782.

Schachter, Stanley, and J. E. Singer. 1962. Cognitive, social, and physiological determinants of emotional state. *Psychological Bulletin* 69:379–399.

Schneider, David J. 1991. Social cognition. *Annual Review of Psychology* 42:527–561.

Schutz, Alfred. 1970. *On Phenomenonology and Social Relations.* Chicago: University of Chicago Press.

Schwartz, Shalom. 1992. Universals in the content and structure of values: Theoretical advances and empirical tests in 20 countries. Pp. 1–65 in *Advances in Experimental Social Psychology,* vol. 25, ed. M. P. Zanna. New York: Academic.

Schwarz, Norbert, Fritz Strack, Denis Hilton, and Gabi Naderer. 1991. Base rates, representativeness, and the logic of conversation: The contextual relevance of "irrelevant" information. *Social Cognition* 9:67–84.

Sherman, Stephen J., Charles M. Judd, and Bernadette Park. 1989. Social cognition. *Annual Review of Psychology* 40:382–386.

Shweder, R. A., and E. J. Bourne. 1982. Does the concept of the person vary cross-culturally? Pp. 158–199 in *Culture Theory: Essays on Mind, Self, and Emotion,* ed. R. S. Shweder and R. A. LeVine. Cambridge, UK: Cambridge University Press.

Snyder, Mark. 1984. When belief creates reality. Pp. 248–306 in *Advances in Experimental Social Psychology,* vol. 18, ed. L. Berkowitz. New York: Academic.

Snow, David A., Rochford E. Burke, Jr., Steven K. Worden, and Robert D. Benford. 1986. Frame alignment processes, micromobilization, and movement participation. *American Sociological Review* 51:464–481.

Sperber, D. 1985. Anthropology and psychology: Towards an epidemiology of representations. *Man* 20:73–89.

Stryker, Sheldon. 1980. *Symbolic Interactionism: A Social Structural Version.* Menlo Park: Benjamin/Cummings.

Stryker, Sheldon, and Avi Gottlieb. 1981. Attribution theory and symbolic interactionism: A comparison. Pp. 425–458 in *New Directions in Attribution Research,* vol. 3, ed. J. H. Harvey, W. Ickes, and R. F. Kidd. Hillsdale, NJ: Erlbaum.

Tajfel, Henri. 1981. *Human Groups and Social Categories: Studies in Social Psychology.* Cambridge, UK: Cambridge University Press.

Tajfel, Henri, Michael Billig, R. P. Bundy, and C. Flament. 1971. Social categorization and intergroup behavior. *European Journal of Social Psychology* 1:149–77.

Tajfel, Henri, and John C. Turner. 1986. The social identity theory of intergroup behavior. Pp. 7–24 in *The Psychology of Intergroup Relations,* ed. S. Worchel and W. G. Austin. Chicago: Nelson-Hall.

Taylor, D. M., and V. Jaggi. 1974. Ethnocentrism and causal attribution in a South Indian context. *Journal of Cross-Cultural Psychology* 5:162–171.

Turner, John C. 1987. *Rediscovering the Social Group: A Self-Categorization Theory.* New York: Blackwell.

Tversky, Amos, and Daniel Kahneman. 1974. Judgment under uncertainty: Heuristics and biases. *Science* 185:1124–1131.

Vallacher, R. R., and D. M. Wegner. 1987. What do people think they're doing? Action identification and human behavior. *Psychological Review* 94: 3–15.

Wagner, David. 1991. Review of *Handbook of Motivation and Cognition: Foundations of Social Behavior. Contemporary Sociology* 20:793–794.

Weber, Max. 1968. *Economy and Society.* New York: Bedminster.

Wegner, D. 1986. Transactive memory: A contemporary analysis of the group mind. Pp. 185–208 in *Theories of Group Behavior,* ed. B. Mullen and G. R. Goethals. New York: Springer-Verlag.

Weiner, Bernard, Dan Russell, and D. Lerman. 1978. Affective consequences of causal ascriptions. Pp. 59–90 in *New Directions in Attribution Research,* vol. 2, ed. J. H. Harvey, W. J. Ickes, and R. F. Kidd. Hillsdale, NJ: Erlbaum.

Wilder, David A. 1986. Social categorization: Implications for creation and reduction of intergroup bias. Pp. 291–355 in *Advances in Experimental Social Psychology,* vol. 19, ed. L. Berkowitz. New York: Academic.

Wong, P. T. P., and Bernard Weiner. 1981. When people ask "why" questions, and the heuristics of attributional search. *Journal of Personality and Social Psychology* 40:650–663.

Wood, Michael R., and Louis A. Zurcher. 1988. *The Development of a Postmodern Self: A Computer-Assisted Comparative Analysis of Personal Documents.* New York: Greenwood.

Yang, Kuo-Shu. 1988. Will societal modernization eventually eliminate cross-cultural psychological differences? Pp. 67–85 in *The Cross-Cultural Challenge to Social Psychology,* ed. M. H. Bond. Newbury Park, CA: Sage.

Yang, Kuo-Shu, and D. Y. F. Ho. 1988. The role of *yuan* in Chinese social life: A conceptual and empirical analysis. Pp. 263–281 in *Asian Contributions to Psychology,* ed. A. C. Paranjpe, D. F. Y. Ho, and R. C. Rieber. New York: Praeger.

Young, T. R. 1990. *The Drama of Social Life: Essays in Post-Modern Social Psychology.* New Brunswick, NJ: Transaction Publishers.

Zajonc, Robert B. 1980. Feeling and thinking: Preferences need no inferences. *American Psychologist* 35:151–75.

Zurcher, Louis A., Jr., and David A. Snow. 1981. Collective behavior: Social movements. Pp. 447–482 in *Social Psychology: Sociological Perspectives,* ed. M. Rosenberg and R. H. Turner. New York: Basic Books.

CHAPTER 5

The Sociology of Affect and Emotion

LYNN SMITH-LOVIN

The glow of pride and satisfaction that we feel after a good lecture makes us respond enthusiastically to the student who comes up to ask a question after class. The guilt and shame after a discovered transgression lead us to change our behavior. The blast of anger from a lover's attentions to another creates an argument, either spurring a useful discussion of the issue or ending the relationship. The grief from a parent's death elicits the caring attentions of others.

Most of the strong emotions that we experience come from our contacts with other people. Sometimes they motivate us to conform to social norms. Other times, they make us respond in ways that seem unpredictable and irrational. We use others' emotional expressions to judge what kinds of people they are and try to control our own expressions to manage others' opinions of us. Exactly how do social situations affect emotions? What part does culture play in determining what we feel and how we express it to others? How do our emotional reactions motivate social action? When do our collective feelings reinforce the existing social order, and when do they spawn changes in social structures?

The mid-1970s saw the development of several theoretical perspectives that focused on these social processes involving affect and emotion (Collins 1975; Heise 1977, 1979; Hochschild 1975, 1979; Kemper 1978; Scheff 1977, 1979; Shott 1979). Before this modern sociology of emotions, however, emotional response was used in many classic sociological works. Durkheim (1912) dealt with the ritual arousal of ecstasy, Simmel (1950)

with gratitude and resentment, Goffman (1956) with embarrassment and shame. Affect was central in substantive areas such as mental health, attitude research, marriage, and family throughout most of the twentieth century. The development of a sociology of emotion in the 1970s marked the first time, however, that researchers attempted to develop general theoretical statements about the social aspects of emotional response, rather than focusing on specific emotions or specific situations.[1]

In this review of the new sociological theories of emotion, I first define a few key terms to limit the range of discussion. I briefly review the treatment of affect and emotions in classic theory and summarize the modern theories of affect and emotion that grow out of these historic roots. To conclude this theoretical discussion, I point out the common ground behind the current formulations and research questions posed by the points of theoretical divergence. I then turn to empirical research in other substantive areas that contributes to our knowledge about affect and emotion. The summary emphasizes the gaps in our current knowledge and fruitful directions for new research.

DEFINITIONS

The terms *affect, emotion, sentiment,* and *mood* are often used interchangeably in the literature. *Affect* is the most general term; it refers to any evaluative (positive or negative) orientation toward an object. It encompasses emotions such as contentment and anger, attitudes such as liking and disliking, and connotative meanings in general. Osgood and colleagues (Osgood, Suci, and Tannenbaum 1957) expanded the definition of *affect* to include three dimensions—evaluation (good versus bad), potency (powerful versus powerless), and activity (lively versus quiet)2. These three dimensions appear to be cross-cultural and to apply to many concepts.

Emotion is a subset of affect, but its boundaries are not clear. In a recent review, Thoits (1989) argued that emotions have four components: (1) appraisals of a situational stimulus; (2) changes in bodily sensations; (3) displays of expressive gestures; and (4) cultural meanings applied to the constellation of the first three elements. She noted that all four elements need not be present for an emotion to be experienced. For example, one can be afraid and not know why. Clearly, Thoits's definition already implies a theoretical statement about the origins and processing of situational contexts that lead to emotions. This is a strength rather than a weakness—definitions are powerful only in the context of a theoretical description. Otherwise, they simply serve as formal statements of colloquial meaning. In this case, Thoits's (1989) definition serves as a condensation of the common elements in most sociological theories of emotions.[3]

Sentiment refers to something more socially constructed and enduring than simple emotional response. Following Cooley (1964, 115), Gordon (1981, 566–567) defined a sentiment as "a socially constructed pattern of sensations, expressive gestures, and cultural meanings organized around a relationship to a social object."[4] Sentiments are enduring, latent tendencies to respond emotionally in the context of a social relationship. In general, we can think of emotions as more situationally determined and sentiments as more enduring, culturally given elements of relationships, identities, or other social elements.

Moods are also more enduring than emotions but are tied more to a person across situations than to a social context or relationship. Perhaps because of their transitual nature, moods have not been studied extensively by sociologists. However, research on mental health is relevant to the antecedents and consequences of mood.

CLASSIC THEORY OF EMOTIONS

The contributions of classic theory to the modern sociology of emotions take two forms. First, there are nonsociological theorists who focused on emotional response in humans. These theorists varied considerably in the degree to which they featured the social nature of that response, but their assumptions often shaped later socially oriented formulations. Second, there are the founding theorists who defined the new discipline of sociology. Emotion often played a role in their social thought, as a motivator of social action or as a source of either solidarity or conflict.

Nonsociological Views of Affect and Emotion

Several important theories created the intellectual climate in which modern sociological theories of emotion have developed. First, of course, came the philosophers. The tendency to place overwhelming emphasis on behavior, cognition, or emotion as the central element in human life has old roots in philosophy, where major thinkers have oscillated between images of the human as a rational actor or an emotional, natural being. Philosophers often concentrated on enumerating the emotions (Aristotle talks of fifteen, Descartes six, Hobbes seven, Spinoza three with forty-eight derivatives, McDougall seven, and Tomkins eight), to the neglect of their situational context (Hochschild 1983, 202).

The first scientific treatment of emotion was Darwin's (1955) *The Expression of the Emotions in Man and Animals*. Darwin looked for common elements in the gestures of humans and animals, documented the emotional expressions of his own children, and surveyed missionaries about the gestures they had observed in other cultures. He developed a theory that some gestures were universal, the residual actions associated with instinctive responses to threat, sexual attraction, and other situations relevant to natural selection. For example, the baring of teeth in anger was a habit associated with the act of biting in combat. Other gestures, he noted, were culturally acquired and learned in a process similar to that of language acquisition.

Darwin's influence on modern theory is present in two forms. First, his suggestion of a scientific study of emotion led the classic sociological thinkers to consider their positions vis-à-vis the social or instinctive nature of emotional response (see Collins 1975, 95 and Hochschild 1983, 208 for different views of Darwin's influence on Durkheim). Second, his ideas reappear roughly a century later in developmental psychology and anthropology as a very active debate about the universality of emotional expression (Ekman 1982; Lutz and White 1986).

The James-Lange theory of emotion had a far more direct impact on modern thought. Originally set out in James's (1950) *The Principles of Psychology,* the theory equated emotions with reflexive bodily changes that occur as an effect of an exciting situation. Emotional experience was a sequence of perception, excitation, and interpretation. What was distinctive about the James-Lange theory was that the physiological changes directly followed the perception of the exciting situation and were *then* subject to cognitive interpretation. The theory sparked great debate among psychologists, philosophers, and (later) sociologists (see an interesting review in Denzin 1984, 17–21). While modern sociological formulations typically emphasize cognitive processing of perceptual inputs to a greater degree than the James-Lange formulation, its stress on direct, unmediated response to events was mirrored in structurally oriented theories like Kemper's (1978) social interactional model. Modern psychological approaches often build on James's ideas (see Candland 1977 for a useful review).

Jean-Paul Sartre's (1962) critique of the James-Lange work from a phenomenological perspective also spawned a modern theoretical branch (e.g., Denzin 1984). Sartre argued that the biological body could not be meaningfully separated from the lived body, a person's consciousness of his/her physical reactions. For Sartre, then, the key question became how emotion as a form of consciousness is lived, experienced, and articulated in everyday life. Emotion was highly contextual, embedded in the field of interaction in which the emotion was experienced. In this phenomenological view, emotion must be studied as a lived, interactional process using subjective techniques.

In addition to James's formulation and Sartre's critiques of it, the major nonsociological force in modern emotion theory is the work of Freud (1938, 1965). The Freudian model of the unconscious and its effects on emotional life directly shaped Scheff's (1979; Scheff and Retzinger 1992) work on catharsis, healing, and ritual; it contributed more indirectly to Hochschild's, Denzin's, and Turner's work. Freud focused on anxiety and fear, suggesting that unconscious sexual drives in childhood are the source of much adult emotionality. Conscious processing could not fundamentally alter emotional reactions; emotions arose in the unconscious and, when inhibited through repression, reappeared as physiological reactions of pain or anxiety. The unconscious provided the meaning of emotion. This meaning resided in the individual's past, rather than in the present social situation (or cognitive processing of that situation).[5]

The ideas of Darwin, James, Lange, Sartre, and Freud formed the intellectual backdrop against which modern sociological theories developed. We can see a much more direct lineage, however, from the classic sociological treatments of emotions as an important feature of the link between social structure and individual experience.

Classic Sociological Theory

Although seldom considered as a distinct topic, emotions occupied a central place in the works of the theorists who defined sociology as a discipline: Marx, Weber, Durkheim, and Simmel. Marx (1983b, esp. 156–178) saw emotional life as molded by social structures. Material economic arrangements led to alienation and disenchantment in the laboring classes; one's emotional experiences were heavily determined by one's class position. Conversely, emotions (including religious fervor and personal alienation) could work to support a repressive class structure (Marx 1983a, 287–323). Hochschild's (1975, 1979, 1983) discussion of the commodity value placed on emotion management in service occupations grew directly from this Marxist tradition.

Weber (Gerth and Mills 1946) and Durkheim (1964) both focused on emotional responses to religious movements as powerful forces for the maintenance and change of structural forms. Weber's analysis of capitalism is based on the emotional responses of individuals to the Protestant religious ideology. Weber argued that once capitalism is in place, rational bureaucracy required emotional management to isolate emotional response to private rather than formal institutional spheres. Weber also analyzed charismatic leadership as an emotion-driven social force in direct opposition to bureaucratic forms of mobilization.

Durkheim stressed the experience of religious ecstasy as a social fact rather than a private experience. He analyzed emotional responses as societal constructions in which the moral sentiments of the group are reaffirmed. Such emotional experiences had a strong coercive element in Durkheim's view; individuals were not free to resist such emotional forces, since they were obligatory for true group membership (Durkheim 1964, 5; see Fisher and Chon 1989). Collins's (1975, 1990) theories of the emotional marketplace build directly on Weber's and especially Durkheim's ideas about how social forces can be unleashed by rituals.

Unlike Marx, Weber, and Durkheim, who dealt with the macrostructural sources and effects of emotional response, Simmel (1924, 1950) emphasized the microstructures of social interaction. His discussion of the emotional instability of dyads created the basis for modern social interactional theories (see Hochschild 1983, 211–222). Simmel's (1924, 357) emphasis on emotional expression in interactions as a bridge to knowledge of

another person leads directly to Goffman's analyses of impression management in public encounters (see below).

Since emotion is one of the main ways that social structures are reflected in our personal experience, it is surprising that the fathers of the symbolic interactionist tradition—especially Dewey and Mead—did not focus on emotion to the same extent that more macrostructural theorists did. Their theoretical statements were organized in opposition to the organismic tradition (exemplified by Darwin, James, Lange, and Freud) and to the behaviorist views of Skinner. The interactionists' ideas focused on the cognitive arena, where they stressed the importance of mind as an active, interactive part of the social milieu. In their efforts to highlight the central place of the mind in human society, Mead (1934) and his followers developed a view of humans as thinking (but not necessarily feeling) actors. However, the interactionists provided a basis for a modern theory of emotion with their emphasis on the uniquely human capacity for symbolization and language. From an interactionist point of view, the problem with the organismic orientation was that it viewed emotional response as a peripheral byproduct rather than an integral element in social interaction. An organismic view failed to note the key difference between animals and humans: humans can symbolize and consciously express an orientation through emotional gestures. The problem with the behaviorist perspective was that it denied the active role of the human actor as an interpreter and constructor of the social situation. Thus, the basic tenets of symbolic interaction provide the basis for a productive social analysis of emotion.

Cooley (1922, 1964) was the only early interactionist to develop this potential. He was one of the first to draw a sharp distinction between biological emotions and social sentiments. His attention to the role of culture in shaping the interpretation of bodily arousal was key to later social constructionist theories of emotion. His emphasis on the communication of feelings through meaningful gestures in social interaction illustrated the potential of the interactionist perspective in the affective domain.

The 1950s and 1960s: Bridges to Modern Theory

Sociology in the middle years of the twentieth century was dominated by functionalists at the macro level and cognitive theorists at the micro level. Affect and emotion were not major concerns. Still, several theoretical insights developed in the 1950s and 1960s provide bridges to modern treatments of affect and emotion.

Parsons's action theory linked affective reactions to social action with three "orientations"— cognitive, cathectic (affective), and evaluative (conative). Parsons and Shils (1962, 5) argued that objects in the actor's situation were "experienced as having positive or negative value to the actor . . . Cathexis, the attachment to objects which are gratifying and rejection of those that are noxious, lies at the root of the *selective* nature of action." Cathectic orientations were emotional responses that motivated action; the evaluative (conative) mode summarized the processes through which the actor allocated his/her energy among objects in attempts to optimize gratification. Following Durkheim and Weber, the Parsonian functionalists developed the motivational aspects of affect and emotion. This use of emotion as an independent, causal variable is still underdeveloped in modern theories (but see Thoits 1989).

Functionalists working with small group interaction stressed that socioemotional work was necessary to maintain harmonious relations in the face of potentially disruptive disagreements or directives while a task was accomplished (Bales 1950, 1953). The key insight was that emotional dynamics were important for the maintenance and performance of even task-oriented, problem-solving groups. The functionalist concern with the role of emotion in maintaining group cohesiveness is continued in modern work by Ridgeway (Ridgeway 1990; Ridgeway and Johnson 1990) and Lawler (1992).

Other scholars who emphasized the management of emotions in groups were the conflict theorists. Lewis Coser (1956, 1967) pointed out that emotion is the basis of group solidarity and is one of the resources that can be mobilized in power conflicts among groups. Coser (1956) argued that experienced hostility from other groups increased in-group solidarity. Such hostility could become violently disruptive (e.g., the Nazi's violent scapegoating of the Jews) unless the social structure allowed safe channels for deprived groups to discharge emotions. Membership in multiple, cross-cutting groups reduced the emotional interest in any single affiliation, buffering the social fabric from dramatic mobilizations of emotional energy. Collins (1975, 1990, 1993) continued the development of conflict theory by blending Coser's ideas with the interaction rituals of Durkheim.

While the functionalists and conflict theorists continued the classic emphasis on the implications of emotion for the group, two other theoretical developments in midcentury emphasized the role of emotions in microinteraction. Homans (1961, 1974) and Blau (1964) built on the behaviorist tradition that dominated psychology during this period. They argued that emotional reactions to social structures had a universal stimulus-response character. Pleasure came from receiving a reward (especially if it was bigger than expected) or not receiving an anticipated punishment (Homans 1974, 39). The emotion motivated behavior to obtain such rewarding feelings and resulted in positive behavior toward the reward provider. When an actor did not received an expected reward, anger and aggressive behavior were the result (Homans 1974, 37). Kemper (1978) later developed a relational version of these exchange ideas as his social interactional theory of emotions.

Homans also had interesting ideas about the formation of feeling rules. He thought unauthentic expressions of emotion were maintained by reinforcers such as social approval (Homans 1961, 380). For example, genuine grief may be rewarded after a calamity; eventually the expression of grief (whether experienced or not) became normative, because it produces social approval in such circumstances.

Other microtheorists reacted against the behaviorist intellectual tradition and tried to build on the alternative posed by the interactionists. Gerth and Mills (1964, xvii) noted the lack of an explicit treatment of emotion in Mead's work and pulled elements of theory from Freud, Weber, and Marx to remedy the gap. They treated interactional context as an important influence on interpreting feelings (as when a jilted girl's mother defines the girl's crying to be anger rather than sadness) (Gerth and Mills 1946, 55). The cultural impact on emotional expression and interpretation is also contained in Mills's (1940) groundbreaking work on vocabularies of motive. The emotional accounts given to support lines of action are cultural prescriptions (in the sense later developed by Hochschild's concept of feeling rules); they provide a cultural description of acceptable emotional responses to situations and a prescriptive motivational framework for linking feelings to actions.

Goffman (1956, 1959) focused his attention on embarrassment and shame. In his early work, especially, he analyzed social life using a dramaturgical perspective, concentrating on the presentation of self through enactment of roles. The emotions of embarrassment and shame resulted from inability to support one's desired self-presentation. Goffman greatly expanded understanding of the place of emotion in social control, viewing feelings as a force motivating the individual to conform to normative and situational pressures. In addition, he introduced the idea of the affective deviant, the actor who is unable or unwilling to maintain the appropriate affective orientation to the situation in which he/she is enmeshed (see Hochschild 1983, 214–218). In his work, we see the emotional responses of the actor as a cue indicating his or her allegiance to the group; rules of social order prescribe feelings as well as actions.

Also influential for interactionists during this period was Schachter and Singer's (1962) two-factor model of emotion: first, environmental events produced generalized arousal, then that arousal was interpreted as a specific emotion depending on the social situation. In a landmark experiment testing their ideas, the researchers varied the two factors: (1) physiological excitation (by injecting undergraduate subjects with epinephrine or a placebo) and (2) the social cues that might allow them to interpret their arousal (exposure to a confederate who acted in a euphoric or angry manner). They found that subjects experienced positive emotion when they were physiologically aroused and exposed to a pleasant social situation; they became angry when aroused and exposed to the unpleasant social cues. When they experienced no physiological arousal or when they were given a physiological explanation for their arousal, they reported little emotional response.

Theorists in sociology, psychology, and anthropology embraced the Schachter and Singer study as evidence of the power of social situations to shape emotional experience. They also viewed it as evidence that physiological arousal was nonspecific, with emotions being differentiated by social rather than physiological factors. Later evidence and interpretations of Schachter and Singer's results support the first but not the second conclusion. Critics of the study pointed out that Schachter and Singer ignored the possibility that the experimental situation aroused spontaneous physiological arousal in their experimental subjects (Kemper 1978; Plutchik and Ax 1967). Later experiments often failed to replicate the finding that emotion was not experienced when initially unaroused subjects are exposed to social cues (see Thoits 1984). More experiments supported the idea that social cues could influence subjects' interpretations of their physiological arousal (Cotton 1981; Manstead and Wagner 1981, Reisenzein 1983). The classic Schachter and Singer (1962) experiment is more important for the attention it focused on the importance of social cues in shaping emotional interpretation than for its statements about the undifferentiated nature of physiological response. However, confusion about the study's implications for the physiology of emotion led to a prolonged debate on the issue.

The Theoretical Heritage: Contributions and Problems

The juxtaposition of nonsociological emotion theories and the early sociological work on emotion makes the contribution of a sociological approach clear. The strength of the nonsociological emotion theories is their attempt to provide an overarching model of how emotional response in humans is generated. Their usefulness is limited because they largely ignored the structured nature of social situations that give rise to emotional responses. They focused instead on a small range of situations presumed to arouse natural, instinctive, or subconscious physiological reactions. This type of analysis, even if useful for a small number of basic emotions, clearly neglected the large, socially differentiated range of emotions that are subdivided by cultural forces. Sartre's critique focused attention on the interactionally embedded nature of emotional experience but failed to develop the structural patterning of the interactional environment. Only sociological theorists have seriously considered how social structure, cultural vocabularies, and interactional situations influence the personal experience of emotion. Only sociologists have considered seriously how emotional responses lead individuals to support or change social structures.

The sociological treatments of emotion, embedded as they are in works centered on other questions, pointed the way toward modern attention to structural, situational, and interactional sources of emotional response. Since the theories are centered around other questions, however, we cannot derive from these treatments a coherent, systematic view of the place of emotions in social life. Discussions of emotions as causal motivators (for either social change or social conformity) and as social effects (of either cultural norms or social structures) are not linked systematically in this literature; they are introduced as needed in the analysis of other questions. Because of this subservience to other topics, we find that the traditional sociological literature has no model of how the emotional experience is related to the structure of the self. The classic theorists do not see the self as actively managing, assessing, and expressing emotions; rather, emotions are a vehicle through which structural forces operate on the individual. Most likely, the lack of development of the emotion-self link is an intellectual outgrowth of the relative inattention to emotional response in interactionist thought, the one intellectual tradition that we would expect to have developed such an orientation. We see from this review that a social psychology of affect and emotion is a relatively modern enterprise, composed of a body of new theory that took emotion as its central concern and of empirical findings that developed from modern fieldwork, survey, and experimental techniques.

Modern social theories of affect and emotion built on the strengths of the sociological insight about the central place of structural and situational sources of emotional response. They also developed interactionist insights about the active role of self-structures in constructing and expressing symbolic meaning. Several of these modern theories also drew explicitly on nonsociological formulations as a description of organismic substrates that were then subject to overlying social dynamics. To these modern theories we now turn.

MODERN THEORIES OF EMOTION

The new developments in the sociology of emotion first reached an open scholarly forum in 1975.[6] Arlie Hochschild (1975) published her first treatment of *feeling rules* in an edited collection of feminist theory, Randall Collins (1975) discussed the ritual production of emotion in *Conflict Sociology,* and Thomas Scheff organized the first session on the sociology of emotion at the 1975 American Sociological Association meetings in San Francisco. Both Hochschild and Collins established an early emphasis on cultural forces in the production of emotional response.

Emotion Culture: Feeling Rules and Emotion Work

Goffman focused attention on rules for expression and engagement in social settings. Hochschild (1975, 1979) expanded this idea, developing the concept of feeling rules, cultural norms that specify the type of emotion, the extent of emotion, and the duration of feeling that are appropriate in a situation. For example, our culture requires that a grieving spouse feel intense unhappiness immediately after the death, but "snap out of it" after a few months.

An example of the excellent qualitative research in this tradition is Clark's (1987) study of the norms governing sympathy. Clark found that people generally believed they deserved sympathy following negative life events. However, the extent of sympathy was tempered by several factors. She likened the limits to sympathy as an "account" (analogous to a bank account) on which people could draw. Their accounts had more sympathy reserves if they had extended sympathy to others in the past, if they were not seen to deserve their plight, and if they did not "overdraw" their sympathy account (e.g., if they did not exaggerate their needs or demand more sympathy than the occasion warranted). High-status people often had trouble drawing on sympathy because they had never needed it in the past. It was understood that recipients of sympathy should be grateful and reciprocate at some later time.

While feeling rules acted as standards for judging others' emotional behavior, Hochschild placed more focus on how these norms were used for interpreting and shaping one's own emotional experience. Feeling rules tell us what we ought to feel, giving us standards for evaluating our own experiences. Hochschild argued that when what we feel differs from the cultural expectation, we actively engage in *emotion management* to create a more appropriate response. Such management can take several forms. *Surface acting* adjusts our expression of emotion to normative patterns; we change the emotional experience "from the outside in" (Hochschild 1990, 120). By pretending an emotion we do not feel, we elicit reactions from others that bolster our performance and may eventually transform it into a genuine one. One of the flight attendants that Hochschild (1983) studied reported pretending to be "up" so that passengers would respond to her as if she were cheery and friendly. The passengers' responses then led to an authentic positive affect. *Deep acting* involves a more basic manipulation of one's emotional state. Through physiological manipulation (deep breathing), shifting perceptual focus (concentrating on a positive aspect of a bad situation), or redefining the situation (thinking of a drunk passenger as a frightened, childlike person), actors can change their feelings "from the inside out" to conform to their ideas of appropriateness.

Thoits (1984, 1985, 1990) argued that when emotions routinely fail to match our cultural expectations and management efforts are ineffective, the emotional deviance would be interpreted as evidence of mental illness. In particular, she noted that self-labeling was likely to occur when an individual frequently found him/herself confronted with unmanageable, counternormative feelings. For example, a woman who finds herself filled with rage at minor slights might interpret these responses as signs of a deeper mental problem.

Such emotional deviance could be created by inadequate socialization or by structurally induced stress. When children are not taught (through modeling and reward) appropriate emotional responses, they display behavioral problems that must be addressed through remedial training (Pollak and Thoits 1989). But even competently socialized actors are likely to experience emotional deviance under some structural conditions: (1) multiple role occupancy, (2) subcultural marginality, (3) role transitions, especially if they are nonnormative in timing or sequence, and (4) rigid rules associated with rituals or other especially restrictive roles. For example, weddings are supposed to be times of joy, but the stresses of coordinating a complex social ritual often lead to negative emotion. Funerals are normatively times of sadness, but renewing acquaintances with relatives and friends at the social functions surrounding death can lead to positive emotion.

In many cases, occupations have well-developed emotional ideologies. Jack Haas (1977), for example, did a participant observation study of how iron workers on the steel framework of high-rise construction projects learned to manage their fear of an obviously dangerous job. The ability to control fear established a worker's reputation as a reliable, predictable partner. In fact, Haas found himself acting calmly in spite of considerable terror in his efforts to gain rapport with and the respect of the workers he was observing. In general, the control of fear in such hazardous occupations actually made the work less dangerous by generating mutual trust and predictable coordinated action. In cases where expressing the fear of dangerous conditions promoted a group goal (e.g., asserting worker autonomy over management in making a decision about whether or not to work in difficult weather conditions), the acknowledgment of danger was normative and unanimous.

Hochschild called emotion management done for a wage *emotional labor.* She linked this type of emotion work to class position, arguing that middle-class service jobs often involve managing one's own feelings to make clients feel good. Professional socialization may train workers explicitly to regulate emotions in dealing with clients.[7] Alienation from authentic feelings may result when emotion management becomes a pervasive part of occupational life.

Hochschild's (1988, 1990) more recent work looked at the relationship between ideology and emotion, arguing that ideologies not only regulated emotion (as in the occupational ideologies described above) but that one could have emotions *about* one's ideological beliefs. Among the couples who participated in Hochschild's (1988) study of gender ideology and household labor, some men and women had underlying feelings that conflicted with their ideological positions (e.g., a husband

who supported his wife's commitment to her job intellectually but felt furious at her engrossment in her work). Goode (1980) pointed out that men who intellectually supported women's equality still might experience negative emotion at having their "gift" of financial support redefined as an equal trade for the household labor of their wives.

Norms about emotional expression and experience are at the heart of what Gordon (1981, 1989b, 1990) called *emotion culture.* Gordon also emphasized two other elements: emotion vocabularies and beliefs about emotion. Emotion vocabularies are the concepts that the culture provides for us to think about, label, and communicate our feelings. This lexicon sensitizes us to some facets of feeling, creating fine distinctions for emotional domains that are important for negotiating social relationships and focusing attention on aspects of emotional life that are culturally valued or especially controlled (Averill 1980; Geertz 1959; Gordon 1990, 155; Kemper 1987). Emotions that we don't have words to describe can be experienced but may be difficult to remember or talk about.

Beliefs about emotions range from basic epistomological differences among societies, to variations across time in the appropriate degree of control exercised over emotional response, to beliefs about the emotions considered appropriate for people in different social positions. Not all cultures share the Western assumption that emotion is internally generated and privately experienced. In some societies, emotions are seen as a public element of social process (Gordon 1990; Lutz and White 1986). Heider (1984), for example, described a tribe in which emotions at funerals shifted markedly each time a new group arrived to participate. The funeral participants were relaxed and sociable until a new group of mourners arrived from another village. They then would fall into dramatic displays of crying and wailing, in concert with the new arrivals. After the display worked to a dramatic close, the scene regained its previous calm sociability. In our culture, this shift is interpreted as lack of "real" sadness, but it did not indicate insincerity in a culture where emotion was conceived as a social rather than internal phenomenon.

Psychologists have generated research on emotion knowledge that is useful for sociologists interested in emotion culture (although typically psychologists begin their work from a intradisciplinary cognitive orientation, rather than an awareness of sociological arguments). Psychologists doing experimental cognitive research concluded that emotion knowledge is typically represented as a sequence of antecedents and emotional reactions, called an *emotion script* (see Russell 1991 for a review of psychological work in this area). Scripts are generic knowledge structures about an emotional episode, typically including a series of subevents. Russell (1990, 1991) argued that emotion scripts have a prototype structure; they represent emotions as stereotypic situations where an antecedent event is followed by an emotional reaction, then perhaps by a response to the emotion. Therefore, our understanding of anger includes a script that encompasses antecedent conditions such as a personal affront or injustice, the physiological symptoms of anger (clenched teeth, red face, taut muscles), and typical behavioral responses, such as getting back at the person who has wronged us. Children begin to learn such emotion scripts at about the age of two (Harris 1989; Saarni and Harris 1990). Clearly, these emotion scripts are closely related to Hochschild's (1983) concept of feeling rules. Averill (1990) went so far as to describe emotions as a type of social role, with organized systems of responses prescribed by cultural scripts.[8]

Researchers have studied *display rules* extensively across cultures (Ekman 1982; Shaver et al. 1987). For example, the Awlad 'Ali (a Bedouin society) should express their sadness only in the company of equals, using formalized poems to tell of their feelings (Abu-Lughod 1986). Display rules are often related to more general beliefs about the beneficial effects of expression. In Western culture, our internal view of emotions leads to a container metaphor that compares strong feelings with steam inside a closed vessel. Ventilation prevents the explosion of the container (Tavris 1984). In other cultures, expression of anger is thought to incur the wrath of God (Briggs 1970).

Cultural studies often have focused on the changes in emotion norms and beliefs over time. In *Anger: The Struggle for Emotional Control in America's History,* Carol Z. Stearns and Peter Stearns (1986) argued that the separation of workplace from the home led to a view of marriage and family as a haven from the stresses of the grueling marketplace. Advice manuals and magazines encouraged women to eliminate expression of anger in the home. In the 1930s and 1940s, the ideal of complete elimination was replaced by management norms imported from the workplace. Anger was to be restrained, vented, or discussed in a managerial style. In the 1960s and 1970s, popular advice books advocated sharing feelings for intimacy, but only in a controlled way. Stearns and Stearns pointed out that there were still rules for expressing anger. Couples were to avoid shouting and physical displays, keep the episodes of anger short, and limit the span of issues on which anger was expressed.

Cancian and Gordon (1988) linked these marital emotion norms to political and cultural trends in larger American society. They used qualitative and quantitative data from women's magazines to argue that during the 1920s and 1960s people challenged the authority of government and other major institutions. During these periods of upheaval, women were encouraged to express more anger, even when such expression challenged their husbands' authority.

Symbolic Interactionist Approaches: From Rule-Based to Generative Models

The groundbreaking work of Hochschild, Gordon, and Thoits emphasized one half of the traditional interactionist approach: the extent to which the social environment influenced how an actor experienced and managed emotional responses. The empirical work using this perspective has focused on the cultural vocabulary and rules that are used to interpret individual experience. It is sometimes less apparent in these culturally oriented social constructionist approaches where the "real" emotion comes from. Authentic emotion is there to be labeled, judged deviant, and managed. But what causes the emotional response in the first place?

Other symbolic interactionist approaches emphasized the other half of the perspective: the active role of the individual in role taking. These approaches gave less attention to the structurally determined epidemiology of emotional experience and placed more emphasis on the motivational aspects of emotions as they impacted the self. These more generative, processual theories argued that emotional reaction depended on the actors' definitions of the situation and the meanings that grow out of these definitions.

Shott (1979), for example, accepted the importance of norms for regulating emotional experience. However, she stressed the individual construction of emotional experience within the limits placed by normative structures. She talked of emotional response as an interplay of impulse, definition, and socialization.[9] Shott discussed two classes of emotions as particularly central to social control: reflexive role-taking emotions and empathic role-taking emotions. *Reflexive emotions* are directed toward oneself (e.g., guilt, shame, pride) and require viewing oneself as object from another's perspective. *Empathic emotions* are evoked by mentally placing oneself in another's position. Both act as motivators of normative and moral conduct. As Shott (1979, 1324) noted, "social control is, in large part, self-control" because of the feelings nonconformity arouse in us. These feelings arise from our ability to take the role of the other, either in viewing our own behavior or in empathetically participating in the experiences of others. Emotions are constructed from ongoing experience using the cultural vocabularies and emotion norms that have built up through social interaction—this is where the cultural and interactionist schools connect. Most important, emotions motivate action since they serve as signals to the social actor about the self-relevance of events (an idea developed by both Hochschild and Shott).

Two structural variants of symbolic interactionist thought—identity theory and affect control theory—focus on social identities that people embrace as a key factor in linking emotional experi-

ence to the self. In identity theory, Stryker (1987) conceptualized the self as a hierarchically organized set of identities. The identities represented commitment to social roles such as wife, mother, lawyer, and athlete. For Stryker, emotions were relevant to this self-structure in several ways. First, they served as motivators: role relationships that generated positive affect would be enacted more frequently and would move upward in the salience hierarchy that constituted one's self-definition. Identity enactments that routinely caused dissatisfaction and pain would move downward in the hierarchy. Therefore, if a manager found himself blocked in his career path at work, he might reorient his activities toward rewarding interactions with family and community organizations.

Second, emotions would result from adequate or inadequate role performances. Emotions therefore served a signal function, indicating how well interactions supported one's sense of oneself in the situation. If a professor feels elation after a classroom interaction with students, the emotion signals that her performance in that identity was above her normal expectations for the role. To Shott's insight about the function of shame and pride in reflecting performance adequacy, Stryker added emotional reaction to the other's performance. Since adequate role performances require coordinated action with our network alters, he pointed out that we could be angry at others as well as ourselves for failed role enactment. He expected emotional outbursts to follow the failure of others to do their part in supporting an identity enactment (Stryker 1987; Stryker and Serpe 1982).

A final insight from identity theory is the sense in which emotions could signal the importance of relationships to the self. Stryker argued that the strength of our emotional reaction to events is a way that we can gauge the centrality of an identity in the self structure. A mother's depression at leaving her child to return to work signals the higher salience of the parental compared to the worker role.[10]

Affect control theory (Heise 1977, 1979; Smith-Lovin and Heise 1988) also took the social identity as its focal point. The theory's distinctive contribution was that it specified which actions make up an adequate role performance and predicted the emotional reactions that accompany adequate and inadequate performances. Affect control theory started by conceptualizing an individual's definition of the situation (including the perception of self, others, behaviors, and settings) as labels with cultural meanings. These meanings (called *fundamental sentiments* to indicate their transituational character) had three dimensions: evaluation (good versus bad), potency (powerful versus powerless), and activity (lively versus quiet).[11] The identity of "mother," for example, is fundamentally nicer, more powerful, and more lively than the identity of "clerk."

The theory then used empirical results from the psychology of impression formation to describe how events can temporarily alter meanings ascribed to self or others (Heise and Smith-Lovin 1981; Smith-Lovin 1987). The extent to which these situational meanings differed from the fundamental sentiments in any situation was called a *deflection.* The event "the mother kissed the child" would create little deflection for mother or child, since this positive, lively behavior would create a situational meaning very close to the culturally appropriate fundamental sentiments. If "the mother abused the child," however, deflection would be high; the negative behavior would cause a big downward shift in the evaluation of the mother, failing to confirm our view of what mothers should be like. The theory predicted that people construct events to *confirm* fundamental meanings about self and others—they expect and enact events that minimize deflections.

In affect control theory, emotions were signals about the extent to which events were confirming or discomfirming identity (Heise 1989; Smith-Lovin 1990; Smith-Lovin and Heise 1988). When deflections were small (i.e., when events were confirming), an actor's emotional response was largely determined by his/her identity (and its fundamental sentiment). When things are going smoothly, mothers feel good, powerful, and lively because they occupy a positive identity. However, when events are disconfirming, the nature of the situation (and

the deflection it causes) heavily determines the character of the emotional response. A mother who has hurt her child typically feels awful. In this case, emotions are powerful motivating forces, signalling the need for social action to restore fundamental affective meanings.

Empirical research has supported affect control theory's assumption about the dimensional structure of emotion terms. Researchers have applied factor analytic and multidimensional scaling techniques to a variety of affect and emotion measures (e.g., semantic differential ratings of mood, self-reports of emotions, similarity ratings of emotion words). Early studies found as many as five to eleven dimensions, but in the early 1980s most researchers settled on a two-dimensional representation (see Watson and Tellegen 1985). The two dimensions were pleasantness-unpleasantness (contrasting happy, euphoric, satisfied feelings with sad, unhappy, upset feelings) and activated-quiet (contrasting excited, tense feelings with relaxed, sleepy ones). A third dimension representing potency or dominance appeared in many studies (Averill 1975; Mehrabian 1980; Osgood 1966) where researchers argued it was necessary to differentiate relatively intense, negative emotions such as fear and anger, from one another.

Some early results were muddied by the inclusion of many terms that did not represent emotions (e.g., tired). After Ortony's and Clore's work in clarifying the boundaries of the emotion lexicon (Clore, Ortony, and Foss 1987; Ortony and Clore 1981; Ortony, Clore, and Foss 1987), recent studies using data from both the United States and Canada have confirmed the three-dimensional structure (Heise and Morgan 1988; MacKinnon and Keating 1989; Shaver et al. 1987). This empirical research supported the three-dimensional view of affect and emotion in affect control theory.

Affect control theory's predictions about behavior were tested using experimental methods. Wiggins and Heise (1987) showed that undergraduate subjects used positive and negative behaviors toward interaction partners to restore their self-esteem after being criticized. A secretary (actually a confederate) berated an undergraduate subject for using incorrect procedures in filling out a questionnaire. The student then had the opportunity to interact with another confederate, who was labeled either another student or a juvenile delinquent. Affect control theory correctly predicted that positive actions would be directed at esteemed interaction partners (the other student), while deviant interaction partners (the juvenile delinquent) would be treated negatively to restore self-esteem.[12]

Other studies tested the emotion predictions of the theory (Adams and Smith-Lovin 1992; Robinson and Smith-Lovin 1992), showing that it accurately mapped emotional responses to a variety of situations. Robinson et al. (1991) showed that people used emotion displays to make inferences about an actor's character after a negative event. When a criminal showed remorse during his confession, he was judged to be less likely to commit another crime and was given a lighter sentence.

Symbolic interactionist approaches like affect control theory differed from the cultural approaches by suggesting a more generative view of feeling rules. Expectations for emotional response were generated by the meanings evoked by identities and actions, rather than being learned as scripts or prescriptions. The generated "rules" could be highly situational: different people would be expected to feel different things under the same circumstances. Identity shaped response and expectation. Most important, actors were expected to experience normative emotions spontaneously *if* they shared the group's meanings and definitions of events. Norms were viewed as the outcome of cultural meanings and interactive process, rather than as a cultural rule system. Only when one did not share cultural meanings (because of inadequate socialization, an externally imposed ideology, or an idiosyncratic view of events) would one experience emotional deviance or need emotion management.

The strength of the identity theories—their generative source of both individual experience and cultural norms—also led to a shortcoming: these theories do not clearly distinguish between feeling rules, experienced emotion, and expressed emotion. While stressing the common source of all

three facets of emotional experience in the meanings individuals give to interaction through their definitions of situations, the theories do not specify the conditions under which felt emotions will be managed or manipulated to convey an impression to others. The identity maintenance perspectives (especially affect control theory) can tell us *what* emotion we should show to maintain a certain impression, but not the conditions under which we will choose to manipulate impressions in this way.

Structural Theories of Emotion

Identity theory and affect control theory emphasized the role of identities in shaping emotional response and the role of emotions in motivating identity enactment. Another branch of sociological theory, more structural in form, posited an even more direct link between social position and emotion.

Kemper (1978, 1987, 1990a) proposed a social relational theory based on social exchange principles (see the discussion of Homans, above). He argued that two dimensions of social relationships —status and power—were universal.[13] Relative positions on these dimensions defined the key aspects of a relationship and determined its emotional character (Kemper and Collins 1990).[14] Changes in status and power led to specific emotional outcomes. For example, loss of power resulted in fear or anxiety; guilt resulted from excess power.

Kemper (1978, 1991) included attributional elements in his theory. He argued that emotional outcomes from status and power changes would depend on the perceived source of the change and, in some cases, whether or not the other person in the interaction was liked or disliked. For example, status loss would result in anger if the loss appeared to be remediable; such anger would be functional in that it motivated action to regain the lost status. If the loss was irredeemable, however, it would lead to sadness and depression, saving energy and acclimating the individual to his/her new lowered state of resources. Status loss by another, if caused by oneself, led to guilt if the other was liked (facilitating group survival by preventing in-group insult). If the other was not liked, his/her status loss would cause happiness.

Kemper (1991) tested ten predictions from his theory using data from forty-eight West German college undergraduates. Each undergraduate was asked to think about situations in which they experienced an emotion (happy, sad, angry, and afraid) and was prompted to answer the following questions: Where did it happen? How long ago was it? Who was involved? What happened? How long did it last? Kemper provided coders trained in status-power judgments and his emotion theory with verbatim descriptions of the four emotion situations given by each undergraduate.[15] The coders classified events in terms of their status and power implications, whether the interactants liked each other, and what emotion the undergraduate had experienced. The theory accurately predicted emotion outcomes in 65 to 75 percent of the situations.

Kemper's theory (1978) analytically distinguished three types of emotions that came from status-power relationships. *Structural emotions* were characteristic of a relationship by virtue of its constellation of relative status and power. These emotions correspond roughly to what others have called "sentiments" in that they are stable affective associations with the relationship; one might feel secure and happy in a relationship where one experiences adequate status and power. *Situational emotions* resulted from changes in status and power as a result of interaction. Finally, *anticipatory emotions* resulted from the contemplation of future interaction. Emotions had a motivational component in interaction as well. Kemper assumed that negative emotions would motivate subsequent attempts to regain lost status or power.

Since Kemper first introduced his theory, much discussion has focused on its positivist assumptions. Kemper proposed that status and power relationships were tied to certain basic emotions through specific physiological reaction.[16] Emotional responses were "prewired" (Kemper 1990a, 213), presumably because they facilitated individual and group survival. Since the socially constructed nature of emotional response was one of the common elements of most other sociological approaches to emotion, theoretical arguments in the sociology of emotions often focused on whether some emotions were physiologically spe-

cific, or whether emotions' character was imparted to an undifferentiated physical substrate by cultural knowledge and social context.

More recently, Kemper (1987) developed a synthetic position. He argued that while some emotions were basic, instinctive, and physiologically distinct, others were differentiated by social and cultural forces. The number and character of emotions that were named and experienced in a culture were determined by the social relationships and interactional outcomes that were central to that group's social fabric. This position was acceptable to most sociologists of emotion, so long as we left open the question of how *many* emotions are basic: the most social constructivist position would argue for just one—undifferentiated arousal; Kemper argued for four basic emotions—anger, happiness, fear, and sadness/depression.

This developing consensus has returned the focus of attention to the other theoretical issues raised by Kemper's work. His model shared many features with affect control theory. Both were general, deductive theoretical formulations that linked abstract situational antecedents to emotion outcomes. Both used a dimensional framework to characterize relationships.[17] Both predicted that emotions will be generated both by the stable features of relationships and by interactional changes in the relative positions of the actors on the dimensions. Culture entered both theories in specifying which actions will cause change in status and power, rather than by specifying rules for feelings or behavior. The two models differed in the emphasis they place on individual interpretation. Starting from an individual's definition of situation, affect control theory gave a greater role to cognitive processing of events. With his emphasis on structural features of interaction, Kemper's social interactional theory stressed the direct effects of structural position and prewired responses to changes in position. This emphasis on direct, unmediated response to social situation is what separated Kemper's social interactional theory from the cultural and interactionist theoretical camps.

Collins (1975, 1981, 1990, 1993; Kemper and Collins 1990) joined Kemper in advocating status and power as the two fundamental dimensions of social interaction. Collins's goal was to account for macrolevel structure and change through aggregating interactions among individuals. He has reconstructed the Weberian theory of stratification on a microlevel, grounding it in microinteraction and emotional motivations. He developed the concept of *emotional energy,* which he argued was released by *interaction ritual chains.* Actors occupy positions by virtue of title or organizational membership,[18] then enact chains of action that maintain shared beliefs. Emotional energies flow through such interaction chains as people in advantaged positions receive positive sentiments from others. Structures are maintained by these emotional responses produced by standardized sequences of interaction. Like the conflict theorists before him, Collins argued that participation cements group membership and (when aggregated over a large number of interactions) supports and constitutes macrostructures. Actors who acquire large amounts of emotional energy from the marketplace of ritual encounters are able to claim property and/or authority. Therefore, stability and change in cultural resources (for producing interaction ritual chains) and emotional energies (emotional rewards and costs in the interactional marketplace) produce the macrostructure, as individual-level interactions are cumulated to create societal forms.

Collins's view was supported by Smith-Lovin and Douglass (1992),[19] who showed that religious rituals developed to produce identity-affirming emotional responses. They looked at services in two churches—a Unitarian Church and a Metropolitan Community Church congregation (a demonination created to serve the gay community). The gay church developed rituals that reaffirmed a positive homosexual identity, while in the Unitarian congregation the ideology and ritual confirmed a deviant status for homosexuals.

Recently, Collins (1993) offered emotional energy as a common element linking different preference hierarchies in rational choice theory. By assuming that people were operating to maximize emotional energy, it was possible to analyze a marketplace of interaction rituals and to predict choices between different spheres of activity. Insti-

tutions and groups that attracted investments and generated positive emotional energy for their participants would survive; other interaction chains would not.

Kemper's and Collins's view of emotion as produced by and mediating change in structural dimensions of status and power firmly linked the sociology of emotion to classic sociological questions about social structure and interaction. In all three of the theoretical perspectives reviewed above—cultural, interactional, and structural—we see a direct connection between the individual and the societal structure in which he/she is embedded. Now we turn to two perspectives that emphasize intraindividual dynamics: the psychodynamic and phenomenological approaches.

The Psychodynamic Perspective

Scheff's (1979, 1988, 1990; Scheff and Retzinger 1992) theory of emotional catharsis was rooted in the Freudian tradition. Scheff thought distressing emotions (e.g., grief, fear, and anger) are universal because the social situations that produce them are universal. For example, attachment losses (e.g., from parental closeness) produced grief and fear. Following Freud, Scheff assumed that emotional discharge was necessary. When society inhibited emotional release, physiological tensions caused neurotic behaviors. Ritual, drama, contests, and other collective emotion-management techniques allowed for the safe discharge of accumulated emotion. These cultural routines allow actors to develop *aesthetic distance* from the sources of their distress by moving back and forth from a focus on the distressing event and a focus on the present ritual enactment. The focus on emotional products elicited by ritual paralleled the attention given such interaction chains by Collins. Here, however, the mechanism and motivation of ritual was quite different. Collins saw interaction ritual chains as producing emotional energies that generated solidarity and structure at the macro level; Scheff saw the rituals as providing a safe outlet for the discharge of emotional distress built up from the common experience of distressing emotions. These rituals were a functional solution to the problem of repressed emotions that Scheff viewed as a necessary element of the human experience.

Like the early interactionists,[20] Scheff (1988) focused on the key roles of pride and shame in producing social conformity. Cultural taboos made the display of these emotions infrequent in interactions, but Scheff argued that they constituted an underlying biosocial substrate to virtually every interaction. Scheff's multimethod research focused on the paradox that his theory posed: how can shame and anger be so fundamental to social control but appear to be so rare in everyday interaction?[21] He (1990) coded facial expressions during recall of distressing events, showing repeated movement from discharge to distance. Scheff and Retzinger (1992) analyzed the moment of revelation on videotapes of the old television show *Candid Camera* for examples of shame. On this show, unsuspecting people were drawn into situations that were not what they seemed. The host then appeared and revealed the joke, recording the naive participants' reactions of surprise and shame.

Scheff argued that unacknowledged shame leads to anger and then back to more shame in a cycle that eventually erupts in violence toward self or another object. Through literary examples of shame-rage cycles in novels (e.g., *The Sufferings of Young Werther* by Goethe) and historic examples of shame and violence (Hitler's rise to power), Scheff and Retzinger (1992) illustrated the underlying cycles of repression and discharge as unacknowledged shame leads to violence.

Although less clinical in his orientation, Jonathan Turner (1987, 1988, 1989, forthcoming) also adopted a melding of the psychoanalytic and interactionist models in his sociological theory of motivation. Turner's view was that individuals were motivated by several basic need states. If these needs were not met, individuals felt deprived and became motivated to avoid the source of deprivation. Anxiety was aroused when needs for group inclusion, ontological security, and self-confirmation were not met. This anxiety, when aroused, fed back into other basic needs for symbolic and material gratification. These need states, if not adequately addressed, fed back into renewed concerns about self-confirmation, group inclusion, and ontological security. Clearly, in Turner's formulation, many emotions that motivated individuals were negative, often representing fears and concerns about what was going wrong with interaction. With Scheff and Retzinger (1992), Turner emphasized the recursive nature of negative emotion; he characterized repression as "a kind of emotional compressor that presses emotions together and . . . makes them a volatile mix of emotional fuel driving the course of an interaction" (Turner forthcoming, 5–6). Fear and anger were transformed into guilt and shame, respectively, when self or others failed to meet expectations. These powerful negative emotions are often intense and self-escalating. This cycling led to a *anger-shame-guilt-fear* cycle modeled closely on Scheff's recursive *shame-anger-shame* formulation. Since the strong negative emotions are socially unacceptable in many situations, they often are repressed with guilt, lowering emotional energy in interaction. On the positive side, satisfaction resulted from meeting or exceeding expectations. This positive emotional energy fed back into situational expectations and needs.

Clearly, Turner's formulation was a composite of several major sociological treatments of emotions. He incorporated Kemper's basic emotions, Scheff's recursive cycles of repressed emotion, and Collins's emotional energies into a model that flows from needs and expectations through emotions (expressed or repressed) to emotional energy, then cycles back into interaction. In this synthesis, Turner placed psychodynamic ideas about repression and distressful emotions back into the context of the social interactions that create them. On the other hand, by focusing on needs he introduced a transitional, personal component to the social structural emphasis of Kemper and Collins. Within Collins's framework, high emotional energy flowed inevitably from high status, rank, and solidarity. For Turner, fear-guilt and anger-shame cycles from unresolved, repressed situations could be carried by high-status actors into situations to moderate their ability to generate positive emotional energy from interaction rituals. Conversely, low-status, low-power people may lower their expectations to lead reasonably satisfied lives. The highly stressed, stymied business executive may be unhappier than the subservient migrant worker.

Denzin's Phenomenological Approach

While Turner incorporated ideas from many different sociological theories of emotion into his synthetic model by adding needs and psychodynamic processes to the structural sources of social experience, the phenomenological approach developed by Denzin (1984, 1985, 1990) explicitly rejected these theoretical attempts to abstract elements of experience. Following Sartre and Peirce (1955), Denzin argued that emotion must be studied as lived experience. Following the interactionists, he put the self at the center of emotional experience. For him, emotions were self-feelings with a threefold structure: (1) a physical sense of experiencing the emotion, (2) a sense of the self feeling the emotion, and (3) a revealing of the inner, moral meaning of this feeling for the self (Denzin 1990, 88). Emotional experiences allowed a person to know himself and others through imagination, sympathy, empathy and self-feelings (Denzin 1984, 245). Any attempt to treat emotion, its antecedents, or its consequences as variables abstracted from lived experience missed the special character of emotion as inner experience. Denzin stated that emotion could not be quantified but should be studied from within. Introspection and thick description of cultural products (e.g., film and television) have been his chosen methods.

Ellis (1991) also advocated the use of introspection as a technique for studying how private and social experience are fused in felt emotions. She used the technique to record the private processing of physiological response, perception, memory, self-dialogue, and behavior that comprised the response to an emotion-eliciting interaction. Ellis pointed out that methods which require people to put their emotions into categories (as many of the empirical tests of deductive theories do) missed the serial nature of many emotions. For example, her intensive interviewing about jealousy episodes found that "the jealous flash may move

from shock and numbness to desolate pain to rage and anger to moral outrage in a very brief time" (Ellis and Weinstein 1986, 367).

In her analysis of her reactions to her lover's illness and death (Ellis, 1988), she focused on the physical sensations that accompanied their intense interactions *and* on her own thoughts about those reactions. In some instances, she talked of making a decision to let go and experience extremely deep, physiologically taxing emotions—holding each other and crying in bed for hours to become physically worn out. Other occasions required heavy emotion management to maintain institutionized interactions with other actors (e.g., bizarrely neutral interactions with doctors who delivered platitudes but could offer no real hope). About one doctor's visit she wrote, "I was scared. How could I feel so numb and like I was exploding at the same time? I suddenly laughed, but covered it with a sigh. How absurd. I felt relief" (Ellis 1988).

Ellis's introspections clearly illustrated the three levels of emotional awareness that Denzin wrote about: the direct experience of physiological sensation, the awareness of a cognitive self experiencing that emotion, and the implications of this lived emotion for the broader relational structure of one's life. Recently, Clark et al. (1990) distinguished three distinct ways of reading the world—cognitive, emotional, and physical—and discussed how people move between them as they build solo and joint realities. This new work reasserts the phenomenological approach's relevance to interaction.

The Modern Theories: Communalities and Questions

The modern sociological theories of emotion make a remarkable addition to the classic treatments reviewed earlier. They offer comprehensive views of the place emotions hold in social life. In particular, they articulate a model of the self who feels, how the social world impacts him/her, and how emotions motivate social action (and, cumulatively, change social structures). From Denzin, who holds that emotionality is the vehicle for both self-knowledge and knowledge of others, to Kemper, who sees emotions as produced by a person's perception of interactional gains and loses, all of these approaches view emotion to some degree as a signal function that connects the individual in a visceral way to the social situation.

Furthermore, there is growing consensus that socialization processes are key to how we experience emotion. While there is still debate about whether or not there are physiological differentiated "basic" emotions, constructionists, interactionists, and structuralists agree that social groups differentiate emotion vocabularies to fit important, recurrent interactions. These emotion vocabularies then shape the interpretation of individual experience, providing a mechanism for encoding and communicating certain emotional reactions more easily than others. Even in the most structural theories, it is the *perception* and interpretation of social interaction that produces emotional response.

The communalities that underlie the growing body of systematic theory make it easier to see interesting questions raised by remaining differences. First, there is the contrast between Denzin's phenomenological view and all of the other views: is it possible to have a traditional social psychology of emotion, or does abstracting the process rob emotionality of its meaning? If we accept abstraction as necessary to a social science of emotion, we face a second contrast between rule-based cultural approaches and more generative models. Social constructionists and cultural theorists do not argue that learned feeling rules determine emotional response in a mechanistic way; far from it—they emphasize emotion management and the lack of fit between spontaneous emotion and cultural prescriptions in many structural positions. But they do argue that cultures impart scripts for emotional response. According to these theorists, we learn rules for what to feel in what situations; part of the meaning of an emotion is a set of beliefs about the typical antecedents and consequences of the feeling. More generative formulations (both interactionist and structural) argue that norms about feelings flow from basic structures of interaction. The interactionists place the affective meanings associated with identities and actions at the center of the process; the structuralists view the status and power associated with structural positions as key to emotional response. Both posit that emotional reactions are responses to (and signals about) the implications of interaction for self and others in interaction. This theoretical distinction between rule/script theories and generative theories has important implications for what is learned in socialization and how emotional responses are regulated by socialized actors.

ADDITIONAL EVIDENCE ABOUT AFFECT AND EMOTIONS

As a relatively young subfield, the sociology of affect and emotion is theoretically rich but short on empirical evidence. Most of our knowledge about affect and emotion comes from research in other disciplines or substantive areas. Much of this research developed quite independently of the sociological theories of emotion and takes on new relevance when viewed in this perspective. Other examples show how the new sociology of emotion is beginning to have an impact on other substantive areas. Therefore, we turn to a brief review of these other research domains before summarizing the current state of the field.

Epidemiology of Emotional Experience

Several theories make strong statements about what types of events should lead to what types of emotional response (e.g., Kemper's prediction that status loss will lead to anger or sadness). They also predict that people occupying certain social positions will experience a different emotional climate than those in other parts of the social structure (e.g., Hochschild's argument that middle-class service workers will be alienated from their genuine emotions by the extensive emotion labor required in their jobs). One would suspect that prototypical cultural beliefs about emotional antecedents and consequences would be related to actual experience.[22] Unfortunately, we have relatively little systematic information about what types of events lead to what emotions or what types of people are more likely to experience certain emotions chronically. One notable exception is a landmark cross-national study by Scherer et al. (1986). Using survey methodology, Scherer asked 779 college students from eight European countries to tell about the antecedents, physiological effects, verbal and nonverbal reactions to situations when they experienced four emotions: joy/happiness, sadness/grief, fear/fright, and anger/rage. The researchers found striking similarities across the countries in emotion distribution and antecedents. Using information about how long it had been since the emotion-eliciting event, Scherer (1986, 174) concluded that anger was the most frequently experienced emotion, followed by joy, sadness, and fear. Anger was also the most likely to have been aroused by social situations; fear was least likely to be social in origin. Anger was most frequently aroused by the failure of friends, relatives, and others to conform to social norms and by the experience of inappropriate rewards for self. Traffic situations, physical aggression, achievement situations, and the unknown led to fear. Relationships with friends (beginning and continuing) and success in achievement situations led to joy. Problems with friends (including the end of relationships through death) most frequently led to sadness. These patterns led Scherer (1986, 175–176) to speculate that three primary concerns—with personal well-being (including physical safety and self-concept), relationships to others, and social order—were cross-cultural needs or goals.

Data on emotion duration from the Scherer et al. (1986) study pointed out the close relationship between emotion and mood. While fear appeared to be a short-lived response (often occurring in strange surroundings with unfamiliar people) and anger appeared to fade after a few minutes or hours, joy and sadness were often transformed into moods that lasted all day. Sadness from relationship loss sometimes lasted for days as the respondents reexperienced the event and their reaction to it more or less continuously.

In general, Scherer and his colleagues found more striking similarities than differences across the European cultural groups. Some differences were noted: the Italian, British, and Spanish respondents showed the highest average intensity; the Germans and Swiss mentioned relationship antecedents most often, while the Southern Europeans mentioned achievement situations. Israelis were more different from the other groups than other nationalities. Clearly, the differences do not fall easily into a stereotypical pattern.

As a survey of college students, the Scherer et al. (1986) study was ill-suited for studying class or other social differences. However, surveys designed to measure the mental health of a general population have given us some clues about the distribution of at least the negative emotions. We turn now to that voluminous literature.

Mental Health, Stress, and Coping

Survey research on reports of social distress has focused more on chronic moods of depression and anxiety than on immediate emotional response to specific situations. However, many of the symptoms used to create depression and anxiety scales are strikingly similar to the physiological manifestations of emotion. Studies in the early 1960s often asked about physical symptoms such as cold sweats and heart palpitations, while more recent studies asked more direct questions about mood (feeling afraid, lonely, or sad)(Mirowsky and Ross 1989). Generally, mental health studies combine distress measures into a single scale; only in a few substantive applications do components such as anxiety and depression show different patterns (but see Mirowsky and Ross 1989; Wheaton 1983).

These mental health studies showed several clear patterns (see Mirowsky and Ross 1989). Women report more distress than men. Unmarried people report more distress than married people. The uneducated poor report more distress than people who have more income and education. African Americans and other minorities show somewhat higher levels of distress, but the pattern gets more complicated if we control for their generally lower socioeconomic status. Poor African Americans suffer considerably more distress than whites, but middle-class African Americans show *less* distress than whites (Kessler and Neighbors 1986). Having children leads to distress; levels of marital satisfaction and well-being drop after a birth and do not return to their prechild levels until after all the children leave home. People who experience undesirable life events (e.g., loss of a job, death of a spouse, sickness, accidents) report more distress than those who do not. Those who claim a weak religious belief are more distressed than those who have strong religious beliefs *or* those who are unbelievers. The young are more depressed and anxious than the middle-aged. Anxiety declines steadily with age, while depression declines from youth to age fifty-five, then increases again in old age. In general, those who have few network contacts and few social roles are more distressed than those who are better integrated into society (Thoits 1986).

How are we to make sense of this wealth of empirical findings? What can they tell us about affect and emotion more generally? Mental health researchers typically interpreted their results in terms of (1) control over life events, (2) inequity or victimization, and (3) availability and usefulness of coping mechanisms. Clearly, disadvantaged persons have fewer resources to avoid negative events and to respond to misfortunes that do occur. This powerlessness puts them at greater risk of stressful circumstances.

Equity research showed that people get angry when they give more than they get (Walster, Walster, and Berscheid 1978). Such victimization also leads to depression because of an implied lack of control: while some people may choose to be exploiters, few choose to be victims. Equity theory also argues that the exploiter in an unfair relationship feels guilt (Homans 1974). Explored in long-term, close relationships, the equity explanation worked quite well: both husbands and wives felt that sharing marital power was more satisfying than usurping it (see Blumstein and Kollock 1988; Hochschild 1988). However, each partner defined the equitable division of marital power as somewhat in his/her favor, so the points of minimum depression/anger were different for both. The actual decision-making structure of families was, in fact, between the husbands' and wives' equity (minimum depression) point, with

the outcome favoring the husbands' view to some extent (Mirowsky 1985; Mirowsky and Ross 1989).

In less personal exchanges, researchers observed little guilt at overreward (but see Hegtvedt 1990). Most people think they earn less than or what they deserve. Occupants of powerful, rewarded positions develop perceptions of themselves as more self-efficacious, competent, and deserving, rather than perceiving themselves as overrewarded (Cook, Hegtvedt, and Yamagishi 1987; Stolte 1983). Given a strong tendency not to perceive overreward, research found that absolute reward level predicted emotional response (satisfaction versus distress) to a greater degree than inequity in most situations (Michaels, Edwards, and Acock 1984). This pattern fits well with Kemper's argument that status gain will produce positive emotion (pride if attributed to self and happiness if attributed to other).

The work on equity and distributive justice points to a much more general relationship between expectations and emotion. When peoples' expectations are not met, they become angry (as in Scherer, Wallbott, and Summerfield's 1986 results); if the situation does not allow remediation, they become depressed. Molm (1991) suggested that this relationship between expectations and affect was one reason why punishment caused stronger affect than reward in exchange experiments: since rewards were much more common in such experiments, punishments had shock value in addition to being negative.

Recently, theory from the sociology of emotions has enriched the interpretation of mental health and distributive justice research (see especially Hegtvedt 1990; Thoits 1984, 1991). Thoits (1991) identified behavioral and cognitive strategies that individuals can use to cope with distressing situations and the emotions they evoke. She argued that perceptions of the controllability of events, and the coping strategies these perceptions evoke, account for some differences in chronic malaise (which can be viewed as the ineffectively managed emotional residue of stressful events). She used data from two hundred undergraduates who wrote detailed descriptions of two emotional experiences that were important to them (one positive, one negative),[23] including information on how they handled the situation and how the situation turned out. Consistent with gender differences in display rules, women were more likely to express their feelings and seek social support. They also were more likely to try to see the situation differently, using a type of emotion management frequently employed by female service workers (Hochschild 1983). Men were more likely to analyze (think through) the situation, accept it as it was, or engage in strenuous exercise to change physiological symptoms. Women mentioned more coping strategies than men in both open-ended and fixed-choice measures. Thoits (1989) concluded that women do not seem to lack coping strategies for dealing with undesirable events; it seemed likely, therefore, that greater exposure to structural stressors (which she could not address with self-report data on one negative event) must be responsible for the greater chronic distress reported by women. It is also possible that the expressive coping strategies women use tend to reinforce distressful emotions, as others respond to the emotional milieu created by the affective displays and social interaction that women seek out to cope with their problems. A problem may continue to be more "real" if its social reality is reinforced by the social environment of supportive others.

Affect and Cognition

The fact that "rethinking" a negative situation is a coping strategy for dealing with distressing events highlights the relationship between cognition and affective response. Psychologists, who rarely attend to our sociological theory, have a separate tradition of research that explores the cognitive bases of affective reaction.[24] Cognitive schemas carry affect as part of their knowledge structure; when they are activated in a new situation, the affective meaning they carry is activated as well (Fiske 1982; Tesser 1978). Thus, recognizing a current situation as akin to a highly unpleasant category of experiences in the past evokes negative affect. Using such schemas frequently tends to con-

solidate their structure and intensify the affect associated with them.

Attributions about the causes of events clearly produce emotional response. If we attribute failure to ourselves, we feel shame; if we attribute it to the actions of others, we feel anger (Weiner, Russell, and Lerman 1978; Weiner et al. 1987; see Kemper 1978 for an application of these findings in sociological theory). Attribution of positive or negative traits as a result of observed behavior clearly indicates the creation of an affective orientation through the encoding of information (see Kelley and Michela 1980).

While the overwhelmingly cognitive focus of modern psychology has led to a presumption that cognitive processing is key to the production of affect, a smaller countermovement espoused the position that affective responses are more basic and can drive cognitive processing (see Zajonc 1984 for a strong statement of this position). Research on the effect of affect on cognition falls into two general camps: (1) the effect of stereotyping on perception, and (2) the influence of mood on cognitive judgments and behavior. In the stereotyping research, strong positive attitudes toward in-groups and negative attitudes toward out-groups influenced the perception of behaviors. For example, white college students described ambiguous behaviors of African-Americans as violent 75 percent of the time while describing the same behaviors by whites as violent in only 17 percent of cases (Duncan 1976). Observers also were more likely to make internal attributions for in-group members' positive behaviors while making external attributions for out-group members' positive acts (Taylor and Jaggi 1974). Granberg and Brown (1989) showed that affective associations with political parties and candidates were stronger, more consistent predictors of voting behavior than the cognitions associated with the parties and candidates. Affect was less stable, however, when not supported by a consistent set of relevant cognitions. Affective expectations also influenced speed of processing in a series of studies by Wilson et al. (1989). When positive affective expectations are met, judgments and behavioral responses came quickly; when they are violated, preferences took longer to form and more cognitive processing of information occurred.

Research on the influence of mood on cognitions typically used mild, positive manipulations of affective state. Isen (1987, 1989) reviewed research that consistently demonstrated that such mild positive affect leads to increased memory and learning of positive material, more positive judgments of a wide variety of stimuli, increased sociability and helping (unless the helping act would be depressing), more receptivity to persuasive communications, more optimistic judgments, and lowered aggressiveness. Positive mood also influenced people's relative assessment of gains and losses (Isen, Nygren, and Ashby 1988). People who were in a good mood showed higher negative subjective utility for losses than control subjects; they did not want a loss to "bring them down" from their positive affective state.

Negative affect appeared to have less systematic effects (Averill 1980; Isen 1987). However, Greenberg and colleagues (1990) found that mortality reminders (which presumably cause a negative, fearful affective state) increased peoples' attraction to in-group members and decreased evaluation of dissimilar, deviant others.[26]

Distributive Justice

One area where the debate between causal direction between cognition and affect has become central to sociological concerns is the literature on equity and distributive justice. Traditional approaches to distributive justice viewed the assessment of inputs and rewards as a cognitive process resulting in an emotional response of satisfaction (if the ratio was appropriate) or anger (if inequity was discerned). Jasso (1993), for example, showed how choices about what to compare, the reference group for comparison, and other cognitive factors influenced emotional responses. Emotion entered the picture only as the *result* of the cognitive evaluation of the situation.

Scher and Heise (1993), on the other hand, proposed that cognitive justice calculations did not normally occur unless the actor first felt a justice-related emotion (e.g., anger or guilt) as a result of

the social interaction. They used affect control theory to show how stereotypically unfair interactions could produce emotions *before* participants made an actual judgment of unfairness. If the emotions can be resolved in other ways (e.g., through identity-confirming action), the situation may never be defined as injust. For example, an employee who repetitively does work that is even a little unpleasant and active came to have situational feelings about the self that were slightly bad, potent, and active. These situational feelings gave rise to anger when they were compared to the fundamentally positive, but not very powerful, identity of employee (Scher and Heise 1993). Good pay could alleviate the feelings of anger by restoring the positive self-image; Scher and Heise argued that if such pay is not forthcoming, cognitive work would occur to reconceptualize the situation as unfair (e.g., the boss is a slavedriver). This argument for the centrality of affective reactions is congruent with experimental work showing that mood affected judgments about fairness and the allocation of rewards (O'Malley and Davies 1984).

Small Group Processes

Researchers have applied the new sociological theories of emotion to small group processes as well. Rather than focusing on emotions as cause or response variables, the group process tradition used emotional response as an intervening process that is triggered by group interaction and motivates behavioral response (Ridgeway 1990). The empirical tradition behind this work begins with Bales (1950, 1953), who noted that task groups needed socioemotional management to maintain solidarity while discussing disagreements about the work at hand. Bales and Slater (1955) found that groups separated the task and socioemotional functions in different people, but later research indicated that one person usually dominated both task and socioemotional interactions (Anderson and Blanchard 1982). Ridgeway and Johnson (1990) offered a new analysis of the task/socioemotional division, based on expectations states theory (see chapter 11) and Kemper's social interactional theory of emotions. Ridgeway and Johnson proposed that when one group member disagreed with an-other, the emotional response to the disagreement would vary depending on the target's position in the group status structure. If someone disagreed with a low-status person, that person would attrib-ute responsibility for the disagreement to his own low-quality task contribution and would respond emotionally with depression (further suppressing task contributions). A high-status person would re-spond by attributing fault to the other group mem-ber (he doesn't know what he's talking about) and emotionally with annoyance or anger. This emo-tional response would likely lead to a sanctioning behavior, negatively reinforcing the disagree-ment response. Positive responses to task behav-iors also caused different emotional reactions, de-pending on the causal attribution (with internal attribution leading to pride and external attribution leading to gratitude), but both types of response led to positive behaviors that reinforced the positive response. The outcome prediction was that both high- and low-status people were likely to show positive socioemotional behaviors, while only high-status people would display negative so-cioemotional acts. Ridgeway and Johnson cited a wide body of evidence that agreed with these pre-dictions (see Anderson and Blanchard 1982).

Robinson and Smith-Lovin (1991) also ap-plied emotion theory to group interaction, arguing that turn taking in group discussions was regulated by the affective identity maintenance processes de-scribed in affect control theory. They found that interruptions were conversational mechanisms used to limit the participation of low-evaluation, low-power members to appropriate levels. Although emotional response was not measured directly, the behavioral patterns predicted by the affective proc-ess were supported.

CONCLUSION

The sociology of affect and emotion is one of the success stories of the discipline. Since its revival as a coherent area of study in the 1970s, an impressive body of theory has developed that centers on the role of emotion in social life. The area has contrib-uted theoretical insights and new directions to im-portant substantive areas such as mental health, distributive justice, and small group processes. The greatest shortcoming in the area now is the paucity of theoretically generated empirical knowledge. The data accumulated from substantive areas often focus on a narrow range of possible social situ-ations and emotions (e.g., the mental health area looks almost exclusively at relatively long-term negative affect, while the affect cognition literature looks at mild, ephemeral positive moods).

There are important theoretical questions that fall between the cracks of the substantive domains. For example, several emotion theories have pre-dictions about the relationship between social position, emotional response, and emotion man-agement (including Hochschild's 1983 statements about middle-class socialization for service jobs, Kemper's 1978 discussion of structural emotions, and Smith-Lovin's 1990 affect control theory pre-dictions about the relationship between identity and emotion). However, we have very little data on how people in different social positions typically feel or the coping strategies they use to regulate their emotions. Most of our data are from under-graduates.

Similarly, the infusion of emotions theory into the substantive areas should be followed by a new wave of data collection. As these theories suggest new affective mechanisms for the explanation of old empirical patterns, more detailed information is needed to assess the contribution. In group proc-esses, affective as well as task information must be collected in new studies. In the mental health area, more detailed emotional response and management data should be obtained from general populations. Distributive justice studies must concentrate their attention on affective as well as cognitive re-sponses.

Finally, we need much more detailed informa-tion on the socialization of emotion. We have two major theoretical schools—a rule-based cultural approach and a more generative interactionist view—that differ in the type of information they see as key to emotional response and the emotional motivation of behavior. What type of information is acquired in the socialization of emotion? How is it used in interaction to shape emotional response? Work with developmental psychologists (see Hoffman's 1983 work on developmental acquisition of emotional empathy) and life course sociologists will be necessary to answer these questions.

NOTES

The development of this chapter was supported by grant SES9008951 from the National Science Foundation. I was aided by two resources that I heartily recommend to all readers: *Syllabi and Instructional Material for the Sociology of Emotions* (ed. David D. Franks and Shelley Ottenbrite in 1989) and the *Bibliography for the ASA Subsection on the Sociology of Emotions* (ed. David D. Franks and Beverly Cuthbertson and indexed by Thomas J. Scheff in 1991). Both publications are available from the ASA Teaching Resources Center, 1722 N Street N.W., Washington DC 20036, (202) 833–3410. I would like to thank Steven Gordon, David Kemper, Miller McPherson, Linda Molm, Peggy Thoits, the editors, and anonymous reviewers for helpful comments on earlier drafts.

1. Early reviews in the newly developing field concentrated on issues of conceptual definition; they firmly established the social nature of emotion (Gordon 1981; Scheff 1983). As comprehensive social theories of emotions developed, later reviews focused on the dimensions that differentiated these theories (Denzin 1984, chap. 1; Hochschild 1983, App. A; Kemper 1981, 1990b; Lutz and White 1986). In particular, the debate between organismic/stimulus-driven formulations and constructionist/interactionist views absorbed much attention in the developing subfield. Recently, reviews concentrated on the strengths and weaknesses of the theoretical traditions in understanding the place of emotion in social life (Gordon 1985; Thoits 1989).

2. Additional dimensions appear to be culture-specific. Only these three were found to apply widely across cultures and concept domains (Osgood, May, and Miron 1975).

3. Psychological researchers also define emotion with reference to its components (Frijda 1986), including behavioral, physiological, and subjective elements. Given the current cognitive emphasis in psychology, many definitions focus on the distinction between affect and cognition, essentially providing a negative definition of emotion as the sources of *non*instrumental behavior or as the *dis*turbance of cognitive processing (Frijda 1986, 2–3). Psycholinguistically oriented researchers often define emotions in terms of what emotion words can appropriately fill a linguistic frame or meet judges' criteria (Clore, Ortony and Foss, 1987; Ortony and Clore 1981; Ortony, Clore, and Foss 1987).

4. Similarly, Heise (1979) defined fundamental sentiments as the cultural affective meanings associated with social identities and actions.

5. As one might expect, Sartre (1962) criticized Freud's ideas along much the same lines as he rejected the James-Lange theory. For Sartre, Freud made the individual too passive, and abstracted emotion out of the lived experience of the moment.

6. As Kemper (1990b, 3–4) noted, the actual work was begun much earlier, and probably has its roots in the intellectual climate of the 1960s.

7. Researchers have studied emotional socialization and management among medical students (A. Smith and Kleinman 1989), nurses (P. Smith 1988), airline attendants (Hochschild 1983), bill collectors (Hochschild 1983), and supermarket checkers (Tolich 1988).

8. Sarbin (1954) and Berger (1963) previously introduced the conceptualization of emotions as roles. Averill (1990) combined this idea with the developing notion of emotion scripts.

9. Ralph H. Turner (1976) earlier developed a distinction between institutional and impulsive orientations that people can hold toward their self-conceptions. Gordon (1989a) employed this conceptualization to study how people embrace emotions as indicative of their "real" selves.

10. Hochschild (1990, 122–123) noted the same phenomenon in the case of a woman who was depressed over having to pass up a promotion at work to handle her behavioral commitment to a husband and two young children. In keeping with her more cultural emphasis, Hochschild analyzed the incident in terms of feeling rules (the woman thought "it was normal to get depressed, but not normal to get *that* depressed").

11. These dimensions correspond to Osgood's three dimensions of affective meaning (Osgood, Suci, and Tannenbaum 1957; Osgood, May, and Miron 1975). Smith-Lovin and Heise (1988) argued that evaluation and potency correspond roughly to the status and power dimensions that Kemper and Collins (1990; Kemper 1978, 1990a) claimed were central, universal elements of all social interaction.

12. Swann and colleagues developed an impressive research program to support an identity maintenance per-

spective developed in psychology. While designed for another purpose, Swann's research results supported affect control ideas. When high- and low-self-esteem subjects were provided with either positive or negative feedback, they preferred further interaction with evaluators who supported their self-views, *not* evaluators who gave them the most positive feedback (Swann et al. 1987). Even people with overall high self-esteem sought out unfavorable feedback pertaining to areas where they held negative self-views (Swann, Pelham, and Krull 1989). The tendency to prefer negative but consistent information was eliminated when subjects were deprived of the ability to retrieve and compare the feedback to the representation of self in memory; when cognitively loaded, both high- and low-self-esteem subjects preferred positive feedback. Swann et al. (1987) emphasized the independence of the cognitive and affective processes, using the metaphor of a war between the two systems for control over behavior. Alternatively, affect control theory argued that affective and cognitive systems are neither parallel nor conflicting systems; instead, they are intricately codependent.

13. In Kemper's theory, status referred to deference that was given voluntarily; power referred to compliance gained through coercion.

14. The dimensions of status and power correspond roughly to the evaluation and potency dimensions used in affect control theory. Kemper and Collins (1990) acknowledge the frequent appearance of a third dimension—activity—in many linguistic studies of identity and emotion terms. They eliminated it from central consideration in their theoretical treatments because they argue that it is not manifestly relational in nature, as are status and power.

15. The episodes were edited to eliminate direct references to the emotion being experienced (e.g., "it made me so angry that . . . ") and to physical symptoms that might directly indicate the emotion (e.g., "I clenched my teeth . . . ").

16. Kemper's argument followed from the classic position of James (1950) that some basic emotions have a specific, universal physiological component. He embraced the position of Funkenstein (1955), who proposed a fourfold differentiation in autonomic response corresponding to basic emotions of fear, anger, and hap-piness/depression (associated with levels of epinephrine, norepinephrine, and acetylcholine, respectively). This differentiation hypothesis was supported by a series of measurements in the 1950s and 1960s (see sympathetic reviews in Kemper 1978, 1987) and by work on autonomic substrates of facial expression (Ekman, Levenson, and Friesen 1983).

17. In affect control theory, identities are characterized on three dimensions. The relational element becomes apparent when the identities are linked in interaction. For example, a judge has high potency and an accused man has low potency, so a judge has greater power in the judge-accused man relationship.

18. Collins (1990, 55) recognized that the basis of status and power would vary from one historical period to another.

19. The Smith-Lovin and Douglass study was designed to test affect control theory's ability to predict interaction chains in religious ritual.

20. Scheff built directly on Cooley (1922) and Goffman (1967).

21. This empirical tradition was developed largely in response to critiques of the empirical relevance of Scheff's (1977) work.

22. Note that causal influence is bidirectional. Common experiences lead to the creation of prototypes, while the existence of prototypical emotion scripts makes us more likely to encode and remember our experiences that fit these cognitive structures.

23. Thoits analyzed only negative events in the study of coping strategies.

24. Some psychologists have argued that cognition comes *after* emotional arousal, however. Mandler (1982, 1990) and Frijda (1986), for example, argued that environmental inputs activated both arousal and action systems. Cognitive appraisal of this activation gave meaning to the arousal and led to labeling of the emotion (see Fridja 1986 for a review of experimental evidence for this formulation).

25. Note the similarity to affect control theory predictions as illustrated in Wiggins and Heise (1987). Negative deflection led to support of positive alters but denigration of negative alters, as others were used as an interactional resource to restore positive self-feelings.

REFERENCES

Abu-Lughod, Lila. 1986. *Veiled Sentiments: Honor and Poetry in a Bedouin Society.* Berkeley: University of California Press.

Adams, Douglas, and Lynn Smith-Lovin. 1992. Emotional reactions to events. Paper presented at ASA meetings, Pittsburgh.

Anderson, Lynn R., and P. Nick Blanchard. 1982. Sex differences in task and social-emotional behavior. *Basic and Applied Social Psychology* 3:109–140.

Averill, James R. 1975. A semantic atlas of emotional concepts. *Catalog of Selected Documents in Psychology* 5:330 (ms 421).

———. 1980. A constructivist view of emotion. Pp. 305–339 in *Emotion: Theory, Research and Experience,* vol. 1, ed. Robert Plutchik and Henry Kellerman. New York: Academic.

———. 1990. Emotions as episodic dispositions, cognitive schemas and transitory social roles: Steps toward an integrated theory of emotions. *Perspectives in Personality* 3:137–165.

Bales, Robert F. 1950. *Interaction Process Analysis: A Method for the Study of Small Groups.* Cambridge, MA: Addison-Wesley.

———. 1953. The equilibrium problem in small groups. Pp. 111–161 in *Working Papers in the Theory of Action,* ed. Talcott Parsons, Robert F. Bales, and Edward A. Shils. Glencoe, IL: Free Press.

Bales, Robert F. and Phillip E. Slater. 1955. Role differentiation in small decision-making groups. Pp. 259–306 in *The Family, Socialization and Interaction Processes,* ed. Talcott Parsons and Phillip E. Slater. Glencoe, IL: Free Press.

Berger, Peter L. 1963. *An Invitation to Sociology: A Humanist Perspective.* New York: Doubleday.

Blau, Peter M. 1964. *Exchange and Power in Social Life.* New York: Wiley.

Blumstein, Philip, and Peter Kollock. 1988. Personal relationships. *Annual Review of Sociology* 14:467–490.

Briggs, J. L. 1970. *Never in Anger.* Cambridge, MA: Harvard University Press.

Cancian, Francesca M., and Steven L. Gordon. 1988. Changing emotion norms in marriage: Love and anger in U.S. women's magazines since 1900. *Gender and Society* 2:308–342.

Candland, D. K. 1977. The persistent problems of emotions. In *Emotion,* ed. D. K. Candland et al., Monterey, CA: Brooks/Cole.

Clark, Candace. 1987. Sympathy biography and sympathy margin. *American Journal of Sociology* 93:290–321.

Clark, Candace, Sherryl Kleinman, and Carolyn Ellis. 1990. Conflicting realities: Dilemmas for interaction. Paper presented at the Sociology and Subjectivity Conference, St. Petersburg, FL.

Clore, Gerald L., Andrew Ortony, and Mark A. Foss. 1987. The psychological foundations of the affective lexicon. *Journal of Personality and Social Psychology* 53:751–766.

Collins, Randall. 1975. *Conflict Sociology: Toward an Explanatory Science.* New York: Academic.

———. 1981. On the micro-foundations of macro-sociology. *American Journal of Sociology* 86:984–1014.

———. 1990. Stratification, emotional energy and the transient emotions. Pp. 27–57 in *Research Agendas in the Sociology of Emotions,* ed. T. D. Kemper. Albany: State University of New York Press.

———. 1993. Emotional energy as the common denominator of rational action. *Rationality and Society* 5:203–230.

Cook, Karen S., Karen A. Hegtvedt, and Toshio Yamagishi. 1987. Structural inequality, legitimation and reactions to inequity in exchange networks. Pp. 291–308 in *Status Generalization: New Theory and Research,* ed. M. Webster and M. Foschi. Stanford: Stanford University Press.

Cooley, Charles Horton. [1909] 1922. *Social Organization.* New York: Scribner's.

———. [1909] 1964. *Human Nature and Social Order.* New York: Scribner's.

Coser, Lewis. 1956. *The Functions of Social Conflict.* New York: Free Press.

———. 1967. *Continuities in the Study of Conflict.* New York: Free Press.

Cotton, J. L. 1981. A review of research on Schachter's theory of emotion and the misattribution of arousal. *European Journal of Social Psychology* 11:365–397.

Darwin, Charles. [1872] 1955. *The Expressions of the Emotions in Man and Animals.* New York: Philosophical Library.

Denzin, Norman K. 1984. *On Understanding Emotion.* San Francisco: Jossey-Bass.

———. 1985. Emotions as lived experiences. *Symbolic Interaction* 8:223–240.

———. 1990. On understanding emotion: The interpretive-cultural agenda. Pp. 85–116 in *Research Agendas in the Sociology of Emotions,* ed. T. D. Kemper. Albany: State University of New York Press.

Duncan, B. L. 1976. Differential social perception and attribution of intergroup violence: Testing the lower limits of stereotyping of blacks. *Journal of Personality and Social Psychology* 34:590–598.

Durkheim, Emile. 1912. *The Elementary Forms of the Religious Life.* London: Allen & Unwin.

———. [1895] 1964. *The Rules of Sociological Method.* New York: Free Press.

Ekman, Paul, ed. 1982. *Emotion in the Human Face.* Cambridge: Cambridge University Press.

Ekman, Paul, R. W. Levenson, and W. V. Friesen. 1983. Autonomic nervous system activity distinguishes among emotions. *Science* 221:1208–1210.

Ellis, Carolyn. 1988. *Final Negotiations.* Unpublished manuscript.

——— . 1990. Sociological introspection and emotional experience. *Symbolic Interaction* 14(1):23–50.

Ellis, Carolyn, and Eugene Weinstein. 1986. Jealousy and the social psychology of emotional experience. *Journal of Social and Personal Relationships* 3: 337–357.

Fisher, Gene A., and Kyum Koo Chon. 1989. Durkheim and the social construction of emotions. *Social Psychology Quarterly* 52:1–9.

Fiske, Susan T. 1982. Schema-triggered affect: Applications to social perception. Pp. 55–78 in *Affect and Cognition: The 17th Annual Carnegie Symposium on Cognition* ed. M. S. Clark and S. T. Fiske. Hillsdale, NJ: Erlbaum.

Freud, Sigmund. 1938. *The Basic Writings of Sigmund Freud.* New York: Random House.

——— . [1900] 1965. *The Interpretation of Dreams.* New York: Avon.

Frijda, Nico H. 1986. *The Emotions.* London: Cambridge.

Funkenstein, D. 1955. The physiology of fear and anger. *Scientific American* 192:74–80.

Geertz, Hildred. 1959. The vocabulary of emotion. *Psychiatry* 22:225–237.

Gerth, H. H., and C. Wright Mills. 1946. Introduction: The man and his work. In *From Max Weber: Essays in Sociology.* ed. and translated by H. H. Gerth and C. Wright Mills. New York: Oxford University Press.

Goffman, Erving. 1956. Embarrassment and social organization. *American Journal of Sociology* 62:264–271.

——— . 1959. *The Presentation of Self in Everyday Life.* New York: Doubleday.

——— . 1967. *Interaction Ritual.* Garden City, NY: Anchor.

Goode, William J. 1980. Why men resist. *Dissent* 27:181–193.

Gordon, Steven L. 1981. The sociology of sentiments and emotion. Pp. 551–575 in *Social Psychology: Sociological Perspectives,* ed. Morris Rosenberg and Ralph H. Turner. New York: Basic Books.

——— . 1985. Micro-sociological theories of emotion. Pp. 133–147 in *Micro-sociological Theory: Perspectives on Sociological Theory,* vol. 2, ed. Horst J. Helle and Samuel N. Eisenstadt. London: Sage.

——— . 1989a. Institutional and impulsive orientations in selectively appropriating emotions to self. Pp. 115–135 in *The Sociology of Emotions: Original Essays and Research Papers.* Greenwich, CT: JAI Press.

——— . 1989b. Socialization of children's emotions: Toward a social constructionist theory. Pp. 38–57 in *Children's Understanding of Emotion,* ed. Carolyn Saarni and Paul Harris. Cambridge, UK: Cambridge University Press.

——— . 1990. Social structural effects on emotions. Pp. 145–179 in *Research Agendas in the Sociology of Emotions,* ed. T. D. Kemper. Albany: State University of New York Press.

Granberg, Donald, and Thad A. Brown. 1989. On affect and cognition in politics. *Social Psychology Quarterly* 52:171–182.

Greenberg, Jeff, Tom Pyszczynski, Sheldon Solomon, Abram Rosenblatt, Mitchell Veeder, Shari Kirkland, and Deborah Lyon. 1990. Evidence for terror management theory, II: The effects of mortality salience on reactions to those who threaten or bolster the cultural world view. *Journal of Personality and Social Psychology* 58:308–318.

Haas, Jack. 1977. Learning real feelings: A study of high steel ironworkers' reactions to fear and danger. *Sociology of Work and Occupations* 4:147–170.

Harris, Paul. 1989. *Children and Emotion: The Development of Psychological Understanding.* New York: Cambridge University Press.

Hegtvedt, Karen A. 1990. The effects of relationship structure on emotional responses to inequity. *Social Psychology Quarterly* 53:214–228.

Heider, Karl. 1984. Emotion: Inner state vs. interaction. Paper presented at American Anthropological Association meetings, Denver.

Heise, David R. 1977. Social action as the control of affect. *Behavioral Science* 22:163–177.

——— . 1979. *Understanding Events.* New York: Cambridge University Press.

——— . 1989. Effects of emotion displays on social identification. *Social Psychology Quarterly* 53:10–21.

Heise, David R., and Richard Morgan. 1988. Structure of emotions. *Social Psychology Quarterly* 51:19–31.

Heise, David R., and Lynn Smith-Lovin. 1981. Impressions of goodness, powerfulness and liveliness from discerned social events. *Social Psychology Quarterly* 44:93–106.

Hochschild, Arlie R. 1975. The sociology of feeling and emotion: Selected possibilities. In *Another Voice:*

Feminist Perspectives on Social Life and Social Science, ed. M. Millman and R. M. Kanter. New York: Anchor.

———. 1979. Emotion work, feeling rules and social structure. *American Journal of Sociology* 85:551–575.

———. 1983. *The Managed Heart: Commercialization of Human Feeling.* Berkeley: University of California Press.

———. 1988. *The Second Shift.* Berkeley: University of California Press.

———. 1990. Ideology and emotion management: A perspective and path for future research. Pp. 117–144 in *Research Agendas in the Sociology of Emotions,* ed. T. D. Kemper. Albany: State University of New York Press.

Hoffman, Martin L. 1983. Empathy, guilt and social cognition. Pp. 1–51 in *The Relationship between social and cognitive development,* ed. W. F. Overton. Hillsdale, NJ: Erlbaum.

Homans, George C. 1961. *Social Behavior: Its Elementary Forms.* New York: Harcourt.

———. 1974. *Social Behavior: Its Elementary Forms,* (rev. ed.) New York: Harcourt, Brace, Jovanovich.

Isen, Alice M. 1987. Affect, cognition and social behavior. Pp. 203–253 in *Advances in Experimental Social Psychology,* ed. L. Berkowitz. New York: Academic.

———. 1989. Some ways in which affect influences cognitive processes: Implications for advertising and consumer behavior. *Advertising and Consumer Psychology,* vol. 20, ed. A. M. Tybout and P. Cafferata. New York: Lexington Books.

Isen, Alice M., Thomas E. Nygren, and F. Gregory Ashby. 1988. Influence of positive affect on the subjective utility of gains and losses: It is just not worth the risk. *Journal of Personality and Social Psychology* 55:710–717.

James, William. [1890] 1950. *The Principles of Psychology.* New York: Dover.

Jasso, Guillermina. 1993. Choice and emotion in comparison theory. *Rationality and Society* 5:231–274.

Kelley, Harold H., and J. L. Michela. 1980. Attribution theory and research. *Annual Review of Psychology* 31:38–57.

Kemper, T. D. 1978. *A Social Interactional Theory of Emotions.* New York: Wiley.

———. 1981. Social constructivist and positivist approaches to the sociology of emotions. *American Journal of Sociology* 87:336–361.

———. 1987. How many emotions are there? Wedding the social and the autonomic component. *American Journal of Sociology* 93:263–289.

———. 1990a. Social relations and emotions: A structural approach. Pp. 207–237 in *Research Agendas in the Sociology of Emotions,* ed. T. D. Kemper. Albany: State University of New York Press.

———. 1990b. Themes and variations in the sociology of emotions. Pp. 3–26 in *Research Agendas in the Sociology of Emotions,* ed. T. D. Kemper. Albany: State University of New York Press.

———. 1991. Predicting emotions from social relations. *Social Psychology Quarterly* 54:330–342.

Kemper, T. D., and Randall Collins. 1990. Dimensions of microinteraction. *American Journal of Sociology* 96:32–68.

Kessler, Ronald C., and Harold W. Neighbors. 1986. A new perspective on the relationships among race, social class and psychological distress. *Journal of Health and Social Behavior* 27:107–115.

Lawler, Edward J. 1992. Affective attachments to nested groups: A choice-process theory. *American Sociological Review* 57:327–339.

Lutz, Catherine, and Geoffrey M. White. 1986. The anthropology of emotions. *Annual Review of Anthropology* 15:405–436.

MacKinnon, Neil J., and Leo J. Keating. 1989. The structure of emotions: A review of the problem and a cross-cultural analysis. *Social Psychology Quarterly* 52:70–82.

Mandler, George. [1975] 1984. *Mind and Body: Psychology of Emotion.* New York: Norton.

———. 1990. A constructivist theory of emotion. Pp. 57–83 in *Psychological and Biological Approaches to Emotions,* ed. N. S. Stein, B. L. Leventhal, and T. Trabasso. Hillsdale, NJ: Erlbaum.

Manstead, A. S. R., and H. L. Wagner. 1981. Arousal, cognition and emotion: An appraisal of the two-factor theory. *Current Psychological Reviews* 1:34–54.

Marx, Karl. [1852] 1983a. From the eighteenth Brumaire of Louis Bonaparte. *The Portable Karl Marx,* ed. E. Kamenka. New York: Penguin.

———. [1888] 1983b. Theses on Feuderbach. *The Portable Karl Marx,* ed. E. Kamenka. New York: Penguin.

Mead, George Herbert. 1934. *Mind, Self and Society.* Chicago: University of Chicago Press.

Mehrabian, Albert. 1980. *Basic Dimensions for a General Psychological Theory.* Cambridge: Oelgeschlager, Gunn & Hain.

Michaels, James W., John N. Edwards, and Alan C. Acock. 1984. Satisfaction in intimate relationships as a function of inequality, inequity and outcomes. *Social Psychology Quarterly* 47:347–557.

Mills, C. Wright. 1940. Situated actions and vocabularies of motives. *American Sociological Review* 5: 904–913.

Mirowsky, John. 1985. Depression and marital power: An equity model. *American Journal of Sociology* 91:557–592.

Mirowsky, John, and Catherine Ross. 1989. *Social Causes of Psychological Distress.* New York: Aldine de Gruyter.

Molm, Linda D. 1991. Affect and social exchange: Satisfaction in power-dependence relations. *American Sociological Review* 56:475–493.

O'Malley, M. N., and D. K. Davies. 1984. Equity and affect: The effects of relative performance and moods on resource allocation. *Basic and Applied Social Psychology* 5:273–282.

Ortony, Andrew, and Gerald L. Clore. 1981. Disentangling the affective lexicon. Paper presented at the Third Annual Conference of the Cognitive Science Society. Berkeley, CA.

Ortony, Andrew, Gerald L. Clore, and Mark A. Foss. 1987. The referential structure of the affective lexicon. *Cognitive Science* 11:341–364.

Osgood, Charles E. 1966. Dimensionality of the semantic space for communication via facial expressions. *Scandanavian Journal of Psychology* 7:1–30.

Osgood, Charles E., W. H. May, and M. S. Miron. 1975. *Cross-Cultural Universals of Affective Meaning.* Urbana: University of Illinois Press.

Osgood, Charles E., George C. Suci, and Perry H. Tannenbaum. 1957. *The Measurement of Meaning.* Urbana: University of Illinois Press.

Parsons, Talcott, and Edward A. Shils. 1962. *Toward a General Theory of Social Action.* New York: Harper and Row.

Peirce, Charles S. 1955. *Philosophical Writings of Peirce.* ed. Justus Buckler. New York: Dover.

Plutchik, Robert, and A. F. Ax. 1967. A critique of the determinants of emotional state by Schachter and Singer. *Psychophysiology* 4:79–92.

Pollak, Lauren H., and Peggy A. Thoits. 1989. Processes in emotional socialization. *Social Psychology Quarterly* 52:22–34.

Reisenzein, Rainer. 1983. The Schachter theory of emotion: Two decades later. *Psychological Bulletin* 94: 239–264.

Ridgeway, Cecilia. 1994. Affect processes. Pp. 54–83 in *Group Processes: Sociological Analyses,* ed. M. Foschi and E. Lawler. Chicago: Nelson-Hall.

Ridgeway, Cecilia, and Cathryn Johnson. 1990. What is the relationship between socioemotional behavior and status in task groups? *American Journal of Sociology* 95:1189–1212.

Robinson, Dawn T., and Lynn Smith-Lovin. 1991. Turn-taking in group conversations: An affect control model. Paper presented at the American Sociological Association meetings, Cincinnati, OH.

———. 1992. Selective interaction as a strategy for identity maintenance: An affect control model. *Social Psychology Quarterly* 55:12–28.

Robinson, Dawn T., Lynn Smith-Lovin, and Olga Tsoudis. 1991. Emotion displays and sentencing in vignettes of criminal trials. Paper presented at the Southern Sociological Society meeting.

Russell, James A. 1990. Culture, scripts and children's understanding of emotion. Pp. 181–209 in *Children's Understanding of Emotions,* ed. C. Saarni and P. L. Harris. Cambridge, UK: Cambridge University Press.

———. 1991. In defense of a prototype approach to emotion concepts. *Journal of Personality and Social Psychology* 60:37–47.

Saarni, Carolyn, and Paul L. Harris, eds. 1990. *Children's Understanding of Emotion.* New York: Cambridge University Press.

Sarbin, Theodore R. 1954. Role theory. Pp. 223–258 in *Handbook of Social Psychology,* ed. Gardner Lindsey and Elliot Aronson. Menlo Park, CA: Addison-Wesley.

Sartre, Jean-Paul. [1939] 1962. *Sketch for a Theory of Emotions.* Translated by P. Mariet. London: Methuen.

Schachter, Stanley, and Jerome E. Singer. 1962. Cognitive, social and physiological determinants of emotional state. *Psychological Review* 69:379–399.

Scheff, Thomas J. 1977. The distancing of emotion in ritual. *Current Anthropology* 18:500–505.

———. 1979. *Catharsis in Healing, Ritual and Drama.* Berkeley: University of California Press.

———. 1983 Toward integration in the social psychology of emotions. *Annual Review of Sociology* 9:333–354.

———. 1988. Shame and conformity: The deference-emotion system. *American Sociological Review* 53: 395–406.

————. 1990. Socialization of emotion: Pride and shame as causal agents. Pp. 281–304 in *Research Agendas in the Sociology of Emotions,* ed. T. D. Kemper. Albany: State University of New York Press.

Scheff, Thomas J., and Susanne Retzinger. 1992. *Shame, Violence and Social Structure: Theory and Cases.* Lexington, MA: Lexington Books.

Scher, Steven J., and David R. Heise. 1993. Affect and the perception of injustice. *Advances in Group Processes,* vol. 10, ed. Edward Lawler, Barry Markovsky, and Jodi O'Brien. Menlo Park, CA: JAI Press.

Scherer, Klaus R. 1986. Emotion experiences across European cultures: A summary statement. Pp. 173–189 in *Experiencing Emotion: A Cross-Cultural study,* ed. Klaus R. Scherer, Harold G. Wallbott, and Angela B. Summerfield. Cambridge, UK: Cambridge University Press.

Scherer, Klaus R., Harold G. Wallbott, and Angela B. Summerfield, ed. 1986. *Experiencing Emotion: A Cross-Cultural Study.* Cambridge, UK: Cambridge University Press.

Shaver, Phillip R., Judith C. Schwartz, D. Kirson, and C. O'Connor. 1987. Emotion knowledge: Further exploration of a prototype approach. *Journal of Personality and Social Psychology* 52:1061–1086.

Shott, Susan. 1979. Emotion and social life: A symbolic interactionist analysis. *American Journal of Sociology* 84:1317–1334.

Simmel, Georg. 1924. Sociology of the senses: Visual interaction. In *Introduction to the Science of Sociology,* ed. Robert E. Park and E. Burgess. Chicago: University of Chicago Press.

————. 1950. *The Sociology of Georg Simmel,* ed. Kurt Wolff. New York: Free Press.

Smith, Allen C. III, and Sherryl Kleinman. 1989. Managing emotions in medical school: Students' contacts with the living and dead. *Social Psychology Quarterly* 5:56–69.

Smith, Pam. 1988. The emotional labor of nursing. *Nursing Times* 84:50–51.

Smith-Lovin, Lynn. 1987. Impressions from events. Pp. 35–70 in *Analyzing Social Interaction: Advances in Affect Control Theory,* ed. L. Smith-Lovin and D. R. Heise. New York: Gordon & Breach.

————. 1990. Emotion as confirmation and disconfirmation of identity: An affect control model. Pp. 238–270 in *Research Agendas in the Sociology of Emotions,* ed. T. D. Kemper. Albany: State University of New York Press.

Smith-Lovin, Lynn, and William T. Douglass. 1992. An affect control analysis of two religious subcultures. In *Social Perspectives on Emotions,* ed. D. Franks and V. Gecas. New York: JAI Press.

Smith-Lovin, Lynn, and David R. Heise, eds. 1988. *Analyzing Social Interaction: Research Advances in Affect Control Theory.* New York: Gordon & Breach.

Stearns, Carol Z., and Peter N. Stearns. 1986. *Anger: The Struggle for Emotional Control in America's History.* Chicago: University of Chicago Press.

Stolte, John. 1983. The legitimation of structural inequality. *American Sociological Review* 48:331–342.

Stryker, Sheldon. 1987. The interplay of affect and identity: Exploring the relationships of social structure, social interaction, self and emotion. Paper presented at the American Sociological Association meetings, Chicago.

Stryker, Sheldon, and Richard Serpe. 1982. Commitment, identity salience and role behavior: Theory and a research example. In *Personality, Roles and Social Behavior,* ed. W. Ickes and E. Knwoles. New York: Springer-Verlag.

Swann, William B., Jr., John J. Griffin Jr., Steven C. Predmore, and Bebe Gaines. 1987. The cognitive-affective crossfire: When self-consistency confronts self-enhancement. *Journal of Personality and Social Psychology* 52:881–889.

Swann, William B., Jr., Brett W. Pelham, and Douglas S. Krull. 1989. Agreeable fancy or disagreeable truth: Reconciling self-enhancement and self-verification. *Journal of Personality and Social Psychology* 57:782–791.

Tavris, Carol. 1984. On the wisdom of counting to ten: Personal and social dangers of anger expression. Pp. 170–191 in *Review of Personality and Social Psychology,* ed. Phillip Shaver. Beverly Hills, CA: Sage.

Taylor, D. M., and V. Jaggi. 1974. Ethnocentrisism and causal attribution in a South Indiana context. *Journal of Cross-Cultural Psychology* 5:162–171.

Tesser, Abraham. 1978. Self-generated attitude change. Pp. 289–338 in *Advances in Experimental Social Psychology,* vol. 11, ed. L. Berkowitz. New York: Academic.

Thoits, Peggy A. 1984. Coping, social support and psychological outcomes: The central role of emotion. Pp. 219–238 in *Review of Personality and Social Psychology,* vol. 5, ed. Phillip Shaver. Beverly Hills, CA: Sage.

———. 1985. Self-labeling processes in mental illness: The role of emotional deviance. *American Journal of Sociology* 92:221–249.

———. 1986. Multiple identities: Examining gender and marital status differences in distress. *American Sociological Review* 51:259–272.

———. 1989. The sociology of emotions. *Annual Review of Sociology* 15:317–342.

———. 1990. Emotional deviance: Research agendas. Pp. 180–206 in *Research Agendas in the Sociology of Emotions,* ed. T. D. Kemper. Albany: State University of New York Press.

———. 1991. Gender differences in coping with emotional distress. Pp. 107–138 in *The Social Context of Coping,* ed. John Eckenrode. New York: Plenum.

Tolich, Martin. 1988. Doing emotion work: The similarities and differences between manual supermarket checkers and Hochschild's airline flight attendants. Paper presented at the Pacific Sociological Association, Las Vegas.

Turner, Jonathan H. 1987. Toward a sociological theory of motivation. *American Sociological Review* 52: 15–27.

———. 1988. *A Theory of Social Interaction.* Stanford: Stanford University Press.

———. 1989. A theory of microdynamics. *Advances in Group Processes* 7:143–156.

———. Forthcoming. A general theory of motivation and emotion in human interaction.

Turner, Ralph H. 1976. The real self: From institution to impulse. *American Journal of Sociology* 81:989–1016.

Walster, Elaine, G. W. Walster, and Ellen Berschied. 1978. *Equity: Theory and Research.* Boston: Allyn and Bacon.

Watson, D., and A. Tellegan. 1985. Toward a consensual structure of mood. *Psychological Bulletin* 98: 219–235.

Weiner, Bernard, J. Amirkhan, V. S. Folkes, and J. A. Verette. 1987. An attributional analysis of excuse giving: Studies of a naive theory of emotion. *Journal of Personality and Social Psychology* 52:316–324.

Weiner, Bernard, Dan Russell, and D. Lerman. 1978. Affective consequences of causal ascriptions. Pp. 59–90 in *New Directions in Attribution Research,* vol. 2, ed. J. H. Harvey, W. J. Ickes, and R. F. Kidd. Hillsdale, NJ: Erlbaum.

Wheaton, Blair. 1983. Stress, personal coping resources, and psychiatric symptoms: An investigation of interactive models. *Journal of Health and Social Behavior* 26:352–364.

Wiggins, Beverly, and David R. Heise. 1987. Expectations, intentions and behavior: Some tests of affect control theory. *Journal of Mathematical Sociology* 13:153–169.

Wilson, Timothy D., Douglas J. Lisle, Dolores Kraft, and Christopher G. Wetzel. 1989. Preferences as expectation-driven inferences: Effects of affective expectations on affective experience. *Journal of Personality and Social Psychology* 56:519–530.

Zajonc, Robert B. 1984. On the primacy of affect. *American Psychologist* 39:117–123.

CHAPTER 6

Language, Action, and Social Interaction

DOUGLAS W. MAYNARD
MARILYN R. WHALEN

At least since Aristotle, language has been seen as distinctively human in its complexity. Ethologists are increasing our appreciation of how other animals—dolphins, chimpanzees, gorillas, and so on —employ sounds to signal one another in sophisticated ways, but humans, in conducting their everyday affairs, rely on spoken and gestural forms of intercourse to an unparalleled degree (Eibl-Eibesfeldt 1989). Despite the centrality of language use in human society, social psychology textbooks often ignore the topic (Clark 1985, 179), and when they do pay attention it is to regard language as a mode of communication or a vehicle whereby humans transmit information, including ideas, thoughts, and feelings, from one to another (cf. Shannon and Weaver 1949). A variety of philosophers and social scientists now dispute that language is a communicative vehicle. Reddy (1979) calls this idea the "conduit metaphor," which is rooted in the common-sense suggestion that, through speech, one person conveys subjective information by inserting it into words and sending them along a communicative channel. People receive the words at the other end and extract the encoded thoughts and feelings from them. The conduit metaphor reinforces the notion that problems of meaning in human society essentially concern how concepts make reference to, correspond with, or represent reality and that language functions to make propositions about the world (Pitkin 1972, 3).

Recently, scholars have approached language as a medium of organized social activity, in which words are "performatives" (Austin 1962) or "deeds" (Wittgenstein 1958, par. 546) involved in the very constitution of social life as such. It is partly through language that humans *do* the social world, even as the world is confronted as the unquestioned background or condition for activity. The conduit metaphor and "picture book" view of language, rather than the more dynamic or activist approach, still heavily influence social psychological theory and research, however. Thus, the literature deserves scrutiny. This chapter begins with a review of general statements in social psychology about language, then examines selected traditional experimental and survey-based research. This is followed by an explication of language as action and the philosophical and social scientific background to this perspective. Rule-based strategies to the so-called "mapping" problem—how utterances become linked to social actions—including sociolinguistics and discourse analysis, are discussed and then cognitive sociology and frame analysis, perspectives in which rules play a less dominant role, are explored. Ethnomethodology and conversation analysis, in which rules are abandoned as explanatory resources and investigators attempt to appreciate the connection between language and action through other means, such as analyzing the sequential organization of talk, are examined. Finally, studies of the relationship between language, action, and social structure broadly conceived are reviewed.

LANGUAGE IN SOCIAL PSYCHOLOGY

In social psychology, symbolic interactionists have been most concerned with language. This is no doubt due to the influence of G. H. Mead (1934), who originated the suggestion that humans employ significant symbols that, when emitted by one party, elicit the same response in that party as in the party to whom the gesture is directed. This suggestion assumes significance in a larger context than social psychology, however. Sociologists regard communication as achieving a solution to "the problem of meaning," which Weber (1947) long ago identified as being at the core of social action, for the defining criterion of such action is that it is a product of the interactive interpretations of society's members. Even while humans engage in sense-making practices to understand one another in immediate association, patterned relationships among large groups, organizations, and institutions depend on these self-same, interactive assemblages of meaningful behaviors and responses.[1] When Mead (1934) proposed the existence of significant symbols and the capacity for "taking the role of the other," it seemed to represent a clear statement of how humans could form common understandings, produce mutual and complementary stances within what he called the "social act," and also thereby provide for larger patterns of social life.

From ideas like Mead's and a more general concern with the problem of meaning, it is easy to see how social psychologists moved to the conduit metaphor when discussing human language, seeing it as a repository of significant symbols in which people package their ideas and feelings.[2] Significant symbols include not only words but gestures as well, although there are two views of gestural communication. In one view, gestures are substituted for words. Thus, a hand wave stands for "hello," a green light suggests "go," a beckoning arm means "come on," and so on (Hertzler 1965, 29–30). In the other view, gestures are regarded as occupying a different "channel of communication"

than words—a *non*verbal one. In either view, the conduit metaphor is preserved. Although it is recognized that gestures and words are arbitrary and conventional and that they take on different senses according to the context in which they appear, individuals' ability to encode their own experiences with them and to assume the attitude of others and thereby appreciate their experience inexorably leads actors to share the same "mental states" (e.g., Hewitt 1991, 43) making collaborative activity possible.

An influential variant of the communicational view of language is the famous Sapir-Whorf, or *linguistic relativity,* hypothesis. Benjamin Whorf, a student of the anthropologist Edward Sapir, performed linguistic studies of American Indians and other groups, discovering that various spoken languages conditioned the members' life experiences. As a straightforward example, Whorf (1956, 216) observes that the Hopi language has one word for everything that flies (except birds, which form another category), whereas English has separate nouns for insect, airplane, aviator, and so on. Thus, according to Whorf (1956, 213), actors "dissect" the world "along lines laid down by our native languages." Despite the relativity it implies, the Whorfian hypothesis is compatible with the conduit metaphor and communicational view of language in that it proposes the very source of an individual's experience. Once individuals have learned the group's language, they have acquired the symbolic means for having emotions, beliefs, perceptions, and so on and transmitting them to one another.

Of course, most social psychologists argue that language and experience reciprocally influence one another. Nevertheless, in studies where language is a prominent variable, it remains as a relatively static repository of meaning[3] that either conditions or is conditioned by those social factors of interest to the investigator. Indeed, we shall show that in traditional studies, *social structure* is often conveyed by the conduit of communication. Overall, then, language has been important to social psychology because it represents a vital medium whereby actors can communicate with one another and thereby set up joint projects according to pre-existing social arrangements. In this view, the manipulation of significant symbols is a precursor to action and behavior is the product of linguistically achieved common understandings. How language and activity are coconstitutive and express a unity within the field of human operation require more appreciation in social psychology. That is, language and action are facets of a single process that participants interactively organize.

EXPERIMENTAL AND SURVEY-BASED LITERATURE ON LANGUAGE AND SOCIAL STRUCTURE

The experimental and survey social psychological literature largely examines how social structural arrangements *condition* language and social interaction. This is evident in four areas of frequent inquiry: (1) social categories and their relation to speech; (2) language in the context of formal organizations, families, and other groups; (3) self-disclosure in dyadic and larger interactions; and (4) the role of affect or emotion in communication.

Social Categories

A great deal of research in the area of language and social psychology has focused on the relationship between social statuses or categories (e.g., race, gender, class, and age) and language. Perhaps the best known work in this area is that of Basil Bernstein (1961, 1972), who proposed that middle-class and working-class children learn two very different linguistic "codes"—an "elaborated" and "restricted" code, respectively, with the features of each determined by the forms of social relations in different communities. The middle-class subculture asserts the primacy of the individual "I" over the collective "we," which results in an elaborated code characterized by flexible organization and a wide range of syntactic options. In contrast, in working-class communities the collective "we" is asserted over the "I," and the result is a restricted code characterized by rigidity, a low level of syntactic and vocabulary selection, and implicit rather

than explicit meanings (Bernstein 1972, 475–476). These two class-based codes, Bernstein argues, help account for middle-class children's success and working-class children's lack of success in school.

Bernstein's argument generated a vigorous response. Portraying Bernstein's analysis of elaborated and restricted codes as a "deficit model," Labov (1972a) demonstrates that the "non-standard English" spoken in U.S. African-American communities is not "restricted" in its flexibility or range of options for syntax or vocabulary and, in certain ways, exhibits impressive linguistic, social, and cultural complexity and competence on the part of the speakers. More recently, Marjorie Goodwin (1990) shows how skilled urban African-American youth are in various linguistic activities (especially disputing) whereby they display and generate "character" and achieve localized social organization. Thus, Labov (1972a) has argued that there is no relationship between language use or "code" in poor and working-class African-American communities and failure in school. Instead, "failure" may lay within the school as a social institution that does not adapt to the cultures of the diverse communities it serves. Controversy about whether linguistic repertoires represent "differences" or "deficits" continues (Edwards 1979; Giles and Robinson 1990).

These early studies of the relationship between language and social stratification are related to numerous comparisons of speech practice-based cross-cultural, gender, and ethnic differences. Perhaps most prominent are investigations of linguistic divergences between women and men (see the bibliography in Thorne, Kramarae, and Henley 1983). Early research suggested that women are more expressive in intonation; that they use more adjectives and intensifiers, including *so, such, quite, vastly,* and *more;* that they make more precise determinations of color (Key 1972); that they employ more fillers, such as *umh* and *you know;* and that they more often use affectionate address terms, such as *dear, honey,* and *sweetie* (see West and Zimmerman 1985, 106). As it turns out, when researchers examine these items as simple markers or indicators of female speech, only two show any consistent patterning: compared to men, women produce speech in phonetically more correct forms (see Thorne and Henley 1975, 17) and vary their pitch and intonation more (e.g., West and Zimmerman 1985, 107). Still, differences between men's and women's speech appear to be enough for Tannen (1990) to propose that males and females speak different "genderlects." Consistent with this is evidence that females are more likely to interpret remarks *indirectly* rather than *directly* (Holtgraves 1991). Research on linguistic differences based on gender, ethnicity, age, and other social categories has proliferated (Giles and Robinson 1990) and no doubt will continue to do so.

Language Use and Group Settings

Another line of research on language and larger social processes or arrangements has examined group settings, such as formal organizations and families. For example, a number of researchers have investigated the frequency and type of communication between minority and majority members in groups (e.g., Hoffman 1985; Kanter 1977a, 1977b; Porter and Roberts 1983; South et al. 1982; Spangler, Gorden, and Pipkin 1978). These studies are especially attentive to variations in the sexual and racial composition of groups, hypothesizing that the relative ratios of members possessing female or minority "master statuses" influence the character of group interaction. Findings suggest that while increases in ratios of women and minorities do not improve the type of interpersonal messages among group members, they do affect the frequency of communication at the organizational level (Hoffman 1985).

If communication in organizational settings, such as workplaces, is related to master statuses or social categories, it is not surprising that features of occupational life appear to affect the intergenerational transmission of verbal facility in family household settings. For example, research by Dunn and Dunn (1981) suggests that mothers' work situations affect the verbal facility of their three- to six-year-old children; specifically, the better paying the mother's job and the more complex her

duties at work, the higher her child's performance on standardized vocabulary and intelligence tests. Verbal facility is thus proposed to be the medium through which inequality is transmitted from mothers to young children (Parcel and Menaghan 1990), an argument similar in form to that advanced by Bernstein.

Studies of communication and conflict in family groups address similar social structural concerns. For example, video and audio field recordings of naturally occurring conflict in families reveal a stable asymmetrical distribution of hostility and boundary maintenance by generation and gender status (Vuchinich 1984). Children are less likely to oppose parents than the reverse, daughters are less likely than sons to oppose parents, children are more likely to oppose mothers than fathers, and parents are more likely to oppose sons than daughters. These patterns, Vuchinich (1984) suggests, reflect wider social structures in which the family is embedded.

Self-Disclosure

Related to research on language use in *groups* are studies of how speech contributes to development and stability in social *relationships*. For example, investigators argue that self-disclosing utterances —vocal actions in which a speaker reveals some aspect of self to cointeractant(s)—index social cohesiveness. The well-established literature on norms of reciprocity (Altman and Taylor 1973; Gouldner 1960; Jourard 1959; for reviews see Chelune 1979; Chaiukin and Derlega 1974) forms the theoretical backdrop for such inquiries, which are largely laboratory-based and typically focus on the level of intimacy contained in subjects' self-disclosures. Theoretically, norms of reciprocity obligate parties in dyadic settings to match the level of intimacy contained in coparticipants' self-disclosing statements. Self-disclosure is hypothesized as the mechanism through which relationships develop from unacquainted to intimate levels (Altman and Taylor 1973).

Interestingly, the pattern seems to be curvilinear, with low levels of self-disclosure in both the unacquainted and intimate phases of a relationship. Studies also indicate that the degree or rate of disclosure decreases with each increase in group size. The research further suggests that there may be gender- and ethnic-based differences in self-disclosing behavior (Won-Doornink 1985). For example, Solano and Dunnman (1985) propose that female subjects disclose less in dyadic groups while male subjects disclose less in larger groups.

The self-disclosure literature concerned with how participants adjust their speech productions to the language behavior and social characteristics of coparticipants has much in common with other social psychological research on strategies through which participants match their verbal pitch, amplitude, code, word selection, and other linguistic markers. While most of the self-disclosure research relies on a vocal mode of exchange, some studies have focused on nonverbal behavior, proposing that increased intimacy by one partner will lead to increased distancing by the other. This implies that participants preserve equilibrium or orient to a principle of compensation (Argyle and Dean 1965; Patterson 1973). Empirical documentation of accent convergence and divergence between speakers in interaction (Giles 1973) also helped in the development of speech accommodation theory (Giles, Taylor, and Bourhis 1973; see Coupland and Giles 1988 for a review).

A number of researchers have attempted to integrate the analysis of verbal and nonverbal interaction (Firestone 1977; Kaplan 1977; Patterson 1976), in part to deal with the incompatibility of findings on nonverbal behavior with the norm of reciprocity. This led to the proposal that there are four rules or norms governing all dyadic interaction: reciprocity, compensation, attraction mediation, and attraction transformation (Kaplan et al. 1983). Attitudinal orientations of participants appear to shift according to the attractiveness of a subject's cointeractant: initial attraction induces a mutual approach while initial negative attitude produces avoidance (Firestone 1977; Kaplan 1977). As interaction moves beyond the initial phase, mutual attraction can be transformed, thus mediating expressions of intimacy and distancing (or, in more technical parlance, disclosure and compensation). The attraction transformation hypothesis has been confirmed with respect to certain nonverbal components of interaction, such as visual gaze, with reciprocity appearing with likable coparticipants and compensation appearing with unlikable ones (Kaplan et al. 1983).

The Social Psychology of Emotions

Experimental social psychologists have also been concerned with social structure, language, and the expression of emotions, although there has been much debate regarding the most appropriate technique and theoretical model for studying emotion (see Winton 1990). Often studying single emotion words, researchers use prototype models to determine which lists of certain stimulus words or terms for emotions (e.g., *anger*) reflect genuine emotional states. For example, it has been demonstrated that most subjects will recurrently reduce a list of 135 emotion terms into just five basic categories: love, joy, anger, sadness, and fear (Clore, Ortony, and Foss 1987; Plutchic 1980; Shaver et al. 1987). Another approach to emotion and language uses naturally produced discourse rather than word lists. For example, tape-recorded conversations are scanned for emotive or affective references (Shimanoff 1985; Winton 1990). As with the conduit model, however, most of the work in the area of emotions relies on a strict distinction between social and expressive meaning and suggests that meaning is transmitted in a unidirectional process which essentially encodes the speaker's emotions for the hearer (see Besnier 1990).

Recently, investigators have come to view the assumption of unidirectional causality as problematic and increasingly conceptualize emotional meaning as taking place within more complex interactional processes. Affect control theory (Heise 1979), for instance, examines how people manage their interpersonal behaviors according to cognitive concepts as represented in language and as containing affective connotations that are especially important in validating reciprocal social identities. Furthermore, anthropologists have actively pursued the relationship between language and emotion as participants in various sociocultural contexts constitute it. Other researchers have come to recognize that emotion pervades virtually all language production and that detailed ethnographic investigation into the social context of language use is needed to document its organization. Because producing emotional expression through experimental design presents ethical and other difficulties, some researchers argue that naturally occurring "conflictual events, conflict-resolution and therapeutic encounters can provide rich ethnographic opportunities for such investigations" (Besnier 1990, 438). The goal would be to focus on microanalytic concerns regarding the relationship between affect and language, which would provide a basis for merging the micro aspects of emotion with the macro aspect of social structure.

LANGUAGE AND ACTION

At the outset, we showed how the conduit metaphor implies that language is largely a vehicle whereby interactants make propositions about the world and that problems of meaning involve how well linguistic concepts refer to, correspond with, and represent reality, including internal thoughts and feelings. This view of language is implicit in traditional social psychological research on language, whether it is concerned with social categories, group behavior, self-disclosure, or emotions. Besides transmitting thoughts and feelings, that is, the linguistic conduit can also convey facets of social structure, such as the actor's class, gender, occupational status, degree of relationship, and so on. The idea that language is a site of social activity, rather than a repository of concepts that somehow makes reference to ideas, emotions, or social structure, stems from developments in what is called ordinary language philosophy. A variety of scholars, including Austin, Ryle, Searle, and Wittgenstein, have taken the position that problems of meaning and reference in traditional philosophy—and, by extension, issues concerning how, under what conditions, and with what frequency interactants communicate with one another—can

be fruitfully recast through investigation of ordinary language practice. This means avoiding the abstracting and generalizing process whereby words serve to index group or interactional structure and appreciating the plurality of internally orderly contexts through which such words achieve intersubjective meaning.

A concern for actual contexts of language use unifies adherents of ordinary language philosophy, but two major strands of this enterprise exert an influence on sociological approaches to language and action: "speech act theory" and "language as form of life." The former is concerned with exposing the underlying rules that make speech acts possible, whereas the latter more strongly promotes investigations of actual linguistic practice—the variety of organized usages through which people assemble courses of activity.

Speech Act Theory

The title of John Austin's famous book, *How to Do Things with Words,* conveys the essence of speech act theory. Austin (1962, 12) questions "an old assumption in philosophy" that to say something is to state something in a propositional sense. Sentences that convey referential information, in Austin's words, form "locutionary" acts, but many utterances do not describe, state, or report anything. That is, they are not true or false, but rather perform actions and are "illocutionary."[4] Examples, paraphrased from Austin (1962, 5), are:

> "I do" (take this woman to be my lawful wedded wife) (as uttered during a marriage ceremony)
> "I name this ship the *Queen Elizabeth*" (as uttered when smashing the bottle against the stem)
> "I give and bequeath my watch to my brother" (as occurring in a will)
> "I bet you it will rain tomorrow"

Such utterances do not report or describe what a person is doing; they actually *do* the activity named.

As Austin (1962, 100) reflected on the characteristics of performatives or illocutionary acts, he came to propose that the "occasion of an utterance matters seriously" and that to understand how it functions, the "context" in which it is spoken must be investigated together with the utterance itself. Austin (1962, 98) argues that when we examine the occasion of locutionary or statement like acts, we will find them being used to ask or answer a question, give assurance or a warning, announce a verdict or intent, and so on, which is to say that they occur in the context of some specific action. The lesson for the "communicational" view of language is that the locutions through which persons provide information about their thoughts, feelings, and ideas occur as part of some context of acting and are, like promising, naming, giving, and so on, illocutionary performances:

> What we need to do for the case of stating, and by the same token, describing and reporting, is to take them a bit off their pedestal, to realize that they are speech-acts no less than all these other speech-acts that we have been mentioning and talking about as performative. (Austin 1961, 249–250)

Thus, Austin abandons the dichotomy between locutionary and illocutionary acts "in favor of more general families of related and overlapping speech acts."

One of Austin's successors, Searle more forcefully states that the "unit of linguistic communication is not, as has generally been supposed, the symbol, word, or sentence . . . but rather the production of the symbol or word or sentence in the performance of a speech act" (1969, 16–17) and that a theory of language therefore needs a theory of action. For Searle, this theory is one in which a set of underlying, constitutive rules specifies how speech acts can be accomplished.

In part, both Austin (1962) and Searle (1969, 22–23) attempt to come to grips with the well-known problem in the philosophy of language that a sentence with a given reference and predication can have an assortment of meanings. In terms of speech act theory, the "same" utterance can perform a variety of different speech acts. Searle's classic example is a wife reporting to her husband at a party, "It's really quite late":

> That utterance may be at one level a statement of fact; to her interlocutor, who has just remarked on how early it was, it may be (and be intended as) an objection; to her husband it may be (and be intended as) a suggestion or even a request ("Let's go home") as well as a warning ("You'll feel rotten in the morning if we don't"). (1969, 70–71)

That there might be underlying rules linking an utterance to a specific action was implied by Austin (1962, 15–24) when he discussed "felicity conditions," or the set of circumstances that allow for the successful completion of a performative. Thus, for an act of promising to be effective, Austin (1962, 22) suggests that the promisor must (a) have been heard by someone and (b) be understood as promising. Searle (1969, 1975) provides a more sophisticated system of rules whereby the "direct" or "indirect" action a given sentence is intended to initiate can be consummated. At the same time, Searle (1969) both incorporates and corrects theories of meaning (e.g., Grice 1957; Strawson 1964) that are based on speakers' intentions and the recognition thereof. For example, rules or conventions, according to Searle (1969, 57–61) specify how an uttered promise is produced, what the preparatory conditions are (e.g., that the promise stipulates an act for someone that would not occur in the normal course of events), that the speaker intends to do the act as an obligation, and that the hearer recognizes the utterance as it was meant. These rules can be related to what Grice (1975) has called "conversational implicature," a set of maxims that underlie and provide for the cooperative use of language (cf. Levinson 1983, 241).

Language as a Form of Life

Another important figure, and perhaps the most influential, in the speech act tradition is Ludwig Wittgenstein, who in his own early work was deeply committed to logical positivism and the idea that the function of language is to represent objects in the world. The fundamental question was the truth or falsity of propositions, and the philosopher's main task was to translate complex sentences into their elementary units (Pitkin 1972, 27–28). Wittgenstein later disavowed this approach to language and instead urged the examination of language practices—how actors employ words and sentences in concrete situations. Thus, in *Philosophical Investigations* and other posthumous publications, Wittgenstein (1958) argues that language, rather than being a vehicle for naming things, conveying information, or even enacting intentions according to rules, is an "activity" or "form of life" in its own right. For example, to analyze a single word in the language, such as *description,* and propose that there is a single definable class of phenomena to which it refers is to neglect that descriptions can be a wide variety of things depending on the various roles the word plays in a multiplicity of "language games" (Wittgenstein 1958, para. 24). To discover the meaning of a word, it is not possible to rely on ostensive or demonstrative definitions; one must examine *contexts* of use to discover similarities that Wittgenstein (1958, para. 67) called "family resemblances." It is in the actual practice of employing words that such resemblances can be traced and the lexical and other components of language appreciated as a *form of life.*

This emphasis on actual practice differs significantly from speech act theory, especially that of Searle. In Wittgenstein's view, just as the word *description* might appear in a variety of language games, so might the word *promise,* but rather than deriving its meaning from some underlying constitutive rules, the illocutionary force of the utterance in which it appears derives from its pragmatics, including both vocal and nonvocal signaling as it occurs within the patterning or "grammar" of diverse language games. From this perspective, an investigator would eschew attempts to derive the rules of illocutionary force or to obtain access to speaker intentions and instead would maintain an interest in the overt expressions and acts through which a word such as *promise* comes to life. Linguistic competence, in other words, consists not in following rules to realize intent but in systematically relating given lexical items to other pieces of

vocal and bodily conduct that signal how such items are produced and understood.

The "Mapping" Problem

According to the speech act theorists, the language that humans use can comprise probably an infinite variety of social actions. Austin (1962, 150) suggests that there are on the order of a thousand or so actions, while Wittgenstein (1958, para. 23) proposes that there are "innumerable" activities in which language plays a constitutive part (see also Searle 1969, 23). A partial list includes "ordering, describing, reporting, speculating, presenting results, telling a story, being ironic, requesting, asking, criticizing, apologizing, censuring, approving, welcoming, objecting, guessing, joking, greeting." This list can be indefinitely extended and shows that, as all the speech act theorists would argue, the communicative function of language, wherein people refer to objects and report their thoughts or feelings about them in a verifiable way, is only one among many modes of linguistic usage.[5]

If social scientists have been taught to regard language in this dynamic sense, as intimately bound with action, a seemingly simple problem still looms large for the investigator: How are we to know what the illocutionary force of an utterance is? It is not tenable that the performative aspect of an utterance is somehow built into its form, for the reason stated above—the "same" utterance can perform a variety of acts. Put differently, the "form" of a sentence or utterance is often misleading as to its status as an activity. For example, Levinson (1983, 275) mentions *imperatives,* which, despite their grammatical structure as commands or requests, rarely appear as such in natural conversation. Rather, they occur "in recipes and instructions, offers *(Have another drink),* welcomings *(Come in),* wishes *(Have a good time),* curses and swearings *(Shut up),* and so on . . ." (Levinson 1983, 275). As Levinson (1983, 274) nicely formulates the problem of knowing the illocutionary force of an utterance, it is one of *mapping* speech acts onto utterances as they occur in actual contexts. We shall see that there are a variety of solutions to this mapping problem.

SOCIOLINGUISTICS AND DISCOURSE ANALYSIS

Although a number of sociologists, anthropologists, and linguists have affiliated with the term *sociolinguistics,* it is, as its name implies, a field linked to linguistics proper. Pioneers in sociolinguistics, such as Gumperz (1972), Hymes (1974), and Labov (1972b), were wrestling with a legacy of theorizing about language that posited its fundamental forms as being cognitive or minded phenomena. This legacy started with Ferdinand de Saussure's (1962) famous distinction between *langue,* which comprises an underlying systematics across variations in social context, and *parole,* which consists of the actual speech that people produce. In de Saussure's (1962) view, the proper focus of study was *langue,* the idea being that human cognition was the seat of linguistic structures and categories that guided people's behavior. In contemporary times, Noam Chomsky (1965) has continued the cognitive legacy with his very influential notion of generative grammar, a set of psychologically based universal structures whose systematic transformations result in an infinite variety of human speech productions. With its emphasis on Cartesian mental properties, structural linguistics has always sought to decontextualize linguistic phenomena in favor of finding certain ideal properties of abstracted sentences. That is, the overwhelming tendency has been to view linguistic structure as extant outside of time and place and hence not subject to social influence.

Sociolinguists, following scholars such as Firth (1935), Malinoswski (1923), and others, were utterly dissatisfied with such a view. As Hymes (1974, 2–3) has argued, the frame of reference of the *social* scientific investigation of language could not be linguistic forms in themselves, and must substitute the community context as a frame. Indeed, Labov (1972b, xiii) resisted the term *sociolinguistics* because he could not conceive of

linguistic theory or method that did not incorporate a social component. The social component would include cultural values, social institutions, community history and ecology, and so on (Hymes 1974, 3).

While sociolinguists agree that social influence is crucial to understanding linguistic structure, there are different perspectives on the relationship between society and language (Grimshaw 1974) and different strategies for investigating this relationship. The earliest sociolinguistic studies used dialect surveys to study speech variation among social networks and communities, finding that dialect variables were an excellent gauge of both social class and ethnic identity (Gumperz 1972, 12). For example, in several classic studies conducted in New York City, Labov (1972b, 44) examined the pronunciation of the phonological variable postvocalic *r,* hypothesizing that "if any two subgroups of New York City speakers are ranked in a scale of social stratification, then they will be ranked in the same order by their differential use of (r)." In his various studies, Labov (1972b) largely confirmed this hypothesis. In general, the use and nonuse of postvocalic *r* in such everyday words as *beer, beard, bare, fire,* and *flowered* is correlated with occupation, education, and income. (The higher one's status, the more one uses the *r* sound.) A large number of survey studies in the United States, Europe, Latin America, and Asia in which investigators ask for respondents' usages of and attitudes toward linguistic markers replicate Labov's findings. In fact, a number of these studies overlap with those reviewed in the section on experimental and survey-based literature. Survey sociolinguistics, being primarily concerned with how language use reflects the backgrounds, origins, and interests of community members (Fishman 1972), takes a "variationist" stance toward its topic—investigating what differs across communities.

An issue concerning language variation has been code switching (Ervin-Tripp 1972), or the manner in which members of a single community juxtapose, in the same situation, speech belonging to different grammatical systems (Gumperz 1982,

59; see also the critical essay by Breitborde 1983 and responses in Fishman 1983). When a group, such as some African-American, Spanish-speaking, or Hindi-speaking minorities in the United States, is basically bilingual, the usual categories of class, ethnicity, education, and so on are not good predictors of code switching. Of course, survey studies can document situational (e.g., home versus work) determinants of code switching in communities but are hard-pressed to explain within-situation exhibits of the phenomenon. *Interpretive* sociolinguists argue that code switching reflects speakers' ability to categorize situations, interlocutors, and social relationships and thereby to make inferences and judgments about the appropriate and relevant speech forms to produce. Whereas the presumption in sociolinguistic survey research is that language usage is normatively guided, interpretive studies propose that ethnographic investigation is necessary to define the *competence* with which interactants manipulate linguistic markers and devices to obtain their ordinary goals in everyday life:

> The analyst's task is to make an in depth study of selected instances of verbal interaction, observe whether or not actors understand each other, elicit participants' interpretations of what goes on, and then (a) deduce the social assumptions that speakers must have made in order to act as they do, and (b) determine empirically how linguistic signs communicate in the interpretation process. (Gumperz 1982, 35–36)

These strategies are compatible with Hymes's (1974) comprehensive outline of the "ethnography of communication" (Gumperz and Hymes 1972), a way of collecting, categorizing, and analyzing the action-oriented linguistic events in a particular community to answer the basic questions of what these events are and how they work.

Sociolinguistics has been occupied with numerous topics related to code switching, including second language learning and the relation of diverse languages to self-concept, personality, and status attitudes. Other classic topics in sociolinguistics are language conflict, loyalty, and mainte-nance and the structure and organization of pidgin and creole languages. Grimshaw (1974, 80) reviews the early literature comprehensively and suggests that sociolinguistics is a "hybrid discipline" that is "largely atheoretical."

Related to sociolinguistics, and representing an effort to become more theoretically sophisticated about the relationship between language and society, is the general category of *discourse analysis.* "Discourse" broadly includes both textual and spoken forms of language and refers to language production as it is organized external to the unitary sentence or clause (Stubbs 1983, 1). That is, discourse analysis is concerned with the orderly connections between clauses and sentences, rather than with the structuring of those units alone. Thus, as Coulthard (1977, 3) notes, discourse analysis overlaps partially with *pragmatics,* a subfield in linguistics that is distinguished from traditional concerns with syntax and semantics by the interest in how language users take the social context into account when producing and understanding speech forms (cf. Levinson 1983).[6] Discourse analysis, however, is multitopical and multidisciplinary, with scholars from anthropology, artificial intelligence, communications, philosophy, psychology, and sociology contributing to the enterprise (Stubbs 1983, 13; van Dijk 1985).

Even if discourse analysis is multidisciplinary, it clearly has its roots in linguistics if only in the attempt to overcome its deficiencies. For instance, Stubbs (1983) identifies three approaches to discourse analysis. In the first two—transcript analysis and ethnography—his impetus is partly to engage, in contrast to the emphasis in traditional linguistics, organizational aspects of language above the level of the sentence (cf. Halliday and Hasan 1976). The third approach is more explicitly linked to the field of linguistics, for the strategy is to analyze very specific "aspects of language which syntax and semantics have had difficulties in explaining" (Stubbs 1983, 67), including adverbs (e.g., admittedly), minimal speech particles (e.g., well), and coordinating conjunctions (e.g, but, nevertheless) (cf. Labov and Fanshel 1977, 34). When such items are embedded in chains of linguistic units larger than the sentence, their discourse structure and function become manifest.

From the linguistic field, an influential study of the chaining of speech acts is Sinclair and Coulthard's (1975, 50) proposed "exchange structure" underlying teacher-student (and other) interactions:

TEACHER: Where's the capital [Initiation]
of the United States?
STUDENT: Washington, D.C. [Response]
TEACHER: Right. [Feedback]

This initiation-response-feedback structure appears to generalize across a variety of pedagogical and testing situations (e.g., Marlaire and Maynard 1990; McHoul 1978; Mehan 1979). Moreover, it is embedded in a hierarchy of acts, moves, and transactions. By way of exchange structure and its embeddedness, teachers and other professionals control talk in the various institutional settings they inhabit (Stubbs 1983, 29).[7]

Another influential approach to establishing connections between utterances is Labov and Fanshel's (1977) "comprehensive" discourse analysis, which initially involves making "expansions" on utterances to reveal their underlying propositions. This strategy might revert to the assumption that speech is communicative of referential meaning in an informational sense, although Labov and Fanshel propose that expansion merely serves the purpose of explicating the analyst's intuitive and other knowledge about the context of an utterance so as to perform the more fundamental task of specifying the rules whereby the speech act force of an utterance is understood as the basis for an appropriate response to it. One of the most straightforward of such rules is "confirmation." A reasonable assumption in regard to a two-party social situation, Labov and Fanshel (1977, 62–63) argue, is that there are A events about which party A but not party B is knowledgeable and B events about which B but not A is knowledgeable (and there are also A-B events, about which each is knowledgeable). The rule of confirmation states, "If A makes a statement about B-events, then it is heard as a request for confirmation" (Labov and Fanshel 1977, 100).

Still another approach to discourse analysis is Grimshaw's (1989) brand of sociolinguistic research, which aims to transcend the linguistically oriented work of Labov and Fanshel by formalizing sociological variables as derived from a more inductive and ethnographic inquiry such as Cicourel's (1974) cognitive sociology (see below). Grimshaw (1981, 1989) models the discourse process as involving a "source," or originator of some manipulative speech move, a "goal," or target of the move, an "instrumentality," which is the speech act itself, and a "result" or outcome that the source pursues. The particular speech act a source employs is constrained according to the three variables of power, affect, and utility. Power has to do with the relative statuses of parties, affect with the emotionality of their relationship, and utility with the value and costs to both the source and target of a speech act in achieving some result. Thus, Grimshaw's (1989, 532–533) approach complements Labov and Fanshel's preoccupation with rules of *discourse* by emphasizing rules deriving from essentially social considerations of *appropriateness* as based on participants' cultural and social knowledge.

Grimshaw's (1989) systematic incorporation of social variables beyond the traditional sociodemographic ones of class, race, ethnicity, and gender is an important advance for discourse analysis. The continuity between his work and others' in this area is clear: speech production and comprehension is *regulated* according to linguistic and social conventions; what differentiates the linguistically oriented from sociologically inclined analysts is the relative emphasis on rules internal to speech act formation versus rules deriving from the speaker's involvement in communal relations. From Grimshaw's (1981) perspective, communal relations provide both social interactional rules having to do with roles, hierarchy, and exchange and sociolinguistic rules regarding the selection of speech resources. Across sociolinguistics and discourse analysis, the solution to the "mapping" problem—how an utterance performs a given speech act—derives from an emphasis on the rule-governed or procedural nature of linguistic interaction. These fields, then, have a clear connection to the speech act theory of Austin, Searle, and others.

COGNITIVE SOCIOLOGY AND FRAME ANALYSIS

As sociologists developed an interest in language, they naturally emphasized the importance of social context. One of the most prominent efforts has been that of Cicourel (1974), who developed the area of *cognitive sociology.* Because cognitive sociology would seem to have much in common with discourse analysis, Cicourel (1980) makes clear that the work of Labov and Fanshel (1977) suffers from an ad hoc, unrestrained, or uncontrolled reference to social context. Accordingly, Cicourel (1981) advocates disciplined ethnographic investigation, including observations of organizational environments and interviews with participants, to analyze ordinary speech fully. For example, in medical settings, researchers need to perform ethnography to penetrate the medical conceptions and theories that lie behind physicians' use of "leading" questions, specialized vocabulary or jargon, and truncated references to patients' medical histories. Likewise, interviews with patients can uncover how their belief systems guide their talk and responses to physicians.

In one study, Cicourel (1982) shows how a patient's experiences with medical bureaucracies are embedded in her challenges to a gynecologist who has diagnosed her with cancer and recommended a treatment regimen of radiation therapy and surgery. Although the patient complies with the doctor's recommendations, because of past experiences she clearly does not fully trust what she had been told about the diagnosis and treatment plan. Patterns of talk in her interaction with the physician attest to her mistrust, but explication of the mistrust and the experiences that caused it become available only through the analytic strategy of interviewing. Ethnographic observation also reveals that despite her beliefs, experiences, and distrust, organizational and interactional pressures constrain her ultimate assent to the doctor's plans. In short, to use Mehan's (1991) terms, interviewing participants to reveal their patterns of common-sense reasoning shows the relation of organizational and other "distal" contexts to local or "proximal" patterns of language use in clinical and other settings.

Cognitive sociology was inspired by phenomenological and ethnomethodological concerns with the presuppositional texture of ordinary interaction. That is, doing ethnographic investigation to analyze common-sense knowledge relates to the proposal that this knowledge and assumptions regarding its social distribution undergird every facet of concerted activity. Indeed, Cicourel uses the linguist Chomsky's metaphor of "basic" and "surface" structures to argue the point. Basic structures are interpretive rules or procedures that enable the actor to "assign meaning or relevance to an environment of objects" (Cicourel 1974, 3) and to decide whether and how more superficial norms and roles are operative in a given social situation. Thus, while discarding the suggestion that speech and interaction are straightforwardly normatively guided, cognitive sociology regards the actors as procedurally matching or linking prosodic and paralinguistic speech clues with presuppositionally based social structural knowledge to interpret utterances (Cicourel 1981). Unlike discourse analysts and sociolinguists, Cicourel (1981) avoids any strict reliance on rules for explaining the active force of utterances; rather, cognitive sociology implies a complex web of presuppositions that are minded or mental phenomena and that enable the "processing" and "screening" activities whereby actors decide the meaning of speech.

In approaching language, action, and social interaction, it seems that sociologists such as Cicourel embrace linguistic metaphors and distance themselves from the linguistic field at the same time. Erving Goffman, a preeminent sociologist of interaction, is another example of this tendency. In studying encounters, for instance, Goffman (1967) claimed not to be interested in the individuals who composed them but in the "syntactical relations" among their acts. In discussing "tie signs" or the evidence that co-participants provide about their relationships, Goffman (1971, 225–226) says, loosely, that they "form a language of relation-ships" or a "ritual idiom." In a variety of places, he strongly dissociates from linguistics per se, but with these linguistic metaphors he clearly means to invoke the rule-governed or normative organiza-tion of everyday life. Like Cicourel, however, Goffman employs a more complicated version of normativity than discourse analysts and sociolin-guists.

To appreciate Goffman's version of social in-teraction, we need to sketch his overall perspective and see how it applies to language in particular. Since people spend most of their daily lives in each other's presence, Goffman (1983) says, such social "situatedness" should have consequences. The do-main of copresent interaction is ceremonial, organ-ized by elaborate rituals that are not a mere effect of "social structure" traditionally conceived, whether the referent of such structure is social relationships, informal groupings, formal institutions, or formal categorizations such as age, ethnicity, gender, and class. As an example, Goffman (1983) refers to a "contact" ritual, such as any service encounter where customers may form a queue as they await their turn at being helped. Although the queue could be organized according to externally structured at-tributes of involved parties (e.g., age, race, gender, or class), normal queuing "blocks" or filters out the effects of such variables in favor of an egalitarian, first-come, first-served ordering principle.

Such an ordering principle belongs to what Goffman (1983, 5) calls the "interaction order," which consists of "systems of enabling conven-tions, in the sense of ground rules for a game, the provisions of a traffic code, or the syntax of a language." Once again, he invokes a linguistic metaphor to portray rulelike organization. While interactional rules are ordinarily upheld, however, violations do not threaten the game or the language as much as they serve as resources for accomplish-ing the very projects that adherence itself involves, including the definition of self and the creation or maintenance of social meaning. For example:

Given that a rule exists against seeking out a stranger's eyes, seeking can then be done as a

means of making a pickup or as a means of making oneself known to someone one expects to meet but is unacquainted with. Similarly, given that staring is an invasion of information preserve, a stare can then be used as a warranted negative sanction against someone who has misbehaved—the misbe-havior providing and ensuring a special signifi-cance to overlong examination. (Goffman 1971, 61)

Thus, Goffman's actors do not range between naive conformity and blatant rule breaking. Rules, says Goffman (1971, 61) make possible a *set* of "nonad-herences," which, according to how we classify the interactional work they do, have a variety of mean-ings.[8]

Though Goffman's corpus of work displays a pervasive concern with rules and normative organi-zation (Burns 1992), rules do not tightly constrain actions; they are more like rough guidelines that permit actors to accomplish a variety of social pro-jects, depending on how they align themselves with respect to those rules or guidelines. This point is most fully developed in *Frame Analysis,* Goff-man's (1974) major treatise on the "organizational premises" of ordinary activity, or, the "reality" of everyday experience. "Primary frameworks" are premises that provide a kind of base meaning to the events and objects of everyday life, but actors transform such frameworks through "keyings" or various types of metacommunication (Bateson 1954) to incorporate more playful and even imagi-nary elements.[9] In other words, much of everyday experience goes beyond literal activity and has nu-merous figurative aspects.

Figurative features of everyday life are espe-cially visible in talk, which is particularly vulner-able to transformation (Goffman 1974, 502). In particular, Goffman (1974, chap. 13) argues that rather than using terms such as *speaking* and *hear-ing* to characterize the production and under-standing of utterances, analysts must see how par-ticipants align themselves to those utterances. A speaker, for instance, may employ a variety of *pro-duction formats* when talking, so that he/she says something as *principal* (one whose position is rep-resented in the talk) or as *animator* (who simply speaks the words representing another's position).

As principal or animator, one can also project a particular identity or *figure* (ranging from that of the speaker to identities of fictitious and actual others). Finally, a speaker can be a *strategist* who acts to promote the interests of an individual on whose behalf he/she is acting. In a way complementary to speakers, hearers also take up different alignments or *participation statuses*—ratified recipient, overhearer, eavesdropper, and so on. Eventually, Goffman (1979) referred to the frame analysis of talk as an investigation of the "footing" or stances that participants constantly change over the course of an utterance's production. Overall, Goffman's (1974, 508) concern is to counter the conduit metaphor, the idea that talk is a vehicle for providing information, with the proposal harking back to his earliest work (Goffman 1959) that talk is how a speaker presents a drama to an audience.

While considerations of frame and footing relate to dramaturgy, they also address another enduring issue for Goffman, raised by speech act theorists among others: how the "same" utterance can change its meaning or active force across different contexts. Goffman (1964) articulated this issue in his earliest extended statement about the sociological study of speech and returns to it in a later, systematic attempt to extend frame analysis. Goffman (1976, 306) takes a conventionalized inquiry—"Do you have the time?"—and lists its many possible meanings according to a classification of possible responses. There are *consensual* responses that are standard ("Yes I do. It's five o'clock.") plus various transformations ("No, I left it with the basil.") and indirect meanings ("Stop worrying. They'll be here."). There are responses that show *procedural* problems ("What did you say?"), *presuppositions* ("Why the formality, love?"), and other laminations that can be placed on the standard and conventional meaning of the utterance. Referring to this classification as a "framework of frameworks," Goffman (1976, 308) insists that this is the object or aim of analysis: ". . . it is some such meta-schema that will allow us to accumulate systematic understanding about contexts, not merely warnings that in another context, meaning could be different." The positing of human

framing activities and the possibility of their systematic capture in a framework of frameworks represent Goffman's ingenious contribution to making sociological sense of the seeming fluidity and artfulness—even slipperiness—of ordinary speech.

Frames, frameworks, metaschemas, and the like are normative systems for the operation of talk, and they return us to the mapping problem once again. In Goffman's view, an utterance gains force as an action according to these systems, which help comprise the "interaction order" of all social situations. Like cognitive sociology, however, Goffman's approach unleashes the strict relations that sociolinguists and discourse analysts suggest exist between some relative combination of linguistic and social rules and speech. As he argued with respect to interactional rules generally, Goffman (1976, 311) proposes that the "framework of conversational constraints" is something "to honor, to invert, or to disregard, depending as the mood strikes." In thus debilitating the force that rules might exert with regard to speech and other conduct, it is as if Goffman opens a "margin," as Burns (1992, 311) put it, where actors can display their character, style, wit, poise, independence, and other attributes of the self. In addition, Goffman's (and Cicourel's) analysis implicitly question the status of rules in sociological theory, for if they have a loose connection to action their value as an explanatory device diminishes accordingly.

ETHNOMETHODOLOGY AND CONVERSATION ANALYSIS

Ethnomethodology proposes that there is a self-generating order in everyday activities (Garfinkel 1967) and takes a unique approach to the problem of mapping utterances onto actions in at least two ways. First, where cognitive sociology and frame analysis relaxed the theoretical hold that rules could have in explaining linguistic conduct, ethnomethodology, arguing that rules can be treated as topics and features of the activities they are said to organize, utterly extricates rules from theory per se. The consequence is to treat rules as resources for actors, who use them for various situated projects and ends of their own; whether abstract conformity or deviance occurs has to do with what works to accomplish these projects and ends. It is not that behavior is unconstrained, disorderly, or arbitrary, however, but that rules, if they are operative at all, figure as part of actors' own practices of reasoning and ways of organizing a social setting. Members are artful users of rules, often invoking them in an ex post facto, rhetorical manner to describe the morality of some way of life. For example, jurors invoke legal standards to depict how they arrive at a verdict, even when the route involves substantial common-sense reasoning (Garfinkel 1967), residents at a halfway house use the "convict code" to account for disregard of the official ways of doing things (Wieder 1974), and staff members at a social welfare agency get their "people processing" job done, in part, through departing from routine policies and still providing a "sense" of having conformed (Zimmerman 1970). Accordingly, in language-oriented research, ethnomethodologists study how "normative assertions" (Maynard 1985) operate in the context of already organized group activities to further such local purposes as accusing, competing, and according membership. Rules, then, are features of actions rather than explanations for them.

Another unique aspect of ethnomethodological research is its concern with "indexical expressions" (Garfinkel 1967; Garfinkel and Sacks 1970), or utterances whose meaning and understandability depend on the context or circumstances in which they appear. That "deictic" utterances, such as "this," "that," "here," "there," and so on, assume particular meaning according to their speech environment is recognized generally, but Garfinkel (1967) argued that all talk is, without remedy, indexical and context-dependent. One major, orderly aspect of "context" is an utterance's sequential placement. Conversation analysis theorizes that an utterance's force as an action of a particular type derives from such placement (see Heritage 1984, 242; Maynard and Clayman 1991, 397–400). Thus, rather than linguistic or social rules, sequential organization has primary analytic utility in describing talk as

action and its relation to "interaction" as well (Schegloff 1991). Overall, ethnomethodology and conversation analysis have close ties to the Wittgensteinian "form of life" approach to the mapping problem, in which actual, orderly linguistic practice (rule usage and sequence organization) is brought to the fore of analytic inquiry.

With its commitment to the study of naturally occurring talk, conversation analysis in particular aims to rebuild sociology as a natural observational science (Sacks 1984, 1992). Indeed, in pursuing this goal, conversation analysts have generated a sizable research literature over the past twenty-five years (Goodwin and Heritage 1990; Heritage 1984, chap. 8; J. Whalen, 1991).

Furthermore, in maintaining a commitment to examining naturally occurring social action, conversation analysis avoids treating language as a variable to be manipulated, tested, or related to other variables (see the section on experimental and survey-based literature). Recall that within such traditional studies, social categories such as gender, race, and class have been correlated with particular language measures such as rates and levels of self-disclosure, degrees of emotionality, and verbal fluency. By this correlational strategy, theorists postulate the relationship between micro patterns and macro structures (but see Boden 1990; Hilbert 1990 for an alternative view).

In contrast, researchers in conversation analysis argue that social theory must be held accountable to the details of naturally occurring interaction to observe the workings of social categories as they are exhibited for and managed by participants on actual social occasions. In other words, if a category or status such as gender, race, or class is relevant to the participants on some occasion, parties will display and manage it contingently within the interaction itself. The point is that such categories and statuses in no way operate "behind the backs" of participants; rather, for such "social structural" matters to be sociologically relevant in analysis of talk, the parties must be embodying them demonstrably and in that way producing the social structure (Schegloff 1991, 51). This conversation analytic stance reflects a principled approach to the "problem of relevance," or how, from all the alternative ways the participants and their actions are to be classified, it is possible rigorously and defensibly to choose one such classification (C. Goodwin and Heritage 1990, 295; Schegloff 1991, 49).

We explore the implications of this stance in the next section. For now, this approach to the problem of relevance means that conversation analysts' major social scientific concern has been with endogenous features of "talk-in-interaction" (Schegloff 1991). There are three principal domains in which the analysis of endogenously structured conversation is grounded: the organization of sequences (Schegloff 1968), turn taking (Sacks, Schegloff and Jefferson 1974), and repair (Schegloff, Jefferson, and Sacks 1977).

Organization of Sequences

It is well established that conversational interaction occurs in a serial fashion, with participants taking turns in an A-B-A-B-A-B . . . ordering. However, parties collaboratively structure the ordering rather tightly. This structure is sequence organization, exemplified in the *adjacency pair*, which includes such conversational objects as question-answer, request-grant/refusal, and invitation-acceptance/declination sequences (Sacks 1992). Adjacency pairs have the following characteristics (Schegloff and Sacks 1973): (1) they are a sequence of two-utterance length, which are (2) adjacent to one another, (3) produced by different speakers, (4) ordered as a first part and a second part, and (5) typed, so that a first part requires a particular second part or a range of second parts.

Moreover, adjacency pairs are characterized by "conditional relevance"—conditional on the occurrence of an item in the first slot, or first pair-part (e.g., the question), the occurrence of an item in the second slot, or second pair-part (e.g., the answer to the question, is expected and required. Consider an example of requesting (Wooten 1981, 62; simplified):

CHILD: Can I have a wee drink while I'm waiting?
MOTHER: Yes, you can.

The absence of a second pair-part may occasion a repeat of the first pair-part and perhaps "warranted inferences" concerning the coparticipant who seems nonresponsive (e.g., they are being evasive). In the next example a child reissues the request for sweets when the mother does not respond to the first request. In other words, a response is expected, and when it does not occur it is noticeably absent (colons denote stretching of the preceding sound) (Wooton 1981, 66 simplified):

CHILD: Mom, I want some swee:::ties.
　　　　[1.4 seconds silence]
CHILD: I want so:me: swee::ties.
　　　　[Child moves rapidly towards sweets; 2.5 seconds silence]
CHILD: [indecipherable talk] There's not any:::: . . .
　　　　[Child finds no sweets in their normal location]
MOTHER: You'll get some after.

The noticeable absence of the mother's reply is evident in the way the child pursues talk and bodily movement until the mother deals with his request.

That second pair-parts are required does not mean answers or replies always occur in a sequential position adjacent to the specific questions or requests (or first pair-parts) they are addressing. Often, participants insert turns between first and second pair-parts, as in invitation sequences, for example, where a recipient may need pertinent details before providing a reply (Schegloff, 1972, 78):

A: Are you coming tonight?
B: Can I bring a guest?
A: Sure.
B: I'll be there.

Similarly, greetings are not always returned immediately and answers are not always given in the turn adjacent to a question. Thus, the structure of adjacency pairs does not represent a "statement of empirical generalization," as speakers do not initiate actions or project outcomes according to statistical probabilities (Heritage 1984, 246). In other words, when a request is not answered, an invitation is probed, or a greeting is unreturned, the producing party does not conclude that it reflects a statistically unlikely roll of the dice. Rather, the absence of the second pair-part is a basis for other actions that are inferentially underway—ignoring insistent demands, obtaining information relevant to answering an invitation, obtaining information about an interlocutor's identity, and so on (for further discussion, see Schegloff 1972, 76, 1991; M. Whalen and Zimmerman 1987; Wilson 1991).

Turn-Taking Organization.

The A-B-A-B serial ordering of sequences also involves a recurring transfer of speakership. The ordering of speaker change, as well as the size and content of a speaker's turn, is not predetermined in ordinary conversation but instead is free to vary (Sacks, Schegloff, and Jefferson 1974). Moreover, change of speakership is so tightly articulated that both gap and overlap are minimized (see Lerner 1989 for elaboration on the social organization of overlap). Consider the following examples, which exhibit extremely close turn transitions (equal signs denote immediate "latching" of one utterance to the other) (Jefferson 1986, 154):

EMMA: G'morning Letitia=
LOTTIE: =uuu-hHow'r YOU=
EMMA: =FI:NE

(Whalen, Zimmerman, and Whalen 1988, 338):

SUPERVISOR: You hafta answer the nurse's questions=
CALLER: =Alright, what are they before she dies, would you please tell me what the hell you want?

This finely tuned coordination by participants is made possible through the projection of possible completion points in any one turn: it is possible for participants to anticipate exactly when their cointeractant might complete an utterance, which enables them to time the start of their own next turn precisely. In the examples above, the possible completion points occur at the end of the first speaker's turn.

The projection of a possible completion point is just one social organizational feature of turn taking, however, which relates to the issue of "who will speak next" on some occasion. To determine this, participants methodically allocate turns of talk through a set of ordered options, including current speaker selecting the next speaker, the next speaker self-selecting, or current speaker continuing to speak (Sacks, Schegloff, and Jefferson 1974). Through projecting the completion points of current turns and precisely timing the start of new turns, participants achieve hearing and understanding as an ongoing feature of ordinary talk.

Organization of Repair

Given this elaborate and systematic organization of sequences and turns within sequences, how are interactional troubles managed? That is, how do participants handle errors, mishearings, glitches in turn transition, problems of meaning, and the like? The answer is that the turn-taking system itself provides resources for understanding as well as "repair" (Levinson 1983; 340–342; Schegloff, Jefferson, and Sacks 1977). In coordinating exchange of speakership and tightly articulating sequences, participants display for one another their sense of a current vocal action in the very next turn at talk. Consider this as a "proof procedure": the second speaker's turn serves as a resource by which the first speaker may check whether a turn was heard correctly. In the next example, Marcia is, according to Schegloff (1992, 1301), explaining to her ex-husband why their son is flying home rather than driving (Schegloff 1992, 1302; simplified):

(1) **MARCIA:** . . . Becuz the top was ripped off of his car which is to say somebody helped themselves.
(2) **TONY:** Stolen.
(3) **MARCIA:** Stolen. Right out in front of my house.

In turn 2, Tony offers a candidate understanding ("stolen") of Marcia's ambiguous reference in turn 1 to the top being "ripped off" their son's car. Then, in turn 3, Marcia confirms Tony's candidate understanding. Had Tony not been correct in his understanding, this is a point at which Marcia could have repaired the trouble. In general, the third turn such as this is a slot that may be taken up with the business of repairing various interactional troubles (Heritage 1984, 254–258; Levinson 1983, 340; Schegloff 1992, 1302). This is not the first opportunity in the sequence for repair initiation, however, for participants might well repair their own utterances in their own first turn at talk or in the transition between turns. Indeed, as Schegloff (1992, 1300–1301) notes about the above episode, Marcia appears to have used "which is to say somebody helped themselves" to clarify "ripped off," a phrase that could be ambiguous as between a literal meaning and an idiomatic expression for robbery. This is termed a "self-initiated self-repair." Also, in the second turn in the sequence it is possible for the second speaker to repair aspects of the first speaker's turn (Schegloff, Jefferson, and Sacks 1977). Thus, turn taking and the organization of repair in the system of turn taking provide a structural basis for the achievement of intersubjectivity (Sacks, Schegloff, and Jefferson 1974; Schegloff 1992).

The explication of these three domains of the social organization of conversation (sequences, turn taking, and repair) provides the basis for much of the vigorous research agenda in conversation analysis and has generated an expansive literature on talk in institutional and organizational settings. We now consider this literature, along with other research on the relation between language, action, and social structure.

LANGUAGE, ACTION, AND SOCIAL STRUCTURE

Thus far, we have implicitly concentrated on *interaction,* suggesting that social psychology benefits from understanding how parties use language in an immediate sense to perform joint endeavors of all sorts. Of course, as parties talk and gesture to one another, more than completely local interests and social organization may be at stake, and this means that questions regarding "social structure" come to the fore.

Following Zimmerman and Boden's (1991) lucid reflections on talk and social structure, we can identify several approaches to probing the interrelation of language, action, and social structure. First, investigators often see social structure as consisting of such forms as age, gender, class, and other sociodemographic categories, as well as culture, institutions, and complex organizations, which condition the use of language in specifiable ways. We call this a *macrodirectional* approach, in which social structural forces are the cause of interactional and linguistic phenomena. "In such a framework," Zimmerman and Boden (1991, 5) remark, "talk and, indeed, all interaction of actual actors in social situations is seen as a *product* of those social forces." As discussed earlier, this is the approach in survey sociolinguistics and in a great number of communication studies, and we will therefore not review the research further.

A second, *dialectical,* approach to talk and social structure involves social structure as cause *and* outcome of spoken interaction; language is the site of the production and reproduction of sociodemographic, cultural, institutional, and organizational forms characteristic of the overall society. It is therefore important to know both the local and broad context in which utterances occur, making it incumbent on the investigator to engage in ethnographic inquiry to complement the analysis of recorded speech. As noted above, this premise is central to cognitive sociology (Cicourel 1981), and it informs the work of students of talk in such institutional settings as preschools (Corsaro 1979), schools (e.g., McDermott, Gospodinoff, and Aron 1978; Mehan 1979; Phillips 1982), universities (Grimshaw 1989), doctor's offices or hospitals (Cicourel 1981; Fisher 1983, Silverman 1987; Strong 1979; Waitzkin 1983), and courts (Danet 1980; Molotch and Boden 1985). As an example of this approach, Mehan (1991) argues that the "social facts" of school systems derive from the "practical work" of educators engaged in interaction with students, parents, and other professionals in a series of "microevents" that occur in the classroom, testing sessions, and meetings. The dialectical approach is also compatible with the work of European theorists such as Bourdieu (1991), Giddens (1984), and Habermas (1979) and their concerns with language, ideology, and social reproduction.[10]

A third approach to the analysis of language, action, and social structure is *reflexive* (cf. Whalen and Zimmerman 1987), in which the interaction order (Goffman 1983) and the institutional order have complex interrelationships not adequately described in causal or even reciprocally causal terms. The interaction order is comprised of mechanisms of turn taking and other sequential organizations, which provide the resources for producing and understanding what is being said and done in concert (Zimmerman and Boden 1991, 9). The interaction order and its constituent devices are basic or primordial in the sense of underlying, preceding, being organized independently of any social structural context in which talk occurs, and being invariant to historical and cultural variation (Drew and Heritage 1992; Heritage 1984; Maynard, 1991; Schegloff 1991; Zimmerman and Boden 1991, 12).

If the interaction order is primordial in this sense, it behooves investigators to analyze its workings as a prelude to explicating the use of language in institutional settings. When investigators do not do so, they risk attributing features of the talk to its institutional surround and missing both the bedrock of orderliness that makes it possible for participants to understand one another at all (no matter what the setting) and the ways in which they display the relevance of social structure through procedural "work" that is visible in the details of their talk (Schegloff 1991). Conversation analysts, who take this position, have shown its implications in various ways. One implication is that the fundamental organization of conversational turn taking may be different in institutional as compared with ordinary settings. Thus, where usually turn size, turn content, and turn order are free to vary and are subject to local management, in settings such as courtrooms (Atkinson and Drew 1979), educational realms (Marlaire and Maynard 1989; McHoul, 1978; Mehan 1979), and news interviews (Clayman 1988, 1989; Greatbatch 1988; Heritage and Greatbatch 1991), this is not the case. It is often attorneys, teachers, and newscasters who

ask questions, and witnesses, students, and interviewees who must answer. From these elemental observations, a wide range of consequences follow in regard to how professionals, in collaboration with lay and other participants, organize such actions as accusing and denying in the courtroom, teaching, testing, and showing learning ability in the classroom, and being "neutral" and expertly informative in the news interview.

It is not just alterations in turn taking that characterize institutional talk. Another implication of regarding conversation as primordial is that some mundane conversational sequences might be imported more or less wholesale as a resource for tasks that actors in institutional settings face recurrently. Thus, in medical settings, physicians and others are occupationally predisposed to having to deliver "bad news" in the form of diagnostic information. Maynard (1991) identified a *perspective display series* that, in ordinary conversation, involves one party asking another about some social object, whereupon the first party presents a report or assessment that is then regularly outfitted to agree with the second party's. This way of producing a report or assessment is an inherently cautious maneuver, in that a speaker can elicit, in a preliminary manner, some display from a recipient of how well the speaker's own information or opinion meshes with the recipient's. Overall, this means that the perspective display series permits delivery of such information or opinion in a way that proposes a mutuality of perspective between speaker and recipient. In medical settings, where severe illness and death are customary topics, the perspective display series and its orderly features can be adapted to handling these topics. Clinicians, rather than presenting a diagnosis or death announcement straightforwardly, often take the more circuitous route of eliciting the view of their recipient before reporting the bad news, and then agreeably shape the news to the recipient's knowledge and beliefs. At the very least, this works to promote the recipient's understanding of what may be technically difficult jargon or terminology. In addition, it coimplicates the recipient's perspective in the presentation of the news, so that clinicians can give a diagnosis in a publicly affirmative and nonconflict-ing manner.

Overwhelmingly, studies of doctor-patient in-teraction stress the power and authority of clini-cians, which limits patients' ability to express their concerns, experience, and ideas. No doubt power and authority are important in understanding the doctor-patient relationship, but without incorporat-ing an investigation of the interaction order of con-versation as such, analysts risk losing sight of the problems, such as delivering and receiving bad news, that can be part of the relationship and also more generic. Furthermore, as Maynard (1991) has argued, if talk in institutional settings is in some ways continuous with that in ordinary life, appreci-ating that continuity can actually help in the techni-cal explication of power and authority, for the rea-son stated above.[11] Such a strategy minimizes the risk of attributing all features of talk to the institu-tional surround and enables the identification of what is "institutional" and what is "interactional" about a particular spate of talk.

Still another implication of treating conversa-tion as a primordial backdrop to institutional lan-guage is that actors can change the ordering of intact sequences of talk in systematic ways. In a comprehensive analysis of openings to ordinary tele-phone calls, Schegloff (1986) distinguished four core opening sequences—the summons/answer sequence (consisting of a ringing phone and its answer), the identification/recognition sequence, the greeting, and the "how are you." After par-ticipants produce these four sequences, they enter into the "first topic" of the call. As Whalen and Zimmerman (1987, 174) compared a corpus of calls to emergency ("9-1-1") dispatch centers with Schegloff's analysis, they noticed that the organi-zation consisting of these four sequences was modified so that (a) identification of the dispatch center occurs as part of answering the summoning phone ring, and (b) the "first topic" (a request for assistance) occurs immediately after the sum-mons answer sequence. Participants dispense with other forms of recognition, with greetings, and with "how are you's." Following Heritage (1984, 238–240), Whalen and Zimmerman (1987, 182)

argue that (a) represents a *specialization* of ordi-nary conversational procedure, and (b) indicates a *reduction* of the core opening sequences.

Thus, the interaction order of talk, what Whalen and Zimmerman (1987, 182) call an "inter-actional machinery," is intimately involved in the means whereby, in institutional settings, partici-pants "exhibit for one another (and for the analyst) their appreciation of who, situationally speaking, they are, and what, situationally speaking, they are up to." That is, in and through modifications to the interaction order, participants also produce the in-stitutional order. These orders are distinct and yet related in complex ways. A reflexive approach to language, action, and social structure, then, means understanding how sequential organization and other aspects of the interaction order can be de-ployed in ways that are sensitive to the contingen-cies and relevances of a society's organizational and institutional settings. This might be through alterations to turn taking, particularized adoption of ordinary conversational sequences and series, discrete changes to the ordering of sequences, and other procedural means yet to be discovered and analyzed.[12]

CONCLUSION

Language is a primary medium of social behavior and, as such, deserves center stage in the panoply of social psychological topics. Indeed, other topics in social psychology, including exchange, bargain-ing, justice, socialization, deviance, health, ethnic relations, and collective behavior, necessarily in-volve interactive speech processes, which makes language use perhaps the most basic of social psy-chological phenomena. This is, we have argued, not so much because language is a vehicle of communi-cation; rather, it is a resource for activity. One activity humans sometimes perform is "communicating" information of various kinds, but this is one among many other activities, such as arguing, promising, requesting, apologizing, joking, and greeting.

Influenced by ordinary language philosophy, recognizing that words do not have stable "mean-ings," and that the "same" utterance has different interpretations according to its context of use, language-oriented researchers therefore wrestle with the basic question of how utterances perform specifiable actions. Sociolinguists and discourse analysts answer this question in one way by suggesting that some combination of linguistic and social *rules* link words and activities together. Cognitive sociologists and frame analysts also presume some normative connection between utterances and actions, while giving freer rein to actors' strategic calculations and decision making in regard to rule-adherence. Ethnomethodologists and conversation analysts argue that in their ongoing conduct, participants themselves are *users* of rules who make normative assertions in the service of performing various activities. Rules, therefore, are only one possible facet of the practices whereby actors order speech productions to accomplish and understand the active force of these utterances.

Moreover, in the conversation analytic view, importance is attached to how actors combine their utterances in a sequenced fashion. That is, the sequential organization of talk-in-interaction is a "primordial site of social action," which implies that this organization needs investigation and explication before the orderliness of conduct and action in institutional and other social structural are-

nas can be analyzed fully. This assertion implies a point of contact between conversation analysts and Goffman's concern with the interaction order. Among sociolinguists, discourse analysts, and cognitive sociologists, however, the argument is that participants' actions are not completely local in terms of either genesis or effect. It behooves the analyst to import the context or setting of talk enthnographically to analyze speech patterning and interactive order properly.

In short, the understanding of spoken language has moved from the conduit metaphor to an "action" orientation, and there is yet considerable controversy on how this orientation is best represented in theory and research. As this controversy continues, ever more realms of language use come under the social psychological microscope. To name just a few, these include discourse "marking" (Schiffrin, 1987)—uses of "well," "and," "so," "y'know," and the like—idiomatic expression (Drew and Holt 1988), gossip (Eder and Enke 1991; Goodwin 1990), narrative (Labov 1972a, Sacks 1992), puns and jokes (Sacks 1992), rhetoric (Atkinson 1984; Billig 1987), and numerous other aspects of the extraordinary human wealth represented in ordinary language, action, and social interaction.

NOTES

We wish to thank Deirdre Boden, Marilyn Carter, William Corsaro, Christopher Fassnacht, Alan Firth, Allen Grimshaw, Robert Moore, Joshua Rossol, and Jack Whalen for extremely helpful comments on an earlier version of this chapter.

1. That actors, through their direct relationships, constitute large-scale social phenomena does not, as Wilson (1970, 59) has observed, "commit the sociologist to a version of psychological reductionism": "Nor do complex patterns of sociological interest need in themselves be meaningful to the actors. For example, the rate of theft in a group may not even be known to the members of the group; nevertheless, an individual act of theft is behavior meaningful to the members, and the rate expresses a regularity in these actions that can be taken as a phenomenon for sociological interest." For extensive discussion of the relationship between interaction and social structure, see Boden and Zimmerman (1991).

2. This is what has been made of Mead's (1934) work, although contemporary scholarship suggests that Mead himself would have a different view of significant symbols. For instance, Joas (1980, 116) argues that Mead's position would be somewhere between the "copy theory" of language (that mind and language reflect reality) and theories of linguistic constitution, such as the Sapir-Whorf hypothesis (see below). Mead, according to Joas was interested in "practical intersubjectivity," or the pragmatic character of meaning, which is derived from individual and bodily embeddedness in the social world of immediate experience.

3. This is true, as Boden (1990, 245) remarks, even in symbolic interactionist studies, which, despite interest in people's *defining* activities, has accorded language very little direct attention.

4. Austin (1962, 102) also discusses "perlocutionary acts," or utterances that are consequential in particular

ways for the behavior of persons to whom they are directed, but this type need not concern us here. The distinction between illocutionary and perlocutionary acts is hazy (see Levinson 1983, 287).

5. In Katriel and Philipsen's (1990) study, informants use "communication" as contrastive with "small talk" to depict speech in relationships that are "close," "supportive," and "flexible."

6. Due to space limitations, we do not discuss the field of pragmatics and its own engagement with such topics as speech act theory, presupposition, and conversational structure. For a thorough account, see Levinson (1983).

7. For appreciation and criticism of the Sinclair and Coulthard exchange model, see Drew and Heritage (1992) and Taylor and Cameron (1987).

8. Indeed, actors' orientation to the interaction order remains moral, resting on commitments that in one way or another (through adherence or violation) enable the self to emerge and be preserved. On this point, see Goffman (e.g., 1971, 185–187); for secondary discussion, see Rawls (1987, 42–44).

9. In addition to keyings, to which all actors in a situation are a party, Goffman (1974, chap. 4) discusses "fabrications" as transformations (of primary frameworks) in which some actors perpetrate deceits or hoaxes on others.

10. A dialectical perspective on childhood socialization, "interpretive reproduction," is discussed in chapter 16 and Corsaro (1992).

11. In regard to the perspective display series and how it affects the "asymmetry" of clinical discourse, see Maynard's (1991) discussion of problems and problem proposals, contrastive displays of knowledge, and rigidity of sequential relationships. These are produced aspects of participants' usage of the perspective display series and show how clinical discourse, rather than being asymmetric in some unadulterated, comprehensive, or total fashion, is only so in particular and specifiable ways.

12. See Drew and Heritage's (1992, 29–53) explication of how speakers display and evoke institutional contexts of their interaction through lexical choice, turn design, sequence organization, overall conversational structure, and distinctive exhibits of "social epistemology."

REFERENCES

Altman, Irwin, and Dalmas Taylor. 1973. *Social Penetration: The Development of Interpersonal Relationships.* New York: Holt, Rinehart & Winston.

Argyle, M., and J. Dean. 1965. Eye-contact, distance, and affiliation. *Sociometry* 28:289–304.

Atkinson, Max. 1984. *Our Masters' Voices: The Language and Body Language of Politics.* London: Methuen.

Atkinson, Max, and Paul Drew. 1979. *Order in Court: The Organisation of Verbal Interaction in Judicial Settings.* London: Macmillan.

Austin, John L. 1961. *Philosophical Papers.* London: Oxford University Press.

———. 1962. *How to Do Things with Words,* 2nd ed. Cambridge: Harvard University Press.

Bateson, Gregory. 1954. A theory of play and phantasy. *Psychiatric Research Reports* 2:39–51.

Bernstein, B. 1961. Social structure, language and learning. *Educational Research* 3:163–176.

Bernstein, B. 1972. A sociolinguistic approach to socialization: With some reference to educability. Pp. 465–511 in *Directions in Sociolinguistics: The Ethnography of Communication,* ed. John J. Gumperz and Dell Hymes. New York: Holt, Rinehart & Winston.

Besnier, Niko. 1990. Language and affect. *Annual Review of Anthropology* 19:419–451.

Billig, Michael. 1987. *Argumentation.* Cambridge: Cambridge University Press.

Boden, Deirdre. 1990. People are talking: Conversation analysis and symbolic interaction. Pp. 244–273 in *Symbolic Interaction and Cultural Studies,* ed. Howard S. Becker and Michal McCall. Chicago: University of Chicago Press.

Boden, Deirdre, and Don H. Zimmerman. 1991. *Talk and Social Structure: Studies in Ethnography and Conversation Analysis.* Cambridge, UK: Polity Press.

Bourdieu, Pierre. 1991. *Language and Symbolic Power.* Cambridge, MA: Harvard University Press.

Breitborde, L. B. 1983. Levels of analysis in sociolinguistic explanation: Bilingual code switching, social relations, and domain theory. *International Journal of the Sociology of Language* 39:5–43.

Burns, Tom. 1992. *Erving Goffman.* London: Routledge.

Chaiukin, Alan, and Valerian J. Derlega. 1974. Liking for the norm-breaker in self-disclosure. *Journal of Personality* 42:117–29.

Chelune, Gorden J. 1979. Reactions to male and female disclosure at two levels. *Journal of Personality* 42:117–129.

Chomsky, Noam. 1965. *Aspects of the Theory of Syntax.* Cambridge, MA: MIT Press.

Cicourel, Aaron V. 1974. *Cognitive Sociology.* New York: Free Press.

———. 1980. Language and social interaction: Philosophical and empirical issues. *Sociological Inquiry* 50:1–30.

———. 1981. Notes on the integration of micro- and macro-levels of analysis. Pp. 51–80 in *Advances in Social Theory and Methodology: Toward an Integration of Micro- and Macro-Sociologies,* ed. Karen Knorr-Cetina and Aaron V. Cicourel. Boston: Routledge and Kegan Paul.

———. 1982. Language and belief in a medical setting. Pp. 48–78 in *Georgetown University Roundtable on Linguistics,* ed. Heidi Burns. Washington, DC: Georgetown University Press.

Clark, Herbert H. 1985. Language use and language users. Pp. 179–231 in *The Handbook of Social Psychology,* vol. 2, ed. Gardner Lindzey and Elliot Aronson. New York: Random House.

Clayman, Steven E. 1988. Displaying neutrality in television news interviews. *Social Problems* 35: 474–492.

———. 1989. The production of punctuality: Social interaction, temporal organization, and social structure. *American Journal of Sociology* 95:659–691.

Clore, G. L., A. Ortony, and M. A. Foss. 1987. The psychological foundations of the affective lexicon. *Journal of Personality and Social Psychology,* 53:751–766.

Coulthard, Malcolm. 1977. *An Introduction to Discourse Analysis.* London: Longman.

Coupland, N., and H. Giles. 1988. Introduction: The communicative contexts of accommodation. *Language and Communication* 8:175–182.

Corsaro, William A. 1979. Young children's conception of status and role. *Sociology of Education* 52: 46–59.

———. 1992. Interpretive reproduction in children's peer cultures. *Social Psychology Quarterly* 55: 160–177.

Danet, Brenda. 1980. Language in the legal process. *Law and Society Review* 14:445–564.

Drew, Paul, and John Heritage, eds. 1992. *Talk at Work: Social Interaction in Institutional Settings.* Cambridge, UK: Cambridge University Press.

Drew, Paul, and Elizabeth Holt. 1988. Complainable matters: The use of idiomatic expressions in making complaints. *Social Problems* 35:398–417.

Dunn, L., and L. Dunn. 1981. *PPVT-R Manual.* Circle Pines, MN: American Guidance Service.

Eder, Donna, and J. Enke. 1991. The structure of gossip: Opportunities and constraints on collective expression among adolescents. *American Sociological Review* 56:495–508.

Edwards, J. 1979. *Language and Disadvantage.* London: Arnold.

Eibl-Eibesfeldt, Irenäus. 1989. *Human Ethology.* Hawthorne, NY: Aldine de Gruyter.

Ervin-Tripp. 1972. On sociolinguistic rules: Alternation and co-occurrence. Pp. 213–250 in *Directions in Sociolinguistics: The Ethnography of Communication,* ed. John J. Gumperz and Dell Hymes. New York: Holt, Rinehart & Winston.

Firestone, I. J. 1977. Reconciling verbal and nonverbal models of dyadic communication. *Environmental Psychology and Nonverbal Behavior* 2:30–44.

Firth, J. R. 1935. The techniques of semantics. *Transactions of the Philological Society* 36–72.

Fisher, Sue. 1983. Doctor talk/patient talk: How treatment decisions are negotiated in doctor-patient communication. Pp. 135–157 in *The Social Organization of Doctor-Patient Communication,* ed. Sue Fisher and Alexandra D. Todd. Washington, DC: Center for Applied Linguistics.

Fishman, Joshua A. 1972. *The Sociology of Language: An Interdisciplinary Social Science Approach to Language in Society.* Rowley, MA: Newbury House.

———. ed. 1983. Levels of analysis in sociolinguistic explanation. *International Journal of the Sociology of Language* 39:5–177.

Garfinkel, Harold. 1967. *Studies in Ethnomethodology.* Englewood Cliffs, NJ: Prentice Hall.

Garfinkel, Harold, and Harvey Sacks. 1970. On formal structures of practical actions. Pp. 338–366 in *Theoretical Sociology,* ed. J. C. McKinney and E. A. Tiryakian. New York: Appleton-Century-Crofts.

Giddens, Anthony. 1984. *The Constitution of Society.* Cambridge, UK: Polity.

Giles, Howard. 1973. Accent mobility: A model and some data. *Anthropological Linguistics* 15:87–105.

Giles, Howard, and W. Peter Robinson. 1990. Prologue. Pp. 1–8 in *Handbook of Language and Social Psychology,* ed. H. Giles and W. Peter Robinson. New York: Wiley.

Giles H., D. W. Taylor, and R. Y. Bourhis. 1973. Towards a theory of interpersonal accommodation through language: Some Canadian data. *Language in Society* 2:177–192.

Goffman, Erving. 1959. *The Presentation of Self in Everyday Life.* Garden City, NJ: Doubleday.

———. 1964. "The neglected situation." *American Anthropologist* 66:133–136.

———. 1967. *Interaction Ritual: Essays on Face-to-Face Behavior.* Garden City, NJ: Doubleday.

———. 1971. *Relations in Public: Microstudies of the Public Order.* New York: Basic Books.

———. 1974. *Frame Analysis.* New York: Harper.

———. 1976. Replies and responses. *Language and Society* 5:357.

———. 1979. Footing. *Semiotica* 25:1–29.

———. 1983. The interaction order. *American Sociological Review* 48:1–17.

Goodwin, Charles, and John Heritage. 1990. Conversation analysis. *Annual Review of Anthropology* 19:283–307.

Goodwin, Marjorie H. 1990. *He-Said-She-Said: Talk as Social Organization Among Black Children.* Bloomington: Indiana University Press.

Gouldner, Alvin W. 1960. The norm of reciprocity: A preliminary statement. *American Sociological Review* 25:161–168.

Greatbatch, David. 1988. A turn taking system for British news interviews. *Language in Society* 17:401–430.

Grice, H. P. 1957. Meaning. *Philosophical Review* 67:377–388.

———. 1975. Logic and conversation. Pp. 41–58, in *Syntax and Semantics 9: Pragmatics,* ed. P. Cole and J. L. Morgan. New York: Academic.

Grimshaw, Allen D. 1974. Sociolinguistics. Pp. 49–92 in *Handbook of Communication,* ed. Ithiel de Sola Pool and Wilbur Schramm. Chicago: Rand McNally.

———. 1981. *Language as Social Resource.* Stanford: Stanford University Press.

———. 1989. *Collegial Discourse: Professional Conversation Among Peers.* Norwood, NJ: Ablex.

Gumperz, John. 1972. Introduction. Pp. 1–25 in *Directions in Sociolinguistics: The Ethnography of Communication,* ed. John J. Gumperz and Dell Hymes. New York: Holt, Rinehart & Winston.

———. 1982. *Discourse Strategies.* Cambridge: Cambridge University Press.

Gumperz, John J., and Dell Hymes, eds. 1972. *Directions in Sociolinguistics: The Ethnography of Communication.* New York: Holt, Rinehart & Winston.

Habermas, Jürgen. 1979. *Communication and the Evolution of Society.* Boston: Beacon Press.

Halliday, M. A. K., and Ruqaiya Hasan. 1976. *Cohesion in English.* London: Longman.

Heise, David R. 1979. *Understanding Events: Affect and the Construction of Social Action.* Cambridge, UK: Cambridge University Press.

Heritage, John. 1984. *Garfinkel and Ethnomethodology.* Cambridge, UK: Polity.

Heritage, John, and David Greatbatch. 1991. On the institutional character of institutional talk: The case of news interviews. Pp. 93–137 in *Talk and Social Structure: Studies in Ethnomethodology and Conversation Analysis,* ed. Deirdre Boden and Don H. Zimmerman. Cambridge, UK: Polity.

Hertzler, Joyce O. 1965. *A Sociology of Language.* New York: Random House.

Hewitt, John P. 1991. *Self and Society: A Symbolic Interactionist Social Psychology,* 5th ed. Needham Heights, MA: Allyn and Bacon.

Hilbert, Richard A. 1990. Ethnomethodology and the micro-macro order. *American Sociological Review* 55:794–808.

Hoffman, Eric. 1985. The effects of race composition on the frequency of organizational cmmunication. *Social Psychology Quarterly* 48:17–26.

Holtgraves, Thomas. 1991. Interpreting questions and replies: Effects of face-threat, question form, and gender. *Social Psychology Quarterly* 54:15–24.

Hymes, Dell. 1974. *Foundations in Sociolinguistics: An Ethnographic Approach.* Philadelphia: University of Pennsylvania Press.

Jefferson, Gail. 1986. Notes on "latency" in overlap onset. *Human Studies* 9:153–183.

Joas, Hans. 1980. *G. H. Mead: A Contemporary Re-Examination of His Thought.* Cambridge, UK: Polity.

Jourard, Sidney M. 1959. Self-disclosure and other cathexis. *Journal of Abnormal and Social Psychology* 59:428–432.

Kanter, Rosabeth Moss. 1977a. *Men and Women of the Corporation.* New York: Basic Books.

———. 1977b. Some effects of proportion on group life: Skewed sex ratios and responses to token women. *American Journal of Sociology* 82:954–990.

Kaplan, K. J. 1977. Structure and process in interpersonal distance. *Environmental Psychology and Non-Verbal Behavior* 1:67–80

Kaplan, Kalman J., Ira Firestone, Kathy Klein, and Charles Sodikoff. 1983. Distancing in dyads: A comparison of four models. *Social Psychology Quarterly* 46:108–115.

Katriel, Tamar, and Gerry Philipsen. 1990. "What we need is communication": "Communication" as a cultural category in some American speech. Pp. 77–93 in *Cultural Communication and Intercultural Contact,* ed. Donal Carbaugh. Hilldale, NJ: Erlbaum.

Key, Mary R. 1972. Linguistic behavior of male and female. *Linguistics* 88:15–31.

Labov, William. 1972a *Language in the Inner City: Studies in the Black English Vernacular.* Philadelphia: University of Pennsylvania Press.

———. 1972b. *Sociolinguistic Patterns.* Philadelphia: University of Pennsylvania Press.

Labov, William, and David Fanshel. 1977. *Therapeutic Discourse: Psychotherapy as Conversation.* New York: Academic.

Lerner, Gene H. 1989. Notes on overlap management in conversation: The case of delayed completion. *Western Journal of Speech Communication* 53:167–177.

Levinson, Stephen C. 1983. *Pragmatics.* Cambridge, UK: Cambridge University Press.

Malinowski, Bronislaw. 1923. The problem of meaning in primitive societies. Pp. 451–510 in *The Meaning of Meaning,* ed. C. K. Ogden and J. A. Richards. London: Kegan Paul.

Marlaire, Courtney L., and Douglas W. Maynard. 1990. Standardized testing as an interactional phenomenon. *Sociology of Education* 63:83–101.

Maynard, Douglas W. 1985. How children start arguments. *Language in Society* 14:1–30.

———. 1991. Interaction and asymmetry in clinical discourse. *American Journal of Sociology* 97:448–495.

Maynard, Douglas W., and Steven E. Clayman. 1991. The diversity of ethnomethodology. *Annual Review of Sociology* 17:385–418.

McDermott, R. P., Kenneth Gospodinoff, and Jeffrey Aron. 1978. Criteria for an ethnographically adequate description of concerted activities and their contexts. *Semiotica* 24:245–275.

McHoul, Alexander. 1978. The organization of turns at formal talk in the classroom. *Language in Society* 7:183–213.

Mead, George H. *Mind, Self and Society.* Chicago: University of Chicago Press.

Mehan, Hugh. 1979. *Learning Lessons.* Cambridge, MA: Harvard University Press.

———. 1991. The school's work of sorting students. Pp. 71–90 in *Talk and Social Structure: Studies in Ethnomethodology and Conversation Analysis,* ed.

Deirdre Boden and Don H. Zimmerman. Cambridge, UK: Polity.

Molotch, Harvey, and Deirdre Boden. 1985. Talking social structure: Discourse, domination and the Watergate hearings. *American Sociological Review* 50:273–288.

Parcel, Toby, and Elizabeth Menaghan. 1990. Maternal working conditions and children's verbal facility: Studying the intergenerational transmission of inequality from mothers to young children. *Social Psychology Quarterly* 53:132–147.

Patterson, M. L. 1973. Compensation in nonverbal immediacy behaviors: A review. *Sociometry* 36:237–262.

———. 1976. An arousal model of interpersonal intimacy. *Psychological Review* 83:235–245.

Phillips, Susan. 1982. *The Invisible Culture: Communication in Classroom and Community on the Warm springs Indian Reservation.* New York: Longman.

Pitkin, Hannah F. 1972. *Wittgenstein and Justice: On the Significance of Ludwig Wittgenstein for Social and Political Thought.* Berkeley: University of California Press.

Plutchic, R. 1980. A general psychoevolutionary theory of emotion. Pp. 3–33 in *Emotion: Theory Research and Experience: Theories of Emotion,* ed. R. Plutchic and H. Kellerman. New York: Academic.

Porter, Lyman W., and Karlene H. Roberts. 1983. Communication in organizations. Pp. 1533–1589 in *Handbook of Industrial and Organizational Psychology,* ed. Marvin D. Dunnette. New York: Wiley.

Rawls, Anne. 1987. The interaction order sui generis: Goffman's contribution to social theory. *Sociological Theory* 5:136–149.

Reddy, Michael J. 1979. The conduit metaphor. Pp. 284–324 in *Metaphor and Thought,* ed. Andrew Ortony. Cambridge, UK: Cambridge University Press.

Sacks, Harvey, 1984. Notes on methodology. Pp. 21–27 in *Structures of Social Action,* ed. J. M. Atkinson and J. Heritage. Cambridge, UK: Cambridge University Press.

———. 1992. *Lectures on Conversation,* vol. I, II. New York: Blackwell.

Sacks, Harvey, Emanuel A. Schegloff, and Gail Jefferson. 1974. A simplest systematics for the organization of turn-taking for conversation. *Language* 50: 696–735.

Saussure, Ferdinand de. 1962. *Cours de Linguistique Générale.* Paris: Payot.

Schegloff, Emanuel A. 1968. Sequencing in conversational openings. *American Anthropologist* 70:1075–1095.

——— . 1972. Notes on conversational practice: Formulation of place. Pp. 75–120 in *Studies in Social Interaction,* ed. David Sudnow. New York: Free Press.

——— . 1986. The routine as achievement. *Human Studies* 9:111–152.

——— . 1991. Reflections on talk and social structure. Pp. 44–70 in *Talk and Social Structure: Studies in Ethnomethodology and Conversation Analysis,* ed. Deirdre Boden and Don H. Zimmerman. Cambridge, UK: Polity.

——— . 1992. Repair after next turn: The last structurally provided defense of intersubjectivity in conversation. *American Journal of Sociology* 97:1295–1345.

Schegloff, Emanuel A., Gail Jefferson, and Harvey Sacks. 1977. The preference for self-correction in the organization of repair in conversation. *Language* 53:361–382.

Schegloff, Emanuel A., and Harvey Sacks. 1973. Opening up closings. *Semiotica* 8:289–327.

Schiffrin, Deborah. 1987. *Discourse Markers.* Cambridge, UK: Cambridge University Press.

Searle, John R. 1969. *Speech Acts: An Essay in the Philosophy of Language.* Cambridge, UK: Cambridge University Press.

——— . 1975. Indirect speech acts. Pp. 59–82 in *Syntax and Semantics, 9: Pragmatics,* eds P. Cole and J. L. Morgan. New York: Academic.

Shannon, C. E., and Weaver, W. 1949. *The Mathematical Theory of Communication.* Urbana: University of Illinois Press.

Shaver, P., J. Schwartz, J., D. Kirson, and C. O'Connor. 1987. Emotion knowledge: Further exploration of a prototype approach. *Journal of Personality and Social Psychology* 52:1061–1086.

Shimanoff, S. B. 1985. Expressing emotions in words: Verbal patterns of interaction. *Journal of Communication* 35:16–31.

Silverman, David. 1987. *Communication and Medical Practice: Social Relations in the Clinic.* London: Sage.

Sinclair, J. McH., and R. M. Coulthard. 1975. *Towards an Analysis of Discourse: The English Used by Teachers and Pupils.* Oxford: Oxford University Press.

Solano, Cecilia H., and Mina Dunnman. 1985. Two's company: Self-disclosure and reciprocity in triads versus dyads. *Social Psychology Quarterly* 48:183–187.

South, Scott J., Charles M. Bonjean, William T. Markham, and Judy Corder. 1982. Social structure and intergroup interaction: Men and women of the federal bureaucracy. *American Sociological Review* 47:587–599.

Spangler, Eve, Marsha A. Gorden, and Ronald M. Pipkin. 1978. Token woman: An empirical test of Kanter's hypothesis. *American Journal of Sociology* 84:160–170.

Strawson, P. F. 1964. Intention and convention in speech acts. *Philosophical Review* 73:439–60.

Strong, Philip M. 1979. *The Ceremonial Order of the Clinic: Parents, Doctors, and Medical Bureaucracies.* London: Routledge & Kegan Paul.

Stubbs, Michael. 1983. *Discourse Analysis: The Sociolinguistic Analysis of Natural Language.* Oxford: Blackwell.

Tannen, Deborah. 1990. *You Just Don't Understand: Women and Men in Conversation.* New York: Ballantine.

Taylor, T., and D. Cameron. 1987. *Analyzing Conversation: Rules and Units in the Structure of Talk.* Oxford: Pergamon.

Thorne, Barrie, and Nancy Henley, 1975. *Language and Sex: Difference and Dominance.* Rowley, MA: Newbury House.

Thorne, Barrie, Cheris Kramarae, and Nancy Henley, eds. 1983. *Language, Gender and Society.* Rowley, MA: Newbury House.

van Dijk, Teun. 1985. *Handbook of Discourse Analysis,* vol. 1–4. London: Academic.

Vuchinich, Samuel. 1984. Sequencing and social structure in family conflict. *Social Psychology Quarterly* 47:217–234.

Waitzkin, Howard. 1983. *The Second Sickness.* New York: Free Press.

Weber, Max. 1947. *The Theory of Social and Economic Organization.* New York: Free Press.

West, Candace, and Don H. Zimmerman. 1985. Gender, language, and discourse. Pp. 103–124 in *Handbook of Social Psychology: Discourse Analysis in Society,* ed. Teun A. van Dijk. London: Academic.

Whalen, Jack. 1991. Conversation analysis. Pp. 303–310 in *Encyclopedia of Sociology,* vol. I, ed. E. F. Borgotta and M. Borgotta. New York: Macmillan.

Whalen, Marilyn, and Don H. Zimmerman 1987. Sequential and institutional contexts in calls for help. *Social Psychology Quarterly* 50:172–185.

Whalen, Jack, Don H. Zimmerman, and Marilyn Whalen. 1988. When words fail: A single case analysis. *Social Problems* 35:335–362.

Whorf, Benjamin. 1956. *Language, Thought, and Reality: Selected Writings of Benjamin Lee Whorf.* Cambridge, MA: MIT Press.

Wieder, D. Lawrence. 1974. *Language and Social Reality.* The Hague: Mouton.

Wilson, Thomas P. 1970. Conceptions of interaction and forms of sociological explanation. *American Sociological Review* 35:697–710.

———. 1991. Social structure and the sequential organization of interaction. Pp. 22–43 in *Talk and Social Structure: Studies in Ethnomethodology and Conversation Analysis,* ed. Deirdre Boden and Don H. Zimmerman. Cambridge, UK: Polity.

Winton, W. M. 1990. Language and emotion. Pp. 33–49 in *Handbook of Language and Social Psychology,* ed. H. Giles and W. Peter Robinson. New York: Wiley.

Wittgenstein, L. 1958. *Philosophical Investigations.* Oxford, UK: Blackwell.

Won-Doornink, Myong Jin. 1985. Self-disclosure and reciprocity in conversation: A cross-national study. *Social Psychology Quarterly* 48:97–107.

Wooten, Anthony J. 1981. The management of grantings and rejections by parents in request sequences. *Semiotica* 37:59–89.

Zimmerman, Don H. 1970. The practicalities of rule use. Pp. 221–238 in *Understanding Everyday Life,* ed. Jack D. Douglas. Chicago: Aldine.

Zimmerman, Don H., and Deirdre Boden. 1991. Structure-in-action: An introduction. Pp. 3–21 in *Talk and Social Structure: Studies in Ethnomethodology and Conversation Analysis,* ed. Deirdre Boden and Don H. Zimmerman. Cambridge, UK: Polity.

CHAPTER 7

Social Interaction

Continuities and Complexities in the Study of Nonintimate Sociality

LYN H. LOFLAND

For many people, especially those in urban spaces, encounters with nonintimates represent most of their interactions. Since by the year 2000 half of the human population is expected to be living in urban spaces and half of those in cities containing a million or more inhabitants (Dogan and Kasarda 1988, 13), nonintimate sociality[1]—sociality among strangers, "mere" acquaintances, habitues of public settings, service workers and their customers, work associates, and so on—will soon be one of the major forms of social intercourse in the world. The goal of this chapter is to review research in sociology (and some sister fields) dealing with these kinds of interactions.

Despite a relative neglect of the topic until about 1960, since then considerable research has accumulated, especially in sociology, but in psychology, geography, anthropology, social history, architecture, and urban planning and design as well. What follows is not an exhaustive review of this material;[2] rather, I focus on seven important themes, which I conceive as being of two sorts. One represents "continuities" with concerns developed quite early in the study of nonintimate sociality and the other adds "complexities" by focusing on sources of variation that were initially overlooked or understressed. Admittedly, there is a certain arbitrariness to this scheme; what I consider a complexity, the reader may consider a continuity, and vice versa. Nonetheless, I think it provides a fruitful way to grasp the extremely large and heterogeneous collection of materials under consideration.

The chapter is organized into three sections: origins and pioneers; continuities; and complexities. A brief conclusion offers observations about where we've been and where we might go next.

ORIGINS AND PIONEERS

The origins of a sociological interest in nonintimate sociality lie in paradox. Those who may justifiably wear the mantle of "fathers" also bear considerable responsibility for the neglect their offspring suffered. For example, Georg Simmel's late nineteenth and early twentieth century essays —"Sociability," "On the Significance of Numbers for Social Life," "The Stranger," "The Metropolis and Mental Life" (K. Wolff 1950)—have served as the starting point for many of the studies we shall encounter in this chapter. Yet those same essays, most particularly "The Metropolis and Mental Life," helped to deflect attention away from nonintimate sociality. When Simmel wrote

> *The psychological basis of the metropolitan type of individuality consists in the* intensification *of nervous stimulation which results from the swift and uninterrupted change of outer and inner stimuli. . . . In . . . [the blasé attitude], the nerves find in the refusal to react to their stimulation the last possibility of accommodating to the contents and form of metropolitan life (1950, 409–410, 415)*

he fathered an extremely influential line of thought that defined city streets as the sites of stimulus overload and psychic shutdown and that dismissed "stranger interaction" as an oxymoron. Similarly, many of the topics and themes with which this chapter is concerned were discussed in the writings of the "Chicago School" (Robert E. Park, W. I. Thomas, Louis Wirth, Ernest W. Burgess, and their students). Yet an immediate and long-term consequence of those writings was the establishment of a sociological agenda that focused almost exclusively on primary groups and relationships. Other social forms (e.g., nonintimate relationships) tended to be ignored, or were bemoaned as indications of (depending on the particular period) social disorganization, alienation, anomie, or personal estrangement. Fortunately for our understanding of modern societies, by midcentury some scholars had begun to "read" Simmel, the Chicago School writers, and others in a rather different manner. They simply bypassed the well-known heritage of neglect, and, in its stead, found encouragement for the idea that they might locate social life in "niches" their immediate predecessors had assumed were barren.

During the 1950s and 1960s, for example, the anthropologist Ray Birdwhistell published a series of works (1952, and the many articles reprinted in 1970) dealing with "kinesics" or body movement communication. He was by no means exclusively concerned with communications among nonintimates; in fact, a good portion of his research dealt with body language as it was used between family members. But at the same time, he argued and demonstrated that body movement is learned in, and patterned by, culture and is therefore available as a means of communication between all members of that culture—whether they are intimates or not, whether they even know one another or not. In the introduction to a collection of his essays (1970, xii), Birdwhistell acknowledged the "determinative influence" of, among other people, Edward T. Hall. Hall, also an anthropologist, interested himself in the "out-of-awareness" aspects of culture, especially space and time. Two of his publications, in particular, were very widely read and cited. In *The Silent Language* (1959) and again in *The Hidden Dimension* (1966), Hall convinced his many readers that the mundane minutiae of everyday

life—how people select where to sit in an airport, how far apart they stand when conversing with someone they don't know well, how they react to inadvertent or intentional body contact from strangers—are neither trivial nor irrelevant matters, but are at the heart and core of any serious study of human group life.

The intellectually revolutionary potential of a focus on minutiae was also the central message in Harold Garfinkel's invitation to his fellow sociologists to partake of the "ethnomethodological" experience. In his pathbreaking "Studies of the Routine Grounds of Everyday Activities" (1964, see also 1967), he reported on a small number of "field experiments" that involved disrupting commonplace scenes in an "attempt to detect some expectancies that lend [such] scenes their familiar, life-as-usual character, and to relate these to the stable social structures of everyday life" (1964, 227). The goal of ethnomethodology, he said, was to learn "something about how the structures of everyday activities are ordinarily and routinely produced and maintained" (1964, 227). While those who responded to Garfinkel's invitation did not all respond in the same way (e.g., Sudnow 1972) many were lured into a fascination with "the routine grounds" of that portion of "everyday activities" occurring in nonintimate settings.

I have thus far mentioned two anthropologists and a sociologist, but psychologists made contributions as well. Michael Argyle's intricate studies of eye contact (Argyle and Cook 1976; Argyle and Dean 1965) and Robert Sommer's detailed empirical studies of personal space (e.g., 1969; Felipe and Sommer 1966) were (among other works) responsible for adding psychology to the list of contributing disciplines.

As we shall see, the concern with the minutiae of social life—with its routines and commonplaces—expressed in the work of Birdwhistell, Hall, Garfinkel, Argyle, and Sommer is a crucial component of most of the research here under review. These scholars, then, certainly qualify as pioneers in the study of nonintimate sociality. But without denigrating the import of their contributions, I think it also fair to say that the lead role can be assigned to only one person: Erving Goffman. We will meet Goffman again and again in the following pages, for a very significant portion of the research I discuss adds to or struggles to reconstruct the foundation he built. Here, only a brief introduction will have to suffice. Beginning with his earliest essays published in the 1950s (collected in the 1967 volume *Interaction Ritual*), proceeding through *The Presentation of Self in Everyday Life* (1959), *Behavior in Public Places* (1963a), *Stigma* (1963b), *Relations in Public* (1971), *Gender Advertisements* (1976), and "The Arrangement between the Sexes" (1977) and culminating in the posthumously published "The Interaction Order" (1983), Goffman shaped most of the agenda, devised most of the analytic strategies, and provided most of the theoretical justification for the flood of studies of social interaction, especially social interaction among nonintimates, that made their appearance in the 1960s, 70s, 80s, and—at least as far as one can judge at this point—the 1990s.[3] He certainly did not see himself as a student of nonintimate sociality, however that topic might be phrased. He was interested in what, in the last essay he wrote, he called the "interaction order": "the study of face-to-face interaction as a naturally bounded analytically coherent field—a sub-area of sociology" (1970, ix). But because a fair amount of the material with which he worked had to do with nonintimates, Goffman (almost inadvertently) focused his enormous talent for microanalysis on instance after instance of face engagements between "strangers, 'mere' acquaintances, habitues of public settings, service workers and their customers, work associates, etc." His analyses offered persuasive testimony for the view that what occurs between two strangers passing on a street is as thoroughly social as what occurs in a conversation between two lovers; that the same concern for the fragility of selves that operates among participants in a family gathering also operates among colleagues in a work setting, among professionals and their clients in modern institutions, and among strangers on an urban beach. And *this* view, as should become clear, is the sine qua non of all the research we look at in the following pages.

CONTINUITIES IN THE STUDY OF NONINTIMATE SOCIALITY

Our first set of topics represent continuations of concerns that initially found expression in the work of these pioneers: (1) principles of stranger interaction, (2) the strategy paradigm, and (3) interaction and inequality.[4]

Principles of Stranger Interaction

In the preceding section, I made a laudatory reference to pioneers learning to find social life in niches that others had assumed to be barren and emphasized the importance of Goffmanian testimony regarding the social character of even stranger interactions. What I had in mind were their challenges to the idea (widespread in the social sciences as late as the 1970s and, among some persons, yet today) that two individuals lacking a personal relationship cannot, in any sociologically meaningful sense, interact; therefore, what goes on in urban public space is of no interest. For example, when I entered graduate school in sociology in the mid-sixties, most textbooks and many professors were still echoing the 1926 views of Nicholas J. Spykman:

> On the street, in the subway, on the bus, [the city dweller] comes in contact with hundreds of people. But these brief incidental associations are based neither on a sharing of common values nor on a co-operation for a common purpose. They are formal in the most complete sense of the term in that they are empty of content. (Spykman 1926, 58)

Spykman was not the only authority on this matter. By the early 1970s, reference could also be made to the contemporary work of Stanley Milgram (1973). Milgram's argument (following Simmel 1950 and Wirth 1938) that the pace and crowding of city street life led to "stimulus overload" and individual psychic "shutdown" was read by many as indicating that social interaction among the urban masses was, if not impossible, at least improbable. What the pioneers accomplished, then, was to chip away at these widespread beliefs. Through their descriptions and analyses of the extraordinarily rich interactional life occurring "on the street, in the subway, on the bus," they demonstrated that in the "incidental associations" Spykman referred to there is, in fact, a good deal of "sharing of common values" and "cooperation for a common purpose." Far from "shutting down," persons in urban space appear to be paying careful attention to what may be conceived of as shared principles of stranger interaction.

The number of relevant studies is enormous, so here I can provide only a small sample. We shall look at research in three areas: order; privacy, disattention, and avoidance; and encounters.

Order among Strangers. Literary and filmic images of the chaotic streets of the city notwithstanding, what strikes those students of social interaction with the discipline and patience necessary for careful observation is the *orderliness* with which city denizens seem to conduct even their most fleeting and ostensibly trivial encounters. The geographer David Seamon's term, "place ballet" (which he introduced in 1979 in an attempt to convey the patterned character of some space use), well captures—through its metaphoric linkage to choreography, to *directed* movement—the tone and flavor of many studies of urban interaction.

Michael Wolff's "Notes on the Behavior of Pedestrians" (1973) and William H. Whyte's *City: Rediscovering the Center* (1988) are representative of this literature. In Wolff's piece, for example, at the same time he was reporting a degree of sociality, of cooperative behavior, that he did not initially anticipate, he was also finding it useful to describe some of what he observed by using a language that hints of the dance: "[A]t higher densities a common behavior . . . was not total detour and avoidance of contact but a slight angling of the body, a turning of the shoulder and an almost imperceptible side-step—a sort of *step-and-slide*" (1973, 39).

The more recent work of William H. Whyte builds on and confirms Wolff's observations of cooperative behavior among pedestrians but is much less timid about the metaphor—speaking quite directly of the "great dance":

If there is a proper place for it, there will be [during the evening pedestrian rush hour] a great dance. . . . Stand on the balcony overlooking the main floor of Grand Central. At left there is a mass of people going the same way. But only for a moment. They split into an infinity of directions. . . . Hundreds of people will be moving this way and that, weaving, dodging, feinting. . . . Almost everyone is on a collision course with someone else, but with a multitude of retards, accelerations and side steps, they go their way untouched. It is indeed a great dance. (Whyte 1988, 67, see also 1980)

The choreography motif can be discerned most readily in studies of pedestrian behavior, but the suggestion of carefully arranged (ordered) movement is also found in research on automobile interaction, seating behavior, queuing, and eye contact.

Privacy, Disattention, and Avoidance among Strangers. According to what we might call the Spykman-Milgram view of the urban world, unacquainted persons are socially irrelevant to one another—they may simultaneously occupy adjacent space, but they are not copresent in any sociological sense. Thus, the absence of verbal and/or visual exchanges among them requires no explanation. It is simply a given of the setting. Those who challenge this view have demonstrated the exact opposite. Far from being a given, the absence of verbal or visual exchanges must be *achieved*. In fact, and paradoxically, privacy, disattention, and avoidance can be accomplished only by means of social interaction. Stated most generally, persons draw on their presumptively shared understandings about body language and appearances, about space-specific appropriate behaviors and identities, and about typical patterns of orderliness, among other matters, to communicate to one another any one or more of the following messages.

"I want my privacy and am not available to be spoken to or encountered in any way."

An individual makes private a public place by making interaction with others impossible or at least highly inconvenient. . . . In the [bus] depot, this end seemed to be effected through two major categories of means: involvement with some activity, and body

position. . . . The most notable use of body position-
ing occurred when all four seats of a set were
occupied. If an individual was seated next to some-
one, he would noticeably adjust his position by
turning himself away from his neighbor. (Hender-
son 1975, 449–450)

"I know you are present and you know I am
   present but we are, of course, each invisible
   to the other."

Protecting oneself via shielding does not stop once
an individual goes into the [pornographic] book-
store . . . Under no circumstances in these stores do
customers make physical or verbal contact with
one another. The normative structure appears to
demand silence and careful avoidance of either eye
or physical contact. (Karp 1973, 439, 449; see also
Cahill et al. 1985)

"I know you are in my visual and audial presence but I am not paying any observable
   attention to you; that is, I am giving you
   'civil inattention.' "

When seated [in subway cars], people usually as-
sume inconspicuous behavior—sitting squarely, at
first turning neither left nor right, and maintaining
expressionless faces. . . . People without books or
papers . . . may begin to stare at fellow passengers,
alternating fleeting or blank stares with an inno-
cent staring off into space. These stares and glances
at fellows are quite restricted and concealed . . .
[as] they are not to be interpreted as invitations . .
. to begin an encounter; they are the behavioral
components of what Goffman . . . has termed "civil
inattention" (Levine, Vinson, and Wood 1973, 210;
see also Karp, Stone, and Yoels 1991, chap. 4).

Encounters among Strangers.   Not only do strangers interact in the manufacture of order, not only
do they interact in the manufacture of privacy,
disattention, and avoidance, they also *interact* in
the more traditional sense of the term. That is, they
engage in fully focused visual and verbal encounters, and they do so for many of the same reasons
acquaintances and intimates encounter one another: for mundane assistance or protection or rescue from danger, for sex, for advice, for reality
checks, for the pleasure of talk, for the defense of

self or companion, and so on. Let us look at what
researchers have to say about three sorts of stranger
face engagements: help-seeking encounters, defensive encounters, and pleasurable sociability encounters.

Help-Seeking Encounters.   The least problematic
stranger encounters are those involving a specifically targeted request for minor help: Could you
tell me the time? Am I on the right street to get to
city hall? May I borrow your newspaper for just a
minute? If you're not going to use the sugar, would
you mind if we moved the bowl to our table?[5] Such
requests are the mundane stuff of everyday stranger encounters—so unremarkable that in many
studies they are mentioned not at all or only in
passing. Receiving far more research attention (because far more problematic) are those situations
where there may be a quite serious need for help
but where requests for it are either not made at all
or not targeted to any specific person or persons.
The multiple field experiments of the psychologists John Darley and Bibb Latané are perhaps the
best known instances of this line of research.[6] They
were interested in why bystanders to an emergency
might fail to help, an interest sparked by the infamous Kitty Genovese case:

> *On a March night in 1964, Kitty Genovese was set*
> *upon by a maniac as she came home from work at*
> *3 A.M. Thirty-eight of her Kew Gardens neighbors*
> *came to their windows when she cried out in ter-*
> *ror—none came to her assistance. Even though her*
> *assailant took over half an hour to murder her, no*
> *one even so much as called the police.*
>
> *This story became the journalistic sensation of*
> *the decade. "Apathy," cried the newspapers. "In-*
> *difference," said the columnists and commentators.*
> *"Moral callousness," "dehumanization," "loss of*
> *concern for our fellow man," added preachers,*
> *professors, and other sermonizers. (Latané and*
> *Darley 1973, 62–63)*

In response to such conventional and moralistic
views, Latané and Darley demonstrated that a bystander's decision to intervene or not was a highly
complex and thoroughly social matter. Bystanders

might do nothing for the simple reason that they fail to notice that anything needs to be done or because they lack the requisite skills to be helpful. But even those who are fully aware that they are witnessing an emergency and who are able to help may not do so if other bystanders are present—a rather remarkable and counterintuitive finding, which the researchers explained as follows:

> *(1) Others serve as an audience to one's actions, inhibiting him from doing foolish things. (2) Others serve as guides to behavior, and if they are inactive, they will lead the observer to be inactive also. (3) The interactive effect of these two processes will be much greater than either alone. . . . (4) The presence of other people dilutes the responsibility felt by any single bystander, making him feel that it is less necessary for himself to act. (Latané and Darley 1970, 125)*

Defensive Encounters.   The line between research dealing with privacy, disattention, and avoidance and research dealing with defensive encounters is difficult to draw. In numerous studies, descriptions of interactions that forestall encounters may gradually shade into descriptions of quite direct defensive interactions. In Margaret Henderson's study of "acquiring privacy in public," for example, a detailed discussion of varying body postures that merely "give off" privacy signals is interrupted by an example of a clearly targeted communication: "A young girl and her boyfriend were seated side by side. The boyfriend left to make a phone call. During the interim, an elderly male approached the apparently vacant seat. At this, the girl *slapped her hand on the seat with a glaring look* and the old man simply shuffled away" (Henderson 1975, 451, emphasis added). The lack of encounters among users is similarly emphasized in Robert Edgerton's study of Southland Beach, as are the body postures and props that communicate a desire to be left alone. Nonetheless, the book is peppered with brief descriptions of defensive encounters: "[M]ost invasions of private space are by small children or dogs. These intrusions almost always take the form of running through another person's territory. The

observed reaction to such occurrence is usually slight, *although it may involve a dirty look or a yell to be more careful*" (Edgerton 1979, 151, emphasis added). I suspect this compounding of indirect and direct interactions is a consequence of the tendency of students of defensive encounters to focus exclusively on the use of body language and "props" to signal displeasure or hostility over spatial invasion or to affirm threatened identities and statuses.[7] This is not to say that verbal defensive encounters have been ignored completely. Snow et al. (1991), for example, detail a series of linguistic strategies used by women to "cool out" men in singles bars and nightclubs (see also Gardner 1988). But there is no question but that we know more about how people "signal" warnings than about how they "symbolize" them.

Pleasurable Sociability Encounters.   Finally, persons may encounter one another for the simple pleasures of sociability. The pleasure may be sensual, as when total strangers have sex in what is common-sensically understood to be a public place. Usually such encounters are managed with the cooperation and support of like-minded others (e.g., Humphreys 1970), but sometimes they occur without "witnesses" aware of what is happening (M. Davis 1983, 20–26; Delph 1978). More frequently, however, the pleasures of the encounter are mundane: passing the time with a chat, sharing an unexpected experience, getting some information on a topic of interest, or basking in the momentary glow of fellow feeling. While there have been attempts to formulate the precise conditions for the initiation of such encounters (e.g, L. Lofland 1985, 168–173), the research record best supports only three quite general principles. First is the principle of the *open person:* individuals who because of inferior (e.g., child, disabled) or occupational (e.g., police officer) status or because of a situationally specific identity (e.g., fellow American in China) are seen as more available for an encounter than others (e.g., Cahill 1990; Gardner 1980; Goffman 1963a, chap. 8). Second is the principle of the *open region:* locations (e.g., drinking establishments, residence lounges of hotels, city streets during carnival, some cafes) in which all the inhabitants are mutually accessible to one another (e.g., Cavan 1966; Goffman 1963a, chap. 8). Third is the principle of *triangulation:* a "process by which some external stimulus provides a linkage between people and prompts strangers to talk to each other as though they were not [strangers]" (W. H. Whyte 1980, 94, 1988, 154–155). Triangulation stimuli may be as mundane as children, dogs, or a period of inclement weather, as esoteric as public place art, or as infrequent as shared emergencies (e.g., Gardner 1986b; Goffman 1963a, chap. 8; Nash 1981; Robins, Sanders, and Cahill 1991).

Many of the researchers whose work I have been discussing have analyzed their data on order, on privacy, disattention, and avoidance, and on encounters in terms of strategies actors use to accomplish one or another of those ends. It is to this "strategy paradigm" that we now turn.

The Strategy Paradigm

While Goffman cannot be said to have invented the "dramaturgical perspective"—the analysis of social life using a theatrical analogy—his 1959 book *The Presentation of Self in Everyday Life* surely can be credited with its ensuing and enthusiastic incorporation by sociologists into their cookbook of analytic techniques.[8] Moreover, in Goffman's hands, two elements of the larger perspective took on special import: the actor and the actor's performance. In *Presentation,* as well as in his later work,[9] Goffman's emphasis was less on the overall analysis of social life in theatrical terms than on understanding how actors accomplish or manage their performances—that is, on understanding the *strategies* they use. It is not surprising, then, that numerous accomplished dramaturgical analyses are simultaneously strategy analyses. Even more important in terms of the literature here under review are the many studies that have adopted a dramaturgically inspired strategy language but discarded most of the other theatrical accouterments. That is, much of what we know about nonintimate

sociality is knowledge derived from research that uses the strategy paradigm.

Goffman is unquestionably the father (or one of the fathers)[10] of the strategy paradigm, but its methodological articulation is largely the work of one of his students, John Lofland. While Lofland utilized the paradigm (although not explicitly identified as such) in his first two books (1966, 1969) and published many strategy analyses during his tenure as founding editor of *Urban Life and Culture,*[11] it was not until the publication of *Doing Social Life* (1976) that he spelled out exactly what it was that, in following Goffman's lead, he and so many others had been up to:

> *Lurking within the sprawling and conflict-ridden world of social science there is a genre of work that seeks to answer the question, "How do people do things?" The question, note, is "How do people do things," not "Why do people do things?" Whatever it is that people feel they want, need, are striving for, are coping with, how do they do it? . . . How do people get across the street? How do people wait for a bus? How do people find their way around? How do people show they are of one or another race or sex? How do people manage to acquire resources? How do adult-people cope with child-people, and vice versa? How do some people get other people happily to do their bidding? How do people rebel? (J. Lofland 1976, 1; see also 1978.)*

In the second edition of *Analyzing Social Settings* (Lofland and Lofland 1984), Lofland advanced the paradigm even further, proposing that the question "What are people's strategies?" is a legitimate coequal of conventionally more esteemed questions about types, structures, frequencies, causes, processes, and consequences. These latter six questions, he argued, all illustrate the "passivist" conception of human social life, and are thus incomplete:

> *[T]here is . . . an additional reality to which we must attend. This is the* activist *approach, in which we view humans as creative and probing creatures who are coping, dealing, designating, dodging, maneuvering, scheming, striving, struggling, . . . who are actively influencing their social settings.*

In the activist view, the focus is on how people construct their actions in various situations. . . . (Lofland and Lofland 1984, 116–117)

Now, of course, the strategy paradigm is hardly limited to the topic of nonintimate sociality, but it does seem to have provided students of secondary interaction with an especially fruitful way of approaching their data. Many of the research pieces discussed or cited in the preceding section utilize it, as do many of the pieces that will be discussed or cited below. Strategy analysis, as we will see, has been especially useful in illuminating the interactional processes involved in stratification.

Interaction and Inequality

Given the centrality of the idea of stratification in sociology more generally, it is hardly surprising that it should also constitute one of the major themes in the study of nonintimate social interaction. Again, while he is hardly the "father" of inequality studies, Goffman must be seen as forging a (perhaps *the*) pivotal link between interaction and stratification. Randall Collins makes the case persuasively:

> *[Goffman] has illuminated . . . the major differences among the immediate day-by-day experiences of social classes. Classes differ because of different kinds and amounts of self-presentational experiences. . . . And the overall structure of stratification, in the final analysis—the distribution of wealth, power, and prestige—is the result of the ongoing activities by which some people idealize themselves better than others in the everyday encounters that make up the world of work and hence the organizational structure of society. . . . Thus well-performed rituals create and re-create the stratified order, and hence underlie the distribution of material, power, and status privileges. . . . It is [also] possible to consider variations in the resources for producing and controlling rituals of various sorts; Goffman connects the Durkheimian to the Weberian and Marxian universes by showing us some of the crucial means of mental production, and the means of emotional production, too. (Collins 1981, 235, 237, 238)*

Collins is discussing what he sees as the import of Goffman's earliest work, especially the essays collected in *Interaction Ritual* (1967b) and, of course, *Presentation* (1959), and he goes on to argue that although the connection between interaction and stratification is present in this material, it is less than explicitly so. Others may or may not agree with Collins on this point, but I suspect few would argue with the observation that in a number of the later writings, that connection became very explicit indeed. *Stigma* (1963b), for example, continues to stand as a prototype analysis of interaction between "superiors" and "inferiors" of all sorts. And *Gender Advertisements* (1976) and "The Arrangement Between the Sexes" (1977), as other examples, provide two of the most graphic depictions of eye-level stratification in the entire literature of social science.

Early on in *Stigma,* Goffman refers to the situation of normals and stigmatized in one another's immediate presence as "one of the primal scenes of sociology" (1963b, 13). If we substitute the words *superiors* and *inferiors* for *normals* and *stigmatized,* we can see that since *Homo sapiens* have managed to use almost all imaginable human differences as bases for judging themselves to be superior, the array of such primal scenes—such inequality situations—available for study is quite breathtaking in its enormity. Thus, once again I must winnow. I will limit myself here to only three types of situations: structural inequality, circumstantial inequality, and normative inequality.

Situations of Structural Inequality. Studies of interaction between structural unequals—persons of different classes, different racial or ethnic groups, different sexes, different ages—yield few surprises in terms of the substance of what they report. We are not amazed to learn, for example, that those in positions of superiority treat their "inferiors" with condescension, cruelty, contempt, coolness, caution, or concern. Nor are we awestruck by the finding that those in positions of inferiority use strategies of subterfuge, silence, sincerity, or silliness when coping with those "above" them. What *is* sociological news emanating from this research is the documentation of, on the one hand, the pervasiveness, the ubiquity, the sheer omnipresence of systems of structural inequality in the moment-by-moment lives of human actors, and, on the other hand, the moment-by-moment creation and recreation of these systems of structural inequality by human actors. That is, what students of interaction and inequality have taught us is that large-scale systems of social stratification are not only continually experienced at the face-to-face level, they are also and at the same time continually fabricated or refashioned there.

Sometimes stratification arrangements are communicated and enacted through nonverbal displays of social distance, as in Elijah Anderson's depiction of "face work" between groups separated by both class and race: "[W]hites of the Village often scowl to keep young blacks at a social and physical distance. As they venture out on the streets of the Village . . . they may plant this look on their faces to ward off others who might mean them harm. Scowling by whites may be compared to gritting by blacks as a coping strategy" (1990, 220–221). Perhaps even more frequently, stratification systems are communicated and enacted not through the maintenance of social distance but through the breach of it. "Encounters between strangers" have uses other than those discussed above; breachings of civil inattention may also serve to flaunt one's superior position. How else are we to interpret reports such as the following?

> In a Santa Fe supermarket, a young woman waits in line with her cart, two young men behind her watching her posterior with appreciation. It is Halloween time. "Bought your punkins yet?" one young man booms to the other, and the young woman shifts uncomfortably. (Gardner 1989, 50)

> I [an African American university professor] was driving. . . . [We] were sitting at an intersection . . . and a group of middle-class looking white boys drives up in a nice car. And they start shouting things at us in a real fake-sounding Mexican American accent, and I realized that they thought we were Mexican Americans. And I turned to look at them, and they started making obscene gestures

> and laughing at the car. And then one of them realized that I was black, and said, "Oh, it's just a nigger." (Feagin 1991, 110)

> It was late afternoon [in Austin, Texas] and the homeless were congregating in front of the [Salvation Army] for dinner. A school bus approached that was packed with Anglo junior high students being bused from an eastside Barrio school to their upper-middle and upper-class homes in the city's northwest neighborhoods. As the bus rolled by, a fusillade of coins came flying out the windows along with a few obscene gestures and injunctions to "get a job." (Snow and Anderson 1993, 198)

Reports of this sort suggest that the following passage, which Spencer Cahill intended merely as a description of the subordinate status of children in public places, actually depicts a far more generic situation. It may, in fact, depict a primal scene between structural unequals of all sorts.

> When in public places, the young always must be mindful of the overwhelming dominance and dictates of their ever watchful elders.
>
> And that is only part of the burden children must bear when in public places. On crowded public transport vehicles and in supermarket check-out queues, adults commonly use nearby children as a temporary source of amusement to break the monotony of their ride or wait. They often visually admire and sometimes smile, wink and make faces at a nearby child in an apparent attempt to provoke some response from her or him. They may even question such a child or otherwise attempt to lure her or him into conversation. All this attention may seem quite innocent, but it just as clearly denies children the right to be let alone when in public places—a right children are continually instructed and encouraged to grant adults. (Cahill 1990, 396–397)

Situations of Circumstantial Inequality.   By "circumstantial inequality," I mean an inequality that is embedded in the nature of the encounter itself rather than in the structural positions of the actors. I am thinking particularly of encounters between workers and those who seek their wares, especially where the participants are—structurally speaking—equals. According to the students of occupationally based interactions, one of the principles of modern social life is that the customer gets to be "king" only if the worker has not already appropriated the crown. Who is the superior and who the inferior depends, that is, on whether or not the "worker" has managed to reinvent him/herself as a "professional" (Hughes 1958). In encounters between service workers and their customers, the customer tends to be top dog. In encounters between professionals and their clients, the positions are reversed.

Service Workers. For service workers, the interactional edge is in the hands of the superordinate customer. As Robert Rothman (1987, 169) reminds us, while customers are encouraged (e.g., by name tags) to address workers by their first names and are given leave to behave rudely, the latter are expected to use honorifics in speaking to customers and to remain calm in the face of insult. Placed in such potentially or actually demeaning interactional situations on a daily basis, many workers cope—as study after study has demonstrated—by developing typologies of troublesome customer types and inventing strategies for coping with them. Fred Davis's classic study of the cabdriver and his attempt to coax tips out of his fares provides one example that can stand for many:

> There exists among drivers an extensive typology of cab users, the attributes imputed to each type having a certain predictive value, particularly as regards tipping. Some of the more common and sharply delineated types are: The Sport . . . The Blowhard . . . The Businessman . . . The Lady Shopper . . . To protect and insure themselves against any unfavorable outcome of tipping, many drivers will . . . employ diverse tactics and stratagems . . . to increase the amount of tip or to compensate for its loss should it not be forthcoming. Certain of these are . . . Making change. . . . The hard-luck story . . . Fictitious charges . . . The "psychological" approach. . . . (Davis 1959, 162–164)

Professionals. Like the worker vis-à-vis his/her customer, professionals, too, may create client typologies, and for the same reason: to help anticipate problems and develop successful strategies for

dealing with them (Mennerick 1974, 399). There is an important difference between workers and professionals, however. The latter, by the very fact that they "are" professionals, have an edge of authority over their clients, tipping the interactional control balance in their favor. Perhaps because medical encounters provide academic researchers with rare challenges to their own "edge of authority," they have spent a fair amount of time looking at health professional-client, especially doctor-patient, interactions. And they have been especially interested in how the former manages to elicit such an extraordinary degree of face-to-face deference and compliance from the latter. Translating the niceties of academic language into everyday prose, the basic question these researchers ask is this: How is it that assured, even arrogant, people are transformed into regular "Uriah Heeps" the minute they walk into a physician's office? This is, of course, the question Talcott Parsons touched on somewhat obliquely in his famous discussion of the "sick role" (1951, 436–437), and it involves what he and many others have described as the institutional discrepancy in power between doctors and patients (e.g., F. Davis 1972, 85). What students of social interaction have been interested in not so much the preencounter definition of the situation of doctor-patient relationships, but the accomplishment and reaffirmation of that definition in the encounter itself. Two examples will have to suffice.

Barney Glaser and Anselm Strauss have shown that one method by which the power differential is accomplished and reaffirmed at the face-to-face level is information management. In their study of patient-hospital staff struggles over knowledge about impending death, Glaser and Strauss described some of the tactics staff use to keep secret from potentially or actually suspicious patients the fact of their dying:

> They will comment favorably on his daily appearance, hoping he will interpret their comments optimistically. . . . They also practice sleight of hand, like magicians, drawing the patient's attention away from a dangerous cue by focusing his atten-

tion on an innocent one.... The physician may even put on diagnostic dramas for him, sending him for irrelevant tests. (Glaser and Strauss 1965, 36)

Candace West's analysis of "talk between doctors and patients" provides examples of other methods for maintaining inequality:

Patterned asymmetries were also evident in the terms of address used by doctors and patients in this collection [of transcripts of one-on-one encounters]. In the third of exchanges containing any form of address, doctors employed familiar terms [e.g., first names] that patients did not return. Moreover, no physician was ever addressed by first name in the 532 pages of transcript. (West 1984, 143–144)

A final note: when circumstantial inequalities (e.g., between doctor and patient) combine with inequalities of a structural sort (e.g., age), we are witness to especially vivid instances of Goffman's primal scenes:

Two persons in "similar" physical condition may be differentially designated dead or not. For example, a young child was brought into the ER [emergency room] with no registering heartbeat, respirations, or pulse—the standard "signs of death" —and was, through a rather dramatic stimulation procedure involving the coordinated work of a large team of doctors and nurses, revived for a period of eleven hours. On the same evening, shortly after the child's arrival, an elderly person who presented the same physical signs, with what a doctor later stated, in conversation, to be no discernible differences from the child in skin color, warmth, etc., "arrived" in the ER and was almost simultaneously pronounced dead, with no attempts at stimulation instituted. (Sudnow 1967, 101)

Situations of Normative Inequality. In his dissection of "stigma," Goffman distinguished between three different types: abominations of the body, blemishes of individual character, and the tribal stigma of race, nation and religion (1963b, 4). Situations of structural inequality may be seen as vaguely analogous to Goffman's third type; what I here call situations of "normative inequal-

ity" are precisely analogous to his types one and two. In this last brief look at interaction and inequality, I am concerned with inequalities that arise out of widely held conceptions of ideal physical and moral states.

Persons who have looked closely at the interactions between and among normative unequals (e.g., "normals" and the "handicapped," or "normals" and "deviants") have displayed a variety of analytic concerns. For example, two of the "classic" studies—Fred Davis's "Deviance Disavowal" (1961) and Goffman's *Stigma* (1963b)—focus analytic attention on the difficult interactional situation created by the inequality and the management techniques (strategies) used to mitigate or avoid the difficulties. Other studies are concerned with such diverse matters as differences in space use demands between normals and the physically handicapped or patterns of accommodation between normals and deviants. Yet I think it is fair to say that one issue, in particular, has proven especially absorbing: the consequences for the self-conceptions or identities of normative "inferiors" of interactions with their normative "superiors."

An entire tradition in the sociology of deviance may be understood in these terms. The so-called "labeling" theory of crime causation argues that it is the action of normals vis-à-vis beginning miscreants that transforms isolated or occasional deviant acts into full-blown deviant identities—which transforms, to put it more concretely, the person who commits a crime into the career criminal (e.g., J. Lofland 1969 and the many works cited therein). Similarly, much work on persons with physical "problems" (illnesses, handicaps, deformities) has as its central theme the psychic costs of repeated demeaning encounters with normals. Writing of the daily tribulations of the chronically ill, for example, Kathy Charmaz explains the common impetus to withdraw from the "judging" eyes (empathetically imagined or directly experienced) of normals:

John Garston's uncontrollable coughing riveted attention on him in public. He said, "But it is, you know, it is embarrassing, no matter what—spitting up and all of that.... But ... I guess possibly one of the reasons why I am reclusive is that . . . it has curtailed social activities. . . ." (Charmaz 1991, 57; see also Gardner 1991).

And as a second and final example, let me point to David Snow's and Leon Anderson's dissection of encounters between the homeless (who suffer both structural and normative inequalities) and the domiciled (who are "superior" on both structural and normative grounds). Though they are writing only about the experience of the homeless, what they say echoes what many researchers tell us is the ordinary and daily experience of the normatively "inferior:"

> *[T]o be homeless in America is . . . to be confronted by gnawing questions and doubts about one's self-worth and the meaning of one's existence. Such vexing existential concerns are not just the psychic fallout of having descended into the streets, however. They are also stoked by varied and sundry encounters with the domiciled that constantly remind the homeless of where they stand in relation to others. . . . [W]herever they turn they are reminded that they are in the basement of the status system and they can fall no further. As Sonny MacCallister lamented shortly after finding himself on the streets, "The hardest thing has been getting used to the way people look down on street people. It's real hard to feel good about yourself when almost everyone you see is looking down on you." (Snow and Anderson 1993, 198, 202; see also Anderson, Snow, and Cress, 1994)*

We have been following the students of nonintimate interaction as they follow, develop, and enlarge upon the work of the field's pioneers. It is time to turn from continuities in a stream of research to work that is forging new channels altogether.

COMPLEXITIES IN THE STUDY OF NONINTIMATE SOCIALITY

Particularly since the late 1970s, researchers have begun to follow a number of threads in the pattern of social interaction that were either unacknowl-

edged or unpursued in earlier work. Three such complicating threads are the complexities of history, of emotion, and of relationship.

Complexities of History

As microsociologists and social historians focus increasing attention on everyday social life in periods other than their own, the rootedness of the study of social interaction in the eternal present has been seriously challenged, sometimes in unexpected ways. It may not be particularly surprising, for example, to learn that when Norbert Elias's 1939 exhaustive work, "The Civilizing Process," was finally published in English (1978, 1982), it moved Goffman's generalizations about embarrassment (e.g., 1967a, 1967b) out of an atemporal ether and relocated them very firmly in the late eighteenthth, nineteenth, and particularly twentieth centuries. It may be somewhat less expected to find that the appearances-oriented "persona" in Goffman's writings[12]—a construct that, according to his critics, is narrowly modern and has no validity outside the mid- to late twentieth century—was alive and well in eighteenth-century Europe (Sennett 1977b), nineteenth-century America (Halttunen 1982), and even, perhaps, sixteenth-century Germany, England, France, and Italy (Elias 1978). That is, the complexities that history brings to the study of nonintimate sociality force us to recognize not only that some patterns we have thought of as timeless are, in fact, peculiar to particular periods, but that some patterns we have thought of as particularly and peculiarly modern are not that at all. Here I describe only two of the complexities that history brings to the study of nonintimate sociality, one having to do with interactional possibilities and the other with interactional proprieties.

Interactional Possibilities. The sheer possibilities for nonintimate sociality may vary historically because the proportion of everyday life spent in public space, parochial space (defined here as the space dominated by nonintimate nonstrangers—neighbors, acquaintances, work associates, and so forth),[13] or private space varies historically. For example, city dwellers in pre-eighteenth-century Europe appear to have been out in public and parochial space far more frequently and regularly than their modern counterparts, and thus appear to have encountered strangers, casual acquaintances, and other nonintimates far more frequently and regularly than their modern counterparts. This was the case because technologies located many of what are now private activities out in public and because those same technologies dictated that most private space was cramped and uncomfortable. To get water, to dispose of wastes and garbage, to learn the news, to speak with someone not in the same house, to purchase goods, to be entertained—all these and many other activities—required that most people had to venture beyond the boundaries of their domiciles. Similarly, to find enough space to socialize with friends or to find enough air and coolness in summer and warmth in winter to be comfortable, most people had to leave home (L. Lofland 1985). In stark contrast, in many parts of the modern world, indoor plumbing, garbage collection services, home delivery of newspapers, efficient postal systems, telephones, computers, television sets, stereo systems, central heating and air conditioning, and a host of other historically recent inventions have transferred a myriad of activities from public and parochial space to private space, thus making possible a level of "privatization" in everyday life that our ancestors would have found inconceivable (Sennett 1970, 1977b).

This change in the proportion of everyday life in urban areas spent in public and parochial versus private space represents a major historical shift, but one can also point to less sweeping variations on the theme. For example, data on early industrialization in Northern Europe and North America suggest that daily toil was first lengthened and intensified, in many settings thereby reducing time available for sociality of any sort, including workplace sociality (Thompson 1963). But as the laboring day was gradually shortened, young working men and women increasingly used their leisure not to return to the intimacy of family life, but to enjoy the pleasures of sociality on the street, at the amusement park or fair, in the saloon, beer garden, or cabaret, or at the music hall or movies.[14] Or, different places may reveal different histories of spatial mixes. Thus, the historian Donald Olsen's argument in *The City as a Work of Art* (1986) that nineteenth-century London was far more "domestic" than were Vienna and Paris in the same period may be translated as saying that in the latter cities, private space represented a smaller proportion of the inhabitants' everyday life space than it did in London.

The possibility for nonintimate sociality may vary historically not simply quantitatively but qualitatively, as well. That is, possibilities may vary in kind because *social spaces* vary in kind. Social spaces may take a built form, as when specific physical settings set the stage for specific forms of social intercourse. The kind of support networks Ruth Stumpe Brent (1981) found among mostly unacquainted elderly women in public restroom lounges in "a northern midwestern city," for example, could not emerge until restroom lounges appeared, and restroom lounges did not appear until nineteenth-century European and North American bourgeois merchants, interested in attracting middle class women to consumerism, invented the department store with all its various amenities (e.g., Barth 1980; Miller 1981). As another example, the strained civil inattention found among nineteenth-century European railroad travellers (as well as many twentieth-century ones) seems particular to the railway compartment per se (which seated three or four persons on one side facing three or four persons on the other side), for it was not visible among earlier patrons of the similarly configured horse-drawn carriage:

> Whenever, in the past, one knew that one was going to pass several hours, sometimes several days, in the company of others [in a horse drawn carriage], one tried to establish a rapport with one's companions that often lasted beyond the duration of the journey. Today [1866] we no longer think about anything but the impatiently awaited and soon reached destination. The traveler one takes one's leave from may get off at the next station where he will be replaced by another. Thus reading becomes a necessity. (quoted in Schivelbusch 1979, 71)[15]

But a social space is not necessarily a physical setting; it may also take the more ephemeral form of a ritual convention. And here we are dealing with the very stuff of historical change. Two examples must stand for many. First, the peculiar sociality involved in the *charivari* (a public and collectively enacted form of community social control that involved an admixture of playful and cruel actions by means of which some perceived wrong was to be "set right"; N. Davis, 1984, 42) can occur only where this particular ritual is practiced:

> *The charivari. . . . begins with a mood of laughter and mockery and with noise that may be sustained throughout. It usually includes a procession or parade of some kind, and may involve costuming. It moves to a reckoning with victims, and, if all goes well, ends in the withdrawal of the crowd, which then turns to drinking and expansive revelry. (N. Davis 1984, 47).*

Similarly, the unique interactions embedded in the *promenade* are to be found only where the promenade exists:

> *Custom and convention in [eighteenth-century urban] England also endorsed the accessibility of the streets to all age and social groups and to both sexes. . . . Walking was . . . an agreeable form of informal entertainment in its own right. The urban promenade was the occasion for the citizens to sally forth to view the sights and each other. . . . (Corfield 1990, 133, 135)*

Interactional Proprieties. Not only the possibilities for nonintimate sociality vary historically, so do the proprieties. The normative regularities that modern students of social interaction have identified are not timeless; they are located in a specific historic period. The principles that guided some of our ancestors in the conduct of their interactions bear little resemblance to the principles that guide ours.

For example, both the understandings about who, routinely, may be expected to be where and the specifics of person-space mismatch that generate tension and anxiety are historically quite variable. In mid-seventeenth-century London, a "respect-able" woman might attend the theater at night and alone (Pipkin 1990, 168); in mid-nineteenth-century New York, she dared not (Kasson 1990, chap. 7; Ryan 1990, chap. 2). In the late nineteenth century, ordinary working-class Parisian women could routinely be found drinking in cafes (Haine 1985b); in the early twentieth century, the American saloon offered no such hospitality to the "gentler sex" (Duis 1983; Rorabaugh 1987). Contemporary middle-class people in the United States view the presence of the homeless on the streets of their cities with deep dis-ease (Anderson, Snow, and Cress, 1994; Snow and Anderson 1993); Victorian gentlemen and ladies in England viewed the "migrating classes" with an easy contempt (Samuel 1973).

Understandings about what constitutes unremarkable behavior among strangers, work associates, acquaintances, and so forth are also variable. Norbert Elias's work on the transformation of manners in Europe from the Middle Ages to the present portrays an interactional world, descriptions of which can set an entire roomful of contemporary middle-class undergraduates wriggling with embarrassment.[16] For example, Elias quotes from Erasmus's *De civilitate morum puerilium*, published in 1530 (think of Erasmus as a sixteenth-century Miss Manners):

> *Listen to the old maxim about the sound of wind. If it can be purged without a noise that is best. But it is better that it be emitted with a noise than that it be held back [because to do so is to risk illness]. . . . Those who, because they are embarrassed, do not want the explosive wind to be heard, simulate a cough. Follow the law of Chiliades: Replace farts with coughs. (Elias 1978, 130; see also Elias 1982, esp. part 2)*

But one does not have to travel so far in time and space to see the routine behavior of the natives as, at minimum, peculiar. Here is John Dollard describing the caste etiquette of "Southerntown" in 1937:

> *A white friend gave me some instructions immediately after I arrived . . . Never . . . address a Negro man or woman as "Mr." or "Mrs." and do not*

refer to them thus in talking to a white person . . . ; don't tip your hat to a Negro, man or woman, but call him or her by the first name whenever you know it. . . . Another form of personal derogation . . . is to apply the special and unfavorable designation "nigger" to them. . . . (1957, 343–345)

Less spectacular variations are no less important. Brian Harrison (1971, 1973) charted the substantial decline of both a tolerance for and, presumably, the occurrence of public drunkenness in England between 1815 and 1872; a similar story could be constructed for the United States (e.g., Monkkonen 1981). Bertram Wyatt-Brown's work on *Southern Honor* details the unspoken and arcane rules of gentlemanly behavior regarding drinking and gambling between and among strangers and acquaintances (violation of which easily eventuated in duels) in the ante- and postbellum American South (1982, chap. 13). And Carol Zisowitz Stearns and Peter N. Stearns (1986) argue persuasively that the "feeling rules" for the expression of anger in all spheres of life have become increasingly repressive over the course of American history and that, especially after about 1920, anger in the workplace was not only proscribed but quite successfully controlled.

Complexities of Emotion

Chapter 5 is entirely devoted to the recently developed sociology of affect and emotion, so here I confine myself to three observations about the complexities that a concern with emotion brings to the study of nonintimate interaction.

First, a concern with emotion adds yet another item to the interactional analyst's already extensive list of matters to take into account, whether he/she is interested in intimate interaction, nonintimate interaction, or both. Consider that even the simplest form of interaction, that between two individuals, includes, among its many ingredients: (1) the self-conceptions (rooted in the historical, cultural, and hierarchical social locations) of each actor; (2) the definitions of the immediate and larger situation and other aspects of their symbolic environments that the actors bring with them (including their understandings of the normative principles that apply

under the circumstances); (3) the invisible cast of reference groups accompanying each actor (Strauss 1959, 56); (4) the actors' respective interactional repertoires, skills, and weaknesses; and (5) the physical/social setting of the interaction itself. The sociology of emotion and affect is teaching us that this list of ingredients, however long and detailed, is not long and detailed enough. If our aim is an adequate analysis of what happens in interaction, we need also to take into account: (1) each actor's emotional repertoire, skills, and weaknesses; (2) the feeling and display rules (Hochschild 1979, 1983) that each sees as appropriate to the situation; (3) each actor's emotional orientation toward self and accompanying invisible characters and toward the other and her/his accompanying invisible characters; (4) each actor's emotional orientation toward the situation more generally; and (5) the "emotional culture" of the setting in which the interaction occurs.

Second, an appreciation for emotion's role in interaction seriously undercuts the cognitive bias of sociology (and of many sister disciplines as well).[17] That the bias is long-standing in sociology, going back to the founding fathers, is a point made forcefully by Arlie Hochschild in her first published call for a "sociology of feeling and emotion":

> *[Max Weber] posits a model of social action that is rational, while action based on emotion, like action based on ignorance or tradition, is nonrational. . . . Take his example of . . . the stock market. He treats deviations from rational behavior as something the sociologist might explain in terms of "irrational emotions" (e.g., panic). But the difference (in terms of feeling and emotion) between the normal stock market and the sudden depression in stocks is the difference between one affective state of stockbrokers and another affective state. It is highly questionable whether emotion enters into the life of stockbrokers only when there is panic, that emotion makes people act only irrationally.*
>
> *Surely emotion and sentiment are active ingredients in rational behavior as well. A normal day at the stock market, not simply during a panic, would amply show that feelings of excitement, anxiety, or glee are all part of a good (rational) day's work. (Hochschild 1975, 285)*

By undercutting sociology's long-standing cognitive bias, a concern with emotion—like a concern with history and culture—complicates our analyses because it invites us to reconsider and reevaluate what we think we already know.

Finally and briefly, note should be made of the fact that a portion of the recent work in the sociology of affect and emotion does something even more complicated (too complicated to discuss here) than adding emotion to the ingredients of the "interaction brew." A number of analysts (e.g., Collins 1990; Hammond 1990; Kemper 1978; Scheff 1990) use specific emotions or emotional states as the "linchpins" (or master variables) in altogether new theories of interaction—intimate and nonintimate.

Complexities of Relationship

Like students of emotion who have complicated (and enriched) the study of nonintimate interaction by challenging the adequacy of sociology's traditional cognitive model of human functioning, students of interpersonal connections have added complexity (and richness) to our understanding of nonintimate interaction by challenging the adequacy of sociology's traditional dyadic conception of human relationships. Since the late 1970s, increasing numbers of researchers, armed with masses of (usually ethnographic) data, have confronted the classic distinction between primary (Cooley 1962b) and secondary (Park 1925) relationships and found that distinction sadly wanting.[18] In its stead they have offered both an expanded vocabulary of relationships and a critique of the presumptively moral superiority (or "primacy") of primary relationships.

Expanding Our Relational Vocabulary. To suggest that much of the challenge to the primary/secondary distinction has occurred recently is not to say that all earlier researchers were insensitive to the analytic problems wrought by such a simple schema. Certainly, scholars who located their inquiries in pubs, taverns, bars, and other drinking settings could not avoid such problems. If the setting were mostly populated by kin or friendship groups with an independent existence, of course, the relationships could, without further ado, simply be coded as "primary." But what of those relationships with limited or no existence outside the setting? What of relationships in which persons who seemed close did not even know one another's surnames, had never been to one another's homes, were not part of one another's intimate networks? In reading some of the older tavern studies (e.g., Mass-Observation 1943; Richards 1964), one is appreciative of the honesty and detail with which the complicating data are presented—this despite, or perhaps because of, the authors' obvious difficulties in knowing what to make of them. However, in terms of contributing to an eventual challenge to the dichotomous tradition, these descriptive studies are far less important than those few pieces of work that—tentatively and hesitantly—moved beyond description and toward a new analytic language. Gregory Stone's depiction of the "personalizing consumer" who "established quasi-primary relationships with the personnel of local independent retail institutions" (1954, 42) is a splendid example, as is Fred Davis's study (1959) of the interaction between cabdrivers and their fares in which he identified the "fleeting relationship" and articulated its noninstrumental components.

More recent research efforts are not so tentative and hesitant in moving beyond description and toward a new analytic language. For example, note the assurance with which Peggy Wireman writes of the "intimate secondary relationship":

> *The term . . . at first appears to contradict itself. This seeming contradiction was a deliberate choice; the concept describes relationships that have the dimensions of warmth, rapport, and intimacy normally connected with primary relationships yet occur within a secondary setting and have some aspects of secondary relationships. The dimensions are: intense involvement, warmth, intimacy, sense of belonging, and rapport; mutual knowledge of character; minimal sharing of personal information; minimal socializing; involvement of the individual rather than the family; a commitment that is*

limited in time and scope and with a relatively low cost of withdrawal; a focus on specific rather than diffuse purposes; consideration of public rather than private matters; and a preference for public meeting places. (Wireman 1984, 2–3)

As a second example, here is my depiction of the "unpersonal/bounded relationship":

I use the term unpersonal *rather than impersonal to describe a relationship that is simultaneously characterized by social distance and by closeness. Persons in these relationships may share little, if any, intimate information about themselves. . . . At the same time, the relationship is experienced as "friendly" or "sociable"—its emotional temperature as being "warm." I use the term* bounded *to convey the restriction of the relationship to public space. . . .*

To review the literature depicting unpersonal/bounded relationships is to confront head-on the extreme over-simplification and distortion inherent in discussions of the "anonymous city" and in the classic contrasts between primary and secondary, gemeinschaft and gesellschaft. The literature tells of elderly persons who tend to congregate in, and to enjoy encounters with, the other customers of downtown restaurants (Pratt 1986). It describes short-term, highly circumscribed, but friendlike relations that emerge again and again in secondhand clothing stores (Wiseman 1979) and laundromats (Kenen 1982). It portrays an unexpected "community on wheels" that developed among riders and with the driver of a suburban commuter bus (Nash 1975). It reports the delimited closeness among airplane passengers (Greenblat and Gagnon 1983) and the similar but longer-term relations among "racetrack buddies" (Rosencrance 1986). It speaks of "cafe friends" (Haine 1985a), of "tavern sociability" (Kingsdale 1973; Thomas 1978) and of restroom lounge "support systems" (Brent 1981). (L. Lofland 1989b, 469–470)

Critiquing the "Primacy" of the Primary.

Within sociology (and in Western thought more generally), there has been more to the opposition of primary and secondary than simply a dichotomy. There has been moral evaluation as well. Primary relationships have been given "primacy"; that is,

they, and the social organizational forms they create (families, friendship groups, neighborhoods, tribes, communities) have been judged to be the *best* relationships and organizational patterns—the sine qua non, as it were, for the creation of "healthy" children and "healthy" adults (e.g., Alexander 1973, 245–246). Conversely, secondary relationships are seen not as different and equally valuable, but as lesser and inferior (though certainly useful) relational forms.[19] Even as Gregory Stone was depicting the "personalizing consumer," for example, he was gently bemoaning her need to find such a poor substitute for more meaningful (read, primary) relationships:

Without access to either formal or informal channels of social participation . . . this type of consumer established quasi-primary relationships with the personnel of local independent retail institutions. . . . The quasi-primary relationships she was forced *to develop on the market compensated for her larger social losses. . . . (1954, 42, emphasis added)*

In challenging the usefulness of the primary/secondary dichotomy, students of nonintimate sociality have attacked not only the oppositional pairing, but the assumption of the "primacy of the primary" that accompanies it.

This critique of the primacy of the primary has two forms. In the more common, the author simply argues that nonintimate relations are worthwhile —that they have value in and of themselves (see, e.g., the quotes from Wireman and L. Lofland, just above). The rarer version of the critique takes more direct aim.

Harvey Farberman and Eugene Weinstein's 1970 discussion of "personalization in lower-class consumer interaction" is an early example of the positive argument form of the critique. The regretful tone of the Stone article discussed above has been replaced by a suggestion of appreciation:

In any event, the general paucity of personalized relationships in consumer contexts increases the importance of those contexts that do support such interaction. For these, as rare as they are, might provide additional enclaves of primacy which con-

tribute to integration and legitimation. (Farberman and Weinstein 1970, 456)

Appreciation is more than "suggested" by Mark Granovetter (1973, 1982) when he argues for the strength of weak ties:

[W]eak ties, often denounced as generative of alienation (Wirth 1938) are here seen as indispensable to individuals' opportunities and to their integration into communities; strong ties, breeding local cohesion, lead to overall fragmentation. (1973, 1378; but see Gans 1974)

Many renditions of the positive argument may also be found in works that detail the beneficial functions of settings in which nonintimate relationships abound—what Ray Oldenburg has called the third place: "a generic designation for a great variety of public places that host the regular, voluntary, informal, and happily anticipated gatherings of individuals beyond the realms of home and work" (1989, 16).

As suggested, most of the critiques of the primacy of the primary are positive arguments. But there is also a small body of work that makes the challenge by addressing the issue of negatives embodied in the primary relationship. One can see a hint of this in the passage from Granovetter quoted above. It can be seen also in the work of the political scientist Glenn Tinder, who has written about community as a "tragic ideal" (1980). David Maines participates in this version of the critique when he reminds us that while "we are more likely to be mugged by a stranger than a friend . . . our friends are more likely than strangers to rape or murder or assault us" (Maines 1989, 194). However, it is Richard Sennett, probably more than any other social scientist, who has taken direct aim on the high value modern Western thought ascribes to intimate and "authentic" relationships. Beginning with *The Uses of Disorder* in 1970, Sennett put forth the argument that in the modern search for homogeneous community, in our avoidance of the painful confrontations of the city's disorder, we Americans were condemning ourselves to retarded psyches—to less than mature psychological lives. Our demands for serenity and authenticity and our locating of them in suburban privatism and intimacy were cause and consequence of our transformation into a nation of psychological adolescents. In his essay, "Destructive Gemeinschaft" the attack is even more direct: "What I want to show is that this celebration of inter-subjectivity is in fact interpersonally destructive: that is, gemeinschaft relations under the conditions of advanced industrial society are mutually destructive to those who want to be open to each other" (1977a, 172). In *The Fall of Public Man* (1977b), Sennett's thesis reaches maturation. The contemporary search for community, our dismissal of urban impersonality as cold and meaningless, our demand for continuous intimacy, are all simultaneously indicators, causes, and consequences of widespread and disabling psychological narcissism and political false consciousness: "[T]he notion of a civilized existence [is one] in which people are comfortable with a diversity of experience and indeed find nourishment in it. . . . In this sense, the absorption in intimate affairs is the mark of an uncivilized society" (1977b, 340).

CONCLUSION

To review any body of work is always, in some sense, to distort it. It is necessarily read through the mind's eye, through the prism of personal biography and private intellectual concerns. That truism aside, I think most scholars of nonintimate interaction would agree that work in the area since the early 1960s—only a portion of which is reviewed here—evinces the following characteristics: (1) an orientation toward generically sociological rather than political or immediately practical problems (e.g., the problem is the homeless as subordinates in interaction with the domiciled, not homelessness in the United States); (2) an appreciation for nuance and complexity (e.g., there are diverse types of interactions and diverse occurrences even in a single instance of one type); (3) a belief that the small, humble pieces of social life are as imbued with significance as the large (e.g., gestures, voice tones, and brief routine encounters are important data); and (4) at the same time, an increasing concern for linking microsociological and macrosociological phenomena (e.g., the system of sexual stratification is enacted and recreated during a three-second exchange between strangers). It seems fair to say that for an area of research that got such a late start, this is a remarkably "mature" and sophisticated set of features.

Where, then, should we go from here? What should be the character of our intellectual agenda? To begin with, we need more of the kinds of studies reviewed in the section on continuities. We may be approaching "theoretical saturation" (Glaser and Strauss 1967) on some topics, but it would be foolhardy to suggest a moratorium until the evidence that we have reached such saturation is irresistible. Certainly there is still much to be learned, for example, not only about the interactional enactment and recreation of systems of inequality, but about the role nonintimate sociality may play in generating and maintaining systems of equality.

The greatest intellectual payoff, however, will likely come from additional work of the sort reviewed in the section on complexities (with the important addition of one complexity I did not discuss—culture). We need to know much more about the role emotions play in nonintimate encounters. Both conventional wisdom and the research record imbue these encounters with potentials for fear and embarrassment, but surely other, more complex and/or more positive emotions are implicated as well. Similarly, we have only begun the task of conceptualizing and appreciating the diversity of relational forms that humans shape from the dough of nonintimate sociality. Generating a taxonomy of such forms should be high on our list of priorities, as should research that illuminates the various social usages (functions) to which these forms are put. But perhaps our greatest challenge is to undertake studies that will help us understand the differences historical and cultural (and subcultural) variations make in how nonintimates interact, how they feel about their interactions, and what patterns of bonding their interactions produce.

NOTES

I am enormously grateful to the colleague "intimates" who read an earlier (and much longer) version of this chapter and who offered supportive but critical commentary and advice: Kathy Charmaz, Carole Joffe, Sherryl Kleinman, and John Lofland. Thanks also to the editors and two anonymous reviewers for their careful readings, editorial suggestions, and patience in the face of intransigence. A special thanks to Ron Ruggiero for his editorial assistance.

1. I use *sociality* here rather than the more familiar *sociability* to avoid the connotations of affability, companionability, or friendliness contained in some dictionary definitions of the latter term. The primary meaning of *sociality* is simply "an instance of social intercourse," thus leaving fully open the question of whether that intercourse is pleasant, unpleasant, a mixture of both states, or emotionally neutral.

2. Space constraints necessitate a very radical restriction of both topics and citations. Even the bibliography of the first version of this chapter, which contained more than five hundred entries, covered only a small fraction of the relevant literature on even the very limited number of topics dealt with.

3. Collins (1981, part 4) provides an assessment of Goffman's impact on sociology more generally. Ditton (1980) dissects important themes in his work. Riggins (1990) is a recent collection of studies inspired—critically or otherwise—by one or another thread in Goffman's work.

4. Because of space constraints, there are three especially glaring omissions here. First, I have omitted almost all mention of the considerable literature on the relation between the built environment and nonintimate interaction. (For a small sampling of this enormously interesting body of work, see Jacobs 1961; L. Lofland, 1988, 1989a; Love, 1973; Michelson 1970, 1977; Newman 1972; Sommer 1972, 1974; W. F. Whyte 1949.) Second, I have ignored the links between research on nonintimate sociality and the highly relevant materials of "social movements and collective

behavior" (see chapter 22). The serious mining of one subfield for insights into the other is both needed and overdue. Third, I have eliminated any discussion of the important complexities that cultural variations bring to the study of nonintimate interaction (but see chapter 15).

5. For an especially insightful analysis of this type of help, see Gardner (1986a). There is some evidence that persons target their requests to strangers whom they perceive to be sufficiently "like me" to be unthreatening (Gardner 1980, 1994; Goffman 1963a, chap. 8).

6. Darley and Latané (1968) has been designated one of the "citation classics" and Latané and Darley (1970) was the winner of the 1968 Socio-Psychological Prize of the American Association for the Advancement of Science and the Century Psychology Prize. For a sample of the extensive research on nonmundane helping, see P. Davis (1991) and Lau and Blake (1976).

7. On responses to spatial invasion, see, for example, Felipe and Sommer (1966), Firestone and Altman (1978), and Jason et al. (1981). On affirming threatened identities and statuses, see Fine et al. (1984). On human territoriality more generally, see Lyman and Scott (1967).

8. Kenneth Burke (1935, 1945, 1950, 1966, 1968) is frequently identified as the "father" of dramatism or dramaturgy, although some scholars (e.g., Hare and Blumberg 1988) note that elements of the perspective may be found in the writings of early symbolic interactionists such as Cooley (1962a) and Mead (1934).

9. One of the selections in *Asylums* (1961), for example, is titled "The Underlife of a Public Institution: A Study of Ways of *Making Out* in a Mental Hospital," and the subtitle of *Stigma* (1963b) is "Notes on the *Management of Spoiled Identity.*" The title of Goffman's 1970 book is even more explicit: *Strategic Interaction.*

10. The strategy paradigm also has deep roots in the reality constructionist perspective and is linked to ethnomethodology, threads of intellectual history I shall not pursue here. On reality construction, see Berger and Luckmann (1967); on ethnomethodology, see Garfinkel (1967).

11. Later titled *Urban Life,* now *Journal of Contemporary Ethnography.*

12. The human at center stage in Goffman's writing is often said to be a poseur, an "inauthentic self," a superficial personality, concerned only with appearances.

13. For more technical definitions of private, parochial, and public space, see L. Lofland (1989b, 454–457). The use of the term *parochial* is borrowed and adapted from Hunter (1985).

14. See, for example, Bailey (1986), Erenberg (1981), Kasson (1978), Peiss (1986), Rosenzweig (1983), and Walton and Walvins (1983).

15. Georg Simmel, too, was intrigued by the changing possibilities for social intercourse brought on by changing modes of transportation in the nineteenth century: "Social life in the large city as compared to the towns shows a great preponderance of occasions to see rather than hear people. Before the appearance of omnibuses, railroads, and street cars in the nineteenth century, men were not in a situation where for periods of minutes or hours they could or must look at each other without talking to one another. Modern social life increases in ever growing degree the role of mere visual impression which always characterizes the preponderant part of all sense relationships between man and man and must place social attitudes and feelings upon an entirely changed basis" (1924, 356–361).

16. Elias's work has been criticized for its linear view of historic change and for the causal model it employs (van Krieken 1989), but to my knowledge no one has challenged its descriptive accuracy.

17. To assert a cognitive bias in sociology is not to suggest that all sociologists have been guilty of it. See, for example, Turner and Killian (1957, chap. 1). On the concern with emotion in history, see Stearns and Stearns (1985, 1988). On the same concern in anthropology, see Levy (1983), Lutz (1988), and White and Kirkpatrick (1985). Firey (1945) provides a very early reminder that emotion is as much a part of the human relationship to space as it is part of the human relationship to other humans.

18. Students of intimate relationships have had similar encounters with the primary/secondary dichotomy, and with similar results. See, for example, Helena Lopata's (1965) discussion of "the secondary features of a primary relationship."

19. To say there is a tendency toward granting primacy to the primary in sociology is not to say that all sociologists have done so. As Ralph Turner has pointed out (personal communication), "Thomas, Park and Wirth all saw the predominance of secondary group relations as an inevitable feature of modern society and viewed it positively as both liberating and enlightening. They also recognized that, like all good things, it had its darker side, and they pointed these out too. And later writers seem often to have paid attention only to that side of their work." It is to "that side of their work" and the "later writers" that modern scholars of nonintimate sociality have reacted.

REFERENCES

Alexander, Christopher. [1967] 1973. The city as a mechanism for sustaining human contact. Pp. 239–274 in *Urbanman: The Psychology of Urban Survival,* ed. John Helmer and N. A. Eddington. New York: Free Press.

Anderson, Elijah. 1990. *StreetWise: Race, Class and Change in an Urban Community.* Chicago: University of Chicago Press.

Anderson, Leon, David A. Snow, and Daniel Cress. 1994. Negotiating the public realm: Stigma management and collective action among the homeless. In *The Community of the Streets,* ed. Spencer E. Cahill and Lyn H. Lofland. Greenwich, CT: JAI Press.

Argyle, Michael, and Mark Cook. 1976. *Gaze and Mutual Gaze.* Cambridge, UK: Cambridge University Press.

Argyle, Michael, and Janet Dean. 1965. Eye contact, distance and affiliation. *Sociometry* 28:289–304.

Bailey, Peter, ed. 1986. *Music Hall: The Business of Pleasure.* Milton Keynes: Open University Press.

Barth, Gunther. 1980. *City People: The Rise of Modern City Culture in Nineteenth-Century America.* New York: Oxford University Press.

Berger, Peter L., and Thomas Luckmann. 1967. *The Social Construction of Reality.* Garden City, NY: Anchor.

Birdwhistell, Ray L. 1952. *Introduction to Kinesics.* Washington, DC: Department of State, Foreign Service Institute.

———. 1970. *Kinesics and Context.* Philadelphia: University of Pennsylvania Press.

Brent, Ruth Stumpe. 1981. Usage of public restroom lounges as support systems by elderly females. *Qualitative Sociology* 4:56–71.

Burke, Kenneth. 1935. *Permanence and Change.* New York: New Republic.

———. 1945. *A Grammar of Motives.* New York: Prentice-Hall.

———. 1950. *A Rhetoric of Motives.* New York: Prentice Hall.

———. 1966. *Language as Symbolic Action.* Berkeley: University of California Press.

———. 1968. Dramatism. Pp. 445–452 in *International Encyclopedia of the Social Sciences,* vol. 7, ed. D. L. Sills. New York: Macmillan.

Cahill, Spencer E. 1990. Childhood and public life: Reaffirming biographical divisions. *Social Problems* 37:390–402.

Cahill, Spencer E. (with William Distler, Cynthia Lachowetz, Andrea Meaney, Robyn Tarallo, and Teena Willard). 1985. Meanwhile backstage: Public bathrooms and the interaction order. *Urban Life* 14:33–58.

Cavan, Sherri. 1966. *Liquor License: An Ethnography of Bar Behavior.* Chicago: Aldine.

Charmaz, Kathy. 1991. *Good Days, Bad Days: The Self in Chronic Illness and Time.* New Brunswick, NJ: Rutgers University Press.

Collins, Randall. 1981. *Sociology since Midcentury: Essays in Theory Cumulation.* New York: Academic.

———. 1990. Stratification, emotional energy, and the transient emotions. Pp. 27–57 in *Research Agendas in the Sociology of Emotions,* ed. Theodore D. Kemper. Albany: State University of New York Press.

Cooley, Charles Horton. [1902] 1962a. *Human Nature and Social Order.* New York: Schocken Books.

———. [1909] 1962b. *Social Organization: A Study of the Larger Mind.* New York: Schocken Books.

Corfield, Penelope J. 1990. Walking the city streets: The urban odyssey in eighteenth-century England. *Journal of Urban History* 16:132–174.

Darley, John M., and Bibb Latané. 1968. Bystander intervention in emergencies: Diffusion of responsibility. *Journal of Personality and Social Psychology* 8:377–383.

Davis, Fred. 1959. The cabdriver and his fare: Facets of a fleeting relationship." *American Journal of Sociology* 65:158–165.

———. 1961. Deviance disavowal: The management of strained interaction by the visibly handicapped. *Social Problems* 9:120–132.

———. 1972. *Illness, Interaction, and the Self.* Belmont, CA: Wadsworth.

Davis, Murray S. 1983. *Smut: Erotic Reality/Obscene Ideology.* Chicago: University of Chicago Press.

Davis, Natalie Zemon. 1984. Charivari, honor, and community in seventeenth-century Lyon and Geneva. Pp. 42–57 in *Rite, Drama, Festival, Spectacle: Rehearsals Toward a Theory of Cultural Performance,* ed. John J. MacAloon. Philadelphia: Institute for the Study of Human Issues.

Davis, Phillip W. 1991. Stranger intervention into child punishment in public places. *Social Problems* 38:227–246.

Delph, Edward William. 1978. *The Silent Community: Public Homosexual Encounters.* Beverly Hills: Sage.

Ditton, Jason, ed. 1980. *The View from Goffman.* London: Macmillan.

Dogan, Mattei, and John D. Kasarda. 1988. Introduction: How giant cities will multiply and grow. Pp. 12–29 in *The Metropolis Era: The World of Giant Cities,* ed. Mattei Dogan and John D. Kasarda. Newbury Park, CA: Sage.

Dollard, John. [1937] 1957. *Caste and Class in a Southern Town,* 3rd ed. Garden City, NY: Doubleday Anchor.

Duis, Perry R. 1983. *The Saloon: Public Drinking in Chicago and Boston 1880–1920.* Urbana: University of Illinois Press.

Edgerton, Robert B. 1979. *Alone Together: Social Order on an Urban Beach.* Berkeley: University of California Press.

Elias, Norbert. [1939] 1978. *The Civilizing Process: The History of Manners.* Translated by Edmund Jephcott. New York: Pantheon.

———. [1939] 1982. *The Civilizing Process: Power and Civility.* Translated by Edmund Jephcott. New York: Pantheon.

Erenberg, Lewis A. 1981. *Steppin' Out: New York Nightlife and the Transformation of American Culture 1890–1930.* Westport, CT: Greenwood.

Farberman, Harvey A., and Eugene A. Weinstein. 1970. Personalization in lower class consumer interaction. *Social Problems* 17:449–457.

Feagin, Joe R. 1991. The continuing significance of race: Antiblack discrimination in public places. *American Sociological Review* 56:101–116.

Felipe, Nancy Jo, and Robert Sommer. 1966. Invasions of personal space. *Social Problems* 14:206–214.

Fine, Gary Alan, Jeffrey L. Stitt, and Michael Finch. 1984. Couple tie-signs and interpersonal threat: A field experiment. *Social Psychology Quarterly* 47:282–286.

Firestone, Ira J., and Irwin Altman. 1978. Interaction territory in public places: Studies of active and passive defense. Pp. 98–108 in *New Directions in Environmental Design Research,* ed. Walter E. Rogers and William H. Itelson. Washington, DC: Environmental Design Research Association.

Firey, Walter. 1945. Sentiment and symbolism as ecological variables. *American Sociological Review* 10:140–148.

Gans, Herbert. 1974. Gans on Granovetter's "Strength of weak ties." *American Journal of Sociology* 80:524–531.

Gardner, Carol Brooks. 1980. Passing by: Street remarks, address rights, and the urban female. *Sociological Inquiry* 50:328–356.

———. 1986a. Public aid. *Urban Life* 15:37–69.

———. 1986b. With child: Opportunities for speech and interaction in public for women accompanied by children." Unpublished manuscript. Indianapolis: Indiana University.

———. 1988. Access information: Public lies and private peril. *Social Problems* 35:384–397.

———. 1989. Analyzing gender in public places: Rethinking Goffman's vision of everyday life. *The American Sociologist* 20:42–56.

———. 1991. Stigma and the public self: Notes on communication, self, and others." *Journal of Contemporary Ethnography* 20:251–262.

———. 1994. A family among strangers: Kinship claims among gay men in public places. In *The Community of the Streets,* ed. Spencer E. Cahill and Lyn H. Lofland. Greenwich, CT: JAI Press.

Garfinkel, Harold. 1964. Studies of the routine grounds of everyday activities. *Social Problems* 11:225–250.

———. 1967. *Studies in Ethnomethodology.* Englewood Cliffs, NJ: Prentice Hall.

Glaser, Barney G., and Anselm L. Strauss. 1965. *Awareness of Dying.* Chicago: Aldine.

———. 1967. *The Discovery of Grounded Theory.* Chicago: Aldine.

Goffman, Erving. 1959. *The Presentation of Self in Everyday Life.* Garden City, NY: Anchor.

———. 1961. *Asylums: Essays on the Social Situation of Mental Patients and Other Inmates.* Garden City, NY: Anchor.

———. 1963a. *Behavior in Public Places: Notes on the Social Organization of Gatherings.* New York: Free Press.

———. 1963b. *Stigma: Notes on the Management of Spoiled Identity.* Englewood Cliffs, NJ: Prentice Hall.

———. [1956] 1967a. Embarrassment and social organization. Pp. 97–112 in *Interaction Ritual: Essays on Face-to-Face Behavior.* Garden City, NY: Anchor.

———. [1955] 1967b. On face-work. Pp. 5–45 in *Interaction Ritual: Essays on Face-to-Face Behavior.* Garden City, NY: Anchor.

———. 1970. *Strategic Interaction.* Oxford, UK: Blackwell.

———. 1971. *Relations in Public: Microstudies of the Public Order.* New York: Harper.

———. 1976. *Gender Advertisements.* London: Macmillan.

———. 1977. The arrangement between the sexes. *Theory and Society* 4:301–331.

———. 1983. The interaction order. *American Sociological Review* 48:1–17.

Granovetter, Mark S. 1973. The strength of weak ties. *American Journal of Sociology* 78:1360–1380.

———. 1982. The strength of weak ties: A network theory revisited. Pp. 105–130 in *Social Structure and Network Analysis,* ed. Peter Marsden and Nan Lin. Beverly Hills: Sage.

Greenblat, Cathy Stein, and John H. Gagnon. 1983. Temporary strangers: Travel and tourism from a sociological perspective. *Sociological Perspectives* 26:89–110.

Haine, W. Scott. 1985a. "Cafe Friend": Friendship and fraternity in Parisian working class cafes 1860–1890. Unpublished manuscript. Washington, DC: American University.

———. 1985b. Neither virtue nor promiscuity: The comportment of working-class women in drinking establishments. Unpublished manuscript. American University, Washington, DC.

Hall, Edward T. 1959. *The Silent Language.* Greenwich, CT: Fawcett.

———. 1966. *The Hidden Dimension.* New York: Doubleday.

Halttunen, Karen. 1982. *Confidence Men and Painted Women: A Study of Middle-Class Culture in America, 1830–1870.* New Haven: Yale University Press.

Hammond, Michael. 1990. Affective maximization: A new macro-theory in the sociology of emotions. Pp. 58–81 in *Research Agendas in the Sociology of Emotions,* ed. Theodore D. Kemper. Albany: State University of New York Press.

Hare, A. Paul, and Herbert H. Blumberg. 1988. *Dramaturgical Analysis of Social Interaction.* New York: Praeger.

Harrison, Brian. 1971. *Drink and the Victorians: The Temperance Question in England 1815–1872.* London: Faber & Faber.

———. 1973. Pubs. Pp. 161–190 in *The Victorian City: Images and Realities,* vol. 1, ed. H. J. Dyos and Michael Wolff. London: Routledge & Kegan Paul.

Henderson, Margaret. 1975. Acquiring privacy in public. *Urban Life and Culture* 3:54–78.

Hochschild, Arlie Russell. 1975. The sociology of feeling and emotion: Selected possibilities. Pp. 280–

307 in *Another Voice: Feminist Perspectives on Social Life and Social Science,* ed. Marcia Millman and Rosabeth Moss Kanter. Garden City, NY: Anchor.

———. 1979. Emotion work, feeling rules, and social structure. *American Journal of Sociology* 85:551–575.

———. 1983. *The Managed Heart: Commercialization of Human Feeling.* Berkeley: University of California Press.

Hughes, Everett C. 1958. *Men and Their Work.* Glencoe, IL: Free Press.

Humphreys, Laud. 1970. *Tearoom Trade: Impersonal Sex in Public Places.* Chicago: Aldine.

Hunter, Albert. 1985. Private, parochial and public social orders: The problem of crime and incivility in urban communities. Pp. 230–242 in *The Challenge of Social Control: Citizenship and Institution Building in Modern Society,* ed. Gerald D. Suttles and Mayer N. Zald. Norwood, NJ: Ablex.

Jacobs, Jane. 1961. *The Death and Life of Great American Cities.* New York: Vintage Books.

Jason, Leonard A., Arnold Reichler, and Walter Rucker. 1981. Territorial behavior on beaches. *The Journal of Social Psychology* 114:43–50.

Karp, David A. 1973. Hiding in pornographic bookstores: A reconsideration of the nature of urban anonymity. *Urban Life and Culture* 1:427–451.

Karp, David A., Gregory P. Stone, and William C. Yoels. 1991. *Being Urban: A Sociology of City Life,* 2nd ed. New York: Praeger.

Kasson, John F. 1978. *Amusing the Million: Coney Island at the Turn of the Century.* New York: Hill & Wang.

———. 1990. *Rudeness and Civility: Manners in Nineteenth-Century Urban America.* New York: Hill & Wang.

Kemper, Theodore D. 1978. *A Social Interactional Theory of Emotions.* New York: Wiley.

Kenen, Regina. 1982. Soapsuds, space, and sociability: A participant observation study of the laundromat. *Urban Life* 11:163–184.

Kingsdale, J. M. 1973. The "Poor man's club": Social functions of the urban workingclass saloon. *American Quarterly* 25:472–489.

Latané, Bibb, and John M. Darley. 1970. *The Unresponsive Bystander: Why Doesn't He Help?* New York: Appleton-Century-Crofts.

———. [1969] 1973. Bystander "Apathy." Pp. 62–91 in *Urbanman:The Psychology of Urban Survival,* ed.

John Helmer and Neil A. Eddington. New York: Free Press.

Lau, S. and B. F. Blake. 1976. Recent research on helping behavior: An overview and bibliography. *Catalogue of Selected Documents in Psychology* 6:69.

Levine, Janey, Ann Vinson, and Deborah Wood. 1973. Subway behavior. Pp. 208–216 in *People in Places: The Sociology of the Familiar,* ed. Arnold Birenbaum and Edward Sagarin. New York: Praeger.

Levy, Robert I., ed. 1983. *Self and Emotion.* Special issue of *Ethos,* vol 11.

Lofland, John F. 1966. *Doomsday Cult: A Study of Conversion, Proselytication, and Maintenance of Faith.* Englewood Cliffs, NJ: Prentice Hall.

———. 1969. *Deviance and Identity.* Englewood Cliffs, NJ: Prentice Hall.

———. 1976. *Doing Social Life: The Qualitative Study of Human Interaction in Everyday Life.* New York: Wiley.

———. 1978. Introduction: The qualitative strategy approach to interaction in everyday life. Pp. 5–15 in *Interaction in Everyday Life: Social Strategies,* ed. John F. Lofland. Beverly Hills: Sage.

Lofland, John F., and Lyn H. Lofland. 1984. *Analyzing Social Settings: A Guide to Qualitative Observation and Analysis,* 2nd ed. Belmont, CA: Wadsworth.

Lofland, Lyn H. [1973] 1985. *A World of Strangers: Order and Action in Urban Public Space.* Prospect Heights, IL: Waveland.

———. 1988. Communication and construction: The built environment as message and medium. Pp. 307–322 in *Communication and Social Structure,* ed. David R. Maines and Carl J. Couch. Springfield, IL: Charles C. Thomas.

———. 1989a. The morality of urban public life: The emergence and continuation of a debate. *Places: A Quarterly Journal of Environmental Design* 6:18–23.

———. 1989b. Social life in the public realm: A review. *Journal of Contemporary Ethnography* 17:453–482.

Lopata, Helena Znaniecki. 1965. The secondary features of a primary relationship. *Human Organization* 24:116–123.

Love, Ruth Leeds. 1973. The fountains of urban life. *Urban Life and Culture* 2:161–209.

Lutz, Catherine A. 1988. *Unnatural Emotions: Everyday Sentiments on a Micronesian Atoll and Their Challenge to Western Theory.* Chicago: University of Chicago Press.

Lyman, Stanford M., and Marvin B. Scott. 1967. Territoriality: A neglected sociological dimension. *Social Problems* 15:236–249.

Maines, David R. 1989. Further dialectics: Strangers, friends, and historical transformations. *Communications Yearbook* 12:190–192.

Mass-Observation. 1943. *The Pub and the People: A Worktown Study.* London: VictorGollancz.

Mead, George Herbert. 1934. *Mind, Self, and Society.* Chicago: University of Chicago Press.

Mennerick, Lewis A. 1974. Client typologies: A method of coping with conflict in the service worker-client relationship. *Sociology of Work and Occupations* 1:396–418.

Michelson, William. 1970. *Man and His Urban Environment: A Sociological Approach.* Reading, MA: Addison-Wesley.

———. 1977. *Environmental Choice, Human Behavior, and Residential Satisfaction.* New York: Oxford University Press.

Milgram, Stanley. [1970] 1973. The experience of living in cities. Pp. 1–22 in *Urbanman: The Psychology of Urban Survival,* ed. John Helmer and Neil A. Eddington. New York: Free Press.

Miller, Michael B. 1981. *The Bon Marche: Bourgeois Culture and the Department Store, 1869–1920.* Princeton: Princeton University Press.

Monkkonen, Eric H. 1981. A disorderly people? Urban order in the nineteenth and twentieth centuries. *The Journal of American History* 68:539–559.

Nash, Jeff. 1975. Bus riding: Community on wheels. *Urban Life* 4:99–124.

———. 1981. Relations in frozen places: Observations on winter public order. *Qualitative Sociology* 4:229–243.

Newman, Oscar. 1972. *Defensible Space: Crime Prevention Through Urban Design.* New York: Macmillan.

Oldenburg, Ray. 1989. *The Great Good Place: Cafes, Coffee Shops, Community Centers, Beauty Parlors, General Stores, Bars, Hangouts and How They Get You Through the Day.* New York: Paragon House.

Olsen, Donald J. 1986. *The City As a Work of Art: London, Paris, Vienna.* New Haven: Yale University Press.

Park, Robert E. 1925. The city: Suggestions for the investigation of human behavior in the urban environment. Pp. 1–46 in *The City,* ed. Robert E. Park, Ernest W. Burgess, and Roderick D. McKenzie. Chicago: University of Chicago Press.

Parsons, Talcott. 1951. *The Social System.* Glencoe, IL: Free Press.

Peiss, Kathy. 1986. *Cheap Amusements: Working Women and Leisure in Turn-of-the-Century New York.* Philadelphia: Temple University Press.

Pipkin, John S. 1990. Space and the social order in Pepys' diary. *Urban Geography* 11:153–175.

Pratt, Lois V. 1986. Social integration of age groups in public settings. Unpublished manuscript. Jersey City, NJ: Jersey City State College.

Richards, C. E. 1964. City taverns. *Human Organization* 22:260–268.

Riggins, Stephen Harold, ed. 1990. *Beyond Goffman: Studies on Communication, Institution, and Social Interaction.* Berlin and New York: Mouton de Gruyter.

Robins, Douglas M., Clinton R. Sanders, and Spencer E. Cahill. 1991. Dogs and their people: Pet-facilitated interaction in a public setting. *Journal of Contemporary Ethnography* 20:3–25.

Rorabaugh, W. J. 1987. Beer, lemonade, and propriety in the gilded age. Pp. 24–46 in *Dining in America 1850–1900,* ed. Kathryn Grover. Amherst: University of Massachusetts Press and Rochester, NY: The Margaret Woodbury Strong Museum.

Rosencrance, John. 1986. Racetrack buddy relations: Compartmentalized and satisfying. *Journal of Social and Personal Relationships* 3:441–456.

Rosenzweig, Roy. 1983. *Eight Hours for What We Will: Workers and Leisure in an Industrial City, 1870–1920.* New York: Cambridge University Press.

Rothman, Robert. 1987. Direct-service work and housework. Chap. 7. *Working: Sociological Perspectives.* Englewood Cliffs, NJ: Prentice Hall.

Ryan, Mary. 1990. *Women in Public: Between Banners and Ballots, 1825–1880.* Baltimore: Johns Hopkins University Press.

Samuel, Raphael. 1973. Comers and goers. Pp. 123–160 in *The Victorian City: Images and Realities,* vol. 1. London: Routledge & Kegan Paul.

Scheff, Thomas J. 1990. *Microsociology: Discourse, Emotion, and Social Structure.* Chicago: University of Chicago Press.

Schivelbusch, Wolfgang. 1979. *The Railway Journey: Trains and Travel in the 19th Century.* Translated by Anselm Hollo. New York: Urizen Books.

Seamon, David. 1979. *A Geography of the Lifeworld: Movement, Rest and Encounter.* New York: St. Martin's Press.

Sennett, Richard. 1970. *The Uses of Disorder: Personal Identity and City Life.* New York: Vintage Books.

———. 1977a. Destructive Gemeinschaft. Pp. 169–197 in *Beyond the Crisis,* ed. Norman Birnbaum. New York: Oxford University Press.

———. 1977b. *The Fall of Public Man.* New York: Alfred A. Knopf.

Simmel, Georg. 1924. Sociology of the senses: Visual interaction. Pp. 356–361 in *Introduction to the Science of Sociology,* ed. Robert E. Park and Ernest W. Burgess. Chicago: University of Chicago Press.

———. [1902–03] 1950. The metropolis and mental life. Pp. 409–424 in *The Sociology of Georg Simmel,* ed. Kurt H. Wolff. Glencoe, IL: Free Press.

Snow, David A., and Leon Anderson. 1993. *Down on Their Luck: A Case Study of Homeless People.* Berkeley: University of California Press.

Snow, David A., Cherylon Robinson, and Patricia McCall. 1991. "Cooling out" men in singles bars and nightclubs: Observations on survival strategies of women in public places. *Journal of Contemporary Ethnography* 19:423–449.

Sommer, Robert. 1969. *Personal Space.* Englewood Cliffs, NJ: Prentice Hall.

———. 1972. *Design Awareness.* San Francisco: Rinehart.

———. 1974. *Tight Spaces: Hard Architecture and How to Humanize It.* Englewood Cliffs, NJ: Prentice Hall.

Spykman, Nicholas J. 1926. A social philosophy of the city. Pp. 55–64 in *The Urban Community: Selected Papers from the Proceedings of the American Sociological Society, 1925,* ed. Ernest W. Burgess. Chicago: University of Chicago Press.

Stearns, Carol Zisowitz and Peter N. Stearns. 1985. Emotionology: Clarifying the history of emotions and emotional standards. *The American Historical Review* 90:813–836.

———. 1986. *Anger: The Struggle for Emotional Control in America's History.* Chicago: University of Chicago Press.

———. eds. 1988. *Emotion and Social Change: Toward a New Psychohistory.* New York: Holmes & Meier.

Stone, Gregory P. 1954. City shoppers and urban identification: Observations on the social psychology of city life. *American Journal of Sociology* 60:36–45.

Strauss, Anselm. 1959. *Mirrors and Masks: The Search for Identity.* Glencoe, IL: Free Press.

Sudnow, David. 1967. *Passing On: The Social Organization of Dying.* Englewood Cliffs, NJ: Prentice Hall.

———. ed. 1972. *Studies in Social Interaction.* New York: Free Press.

Thomas, A. E. 1978. Class and sociability among urban workers: A study of the bar as a social club. *Medical Anthropology* 2:9–30.

Thompson, E. P. 1963. *The Making of the English Working Class.* New York: Pantheon.

Tinder, Glenn. 1980. *Community: Reflections on a Tragic Ideal.* Baton Rouge: Louisiana State University Press.

Turner, Ralph, and Lewis Killian. 1957. *Collective Behavior.* Englewood Cliffs, NJ: Prentice Hall.

van Krieken, Robert. 1989. Violence, self-discipline and modernity: Beyond the "civilizing process." *The Sociological Review* 37:193–218.

Walton, John K., and James Walvin, eds. 1983. *Leisure in Great Britain, 1780–1939.* Manchester: Manchester University Press.

West, Candace. 1984. *Routine Complications: Troubles with Talk Between Doctors and Patients.* Bloomington: Indiana University Press.

White, Geoffrey M., and John Kirkpatrick, eds. 1985. *Person, Self, and Experience: Exploring Pacific Ethnopsychologies.* Berkeley: University of California Press.

Whyte, William Foote. 1949. The social structure of the restaurant. *American Journal of Sociology* 54:302–310.

Whyte, William H. 1980. *The Social Life of Small Urban Spaces.* Washington, DC: The Conservation Foundation.

———. 1988. *City: Rediscovering the Center.* New York: Doubleday.

Wireman, Peggy, 1984. *Urban Neighborhoods, Networks, and Families.* Lexington, MA: Lexington Books.

Wirth, Louis. 1938. Urbanism as a way of life. *American Journal of Sociology* 44:1–24.

Wiseman, Jacqueline P. 1979 Close encounters of the quasi-primary kind: Sociability in urban second-hand clothing stores. *Urban Life* 8: 23–51.

Wolff, Kurt, ed. and trans. 1950. *The Sociology of Georg Simmel.* Glencoe, IL: Free Press.

Wolff, Michael. 1973. Notes on the behavior of pedestrians. Pp. 35–48 in *People in Places: The Sociology of the Familiar,* ed. Arnold Birenbaum and Edward Sagarin. New York: Praeger.

Wyatt-Brown, Bertram. 1982. *Southern Honor: Ethics and Behavior in the Old South.* New York: Oxford University Press.

PART II

Social Relationships and Group Processes

KAREN S. COOK

INTRODUCTION: SOCIAL INTERACTION AND SOCIAL STRUCTURE

Part II focuses on the social processes that occur when individuals interact in groups and networks. Actors in groups and networks cooperate, compete, form coalitions, solve problems, make decisions, work together, allocate rewards and resources, distribute punishment, exercise power, display status, engage in influence tactics and bargaining strategies, win, lose, and even determine what is just and what is not. All of these processes have at various times engaged the minds and sometimes the hearts of social psychologists, especially those trained in the sociological tradition.

Small groups are a "basic unit in the larger organization of society. As such they represent a crucial link between individuals and society" (Ridgeway 1983, 20). Families, teams, work groups, friendship circles, clubs, advisory groups, executive committees, salary review boards, juries, ethics committees, and the president's cabinet represent significant arenas in which the work of society is carried out. Another crucial link between individuals and society is the networks formed by various social relationships (e.g., friendship ties, family ties, professional associations). These networks not only link individuals to one another, but also link groups, organizations, and other subunits of society to each other.

On foundations laid by Simmel, Lewin, Parsons, Bales, Homans, Blau, Goffman, and many others, what were once called "small groups" researchers in sociology have expanded the domain of their intellectual inquiry to embrace social behavior, social interaction, and social structure more broadly construed. The research arena has been expanded to include larger groups, networks of actors, collective actors (e.g., corporate groups), and a more complete treatment of the links between group-level processes and the larger social context.

The Rosenberg and Turner volume included four chapters on group processes: small groups (by Kurt Back), expectation states and interpersonal behavior (by Barbara Meeker), attraction in interpersonal relations (by Carl Backman), and social exchange theory (by Richard Emerson). There were also related chapters on reference groups (by Eleanor Singer) and on role theory (by Jerold Heiss). The theoretical and empirical growth in this general field of inquiry is evidenced by an increase in the number of chapters in this volume devoted to topics that earlier would have fallen under the rubric of "small groups."

Two of the original chapters have been rewritten and expanded in this volume: chapter 8 by Molm and Cook on exchange theory and chapter 11 by Ridgeway and Walker on status and legitimacy. There is theoretical continuity with the past but increased diversity in the range of topics covered, as well as greater integration of theoretical perspectives across the four parts of this volume. For example, there is no chapter on reference groups in the current volume, but reference group notions are now embedded in many chapters, such as those on exchange theory, justice, status structures, and the self. Similarly, role concepts are included in many chapters, particularly in parts I and III.

OVERVIEW

Part II builds on the concepts introduced in part I: self and identity, cognition, attitudes, emotion, and interaction. The social relation is viewed as the primary unit of analysis in these chapters and the foundation of larger social structures. A focus on the individual is replaced by a focus on the social processes and structures generated by social interdependence.

Topics covered in part II have traditionally fallen under the rubric of "small groups" research primarily because many of the processes discussed here have been investigated in the context of small groups. The two chapters on status and justice, for example, focus on topics that have been explored extensively in small groups. How does hierarchy emerge among members of small, task-oriented groups, and how does this status hierarchy determine the exercise of power and influence in such groups? What conceptions of distributive justice are held by individuals, and how do these fairness beliefs affect behavior in group and organizational settings? All of the chapters here, however, move beyond the group level of analysis in their treatment of fairly generic social processes—exchange, power, status differentiation, influence, bargaining, decision making, problem solving, and collective action.

Macrolevel processes often link directly to microlevel processes. Understanding the existence of systems of stratification at the macrolevel in all societies, for example, requires knowledge of how these systems are reproduced and maintained in face-to-face and small group settings and how the larger stratification system affects interaction in groups. Ridgeway and Walker (chapter 11) explore how status structures emerge and are legitimated. The legitimation of status structures (or systems of inequality) gives them a normative quality, and "what is" becomes "what ought to be" (cf. Homans 1961). This legitimation, whether produced by individual beliefs in the desirability or acceptability of the social order (i.e., through internalized rules and norms) or by external authority (validated by the group or collective body), grants normative authority to the existing systems of inequality and the rules and norms that support them.

An important aspect of legitimation of the social order is the extent to which the stratification system is viewed as just or fair. Chapter 10, by Hegtvedt and Markovsky, takes on this central issue. Basic conceptions of distributive justice are presented. Three fundamental principles of just distribution are equality, equity, and need. Allocations based on each of these principles are viewed as fair under different circumstances. Need, for example, is more likely to be viewed as fair as a distribution principle in families or close-knit communities of friends and allies, where longevity and quality of personal relationships are paramount. Equity (i.e., to each according to his/her contributions) is more likely to emerge as a just principle of distribution in settings in which productivity is of prime importance, such as in places of work and sometimes schools (Deutsch 1986). Equality as a justice principle is perhaps the oldest and is often associated with citizenship rights and the allocation of benefits and burdens in many communal associations. The research on these principles is reviewed in chapter 10.

Besides judging the fairness of the actual distribution of rewards, rights, and privileges, members of society also judge the fairness of the procedures by which these allocations are made. This issue of procedural justice is the focus of current research in social psychology (e.g., Lind and Tyler 1990) and legal studies. Hegtvedt and Markovsky review some of this research, as do Hamilton and Rauma (chapter 20).

Molm and Cook (chapter 8) review one of the major theoretical traditions in social psychology, social exchange theory, derived from the work of sociologists Homans, Blau, and Emerson and related to work in both psychology (e.g., Thibaut and Kelley) and microeconomics. As Turner and Rosenberg (1981) noted in their introduction, sociologists have been major contributors to this theoretical tradition. Along with symbolic interactionism, exchange theory is arguably one of the most significant contributions from sociological social psychology since the 1960s.

Exchange arguments are found in the chapters on bargaining (chapter 9), status (chapter 11), justice (chapter 10), group decision making (chapter 13), and social dilemmas (chapter 12). Such arguments often underlie analyses of the social interdependencies found in different forms of social interaction: cooperation, conflict, direct exchange, or simple coordination of action to achieve joint purposes. A fundamental truth is revealed in this analysis: interaction generates social structure (and social change), even as it is conditioned by existing social structures. As Homans made clear, the institutions of interest to macroanalysts are not divorced from the underlying social interactions that create, maintain, alter, and even subvert them. Exchange theory in sociology, however, gives less play to cultural forces, which are treated in more depth in part III. Cultural factors are viewed within the exchange framework as determinants of values and preferences and thus as the source of "meaning" for the actors involved (both individual and collective) and the source of the various "rules" of exchange.

Power is a key sociological concept, and the dominant view of social power in sociology is now primarily relational, based on Emerson's (1962) early discussions of power-dependence relations. In this view power is based on one actor's dependence on another for things (or services) of value to him/her. It is this dependence (or interdependence) that grants power to another, whether the other be another individual, an organization, or the state. Related to the emphasis on power in the chapter on exchange is the notion that exchange relations are embedded in social structures, within groups or networks, and cannot be analyzed meaningfully apart from this context. The earliest work in this tradition was criticized for being too focused on the isolated dyad, or "restricted" exchange (Ekeh 1974). The focus on social structure, most evident in the work of Blau and Emerson, has tended to fuse the interests of the early theorists with the more structural work coming out of the anthropological tradition.

Many of the social processes analyzed in these chapters, such as bargaining and social exchange, occur at various levels in society. The actors involved may be individuals, groups, or entities such as corporations and nation states acting through agents. The context for these forms of interaction thus extends well beyond the "small group." Lawler and Ford, in chapter 9, examine several types of bargaining (e.g., distributive versus integrative, explicit versus tacit) and the conditions under which these types of bargaining are most likely to occur. They review the structural factors that produce conflicts and the strategic implications for the actors involved, providing a comprehensive overview of the social psychology of conflict resolution, a topic central to the sociological analysis of the maintenance of social order. Bargaining is a pervasive form of social interaction engaged in by actors who face a potential or real conflict. Friends, lovers, coworkers, employers and employees, heads of state, and even nations engage in bargaining to achieve collective ends and to avoid conflict.

Negotiation and conflict resolution take different forms, depending on the structure of the bargaining situation and the nature of the actors' incentives to achieve mutual accommodation. Research suggests that the degree to which explicit communication between actors is allowed is important because it opens the door for a wider range of tactical actions, including joint decision making. Another important determinant of the outcomes in bargaining contexts is whether the situation includes much room for common gain (i.e., an integrative setting) or is a strictly win-lose (i.e., distributive bargaining), or "zero-sum," situation. The potential for conflict is higher when there is little room for joint gain.

Yamagishi's chapter on social dilemmas (chapter 12) addresses the fundamental question of what leads individuals to contribute to the larger collective social welfare when each would profit more, at least in the short run, by not contributing. This topic is gaining attention across the social sciences in the face of scarce societal resources, complex collective action problems, and increasing social, economic, and political interdependence (e.g., overuse of nonrenewable resources, pollution, increasing public debt, and general provision of public goods).

Social dilemmas are created by the lack of correspondence between self-interest and the collective interest of a group or community. Such dilemmas are at the heart of long-standing sociological concerns with social order, norms, and sanctioning systems. Social disorganization and the breakdown of community in urban areas, for example, make it more likely that individuals will pursue self-interest at the expense of the collective welfare, akin to the overgrazing of the commons immortalized in the work of Garrett Hardin (1968). Research by social psychologists in psychology and sociology investigates the possible solutions to such dilemmas (e.g., maximization of joint gain, minimization of free riding, resolution of conflict, and enhancement of mutual cooperation).

"Group decision making is a commonplace, everyday phenomenon," as Michener and Wasserman note in chapter 13. From juries to board rooms, important decisions are made in group settings. Not only status and authority affect group decision making (as indicated in chapter 11, by Ridgeway and Walker), so do group composition, the level of group consensus and loyalty, the decision rules used, and the way in which the decisions are framed. The chapter on groups and decisions reviews some of the key concepts, theories, and empirical results on these topics.

Group decision making can be superior in many respects to individual decision making, especially when the discussion leads to broader consideration of the possible alternative courses of action, potential negative as well as positive consequences, and a more thorough treatment of all aspects of a problem. However, groups can produce ill-considered decisions with potentially disastrous consequences if the group process is tainted by those conditions leading to what Janis and colleagues termed *groupthink* (e.g., high cohesion, ideological homogeneity, biased leadership, insulation of the group, and lack of formal decision-making rules). The decision to invade Cuba at the Bay of Pigs and the Watergate coverup are two well-known examples of groupthink in recent political history. Research findings reviewed in chapter 13 suggest ways that groups can mitigate against groupthink. Other important topics reviewed in this chapter include how groups tend to polarize individual opinions, how different decision rules affect the formation of group consensus, and the conditions under which minority opinions influence the majority.

The final chapter in part II reviews the place of gender in the field of social psychology. It could fit into any of the major sections of the volume; we placed it here because Wiley emphasizes the influence of the recent group processes work on current research trends in the study of gender in sociological social psychology.

Wiley distinguishes sex (biologically determined) from sex category (socially assigned) and gender (socially constructed). She describes the evolution of research and theory about gender in social psychology. On the wane are simplistic socialization, sex role, and functionalist explanations of gender differences. On the rise is an emphasis on situational and structural factors. The latter trend has been stimulated by the work on status, legitimacy, power, and stratification-based (as well as cultural) determinants of gender differences. Wiley also describes the related theoretical developments and debates surrounding the "social construction" of gender growing out of the work on the self, language, emotion, attribution, social cognition, and social interaction reported in part I. This chapter clearly reveals the utility of the perspectives presented throughout this volume for analyzing complex topics such as the gendered self and patterns of social interaction and their social structural consequences. Wiley concludes with a brief commentary on the research on gender role attitudes, the link between the structure of work and gender, and the current research on stress and gender, all topics that fall within the domain of social structure and personality, the third face of social psychology.

INTEGRATING THEMES

The threads that link the chapters in part II are many. Social interdependence is the key concept. It derives from the structure of actors' interests, which are determined in part by their positions in the social structure (and system of stratification) and cultural factors. Social interdependence fosters the development of social relations in the form of social networks (linked sets of social relations) and corporate groups or collectivities (e.g., social associations based on kinship and other types of social and economic ties). Within these groups and networks actors engage in exchange, negotiate, bargain, and act strategically to influence others, and pursue their interactional goals. In groups actors become differentiated as a result of status and power dynamics, are part of the majority or a minority, exercise influence, make decisions, and solve problems to accomplish individual and collective purposes. Under some conditions conflict erupts, groupthink occurs, or individuals pursue their independent self-interests and the collectivity suffers as a result. However, under the best of conditions groups make problem solving more efficient, produce superior decisions, distribute resources equitably, and provide for the public good. Based on significant theoretical advances in sociological social psychology, the chapters in this volume have far-reaching theoretical as well as practical consequences. This progress is primarily the result of fruitful programmatic research efforts over the past two decades. Especially notable are the theoretical and empirical advances since the earlier volume was published.

Besides interdependence, another integrative theme that emerges in part II that leads nicely into the chapters which follow is the focus on the micro-macro link or the microfoundations of social structure. Each chapter indicates how the various social processes under consideration tie to macrolevel processes and structures. Recent emphasis on the micro-macro link in sociology (e.g., Alexander et al. 1987) draws attention to the kind of theoretical and empirical work presented here (and in following chapters). How do the macrolevel structures and institutions in society condition interactive processes? How does social interaction at the microlevel form the basis for larger social structures and institutions? How does it constrain, enforce, modify, and support macrolevel structures? Questions like these have come to the forefront in sociology and provide the impetus for rethinking the nature of the contributions of an explicitly sociological social psychology to the social sciences. Part III pursues this set of issues even further.

The distinction between microsociology and social psychology introduced in part I gets blurred in part III because microsociological and social psychological perspectives are integrated in many of the chapters. For example, in the chapter on social exchange there is both an explicit social psychology of the actor and a microsociological conception of social structure that is independent of the "psychology of the actor" involved; in fact, the actor can be conceived as a collective or corporate actor in the theory. Part II sets the stage for the discussions in part III of the effects of social structure on personality. Such effects do not occur in a vacuum. They are usually mediated by interpersonal processes in group and organizational settings. Part II begins to unpack some of the interpersonal processes that generate and perpetuate inequalities at the macrolevel which are embedded in social interaction as well as social structure (see chapter 18). For example, differential access to health services (see chapter 21) is related to social stratification (especially that which is class-, race-, and gender-based), but it is also intimately related to the social dynamics of patient-provider relations. The chapters on exchange processes, status structures, and distributive justice are thus relevant to understanding problems of access to health care.

Integration across the three "faces" of social psychology has been advanced by the explicit efforts of sociological social psychologists to address micro-macro linkages and to develop general theories that explicitly apply across levels of analysis. This integrative mode is evident as well in the increased efforts of sociological social psychologists to use multiple methods of inquiry, recognizing that each method (e.g., experimental, survey, observational, field study) has its own strengths and limitations (see part IV). This peaceful coexistence of the three faces of social psychology, noted in the introduction to this volume, provides an environment conducive to theoretical and empirical progress. In this sense, social psychology in sociology may be entering its "golden age."

REFERENCES

Alexander, Jeffrey C., Bernard Giessen, Richard Munch, and Neil Smelser, eds. 1987. *The Macro-Micro Link.* Berkeley: University of California Press.

Deutsch, Morton. 1985. *Distributive Justice: A Social Psychological Perspective.* New Haven: Yale University Press.

Ekeh, Peter. 1974. *Social Exchange Theory: The Two Traditions.* London: Heinemann.

Emerson, Richard M. 1962. Power-dependence relations. *American Sociological Review* 27:31–41.

Hardin, Garrett. 1968. The tragedy of the commons. *Science* 162:1243–1297.

Homans, George C. 1961. *Social Behavior: Its Elementary Forms.* New York: Harcourt Brace Jovanovich.

Lind, E. Allan, and Tom R. Tyler. 1988. *The Social Psychology of Procedural Justice.* New York: Plenum.

Ridgeway, Cecelia L. 1983. *The Dynamics of Small Groups.* New York: St. Martin's.

Thibaut, John W., and Harold H. Kelley. 1959. *The Social Psychology of Groups.* New York: Wiley.

CHAPTER 8

Social Exchange and Exchange Networks

LINDA D. MOLM
KAREN S. COOK

Social psychology is often defined as the study of how individuals are influenced by social forces. In contrast, social exchange theory takes as its smallest unit the social *relation* and builds upward to groups and social *networks*. It attempts to explain how relations between social actors (both individuals and groups) develop and change, how the structure of networks in which relations are embedded affects processes of interaction, and how processes such as power use and coalition formation lead, in turn, to changes in social structure. Because of its focus on relations rather than individuals, exchange theory holds great promise for bridging the concerns of micro- and macrosociologists.

Compared to some theoretical orientations, social exchange theory is a fairly contemporary perspective. Although its roots lie in the early anthropological studies of Malinowski (1922), Mauss (1925), and Levi-Strauss (1949), it did not emerge as a social psychological perspective until the late 1950s. Then, within a few years of each other, George Homans (1958, 1961), John Thibaut and Harold Kelley (1959), and Peter Blau (1964) published their theories of exchange. While these theories differed in many ways, their similarities were significant enough to signal the emergence of a new and distinctive approach in social psychology. Ten years later, influenced by these works and the controversies that surrounded them, Richard Emerson (1972a, 1972b) published his own theory of social exchange. This highly influential work provided the impetus for further theoretical and empirical development of the approach (Cook 1987).[1]

In a relatively short time, the exchange perspective has matured from a controversial upstart to an established theory with strong empirical support. The early period of development, from 1958 to about 1975, was characterized by considerable controversy over basic theoretical issues and little empirical work. In the last fifteen years, many of these controversies have been laid to rest and a solid foundation of empirical support for the theory has been built. The decade since the publication of the first edition of this volume, in particular, has been a period of sustained, programmatic research.

It is our aim in this chapter to discuss the scope and accomplishments of contemporary theory and research on social exchange in the context of its historical roots and future development. We give particular attention to Emerson's (1972a, 1972b) formulation because his approach, more than that of his predecessors, has shaped the field for the past two decades. The study of power-dependence relations and exchange networks, concepts that Emerson originally developed, dominates current research. At the same time, emerging interest in topics such as commitment, uncertainty, trust, and affective ties suggests the future will continue to bring fresh ideas and new directions to social exchange theory.

THE CHARACTER AND SCOPE OF SOCIAL EXCHANGE THEORY

Even the simplest forms of social interaction involve a myriad of different activities and processes. No single theory can encompass all of these elements in a meaningful way (Emerson 1981). Therefore, different social psychological theories focus their attention on different aspects of interaction: processes of interpretation and meaning, attributions about causality, the development and enactment of roles, and so forth.

Social exchange theory takes as its particular focus the benefits people obtain from, and contribute to, social interaction. This feature of social interaction derives from an obvious characteristic of social life: much of what we value and need in life (e.g., food, companionship, approval, status, and information) can only be obtained from others. People depend on one another for such valued resources, and they provide them to one another through the process of social exchange.

The "theory" of social exchange is actually a general framework or orientation that includes a number of separate but closely related theories. These different exchange theories all share a common set of analytical concepts (e.g., reward, cost, resources, alternatives, value, opportunity, and transactions), borrowed from behavioral psychology and microeconomics. Most exchange theories use a combination of psychological and economic concepts, although the relative emphasis given to one or the other varies.

The conception of social interaction as social exchange is, of course, an extension of the concept of economic exchange. Historically, however, social exchange departed from economic exchange in an important way: whereas classical microeconomic theory typically assumed the absence of long-term relations between exchange partners and the independence of sequential exchange transactions, social exchange theory took as its subject matter and its smallest unit of analysis *the more or less enduring relations that form between specific partners.* Recurring exchanges are necessarily interdependent in these relations, and, as a result, interactions can change over time. This emphasis on the history of relations and the mutual contingency of behaviors reflects the influence of behavioral psychology. What distinguishes contemporary social exchange theory from both psychology and microeconomics, however, is its emphasis on social

structure as the framework within which exchange processes take place and the structural change that results from those processes.

Core Assumptions

All social exchange theories are based, explicitly or implicitly, on a small number of core assumptions, making this a highly parsimonious yet broadly applicable framework. These can be described as assumptions about (1) the structure of exchange relations, (2) the behavior of actors, (3) the process of interaction, and (4) the classes of benefits exchanged. Together, these four assumptions define the scope of the theory.

1. *Exchange relations develop within structures of mutual dependence between actors.* Actors need not be equally dependent on one another, nor do they need to rely on others for all outcomes of value. Some degree of dependence of social actors on one another is a necessary condition for social exchange, however. Actors may be dependent on one another for material goods or services, for socially valued outcomes, or for psychological gratification.

2. *Actors behave in ways that increase outcomes they positively value and decrease outcomes they negatively value.* This assumption includes both "rational action" and "operant behavior" within its scope. Actors may behave "rationally," by weighing the potential costs and benefits of alternative choices of exchange partners and actions, or their choices may reflect the costs and benefits of past behavioral choices, without conscious weighing of alternatives. These two forms of action represent the assumptions of microeconomics and behavioral psychology, respectively, on which various exchange theories have been based.

This assumption does not restrict the theory to egocentric behavior on the part of actors. Actors are self-interested but not necessarily selfish. Actors may value getting rich or providing homeless shelters. The theory makes no assumption about *what* actors value, but it assumes that they will behave in ways that tend to produce whatever it is they do value.

3. *Actors engage in recurring, mutually contingent exchanges with specific partners over time.* This assumption, more than any other, captures the basic premise of exchange theory: Social relations are formed and maintained because actors provide reciprocal benefits to one another over time (Gouldner 1960). If benefits provided for another are not reciprocated (although the reciprocity need not be equal or immediate), the social relation will eventually cease to exist. The contingency of exchange applies both within transactions (i.e., benefits received are contingent on benefits provided) and across transactions (i.e., earlier exchanges affect subsequent exchanges).

4. *All outcomes of value obey a principle of satiation (in psychological terms) or diminishing marginal utility (in economic terms).* Food is more valuable to a hungry person than to one who has just eaten. This assumption is used to define classes of benefits, or value domains. Two outcomes are members of the same class if acquisition of one reduces the unit value of the other (e.g., both bread and apples reduce hunger and thus may be considered members of the class of "food"). The rate of change in value varies for different classes of benefits. Some benefits, such as money, diminish in value much more slowly than others because they can be used to obtain many other classes of benefits. (In economic terms, they have "exchange value," not simply "use value.")

Forms of Social Exchange

Within the scope defined by these four assumptions, several different forms of exchange are possible. The most important distinction is between direct and indirect exchange (Figure 8.1). In *direct exchange,* two actors exchange benefits with each other. In Figure 8.1a, actor A provides benefits to B and receives benefits from B in return. In *indirect exchange* (or generalized exchange), the exchange occurs among three or more actors. A benefit received by A from B is not reciprocated directly by A's giving to B, but indirectly, by A's giving to another actor in the network or group. Some forms of indirect exchange, such as the Kula ring studied

by Malinowski (1922), take a specific form: A gives to B, B gives to C, and C gives to A (a circular exchange pattern, as shown in Figure 8.1b). Other forms of indirect exchange, such as donating blood, giving shower gifts, or reviewing journal manuscripts, do not specify an ordering. In these examples, actors provide a benefit for another with the expectation that at some future time, some other actor—not necessarily the one they benefited—will do the same for them. Norms often emerge in indirect exchange situations to foster the fulfillment of obligations. Work on these two forms of exchange historically followed disciplinary lines, with sociologists concerned more with direct exchange and anthropologists with indirect exchange.

As Emerson (1981) has described, direct exchange can take different forms.[2] *Negotiated direct exchange* involves a joint decision process, such as bargaining, to determine the terms of exchange. In negotiated exchanges, the benefits enjoyed by both exchange partners are easily identified as paired events, called a *transaction*. Both sides of the exchange are agreed on at the same time, even if they do not occur simultaneously. If an agreement is not reached, neither actor benefits. Most economic exchanges (other than fixed-price trades) fit this category, as do many social exchanges (e.g., agreements between husband and wife to go to the ballet this week and the ballgame next week).

In *reciprocal direct exchanges* the contributions to the exchange are separately performed and nonnegotiated. One actor initiates the process (with a small act of consideration or an offer of

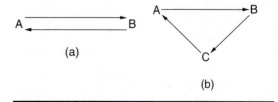

FIGURE 8.1   Direct and indirect forms of exchange; (a) direct exchange, (b) indirect (generalized) exchange.

help) without knowing whether or when the other will reciprocate. If an exchange relation develops, it takes the form of a series of sequentially dependent acts (e.g., neighbors who exchange favors). Reciprocity and contingency characterize the relation over time, rather than on discrete transactions, which may be difficult to identify. Reciprocal exchanges are common outside the economic sphere. In more intimate relations, such as friendships and families, norms curtail the extent of explicit bargaining. Even in political and work organizations, unilateral initiatives are common (e.g., offering help on a project or support for a proposal), and the expectation of reciprocity at some future time is often left implicit.

Finally, Emerson (1976) defined *productive exchange* as a distinct form of exchange in which both (or all) parties contribute to, and benefit from, a single socially produced event. Separately obtained benefits are not possible. If either party fails to contribute, neither will benefit. Examples include coauthored books and many team sports. Productive exchange is equivalent to what other social psychologists have called *cooperation* (Schmitt and Marwell 1975) or *coordination* (Kelley and Thibaut 1978), and it is similar to Barth's (1966) *incorporation*. Groups engage in productive exchange when they act collectively, combining the contributions of group members to form a valued group product. Sometimes productive exchange produces a single product that is appreciated by all group members (e.g., a team trophy), and sometimes the product is a divisible resource that is distributed to group members.

While these various forms of exchange are analytically distinct, they are often found together in relationships. For example, some exchanges between husbands and wives are negotiated and others are reciprocal. Similarly, some relationships involve both direct and productive exchange; that is, the total rewards in a relationship may be based partly on what actors give to each other (direct exchange) and partly on what they jointly produce for both actors (productive exchange). Furthermore, the dominant form of exchange in a relation-

ship may change over time. Relationships originally based on direct exchange may develop into productive exchange relations as the individual actors develop collective interests that can be met only through joint action. Similarly, formal bargaining relations may evolve into broader associations that include nonnegotiated exchanges.

EARLY DEVELOPMENT:
THE CLASSICAL STATEMENTS

The philosophical roots of social exchange theory reflect diverse sources. As Turner (1986) has observed, they begin with the assumptions of utilitarian economics (e.g., Adam Smith, John Stuart Mill, Jeremy Bentham), broaden to incorporate the emergent cultural and structural forces emphasized by classical anthropologists (Levi-Strauss 1949; Malinowski 1922; Mauss 1925), and enter sociology after further input and modification from behavioral psychology. Much of this history has been a dialectic between two different views of social exchange, one emphasizing the motives and strategies of individuals and the other focusing on the structural, institutional forces of collectivities (Befu 1977; Ekeh 1974). In its contemporary form, social exchange theory is beginning to unite these two approaches.

Homans first proposed social exchange as a unique perspective in a 1958 essay and in 1961 expanded these notions in *Social Behavior: Its Elementary Forms* (which he revised in 1974). At the same time, in psychology, John Thibaut and Harold Kelley were developing a theory of group behavior based on very similar ideas, although they did not call it social exchange. A few years later, influenced by Homans and Thibaut and Kelley, as well as by Richard Emerson's classic 1962 article on power-dependence relations, Peter Blau (1964) introduced his own theory of social exchange and power.

Although we do not have the space here to review these works in the depth they deserve, we try to give some sense of the distinct contributions of each and of their influence on the eventual emergence of contemporary forms of social exchange theory. For a more extended analysis, see Turner (1986).

Homans: The Psychology of Exchange

Homans defined social exchange as "an exchange of activity, tangible or intangible, and more or less rewarding or costly, between at least two persons" (1961, 13). He confined his theory to direct exchange in dyads or small groups; his aim was to explain fundamental processes of social behavior, such as power, conformity, status, leadership, and justice. In short, his subject matter was the traditional topics of "small group research." He proposed to show how established empirical propositions in this field could be derived from a small number of general propositions—the "propositions" of behavioral psychology. These concerned the familiar relations between reinforcement, discriminative stimuli, and behavior. Homans also weaved into his analysis ideas from balance theory and microeconomics, including the important concept of distributive justice (see chapter 10).

The most distinctive and controversial feature of Homans's theory was his belief that there is nothing that emerges in social groups that "cannot be explained by propositions about individuals as individuals, together with the given condition that they happen to be interacting" (1974, 12). Homans argued that behavior is a function of payoffs (or reinforcement and punishment), whether the payoffs are provided by the nonhuman environment or by other humans. In short, Homans "explained" social interaction and the forms of social organization that it produced by showing how A's behavior reinforced B's behavior, and how B's behavior reinforced A's behavior, under structural and historical conditions taken as givens. Emerson (1969, 1972a, 1976) and others have criticized this approach, arguing that it conceives of society as the sum of individual behavior and assumes (rather than explains) the conditions sociologists are most interested in understanding, namely the social structure within which individuals interact.

As Turner (1986) has discussed, the most important legacy Homans left was his consider-

able insight into the basic processes of social interaction. Homans provides a convincing view of the ubiquity of exchange processes in social life and of the way they underlie many forms of social structure.

Thibaut and Kelley: Interdependence in Dyads and Groups

Thibaut and Kelley's (1959) work has received less attention from sociologists because of its psychological origins, but in some ways it is more "sociological" than Homans's theory. Thibaut and Kelley also started from basic assumptions about the psychology of behavior, albeit with more of the cognitive flavor of decision theories, but they recognized that social interaction must be predicted from characteristics of the social relation, not just the other person's behavior. In this sense, their approach was social structural, even though the structures they considered were largely dyadic. Individuals' interactions were predicted from the patterns of interdependence in their relations, as determined by their relative control over each other's outcomes.

Three of their contributions are particularly important. First is their analysis of power and dependence, which influenced Emerson's (1962, 1972a, 1972b) subsequent development of these ideas. Second is the concepts of *comparison level* (CL) and *comparison level for alternatives* (CL_{alt}), standards for evaluating outcomes *within* (CL) and *between* (CL_{alt}) relations. Actors evaluate a current relationship by comparing their outcomes from that relationship with their CL, which represents a general level of expectation based on recently experienced outcomes. They decide whether to stay in a current relationship by comparing their outcomes with their CL_{alt}, which represents expected outcomes in their "best alternative." Although Thibaut and Kelley focused primarily on the dyad and never developed the concept of alternatives into the idea of social networks, in which actors have alternative exchange partners, the concept of CL_{alt} laid the foundation for Emerson (1972b) to do so later. Finally, Thibaut and Kelley's introduction of the outcome matrix as a visual tool for describing patterns of interdependence not only aided theory development but stimulated empirical research. The outcome matrix was used in experimental research throughout the 1960s and 1970s to represent patterns of interdependence (see chapter 9). Much of this research, on gaming, bargaining, cooperation, and the like, provided the impetus for later, more sophisticated studies of social exchange.

Blau: Exchange and Social Structure

Blau's approach is the most eclectic of the exchange theorists. Integrated in his analysis are many of the concepts and assumptions of functional, conflict, and interactionist theories, in addition to principles drawn from psychology. Blau also made more use of technical economic analysis (i.e., marginal utility and indifference curves) than Homans or Thibaut and Kelley.[3]

Blau began, like his predecessors, with an analysis of relatively simple, direct exchange relations in dyads or small groups. While his principles are less explicit than those of the other theorists, they share many of the same ideas and concepts. Blau's actors are similar to Thibaut and Kelley's: they engage in goal-oriented behavior, selecting from among alternatives on the basis of expected rewards.

Blau's primary interest, however, was in more complex systems of exchange, at the level of organizations and institutions. In contrast to Homans, Blau recognized that social structures have emergent properties not found in the individual elements: "Emergent properties are essentially relationships between elements in a structure. The relationships are not contained in the elements, though they could not exist without them, and they define the structure" (1964, 3). His aim was to bridge the gap between elementary exchange processes and these emergent structures. He attempted to make this transition by bringing in additional concepts, particularly norms and shared values, which emerge to regulate patterns of indirect exchange in more complex systems. Norms promote stability, while violations of norms create conflict and opposition.

Blau's efforts to bridge the micro-macro gap were not entirely successful, and he later concluded that exchange theory cannot cope adequately with the properties of populations and collectivities (Blau 1987). We believe this dismissal was premature and that exchange theory is currently moving in directions that avoid the discontinuity between different levels of analysis.

Early Controversies and Issues

The publication of the three theories stimulated more theoretical controversy than research. Debate centered around three main issues: rationality, tautology, and reductionism (Emerson 1976). First, exchange theory was accused of assuming an overly rational model of actors. Blau, Thibaut and Kelley, and even Homans (despite his operant base) seemed to describe people making conscious choices based on self-interested deliberation, a view of human behavior that Bierstedt (1965), among others, questioned. Second, numerous critics (e.g., Abrahamsson 1970; Deutsch 1964; Emerson 1976; Turner 1974) accused exchange theorists, particularly Homans, of tautological reasoning. Homans predicted individual exchange behavior from the reinforcement provided by another actor, but behavioral responses and reinforcement do not have independent meaning in operant psychology. A reinforcer is, by definition, a stimulus consequence that increases or maintains response frequency. Third, Blain (1971) and others were critical of Homans's psychological reductionism, a label he defended rather than refuted. Other charges were made as well: exchange theory assumed a hedonistic image of people (Abrahamsson 1970), it dealt only with dyads (Simpson 1972), and it proposed a model of exchange based on individual benefit rather than collective solidarity (Chadwick-Jones 1976; Ekeh 1974).

Many of these criticisms were valid accounts of the weaknesses in the early exchange formulations. Although little theoretical progress was made during this period, the lively debates kept exchange theory highly visible, if somewhat suspect. In 1972, Emerson's exchange formulation laid to rest most of these issues and provided a more explicit, systematic theoretical base for empirical test.

THE EMERGENCE OF CONTEMPORARY SOCIAL EXCHANGE THEORY: EMERSON'S FORMULATION

The publication of Emerson's formulation in 1972 (1972a, 1972b) marked the beginning of a new stage in the development of social exchange theory. Several forces provided the impetus for his work. First, Emerson was interested in using the exchange approach to create a broader framework for his earlier (1962) work on power-dependence relations. As the title of Blau's (1964) volume suggests, a striking feature of exchange theory is the way it directs attention to power and related topics. Second, Emerson believed he could build a theory of social exchange based on operant psychology that would avoid the pitfalls of tautology, reductionism, and rationality that had plagued Homans. Third, and most important, he wanted to develop an exchange theory that could explain social structure and structural change. This was Blau's aim, too, but Emerson used a different strategy. Rather than introducing normative concepts to handle more complex structures, Emerson used social relations and social networks as building blocks that spanned different levels of analysis, combined with the insight that actors could be either individuals or corporate groups, working through agents. While Blau used existing norms to explain how exchange is maintained in complex structures, Emerson described the structural conditions under which norms might initially emerge as part of the process of coalition formation.

Emerson adopted operant psychology for two reasons. First, he recognized that the operant behavior studied by psychologists represented a type of exchange relation between an individual organism and the environment, in contrast with the more internal, individualistic approach of most psychological theories. Second, operant psychology was largely atheoretical and made minimal assumptions about the actor. Emerson believed it provided a broader base than economic theory specifically because it made no assumptions about the rationality of actors. It allowed for conscious calculation but did not assume it.

Although Emerson and others would later bring more cognitive concepts into the theory, the initial absence of assumptions about cognitions or motives facilitated the development of a theory that emphasized structure rather than individuals' thoughts or needs. As social exchange theory has developed, both models of actor behavior have been integrated in the theory. Emerson's last work (1987) was concerned with the conditions under which calculated decisions or long-term conditioning determine behavioral choices. That remains an unfinished task for the future. Other theorists have developed alternative formulations based explicitly on rational choice or expected utility models (e.g., Blalock and Wilken 1979; Coleman 1973; Heath 1976). In contrast to social exchange theory, rational choice models focus primarily on individual decision making. Exchange theory focuses on the interdependence of actors, treating the social relation as the primary unit of analysis.

Whereas Homans began with a set of findings on social behavior in groups and worked downward to explain them in terms of operant principles, Emerson used operant principles of behavior as a base on which to build upward, toward a sociological theory of structure. He believed the problems of tautology and reductionism stemmed not from the psychological base of the theory per se (in fact, he argued that Homans used too little operant psychology, rather than too much), but from the failure to recognize that the concepts of operant behavior, reinforcer, and discriminative stimulus form a single conceptual unit, with each concept defined in terms of the others. Furthermore, their relation to each other is defined only over time, across repeated occurrences of behavior and stimuli. Separating them, and using each to explain the others (e.g., "explaining" behavior by reinforcement), creates the familiar tautology. By maintaining the integrity of this conceptual unit, which represents an exchange relation between an organism and its environment, Emerson established the *social relation,* rather than the individual actor, as the basic unit of analysis of the theory.[4] The relatively enduring relations between specific actors, and the conditions under which they form, change, and end, are the focus of the theory.

Basic Concepts

Before discussing Emerson's most important theoretical ideas—dependence, power, networks, and groups—we define the basic concepts used in the analysis: actors, outcomes, resources, exchange domain, primacy, value, and alternatives.

Actors (designated A, B, C . . . N) refer to either individual persons or corporate groups acting through agents. *Outcomes* are the rewards or costs that actors receive from each other in exchange. Outcomes can have positive value (rewards, reinforcement, utility, benefits) or negative value (costs, punishment, disutility, losses). When an actor has possessions or behavioral capabilities that are valued by other actors, they are *resources* (designated x, y) in the actor's relations with those others. Thus, a resource is "an attribute of an actor's relation to another or set of other actors, whose values define resources" (Emerson 1981, 41). A mother's capacity to offer approval is a resource in her relation with her child but may not be in her relation with someone else's child.

An *exchange domain* is a class of outcomes that are functionally equivalent. Two outcomes are in the same domain if the receipt of one outcome reduces the value of all outcomes in that domain, through the principle of satiation or diminishing marginal utility (as in our earlier example of bread and apples as members of the class of food). The *primacy* of an exchange relation refers to the number of exchange domains the relation mediates. Relations that mediate many domains (e.g., family relations) have high primacy; relations in a single domain (e.g., economic transactions) have low primacy.

Two concepts—the *value* of an exchange relation and the *alternatives* actors have to a particular

exchange relation—are directly involved in determining the major dynamics of exchange relations (i.e., who initiates exchange, the establishment and termination of exchange relations, and the differentiation of power). The value of exchange varies both across and within exchange domains. Across different domains, value refers to an actor's preference ordering of those domains (e.g., an actor's relative preference for friendship, money, and status). Within a single domain, value refers to the magnitude of outcomes that an actor potentially can receive in the relation (e.g., the amount of valued friendship, money, or status a relation offers). What determines people's values and changes in those values remains an unfinished part of the theory (Emerson 1987). At present, values are an exogenous variable in the theory; that is, the theory requires knowledge of what people value and the different magnitudes of value available in relations to make predictions.

The important concept of *alternatives* connects actors to a variety of possible exchange relations in a single exchange domain. An actor's alternatives to any given exchange relation are opportunities to obtain valued outcomes, in the same domain, from other actors (either individual or collective) or from the nonsocial environment. Together, the concepts of value and alternatives converge on the central variable of dependence.

Power and Dependence

With these basic concepts defined, we can discuss the pivotal concept of the theory—dependence. An actor is *dependent* on another to the extent that outcomes valued by the actor are contingent on exchange with the other. Dependence is a function of both value and alternatives. A's dependence on B increases with the value of B's exchange for A and decreases with the availability to A of alternatives to exchange with B (Emerson 1972b). Dependence also increases with primacy, for relations with high primacy mediate a wide range of valued outcomes and have few alternatives.

As Emerson's (1962) earlier work established, actors' mutual dependence provides the structural basis for their power over each other. That is, A's power over B (P_{AB}) derives from and is equal to B's dependence on A (D_{BA}):

$$P_{AB} = D_{BA}$$

An exchange relation is *balanced* when D_{AB} = D_{BA} and imbalanced to the extent that the two actors' power-dependencies are unequal. In an imbalanced relation, the less dependent actor has a power advantage. Defined in this way, *power* is a potential that derives from the structural relations among actors—their relative dependence on one another.[5] *Power use* is the behavioral exercise of this potential to obtain favorable exchange outcomes for the user.

The *cohesion* of the relation, which Emerson treated much more briefly, is defined as the average of the two actors' power-dependencies: (D_{AB} + D_{BA})/2. Thus, cohesion is a measure of the absolute power in a relation and power imbalance is a measure of the relative power of the actors in a relation. Some concept of the absolute power in a relation, as well as its imbalance, is theoretically important because of Emerson's argument that power is fully operative even in balanced relations: "In a highly cohesive relation, both members are significantly controlled 'by the relation.'" (1972b, 76).[6] An example is intense but equal friendships in which both members exert strong influence on each other.

Power imbalance and cohesion are structural attributes of exchange relations and the networks in which they are embedded, not properties of actors. They affect patterns of behavioral interaction in relations and networks, which in turn can stimulate structural change. Several propositions summarize these effects (Emerson 1972a, 1972b). First, the more dependent actor in an imbalanced relation is more likely to initiate exchange. Second, the frequency of exchange in a relation increases with its cohesion. Third, in imbalanced relations, outcome levels change in favor of the less dependent (i.e., more powerful) party. If A has a power advantage, A's power use will increase over time, as evidenced by either increased rewards to A from B or decreased rewards to B from A (i.e., decreased costs

for A). In short, the exchange ratio of the relation changes in favor of the more powerful, less dependent actor until an equilibrium is reached at which B gets no more from A than B can receive from alternative partners. Power use can be purposive, but it need not be: the effects of power imbalance are predicted even in the absence of intent to use power or awareness of power. They are determined by the structure of the relations, not the cognitions of actors.

In both his 1962 article and his 1972 chapters, Emerson focused considerable attention on power-balancing mechanisms. He argued that imbalanced relations are unstable; they create their own impetus toward balance. He defined four balancing operations, representing changes in values and alternatives. If the A—B relation is imbalanced in A's favor, then change toward balance can be produced by a decrease in the value of x for B ("withdrawal from the relation"), an increase in the value of y for A ("status giving" from B to A), an increase in alternatives for B ("network extension"), or a decrease in alternatives for A ("coalition formation" by B with other alternatives for A). The latter two strategies represent changes in networks of relations and receive more attention in Emerson's analysis of exchange networks and groups.

Exchange Networks and Groups

Although the terms *networks* and *groups* are often used interchangeably by sociologists, they represent very different types of structures (Emerson 1972b). Groups are collective actors, while exchange networks are sets of exchange relations among actors, either individual or collective.

More specifically, an exchange network is a set of two or more *connected* exchange relations. The concept of network connection is one of Emerson's most important contributions. Two exchange relations are connected only if the frequency or value of exchange in one relation affects the frequency or value of exchange in another. These connections can be positive or negative and bilateral or unilateral. Network connections are *positive* to the extent that exchange in one relation increases exchange in the other and *negative* to the extent that exchange in one relation decreases exchange in the other. If these effects occur in both directions, the connection is bilateral; if they are one-way only, the connection is unilateral. Mixed networks consist of both positively and negatively connected relations.

For example, consider a three-actor network (B_1—A—B_2) consisting of two potential relations (A—B_1 and A—B_2) connected at A. If B_1 and B_2 (e.g., Bob and Dave) are alternative dating partners for A (e.g., Joan), then the network is negatively connected: the more frequently Joan dates Bob, the less frequently she will date Dave, and vice versa. Now, consider a different three-actor network (B—A—C) consisting of corrupt politicians. If A buys information from B in one exchange and gives that information to C in exchange for C's political support, the network is positively connected: A's exchange of money for information with B facilitates A's exchange of information for political support with C.[7]

Whereas networks are sets of exchange relations among actors, either individual or collective, *corporate groups* are collective actors, composed of two or more persons, that exchange with other actors as a single social unit (Emerson 1972b). Typically, they do so through the relationship of principal and agent; that is, one group member, the "agent," negotiates with other actors (or the other agents of collective actors) on behalf of the "principal," the group as a whole.

A group can thus be one element (an actor) in an exchange network, but embedded within groups are their own internal exchange systems. These internal systems are necessary to regulate and sanction the individual members, to assure that they act on a common policy—that is, collectively—in their exchange with other actors. The collective action of the group members can itself be defined as a mode of exchange, the *productive exchange* described earlier.

Emerson considered coalition formation as a special case of group formation and norm formation, in which the set of actors $B_1B_2 \ldots B_N$ coalesces into a single, collective actor {B}, increasing {B}'s power relative to A's in the process. Collective norms govern the behavior of all B's in their relations with A, and the group members will engage in collective sanctioning if any B violates these norms.

The concepts of exchange networks and corporate actors are the necessary components for a theory of exchange that bridges the gap between individuals or dyads and larger social units, such as organizations or communities. As we discuss shortly, the merger of social exchange theory with developments in social network theory holds the promise of accomplishing that goal.

CONTEMPORARY RESEARCH ON SOCIAL EXCHANGE

Empirical research lagged behind theory development in the early years of the exchange tradition. In contrast, the last two decades have been a time of considerable research activity and substantial progress. While there are many applications of exchange principles to substantive topics such as families and organizations, basic research using experimental methods to test and extend theory has dominated research activity during this period. Experiments on social exchange are typically conducted in standardized settings that aid the cumulation of results across experiments and facilitate the development of theory. While a number of different standardized settings have been used, most are variants of two basic settings, designed for the study of either negotiated or reciprocal exchange.

Standardized Laboratory Settings

Settings for the study of *negotiated exchange* have been developed by Stolte and Emerson (1977), Cook and Emerson (1978), and Bacharach and Lawler (1981). (A variant of the Cook and Emerson setting was subsequently developed by Willer and Patton [1987]). In the Cook and Emerson (1978) setting, exchange is carried out through negotiations in which the subjects bargain over the amounts of valuable resources to be traded, much like two people do when they trade baseball cards or negotiate over pay for hours worked. Subjects complete transactions by agreeing to a specific trade of their resources. If no agreement is reached before the end of a transaction period, then no trade is consummated on that round. For every completed trade between two actors an exchange ratio can be calculated (i.e., the amount of profit one actor obtains in comparison to that obtained by the other—often a constant sum). Subjects earn money by accumulating the profit obtained from a series of transactions. To eliminate the influence of equity concerns on exchange agreements, subjects typically have limited information about the structure of the exchange opportunities beyond their own immediate options, and they usually do not know others' profits.

Other researchers (Burgess and Nielsen 1974; Michaels and Wiggins 1976; Molm 1988; Molm and Wiggins 1979) have developed settings to study *reciprocal exchanges* in which the terms of exchange are not negotiated. In Molm's (1988) setting, subjects individually choose behaviors (adding or subtracting money) that have rewarding or punishing consequences of fixed value for their partners, without knowing in advance whether or to what extent the other will reciprocate. On any given exchange opportunity, a subject might give to another without receiving or receive without giving, or an exchange might be mutual. In the absence of explicit bargaining, actors can influence one another by making their behavioral choices contingent on their partners' previous choices. Exchange ratios are measured only over time (typically several hundred trials), by comparing the relative frequencies of rewarding behaviors two partners perform for one another.

Because of their common foundation in Emerson's theory of exchange, the Cook and Emerson and Molm settings share several features. First, and most important, is the emphasis on the exchange relation as the fundamental unit of analysis. Exchanges between subjects are studied over time in continuing relations, not as one-shot transactions. Second, subjects are typically isolated from one another, with their exchanges mediated through

computers, to assure that their behavior is affected solely by structural characteristics of the exchange relations and not by the actors' personal characteristics. Other researchers, however, have studied exchange in face-to-face interaction settings (e.g., Markovsky, Willer, and Patton 1988; Michener, Cohen, and Sorensen 1977). Finally, virtually all experiments on social exchange use money as the resource to be exchanged, not because of any interest in money per se (the research is concerned with social, not economic, exchange), but because it can be easily quantified, it is generally of value to all subject populations, and it is resistant to satiation effects (or diminishing marginal utility) over the ranges typically offered in experimental sessions. Because Emerson's theory assumes the type of resource is not a critical variable, the results of studies can be generalized theoretically to resources other than money.

In the following sections we review both experimental and nonexperimental research on social exchange in established and emerging areas of inquiry.

Exchange in Dyadic Relations

Understanding the dynamics of social exchange in the dyad was one of the first aims of exchange theorists and is a continuing focus of researchers interested in intimate relations and in the exchange relation as the basic building block of networks. Some of the earliest laboratory tests of Emerson's theory studied the development, maintenance, and disruption of dyadic exchange relations (e.g., Burgess and Nielsen 1974; Michaels and Wiggins 1976; Molm 1980; Molm and Wiggins 1979). These studies, often based explicitly on the operant principles of Emerson's (1972a) original formulation, examined how the course of exchange varied as a function of the rewards for exchange relative to an alternative reward source (an individual task that required only the subject's own behavior), the inequality of rewards within the exchange relation, and changes in the structure and value of exchange over time.

Michaels and Wiggins (1976) demonstrated that for social exchange relations to form, the average value of exchange to both actors must be greater than the average value of their alternatives. As long as that condition is met, mutual (but not necessarily symmetrical) exchange can be maintained even if exchange is inequitable (Burgess and Nielsen 1974; Michaels and Wiggins 1976). However, the structure of direct exchange relations is inherently fragile because of the potential for actors to receive value without reciprocation (Molm and Wiggins 1979). As a result, exchange is more difficult to establish than cooperation (in which both actors must contribute for either one to obtain outcomes) and, once disrupted, more difficult to recover. Disruptions in exchange, produced by changes in the value or structure of the relation, are often severe and permanent for mutually dependent dyads with alternatives, even less rewarding ones (Molm 1984).

Some of the most basic studies on social exchange and power were also conducted on dyads (e.g., Burgess and Nielsen 1974; Molm 1981). Power cannot be studied easily in an isolated dyad in which actors are dependent solely on each other for outcomes they value. However, the use of non-social (individual task) alternatives in these studies allowed researchers to vary actors' dependence on an exchange partner and to study the effect of imbalanced power on exchange outcomes. Results support Emerson's (1962, 1972b) basic prediction that imbalanced power leads to unequal ratios of exchange, in favor of the *less* dependent partner. Lawler and Bacharach (Bacharach and Lawler 1981; Lawler and Bacharach 1987) have also studied power in dyadic relations, integrating structural concepts from Emerson's power-dependence formulation with a tactical approach to explicit bargaining. (For further information on this research program, see chapter 9.)[8]

Researchers studying interpersonal attraction, marital relations, and the family began using the framework of social exchange theory in the 1960s (e.g., Edwards 1969; McCall 1966). Since then, exchange theoretic analyses of such topics as mate selection and relationship formation (Huesmann and Levinger 1976), family power and decision making (e.g., McDonald 1980; Scanzoni 1972), and marital satisfaction and stability/dissolution

(e.g., Levinger 1976; Lewis and Spanier 1982) have proliferated. This research typically employs survey or observational methods. The vast majority of the work draws on the social exchange theories of Homans (1974) and Thibaut and Kelley (1959) and, therefore, tends to be dyadic in focus. Some studies use exchange theory only as a loose framework in which the rewards and costs of relationships are analyzed; others draw on specific concepts such as Thibaut and Kelley's (1959) CL and CL_{alt} to make predictions of marital satisfaction and marital stability/dissolution.

Family power theorists have been most interested in analyzing which exchange resources of the husband and wife are of greater importance for marital decision making, for example, socioeconomic resources, such as income and occupation (Scanzoni 1972), or affective resources, such as love (Safilios-Rothschild 1976). Changes in gender roles (e.g., increases in married women's employment) can alter the relative resources of husbands and wives and shift the distribution of power. Scanzoni's (1972) work is notable for its emphasis on dynamic power processes, such as negotiation, conflict, and hostility, rather than static decision-making outcomes. Gottman's (1979) work also identifies exchange processes as important for predicting the quality and stability of marriages, examining such dimensions as the degree of reciprocity and patterning of both positive and negative exchanges.

Family theorists have led the way in the study of dynamic aspects of exchange relations (e.g., Burgess and Huston 1979). However, the potential of exchange networks for analyzing relations among all family members or between family members and outside agents (e.g., work, kin, friends) has yet to be realized.

Beyond the Dyad: Exchange Networks and Power

One of the most significant developments in contemporary exchange theory has been the effort to extend the theory beyond dyads to apply to networks of exchange relations. This development was driven, in part, by the criticism that the early formulations were too dyadic in focus. As Emerson points out, even Blau's (1964) work employed concepts often drawn from economics (e.g., indifference curves) that tended to "reduce the social situation to a set of dyadic transactions" (1976, 356).

The effort to extend exchange theory beyond dyads to apply to networks of exchange relations is important for two reasons: (1) it links exchange theory to a rapidly developing body of analytical and substantive work on social networks (see Cook 1977; Cook and Emerson 1984; Marsden 1983, 1987) and (2) it establishes the theoretical basis for the analysis of larger and more complex systems of exchange, a key element in the application of exchange theory to macrolevel structures (Emerson 1976).

Network Connections, Power, and Power-Balancing Mechanisms.   The relation between the structure of exchange networks and the distribution of power depends on how relations in the network are connected to one another. The shape of the network alone does not determine exchange processes; these processes are fundamentally different in networks with positive and negative connections (Yamagishi, Gillmore, and Cook 1988). This insight is one of the key contributions of Emerson's concept of network connection.

Most research on power in exchange networks has been conducted on networks with negative connections. In laboratory experiments, negative connections are created by making the choice of partners mutually exclusive; thus, exchange with one partner precludes exchange with another partner for that opportunity or transaction.[9] Negative connections create competition for access to the actors who control the more valuable resources. (For specification of interest and control relations in systems of social exchange, see Coleman 1973, 1990). This competition is at the heart of economic exchanges in market structures. It is also common in networks of social exchange in which valuable resources are in limited supply and access to them is restricted by the opportunity structure (e.g., Marsden 1983). For example, in large families siblings may compete with one another for a parent's attention, or in industry manufacturers may compete with one another for a scarce raw material controlled by a single supplier.

In negatively connected networks, power derives from the dependence relations created by the exchange opportunity structure. Power and dependence can vary as a function of both value and alternatives. In the balanced network shown in Figure 8.2a on page 222, all actors are equally dependent on one another (and equally powerful) because all actors have access to all other actors, and the potential value of exchange in each of these relations is the same. A network of friends might be balanced, for example, if all live in close proximity and find equal enjoyment in each other's company. But in the network shown in Figure 8.2b, power is imbalanced, because A has access to three relations of high exchange value (with B_1, B_2, or B_3), whereas each B_i has access to only one high-value relation, with A. All B_i's can exchange with each other, but those relations are less valuable. Thus, A is less dependent on any one of the B's, while each B is highly dependent on A. A's power advantage is *structurally* determined by A's strategic location in the network. As noted earlier, dating networks and some sales networks often take this form.

Cook and Emerson (1978) found, as this analysis of dependencies predicts, that the balanced network in Figure 8.2a produces an equal distribution of benefits among actors, whereas the imbalanced network in 8.2b produces an unequal distribution of benefit in favor of the less dependent actor, A. Over time, A's benefits increase until B_i is receiving no more from the exchange with A than B_i can receive from exchange with B_j. Numerous other studies confirm the general finding that in negatively connected networks, the power-dependence relations created by the network structure determine the distribution of power (e.g., Cook and Emerson 1978; Cook et al. 1983; Markovsky, Willer, and Patton 1988; Molm 1990; Stolte and Emerson 1977).

In positively connected networks, in contrast, partners in connected relations are not in competition with one another. Instead, resources obtained from one partner facilitate exchange with another. Positive connections are common in settings with a high degree of resource specialization or division

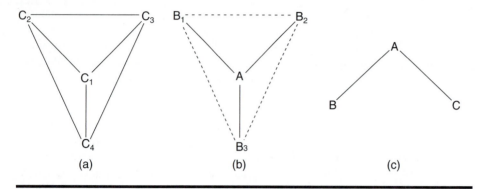

FIGURE 8.2   Exchange networks, illustrating different structures and connections; (a) negatively-connected balanced network; (b) negatively-connected imbalanced network; (c) positively-connected imbalanced network. Note: Solid lines indicate potential relations with *high* exchange value; broken lines indicate potential relations with *low* exchange value.

of labor and in communication networks (Marsden 1982, 1987). For example, the network in Figure 8.2c might represent an arrangement among three small business entrepreneurs who are just starting out in different fields, each with more expertise and experience in a particular sphere of business. Entrepreneur A might have more management skills, B more computer expertise, and C more marketing knowledge. B and C do not know each other, but both know A. A might first exchange management advice for computer expertise with B, and then use the computer expertise acquired from B in a subsequent exchange with C for marketing advice. A could then use this marketing advice, in turn, in another exchange with B.

Because more centrally located actors are ideally placed to act as "brokers" in such an arrangement, they should have greater power (e.g., Marsden 1982, 1987). The research of Yamagishi et al. (1988) supports this analysis. In Figure 8.2c, A is more powerful because only A can obtain both computer and marketing expertise in exchanges with B and C. B and C do not have access to one another in this network except through A.

According to Emerson's (1972b) power-balancing principles, the network in Figure 8.2c could become power-balanced through the process of network extension if a direct connection is estab-

lished between B and C such that their mutual access is no longer mediated by A. Such a network transformation would virtually eliminate A's power advantage and open up options for B and C to set their own terms of trade, decreasing their dependence on A, thereby increasing their relative power.

In the negatively connected network represented in Figure 8.2b, a more likely power-balancing strategy is for B_1, B_2, and B_3 to form a coalition. This would alter the structure of the network by creating a bilateral monopoly (i.e., a dyadic relation with no alternatives) between A and the newly formed "corporate actor" $\{B_1B_2B_3\}$. Research on coalitions (e.g., Cook and Gillmore 1984; Gillmore 1987) confirms this prediction about power-balancing strategies in negatively connected networks.

The insights of social exchange theory have important implications for the study of social networks in general. Most social network research has traditionally assumed that network centrality determines structural power (Freeman 1979). The experimental work reported in Cook et al. (1983) challenged this notion and the findings from a variety of field studies that supported it (e.g., Galaskiewicz 1979; Laumann and Pappi 1976). The key determinant of the nature of the association between centrality and power is whether the exchange relations are negatively or positively connected (Cook and Emerson 1984; Yamagishi, Gillmore, and Cook 1988). In positively connected networks centrality yields power, because central actors can act as "brokers" in cooperative relations. In negatively connected networks, centrality is less important than access to highly dependent actors with few or no alternatives. In essence, actors with few or no alternatives are vulnerable to exploitation.

In addition to centrality, which has been studied extensively, other structural properties of networks, such as density, range, multiplexity, and prominence, may have important implications for the study of exchange processes. For example, what is traditionally referred to as "multiplexity" in the network literature may serve as an adequate operationalization of what Emerson (1972b) called "primacy." Multiplex ties in a social network indicate multiple linkages between actors (i.e., two actors may be related by kinship and also serve as friends and business associates). Primacy is used to indicate that an exchange relation between two or more actors mediates a wide range of valued resources or services. Thus, there is a close correspondence between the theoretical concept, primacy, and the more operational multiplexity. The potential links between network concepts and methods and social exchange theory (Cook 1987) provide fertile ground for further research.

These developments in social exchange theory's analysis of networks are complementary to some of the developments in economics, particularly institutional economics (e.g., Leibenstein 1976; Williamson 1975, 1982), and in organizational theory (e.g., Pfeffer and Salancik 1978). For example, Cook and Emerson (1984) suggest that Williamson's (1975, 1982) distinction between markets and hierarchies can be expressed in exchange theoretic terms. Markets can be viewed as negatively connected networks with multiple foci of power (typically corporate actors like large firms), and hierarchies can be represented as different types of positively connected networks that involve "centralized" power and authority.

Principles of power in exchange networks have also been applied to the analysis of interorganizational relations (Cook 1977, Cook and Emerson 1984). When organizations are "loosely coupled" (Weick 1976), relatively autonomous, and highly competitive, a strong central authority may be difficult to achieve and maintain. An example is the failure of many efforts to establish cooperative networks among hospitals, which have historically been competitors in the delivery of health services (Starkweather and Cook 1987).

Other nonexperimental studies in organizational settings and urban communities further document the significance of exchange network processes (e.g., Fischer 1982). Czako's (1988) study of various Hungarian enterprises, including schools, businesses, and bureaucracies, demonstrates the widespread use of reciprocal transactions among managers to help them cope with persistent shortages of goods and labor and with incomplete markets and other mechanisms of redistribution. Shrum (1990) recently demonstrated that the exchange of favors and information among professionals at different levels in government agencies is structured by network position and status congruence between the actors. Patterns of reciprocal exchange also frequently develop in the form of social support networks in friendship groups and families facing crises, problems of aging and long-term care, or short-term economic difficulties (caused by unemployment, divorce, etc.).

Alternative Approaches to Power in Networks. Over time, other theoretical perspectives have been developed to explain power processes in exchange networks. In addition to the power-dependence tradition derived from Emerson's theory of social exchange (1962, 1972a, 1972b), approaches based on elementary theory (Markovsky, Willer, and Patton 1988; Willer and Anderson 1981), expected value theory (Friedkin 1986, 1992), and game theory (Bienenstock and Bonacich 1992) have been proposed.

Willer and his collaborators (e.g., Markovsky, Willer, and Patton 1988; Willer, Markovsky, and Patton 1989; Willer and Patton 1987) formulated a theory of power in networks based on Willer and Anderson's (1981) "elementary theory of social interactions." Elementary theory derives its name from the idea that complex social structures are generated from simple or "elementary" concepts and social relations (Willer 1981). This theory shares with Emerson's theory of exchange and power-dependence relations an emphasis on social structure as the primary determinant of behavior, but it differs in several key respects.

First, the elementary theory applies to systems in which actors have full and complete information, whereas power-dependence theory makes no assumptions about actors' information, cognitions, or beliefs. Second, the primary focus of elementary theory is on rule-governed interactions, in which exchanges occur only when actors have negotiated agreements or formulated rules that assure actors of reciprocity. In contrast, the scope of power-dependence theory encompasses both negotiated and reciprocal exchange. Third, in empirical tests of the elementary theory and its derivatives (i.e., network exchange theory), the *transaction,* not the exchange relation, is the primary unit of analysis. Because transactions are assumed to be independent, the focus is on power use in transactions, rather than changes in power use over time.[10]

This third feature of elementary theory, more than any other, distinguishes it from theories of social exchange. For Emerson (1972a, 1972b) it is the relatively enduring nature of the exchange relation and the interdependence of *sequential transactions* that sets social exchange theory apart from classical microeconomic models, which treat transactions as independent over time. Willer and Anderson (1981) refer to all exchanges in which actors incur some cost to obtain greater gain as *economic* exchange, reserving *social* exchange to refer to exchanges in which both sides produce benefit for the giver as well as the receiver (Willer 1985; Willer and Anderson 1981).

Markovsky et al. (1988) recently developed a graph analytic theory derived from Willer's elementary theory. The goal of the research is to clarify the conditions under which network structural factors determine the distribution of power in networks of exchange where actors negotiate over the division of a fixed pool of resources. The graph theoretic power index (GPI) developed by Markovsky et al. (1988) formalizes the idea that power derives from "the availability of alternative exchange relations, the unavailability of their relations' alternatives, and so on," consistent with the work of Cook et al. (1983), Bonacich (1987), and Marsden (1987). This formalization is useful as a measure of structural power. (For alternative measures and related debates see Cook, Gillmore, and Yamagishi 1986; Cook and Yamagishi 1992; Markovsky, Willer, and Patton, 1990; Stolte 1988; Willer 1986; Yamagishi and Cook 1990; and *Social Networks* June 1992).

Recent work by Friedkin (1992) challenges the utility of *all* structural measures of power. Instead of pursuing development of a general structural index of power, as have prior investigators, Friedkin (1992) proposes an expected value model of social exchange outcomes for power structures or networks representing opportunities for information flow, interpersonal influence, social support, or social exchange. This model combines network analysis with notions of social influence and power (derived primarily from French 1956), a simple conception of rational action (i.e., actors seek to maximize their net receipt of resources), and the notion that dependency, a component of power, is related to an actor's vulnerability to exclusion from exchange (see Markovsky, Willer, and Patton 1988; Willer and Anderson 1981). This work demonstrates the importance of specifying how the network's structure and the actors' bargaining behavior jointly determine exchange outcomes (see also Molm 1990).

Bases of Power: Coercion in Exchange

Most of the theoretical and empirical work on social exchange relations and networks has assumed as a scope condition the voluntary exchange of rewards or positively valued services and resources. The costs of exchange have been restricted to the costs of the actor's own behaviors (i.e., the "opportunity costs" of rewards foregone from alternatives not chosen) or the costs involved in enacting particular behaviors or engaging in transactions. Costs imposed on the actor by an exchange partner's aversive actions were considered outside the scope of the theory until quite recently.

As Heath (1976) observed, this omission of coercion from the scope of exchange is questionable. The basis for mutual exchange is that it "enables both participants to be better off than they would have been without it . . . they need not necessarily be better off than they were before" (1976, 19). Individuals may remain in aversive relations because alternatives are even less desirable or because leaving the relation would increase rather than decrease punishment from a punitive partner. Women who remain in abusive relations are an example. Even in voluntary relations, motivated primarily by the exchange of rewarding outcomes, negative exchanges are common. Studies of family interaction show that even in close relations based primarily on mutual reward, aversive forms of control are frequently used (e.g., Gottman 1979; Patterson 1982). In organizations, control over both rewards and punishments affects bargaining tactics and outcomes (Bacharach and Lawler 1980; Kanter 1977).

Not surprisingly, the limitation of social exchange to reward-based interaction particularly affects the analysis of power. As Emerson (1981) has noted, power-dependence theory's "soft" interpretation of power distinguishes it from traditional treatments of power as coercive (e.g., Bierstedt 1950). These two conceptions of power—as reward-based or as coercive—have largely been studied within separate literatures, from different theoretical perspectives.

Recently, theorists have shown a renewed interest in integrating theories of reward- and punishment-based forms of power. Blalock and Wilken's (1979) theory of intergroup processes includes an analysis of power that encompasses both reward and punishment. Willer and Anderson (1981) distinguish between exchange and coercion as different types of elementary relations between actors. And Bacharach and Lawler's (1981) theory of bargaining power includes both dependence-based power and punitive power. All of these theorists have maintained the distinction between exchange and coercion, however.

Molm (1987a), in contrast, has argued that control over both rewards and punishments are sources of dependence and can be studied productively within the theoretical framework of social exchange and power-dependence relations. In a series of experiments, she compared these two bases of power in voluntary exchange relations in which actors control varying amounts of both rewarding (positive) and punishing (negative) outcomes for one another (Molm 1988, 1989a, 1989b, 1990). These experiments show that punishment power is rarely used, and that its effects on the frequency and distribution of exchange—while comparable in direction to those of reward power—are much weaker. Molm explains these differences by the greater constraints on the use of coercion in relations of mutual dependence.

This research also suggests that the two bases of power interact in interesting ways. Although socially legitimated forms of coercion are typically used by those in authority (e.g., the state, parents, school authorities), the same is not true of coercion that lacks a normative base. In relations of power and exchange, the actors most likely to use coercive tactics are those who are disadvantaged on reward power (Molm 1989b). This finding is consistent with research in nonexperimental settings, such as Kanter's (1977) analysis of the coercive tactics of midlevel managers who have little access to reward-based resources and the observations of family researchers that aversive actions are most typical of members who are weak on resource-based power (e.g., Patterson, 1982; Raush et al. 1974). At the same time, the dependence of these actors on others for rewards increases the potential costs of using coercion. Thus, risk appears to be an important factor for analyses of coercion in exchange (Molm 1993).

Nonstructural Processes in Social Exchange

Research on how the structure of relationships affects social interaction, particularly power use, and how structural change emerges out of patterns of interaction, has dominated research on social exchange for the past fifteen years. This focus on structure is a defining feature of the theory and will undoubtedly continue. Increasingly, however, researchers are bringing other variables into the theory: strategies of actors, commitments to partners, normative constraints, and affective ties. Sometimes these variables are studied as factors that influence interaction, within the constraints of structure, and sometimes as consequences of long-term exchange relations. Here, we review some of the recent work on these topics.

Strategies of Power Use. In structurally imbalanced exchange networks, the use of power changes in favor of the less dependent actors even if they have no intent to use power or awareness of their potential power. Power use is inherent in the structure of imbalanced reward power. Within the constraints of structural power, however, power can also be used intentionally and strategically. Power strategies have been a central focus of the research tradition initiated by Thibaut and Kelley (1959). More recently, researchers working in Emerson's power-dependence tradition have also begun to investigate strategies. A growing body of research suggests that actual power use may depend on both the structural potential for power and how actors use their power resources in the process of exchange or negotiation.

Researchers have studied the effects of actor strategies in both negotiated and reciprocal forms of exchange. In negotiated exchanges, strategies consist of various decision rules for making offers and counteroffers, and bargaining tactics such as concession making or threats. How bargaining tactics mediate the relation between structure and outcomes, and the conditions under which actors use various tactics of concession making, threats, or punishment, is a central focus of the program of experimental research conducted by Bacharach and Lawler (1981). Markovsky's (1987) computer simulations of negotiated exchange also suggest that actor strategies can alter the eventual distribution of exchange outcomes in the network, independent of structural features of the network.

Molm's work (1987b, 1990) examines how actors' strategies affect power use in reciprocal

exchanges. In the absence of explicit bargaining, actors can influence their partner's behavior by giving or withholding rewards or punishments, contingent on the partner's behavior. This kind of behavioral influence, which requires contingent action over time, can take place only in exchange relations that persist for some time.

The strategies that actors use in nonnegotiated exchange are only weakly related to their structural power (Molm 1990). Therefore, strategies can potentially affect exchange outcomes independent of structure. Within imbalanced power structures, high power users are distinguished from low power users by the stronger and more consistent reinforcement contingencies they create for their partners (Molm 1987b). Strong behavioral strategies are particularly important for actors who lack structural power or whose primary source of power is coercive. Experiments show, for example, that punitive strategies have a stronger effect on exchange outcomes than the structural capacity to punish (Molm 1990).

This line of research is still relatively new, and many questions remain to be answered. Research to date suggests that actor strategies are more important under some conditions than others and that their role varies in different forms and structures of exchange and at different stages of relationships. Further theoretical development is likely to benefit from some of the innovative work on choice behavior and decision making that social psychologists, psychologists, and economists are currently conducting (e.g., Gray and Tallman 1987; Kahneman and Tversky 1984; Machina 1987). This work suggests that actors do not always behave "rationally," but that departures from rationality follow systematic and predictable patterns. Most of this work is based on analyses of individual choice; extending it to exchange relations and networks should produce new insights for both traditions.

Emergent Properties of Exchange Relations. An important feature of the focus on relatively enduring relations in social exchange theory is that it makes change over time a central theoretical concern. Long-term relationships may be characterized by processes that are absent in earlier stages: the emergence of norms of fairness, commitments to specific exchange partners, and the development of trust and affective ties. Some of these processes modify the effects of structure and the outcomes of exchange; others can be conceptualized as new value domains that are of interest in their own right.

Justice Norms.   In reaction to Parsonianism and the overemphasis on normative conceptions of social behavior (Wrong 1961), Homans (1958, 1961) attempted to eliminate, as much as possible, normative considerations from his treatment of social exchange. The one exception was his inclusion of the concept of distributive justice. In contrast, Blau made norms central in his theory, especially norms of fair exchange, which he argued emerge over time to regulate social exchange relations. Such norms establish consensus over the "proper" exchange rate and subsequently eliminate continuous negotiation and potential conflicts over what is a fair return. Thibaut and Kelley (1959) made a similar argument, suggesting that norms emerge to reduce the need to use (and the costs of using) interpersonal power.

The work of Homans on distributive justice and Blau on fair exchange, in addition to the early work of Adams (1965), helped establish an extensive research tradition on distributive justice and equitable exchange (see chapter 10). Of particular interest to exchange theorists is the relation between the structure of exchange and the formation and impact of justice norms. Stolte (1987) proposed that the structure of exchange helps account for the specific justice norms that form; such as equality, need, or equity. Some theorists (e.g., Della Fave 1980; Homans 1976) have argued that those in structural positions of power control this process by imposing their own standards of justice on others, thus legitimating an unequal distribution of benefits.

Experimental research provides mixed evidence on the legitimating effects of power. Several studies show that power-disadvantaged actors perceive unequal outcomes as more unfair than power-advantaged actors; i.e., power does not le-gitimate outcome inequality (e.g., Cook and Hegtvedt 1986; Stolte 1983). Power does affect actors' perceptions of the fairness of their partners' power strategies, however. In particular, targets of coercion perceive their partner's power use as more fair when the partner is advantaged rather than disadvantaged on reward power (Molm, Quist, and Wiseley 1994).

As Cook and Emerson's (1978) work shows, normative concerns over fairness in exchange rates can inhibit the exploitative use of power in exchange networks. When actors in power-imbalanced networks were informed of inequalities in the distribution of profits resulting from exchange, inequality was significantly reduced (but not eliminated) in subsequent exchanges. The issue of the relative strength of structural sources of power versus norms constraining power use is still unresolved, however, and more research is needed (Cook, Donnelly, and Yamagishi 1992).

Commitment.   Commitment between exchange partners in networks may emerge for various reasons, with important consequences for both the structure of the network and the exchange outcomes of the actors. Commitment has a cognitive and emotional component (e.g., loyalty, attraction) as well as a behavioral one. Different approaches to commitment place different emphasis on these components.

Cook and Emerson (1978) focused on the behavioral aspect of commitment, defining two actors as "committed" to the extent that they engaged in repeated exchanges with one another in the face of profitable alternatives. Under conditions of relatively low risk and uncertainty, some actors formed commitments over time, and these commitments impeded power use. Commitment reduced the power-advantaged actors' exchange outcomes because they no longer actively explored their alternatives, but it increased the outcomes of the power-disadvantaged actors for whom commitment was advantageous.

Leik and Leik (1977) proposed that commitment is offered by power-disadvantaged actors as a kind of power-balancing mechanism. In the absence of other resources, these actors offer their continued availability and predictability in exchange for the resources they need or want from their more powerful partners. Because their commitment is not necessarily reciprocated, levels of commitment in the relation can be asymmetrical, in contrast to Cook and Emerson's (1978) definition of commitment as mutually exclusive behavioral exchange.

Recent work by Kollock (1992) suggests that under conditions of greater uncertainty and risk, commitment can be a profit-maximizing strategy for both partners in the exchange. When negotiated agreements are not strictly binding, or the value of exchange resources is unknown or distorted, forming committed relations with trustworthy partners is a way of reducing risk and assuring profit. He argues that both trust and commitment develop from structural conditions of risk.

Lawler and Yoon (1993) take an entirely different approach to commitment, one that emphasizes its link to affective processes. They conceptualize commitment as an expressive outcome that emerges from relations that were originally instrumental. Their study shows that repeated negotiated agreements with the same partner produce positive affect, which in turn fosters behavioral commitment. These commitments may reflect an increase over time in the value of maintaining the relationship for its own sake.

Finally, Tallman et al. (1991) combine behavioral and affective components in their analysis of commitment. They define commitment in behavioral terms but propose that strong commitments, derived from high mutual dependence, can lead to self-sacrifice and altruism for the sake of the relationship.

Affective Ties. While the early exchange theorists (Blau, Homans, and Thibaut and Kelley) devoted considerable attention to affective consequences of exchange relations, those concerns have been noticeably absent from most contemporary work on social exchange. Recently, however, there are signs of a renewed interest in affect. This trend may partly reflect the growing interest in emotions in social psychology (see chapter 5). Whereas many social psychologists view affect as a cause of behavior, however, social exchange theorists study

it primarily as a consequence of exchange structures and processes, including the use of power.

Two recent studies of affect and social exchange, by Molm (1991) and Lawler and Yoon (1993), address the complex relations among exchange structure, exchange processes, and affect. Both suggest that structural power influences affective responses indirectly, through its effects on the processes and outcomes of exchange. The Lawler and Yoon study conceptualizes affect as a mediating variable that links exchange structure with commitment through behavioral processes. Equal power relations produce positive affect (pleasure/satisfaction and arousal/activation) by increasing the frequency of successful exchange transactions. These affective ties represent new domains of exchange, reflected in tendencies to stay with the same partner.

Molm (1991) studies how actors' satisfaction with their exchange relations varies as a function of the structure of power, the base of power, and power strategies. Satisfaction reflects not only actors' evaluations of how "good" or "bad" their relations are, but how those evaluations compare to some standard of expectations (e.g., Thibaut and Kelley's CL). Her work shows that both the outcomes of exchange and the process of exchange (i.e., the power strategies actors use) affect satisfaction and that for both, negative acts affect satisfaction more than equivalent positive acts. All of these effects are modified by actors' power positions in ways that are consistent with an effect of power on expected outcomes.

CONCLUSIONS, UNRESOLVED DEBATES, AND FUTURE DIRECTIONS

Since Emerson's chapter on exchange theory was published in the Rosenberg and Turner (1981) volume, several systematic research programs have provided the necessary empirical base for extension and refinement of the theory. However, some parts of exchange theory have received more empirical attention than others in the various research programs developed since the mid-1970s. The structural determinants of the distribution of power in exchange networks, the dynamics of power use, the impact of different bases of power on exchange relations, and the efficacy of various strategies of power use have been fairly extensively investigated. However, many important topics have received scant attention. Only recently have investigators begun to examine other consequences of exchange in addition to the outcomes received. Research is underway to study the determinants of commitment and solidarity in exchange networks and the development of trust and affective ties between exchange partners. These developments hold the promise of providing the missing ingredients to a fully social theory of exchange.

One impediment to research outside the laboratory on these fundamental exchange processes has been the lack of a fully developed theory of value (see Emerson 1987 for a rudimentary effort). Social exchange theorists, like many economists, presume the existence of values in their theoretical framework. Exchange relations develop primarily because of the complementarity of values and needs among actors in various social systems. But these needs and values are also socially determined. Even consummatory value has a major social component, beyond the basic economic value of the item or service at issue. Marketing research makes this quite clear. Future theoretical and empirical developments in exchange theory will require further investigation of the determinants of value, issues of interpersonal comparison of values (see the exchange between Heckathorn [1983a, 1983b] and Emerson et al. [1983]), and even more complex problems of measurement. Despite the fact that Turner (1987) has argued that the development of a theory of value within the exchange framework moves researchers away from the more sociologically interesting questions and back into intrapsychic phenomenon more characteristic of psychology, resolution of these problems is essential for further development of the theory.

More sociologically interesting are current efforts to expand the theory to include structure and structural change as a dependent variable. Emerson's (1972b) early work on power-balancing mechanisms deals with only a small number of potential change mechanisms in exchange networks (e.g., coalition formation or incorporation and network expansion), and even these have not received extensive empirical treatment. The inclusion of notions being developed in transaction-cost economics (Cook and Emerson 1984) and of power-gaining strategies (see Cook 1991), among others, will be central in the development of a more complete theory of network transformation and structural change. In addition, predicting which types of exchange structures (under what conditions) are more likely to become institutionalized is an important potential outcome that links to some of the early work in anthropology (e.g., Levi-Strauss 1949; Mauss 1925; see also Emerson 1981). This work also may have significant implications for applying exchange notions to the emergence of particular organizational forms.

Recent developments, together with these potential advances in the future, suggest that exchange theory may well be developing in ways that are highly useful for theorizing about micro-macro linkages in society. As Cook (1991) suggested in a discussion of the microfoundations of social structure, no theory can even attempt to bridge the "micro-macro gap" unless it contains both a full conception of agency (i.e., actors with motives, needs, and desires) and a model of social structure that can move from very simple structures (e.g., two-party exchange relations) to complex structures including corporate actors and nested groups. Social exchange theory is moving in directions that make it ideally suited for this task.

NOTES

We gratefully acknowledge research support from the National Science Foundation. We thank Edward Lawler, John Stolte, Lynn Smith-Lovin, Toshio Tamagishi, and our students for valuable suggestions and comments.

1. Many other theorists, including Boulding (1973), Foa and Foa (1974), Gergen (1969), Heath (1976), Kuhn (1963), and Meeker (1971), also contributed to the early development of social exchange theory. Anthropologists

who built on the early pioneering efforts include Barth (1966), Polanyi (1957), and Sahlins (1965a, 1965b).

2. The distinction between negotiation and reciprocation is made only for direct exchange because negotiated agreements are difficult, if not impossible, in indirect exchange relations.

3. See Heath (1976) for a critique of Blau's use of economics and a more extensive application of economic principles to social exchange.

4. In a social exchange relation between A and B, A's reinforcement comes from B's behavior and vice versa; thus, adopting the individual as the unit of analysis necessarily produces tautological reasoning (i.e., predicting behavior from reinforcement when both are defined in terms of one another). This is the error Homans made: he attempted to "explain" A's behavior in terms of the reinforcement B's behavior provides for A, and B's behavior in terms of the reinforcement A provides for B. Adopting the social relation as the unit of analysis avoids this pitfall: one instead attempts to explain the *relation* between A's behavior and B's behavior (i.e., the exchange relation) by the structure of their dependence on one another for reinforcement.

5. Alternative, but similar, conceptions of power have been offered by Coleman (1973, 1977, 1990), Marsden (1983), and others. For example, Coleman defines the dependence of actor A on actor B as the extent to which events (commodities or services) in which actor A is interested are controlled by actor B. An actor's interest in an event in Coleman's theory is equivalent to the value of a resource in Emerson's theory. As Marsden (1983, 1987) noted, however, Emerson's model considers availability of alternative relations, while Coleman's does not because it assumes that any pair of actors can exchange resources with each other—the economic assumption of unrestricted competition.

6. Only a few researchers have examined the effects of what Emerson called "cohesion," and they have referred to it in more neutral terms: "mutual dependence" (Michaels and Wiggins 1976), "total power" (Bacharach and Lawler 1981), or "average power" (Molm 1987a).

7. We adopt Cook and Emerson's (1978) convention of using the same letter (e.g., B_1, B_2, B_3) to designate actors in the same structural position in a network and different letters to designate actors in different structural positions.

8. Gray and associates (e.g., Gray and Griffith 1984; Gray and Tallman 1984) studied dyadic power from a different but related perspective—social power theory. This approach conceptualizes one actor's compliance with another actor's directives as a form of exchange and measures power use as the difference between the two actors' compliance ratios.

9. Markovsky et al. (1988) referred to this procedure as the "one-exchange rule" and studied networks in which actors are not restricted to exchange with a single partner on each opportunity. Allowing actors with n alternative partners to engage in n exchanges on a single opportunity transforms a negatively connected network to one with null connections; that is, exchange in one relation will have no effect on exchange in another.

10. The emphasis on rule-governed exchange is related to Willer and Anderson's (1981) assumption that initiating an exchange involves an actual loss—giving up a material resource that has some value to the actor—over and above the opportunity costs assumed by Emerson (1972a). For these reasons, Anderson and Willer assert that "Any modern economic exchange occurs only if there is a joint agreement on the rate of exchange" (Anderson and Willer 1981, 14). In contrast, theories of social exchange assume that exchanges will be initiated even in the absence of negotiated agreements, because actors' dependence on others for most social rewards is a necessary incentive for undertaking that risk.

REFERENCES

Abrahamsson, H. A. 1970. Homans on exchange. *American Journal of Sociology* 76:273–275.

Adams, J. Stacy. 1965. Inequity in social exchange. Pp. 267–299 in *Advances in Experimental Social Psychology,* vol. 2, ed. Leonard Berkowitz. New York: Academic.

Anderson, Bo, and David Willer. 1981. Introduction. Pp. 1–21 in *Networks, Exchange and Coercion: The Elementary Theory and Its Applications,* ed.

David Willer and Bo Anderson. New York: Elsevier.

Bacharach, Samuel B., and Edward J. Lawler. 1980. *Power and Politics in Organizations.* San Francisco: Jossey-Bass.

———. 1981. *Bargaining: Power, Tactics, and Outcomes.* San Francisco: Jossey-Bass.

Barth, Frederick. 1966. *Models of Social Organization.* London: Royal Anthropological Institute.

Befu, Harumi. 1977. Social exchange. *Annual Review of Anthropology* 6:255–281.

Bienenstock, Elisa Jayne, and Phillip Bonacich. 1992. The core as a solution to exclusionary networks. *Social Networks* 14:231–243.

Bierstedt, Robert. 1950. An analysis of social power. *American Sociological Review* 15:730–738.

———. 1965. Review of Blau's "exchange and power." *American Sociological Review* 30:789–790.

Blain, Robert R. 1971. On Homans' psychological reductionism. *Sociological Inquiry* 41:3–25.

Blalock, Hubert M., Jr., and Paul H. Wilken. 1979. *Intergroup Processes: A Micro-Macro Perspective.* New York: Free Press.

Blau, Peter M. 1964. *Exchange and Power in Social Life.* New York: Wiley.

———. 1987. Microprocesses and macrostructure. Pp. 83–100 in *Social Exchange Theory,* ed. Karen S. Cook. Newbury Park, CA: Sage.

Bonacich, Phillip. 1987. Power and centrality: A family of measures. *American Journal of Sociology* 92:1170–1182.

Boulding, Kenneth E. 1973. *The Economy of Love and Fear: A Preface to Grant's Economics.* Belmont, CA: Wadsworth.

Burgess, Robert L., and Ted L. Huston, eds. 1979. *Social Exchange in Developing Relationships.* New York: Academic.

Burgess, Robert L., and Joyce M. Nielsen. 1974. An experimental analysis of some structural determinants of equitable and inequitable exchange relations. *American Sociological Review* 39:427–443.

Chadwick-Jones, J. K. 1976. *Social Exchange Theory: Its Structure and Influence in Social Psychology.* London: Academic.

Coleman, James S. 1973. *The Mathematics of Collective Action.* Chicago: Aldine.

———. 1977. Social action systems. Pp. 11–50 in *Problems of Formalization in the Social Sciences,* ed. Klemens Szaniawski. Wroclaw: Polskiej Akademii Nauk.

———. 1990. *Foundations of Social Theory.* Cambridge, MA: Harvard University Press.

Cook, Karen S. 1977. Exchange and power in networks of interorganizational relations. *Sociological Quarterly* 18:62–82.

———, ed. 1987. *Social Exchange Theory.* Newbury Park, CA: Sage.

———. 1991. The microfoundations of social structure: An exchange perspective. Pp. 29–45 in *Macro-Micro Linkages in Sociology,* ed. Joan Huber. Newbury Park, CA: Sage.

Cook, Karen S., Shawn Donnelly, and Toshio Yamagishi. 1992. The effect of latent paths on the distribution of power in exchange network structures. Paper presented at the 1992 annual meeting of the American Sociological Association, Pittsburgh.

Cook, Karen S., and Richard M. Emerson. 1978. Power, equity and commitment in exchange networks. *American Sociological Review* 43:721–739.

———. 1984. Exchange networks and the analysis of complex organizations. In *Research in the Sociology of Organizations,* vol. 3, ed. Samuel B. Bacharach and Edward J. Lawler. Greenwich, CT: JAI Press.

Cook, Karen S., Richard M. Emerson, Mary R. Gillmore, and Toshio Yamagishi. 1983. The distribution of power in exchange networks: Theory and experimental results. *American Journal of Sociology* 89:275–305.

Cook, Karen S., and Mary R. Gillmore. 1984. Power, dependence, and coalitions. Pp. 27–58 in *Advances in Group Processes,* vol. 1, ed. Edward J. Lawler. Greenwich, CT: JAI Press.

Cook, Karen S., Mary R. Gillmore, and Toshio Yamagishi. 1986. Point and line vulnerability as bases for predicting the distribution of power in exchange networks: Reply to Willer. *American Journal of Sociology* 92:445–448.

Cook, Karen S., and Karen A. Hegtvedt. 1986. Justice and power: An exchange analysis. Pp. 19–41 in *Justice in Social Relations,* ed. Hans Werner Bierhoff, Ronald L. Cohen, and Jerald Greenberg. New York: Plenum.

Cook, Karen S., and Toshio Yamagishi. 1992. Power in exchange networks: A power-dependence formulation. *Social Networks* 14:245–265.

Czako, Agnes. 1988. Manager's reciprocal transaction. *Connections* 11:23–32.

Della Fave, L. R. 1980. The meek shall not inherit the earth. *American Sociological Review* 45:955–971.

Deutsch, Morton. 1964. Homans in the Skinner box. *Sociological Inquiry* 34:156–165.

Edwards, J. 1969. Familial behavior as social exchange. *Journal of Marriage and the Family* 31:518–526.

Ekeh, Peter. 1974. *Social Exchange Theory: The Two Traditions.* Cambridge, MA: Harvard University Press.

Emerson, Richard M. 1962. Power-dependence relations. *American Sociological Review* 27:31–41.

————. 1969. Operant psychology and exchange theory. Pp. 379–405 in *Behavioral Sociology,* ed. Robert L. Burgess and Don Bushell. New York: Columbia University Press.

————. 1972a. Exchange theory, part I: A psychological basis for social exchange. Pp. 38–57 in *Sociological Theories in Progress,* vol. 2, ed. Joseph Berger, Morris Zelditch, Jr., and Bo Anderson. Boston: Houghton-Mifflin.

————. 1972b. Exchange theory, part II: Exchange relations and networks. Pp. 58–87 in *Sociological Theories in Progress,* vol. 2, ed. Joseph Berger, Morris Zelditch, Jr., and Bo Anderson. Boston: Houghton-Mifflin.

————. 1976. Social exchange theory. *Annual Review of Sociology* 2:335–362.

————. 1981. Social exchange theory. Pp. 30–65 in *Social Psychology: Sociological Perspectives,* ed. Morris Rosenberg and Ralph H. Turner. New York: Basic Books.

————. 1987. Toward a theory of value in social exchange. Pp. 11–46 in *Social Exchange Theory,* ed. Karen S. Cook. Newbury Park, CA: Sage.

Emerson, Richard M., Karen S. Cook, Mary R. Gillmore, and Toshio Yamagishi. 1983. Valid predictions from invalid comparisons: Response to Heckathorn. *Social Forces* 61:1232–1247.

Fischer, Claude S. 1982. *To Dwell Among Friends: Personal Networks in Town and City.* Chicago: University of Chicago Press.

Foa, Uriel G., and Edna B. Foa. 1974. *Societal Structures of the Mind.* Springfield, IL: Charles C. Thomas.

Freeman, Linton C. 1979. Centrality in social networks: Conceptual clarification. *Social Networks* 1:215–239.

French, John R. P., Jr. 1956. A formal theory of social power. *Psychological Review* 63:181–194.

Friedkin, Noah E. 1986. A formal theory of social power. *Journal of Mathematical Sociology* 12:103–126.

————. 1992. An expected value model of social power: Predictions for selected exchange networks. *Social Networks* 14:213–229.

Galaskiewicz, Joseph. 1979. *Exchange Networks and Community Politics.* Beverly Hills, CA: Sage.

Gergen, Kenneth J. 1969. *The Psychology of Behavior Exchange.* Reading, MA: Addison-Wesley.

Gillmore, Mary R. 1987. Implications of generalized versus restricted exchange. Pp. 170–189 in *Social Exchange Theory,* ed. Karen S. Cook. Newbury Park, CA: Sage.

Gottman, John M. 1979. *Marital Interaction: Experimental Investigations.* New York: Academic.

Gouldner, Alvin W. 1960. The norm of reciprocity: A preliminary statement. *American Sociological Review* 25:161–178.

Gray, Louis N., and W. I. Griffith. 1984. On differentiation in small group power relations. *Social Psychology Quarterly* 47:391–396.

Gray, Louis N., and Irving Tallman. 1984. A satisfaction balance model of decision making and choice behavior. *Social Psychology Quarterly* 47:146–159.

————. 1987. Theories of choice: Contingent reward and punishment applications. *Social Psychology Quarterly* 50:16–23.

Heath, Anthony F. 1976. *Rational Choice and Social Exchange: A Critique of Exchange Theory.* Cambridge, UK: Cambridge University Press.

Heckathorn, Douglas D. 1983a. Extensions of power-dependence theory: The concept of resistance. *Social Forces* 61:1206–1231.

————. 1983b. Valid and invalid interpersonal comparisons: Response to Emerson, Cook, Gillmore, and Yamagishi. *Social Forces* 61:1248–1259.

Homans, George C. 1958. Social behavior as exchange. *American Journal of Sociology* 62:597–606.

————. [1961] 1974. *Social Behavior: Its Elementary Forms.* New York: Harcourt Brace & World.

————. 1976. Commentary. Pp. 231–244 in *Advances in Experimental Social Psychology,* vol. 9, ed. Leonard Berkowitz and Elaine Walster. New York: Academic.

Huesmann, L., and George Levinger. 1976. Incremental exchange theory: A formal model for progression in dyadic social integration. Pp. 151–193 in *Advances in Experimental Social Psychology,* vol. 9, ed. Leonard Berkowitz and Elaine Walster. New York: Academic.

Kahneman, Daniel, and Amos Tversky. 1984. Choices, values, and frames. *American Psychologist* 39:341–350.

Kanter, Rosabeth Moss. 1977. *Men and Women of the Corporation.* New York: Basic Books.

Kelley, Harold H., and John W. Thibaut. 1978. *Interpersonal Relations: A Theory of Interdependence.* New York: Wiley.

Kollock, Peter. 1992. The emergence of exchange structures: An experimental study of uncertainty, commitment, and trust. Paper presented at the 1992 annual meeting of the American Sociological Association, Pittsburgh.

Kuhn, Alfred. 1963. *The Study of Society: A Unified Approach.* Homewood, IL: Irwin-Dorsey.

Laumann, Edward O., and Franz Urban Pappi. 1976. *Networks of Collective Action.* New York: Academic.

Lawler, Edward J., and Samuel B. Bacharach. 1987. Comparison of dependence and punitive forms of power. *Social Forces* 66:446–462.

Lawler, Edward J., and Jeongkoo Yoon. 1993. Power and the emergence of commitment behavior in negotiated exchange. *American Sociological Review* 58:465–481.

Leibenstein, Harvey. 1976. *Beyond Economic Man: A New Foundation for Micro Economics.* Cambridge MA: Harvard University Press.

Leik, Robert K., and Sheila K. Leik. 1977. Transition to interpersonal commitment. Pp. 299–322 in *Behavioral Theory in Sociology,* ed. Robert L. Hamblin and John H. Kunkel. New Brunswick: Transaction.

Levinger, George. 1976. A social psychological perspective on marital dissolution. *Journal of Social Issues* 32:21–47.

Levi-Strauss, C. 1949. *Les Structures Elementaires de la Parente.* Paris: Presses Universitaires de France.

Lewis, Robert A., and Graham B. Spanier. 1982. Marital quality, marital stability, and social exchange. Pp. 49–66 in *Family Relationships: Rewards and Costs,* ed. F. Ivan Nye. Beverly Hills, CA: Sage.

Machina, Mark J. 1987. Choice under uncertainty: Problems solved and unsolved. *Economic Perspectives* 2:121–154.

Malinowski, Bronislaw. 1922. *Argonauts of the Western Pacific.* New York: E.P. Dutton.

Markovsky, Barry. 1987. Toward multilevel sociological theories: Simulations of actor and network effects. *Sociological Theory* 5:101–117.

Markovsky, Barry, David Willer, and Travis Patton. 1988. Power relations in exchange networks. *American Sociological Review* 53:220–236.

———. 1990. Theory, evidence, and intuition. *American Sociological Review* 55:300–308.

Marsden, Peter V. 1982. Brokerage behavior in restricted exchange networks. Pp. 201–218 in *Social Structure and Network Analysis,* ed. Peter V. Marsden and Nan Lin. Beverly Hills, CA: Sage.

———. 1983. Restricted access in networks and models of power. *American Journal of Sociology* 88:686–717.

———. 1987. Elements of interactor dependence. Pp. 130–148 in *Social Exchange Theory,* ed. Karen S. Cook. Newbury Park, CA: Sage.

Mauss, Marcel. 1925. *Essai sur le Don en Sociologie et Anthropologie.* Paris: Presses Universitaires de France.

McCall, M. 1966. Courtship as social exchange: Some historical comparisons. Pp. 190–200 in *Kinship and Family Organization,* ed. Bernard Farber. New York: Wiley.

McDonald, Gerald W. 1980. Family power: The assessment of a decade of theory and research, 1970–1979. *Journal of Marriage and the Family* 42:841–854.

Meeker, Barbara F. 1971. Decisions and exchange. *American Sociological Review* 36:485–495.

Michaels, James W., and James A. Wiggins. 1976. Effects of mutual dependency and dependency asymmetry on social exchange. *Sociometry* 39:368–376.

Michener, H. Andrew, Eugene D. Cohen, and Aage B. Sorensen. 1977. Social exchange: Predicting transactional outcomes in five-event, four-person systems. *American Sociological Review* 42: 522–535.

Molm, Linda D. 1980. The effects of structural variations in social reinforcement contingencies on exchange and cooperation. *Social Psychology Quarterly* 43:269–282.

———. 1981. The conversion of power imbalance to power use. *Social Psychology Quarterly* 16:153–166.

———. 1984. The disruption and recovery of dyadic social interaction. Pp. 183–227 in *Advances in Group Processes,* vol. 1, ed. Edward J. Lawler. Greenwich, CT: JAI Press.

———. 1987a. Extending power-dependence theory: Power processes and negative outcomes. Pp. 171–198 in *Advances in Group Processes,* vol. 4, ed. Edward J. Lawler and Barry Markovsky. Greenwich, CT: JAI Press.

———. 1987b. Linking power structure and power use. Pp. 101–129 in *Social Exchange Theory,* ed. Karen S. Cook. Newbury Park, CA: Sage.

———. 1988. The structure and use of power: A comparison of reward and punishment power. *Social Psychology Quarterly* 51:108–122.

———. 1989a. An experimental analysis of imbalance in punishment power. *Social Forces* 68:178–203.

———. 1989b. Punishment power: A balancing process in power-dependence relations. *American Journal of Sociology* 94:1392–1428.

———. 1990. Structure, action, and outcomes: The dynamics of power in social exchange. *American Sociological Review* 55:427–447.

———. 1991. Affect and social exchange: Satisfaction in power-dependence relations. *American Sociological Review* 56:475–493.

———. 1993. When coercive power fails: Incentive and risk in social exchange. Paper presented at the 1993 annual meeting of the American Sociological Association, Miami.

Molm, Linda D., Theron M. Quist, and Phillip A. Wiseley. 1994. Imbalanced structures, unfair strategies: Power and justice in social exchange. *American Sociological Review* 49:98–121.

Molm, Linda D., and James A. Wiggins. 1979. A behavioral analysis of the dynamics of social exchange in the dyad. *Social Forces* 57:1157–1179.

Patterson, Gerald R. 1982. *Coercive Family Process.* Eugene, OR: Castalia.

Pfeffer, Jeffrey, and Gerald R. Salancik. 1978. *The External Control of Organizations: A Resource Dependence Perspective.* New York: Harper & Row.

Polanyi, Karl. 1957. *Trade and Market in the Early Empires.* New York: Free Press.

Raush, Harold L., W. A. Barry, R. K. Hertel, and M. A. Swain. 1974. *Communication, Conflict, and Marriage.* San Francisco: Jossey-Bass.

Rosenberg, Morris, and Ralph H. Turner. 1981. *Social Psychology: Sociological Perspectives.* New York: Basic Books.

Safilios-Rothschild, Constantina. 1976. A macro- and micro-examination of family power and love: An exchange model. *Journal of Marriage and the Family* 37:355–362.

Sahlins, Marshall D. 1965a. Exchange value and the diplomacy of primitive trade. Pp. 95–129 in *Proceedings of the American Ethnological Society.* Seattle: University of Washington Press.

———. 1965b. On the sociology of primitive exchange. Pp. 139–236 in *The Relevance of Models for Social Anthropology,* ed. Michael P. Banton. New York: Praeger.

Scanzoni, John. 1972. *Sexual Bargaining: Power Politics in American Marriage.* Englewood Cliffs, NJ: Prentice Hall.

Schmitt, David R., and Gerald Marwell. 1975. *Cooperation: An Experimental Analysis.* New York: Academic.

Shrum, Wesley. 1990. Status incongruence among boundary spanners: Structure, exchange, and conflict. *American Sociological Review* 55:496–511.

Simpson, Richard L. 1972. *Theories of Social Exchange.* Morristown, NJ: General Learning Press.

Starkweather, David, and Karen S. Cook. 1987. Managing organization-environment relations. Pp. 344–378 in *Health Care Management: A Text in Organizational Theory and Behavior,* ed. Stephen M. Shortell and Arnold D. Kaluzny. New York: Wiley.

Stolte, John R. 1983. The legitimation of structural inequality: The reformulation and test of the self-evaluation argument. *American Sociological Review* 48:331–342.

———. 1987. The formation of justice norms. *American Sociological Review* 52:774–784.

———. 1988. From micro- to macro-exchange structure: Measuring power imbalance at the exchange network level. *Social Psychology Quarterly* 51: 357–364.

Stolte, John R., and Richard M. Emerson. 1977. Structural inequality: Position and power in network structures. Pp. 117–138 in *Behavioral Theory in Sociology,* ed. Robert L. Hamblin and John Kunkel. New Brunswick, NJ: Transaction.

Tallman, Irving, Louis Gray, and Robert K. Leik. 1991. Decision, dependency, and commitment: An exchange based theory of group formation. Pp. 227–257 in *Advances in Group Processes,* vol. 8, ed. Edward J. Lawler, Barry Markovsky, Cecilia Ridgeway, and Henry A. Walker. Greenwich, CT: JAI Press.

Thibaut, John W., and Harold H. Kelley. 1959. *The Social Psychology of Groups.* New York: Wiley.

Turner, Jonathan H. [1974] 1986. *The Structure of Sociological Theory.* Homewood, IL: Dorsey.

———. 1987. Social exchange theory: Future directions. Pp. 223–238 in *Social Exchange Theory,* ed. Karen S. Cook. Newbury Park, CA: Sage.

Weick, Karl. 1976. Educational organizations as loosely coupled systems. *Administrative Science Quarterly* 21:1–19.

Willer, David. 1981. The basic concepts of the elementary theory. Pp. 25–53 in *Networks, Exchange and Coercion: The Elementary Theory and Its Applications,* ed. David Willer and Bo Anderson. New York: Elsevier.

———. 1985. Property and social exchange. Pp. 123–142 in *Advances in Group Processes,* vol. 2, ed. Edward J. Lawler. Greenwich, CT: JAI Press.

———. 1986. Vulnerability and the location of power positions. *American Journal of Sociology* 92: 441–448.

Willer, David, and Bo Anderson. 1981. *Networks, Exchange and Coercion: The Elementary Theory and Its Applications.* New York: Elsevier.

Willer, David, Barry Markovsky, and Travis Patton. 1989. Power structures: Derivations and applications of elementary theory. Pp. 313–353 in *Sociological Theories in Progress: New Formulations,* ed. Joseph Berger, Morris Zelditch, Jr., and Bo Anderson. Newbury Park, CA: Sage.

Willer, David, and Travis Patton. 1987. The development of network exchange theory. Pp. 199–242 in *Advances in Group Processes,* vol. 4, ed. Edward J. Lawler and Barry Markovsky. Greenwich, CT: JAI Press.

Williamson, Oliver E. 1975. *Markets and Hierarchies.* New York: Free Press.

———. 1982. The economics of organization: The transaction cost approach. *American Journal of Sociology* 87:548–577.

Wrong, Dennis H. 1961. The oversocialized conception of man in modern sociology. *American Sociological Review* 26:183–193.

Yamagishi, Toshio, and Karen S. Cook. 1990. Power relations in exchange networks: Comment on "network exchange theory." *American Sociological Review* 55:297–300.

Yamagishi, Toshio, Mary R. Gillmore, and Karen S. Cook. 1988. Network connections and the distribution of power in exchange networks. *American Journal of Sociology* 93:833–851.

CHAPTER 9

Bargaining and Influence in Conflict Situations

EDWARD J. LAWLER
REBECCA FORD

Bargaining subsumes a diverse range of phenomena approached by a variety of academic disciplines. Economists have studied how labor-management bargaining affects wage rates (Chamberlain 1955; Dunlop 1950; Young 1975; Zeuthen 1930); mathematicians and game theorists have tried to find predictive (or prescriptive) mathematical solutions to explain how actors will "split the difference" when they bargain (Harsanyi 1977; Luce and Raiffa 1957); political scientists have studied international alliances, the onset of wars, and deterrence processes (Morgan 1977; Schelling 1960); and social psychologists have examined the influence tactics of actors in conflict and bargaining (Deutsch 1969; Pruitt 1981; Rubin and Brown 1975). Sociologists, only recently interested in bargaining, bring an emphasis on structure (power) and process (tactics) in bargaining (e.g., Bacharach and Lawler 1981; Cook and Emerson 1978; Patchen 1988; Strauss 1978).

This chapter examines bargaining as an influence process through which actors attempt to resolve a social conflict. Conflict occurs when two or more interdependent actors have incompatible preferences and perceive or anticipate resistance from each other (Blalock 1989; Kriesberg 1982). Bargaining is a basic form of goal-directed action that involves both intentions to influence and efforts by each actor to carry out these intentions. Tactics are verbal and/or nonverbal actions designed to maneuver oneself into a favorable position vis-à-vis another or to reach some accommodation. Our treatment of bargaining subsumes the concept of "negotiation" (see Morley and Stephenson 1977).[1]

This chapter focuses on social psychological theory and research on bargaining and adopts a sociological perspective. We attempt a conceptual synthesis rather than a thorough review, and thus selectively emphasize fundamental theoretical ideas and classic empirical work. Our sociological perspective is captured by five basic assumptions. (1) Conflict has a social structural foundation, meaning that actors in a bargaining situation tend to occupy social positions with different interests. Conflicts are likely to emerge time and time again, regardless of who occupies these positions, as long as the social structure remains unchanged (Lawler 1992). (2) Incentives, utilities, or payoffs that stimulate bargaining are embedded in social structures allocating power and status across social positions and roles. Some structures create incentives for actors to accommodate and some create incentives to gain advantage. (3) Actors are at best "boundedly rational," because they not only face substantial ambiguity and uncertainty about each other's intentions but also have incentives to withhold information, bluff, and otherwise manipulate each other's cognitions and behavior. (4) Social interaction in the bargaining process is "tactical action." Tactics are time-bound patterns of action that can be directed at various goals, such as to punish the other, test the other's resolve, and gain information (Lawler 1992; Pruitt 1981; Strauss 1978). Actors imperfectly assemble their tactics into strategies. (5) The bargaining process consists of tactical-countertactical patterns of action that produce emergent effects on the results of bargaining (Bacharach and Lawler 1981). The social structure shapes actors' definitions of the bargaining context, but the bargaining process takes on a "life of its own" once initiated.

Bargaining tends to occur under two conditions. First, two or more actors (individuals, groups, organizations) have a conflict of interest, manifest in expected or actual negative acts toward one another (Blalock 1989). The negative acts may range from snide comments among friends to military force among nations. Second, actors wish to influence each other, either to get their own way or, failing this, to reach a mutual accommodation. Getting their own way could involve what movie to attend on a Friday night or how member nations are to interpret a rule of the European Economic Community. Mutual accommodation could involve opting for everybody's second choice among movie options or interpreting a given rule of the European Economic Community so that all members suffer an equal decrement in national autonomy. Structurally, bargaining presupposes a relationship in which actors are at least minimally interdependent on one another. If interdependence between actors is so low that each can readily avoid the other, or if they prefer other relationships anyway, a conflict will likely trigger a breakdown of the relationship prior to any bargaining. The structure of interdependence produces sufficient incentives to bargain when the costs of continuing the conflict are greater than the costs to actors of compromise agreements involving something less than their most preferred solution (Raiffa 1982).

When bargaining occurs, the mutual efforts of actors to influence one another other results in a joint (collective) product (Bacharach and Lawler 1981; Walton and McKersie 1965). One aspect of this joint product is simply whether conflict resolution (agreement) occurs or not; another is the exact nature of the agreement reached. These are distinguishable dependent variables that receive varied emphasis in the bargaining literature. In game theoretical work, for example, the likelihood of agreement typically is assumed to be 100 percent (given rational actors) and the focus is the nature of the agreement (Luce and Raiffa 1957; Rapoport 1966). In social psychological and sociological work, conflict resolution is assumed to be more highly prob-

lematic, so greater attention is given to the structural and processual conditions likely to promote or inhibit agreements (Bacharach and Lawler 1981; Blalock 1989; Cook and Emerson 1978; Dahrendorf 1959; Lawler 1992; Rubin and Brown 1975; Strauss 1978).

This chapter is organized around a conceptual framework that distinguishes basic types of bargaining contexts. We begin by introducing the framework and then present an overview of and analyze theoretical and empirical work on each type of bargaining context.

CONCEPTUAL FRAMEWORK

Conceptualizing the varied contexts of bargaining is useful, heuristically, to understand the structural constraints and opportunities in different bargaining settings. Two contrasts form the foundation for a fourfold typology of bargaining contexts (see Bacharach and Lawler 1980 for an earlier version): tacit versus explicit, and distributive versus integrative bargaining. The first refers to the nature and use of verbal communication between actors (Schelling 1960) and the second to the potential for actors to increase their joint benefit from conflict resolution (Pruitt 1981; Walton and McKersie 1965). Our theoretical strategy is to abstract the prototypical features of diverse bargaining contexts by sharpening and interrelating these contrasts.[2]

Tacit versus Explicit Bargaining

Schelling (1960) first introduced and developed the distinction between tacit and explicit bargaining. Tacit bargaining occurs when interdependent actors perceive a conflict and anticipate each other's behavior without open communication. The moves and countermoves tend to be nonverbal and to occur at a distance, because the social structure obstructs opportunities to communicate, makes explicit bargaining normatively inappropriate, or fosters too much distrust for actors to use existing channels of communication to deal with conflict openly and constructively.

The task actors face in *tacit* bargaining depends on the priority they give to the cooperative or competitive sides of the mixed-motive dilemma. If cooperation is stressed, the dilemma is how to reach a jointly beneficial result without overtly communicating. For example, two shoppers who become separated from one another in a busy mall must tacitly coordinate their efforts to reunite (Schelling 1960). If competition is emphasized, tacit bargaining involves tactical efforts to outmaneuver the other and achieve an advantage, or at least avoid a disadvantage. Examples include a nation that preemptively occupies a strategic location in an international conflict, a motorist who swerves in front of another to be the first through an intersection, and a sales manager who proposes an organizational policy that favors sales over production.

Explicit bargaining differs from tacit bargaining in three primary respects (Bacharach and Lawler 1980, 108–116). First, actors acknowledge a conflict and consent to bargain. Second, lines of communication are direct, verbal, and open enough to permit a series of offers and counteroffers, that is, provisional compromises that are not fixed until both agree. Third, the actors perceive a potential for compromise—solutions that give each party benefits greater than those derived from nonagreement. The task is to converge on an explicit and often formal agreement. These three properties of explicit bargaining contexts are manifest in international peace treaties, corporate mergers, labor-management wage negotiations, prenuptial agreements, and even child custody settlements.

Distributive versus Integrative Bargaining

The contrast between distributive and integrative bargaining concerns the nature of the issues under negotiation. An issue is defined as a single dimension with a range of possible solutions that produce payoffs for each actor. The range of possible solutions includes a subset referred to as the "contract zone," which provides each actor payoffs better than nonagreement and constitutes the incentive to bargain in the first place. The ends of the contract zone are anchored by each actor's "resistance points," such as the highest wage an organization will pay versus the lowest wage a union will accept (Walton and McKersie 1965).

In their classic statement, Walton and McKersie (1965) define *distributive bargaining* in terms of issues that involve a *fixed* amount of benefit to divide and integrative bargaining in terms of *variable-sum* issues. In distributive bargaining over wages, for example, an increase in wage rates for labor entails a gain for labor and a cost to management. This zero-sum aspect of the issue exerts pressure toward competition and hostility, whereas the opportunity costs associated with nonagreement exert pressure toward cooperation and conciliation (Bacharach and Lawler 1981; Luce and Raiffa 1957; Walton and McKersie 1965). These competing pressures make the overall situation a classic mixed-motive one; that is both incentives to compete and incentives to cooperate are present. Each actor wants an agreement (the incentive to cooperate), but each also wants an agreement giving them as much of the fixed benefit as possible (the incentive to compete).

In integrative bargaining, some agreements produce more total benefit than others, and there is therefore a potential for joint problem solving. The prototypical integrative bargaining context is one in which there are multiple issues under negotiation and bargainers assign complementary priorities to them. Take the example of a union and management negotiating a wage and fringe benefits package. If the union gives higher priority to wages than fringe benefits while management gives higher priority to fringe benefits, then separate "split-the-difference" solutions on each issue produce less benefit for each party than trading off a larger wage increase for a less generous fringe benefits package. Integrative bargaining contexts contain underlying compatible interests or goals that enable actors to develop solutions that increase their joint benefit beyond what "split-difference agreements" would provide (Pruitt 1981; Walton and McKersie 1965).

Bargainers typically do not have perfect information about the other's payoffs and priorities, so they often approach integrative contexts as if the issues were distributive (Neale and Bazerman 1991). For integrative issues to promote conflict resolution, the actors must perceive the structural conditions that create an underlying common interest. Thus, research on integrative bargaining focuses on the conditions giving rise to such perceptions (Neale and Bazerman 1991). The task in integrative bargaining is for actors to discover how to integrate their interests by, for example, exchanging information about their preferences (e.g., Pruitt 1981).

A Typology

Cross-classifying tacit-explicit and distributive-integrative dimensions yields a two-by-two typology of bargaining contexts (Bacharach and Lawler 1980). This typology is important for a number of reasons. It captures some key differences of focus across different theoretical traditions in sociology. Symbolic interactionist theories of identity and "negotiated order" analyze the subtle ways actors develop complementary, mutually shared self-other definitions, and this implies a concern with tacit-integrative bargaining (Strauss 1978). Social exchange theories of power analyze how structural power positions affect bargaining process and outcomes, focusing primarily on explicit-distributive bargaining (Bacharach and Lawler 1981; Cook and Emerson 1978; Heckathorn 1983; Lawler 1992; Markovsky, Willer, and Patton 1988).[3] Economic models also emphasize explicit-distributive contexts (e.g., Chamberlin 1955; Zeuthen 1930). Cognitive theories focus on explicit-integrative bargaining and analyze how decision heuristics and biases shape actors' definitions of and response to issues and payoff structures (Neale and Bazerman 1991; Pruitt 1981). Finally, game theories of strategic interaction in choice matrices reveal principles of special relevance to tacit-distributive bargaining (Harsanyi 1977; Luce and Raiffa 1957; Rapoport 1966).[4]

The typology also has implications for the type of setting—experimental or natural—appropriate to test or apply a theory. A theory directed at explicit-distributive bargaining would require a somewhat different context than one directed at explicit-integrative or tacit-distributive bargaining. In fact, different research traditions tend to use different experimental settings tied to the particular conditions required for a theoretical approach, but little effort has been made to conceptualize these different settings abstractly. We contend that the different experimental settings found in the bargaining literature create distinct social contexts that correspond to one of the above types and that these represent unrecognized and unspecified assumptions about social context implied by various research traditions.

A similar point is made by Stryker (1977), who suggests more generally that social psychological researchers are not sensitive enough to the implicit social structures and definitions of the situation they create in the laboratory. One implication for bargaining is that a matrix game is likely to be a different social context than other experimental games, therefore creating different definitions of the situation. In research using matrix games, choices are dichotomous and made simultaneously without verbal communication, which reflects major features of a tacit-distributive context. In a buyer-seller game (bilateral monopoly), actors have a wide range of possible compromise solutions and can make offers and counteroffers across a number of bargaining rounds, which reflects major features of explicit-distributive bargaining. Such contexts are likely to foster different definitions of the situation and lead to different kinds of tactical action (Morley and Stephenson 1977; Nemeth 1970; Stryker 1977).

Of the four types of bargaining, tacit-distributive bargaining is the most conflictual: there are fundamental incompatibilities in actors' goals; there are few viable compromise solutions; and tactical options are highly constrained. Explicit-distributive bargaining conforms to most common-sense conceptions of bargaining. The bargaining is mutually recognized, the issues involve a fixed sum, and a wide range of possible solutions or compromises allow an offer-counteroffer sequence. A wider range of solutions expands the range of tactical options (e.g., concession patterns).

In tacit-integrative bargaining, actors have underlying compatible goals, a variable sum issue, and constraints on their verbal communication that limit tactical options. They coordinate their behavior without appearing to negotiate or having to acknowledge the conflict or define the relationship in bargaining terms. Much of the bargaining in organizations takes this subtle, informal, and cooperative form (Bacharach and Lawler 1980). Explicit-integrative bargaining, in contrast, combines a mutually acknowledged conflict with underlying common interests and a problem-solving approach. There are a range of possible issues and solutions from which actors overtly construct integrative solutions that enhance the joint sum of benefits. In the following sections, we subsume disparate research traditions under the four types of bargaining context.

TACIT-DISTRIBUTIVE BARGAINING

We argue that social psychological research on matrix games essentially involves a tacit-distributive context. The standard matrix game used in research consists of two actors, who may choose to compete or cooperate, and a payoff structure (the matrix). Each actor's payoffs are contingent on both his/her own and the other's choice (Rapoport 1966); the contingent nature of the payoffs is the source of their interdependence. In addition, communication opportunities are limited, and the meaning of concession and compromise is unclear in these settings, which gives the issue a "win-lose" appearance (Boyle and Lawler 1991; Nemeth 1972). Actors do not necessarily define their action as bargaining, and conflict resolution involves implicit coordination.

It is important to emphasize that matrix games have been used as both generalized analytic devices and concrete research settings. As analytic devices, they provide insightful, fundamental ideas about the logic of conflict underlying all four types of bargaining context (e.g., Hamburger 1979; Rapoport 1966). In this section, we deal only with their use as experimental research settings (see Pruitt 1981; Rubin and Brown 1975 for extensive reviews).

Of innumerable types of choice matrices (e.g., Hamburger 1979), two have been particularly prominent in research by social psychologists—the prisoner's dilemma and chicken games. We use these to examine the dynamics of tacit-distributive contexts.

Abstract examples of a prisoner dilemma and chicken payoff structures are shown in Figure 9.1. Assuming that each actor wants to maximize his/her own payoff and is making simultaneous choices to cooperate or compete, each matrix creates a different problem for actors. In the prisoner's dilemma, each individual has an incentive to choose the competitive choice, because he/she receives more from competition than from cooperation regardless of what the other person does—in Figure 9.1, actor A receives ten instead of three (if B cooperates) and zero instead of minus five units of payoff (if B competes). This is called a "dominant strategy," a choice that gives an actor more payoff regardless of what the other does (Rapoport 1966). As a dominant strategy, competition is the rational choice for each individual. However, if both actors adopt this choice in a prisoner's dilemma, the result is that they get less than they would if they both cooperated (see chapter 12 for further discussion of this paradox). Furthermore, once they start choosing competitive lines of behavior, it is quite difficult for them to arrive at a tacit agreement to cooperate mutually, because neither will trust the other to keep such a tacit agreement. Conflict resolution is quite difficult to accomplish in a prisoner's dilemma.

A chicken setting does not contain a dominant strategy, as the example in Figure 9.1 illustrates. Actor A gets more from competition only if the other cooperates (ten versus three units of payoff); if the other competes, A gets more from cooperating rather than competing (zero versus minus five units of payoff). In addition, if both actors adopt the competitive choice, each receives his/her *worst* payoff; therefore, the payoff structure involves stronger incentives to resolve the conflict than in a prisoner's dilemma. Note that in a prisoner dilemma structure, the payoff from mutual competition is still better than the payoff from cooperating while the other competes.

PRISONER'S DILEMMA

ACTOR A

		Cooperate	*Compete*
ACTOR B	*Cooperate*	3 / 3	10 / −5
	Compete	−5 / 10	0 / 0

CHICKEN STRUCTURE

ACTOR A

		Cooperate	*Compete*
ACTOR B	*Cooperate*	3 / 3	10 / 0
	Compete	0 / 10	−5 / −5

FIGURE 9.1   Prisoner's dilemma and chicken game matrices. Numbers in each cell are units of payoff resulting from the conjoint choices of each actor. The numbers in the upper right positions are A's payoffs and those below are B's payoffs.

An arms race between two nations typically involves a prisoner's dilemma structure. The cooperative choice for each is to disarm; the competitive choice to arm. In the arms race, the worst result for each actor occurs if they cooperate (disarm) while the other competes (arm). Continuing to compete (arm) is better than risking unreciprocated disarmament. Given the underlying prisoner's dilemma structure, arms races are difficult to stop. However, they sometimes continue for long periods of time without producing actual hostilities, because the decision to start or not start a war is embedded in a chicken structure. This is true if the nations suffer their *worst* payoffs when both choose mutual competition (war). Overall, chicken structures should produce more cooperative action, whatever its specific form, than a prisoner's dilemma structure. Classic comparisons of prisoner's dilemma and chicken structures by Rapoport and Chammah (1965) support this general conclusion.

Competition is clearly and unequivocally the rational choice in a single-play (one choice or one trial) prisoner's dilemma. Empirical research confirms that a large proportion of persons in an experimentally created, one-trial prisoner's dilemma choose the competitive option (Murnighan and Roth 1978). Repeated (iterative) prisoner dilemmas are more interesting, however, because most conflicts occur in continuing social relationships. Competition typically remains the "rational" choice (i.e., dominant strategy) in ongoing relations of a prisoner's dilemma form, but theorists such as Luce and Raiffa (1957) and Axelrod (1984) suggest that over time actors develop tacit agreements to cooperate, thereby avoiding the costs of continued mutual competition. In an ongoing relationship, choices at one point have as one purpose influencing the subsequent or later choices of the other.

However, research suggests while rates of cooperation may increase with repeated play over time, the rate of cooperation does not approach 100 percent; in fact, there is often a higher rate of competitive than cooperative behavior at the end of studies with one hundred to two hundred repeated plays of the same payoff structure (Gallo and McClintock 1965; Nemeth 1970; Rapoport and Chammah 1965). An interesting and important reason is that parties often have knowledge of when the game ends, which produces an infinite regress (Murnighan and Roth 1978; Rapoport 1966). If on the last trial there is no chance of influencing future behavior, both realize the competitive choice is most profitable, as in a one-choice or one-trial game. As long as the outcome of this last trial is known, each actor also knows he/she cannot influence future behavior on the *next-to-last* trial, which suggests a competitive choice on that trial as well. Since the outcome of the second-to-last trial is now known, each actor anticipates that his/her choice on the *third-to-last trial* also cannot influence future trials, and so on, until both are led, theoretically, to choose competitively on each and every trial (Rapoport 1966). In support, Murnighan and Roth (1978) found that parties are more cooperative if there is a high probability the game will continue.

The Opponent's Strategy

One of the major topics of research—the use of particular strategies to induce more cooperation by the other—results from the fact that cooperation doesn't emerge naturally in a prisoner's dilemma. A two-by-two matrix (two actors, two choice options) allows two fundamental strategies with a number of variants: (1) an unconditional strategy, involving consistent cooperation or competition, not contingent on the opponent's behavior; and (2) a conditional strategy, involving competition or cooperation contingent on the opponent's behavior. Early research on the prisoner's dilemma indicated that conditional strategies of one sort or another produce more cooperation than unconditional cooperation or competition (e.g., Oskamp 1971; Sermat 1964; Solomon 1960). A conditional strategy is relatively successful because it rewards the other for cooperating and retaliates in response to competition. Unconditional competition engenders a "lock-in" of mutual conflict, while unconditional cooperation produces exploitation of those who use it (e.g., Solomon 1960).

Applied to a chicken structure, however, unconditional competition puts the opponent in the bind of accepting mutual high costs or lower costs that allow the other to do better. In an interesting study, Sermat (1964) observed that in a chicken game a 100 percent competitive strategy (i.e., competition on all trials) was more effective in eliciting cooperation than a 100 percent (unconditional) cooperative strategy. In a subsequent study, Sermat (1967) showed that a chicken structure, compared to a prisoner's dilemma, makes actors more responsive to the opponent. In one condition, subjects were told their opponent could freely play the game; in a second condition they (knowingly) faced a machine with a preprogrammed strategy. In the prisoner's dilemma, the subjects' rate of cooperation was unaffected by the kind of opponent, but in the chicken structure the type of opponent made a significant difference. When facing an opponent choosing competition 100 percent of the time, subjects knowingly interacting with the machine made more cooperative choices than those interacting with the "freely playing" opponent. One interpretation is that for reasons of face subjects became more concerned with preventing the other from gaining an advantage when interacting with a real other.

Most research indicates overall that a tit-for-tat strategy—reciprocating the choices of the other—produces the greatest cooperation by an opponent (Marinoff 1992; Oskamp 1971; Rapoport and Chammah 1965; Wilson 1971). In a highly influential analysis of strategies, Axelrod (1984) asked scholars of bargaining to submit strategies for a series of computer tournaments using a prisoner's dilemma. Many of these strategies were highly complex variants of conditional cooperation. The results showed that the best strategy was a simple tit-for-tat one involving a cooperative choice on the first trial and reciprocation of the opponent's last choice on all subsequent trials. This strategy did better than or as well as any other strategy entered in the tournaments (Axelrod 1984). Axelrod explains the success of tit for tat as due to the fact that it never provokes an opponent into competition yet cannot be taken advantage of, because it always reciprocates the opponent's last move and therefore punishes unprovoked competition. Because it is a simple strategy, tit for tat is easily recognized and adapted to by others (Axelrod 1984).

The tit-for-tat strategy also has several important limitations. First, as Axelrod himself points out, in a multiactor setting tit for tat needs other cooperators. A completely hostile environment, where everyone chooses competitively all of the time, will not be affected by the tit-for-tat strategy. In fact, there is evidence that tit for tat is not a very robust strategy if any of Axelrod's assumptions are relaxed (Hirshleifer and Coll 1988). Second, one party may not wish to "learn" to be cooperative, or as Blalock (1989) observes, one party may detest the other and wish him/her dead. Third, tit for tat may create competitive deadlocks. If the first cooperative gesture is not reciprocated, it will produce an impasse or lock-in of mutual competition (Axelrod 1984). Overall, a tit-for-tat strategy may be useful only to prevent a lock-in at mutual competition.

Axelrod's work is directed solely at a prisoner's dilemma, but Patchen (1987) suggests two reasons why a tit-for-tat strategy should be even more effective in a chicken structure. First, B's knowledge that A will reciprocate competition effectively removes B's temptation to compete, because doing so would result in B receiving his/her lowest payoff. Second, since B does not expect A to compete, B has little incentive to try to be the first to compete. Consistent with our earlier discussion, the chicken structure has more built-in push toward mutual cooperation, and a tit-for-tat strategy should capitalize on this.[5]

Conditions for Cooperation

A tit-for-tat strategy should induce an "expectation of cooperation" by the other, which can be interpreted in terms of Pruitt and Kimmel's (1977) goals/expectations theory of cooperation. They identify two conditions that foster the development of mutual cooperation: (1) each actor adopts a goal of establishing or maintaining mutual cooperation; and (2) each expects the other to engage in cooperation in response to his/her cooperation. Goals of cooperation ostensibly emerge if people take a longer-term view of the relationship, perceive that they are highly dependent on the other, and believe each other are not likely to cooperate unilaterally. In general, a chicken structure should be more likely

than a prisoner's dilemma to produce a goal of mutual cooperation, simply because mutual competition produces the worst payoffs. Mutual competition in a prisoner's dilemma may produce a goal of mutual cooperation, but acting on that goal is more difficult because to reach it actors have to risk receiving their worst possible payoffs, those from cooperating when the other competes. This is the problem Axelrod's tit-for-tat strategy addresses.

However, Axelrod's (1984) solution to the prisoner's dilemma neglects an important implication of the goal criterion—that each actor perceives the other's cooperative behavior as reflecting a goal of mutual cooperation. A pattern of mutual cooperation is likely to be unstable unless each actor comes to believe that the other also has a goal of mutual cooperation. This is important to "trust," a problem that is particularly severe when actors establish a lock-in of mutual competition.

Such an impasse might be broken by applying Osgood's (1962) idea of graduated and reciprocated initiatives in tension reduction (GRIT strategy) (Lindskold 1978). Osgood proposes that if one actor makes a series of small, unilateral gestures without an expectation of immediate reciprocity, the other will come to reciprocate conciliatory behavior. A GRIT strategy goes beyond tit for tat by making a unilateral switch to cooperation in the context of an extended pattern of mutual competition. Along with such a switch, the strategy involves verbal affirmations of conciliatory intent. Presumably, such a strategy promotes trust, or expectations of cooperation (Pruitt 1981), and treats a problem that cannot be addressed by Axelrod's tit-for-tat strategy.

Several studies have explored the effectiveness of GRIT strategy at eliciting cooperation. Lindskold and Collins (1978) report that GRIT elicited more cooperation than tit for tat and a 50 percent cooperation control condition. Furthermore, Lindskold (1978) analyzed GRIT's effectiveness against opponents classified as either cooperators or competitors and found that it was equally effective with both. Overall, it appears that unilateral gestures are potentially effective to resolve an impasse in tacit-distributive bargaining, but these initiatives must meet certain conditions or users risk exploitation (see Boyle and Lawler 1991; Lindskold 1978).

To conclude, in tacit-distributive bargaining, social structures create incompatible goals and limit the degree to which actors are able or willing to communicate with each other overtly and explicitly about the conflict. Each independently and simultaneously pursues his/her own interests and adopts cooperative or competitive lines of action. The choices of action are based on incentives created and maintained by the social structure, and individuals' choices produce collective results that are often unintended. Avoiding a mutually destructive pattern of mutual conflict and reaching mutual cooperation requires tacit coordination. As a whole: (1) chicken structures are more likely to produce such coordination than prisoner's dilemma structures; (2) tit for tat is the most promising interpersonal strategy for promoting cooperation by others; and (3) unilateral initiatives, including noncontingent cooperation, can mitigate conflict when a lock-in of mutual competition occurs.

TACIT-INTEGRATIVE BARGAINING

In tacit-integrative bargaining, actors do not acknowledge a conflict but can coordinate their behavior because of underlying common interests. In many instances, the structure and norms of the relation or the larger group discourage or even prohibit the actors from acknowledging the conflict. A perception of common interest means that actors have a "dual concern" for self's and other's outcomes (Blake and Mouton 1979; Pruitt 1983).

Tacit-integrative, as opposed to tacit-distributive, contexts inherently satisfy one of the conditions for cooperation identified by Pruitt's goals/expectations theory—each actor already has a goal of mutual cooperation. The dilemma actors face is that they don't know whether joint benefit is a goal for the other, making trust a problem. Actors can't be certain, for example, that they define their relationship or the issues at hand similarly, and these sort of judgments require significant "cognitive work."

Three specific types of tacit-integrative settings can be distinguished: (1) actors are unable to communicate either verbally or nonverbally (i.e., they are completely out of contact); (2) actors are unable to communicate verbally, but they can observe and interpret each other's behavior; (3) actors communicate verbally and nonverbally but fail to (or cannot) talk about the underlying conflict or disagreement. Structural constraints on actors' patterns or forms of communication could be due to geographical distance, cultural barriers (e.g., language), different knowledge bases (e.g., training, expertise), or divergent definitions of the situation based on positions in a larger structure (e.g., status, authority). Related constraints on their propensity to communicate about the conflict could be based on interpersonal distrust or collective norms that discourage definitions of group relations as bargaining. Tacit-integrative bargaining is particularly common in informal organizations and groups because it serves to emphasize collective purposes, keep conflict latent, and enable people with conflicting interests to "get the work done" in relative harmony.

There is no systematic, cumulative body of theory and research on tacit-integrative bargaining contexts, although instances of such bargaining are common, everyday experiences in organizations (Bacharach and Lawler 1980). One can nevertheless extrapolate from some tacit-distributive research, because the "solutions" for tacit-integrative bargaining are likely to be the most cooperatively-oriented ones in tacit-distributive bargaining. In particular, unilateral gestures or "testing the waters" (Ward 1989) should be a prime way for actors in tacit-integrative bargaining to communicate and affirm their goals of mutual accommodation. In a tacit-integrative context, unconditional (100 percent) cooperation by one actor should generate reciprocal cooperation without the safeguards against exploitation needed in tacit-distributive contexts (Axelrod 1984; Lindskold 1978; Osgood 1962).

Schelling's (1960) analysis of the role of "prominent" solutions adds to our understanding of conflict resolution in tacit-integrative contexts. A prominent solution is conspicuous in some way, so that both actors independently conclude that it is the most likely solution (Pruitt 1981; Schelling

1960). Solutions such as midpoints of issue continua or equal trades of complementary benefits often have prominence. Actors arrive at prominent solutions by taking the other's role, so familiarity with the other actor or the situation increases the success of settling on a prominent solution. Available research suggests, for example, that prominence may stem from perceptual salience (e.g., size, centrality, order), normative standards (e.g., distributive justice), or interpretation of the other's likely intentions (Murnighan 1991; Pruitt 1981). Actors also may converge on a single solution, even without much knowledge of the other or any capability to communicate.

It is important to emphasize that a prominent solution channels behavior only to the extent that it produces shared expectations perceived as shared by the actors themselves. Where actors cannot verbally or nonverbally communicate, the expectations are based solely on what each can assume about the other, and they are unable to validate their expectations until the desired outcome occurs or fails to occur at the appropriate time or place. If actors can monitor the other's behavior nonverbally, they can "test" their expectations along the way and can send signals if one gets off-track. For example, pedestrians and motorists can generally coordinate their behavior so that both get through an intersection. If one gets off-track, they can realign their actions by observing facial expressions and other nonverbal behaviors (e.g., hand gestures) (Couch 1979; Garfinkel 1964).

If actors are engaged in verbal interaction, their larger relationship expands opportunities for coordination with the other. Stein (1967) describes a "game" that takes place between doctors and nurses. The primary goal of this game is to avoid open conflict over patient treatment through a subtle negotiation process in which nurses make recommendations to doctors without appearing to do so and physicians accept these recommendations without appearing to do. This requires careful monitoring of the other's nonverbal and verbal communications. Success at this game provides rewards to both "players." The doctor can use the nurse's expertise and the nurse gains self-esteem and profes-

sional satisfaction. The "negotiated order" perspective in symbolic interaction theory (Strauss 1978) suggests the sort of social processes underlying such tacit coordination (Couch 1979; Strauss 1978).

To conclude, tacit-integrative bargaining occurs in social structures that create incentives for mutual cooperation but discourage explicit bargaining by blocking opportunities for open communication or by defining explicit bargaining as normatively inappropriate. The integrative side of a tacit-integrative context creates common interests, while the tacit side can make it difficult for the actors to accomplish their objectives. However, all things equal, tacit-integrative contexts are more likely to produce conflict resolution in the form of tacit coordination than tacit-distributive ones. While actors may misread the each other's intentions or goals, as long as each believes the other also perceives common interests and has a goal of mutual cooperation, unilateral actions are less risky and settling on prominent solutions is more feasible.

EXPLICIT-DISTRIBUTIVE BARGAINING

A bilateral monopoly game (Siegel and Fouraker 1960) is the laboratory prototype of an explicit-distributive bargaining context. Actors are buyers or sellers negotiating the price of a commodity; they consensually define their interaction as bargaining; there is a wide range of possible solutions (prices); and they make offers and counteroffers over time to reach an agreement. Each perceives an incentive to reach an agreement—the payoffs are higher from agreement than nonagreement—but each also wants an agreement favorable to his/her own interests.

A major contribution of sociologists and social psychologists to the literature on bargaining is to pick up where economists and game theorists tend to leave off, by relaxing some highly stringent assumptions and focusing on the process of explicit bargaining (e.g., Bacharach and Lawler 1981; Cook et al. 1983; Heckathorn 1983; Hegtvedt and Cook 1987; Willer, Markovsky, and Patton 1989). The result is that bargaining tactics (e.g., toughness), structurally based power relations, perceptions of power, and impression management become central to explanations of bargaining process. Two classes of tactics have received substantial attention: concession tactics (Chertkoff and Esser 1976; Murnighan 1991) and coercive tactics (Deutsch and Krauss 1962; Lawler 1986; Michener and Cohen 1973). Both are tied to essential features of the explicit-distributive context, the offer-counteroffer sequence.

Concession Tactics

Research on concession tactics is generally concerned with how various facets of a bargainer's concession behavior—the initial offer, concession magnitude, or concession frequency—are related to the opponent's concession behavior. Most of this research is organized around two somewhat divergent theoretical foci—aspiration levels (Komorita and Brenner 1968; Siegel and Fouraker 1960) and the norm of reciprocity or fairness (Chertkoff and Esser 1976; Gouldner 1960). *Level of aspiration theory* assumes that actors develop target points (aspirations) for a solution: the higher their targets (aspirations) the less they yield in the bargaining (Chertkoff and Esser 1976; Osgood 1962; Siegel and Fouraker 1960). Normative theories suggest that actors' pursuit of individual gain is constrained by norms, such as reciprocity, that they invoke in the bargaining: the stronger these norms, the more actors yield and, in particular, the more responsive they are to the other's yielding (see Hegtvedt and Cook 1987 for a recent discussion).

Toughness versus Softness.   As tactics, concessions are important because of the impressions they give. Level of aspiration theory stresses the importance of giving an impression of toughness (or avoiding an impression of weakness), whereas normative theories stress the importance of giving an impression of fairness (or avoiding an impression of unfairness). Both theoretical traditions assume that aspirations and norms are malleable or manipulable in the bargaining process (i.e., not fixed). Further, when these sorts of processes operate,

game theory predictions for the likelihood and nature of agreement (Nash 1950) will not reliably occur, meaning that the variance around predicted (determinate) solutions should be larger and nonagreements more frequent than expected, not because actors are nonrational but because of their interpretation of the situation and the meaning they attach to the other's concession behavior (Bacharach and Lawler 1981, chap. 1, 6; Bartos 1977).

Applied to concession tactics in explicit bargaining, level of aspiration and reciprocity theories make opposite predictions. Level of aspiration theory indicates that substantial concessions by actor A raise actor B's level of aspiration and, therefore, reduce B's concessions. The tougher or firmer A's concession pattern, the lower B's aspirations and the greater B's concessions. Reciprocity theories, in contrast, suggest that significant concessions by actor A activate a reciprocity norm, which exerts subtle pressure on B to make comparable concessions, whereas toughness by A begets toughness by B. Thus, tougher concession tactics produce impasses and softer ones reciprocal concessions.

Several studies have tested one or both of these theoretical standpoints, with each receiving some empirical support. In the initial test of level of aspiration, Siegel and Fouraker (1960) found that parties with higher aspirations adopted tougher concession tactics, which yielded them more profitable agreements. Also supporting level of aspiration theory, Bartos (1970) found a negative correlation between each actor's toughness (measured by average demand), suggesting that a tougher stance produced more yielding and a soft stance less. However, while toughness produced higher payoffs from the bargaining when agreement occurred, it decreased the prospects for reaching agreement.

Like Bartos (1970), Komorita and Brenner (1968) found an inverse relationship between the concessions of one party and those of the opponent. Contrary to the reciprocity notion, they also revealed that a large initial offer at the midpoint of the issue continuum, combined with no further concessions, produced the least amount of yielding by the opponent. Beginning negotiations with a "fair" offer that one expects to settle on was highly ineffective, presumably because it increased the other's aspirations. These findings dovetail with several other studies, indicating that tough initial offers produce better outcomes for a bargainer than soft initial offers (Benton, Kelley and Liebling 1972; Chertkoff and Conley 1976; Liebert et al. 1968; Yukl 1974). In sum, research on *initial* offers shows fairly consistent support for level of aspiration theory.

Other research indicates that beyond the initial period of bargaining, more concession making than suggested by level of aspiration theory is necessary to prevent an impasse (Chertkoff and Esser 1976; Hegtvedt and Cook 1987; Lawler and MacMurray 1980). Reciprocity theory tends to receive the strongest overall empirical support (Bacharach and Lawler 1980, 120–127; Chertkoff and Esser 1976). For example, Esser and Komorita (1975) compared a concession tactic conceding about 75 percent of what the subject concedes to complete (100 percent) reciprocity and found that complete reciprocity produced larger final offers by the subject. Hamner (1974) found that following an impasse, a 100 percent reciprocity tactic produced more concessions than did tougher tactics. The emergence or activation of the reciprocity norm is a plausible interpretation for these results because the social context implicit in explicit bargaining encourages parties to respect each other's preferences and to search for a mutually acceptable solution.

Overall, the research points to deficiencies in each theoretical standpoint. Level of aspiration theory fails to account for the fact that toughness backfires if it fosters impressions of unfairness or unreasonableness, and reciprocity fails to account for observations that larger concessions often yield lower concessions in response (i.e., exploitation). Osgood's GRIT theory, however, provides a basis for integrating the theories. Temporarily adopting a soft concession tactic (i.e., greater than 100 percent reciprocity) should elicit reciprocal concessions following an impasse. Exploitation will not occur because the impasse demonstrates each actor's re-

solve, and once reciprocal concession making starts it can escalate gradually and produce quicker, more mutually satisfying agreements than otherwise (Boyle and Lawler 1991).

To test this idea, Boyle and Lawler (1991) induced an impasse by having a programmed "other" make no concessions and inflict punitive damage during the first five of twenty rounds. Following the impasse, the programmed other either made a series of unilateral concessions across five rounds or reciprocated (100 percent matching) concessions by the subject. The results indicate that unilateral initiatives increased the actor's concessions and reduced their use of punitive tactics more than reciprocal concession making (Boyle and Lawler 1991). These results support the GRIT hypothesis. Thus, if initial toughness produces an impasse, a series of small unilateral concessions can break it. More generally, *firm but fair* concession tactics are most effective with or without an impasse (Chertkoff and Esser 1976; Lawler and MacMurray 1980).

Explicit negotiations often take place among the same actors over time, yet almost all of the research on explicit bargaining involves a "one shot" negotiation session. In recent work, Lawler and Yoon (1993) show how power affects the emergence of a positive relation among actors who negotiate repeatedly with each other. They had subjects bargain with each other in ten independent negotiations. Equal power produced more frequent agreements than unequal power, and more frequent agreements in turn aroused positive emotions or feelings. These emotions lead actors to give each other gifts and to stay in their relation despite equal or better alternatives. Lawler and Yoon (1993) suggest that a subtle commitment formation process often occurs when the same two persons engage in explicit bargaining over time, and this has an emotional/affective foundation.

Power Relations and Toughness. Social exchange theory and research suggests the following basic conclusions about the impact of power relations on the use of toughness in explicit bargaining.

First, in an unequal power relationship, higher-power actors are likely to adopt tougher concession tactics and lower-power actors softer ones (e.g., Cook et al. 1983; Markovsky, Willer, and Patton 1988; Michener et al. 1975). Second, unequal-power relations create more of an obstacle to concession making than equal-power relations, because actors tend to dispute the appropriate connection between their power differences and their relative yielding (Bacharach and Lawler 1981; Hegtvedt and Cook 1987; Komorita and Chertkoff 1973; Lawler 1992; Lawler and Yoon 1993). Third, in an equal-power relation, greater total power or mutual dependence softens the concession tactics of each actor and increases the likelihood of conflict resolution (Lawler 1992; Lawler and Ford 1993).[6] (See chapter 8 for a discussion of power in exchange networks.)

Coercive Tactics

Coercive tactics take the form of threats and damage and presuppose a coercive capability anchored in actors' positions in a social structure (Lawler 1992). Threats express intent to do harm and implicitly or explicitly contain an "if-then" contingency (i.e., "If you do X, then I'll do Y") (Deutsch 1973; Tedeschi, Schlenker, and Bonoma 1973). These threats can be verbal or nonverbal and vary in specificity or clarity about what the target can do or not do to avoid actual damage (Schelling 1960). Damage tactics actually inflict punishment and may follow through on prior threats or constitute an implicit threat of future harm (Lawler 1986; Schelling 1960; Tedeschi, Schlenker, and Bonoma 1973). In explicit-distributive bargaining, coercive tactics are generally used to extract concessions or forestall the other's use of coercive tactics.

Two theory and research traditions—conflict spiral and deterrence—make competing predictions about when actors use coercive tactics. The conflict spiral tradition stems from Deutsch and associates' seminal work on threats (Deutsch 1973; Deutsch and Krauss 1960, 1962; Krauss and Deutsch 1966), and the deterrence tradition in social psychology can be traced to Hornstein (1965), Michener and

Cohen (1973), and a series of studies by Tedeschi and associates (Horai and Tedeschi 1969; Tedeschi, Schlenker, and Bonoma 1973).

The basic implication of the spiral tradition is that the availability of coercive capabilities leads to their use, and use by one actor begets counteruse by the other, resulting in a costly use-counteruse spiral. The theoretical rationale is that the mere presence of a coercive capability creates a temptation to use it, while at the same time actors are unlikely to yield because of costs associated with loss of face. Conflict spiral effects are reported by Deutsch and Krauss (1962), who found that bilateral power conditions (where both actors can damage the other's outcomes) produced more hostile power use than unilateral (only one party has a coercive capability) or no power conditions.

In contrast, the basic implication of the deterrence tradition is that actors are unlikely to take hostile action against someone with a larger coercive capability because of the retaliation costs the other can levy. The more powerful the other becomes, the less likely an actor is to initiate coercive tactics. This implies that if both actors have large coercive capabilities that make threats of retaliation credible, then each will use threat and damage tactics less frequently than otherwise (Schelling 1960; Tedeschi, Schlenker, and Bonoma 1973). Tests of this deterrence notion have focused on conditions of unilateral or bilateral coercive capability. Tedeschi and colleagues (Tedeschi, Schlenker, and Bonoma 1973) conducted a large number of studies in which a programmed other (with a coercive capability) could levy threats and punishments of varying magnitude against a subject without a coercive capability (unilateral condition). Larger magnitudes of coercive capability by the programmed other produced greater compliance on the part of the target (Horai and Tedeschi 1969; Schlenker et al. 1970; Tedeschi, Schlenker, and Bonoma 1973; also see Michener and Cohen 1973).

Studies of explicit bargaining find support for deterrence notions when both parties have a coercive capability. Hornstein (1965) contrasted low, medium, and high levels of equal coercive capability and found that the lowest frequency of threat and damage tactics occurred when both parties had high levels of power. Bacharach and Lawler (1981, chap. 5) corroborate these results, showing that larger magnitudes of coercive capability for both actors (with equal power held constant) reduced the rate of damage tactics by both. The results of these studies contradict hypotheses of the conflict spiral tradition.

Lawler (1986) formulated contrasting theories designed to explicate and systematize bilateral deterrence and conflict spiral notions. The theories use slightly different intervening cognitions to explain how "total power" (the sum of each actor's coercive capability) and "relative power" (the degree of power difference between the actors) affect the use of coercive tactics in explicit-distributive bargaining (Lawler 1986, 1992). Bilateral deterrence theory predicts that given equal power, increases in power capability across both actors leads both to have higher fear of retaliation and a lower expectation of attack, which in turn reduces use of coercive tactics. In contrast, conflict spiral theory predicts that increases in power for both leads both to be more tempted to use power and to develop higher expectations of attack, which increases use of coercive tactics.

Bilateral deterrence theory stipulates further that unequal power produces more use of coercive tactics than equal power, because high- and low-power actors assess a power difference differently. Higher-power actors emphasize the higher costs of retaliation, while lower-power actors stress the greater expectation of attack. Thus, higher-power actors use more coercive tactics because they have less to fear, and lower-power actors use more coercive tactics than would be predicted from their power position because they expect higher-power actors to take coercive measures against them. Bargaining theory and research suggest that expectations of attack often produce hostile action in advance of the expectations being fulfilled (Lawler 1986; Morgan 1977; Schelling 1960; Tedeschi, Bonoma, and Novinson 1970). Conflict spiral theory predicts the opposite: higher-power actors respond primarily to reduced expectation of attack

and use fewer coercive tactics, while lower-power actors are less tempted to use coercive tactics.

Recent research pitting bilateral deterrence against conflict spiral predictions supports Lawler's (1986) bilateral deterrence formulation. Two experiments demonstrated that where both actors have greater coercive capability, they use damage tactics less frequently (e.g., administering punishments) in explicit-distributive bargaining (Lawler and Bacharach 1987; Lawler, Ford, and Blegen 1988). Also, actors used damage tactics less frequently if they had equal rather than unequal coercive capability, and higher- versus lower-power actors did not use damage tactics at different rates. Consistent with the theory, those with lower yet "significant" absolute power resisted efforts to dominate.

To conclude, explicit-distributive bargaining is most likely where social structures create positions with divergent interests involving fundamental goal incompatibilities, while also facilitating direct efforts to acknowledge and deal with social conflict. Actors who occupy such structural positions aren't able to reconcile their interests, except through a process of concession and compromise. By tactically using concession and coercive tactics, the actors attempt to maximize the other's yielding yet reach agreement. Overall, the research on explicit-distributive contexts suggests that concession tactics that combine firmness with fairness are most effective, and if each has equal or large coercive capabilities the rate of coercive tactics in the relation will be lower than otherwise, making conflict resolution somewhat easier.

EXPLICIT-INTEGRATIVE BARGAINING

Integrative bargaining research assumes a distinction between "compromise solutions" involving a split-the-difference principle and "integrative solutions" based on elements of common interest (Neale and Bazerman 1991; Pruitt 1981; Walton and McKersie 1965). A compromise solution (splitting the difference) involves each actor converging on agreements that fall on a fixed contract zone bordered by their "most preferred" agreement points.

Integrative solutions reshape the contract zone by essentially adding net benefits to some or all of the possible agreement points via a social exchange process. This is possible mainly when an issue can be subdivided into distinct components or when two or more issues are already on the bargaining table (see Murnighan 1991; Neale and Bazerman 1991; Pruitt 1981; Thompson and Hastie 1990). Explicit-integrative bargaining implies a social context where actors have common interests or goals based on common organizational memberships but also find themselves in conflict based on the positions they occupy in the larger structure. The conflict is likely to be over means rather than fundamental goals.

To illustrate, consider Follet's (1940) example of two actors (A and B) who both want an orange, but have only one available. Each would like to have the entire orange, but given that this is not feasible the obvious compromise is to cut the orange in half. In the course of argument, however, they realize that they give priority to different parts of the orange. A wants the juice more than the peel, B wants the peel more than the juice. The integrative solution is to give A all of the juice and B all of the peel; that is, each gives up what they value least in exchange for what they value most. Notice that splitting the difference (i.e., the orange) would lead to a suboptimal solution. The actors in this example essentially decompose a distributive issue into two subissues (juice and peel) and then trade off. To accomplish this, actors have to exchange accurate information on their preferences, which those in conflict are often reluctant to do.[7]

In an influential analysis of integrative bargaining, Pruitt (1981, 1983) sets forth five ways for bargainers to move from distributive (compromise) to integrative (problem solving) forms of negotiation. The most basic strategy is "logrolling," defined as a trade-off or exchange across two or more issues in which each actor receives a good agreement on his/her higher-priority issue at the expense of a poor agreement on his/her lower-priority issue. Logrolling is common in negotiations involving a large number of complex issues facing actors in the same organization or group (Neale and Bazerman 1991).

Some of the other strategies overlap with logrolling. A "bridging" strategy redefines an issue, revealing a new option that satisfies actors' most valued goals. Bridging requires actors to analyze and set priorities among the interests producing their current demands and to eliminate less important ones. It can lead to the decomposition of a single issue into components, the initial step toward logrolling in the example of two persons arguing over an orange.

In "nonspecific compensation" one actor commits future compensation to another in exchange for concessions on the issues currently under negotiation. For example, in exchange for ending a prison riot, prison authorities might agree to form a joint committee of prisoners and guards to propose changes in policies and procedures. Solutions to intense public conflicts often arrange "face-saving" devices involving nonspecific compensation of various sorts, with the specifics to be worked out later. A related strategy, "cost cutting" involves specific compensation for the cost one actor incurs as a result of an agreed-upon solution. Finally, "expanding the pie" involves, for example, planting an orange tree in the above example. This is tantamount to adding a constant to the payoffs along the distributive contract zone. If workers in a subunit negotiate for more discretion over how they accomplish their tasks, the local managers can spend less time on supervision and more time on planning and other activities that raise their own prospects for promotion (Kanter 1977). In developing explicit understandings about who is responsible for what, both workers and managers might "win" by expanding the "total control" pie (Tannenbaum 1968).

In reviews of research on integrative bargaining, Pruitt (1981; Pruitt and Lewis 1977) suggests that integrative agreements are more likely if actors consider multiple issues simultaneously rather than sequentially, because package deals (trade-offs) are more salient and easier to arrange. A mutual problem-solving orientation also is important, because parties are more likely to exchange detailed information about their intentions and priorities under such conditions. Lower accountability to constituents allows representatives the flexibility and autonomy to exchange information as necessary and to make other strategic adjustments at the bargaining table (Carnevale 1985, 1989). Pruitt (1983) also suggests that actors who adopt a firm but flexible bargaining stance are likely to come closest to reaching whatever integrative potential is available in the context.

Negotiator Heuristics

Finding integrative solutions that are structured into the context may require actors to penetrate beneath the surface features of the issues under negotiation. The need for more "cognitive work" raises the question of how judgment heuristics shape or bias an individual's cognitions. Bazerman and associates recently applied ideas from the heuristics literature (Kahneman, Slovic, and Tversky 1982) to the individual negotiator as decision maker (e.g., Bazerman and Neale 1983; Neale, Huber, and Northcraft 1987; Neale and Bazerman 1991; Thompson and Hastie 1990). They focus on four cognitive heuristics: framing, anchoring, availability, and overconfidence (Neale and Bazerman 1991).

Framing refers to whether the negotiator interprets variations in payoffs in terms of losses or gains. In a labor-management dispute, negotiators could regard the other's concession as a loss from what would like to get or as a gain, using the opponent's previous offer or the current contract as a reference point. The hypothesis is that interpreting payoff variations in terms of losses leads the negotiator to take more risks in bargaining (i.e., risk seeking), while interpreting it as a gain leads the actor to be risk-averse.

Positively framed actors should be more conciliatory and negatively framed actors more hostile and competitive. Several studies support this hypothesis. Neale and Bazerman (1985) examined the impact of framing in collective bargaining and report that actors with a positive frame made more concessions, reached more agreements, and perceived the bargaining outcomes as more fair than did those with a negative frame. Bazerman et al. (1985) found that positively framed negotiators made more profit than negatively framed negotiators. Framing clearly affects the prospects of resolving conflict.

Anchoring occurs when people use information at hand as a reference point to estimate values for other events. Neale and Bazerman (1991) indicate that goals impact bargainers in part as cognitive anchors and suggest goal difficulty as an important factor. Huber and Neale (1986) examined the connection between the difficulty of a goal set initially by a constituent and the difficulty of subsequent self-determined goals. They found that negotiators who were assigned difficult goals by constituents achieved more integrative agreements.

The availability bias refers to errors in estimating the frequency of an event and is affected by the degree to which the information is vivid or easy to recall. One implication is that negotiation outcomes are affected by the presentation of information. For example, if the costs of nonagreement are made personally relevant, negotiators are slower to settle, but if the costs of third-party intervention are made salient, negotiators are quicker to settle (see Neale and Bazerman 1991). Finally, overconfidence biases are reflected in the fact that actors tend to overestimate probabilities of good outcomes or positive performance (Bazerman and Neale 1983).

Explicit-integrative bargaining presupposes a structure that creates underlying common goals and facilitates open communication to resolve differences when they arise. In such contexts, actors mutually acknowledge a conflict and have issues that can be interrelated or reshaped. In explicit-integrative bargaining, offers and counteroffers are part of an effort to share information about priorities, but various cognitive heuristics can impede the process of conflict resolution.

CONCLUSION

Bargaining and negotiation is an interdisciplinary area in which psychologists, mathematicians, economists, political scientists, and sociologists have made a mark. Each discipline approaches the phenomenon of bargaining from a distinct metatheory—a unique set of concepts, assumptions, and theoretical questions—and each generates research based in part on metatheories about the phenomenon and how to study it. One result is that the bargaining literature contains a rich mix of theoretical approaches and research strategies; another is that it has some frustrating ambiguities, gaps, and inconsistencies.

We focused here on one part of the literature, the social psychological tradition, and have taken a sociological perspective that highlights the social-structural context of bargaining. The fourfold classification of bargaining contexts presented here is based on the distinctions between tacit versus explicit and distributive versus integrative bargaining (Bacharach and Lawler 1980; Schelling 1960; Walton and McKersie 1965). Each social context has structural and cognitive dimensions, and each is likely to develop out of the conjoint effects of the social structure, actors' definition of their relationship, and their tactical action. Explicit bargaining is possible only where the social structure allows open communication between the actors and they choose to deal directly and explicitly with a conflict. Integrative bargaining is possible only where the social structure creates sufficient overriding common interest and the actors perceive and choose to act on these common interests. The typology has the heuristic advantage of subsuming and organizing a vast range of research literature on bargaining; it pulls together disparate threads.

Different theoretical traditions (e.g., symbolic interaction, social exchange theory, cognitive theory, game theory) focus on and assume different types of bargaining contexts. For the most part, these theoretical perspectives complement each other. One way sociologists can contribute is by specifying and elaborating the structural aspects of bargaining contexts and showing how these shape bargaining processes (e.g., actors' definitions of the situation, tactical choices) and the prospects for conflict resolution. The precise nature of problems actors face is different across contexts, as are the tactical options available and the prerequisites of conflict resolution. Future work should attempt to distinguish theoretical principles that apply across contexts from those that are context-specific.

There are several promising directions for future work. First, tacit-integrative bargaining warrants more systematic attention because it can capture how people negotiate their way through daily conflicts and tensions (see Strauss 1978). Conversational analyses will be useful here. Second, most social psychological work on explicit-distributive bargaining has been limited to isolated two-party bargaining, but recent exchange network and power dependence theories place dyads in a larger network of relations (e.g., Cook et al. 1983; Markovsky, Willer, and Patton 1988). Such work offers a structural approach to bargaining, focusing on power relations (Lawler 1992), and there is much to be done here (see chapter 8). Third, research on explicit-integrative contexts has used principles of cognitive psychology to understand how cognitive biases affect negotiators' decisions. Future efforts should address the emotional responses of negotiators and interweave the emotional with the cognitive, because positive and negative frames, for example, should have emotional as well as cognitive effects on negotiators. Finally, research on tacit-distributive contexts, as we define it, is voluminous but also in need of new direction, because the two-party matrix game has probably outlived its usefulness as a research setting. Issues surrounding the social dilemma represent a promising new direction that ties this form of bargaining to larger sociological questions about the foundation of social order (see chapter 12). Overall, social psychological work on bargaining and negotiation offers a fertile basis for more systematic sociological theorizing about conflict and resolution.

NOTES

1. A common theme of the definitions is that bargaining involves a process of exchanging demands, bids, or offers, while negotiation is either the broader social interaction or relationship within which such exchange takes place (Gulliver 1979; Strauss 1978) or simply efforts to transcend the conflict and promote more cooperative decision making (Morley and Stephenson 1977; Pruitt 1981). Our definition of bargaining, taken from Schelling

(1960) and Bacharach and Lawler (1980, 1981), distinguishes it from conflict but not negotiation.

2. In Kelley and Thibaut's (1978) terms, actors in each bargaining context have significant degrees of fate control and behavioral control over each other. The former encourages them to bargain and the latter encourages them to attend to each other's behavior.

3. The line of research by Linda Molm on social exchange exemplifies a nonbargaining context (Molm 1987, 1989, 1990), although the setting contains some elements of what we call a tacit-integrative context.

4. We acknowledge that game theories provide fundamental theoretical analyses that apply to all forms of two-party bargaining (Rapoport 1966). Our point here is simply that taking the conditions assumed by game theoretical models as a whole (e.g., simultaneous choices involving two options—cooperation versus competition—and no verbal communication), the research based on these models is directed primarily at the tacit-distributive cell of our typology.

5. Compared to a chicken setting, actors in a prisoner's dilemma find it more difficult to avoid conflict spirals and require more safeguards (i.e., monitoring) to move from a pattern of mutual competition to mutual cooperation. Solutions often require sanction systems, punishing competition or rewarding cooperation to such an extent that the original prisoner's dilemma is transformed into a "positive sum" payoff matrix (Rapoport 1966), where each actor's highest payoffs are attached to mutual cooperation. Sanction systems are important because they provide actors "mutual assurances" of cooperation (e.g., Hechter 1990).

6. Heckathorn (1983; see also Willer, Markovsky, and Patton 1989) proposes a resistance model of the bargaining process in which each actor's resistance to a concession at each point of the bargaining process is a function of the ratio of the difference in utility attached to the actor's most preferred solution (i.e., "best hope") and the other's current offer to the difference between their "best hope" and the conflict point (i.e., their maximum net gain). The actor with the least resistance will make a concession at each point in the bargaining process; power relations are key determinants of this process (see also Willer, Markovsky, and Patton 1989).

7. Game theorists have identified as the "best" solution those intermediate points that maximize the product of each actor's net utility from the agreement (Nash 1950; Rapoport 1966). These theoretical models would reduce the multiple issues of integrative bargaining to a single set of overall utilities. From this standpoint, each actor in this example has to give up only a little to reach a mutually beneficial result. An underlying distributive dimension remains, unless actors ascribe no value to what is given up.

REFERENCES

Axelrod, R. 1984. *The Evolution of Cooperation.* New York: Basic Books.

Bacharach, S. B., and E. J. Lawler. 1980. *Power and Politics in Organizations.* San Francisco: Jossey-Bass.

———. 1981. *Bargaining: Power, Tactics, and Outcomes.* San Francisco: Jossey-Bass.

Bartos, O. 1970. Determinants and consequences of toughness. Pp. 45–68 in *The Structure of Conflict,* ed. P. Swingle. New York: Academic.

Bartos, O. J. 1977. A simple model of negotiation: A sociological point of view. *Journal of Conflict Resolution* 21:565–580.

Bazerman, Max, T. Magliozzi, and M. Neale. 1985. The acquisition of an integrative response in a competitive market. *Organizational Behavior and Performance* 34:294–313.

Bazerman, Max, and Margaret Neale. 1983. Heuristics in negotiation: Limitations to dispute resolution effectiveness. Pp. 51–67 in *Negotiating in Organiza-* *tions,* ed. M. H. Bazerman and R. S. Lewicki. Beverly Hills: Sage.

Benton, A. A., H. H. Kelley, and B. Liebling. 1972. Effects of extremity of offers and concession rate on the outcomes of bargaining. *Journal of Personality and Social Psychology* 1:73–83.

Blake, R. R., and J. S. Mouton. 1979. Intergroup problem solving in organizations: From theory to practice. In *The Social Psychology of Intergroup Relations,* ed. W. G. Austin and S. Worchel. Monterey, CA: Brooks/Cole.

Blalock, H. M. 1989. *Power and Conflict: Toward a General Theory.* Newbury Park, CA: Sage.

Boyle, E. H., and E. J. Lawler. 1991. Resolving conflict through explicit bargaining. *Social Forces* 69: 1183–1204.

Carnevale, P. J. D. 1985. Accountability and the dynamics of group representation. Pp. 227–248 in *Advances in Group Processes,* vol. 2, ed. E. J. Lawler. Greenwich, CT: JAI Press.

———. 1989. Determinants of mediator behavior: A test of the strategic choice model. *Journal of Applied Social Psychology* 19:481–498.

Chamberlain, N. W. 1955. *A General Theory of Economic Process.* New York: Harper & Row.

Chertkoff, J., and M. Conley. 1967. Opening offer and frequency of concession as bargaining strategies. *Journal of Personality and Social Psychology* 7: 181–185.

Chertkoff, J., and J. K. Esser. 1976. A review of experiments in explicit bargaining. *Journal of Experimental Social Psychology* 12:487–503.

Cook, K., and R. Emerson. 1978. Power, equity, and commitment in exchange networks. *American Sociological Review* 43:721–739.

Cook, K. S., R. M. Emerson, M. R. Gillmore, and T. Yamagishi. 1983. The distribution of power in exchange networks: Theory and experimental results. *American Journal of Sociology* 89:275–305.

Couch, C. 1979. Economic exchange, bargaining and civilization. Pp. 377–398 in *Studies in Symbolic Interaction,* vol. 2, ed. N. K. Denzin. Greenwich, CT: JAI Press.

Dahrendorf, R. 1959. *Class and Class Conflict in Industrial Society.* Stanford: Stanford University Press.

Deutsch, M. 1969. Conflicts: Productive and destructive. *Journal of Social Issues* 25:7–41.

———. 1973. *The Resolution of Conflict.* New Haven: Yale University Press.

Deutsch, M., and R. M. Krauss. 1960. The effect of threat upon interpersonal bargaining. *Journal of Abnormal and Social Psychology* 61:181–189.

———. 1962. Studies of interpersonal bargaining. *Journal of Conflict Resolution* 6:52–76.

Dunlop, J. T. 1950. *Wage Determination Under Trade Unions.* New York: A.M. Kelley.

Esser, J. K., and S. S. Komorita. 1975. Reciprocity and concession making in bargaining. *Journal of Personality and Social Psychology* 31:864–872.

Follet, M. P. 1940. Constructive conflict. Pp. 30–49 in *Dynamic Administration: The Collected Papers of Mary Parker Follet,* ed. H. C. Metcalf and L. Urwick. New York: Harper.

Gallo, P. S., Jr., and C. G. McClintock. 1965. Cooperative and competitive behavior in mixed motive games. *Journal of Conflict Resolution* 9:68–78.

Garfinkel, H. 1964. *Studies in Ethnomethodology.* Englewood Cliffs, NJ: Prentice Hall.

Gouldner, A. 1960. The norm of reciprocity: A preliminary statement. *American Sociological Review* 25: 161–179.

Gulliver, P. H. 1979. *Disputes and Negotiations: A Cross-Cultural Perspective.* New York: Academic.

Hamburger, H. 1979. *Games as Models of Social Phenomena.* San Francisco: Freeman.

Hamner, W. C. 1974. Effects of bargaining strategy and pressure to reach agreement in a stalemated negotiation. *Journal of Personality and Social Psychology* 30:458–467.

Harsanyi, J. C. 1977. Rational Behavior and Bargaining Equilibrium in Games and Social Situations. New York: Cambridge University Press.

Hechter, M. 1990. The emergence of cooperative social institutions. Pp. 13–34 in *Social Institutions: Their Emergence, Maintenance, and Effects,* ed. Michael Hechter, Karl-Dieter Opp, and Reinhard Wippler. New York: Aldine de Gruyter.

Heckathorn, D. D. 1983. Extensions of power-dependence theory: The concept of resistance. *Social Forces* 61:1206–1231.

Hegtvedt, K. A., and K. S. Cook. 1987. The role of justice in conflict situations. Pp. 109–136 in *Advances in Group Processes,* ed. E. J. Lawler and B. Markovsky. Greenwich, CT: JAI Press.

Hirshleifer, J., and J. C. M. Coll. 1988. What strategies can support the evolutionary emergence of cooperation. *Journal of Conflict Resolution* 32:367–398.

Horai, J., and J. T. Tedeschi. 1969. Effects of credibility and magnitude of punishment on compliance to threats. *Journal of Personality and Social Psychology* 12:164–169.

Hornstein, H. A. 1965. The effects of different magnitudes of threat upon interpersonal bargaining. *Journal of Experimental Social Psychology* 1: 282–293.

Huber, V. L., and M. A. Neale. 1986. Effects of cognitive heuristics and goals on negotiator performance and subsequent goal setting. *Organizational Behavior and Human Decision Processes* 38:342–169.

Kahneman, D. P. Slovic, and A. Tversky, A. 1982. *Judgment Under Uncertainty: Heuristics and Biases.* Cambridge: Cambridge, University Press.

Kanter, R. M. 1977. *Men and Women of the Corporation.* New York: Basic Books.

Kelley, H. H., and J. T. Thibaut. 1978. *Interpersonal Relations: A Theory of Interdependence.* New York: Wiley.

Komorita, S. S., and M. Barnes. 1969. Effects of pressures to reach agreement in bargaining. *Journal of Personality and Social Psychology* 3:245–252.

Komorita, S. S., and A. R. Brenner. 1968. Bargaining and concession making under bilateral monopoly. *Journal of Personality and Social Psychology* 9: 15–20.

Komorita, S. S., and J. Chertkoff. 1973. A bargaining theory of coalition formation. *Psychological Review* 80:149–162.

Krauss, R. M., and M. Deutsch. 1966. Communication in interpersonal bargaining. *Journal of Personality and Social Psychology* 4:572–577.

Kriesberg, L. 1982. *The Sociology of Social Conflict.* Englewood Cliffs, NJ: Prentice Hall.

Lawler, E. J. 1986. Bilateral deterrence and conflict spiral: A theoretical analysis. Pp. 107–130 in *Advances in Group Processes,* vol. 3, ed. E. J. Lawler. Greenwich, CT: JAI Press.

———. 1992. Power processes in bargaining. *Sociological Quarterly* 33:17–34.

Lawler, E. J., and S. B. Bacharach. 1987. Comparison of dependence and punitive forms of power. *Social Forces* 66:446–462.

Lawler, E. J., and R. Ford. In press. Metatheory and friendly competition in theory growth: The case of power processes in bargaining. Pp. 172–210 in *Theoretical Research Programs: Studies in Theory Growth,* ed. J. Berger and M. Zelditch, Jr. Stanford: Stanford University Press.

Lawler, E. J., R. Ford, and M. Blegen. 1988. Coercive capability in conflict: A test of bilateral deterrence versus conflict spiral theory. *Social Psychology Quarterly* 51:93–107.

Lawler, E. J., and B. MacMurray. 1980. Bargaining toughness: A qualification of level of aspiration and reciprocity hypotheses. *Journal of Applied Social Psychology* 10:416–430.

Lawler, E. J., and J. Yoon. 1993. Power and the emergence of commitment behavior in negotiated exchange. *American Sociological Review* 58:465–481.

Liebert, R. M., W. P. Smith, J. H. Hill, and M. Keiffer. 1968. The effects of information and magnitude of initial offer on interpersonal negotiation. *Journal of Experimental Social Psychology* 4:431–441.

Lindskold, S. 1978. Trust development, the GRIT proposal, and the effects of conciliatory acts on conflict and cooperation. *Psychological Bulletin* 85: 772–793.

Lindskold, S., and M. G. Collins. 1978. Inducing cooperation by groups and individuals. *Journal of Conflict Resolution* 22:679–690.

Luce, R. D., and H. Raiffa. 1957. *Games and Decisions: Introduction and Critical Survey.* New York: Wiley.

Marinoff, L. 1992. Maximizing expected utilities in the prisoner's dilemma. *Journal of Conflict Resolution* 36:182–216.

Markovsky, B., D. Willer, and T. Patton. 1988. Power relations in exchange networks. *American Sociological Review* 53:220–236.

Michener, H. A., and E. D. Cohen. 1973. Effects of punishment magnitude in the bilateral threat situation: Evidence for the deterrence hypothesis. *Journal of Personality and Social Psychology* 26:427–438.

Michener, H. A., J. J. Vaske, S. L. Schleifer, J. G. Plazewski, and L. J. Chapman. 1975. Factors affecting concession rate and threat usage in bilateral conflict. *Sociometry* 38:62–80.

Molm, L. 1990. Structure, action, and outcomes: The dynamics of power in social exchange. *American Sociological Review* 55:427–447.

———. 1987. Power-dependence theory: Power processes and negative outcomes. Pp. 171–198 in *Advances in Group Processes,* vol. 4, ed. E. J. Lawler and B. Markovsky. Greenwich, CT: JAI Press.

———. 1989. Punishment power: A balancing process in power-dependence relations. *American Journal of Sociology* 94:1392–1418.

Morgan, M. P. 1977. *Deterrence: A Conceptual Analysis.* Beverly Hills: Sage.

Morley, I., and G. Stephenson. 1977. *The Social Psychology of Bargaining.* London: Allen & Unwin.

Murnighan, J. K. 1991. *The Dynamics of Bargaining Games.* Englewood Cliffs, NJ: Prentice Hall.

Murnighan, J. K., and A. Roth. 1978. Expecting continued play in prisoner's dilemma games. *Journal of Conflict Resolution* 27:279–300.

Nash, J. F., Jr. 1950. The bargaining problem. *Econometrica* 18:155–162.

Neale, M., and M. Bazerman. 1985. The effects of framing and negotiator overconfidence on bargainer behavior. *Academy of Management Journal* 28:34–49.

———. 1991. *Cognition and Rationality in Bargaining.* New York: Free Press.

Neale, M. A., V. L. Huber, and G. B. Northcraft. 1987. The framing of negotiations: Context versus task frames. *Organizational Behavior and Human Decision Processes* 39:228–241.

Nemeth, C. 1970. Bargaining and reciprocity. *Psychological Bulletin* 74:128–140.

Osgood, C. 1962. *An Alternative to War or Surrender.* Urbana: University of Illinois Press.

Oskamp, S. 1971. Effects of programmed strategies on cooperation in the prisoner's dilemma and other mixed motive games. *Journal of Conflict Resolution* 15:225–259.

Patchen, M. 1987. Strategies for eliciting cooperation from an adversary. *Journal of Conflict Resolution* 31:164–185.

———. 1988. *Resolving Disputes between Nations.* Durham, NC: Duke University Press.

Pruitt, D. G. 1981. *Negotiation Behavior.* New York: Academic.

———. 1983. Achieving integrative agreements. Pp. 35–50. in *Negotiating in Organizations,* ed. M. Bazerman and R. Lewicki. Beverly Hills: Sage.

Pruitt, D. G., and M. J. Kimmel. 1977. Twenty years of experimental gaming: Critique, synthesis, and suggestions for the future. *Annual Review of Psychology* 28:363–392.

Pruitt, D. G., and S. A. Lewis. 1977. The psychology of integrative bargaining. In *Negotiations: Social Psychological Perspectives,* ed. D. Druckman. Beverly Hills: Sage.

Raiffa, H. 1982. *The Art and Science of Negotiation.* Cambridge, MA: Harvard University Press.

Rapoport, A. 1966. *Two Person Game Theory: The Essential Ideas.* Ann Arbor: University of Michigan Press.

Rapoport, A., and A. M. Chammah. 1965. *Prisoner's Dilemma: A Study of Conflict and Cooperation.* Ann Arbor: The University of Michigan Press.

Rubin, J. Z., and B. R. Brown. 1975. *The Social Psychology of Bargaining and Negotiation.* New York: Academic.

Schelling, T. C. 1960. *The Strategy of Conflict.* New York: Oxford University Press.

Schlenker, B., T. V. Bonoma, J. Tedeschi, and W. P. Pivnik. 1970. Compliance to threats as a function of the threat and the exploitiveness of the threatener. *Sociometry* 33:394–408.

Siegel, S., and L. Fouraker. 1960. *Bargaining and Group Decision-Making: Experiments in Bilateral Monopoly.* New York: McGraw-Hill.

Sermat, V. 1964. Cooperative behavior in a mixed motive game. *The Journal of Social Psychology* 62:217–239.

———. 1967. The possibility of influencing the other's behavior and cooperation: Chicken versus prisoner's dilemma. *Canadian Journal of Psychology* 21:204–219.

Solomon, L. 1960. The influence of some types of power relationships and game strategies upon the development of interpersonal trust. *Journal of Abnormal and Social Psychology* 61:223–230.

Stein, L. J. 1967. The doctor-nurse game. *Archives of General Psychiatry* 16:699–703.

Strauss, A. 1978. *Negotiations: Varieties, Contexts, Processes, and Social Order.* San Francisco: Jossey-Bass.

Stryker, S. 1977. Developments in "two social psychologies": Toward an appreciation of mutual relevance. *Sociometry* 40:145–160.

Tannenbaum, A. S. 1968. *Control in Organizations.* New York: McGraw-Hill.

Tedeschi, J. T., T. V. Bonoma, and N. Novinson. 1970. Behavior of a threatener: Retaliation versus fixed opportunity costs. *Journal of Conflict Resolution* 14:69–76.

Tedeschi, J. T., B. Schlenker, and T. V. Bonoma. 1973. *Conflict, Power, and Games.* Chicago: Aldine.

Thompson, L., and R. M. Hastie. 1990. Social perception in negotiation. *Organizational Behavior and Human Decision Processes* 47:98–123.

Walton, R. E., and R. B. McKersie. 1965. *A Behavioral Theory of Labor Negotiations: An Analysis of a Social Interaction System.* New York: McGraw-Hill.

Ward, H. 1989. Testing the waters: Taking risks to gain reassurance in public goods games. *Journal of Conflict Resolution* 33:274–308.

Willer, D., B. Markovsky, and T. Patton. 1989. Power structures: Derivations and applications of elementary theory. Pp. 313–353 in *Sociological Theories in Progress: New Formulations,* ed. J. Berger, M. Zelditch, Jr., and B. Anderson. Newbury Park, CA: Sage.

Wilson, W. 1971. Reciprocation and other techniques for inducing cooperation in the prisoner's dilemma game. *Journal of Conflict Resolution* 15: 167–195.

Young, O. R., ed. 1975. *Bargaining: Formal Theories of Negotiation.* Chicago: University of Illinois Press.

Yukl, G. A. 1974. Effects of the opponent's initial offer, concession magnitude, and concession frequency on bargaining behavior. *Journal of Personality and Social Psychology* 3:323–335.

Zeuthen, F. 1930. *Problems of Monopoly and Economic Warfare.* London: Routledge & Kegan Paul.

CHAPTER 10

Justice and Injustice

KAREN A. HEGTVEDT
BARRY MARKOVSKY

Justice research, in its several conceptual guises, touches on a wide variety of theoretical and practical issues related to both interpersonal and societal levels of analysis. The centrality of justice processes in small as well as large groups stems from its relevance to any situation in which benefits or burdens are distributed. Evaluations of the fairness of resulting distributions are the purview of distributive justice, whereas procedural justice focuses on the fairness of the processes leading up to the distribution. Thus to understand justice sentiments is to understand something that touches everyone's lives in overt and often profound ways. Most people can readily recount salient personal experiences of either distributive or procedural injustice. And, as philosophers have long contended, issues of justice and injustice are fundamental problems inherent in the maintenance of social order, the existence of inequality, and the fomenting of social change.

At the individual level, people raise cries of injustice when the benefits they receive are not what they expected or fall short of what they felt they deserved. Expectations derive from knowledge of the normative rules governing distributions or the relevant procedures, perceptions, and cognitions about the situation, as well as comparisons to past experiences, to other individuals, or to reference groups. Substantively, for example, individuals may feel unfairly treated when their pay level is lower than that of coworkers with equivalent experience and hours worked. Or women may claim unfair treatment when they find themselves working full-time as well as carrying full responsibility for domestic chores while their husbands participate in the paid labor force and do little at home. That some women accept such a division of labor as fair, however, highlights the subjective nature of justice evaluations and the necessity of understanding the various roles of rules, perceptions, and comparisons in justice assessments.

At the societal level, subjective evaluations have long colored what is considered fair in the interrelated spheres of politics and economics. Historical variation in the distribution of rights to vote or own property has often reflected the interests of power holders. Such interests continue to influence the policies promulgated by political parties in the United States. For example, the Democratic Party, whose membership traditionally includes a higher percentage of the working class and minority group members, frequently emphasizes government intervention to maintain minimal standards of living, whereas the Republican Party, whose members tend to be wealthier and involved in business, often advocates reliance on market forces to ensure minimal standards. Disparity in living standards or, more generally, income and wealth among people constitutes concerns with economic justice or the fairness of stratification systems.

Given the multiple levels of analysis and the centrality of questions of justice, approaches to the study of justice and injustice are many and varied.[1] We first anchor our discussion in the philosophical literature, demonstrating connections between these age-old, abstract, prescriptive views and current conceptualizations of justice in social psychology. We then turn to more specific analyses of theories and research on distributive justice. We attempt to delimit the status of knowledge concerning the development of justice rules, the experience of injustice, and responses to perceived injustice. In the third section we provide a brief overview of procedural justice issues, many of which parallel those in distributive justice. We conclude by outlining current trends in both basic and applied research.

CONCEPTIONS OF JUSTICE

Philosophers have long analyzed Plato's question, "What is justice?" (see Solomon and Murphy 1990). Although highly abstract and prescriptive, oriented toward describing what a just society ought to be, the imprint of philosophers' analyses is visible in discussions about justice in the social sciences (see Cohen 1986; Scherer 1992). In social psychology, in particular, emphasis tends to be more on beliefs about justice, with consequences for individuals and groups, rather than on prescriptions for societal organization. Despite this variation, there is indeed correspondence between some of the major philosophical approaches and those developed in social psychology (Hegtvedt 1992b).

The philosopher Plato (*The Republic*, Book IV) defined justice in effect as performing one's own role and the utilitarian John Stuart Mill as "the greatest good for the greatest number." These conceptualizations are rarely echoed in social psychological approaches to justice. In contrast, the ideas of Aristotle, social contractarian philosophers, Rawls (1971), and, most recently, Barry (1989) more prominently shape social psychological approaches to justice and injustice.

Aristotle's arguments in *Nicomachean Ethics* (Book V) cast the development of justice into the less abstract realm of fair exchange. His admonishment to treat equals equally and to treat unequals unequally relies on a proportional definition of justice: a just distribution is one in which people receive rewards and honors in proportion to what they deserve or merit. In addition, he specifies that

determination of just desserts relies on comparisons between individuals. These notions clearly underlie approaches that define justice as the equivalence of the ratio of outcomes to inputs for two actors (e.g., Adams 1965; Homans 1974; Walster, Walster, and Berscheid 1978). What constitutes "desserts," however, is a fundamental issue in some of the modern approaches to justice.

The social contractarian philosophers of the seventeenth and eighteenth centuries (e.g., Thomas Hobbes, John Locke, and Jean-Jacques Rousseau) recognized the limitations of a conception of justice based on assessments of individual desserts vis-à-vis others. They argued that if individuals believe they deserve what is in their own interests and pursue those interests, civilized society becomes impossible. Alternatively, they proposed that a just society is one in which rational people come to see their way to compromising their often divisive self-interests to establish a system in which their own and others' self-interest would be maximized (Solomon and Murphy 1990). In their formulations, emphasis shifts away from the exclusive focus on individual desserts to the collective good. This theme emerges in social psychologists' claims that justice fosters effective social cooperation to promote individual well-being (Deutsch 1975) and that a justice principle is one for which people share the perception that the rule promotes mutually agreeable exchange or allocations (Reis 1986).

Revitalizing discussions of justice in the late twentieth century, Rawls (1971) modifies the social contractarian approach by focusing on the means to ensure the welfare of the collectivity. Presumably, when self-interested, rational individuals occupy the "original position" behind a "veil of ignorance," so that they do not know their position in society (in terms of class, status, or natural abilities), they are likely to agree on equal rights to liberties and to promote a distribution principle that arranges inequalities to the greatest benefit of the least advantaged members of society and ensures equal opportunity. This approach circumvents the issue raised by Marx that justice is little

exchange—an argument that stems from the assumptions of the exchange approach to interaction (see chapter 8). Microexchange approaches to distributive justice (Adams 1965; Blau 1964; Homans 1974; Walster, Walster, and Berscheid 1978) assume that individuals attempt to secure rewards from their relationships. They are therefore likely to maintain rewarding relationships and discontinue unrewarding ones.

Drawing on the work of Aristotle, Homans (1961) asserts that "the rule of justice says that a man's rewards in exchange with others should be proportional to his investments" (p. 235). Investments may be ascribed characteristics, such as race or sex, or achieved characteristics, including those that have gained value over time (e.g., seniority on a job) and those contributed to the immediate exchange (e.g., hours worked, widgets produced). Distributive justice exists when rewards align with investments, except where participation in the exchange involves costs beyond those investments. Taking into account costs, Homans suggests that distributive justice obtains when the profits (rewards minus costs) of two actors are equal. To the extent that numerical quantities are difficult to assess, justice exists when each actor's reward rank is also his/her rank on costs and investments. This "ordinal equality" principle ensures congruence between status and rewards.

Presumably, this distribution principle stems from beliefs regarding the links between investments and profits, as well as repeated experiences involving congruent distributions (Homans 1974). As a consequence, people come to generalize from what is to what ought to be. Blau (1964) casts the analyses of reward-to-investment comparisons in the context of society's need for what the person contributes to the exchange, based on the actual contribution and the investments necessary to produce it. He thus emphasizes that those who invest a great deal of resources to supply society with what it needs ought to receive correspondingly high rewards. Recent work by Stolte (1987), however, suggests that acceptance of proportionality as the justice principle in exchange may depend on an assumption of power inequality between actors. In

his theoretical analysis, Stolte demonstrates that in exchange among power equals, equality may emerge as the fair principle. Regardless of the justice rule guiding exchange, complications arise if individuals' views of what legitimately constitutes investments, costs, or rewards, and how people are to be ranked on each, differ.

In the absence of any absolute standard of what is fair, people assess whether or not they are receiving their just desserts by comparing themselves to similar others, especially those with whom they are in direct exchange. If a person receives less (or more) than he/she expects, as determined by comparison to a similar other, then injustice obtains. Homans (1974) suggests that when a reward is lower than expected, the recipient is likely to feel anger and display some form of aggressive behavior toward the source or beneficiary of the injustice. Such aggressive responses are more likely when the victim of the injustice perceives that he/she is not at fault. In contrast, the person who benefits unexpectedly from the exchange may feel guilty and, as a consequence, increase what he/she offers in subsequent exchanges.

Adams (1965) builds on Homans's work by providing more precise specifications of the justice rule, the processes giving rise to felt injustice, and the actions people take to redress injustice. Similar to Homans's conception of distributive justice, Adams asserts that equity exists for a person (A) when he/she perceives equality between the ratio of his/her outcomes (O) to inputs (I) and the ratio of another's (B) outcomes to inputs:

$$\frac{O_A}{I_A} = \frac{O_B}{I_B}$$

Outcomes are positive or negative receipts from the exchange, and inputs are what the individual invests in or contributes to the exchange. Individuals must recognize and perceive contributions as relevant if they are to exist as exchange inputs; these criteria apply similarly to exchange outcomes. Problems of inequity arise, however, if only the possessor of a particular investment considers it relevant or if the actors differentially weigh relevant inputs (or outcomes).

Like Homans, Adams claims that normative expectations of fairness stem from observed correlations between outcomes and inputs for reference individuals and groups and that people learn these correlations during socialization. Inequity obtains whenever a person perceives an *inequality* between his/her outcome/input ratio and that of another—an inequality that violates normative expectations. If A's ratio is smaller than B's, A feels underrewarded; if A's ratio is larger than B's, A feels overrewarded. Although Adams assumes that the magnitude of experienced inequity increases with the size of the discrepancy between the outcome/input ratios, he does not explore this relationship, as do some of the sociologists discussed below. He notes, however, that the threshold for inequity experiences is probably higher for overreward than for underreward.

Adams draws on cognitive dissonance theory to describe the experience of inequity and to explain reactions to injustice. He posits that violation of the equity rule creates tension or distress in an individual, presumably in proportion to the magnitude of the inequity. The unpleasantness of the felt tension then motivates the actors to resolve the injustice and thereby diminish the distress. Adams (1965) offers six means by which individuals can eliminate the tension arising from inequity: they may (1) alter their inputs; (2) alter their outcomes; (3) cognitively distort either their inputs or their outcomes; (4) leave the situation; (5) cognitively distort either the inputs or the outcomes of the exchange partner; or (6) change the object of comparison. Use of the first two strategies depends on whether the person has been over- or underrewarded. Overrewarded individuals can increase their inputs or decrease their outcomes to restore equal ratios, whereas underrewarded people must decrease their inputs or increase their outcomes. Similarly, the nature of cognitive distortions of inputs or outcomes depends on the type of inequity.

According to Adams, individuals choose an equity-restoration method that maximizes positive outcomes with the least expenditure of real or psychological costs. If distortion must occur, actors will be more likely to focus on the other person's inputs or outcomes before distorting their own, especially if such distortion threatens their self-esteem. Leaving the situation and changing the comparison other involve the highest costs, because they disrupt the status quo and violate justice beliefs. As a consequence, people are likely to opt for those methods only when the experienced inequity is intense and other means of redress are unavailable.

In an attempt to refine and extend Adams's formulation of equity theory, Walster et al. (1978) offer explicit propositions for the development of equity as a justice principle, the perception of inequity, and reactions to perceived injustice. Beginning with the proposition that "individuals will try to maximize their outcomes," they argue that groups try to maximize their rewards by developing systems of equitable apportionment and inducing members to adhere to the system by rewarding those who act equitably and punishing those who do not. Like Adams, they propose that people in inequitable relationships become distressed in proportion to the degree of inequity. To eliminate the distress, actors attempt to restore equity—either psychologically, through perceptual distortion methods, or through actual changes in inputs and outcomes. Walster et al. contend that their approach improves on Adams's. For instance, they refine the equity formula to account ostensibly for negative inputs:

$$\frac{O_A - I_A}{|I_A|^{k_A}} = \frac{O_B - I_B}{|I_B|^{k_B}}$$

The numerator is what Homans refers to as "profit," and the denominator adjusts for the positive or negative sign of the inputs. Each k takes on the value of either +1 or -1, as determined by each person's sign (I) × sign (O − I). Other researchers, however, have uncovered serious problems with this formula when individuals have opposite-signed inputs (Alessio 1980; Harris 1976; Moschetti 1979). Another improvement claimed by Walster et al. is the application of their theory to a wide variety of relationships, such as business, intimate, exploiter/victim, and philanthropist/recipient. For example, in exploiter/victim relationships, the exploiter presumably experiences the distress of overreward and may take steps to restore justice through compensations such as confession or self-deprivation, reparations to the victim, or justifications (e.g., blaming the victim or denying responsibility for the act). The victim, in turn, may choose to retaliate, demand compensation, or justify the inequity and learn to live with it. Furthermore, Walster et al. note the possibility of intervention by outside agents who are mandated to maintain and/or restore justice or who take it upon themselves to do so. Perhaps with the exception of the intervention of outside agents, Walster et al.'s analyses of injustice reactions represent concrete examples of Adams's more abstract assertions. Unfortunately, as described below, empirical work examines few of the response alternatives set forth by either Adams or Walster et al.

Microexchange Research. Although the microexchange theorists address the development of equity principles, most equity research focuses on reactions to interpersonal input and outcome comparisons. For the most part, questions of the recognition and relevance of outcomes and inputs—especially as they differ across individuals—remain unaddressed. These questions, coupled with issues raised by the research on reactions, however, provide a basis for recent efforts to integrate social perception and equity approaches. These integrative theories spell out more explicitly the cognitive processes linking the experience of injustice with subsequent behaviors to restore justice.

A number of studies have examined Adams's (1965) and Walster et al.'s (1978) proposition that inequity creates distress, despite the elusiveness of a definition of distress. The ground-breaking study by Austin and Walster (1974) measured distress using self-reports of feelings and galvanic skin response (GSR), an indicator of physiological arousal. Self-reports showed that underrewarded subjects expressed more distress than equitably rewarded subjects. The GSR results were statistically nonsignificant, though in the predicted direction. More recently, Markovsky (1988b) found heightened GSR

in underreward and overreward conditions relative to an equitable baseline condition.

Studies of both impersonal relationships (e.g., Hegtvedt 1990) and intimate couples (e.g., Sprecher 1986) consistently indicate that equitably rewarded individuals report feeling more content than inequitably rewarded individuals. There is some evidence, however, that overrewarded members of couples express as much relationship satisfaction as equitably rewarded members (Davidson 1984). Similarly, slightly overrewarded individuals in businesslike relations express quite positive emotions (Hegtvedt 1990).

These findings on the emotional responses of overrewarded people cast some doubt on Homans's (1974) prediction that such individuals would feel guilty while underrewarded ones would feel angry. Findings regarding the expression of anger by underrewarded individuals are very consistent (e.g., Gray-Little and Teddlie 1978; Hegtvedt 1990), whereas evidence for the expression of guilt is inconsistent. Gray-Little and Teddlie (1978) find no differences across levels of reward in feelings of guilt. In contrast, Hegtvedt's (1990) results demonstrate expected differences across reward level, but the absolute level of guilt was extremely low and dependent on the actor's power position.

Working with the assumption that distress follows inequity, most research on reactions to inequity comes from "productivity" or "reallocation" experiments. The prototypical productivity experiment (e.g., Adams and Rosenbaum 1962) leads subjects to believe they are underpaid, equitably paid, or overpaid compared to one or more other workers (based on inputs of time or amount of work completed), then provides subjects an opportunity to raise or lower their productivity in a subsequent work session. Adams's hypothesized response in terms of altering inputs is that an overrewarded actor will produce more while an underrewarded actor will produce less to restore equity. Studies generally confirm the prediction that overrewarded subjects will raise their productivity. In contrast, support is more equivocal for the predicted response of underrewarded subjects, perhaps owing to their fear that lower inputs will result in even lower outcomes (see Cook and Hegtvedt 1983).

The typical reallocation experiment examines alteration in outcomes as a reaction to inequity (e.g., Leventhal, Allen, and Kemelgor 1969). Individuals who are underpaid, equitably paid, or overpaid on a task receive additional money to distribute after a second task. According to Adams, underrewarded subjects will allocate more to themselves than to their partners to compensate for their lower rewards on the first task; overrewarded subjects allocate less to themselves to create equity. Empirical investigations typically bear out these predictions (see Cook and Hegtvedt 1983).

Despite the number of studies on reactions to inequity, few have studied factors assumed to affect the selection of one form of equity restoration over another or the conditions under which individuals choose not to respond to inequity. The absence of a behavioral reaction to inequity does not necessarily imply lack of concern about justice. For example, Lerner (1980) suggests that if people construe events in ways that enable them to believe individuals get what they deserve, they may be unlikely to respond to injustice. His notion of a "belief in the just world" allows rationalization of one's own or others' inequitable outcomes: victims are held responsible for their own misfortunes. Failures to respond may also stem from different interpretations of relevant inputs and outcomes in a situation. A critical omission in early theoretical and empirical work is the failure to investigate underlying psychological processes and perceptions relevant to coping with inequity.

Microexchange and Social Perception: Theory and Research. To augment the equity approach, Utne and Kidd (1980) provide an analysis of the cognitive processing underlying individuals' responses to injustice. This analysis centers on attributions. Utne and Kidd propose that people deal with the distress accompanying inequity by analyzing the causes of the inequity. Such causal attributions allow individuals to assess the relative costs of various justice restoration methods, providing a basis for a more rational choice. Earlier work (Garrett and Libby 1973) shows that when individuals attribute the inequity to chance rather than intention, they are unlikely to expend further effort to restore equity. Thus Utne and Kidd emphasize the general importance of intention by arguing that individuals who perceive another person as the perpetrator of an inequitable underreward are more distressed than those who ascertain that the inequity stems from forces external to the relationship. By identifying another person as the cause of the inequity, individuals gain information regarding the most effective means to restore equity. Situational factors, however, may make direct appeals to the cause of the inequity costly, thus individuals may opt for alternative methods. For example, when a person feels little control in the situation, perhaps resulting from power inequalities between him/herself and the perpetrator of the inequity, he/she may simply respond with resignation. In contrast, one who feels control may actively attempt to create a just situation.

Recent work on attributions and responses to inequity confirm some of Utne and Kidd's reasoning. Hassebrauck (1987) demonstrates that when individuals misattribute their distress to a neutral source, they are unlikely to attempt to redress inequity. A study by Hegtvedt et al. (1993) indicates that attributions do mediate responses to inequity under certain conditions. In a single-exchange transaction between partners of unequal power, attributions to self mediate responses to inequity in mixed sex dyads but not in female dyads, suggesting that sex composition of the dyad affects the nature of cognitive and behavioral reactions to inequity.

Whereas Utne and Kidd's analysis pertained mainly to attributions in situations of social exchange, Folger's (1986) referent cognitions approach includes a wider variety of cognitions in allocation as well as exchange situations. Folger argues that a gap in equity theory pertains to how reward distributions are made and that an understanding of this process is necessary to predicting reactions to inequity. He weaves together three cognitive elements to address this gap. First, referent outcome level represents the "distance" between actual outcome and referent outcome. People with high referent outcomes—the most favorable imaginable outcomes—are more likely to find inequity distressing than those with lower referent outcomes. Second, the greater the perceived likelihood of remedying the inequity situation, the less likely are individuals to express inequity distress. The ability to remedy the situation diminishes its apparent severity. A discrepancy between actual and referent outcome levels may result in dissatisfaction, but the extent to which the result is justifiable—the third element—determines whether resentment over the inequity emerges.

Folger suggests that perceivers examine the procedures or "instrumentalities" responsible for their outcomes. Actual instrumentalities refer to procedures people perceive as responsible for their outcomes, and referent instrumentalities are what they imagine could have been employed. Comparing actual and referent instrumentalities helps actors to evaluate and/or justify reward distributions. For example, if referent instrumentalities seem more reasonable than actual procedures, then the latter will seem unjustified. That judgment, coupled with dissatisfaction over outcomes, results in strong feelings of resentment (Folger and Martin 1986). Variation in referent outcome levels or instrumentalities may lead two individuals to different assessments and affect the likelihood of observable reactions to injustice.

The notion of referent outcomes complements the interpersonal comparison inherent in the equity formula. These comparisons, however, are not the only types relevant to justice evaluations. Sociological contributions to distributive justice consider additional types of comparisons.

Sociological Contributions

Sociological contributions to justice theorizing and research extend the interpersonal level social psychological approaches in several ways. First, they specify the importance of comparisons to reference groups as well as to specific other individuals or to one's own past experience. Second, they highlight the subjective nature of the experience of injustice. And third, by anchoring justice evaluations

in group rather than individual contexts, they provide insights into collective reactions to injustice. Below we review relative deprivation theory, status value theory, and their hybrids and conclude with a review of the relevant empirical findings.

Relative Deprivation Approaches. Relative deprivation approaches draw attention to group-level comparisons as an important component in determining reward evaluations. Stouffer et al. (1949) introduced the idea to explain why people who are better off than others in an objective sense often still feel deprived. He noted that such feelings occur when comparing one's rewards to those of others in a "comparison group," rather than to rewards in a broader system. Merton and Rossi (1968) refined the idea by tying in the concepts of group membership and reference groups.

Davis (1959, 1963) offers a formal theory that examines the reward comparison processes in the relative deprivation argument. Relative deprivation and gratification are seen as subjective feelings that stem from reward comparisons within one's group. In contrast, relative subordination and superiority are attitudes stemming from reward comparisons with other groups.

In his own version of the relative deprivation argument, Davies (1962, 1969) focused on patterns of change in reward expectations rather than reward levels. He predicted that revolution is most likely when, following a prolonged period of rising expectations and gratifications, the latter sharply declines. The consequent widespread frustration results in violent collective actions. When graphed, such changes in gratification over time resemble a rotated letter *J,* hence the so-called "J-curve theory of relative deprivation." The testability of the J-curve notion has been questioned, however, because Davies does not specify how severe the curve in the *J* must be to produce collective action, or whose deprivation matters—the group's or its individual members' (Miller, Boyce, and Halligan 1977). To rectify some of these problems, Gurr (1970) offers a typology of J-curves and Geschewender (1968) develops Davies' idea of deprivation as a form of cognitive dissonance.

Runciman's (1966) greatest contribution was to distinguish two types of relative deprivation: egoistic and fraternal. Egoistic deprivation refers to one's own situation; fraternal deprivation is experienced on behalf of one's group. The major consequence of this distinction is the recognition that fraternal deprivation is more likely to lead to collective action than is egoistic deprivation (Dubé and Guimond 1986).

Williams (1975) refines relative deprivation theory considerably and makes its claims more specific. For example, he notes that deprivation follows from receiving less than one desires; disappointment from receiving less than one expects; and injustice from receiving less than is socially mandated. He further analyzes the causes of social comparison choices (e.g., salience, social proximity, information availability) and the responses produced by egoistic and fraternalistic deprivation (e.g., individual versus collective responses). Although Williams's review and synthesis is impressive, it has been largely ignored by other theorists. This may be due in part to its complexity and a tendency to conflate highly abstract with very concrete assertions. It was mentioned favorably, however, in an otherwise critical review of relative deprivation theory by Walker and Pettigrew (1984), a review that itself provided a cogent analysis and integration of relative deprivation and social identity theories.

Whereas Williams (1975) emphasizes fraternalistic deprivation, Crosby (1976) focuses exclusively on egoistic relative deprivation in her attempt to provide the most rigorous theory to date. Using a causal diagram, she establishes a set of necessary and sufficient "preconditions" on the subjective experience of deprivation to the final behavioral outcomes. A more recent refinement (Crosby 1982) focuses attention on two conditions: egoistic relative deprivation will occur if there are perceived discrepancies between (1) actual outcomes and desired outcomes and (2) actual outcomes and entitled outcomes. Both desired and entitled outcomes are affected by comparative referents and expectations.

The most recent theoretical developments in relative deprivation theory are for the most part efforts to build conceptual bridges between it and other social psychological approaches (Masters and Smith 1987), such as social comparison formulations (e.g., Atkinson 1986) and Folger's (1986) referent cognitions theory. These recent developments help resolve ambiguities surrounding claims that "similar" others serve as comparative referents by specifying the conditions under which different individuals choose different bases of comparison. Atkinson (1986), for example, uses social identification and judgment heuristics theories to show how group membership and information contexts affect perceptions of similarity. Folger's referent cognitions theory asserts that people compare actual outcomes to referent outcomes, which stem from mental simulations of possible situations. When perceived and referent outcomes are at variance, dissatisfaction and resentment emerge. Such negative reactions are less likely if individuals perceive the situation as easily remedied.

In some ways, relative deprivation theory, especially its egoistic side, is a weaker version of the microexchange approaches: it excludes input factors known to affect reward comparisons. Although it may be the case that not all reward comparisons require input comparisons, relative deprivation theorists do not provide explicit guidelines for when this condition applies. Remarkably few theorists and researchers associated with the relative deprivation tradition have recognized this simple fact, much less addressed it. On the other hand, the strength of relative deprivation theory is its appreciation for the social comparison processes that underlie all justice evaluations (e.g., Masters and Smith 1987; Singer 1981) and its focus on collective reactions (e.g., Dubé and Guimond 1986; Williams 1975).

Status Value Theory. Like relative deprivation, the status value theory of distributive justice (Berger, Fisek, Norman and Wagner 1983; Berger, Zelditch, Anderson and Cohen 1972) highlights the importance of reference standards for justice evaluations. Unlike relative deprivation approaches, however, it considers input levels as well as reward levels. Moreover, both of these components are viewed in terms of their status values or prestige ratings, rather than their consummatory or economic values, as in microexchange approaches. Berger et al. (1972) suggest that people develop stereotyped conceptions of linkages between social characteristics and particular rewards or goal objects. Akin to Homans's emphasis on status congruence, the authors argue that people expect consistency between the status values of an actor's social characteristics and the rewards received by that actor.

In status value theory the concept, "referential structure," is used to capture this assumed reward/characteristic value consistency. The referential structure is a shared conception of how the social characteristics of generalized others correspond to their social rewards. When a situation activates a referential structure, participants expect social characteristics and rewards to correspond in the "local situation" as they do in the referential structure. Thus, for example, a particular electrician's wages are expected to align with some notion of the wages earned by electricians *in general*. Thus, status value theory asserts that fairness obtains "when you and I receive what people like us generally get." Activation of reward expectations based on a particular referential structure may stem from task expectations in the situation (Cook 1975).

Including the concept of referential structure in the development of justice evaluations reveals a major shortcoming of the exchange formulations of justice: their exclusive emphasis on comparisons between individuals. Such purely local comparisons exclude from consideration general social standards by which outcomes may also be evaluated. Referential comparisons put individual rewards and social characteristics in a broader perspective. For instance, given two differentially rewarded actors in a relationship and no referential information, all that either person may infer is that he/she received more or less than the other. With a referential structure, however, both individuals

may judge themselves against a more general standard. In fact, whatever their relative reward, it is possible for both to feel unjustly under- (or over-) rewarded if people like themselves in similar circumstances are believed to receive higher (or lower) rewards. A state of collective injustice can thus emerge, in contrast to the self-oriented evaluations of the strictly interpersonal level theories.

Sociological Hybrids. Some researchers combine elements of the different theoretical formulations in attempts to understand more clearly the complexities of justice evaluations and reactions. These "hybrids" integrate and extend the analyses of relative deprivation, status value, and exchange theories.

Törnblom (1977), for example, integrates aspects of exchange and status value theories by examining combinations of local and referential comparisons that underlie justice evaluations. He notes that individuals may also compare their rewards to internal standards. Törnblom first develops a typology of interpersonal comparisons, showing how a person's inputs and outcomes may be greater than, equal to, or less than another person's inputs and outcomes. He then couples these nine types of local comparisons with a referential standard of inputs and outcomes that likewise may be greater than, equal to, or less than those of the actors represented in the local comparison. A set of propositions permits the ordering of the various injustice types in terms of perceived severity, arguing that more severe types of injustice produce a stronger motivation to redress injustice.

Jasso's (1980) "new theory of distributive justice" also provides a model for degrees of perceived injustice. Critical to Jasso's analysis is her justice evaluation (JE) formula:

$$JE = \ln (\text{actual share/just share})$$

The actual share is analogous to Adam's "outcomes," and just share is the reward the evaluator considers to be just. In contrast to the earlier justice equations of Adams and Walster et al., Jasso explicitly focused on the mathematical form of injustice experiences—departures of various magnitudes from the state of perfect justice. This permits more refined predictions for injustice experiences. More important for Jasso, however, is that this model and its variants (e.g., Jasso 1986) are readily extended to group-level phenomena. Jasso relates patterns of justice evaluations across members of a social group to a variety of group consequences, such as the likelihood of revolution and the rates of crime and mental illness.

Markovsky's (1985) "multilevel justice theory" builds on several notions that appeared in Jasso's (1980) theory, Berger et al.'s (1972) status-value theory, relative deprivation, and equity approaches. First, individuals' justice evaluations are modeled from the point of view of actors in exchanges, or empathic observers. Second, the actor on whose behalf a justice evaluation is being made may be either an individual or group. And, third, the comparison standard against which rewards are assessed may be a reward value associated with an individual, the evaluator at another point in time, a group, an abstract standard, a generalized other, and so on. As a consequence, the theory does not restrict the reference standard to either specific or generalized others or to either individuals or groups as do some prior formulations. Finally, the multilevel theory of justice introduces the unique idea of "justice indifference," representing the degree to which the evaluator is indifferent as to whether justice or injustice holds for the subject of the evaluation. More recent work by Markovsky (1988a) and Jasso (1990, 1993) elaborates on these ideas.

The mathematical modeling of justice represents evolutionary progress in terms of logical and empirically driven revisions as well as recognition of the need to integrate sociological phenomena into the original psychological model. Moreover, this progression epitomizes the extent to which perceptions of justice and injustice are socially constructed. The next logical step is to integrate these considerations with an understanding of reactions to injustice.

Research on Sociological Approaches. The sociological contributions draw attention to social comparisons, subjective assessments of injustice, and collective responses to injustice. The first and third of these issues have received the most empirical attention. Studies reviewed above on perceptions of inputs relevant to allocation preferences or distribution evaluations also bear indirectly on the second issue.

Empirical attention to variation in the type of comparison—internal, local, referential, or group—stems from Berger et al.'s and Törnblom's theoretical approaches as well as from the relative deprivation framework. Although little empirical research addresses choices of comparison standards, Austin (1977) suggests that these choices are affected by proximity, similarity, and instrumentality. Moreover, Masters and Smith (1987) argue that individuals typically prefer no single comparison across situations but rather the comparison depends on the type of evaluation at issue and the social context.

Markovsky (1985) empirically examines the impact of several of the types of comparisons set forth in his theoretical formulation. His experiment allowed interpersonal, intergroup, and mixed comparisons of rewards. Initial results showed that individual responses to injustice based on interpersonal comparisons were more frequent and forceful than responses based on intergroup comparisons. Increasing group identification, however, reversed this effect, and subjects responded more frequently and forcefully on behalf of their groups than on their own behalf.

The availability of multiple and different reference group comparisons complicates assessments of justice. For example, Gartrell's (1985) model accommodates gross patterns of social comparisons and injustice experiences across members at different levels of multitiered systems. These patterns turn out to be rather complex and, as yet, are not predictable by any justice theory. Martin and Petersen's (1987) research indicates that when new workers in a lower wage tier have two referential comparisons—their own wage tier and that of co-workers in a higher wage tier—they evaluate the distribution of wages as more unfair than when their only comparison consists of other workers in the lower wage tier. Differential pay evaluations made by males and females also draws attention to the effects of various referential structures. Moore (1990) shows that women in a female-typed occupation use members of that occupation as referential comparisons and perceive little injustice. In contrast, women working in male-typed occupations express feelings of injustice when they compare themselves to others in the occupational group but not when they use other women as a reference group.

Input and outcome comparisons are further complicated by the presence of ancillary and even irrelevant information in the social context of justice evaluations. Markovsky (1988a) shows how the salience and nature of such informational "anchors" systematically bias judgments of what rewards would be fair and of the fairness of given reward amounts. Alwin (1987) further demonstrates how the subjectively anchored sense of injustice about family income predicts material satisfaction. His results, however, provide only a hint of support for Jasso's contention that degrees of underreward exert more potent effects than those of overreward.

The use of fraternal comparisons in relative deprivation theory or of referential comparisons in status value theory is a necessary precursor to the shared perceptions that underlie collective reactions to injustice. When members of a group feel unjustly treated and recognize that others share their plight, the potential emerges for them to coalesce into a solid group that is better able to redress collective injustice. Although not addressed by relative deprivation and status value approaches, collective reactions to injustice also depend on group-level power processes, resource mobilization, the development of organizational tactics, and leadership among the less powerful group (deCarufel 1981). As a consequence, collective reactions highlight a relationship between power and justice (Cook and Hegtvedt 1986) that is scarcely considered by exchange approaches to individual reactions. Power imbalances between groups resulting in lower rewards for the disadvantaged may stimulate a collective response, while shared feel-

ings of justice cement the solidarity of the deprived group.

Research in the relative deprivation tradition, though less abundant or systematic than that in other justice areas, spans decades and levels of analysis. The earlier work focuses on the basic relative deprivation phenomenon: discontentedness among members of (usually) large groups or social categories following the selection of advantaged reference groups. For example, Martin and Murray (1983) review research that finds this effect among American soldiers, English workers, northern African Americans who moved south, blue-collar workers, and urban voters. Later research more pointedly addresses theoretical nuances. Crosby (1982) studies working women and finds evidence for her two-factor model; Martin (1986) develops conditions under which various social comparison choices are made; Walker and Mann (1987) find fraternalistic relative deprivation associated with social protest and egoistic relative deprivation associated with individual stress symptoms. Most of today's research on relative deprivation, however, generally does not test new theoretical developments, but rather applies existing formulations to new data. For example, Van Dyk and Nieuwaudt (1990) and Krahn and Harrison (1992) use relative deprivation ideas to interpret attitudes of, respectively, rural Afrikaans-speaking women in South Africa and recession victims in Alberta, Canada.

Although Berger et al. (1972) assert that referential standards are necessary for determining collective injustice, their status value approach has only indirectly guided empirical research on collective responses. Some experimental studies show that when two "weak" or subordinate members believe a leader has treated them unfairly, they are likely to form "revolutionary" coalitions against the leader (Lawler 1975; Webster and Smith 1978). Moreover, consistent with Utne and Kidd's (1980) arguments about the role of attributions in responses to injustice, subordinates who attribute high responsibility to their leader for the inequity are more likely to revolt than those who perceive their leader to have low responsibility (Lawler and

Thompson 1978). Other beliefs also shape reactions to the status quo. Group members may attempt to overthrow the distribution rule promoted by a legitimate authority (especially an equality rule) if they consensually agree that another rule enhances their collective benefit (Martin and Sell 1986). If individuals must choose between their own interests and those of other group members, rejection of an authority's rule becomes more difficult. Collective reactions to injustice are thus most likely to emerge when self- and group interests coincide—when local and referential comparisons create consistent feelings of injustice.

Summary: Distributive Justice Evaluations

Social psychological and sociological approaches focus on several points in the justice evaluation process: the development and application of justice standards; the perception of inputs and outcomes and comparisons of them to those of reference individuals or groups; and the enactment of various responses to injustice. In spite of these successful theoretical inroads, however, most of the theories reviewed underestimate the extent of differential perceptions of justice and injustice.

The work of Mikula and his associates (e.g., Mikula, Petri, and Tanzer 1989) describes factors in natural settings not yet accounted for in theory that underlie differential perceptions of justice. Here we categorize these factors and specify other research domains that may inform our understanding of justice evaluations. In general, people's differential evaluations of justice stem from differences in perceptions, comparisons, and emotions about the situation.

The perceptual component of justice evaluations primarily pertains to the level of rewards and the comparison standard for those rewards. If individuals select different comparison standards, they may be likely to arrive at different justice evaluations. Systematic research is needed to determine the conditions under which individuals select a given comparison and use it to determine a justice evaluation. The comparison process, furthermore,

requires cognitive processing of inputs and outcomes to determine their relative weights as well as causal sources. To the extent that errors and biases pervade human judgments (e.g., Nisbett and Ross 1980), individuals may diverge in their assessment of the fairness of a distribution. In addition, the comparison and cognitive processes may elicit or be affected by emotions that ultimately color the justice evaluation. A negative emotional response to the result of the comparison process is likely to lead to a stronger evaluation of injustice than a positive response. Insofar as emotions are multidimensional, not simply positive or negative, and situational circumstances inhibit or facilitate types of emotional experiences (see Kemper 1990), emotions may differentially affect individuals' evaluations of justice. Thus developments in cognitive psychology and the sociology of emotions are relevant to further our understanding of justice evaluations.

Greater sensitivity to the perceptual, cognitive, and emotional issues involved in justice evaluations may also provide a basis for understanding various reactions to distributive injustice. These same components appear also to underlie evaluations of procedural injustice, despite the current separation of the domains of distributive and procedural justice.

PROCEDURAL JUSTICE

Procedural justice refers to fairness in the means by which distributions are made. Although social psychological approaches to distributive justice originally focused on pay evaluation in small groups, theories of procedural justice were initially applied to issues in the legal arena. The earliest researchers, Thibaut and Walker (1975), focused on legal means or strategies of conflict resolution (see also chapter 20). More recent work (Leventhal, Karuza, and Fry 1980; Lind and Tyler 1988) emphasizes the importance of procedural issues in organizational, political, and interpersonal contexts. In our brief review of the dominant perspectives and key research on the social psychology of procedural justice, we highlight theoretical parallels between distributive and procedural justice.

Thibaut and Walker (1975) examine the development of procedural justice rules in conflict situations, much like exchange theorists study the rationale for equity as a normative principle. Starting with the exchange assumption of outcome maximization, Thibaut and Walker argue that people desire control over the decisions that affect their outcomes. Moreover, they argue that procedures used to resolve conflicts should promote an equitable distribution. Their work thus focuses on conflict resolution: how parties to a dispute gain more or less control over the process by which outcomes are determined. Research demonstrates that individuals prefer, and judge as more fair, those resolution procedures that allow disputants to explain their positions to a third party. Of course, as in allocation preferences, disputants may present information in a manner favorable to themselves. Lind and Tyler (1988) criticize this formulation of procedural justice for its emphasis on how concern with outcomes determines just procedures. They cite recent research that indicates fair procedures are important even independent of outcome evaluations.

More generally, Leventhal et al. (1980) call attention to a number of procedural justice rules that are not limited to conflict resolution. As in their expectancy approach to allocation preferences, they argue that individuals prefer procedural rules that fulfill the most important situational goals, such as: (1) consistency of procedures across persons and across time; (2) suppression of bias; (3) accuracy of information; (4) mechanisms to correct bad decisions; (5) representativeness of the participants to a decision; and (6) ethicality of standards.

A number of studies outside the legal context demonstrate the importance of consistency and representativeness (see Lind and Tyler 1988). Particularly important is representativeness of the participants to a decision, which allows them to "voice" their opinions on issues that affect them (e.g., Folger 1977). Some evidence demonstrates that ability to express opinions without instrumen-

tal purpose increases feelings of inclusion and enhances procedural justice evaluations (see Lind and Tyler 1988). Providing a rationale for a decision that emphasizes mitigating circumstances has a similar effect on inclusion and justice evaluations, perhaps by allowing evaluators to make more accurate attributions about the situation (Bies and Shapiro 1987). Thus, even in the absence of control over outcomes, voice and two-way communication may fulfill individuals' desires to have their views considered.

Such considerations underlie a recent model of procedural justice offered by Lind and Tyler (1988; Tyler 1989). Distinct from the self-interest model inherent in the work of Thibaut and Walker (1975), their group value model stresses the importance of group membership and the group's influence on values and behavior. Individuals judge as fair procedures consistent with those values, which in turn solidifies the group by regulating its structure and process. Besides predicting the nature of fair procedures, the model extends its scope to include violations of procedural justice. Given the centrality of procedures to group life, violations should engender strong feelings of anger and dislike toward the perpetrators of procedural injustice.

With the exception of the group value model of procedural justice, the theoretical perspectives focus primarily on the development of procedural principles. These perspectives in effect establish comparison standards necessary for evaluations of procedural justice. Issues relating to cognitive processing and emotional experiences as described for distributive justice may also affect the assessment of procedural justice. Empirical examination of these issues, however, is far less developed in the realm of procedural justice than in the case of distributive justice, although some research calls attention to the role of attributions on evaluations. In light of the similarity of the theoretical questions underlying both procedural and distributive justice evaluations, the "separate routes" representing the prior developments in distributive and procedural justice are clearly converging (Hegtvedt 1993).

The theoretical correspondence between the two types of justice emerges in consideration of practical justice issues.

FUTURE DIRECTIONS AND APPLICATIONS

The popular appeal of the topic of justice and the ubiquity of personal accounts of injustice experiences belie the complexity of justice and injustice processes. The interrelated questions of what constitutes justice, what activates perceptions of injustice, and how individuals and groups respond to injustice generally guide both basic and applied research. Our summary of the distributive justice literature highlights a number of issues for basic research and notes substantive connections to other social psychological domains. Here we specify several related directions for future work on basic theory and research and illustrate applications to concrete social issues. Though not exhaustive or detailed, this discussion demonstrates the expansiveness of justice issues and reveal gaps in our current knowledge. Justice theorizing and research are sure to continue along numerous paths and to branch out to new ones. We expect, however, that at least two of these paths will converge rather than continue to digress: procedural justice and distributive justice. Our brief review of the procedural justice literature attests to its concentration on the question of what constitutes fair procedural rules, but little work addresses the equally important questions of perception of and reaction to injustice or the links between procedures and outcomes. Folger's (1986) referent cognitions theory is a preliminary and unifying step in this direction.

Similarly, cognitive approaches are likely to play a major role in understanding the inevitable variation in beliefs about justice arising in complex societies. Thus, a second avenue for future research is the study of disagreement about what is just. Such disagreement is likely to arise when individuals in different structural positions have multiple relationships providing different sources of information. Perceptions are sensitive to contexts, so the more variable the informational context provided by structures and relations, the more variable the justice evaluations. Disagreements about what is just may then influence the way people respond to injustice. Recent work on "justice conflict" emphasizes the roles of social psychological processes of power and bargaining as a means to justice conflict resolution (Hegtvedt 1992a; Lamm 1986). Disagreement may result in the discontinuation of the relationship (i.e., withdrawal as a means to restore justice) or may result in the development of new conceptions of justice through negotiation and the formation of groups of like-minded members who challenge other groups in fomenting social change.

The dynamics of power and negotiation also influence the struggle for social change by groups promoting new conceptions of justice. Although most of this chapter focuses on the perceptions, evaluations, and reactions of individuals, a third major issue for future research is the link between the individual and the group. To understand collective experiences of injustice requires a knowledge of more than individual sentiments or coalitional mechanisms. Research should also consider issues of group identity (Hogg and Abrams 1988) and network dynamics (e.g., Burt 1982). Moreover, the relevance of studies of stratification and the perception of income inequalities (e.g., Huber and Form 1973; Robinson and Bell 1978) grows when emphasis shifts from the individual to the group level, with attention focused on social change.

Theoretical developments stemming from basic research may also guide evaluation research and interventions in real-world contexts. Researchers, administrators, politicians, and others employ the rhetoric of justice and injustice in virtually all situations where benefits or burdens are distributed. Justice applications rely to varying degrees on the systematic theory and empirical work discussed above, however. Here we briefly present two applications that use theory to a different extent and illustrate the relevance of the above directions for future research.

First, the application that draws most directly on existing theory is that of justice in organizations, where both distributive and procedural justice issues frequently arise.[2] A number of studies focus on justice as a means to understand other phenomena, such as employee satisfaction with jobs and pay, work attitudes, turnover rates, organizational commitment, performance appraisals, and employer-employee relations. For example, McFarlin and Sweeney (1992) show that distributive justice is more important than procedural justice in determining individual pay and job satisfaction ratings. With regard to organizational outcomes, however, findings suggest that the combination of unfair procedures and low distributive justice produces the lowest levels of organizational commitment and the lowest evaluations of supervisors. The authors interpret these findings as consistent with referent cognitions theory (Folger 1986). Other research examines justice as an end in itself. Sheppard and Lewicki (1987) surveyed business managers to understand the principles they use to judge both procedural and distributive fairness. The principles corresponded with those offered by Leventhal et al. (1980)—consistency, representativeness, and ethicality—and with Folger's (1977) emphasis on voice. Such results may be useful in structuring organizational policy to ensure that goals are achieved and workers and employers alike are satisfied.

Recent applications of justice research in the policy arena also bear on organizational issues. A second major research area applies to work-related policies such as affirmative action, designed to address racial and gender discrimination in hiring, and comparable worth policies, designed to equalize pay for jobs of similar worth performed by different categories of workers, (e.g., males and females).[3] These applications raise the general question of the fairness of a social policy, albeit not always with reference to existing theory and research.

By identifying the issues and examining different sides of the debate, these applications reveal in practice the second research direction cited above: justice conflict. Proponents view the role of affirmative action as redressing injustice and securing equal opportunities. Opponents argue that the policy unfairly penalizes nonbeneficiaries—usually white men—and may stigmatize beneficiaries. Justice theories may provide insights into these differences. For example, Tougas and Beaton (1992) explain variation among women in their support of affirmative action in terms of relative deprivation. Women who invoke fraternal comparisons tend to support the policy, inferring that women as a group are disadvantaged compared to men.

Hegtvedt (1989) analyzes the comparable worth debate in terms of conflict between relatively powerful business owners and less powerful groups of workers, such as women and minorities. Owners prefer to rely on market mechanisms for setting wages. Workers argue that market mechanisms fail to redress existing pay inequalities for jobs requiring similar levels of skill, effort, and responsibility. In addition, her analysis casts the determination of job worth as questions of procedural justice and equity: How bias-free is the available information for job worth? How representative of the organization are those who compile the information? What elements of job worth (i.e., inputs) are relevant and how are they combined? How does input value correspond with outcomes (i.e., pay)? These questions reveal the importance of microlevel organizational dynamics in wage setting—dynamics that may redress the wage gap between men and women. In other words, the comparable worth issue links individual fairness with societal fairness and raises the possibility of social change based on justice beliefs.

To understand issues of justice and injustice demands that we consider a variety of distinct but interrelated processes. Other social psychological and sociological perspectives will ultimately contribute to this understanding. In addition, questions raised in the applications of justice theory and research to concrete issues may hasten theoretical progress. To the extent that justice concerns pervade most aspects of social life, working out the theoretical complexities of justice processes on all levels—intrapersonal, interpersonal, and systemic—is not only of scientific importance but also of practical and humane interest.

NOTES

1. See edited volumes on justice and related issues: Berkowitz and Walster (1976), Bierhoff et al. (1986), Cohen (1986), Folger (1984), Greenberg and Cohen (1982), Lerner and Lerner (1981), Masters and Smith (1987), Messick and Cook (1983), Mikula (1980a), Scherer (1992), Vermunt and Steensma (1990).

2. Two journals have devoted special issues to questions of justice in organizations. *Social Justice Research,* volume 1, number 2 (1987), concentrates on procedural justice in organizations. *Administrative Science Quarterly,* volume 37, number 2 (1992), focuses on the distribution of rewards in organizations.

3. See special issues of *Social Justice Research,* volume 5, number 3 (1992), for a discussion of affirmative action and the *Journal of Social Issues,* volume 45, number 1 (1989), for various articles on comparable worth.

REFERENCES

Adams, J. Stacy. 1965. Inequity in social exchange. *Advances in Experimental Social Psychology* 2:267–299.

Adams, J. S., and W. B. Rosenbaum. 1962. The relationship of worker productivity to cognitive dissonance about wage inequalities. *Journal of Applied Psychology* 46:161–164.

Alessio, J. C. 1980. Another folly for equity theory. *Social Psychology Quarterly* 43:336–340.

Alves, W. M., and Peter H. Rossi. 1978. Who should get what? Fairness judgments of the distribution of earnings. *American Journal of Sociology* 84:541–565.

Alwin, Duane. 1987. Distributive justice and satisfaction with material well-being. *American Sociological Review* 52:83–95.

Atkinson, Michael. 1986. The perception of social categories: Implications for the social comparison process. Pp. 117–134 in *Relative Deprivation and Social Comparison,* ed. J. M. Olson, C. P. Herman, and M. P. Zanna. Hillsdale, NJ: Erlbaum.

Austin, William. 1977. Equity theory and social comparison processes. Pp. 279–305 in *Social Comparison Theory,* ed. J. Suls and R. Miller. Washington, DC: Hemisphere.

Austin, William, and Elaine Walster. 1974. Reactions to confirmation and disconfirmation of equity and inequity. *Journal of Personality and Social Psychology* 30:208–216.

Barry, Brian. 1989. *Theories of Justice.* Berkeley: University of California Press.

Berger, Joseph, Morris Zeldritch, Jr., Bo Anderson, and Bernard P. Cohen. 1972. Structural aspects of distributive justice: A status value formation. Pp. 119–146 in *Sociological Theories in Progress,* ed. J. Berger, M. Zelditch, and Bo Anderson. Boston: Houghton Mifflin.

Berger, Joseph, Hamit Fisek, Robert Z. Norman, and David G. Wagner. 1983. The formation of reward expectations in status situations. Pp. 127–168 in *Equity Theory: Psychological and Sociological Perspectives,* ed. D. Messick and K. S. Cook. New York: Praeger.

Berkowitz, Leonard, and Elaine Walster, eds. 1976. Equity theory: Toward a general theory of social interaction. In *Advances in Experimental Social Psychology.* New York: Academic.

Bierhoff, Hans Werner, Ronald L. Cohen, and Jerald Greenberg, eds. 1986. *Justice in Social Relations.* New York: Plenum.

Bies, Robert J., and Debra L. Shapiro. 1987. Interactional fairness judgments: The influence of causal accounts. *Social Justice Research* 1:199–218.

Blau, Peter. 1964. *Exchange and Power in Social Life.* New York: Wiley.

Burt, Ronald S. 1982. *Toward a Structural Theory of Action.* New York: Academic.

Cohen, Ronald L. 1982. Perceiving justice: An attributional perspective. Pp. 119–160 in *Equity and Justice in Social Behavior,* ed. J. Greenberg and R. L. Cohen. New York: Academic.

———. ed. 1986. *Justice: Views From the Social Sciences.* New York: Plenum.

Cohen, Ronald L., and Jerald Greenberg. 1982. The justice concept in social psychology. Pp. 1–42 in *Equity and Justice in Social Behavior,* ed. J. Greenberg and R. L. Cohen. New York: Academic.

Cook, Karen S. 1975. Expectations, evaluations and equity. *American Sociological Review* 48:372–388.

Cook, Karen S., and Karen A. Hegtvedt. 1983. Distributive justice, equity, and equality. *Annual Review of Sociology* 9:217–241.

———. 1986. Justice and power: An exchange analysis. Pp. 19–41 in *Justice in Social Relations,* ed. H. W.

Bierhoff, R. L. Cohen, and J. Greenberg. New York: Plenum.

Cook, Karen S., and Toshio Yamagishi. 1983. Social determinants of equity judgments: The problem of multidimensional input. Pp. 95–126 in *Equity Theory: Psychological and Sociological Perspectives,* ed. D. M. Messick and K. S. Cook. New York: Praeger.

Crosby, Faye. 1976. A model of egoistical relative deprivation. *Psychological Review* 83:85–113.

———. 1982. *Relative Deprivation and the Working Woman.* New York: Oxford University Press.

Davidson, Bernard. 1984. A test of equity theory for marital adjustment. *Social Psychology Quarterly* 47:36–42.

Davies, James C. 1962. Toward a theory of revolution. *American Sociological Review* 27:5–18.

———. 1969. The J-curve of rising and declining satisfaction as a cause of some great revolutions and a contained rebellion. Pp. 690–731 in *The History of Violence in America,* ed. H. D. Graham and T. R. Gurr. New York: Bantam.

Davis, James A. 1959. A formal interpretation of the theory of relative deprivation. *Sociometry* 22: 280–296.

———. 1963. Structural balance, mechanical solidarity, and interpersonal relations. *American Journal of Sociology* 68:444–462.

deCarufel, Andre. 1981. The allocation and acquisition of resources in times of scarcity. Pp. 317–343 in *The Justice Motive in Social Behavior,* ed. M. J. Lerner and S. C. Lerner. New York: Plenum.

Deutsch, Morton. 1975. Equity, equality, and need: What determines what value will be used as the basis for distributive justice? *Journal of Social Issues* 31:137–150.

———. 1985. *Distributive Justice: A Social Psychological Perspective.* New Haven: Yale University Press.

Dubé, Lise, and Serge Guimond. 1986. Relative deprivation and social protest: The personal-group issue. Pp. 201–216 in *Relative Deprivation and Social Comparison,* ed. J. M. Olson, C. P. Herman, and M. P. Zanna. Hillsdale, NJ: Erlbaum.

Folger, Robert. 1977. Distributive and procedural justice: Combined impact of "voice" and improvement on experienced inequity. *Journal of Personality and Social Psychology* 35:108–119.

———. ed. 1984. *The Sense of Injustice: Social Psychological Perspectives.* New York: Plenum.

———. 1986. Rethinking equity theory: A referent cognition model. Pp. 145–163 in *Justice in Social Re-*

lations, ed. H. Bierhoff, R. L. Cohen, and J. Greenberg. New York: Plenum.

Folger, Robert, and Chris Martin. 1986. Relative deprivation and referent cognitions: Distributive and procedural justice effects. *Journal of Experimental Social Psychology* 22:531–546.

Form, William, and Claudine Hanson. 1985. The consistency of stratal ideologies of economic justice. *Research in Social Stratification and Mobility* 4:239–269.

Frohlich, Norman, Joe A. Oppenheimer, and Cheryl L. Eavey. 1987. Choices of principles of distributive justice in experimental groups. *American Journal of Political Science* 31:606–636.

Garrett, J., and W. L. Libby. 1973. Role of intentionality in mediating responses to inequity in the dyad. *Journal of Personality and Social Psychology* 28: 21–27.

Gartrell, David. 1985. Relational and distributional models of collective justice sentiments. *Social Forces* 64:64–84.

Geschwender, James A. 1968. Explorations in the theory of social movements and revolutions. *Social Forces* 47:127–135.

Gray-Little, Bernadette, and Charles B. Teddlie. 1978. Racial differences in children's responses to inequity. *Journal of Applied Social Psychology* 8:107–117.

Greenberg, Jerald, and Ronald L. Cohen, eds. 1982. *Equity and Justice in Social Behavior.* New York: Academic.

Gurr, Ted. 1970. *Why Men Rebel.* Princeton, NJ: Princeton University Press.

Harris, R. J. 1976. Handling negative inputs: On the plausibility of equity formulae. *Journal of Experimental Social Psychology* 12:194–209.

Hassebrauck, Manfred. 1987. The influence of misattributions on reactions to inequity: Towards a further understanding of inequity. *European Journal of Social Psychology* 17:295–304.

Hegtvedt, Karen A. 1987. When rewards are scarce: Equal or equitable distributions? *Social Forces* 66:183–207.

———. 1989. Fairness conceptualizations and comparable worth. *Journal of Social Issues* 45:81–97.

———. 1990. The effects of relationship structure on emotional responses to inequity. *Social Psychology Quarterly* 53:214–228.

———. 1992a. Bargaining for justice: A means to resolve competing justice claims. *Social Justice Research* 5:155–172.

———. 1992b. When is a distribution rule just? *Rationality and Society* 4:308–331.

———. 1993. Approaching distributive and procedural justice: Are separate routes necessary? Pp. 195–221 in *Advances in Group Processes*, vol. 9, ed. E. J. Lawler, B. Markovsky, J. O'Brien, and K. Heimer. Greenwich, CT: JAI Press.

Hegtvedt, Karen A., Elaine A. Thompson, and Karen S. Cook. 1993. Power and equity: What counts in explaining exchange outcomes? *Social Psychology Quarterly* 55.

Hogg, Michael A., and Dominic Abrams. 1988. *Social Identifications.* London: Routledge.

Homans, George C. [1961] 1974. *Social Behavior: Its Elementary Forms.* New York: Harcourt, Brace & World.

Huber, Joan, and William H. Form. 1973. *Income and Ideology.* New York: Free Press.

Jasso, Guillermina. 1980. A new theory of distributive justice. *American Sociological Review* 45:3–32.

———. 1986. A new representation of the just term in distributive justice theory: Its properties and operation in theoretical derivation and empirical estimation. *Mathematical Sociology* 12:251–274.

Jasso, Guillermina, and Peter H. Rossi. 1977. Distributive justice and earned income. *American Sociological Research* 42:639–651.

———. 1990. Methods for the theoretical and empirical analysis of comparison processes. Pp. 369–419 in *Sociological Methodology*, ed. C. C. Clogg. Washington, DC: American Sociological Association.

———. 1993. Choice and emotion in comparison theory. *Rationality and Society* 5:231–274.

Kahn, A., R. E. Nelson, W. Gaeddert, and J. L. Hearn. 1982. The justice process: Deciding upon equity or equality. *Social Psychology Quarterly* 45:3–8.

Kashima, Yoshihisa, Michael Siegal, Kenichiro Tanaka, and Hiroko Isaka. 1988. Universalism in lay conceptions of distributive justice: A cross-cultural examination. *International Journal of Psychology* 23:51–64.

Kemper, Theodore D., ed. 1990. *Research Agendas in the Sociology of Emotions.* Albany: State University of New York Press.

Kernis, M. H., and H. T. Reis. 1984. Self-consciousness, self-awareness, and justice in reward allocation. *Journal of Personality* 52:58–70.

Kluegel, James R., and Eliot R. Smith. 1986. *Beliefs about Inequality.* New York: Aldine.

Krahn, Harvey, and Trevor Harrison. 1992. "Self-referenced" relative deprivation and economic beliefs: The effects of the recession in Alberta. *Canadian Review of Sociology and Anthropology* 29:191–209.

Lamm, Helmut. 1986. Justice considerations in interpersonal conflict. Pp. 43–63 in *Justice in Social Relations,* ed. H. Bierhoff, R. L. Cohen, and J. Greenberg. New York: Plenum.

Lawler, Edward J. 1975. An experimental study of factors affecting the mobilization of revolutionary coalitions. *Sociometry* 38:163–179.

Lawler, Edward J., and Martha E. Thompson. 1978. Impact of leader responsibility for inequity on subordinate revolts. *Social Psychology* 41:265–268.

Lerner, Melvin J. 1980. *The Belief in a Just World: A Fundamental Delusion.* New York: Plenum.

Lerner, Melvin J., and Sally C. Lerner, eds. 1981. *The Justice Motive in Social Behavior.* New York: Plenum.

Leung, Kwok, and Michael H. Bond. 1984. The impact of cultural collectivism on reward allocation. *Journal of Personality and Social Psychology* 47:793–804.

Leventhal, Gerald S. 1976. Fairness in social relations. Pp. 211–239 in *Contemporary Topics in Social Psychology,* ed. J. W. Thibaut, J. T. Spence, and R. C. Carson. Morristown, NJ: General Learning Press.

Leventhal, Gerald S., J. Allen, and B. Kemelgor. 1969. Reducing inequity by reallocating rewards. *Psychonomic Science* 14:295–296.

Leventhal, Gerald S., J. Karuza, Jr., and W. R. Fry. 1980. Beyond fairness: A theory of allocation preferences. Pp. 167–218 in *Justice and Social Interaction,* ed. G. Mikula. New York: Springer-Verlag.

Leventhal, Gerald S., and James W. Michaels. 1969. Extending the equity model: Perceptions of inputs and allocations of reward as a function of duration and quantity of performance. *Journal of Personality and Social Psychology* 12:303–309.

Lind, E. Allan, and Tom R. Tyler. 1988. *The Social Psychology of Procedural Justice.* New York: Plenum.

Major, Brenda, and J. B. Adams. 1983. Role of gender interpersonal orientation and self presentation in distributive justice behavior. *Journal of Personality and Social Psychology* 45:598–608.

Major, Brenda, Wayne H. Bylsma, and Catherine Cozzarelli. 1989. Gender differences in distributive justice preferences: The impact of domain. *Sex Roles* 21:489–497.

Major, Brenda, and Kay Deaux. 1982. Individual differences in justice behavior. Pp. 43–76 in *Equity and Justice in Social Behavior,* ed. J. Greenberg and R. L. Cohen. New York: Plenum.

Markovsky, Barry. 1985. Toward a multilevel distributive justice theory. *American Sociological Review* 50:822–839.

———. 1988a. Anchoring justice. *Social Psychology Quarterly* 51:213–224.

———. 1988b. Injustice and arousal. *Social Justice Research* 2:223–233.

Martin, Joanne E. 1986. The tolerance of injustice. Pp. 217–242 in *Relative Deprivation and Social Comparison,* ed. J. M. Olson, C. P. Herman, and M. P. Zanna. Hillsdale, NJ: Erlbaum.

Martin, Joanne E., and Alan Murray. 1983. Distributive injustice and unfair exchange. Pp. 169–205 in *Equity Theory: Psychological and Sociological Perspectives,* ed. David M. Messick and Karen S. Cook. New York: Praeger.

Martin, Joanne E., and M. M. Petersen. 1987. Two-tier wage structures: Implications for equity theory. *Academy of Management Journal* 30:297–315.

Martin, Michael W., and Jane Sell. 1986. Rejection of authority: The importance of type of distribution rule and extent of benefit. *Social Science Quarterly* 67:855–868.

Masters, John C., and William P. Smith, eds. 1987. *Social Comparison, Social Justice, and Relative Deprivation.* Hillsdale, NJ: Erlbaum.

McFarlin, Dean B., and Paul D. Sweeney. 1992. Distributive and procedural justice as predictors of satisfaction with personal and organizational outcomes. *Academy of Management Journal* 35: 626–637.

Merton, Robert K., and Alice Rossi. [1957] 1968. Contributions to the theory of reference group behavior. Pp. 279–334 in *Social Theory and Social Structure,* ed. R. K. Merton. New York: Free Press.

Messé, Lawrence, A., Robert W. Hymes, and Robert J. MacCoun. 1986. Group categorization and distributive justice decisions. Pp. 227–248 in *Justice in Social Relations,* ed. H. Bierhoff, R. L. Cohen, and J. Greenberg. New York: Plenum.

Messick, David M., and Karen S. Cook, eds. 1983. *Equity Theory: Psychological and Sociological Perspectives.* New York: Praeger.

Messick, David M., and Kenneth P. Sentis. 1979. Fairness and preference. *Journal of Experimental Social Psychology* 15:416–434.

Mikula, Gerold, ed. 1980a. *Justice and Social Interaction.* New York: Springer-Verlag.

———. 1980b. On the role of justice in allocation decisions. Pp. 127–166 in *Justice and Social Interaction,* ed. G. Mikula. New York: Springer-Verlag.

Mikula, Gerold, Birgit Petri, and Norbert K. Tanzer. 1989. What people regard as unjust: Types and structures of everyday experiences of injustice. *European Journal of Social Psychology* 20: 133–149.

Miller, A., L. Boyce, and M. Halligan. 1977. The J-curve theory and black urban riots. *American Political Science Review* 71:964–982.

Moore, Dahlia. 1990. Discrimination and deprivation: The effects of social comparisons. *Social Justice Research* 4:49–64.

Moschetti, G. J. 1979. Calculating equity: Ordinal and ratio criteria. *Social Psychology Quarterly* 42:172–176.

Murphy-Berman, V., J. J. Berman, P. Singh, A. Pachauri, and P. Kumar. 1984. Factors affecting allocation to needy and meritorious recipients: A cross-cultural comparison. *Journal of Personality and Social Psychology* 46:1267–1272.

Nisbett, Richard, and Lee Ross. 1980. *Human Inference: Strategies and Shortcomings of Social Judgment.* Englewood Cliffs, NJ: Prentice Hall.

Nozick, Robert. 1974. *Anarchy, State, and Utopia.* New York: Basic Books.

Prentice, Deborah A., and Faye Crosby. 1987. The importance of context for assessing deserving. Pp. 165–182 in *Social Comparison, Social Justice, and Relative Deprivation,* ed. J. C. Masters and W. P. Smith. Hillsdale, NJ: Erlbaum.

Rawls, John. 1971. *A Theory of Justice.* Boston: Harvard University Press.

Reis, Harry T. 1981. Self presentation and distributive justice. Pp. 269–291 in *Impression Management Theory and Social Psychological Theory,* ed. J. T. Tedeschi. New York: Academic.

———. 1986. Levels of interest in the study of interpersonal justice. In *Justice in Social Relations,* ed. H. Bierhoff, R. L. Cohen, and J. Greenberg. New York: Plenum.

Robinson, Robert V. 1983. Explaining perceptions of class and racial inequality in England and the United States. *British Journal of Sociology* 34: 344–366.

Robinson, Robert V., and Wendell Bell. 1978. Equality, success, and social justice in England and the

United States. *American Sociological Review* 43: 125–143.

Runciman, William. 1966. *Relative Deprivation and Social Justice.* London: Routledge & Kegan Paul.

Scherer, Klaus R., ed. 1992. *Justice: Interdisciplinary Perspectives.* Cambridge, UK: Cambridge University Press.

Schwinger, Thomas. 1980. Just allocation of goods: Decisions among three principles. Pp. 95–125 in *Justice and Social Interaction,* ed. G. Mikula. New York: Springer-Verlag.

Shepelak, Norma J., and Duane F. Alwin. 1986. Beliefs about inequality and perceptions of distributive justice. *American Sociological Review* 51:30–46.

Sheppard, Blair H., and Roy J. Lewicki. 1987. Toward general principles of managerial fairness. *Social Justice Research* 1:161–176.

Singer, Eleanor. 1981. Reference groups and social evaluations. Pp. 66–93 in *Social Psychology: Sociological Perspectives,* ed. Morris Rosenberg and Ralph H. Turner. New York: Basic Books.

Solomon, Robert C., and Mark C. Murphy, eds. 1990. *What Is Justice? Classic and Contemporary Readings.* Oxford, UK: Oxford University Press.

Sprecher, Susan. 1986. The relationship between inequity and emotions in close relationships. *Social Psychology Quarterly* 49:309–321.

Stolte, John F. 1983. The legitimation of structural inequality: Reformulation and test of the self-evaluation argument. *American Sociological Review* 48: 331–342.

———. 1987. The formation of justice norms. *American Sociological Review* 52:774–784.

Stouffer, Samuel A., Edward A. Suchman, Leland C. DeVinney, Shirley A. Star, and Robin M. Williams. 1949. *The American Soldier: Adjustment During Army Life.* Princeton, NJ: Princeton University Press.

Thibaut, John, and Laurens Walker. 1975. *Procedural Justice: A Psychological Analysis.* Hillsdale, NJ: Erlbaum.

Törnblom, Kjell Y. 1977. Distributive justice: Typology and propositions. *Human Relations* 31:1–24.

———. 1992. The social psychology of distributive justice. Pp. 177–236 in *Justice: Interdisciplinary Perspectives,* ed. K. Scherer. Cambridge, UK: Cambridge University Press.

Tougas, Francine, and Ann M. Beaton. 1992. Women's views on affirmative action: A new look at preferential treatment. *Social Justice Research* 5:239–248.

Tyler, Tom R. 1989. The psychology of procedural justice: A test of the group-value model. *Journal of Personality and Social Psychology* 57:830–838.

Utne, M. K., and R. F. Kidd. 1980. Equity and attribution. Pp. 63–93 in *Justice and Social Interaction,* ed. G. Mikula. New York: Springer-Verlag.

Van Dyk, Alta C., and Johan M. Nieuwaudt. 1990. The relationship between relative deprivation and the attitudes of rural Afrikaans-speaking women toward blacks. *Journal of Psychology* 124:513–521.

Vermunt, Reil, and H. Steensma, eds. 1990. *Social Justice in Human Relations.* New York: Plenum.

Walker, Iain, and Leon Mann. 1987. Unemployment, relative deprivation, and social protest. *Personality and Social Psychology Bulletin* 13:275–283.

Walker, Iain, and Thomas F. Pettigrew. 1984. Relative deprivation theory: An overview and conceptual critique. *British Journal of Social Psychology* 23: 301–310.

Walster, Elaine, G. William Walster, and Ellen Berscheid. 1978. *Equity: Theory and Research.* Allyn and Bacon.

Watts, B. L., R. R. Vallacher, and L. A. Messé. 1982. Toward understanding sex differences in pay allocations: Agency, communion, and reward distribution behavior. *Sex Roles* 12:1175–1188.

Webster, Murray, Jr., and Le Roy F. Smith. 1978. Justice and revolutionary coalitions: A test of two theories. *American Journal of Sociology* 84: 267–292.

Williams, Robin M., Jr. 1975. Relative deprivation. Pp. 355–378 in *The Idea of Social Structure: Papers in Honor of Robert K. Merton,* ed. Lewis A. Coser. New York: Harcourt Brace Jovanovich.

Wittig, M. A., G. Marks, and G. A. Jones. 1981. Luck versus effort attributions: Effect on reward allocations to self and other. *Personality and Social Psychology Bulletin* 7:71–78.

CHAPTER 11

Status Structures

CECILIA L. RIDGEWAY
HENRY A. WALKER

Status structures are patterned inequalities of respect, deference, and influence among a group of people. Some in the group are "looked-up to," treated as more important, and have more privileges and power than others. In all known societies people exhibit regular patterns of differentiation on the basis of status. Observation of American society suggests that everyone from teenagers to corporate executives jockeys for a position of respect among those they deal with. Indeed, the development of status hierarchies is an enduring feature of human interaction and a fundamental aspect of the organization of social behavior. Explaining why or how they emerge and what their consequences are is essential to the sociological problems of inequality and social order.

To understand status relations, it is important to distinguish between status structures and status value. The word *status* has two traditional meanings in sociology. Linton (1936) used the term to mean a position in a social system, much like a role. For Veblen (1953), status was a position of value or worth in the community that was communicated through the cultural symbolism of one's possessions and consumption. Contemporary usage draws on both meanings but casts them differently into status structures and status value. In both contemporary concepts status refers to a position in a set of things that are rank-ordered by a standard of value. *Status structures* are rank-ordered relationships among *actors*. They describe the interactional inequalities formed from actors' implicit valuations of themselves and one another according to some shared standard of value. Status structures are inherently relational in that one actor is only high or low status in comparison to another. The actors can be individuals or corporate actors, such as nations or businesses; in this chapter we focus on individuals.

Anything that a society's or group's cultural beliefs associate with standing in status structures can take on *status value* in that collectivity. With status value, things become cultural symbols of worthiness in the collectivity. As sociologists since Veblen (1953) and Weber (1946) have observed, occupations, ethnic groups, genders, dress, automobiles, accents, and neighborhoods can all carry differential status value according to shared cultural beliefs. Some beliefs that rank-order the status value of certain things are widely held in entire societies (e.g., occupational prestige in the United States). Others are particular to smaller groups (e.g., dress styles among teenagers) and differ from one group to another.

Whatever their social basis, the principle effect of status value beliefs is on the behavior of actors who hold them. As we shall see, actors employ shared beliefs about the status value of their attributes, possessions, and behavior, and the social groups they belong to establish and maintain their own and others' positions in a given status structure. Thus it is status structures themselves—the interactional hierarchies of esteem, deference, and influence that actors form—that are at the heart of sociological questions about status.

Since high-status members of these hierarchies are those more highly respected by a group standard, status creates the capacity to influence others in the structure. As a result, status structures are hierarchies of informal power as well as prestige. High-status members "call the shots" for the group in a way that low-status members do not. In fact, status structures, as influence hierarchies, are the central means by which groups of interactants organize their behavior and make collective decisions. This is what makes status structures important for understanding social order.

Although status structures are based in the person-to-person relationships of interaction, they are an important element in the larger, less personal process of social stratification in society. We have noted that the status significance society attaches to the social groups (e.g., economic, ethnic, sexual) to which a person belongs has an important impact on the status and influence a person achieves among a group of interactants. In turn, the influence and status a person achieves in interactional contexts has a powerful effect on his/her access to valued positions in organizations and to economic resources. Access to jobs, promotions, and economic opportunities are frequently mediated by interpersonal networks, encounters, and interviews where status processes operate and affect the outcome. Similarly, the actions of decision-making groups such as committees, panels, boards, councils, and ruling cliques reflect their status structures and, consequently, are likely better to represent the interests of their high- rather than low-status members or constituents. In fact, interactional status structures are the context in which many of the advantages and slights indicated by society's stratification system are actually delivered to the individual.

For a stratification system to persist, it must be enacted and supported in a variety of interactional contexts. There is an interdependence between society-level systems of stratification, formal hierarchies of power in a variety of organizations, and interactional status structures. The interdependence of these systems of status, power, and stratification is an important component of their legitimation, the process by which patterns of social action acquire a normative character. Within a legitimated status structure the deference and demeanors by which high- and low-status actors enact their posi-

tions take on a normative, ritual quality (E. Goffman 1956).

Legitimation can occur in systems of almost any size, from interactional status structures to formal organizations to systems of government. Legitimation transforms differences in status, influence, or power into systems of rights and obligations. As an example, actors whose exercise of power acquires legitimacy have the right to demand compliance from low-status actors, and low-status actors have the obligation to comply as long as the exercise of power is in accord with the accepted norms. Furthermore, those for whom high status has been legitimated can call on collective support to back up their directives, thereby increasing the level of compliance to their demands. Ironically, legitimate authorities are less likely to exercise power, since most actors voluntarily comply with normatively appropriate directives.

When status structures in interactional contexts reproduce patterns that exist in larger systems of stratification, they help maintain the legitimacy of those systems. Actors' deference and demeanor in the status structure affirms the apparent moral order of the larger system. Similarly, the stratification of groups on the basis of qualities such as race, gender, or occupational status is an important source of legitimacy for interactional status structures that include members of such groups.

As our discussion suggests, both status-organizing processes and legitimation processes are inherently multilevel processes in complex societies. The study of status structures—how they emerge, the factors that account for their stability, how they change, and the manner in which they influence the behavior of individuals and groups—is an exciting convergence of work at the social structural and individual levels of investigation.

This chapter is divided into two major sections. The first addresses the nature of status structures—how they develop and achieve stability. The second section examines the importance of legitimation processes to an analysis of status structures. We begin with early research and describe the emergence and consequences of status hierarchies in interacting groups. Then we discuss the major theoretical perspectives that have been brought to bear on these early findings—exchange theory, functionalism, symbolic interactionism, and dominance theory. Together, they raise issues about the competitive versus cooperative bases of hierarchies. Next we turn to expectation states theory, a systematic theory of status processes that draws on several of these perspectives. We examine the theory's accounts of the formation of hierarchies and their impact on verbal and nonverbal behavior, external status characteristics, and rewards, and evidence for these accounts. The section concludes with a critical assessment of the expectation states account of status structures.

The discussion of legitimacy and status structures begins with an overview of the general conception of legitimacy and legitimation processes, followed by an examination of the importance of legitimation processes to the emergence and shape of interactional status structures, to the replication of societal level patterns of stratification in the interactional situation, to the influence of those with authority and status, and in ensuring the stability of existing structures.

We focus throughout on the theoretical issues raised by status structures and their legitimation. We attempt a broad coverage of the empirical literature on status but do not try to be encyclopedic. Instead, our emphasis is on empirical findings that are especially informative about the theoretical issues of concern.

STATUS STRUCTURES

Early Research

Contemporary theories of status structures developed in response to a series of studies conducted from 1930 through the 1950s (e.g., Bales 1950; Roethlisberger and Dickson 1939; Whyte 1943). These studies provided a systematic empirical record of the emergence and operation of status hierarchies. They describe the behaviors by which status structures are enacted and some of the factors and circumstances out of which they emerge. Both for their descriptive value and because they

provide the data that subsequent theories sought to explain, they offer a useful starting point.

Most influential were the observational studies of decision-making groups conducted by Bales (1950) and associates. Bales developed (1950, 1970) interaction process analysis, a scheme for coding behavior in task- or goal-oriented groups, that classifies each speech act in terms of who said it, to whom it was directed, and its instrumental (e.g., task suggestions, questions, and answers) or social-emotional content (i.e., positive and negative comments and reactions). Using this scheme, Bales developed empirical profiles of interaction in groups of three to seven previously unacquainted male undergraduates who met for several one-hour sessions to discuss and decide on human relations problems.

These groups are notable for two reasons. They began interaction with no structure imposed from the outside, since the members had no prior relationships with one another and no leader was appointed. Second, the members of the groups were homogeneous with respect to age, background, and social status. One of Bales's most striking findings was that despite this initial equality and lack of structure, these groups developed stable inequalities in participation by the end of the first one-hour session (Bales 1950, 1953). This finding has been replicated in several subsequent studies (e.g., Fisek and Ofshe 1970).

The inequalities that emerged were reflected in a series of correlated behaviors. First, the most talkative group member usually talks considerably more than the others, often accounting for upwards of 40 percent of the total speech acts (Bales 1970, 467–470). Second, the other group members are most likely to direct their own speech to the most talkative person. Finally, the higher a member's participation rank in the group, the more likely that member is to be rated by the others as having the best ideas and doing the most to guide and influence the group. Once these inequalities develop, they tend to persist over future group sessions.

While clear behavioral hierarchies emerged in his studies, Bales noted two complications. First, in an occasional group, an apparent power struggle resulted in a lack of consensus on who had the best ideas, slowing the development of a stable hierarchy. Second, Bales (1953; Bales and Slater 1955) and Slater (1955) argued that the most talkative, "best ideas" member was not always the best liked. Consequently, another member, usually the second most talkative, became the best-liked "social leader," while the most talkative was the "task leader." Although these studies are often cited, the extent to which Bales's and Slater's data support this interpretation has been challenged (Bonacich and Lewis 1973; Lewis 1972; Riedesel 1974). Subsequent research shows that the separation of task and social leadership occurs primarily when the task leader lacks legitimacy (Burke 1967, 1968, 1971). We return to this research later.

If stable inequalities emerge rather quickly in unstructured groups of initial equals, they are likely to develop in almost any group. In most actual groups, interactors differ somewhat in their social characteristics or background. Other early research focused on groups of this sort (Strodtbeck, James and Hawkins 1957; Strodtbeck and Mann 1956; Torrance 1954). Typical is Strodtbeck et al.s' (1957) study of simulated juries composed of men and women selected from actual jury pools. In these groups, too, clear participation hierarchies developed, with the top two or three members doing half the talking. The most active members were also the most influential in the jury decisions. The most interesting finding, however, was that jurors' status in the larger society, as indicated by their occupations and sex, predicted how active and influential they became. It also predicted their likelihood of being chosen foreperson and how competent and helpful their fellow jurors perceived them to be. Clearly, standing in the outside society was translated into standing in the behavioral status order that emerged in the face-to-face group.

Studies of the emergence of status structures were supplemented by other early research documenting the consequences of established structures. As we have seen, members perceived to have higher standing in a group participate more and are more influential. Additional research demonstrated that standing in the group also determines how a mem-

ber's contributions are evaluated by other members. Riecken (1958) found that the same idea expressed by a talkative member of a group was perceived to be more valuable than when it came from a less talkative member. Sherif et al. (1955; Harvey 1953) showed that group members overestimated the quality of performances by high-status members and underestimated those of low-status members, so that high-status members were seen as the better performers independent of their actual performances. Finally, and most dramatically, Whyte (1943) found that group members pressured one another to perform better or worse, to keep the quality of their contributions in line with their standing in the group. The status hierarchy, then, is an important regulator of the number, quality, and evaluation of members' contributions to group activities.

Whyte's (1943) classic study of the Nortons, a street-corner gang in Depression-era Boston, provides an excellent illustration of the way a status hierarchy regulates members' performances at group activities. Bowling was an important activity for the Nortons. Whyte observed that when they bowled together, the members' scores lined up almost perfectly with their positions in the gang's status hierarchy. The leader, "Doc," almost always scored the highest; "Alec," at the bottom of the hierarchy, always scored poorly. The interesting thing was that when he bowled alone, Alec was a good bowler, often outscoring Doc's average. But he could not perform well with the gang.

On one occasion, Doc staged a bowling competition among the gang members, offering prize money to the top scorers. Alec announced his intentions to win. When after the first few frames Alec was indeed ahead, the rest of the gang began to heckle him in a hostile fashion. He began to make mistakes and then began going out for drinks between turns. By the end, Alec's bowling score fell from first to last place. The gang members said it would not have been right if Alec had won.

After his defeat, Alec started challenging the number two man in the gang, "Long John," to bowl. He regularly defeated him. Hearing of this, Doc took Long John aside and told him that he must try harder, that he couldn't allow himself to be embarrassed by Alec. Long John's bowling began to improve and Alec no longer defeated him on a usual basis. Clearly, the Norton gang status hierarchy controlled its members' bowling performances almost independent of their actual skills. It appears to have done so through the positive and negative expectations the gang members held for one another and the social support (or discouragement) this provided for the individual member.

This early research record clearly shows that when people interact (particularly if the interaction is goal-oriented), a hierarchy of participation, evaluation, performance, and influence quickly develops, stabilizes, and shapes future behavior. Members' goal-related behaviors and their evaluations of one another are particularly governed by the hierarchy. Such status structures develop whether group members are similar or different in social background or characteristics, although when such differences occur they shape the status structure. But the questions that remained were the theoretical ones before us here: Why and how do status structures emerge in interaction? Through what social processes do they operate?

Theoretical Approaches to Status Hierarchies

At least four theoretical perspectives have been used to explain the emergence of status structures: exchange theory, functionalism, symbolic interactionism, and conflict-dominance approaches. Exchange theory (e.g., Blau 1964; Homans 1961) views status as a reward that one actor grants to another by deferring to the other and accepting his/her influence. Status is granted in exchange for the recipient engaging in behaviors that produce rewards for other group members. In a goal-oriented group, for instance, status might be exchanged for a member's efforts to help the group attain its goal, since goal attainment provides rewards for all. If one member's contributions are thought to be more valuable to the group than another's, the first member will be granted greater deference and influence than the other, creating a hierarchy based on perceived value. In exchange theory, then, hierarchies develop from actors' ra-

tional interests in maximizing collective rewards by offering incentives for valuable contributions to collective activities.

The functionalist approach explains status hierarchies as a necessary mechanism that groups develop to adapt and survive in their environment (Bales 1953; Hare, Borgatta, and Bales 1955; Parsons and Bales 1955). It argues that to persist, groups must develop means of adapting to the outside environment, attaining collective goals, achieving internal cohesion, and maintaining organizational patterns. Status hierarchies address the first two functions. They provide a structure by which individual efforts are organized for effective decision making and collective action in regard to group goals and the environment. When more competent members are given higher status, the group adapts and survives more successfully.

Bales (1953) further argued that while status hierarchies are functionally necessary, the invidious distinctions they create cause problems for internal cohesion that the group must also address, maintaining an equilibrium between the two contending concerns. Because there is a tension between status processes and internal cohesion, the implication is that the social or affective processes by which cohesion is maintained will be distinct from status processes and operate differently. While never clearly tested, this argument has been quite influential. Most contemporary approaches to status focus exclusively on the goal (task)-oriented behavior on which the hierarchy seems to turn, excluding affective behavior as a separate domain (but see Clark 1991 for an exception).

Symbolic interactionism, the third theoretical approach, views interaction as a process by which actors construct shared meanings (Blumer 1969; Mead 1934; Stryker and Statham 1985). Within this context, status is understood as the meaning and relative value attached to each actor's self as it is socially constructed in the situation (Alexander and Wiley 1981; Clark 1991). Each actor attempts to present and have accepted a valued social "face" (E. Goffman 1959, 1967), but each depends on the support of others to enact that face successfully in the group. As a result, the status order is negotiated through interaction as actors' face claims, reactions, and counterreactions mutually construct one another's selves in the situation (Alexander and Wiley 1981; E. Goffman 1956). According to this view, then, status hierarchies arise jointly out of the need to create shared definitions of the self for interaction and each actor's desire to be defined in the most valued way possible.

Exchange, functionalist, and symbolic interactionist perspectives all view status processes as essentially cooperative in nature. Each emphasizes the goal-oriented nature of interaction and the *positive interdependence* this creates among the actors. Because of their interdependence, they must cooperatively exchange deference for something they jointly want or need (rewards, functional task organization, a shared system of meaning). As a result, status is more *given* than *taken.*

This cooperative view contrasts with the more competitive perspective of the conflict-dominance approach (e.g., Archibald 1976; Keating 1985; Lee and Ofshe 1981; Mazur 1973; Wilson 1975) . Traditionally, dominance analyses explain status hierarchies as a result of competition over scarce resources (e.g., food, mates, rewards, power), a type of *negative interdependence.* Individuals try to intimidate one another in a series of dominance contests to establish each other's rank in the hierarchy and, thus, access to resources. Once established, these hierarchies tend to stabilize because of individuals' shared interest in avoiding continual, destructive fighting. Thus, dominance approaches emphasize resource distribution rather than resource production (i.e., goal attainment) as the primary basis of status hierarchies. Most dominance approaches seek similarities between animal and human hierarchies and some posit biological factors that contribute to an individual's standing in a hierarchy (e.g., Mazur 1985).

Cooperative versus Competitive Hierarchy Formation

Evidence indicates that most status allocation is uncontested (Mazur 1973). Consequently, recent dominance analyses of humans and other primates have moderated the traditional emphasis on agonistic competition and granted a role for cooperative as well as competitive processes in the development of hierarchies (Mazur 1985; Mitchell and Maple 1985). But why should cooperative status processes predominate? What happens to self-interest? The conflict-dominance approach raises basic issues about hierarchy formation that must be considered, especially because the traditional dominance perspective has been widely popularized and affects much everyday thinking about status structures.

According to recent analyses, there may be structural reasons why status allocation in goal-oriented interaction is not purely competitive (Ridgeway and Diekema 1989). In a goal-oriented setting, actors have a cooperative interest in deferring to one another on the basis of expected contributions to the goal to achieve maximum collective rewards. On the other hand, they also have a competitive interest in dominating others to increase their personal share of the rewards. Given these conflicting possibilities, it is instructive to consider that the actors' dependence on one another to accomplish the goal also creates a third set of interests. It makes it in each actor's interest that all *other* actors grant status on the basis of expected contributions to the goal, so that there will be some collective rewards to claim. This suggests that actors are likely to pressure others to defer on the basis of expected contributions, whatever they seek for themselves. As a result, even if each actor pursues personal dominance above all, each is likely to face a coalition of others unwilling to see status granted on any basis other than expected contributions.

As Emerson notes (1972), this implicit coalition effectively creates norms that make deference on the basis of expected contributions the acceptable, legitimate basis for status in goal-oriented settings. Claims to status on any other basis, including pure dominance (i.e, threatening behavior), are subject to collective sanction. Tests of this argument, in fact, show that group members intervene to sanction a member who claims status through threatening dominance behaviors (a raised voice with a dismissive, commanding, interrogating manner and intrusive gestures, such as pointing), and the domineering member fails to gain influence (Ridgeway 1987; Ridgeway and Diekema 1989). Because of this normative control process, dominance alone is an ineffective means of gaining status in goal-oriented interaction.

It appears, then, that positive interdependence with respect to a goal creates implicit norms that coerce actors from pursuing purely competitive claims to status without regard to contributions to the collective. However, this doesn't eliminate individuals' competitive interests from the status process. Rather, these norms redirect individual competition to the arena of the shared goal, so that actors compete to appear competent in regard to the goal to "deserve" a more rewarding position in the status order. It is through these processes that status hierarchies become collective instruments of resource production as well as resource distribution. These processes highlight the importance of legitimating norms in the operation of status structures.

Systematic Theories of Status

The theoretical perspectives of exchange, functionalism, symbolic interaction, and conflict-dominance offer distinctive insights about status hierarchies. Yet none, by itself, has yielded a specific theory of status processes that can fully account for the existing empirical evidence on status structures. As Meeker (1981) notes, a strict exchange approach can explain much but has difficulty accounting for evidence that group members distort their perceptions of the quality of contributions by high- and low-status members. The functionalist explanation gives important attention to the role of the status order in accomplishing collective goals but seems to assume that merely because a behavior is "adaptive" it will occur. Symbolic interactionism points out the negotiated nature of status orders and the need for a shared definition of the situation for coordinated interaction to occur. But, perhaps because it focuses on selves rather than group structure, it has not yet produced a specific theory of

status that can predict the structural form of hierarchies in differing situations. Finally, dominance theory reminds us of the role of competition and coercion in status process but must deal with the evidence that most status relations are cooperative and uncontested (Mazur 1973).

From such a diversity of insights and weaknesses, a variety of rather different systematic theories of status could be constructed. In fact, empirical studies of status have continued with a variety of approaches, such as symbolic interaction and conversational analysis (Kollock, Blumstein, and Schwartz 1985; West 1984; West and Garcia 1988) and dominance (Mazur and Cataldo 1989). However, *expectation states theory* has become the dominant systematic account. As the most conceptually developed and empirically verified theory of status-organizing processes available, it has been the focus of most recent research in the area. The intellectual roots of the theory are diverse, but it draws primarily on the concepts and insights of exchange theory, functionalism, and symbolic interactionism. As this suggests, it views the emergence of status orders as an essentially cooperative process arising from interactants' positive interdependence with respect to some collective goal.

Expectation States Theory

Expectation states theory developed in an explicit effort to explain the empirical findings of early status research (J. Berger, Wagner, and Zelditch 1985). Berger and colleagues (J. Berger, Conner, and Fisek 1974) proposed that the correlations demonstrated among speaking, being spoken to, evaluations of members and their contributions, and influence occurred because each of these behaviors is an observable indicator of a single, underlying phenomenon, a *power and prestige order.* The best way to understand how power and prestige (i.e., status) order emerges and operates, Berger et al. argue, is to separate the status process from other interactional processes analytically and study it on its own. Once status dynamics are understood they can then be placed back in context and analyzed in relation to other processes, such as conformity or affect, that occur simultaneously in face-to-face interaction. Following this strategy, the theory limits its focus to the behavioral indicators of power and prestige, which in goal-oriented settings are goal- or task-related behaviors and evaluations. The theory's basic argument is that the dynamics of a power and prestige order arise out of group members' expectations about the value of their own and others' contributions to group activities and the way those expectations, called *performance expectations,* affect their task-related behavior toward one another.

Expectation states theory is distinctive in that it adopts a formal approach to theory construction, testing, and application. Explicit scope conditions specify the range of the phenomena the theory claims to explain, so that negative results can be clearly interpreted (Walker and Cohen 1985). The theory itself is stated in formal postulates that are usually linked with a mathematical calculus for expressing the stated relationships and deriving testable hypotheses. While theoretical postulates are often proposed to account for existing empirical evidence, they are subjected to independent tests in controlled experiments. Many of these experiments use a standardized experimental setting to allow clear comparisons of results across multiple experiments. While this theoretical and methodological strategy can make the theory seem forbidding to an outsider, it has been the secret of its success. It has enabled expectation states theory to generate a cumulative body of evidence with which to refine and expand its analysis. The resulting theory has been better able than its alternatives to predict and explain status processes both in controlled studies and applied settings, such as the classroom (E. Cohen 1982), and in corporate research and development teams (B. Cohen and Zhou 1991).

Expectation states theory takes the interactional *encounter,* rather than individuals, as its unit of analysis (J. Berger et al. 1985). It limits its scope to those encounters where actors are oriented toward the accomplishment of a shared goal or task for which they have a sense of success and failure and for which it is appropriate to take one another's opinions into account to achieve the best task outcome. An encounter can meet these conditions either because it is the meeting of an explicit task group, such as a committee, or because people interacting on another basis turn their attention to a collective task or decision.

The theory argues that when these conditions occur a *status organizing process* is activated by the actors' efforts to evaluate their own and others' task suggestions, to reach a successful collective decision about the task. To decide how to act, whether to speak up, who to listen to, and who to agree with when conflicts develop, actors look for a way to anticipate the likely usefulness of their own and each other's suggestions. In doing so, they form performance expectations for themselves compared to each other actor in the setting. Performance expectations are generally not conscious judgments, but rather implicit, unaware hunches about whose suggestions are more likely to be better. Because they are often implicit, the theory treats performance expectations as an unobserved theoretical construct that mediates changes in observable factors. The theory assumes that actors follow similar cognitive principles in forming performance expectations. Consequently, as long as interactants have roughly similar cultural beliefs and information about one another, the expectations they develop are shared, creating a roughly consensual *order of performance expectations* in the encounter.

Self-other performance expectations are important because they tend to guide behavior in a self-fulfilling manner. If an actor has a higher expectation for him/herself than for another, the actor is more likely to speak up, offer opinions, and stick to them if challenged. If the same actor has lower expectations for him/herself than for the other, the actor is more likely to hesitate in making suggestions, to ask for and respond positively to the other's opinions, and to assume that he/she is wrong when another disagrees. Thus, the theory proposes that the higher the expectations held for one actor compared to another: (1) the more opportunities the other will give the actor to participate; (2) the more task suggestions the actor will offer; (3) the more likely these suggestions are to be positively evaluated by the others; and (4) the more influential the actor will be over the others.

In this way, self-other performance expectations determine the inequalities in action opportunities, performance outputs, positive and negative evaluations, and influence that constitute the observable power and prestige order of the setting. Assuming a shared order of performance expectations, each actor's behaviors confirm the others' expectations. As a result, once formed, differentiated performance expectations tend to magnify and stabilize the behavioral differences between self and other in a manner consistent with expectations, stabilizing the power and prestige order. This argument is expressed in the theory's principal postulate (J. Berger et al. 1977, 130):

> *Once actors have formed expectations for self and other(s), their power and prestige positions relative to the others will be a direct function of their expectation advantage over (or disadvantage compared to) those others.*

For this postulate to be useful, however, we must ask: How and on what basis do actors form higher performance expectations for one person rather than another? Can the processes by which expectations are formed predict when there will be very large power and prestige differences among group members and when these differences will be relatively small? Much of expectation states theory is directed toward answering the first question in a manner that allows it to answer the second. Thus far, a variety of factors that create or change performance expectations and, consequently, positions in a power and prestige order have been analyzed. These include task-directed behaviors, nonverbal behaviors, status-valued characteristics of actors, evaluations from an outside source, and rewards. The theory's argument about each of these factors follows a similar form, expressed in its four additional postulates (J. Berger et al. 1977, 91–134; Fisek, Berger, and Norman 1991). It is this shared logical form that allows the theory to combine the effects of multiple factors on expectations to make predictions about the differing structures

of power and prestige orders in different situations. A brief review of this logical form is useful before turning to the analysis of specific factors.

According to the second postulate, for any behavior, characteristic, reward, or other factor to affect expectations, it must first become *salient* in the situation. Factors become salient when they either provide a contrast among actors in the situation (e.g., gender in a mixed-sex setting) or are perceived to be relevant to the shared task. Because of this assumption, expectation states theory takes a *situational* approach to status orders. Although actors carry some of the same attributes from one situation to the next, whether they affect the status order in a given situation and, if so, how they affect it depends on other factors in the situation. Thus status orders are always socially constructed in the situation itself and never merely imported unchanged from outside the setting.

The third postulate states that when a factor is salient, unless it is specifically disassociated from the task, actors will use cultural beliefs about its status value in forming their expectations, even if the factor is logically irrelevant to the task. This is called the *burden-of-proof process,* because actors act as if the burden of proof lies in showing that a salient factor is not relevant to task competence rather than that it is relevant. Because of this postulate, the theory predicts that socially evaluated characteristics, such as race or gender, or behaviors that may be entirely unrelated to objective competence, such as talking more, still affect expectations for performance and, thus, power and prestige, when the members differ on them. Thus the theory predicts that power and prestige orders may be quite unmeritocratic sometimes, despite being based on expectations for performance, because of the way status valued but logically irrelevant factors can bias perceptions of competence.

The fourth postulate states that whenever a new factor becomes salient in a situation, it becomes connected to all the other factors already salient, either strengthening or counteracting their implications for expectations. This is called the *structure completion* postulate, in reference to the formal graph structures by which the theory represents the impact all salient factors have on expectations in the setting (J. Berger et al. 1977). These graphs represent the actors' definition of the situation with respect to the task, themselves, and each other. The theory analyzes them by means of graph theory to produce precise metric predictions for a given setting of each actor's expectation advantage or disadvantage compared to the others.

The fifth postulate, *aggregation,* states that the impacts of all salient factors are combined to produce aggregated expectations for each actor compared to the others. Specifically, the negative implications of all factors are weighted by their perceived relevance to task performance, combined, and then subtracted from the weighted and combined positive implications of all factors to produce aggregated expectation states for each actor. The principal postulate, stated earlier, then takes over to state that power and prestige positions will be a direct function of these aggregated expectations. For the exact formulas and procedures for analyzing graphs, calculating aggregated expectations, and making metric predictions of observable power and prestige positions, see J. Berger et al. (1977, 91–134), Fisek et al. (1991), and Balkwell (1991a).

One implication of aggregation is that the theory can make predictions about the situations in which power and prestige differences between actors are likely to be large and those in which they will be slight (Humphreys and Berger 1981). When salient factors have inconsistent implications for task competence, power and prestige differences will be less than if the same number of factors have consistent implications for competence. Status orders where status characteristics, behavior, and rewards cross-cut are more likely to be egalitarian, then, than status orders where these factors are all aligned.

The five postulates of expectation states theory paint a picture of status processes as an outcome of the ongoing process of constructing a social definition of reality in a task-oriented setting to accomplish the shared goal. To figure out how to act, actors look for information with which to create differential expectations for self and other, us-ing whatever becomes salient. They notice differences in appearance or manner that indicate the social categories (e.g., gender or social class) each belongs to. They respond to the confidence or assertiveness of each other's eye gaze, speech, and overall demeanor. They notice distinctions in the socially valued possessions or rewards each controls. Aggregating all such information, actors form implicit expectations that self will have more (or less) to contribute to the situation than given others. Each then acts on these expectations by speaking up or hesitating, acting confident or nervous, arguing or deferring. In doing so, self and others jointly create a behavioral power and prestige order that implicitly fulfills their expectations. Although this power and prestige order tends to stabilize, new information and discordant events can modify expectations and alter the order.

With this framework in mind, let us turn to specific factors that affect expectations and power and prestige. Due to space limitations we focus on verbal and nonverbal behavior, status characteristics, and rewards, although other factors, such as sources of evaluation, have also been shown to affect expectations (Webster and Sobieszek 1974). We begin with the role of behavior enacted in the setting to illustrate the theory's analysis of how a power and prestige order is negotiated through interaction.

Behavior and Performance Expectations

We know that status hierarchies form quickly even in homogeneous groups, where participants are initially status equals. In such groups, actions and demeanor are the only bases participants have to form differential judgments about one another. The theory proposes that such behavior itself creates differentiated performance expectations, even though, once formed, expectations then drive behavior (J. Berger and Conner 1974; Fisek, Berger, and Norman 1991).

At the core of goal-oriented interaction are the behavioral cycles in which participants offer task suggestions and have them accepted or rejected by others. In the simplest such *behavioral sequence,* an actor is given or takes an opportunity to speak (an action opportunity) and makes a task suggestion (a performance output), and others react positively or negatively to it. However structured, the sequence concludes when the actors jointly accept (positively evaluate) or reject (negatively evaluate) the task suggestion. If joint acceptance or rejection comes about because one actor changes his/her evaluation of the task suggestion to agree with the evaluation of another actor, then influence has occurred.

In their early formulation, Berger and Conner (1974; Berger, Conner, and McKeown 1974) postulated that every time a task suggestion is positively or negatively evaluated or influence occurs, there is some probability that self and other(s) will form expectation states for one another corresponding to the evaluation or influence. This means the more task suggestions an actor makes compared to another, or the more positive evaluations he/she receives for those suggestions, the more likely it is that both the actor and the other will form higher expectations for the actor than the other. This prediction of the theory is consistent with evidence that participation levels are associated with perceived competence and influence.

Subsequent research has shown that whether an actor's task suggestions are accepted by others is also affected by nonverbal demeanor during interaction. Taking a seat at the head of the table, having an upright, relaxed posture, speaking up without hesitation in a firm, confident tone, and maintaining direct eye contact all make a group member's suggestions "sound better" and increase the likelihood that he/she will be influential (see Dovidio and Ellyson 1985; Ridgeway 1987; Ridgeway, Berger, and Smith 1985). Joseph Berger et al. (1986) refer to these demeanor variables as *task cues* because actors appear to read them as cultural signs of confidence and competence at the task.[1]

Recently, Fisek et al. (1991) incorporated task cues into an expanded account of behavior and performance expectations that recasts the argument in terms of the theory's basic postulates. They note that evaluative reactions tend to encourage or dis-courage future suggestions from an actor and affect the actor's confidence and demeanor. Also, having one suggestion positively or negatively evaluated by others increases the chance that the actor's next suggestion will be similarly evaluated. Consequently, behavior sequences in a group tend to develop into stable patterns of interchange, as others have shown (Burke 1974). Fisek et al. define these *behavior interchange patterns* as sets of behavioral sequences that are consistent in their power and prestige significance with respect to the actors.

Consistently making more task suggestions or speaking in a forceful manner attracts attention. Consequently, Fisek et al. argue that actors implicitly recognize interchange patterns when they develop. They notice at some level that one actor is consistently speaking up while another only agrees. When recognized, interchange patterns make salient *status typifications,* which are socially constructed beliefs about what high-status and low-status, "leader-follower," behaviors and demeanors are like (this is the salience postulate of the theory). These cultural beliefs associate people who enact high-status behavioral cues with higher levels of ability or competence than those who display low-status behavioral cues. This, in turn, leads actors to expect more useful contributions to the task at hand from people who act high-status than from people who act low-status (the burden-of-proof postulate). This is how the theory explains the impact of demeanor on perceptions of competence. Through this sequence, interchange patterns lead to differentiated performance expectations. Every time a new interchange pattern becomes salient, it either strengthens or replaces the implications of the former pattern, creating a dynamic process (the structure completion postulate). Dynamic changes in performance expectations, in turn, produce changes in observable indicators of power and prestige, such as participation rates and nonverbal task cues (the principle postulate).

This sequence is represented in graph-theoretic terms so the effects of interchange patterns can be combined with other factors salient in the setting to predict aggregated expectation advantages and consequent differences in participation and other behaviors. Fisek et al. evaluate the model's ability to account for participation rates in open interaction groups by fitting it to several existing data sets, including Bales's (1970) original data from 208 groups. The rates of participation predicted by the model accounted for 89 to 99 percent of the variance of the actual observed participation rates. Thus the model can indeed describe the inequalities in participation that develop among actors in an open interaction setting.

Status Characteristics

Strodtbeck et al.'s (1957) jury study clearly demonstrated that characteristics that carry status value in society, such as occupation and gender, have a powerful impact on a person's behavior and position in a power and prestige order. But as they noted, the means or mechanism by which the status of the social categories to which one belongs affects one's behavior and standing in interaction were unknown. Expectation states theory sought to answer this question in its *status characteristics theory* (see J. Berger et al. 1977 for a formal statement; Webster and Foschi 1988, 1–20 for a brief review). The theory proposes that status characteristics, when salient in the situation, create performance expectations in goal-oriented settings and these shape the actors' behavior and, thus, rank in the power and prestige order (J. Berger, Cohen, and Zelditch 1972; J. Berger et al. 1977; Webster and Foschi 1988).

A status characteristic is defined as an attribute on which individuals vary that is associated in society with widely held beliefs according greater esteem and worthiness to some states of the attribute (e.g., being male or a proprietor) than other states of the attribute (e.g., being female or a laborer). Because it is based in consensual beliefs, the status value of an attribute can change over time and vary among populations. The theory's most important insight is that the cultural beliefs that attach status value to a characteristic also associate it with implicit expectations for competence. Worthiness becomes presumed competence. Occu-

pation, educational attainment, race, gender, and age are some of the status characteristics that carry such beliefs in the United States.

Status characteristics range from specific to diffuse, depending on the specificity of the competence associations they carry. Specific status characteristics are socially valued skills, expertise, or social accomplishments that imply a specific and bounded range of competencies. Computer skills are an example. Most interesting are diffuse status characteristics such as gender or race. These, too, are culturally associated with some specific skills but also carry general expectations for competence that are diffuse and unbounded in range. Yes, men are presumed by cultural stereotypes to be better at mechanics and worse at sewing than women, but they are also expected to be diffusely more able than women at almost any new task. This gives diffuse status characteristics a wide-ranging power to affect status relations in interaction.

Like any other factor, to affect power and prestige status characteristics must become salient in the setting either by discriminating among actors or by being perceived as task relevant. This suggests that whether or not a given status characteristic affects an individual's power and prestige in a setting depends on the goals of the setting and how the characteristic compares with those of the other participants. A characteristic (e.g., a B.A. degree) that gives an actor an edge in one setting (with college dropouts) can have no effect in another (where others have B.A.s also and it is not task-relevant) or be a disadvantage in a third setting (where others have Ph.D.s). So the impact of status characteristics is situationally specific. By this account, there are no "master statuses" that doom a person to low status or guarantee high status in all situations.

Once a status characteristic is salient, its competence associations generalize to affect actors' expectations about their own and other's abilities at the specific task at hand. If the status characteristic is actually relevant to the task, it will have a very strong impact on performance expectations. But even if it is completely irrelevant it will have a significant, if weaker, impact on expectations (the burden-of-proof process). This is what makes status characteristics prejudicial. It means, for instance, that in a mixed-sex setting, general beliefs about men's greater overall competence will generalize to affect reactions to an idea offered by a man rather than a woman even if the task is unrelated to gender. Both men and women are likely to assume the idea is better if it comes from a man. Such unfortunate effects persist despite official ideologies of equality because they usually operate as unaware judgments made "without thinking." Part of the power of expectation states theory is its ability to explain these effects.

Several studies have demonstrated this *status generalization* process (see J. Berger et al. 1985). Many use expectation states theory's standardized experimental setting, where participants are placed in separate rooms and given controlled feedback about one another's characteristics. Then they work together on an ambiguous task by pushing buttons on a console to exchange opinions and agree on a decision over a series of trials. Although they believe they are working together, each participant actually receives preprogrammed feedback that shows their partner disagreeing with them on many trials. They then must stick to their own choice or change to agree with their partner, in effect accepting influence from the partner. This controlled setting allows the investigator to test whether knowledge of self and other's status characteristics alone will affect the participants' willingness to accept or reject influence from the other. Using this setting, studies have shown that status characteristics as diverse as educational attainment (Moore 1968), gender (Pugh and Wahrman 1983; Wagner, Ford, and Ford 1986), military rank (J. Berger, Cohen, and Zelditch 1972), race (Webster and Driskell 1978), age (Freese and Cohen 1973), and specific abilities (Webster 1977) affect rates of influence even when they are completely irrelevant to the task.

The theory has also accurately predicted status generalization effects in open interaction settings (E. Cohen and Roper 1972; Carli 1990, 1991; Fisek, Berger, and Norman 1991; Lockheed and Hall 1976; Ridgeway 1982). In one such study, Wood and Karten (1986) demonstrated that the

reason gender affected participation rates and other task behaviors in mixed-sex interaction was that it affected expectations for competence at the task, just as the theory argues. When these expectations were controlled, gender effects on task behaviors disappeared. Driskell and Mullen's (1990) meta-analysis of status generalization studies similarly shows that status characteristics affect influence by affecting perceived competence.

Other open interaction studies have shown that status generalization shapes nonverbal task cues in the manner the theory predicts (Dovidio et al. 1988; Leffler, Gillespie, and Conaty 1982; Ridgeway, Berger, and Smith 1985; Smith-Lovin and Brody 1989). When a status characteristic places a person at an advantage in a given interaction, he/she becomes nonverbally assertive, as indicated by speech initiations, direct eye contact, looking at the other while speaking rather than while listening, gesturing, and interrupting. But when the same characteristic puts the person at a disadvantage in another interaction, his/her task cues become less assertive than those of others present. In a particularly clear demonstration of the theory's predictions, Dovidio et al. (1988) showed that when mixed-sex dyads shifted from a gender-neutral task, where the man had a status advantage, to a stereotypically feminine task, where the woman had a status advantage, the observable power and prestige orders reflected in their participation and nonverbal task cues reversed from one favoring the man to one favoring the woman.

Status Characteristics in Enduring Groups. Most studies of status generalization have focused on relatively short-lived groups, where members have limited opportunities to get to know one another and discover their actual abilities and interests in the group. Knowledge of actual abilities will have a stronger impact on performance expectations and power and prestige than diffuse status characteristics, since it is more directly relevant to task performance. Does this mean status generalization is likely to affect only the initial period of hierarchy formation? Do status characteristics play a significant role in enduring groups?

The most powerful impact of observable status characteristics, such as gender and race, is at the beginning of interaction, when actors know little else about one another. However, status characteristics usually have a long-lasting impact on a power and prestige structure because, by affecting initial expectations and opportunities to participate, they shape the subsequent information actors are able to introduce about themselves. Also, as Whyte's (1943) study of the Nortons showed, expectations, shaped by status characteristics, can powerfully constrain actors' ability actually to perform well at group activities, regardless of their real skills. Thus, it is difficult, although not impossible, for actors to break out of the power and prestige position into which they are cast initially by the status generalization process (see E. Cohen 1982; Ridgeway 1982 for discussions of how status generalization may be overcome). Consequently, as Bernard Cohen and Xueguang Zhou's (1991) study of corporate research and development teams demonstrates, the power and prestige structures of most enduring groups continue to reflect the impact of status characteristics.

Recently, Foschi (1989, 1991) showed that status characteristics may have such a pervasive impact on power and prestige because, in addition to shaping performance expectations, they also create double standards for judging success and failure. Performance expectations make it unlikely that the same contribution from a status-advantaged and a status-disadvantaged person will be perceived to be of the same quality. But double standards mean that even if they are, a contribution of that quality will be seen as stronger evidence of genuine task ability (or weaker evidence of incompetence) for the status-advantaged person than the status-disadvantaged person. Double standards are another way the effects of status characteristics in interaction can become self-fulfilling.

Multiple Status Characteristics.   Our discussion thus far has dealt with single status characteristics, such as gender, skills, or race. But what about gender *and* skills *and* race? No individual is only a man or a woman, African American or white, and

not also a variety of other status characteristics. In open interaction, participants often differ simultaneously on multiple status characteristics, and these characteristics can have inconsistent implications for power and prestige. There was a debate at one time about whether interactants would deal with inconsistent status characteristics by ignoring one or more of the characteristics, perhaps the least flattering or least task-relevant ones (Freese and Cohen 1973; I. Goffman 1957; Sampson 1969). The evidence suggests that this is not the case (Webster and Driskell 1978; Zelditch, Lauderdale and Stublarec 1980). As the theory predicts, people act as though they create aggregated expectations for themselves and others by weighting positive and negative characteristics by task relevance and combining them (Balkwell 1991b; Berger et al. 1977).

Such weighted combining indicates that the competence expectations and power and prestige of a woman doctor in a mixed-sex medical setting will be more strongly affected by her occupational status than her gender, but gender will still have an effect. She is likely to have slightly lower power and prestige than a similar male doctor (cf. Floge and Merrill 1986). However, it also implies that a woman might have equal or higher power and prestige than some men in the setting if she is higher than them on enough relevant skills or other status characteristics, as a number of studies have demonstrated (E. Cohen and Roper 1972; Dovidio et al. 1988; Pugh and Wahrman 1983). Because people are complex packages of skills and status characteristics, the status structures people construct through interaction reflect that complexity. They are not merely mirror images of the stratification of the larger society, despite being strongly affected by that stratification.

An interesting implication of this is that people may experience power and prestige structures that challenge their usual expectations for individuals with given diffuse status characteristics. When this happens, the experience can transfer to the way they treat the next person they encounter with that characteristic. Studies have shown that a man's experience working with a woman clearly more competent than he causes him to have somewhat higher performance expectations for the next woman he works with (Markovsky, Smith, and Berger 1984; Pugh and Wahrman 1983). While the effects diminish with each transfer, sufficient "reversal" experiences could moderate the cultural beliefs that associate competence with the characteristic and reduce its biasing effect on power and prestige structures.

Rewards and Performance Expectations

As noted earlier, status hierarchies are both a result of actors' efforts to organize the production of collective rewards and systems for reward distribution. Not surprisingly, in established hierarchies rewards tend to be distributed in accordance with rank and help maintain the relative power of those ranks (Homans 1961). But rewards have more subtle effects as well that show their integral role in status processes. Rewards can affect the creation of status hierarchies, modify positions in an existing hierarchy, and produce judgments about the justice or injustice of the status system. We leave the justice issue for chapter 10, focusing instead on the way rewards shape status positions.

It is a common observation that distributing rewards equally in a group reduces the apparent status differences among the members, while unequal distribution tends to increase status differences (e.g., Lerner 1974). This suggests that rewards are interdependent with other sources of power and prestige in a group. Expectation states theory captures this idea by arguing that actors' expectations for rewards in a task setting are interdependent with their performance expectations and, so, power and prestige positions (Berger, Fisek, et al. 1985; Cook 1975). In an experimental test of this argument, Cook (1975) showed that when a third party gave differential rewards to subjects who had no other basis for evaluating their performances on a shared task, the subjects used the reward differences to infer ability differences. Those who receive higher rewards are presumed to have greater task ability than those with lower rewards, even when there is no explicit connection between the distribution of rewards and

level of ability (Harrod 1980; Stewart and Moore 1992).

This important point highlights how the power or good luck represented in the unequal possession of rewards becomes legitimate status. Through the creation of performance expectations, the unequal rewards appear to be "deserved," and thus legitimately and justly bring respect, deference, and influence. It also suggests an association between possession of rewards and membership in a given racial, ethnic, or other social category may be one means by which such membership becomes or remains a status characteristic in society (Ridgeway 1991).

Expectation states theory considers rewards, like status characteristics and behavior, to be an additional factor that interactants include in their formation of aggregated performance expectations. These performance expectations, in turn, affect expectations for future rewards, with the result that interactants generally distribute future awards in accord with their standing in the power and prestige order.

A Critical Assessment

It is clear that expectation states theory is a powerful, well-documented theory that can successfully account for many of the structural forms and interactional dynamics of status orders in goal-oriented settings. But there are important questions about status orders that it has not yet addressed. One of the most obvious is to account for status orders in interactional settings not characterized by explicit goals, which expectation states theorists have only begun to discuss (Johnston 1988). Unfortunately, this problem has not been systematically addressed by other theories either, although McWilliams and Blumstein (1991) have offered some interesting initial thoughts on it. As they note, status characteristics, assertive behavior, and rewards are likely to be important to power and prestige in such settings also. But exactly how do they work? More important, does a weaker goal orientation in interaction reduce the importance or extent of status dynamics? Certainly this is the implication of the exchange and functionalist approaches to status that have dominated sociological analyses of status structures, including the expectation states theory.

A second important question is the role of expressive, emotionally oriented behavior in status dynamics. The organization of affective relations may indeed be a separate process, as Bales (1950) suggested. However, recent analyses suggest that, at the very least, status dynamics shape emotional reactions during interaction in ways that control and direct positive and negative expressive behavior (Clark 1991; Ridgeway and Johnson 1990; Smith-Lovin and Heise 1988). Other analyses indicate that affective relations moderate or magnify power and prestige differences (Shelly 1988). Much more data are needed to assess these ideas properly and understand the relationship between affect and status.

Finally, there is the problem of the role of conflict in status hierarchies. Expectation states theory focuses on consensual allocation, which evidence indicates predominates (Mazur 1973). But conflict does occur, and it needs to be explicitly addressed. Since status conflicts usually elicit emotions (Bales 1953; Ridgeway and Johnson 1990), the problem of conflict is related to the need to understand affect and status.

LEGITIMACY AND STATUS STRUCTURES

Despite some gaps, theory and research has given us a reasonably clear picture of the way actors, often without being aware of it, construct status structures when they interact to pursue a common goal. They respond to each other's social attributes, rewards, demeanor, and actions and the cultural assumptions of status value and competence these evoke, to form rank-ordered expectations about the likely value of the contributions of each to the effort. These often unconscious expectations shape their own and others' participation, demeanor (whether confident or insecure), evaluative responses, and influence, creating a behavioral status order.

As status orders develop, the actors must confront an additional set of issues, concerning legitimacy. Recall that a status order acquires legitimacy when it becomes normative. Questions affecting the development of legitimacy can enter into interactional status dynamics in at least three interrelated ways: different actors can be seen as more or less legitimate candidates for high status in the setting; different sorts of actions (e.g., highly task-oriented or dominating behaviors) can be seen as more or less legitimate; and the structure of inequality itself can be viewed as more or less legitimate (Walker, Rogers, and Zelditch 1989; Walker, Thomas, and Zelditch 1986).

Legitimacy transforms a status structure from a system of behavioral inequalities (what is) into a system of rights and obligations (what ought to be). In a legitimated structure, the actions and demeanors by which high- and low-status actors enact their positions become status markers that signify the order for the members, giving status relations a ritual quality (E. Goffman 1956; Ridgeway and Berger 1986). Behaviors on the part of either high- or low-status actors that contradict the legitimated order become status violations that are subject to sanction by other members. Thus legitimation processes play an important role in creating stability in newly formed status structures and in maintaining the stability of existing structures. They are also crucial to the process by which macrolevel systems of stratification are reproduced and maintained in face-to-face settings.

Classic Approaches

Theory and research on the legitimacy of status structures represents the convergence of two distinct research traditions. It is an amalgam of work that examines the general issue of the legitimation of social behavior and research on status structures. It is difficult to characterize any single line of empirical inquiry as having played a dominant role in the development of this area of investigation; several collections of studies examine basic issues of direct relevance to the study of legitimacy and status structures. Our discussion focuses on three areas of investigation that have benefitted from the application of ideas about legitimacy to the study of status structures: the study of the emergence of status differentiation and the organization of status structures; studies of compliance to authority and deference to status; and studies on the determinants of the stability of status structures. We discuss legitimizing processes in general terms before proceeding with an examination of these specific issues.

Legitimation is a central—and often ill-defined—social process. Various authors use the idea to mean the process through which patterns of beliefs or behaviors acquire social support (Parsons 1951), the process by which actions are justified (Weber 1968), or the process that generates explanations or accounts of phenomena (P. Berger and Luckmann 1966). The term is also used to refer to specific justifications or accounts (P. Berger and Luckmann 1966; Weber 1968). Despite the conceptual imprecision, there is an extensive literature on legitimacy and legitimation processes, much of it relevant to our examination of status structures.

There are two major streams of work on legitimacy and legitimation processes, both of which can be traced to an ambiguity in the work of Max Weber (1968). Weber defined a legitimate social order as one that actors treat as a desirable model of action or that actors believe is valid. In turn, validity was defined as the belief that the operating norms (or rules) are binding on members of the collectivity.

Weber's contention that legitimate social orders represent desirable models of action is exemplified by one branch of legitimation research. Investigators who take this perspective define legitimacy in terms of the orientations of focal actors to rules and norms and study the effects of such orientations on their behavior. Legitimate norms are those believed by some focal actor to be desirable or acceptable. Internalization—an individual's acceptance of a set of norms as desirable and proper —plays a central role in this perspective on legitimation processes. Actors who internalize norms are presumed to exhibit a greater likelihood of conformity with norms than those who have not accepted them as standards of desirable conduct.

If the first branch of legitimation research can be described as individual-centered, the second branch is focused on the collective nature of legitimacy and legitimation processes. In this conception legitimacy refers to the validity of norms. Valid norms are those that group members believe they are compelled to obey, whether they internalize them or not. As such, the mechanisms that produce adherence to valid norms are external to the individual. Research guided by this perspective has generally focused on the social conditions that influence the collective validation of group standards of behavior and the effects such standards have on individual and collective action.

Recent Formulations

Dornbusch and Scott (1975) effected a conceptual separation of the two ideas described above and offered arguments that unite them. The Dornbusch-Scott conception of legitimacy is embedded in their theory of formal authority. Therefore, their discussion is organized around the hierarchical arrangement of persons in formal organizations and the control rights associated with positions in systems of formal authority. Dornbusch and Scott envision authority relations as involving, at a minimum, three levels of status or authority, A, B, and C. Persons at level C are subordinate to both B and A; those at level B are higher in status and power than those at level C but subordinate to persons at level A.

Dornbusch and Scott introduced the term *propriety* to refer to any individual's belief that rules and norms of conduct describe desirable patterns of action. They reserved the term *validity* to refer to norms that are obligatory for group members even when they do not personally approve of them. The Dornbusch-Scott theory describes how individual judgments about the propriety of standards of conduct, the aggregation of individual judgments about such standards, and the validity of those standards are related.

An actor's belief that regularized patterns of conduct possess propriety is presumed to have direct effects on his/her behavior. Standards to which interactants attribute propriety serve an evaluative function. The desirability of enacted behaviors and alternative standards of behavior is determined by comparison with proper standards. The more similar alternative behaviors are to those that possess propriety, the more likely are alternative behaviors to acquire propriety.

Actors are expected to enact behaviors to which they attribute propriety. For example, interactants who believe it is desirable for one member of the group to take control of group activity are expected not to object when a (qualified) member of the group attempts to exercise control. On the other hand, persons who do not attribute propriety to such actions are presumed to be less likely to comply with the demands of an actor who attempts to direct or control group activity.

Valid rules influence behavior through a very different set of processes. Awareness of valid norms establishes a sense of obligation among group members. Group members comply not because they believe the enacted behaviors to be desirable or morally correct but because "that is the way things are supposed to be done."

Valid norms serve as powerful constraints on group life, but their effects are not limited to the direct effects just described. They influence group members in an indirect way as well by promoting or enhancing a belief in the norm's propriety. The Dornbusch-Scott theory implies that group members confronted with valid standards of behavior are more likely to develop a belief that the standards are desirable (i.e., to internalize them) than persons who encounter standards that are not valid.

While propriety serves evaluative purposes, validity serves both evaluative and constitutive functions. Valid standards of conduct are constitutive because they describe ways of behaving required of persons who occupy particular stations in life. Indeed, acting in a manner that is consistent with valid norms is one aspect of what it means to occupy a particular social position. To do otherwise

is not only unthinkable but strips the meaning from group life as it is known and commonly experienced (Walker et al. 1991). As an example, a pauper may come to occupy the position of prince, but he will not be a prince until his behavior conforms with the standards princes are obliged to meet.

The validity and propriety of norms and rules are bolstered by two other factors, which Dornbusch and Scott label *endorsement* and *authorization*. Both concepts refer to the support or approval for specific patterns of action or standards of conduct. Endorsement refers to the support or approval of group members who are at a level equal to or lower than that of a focal actor. As an example, assume that B_1 is a supervisor in an automobile assembly plant and C_1 works on the assembly line. If other B's and C's in the plant support B_1's sanctioning of C_1 for drinking on the job, B_1's behavior is endorsed.

Authorization refers to demonstrations of support by persons who occupy positions that are superordinate to a focal actor. When applied to the previous example, B_1's behavior is authorized if it is supported by higher-level supervisors (A's).

Zelditch and Walker (1984; Walker, Rogers and Zelditch 1988; Walker, Thomas, and Zelditch 1986) have revised and extended the Dornbusch-Scott formulation in two ways. First, Zelditch and Walker (1984) argue that Dornbusch and Scott's arguments are applicable to groups that do not have three-level hierarchies. Second, they argue that at least three features of social situations are objects of legitimation: persons, positions or roles that persons occupy, and the relations or institutions in which positions are embedded, can each serve as objects of legitimation.

To this point we have described the complexity entailed by the idea of legitimacy. There are individual and collective aspects of legitimacy; standards of conduct can possess propriety and/or validity. Furthermore, legitimacy is both evaluative and constitutive. Legitimate standards provide a basis for comparing and evaluating specific behaviors but also establish the meaning of determinate features of social life. Finally, legitimacy is buttressed by endorsement and authorization. We can employ these basic ideas in our application of theories of legitimacy and legitimation processes to the study of status structures.

Legitimacy and the Emergence of Status Structures

The importance of legitimacy—or its absence—to shaping patterns of action can be illustrated by two quite different phenomena identified with the emergence of status structures. First is the emergence of status hierarchies and the observation that some groups develop distinct positions of task and socioemotional leadership. Second is duplication of societal level stratification systems in small groups of interactants.

Emergence of Status Hierarchy. Legitimacy arguments have been employed to further our understanding of the processes by which status hierarchies emerge in face-to-face groups. We have noted that functional theories of role differentiation (Bales 1953; Bales and Slater 1955; Zelditch 1955) contend that hierarchical status structures facilitate the accomplishment of collective goals. These theories also imply that strong hierarchies of status and influence are more typical of some groups than others; for example, mixed-gender and all-male groups are presumed to be more hierarchical than all-female groups. Some investigators (Fennell et al. 1978; Meeker and Weitzel-O'Neill 1977) suggest that this difference in patterns of status organization can be explained as a function of legitimation processes.

Fennell et al. (1978) argue that what is empirically usual in a society is duplicated in particular formal organizations and the argument can be easily extended to smaller groups. Although empirical usuality is not rigorously defined, the idea is clear. Actors learn which roles they may legitimately occupy, which behaviors are valid (i.e., expected and obligatory), and which roles are not valid. While it can be presumed that some actors come to believe that what is empirically usual is desirable or proper, Fennell et al.'s general statement is not clear on this point.

Meeker and Weitzel-O'Neill (1977) offer a similar but more rigorous theory. They use ideas from status characteristics theory and several other frameworks to construct their arguments. They contend that actors whose performance outputs are not contested are perceived as raising their status. Attaining high status is presumed to be a legitimate objective for group members with high external status and illegitimate for persons with low external status. Meeker and Weitzel-O'Neill's notion of legitimacy implies both propriety and endorsement.

Both arguments have been applied to the study of gender differences in patterns of status organization. Meeker and Weitzel-O'Neill argue that members of low-status groups expect, and are expected, to retain their station in life; that is, it is empirically usual for members of their group to be subordinate to members of higher-status groups. They also expect, and are expected, to be excluded from high-status positions and roles. Similarly, Fennell et al. argue that women are less likely to organize hierarchically than men because it is not valid (i.e., empirically usual) for women to occupy positions of high status. Consequently, they are reluctant to assume such positions.

The theories have somewhat different implications for the behavior of males. Males are likely to engage in contests for high-status positions because it is legitimate for males to occupy such positions. Given the initial status equality of members of all-male and all-female groups, all-male groups might be expected to develop strongly hierarchical structures more often than all-female groups. Fennell et al. (1978) reported findings that generally support this argument, although the number of groups they studied is small and the study has not been replicated.

The basic approach exemplified in this research is also consistent with the observation that, in some instances, homogeneous groups experience more difficulty in completing tasks than heterogeneous groups. If hierarchy improves efficiency, the proficiency of groups should be reduced if the formation of status structures is impeded.

There is some evidence that homogeneous groups take longer to complete some tasks than do heterogeneous groups. Eskilson and Wiley (1976) employed legitimation arguments to suggest that all-female groups experience difficulty at task completion because their members resist taking leading roles with respect to task activity. On the other hand, all-male groups are presumed to experience similar troubles as a result of excessive competition for high-status positions. Although the evidence is limited, it appears that the problem is rectified in all-female groups when task leadership is authorized by the experimenter (Eskilson and Wiley 1976).

Theories of legitimation have also been used to explain why some groups develop task and socioemotional leaders while in other groups one person occupies both positions. Verba (1961) modified Bales's (1950) functional theory of differentiation to argue that the emergence of dual leadership structures is, in part, a result of the extent to which task activity and the behavior of task leaders is legitimate. Verba's arguments imply that actors are less likely to challenge task leaders' actions when task activity is valid and/or proper or if the person assuming task leadership behaves in valid or proper ways. The diminished challenge to the actions of task leaders and to task activity in general is presumed to obviate the need for a separate socioemotional specialist. As a consequence, separate task and socioemotional leadership structures are less likely in groups in which task activity and task leaders are legitimized.

Burke (1967, 1968, 1971) tested Verba's ideas experimentally. In an early study (Burke 1967), legitimacy was measured as endorsement, the extent to which group members were oriented to engage in task activity. Burke reported, consistent with Verba's arguments, that groups were less likely to have separate task and socioemotional leaders when task activity was endorsed. Inequality of participation was weakly correlated with role differentiation in groups in which task activity was strongly endorsed. On the other hand, inequality of task activity was highly correlated with role differentiation when task activity was not endorsed.

Burke also found that task activity was negatively correlated with liking, but only when task activity was weakly endorsed. Task leadership did not reduce the leader's approval ratings when task activity was endorsed.

In another study (Burke 1968), the legitimacy of task activity was established by authorization. Burke reported that the emergence of dual leadership was not significantly correlated with levels of task activity when achieving consensus and task activity were authorized by the experimenter. The emergence of differentiated leadership roles was highly correlated with task activity when the importance of consensus and task activity were not stressed by the experimenter. There was also a positive correlation between actors' levels of task and socioemotional activity in the high-legitimacy treatment. That is, there was a tendency for the same person to occupy the roles of task and socioemotional leader.

Burke's findings provide strong empirical support for the modified functional theory of role differentiation. They are also consistent with the finding that task and socioemotional leadership are claimed by the same persons in a relatively large proportion of the ad hoc task groups studied by Bales and others (Lewis 1972; Riedesel 1974). It is plausible to assume that the legitimacy of task activity plays an important role in the failure of many groups to develop differentiated structures of task and socioemotional leadership. When task activity is valid, group members are less likely to challenge the performance outputs of persons taking leadership roles. Also, actors for whom the behavior of the task leader is proper are less likely to challenge and more likely to support the leader's actions.

Emergence of Hierarchy in Heterogeneous Groups.   A second example of how legitimacy and legitimation processes affect the creation of emergent status hierarchies can be taken from the study of status-organizing processes in heterogeneous groups. It is generally well known that status structures emerge almost instantaneously in groups in which the members are differentiated on the basis of attributes that are consistently ranked by members of the society at large. Furthermore, the rankings of interactants are highly correlated with the rankings of the groups of which they are members (Berger, Cohen, and Zelditch 1972). As we have pointed out, status characteristics theory is the best general explanation for the duplication of societal level status structures in the small group.

Meeker and Weitzel-O'Neill (1977) attempted to integrate status characteristics theory and ideas about legitimacy to explain this process more fully. The reproduction of society-level status structures at the level of small groups is implied by their arguments (as well as those of Fennell et al. 1978). Members of both higher- and lower-status groups might be expected to take on duties and responsibilities that are legitimized for members of their respective status groups in heterogeneous small groups or organizations. As a result, we would expect macrosocial status structures to be replicated at the level of the small group. To our knowledge, no empirical investigations have explicitly tested the implications of these arguments for the general problem of the relationship between status structures in small groups and formal organizations and the legitimacy of stratification systems in the larger society. However, expectation states theorists increasingly incorporate ideas from legitimation theory into their formulations (Fisek, Berger, and Norman 1991; Ridgeway and Berger 1986).

Status, Legitimacy, and Compliance

As we noted in our introduction, status structures are not simply patterns of respect or honor established by group members. Status differences establish a foundation for the emergence of patterns of dominance and influence. Persons with high status generally exert more influence than persons of lower status, are more likely to dominate low-status persons, and are more likely to exact deference from persons of lower status. One implication of the legitimation of status structures is the strengthening of patterns of influence. Theories of legitimacy imply that legitimate occupants of high-status positions are more influential than similarly placed (but not legitimate) occupants of such posi-

tions. A number of studies provide strong support for this.

Early studies conducted by Raven and French (1958a, 1958b) provide equivocal support for the effects of endorsement on compliance. Their initial study (Raven and French 1958a) found that group members were more likely to comply with leaders who were endorsed than leaders who were not. A second study (Raven and French 1958b) found a relatively weak effect of endorsement on compliance. Among criticisms of that work is the observation that their experimental treatments confounded power and legitimacy (Schopler 1965; Walker, Thomas, and Zelditch 1986).

Michener and Burt (1975) used an ingenious experiment to study the effects of endorsement and validity on compliance. Group members were assigned a high- or low-status position in an organization. The scope of the high-status actor's authority (i.e., the range of fines he could assess) was set by an election procedure. Michener and Burt failed to find significant effects of endorsement on compliance. However, they found a substantial effect of validity. Subjects were less likely to pay their assessed fines when high-status actors behaved invalidly (i.e., by assessing fines greater than the standard established by the collectivity).

More recently Walker et al. (1989) demonstrated that actors are less likely to comply with the directives of a high-status actor if the authority relation is not valid. Persons who were assessed fines by a high-status actor whose right to penalize them had not been established by valid procedures (i.e., an election) refused to pay the fines. Those who were fined when the right to penalize them was made valid proffered the fines on demand. The robustness of the finding is indicated by the fact that subjects paid fines despite the experimenter's instruction that neither their payment nor refusal to pay fines could be monitored by the high-status actor or the experimental staff. Finally, Ridgeway's recent studies (Ridgeway 1987; Ridgeway and Diekema 1989; Ridgeway, Johnson, and Diekema 1994) of responses to dominating behavior suggests that those perceived to be making demands illegitimately are less likely to receive compliance than those perceived to have a legitimate right to make such demands.

Legitimacy and the Stability of Status Structures

The above discussion demonstrates that legitimizing status structures has important effects on the level of compliance to group norms and to the directives of leaders. The failure of newly formed status structures to secure the compliance of their members is a source of conflict and instability. How do newly formed status structures acquire legitimacy? How do existing structures maintain it?

Stability is a problem for any newly created social structure, and status structures are no exception. An actor may ascend to the most influential position in a group, but his/her position and the integrity of the group may be threatened if he/she or his/her performance is not recognized as legitimate. Ridgeway and Berger (1986; Ridgeway 1988) argue that emergent behavioral inequalities are legitimated as a function of referential beliefs held by group members. Referential beliefs are assumptions about the types of actors who typically hold higher- or lower-status positions in society. When referential beliefs are activated, group members use them to form status expectations for self and others. The strength of status expectations varies with the number of referential beliefs that are activated and the consistency of the belief structures (i.e., the degree to which different referential beliefs generate the same status expectations). The more congruent the ordering of behavioral inequalities and status expectations, the more likely group members are to accept and comply with the actions of high-status actors. The greater the level of acceptance of the actions of high-status persons, the more likely the behavioral order is to acquire validity (Fisek, Berger, and Norman 1991). The general argument has been applied to the issue of gender differences in the enactment of task and socioemotional behaviors (Ridgeway 1988) and to the issue of compliance with persons who exhibit dominance behavior (Ridgeway, Johnson, and Diekema 1994). The findings of Ridgeway et al. (1994) are consistent with theoretical predictions.

Subjects in their experiment were less likely to comply with dominating persons when referential beliefs led to consistent status expectations than when such beliefs led to inconsistent status expectations.

Legitimacy and the Maintenance of Status Structures

When positions in a group acquire status significance, some group members will be more influential and garner more scarce resources than others. Inequalities in the distribution of scarce resources (e.g., income or power) can lead to pressure to reorganize status rankings. Indeed, it is plausible to assume that low-status actors have a vested interest in revolt (i.e., in overturning the existing placement of persons in status structures). Those in inferior positions should aspire to hold the top positions.

Despite the strains inherent in status structures, they are remarkably stable (Bales and Slater 1955; Walker et al. 1991). A number of arguments have been called on to explain the stability of status and reward structures. Theories of power and influence make the case that the superior resources of high-status actors are used to maintain existing status arrangements. Conflict theories imply that, in addition to the effects of differences in power, status arrangements remain stable as a result of the false consciousness of lower-status actors. A number of arguments attribute the stability of status structures to their legitimacy and the operation of legitimation processes.

Two general classes of arguments have been applied to the relationship between legitimacy and the stability of extant status structures. The first has been called the self-evaluation argument and depends on propriety as a stabilizing factor (Della Fave 1980, 1986; Stolte 1983). The second relies on validity as well as propriety (Dornbusch and Scott 1975; Zelditch and Walker 1984).

Self-Evaluation and Stability. The self-evaluation argument (Della Fave 1980, 1986; Stolte 1983) suggests that low-status persons fail to initiate actions to overturn status structures because they believe such structures possess propriety. In situations where some actors receive fewer and lower-quality rewards than others, actors who receive low rewards are presumed to adjust their self-evaluations to make them consistent with the relatively lower rewards they receive. Ultimately, low-status actors are expected to exhibit lower self-evaluations than actors who receive more and higher-quality rewards. As self-evaluations become increasingly aligned with rewards, neither low- nor high-status persons should be inclined to believe that the reward distributions are unfair or undeserved. The reorganized self-evaluations of group members and the concomitant reduction in the sense that injustice exists is presumed to result in actors' making attributions of propriety to their stations in life and of the rewards their positions bring. As a result, any impetus for change is checked.

The evidence that propriety enhances the preservation of status structures is incontrovertible (Walker et al. 1991; Walker, Rogers, and Zelditch 1988; Walker, Thomas, and Zelditch 1986; Zelditch and Walker 1984). However, it is not clear that lower-status actors accord greater propriety to the status structures they inhabit as a result of their having low self-evaluations. Stolte (1983) investigated the self-evaluation hypothesis with mixed results. He varied the status (measured as positional power) of actors in an exchange situation and collected data on the outcomes actors received from a series of exchanges, the actors' sense of self-efficacy, and their evaluations of the fairness of the outcomes. While he found that actors' evaluations of their self-efficacy varied with their (low or high) status, their evaluations of the fairness of outcomes also varied with status. The second finding is inconsistent with the self-evaluation hypothesis. Karen Cook et al. (1988) replicated Stolte's results but found evidence to suggest that low-power actors accept their positions because they perceive the structure to be beyond their control, even if unfair. If Cook et al. are correct in their interpretation, low-power actors are constrained more by validity than by propriety.

In a more recent investigation, Choe (1991) varied the specific self-evaluations of experimental subjects by providing them fictitious scores for an uncommon skill. In the second phase of the study they received rewards that were lower than, higher than, or consistent with their level of skill. Choe reports evidence that fairness judgments are influenced by self-evaluations. However, it must be noted that Choe's status indicator is based on a functional criterion (i.e., skill). In that respect, Stolte's measure of status as social position is more consistent with the concerns addressed by Della Fave's and Stolte's versions of the self-evaluation hypothesis. That is, when persons receive low rewards as a result of their social position as determined by class, gender, or race—factors that should be independent of reward allocation—they might be expected to raise issues of inequality more often than persons whose rewards are based on performance criteria such as skill or competence.

Validity and Stability.   The argument that validity enhances the stability of status structures proposes fundamentally different mechanisms than the self-evaluation argument. If group members believe compliance with norms and rules is obligatory, legitimately constituted status structures should be quite stable. Validity implies the support of collectivity members (i.e., endorsement) and superordinate persons through the mechanism of authorization. Consequently, any group member, whether he/she believes a status structure possesses propriety or not, should be less likely to engage in destabilizing activity if the relevant structure is valid.

Thomas et al. (1986) designed a laboratory experiment to document the constitutive effects of validity—effects that flow from the legitimacy of meaning. The experimenters authorized continued use of an inequitable task structure for one-half the experimental subjects by giving them information that suggested that changing the structure would make the study meaningless. The remaining subjects were not given that information. Thomas et al. report that subjects in the authorization treatment were significantly less likely to propose action to change it. Replications of the study support these findings (Walker et al. 1991; Walker, Rogers, and Zelditch 1988).

In a study of effects of propriety on stability, Lineweber et al. (1982) describe evidence that is consistent with a validity effect. Experimental subjects were less likely to change an inequitable reward structure when the experimenter declared the structure equitable, compared to the absence of such a declaration. Subjects reported in postsession interviews that they refused to change the structure because they surmised that the experimenter believed the structure to be equitable. Authorization appeared to have bolstered the validity of the structure.

Endorsement and Stability.   Endorsement is the last of the mechanisms proposed by Dornbusch and Scott. The Dornbusch-Scott theory assumes that group support increases compliance to standards of conduct. Walker et al. (1986) studied the effects of endorsement on the stability of communication structures. Low-status subjects were provided a mechanism for altering a status structure in instances in which doing so would substantially improve their level of reward relative to a high-status actor. There were significantly fewer attempts to change the status structure when the structure was endorsed.

Summary

Current findings suggest that legitimacy plays an important role in the life of status structures. Legitimizing task activity and leadership functions appears to raise the likelihood that groups will develop hierarchical status structures. It also retards the emergence of dual task and socioemotional leadership structures. Recent syntheses of legitimation and expectation states theories (Fisek, Berger, and Norman 1991; Meeker and Weitzel-O'Neill 1977) have been employed to explain how the legitimation process facilitates the reproduction of macrolevel stratification systems in face-to-face situations. While they have not been extensively tested, some evidence is supportive (Carli 1990; Ridgeway 1982).

Finally, legitimacy plays a significant role in creating stability in emergent status structures and in maintaining the stability of existing structures. Both propriety and validity contribute to stability,

but the latter is the more powerful force in preventing the destabilization of status structures. Validity establishes the constitutive meaning of social behavior; it implies both authorization and endorsement and facilitates a belief in the propriety of social action and status arrangements. In turn, each of these factors has a demonstrable effect on the maintenance of status structures in informally organized groups (Thomas, Walker, and Zelditch 1986; Walker, Thomas, and Zelditch 1986).

CONCLUSION

As evaluative hierarchies of respect, deference, and influence among actors, status structures are a persistent feature of human interaction. They develop whenever actors must coordinate their behavior toward some collective end. Given the social nature of human life and our frequent dependence on others, most interaction contains some of the elements of positive interdependence out of which status structures emerge. Theory and research on status structures has focused on a subset of these interactions that are clearly goal- or task-oriented. In such situations, status dynamics are starkly highlighted, and fifty years of research, aided by systematic theoretical programs such as expectations states theory, has provided a reasonably clear account of their operation.

Status structures develop out of actors' efforts to construct a social definition of one another in relation to their shared goal. Actors notice, at some level, social attributes and possessions, demeanor, and actions that distinguish them from one another. From the cultural assumptions of status value and competence these evoke, they form rank-ordered expectations about the value of each actor's contributions to the goal. These often unconscious expectations govern actors' willingness to assert themselves, to listen to others, and to accept or reject others' opinions when they conflict with their own or to wield or accept influence.

In this way, often without thinking about it, actors construct a hierarchy of influence by which they organize their behavior and direct it toward the collective goal. As a result, status hierarchies are an organizational means by which groups of actors produce collective rewards through goal attainment. But status hierarchies are systems of reward distributions as well, and among the rewards distributed is the honor of high status. So status structures involve members' competitive interests, too.

To manage competitive interests while maintaining a cooperative goal effort, actors often effectively construct legitimating norms that define their status relations and sanction violations of them. Issues of legitimacy and legitimation arise in the emergence, enactment, and maintenance or change of a status structure. When they acquire legitimacy, status structures, in addition to being systems for the production and distribution of rewards, become systems for the maintenance of shared meanings.

We have seen that legitimation is a complex, collective process involving validity, propriety, authorization, and endorsement in the construction of normative definitions of the status order. It affects how differing actors' bids for status in the group will be received (e.g., those with low- versus high-status characteristics), whether high-status actors can be assertively task-directed and still be liked, the effectiveness of dominance behaviors such as commands, and actors' willingness to accept the inequality the status order entails and, consequently, the persistence and stability of the status order.

In complex societies, both the processes by which status structures are organized and those by which they are legitimated are inherently multilevel. In the status-organizing process, cultural status value beliefs are evoked by interactional events and complexly combined to create expectations in the setting. In the legitimizing process, cultural beliefs about what is empirically usual, referentially true, or supported by authority in a larger social framework are brought to bear in defining what should occur in the interactional setting.

If the larger social framework plays an important (but not entirely determinative) role in constituting interactional status structures, they, in turn, are a significant means by which larger systems of stratification are enacted and maintained. Interactional status orders mediate much individual access to valued organizational positions and economic resources. They govern the principal decision-making entities (e.g., boards, committees, interest groups) in complex societies. When interactional status structures reproduce the patterns of larger systems of stratification, they help maintain those systems and affirm their moral order. As face-to-face systems of inequality, status structures reflect, enhance, and facilitate the organization of inequality in societies at large.

NOTE

1. Some researchers have argued that these findings indicate a very different status process altogether, one based on behavioral dominance rather than task expectations (Lee and Ofshe 1981; Rosa and Mazur 1979). However, other evidence indicates that task cues, which convey confidence and competence, can be distinguished from dominance cues that portray threat. It is task cues, not dominance cues, that aid influence (Ridgeway 1987).

REFERENCES

Alexander, C. Norman Jr., and Mary Glenn Wiley. 1981. Situated activity and identity formation. Pp. 269–289 in *Social Psychology: Sociological Perspectives,* ed. M. Rosenberg and R. H. Turner. New York: Basic Books.

Archibald, W. Peter. 1976. Face-to-face: The alienating effects of class, status, and power divisions. *American Sociological Review* 41:819–837.

Bales, Robert F. 1950. *Interaction Process Analysis: A Method for the Study of Small Groups.* Cambridge, MA: Addison-Wesley.

———. 1953. The equilibrium problem in small groups. Pp. 111–161 in *Working Papers in the Theory of Action,* ed. T. Parsons, R. F. Bales, and E. A. Shils. Glencoe, IL: Free Press.

———. 1970. *Personality and Interpersonal Behavior.* New York: Holt, Rinehart & Winston.

Bales, Robert F., and Philip E. Slater. 1955. Role differentiation in small decision-making groups. Pp. 259–306 in *The Family, Socialization, and Interaction Processes,* ed. T. Parsons and R. F. Bales. Glencoe, IL: Free Press.

Balkwell, James W. 1991a. From expectations to behavior: An improved postulate for expectation states theory. *American Sociological Review* 56:355–369.

———. 1991b. Status characteristics and social interaction: An assessment of theoretical variants. Pp. 135–176 in *Advances in Group Processes,* vol. 8, ed. E. Lawler, B. Markovsky, C. Ridgeway, and H. Walker. Greenwich, CT: JAI Press.

Berger, Joseph, Bernard P. Cohen, and Morris Zelditch, Jr. 1972. Status characteristics and social interaction. *American Sociological Review* 37:241–255.

Berger, Joseph, and Thomas L. Conner. 1974. Performance expectations and behavior in small groups: A revised formulation. Pp. 85–110 in *Expectation States Theory: A Theoretical Research Program,* ed. J. Berger, T. Conner, and M. H. Fisek. Cambridge, MA: Winthrop.

Berger, Joseph, Thomas L. Conner, and M. Hamit Fisek. 1974. *Expectation States Theory: A Theoretical Research Program.* Cambridge, MA: Winthrop.

Berger, Joseph, Thomas L. Conner, and William L. McKeown. 1974. Evaluations and the formation and maintenance of performance expectations. Pp. 27–51 in *Expectation States Theory: A Theoretical Research Program,* ed. J. Berger, T. Conner, and H. M. Fisek. Cambridge, MA: Winthrop.

Berger, Joseph, M. Hamit Fisek, Robert Z. Norman, and David G. Wagner. 1985. The formation of reward expectations in status situations. Pp. 215–261 in *Status, Rewards, and Influence,* ed. J. Berger and M. Zelditch. San Francisco: Jossey-Bass.

Berger, Joseph, M. Hamit Fisek, Robert Z. Norman, and Morris Zelditch, Jr. 1977. *Status Characteristics in Social Interaction: An Expectation States Approach.* New York: Elsevier.

Berger, Joseph, David G. Wagner, and Morris Zelditch, Jr. 1985. Expectation states theory: Review and assessment. Pp. 1–72 in *Status, Rewards, and Influence,* ed. Joseph Berger and Morris Zelditch. San Francisco: Jossey-Bass.

Berger, Joseph, Murray Webster, Jr., Cecilia Ridgeway, and Susan J. Rosenholtz. 1986. Status cues, expectations and behavior. Pp. 1–22 in *Advances in Group Processes,* vol. 3, ed. E. Lawler. Greenwich, CT: JAI Press.

Berger, Peter L., and Thomas Luckmann. 1966. *The Social Construction of Reality.* Garden City, NY: Doubleday.

Blau, Peter. 1964. *Exchange and Power in Social Life.* New York: Wiley.

Blumer, Herbert. 1969. *Symbolic Interactionism: Perspective and Method.* Englewood Cliffs, NJ: Prentice Hall.

Bonacich, Philip, and Gordon H. Lewis. 1973. Function specialization and sociometric judgment. *Sociometry* 36:31–41.

Burke, Peter J. 1967. The development of task and social-emotional role differentiation. *Sociometry* 30:379–392.

———. 1968. Role differentiation and the legitimation of task activity. *Sociometry* 31:404–411.

———. 1971. Task and socioemotional leadership role performance. *Sociometry* 34:22–40.

———. 1974. Participation and leadership in small groups. *American Sociological Review* 39:832–843.

Carli, Linda L. 1990. Gender, language, and influence. *Journal of Personality and Social Psychology* 59:941–951.

———. 1991. Gender, status, and influence. Pp. 89–114 in *Advances in Group Processes,* vol. 8, ed. E. Lawler, B. Markovsky, C. Ridgeway, and H. Walker. Greenwich, CT: JAI Press.

Choe, Joon Young. 1991. *Self-evaluations and the sense of injustice.* Ph. D. diss., Department of Sociology, Iowa City, IA: University of Iowa.

Clark, Candace. 1991. Emotions and micropolitics in everyday life: Some patterns and paradoxes of "place." Pp. 305–333 in *Research Agendas in the Sociology of Emotions,* ed. T. D. Kemper. Albany: State University of New York Press.

Cohen, Bernard P., and Xueguang Zhou. 1991. Status processes in enduring work groups. *American Sociological Review* 56:179–188.

Cohen, Elizabeth G. 1982. Expectation states and interracial interaction in school settings. *Annual Review of Sociology* 8:209–235.

Cohen, Elizabeth G., and Susan S. Roper. 1972. Modification of interracial interaction disability: An application of status characteristics theory. *American Sociological Review* 37:643–657.

Cook, Karen S. 1975. Expectations, evaluations, and equity. *American Sociological Review* 40:372–388.

Cook, Karen S., Karen A. Hegtvedt, and Toshio Yamagishi. 1988. Structural inequality, legitimation, and reactions to inequity in exchange networks. Pp. 291–308 in *Status Generalization,* ed. Murray A. Webster and Martha Foschi. Stanford, CA: Stanford University Press.

Della Fave, L. Richard. 1980. The meek shall not inherit the earth. *American Sociological Review* 45:955–971.

———. 1986. Toward an explication of the legitimation process. *Social Forces* 65:477–500.

Dornbusch, Sanford M., and W. Richard Scott. 1975. *Evaluation and the Exercise of Authority.* San Francisco: Jossey-Bass.

Dovidio, John F., Clifford E. Brown, Karen Heltman, Steven L. Ellyson, and Caroline F. Keating. 1988. Power displays between women and men in discussions of gender-linked tasks: A multichannel study. *Journal of Personality and Social Psychology* 55:580–587.

Dovidio, John F., and Steven L. Ellyson. 1982. Decoding visual dominance behavior: Attributions of power based on relative percentages of looking while speaking and looking while listening. *Social Psychology Quarterly* 45:106–113.

———. 1985. Patterns of visual dominance behavior in humans. Pp. 129–150 in *Power, Dominance, and Nonverbal Behavior,* ed. S. Ellyson and J. Dovidio. New York: Springer-Verlag.

Driskell, James E., and Brian Mullen. 1990. Status, expectations, and behavior: A meta-analytic review and test of the theory. *Personality and Social Psychology Bulletin* 16:541–553.

Emerson, Richard M. 1972. Exchange theory, II: Exchange relations and networks. Pp. 58–87 in *Sociological Theories in Progress,* vol. 2, ed. J. Berger, M. Zelditch, and B. Anderson. Boston: Houghton Mifflin.

Eskilson, Arlene, and Mary G. Wiley. 1976. Sex composition and leadership in small groups. *Sociometry* 39:183–194.

Fennell, Mary L., Patricia R. Barchas, Elizabeth G. Cohen, Anne M. McMahon, and Polly Hildebrand. 1978. An alternative perspective on sex differences in organizational settings: The process of legitimation. *Sex Roles* 4:589–604.

Fisek, M. Hamit, Joseph Berger, and Robert Z. Norman. 1991. Participation in heterogeneous and homogeneous groups: A theoretical integration. *American Journal of Sociology* 97:114–142.

Fisek, M. Hamit, and Richard Ofshe. 1970. The Process of status evolution. *Sociometry* 33:327–346.

Floge, Liliane, and Deborah M. Merrill. 1986. Tokenism reconsidered: Male nurses and female physicians in a hospital setting. *Social Forces* 64:925–947.

Foschi, Martha. 1989. Status characteristics, standards, and attributions. Pp. 58–72 in *Sociological Theories in Progress: New Formulations,* ed. J. Berger, M. Zelditch, and B. Anderson. Newbury Park, CA: Sage.

———. 1991. Gender and double standards for competence. *In Gender, Interaction, and Inequality,* ed. C. Ridgeway. New York: Springer-Verlag.

Freese, Lee, and Bernard P. Cohen. 1973. Eliminating status generalization. *Sociometry* 36:177–193.

Goffman, Erving. 1956. The nature of deference and demeanor. *American Anthropologist* 58:473–502.

———. 1959. *The Presentation of Self in Everyday Life.* New York: Doubleday.

———. 1967. *Interaction Ritual.* New York: Anchor.

Goffman, Irwin W. 1957. Status consistency and preference for change in power distribution. *American Sociological Review* 22:275–281.

Hare, A. Paul, Edgar F. Borgatta, and Robert F. Bales, eds. 1955. *Small Groups: Studies in Social Interaction.* New York: Knopf.

Harrod, Wendy J. 1980. Expectations from unequal rewards. *Social Psychology Quarterly* 43:126–130.

Harvey, O. J. 1953. An experimental approach to the study of status reactions in small groups. *American Sociological Review* 18:357–367.

Homans, George C. 1961. *Social Behavior: Its Elementary Forms.* New York: Harcourt Brace.

Humphreys, Paul, and Joseph Berger. 1981. Theoretical consequences of the status characteristics formulation. *American Journal of Sociology* 86:953–983.

Johnston, Janet R. 1988. The structure of ex-spousal relations: An exercise in theoretical integration and application. Pp. 309–326, 509–510 in *Status Generalization: New Theory and Research,* ed. M. Webster, Jr., and M. Foschi. Stanford, CA: Stanford University Press.

Keating, Caroline F. 1985. Human dominance signals: The primate in us. Pp. 89–108 in *Power, Dominance, and Nonverbal Behavior,* ed. S. L. Ellyson and J. F. Dovidio. New York: Springer-Verlag.

Kollock, Peter, Philip Blumstein, and Pepper Schwartz. 1985. Sex and power in interaction. *American Sociological Review* 50:34–47.

Lee, Margaret T., and Richard Ofshe. 1981. The Impact of behavioral style and status characteristics on social influence: A test of two competing theories. *Social Psychology Quarterly* 44:73–82.

Leffler, Ann, Dair L. Gillespie, and Joseph C. Conaty. 1982. The effects of status differentiation on nonverbal behavior. *Social Psychology Quarterly* 45:153–161.

Lerner, Melvin J. 1974. The justice motive: "Equity" and "parity" among children. *Journal of Personality and Social Psychology* 29:539–550.

Lewis, Gordon H. 1972. Role differentiation. *American Sociological Review* 37:424–434.

Lineweber, David, Dorine Barr-Bryan, and Morris Zelditch, Jr. 1982. Effects of a legitimate authority's justification of inequality on the mobilization of revolutionary coalitions. Technical Report #84, Laboratory for Social Research, Stanford University.

Linton, Ralph. 1936. *The Study of Man: An Introduction.* New York: Appleton.

Lockheed, Marlaine E., and Katherine P. Hall. 1976. Conceptualizing sex as a status characteristic. *Journal of Social Issues* 32:111–124.

Markovsky, Barry, LeRoy F. Smith, and Joseph Berger. 1984. Do Status interventions persist? *American Sociological Review* 49:373–382.

Mazur Allan. 1973. Cross-species comparison of status in established small groups. *American Sociological Review* 38:111–124.

——— . 1985. A biosocial model of status in face-to-face primate groups. *Social Forces* 64:377–402.

Mazur, Allan, and Mima Cataldo. 1989. Dominance and deference in conversation. *Journal of Social Biology and Structure* 12:87–99.

McWilliams, Susan, and Philip Blumstein. 1991. Evaluative hierarchy in personal relationships. Pp. 67–88 in *Advances in Group Processes,* vol. 8, ed. E. Lawler, B. Markovsky, C. Ridgeway, and H. Walker. Greenwich, CT: JAI Press.

Mead, George H. 1934. *Mind, Self, and Society,* ed. Charles C. Morris. Chicago: University of Chicago.

Meeker, Barbara F. 1981. Expectation states and interpersonal behavior. Pp. 290–319 in *Social Psychology: Sociological Perspectives,* ed. M. Rosenberg and R. H. Turner. New York: Basic Books.

Meeker, Barbara F., and P. A. Weitzel-O'Neill. 1977. Sex roles and interpersonal behavior in task oriented groups. *American Sociological Review* 42:91–105.

Michener, H. Andrew, and Martha R. Burt. 1975. Components of "authority" as determinants of compli-

ance. *Journal of Personality and Social Psychology* 31:600–614.

Mitchell, G., and Terry L. Maple. 1985. Dominance in nonhuman primates. Pp. 49–68 in *Power, Dominance, and Nonverbal Behavior,* ed. S. Ellyson and J. Dovidio. New York: Springer-Verlag.

Moore, James C., Jr. 1968. Status and influence in small group interactions. *Sociometry* 31:47–63.

Parsons, Talcott. 1951. *The Social System.* New York: Free Press.

Parsons, Talcott, and Robert F. Bales. 1955. *Family, Socialization, and Interaction Process.* New York: Free Press.

Pugh, Meredith D., and Ralph Wahrman. 1983. Neutralizing sexism in mixed-sex groups: Do women have to be better than men? *American Journal of Sociology* 88:746–762.

Raven, Bertram J., and John R. P. French, Jr. 1958a. Group support, legitimate power, and social influence. *Journal of Personality* 26:400–409.

——— . 1958b. Legitimate power, coercive power, and observability in social influence. *Sociometry* 21:83–97.

Ridgeway, Cecilia L. 1982. Status in groups: The importance of motivation. *American Sociological Review* 47:76–88.

——— . 1987. Nonverbal behavior, dominance, and the basis of status in task groups. *American Sociological Review* 52:683–694.

——— . 1988. Gender differences in task groups: A status and legitimacy account. Pp. 188–206 in *Status Generalization,* ed. Murray Webster and Martha Foschi. Stanford, CA: Stanford University Press.

——— . 1991. The social construction of status value: Gender and other nominal characteristics. *Social Forces* 70:367–386.

Ridgeway, Cecilia L., and Joseph Berger. 1986. Expectations, legitimation, and dominance behavior in task groups. *American Sociological Review* 51:603–617.

——— . 1988. The legitimation of power and prestige orders in task groups. Pp. 207–231 in *Status Generalization,* ed. Murray A. Webster and Martha Foschi. Stanford, CA: Stanford University Press.

Ridgeway, Cecilia L., Joseph Berger, and LeRoy Smith. 1985. Nonverbal cues and status: An expectation states approach. *American Journal of Sociology* 90:955–978.

Ridgeway, Cecilia L., and David Diekema. 1989. Dominance and collective hierarchy formation in male and female task groups. *American Sociological Review* 54:79–93.

Ridgeway, Cecilia L., and Cathryn Johnson. 1990. What is the relationship between socioemotional behavior and status in task groups? *American Journal of Sociology* 95:1189–1212.

Ridgeway, Cecilia L., Cathryn Johnson, and David Diekema. 1994. External status, legitimacy, and compliance in male and female groups. *Social Forces:* 72 (June).

Riecken, Henry W. 1958. The effect of talkativeness on ability to influence group solutions of problems. *Sociometry* 21:309–321.

Riedesel, Paul L. 1974. Bales reconsidered: A critical analysis of popularity and leadership differentiation. *Sociometry* 37:557–564.

Roethlisberger, Fritz, and William J. Dickson. 1939. *Management and the Worker.* Cambridge, MA: Harvard University Press.

Rosa, Eugene, and Allan Mazur. 1979. Incipient status in small groups. *Social Forces* 58:18–37.

Sampson, Edward E. 1969. Studies in status congruence. Pp. 225–270 in *Advances in Experimental Social Psychology,* vol. 4, ed. Leonard Berkowitz. New York: Academic.

Schopler, John. 1965. Social power. Pp. 177–218 in *Advances in Experimental Social Psychology,* vol. 2, ed. Leonard Berkowitz. New York: Academic.

Shelly, Robert K. 1988. Social differentiation and social integration. Pp. 366–376 and 512–515 in *Status Generalization: New Theory and Research,* ed. M. Webster, Jr. and M. Foschi. Stanford, CA: Stanford University Press.

Sherif, Muzafer, B. Jack White, and O. J. Harvey. 1955. Status in experimentally produced groups. *American Journal of Sociology* 60:370–379.

Slater, Philip E. 1955. Role differentiation in small groups. *American Sociological Review* 20:300–310.

Smith-Lovin, Lynn, and Charles Brody. 1989. Interruptions in group discussions: The effects of gender and group composition. *American Sociological Review* 54:424–435.

Smith-Lovin, Lynn, and David R. Heise. 1988. *Analyzing Social Interaction: Advances in Affect Control Theory.* New York: Gordon & Breach.

Stewart, Penni A., and James C. Moore, Jr. 1992. Wage disparities and performance expectations. *Social Psychology Quarterly* 55:78–85.

Stolte, John F. 1983. The legitimation of structural inequality: Reformulation and test of the self-evalu-

ation argument. *American Sociological Review* 48:331–342.

Strodtbeck, Fred L., Rita M. James, and Charles Hawkins. 1957. Social status in jury deliberations. *American Sociological Review* 22:713–719.

Strodtbeck, Fred L., and Richard D. Mann. 1956. Sex role differentiation in jury deliberations. *Sociometry* 19:3–11.

Stryker, Sheldon, and Anne Statham. 1985. Symbolic interaction and role theory. Pp. 311–378 in *The Handbook of Social Psychology,* 3rd. ed., vol. 1, ed. G. Lindzey and E. Aronson. New York: Random House.

Thomas, George M., Henry A. Walker, and Morris Zelditch, Jr. 1986. Legitimacy and collective action. *Social Forces* 65:378–404.

Torrance, E. Paul. 1954. Some consequences of power differences in decision making in permanent and temporary three-man groups. Pp. 600–609 in *Small Groups,* ed. A. P. Hare, E. F. Borgatta, and R. F. Bales. New York: Knopf.

Veblen, Thorstein. [1899] 1953. *The Theory of the Leisure Class: An Economic Study of Institutions,* rev. ed. New York: New American Library.

Verba, Sidney. 1961. *Small Groups and Political Behavior.* Princeton, NJ: Princeton University Press.

Wagner, David G., Rebecca S. Ford, and Thomas W. Ford. 1986. Can gender inequalities be reduced? *American Sociological Review* 51:47–61.

Walker, Henry A., and Bernard P. Cohen. 1985. Scope statements: Imperatives for evaluating theory. *American Sociological Review* 50:288–301.

Walker, Henry A., Larry Rogers, George M. Thomas, and Morris Zelditch, Jr. 1991. Legitimating collective action: Theory and experimental results. Pp. 1–25 in *Research in Political Sociology,* vol. 5, ed. Philo C. Wasburn. Greenwich, CT: JAI Press.

Walker, Henry A., Larry Rogers, and Morris Zelditch, Jr. 1988. Legitimacy and collective action: A research note. *Social Forces* 67:216–228.

———. 1989. All or nothing: Effects of the legitimacy of persons, positions and acts. Paper presented at the Annual Meeting of the Midwest Sociological Society, St. Louis.

Walker, Henry A., George M. Thomas, and Morris Zelditch, Jr. 1986. Legitimation, endorsement and stability. *Social Forces* 64:620–643.

Weber, Max. [1921] 1946. Class, status, and party. Pp. 180–195 in *From Max Weber: Essays in Sociology,* translated and ed. H. Gerth and C. W. Mills. New York: Oxford University Press.

———. 1968. *Economy and Society,* ed. Guenther Roth and Claus Wittich. Berkeley: University of California Press.

Webster, Murray, Jr. 1977. Equating characteristics and social interaction: Two experiments. *Sociometry* 40: 41–50.

Webster, Murray, Jr., and James E. Driskell. 1978. Status generalization: A review and some new data. *American Sociological Review* 43:220–236.

Webster, Murray, Jr., and Martha Foschi. 1988. *Status generalization: New theory and research.* Stanford, CA: Stanford University Press.

Webster, Murray, Jr., and Barbara I. Sobieszek. 1974. *Sources of Self-Evaluation: A Formal Theory of Significant Others and Social Influence.* New York: Wiley.

West, Candace. 1984. When the doctor is a "lady": Power, status and gender in physician-patient exchanges. *Symbolic Interaction* 7:87–106.

West, Candace, and Angela Garcia. 1988. Conversational shift work: A study of topical transition between men and women. *Social Problems* 35:551–575.

Whyte, William F. 1943. *Street Corner Society.* Chicago: University of Chicago Press.

Wilson, Edward O. 1975. *Sociobiology: The New Synthesis.* Cambridge, MA: Harvard University.

Wood, Wendy, and Steven J. Karten. 1986. Sex differences in interaction style as a product of perceived sex differences in competence. *Journal of Personality and Social Psychology* 50:341–347.

Zelditch, Morris, Jr. 1955. Role differentiation in the nuclear family: A comparative study. Pp. 307–352 in *Family, Socialization and Interaction Processes,* ed. Talcott Parsons and Robert F. Bales. Glencoe, IL: Free Press.

Zelditch, Morris, Jr., Patrick Lauderdale, and Stephen Stublarec. 1980. How are inconsistencies between status and ability resolved? *Social Forces* 58:1025–1043.

Zelditch, Morris, Jr., and Henry A. Walker. 1984. Legitimacy and the stability of authority. Pp. 1–25 in *Advances in Group Processes,* vol. 1, ed. Edward J. Lawler. Greenwich, CT: JAI Press.

CHAPTER 12

Social Dilemmas

TOSHIO YAMAGISHI

The term *social dilemmas* may be unfamiliar to some readers, but the various problems to which it refers, such as environmental pollution, overexploitation of natural resources, desertification of farm land, and protectionist trading practices, are familiar to us all. Central to the problems we call social dilemmas is that we (as individual actors or as collective actors, such as corporations or countries) often impose the costs of our own "selfish" behavior on others. We often pursue our own self-interest without regard to others. Ironically, as a result of such selfish behavior, we create situations in which all eventually suffer.

In this chapter, we begin with an overview of social dilemmas and then address whether cooperation is possible among egoists in such situations, a question that is critical in distinguishing the various approaches to research on social dilemmas. We examine possible answers to this and related questions and conclude with a proposal for future research. Since our discussion focuses on only a few theoretically relevant issues, we do not cover the range of empirical findings concerning social dilemmas. Interested readers are referred to various reviews on this topic: Dawes (1980), Edney and Harper (1978a), Messick and Brewer (1983), Orbell and Dawes (1981), Stroebe and Frey (1982), and Yamagishi (1989a).

SOCIAL DILEMMAS AND RELATED ISSUES

An example will help illustrate the nature of a social dilemma. In mainland China, the phrase "rice in big pot" is often used to describe the attitude of state workers. When the pot is big enough,

the amount of rice one person eats does not seem to affect the amount left in the pot to be shared with everyone else. "Big Pot" is an analogy for the state or government. In China (at least until the recent economic reform) pay is guaranteed to workers by the government regardless of the factory's productivity: the factory will not go bankrupt, nor will workers be fired for lack of productivity. There is no individual (at least material) incentive for laborers to work hard. Most of the workers would prefer to have a higher standard of living, which is possible if they all work harder. However, a single worker's hard work will not make any difference in his/her standard of living, and thus he/she has no material incentive to work harder. As a result, single workers fail to achieve a higher standard of living despite their individual willingness to work harder to achieve it. Most of us, some of the time, eat rice from a big pot. For example, when we use hair spray that contains aerosols, we are eating rice from the big pot we call Earth.

Formally, a social dilemma is defined as a group structure

> . . . *involving individually dominating strategies that converge on a deficient equilibrium. A strategy is dominating if its personal payoffs are superior to those of all other strategies no matter what others do; an outcome is "deficient" when that outcome is less preferred by* all *choosers to some other outcomes; such an outcome in a social dilemma will, however, be in equilibrium because no individual chooser has an egoistic incentive to depart from selecting a dominating strategy. (Dawes 1991).*

In the above example, not working hard is the dominant strategy (individual workers have no incentive to work harder), which leads to the deficient equilibrium of sharing the lower standard of living (which is less preferred than a higher standard of living).

Since the definition of social dilemmas introduced above is highly abstract, it applies to a wide range of social problems. On the other hand, each social problem, while fitting this definition of a social dilemma, has its own special twist. As a result, social dilemmas have been studied from different perspectives, often under different rubrics. We review these divergent perspectives below.

Tragedy of the Commons and the Resource Dilemma

The single greatest influence on the subsequent development of social dilemmas research is G. Hardin's "The Tragedy of the Commons" (1968), based on earlier work on the overgrazing of common pastures in England by Lloyd (1977; originally published in 1833). In it, Hardin articulated the logic of social dilemmas. Like "rice in big pot," Hardin's tragedy of the commons concerns a collective disaster resulting from individuals pursuing their own self-interest: herders increase the number of livestock that graze on a common pasture for their own profit until the commons can no longer sustain the animals, destroying the ecological stability of the pasture. Because many contemporary environmental problems are concerned with the proper use of the commons—air, water, forest, and so on—this essay stimulated the development of social dilemmas research in various fields. More recent research using the commons paradigm is called "commons dilemma" or "resource dilemma" research. In many experiments using this paradigm, subjects freely consume a regenerating common resource (e.g., Allison and Messick 1985; Baird 1982; Brann and Foddy 1988; Brechner 1977; Brewer and Kramer 1986; Cass and Edney 1978; Kramer and Brewer 1984, 1986; Kramer, McClintock, and Messick 1986; Messick and McClelland 1983; Messick et al. 1983; Samuelson and Messick 1986a, 1986b; Samuelson et al. 1984; Sato 1985, 1987; Sato, Toda, and Yamagishi 1985; Stern 1978;

Umino, Iwamoto, and Ueda 1985; Wit 1989; Wit and Wilke 1988).

Provision of Public Goods and the Free Rider Problem

The provision of a public good often involves a social dilemma. A public good is something everyone can enjoy regardless of whether he/she has contributed to its provision. Examples are a pollution-free environment and a social movement organized to halt pollution. Everyone who lives in an unpolluted area can enjoy the clean environment whether or not he/she has worked to stop pollution. Public broadcasting is another example. People need not subscribe to public broadcasting programs to enjoy them. One way of looking at the relationship between the provision of public goods and social dilemmas is by considering the "free rider problem." When an individual's action is not critical to the provision of a public good, each individual is tempted to free ride on other members' efforts to provide and maintain the public good. However, if everyone tries to free ride while expecting others will do the necessary work, the public good will not be provided. That is, in the provision of a public good, free riding (not contributing to the provision of a public good) is an individually dominant choice, but the outcome (e.g., a polluted environment, a failed social movement, or lack of funding for public broadcasting) of individuals taking the dominant choice is a deficient choice.

The provision of a public good may not always involve a social dilemma. Consider, for example, industrial pollution in a society where penalties for pollution do not exist or are not strong enough to deter pollution. Two groups of people are involved: those who benefit from pollution (industrialists) and those who suffer (the general public). This is a one-sided game; only the first group can choose whether or not to control pollution. Although the general public benefits from pollution control, and the total benefit far exceeds the total cost of controlling pollution, those who have a choice (whether or not to control pollution) do not face a social dilemma. The few industrialists can solve the problem, but the general public cannot. In contrast, pollution caused by most everybody—such as water pollution caused by the use of household detergents—constitutes a social dilemma. Everyone who shares a closed water system has the capacity and incentive to pollute (e.g., to use detergent to wash clothes). Each benefits a little bit (i.e., spending less time for cleaner outputs) from using chemical detergent rather than a less polluting soap. Furthermore, if each pursues this individual benefit, the water system will be polluted, causing everyone to suffer.

Collective Action

As indicated above, industrial pollution need not constitute a social dilemma, because the general public that suffers from the pollution is not causing it. However, the public may organize a movement against industrial pollution. They may negotiate with the polluters or influence the legislature to create laws against pollution. Organizing a social movement, however, involves a social dilemma. In fact, the terms *collective action* and *social dilemmas* are functionally equivalent, the former commonly used by political scientists and sociologists and the latter by social psychologists. In our example, the collective action problem of organizing a social movement is subject to the dynamics of a social dilemma. Everyone in the polluted area benefits if a sufficient number of people join the movement to stop pollution. Failure of the movement is a deficient outcome; that is, it is better to participate and live in a cleaner environment than not to participate and live in a polluted environment. However, once a sufficient number of people have participated and succeeded in controlling pollution, every one, even those who have not participated in the movement, can enjoy the cleaner environment. This sufficient number is often called a "provision point." (For the effect of provision points, see Dawes, Orbell, and van de Kragt 1986; Marwell and Ames 1979; van de Kragt, Orbell, and Dawes 1983; Yamagishi and Sato 1986.) People who went on vacation while others were demon-

strating will enjoy the cleaner environment as much as those who participated, expending their time, resources, and energy. And what if the movement failed? Everyone suffers, but those who participated suffer more because they wasted their time, resources, and energy. Thus *not* joining the movement is a dominant choice. But if people take the dominant choice (i.e., not to participate), the movement will fail and they will suffer from a polluted environment. Most social movements or collective actions based on voluntary participation involve this type of social dilemma.

While the theory of social dilemmas is largely abstract and laboratory-tested, social movements research is commonly substantive. Marwell, Oliver, and associates (Marwell and Oliver 1984; Marwell, Oliver, and Prahl 1988; Oliver 1980, 1984; Oliver and Marwell 1988; Oliver, Marwell, and Teixeira 1985) attempted to integrate these two lines of research.[1] Social dilemmas and social movements may be linked especially by the resource mobilization perspective, which attempts to account for the incentive problems associated with participation (Klandermans 1984; Klandermans and Oegema 1987).

Demand Revelation

Public broadcasting, as mentioned above, is an example of a public good. Often, people who watch public television programs do not pay the subscription fee. A unique situation exists in Japan, where those who own a television set are required by law, whether or not they actually watch public television programs, to pay a subscription fee to the public television station, and the majority do pay this fee. The free rider problem is thus relatively minor. However, mandatory subscription to the public television station creates another problem: it is not fair for a person who owns a television set but never watches public television programs to be required to pay for them. Voluntary subscription in the United States creates the problem of free riding; mandatory subscription in Japan, while solving the problem of free riding, is unfair. One way of solving this dilemma between free riding and fairness is mandatory subscription with variable rates of payment. People would be required to pay, but the level of payment would be determined by how often they watch the programs. More generally, all members of a group are "taxed" for the provision of a public good, but the amount of tax is determined by the individual's "demand" for it. If this method is used, no one can free ride (since cooperation is mandatory) and anyone who does not benefit (or benefits less) from the public good will not be excessively "taxed." This method works only if each member honestly reveals his/her demand for the public good. However, each can evade or lower his/her "tax" by underreporting his/her true demand. A person who actually enjoys public television programs may still say that he/she seldom watches them and therefore be required to pay little or nothing. If people underreport their true demand, fair allocation of the cost for provision of the public good becomes impossible. The issue of demand revelation has been addressed primarily by economists.

Social Traps

Thus far we have examined social dilemmas and related problems from the point of view of rational decision making. Some people consider the same problem from the point of view of learning theory. Rather than concentrating on the decision processes that unfold in a social dilemma, behaviorists try to avoid the cognitive "black box" altogether. They draw our attention instead to the patterns of reinforcers inherent in a dilemma that rewards defecting behavior and punishes cooperative behavior (Cross and Guyer 1980; Platt 1973). Distinct from a cognitive model, it is the actor's behavioral experience that determines future behavioral choices. In social traps, people are reinforced to take actions that are immediately rewarding but indirectly punishing. Because the punishment is indirect, it does not deter people from taking action. The indirectness is sometimes a result of aggregation effects (e.g., the hair spray one uses barely affects one's own health) and sometimes a result of temporal effects (e.g., it is not us but our children who suffer the consequences of an enlarged ozone hole). An

experiment by Messick and McClelland (1983) showed that when temporal effects are added to social dilemmas, the problem becomes more difficult to resolve.

Although learning theoretic perspectives have played a relatively minor role in social dilemmas research, a series of recent studies by Macy (1989, 1991a, 1991b) suggests the potentially critical role of learning. Macy demonstrated, theoretically and through a series of computer simulations, that it is sometimes possible for actors to escape from a social trap when they act on the basis of a learning theoretic principle of "win-stay, lose-change" (i.e., when they change their choices only if the reward they receive fails to reach a certain level).

Social Loafing

The lack of cooperative behavior in social dilemmas has often been interpreted in terms of a motivational loss, rather than the response to individually dominant incentives. "Social loafing" refers to a decrease in effort by individuals while performing a joint task, as compared to the situation in which they perform individually. In Ringelmann's original study (1913), it was noted that subjects did not pull as hard on a rope when several subjects pulled together as when they pulled alone. Several studies have demonstrated this effect in a variety of situations involving both cognitive and physical tasks (see Harkins and Szymanski 1987 for a review). The dynamic is important and related to social dilemmas because it offers another perspective on free riding behavior (see Kerr 1983 for the relationship between social dilemmas and social loafing).

Helping

What is called "diffusion of responsibility" in social psychological studies of helping behavior may be interpreted as a social dilemma, as suggested by Fleishman (1980).[2] If we adopt the theoretical position that cooperation in social dilemmas is basically an altruistic behavior (i.e., behavior based on concern for others' well-being), then social dilemma research is actually the study of altruistic behavior. What distinguishes social dilemmas research from the study of helping behavior? Social dilemmas researchers typically emphasize nonaltruistic behavior as a source of cooperation, whereas those who study helping behavior are more concerned with altruism. The focus of helping research is understanding and predicting altruistic behavior: the voluntary and intentional act of rewarding others in spite of the cost of such behavior. In a recent discussion of altruism, Piliavin and Charng (1990) concluded that a paradigm shift occurred in the 1980s regarding the place of altruism research in social psychology. The existence of altruism as a motive independent of self-interest is less questioned, and the focus has turned toward identifying the emergence of altruism (sociologically) and the social psychological factors that promote or inhibit altruistic behavior. Although some social dilemmas researchers are interested in finding and explaining individual differences in the degree to which people care for others (discussed below), the trend in recent research is toward explaining self-interested sources of cooperation.

MAJOR TYPES OF SOCIAL DILEMMAS: PRISONER'S DILEMMA, CHICKEN, AND ASSURANCE

The core of the social dilemmas problem is in the incentive structure. Group members end up with a less desirable consequence collectively insofar as they individually pursue their own self-interest. This incentive structure, which characterizes social dilemmas, is often called a mixed-motive situation. Although systematic studies of social dilemmas began fairly recently (about the mid-1970s), research on the two-person, mixed-motive situation has a long history in the form of experimental gaming research, especially research on the "prisoner's dilemma," named for the mixed-motive situation illustrated by the following story (Luce and Raifa 1957, 95):

Two suspects are taken into custody and separated. The district attorney is certain that they are guilty of a specific crime, but he does not have adequate evidence to convict them at a trial. He points out to each prisoner that each has two alternatives: to

confess to the crime the police are sure they have done, or not to confess. If they both do not confess, then the district attorney states he will book them on some very minor trumped-up charge such as petty larceny and illegal possession of a weapon, and they will both receive minor punishments; if they both confess they will be prosecuted, but he will recommend less than the most severe sentence; but if one confesses and the other does not, then the confessor will receive lenient treatment for turning state's evidence whereas the latter will get 'the book' slapped at him.

An example of the consequences of the two suspects' actions is shown in Figure 12.1 on page 316. Each cell of this matrix shows what will happen to each (the lower-left entry of each cell is A's outcome and the upper-right represents B's outcome) when they independently decide whether or not to confess. It is clear that each gets a lighter sentence for confessing than for not confessing, no matter what the other does. The pure self-interest of each suspect, leaving aside his fear of personal retaliation or guilt for betraying his partner, is thus to confess; that is, confessing is a *dominant strategy* for each suspect. If they both care only about their own interests and decide to confess, each will get a sentence of ten years. This is, of course, not as desirable for each as the sentence of only two years that each could obtain if neither confessed. The outcome of this prisoner's dilemma, which is in equilibrium, is thus *deficient*.

Substituting a nation for the individual actor, two equally powerful countries may become locked in an arms race due to the prisoner's dilemma dynamic. The noncooperative choice of military buildup unfortunately becomes the individually preferred strategy. While both countries would like to see mutual arms reduction, neither can unilaterally reduce its own spending in fear that the other will not, in which case the country's safety would be threatened.

Not all mixed-motive situations between two people are represented by a prisoner's dilemma. In the following discussion, C refers to a cooperative action and D to a noncooperative (or defecting) action. A combination of the two letters indicates the outcome of the joint actions for the first person;

B'S CHOICE

	C: Not Confess	D: Confess
A'S CHOICE C: Not Confess	2 years / 2 years	1 year / 99 years
D: Confess	99 years / 1 year	10 years / 10 years

FIGURE 12.1 An example of a prisoner's dilemma payoff matrix. Entries of the cells are different from the matrix presented by Luce and Raifa (1957).

that is, CD is the outcome for the one who cooperates when the other does not, DC is the outcome for the one who does not cooperate when the other does, and so on. The prisoner's dilemma is formally defined as a situation that satisfies the following two conditions: (1) CC > DD (i.e., mutual cooperation is more beneficial than mutual noncooperation); (2) DC > CC and DD > CD (i.e., each is better off for not cooperating than for cooperating, regardless of the other's action). All mixed-motive situations meet the first condition: mutual cooperation is better than mutual noncooperation. However, the second condition is met only partially in some mixed-motive situations.

For example, in the mixed-motive situation called a "chicken game," (noncooperation) is an individually better choice than C (cooperation) when the other actor cooperates. However, the direction of this inequality is reversed when the other does not cooperate. Here, DC > CC but DD < CD. Of course, the first condition, CC > DD, exists in a chicken game as well. The name "chicken" comes from the old game played by rebellious teenagers: two cars race at high speed toward each other and the first to swerve out of the way is deemed the loser. Although both swerving (CC) is not very desirable for either, it is better than DD, a lethal crash. A driver waits until the last moment for some sign that the other is going to swerve. If he/she sees such a sign, he/she will not swerve (i.e., choose D), because DC (the driver wins the game and the

respect of his/her peers) is better than a draw. On the other hand, if he/she does not see a sign that the other is going to swerve, he/she will swerve at the last moment to avoid the crash, since CD (being ridiculed as a chicken) is better than DD (being killed in a crash).

In a chicken game, one of the two inequalities in the second condition of the prisoner's dilemma is reversed. In another mixed-motive situation, called an "assurance game," this reversal occurs in the other inequality. In an assurance game, D is a better choice than C when the other actor does not cooperate; however, when the other cooperates, C becomes a better choice than D. That is, DD > CD but DC < CC. The earlier story of the prisoner's dilemma becomes an example of an assurance game if the district attorney cannot book the suspects for minor charges: if they both refuse to confess, they will be acquitted. If the suspects trust that their partner will not confess, it is in their own interest not to confess (CC > DC). However, if they do not trust their partner, it is better for them to confess (DD > CD). Whether or not the suspects can trust each other is critical. The "bandwagon effect" provides an example of an N-person assurance game. A return for the money or time one contributes to an election campaign can be expected only when the candidate wins; otherwise the contribution is wasted. An individual's payoff resulting from his/her contribution to an election campaign thus depends on how many others are expected to contribute to the campaign. An assurance that many others will contribute is critical.

The distinction between prisoner's dilemmas, chicken games, and assurance games can be based on the temptation for free riding. Whether or not the temptation to free ride always exists distinguishes N-person prisoner's dilemmas from other forms of social dilemmas. Consider the collective maintenance of an irrigation system in a small village where every villager's cooperation is necessary. If one villager stops cooperating, the system will not be maintained properly. As a result, all villagers will suffer, including those who failed to cooperate. This is an example of an N-person assurance game. It is impossible to free ride on the maintenance of the irrigation system, since the public good (the irrigation system) is destroyed as soon as one person stops cooperating. The very act of free riding (i.e., not cooperating in the maintenance of the system) destroys the public good. Therefore, each villager is no longer tempted to free ride.[3] In contrast, the temptation to free ride in an N-person chicken game is even greater than in an N-person prisoner's dilemma. Imagine an abalone fishing village in which each villager has two choices: voluntarily limiting his/her own harvest (C) or harvesting as much as he/she wishes (D). If no one cooperates and all villagers harvest as much as they wish, there will soon be very little abalone left in the area, and fishing will no longer be desirable. Villagers will find jobs other than fishing. This means cooperation (not to fish abalone) is preferable to noncooperation (to fish) when everyone defects. On the other hand, if everyone voluntarily restrains him/herself, there will be plenty of abalone in the area, and each villager will be very much tempted to harvest a lot since it is easy to do so.

Social dilemmas have often been conceived as N-person prisoner's dilemmas (Dawes 1980) in which noncooperation is the dominant choice. Recently, however, the concept of social dilemmas has been extended to include situations that do not strictly meet these two conditions. In particular, some social dilemmas have the structure of a chic-

ken or assurance game, rather than that of a prisoner's dilemma (Liebrand 1986; Taylor 1987; Yamagishi 1991, 1993b).

COOPERATION AMONG EGOISTS

The Fundamental Question and Major Theoretical Approaches

One of the most fundamental theoretical issues surrounding social dilemmas is whether or not cooperation is possible among egoists. Do people need to be concerned with the welfare of others to act cooperatively (i.e., in a way that improves others' welfare)? In other words, do we need to be altruistic to be cooperative? This is the fundamental question in the research on social dilemmas. How it is answered distinguishes the major theoretical approaches to social dilemmas.[4]

If the answer to this question is negative, that is, if it is assumed that people cooperate in a social dilemma situation only to the degree they care for others, then the relevant research questions are either (1) about the individual or situational differences in altruism (i.e., in the degree to which people care for others' well-being vis-à-vis their own) or (2) about the effect of changes in the incentive structure on people's cooperative behavior. The first is the question addressed by researchers interested in *social motivation* or *social orientation*. This is the *motivational approach* to social dilemmas. The second is the question addressed primarily by economists. Economists tend to assume that people are not altruistic and therefore are inherently uncooperative in situations that are not self-beneficial. For them, the only possible way to resolve the problem posed by social dilemmas is to alter the incentive structure of the dilemma by, for example, rewarding cooperators and punishing noncooperators. Identifying the kinds of structural changes that are easy to introduce and effective in resolving a social dilemma, then, becomes the central task. This is the *structural approach* to social dilemmas.

On the other hand, there are researchers who answer to the fundamental question positively.

These researchers assume cooperation is possible in a social dilemma even when actors are purely self-interested. This positive response is based on one of the following three, theoretically distinct, approaches. First, even egoists can and do act cooperatively if they understand the need for mutual cooperation to ensure their own self-interest and, at the same time, can trust each other. This is the *goal/expectation approach,* based on the theory proposed by Pruitt and Kimmel (1977). Second, egoists may act cooperatively as a means to induce others to cooperate when the benefits generated by others' induced cooperation outweigh the costs of their own cooperation. This is the *strategy approach.* Finally, egoists may act cooperatively when they sanction each other, forcing each other into cooperation. This is called the *norm-formation approach,* since voluntarily based mutual sanctioning constitutes the core of the social norm. The goal/expectation approach and the strategy approach are discussed here and the motivational approach below. Issues related to the structural approach and the norm-formation approach are discussed later in the chapter.

One-Shot and Iterated Dilemmas

The last three approaches introduced above assume that cooperation is possible among egoists. They also assume that the same group members repeatedly face the same social dilemma. In other words, the relevance of these approaches is greatly reduced in "one-shot" social dilemmas, those that take place only once among the same set of people. Let us examine the significance of whether a social dilemma is one-shot or "iterated" (i.e., repeated). Imagine that you are participating in the following experiment of a dyadic prisoner's dilemma. You are given $5 as a reward for your participation. Then you are asked whether or not you would like to give the $5 to your partner. If you give the $5 to your partner, the experimenter will match the money and your partner will receive $10. Your partner also makes the same decision. If both you and your partner decide to give, each will get $10. That is, CC = 10. This is better than the DD out-

come of $5, in which neither gives. You will never see your partner, before, during, or after the experiment. Each person makes the decision independently, without knowledge of the other's decision. What would be your decision: to cooperate and give your $5, or not to cooperate and keep your money?

Suppose you are a purely egoistic person, who has no sympathy or compassion for others. Then you will not cooperate. Cooperation among egoists in this experimental situation is theoretically impossible. In other words, you are not a pure egoist if you decide to cooperate in this situation. You may be altruistic (meaning you are concerned with your partner's well-being), or your decision may be influenced by a social norm that prescribes cooperation in such a situation.

But what if you are told you will face the same decision task many times? You and your partner will make the decision once a day until one of the two of you dies. If you defect while your partner cooperates, you can free ride and get $15 instead of $10. However, this kind of exploitive relationship will not last long since your partner, noticing that his/her good will is being exploited, will soon stop cooperating, either in retaliation or in self-defense. Pruitt and Kimmel's (1977) theory explains what will happen when people experience mutual defection and wish to get out of the vicious cycle of mutual defection.

Goal/Expectation Approach

Pruitt and Kimmel (1977), after reviewing over a thousand experimental gaming studies, proposed the goal/expectation theory. This theory is based on their examination of experimental studies in which subjects repeatedly faced a prisoner's dilemma-like situation with the same partner. Typically, subjects in such experiments become less cooperative as they repeatedly experience the prisoner's dilemma-like situation. During this initial phase, Pruitt and Kimmel argue, subjects are directly responding to the incentive structure typically represented by a payoff matrix such as the one shown in Figure 12.1. That is, subjects tend to isolate each trial, in the early phases, as if it were a one-shot game. Since defection is the dominant strategy of a one-shot game, subjects eventually face a situation of mutual defection. When they experience this absurd and frustrating situation of mutual defection, they come to realize that mutual cooperation is a must. They also realize mutual cooperation is impossible to achieve insofar as their partner is unwilling to cooperate, and that their partner will not cooperate insofar as they themselves are unwilling to cooperate. That is, having experienced the absurdity of mutual defection, subjects come to adopt the goal of mutual cooperation, rather than the goal of exploitation. They also come to realize that their own cooperation is necessary to achieve that goal.

That people who have realized the absurdity of mutual defection eventually adopt a goal of mutual cooperation does not mean they became altruistic. They cooperate not because they become concerned with their partner's well-being, but because they believe cooperation will produce better outcomes for themselves than defection. For example, however much you hate your enemy, maintaining nuclear peace is better than starting a mutually destructive nuclear war. This is one basis for cooperation among egoists; each egoist realizes that his/her own cooperation is a necessary condition for mutual cooperation, which is better than mutual defection.

However, this is not enough to move them to act cooperatively. They may be afraid their cooperative move to achieve mutual cooperation will be wasted or, even worse, exploited if the partner is not willing to cooperate as well. Using Arneson's (1982) terms, by experiencing the absurd situation of mutual defection, subjects in repeated prisoner's dilemma games become "reluctant" or "nervous" cooperators. Nervous and reluctant cooperators recognize the importance of mutual cooperation in mixed-motive situations but are hesitant to cooperate when others are not cooperating.

There are two possible reasons for this. First, they may be afraid their efforts for acting cooperatively may be wasted if others do not cooperate. For example, people will join the election campaign of a candidate who seems unlikely to attract much support. Arneson (1982) calls these people "nervous cooperators." Second, they may be afraid their cooperative initiatives will be exploited by noncooperators. For example, a price-fixing cartel (although it is illegal in many countries) will fail if members are afraid others would undersell. If some corporations lower their prices, those that do not will lose their share and eventually be driven out of the market. Arneson (1982) calls those who are afraid they may be exploited by noncooperators "reluctant cooperators." As long as nervous or reluctant cooperators are convinced that others will cooperate, they will cooperate. If they cannot trust others, they will not cooperate. Results of many experimental studies show that trust (and expectations that others cooperate) has a strong effect in promoting cooperation in social dilemmas (Dawes, McTavish, and Shaklee 1977; Marwell and Ames 1979; Messick et al. 1983; Sato and Yamagishi 1984; Tyszka and Grzelak 1976; Yamagishi 1986a, 1988c; Yamagishi and Sato 1986). However, there is some evidence that the effect of trust diminishes as subjects repeatedly experience other subjects' real actions and as group size increases (J. Fox and Guyer 1977; Sato 1988).

Sociologists may see the similarity of Pruitt and Kimmel's goal/expectation theory to the logic Hobbes (1965) used to explain the origin of government, at least as it is interpreted by Taylor (1976, 1982). The "war of all against all" assumed by Hobbes to be the logical state of anarchy without a central authority or Leviathan is a good example of a social dilemma. In this social dilemma, attacking or exploiting others whenever there is an opportunity to do so is the noncooperative choice and refraining from doing so even when there is an opportunity is the cooperative choice. This state of ubiquitous civil war as a social dilemma is not desirable. Using our terms, people prefer mutual cooperation over mutual defection; people are willing to disarm themselves and refrain from attacking others insofar as others do the same and the threat of being attacked by others is removed. The guarantee that others will also cooperate is critical. This guarantee is based on trust for Pruitt and

Kimmel. It is generated by the government for Hobbes.

Strategy Approach

We have now examined one positive answer to the fundamental question, based on the goal/expectation approach. Are other positive answers possible? In other words: Is cooperation possible among egoists when they cannot trust each other? A positive answer to this question is provided by the strategy approach.

Suppose you are a nervous or reluctant cooperator. You understand that an attempt to free ride on your partner will lead to mutual defection. You also understand that the only way out of this mutual defection is to achieve mutual cooperation. You are willing to cooperate to achieve mutual cooperation if you are guaranteed that your partner will not exploit your cooperation. However, you don't trust your partner. What can you do? You need a guarantee that your partner will also cooperate. This guarantee may come from trusting your partner, if you can trust him/her. Alternatively, it could come from your power to control your partner's action. If you have the power to force your partner to cooperate, you don't need to trust him/her. The question is: Can you force or induce your partner to cooperate? Let us call actions intended to affect a partner's choice "strategic action."

There is a large body of literature on the effectiveness of various strategies for achieving mutual cooperation in prisoner's dilemmas. Strategies are decision rules prescribing when to cooperate and when to defect. One of the simplest strategies is an unconditional cooperation strategy: "Always cooperate, no matter what." Another simple strategy is the unconditional defection strategy: Always defect. Other strategies are conditional cooperation strategies: Cooperate when certain conditions exist; otherwise, do not cooperate. Conditional cooperation strategies are meaningful only in iterated (repeated among the same members) social dilemmas or, using the game theoretic term, in *supergames*. The term *supergame* implies that people apply their strategies to a series of decisions as they go through a social dilemma "game" repeatedly, rather than responding to each game separately and independently from other games in the series.

One of the simplest conditional cooperation strategies is called the *tit-for-tat* strategy, which states: "Cooperate when and only when the partner cooperated on the previous round; otherwise, do not cooperate." This strategy, despite its simplicity, has proven very effective in inducing the partner to take cooperative actions (cf. Axelrod 1984; Oskamp 1971; Wilson 1971). The key to the success of the tit-for-tat strategy is that it removes CD and DC outcomes from the payoff matrix; the tit-for-tat strategy responds with D to the partner's D and with C to the partner's C. Adhering to the tit-for-tat strategy, the practical choice for the partner is reduced to CC and DD. Using Yamagishi's (1986b) terminology, an *action interdependency* is introduced between the partner's action and your action by using the tit-for-tat strategy. By sticking with the tit-for-tat strategy, you alter the incentive structure for your partner such that the cooperative choice is more beneficial than the noncooperative choice to the partner him/herself.

The use of conditional cooperation strategies such as the tit-for-tat strategy can thus be one source of a positive answer to the fundamental question. Even if people do not trust each other, they may still achieve mutual cooperation if they adopt a conditional cooperation strategy such as tit for tat in a social dilemma supergame. Of course, you cannot exploit your partner with the tit-for-tat strategy, but what you, as a nervous or reluctant cooperator, achieve is the sought-after mutual cooperation.

The effectiveness of the tit-for-tat strategy is based on its capability to transform the incentive structure (Watabe 1992b; Yamagishi 1993b). Suppose two people, A and B, face the repeated prisoner's dilemma situation represented in Figure 12.2a. Between C and D, D is the dominant choice. However, if people give up unconditional cooperation (C) and replace it with the tit-for-tat strategy, the long-term outcomes of the choice of tit-for-tat and D (instead of C and D) is now represented in Figure 12.2b. In this figure, which represents the long-term outcomes of choosing between the tit-for-tat

B'S CHOICE

		C	D
A'S CHOICE	C	2, 2	0, 3
	D	3, 0	1, 1

FIGURE 12.2a   Original prisoner's dilemma.

B'S CHOICE

		TFT	D
A'S CHOICE	TFT	2, 2	1, 1
	D	1, 1	1, 1

FIGURE 12.2b   The long-term payoff structure when tit for tat is applied.

strategy and the unconditional defection strategy, tit-for-tat is clearly a better choice than D. The tit-for-tat strategy is effective in producing mutual cooperation because it transforms the incentive structure with regard to the long-term outcomes.

Limitations of Strategies as a Solution to the Social Dilemmas.   Achieving mutual cooperation among egoists through the use of strategies such as tit for tat has several serious limitations. First, there must be the expectation of a long-term relationship between the partners. Strategic actions are meaningful only in supergames; if there is no future in the relationship, there is no chance you will be repaid for favors given to your partner. Second, as Dawes (1980) points out, the effectiveness of the strategic solution is primarily limited to dyadic relations. When there are more partners it is difficult to detect who is cooperating and who is defecting. Furthermore, the effectiveness of one's action is distributed across many partners so that it does not have a strong impact on specific others. Finally, strategic actions may have negative "externalities" (Yamagishi 1989b). If you decide to defect to punish a defector, other cooperators might interpret your strategic action as exploitive and might try to punish you by defecting themselves.

Trigger Strategy.   The above discussion leads to the conclusion that the effectiveness of strategic actions—actions aimed at achieving one's goal by inducing changes in other people—is mainly limited to dyadic relations. However, some game theorists believe an effective conditional cooperation

strategy can be developed for N-person social dilemmas (Friedman 1986; Taylor 1976, 1982). One possible strategy might be the *trigger strategy* (Friedman 1986): "Cooperate if and only if all others cooperate; otherwise, do not cooperate." This is similar to the tit-for-tat strategy in the sense that if everybody else has adopted this strategy, it is individually better for one to cooperate than not. Any attempt to free ride, then, triggers an avalanche of defection and immediately produces unanimous defection. In addition, once unanimous cooperation is achieved, no one has an incentive to defect. This is called the *Nash equilibrium* in game theory; no one has an incentive unilaterally to change his/her own action. Furthermore, the risk of being exploited does not exist with this strategy. When there is at least one other member who is not willing to cooperate, you will not cooperate either; then you will not be exploited by the free riders.[5]

In an experiment using a ten-person group lasting over ten days, Watabe (1992a) demonstrated that many subjects, after experiencing a decline in the cooperation level, began to adopt an unconditional cooperation strategy. However, this invited free riding of a few group members, and the general cooperation level declined again, presumably in response to the few free riders. After this failure of the unconditional cooperation strategy, group members started to adopt "tougher" conditional cooperation strategies (requiring that a sizable majority cooperate before cooperating oneself). These strategies approximate the trigger strategy. However, follow-up studies (Watabe 1992b) indicate that the trigger strategy is not always likely to be adopted voluntarily by group members in a social dilemma supergame because many are afraid there will be some "unreasonable" people who would not cooperate even under the "trigger" incentive structure. Requiring everyone to cooperate as a mandate for the provision of a public good can effectively eliminate the incentive for free riding, but for many subjects it is too risky, since one person's defection can change unanimous cooperation into unanimous defection. In sum, the trigger strategy may be effective beyond dyadic relations, but people are not likely to adopt it since it is so precarious.

Prisoner's Dilemma Network. As discussed above, the effectiveness of conditional cooperation strategies such as tit for tat may not be generalized easily beyond mutually committed, long-term dyadic relations. In general, experimental studies have not deviated from this narrow sphere. Typically, two subjects are forced to interact repeatedly, without the opportunity to leave the relation or change partners (for exceptions see Marwell and Schmitt 1972; Orbell and Dawes 1992; Schuessler 1989). However, a new interest is emerging that examines dyadic relations embedded in a larger network of group members. Sometimes two parties are locked into an isolated dyadic relationship in which neither has alternatives, as were the United States and the Soviet Union during the Cold War. More commonly, we choose to interact with our partners even when the dyadic relationship is mutually committed and long-lasting, such as in marriage. Two parties form a relationship by mutual choice, and each is free to leave the relationship. In an experiment on a "prisoner's dilemma network," Jin et al. (1993) allowed subjects to choose their partners for a prisoner's dilemma game from the other three members in a four-person group. One interesting finding is that the subjects who succeeded in forming a mutually committed relationship with another subject maintained an extremely high level of cooperation. But only a slight deviation from this high level of mutual cooperation was enough to terminate the committed relationship. In other words, a substantial proportion of subjects in Jin et al.'s experiment adopted a special form of tit

for tat, using both cooperation-defection and choice of partners as alternatives: "If you keep cooperating, I will keep choosing you as my partner and cooperate; if you fail to cooperate, I will turn to someone else."[6] In a series of computer simulations of strategies in prisoner's dilemma networks, Hayashi and associates (Hayashi 1993; Yamagishi, Hayashi, and Jin 1992) found that choosing the proper partner (which she calls the *selection strategy*) is more important than how one interacts with the chosen partner (which she calls the *action strategy*). By treating dyadic relations as embedded in a network structure, a new dimension is added to the strategy approach.

INDIVIDUALISTS, COMPETITORS, AND COOPERATORS

We all know from everyday experience that some people are more cooperative than others. The literature on social orientation or social motivation examines individual differences in cooperativeness. There are two distinct perspectives to interpreting individual differences: the *motivational view* and *cognitive-strategic view*. The social orientation or social motivation literature generally represents the motivational approach.

Social Orientation

Social orientation is defined as an attitude taken toward self and an interdependent other. It is usually represented by a combination of positive and negative attitudes toward self and other: how strongly one is concerned with one's own welfare and with other's welfare. Three major types of social orientation have been extensively studied. (1) *Individualists* are concerned with their own welfare but have little or no concern with other's welfare (positive toward self and neutral or indifferent toward other). Given a choice, they typically take an action that improves their own welfare without considering whether such an action improves or jeopardizes the other's welfare. (2) *Cooperators* are concerned with the welfare of both self and other (positive toward both self and other).

They typically take an action that improves joint gain (the sum of own and other's welfare) rather than an action that improves own gain, but not joint gain. (3) *Competitors* prefer positive outcomes for self and negative outcomes for other. They typically take an action that maximizes the difference between own gain and other's gain. Theoretically, other types of social orientation can exist, depending on the combination of attitudes toward self and other. However, studies of social dilemmas have repeatedly shown that these three types are the dominant modes of social orientation, while others appear infrequently (Kuhlman and Marshello 1975; Messick and McClintock 1968).

One interesting finding concerning individual differences between cooperators and competitors involves the difference in the way they perceive others. In general, people tend to perceive others as similar to themselves. Cooperators tend to see most people as cooperative, competitors tend to see most others as competitive, and individualists tend to see most others as individualistic (Kuhlman and Wimberley 1976). However, Kelley and Stahelsky (1970) found this to be true only for competitors. Cooperators tend to think some people are cooperative and others are not and would adjust their choices accordingly. Kelly and Stahelski suggested that this difference may be related to the authoritarian personality of competitors.

Differences in the perception of others between cooperators and competitors was explored further by Beggan and Messick (1988), Kuhlman et al. (1986), and Liebrand et al. (1986). One major finding of these studies is that competitors tend to view actions along a potency dimension (strong-weak), whereas cooperators view actions along an evaluative dimension (good-bad) (Liebrand et al. 1986). For example, against a cooperator, competitors tend to think that they cooperated because the cooperator was not strong enough to pursue own interest, whereas cooperators tend to think that the other cooperator cooperated because he/she cared for others.

Orbell and Dawes (1992) examine an interesting and potentially very important implication of the differential perceptions of cooperators and competitors. What would happen if cooperators and competitors were given an alternative to stay out of a social dilemma situation besides the ordinary alternatives of making a cooperative or non-cooperative choice? Cooperators would join the social dilemma situation in which they expect mutual cooperation. On the other hand, competitors would stay away from the social dilemma situation in which the expected outcome is mutual defection. Due to this "self-selection bias," only cooperators will face the social dilemma situation, and consequently, the cooperators' expectation that others are cooperative as well will be substantiated. Orbell and Dawes (1992) demonstrated this effect in an experiment.

A Strategic View of Social Orientation

The findings mentioned above suggest the possibility that the cooperator-competitor distinction may not reflect a difference in motivation. That is, cooperators, individualists, and competitors may in fact be quite similarly motivated. According to the *strategic view* of social orientation suggested by Kuhlman et al. (1986), the stable differences found among different groups of people "is due to differences in beliefs as to the best way to maximize one's own welfare rather than to differences in preferences as to what to maximize" (Kuhlman, Camac, and Cunha 1986, 164). We have already learned that nervous or reluctant cooperators would cooperate if they expect others will also cooperate. Whether they cooperate or not in a particular situation does not reflect the degree to which they care about other's well-being vis-à-vis their own well-being but, rather, their expectation of others. According to this view, competitors are nervous or reluctant cooperators who consider mutual cooperation a "highly desirable, but impossible dream" (Kuhlman, Camac, and Cunha 1986).

Factors Promoting Group-Regarding Motivations

Based on the motivational approach, the most relevant research issue is the identification of factors that promote other- or group-regarding motivations, including both cooperative and altruistic motivations. Several factors have been investigated thus far.

Social Identity. We care greatly about family members and close friends as well as other members of our primary groups, such as community groups or work groups. More generally, we care for each other in highly cohesive groups. Therefore, any factor that enhances group cohesiveness should improve group-regarding motivation. In addition, social identity theory (Tajfel 1978; Turner 1981) posits that simply belonging to a group or social category promotes group-regarding motivation. Applying this theory to social dilemmas, Brewer and Kramer (1986; Kramer and Brewer 1984, 1986) found that subjects who identified with a seemingly superficial social category show a higher level of cooperation.

Intergroup Competition. Group cohesiveness that enhances group-regarding motivation is raised by intergroup competition (e.g., Sherif et al. 1961). Groups in competition with other groups, then, should be able to elicit a higher level of cooperation from its members. The effect of intergroup competition on cooperation in social dilemmas was investigated by Bornstein, Rapoport, and associates (Bornstein and Rapoport 1982; Rapoport and Bornstein 1987, 1989; Rapoport, Bornstein, and Erev 1988). In these studies, two groups competed for a bonus that was equally provided to all members of the winning group. Each group member contributed his/her own resource to the group, and the group in which the total contribution by its members was greater won the bonus. The bonus was a public good to be shared by all members, regardless of their contribution. The results show that intergroup competition promotes intragroup cooperation for the provision of a public good.

Communication. Another common factor with potential for enhancing other-regarding motivation is communication and/or face-to-face interaction. The positive effect of communication and/or face-to-face interaction for promoting cooperation in social dilemmas has been well documented (Bixenstein, Levitt, and Wilson 1966; Brechner 1977; Dawes, McTavish, and Shaklee 1977; Edney and Harper 1978b, 1978c; Jerdee and Rosen 1974; Jorgenson and Papciak 1981; Rapoport et al. 1962; Yamagishi and Sato 1986). Results of a study by Dawes et al. (1977) indicate that communication per se does not improve mutual cooperation; improvement in the level of cooperation resulted when the content of communication was relevant to the social dilemma. Based on a series of more recent experiments investigating the effects of communication in social dilemma situations (Orbell, van de Kragt, and Dawes 1988; van de Kragt, Orbell, and Dawes 1983), Dawes (1991) suggests that communication is important because it enhances group identity among members.

MUTUAL SANCTIONS AND SOCIAL NORMS

We learned earlier that the voluntary use of strategies, despite their effectiveness in dyadic relationships, is not likely to lead to high levels of cooperation in N-person social dilemmas. This is because one's action affects all other members' outcomes in the same way, such that if one cooperates defectors as well as cooperators are rewarded, and if one defects cooperators as well as defectors are punished. This implies that if strategic actions aimed at influencing a specific other's choice (by either punishing or rewarding him/her) can be focused on that specific target, strategic actions will be effective in N-person social dilemmas as well. One way to make this possible is to separate sanctioning actions from cooperation-defection choices. If people are capable of sanctioning other members by punishing defectors and/or rewarding cooperators independent of their choices of cooperation-defection, then that kind of strategic action (or sanctioning) will be as effective as it is in dyadic relations.

Cost and Benefit of Selective Incentives

The administration of "selective incentives" is considered the standard approach by economists to solve free riding (e.g., Olson 1965). Economists use the term *selective incentives* to refer to positive and negative sanctions given to cooperators and/or defectors. Some selective incentives are monetary or material rewards, such as a program guide provided to public television subscribers. Some are social or psychological, such as prestige and praise given to cooperators. Administration of such selective incentives helps resolve social dilemmas by altering the incentive structure itself. It is rational for each actor to cooperate if the extra cost or benefit associated with the selective incentive (or sanction) exceeds the cost of cooperation. For example, if all public television subscribers were provided a $100 refund check while the subscription fee is $50, most everyone would subscribe.

The above example points to one problem with the administration of selective incentives or sanctions as a solution to social dilemmas. First, as discussed by Tullock (1977) and others, the cost of selective incentives ($100 per subscriber in the above example) may exceed the benefit derived from making people cooperative (i.e., revenue generated by the $50 subscription fee). The cost of administering selective incentives or sanctions includes the cost for monitoring members' behavior and actually providing sanctions (cf. Hechter 1984, 1987). Whether the benefit of sanctioning exceeds its cost depends on the size of the benefit generated by cooperation and the size of the cost of administering selective incentives. For example, a trade union provides financial support to striking members so they can maintain the strike. The total benefit derived from a successful strike (increased wage and benefits to all members) usually exceeds the total cost to the union for the support. On the other hand, excessive regulations and bureaucratic red tape often could be more costly than beneficial to group members.

Second-Order Dilemma

The use of selective incentives or mutual sanctions faces another problem even when the benefits exceed the costs. Let us assume a social dilemma where the total cost of administering selective in-

centives is less than the benefit generated by it. If an agency already exists that is capable of taxing a portion of the extra benefit generated by the administration of selective incentives to fund its operation, the only remaining problem is how to assess fair taxes. This involves the demand revelation problem, as briefly introduced early in the chapter. In our society, the government at various levels (local, state, and national) fulfills this function.

Let us remember the question raised earlier in the chapter: Is cooperation possible among egoists? The possible answers to this question examined thus far are based on mutual trust or the use of strategies. Now, we add the third answer: Cooperation among egoists is possible if there exists an agency to administer selective incentives (and the total benefit derived from it exceeds the total cost).

Many social dilemmas exist in the absence of such an agency, but people may still provide selective incentives or sanction each other to make others cooperate, or they may get together and create such an agency. This raises the next question: Is cooperation among egoists possible if people are capable of monitoring each other and sanctioning each other? In other words, can the necessary selective incentives be voluntarily provided by group members without a central authority? The answer to this question depends on how we deal with the problem of the second-order dilemma.

Suppose that people begin cooperating after they have started monitoring and sanctioning each other. This is typical in small traditional communities. Most people in a village know what others are doing and will pressure deviants to conform. In many other situations, however, people may not voluntarily monitor and sanction each other, especially since such activities often involve substantial costs. If you remind your colleague who is always late for meetings that he/she should not be late, you might become disliked by this colleague. In this example, the cost is relatively minor. However, if this colleague was your boss, the cost of such sanctioning might rise dramatically.

Now, we are faced with a second-order social dilemma that concerns the provision of mutual monitoring and sanctioning. If many people monitor and sanction their neighbors, the majority will cooperate and, as a result, everyone will profit. But the fruit of mutual monitoring and sanctioning can also be enjoyed by those who do not participate in such activities. The increase in the overall cooperation level due to mutual monitoring and sanctioning is thus a public good in and of itself. People can free ride on others' effort to monitor and sanction defectors. Yamagishi (1986b) used the term *instrumental cooperation* to refer to people's effort to monitor and sanction each other and the term *elementary cooperation* for their cooperation in the original social dilemma. The question raised here is: Will people who do not cooperate in the original social dilemma cooperate in the second-order dilemma?

The series of experiments conducted by Yamagishi and associates indicate that people who do not cooperate in the original social dilemma often do cooperate in the second-order dilemma. In one experiment (Yamagishi 1986a), participants were classified in advance as high trusters or low trusters, based on their responses to a questionnaire on trust (i.e., a trust scale). The dilemma situation was constructed such that a contribution made by each member is doubled or tripled (depending on the condition) and distributed among the other three members of a four-person group. Trust had a strong effect in this experiment, with high trusters (who scored high in the preexperimental measurement of trust on the trust scale) contributing almost 50 percent more than low trusters. Half of the groups in each condition were then given the opportunity to contribute to the establishment of a sanctioning system. In this condition, twice the total amount contributed by the members to the sanctioning system was subtracted from the lowest elementary contributor's cumulative profit. Interestingly, low trusters rather than high trusters contributed more in the second-order dilemma; as a result, the difference in the levels of elementary cooperation between the two trust groups disappeared. The results of this and other studies (Rutte 1989; Yamagishi 1988b, 1988c, 1993a) indicate that some factors that enhance elementary cooperation sometimes depress instrumental cooperation.

Loss of Intrinsic Motivation for Cooperation

A solution to the social dilemmas problem based on mutual sanctioning still involves an important problem. Voluntarily supported mutual sanctioning, "mutual coercion mutually agreed upon," was originally suggested by Hardin (1968) when he introduced the tragedy of the commons. This solution, however, was immediately criticized by Crowe (1969) and others because of its "totalitarian" connotations (for similar criticisms see Fox 1985; Lynn and Oldenquist 1986; Stillman 1975; Taylor 1976, 1982). Following this line of criticism, Yamagishi (1989b) argued that people will lose their "intrinsic" motivation for cooperation when they are forced to cooperate by pressure from others (see Yamagishi 1988a, 1988b, for experiments indirectly "testing" this idea).

Explaining Norms

The second-order dilemma discussed above has stimulated a considerable amount of interest among sociologists and political scientists, because the notion of voluntarily supported mutual sanctioning is very close conceptually to the notion of social norms. Among the three types of definitions of norms—based on expectations, values, and behavior—as suggested by Axelrod (1986), the existence of mutual sanctioning is central to the behavioral definition of norms. According to Axelrod, a norm is said to "exist in a given social setting to the extent that individuals usually act in a certain way and are often punished when seen not to be acting in this way" (p. 1097).

Although the concept of social norms has played an important role in sociology, no satisfactory explanation of the existence of social norms has been proposed. Often social norms are treated as a given and people are simply assumed to internalize them (cf. Wrong 1961). When social norms have been "explained," it has been from a functional perspective (e.g., Ullman-Margalit 1977)—a norm exists in a society because it serves an important function in that society. Functional "explanations" do not specify how "functional" norms emerge; they assume that what is desirable in society will somehow come to exist. That "somehow" is usually left out of a functionalist explanation as a black box. The content of a norm may be functionally explained, but its existence needs to be explained by some other perspective. If we can explain how and why people voluntarily sanction each other, we will be much closer to explaining how norms come to exist.

Rational Theoretic Explanation of Norms

Some researchers (e.g., Heckathorn 1988, 1989) think people can voluntarily provide mutual sanctions if their individual regulatory interest is larger than the individual cost of sanctioning. Regulatory interest is the benefit derived from making other people more cooperative through sanctioning. It is rational for one to sanction others if the extra benefit gained by the improved cooperation of others exceeds the cost of sanctioning. This situation will be rare, however, in relatively large groups, where one actor's sanctioning activities have a barely noticeable effect on the group's general cooperation level. In these situations, the cost of sanctioning usually exceeds the regulatory interest. As a result of this second-order dilemma, rational actors will not voluntarily engage in sanctioning. One way to avoid this second-order dilemma is to impose collective sanctions (Heckathorn 1988). If a group, rather than individual defectors, is sanctioned for harboring defectors in the group, group members will have a strong regulatory interest in sanctioning each other. In such a situation, rational actors will voluntarily sanction each other. Another situation where voluntary mutual sanctioning is likely to emerge is in the N-person assurance situation (Yamagishi 1991). If almost unanimous cooperation is required for the provision of a public good, it will be relatively costless to detect and sanction a few defectors, whereas the benefit is substantial.

Except for these special occasions, mutual sanctions are not likely to be provided by rational actors due to the second-order dilemma problem. The rational choice approach to explaining social norms (as voluntarily supported mutual sanctioning) is thus very limited in scope, if not impossible.

The Evolutionary Explanation of Norms

The fundamental problem addressed earlier—whether or not cooperation is possible among egoists—has a close logical similarity to a problem central to sociobiology—how to explain the cooperation of social animals. The only mechanism by which cooperative behavior among social animals could develop, according to sociobiologists, is through proliferation of genes responsible for that behavior (Maynard-Smith 1982). What is promising about the sociobiological explanation of cooperative behavior among social animals is that seemingly self-sacrificing behavior (i.e., behavior that operates against an individual's own survival) has been successfully shown to have resulted from individual-level selection rather than from group selection. That is, some animals self-sacrifice for the benefit of the species not because it helps the species to survive (this "functionalistic" notion of the survival of the group has practically no place in modern evolutionary biology), but because it helps the gene responsible for such behavior to proliferate.

This seeming paradox of the proliferation of the self-sacrificing gene among some social animals prompted researchers to apply a similar logic and research methodology of computer simulation to studying cooperation in social dilemmas. The pioneer in this endeavor is Axelrod (1984). A series of simulation studies demonstrated the power of the strategy approach in the iterated two-person prisoner's dilemma. Another computer simulation by Axelrod (1986), which deals with a twenty-person social dilemma situation rather than dyadic relations, is more relevant to the current issue of social norms. Axelrod endowed each "member" of a twenty-person group a "gene" for "boldness." The bolder a member, the more frequently he/she would defect. The members who accumulated the highest scores during a "generation" reproduced the most children, who were endowed with the same boldness level. The result of this simulation is simple and dismal, and perfectly reflects the logical consequence of the social dilemma problem. After one hundred generations, everyone in the group became extremely bold and practically no one cooperated. Then Axelrod introduced another "gene" responsible for mutual sanctioning behavior, which he termed "vengefulness." The more vengeful a member, the more likely he/she would punish a defector when found. The punishment, of course, required a certain cost. The purpose of the second simulation was to determine whether mutual sanctioning would "evolve." It did not. This result of the second simulation can be attributed to the second-order dilemma problem (i.e., free riding in the provision of mutual sanctioning).

Does the result of Axelrod's second simulation imply that voluntarily provided mutual sanctioning, which Axelrod (1986) terms a social norm, cannot be produced through the "evolutionary" process? Not necessarily, Axelrod thinks. He argues further that the sanctioning of nonsanctioners is the only needed ingredient for a social norm of cooperation to develop. In his next simulation, Axelrod (1986) let "vengeful members" punish nonpunishers (the ones who do not punish noncooperators) as well as noncooperators. The vengefulness level was kept high and the boldness level low, and the cooperation level was high after one hundred "generations." The general implication of this simulation is that social norms develop and are maintained only when the norms include sanctions against apathy (which Axelrod calls "metanorms") as well as against deviant behavior.

Axelrod's interpretation of the result of this simulation (1986), however, is challenged by Yamagishi (1992). He claims that what is needed for the "evolution" of voluntary mutual sanctioning is the linkage between actions (cooperation-defection) at one level and those one level higher. In Axelrod's simulation, the group member who punishes defectors also punishes nonpunishers, and the one who does not punish defectors does not punish nonpun-

ishers. Thus, the action in the second-order dilemma (whether or not to punish defectors) is linked with the action in the third-order dilemma (whether or not to punish nonpunishers). According to Yamagishi (1992), it is this linkage, not metanorms per se, that explains the success of "metanorms" in Axelrod's (1986) simulation. Mutual cooperation emerges insofar as one level of action is linked with a higher-level action, whether the linkage is between the second- and third-order dilemmas, as in Axelrod's simulation, or between the first- and second-order dilemmas. Results of Yamagishi's simulations demonstrate an evolution of mutual sanctioning when the action in the original dilemma (whether to cooperate or defect) is linked with the action in the second-order dilemma (whether or not to punish defectors). That is, norms evolved even without metanorms in these simulations. Yamagishi's simulations further indicate that this linkage itself also evolves under certain conditions.

SUMMARY AND FUTURE RESEARCH TOPICS

Recent research on social dilemmas has been introduced as we successively asked questions and examined answers above. The first question was whether cooperation is possible among egoists. Two positive answers to this question were examined, both assuming that people facing iterated social dilemmas come to realize the need for mutual cooperation and are willing to cooperate insofar as others cooperate as well. What they need is a guarantee that others will cooperate, which may come either through trust of others or through power to induce others to cooperate. Therefore, the first answer to the fundamental question is that nervous or reluctant cooperators will cooperate if they can trust others. The second answer is that nervous or reluctant cooperators will cooperate if, through their own strategic actions, they can induce others to engage in mutual cooperation.

When we raised the above question, we implicitly assumed that cooperation among people is likely if each cares about the well-being of others. That is, cooperation is likely among altruists. We then examined individual differences in cooperativeness, and a third answer to the above question was suggested: Egoists will cooperate if selective incentives are effectively administered by a central agency. We reformulated the question and asked whether cooperation among egoists is possible without a central authority. The first two answers to the original question, trust and strategy, are not likely to apply in large-scale social dilemmas. A possible answer to the question is mutual sanctioning, but this involves a second-order dilemma as well as other problems. Two further possible solutions to the second-order dilemma are the rational choice theoretic solution and the evolutionary solution.

In conclusion, I would like to discuss briefly the important current issues in social dilemmas research, especially those that have been discussed not at all or only tangentially here.

Subjective and Objective Transformation of Incentive Structures

Some of the approaches to the social dilemmas problem discussed in this chapter may be reinterpreted from the point of view of the subjective or objective transformation of the incentive structure. First, it is possible to interpret Pruitt and Kimmel's (1977) goal/expectation theory as a theory of the subjective transformation of a prisoner's dilemma structure to an assurance game structure; nervous and reluctant cooperators are those who perceive an iterated prisoner's dilemma as an assurance supergame. Considering the long-term benefit, it is better to cooperate insofar as the partner is cooperative; otherwise it is better not to cooperate. The consistent empirical finding of the correlation between own action and expectations of other people's actions, as discussed earlier, may reflect the tendency to define a prisoner's dilemma subjectively as an assurance game. Second, adoption of certain strategies, such as the tit-for-tat strategy or the trigger strategy, objectively transforms a prisoner's dilemma into a structure similar to an assurance game. Third, the linkage between cooperation and sanctioning discussed above also objectively transforms the prisoner's dilemma incentive struc-

ture into an assurance game structure. In fact, this is why the linkage has a positive effect on the "evolution of norms" (see Yamagishi 1992 for the analysis of this transformation). Finally, actors in the simulation of critical mass models of collective action (see note 1) are assumed to treat the prisoner's dilemma structure as if it were an assurance game. Transformation of the prisoner's dilemma into an assurance game in these instances does not require large costs. This is in sharp contrast to the substantial cost of administering selective incentives, which transform the prisoner's dilemma structure into the no-dilemma structure (in which cooperation is a dominant choice). What is suggested here is the possibility that solving social dilemmas may not require that the dilemma be completely removed; a partial transformation of the incentive structure into an assurancelike structure may be sufficient. This idea of the partial transformation of the incentive structure may provide a bridge between the structural approach and other approaches.

Emotion and Rationality

A conflict spiral may occur among group members who are angered by the existence of a few free riders (see chapter 9 for a discussion of conflict spirals). In anger, otherwise cooperative group members stop cooperating to retaliate. This anger-based retaliatory action may actually promote mutual cooperation in two-person prisoner's dilemmas if the anger disappears after one retaliation, since such anger-based, short-term retaliatory action can lead to the tit-for-tat strategy, which has proven useful in dyadic prisoner's dilemmas. However, if the retaliation continues for several trials, it will start a conflict spiral that promotes mutual defection. In addition, in N-person groups rather than dyadic relationships, even retaliatory actions (noncooperation) based on short-lived anger are more likely to start a conflict spiral than to promote mutual cooperation (see the earlier discussion of the limitations of strategic actions). Anger in social dilemma situations, therefore, is likely to produce an outcome that is counter to one's own benefits. In this sense, emotional behavior is "irrational" in social dilemmas. Emotional actions could have a positive role, however, in resolving the second-order dilemma. That is, anger-driven sanctioning behavior could provide a solution to the second-order dilemma. People often punish noncooperators in anger and pay little attention to the cost of such behavior. In such a case, emotional behavior may provide an avenue for individuals to escape the trap of short-term rationality in the second-order dilemma, eventually leading to improved long-term benefits. In this case, emotional behavior could then be seen as "rational." Despite the seeming importance of the role emotional behavior plays in social dilemmas, not much research has been conducted on this issue. The role emotional behavior plays in social dilemmas at both levels (the original dilemma and the second-order dilemma) needs further investigation.[7]

Social Orientation, Strategy, Trust, and Norms

We saw earlier that there are two distinct approaches to interpreting cooperative behavior in social dilemmas—the motivational approach and the strategy approach. According to the motivational approach, a person cooperates because he/she is altruistic (i.e., cares about other people's well-being). According to the strategy approach, a person cooperates because he/she thinks that it will produce a better long-term outcome. These two approaches have more than theoretical implications; they also have important practical implications. For example, should we emphasize the moral value of altruistic social motivation (e.g., it is morally right to be concerned with others) in children's education rather than long-term self-interest (e.g.,

to be cooperative will pay in the long run)? On the other hand, the motivational and the strategic approaches may not be as distinct as they appear to be. First, as suggested in the section on social orientation, what has traditionally been considered other-regarding motivation may simply reflect people's expectations of others' behavior or their trust. Even egoists are willing to cooperate if they understand the long-term consequences of noncooperative behavior and, at the same time, trust others (Kuhlman, Camac, and Cunha 1986; Pruitt and Kimmel 1977). Second, as discussed in the section on the second-order dilemma, rational choice theoretic and evolutionary explanations of social norms or mutual sanctions against defectors raise the question of how important morality is in social norms. The moral component of social norms, in fact, is not critical according to these approaches, implying that other-regarding motivations need not be given special status in a society's moral code for that society to develop a system of mutual control. According to this point of view, morality is shorthand or heuristic, representing an explanation of long-term outcomes of own behavior in interdependent situations. On the other hand, most sanctioning behavior against noncooperators in the real world seems to be accompanied by rather strong moral outrage. Any attempt to explain norms will have to be able to explain the correlation between sanctioning behavior and morality.

These are a few of the problems of relevance to sociology that extend beyond the realm of social dilemmas research. Studies of social dilemmas introduced in this chapter, I hope, can and will provide useful conceptual tools for analyzing these and other important sociological problems.

NOTES

1. Marwell and associates' study of collective action deviates from the majority of social dilemmas research (especially research conducted by social psychologists) in the basic assumptions of individuals' decision principles. In the study of critical mass (Marwell, Oliver, and Prahl 1988; Oliver and Marwell 1988; Oliver, Marwell,

and Teixeira 1985), it is assumed that individuals join a collective action when the total benefit they receive is greater than the cost of participation. In contrast, the idea of a dominant strategy often adopted in social dilemmas research is based on the assumption that individuals contribute (or join a collective action) when the increment in the benefit produced by his/her contribution, not the total benefit of which the increment is a small portion, is greater than the cost. Despite the importance of this distinction, no systematic study has been conducted to explore the implications of these two assumptions.

2. Diffusion of responsibility typically involves an N-person chicken game rather than N-person prisoner's dilemma.

3. Individuals facing an assurance game are not tempted to free ride and do not need to be afraid that others will free ride insofar as they are sure that others are "rational." On the other hand, they may not cooperate if they are afraid some of the other members are "irrational" or have a competitive social motivation, as demonstrated in Watabe's (1992b) study. (See the section on individualists, competitors, and cooperators.)

4. This question, however, is irrelevant in the learning theoretic approach to social dilemmas (see the section on social traps), because the fundamental driving force of individuals' actions assumed in the learning theoretic approach is not the pursuit of self-interest. Similarly, this question is not fundamental in the critical mass theory of collective action, in which the fundamental decision principle of individuals is different from the one assumed in most social dilemma research. (See also note 1.)

5. This strategy, called out for tat (Yamagishi, Hayashi, and Jin 1992), is also consistent with the learning theoretic strategy applied in a simulation of N-way prisoner's dilemma by Macy (1991a).

6. There are currently at least two more lines of research investigating the role of network structures in social dilemmas. First, Marwell et al. (1988) study the role of a preexisting network structure among group members for organizing members into a collective action. This line of research is based on a theory of critical mass (Oliver and Marwell 1988; Oliver, Marwell, and Teixeira 1985) that assumes that group members' propensity to contribute depends on the total profit, not the marginal gain resulting from their contributions. In this sense, the collective action problem they study has the form of an N-person assurance game rather than an N-person prisoner's dilemma. The second line of research involves the generalized exchange of unilateral contributions (Yamagishi 1989b; Yamagishi and Cook 1992). Generalized exchange, in which transactions of valued resources are indirect rather than between two specific partners, inevitably involves social dilemmas (Yamagishi 1991; Yamagishi and Cook 1992), and the shape of the network affects the level of generalized exchange (and the total value produced through generalized exchange) in the whole system.

7. The role of emotion as a "strategy" to deal with problems related to social dilemmas is investigated by Frank (1988). He argues that having a reputation of being "emotional" or "irrational" provides an advantage in certain social situations. In addition to such individualistic advantages, emotions may provide an avenue of organizing a collective endeavor to resolve a social dilemma.

REFERENCES

Allison, Scott T., and David M. Messick. 1985. Effects of experience on performance in a replenishable resource trap. *Journal of Personality and Social Psychology* 49:943–948.

Arneson, R. J. 1982. The principle of fairness and free-rider problem. *Ethics* 92:616–633.

Axelrod, Robert. 1984. *The Evolution of Cooperation.* New York: Basic Books.

———. 1986. An evolutionary approach to norms. *American Political Science Review* 80:1095–1111.

Baird, John S. 1982. Conservation of the commons: Effects of group cohesiveness and prior sharing. *Journal of Community Psychology* 10:210–215.

Beggan, James K., and David M. Messick. 1988. Social values and egocentric bias: Two tests of the might over morality hypothesis. *Journal of Personality and Social Psychology* 55:606–611.

Bixenstein, V. Edwin, Clifford A. Levitt, and Kellogg V. Wilson. 1966. Collaboration among six persons in a prisoner's dilemma game. *Conflict Resolution* 10:488–496.

Bornstein, Gary, and Amnon Rapoport. 1982. Intergroup competition for the provision of step-level public goods: Effects of preplay communication. *European Journal of Social Psychology* 18:125–142.

Brann, P., and M. Foddy. 1988. Trust and the consumption of a deteriorating common resource. *Journal of Conflict Resolution* 31:615–630.

Brechner, Kevin C. 1977. An experimental analysis of social traps. *Journal of Experimental Social Psychology* 13:552–564.

Brewer, Marilynn B., and Roderick M. Kramer. 1986. Choice behavior in social dilemmas: Effects of social identity, group size, and decision framing. *Journal of Personality and Social Psychology* 50: 543–549.

Cass, Robert C., and Julian J. Edney. 1978. The commons dilemma: A simulation testing the effects of resource visibility and territorial division. *Human Ecology* 6:371–386.

Cross, John G., and Melvin J. Guyer. 1980. *Social Traps.* Ann Arbor: University of Michigan Press.

Crowe, Beryl L. 1969. The tragedy of the commons revisited. *Science* 166:1103–1107.

Dawes, Robyn M. 1980. Social dilemmas. *Annual Review of Psychology* 31:169–193.

———. 1991. Social dilemmas, economic self-interest, and evolutionary theory. Pp. 53–79 in *Frontiers of Mathematical Psychology: Essays in Honor of Clyde Coombs,* ed. Donald R. Brown and J. E. Keith Smith. New York: Springer-Verlag.

Dawes, Robyn M., Jeanne McTavish, and Harriet Shaklee. 1977. Behavior, communication and assumptions about other people's behavior in a commons dilemma situation. *Journal of Personality and Social Psychology* 35:1–11.

Dawes, Robyn M., John Orbell, R. T. Simmons, and Alphons J. C. van de Kragt. 1986. Organizing groups by promising contributors they won't lose and by requiring "fair share" contributions. *American Political Science Review* 80:1171–1185.

Edney, Julian J., and Christopher S. Harper. 1978a. The commons dilemma: A review of contributions from psychology. *Environmental Management* 2:491–507.

———. 1978b. The effects of information in a resource management problem: A social trap analog. *Human Ecology* 6:387–395.

———. 1978c. Heroism in a resource crisis: A simulation study. *Environmental Management* 2:523–527.

Fleishman, John A. 1980. Collective action as helping behavior: Effects of responsibility diffusion on contributions to a public good. *Journal of Personality and Social Psychology* 38:629–637.

Fox, D. R. 1985. Psychology, ideology, utopia, and the commons. *American Psychologist* 40:48–58.

Fox, John, and Melvin Guyer. 1977. Group size and others' strategy in an N-person game. *Journal of Conflict Resolution* 21:323–338.

Frank, Robert H. 1988. *Passions within Reason: The Strategic Role of the Emotions.* New York: Norton.

Friedman, J. W. 1986. *Game Theory with Applications to Economics.* New York: Oxford University Press.

Hardin, Garrett. 1968. The tragedy of the commons. *Science* 162:1243–1297.

Harkins, G., and K. Szymanski. 1987. Social loafing and social facilitation: New wine in old bottles. Pp. 167–188 in *Review of Personality and Social Psychology: Group Processes and Intergroup Relations,* vol. 9, ed. C. Hendrick. Newbury Park, CA: Sage.

Hayashi, Nahoko. 1993. From TIT-FOR-TAT to OUT-FOR-TAT. *Sociological Theory and Methods* 8: 19–32. (in Japanese)

Hechter, Michael. 1984. When actors comply: Monitoring costs and the production of social order. *Acta Sociological* 27:161–183.

———. 1987. *Principles of Group Solidarity.* Berkeley: University of California Press.

Heckathorn, Douglas D. 1988. Collective sanctions and the creation of prisoner's dilemma norms. *American Journal of Sociology* 94:535–562.

———. 1989. Collective action and the second order free rider problem. *Rationality and Society* 1:78–100.

Hobbes, Thomas. [1651] 1965. *Leviathan.* Oxford: Clarendon Press.

Jerdee, T. H., and B. Rosen. 1974. Effects of opportunity to communicate and visibility of individual decisions on behavior in the common interest. *Journal of Applied Social Psychology* 59:712–716.

Jin, Nobuhito, Nahoko Hayashi, and Hiromi Shinotsuka. 1993. An experimental study of prisoner's dilemma network: Formation of committed relations among PD partners. *Japanese Journal of Experimental Social Psychology.* (In press, in Japanese)

Jorgenson, Dale O., and Anthony S. Papciak. 1981. The effects of communication, resource feedback, and identifiability on behavior in a simulated commons. *Journal of Experimental Social Psychology* 17: 373–385.

Kelley, Harold H., and A. J. Stahelsky. 1970. The social interaction basis of cooperators' and competitors' beliefs about others. *Journal of Personality and Social Psychology* 16:66–91.

Kerr, Norbert L. 1983. Motivational losses in small groups: A social dilemma analysis. *Journal of Personality and Social Psychology* 45:819–828.

Klandermans, Bert. 1984. Mobilization, and participation: Social psychological expansions of resource mobilization theory. *American Sociological Review* 49:583–600.

Klandermans, Bert, and Dirk Oegema. 1987. Potentials, networks, motivations, and barriers: Steps towards participation in social movements. *American Sociological Review* 52:519–531.

Kramer, Roderick M., and Marilynn B. Brewer. 1984. Effects of group identity on resource use in a simulated commons dilemma. *Journal of Personality and Social Psychology* 46:1044–1056.

———. 1986. Social group identity and the emergence of cooperation in resource conservation dilemmas. Pp. 205–234 in *Experimental Social Dilemmas,* ed. Henk A. M. Wilke, David M. Messick, and Christel G. Rutte. Frankfurt: Verlag Peter Lang.

Kramer, Roderick M., C. G. McClintock, and David M. Messick. 1986. Social values and cooperative response to a simulated resource conservation crisis. *Journal of Personality* 54:576–592.

Kuhlman, D. M., C. R. Camac, and D. A. Cunha. 1986. Individual differences in social orientation. Pp. 151–176 in *Experimental Social Dilemmas,* ed. Henk A. M. Wilke, Dave M. Messick, and Christel G. Rutte. Frankfurt: Verlag Peter Lang.

Kuhlman, D. M., and A. F. J. Marshello. 1975. Individual differences in game motivation as moderators of programmed strategy effects on prisoner's dilemmas. *Journal of Personality and Social Psychology* 32:922–931.

Kuhlman, D. M., and D. L. Wimberley. 1976. Expectations of choice behavior held by cooperators, competitors, and individualists across four classes of experimental games. *Journal of Personality and Social Psychology* 34:69–81.

Liebrand, Wim B. G. 1986. The ubiquity of social values in social dilemmas. Pp. 113–133 in *Experimental Social Dilemmas,* ed. H. A. M. Wilke, D. M. Messick, and C. G. Rutte. Frankfurt: Verlag Peter Lang.

Liebrand, Wim B. G., R. Jansen, V. Rijken, and C. Suhre. 1986. Might over morality: Social values and the perception of other players in experimental games. *Journal of Experimental Social Psychology* 22:203–215.

Lloyd. [1833] 1977. On the checks to population. Pp. 8–15 in *Managing the Commons,* ed. Garrett Hardin and John Baden. San Francisco: Freeman.

Luce, Duncan, and Howard Raifa. 1957. *Games and Decisions.* New York: John Wiley.

Lynn, M., and A. Oldenquist. 1986. Egoistic and nonegoistic motives in social dilemmas. *American Psychologist* 41:529–534.

Macy, Michael W. 1989. Walking out of social traps: A stochastic learning model for prisoner's dilemma. *Rationality and Society* 1:197–219.

———. 1991a. Learning to cooperate: Stochastic and tacit collusion in social exchange. *American Journal of Sociology* 97:808–843.

———. 1991b. Learning theory and the logic of critical mass. *American Sociological Review* 55:809–826.

Marwell, Gerald, and Ruth E. Ames. 1979. Experiments on the provision of public goods, I: Resources, interest, group size, and the free-rider problem. *American Journal of Sociology* 84:1335–1360.

Marwell, Gerald, and Pamela Oliver. 1984. Collective action theory and social movements research. *Research in Social Movements, Conflicts and Change* 7:1–28.

Marwell, Gerald, Pamela E. Oliver, and Ralph Prahl 1988. Social networks and collective action: A theory of critical mass, III. *American Journal of Sociology* 94:502–534.

Marwell, Gerald, and David R. Schmitt. 1972. Cooperation in a three-person prisoner's dilemma. *Journal of Personality and Social Psychology* 21:376–383.

Maynard-Smith, J. 1982. *Evolution, and the Theory of Games.* Cambridge, UK: Cambridge University Press.

Messick, David M., and Marilynn B. Brewer. 1983. Solving social dilemmas: A review. Pp. 11–14 in *Review of Personality and Social Psychology,* vol. 4, ed. L. Wheeler. Beverly Hills: Sage.

Messick, David M., and Carol L. McClelland. 1983. Social traps and temporal traps. *Personality and Social Psychology Bulletin* 9:105–110.

Messick, David M., and Charles G. McClintock. 1968. Motivational bases of choice in experimental games. *Journal of Experimental Social Psychology* 4: 1–25.

Messick, David M., Henk Wilke, Marilynn B. Brewer, Roderick M. Kramer, Patricia English Zemke, and Layton Lui. 1983. Individual adaptations and structural change as solutions to social dilemmas. *Journal of Personality and Social Psychology* 44:293–309.

Oliver, Pamela. 1980. Rewards and punishments as selective incentives for collective action: Theoretical investigations. *American Journal of Sociology* 85: 1356–1375.

———. 1984. If you don't do it, nobody else will: Active and token contributors to local collective action. *American Sociological Review* 49:601–610.

Oliver, Pamela, and Gerald Marwell. 1988. The paradox of group size in collective action: A theory of the critical mass, II. *American Sociological Review* 53: 1–8.

Oliver, Pamela, Gerald Marwell, and Ruy Teixeira. 1985. A theory of the critical mass, I: Interdependence, group heterogeneity, and the production of collective action. *American Journal of Sociology* 91:522–556.

Olson, Mancur. 1965. *The Logic of Collective Action.* Cambridge, MA: Harvard University Press.

Orbell, John, and Robyn M. Dawes. 1981. Social dilemmas. Pp. 37–65 in *Progress in Applied Social Psychology,* vol. 1, ed. G. Stephenson and J. H. Davis. Chichester: Wiley.

———. 1992. Optimism about others as cooperators' advantage: Experimental evidence. Paper presented at the 87th Annual Meeting of the American Sociological Association, Pittsburgh.

Orbell, John, Alphons J. C. van de Kragt, and Robyn M. Dawes. 1988. Explaining discussion-induced cooperation. *Journal of Personality and Social Psychology* 54:811–819.

Oskamp, S. 1971. Effects of programmed strategies on cooperation in the Prisoner's Dilemma and other mixed-motive strategies. *Journal of Conflict Resolution* 15:225–269.

Piliavin, J. A., and H. W. Charng. 1990. Altruism: A review of recent theory and research. *Annual Review of Sociology* 16:27–65.

Platt, John. 1973. Social traps. *American Psychologist* 28:641–651.

Pruitt, Dean G., and Melvin J. Kimmel. 1977. Twenty years of experimental gaming: Critique, synthesis, and suggestions for the future. *Annual Review of Psychology* 28:363–392.

Rapoport, Amnon, and Gary Bornstein. 1987. Intergroup competition for the provision of binary public goods. *Psychological Review* 94:291–299.

———. 1989. Solving public good problems in competition between equal and unequal size groups. *Journal of Conflict Resolution* 33:460–479.

Rapoport, Amnon, Gary Bornstein, and Ido Erev. 1988. Intergroup competition for public goods: Effects of unequal resources and relative group size. IPDM Report no.68, University of Haifa.

Rapoport, Anatol, A. Chammah, J. Dwyer, and J. Gyr. 1962. Three-person non-zero-sum nonnegotiable games. *Behavioral Science* 7:30–58.

Ringelmann, M. 1913. Recherches sur les moteurs animes: Travail de l'homme. *Annales de l'Institut National Agronomique* 12:1–40.

Rutte, Christel G. 1989. Elementary and instrumental cooperation in social dilemma situations. Ph.D. diss, Dept. of Psychology, University of Groningen.

Samuelson, Charles D., and David M. Messick. 1986a. Alternative structural solutions to resource dilemmas. *Organizational Behavior and Human Decision Processes* 37:139–155.

———. 1986b. Inequities in access to and use of shared resources in social dilemmas. *Journal of Personality and Social Psychology* 51:960–967.

Samuelson, Charles D., David M. Messick, Christel G. Rutte, and Henk Wilke. 1984. Individual and structural solutions to resource dilemmas in two cultures. *Journal of Personality and Social Psychology* 47:94–104.

Sato, Kaori. 1985. An experimental simulation of the tragedy of the commons. *Japanese Journal of Experimental Social Psychology* 24:149–159. (in Japanese)

———. 1987. Distribution of the cost of maintaining common resources. *Journal of Experimental Social Psychology* 23:19–31.

———. 1988. Trust and group size in a social dilemma. *Japanese Psychological Research* 30:88–93.

Sato, Kaori, Masanao Toda, and Toshio Yamagishi. 1985. A time series analysis of behavior in a social dilemma. *Japanese Journal of Psychology* 56:277–287. (in Japanese)

Sato, Kaori, and Toshio Yamagishi. 1984. Two psychological factors in the problem of public goods. *Japanese Journal of Experimental Social Psychology* 26:89–95. (in Japanese)

Schuessler, Rudolf. 1989. Exit threats and cooperation under anonymity. *Journal of Conflict Resolution* 33:728–749.

Sherif, M., O. Harvey, B. White, W. Hood, and C. Sherif. 1961. Intergroup conflict and cooperation: The Robber's Cove experiment. Norman: Institute of Group Relations, University of Oklahoma.

Stern, Paul C. 1978. When do people act to maintain common resources? A reformulated psychological question for our time. *International Journal of Psychology* 13:139–158.

Stillman, P. G. 1975. The tragedy of the commons: A reanalysis. *Alternatives* 4:12–15.

Stroebe, Wolfgang, and Bruno S. Frey. 1982. Self-interest and collective action: The economics and psychology of public goods. *British Journal of Social Psychology* 21:121–137.

Tajfel, H. 1978. Social categorization, social identity, and social comparison. Pp. 61–76 *Differentiation between Social Groups,* ed. H. Tajfel. London: Academic.

Taylor, Michael. 1976. *Anarchy, and Cooperation.* London: Wiley.

———. 1982. *Community, Anarchy, and Liberty.* Cambridge, UK: Cambridge University Press.

———. 1987. *The Possibility of Cooperation: Studies in Rationality and Social Change.* Cambridge, UK: Cambridge University Press.

Tullock, G. 1977. The social cost of reducing social cost. Pp. 147–156 in *Managing the Commons,* ed. G. Hardin and J. Baden. San Francisco: Freeman.

Turner, J. C. 1981. The experimental social psychology of intergroup behavior. Pp. 66–101 in *Intergroup Behavior,* ed. J. C. Turner and H. Giles. Chicago: University of Chicago Press.

Tyszka, Tadeusz, and Janusz L. Grzelak. 1976. Criteria of choice in non-constant zero-sum games. *Journal of Conflict Resolution* 20:357–376.

Ullman-Margalit, Edna. 1977. *The Emergence of Norms.* Oxford, UK: Oxford University Press.

Umino, Michio, Takeyoshi Iwamoto, and Hiroko Ueda. 1985. An experimental study of social ant lion's trap: Effects of time-lags. Pp. 141–148 in *Developments in Mathematical Sociology,* ed. Junsuke Hara, Michio Umino, and Shuichi Wada. Tokyo: Suri Sakaigaku Kenkyukai. (in Japanese)

van de Kragt, Alphons J. C., John M. Orbell, Robyn M. Dawes. 1983. The minimal contributing set as a solution to public goods problems. *American Political Science Review* 77:112–122.

Watabe, Motoki. 1992a. Choice of strategies in a social dilemma. *Japanese Journal of Experimental Social Psychology* 32:171–182. (in Japanese)

———. 1992b. Choice of strategies in social dilemma supergames. Paper presented at the Fifth International Conference on Social Dilemmas, Bielefeld, Germany.

Wilson, W. 1971. Reciprocation and other techniques for inducing cooperation in the prisoner's dilemma game. *Journal of Conflict Resolution* 15:167–195.

Wit, A. P. 1989. Group efficiency and fairness in social dilemmas: An experimental gaming approach. Ph.D. diss., University of Groningen.

Wit, A. P., and H. A. M. Wilke. 1988. Subordinates' endorsement of an allocating leader in a commons dilemma: An equity theoretical approach. *Journal of Economic Psychology* 9:327–333.

Wrong, Dennis. 1961. The over-socialized conception of man in modern sociology. *American Sociological Review* 26:183–193.

Yamagishi, Toshio. 1986a. The provision of a sanctioning system as a public good. *Journal of Personality and Social Psychology* 51:110–116.

———. 1986b. The structural goal/expectation theory of cooperation in social dilemmas. Pp. 51–87 in *Advances in Group Processes,* vol. 3, ed. E. J. Lawler. Greenwich, CT: JAI Press.

Yamagishi, Toshio. 1988a. Exit from the group as an individualistic solution to the free-rider problem in the United States and Japan. *Journal of Experimental Social Psychology* 24:530–542.

———. 1988b. The provision of a sanctioning system in the United States and Japan. *Social Psychology Quarterly* 51:32–42.

———. 1988c. Seriousness of social dilemmas and the provision of a sanctioning system. *Social Psychology Quarterly* 51:32–42.

———. 1989a. Major theoretical approaches in social dilemmas research. *Japanese Psychological Review* 33:64–96. (in Japanese)

———. 1989b. Unintended consequences of some solutions to the social dilemmas problem. *Sociological Theory and Method* 4:21–47. (in Japanese)

———. 1991. Social exchange and social dilemmas. Pp. 227–257 in *The Problem of Social Order and Social Dilemmas,* ed. Kazuo Seiyama and Michio Umino. Tokyo: Harvest Press. (in Japanese)

———. 1992. Evolution of norms without metanorms. Paper presented at the 5th International Conference on Social Dilemmas, Bielefeld, Germany.

———. 1993a. Group size, and the provision of a sanctioning system in a social dilemma. In *A Social Psychological Approach to Social Dilemmas,* ed. W. B. G. Liebrand, D. M. Messick, and H. A. M. Wilke. New York: Pergamon Press.

———. 1993b. Transformation of the incentive structure and the emergence of norms. *Sociological Theory and Methods* 8:51–68. (in Japanese)

Yamagishi, Toshio, and Karen S. Cook. 1992. Generalized exchange and social dilemmas. Mimeo. University of Washington.

Yamagishi, Toshio, Nahoko Hayashi, and Nobuhito Jin. 1992. Prisoner's dilemma network: Winning strategies and emerging structures. Paper presented at the 87th Annual Meeting of the American Sociological Association, Pittsburgh.

Yamagishi, Toshio, and Kaori Sato. 1986. Motivational bases of the public goods problem. *Journal of Personality and Social Psychology* 50:67–73.

CHAPTER 13

Group Decision Making

H. ANDREW MICHENER
MICHELLE P. WASSERMAN

Many groups in society make decisions. The management team of a business, for instance, decides to phase out an old product line and to introduce a new one. A family, after some discussion, decides to take its annual vacation at one location (seashore) rather than another (mountains). A jury hears evidence about a felony, deliberates at length, and finally reaches a verdict to acquit. A personnel committee scrutinizes applicants for a job, then selects what it considers to be the best one and hires accordingly.

This chapter reviews current social psychological research and theory on group decision making. Throughout this chapter, the term *group* refers to a social unit consisting of two or more persons who (1) share a goal (or goals) that they pursue through coordinated activity, (2) communicate with and influence one another, (3) share a set of normative expectations (i.e., rules and roles) that regulate behavior, and (4) consciously view themselves and are viewed by others as members of the social unit. Groups are collective actors that can make decisions and take actions vis-à-vis their environment.

GROUPS AND DECISIONS

Social psychologists have investigated group decision making for many years. In fact, social psychology includes a tradition of work dating back to the early 1900s on various aspects of group performance, including performance on information-processing tasks such as judgments and decisions. Groups face many types of informa-tion-processing tasks. One approach categorizes them as follows:

1. Group problem solving (intellective tasks). Intellective tasks are those that have demonstrably correct or easily verifiable answers within a verbal or mathematical conceptual system. In problem solving, the group's goal is to find an accurate solution to the problem through the use of insight and logic (Laughlin 1980; Restle and Davis 1962).

2. Group judgment and categorization. Judgment tasks require a group to appraise or assess an object's attributes. Some problems of this type have objectively correct answers, but many do not. The group's goal is to make accurate judgments and/or to resolve cognitive conflicts stemming from different conceptions of reality held by members (Asch 1956; Brehmer 1976; Hastie 1986).

3. Group idea generation and brainstorming. Idea-generation tasks require a group to develop or create novel ideas. Usually, the group's goal is to generate as many original ideas as possible (on some specified issue, within some specified time period). Members hope the novel ideas will be of high quality and will serve as guides to action or solutions to problems (Delbecq, Van de Ven, and Gustafson 1975; Diehl and Stroebe 1987).

4. Group decision making. Decision-making tasks require a group to make a choice among options (i.e., mutually exclusive alternatives) on the basis of preferences or values. Usually, the group's goal is to reach agreement about which option is most preferred (Brandstatter, Davis, and Stocker-Kreichgauer 1982; Collins and Guetzkow 1964;

Hwang and Lin 1987; Janis and Mann 1977; Swap et al. 1984).

This chapter focuses primarily on tasks of the last type—group decision making—although it also discusses some studies of group judgment.

Topics in Group Decision Making

Investigators distinguish between the decisional process or procedure followed by the group when making a decision and the outcome or product resulting from the process (i.e., the choice made). In the earliest studies of group decision making, investigators focused on the quality of group decisions and addressed questions such as whether groups make better decisions than individuals (Burtt 1920; Johnson et al. 1981; Watson 1928). Over the years, however, investigators increasingly realized that the study of quality of decisions is very difficult and profoundly problematic. Many decisions cannot be evaluated unequivocally in terms of success or failure. Often there is no unequivocally superior option, because some (short-term and long-term) effects of the available options are simply unknown (and perhaps unknowable). As Janis and Mann (1977) point out, to evaluate the quality of a decision fully, an investigator would need to take into account all the positive consequences of the decision made, all the positive consequences that would have resulted if each of the other options had been selected instead, all the negative consequences of the decision made, and all the negative consequences that would have resulted if each of the other options had been selected instead. In most situations, taking all these effects into account is impossible.

On the other hand, it is quite feasible to study the processes and procedures used by a group when making decisions. Thus, it is not surprising that recently, social psychologists have focused more on the processes of group decision making than on the quality of the decisions that result from these processes. There is at least some agreement regarding what constitutes an effective decision-making process. For instance, Janis and Mann

(1977, chap. 14) outline steps taken by effective decision makers:

1. They thoroughly survey a wide array of possible courses of action (options).
2. They survey the full range of objectives to be fulfilled and the standing of each option with respect to each of these objectives.
3. They carefully weigh whatever they know about the costs and risks of the negative consequences that could result from each option.
4. They search intensively for new information relevant to further evaluation of the options.
5. They carefully assimilate any new information or expert judgment to which they are exposed, even when the information or judgment does not support the option they initially prefer.
6. Before making a final choice, they reexamine the positive and negative consequences of all known options, including those originally regarded as unacceptable.
7. They make detailed provisions for implementing the chosen option, paying special attention to contingency plans that might be required if various risks were to materialize.

While some decision-making groups adopt procedures such as these, others do not. In many groups, the members' real objective is not to select the "best" option but to achieve sufficient consensus regarding the choice. Because group members often differ in their preferences, reaching consensus can prove difficult and may entail processes (e.g., withholding information or demanding conformity) that actually defeat careful decision-making.

Social psychologists have studied a variety of factors that affect the decision-making processes in groups. Since the 1970s, they have concentrated heavily on four key topics: (1) groupthink; (2) polarization and choice shift; (3) social decision rules; and (4) minority influence in group decisions. Each of these topics highlights some aspect of group structure or interaction (i.e., conformity pressures, information exchange, minority dissent, established decision rules, and level of cohesion) as it impacts group decision-making processes. Because these topics are important and central, the following discussion is structured in terms of them.

GROUPTHINK

In *Victims of Groupthink* (1972), Irving Janis analyzed the impact of U.S. governmental decision making on foreign policy blunders. He focused on four decisions made by the president's cabinet that led to poor outcomes: the decision to invade Cuba at the Bay of Pigs, the decision to invade North Korea during the Korean War, the failure to defend Pearl Harbor adequately on the eve of World War II, and the decision to escalate the Vietnam War. In a later edition of the book, Janis (1982) added another, the Watergate coverup. For contrast, he also considered two instances of cabinet decision making that led to good outcomes: the Cuban Missile Crisis and the Marshall Plan after World War II. To discover why some high-level decisions led to poor foreign policy outcomes while others led to more favorable results, Janis analyzed these cases and looked for common elements. He concluded that poor foreign policy decisions resulted from aberrant processes of social interaction in the decision-making group, a phenomenon he labeled *groupthink*.

Groupthink Theory

The term *groupthink* refers to a mode of thought wherein pressures toward unanimity in a group overwhelm the members' motivation to appraise realistically the available options. Groupthink is a form of premature consensus seeking. It produces an incorrect assessment of the options, which often leads to ill-considered decisions that eventuate in significant failure.

Symptoms of Groupthink. According to Janis (1972, 1982), when groupthink occurs in a group, it manifests itself through various *symptoms,* including:

1. Illusions of invulnerability. Group members may think they are invulnerable and cannot fail,

and therefore they display excessive optimism and take excessive risks.

2. Illusions of morality. Members may display an unquestioned belief in the group's inherent superior morality, and this may incline them to ignore (undesirable) ethical consequences of their decisions.

3. Collective rationalization. Members may discount warnings that, if heeded, would cause them to reconsider their (incorrect) assumptions.

4. Stereotyping of the adversary. Especially in the political sphere, the group may develop a stereotyped view of enemy leaders as too evil to warrant genuine attempts to negotiate or too weak to mount effective counteractions.

5. Self-censorship. Members may engage in self-censorship to avoid deviating from the apparent group consensus; specifically, each member may incline to minimize the importance of his/her own doubts.

6. Pressure on dissenters. The majority may exert direct pressure on any member who dissents or argues against any of the group's stereotypes, illusions, or commitments.

7. Mindguarding. There may emerge in the group one or several self-appointed "mind guards"—members who protect against information that might shatter the complacency about the effectiveness and morality of the group's decisions.

8. Apparent unanimity. Despite personal doubts, members may share an illusion that the decision is unanimous.

Causes of Groupthink. Although these symptoms indicate the occurrence of groupthink, they are not causes of it. Janis's (1972, 1982) theory identifies several factors that cause groupthink. Foremost among these is group cohesion. A cohesive group is one whose members stick together and remain unified in pursuit of the group's goals (Carron 1982; Mudrack 1989). Cohesive groups are marked by strong ties among members and a tendency for members to perceive events in similar terms (Braaten 1991; Evans and Jarvis 1980). Janis's theory states that groupthink is more likely to occur in groups with high cohesion than in groups with low cohesion; moreover, cohesion interacts (in the statistical sense) with other factors to intensify groupthink.

Janis (1982) identifies two classes of factors that cause groupthink—structural faults in the group and provocative situational contexts. The structural faults hypothesized to cause groupthink are: (1) biased, promotional leadership in the group; (2) homogeneity of members in background and ideology; (3) insulation of the group from outside agents; and (4) lack of rules in the group that establish formal methods for making decisions.

The provocative contexts hypothesized to induce groupthink include (1) situations that impose a high level of stress on the group and (2) situations that lower the self-esteem of group members. Although stress is neither necessary nor sufficient to induce groupthink, Janis states that it increases the probability of groupthink. One source of stress is time pressure imposed by a deadline; another is a threat to the group from external forces or agents.

Consequences of Groupthink. The theory holds that when groupthink occurs, it leads to defective decision making. Indicators of defective group decision making include: (1) an incomplete survey of available options, causing the group's discussion to focus on only a few options; (2) an incomplete survey of the attributes or properties of the various options, including the risks associated with the various options; (3) poor information search, including failure to seek advice of experts; (4) selective bias by members in processing information; (5) failure to reappraise any options that were discarded or rejected in the early stages of decision; (6) failure to reappraise the group's initially preferred option (to see whether members have changed their preferences); and (7) failure to formulate contingency plans that take into account how external groups might react to the option selected by the focal group (Janis 1972, 175).

Groupthink can reduce stress and increase consensus, but it does this at the price of suppressing critical analysis. Lack of critical analysis means an inaccurate appraisal of options, which often produces suboptimal decisions. Of course,

the linkage between groupthink and deficient decisions is probabilistic, not deterministic; groupthink will often produce poor decisions and unfavorable outcomes, but it need not do so in all cases.

Influence Processes in Groupthink. Many analysts distinguish between *public compliance* and *private acceptance,* modes of response by an influence target (Allen 1965; Festinger 1953; Nail 1986). Public compliance occurs when a member goes along publicly with the position advocated by others; private acceptance occurs when a member changes beliefs and accepts the others' position. Even if a member complies publicly with a decision or judgment, he/she may not accept it privately.

While strong pressure for uniformity underlies groupthink, the nature of this pressure is not entirely clear. Janis (1982, 247–48) apparently views groupthink as entailing both public compliance and private acceptance. He states that groupthink is likely to occur under high cohesion because group members are especially receptive to persuasion under this condition. However, McCauley (1989) argues that certain frequently cited instances of groupthink involve elements of public compliance without private acceptance. For example, during decision making for the Bay of Pigs invasion, some cabinet members engaged in self-censorship and refrained from expressing their reservations publicly; similarly, with respect to decisions to escalate the Vietnam conflict, expressions of dissent were generally viewed as indicating personal disloyalty to the president.

Research Findings on Groupthink

Writers have criticized various aspects of Janis's groupthink theory. Longley and Pruitt (1980) criticized the theory as failing to provide an adequate conception of the conditions under which cohesion will lead to groupthink. Steiner (1982) suggested that cohesion may, in reality, be a consequence of groupthink, not an antecedent. Whyte (1989) noted that the theory omits important variables that affect decisional outcomes. Despite these criticisms, groupthink theory is plausible and interesting. An immediate question, then, is whether the theory is empirically accurate. To date, investigators have conducted only a moderate number of studies—laboratory experiments and case studies—to test the theory (Park 1990). While certain hypotheses have been tested in depth, others remain untested. Nevertheless, the information available is sufficient to permit a preliminary assessment.

Some studies of groupthink focus on whether groupthink actually leads to poor decisions. Virtually all studies addressing this issue have been archival investigations or case studies (e.g., Esser and Lindoerfer 1989; Herek, Janis, and Huth 1987; Moorhead, Ference, and Neck 1991; Tetlock 1979). Although few in number, these studies report findings consistent with the hypothesis that groupthink produces inferior decisions and poor outcomes.

Other groupthink studies focus on factors that cause the onset of groupthink. The main dependent variable(s) in these studies is the extent to which symptoms of groupthink occur during group interaction. The results of these studies support some, but not all, of the hypotheses from groupthink theory. Following are some key findings.

Effects of Promotional Leadership on Groupthink. Promotional leadership occurs if a group's leader (or leaders) strongly advocates a particular option and opposes other options. Several case studies support the hypothesis that promotional leadership causes symptoms of groupthink. McCauley (1989) reanalyzed the foreign policy events (Bay of Pigs, Vietnam escalation, North Korea invasion, etc.) discussed by Janis. Results indicate that promotional leadership was usually present in the situations resulting in foreign policy failures but absent from those resulting in favorable outcomes. In a similar vein, Hensley and Griffin (1986) analyzed the controversy that erupted in 1977 at Kent State University when the board of trustees elected to build a new gymnasium on a site that many considered to be hallowed ground. The analysis suggests that many symptoms of groupthink were present when the board made this decision. The trustees were exposed to strong pro-

motional leadership that advocated one site for the gym and discouraged inquiry into alternative sites.

Findings from several laboratory studies also support the hypothesis that promotional leadership induces symptoms of groupthink. Leana (1985) found that four-person groups with a directive leader discussed fewer alternative solutions and more often accepted the solution advocated by the leader than did groups with a participative leader. Flowers (1977) studied four-person groups in which a trained upper-class student served as the group's leader. Depending on experimental treatment, this person enacted an open (nondirective) or a closed (directive) style of leadership. Consistent with the theory, groups with a closed-style leader developed fewer possible solutions to the problem, used fewer outside sources of information, and rationalized more after the decision. Moorhead and Montanari (1986) investigated forty-five decision-making teams of three to five persons in a business school context. Using measures developed previously (Montanari and Moorhead 1989; Moorhead and Montanari 1982), they constructed a path analytic model of the decisional processes in these groups. The results were mixed, but consistent with the theory they show that promotional leadership caused members to discourage dissent and express strong feelings of in-group morality. Fodor and Smith (1982) investigated the impact of a leader's power motivation (measured via the Thematic Apperception Test) on groupthink in five-person groups. Groups headed by leaders high in power motivation introduced less factual information and considered fewer action proposals than groups headed by leaders low in power motivation. Leaders with high power motivation fostered a group atmosphere that discouraged creative thinking by members and produced more symptoms of groupthink. Overall, these studies support the hypothesis that promotional leadership induces symptoms of groupthink in decision-making groups.

Effects of Insulation on Groupthink. Another hypothesis from the theory is that insulation of the group from its environment increases groupthink symptoms. Studies to date support this hypothesis. McCauley's (1989) reanalysis of the foreign policy decisions reveals that groups were insulated in four of the six groupthink cases but were not insulated in the two nongroupthink cases. Hensley and Griffin (1986) concluded that during the Kent State controversy, the board of trustees was highly insulated from outside sources of information and opinion. Manz and Sims (1982) proposed that "autonomous" (i.e., insulated, self-managing) work groups are especially vulnerable to groupthink. They found that autonomous work groups in a nonunionized battery assembly plant frequently manifested such groupthink symptoms as self-censorship, illusions of unanimity, collective rationalization, and shared stereotypes. Moorhead and Montanari (1986) also found evidence that insulation produces groupthink. Insulation caused groups to rely more on expert advice, to generate fewer decisional alternatives, and to perform poorly on decision tasks.

Effects of Stress on Groupthink. Janis's theory predicts that high levels of stress will produce symptoms of groupthink. Similarly, some investigators (Callaway, Marriott, and Esser 1985) view groupthink as a stress-reduction process; that is, group members reduce stress by suppressing critical inquiry during discussion prior to decision making. However, empirical studies investigating this hypothesis have produced mixed findings. While some studies support this hypothesis, others do not.

Courtright (1978) manipulated decisional stress by varying time pressure and normative instructions from the experimenter. The dependent variable was relative absence of disagreements, a symptom of groupthink. Highly cohesive groups disagreed more in the high-stress condition than in the low-stress condition. This result supports the theory. Hensley and Griffin (1986) concluded that the Kent State board of trustees, which displayed several symptoms of groupthink, experienced stress from external sources throughout the gymnasium controversy.

In contrast, McCauley (1989) concluded from a reanalysis of the foreign policy cases that stress did not reliably produce symptoms of groupthink.

Specifically, such factors as time pressure, external threat, perceived difficulty of decision, and recent group failure were not related to poor decisional outcomes. Overall, the findings regarding effects of stress on groupthink are inconsistent and do not support the theory unequivocally.

Effects of Cohesion on Groupthink. Although cohesion occupies a central place in groupthink theory, evidence regarding the effects of cohesion is mixed, even disconfirmatory. In support of the theory, several studies (including some of those discussed above) have shown that groups with high cohesion display more groupthink symptoms than groups with low cohesion. Courtright (1978) manipulated cohesion by giving members in some groups an opportunity to become acquainted and by telling them they had especially compatible personalities. Groups in the condition predicted to induce groupthink (i.e., high cohesion plus high stress) did display significantly less disagreement than groups in other conditions. However, results showed no main effect of cohesion on disagreements, and other dependent measures in this study (e.g., number of solutions proposed during discussion) did not show the predicted effect. Callaway and Esser (1984) manipulated cohesion in groups of college students by telling some they were high in similarity and compatibility (high cohesion) and others they were low in similarity and compatibility (low cohesion). This design also manipulated the procedural norms governing decision making in the groups. Some groups received instructions that encouraged consideration of all options and discouraged consensus (procedures present), while other groups did not receive these instructions (procedures absent). In the condition expected to produce groupthink (i.e., high cohesion with procedures absent), the quality of the group's decision was poorest, disagreement among members was lowest, and confidence in the decision was strongest. These findings support predictions based on groupthink theory.

On the other hand, several studies have found that cohesion does not significantly affect symptoms of groupthink. Flowers (1977) compared groups of acquaintances (high cohesion) with groups of strangers (low cohesion). Results revealed no difference between high-cohesion and low-cohesion groups in the quantity of groupthink symptoms. Fodor and Smith (1982) gave some groups an opportunity to earn a reward by performing well on a decision problem (high cohesion) but gave other groups no such opportunity (low cohesion). Results indicated that cohesion had no effect on the group decision-making process. Leana (1985) compared high-cohesion groups (four-person groups with fifteen weeks of experience working together) with low-cohesion groups (ad hoc groups of strangers). Results showed that subjects in the high-cohesion groups were more prone to share information and to analyze facts critically than subjects in low-cohesion groups. Postsession questionnaires showed that members of high-cohesion groups engaged in less self-censorship of information than did members of low-cohesion groups. These findings do not support groupthink theory.

Moorhead and Montanari (1986) reported mixed findings on cohesion. Consistent with the theory, the results show that high-cohesion groups discouraged dissent more than low-cohesion groups. Contrary to the theory, however, the results show less self-censorship and more evaluation of options in highly cohesive groups. Tetlock et al. (1992) used a statistical model (LISREL) to assess the causes of groupthink in the foreign policy cases discussed by Janis. They found that neither group cohesion nor provocative situations had any significant causal impact on concurrence seeking or groupthink symptoms.

Overall, findings are inconsistent regarding the effect of cohesion on the symptoms of groupthink. Two studies support the theory's predictions (Callaway and Esser 1984; Courtright 1978), but numerous others do not (Flowers 1977; Fodor and Smith 1982; Leana 1985; Moorhead and Montanari 1986; Tetlock et al. 1992). This inconsistency may arise, in part, from differences in the manipulations and/or measurements of cohesion. The supportive studies (Courtright; Callaway and Esser) manipulated cohesion by varying members' expectations regarding the extent to which they would be compatible with other members. In contrast, two of the nonsupportive studies (Flowers; Leana) manipulated cohesion by varying acquaintanceship: groups of acquaintances were considered to be high in cohesion, while groups of strangers were considered low in cohesion. Another nonsupportive study (Fodor and Smith) manipulated cohesion by varying joint fate: groups given an opportunity to achieve a group reward were considered high in cohesion, while those not given this opportunity were considered low in cohesion. The remaining nonsupportive studies (Moorhead and Montanari; Tetlock et al.) measured cohesion and did not manipulate it. Given these differences in procedure, the divergent findings regarding cohesion and groupthink are, perhaps, not surprising.

Moreover, there is some doubt that the level of cohesion achieved in the experimental studies is sufficiently high to test the theory fairly. In the laboratory studies, cohesion usually ranges from moderate to low. This is troublesome because most of the naturally occurring groups that Janis considered were highly cohesive. There is opportunity here for more research; the definitive study of cohesion and groupthink has yet to be conducted.

CHOICE SHIFT AND POLARIZATION

In 1961, a study by James Stoner showed that decisions made by a group are riskier than decisions on the same issues made previously by the group's members (Stoner 1961). Specifically, if individuals first decide on some level of risk as appropriate for a particular venture and then join together in a group to discuss that venture, after discussion they will choose a greater level of risk than what they preferred, on average, before discussion. This finding attracted considerable attention, for it contradicted the prevailing wisdom that a group's opinion corresponded closely to the average of the opinions of its constituent members. The tendency of members to favor riskier decisions after group discussion was labeled the *risky shift*.

Over the years, many studies have replicated Stoner's original finding that decision-making groups shift toward risk (Cartwright 1971). Other studies, however, have revealed an opposite effect.

On certain issues where members are initially risk-avoidant, group discussion will cause them to become even more cautious. This tendency has been termed the *cautious shift* (Fraser, Gouge, and Billig 1971; Stoner 1968; Wallach, Kogan, and Bem 1962). Both the risky shift and the cautious shift are special cases of a more general phenomenon, the *choice shift*.

Choice Dilemmas

Many investigations of choice shift have used stimulus materials called *choice dilemmas*. In the typical experiment with choice dilemmas, the subjects' task is to advise a fictional character regarding how much risk to take on an important issue. The following item (Kogan and Wallach 1964) illustrates this task:

> *Mr. A, an electrical engineer who is married and has one child, has been working for a large electronics corporation since graduating from college five years ago. He is assured of a lifetime job with a modest, although adequate, salary and liberal pension benefits upon retirement. On the other hand, his salary will probably not increase much before he retires. While attending a convention, Mr. A is offered a job with a small, newly founded company which has a highly uncertain future. The new job would pay more to start and would offer the possibility of a share in the ownership if the company survived the competition of the larger firms.*

Imagine that you are advising Mr. A. Listed below are several probabilities or odds of the new company proving financially sound. Please check the lowest probability that you would consider acceptable to make it worthwhile for Mr. A to take the new job.

> _____ *The chances are 1 in 10 that the company will prove financially sound.*

> _____ *The chances are 3 in 10 that the company will prove financially sound.*

> _____ *The chances are 5 in 10 that the company will prove financially sound.*

> _____ *The chances are 7 in 10 that the company will prove financially sound.*

> _____ *The chances are 9 in 10 that the company will prove financially sound.*

> _____ *Place a check here if you think Mr. A should not take the new job no matter what the probabilities.*

Other choice dilemmas are similar. One example: A captain of a college football team, in the final seconds of a game with the college's traditional rival, can choose a conservative play or a risky play. The conservative play would produce a tied score, while the risky play would lead either to victory (if successful) or defeat (if unsuccessful). Another example: A low-ranking participant in a national chess tournament, playing an early match against the top-ranked competitor, faces a decision whether to play conservatively or to attempt a risky maneuver. If undetected by the top player, the risky maneuver could lead to quick victory; if detected, it would lead to defeat (Wallach, Kogan, and Bem 1962).

In the typical choice dilemma study, subjects first complete a questionnaire and indicate what probability of success they would require before recommending the risky alternative to the decision maker. The average of these recommendations is the pretest group mean. Next, the subjects assemble in a group (e.g., five members) and discuss each item until they reach a (unanimous) consensus regarding the appropriate level of risk. Finally, each subject is retested individually on the items; this produces the posttest group mean. Using this procedure, many studies have shown that the group consensus and the posttest group mean are in the same direction as, but more extreme than, the pretest group mean. In some cases, this is a shift toward risk (Cartwright 1971; Dion, Baron, and Miller 1970); in others, it is a shift toward caution (Fraser, Gouge, and Billig 1971).

Group Polarization

Today, social psychologists view the choice shift as just one manifestation of a more general phenomenon, *group polarization* (Moscovici and Zavalloni 1969; Myers and Lamm 1976). Group polarization is the tendency of group discussion (or some related manipulation) to move the prevailing response in the group toward an extreme. Although first observed in decisions involving risk, group polarization has also been noted on a wide variety of other measures. Polarization occurs, for instance, in the level of guilt attributed to defendants by juries, in judgments of autokinetic movements (distance), and in judgments of physical attractiveness (Isenberg 1986; Isozaki 1984; Myers and Kaplan 1976). It also occurs on attitudinal measures, such as those tapping racial prejudice and reactions to civil disobedience (Cvetkovich and Baumgardner 1973; Myers and Bishop 1970). With polarization, the mean response of members after discussion tends to be in the same direction as, but more extreme than, the average of the members' individual responses before discussion. (For reviews of research on polarization, see Clark 1971; Dion, Baron, and Miller 1970; Isenberg 1986; Lamm 1988; Lamm and Myers 1978; Myers and Lamm 1976; Pruitt 1971; Vinokur 1971.)

Why does group polarization occur? It cannot be explained by traditional conformity theory, unaided by other constructs (Allen 1965; Asch 1951, 1956; Deutsch and Gerard 1955). While social influence and conformity processes will reduce the dispersion in members' responses, they should cause members' responses to converge toward the pretest group mean. Such convergence does not explain why the posttest mean actually shifts from the pretest mean toward an extreme. For this reason, social psychologists have developed various theories of polarization that emphasize processes other than conformity.

Theories of Group Polarization

To date, three midrange theories have emerged as especially plausible explanations of polarization (Isenberg 1986; Myers and Lamm 1976). These include (1) social comparison theory, (2) persuasive arguments theory, and (3) self-categorization theory.

Social Comparison Theory. The *social comparison theory* maintains that merely exposing group members to one another's preferences activates a process of interpersonal comparison that results in group polarization (Goethals and Zanna 1979; Jellison and Riskind 1970; Levinger and Schneider 1969). This theory assumes that people often value attitudinal positions that are more extreme than those they personally advocate. They do not advocate these extreme positions on the pretest because they fear being rejected or labeled deviant by other persons. However, on participating in discussion, the members can compare their positions; the moderate members then come to realize that opinions held by others are more extreme and, hence, closer to the ideal position than their own opinions.

This realization will produce any of several effects. It may banish *pluralistic ignorance* and liberate the moderates from the fear of appearing too extreme or deviant (Levinger and Schneider 1969; Pruitt 1971). Alternatively, it may motivate the moderates to engage in a status competition with the more extreme members. This so-called *bandwagon effect* would result if members want to present themselves as different from and superior to others by espousing a position closer to the ideal (Brown 1974; Jellison and Arkin 1977; Myers, Wojcicki, and Aardema 1977).

Whatever the case, the realization obtained through social comparison will motivate the moderates to adopt positions more extreme than those they advocated on the pretest. There is, however, no corresponding pressure on the extreme members to adopt more moderate positions. The net result will be a mean shift in attitudes toward a more extreme position (i.e., polarization) (Sanders and Baron 1977).

Numerous empirical studies have reported findings that support social comparison theory. First, research has shown that if, after responding to the choice dilemmas for the first time, subjects go back over the items and guess how the average member would respond, they estimate the average response as less extreme than their own response. If they then go over the items another time to indicate what response they would admire most, they select as ideal a response in the same direction as, but more extreme than, their own (McCauley, Kogan, and Teger 1971; Myers and Lamm 1976).

Thus, the subjects' position is located more extremely in the socially desirable direction than the estimated average response, but less extremely than the ideal response.

Second, studies have shown that subjects perceive group members whose responses are more extreme than their own in the direction of their ideal as more socially desirable than members whose responses are not more extreme than their own (Baron, Monson, and Baron 1973; Jellison and Davis 1973). Third, studies have shown that merely receiving information about the positions of other members is sufficient to produce polarization. In other words, even without argument-rich communication among members, information that enables members to compare their positions will induce polarization (Baron and Roper 1976; Blascovich, Ginsburg, and Veach 1975; Myers et al. 1980). All of these findings support social comparison theory.

Other findings, however, are not consistent with the theory. Research has not supported the motivational postulate that members engage in status competition and try to differentiate themselves from others. If anything, findings suggest that members tend to conform—that is, to converge to a (more extreme) position—and to become increasingly similar to one another in their views. They do not become more highly differentiated, as would be predicted from status competition. For instance, some polarization studies have shown that persons exposed to a manipulated group norm (either pro or con the cultural value) shift in the direction of the fake norm (Baron et al. 1971; Blascovich and Ginsburg 1974). In addition, Singleton (1979) found that while members who were moderate on the pretest shifted toward a more extreme position after discussion, some members who were extreme on the pretest shifted back toward a moderate position. This pattern is consistent with a convergence (conformity) process, not a differentiation (status competition) process.

Persuasive Arguments Theory.   The second major explanation of group polarization is *persuasive arguments theory* (Burnstein 1982; Burnstein and

Vinokur 1973, 1977; Madsen 1978). Fundamentally, this theory holds that polarization results from a process of informational influence (i.e., persuasion based on factual argument.) According to this theory, there exists a "cultural pool" of persuasive arguments, both pro and con, for any given issue. Subjects sample arguments from this pool and consider them when making judgments on the pretest. The theory assumes that if these initial judgments favor one direction (say, pro risk taking), then most of the remaining arguments in the pool also favor that direction.

When members come together in a group, they discuss the issue and exchange arguments from the cultural pool. Through this process, members shift their views into line with positions advocated by others. Since the preponderance of arguments in the pool run in the direction favored by the subjects' pretest judgments, the group discussion will produce polarization in that direction.

What is important, however, is not the sheer number of arguments during discussion, but the number of compelling arguments. For an argument to be compelling, members must construe it as *valid* and *novel.* An argument is valid when it is logically coherent and consistent with established facts; it is novel when it contains new facts or offers new ways to organize information. When arguments presented in a group discussion are valid and novel, they challenge the views of members who initially held moderate or neutral positions and cause them to adopt more extreme positions.

Certain empirical findings support the persuasive arguments theory. First, numerous studies have shown that polarization does result from the exchange of persuasive arguments and that it is a function of the group's initial information pool. The greater the number of novel and valid arguments exchanged during discussion, the greater the influence of those arguments on members and the greater the magnitude of polarization (Kaplan 1977; Vinokur and Burnstein 1974, 1978).

Second, studies have shown a relation between the preponderance of pro and con arguments advanced by members and the amount of subsequent polarization (Ebbesen and Bowers 1974; Lamm 1988; Madsen 1978). For instance, several studies have manipulated the proportion of arguments favoring a particular position (either pro or con) on some issue. The greater the proportion favoring a particular position, the greater is the shift of opinion in that direction (Burnstein and Vinokur 1973; Kaplan and Miller 1977; Laughlin and Earley 1982). Thus, subjects exposed primarily to arguments advocating risk will shift toward risk, whereas those exposed primarily to arguments advocating caution will shift toward caution.

Third, some studies have provided correlational evidence consistent with predictions from the theory. The theory holds that if members' pretest judgments favor one direction (say, pro risk taking), then most of the arguments in the pool will run in the same direction. In support of this, Myers and Lamm (1976) found that the direction of the pretest judgments predicts the direction of most arguments advanced during group discussion. Moreover, the majority of high-quality arguments offered during discussion favor the predominant extreme (Vinokur and Burnstein 1974).

Despite this empirical support, there are two strong reservations regarding persuasive arguments theory. First, some studies have shown that polarization can occur without an exchange of persuasive arguments (Baron and Roper 1976; Blascovich, Ginsburg, and Veach 1975; Cotton and Baron 1980; Myers 1982). Thus, persuasive argumentation and information exchange are sufficient, but apparently not necessary, for polarization to occur. Second, persuasive arguments theory is incomplete because it does not specify what mechanism actually brings about polarization (Kaplan 1977; Sanders and Baron 1977). Persuasive arguments theory holds that the underlying cultural pool includes arguments, both pro and con, in a certain ratio, and that group members advance these arguments in that ratio during discussion. If this were so, the group would converge on the position defined by the pro-to-con ratio. But this position is exactly the same as the mean of the pretest judgments. Thus, it is difficult to see how

discussing the issue would produce a shift in position toward an extreme, rather than convergence on the pretest mean. Although several mechanisms have been proposed to address this problem (Kaplan 1977; Lamm and Myers 1978; Vinokur and Burnstein 1974), it is still unresolved.

Self-Categorization Theory. The third major explanation of group polarization stems from *self-categorization theory* (Turner et al. 1987; Turner and Oakes 1986, 1989; Wetherell 1987). Self-categorization theory is a comparatively new cognitive approach that emphasizes social identity. It holds that people can categorize themselves as individual persons (defined by their differences from other persons) or as members of some social group (defined by its differences vis-à-vis one or more outgroups). In everyday life, most persons categorize themselves both as individuals and as group members. Depending on conditions, one or another of these self-categorizations will predominate at any given time (Oakes 1987). If a person categorizes him/herself primarily as a member of a specific group, then he/she will engage in a process of self-stereotyping; that is, he/she will adopt the attributes characteristic of the group and conform to its standards.

Group behavior, from the vantage of self-categorization theory, consists of persons enacting their shared group identities, rather than their individual identities. Some studies have shown that groups to which persons view themselves as belonging (i.e., in-groups) influence their behavior more than groups to which they do not view themselves as belonging (out-groups) (Abrams et al. 1990; Mackie and Cooper 1984; Wilder 1990). Other studies have shown that people conform more to group norms when social identity is salient than when it is not (Reicher 1984; Wilder and Shapiro 1984).

Self-categorization theory explains group polarization as resulting from members' conformity, through self-categorization, to an extreme group norm. This norm, however, is not the average of members' positions on the pretest measure but the *prototypical position* of the group, a cultural construct. The prototype is that position (on some issue) which best delineates what the group's members have in common compared to relevant out-groups. As such, it functions as a boundary-defining norm.

During discussion, group members exchange views and compare their positions with those of others. They also compare their own group with various out-groups to ascertain the relevant prototype that best defines their group as unique. The prototype serves as a frame of reference in terms of which members assess the validity (or invalidity) of arguments advanced during group discussion. This conformity process, rooted in group identity, causes members to shift toward the prototype.

In principle, the group's prototype can be either more extreme or less extreme than the mean of the pretest positions of the members. When the prototype is more extreme, convergence on the prototype will result in group polarization; when the prototype is less extreme, convergence will result in "depolarization." Of these two possibilities, however, polarization seems to be more common. Several studies have reported cases where prototypes are more extreme than the pretest mean (Hogg, Turner, and Davidson 1990; Turner, Wetherell, and Hogg 1989).

Because self-categorization theory is relatively new, researchers are still actively investigating its predictions about polarization. Empirical research to date provides support for several propositions in the theory. Several studies have shown that categorization of self as a group member leads to attitude polarization in the direction of the group's norm. In one study (Mackie and Cooper 1984), subjects listened to a tape-recorded discussion ascribed either to a group the subject was about to join (in-group) or to a group against which the subject's own group was about to compete (out-group). The subjects' attitudes polarized in the direction advocated on the tape in the in-group condition but not in the out-group condition. Movement toward the in-group norm resulted from private acceptance (attitude change), not public compli-

ance. In a subsequent study, Mackie (1986) established different levels of salience of in-group membership for subjects by varying conditions of intergroup competition and intragroup competition. When in-group membership was most salient (intergroup competition), the subjects perceived group attitudes as extremitized, and their attitudes shifted toward the extreme (i.e., polarized). In contrast, when in-group membership was least salient (intragroup competition), the subjects did not perceive group attitudes as extremitized, and their attitudes shifted to a neutral position. These findings support the view that polarization results from conformity by members to extreme group norms.

Turner et al. (1989) demonstrated that the way subjects are induced to categorize themselves—either as group members or as individuals—plays an important role in polarization. Labeling subjects as members of either risky groups or cautious groups produced a shift in response in line with the normative tendency that defined the group; that is, subjects in stereotypically risky groups polarized toward risk, while subjects in stereotypically cautious groups polarized toward caution. In contrast, labeling the subjects either as risky or cautious individuals (versus labeling them as risky or cautious group members) produced no such shift in response.

Self-categorization theory maintains that changing the particular out-group against which members make comparisons will change the group's prototypical position. In turn, this will change the direction and/or amount of shift in members' judgments following discussion. Therefore, by manipulating the out-group that serves as the group's frame of reference, it should be possible to change the direction of polarization on choice-dilemma items. Consistent with this hypothesis, Hogg et al. (1990) found that when confronted by a cautious out-group, subjects perceived their group's prototypical position as riskier than their mean pretest score, but when confronted by a risky out-group, subjects perceived their group's prototypical position as more cautious than their pretest mean. In other words, a group will polarize either toward risk or toward caution, depending on which out-group serves as the reference.

SOCIAL DECISION RULES

The topics reviewed to this point—groupthink and polarization—emphasize behavior during the discussion phase, before the group actually makes its choice. Groups differ, however, not only in their style of discussion, but also in the procedures they use to combine preferences and reach collective decisions (Lehrer 1979; Wood 1984). Some groups rely on *discussion to consensus*; that is, they discuss the issue until some members change opinions and move toward (unanimous) agreement. Other groups rely on *voting* to combine preferences into a decision; although voting mechanisms differ in various respects, they always permit members' preferences to be formally expressed and counted. Still other groups use *delegation,* wherein members cede power to an individual or subgroup who decides for the entire group. Finally, some groups rely on *mathematical amalgamation* of members' preferences. In this case, the group uses some explicit formula (e.g., an average or weighted average) to combine individual preferences and determine the group's choice or preference.

Groups differ also in the level of agreement they require to make a collective decision. Some groups require a very high level of agreement among members to reach a decision, while others require only a moderate level. Groups usually implement the desired strictness through a decision rule. Formally, a *social decision rule* is a group norm that specifies what level of agreement is required to reach a (binding) group decision with respect to a set of options. Examples of decision rules are the simple majority rule, the two-thirds majority rule, and the unanimity rule.

Theorists distinguish between two types of decision rules—explicit and implicit (Davis 1973). An explicit decision rule is a formal, publicly acknowledged norm that stipulates the level of agreement required to reach agreement. In a jury, for example, the explicit decision rule might be unanimity (e.g., twelve out of twelve). An implicit

decision rule is a tacit norm that describes the method by which a group actually arrives at a decision. In that same jury, the implicit decision rule might be the ten-twelfths majority rule: if ten out of twelve jurors support a verdict, the other two will set aside their objections and acquiesce to the majority.

This section focuses primarily on explicit decision rules. The central issue is: In what ways does the use of one explicit decision rule (rather than another) influence the outcomes of group decision making? Social decision rules do affect the deliberations and decisions by groups. This was demonstrated, for instance, by Saks's (1977) experimental simulation of jury decision making. In this study (experiment 2), 461 jurors served on fifty-eight experimental juries. The study used a two-by-two factorial design that crossed decision rule (unanimity versus two-thirds majority) with jury size (twelve-person versus six-person). The trial, which was presented to jurors via a one-hour videotape plus written instructions from the judge, concerned a felony (burglary of an inhabited dwelling).

The results of this study showed that among those juries reaching a decision, the distribution of verdicts (convict or acquit) did not differ as a function of decision rule. However, juries using the unanimity rule failed to reach any decision (i.e., hung) more often than juries using the two-thirds majority rule; the greater frequency of hung juries implies that dissenting minorities are more effective in blocking the majority under the stricter decision rule (unanimity). Postdeliberation questionnaires showed that members of juries that convicted the defendant were more certain of the defendant's guilt when they used the unanimity rule than when they used the two-thirds majority rule; that is, aggregate certainty about the correctness of the decision was higher under unanimity than under two-thirds majority.

The outcomes in this study were also affected by jury size. Jurors in the large (twelve-person) juries communicated more and recalled testimony better than did jurors in the small (six-person) juries. However, jury size did not affect the conviction-to-acquittal ratio or the proportion of hung juries.

Nor did jury size affect the jurors' postdeliberation certainty about the correctness of their decisions.

Consensus Models Incorporating Decision Rules

To study how members' preferences are combined into a group decision, theorists have developed a variety of formal models (Penrod and Hastie 1979; Stasser, Kerr, and Davis 1989). Most of these are highly complex computer simulations involving many variables. Among them are DICE (Penrod and Hastie 1980), JUS (Hastie, Penrod, and Pennington 1983), SIS (Stasser and Davis 1981), and DISCUSS (Stasser 1988). Analysts have used predictions from these models to study various decision-making groups, most notably juries.

All of these models assume that a group consists initially of members with some given distribution of preference or sentiment and that the members interact with and influence one another. Thus, the models treat group decision making as sequences of opinion changes by members that lead either to a decision (if there is sufficient convergence of opinion) or to a stalemate (if there is insufficient convergence).

Typical independent variables in these models are: social decision rule (e.g., unanimity, two-thirds majority, simple majority), group size (e.g., twelve members, six members, etc.), initial distribution of members' preferences regarding options (e.g., the percentage of members favoring one option rather than another), and member persuadability (a parameter indicating how readily members change their opinions). Dependent variables in these models include the predicted distribution of group decisions and the members' confidence in the decision.

A typical computer simulation begins by sampling (hypothetical) groups of a given size from a population having some specified distribution of individual preferences. Then, through iterative looping, the model implements the process by which members interact and attempt to influence one another. Influence is based on some version of the *strength-in-numbers postulate,* which holds that

the probability of a member shifting his/her preference to a new position increases directly as a function of the number of other members advocating that position. Based on the idea that larger factions produce more arguments and exert more normative pressure, this postulate has received support in many empirical studies (e.g., Kerr et al. 1987; Latane 1981; Latane and Wolf 1981).

Although the DICE, JUS, SIS, and DISCUSS models implement the strength-in-numbers postulate differently, they share the notion that some initial configuration of sentiment in a group (e.g., eight advocating guilty and four advocating not guilty in a twelve-person jury) constitutes the starting point for social influence. These models calculate the probabilities of opinion change based on the sizes of existing factions and the persuadability parameter; they then determine which members change opinions at any given stage of the discussion. Through this method, the models simulate how a group moves from its initial configuration of preferences to its final configuration and, subsequently, to a group decision.

By specifying parameters in advance, analysts can use these simulation models to predict outcomes for specific cases. Indeed, the DICE, JUS, and SIS models account for a wide range of data on jury decisions (Hastie, Penrod, and Pennington 1983; Penrod and Hastie 1980; Stasser and Davis 1981). Analysts can also use these simulation models to explore heuristically the impact of changes in various independent variables. The models generate testable predictions about the effects of different decision rules on group outcomes.

For instance, Stasser and Davis (1981) used the SIS model to predict the effects of decision rule and jury size on the verdict and postdeliberation juror confidence. The SIS model predicts that more hung juries will occur under the unanimity rule than under the two-thirds majority rule. It also predicts that jurors' confidence in the verdict will be greater in larger juries that use more stringent decision rules (e.g., unanimity rule rather than two-thirds majority rule).

Penrod and Hastie (1980) used the DICE model to predict the effects of decision rule and jury size on verdict and average deliberation time. They contrasted the unanimity rule against a nonunanimity rule (ten-twelfths majority). The DICE model predicts a greater frequency of hung juries under unanimity than under nonunanimity in six-person juries but no difference in twelve-person juries. It also predicts that deliberation time will be greater in unanimous-rule juries than in nonunanimous-rule juries and in twelve-person juries than in six-person juries.

Research Findings on Decision Rules

Numerous experiments have been conducted to ascertain how social decision rules affect the choices and verdicts made by groups. Most of these investigate mock juries in laboratory settings; many contrast the unanimity rule with some variant of the majority rule. Dependent variables in these studies include the nature of the decision reached (e.g., guilty, innocent, hung jury), deliberation time required, care taken in reaching a decision (i.e., scrutiny of facts, fullness of deliberation, etc.), the extent of members' participation in the discussion, and level of members' satisfaction with the final decision. (For reviews of this research, see Davis 1980; Davis, Bray, and Holt 1977; Miller 1989; Vollrath and Davis 1980.)

The discussion below summarizes some empirical generalizations about the effects of the unanimity rule and the majority rule. First, consistent with predictions from the SIS and DICE models, some experiments show that groups using the unanimity rule fail more often to reach a decision than groups using versions of the majority rule. Many studies of mock juries have demonstrated this effect (Buckhout et al. 1977; Foss 1981; Hastie, Penrod, and Pennington 1983; Padawer-Singer, Singer, and Singer 1977). Although not large in magnitude, the effect is reliable. The reason for it seems straightforward. The unanimity rule gives every member a veto, whereas the majority rule does not. Under unanimity, it takes only a single dissenting member to produce a hung jury.

In situations where groups choose between exactly two options, the decision rule per se does not affect the substantive nature of the outcome.

For example, in jury decisions where the choice is between guilty and not guilty, the decision rule (i.e., unanimity or majority) does not affect the verdict distribution. Several studies of mock juries have shown that the use of one decision rule or another does not bias the decision either toward guilty or toward not guilty (Davis et al. 1975; Grofman 1976; Nemeth 1977).

However, in situations where groups choose among more than two options, the unanimity and majority rules can produce different outcomes. For decisions of this type, the options frequently can be ranked according to some underlying dimension or continuum (e.g., degree of riskiness). When there are many options, the unanimity rule leads to compromise more often than the majority rule. This happens because under unanimity, members must compromise with one another (i.e., shift positions along a dimension) or face the possibility that the group will fail to reach a decision. Under majority rule, the group's eventual choice is usually the option favored initially by a majority of members; the majority has little need to compromise with minority members because the minority has no veto (Birnberg and Pondy 1971; Harnett 1967; Kaplan and Miller 1987).

Groups tend to make decisions more carefully under the unanimity rule than under the majority rule. Unanimity-rule groups deliberate more fully and examine evidence more thoroughly than majority-rule groups (Bower 1965; Hastie, Penrod, and Pennington 1983; Holloman and Hendrick 1972). Alternative viewpoints come into play, and members of minority factions participate more fully in discussions under the unanimity rule than under majority rule (Foss 1981; Hastie, Penrod, and Pennington 1983; Nemeth 1977).

The stricter the decision rule, the greater the time spent in discussion before making a choice. For instance, discussion time under the unanimity rule is greater than that under the two-thirds majority rule, which in turn is greater than that under the simple majority rule. Mock juries under the unanimity rule take longer to reach a decision than mock juries under majority rule (Davis et al. 1975; Foss 1981; Hastie, Penrod, and Pennington 1983; Kerr et al. 1976; Saks 1977). This pattern accords with the DICE model, which predicts greater deliberation time in unanimity-rule juries than in nonunanimity-rule juries.

The group's decision rule also affects who participates in discussion. Members holding a minority viewpoint tend to participate more in the discussion under the unanimity rule than under the majority rule. Similarly, majority members dominate the discussion less under the unanimity rule than under various forms of the majority rule (Hastie, Penrod, and Pennington 1983).

In groups that actually reach decisions (i.e., do not hang), members on average express more satisfaction about decisions made under unanimity rule than about those made under majority rule (Kaplan and Miller 1987; Kerr et al. 1976; Nemeth 1977). Under majority rule, members who dissent from the majority's position tend to be more dissatisfied than those who vote with the majority. Not surprisingly, members are usually more satisfied with collective decisions when they agree with them personally (Hastie, Penrod, and Pennington 1983; Miller and Anderson 1979; Miller et al. 1987).

MINORITY INFLUENCE IN GROUP DECISIONS

A minority coalition within a larger group cannot outvote the majority or compel the majority to change its viewpoint. Still, a minority can affect group decisions in several ways. First, it can serve as a liberating model that enables members to resist social pressure from the majority and to express their preferences more freely. Second, it can often modify the majority's thought processes, causing majority members to reconceptualize the options or see the objectives in a different light.

Resisting Pressure from the Majority

In decision-making groups, majorities usually attempt to influence dissenting members and bring them into line. This pressure is especially great when a group is operating under the unanimity rule or when the majority needs a few more votes to meet the group's quorum. If, for example, the first ballot splits eleven to one in a twelve-person jury

operating under unanimity, the majority will surely pressure the lone dissenter to change his/her vote.

Members who disagree with a unified majority may have difficulty resisting pressures for conformity. As research in the tradition of Asch has shown, subjects frequently acquiesce even if they do not truly accept the majority's view (Allen 1965; Asch 1956; Kiesler and Kiesler 1969). Individuals' tendency to comply publicly increases directly, up to some threshold, as a function of the size of the unified majority (Asch 1951; Gerard, Wilhelmy, and Conolley 1968; Rosenberg 1961).

If a dissenting subject faces the majority without a single ally, he/she will have to bear the total brunt of pressure from the majority. However, if a minority coalition exists within the group and the dissenting subject agrees with the minority's position, he/she will receive some relief. Pressure from the majority will be diffused across several persons, and the minority will provide social support (in effect, it will exercise counterinfluence on the dissenter). This will tend to reduce conformity by the dissenter to the majority (Latane and Wolf 1981; Levine, Sroka, and Snyder 1977; Tanford and Penrod 1984; Wolf 1985).

Even if the dissenter does not agree with the minority coalition or wish to join it, the presence of that coalition will still promote independent thought and judgment. Any breach in unanimity—even in the direction opposite to that of the dissenter's own position—will raise questions about the correctness of the majority's position. Studies report less conformity by subjects when a confederate breaks from the majority than when a confederate does not break from the majority, irrespective of the direction of that break (Allen and Levine 1968, 1971; Morris and Miller 1975). Similarly, the presence of a minority coalition will liberate others from majority pressure (Kiesler and Pallak 1975).

Influencing the Majority

Although minority coalitions may liberate dissenters from majority pressure, they frequently have little impact on the majority itself. This lack of influence is readily apparent in voting groups and juries. For instance, one study (Kalven and Zeisel

1966, chap. 38) compared the jury's first-ballot voting pattern with its final verdict in twelve-person juries. When a majority of jurors (i.e, seven to eleven persons) favored guilty on the first ballot, the jury, on deliberation, returned a verdict of guilty in 86 percent of the cases. In contrast, when only a minority of jurors (i.e., one to five persons) favored guilty on the first ballot, the jury returned a verdict of guilty in just 2 percent of the cases. Thus, the majority's initial opinion usually determined the verdict of the jury, and the minority influenced the verdict only rarely. Other studies show that if a significant majority (e.g., two-thirds or more of the members) favors a particular position on the first ballot, the jury most often returns that verdict (Davis, Bray, and Holt 1977; Hastie, Penrod, and Pennington 1983).

Nevertheless, a resolute minority may occasionally cause a jury to hang, or it may even persuade the majority to change its position. Experimental studies have shown that a dissenting minority can influence the judgments and decisions of majority members in certain cases. Reviews of research on minority influence, much of which focuses on group judgments rather than group decisions, appear in Moscovici and Mugny (1983), Maass and Clark (1984), Mugny (1984), and Levine and Russo (1987).

For present purposes, the central question is: What factors affect a minority coalition's capacity to change the majority's view and, hence, the group's decision? One factor is sheer size. Some computer models predict that the influence of a minority coalition will increase as that coalition increases in size relative to the majority. The DICE model, for instance, predicts that a minority's influence grows exponentially with size (Penrod and Hastie 1980; Tanford and Penrod 1983). Empirical research has addressed minority size, although there does not appear yet to exist a precise test of DICE's exponential prediction. One study (Arbuthnot and Wayner 1982) found that a minority of two is more effective than a minority of one. Another study (Nemeth, Wachtler, and Endicott 1977) fixed the size of the majority at six persons and varied the size of the minority; results showed that

a minority of three or four is more influential than a minority of one or two.

According to *minority influence theory* (Moscovici 1976; Moscovici and Faucheux 1972), a minority coalition has a greater chance of influencing majority opinion when its position is consistent over time than when its position is inconsistent. This hypothesis has received support in many empirical studies. Experiments using a color-perception paradigm have reported confirmation (Moscovici, Lage, and Naffrechoux 1969; Nemeth, Swedlund, and Kanki 1974; Nemeth, Wachtler, and Endicott 1977), as have studies using a jury-award paradigm (Levine and Ranelli 1978; Levine, Saxe, and Harris 1976; Nemeth and Wachtler 1974; Wolf 1979).

Minority influence theory proposes that consistent behavior confers influence because others will attribute more confidence (i.e., certainty of outlook) and competence (i.e., judgmental skill) to a consistent minority than to an inconsistent one. Experimental studies show that, in general, other members perceive a consistent minority as more confident than an inconsistent one (Bray, Johnson, and Chilstrom 1982; Moscovici and Lage 1976; Nemeth and Wachtler 1973, 1974). To a lesser extent, they also see a consistent minority as more competent than the group's majority (Moscovici, Lage, and Naffrechoux 1969; Moscovici and Neve 1973).

If the majority attributes the minority's consistent behavior to confidence and competence, it may be willing to accept influence from the minority. However, if the majority attributes the minority's consistent behavior to personal idiosyncrasies and subjective biases, it will avoid the minority and reject influence from it. To be seen as competent and confident, the minority must do more than merely state its position repetitively; it must demonstrate a capacity to react in a principled manner to changing conditions. This means that to be influential, the minority must display openness in negotiations with the majority and avoid rigidity and dogmatism (Mugny 1982; Nemeth, Swedlund, and Kanki 1974; Papastamou and Mugny 1985).

Some theorists have suggested that minorities and majorities influence their targets in different ways. The *dual-process model* (Moscovici 1980, 1985; Nemeth 1985, 1986) maintains that while majorities influence their targets directly, often producing compliance, minorities influence their targets indirectly, producing both compliance and acceptance (ie., conversion). Thus, the model suggests that the impact of the majority is direct, immediate, and public, whereas the impact of the minority is indirect, delayed, and private.

The indirect nature of minority influence is apparent in a study of decisions by five-person mock juries (Nemeth and Wachtler 1974). These groups had to decide on appropriate awards in a simulated personal injury case. The groups contained a member (a confederate) who argued consistently for an award ($3000) that was far below the mean amount favored by the majority ($14,670). Despite these arguments, the majority's position changed very little on the final vote. But when the group turned to a second case, the subjects awarded significantly smaller amounts than did subjects in control groups that did not contain a dissenting confederate; this pattern was especially clear when the confederate occupied the head seat at the table. The influence process in this case appears to be acceptance and not just compliance, a finding consistent with the dual-process model. Although the dual-process model is not universally accepted, many studies have reported results that support it (Maass and Clark 1983, 1984; Mugny 1975, 1976; Nemeth and Kwan 1985, 1987).

SUMMARY

This chapter reviewed theory and research on four topics in group decision making—groupthink, polarization and choice shift, social decision rules, and minority influence.

Groupthink

Groupthink is a mode of thought whereby pressures toward unanimity overwhelm group members' motivation to appraise the available options realistically. Eight behavioral symptoms indicate when groupthink is occurring. According to Janis's

theory, groupthink is produced by high levels of group cohesion in conjunction with conditions such as promotional leadership, homogeneity of members, insulation of the group from the environment, and the lack of procedural norms governing decision making.

Research findings to date support some hypotheses from groupthink theory but disconfirm others. There is strong support for the hypothesis that promotional leadership heightens the occurrence of groupthink symptoms and moderate support for the hypothesis that insulation of a group from its environment increases the occurrence of groupthink symptoms. However, research does not consistently substantiate the hypothesis that high stress produces symptoms of groupthink. Nor does research offer much support for the hypothesis that group cohesion, in interaction with other factors, causes groupthink. Data available at this time suggest that the primary causes of groupthink are promotional leadership and insulation, not cohesion.

With respect to future research on groupthink, several points seem evident. First, there is currently no standard or unified research paradigm for groupthink (in the sense that the choice dilemma task is a standard in polarization research or the Asch line-judgment paradigm is a standard for conformity research). Refinement of groupthink theory would accelerate if investigators developed and used a standard research paradigm. Second, investigators have used a diversity of (possibly unrelated) manipulations and measures of cohesion in groupthink studies. More research is needed to clarify the impact of cohesion on groupthink, and comparison across studies would be facilitated if investigators were to establish standard measures and manipulations of this variable.

Choice Shift and Polarization

Polarization occurs if members who tend initially in a given direction on some issue shift to an extreme position in the same direction after discussion. One form of polarization is choice shift. Theorists have proposed three major explanations of group polarization. Social comparison theory explains polarization as resulting from interpersonal comparisons among members regarding their respective positions. Persuasive arguments theory explains polarization as resulting from novel and valid arguments advanced during discussion. Self-categorization theory explains polarization as resulting from a shift by members toward the group's (extreme) prototypical position. Although empirical studies support each of the theories, the support is not unequivocal. Persuasive argumentation may explain a greater proportion of the variation in choice shift than does social comparison (Isenberg 1986). Self-categorization theory is comparatively new and merits further investigation in the future.

Social Decision Rules

Groups differ in the procedures they use to combine members' preferences when making a collective decision. Typical procedures include discussion to consensus, voting, delegation, and averaging. Groups differ also in the level of agreement they require to finalize a collective decision. The desired level of strictness is usually implemented by a decision rule. Widely used decision rules include unanimity, two-thirds majority, and simple majority.

Several computer simulation models (DICE, JUS, SIS, and DISCUSS) address the impact of decision rules on the choices made by groups. These simulations describe how groups move from their initial configurations of preference to their final configurations, and they predict the effects of various decision rules on decisional outcomes.

Research shows that groups operating under unanimity rule make decisions more deliberately than those operating under majority rule. Time spent on discussion before decision increases as a function of the strictness of the decision rule. Members who hold a minority view are more likely to participate in the discussion under unanimity rule than under majority rule. The unanimity rule more often results in failure to reach a decision (i.e., a hung jury) than do variants of the majority rule.

The heavy reliance on computer simulation models in research on social decision rules is especially noteworthy. This style of work will surely continue in the future, and researchers investigating other topics in group decision making may eventually adopt it as well. Computer simulation provides an excellent medium in which to formulate complex models that make explicit, testable predictions.

Minority Influence in Group Decisions

Changing the position favored by a group's majority is difficult for even the staunchest minority. Minority influence, however, varies as a function of several factors. Other things equal, a large minority will be more influential than a small one. As predicted by minority influence theory, a consistent minority will generally be more influential than an inconsistent one. Use of a flexible negotiating style will afford the minority greater influence than a rigid style.

The dual-process model, which extends minority influence theory, maintains that influence by a majority often produces public compliance, while influence by a minority coalition (if effective) produces belief change and private acceptance. Research findings support the primary thrust of the dual-process model: minority influence operates largely via cognitive activity (a validation process) on the part of the target and, hence, depends heavily on private acceptance.

REFERENCES

Abrams, D., M. S. Wetherell, S. Cochrane, M. A. Hogg, and J. C. Turner. 1990. Knowing what to think by knowing who you are: Self-categorization and the nature of norm formation, conformity and group polarization. *British Journal of Social Psychology* 29:97–119.

Allen, V. L. 1965. Situational factors in conformity. Pp. 133–175 in *Advances in Experimental Social*

Psychology, vol. 2, ed. L. Berkowitz. New York: Academic.

Allen, V. L., and J. M. Levine. 1968. Social support, dissent, and conformity. *Sociometry* 31:138–149.

———. 1971. Social support and conformity: The role of independent assessment of reality. *Journal of Experimental Social Psychology* 7:48–58.

Arbuthnot, J., and M. Wayner. 1982. Minority influence: Effects of size, conversion, and sex. *Journal of Psychology* 111:285–295.

Asch, S. E. 1951. Effects of group pressure upon the modification and distortion of judgments. Pp. 177–190 in *Groups, Leadership, and Men,* ed. H. Guetzkow. Pittsburgh: Carnegie.

———. 1956. Studies of independence and conformity: A minority of one against a unanimous majority. *Psychological Monographs: General and Applied* 70:1–70.

Baron, R. S., K. L. Dion, P. H. Baron, and N. Miller. 1971. Group consensus and cultural values as determinants of risk-taking. *Journal of Personality and Social Psychology* 20:446–455.

Baron, R. S., T. C. Monson, and P. H. Baron. 1973. Conformity pressure as a determinant of risk taking: Replication and extension. *Journal of Personality and Social Psychology* 28:406–413.

Baron, R. S., and G. Roper. 1976. Reaffirmation of social comparison views of choice shifts: Averaging and extremity effects in an autokinetic situation. *Journal of Personality and Social Psychology* 33:521–530.

Birnberg, J., and L. Pondy. 1971. An experimental study of three voting rules. Pp. 225–242 in *Social Choice,* ed. B. Lieberman. New York: Gordon & Breach.

Blascovich, J., and G. P. Ginsburg. 1974. Emergent norms and choice shifts involving risk. *Sociometry* 37:205–218.

Blascovich, J., G. P. Ginsburg, and T. L. Veach. 1975. A pluralistic explanation of choice shifts on the risk dimension. *Journal of Personality and Social Psychology* 31:422–429.

Bower, J. L. 1965. Group decision making: A report of an experimental study. *Behavioral Science* 10:277–289.

Braaten, L. J. 1991. Group cohesion: A new multidimensional model. *Group* 15:39–55.

Brandstatter, H., J. H. Davis, and G. Stocker-Kreichgauer, eds. 1982. *Group Decision Making.* New York: Academic.

Bray, R. M., D. Johnson, and J. T. Chilstrom. 1982. Social influence by group members with minority opinions: A comparison of Hollander and Moscovici. *Journal of Personality and Social Psychology* 43:78–88.

Brehmer, B. 1976. Social judgment theory and the analysis of interpersonal conflict. *Psychological Bulletin* 83:985–1003.

Brown, R. 1974. Further comment on the risky shift. *American Psychologist* 29:468–470.

Buckhout, R., S. Weg, F. Reilly, and R. Frohboese. 1977. Jury verdicts: Comparison of 6- vs. 12-person juries and unanimous vs. majority decision rule in a murder trial. *Bulletin of the Psychonomic Society* 10:175–178.

Burnstein, E. 1982. Persuasion as argument processing. Pp. 103–124 in *Contemporary Problems in Group Decision-Making,* ed. H. Brandstatter, J. H. Davis, and G. Stocker-Kreichgauer. New York: Academic.

Burnstein, E., and A. Vinokur. 1973. Testing two classes of theories about group-induced shifts in individual choice. *Journal of Experimental Social Psychology* 9:127–137.

———. 1977. Persuasive argumentation and social comparison as determinants of attitude polarization. *Journal of Experimental Social Psychology* 13:315–332.

Burtt, H. E. 1920. Sex differences in the effect of discussion. *Journal of Experimental Social Psychology* 3:390–395.

Callaway, M. R., and J. K. Esser. 1984. Groupthink: Effects of cohesiveness and problem-solving procedures on group decision making. *Social Behavior and Personality* 12:157–164.

Callaway, M. R., R. G. Marriott, and J. K. Esser. 1985. Effects of dominance on group decision making: Toward a stress-reduction explanation of groupthink. *Journal of Personality and Social Psychology* 49:949–952.

Carron, A. V. 1982. Cohesiveness in sports teams: Implications and considerations. *Journal of Sport Psychology* 4:123–138.

Cartwright, D. 1971. Risk taking by individuals and groups: An assessment of research employing choice dilemmas. *Journal of Personality and Social Psychology* 20:361–378.

Clark, R. D., III 1971. Group-induced shift toward risk: A critical appraisal. *Psychological Bulletin* 76:251–270.

Collins, B. E., and H. Guetzkow. 1964. *A Social Psychology of Group Processes for Decision Making.* New York: Wiley.

Cotton, J. L., and R. S. Baron. 1980. Anonymity, persuasive arguments and choice shifts. *Social Psychology Quarterly* 43:391–404.

Courtright, J. A. 1978. A laboratory investigation of groupthink. *Communications Monographs,* 45: 229–246.

Cvetkovich, G., and S. R. Baumgardner. 1973. Attitude polarization: The relative influence of discussion group structure and reference group norms. *Journal of Personality and Social Psychology* 26:159–165.

Davis, J. H. 1973. Group decision and social interaction: A theory of social decision schemes. *Psychological Review* 80:97–125.

———. 1980 Group decision and procedural justice. Pp. 157–229 in *Progress in Social Psychology,* vol. 1, ed. M. Fishbein. Hillsdale, NJ: Erlbaum.

Davis, J. H., R. M. Bray, and R. W. Holt. 1977. The empirical study of decision processes in juries: A critical review. Pp. 326–361 in *Law, Justice, and the Individual in Society: Psychological and Legal Issues,* ed. J. L. Tapp and F. J. Levine. New York: Holt, Rinehart & Winston.

Davis, J. H., N. Kerr, R. S. Atkin, R. Holt, and D. Meek. 1975. The decision process of 6- and 12-person mock juries assigned unanimous and two-thirds majority rules. *Journal of Personality and Social Psychology* 32:1–14.

Delbecq, A. L., A. H. Van de Ven, and D. H. Gustafson. 1975. *Group Techniques for Program Planning.* Glencoe, IL: Scott, Foresman.

Deutsch, M., and Gerard, H. B. 1955. A study of normative and informational social influences upon individual judgment. *Journal of Abnormal and Social Psychology* 51:629–636.

Diehl, M., and W. Stroebe. 1987. Productivity loss in brainstorming groups: Toward the solution of a riddle. *Journal of Personality and Social Psychology* 53:497–509.

Dion, K. L., R. S. Baron, and N. Miller. 1970. Why do groups make riskier decisions than individuals? Pp. 305–377 in *Advances in Experimental Social Psychology,* vol. 5, ed. L. Berkowitz. New York: Academic.

Ebbesen, E. B., and R. J. Bowers. 1974. Proportion of risky to conservative arguments in a group discussion and choice shifts. *Journal of Personality and Social Psychology* 29:316–327.

Esser, J. K., and J. S. Lindoerfer. 1989. Groupthink and the space shuttle challenger accident: Toward a quantitative case analysis. *Journal of Behavioral Decision Making* 2:167–177.

Evans, N. J., and P. A. Jarvis. 1980. Group cohesion: A review and reevaluation. *Small Group Behavior* 11: 359–370.

Festinger, L. 1953. An analysis of compliant behavior. Pp. 232–256 in *Group Relations at the Crossroads,* ed. M. Sherif and M. O. Wilson. New York: Harper.

Fisher, B. A. 1980. *Small Group Decision Making,* 2nd ed. New York: McGraw-Hill.

Flowers, M. L. 1977. A laboratory test of some implications of Janis' groupthink hypothesis. *Journal of Personality and Social Psychology* 35:888–896.

Fodor, E. M., and T. Smith. 1982. The power motive as an influence on group decision making. *Journal of Personality and Social Psychology* 42:178–185.

Foss, R. D. 1981. Structural effects in simulated jury decision making. *Journal of Personality and Social Psychology* 40:1055–1062.

Fraser, C., C. Gouge, and M. Billig. 1971. Risky shifts, cautious shifts, and group polarization. *European Journal of Social Psychology* 1:7–30.

Gerard, H. B., R. A. Wilhelmy, and E. S. Conolley. 1968. Conformity and group size. *Journal of Personality and Social Psychology* 8:79–82.

Goethals, G. R., and M. P. Zanna. 1979. The role of social comparison in choice shifts. *Journal of Personality and Social Psychology* 37:1469–1476.

Grofman, B. 1976. Not necessarily twelve and not necessarily unanimous: Evaluating the impact of Williams v. Florida and Johnson v. Louisiana. Pp. 149–168 in *Psychology and the Law,* ed. G. Bermant, C. Nemeth, and N. Vidmar. Lexington, MA: DC Heath.

Harnett, D. L. 1967. A level of aspiration model for group decision making. *Journal of Personality and Social Psychology* 5:58–66.

Hastie, R. 1986. Review essay: Experimental evidence on group accuracy. Pp. 129–157 in *Information Pooling and Group Decision Making,* ed. G. Owen and B. Grofman. New York: Grune & Stratton.

Hastie, R., S. D. Penrod, and N. Pennington. 1983. *Inside the Jury.* Cambridge, MA: Harvard University Press.

Hensley, T. R., and G. W. Griffin. 1986. Victims of groupthink: The Kent State University Board of Trustees and the 1977 gymnasium controversy. *Journal of Conflict Resolution* 30:497–531.

Herek, G., I. L. Janis, and P. Huth. 1987. Decisionmaking during international crisis: Is quality of process related to outcomes? *Journal of Conflict Resolution* 31:203–226.

Hogg, M. A., J. C. Turner, and B. Davidson. 1990. Polarized norms and social frames of reference: A test of the self-categorization theory of group polarization. *Basic and Applied Social Psychology* 11:77–100.

Holloman, C. R., and H. W. Hendrick. 1972. Adequacy of group decisions as a function of the decision-making process. *Academy of Management Journal* 15:175–184.

Hwang, C-L., and M-J. Lin. 1987. *Group Decision Making under Multiple Criteria.* Berlin: Springer-Verlag.

Isenberg, D. J. 1986. Group polarization: A critical review and meta-analysis. *Journal of Personality and Social Psychology* 50:1141–1151.

Isozaki, M. 1984. The effect of discussion on polarization of judgments. *Japanese Psychological Research* 26:187–193.

Janis, I. L. 1972. *Victims of Groupthink.* Boston: Houghton Mifflin.

———. 1982. *Groupthink,* 2nd ed. Boston: Houghton Mifflin.

Janis, I. L., and L. Mann. 1977. *Decision Making: A Psychological Analysis of Conflict, Choice, and Commitment.* New York: Free Press.

Jellison, J., and R. Arkin. 1977. Social comparison of abilities: A self-presentation approach to decision-making in groups. Pp. 235–258 in *Social Comparison Processes: Theoretical and Empirical Perspectives,* ed. J. Suls and R. Miller. Washington, DC: Hemisphere.

Jellison, J., and D. Davis. 1973. Relationships between perceived ability and attitude extremity. *Journal of Personality and Social Psychology* 27:430–436.

Jellison, J., and J. Riskind. 1970. A social comparison of abilities interpretation of risk-taking behavior. *Journal of Personality and Social Psychology* 15: 375–390.

Johnson, D. W., G. Maruyama, R. Johnson, D. Nelson, and L. Skon. 1981. Effects of cooperative, competitive, and individualistic goal structures on achievement: A meta-analysis. *Psychological Bulletin* 89:47–62.

Kalven, H., Jr., and H. Zeisel. 1966. *The American Jury.* Boston: Little, Brown.

Kaplan, M. F. 1977. Discussion polarization effects in a modified jury discussion paradigm: Informational influences. *Sociometry* 40:262–271.

Kaplan, M. F., and C. E. Miller. 1977. Judgments and group discussion: Effects of presentation and memory factors on polarization. *Sociometry* 40:337–343.

———. 1987. Group decision making and normative versus informational influence: Effects of type of issue and assigned decision rule. *Journal of Personality and Social Psychology* 53:306–313.

Kerr, N. L., R. S. Atkin, G. Stasser, D. Meek, R. Holt, and J. H. Davis. 1976. Guilt beyond a reasonable doubt: Effects of concept definition and assigned decision rule on the judgments of mock jurors. *Journal of Personality and Social Psychology* 34: 282–294.

Kerr, N. L., R. J. MacCoun, C. H. Hansen, and J. A. Hymes. 1987. Gaining and losing social support: Momentum in decision-making groups. *Journal of Experimental Social Psychology* 23:119–145.

Kiesler, C. A., and S. B. Kiesler. 1969. *Conformity.* Reading, MA: Addison-Wesley.

Kiesler, C. A., and M. S. Pallak. 1975. Minority influence: The effect of majority reactionaries and defectors, and minority and majority compromisers, upon majority opinion and attraction. *European Journal of Social Psychology* 5:237–256.

Kogan, N., and M. A. Wallach. 1964. *Risk-Taking: A Study in Cognition and Personality.* New York: Holt, Rinehart & Winston.

Lamm, H. 1988. A review of our research on group polarization: Eleven experiments on the effects of group discussion on risk acceptance, probability estimation, and negotiation positions. *Psychological Reports* 62:807–813.

Lamm, H., and D. G. Myers. 1978. Group-induced polarization of attitudes and behavior. Pp. 145–195 in *Advances in Experimental Social Psychology,* vol. 11, ed. L. Berkowitz. New York: Academic.

Latane, B. 1981. Psychology of social impact. *American Psychologist* 36:343–356.

Latane, B., and S. Wolf. 1981. The social impact of majorities and minorities. *Psychological Review* 88:438–453.

Laughlin, P. R. 1980. Social combination processes of cooperative problem-solving groups on verbal intellective tasks. Pp. 127–155 in *Progress in Social Psychology,* vol. 1, ed. M. Fishbein. Hillsdale, NJ: Erlbaum.

Laughlin, P. R., and C. Earley. 1982. Social combination models, persuasive arguments theory, social comparison theory, and choice shift. *Journal of Personality and Social Psychology* 42:273–281.

Leana, C. R. 1985. A partial test of Janis' groupthink model: Effects of group cohesiveness and leader behavior on defective decision making. *Journal of Management* 11:5–17.

Lehrer, K. 1979. Consensus and comparison: A theory of social rationality. Pp. 283–309 in *Foundations and Applications of Decision Theory*, vol. 1, ed. C. A. Hooker, J. J. Leach, and E. F. McClennen. Dordrecht, Holland: Reidel.

Levine, J. M., and C. J. Ranelli. 1978. Majority reaction to shifting and stable attitudinal deviates. *European Journal of Social Psychology* 8:55–70.

Levine, J. M., and E. M. Russo. 1987. Majority and minority influence. Pp. 13–54 in *Group Processes,* ed. C. Hendrick. Newbury Park, CA: Sage.

Levine, J. M., L. Saxe, and H. J. Harris. 1976. Reaction to attitudinal deviance: Impact of deviate's direction and distance of movement. *Sociometry* 39: 97–107.

Levine, J. M., K. R. Sroka, and H. N. Snyder. 1977. Group support and reaction to stable and shifting agreement/disagreement. *Sociometry* 40:214–224.

Levinger, G., and D. J. Schneider. 1969. Test of the "risk is a value" hypothesis. *Journal of Personality and Social Psychology* 11:165–169.

Longley, J., and D. G. Pruitt. 1980. Groupthink: A critique of Janis's theory. Pp. 74–93 in *Review of Personality and Social Psychology*, vol. 1, ed. L. Wheeler. Beverly Hills: Sage.

Maass, A., and R. D. Clark III. 1983. Internalization versus compliance: Differential processes underlying minority influence and conformity. *European Journal of Social Psychology* 13:197–215.

———. 1984. Hidden impact of minorities: Fifteen years of minority influence research. *Psychological Bulletin* 95:428–450.

Mackie, D. M. 1986. Social identification effects in group polarization. *Journal of Personality and Social Psychology* 50:720–728.

Mackie, D., and J. Cooper. 1984. Attitude polarization: The effects of group membership. *Journal of Personality and Social Psychology* 46:575–585.

Madsen, D. B. 1978. Issue importance and choice shifts: A persuasive arguments approach. *Journal of Personality and Social Psychology* 36:1118–1127.

Manz, C. C., and H. P. Sims. 1982. The potential for "groupthink" in autonomous work groups. *Human Relations* 35:773–784.

McCauley, C. 1989. The nature of social influence in groupthink: Compliance and internalization. *Journal of Personality and Social Psychology* 57: 250–260.

McCauley, C., N. Kogan, and A. I. Teger. 1971. Order effects in answering risk dilemmas for self and others. *Journal of Personality and Social Psychology* 20:423–424.

Miller, C. E. 1989. The social psychological effects of group decision rules. Pp. 327–355 in *Psychology of Group Influence*, 2nd. ed., ed. P. B. Paulus. Hillsdale, NJ: Erlbaum.

Miller, C. E., and P. D. Anderson. 1979. Group decision rules and the rejection of deviates. *Sociometry* 42: 354–363.

Miller, C.E., P. Jackson, J. Mueller, and C. Schersching. 1987. Some social psychological effects of group decision rules. *Journal of Personality and Social Psychology* 52:325–332.

Montanari, J. R., and G. Moorhead. 1989. Development of the Groupthink Assessment Inventory. *Educational and Psychological Measurement* 49: 209–219.

Moorhead, G., Ference, R., and Neck, C. P. 1991. Group decision fiascoes continue: Space shuttle Challenger and a revised groupthink framework. *Human Relations* 44:539–550.

Moorhead, G., and J. R. Montanari. 1982. Groupthink: A research methodology. Pp. 380–382 in *Proceedings of the 14th Annual Meeting of the American Institute for Decision Sciences.* San Francisco.

———. 1986. An empirical investigation of the groupthink phenomenon. *Human Relations* 39:399–410.

Morris, W. N., and R. S. Miller. 1975. The effects of consensus-breaking and consensus-preempting partners on reduction of conformity. *Journal of Experimental Social Psychology* 11:215–223.

Moscovici, S. 1976. *Social Influence and Social Change.* London: Academic.

———. 1980. Toward a theory of conversion behavior. Pp. 209–239 in *Advances in Experimental Social Psychology,* vol. 13, ed. L. Berkowitz. New York: Academic.

———. 1985. Innovation and minority influence. Pp. 9–51 in *Perspectives on Minority Influence,* ed. S. Moscovici, G. Mugny, and E. Van Avermaet. Cambridge, UK: Cambridge University Press.

Moscovici, S., and C. Faucheux. 1972. Social influence, conforming bias, and the study of active minorities. Pp. 149–202 in *Advances in Experimental Social Psychology,* vol. 6, ed. L. Berkowitz. New York: Academic.

Moscovici, S., and E. Lage. 1976. Studies in social influence, III: Majority vs. minority influence in a group. *European Journal of Social Psychology* 6:1 49–174.

Moscovici, S., E. Lage, and M. Naffrechoux. 1969. Influence of a consistent minority on the responses of a majority in a color perception task. *Sociometry* 32:365–379.

Moscovici, S., and G. Mugny. 1983. Minority influence. Pp. 41–64 in *Basic Group Processes,* ed. P. B. Paulus. New York: Springer-Verlag.

Moscovici, S., and P. Neve. 1973. Studies in social influence, II: Instrumental and symbolic behavior. *European Journal of Social Psychology* 3: 461–474.

Moscovici, S., and M. Zavalloni. 1969. The group as a polarizer of attitudes. *Journal of Personality and Social Psychology* 12:125–135.

Mudrack, P. E. 1989. Defining group cohesiveness: A legacy of confusion? *Small Group Behavior* 20: 37–49.

Mugny, G. 1975. Majorité et minorité: Le niveau de leur influence (Majority and minority: The level of their influence). *Bulletin de Psychologie* 28:831–835.

———. 1976. Quelle influence majoritaire? Quelle influence minoritaire? (What majority influence? What minority influence?) *Revue Suisse de Psychologie Pure et Appliquee* 4:255–268.

———. 1982. *The Power of Minorities.* London: Academic.

———. 1984. The influence of minorities: Ten years later. Pp. 498–517 in *The Social Dimension: European Developments in Social Psychology,* vol. 2, ed. H. Tajfel. Cambridge, UK: Cambridge University Press.

Myers, D. G. 1982. Polarizing effects of social interaction. Pp. 125–161 in *Group Decision Making,* ed. H. Brandstatter, J. H. Davis, and G. Stocker-Kreichgauer. New York: Academic.

Myers, D. G., and G. D. Bishop. 1970. Discussion effects on racial attitudes. *Science* 169:778–789.

Myers, D. G., J. B. Bruggink, R. C. Kersting, and B. A. Schlosser. 1980. Does learning others' opinions change one's opinion? *Personality and Social Psychology Bulletin* 6:253–260.

Myers, D. G., and M. F. Kaplan. 1976. Group-induced polarization in simulated juries. *Personality and Social Psychology Bulletin* 2:63–66.

Myers, D. G., and H. Lamm. 1976. The group polarization phenomena. *Psychological Bulletin* 83:602–627.

Myers, D. G., S. B. Wojcicki, and G. C. Aardema. 1977. Attitude comparison: Is there ever a bandwagon effect? *Journal of Applied Social Psychology* 7: 341–347.

Nail, P. R. 1986. Toward an integration of some models and theories of social response. *Psychological Bulletin* 100:190–206.

Nemeth, C. 1977. Interactions between jurors as a function of majority vs. unanimity decision rules. *Journal of Applied Social Psychology* 7:38–56.

———. 1985. Dissent, group process, and creativity: The contribution of minority influence. Pp. 57–75 in *Advances in Group Processes,* vol. 2, ed. E. J. Lawler. Greenwich, CT: JAI Press.

———. 1986. Differential contributions of majority and minority influence. *Psychological Review* 93:23–32.

Nemeth, C. J., and J. L. Kwan. 1985. Originality of word associations as a function of majority vs. minority influence processes. *Social Psychological Quarterly* 48:277–282.

———. 1987. Minority influence, divergent thinking and detection of correct solutions. *Journal of Applied Social Psychology* 17:788–799.

Nemeth, C., M. Swedlund, and B. Kanki. 1974. Patterning of the minority's responses and their influence on the majority. *European Journal of Social Psychology* 4:53–64.

Nemeth, C., and J. Wachtler. 1973. Consistency and modification of judgment. *Journal of Experimental Social Psychology* 9:65–79.

———. 1974. Creating the perceptions of consistency and confidence: A necessary condition for minority influence. *Sociometry* 37:529–540.

Nemeth, C., J. Wachtler, and J. Endicott. 1977. Increasing the size of the minority: Some gains and some losses. *European Journal of Social Psychology* 7: 15–27.

Oakes, P. J. 1987. The salience of social categories. Pp. 117–141 in *Rediscovering the Social Group: A Self-Categorization Theory,* ed. J. C. Turner, M. A. Hogg, P. J. Oakes, S. D. Reicher, and M. S. Wetherell. Oxford, UK: Blackwell.

Padawer-Singer, A. M., A. N. Singer, and R. L. J. Singer. 1977. An experimental study of twelve vs. six member juries under unanimous vs. nonunanimous decisions. Pp. 77–86 in *Psychology in the Legal Process,* ed. B. D. Sales. New York: Spectrum.

Papastamou, S., and G. Mugny. 1985. Rigidity and minority influence: The influence of the social in social influence. Pp. 113–136 in *Perspectives on Minority Influence,* ed. S. Moscovici, G. Mugny, and E. Van Avermaet. Cambridge, UK: Cambridge University Press.

Park, W-W. 1990. A review of research on groupthink. *Journal of Behavioral Decision Making* 3:229–245.

Penrod, S., and R. Hastie. 1979. Models of jury decision making: A critical review. *Psychological Bulletin* 86:462–492.

———. 1980. A computer simulation of jury decision making. *Psychological Review* 87:133–159.

Pruitt, D. G. 1971. Choice shifts in group discussion: An introductory review. *Journal of Personality and Social Psychology* 20:339–360.

Reicher, S. D. 1984. Social influence in the crowd: Attitudinal and behavioural effects of de-individuation in conditions of high and low group salience. *British Journal of Social Psychology* 23:341–350.

Restle, F., and J. H. Davis. 1962. Success and speed of problem solving by individuals and groups. *Psychological Review* 69:520–536.

Rosenberg, L. A. 1961. Group size, prior experience, and conformity. *Journal of Abnormal and Social Psychology* 63:436–437.

Saks, M. J. 1977. *Jury Verdicts.* Lexington, MA: DC Heath.

Sanders, G. S., and R. S. Baron. 1977. Is social comparison irrelevant for producing choice shifts? *Journal of Experimental Social Psychology* 13:303–314.

Singleton, R., Jr. 1979. Another look at the conformity explanation of group-induced shifts in choice. *Human Relations* 32:37–56.

Stasser, G. 1988. Computer simulation as a research tool: The DISCUSS model of group decision making. *Journal of Experimental Social Psychology* 24: 393–422.

Stasser, G., and J. H. Davis. 1981. Group decision making and social influence: A social interaction sequence model. *Psychological Review* 88:523–551.

Stasser, G., N. L. Kerr, and J. H. Davis. 1989. Influence processes and consensus models in decision-making groups. Pp. 279–326 in *Psychology of Group Influence,* 2nd ed., ed. P. B. Paulus. Hillsdale, NJ: Erlbaum.

Steiner, I. D. 1982. Heuristic models of groupthink. Pp. 503–524 in *Group Decision Making,* ed. H. Brandstatter, J. H. Davis, and G. Stocker-Kreichgauer. San Diego: Academic.

Stoner, J. A. F. 1961. A comparison of individual and group decisions involving risk. Master's thesis, Massachusetts Institute of Technology, Cambridge, MA.

———. 1968. Risky and cautious shifts in group decisions: The influence of widely held values. *Journal of Experimental Social Psychology* 4:442–459.

Swap, W. C., and associates, eds. 1984. *Group Decision Making.* Beverly Hills: Sage.

Tanford, S., and S. Penrod. 1983. Computer modeling of influence in the jury: The role of the consistent juror. *Social Psychology Quarterly* 46:200–212.

———. 1984. Social influence model: A formal integration of research on majority and minority influence processes. *Psychological Bulletin* 95:189–225.

Tetlock, P. E. 1979. Identifying victims of groupthink from public statements of decision makers. *Journal of Personality and Social Psychology* 37: 1314–1324.

Tetlock, P. E., R. S. Peterson, C. McGuire, S-J. Chang, and P. Feld. 1992. Assessing political group dynamics: A test of the groupthink model. *Journal of Personality and Social Psychology* 63:403–425.

Turner, J. C., M. A. Hogg, P. J. Oakes, S. D. Reicher, and M. S. Wetherell. 1987. *Rediscovering the Social Group: A Self-Categorization Theory.* Oxford, UK: Blackwell.

Turner, J. C., and P. J. Oakes. 1986. The significance of the social identity concept for social psychology with reference to individualism, interactionism, and social influence. *British Journal of Social Psychology* 25:237–252.

———. 1989. Self-categorization theory and social influence. Pp. 233–275 in *Psychology of Group Influence,* 2nd ed., ed. P. B. Paulus. Hillsdale, NJ: Erlbaum.

Turner, J. C., M. S. Wetherell, and M. A. Hogg. 1989. Referent informational influence and group polarization. *British Journal of Social Psychology* 28: 135–147.

Vinokur, A. 1971. A review and theoretical analysis of the effects of group processes upon individual and group decisions involving risk. *Psychological Bulletin* 76:231–250.

Vinokur, A., and E. Burnstein. 1974. Effects of partially-shared persuasive arguments on group-induced shifts: A group-problem-solving approach. *Journal of Personality and Social Psychology* 29: 305–315.

————. 1978. Novel argumentation and attitude change: The case of polarization following group discussion. *European Journal of Social Psychology* 8:335–348.

Vollrath, D. A., and J. H. Davis. 1980. Jury size and decision rule. In *The Jury: Its Role in American Society,* ed. R. J. Simon. Lexington, MA: Lexington Books.

Wallach, M., N. Kogan, and D. Bem. 1962. Group influence on individual risk taking. *Journal of Abnormal and Social Psychology* 65:75–86.

Watson, G. 1928. Do groups think more effectively than individuals? *Journal of Abnormal and Social Psychology* 23:328–336.

Wetherell, M. S. 1987. Social identity and group polarization. Pp. 142–170 in *Rediscovering the Social Group: A Self-Categorization Theory,* ed. J. C. Turner, M. A. Hogg, P. J. Oakes, S. D. Reicher, and M. S. Wetherell. Oxford, UK: Blackwell.

Whyte, G. 1989. Groupthink reconsidered. *Academy of Management Review* 14:40–56.

Wilder, D. A. 1990. Some determinants of the persuasive power of in-groups and out-groups: Organization of information and attribution of independence. *Journal of Personality and Social Psychology* 59:1202–1213.

Wilder, D. A., and P. N. Shapiro. 1984. The role of outgroup cues in determining social identity. *Journal of Personality and Social Psychology* 47:342–348.

Wolf, S. 1979. Behavioral style and group cohesiveness as sources of minority influence. *European Journal of Social Psychology* 9:381–395.

————. 1985. Manifest and latent influence of majorities and minorities. *Journal of Personality and Social Psychology* 48:899–908.

Wood, J. T. 1984. Alternative methods of group decision making: A comparative examination of consensus, negotiation, and voting. Pp. 3–18 in *Emergent Issues in Human Decision Making,* ed. G. M. Phillips and J. T. Wood. Carbondale: Southern Illinois University Press.

CHAPTER 14

Sex Category and Gender in Social Psychology

MARY GLENN WILEY

Sex category and gender are pervasive principles of social organization in all known societies. Although wide variation exists with regard to expectations held for women and men, the traits and jobs assigned to them, and the rights accorded them,[1] all societies posit a difference in status and attendant expectations and privileges due to sex category assignment. Social structure and culture interact to construct a hierarchy that empowers men and disadvantages women (Epstein 1988), despite the small number of documented physical and psychological differences between women and men and the great variation within each group (Deaux 1984; Eagly 1983; Maccoby and Jacklin 1974).

This distinction between women and men is so pervasive that it affects the approach to research and the structure of theory in social psychology just as it affects other areas of social science (Epstein 1988). Obviously such a ubiquitous factor deserves attention apart from specific topics of social psychological interest. The purpose of this chapter is to review and identify trends in the treatment of sex category and gender in each of the three broad areas of sociological social psychology covered in this volume.

SEX OR GENDER?

For the last two decades, feminist writers (e.g., Deaux and Kite 1987; Lorber 1987; Unger 1985) have stressed the importance of distinguishing between sex which is physiologically or biologically determined and gender which is socially constructed and culturally determined.[2] Although this distinction is useful, it does not cover sex as an appearance characteristic. For this reason, I employ the three category scheme—sex, sex category, and gender—suggested by West and Zimmerman (1987). In this scheme, *sex* refers to the physiological and reproductive differences between humans. One's sex can be determined unequivocally only by genetic testing, but this is rarely done. In the absence of empirical evidence, however, we act as if we know the biological sex of others based on their appearance. *Sex category* refers to this appearance of an individual that results in labeling as male or female by oneself and/or others.[3] We base these judgments on factors such as height, weight, hair length, clothes, voice, and so on. This sorting of individuals on the basis of physical configuration allows a sex-linked label of identification (Goffman 1977). Since this is a social classification, the variables used and their relationship to the categories depend on one's culture. Further, perfect congruence between sex and sex category is not necessary even though we act as if it exists. Regardless of appearance, individuals may lay claim to a masculine or feminine identity via their actions. The presentation of these claims in social interaction result in one's gender identification. *Gender* consists of the expression of those traits, attitudes, beliefs, and behaviors that support a claim on the descriptive dimensions of masculinity and femininity. By expression, I mean those actions taken by individuals in attempting to support a gender identity claim. Making successful gender claims is highly dependent on an understanding of the culture's normative definition of masculine and feminine and the agreement of others as to these definitions and the legitimacy of the claim. Thus, gender is a product of social interaction.

Distinguishing sex category from gender is especially useful, since sex category, rather than sex or gender, is the actual basis of most social organization. Thus, sex category may be profitably treated as a stratification variable (Lipman-Blumen and Tichamyer 1975). Although sex category assignment is independent of genetic or physiological sex, in everyday interaction people act as if these socially constructed categories are physiologically determined and reflect real differences. For these reasons, the term *sex category* is particularly appropriate for describing a stimulus characteristic or a category of research participant.

TRENDS IN THE TREATMENT OF SEX CATEGORY AND GENDER

During the 1970s and 1980s, there has been an evolution in sex category and gender research and theory in social psychology. The field has moved away from sex role or sex role socialization explanations of sex category differences in behavior or attitudes. With the decline of functionalist explanations, there has been an increased emphasis on situational and structural factors, best reflected in the work that treats sex category as a stratification variable. Similarly, there has been a burgeoning of theory and research on the social construction of gender, resulting in a clearer separation between the concepts of sex category and gender as well as necessitating the use of qualitative methodologies.

These changes represent a reaction to criticisms by feminists and others of sociology's treatment of women and gender. The central, and most consequential, criticism concerns the influence of functionalism on theoretical perspectives (Bernard 1973; Stacey and Thorne 1985). Although the impact of functionalism is greater in some areas of social psychology than others, there is certainly evidence of a deeply ingrained tendency to separate instrumental and socioemotional functions and to assign these functions to men and women, respectively. The danger of this division of roles is the attendant implication that sex category differences associated with these roles, even if socialized, are necessary or inevitable (Stacy and Thorne

1985). The move away from sex role socialization explanations toward status- and stratification-based explanations of social process and the increased emphasis on the social construction of gender indicate a waning of this functionalist influence.

Attacks leveled against the prevailing methodological approaches associated with functionalism have also been conducive to changes in the treatment of sex category and gender issues in social psychology. One such criticism is the disproportionate use of quantitative methods (Millman and Kanter 1975; Stacey and Thorne 1985). Despite the existence of a strong and healthy tradition of employing nonquantitative methods, especially among symbolic interactionists, there has been a heavy dependence on quantitative methodology in many areas of social psychology. This dependence can lead researchers to ignore the impact of situational factors, including the researchers themselves. Of late there has been an increasing body of qualitative work, especially on the social construction of gender, and evidence of increased attention to contextual variables in quantitative work.

A closely related criticism is the tendency to treat society as a single generalizable entity (i.e., men and women are substitutable) (Millman and Kanter 1975). To assess the relevance of this criticism for social psychology, I reviewed the 923 articles published from 1966 to 1990 in *Social Psychology Quarterly*,[4] an official publication of the American Sociological Association. The validity of this criticism is supported by the fact that women and men are treated as if they are substitutable—almost half of the published studies either fail to indicate the sex category of the participants (17 percent) or use only one sex category (30 percent). However, social psychology does not appear as vulnerable to the criticism of being a "science of male society" (Bernard 1973)—19 percent of the articles used only men and 11 percent used only women. Perhaps reflecting a response to these concerns about generalizability, there has been a steady increase in the proportion of articles published in *Social Psychology Quarterly* over the past twenty-five years that use both women and men

(41 percent from 1966 to 1970 and 66 percent from 1986 to 1990). In all fairness I should point out that this pervasive tendency to generalize research results inappropriately is not restricted to sex category. In fact, most of the research on which this chapter is based ignores distinctions of race category, class, age, and sexual orientation.

Even if studies employ both women and men in their samples, there remains the question of whether sex category is simply used as a control or is treated as a theoretical or social category (Bernard 1973; Stacey and Thorne 1985). (In fact, only 32 percent of the empirical studies in *Social Psychology Quarterly* even include sex category in the analysis.) Treating sex category as a control is problematic, since it frequently reflects the unstated assumption that it is a property of individuals and leads to the attribution of any effects associated with sex category to "sex differences" (West and Zimmerman 1987) rather than to principles of social organization (Stacey and Thorne 1985). The sex differences/sex role socialization perspective informing past work in social psychology can also lead researchers to treat sex category as a control rather than a theoretical or social category.[5] As later sections of this chapter show, social psychologists are moving away from a sex difference perspective toward more constructed and stratification based approaches.

In this chapter, I trace the evolution of the treatment of sex category and gender in the three broad areas of social psychology treated in this volume. Since gender and sex category have not been systematically investigated in all areas of social psychology, the coverage of various fields is selective. Due to sociological social psychology's unique contribution to the discourse concerning the social construction of gender, I devote more space to the treatment of sex category and gender in investigations of the self and social interaction. Group processes are also highlighted, due to the pivotal contribution theory and research in this area played in the progression from a functionalistic view that demanded sex differences to a conception of sex category as a status variable. Due to space limitations, the section on the individual and social structure treats only a few major areas in which social psychologists have looked at gender and sex category.[6]

THE SELF AND SOCIAL INTERACTION

The concept of self, as well as its relationship to gender and sex category, has changed radically over the last twenty-five years. Here I consider changes in how social psychologists relate sex category and gender to the self, how a gendered self is acquired, and how sex category and gender are related to self-esteem.

A Gendered Self

Three changes in the treatment of self reflect a general transformation in the social psychological study of sex category and gender: the evolution of research on masculinity and femininity into a concern with cognitive categories, the development of a social construction approach to the gendered self, and the development of models that tie a constructed self to social structural factors.

Masculinity and Femininity. In contrast to the mutable nature of the constructed self proposed by many feminists and symbolic interactionists, a substantial number of psychologists posit a relatively stable gendered self. This is reflected in the long and robust research tradition assessing gender (masculinity/femininity) or sex roles. Initially measures of gender consisted of personality traits that empirically differentiated individuals on the basis of sex category but had no theoretical connection to conceptions of gender.

In the 1970s, a theoretical model emerged with two *independent* factors representing masculinity and femininity, such as the Bem Sex Role Inventory (Bem 1974) and the Personal Attributes Questionnaire (Spence, Helmreich, and Stapp 1974). This move to independent scales for masculinity and femininity reflects a philosophy that exalts androgyny as the ideal. Instead of using items that empirically distinguish between men and women, as previous instruments had, both of these measures employ traits for masculinity scales that represent stereotypical aspects of maleness and stereotypically female traits in the construction of femininity scales.

Despite this new approach, these scales proved to be predictive only of role behaviors that are directly connected with agentic self-assertive traits and expressive, interpersonally oriented traits. These measures do not tap other dimensions believed associated with masculinity and femininity.

Gender Schema, Cognitive Schema, and Gender Identity.   This failure, combined with the lack of relationship between these scores and men's and women's self-ratings on masculinity and femininity, led to the rethinking of this concept (Spence 1984). Both Bem and Spence have moved to more global concepts—gender schema and gender identity—that reflect a return to a bipolar conception of gender.

Bem's gender schema theory (Bem 1981, 1984) contends that children learn society's definitions of femaleness and maleness (femininity and masculinity) from the sex-differentiated practices in society. These definitions are much broader than the anatomical or biological differences between men and women.

Unique to this gender schema perspective is the contention that once a gender schema is learned, this cognitive structure organizes and guides an individual's perception of the social world. This is similar to the arguments of labeling theorists who contend that social categories structure perception and attendant evaluations. The unique contribution of this approach is the link to general theories of cognitive processing. It also allows for variance among societies in the content and organization of gender schemata and within societies for variation among individuals in the actual structure of their gender schemata and the degree to which self is schematized.

Markus and associates (1982) propose a more comprehensive conceptualization of cognitive schemata and gender. They do not limit cognitive schema to sex typing in the sense of simple categories of maleness and femaleness. Instead, individu-

als may have both an androgynous self-schema and a firm belief that they are male or female. This conceptualization challenges the combination of sex typing and general cognitive schemes. Their perspective leads to the conclusion that there may be a difference between conception of one's sex category and gender.

Janet Spence (1984; Spence and Sawin 1985) proposed yet a third construction of gender. She applies the concepts of masculinity and femininity only to that portion of an individual's self-concept that she labels *gender identity,* "a basic phenomenological sense of one's maleness or femaleness that parallels awareness and acceptance of one's biological sex" (Spence 1984, 79–80). Thus the actual content of a person's self-concept is not adequately represented or determined by his/her gender identity. Rather, as in Markus's view, this construction of gender identity accommodates a great deal of diversity in the characteristics and behavior of women and men without threatening their basic sense of maleness or femaleness.

Despite this recent tendency for psychologists to view gender as a product of social interaction, they still view a gendered self as relatively static. Early childhood learning and labeling are emphasized. In contrast, current sociological work stresses the potential for change in gender throughout life in every social interaction.

Social Construction of Gender.   The works of Goffman (1977, 1979) and West and Zimmerman (1987) epitomize the social construction approach to gender and sex category championed by symbolic interactionists and feminists.[7] In contrast to a sex differences approach, "gender [sic] categories . . . are analyzed to see how different social groups define them, and how they construct and maintain them in everyday life and in major social institutions" (Lorber and Farrell 1991, 1).

Goffman (1977) argues that all societies sort their members at birth into sex-linked categories on the basis of physical appearance, which results in differential treatment from that point on. The importance of this sorting is that societies develop their own definition of the characteristics essential to these two groups. According to Goffman (1977), society's impact on the construction of gender is accomplished through "institutionalized reflexivity." This is the process whereby features of social organization are arranged such that they permit a display of our "essential" gender while also confirming our gender stereotypes and the prevailing "arrangement" between the sexes. From this perspective, the maintenance of a proper gender identity is of particular importance in all interaction. Regardless of our biological sex, the overriding concern is with the acceptance of our gender identity claims. Gender is not just a label, but the essence of the relationship between the two types of people supposedly represented by the two genders. Among the aspects of this relationship communicated in interaction are relative power, sexuality, and maturity (Goffman 1979).

Building on Goffman's idea that gender is an expression of what society has defined as our "essential natures," West and Zimmerman (1987) draw an excellent blueprint of how one goes about constructing gender in social interaction. The actual performance and construction of gender may vary widely from culture to culture or time to time, even though gender is a pervasive aspect of social organization with no specific site or organizational context. They also argue that there is no such thing as a gender role: "Roles are *situated* identities—assumed and relinquished as the situation demands—rather than *master identities*" (West and Zimmerman 1987, 128). Berk (1985) provides an excellent example of how construction of gender affects the organization of a specific social activity—the division of household labor.

Feminist researchers who adopt a social construction perspective view this approach as inherently structural (Lorber and Farrell 1991). They consider gender as one of the organizing principles of every social order. The continual construction and reconstruction of sex categories and genders is considered essential to any given society's power and status hierarchy. Regardless of other constructed category similarities (e.g., race, age), sex category results in differential valuation.

One major strength of this social construction approach is its recognition of the complexities involved in the continual construction of gender. Although context is given a great deal of attention, the structural constraints on behavior are not yet well articulated. In particular, the potential conflicts between the demands of claiming and maintaining a gender identity and the claiming and maintenance of other identities and their resolution is not adequately addressed. Gender identity claims are only *one* of many interaction goals. Further, this approach still lacks a systematic way of assessing the contents of sex category and gender and their implications for future performance.

Specifically, how does the social structure affect the construction of sex categories and gender? In contrast to the position of West and Zimmerman (1987), other sociologists, including some symbolic interactionists, claim that conceiving of gender either as a set of traits or as a role is essential for providing the connection between social structure and gender.

Roles, Traits, and Sex Category.   Structural symbolic interactionists also view interaction as the mechanism whereby gender and sex category are created and see these constructions as subject to change. Peter Burke's work on gender identity (1989) best exemplifies this approach. According to Burke, identities are defined along trait dimensions in contrast to counterpositions in the social structure. Therefore, the male and female genders are defined in contrast to each other. Further, the content of these identities has to be defined in terms of the persons involved, since their content is a product of social consensus and subject to change. However, social structure establishes (through interaction) expectations for behavior based on various roles and positions in society. Gender identity is embedded in this web of societal roles. Since the maintenance of these identities is important for smooth interaction and the receipt of rewards in interaction, identities are relatively stable and their maintenance is a source of motivation.

One additional contribution of structural symbolic interactionism is the idea that identities are ranked in a hierarchy and actions that maintain or claim a particular identity may undermine another identity claim. For that reason, Stryker (1987) argues that despite situational demands individuals may disagree about what identity it is most important to portray. In fact, women and men may have different rankings (Santee and Jackson 1982). The demands of the setting are assumed to be predominant except when there is an overwhelming need to maintain a particular identity across situations.

Interestingly, Gecas and associates (Gecas, Thomas, and Weigert 1973) report that gender emerged as the most prominent social identity for both men and women in a study of adolescents in three societies. It appears that at least during some periods of life, gender plays such an important role in the identity hierarchy that it pervades all interaction settings. Whether this is true across the life cycle is a question for future research.

Two additional factors deserve attention in future research on the construction of a gendered self. The first concerns the links between actions and identity attributions. These links may well differ, depending on the sex category of the actor or the attributor (Santee and Jackson 1982). The second is the potential role of social networks in determining behaviors. For example, research by Risman (1987) illustrates the impact of differences in social networks on men's and women's parenting behaviors.

Summary. Although psychologists' recent cognitive approaches allow for a greater flexibility in the gendered self, they still envision it as more stable than do many sociologists. However, the most recent psychological models are similar to those developed by sociologists in that the content of a gendered self-conception is viewed as socially defined and personally variable. Perhaps the most important trend is that sociologists are attempting to link the process of gendered self construction to social structure. The jury is not yet in as to which of these formulations will be most influential. The present contest among divergent models reflects a healthy intellectual climate for the development of a more comprehensive theory of gender.

Acquisition of a Gendered Self

Regardless of whether a gendered self is conceived of as relatively stable or as an ever-changing social construction, the acquisition of such a self is a central concern. In the past, many sociologists cited sex role socialization as the mechanism that created differences in the behaviors of women and men. However, these explanations failed to isolate the specific practices responsible for any differences, assuming instead that girls and boys were treated differently and that they identified with same-sex models. This conception of a stable sex role that is learned early and unchanging does not appear viable to most sociologists today. They, in turn, have emphasized the importance of language and social structure in the acquisition and maintenance of a gendered self.

Impact of Early Social Relationships. Possibly the most famous current advocate for the early acquisition of a stable gendered self is Chodorow (1978, 1989). Employing a psychoanalytic perspective, Chodorow stresses the impact of early interaction with the mother on the development of sex category-differentiated personalities. She argues that the mother-daughter relationship results in daughters with a desire to mother and with personalities that lack differentiation and feature connectedness. In contrast, sons' early interactions with their mothers result in personalities that feature separation and repressed nurturant capacities and needs. Chodorow views social structural factors as supporting these differences but claims the mother-child relationship is the basis for differences in women's and men's personalities.

Importance of Language and Social Interaction. In contrast, a very fluid model of gender acquisition has evolved from Goffman's conception that expressions of gender are expressions of "essential" nature. According to this view, behavioral conditioning plays a role in a child's learning prior to the acquisition of language. However, language acquisition transforms the infant from an acquiescent recipient of a conveyed identity to an active if unwitting participant in his/her own socialization. Although the early acquisition of gender identity may be based on the actions of significant others toward the child (Seavey, Katz, and Zalk 1975; Sidorowicz and Lunney 1980), Cahill (1980) argues that the child (and his/her peers) also plays an important role. In this view, the child is seen as an active agent who seeks to confirm his/her gender identity through social interaction. It is through the acquisition of language categories that children become linked to the social whole (Cahill 1986a, 1986b), since these categories not only are labels but also reflect values.

Thorne (1990) claims that language categories have even colored research on the acquisition of gender. Due to the sex-based dichotomies of language, researchers focus on the evidence of division into groups of boys and girls and on behaviors on which they differ, if only statistically. Thorne argues that instead the study of children's gender should begin by looking at social relations and should emphasize contexts and meanings, thereby creating a more fluid and situated approach to gender. Further, researchers should attend to the contextual and situational factors that decrease as well as reinforce the salience of gender. Her work illustrates how treating children as agents and the use of multiple standpoints can help researchers avoid the pitfalls of a dichotomous perspective.

Impact of Social Structure.　There is also research that focuses on the role of social structure in gender acquisition. Lever's work (1978) on the structure of children's games provides an excellent example of how social structure, as communicated through others' responses, teaches children what they need to know and how to behave to meet the demands of their sex category-based social positions. Lever argues that the documented differences in the games played by boys and girls on dimensions of complexity, role differentiation, in-

terdependence, size of play group, explicitness of goals, number of rules, and team formation derive from society's stereotypes. Further, these differences give boys and girls differential experience with social organizations that reflect the complexity of occupational settings of the adult world.

Summary.　Although there are several approaches to the acquisition of a gendered self, almost all recent approaches reflect the impact of the changing social roles of men and women. This focus on change and mutability is obvious both in the heavy emphasis on ongoing interaction and social arrangements by symbolic interactionists and in the deconstruction strategies employed by ethnomethodologists. Even those sociologists who promulgate an individualistic view that stresses the internalization of stable personality traits no longer subscribe to a sex role model that completely forms an individual for all later social interaction.

Self-Esteem

We now turn from a consideration of the gendered content of self-conceptions to the links between sex category and gender and the evaluative and emotional dimensions of self-concept. The predominant view in sociology is that self-evaluations reflect the responses and appraisals of others. In addition, self-perception and social comparisons are posited to play a role in guiding self-evaluations.

Differences in Self-Esteem.　At first glance it appears that all three sources of self-esteem would result in sex category differences: in current Western cultures, society evaluates women less positively (reflected appraisals); women occupy less-esteemed and less-powerful positions in society (self-perception); and women achieve less of value (success, rewards) in many social arenas than do men (social comparison). All of these factors should lead women to devalue the self, yet, just as with minority group members, women do not differ significantly from men in *global* self-esteem (Gecas 1982; Mackie 1983; Wylie 1979). There is, however, some evidence of sex category differences among adolescents in certain components of self-esteem (Elliott 1988; Rosenberg and Simmons 1975; Simmons and Rosenberg 1975). One possible explanation for these findings is that women's and men's selves have different bases.

Different Bases of Self-Esteem. This idea has recently been restated in the writings of Chodorow (1978), Gilligan (1982), and McGwire (1984). Women's self-concepts are purported to be based more on relationships, whereas men's are more dependent on individuation and instrumental action. Research by Schwalbe and Staples (1991) provides limited support for this distinction. Despite women's and men's identical ranking of the importance of the three sources of self-esteem (reflected appraisals being most important for both), reflected appraisals are more important for women than men and social comparisons are more important for men. In adolescence, this pattern may be much more discernable. Rosenberg and Simmons (1975) report sharp differences between boys and girls in their sensitivity to the impression they are making on others. Their contention that during adolescence girls focus on *pleasing others* whereas boys center on *accomplishment and achievement* is similar to the pattern hypothesized by Chodorow, Gilligan, and McGwire.

Sex Category as a Status Variable. Viewing sex category as a status variable provides an alternative explanation for current findings on self-esteem. For example, research on the combined impact of race and sex category (Simmons and Rosenberg 1975) indicates that white girls have lower self-esteem than white boys or African-American girls. Rather than simply attributing this pattern to different bases of self-esteem, a status perspective might hypothesize that different standards of self-judgment are employed by different groups, due to their position in the social structure.

Self-Esteem and Gender. Perhaps global self-esteem is linked to gender rather than sex category (Whitley 1983; Wylie 1979). Whitley (1983) found a slight relationship between self-attributed masculine traits and self-esteem for both men and women. This may be due to the high social desirability of both the masculine traits employed in the measures of gender role orientation and the traits and behaviors included in the various self-esteem scales.

Summary. The evolution from a sex differences to a more social structural approach is not as obvious in the work on self-esteem as it is in other research areas related to the self. However, the reported impact of race and sex category indicates that recasting the analysis of sex category differences in status terms could well clarify the confusing patterns uncovered by prior research. A second conclusion that can be drawn from the research on self-esteem is the need to disentangle the effects of sex category and gender. Separating these concepts may eliminate the contradictions in some reported findings (Whitley 1983).

To this point we have focused on research and theory concerned with the self and interaction. Now we turn to a consideration of how the content, processes, and contexts of interaction relate to sex category and gender.

SOCIAL RELATIONSHIPS AND GROUP PROCESSES

A sizable literature reports "sex differences" in such important areas as leadership style, causal attribution, conformity, help giving, verbal productivity, and so on (see Freize et al. 1982; Meeker and Weitzel-O'Neill 1977; O'Leary, Unger, and Wallston 1985). However, developing a theory to explain the confusing and often contradictory findings of this research is much like attempting to shoot a moving target. Sex category effects have a "now you see it, now you don't" quality.

The most valid statement that can be made at present is that contextual and situational variables have a major effect on the occurrence of such differences. I will therefore not attempt to review the findings in this area; rather, I will concentrate on how sex category and gender are treated in research on group processes and attribution and evaluate the relative merits of the various theoretical approaches.

Group Processes

Due to the variability and complexity of reported sex category and gender effects on group processes, there are more explanations offered for these effects in this than in other areas of social psychology. Here, too, the functionalist influence is evident, but regardless of its strength the general trend is away from a sex differences/socialization view to a more stratification-based explanation of sex category effects.

Sex Role Differentiation and Socialization.   The classic functionalist perspective (Bales 1949, 1953) articulates a dualistic conception of group goals: task and social. Using the family as the preeminent example of a small group, functionalists attribute the allocation of socioemotional work to women to their childbearing and nursing (Parsons and Bales 1955). Men, biologically excluded from these responsibilities, concentrate on instrumental tasks in the family. Through the mechanism of sex-differentiated socialization, these different competencies (instrumental and socioemotional expertise) are supposedly instilled in the fundamental personalities of individuals. Once established in the personality, the hypothesized pattern of "sex-role differentiation" is expected to generalize to contexts outside the family (Wagner 1988).

Much of the research on group processes, whether guided by functionalist perspectives or not, relies on sex role socialization to explain any sex category differences. For example, most of the work that involves mixed-motive settings (those requiring both cooperation and competition) attributes differences in the bargaining strategies of women and men to differences in the emphasis placed on cooperation and competition for girls and boys (Wiley 1973). Whether or not researchers view this differentiation as function or inevitable, many

agree it results from existing socialization practices.

Although the functionalist legacy persists in the study of group processes (note especially the widespread use of the labels "instrumental" and "socioemotional"), the plethora of later research does not support the predicted difference in concentration on instrumental and socioemotional activity in task groups (Meeker and Weitzel-O'Neill 1977; Ridgeway 1988). Similarly, the assumed fundamental differences in men's and women's personalities due to sex-differentiated socialization lacks empirical substantiation. Further, a functionalist or sex role socialization approach is incapable of explaining situational variability in men's and women's task and socioemotional behavior (Ridgeway 1988).

Turning to a structural rather than a functionalist perspective, we find approaches that can be loosely categorized into three groups on the basis of the aspect of social structure central to each: position, social role, or status. Although these theoretical and empirical perspectives vary in their focal point, they are quite similar in their basic arguments and in the limited role accorded an individual's socialization history.

Sex Category as Position.   Kanter's (1977a) work on the corporation illustrates the focus on position. She argues that differences in the behavior of men and women in corporations are due to their positions in the organizational structure and their relative numbers, rather than to other variables. Positions are important because they represent access to structural sources of power and status. An increasing body of evidence supports the hypothesized effect of minority/majority status (Johnson and Schulman 1989), but the effect of relative numbers of women and men may not be quite as Kanter (1977b) portrays it. Yoder (1991) finds that Kanter's propositions regarding tokenism apply only to women (not men) in sex category-inappropriate occupations. Despite these weaknesses, Kanter's work focuses attention on structural rather than individual-level variables.

Another influence in the move away from socialization explanations comes from research on social exchange. This approach also fosters a position-based treatment of sex category. Sex category has not been a primary focus of research in the area of power-dependence, the major articulation of exchange theory in group processes research. The power-dependence studies that do consider sex category as a variable often employ same-sex dyads and use sex category as a control (Cook and Emerson 1978; Molm 1981, 1985b). However, the premise that position in an exchange structure affects access to power, which in turn affects behavior, has important implications for the study of sex category effects in group processes. Since women's social positions are often lower in power relative to men's, an exchange perspective predicts differences in behavior. Thompson (1981) argues that differences in power-dependence positions, not sex category, are responsible for observed differences between women and men in groups, such as women's tendency to be more sensitive to others, to change their behavior more often, and to make sacrifices for others as evidence of their low-power position.

Outside the experiment-based power-dependence research, exchange principles have been reinterpreted and expanded recently to explain variations in marital power and gender inequity. For example, England and Kilbourne (1990) emphasize the role of cultural values in determining the relative exchange value of men's and women's contributions in a marital relationship. Not only does American culture value men's contributions more, but women's contributions are more relation-specific and less liquid (i.e., depend on a specific marital relationship). In addition, many of women's contributions profit children rather than their partner. These factors all operate to advantage men in marital power relationships.

These recent developments can be seen as introducing flexibility into position-based explanations via cultural values and types of exchanges. Such developments appear more likely to be successful in explaining women's and men's behaviors than do previous versions of this approach that ignore the role of meaning in assessing the impact of position.

Viewing sex category as position reduces the importance of sex role socialization in explanations of differences in women's and men's behavior. Further, it interprets sex category effects as instances of more general processes of power-dependence and organizational structure. It also goes a long way toward rejecting biological causes for sex category and gender differences, but in so doing it virtually ignores all the variables associated with the actor and downplays the role of transituational societal norms and beliefs.

Sex Category as Social Role.   Some psychologists also employ structural approaches to sex category differences in social behavior. A prime example is found in the work of Eagly (1987; Eagly and Steffen 1984), who argues that sex category differences in social behavior result from the unequal distribution of men and women to social roles, which vary in both status and emphasis on agentic and communal skills. The impact of this sex category-based allocation of roles, she contends, is mediated by gender roles, as well as by learned (socialized) sex-typed skills and beliefs. This social role position does not rule out the potential impact of sex category-differentiated socialization or biology on the sex category-differentiated organization of society. Eagly, however, focuses on the differences in the values attached to the roles men and women are assigned in a society and the traits or attributes (agentic or communal) required by those roles. To date, Eagly has employed her social role perspective in explaining sex category stereotypes as well as a variety of social behaviors, including conformity, influenceability, nonverbal behavior, helping behavior, and aggression (Eagly 1987).

This perspective may be helpful in looking at a few categorical bases for divisions in society that are built on differential participation in the structure of society. However, the scheme it provides is not as generalizable as that provided by the view of sex category as position or as a status characteristic.

Sex Category as a Status Variable.   Expectation states theory (Berger et al. 1977) asserts that performance expectations provide the basis for status and power structures in task-oriented groups. One important type of information that can differentiate the expected performances of individuals comes from diffuse status characteristics. A diffuse status characteristic: (1) consists of a dimension on which people may be ranked and for which the high state is more desirable; (2) is associated with a set of attributes or stereotypes concerning expected performance on specific tasks; and (3) creates a general expectation state that leads to expectations of diffuse differences in competence. Obviously, sex category fits this definition. Thus, in this culture and in the absence of any information clearly relevant to task performance, both men and women assume men will provide more valued contributions to the group process and will act on that assumption until or unless task-relevant evidence is available.[8] Based on an extensive review of group processes research, Meeker and Weitzel-O'Neill (1977) conclude that sex category does operate as a status variable affecting interaction in task-oriented groups.

Although expectation states research provides the basis for this perspective, elaborations have come from work on status generalization. For example, Foschi and Foddy (1988; Foschi 1991) link the development of differential standards to rank on diffuse status characteristics. Standards are viewed as filters through which performances are assessed (Foschi 1991), such that variable standards result in different attributions for identical performances. The connection of this theoretical elaboration to the imposition of double standards on the basis of sex category is fascinating and suggests a fruitful new approach to inequity.

Despite the success of a status processes model in explaining sex category effects in instrumental behavior, it does not address variability in socioemotional behavior (Ridgeway 1988). Ridgeway (1988; Ridgeway and Berger 1986; see also chapter 11) suggests that socioemotional behaviors are linked to legitimacy rather than status processes. By recasting legitimacy processes in terms compatible with those used to describe status processes, she succeeds in developing a coherent model for the prediction of men's and women's behavior, both instrumental and socioemotional, under varying situational conditions.

There are several major advantages for social psychologists interested in group processes to view sex category as a status characteristic. Not only does this perspective allow for the operation of other processes, such as gender role socialization (Gigliotti 1988), it also bases the definition of valued states on currently held attitudes and stereotypes (Wagner, Ford, and Ford 1986). Thus sex category may operate as a status variable in most current societies, but it need not do so if attitudes and stereotypes change (Stewart 1988).

Such a conceptualization also allows for a connection with larger social structures (by employing society-based differentiating factors as potential bases of power and status structures) and for the incorporation of other status characteristics. Perhaps this is why researchers in quite different theoretical traditions have integrated the conception of sex category as status into their own theoretical perspectives.

Finally, treating sex category as a status variable links it to an established body of applied research. This work has successfully reduced the impact of status variables on performance expectations and may provide a blueprint for programs designed to reduce discrimination based on sex category (Pugh and Wahrman 1985; Stewart 1988; Wagner, Ford, and Ford 1986).

Socialization, Position, Status, or Attribution?
Molm's work (Molm 1985a, 1986, 1988) on power and resources pushes the boundaries of present formulations by assessing the utility of socialization, structural (power-dependence), expectation states, and attribution perspectives in contexts drawn from power-dependence theory. Unlike contexts employed in expectation states research, participants are not collectively oriented. Under these conditions, Molm finds little support for expectation states predictions. In contrast, she finds strong support for structural theory and some support for

attribution theory. One obvious implication of this comparative work is that theories that are broader than any of the present perspectives must be developed.

Summary.   The functionalist legacy of sex-differentiated roles served as an impetus for the study of mixed-sex groups in this area of social psychology. Otherwise, the prevailing tendency to enhance internal validity might have resulted in the exclusive study of homogeneous (single-sex) groups. However, researchers and theorists studying group processes did not find a sex role socialization explanation sufficient and moved on to conceptions of sex category as instances of a more general social phenomena, such as positions, roles, or statuses. This transition has transported research on sex category into the mainstream of theoretical development in social psychology. By treating sex category as one example of a status, power or organizational position, or role, research profits from the theoretical advances in the general areas of stratification, organizations, and status processes. Further, sex category is no longer seen as a biologically determined category that results in interaction deficiencies for one or the other group; it is treated instead as a label, role, or position that determines expectations, standards, and performance.

Attribution Processes

Reflecting the recent resurgence of interest in cognitive processes, attribution theory has been a focus of a great deal of attention since the mid-1970s. Attribution concepts and theory represent an attempt to systematize the study of the causal interpretations people give to events in their environment. Although attribution theory is usually the province of psychologists, sociologists have long been concerned with subjective understandings (Crittenden 1983). Some important parallels have been drawn between attribution theory and symbolic interactionism (Crittenden 1983; Stryker and Gottlieb 1981). Although this convergence of psychological and sociological approaches is impor-

tant, the frequent inclusion of sex category as a variable in attribution research is more important for present purposes (Deaux 1976; Hansen and O'Leary 1985).

Achievement is the primary phenomenon to which researchers apply attribution theory. Much of this work concentrates on how one's sex category affects attributions of one's own success or failure. As in research on group processes, the many inconsistent findings on sex category effects in the attribution literature has resulted in a proliferation of explanations (Frieze et al. 1982).

Unlike the research on group processes, there is no evolution from a functionalist to a more structural, stratification-based model. Perhaps due to the influence of psychologists, we find instead a transition from models that propose stable or fixed patterns of sex category-differentiated attributions to models that consider sex category as only one of many bases for expectancies and, therefore, attributions. Let us first consider the fixed models.

Sex Category Differences and Socialization. Frieze and associates (1982) isolated three models that purport to explain sex category differences in attributions of success and failure: (1) general externality—women tend to make external attributions for both success and failure; (2) self-derogation—women tend to attribute their successes to external factors and their failures to internal factors; and (3) low expectancy—women, due to low expectations of success in achievement situations, have unstable attributions for success and stable attributions for failure. Even based on these limited descriptions, it is evident that these models all assume that women and men differ in their attributions of their own achievements *and,* most important, that these differences are not situation-specific.

There is also considerable research on the differences in observers' causal attributions for women's and men's performances. Again, the pattern of sex category effects is unclear. One thing that emerges is that men and women agree that their identical performances are due to *different* causes (Deaux 1976). Researchers share this belief.

This focus on differences implies that sex-differentiated socialization is the source of sex category differences in attributional patterns of both actors and observers. Deaux's report (1976) of sex category differences in attribution at ages as young as ten indicates that these patterns are established early in the life cycle. The remaining question is how these patterns are learned. Deaux suggests that these early differences result from different patterns of reinforcement, but this claim has yet to be tested.

Not only have researchers not detailed the reinforcement patterns or other socialization mechanisms posited to create sex category differences, but their reliance on distinct universal patterns for women and men fails to address the complexity of social life. As in other areas of social psychology, transituational (socialization) models of sex category differences do not adequately explain existing data (McHugh, Frieze, and Hanusa 1982). Although socialization may play an important role, future formulations need to include contextual variables in any conceptualization of attribution processes and need to specify the socialization mechanisms that are linked to sex differences in attribution patterns.

Sex Category-Based Expectancies. Deaux's (1976) attribution model, which treats sex category as the source of a category-based expectancy, illustrates how contextual variability can be included in an attribution model. A category-based expectancy is one that "derives from the perceiver's knowledge that the target person is a member of a particular class, category, or reference group" (Jones and McGillis 1976, 393). This is in contrast to target-based expectancies that "derive from prior information about the specific individual actor" (Jones and McGillis 1976, 394). Category-based expectancies originate in social interaction, but the exact process of creation has not yet been delineated. The social nature of expectancies allows for variability across culture as well as potential change. One source of category-based expectancies—stereotypes—illustrates the connection of expectancies to societal values.

Deaux's model posits that the relationship of expectancies to actual performances determines attributions. For example, inconsistency between an actual performance and expectancies is predicted to result in an attribution to variable causes for the performance, whereas consistency is expected to result in an attribution to stable causes. Thus, differential attributions on the basis of sex category, for either one's own or another's performance, preserve stereotypical beliefs about the competencies of men and women.

Since expectancies vary across situations, the model can be expanded to include situational factors, such as sex categorization of the task. For example, a task that is associated with men might result in attributions of ability to successfully performing men and attributions of effort to successfully performing women. A different pattern would result if the task were associated with women.

Another strength of the category-based model is its ability to address the normative aspects of public attributions (Crittenden and Wiley 1985; Tetlock 1981). For example, there are category-based norms that guide women's and men's public explanations of their behavior (e.g., women are expected to give more modest attributions of their successes than are men) (Deaux and Major 1989; Gould and Sloan 1982). Further expansion of a category-based model to specify the role of self-presentational norms would forge an important link to sociological views of interaction.

Although this model appears to satisfy many of the criticisms leveled at previous models, it does not adequately describe the process by which category-based expectancies are acquired. In addition, it does not address explicitly the different functions of attributions.

Summary. Initial attribution models proposed several transituational patterns of sex category differences due to differential socialization. In contrast, the later category-based expectancy model allows for situational variation due to the inclusion of situation-specific social norms and values. This transition reflects a broadening of focus from the strictly personal function of attributions (i.e., the impact of attribution on motivation) to a view that encompasses both personal and interpersonal functions of attribution. By expanding the approach to include interpersonal functions, new and interesting research possibilities arise, such as the role attributional patterns play in the maintenance of valued self-images. The interpersonal function of attribution promises to be a profitable area for collaboration between sociology and psychological social psychologists.

One area that has yet to be investigated is the impact of gender on attributions. Since past research has not measured gender, it is impossible to separate gender effects from sex category effects. In fact, Hansen and O'Leary (1985) suggest that given the distribution of masculinity and femininity across sex categories, sex category effects on self-attributions may be gender effects. Thus a particularly profitable line of investigation might focus on the impact of differences in gendered selves on attributions that serve an interpersonal function.

SOCIAL STRUCTURE AND THE INDIVIDUAL

The area of social structure and the individual, with its concentration on the link between micro- and macrolevels, is a relatively underdeveloped "face" of social psychology (House and Mortimer 1990) but an ideal area in which to investigate the effects of sex category and gender. In fact, sex category is one of the prime hierarchical dimensions of social structure (macrolevel) that is central to research and theory in this area. On the other hand, gender, a microlevel variable, has been given little attention.

Despite the importance of the micro-macro link, research in the area of social structure and personality has frequently been diluted or sidetracked by its isolation in topic areas, such as that of work (House and Mortimer 1990). Therefore the material presented here does not provide the same coherence of theoretical and research trends as do the two other areas of social psychology. For that reason, I will focus on three separate topics: the relationship of gender and gender role attitudes to structural variables, the impact of sex category and gender on the relationship between the structure of

work and the self, and the relationship of sex category and gender to stress.

Gender Role Attitudes, Sex Category, and Gender

Since it is quite common in the area of social structure and the individual to look at the relationship between social structural position and attitudes or beliefs, gender role attitudes have received much attention. The anomaly in these studies is that researchers ignore sex category as a social structural variable; rather, they have concentrated on how other indicators of social location, such as type of employment and work force participation, affect attitudes. Using a wide variety of measures, researchers have demonstrated an association between labor force participation and gender role attitudes (e.g., Mason, Czajka, and Arber 1976; Miller and Garrison 1982; Talichet and Willits 1986), but they have yet to specify the components of labor force participation that directly affect gender role attitudes. Perhaps characteristics of the job may mediate the impact of employment on gender role attitudes, just as they affect other attitudes (Kanter 1976, 1977a; Kohn and Schooler 1973).

To those interested in social change, important topics of research include historical changes in gender role attitudes and their relation to structural variables such as age, education, and labor force experience. Reviewing a sample of this research reveals that both men and women have become more nontraditional and egalitarian in their attitudes over time and that there is more consistency in their attitudes across domains such as work and family (Cherlin and Walters 1981; Mason, Czajka, and Arber 1976; Mason and Lu 1988). Of particular interest is the apparent link between structural variables and gender role attitudes, with more traditional views being related positively to age and negatively to education and income (Morgan and Walker 1983).

What little work has been done in this area using sex category as a structural variable challenges the assumption that structural variables such as race category and sex category act independently

(Dugger 1988). This should encourage researchers to investigate the potential impact of interactions between sex category and other structural variables (House and Mortimer 1990).

Summary.   Research in this area has generally treated sex category as an individual-level variable, with the patterns of men's and women's attitudes linked to their socialization experience. A major advance in attempts to model gender role attitudes might be to reinterpret prior findings within a framework that treats sex category as a status or stratification variable. This area would also benefit from a clear distinction between gender and sex category. Clearly distinguishing between self-attitudes and gender role expectations could prove a major asset in understanding patterns of gender role and other attitudes.

Work, Sex Category, and Gender

Research on work, especially job satisfaction, provides an excellent context in which to assess the utility of a social structure and personality perspective, not only because of the volume of research in this area but because sex category is frequently included as a variable. Although many models treating the structural and psychological variables related to work have been proposed, I will consider two distinct classes of explanation that are especially relevant to the way sex category is expected to affect job satisfaction.

Job and Gender Models.   In consideration of job commitment, Lorence (1987) distinguishes between job and gender models. This distinction applies equally well to the models offered to explain job satisfaction. What Lorence calls the *gender model* is very similar to the gender role/socialization explanations discussed earlier. In its most general form, this model asserts that men are raised to believe it is their responsibility to provide economic support for their families, whereas women are taught that the family is their preeminent responsibility. Due to this essential difference in the socialization of women and men, they view their

work role differently (Bernard 1981; Bielby and Bielby 1984). Thus, the gender model predicts sex category differences in job orientation (satisfaction and commitment).

Other researchers have proposed a more restricted model that predicts that men's and women's job satisfaction is determined by different aspects of the job, with the emphasis on the relationship of the job to family responsibilities. Work is defined as essential for the fulfillment of men's family responsibilities, but for women it represents a more complex lifestyle choice due to the possible conflicts between occupational and family responsibilities (Bernard 1981). For example, several versions of this model predict that women will be more interested in the work environment, interpersonal relationships on the job, proximity of the work site to home, and scheduling, whereas men will be concerned with career achievement, self-expression, autonomy, and their influence in decision making (Bokemeier and Lacy 1987; Hodson 1989; R. Kessler and McRae 1982; Miller 1980).

Whereas the gender model is quite similar to socialization explanations, the job model is similar to structural explanations and demonstrates the contribution of a social structure and personality perspective. The basic premise of the job model is that the relative status of positions filled by women and men in the economic sector, as well as the characteristics of jobs and their settings, result in differences between women and men in job satisfaction and commitment (Kanter 1977a; Kohn and Schooler 1973). Kanter (1976, 1977a) claims that power, opportunity, and the proportional representation of women are the most important determinants of work attitudes, including satisfaction. In fact, there is considerable evidence that work conditions have a similar impact on women's and men's job satisfaction (Bokemeier and Lacy 1987; Lacy, Bokemeier, and Shepard 1983; Mannheim 1983; Miller 1980; Miller et al. 1979).

Sex Category as a Structural Variable.   Despite this evidence that the conditions of employment have similar effects on women's and men's job satisfaction and commitment, unexplained differences remain. For example, when conditions of employment are controlled, women are frequently more satisfied with their jobs than men (Crosby 1982; Hodson 1989; Summers and DeCotiis 1988).

Crosby (1982) argues that the explanation for this difference lies in the theory of relative deprivation. Women are less dissatisfied than men despite lower pay, less potential for advancement, and less fulfilling jobs because satisfaction is determined by the discrepancy between what they have, what they want, and what they think they deserve. The value of this perspective lies in its focus on expectancies. In addition to the impact of job conditions, differences in the expectancies associated with an individual's sex category are predicted to have an effect on job satisfaction. A model that incorporates expectancies derived from sex category, occupational position, and other status categories (e.g., race and age), as well as more traditional job condition measures, may result in a more parsimonious explanation of job satisfaction than any of the prior job or gender models.

Gender as an Individual-Level Variable. Job satisfaction is also affected by the importance of the job to the individual's self-conception. Mortimer and Lorence (1989) demonstrate the usefulness of assessing individuals' role identity hierarchies in their consideration of the relationship of job satisfaction to job involvement over time. Gender may play a role in this aspect of the model. For example, the congruence between a person's gender and his/her job may combine with the position of gender in the hierarchical structure of the self to affect satisfaction. There is some preliminary evidence to support the potential value of including gender in the model. For example, gender attitudes and beliefs are related to women's work behavior (Bielby and Bielby 1984). The relationship between the self and work role identities offers a fertile field for future inquiry.

Summary. Reflecting the renewed interest in micro-macro linkages, research on the relationship between job satisfaction and sex category has moved from a gender- or socialization-based model to a job- or stratification-based model. Although this is consistent with trends in other areas, still lacking is the inclusion of sex category as one of the stratification variables in the model.[9] Certainly the role of job characteristics is important, but ignoring other important indicators of status or position, such as sex category, is unwarranted (Mortimer, Finch, and Maruyana 1988). It is also clear that gender plays an important role in this equation and warrants inclusion in future models.

Stress

Let us consider another individual-level variable, stress. Sociologists working in this area generally employ a social structure and personality approach and also consider sex category as a major variable (Aneshensel 1992). Results indicate that women have higher rates of psychological distress than men. This has led some writers to posit a biological explanation, but social structural explanations appear appropriate since the greater incidence of psychological distress among women is consistent with a general pattern of greater distress among lower-status individuals (McLeod and Kessler 1990).

Sex Role Differentiation and Socialization. The early explanations of sex category differences in stress depend on sex role differentiation and differential socialization (Gove 1972, 1984; Gove and Tudor 1973; Tweed and Jackson 1981). Interestingly, there is a typical division between instrumental and socioemotional emphases in such explanations. For example, Wheaton (1990) argues that contextual factors that affect reactions to crucial life transitions vary by sex category, with women experiencing more relational stress and men experiencing more work-related stress.

Other approaches have also posited a stable individual-difference model based on socialized sex role attitudes. For example, Ross et al. (1983) report that gender role attitudes play an important role in mediating the distress of married men and women. This is a major contribution, since it may result in the addition of gender to the model.

Despite these contributions, the lack of stable sex category differences in reactions to stress (Turner and Avison 1989 as cited by Aneshensel 1992; Newmann 1986) leads some researchers to doubt the value of models that concentrate on individual differences. Rather, they consider factors related to men's and women's position or status to explain the confusing pattern of sex category differences in stress reactions, because role or position may determine exposure to risk factors.

Sex Category as a Structural Variable. The concept of role provides a link to social structure for many stress researchers. Initially, researchers predicted both positive and negative correlations between the number of roles occupied and amount of stress (Sieber 1974). Since available data do not support a simple relationship in either direction between number of roles and psychological distress (Menaghan 1989; Radloff 1975), explanations that attribute women's greater level of stress to the number of roles they occupy appears inadequate. Recent models have suggested the need to introduce intervening variables. For example, Thoits (1983) reports that the impact of role identity gains and losses is mediated by the individual's level of social integration, one possible determinant of which is position in the social structure.

Even if women and men occupy the same roles, they may experience different stressors, due to their different structural positions (R. Kessler 1982). The demands and limitations placed on their actions may vary (Pearlin 1975). In fact, specific roles, such as employment, marriage, and parenthood, have different meanings for men and women (Aneshensel and Pearlin 1987; Barnett and Baruch 1987; Gore and Mangione 1983). For that reason women and men are seen to experience unique stressors (R. Kessler and McLeod 1984; Wethington, McLeod, and Kessler 1987).[10]

Not only may stress vary with the meaning of various roles, but stress levels may be linked to specific role combinations (Gore and Mangione 1983; Menaghan 1989; Thoits 1986). This proposal requires consideration of the relationship between specific role configurations and the normative, expected pattern for a person with specific social characteristics (e.g., sex category).

Recently, some researchers (Thoits 1986, 1991; Wiley 1991) have advocated the use of concepts drawn from identity theory (Burke 1980, 1989; Burke and Reitzes 1981; Stryker 1968, 1980, 1987) to explain the different implications of specific roles and role combinations for stress. Using this approach, Thoits (1991) proposes a general model that will explain not just sex category differences but the extensive data on status differences in stress and stress responses. She argues that self-conceptions are built on positions in the social structure (wife, mother, attorney, etc.). Each individual possesses many positions (identities), but they differ in value depending on their importance to the individual's self-conception. For that reason, Thoits argues, events that threaten highly valued identities will result in greater stress and potential for psychological distress. Since the selves of men and women may well differ in both content and importance of role identities, stress and psychological distress are expected to vary. Although Thoits (1992) recently reported that identity salience by itself does not have a significant impact on psychological well-being, the combinations of identities held by men and women appears to be important.

Summary. Here we see an evolution of the treatment of sex category differences in stress from relatively simple sex role differentiation and socialization explanations to much broader conceptualizations that consider the relationship among roles, the uneven distribution of valued roles depending on sex category, and the salience of role identities in the self. A model of the latter type is of particular importance to researchers interested in sex category and gender because it includes social structural and normative aspects of the current social situation that have not been considered in other formulations. From a social psychological perspective, the identity approach appears promising because it incorporates aspects of many earlier explanations and provides a link to both the macrolevel of social structure and the microlevel of the self.

Conclusion

The major contribution of a social structure and personality perspective to the study of sex category and gender is in fostering the view of sex category as a structural variable. Explanations adopting this perspective not only mirror the current trends in other fields of social psychology but are more consistent with available data. Although this treatment of sex category is not fully developed, it is promising.

There is a bias in the social structure and personality approach—concerning the direction of the influence—that needs to be addressed in future research. Most research in this area (House and Mortimer 1990) emphasizes the impact of social structure on the individual, rather than the impact of the individual on social structure. This is especially true with regard to research on sex category and gender.

Gender is absent or given little attention by most researchers in this area. Considering the key role gender may play, for example in role salience, future research should incorporate this variable.

SOCIAL PSYCHOLOGICAL TREATMENT OF SEX CATEGORY AND GENDER: PAST, PRESENT, AND FUTURE

General Trends

Although only a small portion of the work on sex category and gender in social psychology is reviewed here, it is sufficiently broad to permit some general statements about the current state of the field. One of the patterns discernible in the literature is a move away from the automatic attribution of sex category differences to sex role differences without further elaboration. Initially, sex category differences were treated as explanatory rather than descriptive, reflecting "strong underlying (and unexamined) assumptions about the biological causality of sex differences" (Unger 1979, 1087). This use of sex differences evolved over time into a use of sex roles as an explanation (Hess and Ferree 1987). Although this change might have encour-

aged investigation of social factors that result in specific role requirements, instead it served as a complete explanation. Gender/sex role explanations did not result in attempts to isolate the components of social roles or the aspects of socialization that resulted in the differences between women and men. Frequently these explanations also ignored the question of the social construction and learning of these roles. Thus, the attribution of any sex category difference to sex or gender roles is simplistic whether sex/gender roles are understood to be biologically or socially determined.

One step removed from gender/sex role explanations are those that attribute sex category differences to socialization. These represent only a slight improvement over role explanations because researchers frequently fail to specify the causal connection between specific socialization practices or experiences and the behaviors under consideration. This is not to deny the potential role of socialization in the creation of sex category-based differences; rather, it emphasizes the importance of specifying the components of the socialization process both to predict sex category and gender effects and to allow for empirical tests of any such predictions.

The inadequacy of simplistic social role and socialization explanations has led researchers to look for more proximal causes for sex category differences. It also encouraged an increased concern with the impact of situational variables and structural factors on sex category-linked behavior. At the same time, this change in theoretical approach to sex category represents a departure from a basically functionalist perspective. It has freed researchers to look at sex category as an instance of much broader social phenomena, such as status processes and hierarchical structure.

Not only does this increased emphasis on situational and structural factors link current work on sex category to the large body of research on stratification, it also underscores the importance of linking micro- and macrolevel conceptualizations of significant issues. In fact, the current trend in social psychology that views sex category effects as due to either differential status or position implicitly treats sex category as a stratification variable. This is a perspective Lipman-Blumen and Tickamyer (1975) urged sociologists to adopt almost two decades ago.

The final trend of note is the separation of sex category from gender. This change accompanies the burgeoning of research on the social construction of gender. Since social construction has been an important perspective in sociological social psychology from its inception, it is surprising that this perspective has not had greater influence in the past. The view of gender as socially constructed is not incompatible with the theoretical conception of sex category as a status or stratification variable. It simply reinforces the notion that schemes of social categorization are not necessarily based on "real" differences. Sex category may well trigger differential socialization (differential treatment and expectations). In turn, an individual's gender is, in part, the product of the differential expectations and treatment associated with sex category (e.g., girls do not hit people, boys do not cry). Once gender identity is developed it also has the potential to affect behavior.

Cautionary Notes

This review illustrates the importance of including gender and sex category in the analyses done in almost all research in sociological social psychology. This is not to imply that differences should be the focus of research but rather that the impact of sex category and gender on phenomena of sociological interest continues to be an empirical question. In fact, one of the problems with past research on sex category effects is the emphasis on differences rather than similarities. The tendency for researchers to report and editors to publish results only when there are differences may explain the apparently infrequent use of sex category as a variable in the research published in *Social Psychology Quarterly*. If sex category were routinely included in research designs and reported, a more balanced picture of sex category effects would be available.

An important warning that bears repeating here is that the use of a single-sex category or skewed samples limits researchers' ability to generalize. Whether the limitation of samples is due to beliefs in substitutability, concerns with internal validity, or beliefs about the relative importance and applicability of particular issues to women or men, the result is the same—a very inadequate and ungeneralizable model of human behavior. Researchers are encouraged to include sufficient women and men in their samples to allow for generalization.

It is also imperative for researchers to separate sex category from gender in theoretical conceptualizations and empirical investigations. It is evident from this review that gender is frequently not assessed. Researchers assume a high correlation between these variables, but the degree of congruity remains a research question. Even if gender and sex category are highly congruent, gender may have effects that are quite distinct. If researchers untangle these two concepts in their models, they may well achieve a measure of clarity that has escaped them in the past.

Finally, while including sex category and gender in their research, social psychologists must keep foremost in their minds the social origins of sex category and gender differences.[11] As Epstein (1988) has thoroughly documented, the differences between women and men are deceptive distinctions. We must avoid the trap of dichotomous thinking, a tendency that frequently results in hierarchical ordering and the tendency to treat differences, whether in style or status, behavior or thought, as natural, necessary, or inevitable.

Summary

Current trends that place greater emphasis on proximate causes, particularly structural ones, apply a stratification perspective to the treatment of issues related to sex category, separate the concepts of sex category and gender, and recognize the socially constructed quality of gender foreshadow important contributions of work on sex category and gender to the advancement of sociological social psychology and sociology in general. The importance and centrality of social psychological theory and research related to sex category and gender is obvious. There is much to be done, but there are many productive scholars in this area.

NOTES

1. There is even variation in the number of genders depending on the society. Some define as many as four (Martin and Voorhies 1975).

2. The choice of either term has major implications for scholarship, since the use of a particular label may well bias the interpretation social psychologists draw from their work. For example, the use of *sex* when describing differences may lead us, perhaps unconsciously, to attribute any variation in the behavior of women and men to biological origins because *sex* implies biological mechanisms (Unger 1979).

3. Goffman (1977) also warns us that it is a "dangerous economy" not to specify sex class (or sex category) continually when we speak or write of sex class-linked behaviors and so on, because the use of the shorter term *sex* fits our cultural stereotypes.

4. *Social Psychology Quarterly* was published previously under the names *Social Psychology* and *Sociometry*.

5. This focus on differences also reflects a general bias against the finding of no difference that results in an overemphasis on differences in the published literature (Tresemer 1975).

6. Two major issues not addressed in this chapter are the role of biological/physiological factors (see chapter 2) and the differences in the experiences of minority and majority men and women.

7. Ethnomethodologists have also devoted considerable time to the construction of gender (e.g., S. Kessler and McKenna 1978).

8. Lockheed (1985) found strong evidence of the impact of sex category and support for the prediction that task-relevant information, when available, would be given more weight than would sex category.

9. The meanings and demands of work and family roles undoubtedly vary for men and women depending on race, ethnicity, age, and socioeconomic status (Baca Zinn 1990; Reskin and Coverman 1985).

10. There is an important body of literature on the division of household labor and its social psychological consequences (e.g., Berk 1985).

11. Future research must also be cognizant of the impact of biological factors (see chapter 2).

REFERENCES

Aneshensel, Carol S. 1992. Social stress: Theory and research. Pp. 15–38 in *Annual Review of Sociology,* vol. 18, ed. J. Blake and J. Hagan. Palo Alto: Annual Reviews.

Aneshensel, Carol S., and Leonard I. Pearlin. 1987. Structural contexts of sex differences in stress. Pp. 75–95 in *Gender and Stress,* ed. R. C. Barnett, L. Biener, and G. K. Baruch. New York: Free Press.

Baca Zinn, Maxine. 1990. Family, feminism, and race in America. *Gender & Society* 4:68–82.

Bales, Robert F. 1949. *Interaction Process Analysis: A Method for the Study of Small Groups.* Cambridge: Addison Wesley.

———. 1953. The equilibrium problem in small groups. Pp. 111–161 in *Working Papers in the Theory of Action,* ed. Talcott Parsons, Robert F. Bales, and Edward Shils. Glencoe, IL: Free Press.

Barnett, Rosalind C., and Grace K. Baruch. 1987. Social roles, gender, and psychological distress. Pp. 122–143 in *Gender and Stress,* ed. R. C. Barnett, L. Biener, and G. K. Baruch. New York: Free Press.

Bem, Sandra. 1974. The measurement of psychological androgyny. *Journal of Consulting and Clinical Psychology* 42:155–162.

———. 1981. Gender schema theory: A cognitive account of sex typing. *Psychological Review* 88:369–371.

———. 1984. Androgyny and gender schema theory: A conceptual and empirical integration. Pp. 180–226 in *Nebraska Symposium on Motivation 1984,* vol. 34, ed. Theo B. Sonderegger. Lincoln: University of Nebraska Press.

Berger, Joseph, M. Hamet Fisek, Robert Z. Norman, and Morris Zelditch, Jr. 1977. *Status Characteristics and Social Interaction: An Expectation-States Approach.* New York: Elsevier.

Berk, Sara Fenstermaker. 1985. *The Gender Factory: The Apportionment of Work in American Households.* New York: Plenum.

Bernard, Jessie. 1973. My four revolutions: An autobiographical history of the ASA. Pp. 11–29 in *Changing Women in a Changing Society,* ed. Joan Huber. Chicago: University of Chicago Press.

———. 1981. The good-provider role: Its rise and fall. *American Psychologist* 36:1–12.

Bielby, Denise D., and William T. Bielby. 1984. Work commitment, sex role attitudes, and women's employment. *American Sociological Review* 49:234–247.

Bokemeier, Janet L., and William B. Lacy. 1987. Job values, rewards, and work conditions as factors in job satisfaction among men and women. *The Sociological Quarterly* 28:189–204.

Burke, Peter J. 1980. The self: Measurement requirements from an interactionist perspective. *Social Psychology Quarterly* 43:18–29.

———. 1989. Gender identity, sex, and school performance. *Social Psychology Quarterly* 52:159–169.

Burke, Peter J., and Donald C. Reitzes. 1981. The link between identity and role performance. *Social Psychology Quarterly* 44:83–92.

Cahill, Spencer. 1980. Directions for an interactionist study of gender development. *Symbolic Interaction* 3:123–138.

———. 1986a. Childhood socialization as a recruitment process: Some lessons from the study of gender development. Pp. 163–186 in *Sociological Studies of Child Development,* vol. 1, ed. Patricia A. Adler and Peter Adler. Greenwich, CT: JAI Press.

———. 1986b. Language practices and self definition: The case of gender identity acquisition. *The Sociological Quarterly* 27:295–311.

Cherlin, Andrew, and Pamela Barnhouse Walters. 1981. U.S. men's and women's sex-role attitudes: 1972–1978. *American Sociological Review* 46:453–474.

Chodorow, Nancy. 1978. *The Reproduction of Mothering.* Berkeley: University of California Press.

———. 1989. *Feminism and Psychoanalytic Theory.* New Haven: Yale University Press.

Cook, Karen S., and Richard M. Emerson. 1978. Power, equity, commitment in exchange networks. *American Sociological Review* 43:721–739.

Crittenden, Kathleen S. 1983. Sociological aspects of attribution. *Annual Review of Sociology* 9:425–446.

Crittenden, Kathleen S., and Mary Glenn Wiley. 1985. When egotism is normative: Self-presentational norms guiding attributions. *Social Psychology Quarterly* 48:360–365.

Crosby, Faye J. 1982. *Relative Deprivation and Working Women.* New York: Oxford University Press.

Deaux, Kay. 1976. Sex: A perspective on the attribution process. Pp. 335–352 in *New Directions in Attribution Research,* vol. 1, ed. John H. Harvey, William John Eckes, and Robert F. Kidd. Hillsdale, NJ: Lawrence Erlbaum.

———. 1984. From individual differences to social categories: Analysis of a decade's research on gender. *American Psychologist* 39:105–116.

Deaux, Kay, and Mary E. Kite. 1987. Thinking about gender. Pp. 92–117 in *Analyzing Gender,* ed. Beth B. Hess and Myra Marx Ferree. Newbury Park, CA: Sage.

Deaux, Kay, and Brenda Major. 1989. Putting gender into context: An interactive model of gender-related behavior. *Psychological Review* 94:369–389.

Dugger, Karen. 1988. Social location and gender-role attitudes: A comparison of black and white women. *Gender & Society* 2:425–448.

Eagly, Alice H. 1983. Gender and social influence: A social psychological analysis. *American Psychologist* 38:971–981.

———. 1987. *Sex Differences in Social Behavior: A Social-Role Interpretation.* Hillsdale, NJ: Erlbaum.

Eagly, Alice H., and Valerie J. Steffen. 1984. Gender stereotypes stem from the distribution of women and men into social roles. *Journal of Personality and Social Psychology* 46:735–754.

Elliott, Gregory C. 1988. Gender differences in self-consistency: Evidence from an investigation of self-concept structure. *Journal of Youth and Adolescence* 17:41–57.

England, Paula, and Barbara Stanek Kilbourne. 1990. Market, marriages, and other mates: The problem of power. Pp. 163–188 in *Beyond the Marketplace: Rethinking Economy and Society,* ed. Riger Friedland and A. F. Robertson. New York: Aldine de Gruyter.

Epstein, Cynthia Fuchs. 1988. *Deceptive Distinctions.* New Haven: Yale University Press.

Foschi, Martha. 1991. Gender and double standards for competence. In *Gender, Interaction, and Inequality,* ed. Cecilia L. Ridgeway. New York: Springer-Verlag.

Foschi, Martha, and Margaret Foddy. 1988. Standards, performances, and the formation of self-other expectations. Pp. 248–260 in *Status Generalization,* ed. Murray A. Webster, Jr., and Martha Foschi. Stanford: Stanford University Press.

Frieze, Irene Hanson, Bernard E. Whitley, Jr., Barbara Hartman Hanusa, and Maureen C. McHugh. 1982. Assessing the theoretical models for sex differences in causal attributions for success and failure. *Sex Roles* 8:333–343.

Gecas, Viktor. 1982. The self-concept. *Annual Review of Sociology* 8:1–33.

Gecas, Viktor, Darwin L. Thomas, and Andrew J. Weigert. 1973. Social identities in Anglo and Latin adolescents. *Social Forces* 51:477–484.

Gigliotti, Richard J. 1988. Sex differences in children's task-group performance: Status/norm or ability? *Small Group Behavior* 19:273–293.

Gilligan, Carol. 1982. *In a Different Voice.* Cambridge, MA: Harvard University Press.

Goffman, Erving. 1977. The arrangement between the sexes. *Theory and Society* 4:301–331.

———. 1979. *Gender Advertisements.* Cambridge, MA: Harvard University Press.

Gore, S., and T. W. Mangione. 1983. Social roles, sex roles and psychological distress: Additive and interactive models of sex differences. *Journal of Health and Social Behavior* 24:300–312.

Gould, Robert J., and Caroline G. Slone. 1982. The "feminine modesty" effect: A self-presentational interpretation of sex differences in causal attribution. *Personality and Social Psychology Bulletin* 8:477–485.

Gove, Walter R. 1972. The relationship between sex roles, marital status, and mental illness. *Social Forces* 51:34–44.

———. 1984. Gender differences in mental and physical illness: The effects of fixed roles and nurturant roles. *Social Science and Medicine* 19:77–91.

Gove, Walter R., and Jeanette F. Tudor. 1973. Adult sex roles and mental illness. *American Journal of Sociology* 78:812–835.

Hansen, Ranald D., and Virginia E. O'Leary. 1985. Sex-determined attributions. Pp. 67–99 in *Women, Gender, and Social Psychology,* ed. Virginia E. O'Leary, Rhoda Kesler Unger, and Barbara Strudler Wallston. Hillsdale, NJ: Erlbaum.

Hess, Beth B., and Myra Marx Ferree, eds. 1987. *Analyzing Gender.* Newbury Park, CA: Sage.

Hodson, Randy. 1989. Gender differences in job satisfaction: Why aren't women more dissatisfied? *The Sociological Quarterly* 30:385–399.

House, James S., and Jeylan T. Mortimer. 1990. Social structure and the individual: Emerging themes and new directions. *Social Psychology Quarterly* 53:71–80.

Johnson, Richard A., and Gary I. Schulman. 1989. Gender-role composition and role entrapment in decision-making groups. *Gender & Society* 3:355–372.

Jones, Edward E., and Daniel McGillis, 1976. Correspondent inferences and the attribution cube: A comparative reappraisal. Pp. 389–420 in *New Directions in Attribution Research,* vol. 1, ed. John H. Harvey, William John Eckes, and Robert F. Kidd. Hillsdale, NJ: Erlbaum.

Kanter, Rosabeth Moss. 1976. The impact of hierarchical structures on the work behavior of women and men. *Social Problems* 23:415–430.

———. 1977a. *Men and Women of the Corporation.* New York: Basic Books.

———. 1977b. Some effects of proportions on group life: Skewed sex ratios and responses to token women. *American Journal of Sociology* 82:965–990.

Kessler, Ronald C. 1982. A disaggregation of the relationship between socioeconomic status and psychological distress. *American Sociological Review* 47:752–764.

Kessler, Ronald C., and Jane D. McLeod. 1984. Sex differences in vulnerability to undesirable life events. *American Sociological Review* 49:620–631.

Kessler, Ronald C., and James A. McRae, Jr. 1982. The effect of wives' employment on the mental health of married men and women. *American Sociological Review* 47:216–227.

Kessler, Suzanne, and Wendy McKenna. 1978. *Gender: An Ethnomethodological Approach.* New York: Wiley.

Kohn, Melvin L., and Carmi Schooler. 1973. Occupational experience and psychological functioning: An assessment of reciprocal effects. *American Sociological Review* 38:97–118.

Lacy, William B., Janet L. Bokemeier, and Jon M. Shepard. 1983. Job attribute preferences and work commitment of men and women in the United States. *Personnel Psychology* 36:315–329.

Lever, Janet. 1978. Sex differences in the complexity of children's play and games. *American Sociological Review* 43:471–483.

Lipman-Blumen, Jean, and Ann R. Tickamyer. 1975. Sex roles in transition: A ten-year perspective. *Annual Review of Sociology* 1:297–337.

Lockheed, Marlaine E. 1985. Sex and social influence: A meta-analysis guided by theory. Pp. 406–429 in *Status, Rewards, and Influence,* ed. Joseph Berger and Morris Zelditch, Jr. San Francisco: Jossey-Bass.

Lorber, Judith. 1987. From the editor. *Gender & Society* 1:123–124.

Lorber, Judith, and Susan A. Farrell. 1991. *The Social Construction of Gender.* Newbury Park, CA: Sage.

Lorence, Jon. 1987. A test of "gender" and "job" models of sex differences in job involvement. *Social Forces* 66:121–142.

Mackie, Marlene. 1983. The domestication of self: Gender comparisons of self-imagery and self-esteem. *Social Psychology Quarterly* 46:343–350.

Mannheim, Bilha. 1983. Male and female industrial workers: Job satisfaction, work role centrality, and work place preference. *Work and Occupations* 10: 413–436.

Markus, Hazel, Marie Crane, Stan Bernstein, and Michael Siladi. 1982. Self-schemas and gender. *Journal of Personality and Social Psychology* 42: 38–50.

Martin, M. Kay, and Barbara Voorhies. 1975. *Female of the Species.* New York: Columbia University Press.

Mason, Karen Oppenheimer, John L. Czajka, and Sara Arber. 1976. Change in U.S. women's sex-role attitudes, 1964–1974. *American Sociological Review* 41:573–596.

Mason, Karen Oppenheim, and Yu-Hsia Lu. 1988. Attitudes toward women's familial roles: Changes in the United States, 1977–1985. *Gender & Society* 2:39–57.

McGwire, W. J. 1984. Search for self: Going beyond self-esteem and the reactive self. Pp. 72–120 in *Personality and the Prediction of Behavior,* ed. Robert A. Zucker, Joel Aronoff, and A. I. Rabin. New York: Academic.

McHugh, Maureen C., Irene Hanson Frieze, and Barbara Hartman Hanusa. 1982. Attributions and sex differences in achievement: Problems and new perspectives. *Sex Roles* 8:467–479.

McLeod, Jane D., and Ronald C. Kessler. 1990. Socioeconomic status differences in vulnerability to undesirable life events. *Journal of Health and Social Behavior* 31:162–172.

Meeker, Barbara F., and Patricia A. Weitzel-O'Neill. 1977. Sex roles and interpersonal behavior in task oriented groups. *American Sociological Review* 42: 91–105.

Menaghan, Elizabeth G. 1989. Role changes and psychological well-being: Variations in effects by gender and role repertoire. *Social Forces* 67:693–714.

Miller, Joanne. 1980. Individual and occupational determinants of job satisfaction: A focus on gender differences. *Sociology of Work and Occupations* 7:337–366.

Miller, Joanne, and Howard H. Garrison. 1982. Sex roles: The division of labor at home and in the workplace. *Annual Review of Sociology* 8:237–262.

Miller, Joanne, Carmi Schooler, Melvin L. Kohn, and Karen A. Miller. 1979. Women and work: The psychological effects of occupational conditions. *American Journal of Sociology* 85:66–94.

Millman, Marcia, and Rosabeth Moss Kanter. 1975. *Another Voice,* pp. vii–xviii. Garden City, NY: Anchor/Doubleday.

Molm, Linda D. 1981. The conversion of power imbalance to power use. *Social Psychology Quarterly* 44:151–163.

———. 1985a. Gender and power use: An experimental analysis of behavior and perceptions. *Social Psychology Quarterly* 48:285–300.

———. 1985b. Relative effects of individual dependencies: Further tests of the relation between power imbalance and power use. *Social Forces* 63:810–837.

———. 1986. Gender, power, and legitimation: A test of three theories. *American Journal of Sociology* 91:1356–1386.

———. 1988. Status generalization in power-imbalanced dyads: The effects of gender on power use. Pp. 86–109 in *Status Generalization,* ed. Murray A. Webster, Jr., and Martha Foschi. Stanford: Stanford University Press.

Morgan, Carolyn Stout, and Alexis J. Walker. 1983. Predicting sex role attitudes. *Social Psychology Quarterly* 46:148–151.

Mortimer, Jeylan T., Michael D. Finch, and Geoffrey Maruyama. 1988. Work experience and job satisfaction: Variation by age and gender. Pp. 109–155 in *Work Experience and Psychological Development Through the Life Span,* ed. Jeylan T. Mortimer and Kathryn M. Borman. Boulder: Westview.

Mortimer, Jeylan T., and Jon Lorence. 1989. Satisfaction and involvement: Disentangling a deceptively simple relationship. *Social Psychology Quarterly* 52:249–265.

Newmann, J. P. 1986. Gender, life strains and depression. *Journal of Health and Social Behavior* 27: 161–178.

O'Leary, Virginia E., Rhoda Kesler Unger, and Barbara Strudler Wallston. 1985. *Women, Gender, and Social Psychology.* Hillsdale, NJ: Erlbaum.

Parsons, Talcott, and Robert F. Bales. 1955. *Family, Socialization, and Interaction Process.* New York: Free Press.

Pearlin, Leonard I. 1975. Sex roles and depression. Pp. 191–207 in *Lifespan Developmental Psychology: Normative Life Crises,* ed. N. Datan and L. Ginsberg. New York: Academic.

Pugh, M. D., and Ralph Wahrman. 1985. Neutralizing sexism in mixed-sex groups: Do women have to be better than men? *American Journal of Sociology* 88:746–762.

Radloff, Leonore. 1975. Sex differences in depression: The effects of occupation and marital status. *Sex Roles* 1:249–265.

Reskin, Barbara F., and Shelley Coverman. 1985. Sex and race as determinants of psychophysical distress: A reappraisal of the sex-role hypothesis. *Social Forces* 63:1038–1059.

Ridgeway, Cecilia L. 1988. Gender differences in task groups: A status and legitimacy account. Pp. 188–206 in *Status Generalization,* ed. Murray A. Webster, Jr., and Martha Foschi. Stanford: Stanford University Press.

Ridgeway, Cecilia L., and Joseph Berger. 1986. Expectations, legitimation, and dominance behavior in task groups. *American Sociological Review* 51: 603–617.

Risman, Barbara J. 1987. Intimate relationships from a microstructural perspective: Men who mother. *Gender & Society* 1:6–32.

Rosenberg, Florence R., and Roberta G. Simmons. 1975. Sex differences in the self-concept in adolescence. *Sex Roles* 1:147–159.

Ross, Catherine E., John Mirowsky, and Joan Huber. 1983. Dividing work, sharing work, and in-between: Marriage patterns and depression. *American Sociological Review* 48:809–823.

Santee, Richard T., and Susan E. Jackson. 1982. Identity implications of conformity: Sex differences in normative and attributional judgments. *Social Psychology Quarterly* 45:112–125.

Schwalbe, Michael L., and Clifford L. Staples. 1991. Gender differences in sources of self-esteem. *Social Psychology Quarterly* 54:158–168.

Seavey, Carol A., Phyllis A. Katz, and Sue Rosenberg Zalk. 1975. Baby X: The effect of gender labels on adult responses to infants. *Sex Roles* 1:103–109.

Sidorowicz, Laura S., and G. Sparks Lunney. 1980. Baby X revisited. *Sex Roles* 6:67–73.

Sieber, Sam. 1974. Toward a theory of role accumulation. *American Sociological Review* 39:567–578.

Simmons, Roberta G., and Florence Rosenberg.1975. Sex, sex roles, and self image. *Journal of Youth and Adolescence* 4:229–258.

Spence, Janet T. 1984. Gender identity and its implication for the concepts of masculinity and femininity. Pp. 60–95 in *Nebraska Symposium on Motivation, 1984,* vol. 34, ed. Theo B. Sonderegger. Lincoln: University of Nebraska Press.

Spence, Janet T., Robert L. Helmreich, and Joy Stapp. 1974. The personal attributes questionnaire: A measure of sex-role stereotypes and masculinity-femininity. *JSAS Catalog of Selected Documents in Psychology* 4:43–44, ms 617.

Spence, Janet T., and Linda L. Sawin. 1985. Images of masculinity and femininity: A reconceptualization. Pp. 35–66 in *Women, Gender, and Social Psychology,* ed. Virginia E. O'Leary, Rhoda Kesler Unger, and Barbara Strudler Wallston. Hillsdale, NJ: Erlbaum.

Stacey, Judith, and Barrie Thorne. 1985. The missing feminist revolution in sociology. *Social Problems* 32:301–316.

Stewart, Penni. 1988. Women and men in groups: A status characteristics approach to interaction. Pp. 69–85 in *Status Generalization,* ed. Murray A. Webster, Jr., and Martha Foschi. Stanford: Stanford University Press.

Stryker, Sheldon. 1968. Identity salience and role performance: The relevance of symbolic interaction theory for family research. *Journal of Marriage and the Family* 30:558–564.

———. 1980. *Symbolic Interactionism: A Social Structural Version.* Menlo Park, CA: Benjamin/Cummings.

———. 1987. Identity theory: Developments and extensions. Pp. 83–103 in *Self and Identity: Psychosocial Perspectives,* ed. Krysia Yardley and Terry Honess. New York: Wiley.

Stryker, Sheldon, and Avi Gottlieb. 1981. Attribution theory and symbolic interactionism: A comparison. Pp. 425–458 in *New Directions in Attribution Research,* vol. 3. Hillsdale, NJ: Erlbaum.

Summers, Timothy P., and Thomas A. DeCotiis. 1988. An investigation of sex differences in job satisfaction. *Sex Roles* 18:679–689.

Talichet, Suzanne E., and Fern K. Willits. 1986. Gender-role attitude change of young women: Influential factors from a panel study. *Social Psychology Quarterly* 49:219–227.

Tetlock, Philip E. 1981. The influence of self-presentation goals on attributional reports. *Social Psychology Quarterly* 44:300–311.

Thoits, Peggy A. 1983. Multiple identities and psychological well-being: A reformulation and test of the social isolation hypothesis. *American Sociological Review* 48:174–87.

———. 1986. Multiple identities: Examining gender and marital status differences in distress. *American Sociological Review* 51:259–272.

———. 1991. On merging identity theory and stress research. *Social Psychology Quarterly* 54:101–112.

———. 1992. Identity structures and psychological well-being: Gender and marital status comparisons. *Social Psychology Quarterly* 55:236–256.

Thompson, Martha E. 1981. Sex differences: Differential access to power or sex-role socialization? *Sex Roles* 7:413–424.

Thorne, Barrie. 1990. Children and gender: Constructions of difference. Pp. 100–113 in *Theoretical Perspectives on Sexual Difference,* ed. Deborah L. Rhode. New Haven: Yale University Press.

Tresemer, David. 1975. Assumptions made about gender roles. Pp. 308–339 in *Another Voice,* ed. Marcia Millman and Rosabeth Moss Kanter. Garden City, NY: Anchor/Doubleday.

Tweed, Dan L., and David J. Jackson. 1981. Psychiatric disorder and gender: A logit analysis. *Social Forces* 59:1200–1216.

Unger, Rhoda Kesler. 1979. Toward a redefinition of sex and gender. *American Psychologist* 34:1085–1094.

———. 1985. Epilogue: Toward a synthesis of women, gender, and social psychology. Pp. 349–358 in *Women, Gender and Social Psychology,* ed. Virginia E. O'Leary, Rhoda Kesler Unger, and Barbara Strudler Wallston. Hillsdale, NJ: Erlbaum.

Wagner, David G. 1988. Gender inequalities in groups: A situational approach. Pp. 55–68 in *Status Generalization,* ed. Murray A. Webster, Jr., and Martha Foschi. Stanford: Stanford University Press.

Wagner, David G., Rebecca S. Ford, and Thomas W. Ford. 1986. Can gender inequalities be reduced? *American Sociological Review* 51:47–61.

West, Candace, and Don H. Zimmerman. 1987. Doing gender. *Gender & Society* 1:125–151.

Wethington, Elaine, Jane D. McLeod, and Ronald C. Kessler. 1987. The importance of life events for explaining sex differences in psychological distress. Pp. 144–156 in *Gender and Stress,* ed. R. C. Barnett, L. Biener, and G. K. Baruch. New York: Free Press.

Wheaton, Blair. 1990. Life transitions, role histories, and mental health. *American Sociological Review* 55:209–223.

Whitley, Bernard E. Jr., 1983. Sex role orientation and self-esteem: A critical meta-analytic review. *Journal of Personality and Social Psychology* 44:765–778.

Wiley, Mary Glenn. 1973. Sex roles in games. *Sociometry* 36:526–541.

———. 1991. Gender, work, and stress: The potential impact of role identity salience and commitment. *Sociological Quarterly* 32:495–510.

Wylie, Ruth C. 1979. *The Self-Concept,* vol. 2. Lincoln: University of Nebraska Press.

Yoder, Janice D. 1991. Rethinking tokenism: Looking beyond the numbers. *Gender & Society* 5:178–192.

PART III

Social Structure, Relationships, and the Individual

JAMES S. HOUSE

INTRODUCTION: SOCIAL STRUCTURE AND PERSONALITY: PAST, PRESENT, AND FUTURE

Where part I focused on the psychology and behavior of individuals in proximate, largely face-to-face, interaction with others and part II on processes at the level of small groups and networks of individuals, part III focuses on more macroscopic social phenomena and processes in relation both to individual psychology and behavior and to small groups and networks. This constitutes the domain of what I and others have termed the study of social structure and personality. It is important to recognize, however, the close interrelations of work in part III with that in parts I and II. Chapters in those sections in varying degrees consider macrosocial influences on more psychological, microsocial, and mesosocial phenomena. Similarly, the chapters here must and do draw heavily on our understanding of psychological, interactional, and group processes for analyzing the mutual relationships between individuals or small groups and more macrosocial structures or processes.

I have argued for some time, including in the predecessor to this volume, that macrosocial structures and processes must be central to social psychology, especially in its more sociological forms (House 1977, 1981). All individual psychology and behavior occurs in and is influenced by macrosocial structures and processes. Thus, to the extent that social psychology seeks to understand individual psychology and behavior, it must understand the macrosocial influences thereon. This is being increasingly recognized, even among psychological social psychologists, as is evident in the revival of cross-cultural psychology since the late 1970s and the growing recognition that basic cognitive processes (e.g., attribution, the self, moral development) once considered potential human universals may vary across gender, racial/ethnic/national, or socioeconomic lines as a function of the differing cultures or social structures of such groups (see chapters 2, 4, and 14 in parts I and II and chapter 15 in this part). The functioning of interpersonal relations and small groups may be similarly socioculturally contextualized (see chapters 11 and 12).

Since macrosocial structures and processes are ultimately the product of patterns of behavior and belief among sets of individuals, social psychology must also consider how individual psychology and behavior may shape macrosocial structures and processes. Hence, social psychology should be a major component of, or contributor to, the social science disciplines that have macrosocial phenomena as their focal concern, most notably sociology but also economics, political science, and anthropology. Since the mid-1970s and especially since the mid-1980s, there has been a major increase in attention across the social sciences to the influence of individuals on larger social structures and processes—what in sociology has been termed the "micro-macro link" (Alexander et al. 1987; Huber 1991). Similar trends have been evident in social psychology, but the opportunity these developments provide for interchange between social psychology and more macrosocial analyses have been only partially realized.

The substantial development since the late 1970s in the study of the relation between macrosocial structures and processes and individual psychology and behavior is well reflected in the chapters in part III. Miller-Loessi (chapter 15) shows that cross-national or comparative studies have played and must continue to play a major role in this process. Though such work confronts important methodological and theoretical problems, it also provides a unique means of comparing and contrasting the role of cultural values versus social structural constraints in shaping individual psychology and behavior. Miller-Loessi delineates how the cross-national work of sociological social psychologists has demonstrated that similar social and occupational structures produce similar effects on individuals in societies with very different cultural heritages or economic systems. She also suggests that cultural heritage is receiving and should receive renewed attention in current and future work.

Chapters 16 and 17 suggest that the study of socialization and development has broadened in time and space, and become a lively locus of interdisciplinary interchange among sociology, psychology, anthropology, and even biology, with social psychology at the center. Corsaro and Eder (chapter 16) demonstrate that childhood socialization and development occurs in a broad context, with peer relationships playing important roles at early ages as well as in later childhood and adolescence. This reflects in part the increased exposure of young children to peers through day care and formal early childhood education, which have become much more common recently in American and other societies. Elder and O'Rand (chapter 17) show that socialization and development are lifelong processes, not just the province of childhood and adolescence. Further, these processes are significantly shaped by the social, cultural, and historical contexts in which they occur. The Great Depression and World War II, for example, created powerful contexts in which children and families developed, with the nature of that context and development differing greatly as a function of gender and socioeconomic status. The Vietnam War created still another context shaping human development, as may have the prolonged economic malaise of the 1970s and 1980s, the full nature and dimensions of which are just now becoming manifest.

Social psychological analysis has come to play a new or revitalized role in the study of a number of phenomena previously analyzed more in terms of purely macrosocial or demographic factors. Education and work are central experiences in the lives of almost every human. In chapter 18, Kerckhoff indicates how the stratification system of society comes to affect the life choices and social mobility of individuals in the educational and occupational spheres and how social psychological analysis is essential to understanding how and why individuals experience the kind of educational, occupational, and income attainments and trajectories they do. Race, gender, and socioeconomic origins influence not only what individuals bring with them into the world of school or work, but also how the organizations and institutions of education and employment respond to these individuals. Understanding these interactions between individuals and occupational and educational institutions is essential if individuals and the larger society are to develop to their full potential.

Chapter 19 (by Mortimer and Lorence) shows that work organizations and individual workers can reciprocally influence each other. Organizations are affected by the nature of the individuals who come to work in them, but these organizations even more powerfully influence their workers. Work experience and the way work is organized have pervasive impacts on worker attitudes such as job satisfaction and work commitment. Though these attitudes are also influenced by individual and other contextual factors, Mortimer and Lorence demonstrate that work conditions, such as worker autonomy and style of supervision, have quite similar psychological effects, irrespective of cultural variation and individual characteristics (e.g., age, gender, and race).

In chapter 20, Hamilton and Rauma suggest that the study of deviance and law has in some ways turned back toward social psychological analyses from more recent economic, demographic, and even engineering approaches. Social psychology, like the theories of recent economics Nobel Prize winner Gary Becker, suggests that the behavior of deviants and criminals and of those who label and sanction such behavior is governed by the same laws that govern more "normal" behavior. And we now recognize that "normal" behavior can be criminal or deviant, as in "organizational" and "white-collar" deviance or crime and in "crimes of obedience." Such phenomena are increasingly prominent in daily news reports from around the world and in Hamilton and Rauma's characterization of the social psychology of deviance and law.

In chapter 21, Kessler, House, Anspach, and Williams document that social psychology over the last several decades has come to play a major role in our understanding of the etiology and course of physical as well as mental health and illness. Health promotion and disease prevention are now national goals, involving not only smoking, diet, and exercise but also stress, social relationships and supports, and feelings of self-efficacy. Even health and illness behaviors, ranging from smoking to risk taking to adhering to medical regimens, are now analyzed as social psychological phenomena, affected by macrosocial as well as microsocial and psychological factors.

Snow and Oliver suggest in chapter 22 that the 1980s saw the study of social movements and related aspects of collective behavior (e.g., crowds) go from, in the words of one analyst, a view of social psychological analyses as "stultifying" to a view that "the major questions animating contemporary work on social movements are intrinsically social psychological." After a period in which organizational analysis dominated the study of social movements, analyses deriving from all faces (psychological, symbolic interactionist, and social structure and personality) and methods (observational, historical, experimental, and survey) of social psychology have illuminated the processes of recruitment, commitment, and action inherent in all social movement and collective behavior activity, whether their focus is civil rights, abortion, or religion.

While each of the chapters is valuable in its own right, considered as a group and in relation to broader developments in social psychology, they suggest the directions taken by the study of social structure and personality since the publication of the predecessor to this volume in 1981. Let me briefly sketch some of these lines of development, suggesting the many ways they have been and are salutary for the study of social structure and personality, social psychology, and social science, but also noting some potential problems and gaps in this generally positive pattern of development.

SOCIAL STRUCTURE AND PERSONALITY: THEMES AND DIRECTION

In 1981 I suggested several directions for the development of theory and research on social structure and personality. One was to continue the development of better theories and data regarding the microsocial and psychological processes through which macrosocial processes and individual behavior are linked. I saw this as requiring better theoretical specification and empirical assessment of (1) the *components* of complex macrosocial phenomena, (2) the *proximate* microsocial interactions and stimuli through which these components impinge on individuals, and (3) the *psychological processes* that govern how individuals perceive and respond to proximate social interactions and stimuli. These issues have indeed received increased attention from both social psychologists, as manifest in these chapters, and the work of micro-macro theorists in sociology.

I also noted in 1981 that increased attention should be directed to understanding the potential and actual effects of individuals on social structures, as well as continuing study of the impact of social structures on individuals. As the chapters in part III suggest, increased focus on the impact of the individual on society is evident in social psychological analysis of many aspects of social structure and personality. This concern has been given special impetus by the desire of micro-macro theorists to understand how individual human action and agency affect and help to explain stability and change in social structure (cf. Sewell 1992). The tendency in this literature to speak of the micro-macro link, rather than the macro-micro link, reflects the priority given to understanding how micro affects macro as well as how macro affects micro.

Finally, I noted in 1981 that the terms *social structure* and *culture* were often used broadly and diffusely to refer to all aspects of a social system. In this sense, the study of social structure and personality (or of culture and personality) refers to the relationship of any macrosocial phenomenon to individual psychology and behavior. However, I also sought to distinguish between narrower and more precise conceptions of culture versus social structure and cultural versus structural explanations of the existence and persistence of patterns of individual behavior. In these narrower terms, social structure refers descriptively to persisting and bounded patterns of behavior and interaction among people or positions and dynamically to the tangible or material forces that tend to maintain such patterns (e.g., physical, biological, or social resources and power deriving therefrom). This narrower conception of structure is counterposed to a narrower conception of culture as cognitive and evaluative beliefs shared among members of a social system and generally developed and maintained through processes of socialization.

Analyses in the micro-macro tradition have generally used *structure* in its broader sense as referring to all aspects of a social system. However, they also have distinguished between two components of structure, called "rules and resources" by Giddens (1984) or "schemas and resources" by Sewell (1992), which are analogous to my narrower definitions of culture and social structure, respectively. What is important is not the semantic labels, but the recognition that these are two separable components of any social system, that each may affect the other, and that one or the other may be more important as a cause or explanation of any observed individual behaviors or patterns of behavior among members of a social system.

In 1981 I suggested that cultural explanations are probably more congruent with the psychological nature of members of at least our society and with our sociocultural context, and that such explanations had predominated in the study of the relation of macrosocial phenomena to individual psychology and behavior through the 1950s, as, for example, in theories of cultural or national character as explanations for the behavior of ethnic or national groups (e.g., Germans versus Americans). However, I saw structural explanations as becoming increasingly prevalent and important during the 1960s and 1970s. The 1980s, however, saw a resurgence of cultural explanations both in analyses of micro-macro linkages and, more generally, as indicated in chapter 15.

These three developments—(1) increasing analysis of linkages between macrosocial phenomena and individual behavior, (2) increased attention to the influence of individuals on macrosocial phenomena, and (3) increasing focus on culture and cultural explanations—are both promising and problematic for our understanding of the relations between macrosocial phenomena and individual psychology and behavior, and hence for the study of social structure and personality in social psychology. Let us consider each development a bit further and then assess their implications.

LINKAGES BETWEEN INDIVIDUALS AND SOCIAL STRUCTURE

The 1980s saw an increasing focus on the mesosocial, microsocial, and psychological processes linking a variety of macrosocial phenomena to individual psychology and behavior. This has involved recognition of the relevance of a wide range of social psychological theory and research to analyses where social psychological processes previously had been deemed virtually irrelevant or counterproductive or had constituted nothing more than a large "black box" between macrosocial phenomena and individual psychology and behavior. Further, many of these analyses have delineated the ways in which the relation between macrosocial phenomena and the individual are highly contingent, contextualized, and constructed, thus suggesting ways individuals may affect social structure, as well as vice versa.

Snow and Oliver, in chapter 22, identify and illustrate these trends in their overview of social psychological dimensions and considerations in the study of crowds and especially social movements. Their integration of recent literature shows that mesosocial, microsocial, and psychological processes are central in the genesis and development of crowds and especially social movements, and that the influence processes are reciprocal. The involvements of individuals in crowds and social movements are influenced by pre-existing cognitions, affects, values, identity, and networks of socialization and social relations. Conversely, crowds and social movements shape individuals' psychological attributes and social networks. Thus movements both recruit sympathetic participants and mobilize them to sympathetic action.

Analysis of the socialization and development of individuals over the life course, both generally and more particularly in the realm of education and labor force participation and status attainment, has placed increased emphasis both on analysis of mesosocial, microsocial, and psychological processes that relate macrosocial phenomena to individual psychology and behavior and on the contingent, contextual, and constructed nature of these processes. Corsaro and Eder document considerable interdisciplinary convergence in the study of socialization and human development, with psychologists increasingly cognizant of the impact of collective action and social structure on individual development and sociologists becoming more open to the importance of biogenetic factors and individual cognition and behavior. Constructivist approaches to developmental psychology (e.g., Piaget, Vygotsky) and interactionist and interpretive sociological social psychology have intersected and complemented each other in portraying individuals as more active agents in constructing their development, both individually and collectively, in relationships with family, peers, and formal organizations. Similarly, Elder and O'Rand show how the impact of aging, the current social environment, and individuals' prior life experiences as members of particular birth cohorts combine in complex ways to influence their psychological development and social action over the life course. Again, individuals and groups are active agents in constructing their behavior in relation to particular historical and social contexts.

The study of power and inequality has increasingly been illuminated by more explicit social psychological analyses, as evident in chapters 7, 8, and 11 as well as chapters in part III. Chapter 15 by Mortimer and Lorence and Chapter 19 by Miller-Loessi review the continuing program of research by Kohn, Schooler, Slomezynski, and colleagues linking higher-level positions in class or stratification systems to more autonomous and self-directed individual values. In chapter 18, Kerckhoff documents the actual and potential value of more in-depth qualitative and quantitative studies of the relation between individuals and the social structures of education and the labor market in understanding processes of status attainment and social mobility in American and other societies. Such studies have, for example, illuminated the mechanisms through which social structures often impede the educational, occupational, and income attainments and mobility of women, racial and ethnic minorities, and persons of lower socioeconomic origins. One of the major new directions in research on race and ethnicity involves the direct study of processes of discrimination, both intentional and unintentional, from the perspective of both majority and minority group members (e.g., Feagin 1991; Kirschenman and Neckerman 1991). In chapter 20, Hamilton and Rauma illuminate the psychological and interactional processes of individual actors that underlie malevolent acts by corporate actors and structures of authority. The commission of "crimes of obedience" or "corporate crimes" requires that individuals feel constrained or enabled by their social roles and contexts to engage in acts they otherwise might eschew on moral grounds.

Finally, chapter 21 (Kessler et al.) and chapter 1 (Piliavin and LePore) suggest that the study of linkages between individuals and social structures must increasingly include biological and physiological as well as psychological processes. In both animals and humans, deprivation of power and control or of social relationships and supports leads to psychoneuroendocrine arousal and/or immune suppression that, if sustained, can be productive of disease. However, physiological as well as psychological and behavioral responses to potentially stressful situations are contingent on social psychological processes of cognitive appraisal and behavioral response, which have become a focus of social psychological research on health.

THE MICRO-MACRO LINK

All of this work extends and amplifies the long-standing symbolic interactionist position that social interactions, organizations, and systems are constructed and negotiated orders (cf. Maines 1977). In their acts and interactions, individuals simultaneously are constrained by the existing social structure and contribute in varying degrees to its perpetuation or its modification and change (Stryker and Statham 1985). This has also been the concern of micro-macro theorists, though they have shown at best partial recognition of the contributions of symbolic interactionists and other social psychologists to these issues.

Some micro-macro analysts (e.g., Coleman 1990; Hechter 1987) have looked to other related traditions of social science and social psychology—rational choice theory and, to a lesser degree, exchange theory (cf. Cook 1991; chapter 8)—to understand how individual action creates, maintains, and changes macrosocial structures and processes. Such theories, however, often recognize a very limited range of individual motivations, goals, and purposes—mainly economic ones—or tautologically attribute utility or rationality to goals or acts, since actors do only what is in their interest. As Molm and Cook argue in chapter 8, however, exchange and rational choice theories can and must increasingly take account of the full range of human values and purposes, both individual and collective, and of the processes through which objects and acts acquire value. What is needed is a broader social psychological analysis of the nature of action, derivable from some combination of Weber's original analysis of social action, symbolic interactionism, field theory, and other constructivist social psychologies (cf. Diamond 1992; House and Mortimer 1990; Swanson 1992).

The development of such a broader social psychological analysis of social action and the impact of individual actors on social structure is still very much ongoing, but the chapters in this volume suggest that we have moved a long way recently. Snow and Oliver come closest to achieving such a synthesis in their analysis of crowds and social movement, while Corsaro and Eder and Elder and O'Rand illustrate continuing advances in this direction in the development of life course theories of child and adult development. Studies of race as well as gender and class increasingly discover the ways disadvantaged individuals, acting individually and collectively, have been the prime movers in changing long-standing social structures of power and privilege, though these processes of social change are far from complete.

The growing recognition of biological influences on individual and social behavior, noted by Kessler et al., made focal by Piliavin and LePore in chapter 1, and picked up on in other ways in more essentialist feminist analyses (see chapter 14), represents a different way that individuals impact on sociocultural systems. As Piliavin and LePore cogently argue, however, genes and biology create only tendencies or potentials. How they actualize or manifest themselves are a function of the social psychological context in which they operate. Such biological imperatives need to be considered in any thorough analyses of the impact of individuals on their social order.

CULTURE VERSUS SOCIAL STRUCTURE

Psychologists (especially psychoanalysts) and anthropologists dominated the study of the relation of macrosocial phenomena to personality from the 1920s through the 1950s (House 1981, 530–536), focusing on the role of culturally shared beliefs and values in explaining patterned differences in behavior between individuals in different ethnic or national groups. By the 1960s, as Miller-Loessi shows in chapter 15, sociologists had become increasingly involved in international and intranational research on differences in personality and behavior between different socioeconomic, ethnic, and national groups. For example, Inkeles and colleagues documented how industrialization, urbanization, and education combined to create "modern" patterns of attitudes and behaviors in individuals in widely varying nations or cultures and to account for differences across nations or cultures. Similarly, Kohn and Schooler and colleagues analyzed how and why education and occupational conditions affect a wide range of psychological orientations, again with substantial similarity in these processes across nations or cultures.

The 1980s and 1990s have again seen increased involvement of psychologists and anthropologists in the study of cross-cultural psychology, also discussed in chapter 15 by Miller-Loessi, and increased use of cultural as opposed to structural explanations of differences in the psychological attributes or behaviors of members of different socioeconomic, ethnic, and regional groups. These developments are part of a larger growth in cultural analysis in the social sciences. This increasing turn toward cultural explanations appears throughout this volume, though a healthy emphasis on social structure and structural explanations is retained. Miller-Loessi recognizes the rise of more cultural analyses of cross-national differences, while also arguing for the continuing validity of structural explanations thereof. Gecas and Burke (chapter 2) also discuss the recent work of Markus and Kitayama (1991) on cross-cultural differences in the nature of the self, and Corsaro and Eder note the growing attention to culture in the study of socialization and childhood. There has also been a substantial shift back toward cultural models of race and ethnic relations, for example in notions of the underclass (Jencks and Peterson 1991) or symbolic racism (Kinder and Sears 1981). Many of these developments represent needed antidotes to overly structural analyses, but, as many chapters suggest, social psychology and social science more generally need to guard against a neglect of structure.

CONCLUSIONS

Overall, the recent trends in analyses of social structure and personality place more emphasis on the role of individuals as active agents in shaping their own behavior and even larger social structures, often guided by cultural values and beliefs. These increased emphases on linkages between macrosocial phenomena and individuals, on the impact of individuals on macrosocial phenomena, and on cultural explanations represent a shift away from a focus on the impact of social structure on individuals to a focus on individuals as constituting and constructing structures within systems of cultural meaning. These developments are promising in reflecting increased attention to issues and approaches that received too little emphasis a decade ago. They also reflect increased integration among different methods and faces of social psychology and an opportunity to intersect with a major focus of mainstream sociology on the micro-macro link.

These trends may also, however, represent a response to a sociocultural context that emphasized individual autonomy and responsibility and long-established cultural belief systems, rather than structural properties of social organizations, as the major determinants of both individual psychology and behavior and more macrosocial phenomena. Similarly, increased interest in biogenetic determinants of individual psychology and behavior and hence of culture and social structure may reflect both prior gaps in our science and a receptive sociocultural milieu.

Despite the promise in these developments, there is also a danger of throwing out the baby with the bath water. In focusing on processes linking macrosocial phenomena and individuals and on the potential impact on social structure of individuals constructing their actions within cultural systems of meaning, we may lose sight of the nature and power of social structures as constraints on and determinants of individual psychology and behavior, and collective patterns thereof. Fine (1991) has also suggested that the turn toward microsociology must recognize the strong constraints and influence that social structure exerts on individual behavior and personality and microsocial interaction. Such structural effects are especially crucial to social psychology's and social science's efforts to understand the persisting and pervasive impact of race, class, and gender on social life. Thus, it is an opportune time to focus increased attention again on the place of social structure in social psychology and to seek balanced consideration of how it both affects and is affected by the psychology and behavior of human actors.

REFERENCES

Alexander, Jeffrey C., Bernard Giesen, Richard Munch, and Neil J. Smelser, ed. 1987. *The Micro-Macro Link.* Berkeley: University of California Press.

Coleman, James. 1990. *Foundations of Social Theory.* Cambridge, MA: Belknap Press of Harvard University Press.

Cook, Karen S. 1991. The microfoundations of social structure: An exchange perspective. Pp. 29–45 in *Macro-Micro Linkages in Sociology,* ed. Joan Huber. Newbury Park, CA: Sage.

Diamond, George Andrade. 1992. Field theory and rational choice: A Lewinian approach to modeling motivation. *Journal of Social Issues* 48:79–94.

Feagin, Joe R. 1991. The continuing significance of race: Anti-black discrimination in public places. *American Sociological Review* 56:101–116.

Fine, Gary Alan. 1991. On the macrofoundations of microsociology: Constraint and the exterior reality of structure. *The Sociological Quarterly* 32:161–177.

Giddens, Anthony. 1984. *The Constitution of Society: Outline of the Theory of Structuration.* Berkeley: University of California Press.

Hechter, Michael. 1987. *Principles of Group Solidarity.* Berkeley: University of California Press.

House, James S. 1977. The three faces of social psychology. *Sociometry* 40:161–177.

———. 1981. Social structure and personality. Pp. 525–561 in *Sociological Perspectives on Social Psychology,* ed. Morris Rosenberg and Ralph Turner. New York: Basic Books.

House, James S., and Jeylan T. Mortimer. 1990. Social structure and the individual: Emerging themes and new directions. *Social Psychology Quarterly* 53:71–80.

Huber, Joan, ed. 1991. *Macro-Micro Linkages in Sociology.* Newbury Park, CA: Sage.

Jencks, Christopher, and Paul C. Peterson. 1991. *The Urban Underclass.* Washington, DC: Brookings Institution.

Kinder, Donald R., and David O. Sears. 1981. Prejudice and politics: Symbolic racism versus racial threats to the good life. *Journal of Personality and Social Psychology* 40:414–431

Kirschenman, Joleen, and Kathryn Neckerman. 1991. We'd love to hire them, but . . . : The meaning of race for employers. Pp. 203–232 in *The Urban Underclass,* ed. Christopher Jencks and Paul E. Peterson. Washington, DC: Brookings Institution.

Maines, David R. 1977. Social organization in symbolic interactionism. Pp. 235–259 in *Annual Review of Sociology,* vol. 3., ed. A. Inkeles, J. Coleman, and N. Smelser. Palo Alto, CA: Annual Reviews.

Markus, Hazel, and Shinobu Kitayama. 1991. Culture and the self: Implications for cognition, emotion, and motivation. *Psychological Review* 98:224–253.

Sewell, William H. Jr. 1992. A theory of structure: Duality, agency, and transformation. *American Journal of Sociology* 98:1–29.

Stryker, Sheldon, and Anne Statham. 1985. Symbolic interaction and role theory. Pp. 311–389 in *The Handbook of Social Psychology,* 3rd ed., vol. 1, ed. Gardner Lindzey and Elliott Aronson. New York: Random House.

Swanson, Guy E. 1992. Doing things together: Some basic forms of agency and structure in collective action and some explanations. *Social Psychology Quarterly* 55:94–117.

CHAPTER 15

Comparative Social Psychology
Cross-Cultural and Cross-National

KAREN MILLER-LOESSI

The comparative perspective in social psychology has a long and distinguished history, traceable to the comparative social psychological concerns of Max Weber.[1] Over the years, comparative research has made major contributions to the development of social psychology. Research projects have varied in scope and subject, from relatively small-scale studies comparing two cultures or nations on a few variables to relatively large-scale, multivariable, multicountry research programs. This chapter reviews issues, trends, and selected findings from this body of research.

Interest in the issues surrounding comparative research has recently intensified because of several current far-reaching trends: the increasingly global interconnectedness of social, political, and economic life; increased recognition of cultural and ethnic diversity within and among societies; and broad philosophical and methodological trends, such as postmodernism and deconstruction, in the humanities and social sciences. These trends have led many social psychologists to a fresh evaluation of the need for culturally and nationally comparative approaches in social psychology. In the course of much recent dialogue and debate, questions have been raised about the fundamental purposes of comparative research, what we can learn from it, whether it is worth doing—or whether any other kind of research is worth doing.

In this chapter, I examine comparative research in social psychology. After first assessing the unique advantages of a comparative perspective, I highlight fundamental theoretical and methodological issues associated with comparative research. I then discuss some of the special problems of comparative social psychological research. I conclude with an intensive review of research in social structure and personality, an area that is particularly well informed by a comparative perspective.

UNIQUE ADVANTAGES OF THE COMPARATIVE PERSPECTIVE IN SOCIAL PSYCHOLOGY

In the view of its proponents, comparative research helps to expose bias in social psychology caused by "the blinders and filters of our culture" (Triandis 1988). Social psychology is itself a cultural product, much as religions, political structures, or legal systems are cultural products (Hogan and Emler 1978; Triandis 1988). Furthermore, people tend to seek out information that confirms their already-established constructions of reality (Swann and Read 1981a, 1981b), whether these be culturally or otherwise determined, and social psychologists, like other humans, may operate with unconscious cultural biases. As Hofstede (1980, 374) aptly puts it: "If we begin to realize that our own ideas are culturally limited . . . we can never be self-sufficient again. Only others with different mental programs can help us find the limitations of our own."

One of the biases most often identified as afflicting social psychology as a discipline is an indivuocentric bias, resulting from the discipline's major development and practice in the Western cultural context (Gabrenya 1988; Hogan and Emler

1978; Jahoda 1988). This bias locates the source of behavior within the individual and ignores or de-emphasizes the normative or social structures within which behavior occurs. Hogan and Emler (1978) argue that individualism and rationalism are among the important values that Western social psychologists use without conscious awareness. These values result in underestimation of the influence of groups, norms, culture, and emotion or impulse on social behavior (Triandis 1988).

Comparative research may challenge this focus on the individual. For example, Gecas and Burke (chapter 2) discuss Markus and Kitayama's (1991) review showing that our theoretical paradigms of the self have mostly been developed from, and are most applicable to, Western cultures. The dominant paradigm of the self as bounded, independent, and autonomous is challenged by cross-cultural research, with major and fundamental ramifications for theories about the self. For example, cognitive consistency may be an important self-dynamic only in the West. The Japanese do not expect consistency between feelings and actions; rather, they consider the expression of one's true feelings to be a sign of immaturity (Doi 1986, 240). Americans, in contrast, see consistency between emotions and their expression as critical for self-authenticity (Hochschild 1983). Self-esteem as a motive may also operate quite differently in the East than in the West, again challenging some fundamental aspects of the dominant theoretical paradigm of self and identity.

The numerous actual or potential contributions of the comparative perspective to social psychological theory are discussed at length below. But there are other advantages of comparative research as well. One is that cross-national research brings in the international sphere as a source of important social knowledge (Cole 1984; Gabrenya 1988). Ragin (1989, 64) suggests that the altered geopolitical context of the late twentieth century "makes intensive work on the United States (or any other country) seem incomplete in the absence of background knowledge of cross-national variation and of global patterns and trends."

Finally, an understanding of cultural and national differences is one of the main contributions social psychology can make to practical policy makers in today's world (Hofstede 1980, 9). As we interact in an increasingly global environment, cross-cultural and cross-national social psychology have great potential applied usefulness for government, business, and higher education.

The realization of the many unique advantages of a comparative approach requires attention to important theoretical and methodological issues, to which I now turn.

THEORETICAL ISSUES

I discuss three major theoretical issues. First, central concepts, such as culture, social structure, and nation, must be clearly defined. A second issue is how entities chosen for comparison should be treated as explicit elements in research. Finally, I discuss how comparative work can contribute to building theory in social psychology.

Culture, Social Structure, and Nation

Culture, social structure, and nation are major concepts in comparative social psychological research. Historically, comparative social psychological researchers, depending on their disciplinary background, have tended to be most interested in culture or social structure while often actually analyzing data from nations, political entities that have both structural and cultural elements. The dominance of anthropology and psychology in comparative research in the first half of the twentieth century led to an emphasis on culture. Beginning in the 1950s sociologists became more heavily involved in comparative research, bringing with them a more structural emphasis. Recently, psychologists and anthropologists have again become more involved in comparative social psychological research, instigating a resurgence of interest in culture.

A primary theoretical task is to develop a workable definition of *culture*. It is often defined very broadly, more so by anthropologists than by sociologists (De Vos and Hippler 1969, 323). For example, the noted anthropologists Alfred Kroeber and Clyde Kluckhohn (1952, 181) formulated the concept of culture as follows:

> Culture consists of patterns, explicit and implicit, of and for behavior, acquired and transmitted by symbols constituting the distinctive achievement of human groups, including their embodiment in artifacts; the essential core of culture consists of traditional (i.e., historically derived and selected) ideas and especially their attached values; culture systems may, on the one hand, be considered as products of action, on the other as conditioning elements of future action.

By this definition, culture seems somewhat "breathtaking in its scope of reference" (Tedeschi 1988a, 21), referring to a large complex of variables, including institutions, roles, norms, and physical artifacts. For our purposes, however, it is useful to narrow it down by following House's (1981) distinction among social system, culture, and social structure. According to House (1981, 542):

> A social system, or what Inkeles and Levinson (1969) term a sociocultural system, is a set of persons and social positions or roles that possess both a culture and a social structure. A culture is a set of cognitive and evaluative beliefs—beliefs about what is or what ought to be—that are shared by the members of a social system and transmitted to new members. A social structure is a persisting and bounded pattern of social relationships (or pattern of behavioral interaction) among the units (that is, persons or positions) in a social system.

Thus, according to House, culture represents what members of a social system collectively believe, and social structure represents what members of a social system collectively do.

This distinction between culture and social structure is fundamental. Although they are highly related dimensions and both may operate simultaneously, culture and social structure are analytically separable. For example:

> One of the major differences between cultural and structural explanations is in how they account for,

> or explain, persisting patterns of overt behavior. A cultural explanation . . . sees persisting patterns of social behavior as emanating from shared beliefs and values. A structural explanation, in contrast, need only assert that contemporaneous situational contingencies and constraints exist that motivate the behavior . . . For example, the recurrent flow of people in our society into work organizations between 7:00 and 10:00 A.M. on Mondays could be explained by the combination of inducements for going to work and penalties for not working that are imposed in our society. This pattern of inducements and constraints might emanate from and largely reinforce a widely shared cultural value, but it might equally well emanate from the power that the owners and managers of business have to set work regulations. (House 1981, 543)

Furthermore, culture and social structure may impinge on the individual through different proximal stimuli and they may be incorporated by individuals through different psychological processes (House 1981). Thus, the distinction between the two has important implications for theory.

Even when culture is clearly distinguished from social structure, it is a broad, pervasive, and somewhat messy concept. At least one, and often more than one, cultural milieu impinges on every concrete instance of a social psychological phenomenon. Subcultures exist within cultures. Individuals may exist in different cultures over time or at the same time, carrying with them varying residues of each culture they have experienced.

Partly because of these complexities and difficulties in conceptualizing and measuring culture, the nation, or more precisely the nation-state, is the comparative entity preferred by some researchers (see Rokkan 1970). For example, Kohn (1989b) finds it conceptually advantageous to study phenomena within nation-states rather than cultures, because *nation-state* has a relatively unambiguous meaning, whereas *culture* does not. In making this distinction, Kohn points out that there can be different cultures within a nation and different nations can share a similar culture. Often nations can be used to compare cultures, assuming that their cultures make for a useful comparison. (It should be noted that using nation as a "stand-in" for culture makes more sense the more culturally homogeneous the nation.) Studying nations with similar cultures also can allow a comparison of the effects of different political and economic systems; that is, one can analytically separate structural from cultural factors as explanatory variables.

In fact, much "cross-cultural" research in social psychology compares social psychological phenomena in different nation-states, while not always being analytically clear about the structural and cultural aspects of these entities that impinge on the research situation and/or that are relevant to the research question. Furthermore, few empirical cross-cultural studies have been explicitly designed to test the competing effects of culture and social structure on psychological phenomena. Thus, the culture/social structure distinction has not received the attention it deserves in social psychology.

The usefulness of distinguishing between culture and social structure is illustrated by Lincoln and Kalleberg's (1990) study of work organization and work attitudes in the United States and Japan. Their study design enabled them to test two competing explanations—one structural, the other cultural—of the greater work commitment of Japanese compared to American employees. They hypothesized that welfare-corporatist types of work organization, common in Japanese firms, explain the high work commitment of Japanese workers. Their alternative hypothesis was that Japanese workers' commitment is not to a significant degree a function of the organization of Japanese firms, but rather is due to the values and beliefs of the relatively homogeneous Japanese culture.

Lincoln and Kalleberg (1990) find essentially similar antecedents of work attitudes among Japanese and U.S. employees, thus providing support for the structural hypothesis of "a universally applicable commitment-maximizing organizational form" (Lincoln and Kalleberg 1990, 251). They are further able to specify the role of culture:

> While the role of culture is not trivial, it is primarily: (a) indirect through the role it presently plays and the residues it has historically left in the concrete organization of Japanese firms; and (b) additive in the sense that it contributes to attitude and behavioral differences between Japanese and U.S. workers but does not markedly condition the ways employees respond to their jobs or other facets of their employment. (Lincoln and Kalleberg 1990, 251)

This specification of the relative roles of culture versus organizational structure in explaining values represents an important advance in our ability to disentangle the effects of culture and structure on social psychological processes.

Comparison in Social Psychological Research

Although much of social science is inherently comparative, when we speak of comparative social psychological research we generally mean comparisons across different cultures or nations. How culture or nation is incorporated into research involves, first, one's position on a set of fundamental philosophical issues that can be crystallized as the emic versus etic positions. I discuss these distinct approaches and their philosophical implications and then uses of culture or nation in research that follow from the philosophical position taken: culture or nation can be treated as context or as the specific focus of the research.

Emic versus Etic Approaches.   Comparative research can be used to search for differences or similarities. Kagitcibasi and Berry (1989), in reviewing recent research in cross-cultural psychology, identify distinct trends in two opposite directions: the intensive study of psychological phenomena within separate cultures—the indigenous or emic approach; and the quest for commonalities across many or all cultures—the universalist or etic approach. The terms *emic* and *etic* are taken from linguistic terminology (Berry 1969; Pike 1967). The emic approach involves studying behavior from within the system, examining only one culture at a time, discovering rather than imposing structure, and using criteria relative to internal characteristics. The etic approach involves studying behavior from a position outside the system, examining two or more cultures and comparing them, imposing a structure created by the analyst, and using criteria that are considered absolute or universal (Berry 1969). The emic approach has traditionally been used by anthropologists in their quest to understand what is unique to each culture. On the other hand, the thrust of sociology as a discipline has generally been etic, a search for general relationships that transcend particular circumstances. In social psychology, the two approaches to comparative work constitute two different streams of research, with clear and fundamental differences in epistemological assumptions.

The emic approach has historically been the minority view in comparative social psychology, yet it is an increasingly significant trend in research and can be related to more general contemporary theoretical trends such as poststructuralism, postmodernism, and critical theory (Agger 1991). It challenges—sometimes radically—the assumptions of the mainstream etic approach. Social psychological theorists such as Gergen (1973, 1978, 1985; Gergen and Davis 1985), Sampson (1978, 1985, 1988), Harre (1981), and Kukla (1988) have questioned the positivist, empiricist, modernist epistemology—the belief that knowledge about social psychological phenomena can be obtained through theoretical analysis and empirical observation aimed at formulating general laws of human behavior—underlying social psychology in general and comparative social psychology in particular. Rather, they have emphasized the contextual, historically bound, socially constructed nature of human psychology. When taken to their logical conclusions, these views lead to radical cultural relativism (Kagitsibasi and Berry 1989)—the position that there are no social psychological universals that transcend specific cultures and that universal laws of human behavior cannot be identified. Without necessarily taking this extreme position, a considerable amount of empirical research has been done explicitly arising from, and specific to, particular cultures and nations (e.g., Sinha 1983; for reviews see Backman 1990; Kagitsibasi and Berry 1989).

The more common, "mainstream" approach in cross-cultural social psychology has been to search for universals (Lonner 1980). Faucheux (1976) takes the position that unless we define *cultural* as particular, accidental, and contingent, it should theoretically be possible to develop universal theories that incorporate cultural dimensions. This goal, though far from attainment, underlies most comparative research in social psychology.

There appears to be a basic conflict between the emic and the etic approaches, yet Kagitcibasi and Berry (1989) believe cross-cultural psychology can progress only through a dialectic of the two. A synthesis of sorts may come about in the recognition that "emic (indigenous) knowledge is necessary for a truly universal psychology, since universals may simply be the common patterns among various emic realities" (Kagitcibasi and Berry 1989, 519). In other words, it may be necessary for social psychology fully to understand diverse realities in order to understand their commonalities, a point developed by Faucheux (1976).

Treatments of Culture or Nation in Research
Culture or Nation as Context. The most common usage of comparative research in social psychology, as noted above, is to test the generality or universality of psychological phenomena. Kohn (1989b, 21) sees cross-national studies that primarily test the generality of findings and interpretations as using the nation as context, to borrow Scheuch's (1967) phrase. Most of these studies do not treat different nations as theoretically specified sets of variables but, because of their diversity, as tests of the generalizability of hypothesized relationships. Examples of such studies that attempt to maximize the number and diversity of contexts include Schwartz and colleagues' search for universals in the content and structure of values, using samples of respondents from twenty countries (Schwartz 1992), and Eysenck and colleagues' search for universal personality dimensions in twenty-four cultures (Eysenck 1986). The research on psychological modernity in six nations by Inkeles and colleagues (Inkeles 1969; Inkeles and Smith 1974),

discussed at length below, also fits into this category, as does Form's (1976) study of the impact of technology and work organization on attitudes and beliefs of auto workers in India, Argentina, Italy, and the United States.

Another similar use of culture or nation as context is the cross-cultural replication of results found in only one setting (usually the United States). According to Finifter (1977): "The maturity of an area of empirical investigation can be gauged in part by the amount, probativeness, and informativeness of its replication research" (p. 173). Yet there is a relative scarcity of such studies in social psychology (Finifter 1977; Sharon and Amir 1988). One of the reasons for this is that journal editors tend to reject replications, apparently preferring previously untested ideas. This general policy extends to comparative research, such that there are relatively few replications of nation- or culture-specific findings in different nations or cultures (Sharon and Amir 1988; see also Rodrigues 1982). One exception is Crittenden and Lamug's (1988) cross-cultural replication in the Philippines of the learned helplessness model of depression (Seligman et al. 1979), originally tested on U.S. subjects. The Philippine replication points to the possible confounding influence of overall attributional style on depressive symptoms. Another notable exception is the replication of the U.S. findings on work and personality of Kohn, Schooler, and colleagues (Kohn and Schooler 1983), in Poland by Slomczynski et al. (1981), and in Japan by Atsushi Naoi and Carmi Schooler (1985). Other replications of the Kohn-Schooler research are reviewed in Kohn and Schooler (1983, chap. 12), and this body of research is discussed at greater length below.

Faucheux (1976) takes a critical stance toward the value of cross-cultural replication in experimental social psychology. He argues strongly that there is no point in conducting cross-cultural replications unless there is some theoretical justification for doing so, requiring in advance knowledge of theoretically relevant cultural differences. According to Faucheux (1976, 279): "Unless the theory itself implies possible cultural differences, there is no legitimate reason to attribute a particular value to a replication carried out in Paris rather than New York of an experiment originally performed in Boston." To Faucheux (1976, 278), "a theory of culture is not only possible but essential to the social psychologist." Faucheux reacts against what he sees as rampant empiricism, a relative lack of theory-driven research, and "the accumulation of superficial findings" in experimental social psychology.

Yet comparative research can give us much more than "catalogues of social-psychological factlets," in Messick's apt phrase (Messick 1988b)—it can help in the building of theory. According to Messick (1988b, 42), the central question that we must keep before us is: What is the value of comparative empirical information with regard to understanding the causes of the phenomenon? Kohn (1989a) argues that cross-national research may force us to revise our interpretations to take account of cross-national differences and inconsistencies that could never be uncovered in single-nation research. Giving examples from his and his colleagues' cross-national research program, discussed at length below, Kohn concludes that when confronted with theoretically unexpected cross-national differences in relationships, the ultimate goal is "to include the discrepant findings in a more comprehensive interpretation, by reformulating the interpretation on a more general level that accounts for both similarities and differences. Thus, although the discovery of cross-national differences may initially require that we make a less sweeping interpretation, in time and with thought it can lead to more general and more powerful interpretations" (Kohn 1989a, 85–86).

Culture or Nation as Theoretical Focus.   Culture and nation are elements of the context in which social psychological phenomena occur. As such, they can be characterized and analyzed as to their dimensions (Foschi 1980). This is not, however, an easy task. Kohn (1989b) points to some of the difficulties in abstracting dimensions of nations for analysis; his argument is just as relevant to cultures. Kohn (1989b, 23) sees research in which nation is treated as context as a "way station" toward analyses in which the distinguishing characteristics of nations become variables in the analysis. Kohn is cautious about our ability at this point to translate "nations" into "variables," noting that several steps are required: identifying which of the many differences between countries are the pertinent analytic variables; formulating meaningful hypotheses at the appropriate level of abstraction; and having sufficiently high-quality data from a sufficient number of countries to test these hypotheses.

Although it is certainly true that the task of abstracting dimensions of either nation or culture and testing them empirically is formidable, many see this as vital for progress in cross-cultural social psychological research. Foschi and Hales (1979) argue that we must break culture into operationalizable elements if we are ever going to be able to build a theoretical structure to explain cross-cultural differences in behavior. A few have taken up this challenge.

Hofstede (1980) was among the first survey researchers to attempt to identify cultural dimensions empirically on a massive scale, aiming explicitly to identify major elements of which cultures are composed. Using survey data from employees of a multinational corporation in forty countries, he derived, using factor analysis, four main dimensions along which dominant value systems in the different cultures could be ordered. He labeled these dimensions power distance (the extent to which the less powerful members of groups accept power inequalities); individualism (responsibility for oneself and one's family rather than a larger collective); uncertainty avoidance (the extent to which people feel threatened by ambiguous situations); and masculinity (the extent to which the dominant values in society are success, money, and things). Although Hofstede's focus was on work-related values, he saw the four dimensions that emerged from his analysis as having more general cultural relevance. Although not without its limitations (Triandis 1982), Hofstede's study has been highly influential, stimulating some to use his factors in further research and others to attempt to expand or modify his conceptualization.

Among those using Hofstede's work as a starting point is Shalom Schwartz (in press), whose ambitious study of values in twenty countries yielded a set of culture-level value dimensions that are somewhat related to Hofstede's. Schwartz's dimensions are collectivism, hierarchy, mastery, affective individualism, intellectual individualism, social concern, and harmony. Although Schwartz, like Hofstede, was looking for universal elements of culture, he points out that neither study can claim to have found a definitive set of dimensions because neither study includes all nations, all relevant samples within nations, or multiple time periods.

On a theoretical level, Triandis (1988) explores the question of the likely differential validity of social psychological theories in different cultures. He identifies three cultural dimensions that will likely moderate the generality of social psychological theories: simplicity versus complexity of the culture, individualism/collectivism, and tightness (behavior must conform exactly to norms)/looseness (behavior can deviate a good deal from norms). In their review of recent research in cross-cultural psychology, Kagitcibasi and Berry (1989) confirm that individualism/collectivism stands out as a universal and important cultural dimension, affecting many basic psychological processes. For example, attribution processes may operate somewhat differently in individualistic versus collectivist cultures (Al-Zahrani and Kaplowitz 1993; Bond 1983; Bond and Hwang 1986; Bond et al. 1982; Crittenden 1989, 1991; Kashima and Triandis 1986). These differences may involve even the extent to which attributions are actually made. Bond (1983) points out that the separate person is central to all theories of attribution and that people in collectivistic cultures, in which the individual personality is not of major concern, may not engage much in attribution because they feel relatively little need to explain individual behavior. To the extent that they do construct explanations for individual behavior, they tend more to attribute behavior to causes external to the person (Al-Zahrani and Kaplowitz 1993; Crittenden 1989). In contrast, in individualistic cultures, individual action is seen as more problematic and in need of explanation and behavior is more likely to be attributed to causes internal to the individual. While the cultural characteristic of individualism/collectivism may indeed have powerful consequences for a range of social psychological processes (Bond and Hwang 1986), Kagitcibasi and Berry (1989) warn that further refinement of the individualism/collectivism concept is needed— for example, it needs to be determined whether these are opposite poles of the same dimension or two independent factors—before further conceptual progress and sophistication can be achieved (see also Leung and Bond 1989). In subsequent work, Triandis (1990) further reviews and elaborates the individualism/collectivism dimension (see also Oyama 1990) and Schooler (1990b) examines individualism in historical and social structural context.

The Chinese Culture Connection (1987) also attempts to abstract important theoretical dimensions from different cultures, but it proceeds from a non-Western, emic premise, unlike most other research in social psychology. That is, the researchers created an instrument based on the Chinese tradition, a survey written in Chinese and reflecting indigenous themes and concerns of Chinese culture. This was translated into the appropriate language and administered to more than two thousand university students in twenty-two countries, representing major geographic and cultural groups of the world. The means for each country were factor-analyzed (as well as analyzed with nonmetric multidimensional scaling to correct for the small N). Four factors emerged: integration (including, for example, tolerance of others, harmony and solidarity with others, and noncompetitiveness); Confucian work dynamism (including, for example, ordering relationships by status and observing this order, thrift, persistence, and having a sense of shame); human-heartedness (including, for example, kindness, patience, and courtesy); and moral discipline (including, for example, moderation, keeping oneself disinterested and pure, and having few desires). With the exception of Confucian work dynamism, the factors correlate well with Hofstede's (1980) four dimensions. The Chi-

nese Culture Connection considers integration and moral discipline to be forms of collectivism, in that each pits narrow self-seeking against the maintenance of group integrity. They relate human-heartedness to Hofstede's femininity dimension. Finally, the Confucian work dimension differentiates Asian cultures from the rest of the world and is highly correlated over all countries in the study with gross national growth over the past twenty years. Thus, this non-Western instrument may have identified an important cultural dimension that would not have been discovered using a Western instrument.

Comparative Work and Theory Building in Social Psychology

Comparative work can contribute to building theory in social psychology in at least two ways. First, it can help to set scope conditions for theories. Second, it can serve as an important source of theoretical insight.

The Setting of Scope Conditions.   The setting of scope conditions is an important part of theory construction (Foschi 1980; Nowak 1989; Walker and Cohen 1985). Foschi gives a useful definition: "Scope conditions are general statements specifying when a theory (or a single theoretical relationship) is assumed to be valid, or the range of values that certain variables may take on without altering the predictions of the theory. The range may consist of only one value or it may be fairly wide. It cannot, however, be limitless. This would be the equivalent of removing the scope condition . . ." (1980, 94). Culture can theoretically be broken down into a set of elements that are specified as scope conditions for theories. Alternatively, culture can be built into the theory itself: this requires the specification of specific elements of culture that affect social psychological processes, as well as the mechanisms by which the effect(s) take place. Unfortunately, social psychologists have rarely used cultural elements either as scope conditions or as integral components of theories, mainly because their research has generally been conducted with limited populations (mostly U.S. college students) and under restricted conditions (e.g., laboratory experiments) (Tedeschi 1988b).

Theoretical Insight.   Comparative research may also generate theoretical insights in social psychology. Faucheux (1976, 293) asserts that "without others (other cultures, other worldviews) . . . we might not be able to break out of our cultural 'taken for granted' which is a basic condition for progress in knowledge." Cole (1984) describes how experience in another culture—immersion in its assumptions, relationships, its whole gestalt—may give us wholly different ways to think about things. This kind of new perspective may radically alter our theories or even our views of what is important to explain in the first place.

Examples of how work initiated in other cultural perspectives can radically alter social psychological theories originally derived in the Western cultural context are the work on the self reviewed in chapter 2 and the work on major dimensions of culture discussed above (Chinese Culture Connection 1987). Another example is Kumagai's (1988) theoretical analysis of George Herbert Mead's concept of the self based on the Japanese linguistic term *ki,* which identifies "an emotion in the self that hitherto has been bypassed by Western social scientists and locates that emotion (via 'I') unambiguously in the social act" (Kumagai 1988, 177). Kumagai's work raises questions about Mead's exclusion from the self of affective elements and about his view that impulse is passive in social interaction, thus suggesting limitations on the cultural universality of Mead's theory.

All of the above are instances in which theoretical insight was directly derived from a non-Western cultural context, just as most of the theoretical insights now extant in social psychology were derived from the Western cultural context. The point—which is perhaps still controversial—is that no theoretical insight derived from a single cultural tradition can be assumed to be universal.

It can be argued in general that the gradual accumulation of empirical research findings about how things operate in different cultures can contribute to theoretical insight. Those taking a strong deductive stance toward theory construction (e.g., Faucheux 1976) might disagree. But if we accept as necessary an interplay between deductive theory construction and inductive reasoning from empirical results, it follows that finding unexpected cross-cultural differences can lead to progress in theory building.

METHODOLOGICAL ISSUES

I have outlined theoretical issues concerning the incorporation of different cultures or nations into social psychological research. As with any social psychological research, theoretical considerations should dictate methodological decisions in comparative social psychological research. Ideally, once we determine how our knowledge of social psychology will be advanced by addressing the questions of the research, methodological decisions will follow.

All researchers, whether comparative or not, face a common set of methodological concerns: issues of planning and funding, measurement of concepts, type of design, sampling, and methods of data analysis. Incorporating a diversity of nations or cultures introduces additional complexities, however, and there is a large body of literature addressing specifically the problems of comparative research. As Form (1979, 3) noted, "probably no field has generated more methodological advice on a smaller data base with fewer results than has comparative sociology." His point is that, although it is important to heed the numerous methodological caveats in the literature, the methodological problems of cross-cultural or cross-national research can be made to seem so formidable that researchers are discouraged from even attempting to find solutions to methodological problems, or they abandon comparative research altogether (see also Kuechler 1987). As Lincoln and Kalleberg (1990, 49) point out: "While the obstacles to careful comparative research are severe, they are hardly unique. In numerous ways, such problems also manifest themselves in studies limited to a single country, though they tend not to attract the attention and concern evoked in the context of comparative work." Comparative research is based on the same principles of scientific method as any research, with the major issues boiling down to issues of validity, reliability, generality, and theoretical consequences (Finifter 1977).

I agree with Scheuch's (1989) comment that "in terms of methodology in *abstracto* and on issues of research technology, most of all that needed to be said has already been published" (p. 148). For useful, comprehensive discussions of cross-cultural methodology that are relevant to social psychological research I refer the reader to Przeworski and Teune (1970), Brislin et al. (1973), Armer and Grimshaw (1973), Elder (1976), Triandis and Berry (1980), and Lonner and Berry (1986). Among the useful articles on somewhat more specialized methodological topics are those by Kuechler (1987) on the utility of surveys for cross-national research; Archer (1987) and Kuechler (1987) on sources of data for cross-national research; and Finifter (1977) on strategies for evaluating the robustness of cross-cultural findings and making our knowledge more genuinely cumulative through careful replication and extension in subsequent research.

Two methodological techniques currently receiving widespread attention in sociology and social psychology are highly relevant to comparative research and merit special mention in this chapter. These are the use of confirmatory factor analysis and the analysis of statistical interactions.

Confirmatory factor analysis techniques can be extraordinarily useful in addressing one of the central issues in cross-cultural research—measurement validity. Joanne Miller et al. (1981) demonstrate how confirmatory factor analytic techniques can be used to address the dilemma posed by Berry (1969): that both emic (within-culture) and etic (across-cultures) validity must be considered for overall construct validity, and these may be in conflict. In other words, the best measurement of a

concept in one culture may not be "identical" to the best measurement of that concept in another culture, yet if we wish to claim that we are measuring the "same" concept in the two cultures we need to test the conceptual equivalence of our measures (see Berry 1980 for discussion). Berry (1969) proposes that this problem can be resolved by first imposing an etically derived construct on a given culture, then modifying it to make it valid in that culture. The resulting construct for a given culture would then be composed of both emic (culturally specific) and etic (cross-cultural) elements. Joanne Miller et al. (1981) demonstrate in detail how confirmatory factor analysis can be a useful statistical tool for constructing and evaluating such distinct yet overlapping measures of a given concept in different cultures. They illustrate this by constructing and testing indexes of the concept of authoritarian conservatism in the United States and Poland.

Just as confirmatory factor analysis is becoming widely used in social psychology, interaction effects are receiving increased attention (Aiken and West 1991; Jaccard, Turrisi, and Wan 1990). In the past, interaction effects were often ignored in sociological analyses (Aiken and West, 1991, 4; Jaccard, Turrisi, and Wan 1990, 8). House (1981), for example, noted this deficiency in research on social structure and personality. The need for attention to interactions is especially clear with respect to cross-cultural research, in that one of the most fundamental questions posed is how culture moderates or conditions the effects of other major determinants of human behavior.

There are various approaches to specifying cultural interaction effects. One is to compare regression effects of various independent variables across culture-specific samples (as is done, for example, by Lincoln and Kalleberg 1990). Ayala Cohen (1983) discusses some of the possible pitfalls of this approach. Another approach is to compare structural coefficients using linear structural equation models, for example by using LISREL (Joreskog and Sorbom 1988, 1989). Aiken and West (1991, 151–153) discuss this approach and others. The increased attention to the various methods and issues associated with interaction analysis will be salutary for comparative research.

PROBLEMS

Having reviewed the unique advantages, major theoretical issues, and some of the methodological issues associated with comparative research, I now assess the special problems of this approach to social psychological research. I begin with a somewhat curious observation. As a proportion of all social psychological research, comparative research occupies a modest place (Gabrenya 1988; Messick 1988a; Tedeschi 1988a). For example, a search of *Social Psychology Quarterly* for the twelve-year period from 1980 through 1991 yielded only twelve articles (less than 4 percent of all articles) that were in any way cross-cultural or cross-national. Furthermore, comparative work is ghettoized: its results only rarely inform the dominant activities through which social psychologists strive for general theory (Cole 1984; Messick 1988a, 1988b). Although there are influential comparative studies that have made major contributions to the development of social psychology, they are few relative to the whole body of social psychological research. Why isn't there more comparative research in social psychology? And why isn't the comparative perspective an integral part of mainstream activity in social psychology?

One of the reasons involves the methodological difficulties inherent in comparative research. Some see comparative work as somewhat suspect, partly because it often involves methodological compromises that make its results potentially invalid in mainstream eyes (Cole 1984; Messick 1988a, 1988b). Yet, as discussed above, many of the methodological problems of cross-cultural or cross-national research are shared by social psychological research in general; they are just more noticeable and more difficult to ignore in comparative research (Lincoln and Kalleberg 1990, 49).

While some believe the reason for the relative paucity of comparative research resides in the inherent problems of the research itself, others (e.g.,

Faucheux 1976; Pepitone 1986) argue that many social psychologists have simply assumed that what is valid in their culture is valid everywhere. This view is exemplified by the following assertion:

> *Human beings are human beings and social influence phenomena occurring anywhere and at any time can be interpreted within the same basic conceptual framework ... Given the abiding faith in basic universals of humankind, the social psychologist might just as well work within the subject population he knows something about and that is close at hand—the students in his classes. (Gerard and Conolley 1972, 242).*

Jahoda (1988) vigorously criticizes this view and asserts that it is widespread, stating:

> *Much of the journal literature in experimental social psychology deals with issues that are both trivial in a wider context and specific to contemporary American culture. In spite of this provincialism, limitations to generality are hardly ever acknowledged, and cross-cultural verification of claims is not only seldom attempted, but the need for it is not even recognized. (90)*

Rebutting this accusation that unexamined ethnocentrism is rampant among researchers, Messick (1988a) argues that the reason many social psychologists do not do cross-cultural research is not necessarily because they have never bothered to question the universality of their results, but rather because of limitations in terms of time, budgets, and international contacts (see also Sarapata 1985). Kohn (1989a), while arguing that cross-national research is potentially invaluable and underutilized as a research strategy, reiterates its drawbacks: it is costly in time and money; it is difficult to do; and it often seems to raise more interpretive problems than it solves. His general advice is: "Unless one has a good reason why research should be cross-national, it generally isn't worth the effort of making it cross-national" (Kohn 1989a, 97) Faucheux (1976) agrees that cross-cultural research should only be done if it is theoretically motivated.

Another reason for not engaging in cross-cultural research is that some of what it reveals may be learned just as effectively by other means. Messick (1988b, 47) makes the interesting point that "to the extent that different norms or expectations for behavior characterize different cultures, one can presumably study the impact of cultures, that is, norms and expectations, on behavior within a single laboratory. Was it not Milgram's (1974) goal in his famous obedience studies to teach us something about the 'culture' of the Third Reich?" In a related vein, Nowak (1989) points out that "overall characteristics" of a nation or cultural group may not have the same impact on all members of a given society, and variations in intensity of these contextual variables may be tested intraculturally, saving the expense and labor of a cross-national study. Both Messick's and Nowak's suggestions depend, of course, on understanding the relevant dimensions of culture that can be tested in an experiment or in a given group, an important theoretical issue discussed earlier.

Other reasons for the relative paucity and ghettoization of cross-cultural research in social psychology are the ethical and political dilemmas it poses (see Warwick 1980). Some have raised ethical questions of whose interests cross-cultural research serves and whether subjects become victims of exploitation (Kohn 1989a, 92; Portes 1975; Scheuch 1967; Sinha 1983; Trimble 1988). One of the worst cases of ethical abuse of cross-cultural collaboration is that of the infamous Project Camelot (Horowitz 1967; discussed at length in Warwick 1980), whose findings were to be used for political oppression. Although few research projects become directly implicated as tools of oppression, many view comparative research as an extension of American dominance: the United States dominates social psychological research in number of publications, and any research project involving U.S. and non-U.S. collaborators is likely to be on American terms (Bond 1988, 11). An unfortunate potential concomitant of this is the attitude that U.S. social psychology has little to learn in terms of theory and method from the rest of the world (see Cole 1984 for discussion). All of these concerns need to be addressed. Kohn (1989a, 92) takes the position that "the theoretical and policy issues to be ad-

dressed in cross-national research can be—in principle, ought to be—equally important for sociologists of all countries concerned." If this is not the case, however, should the research be done? This question should be considered seriously and fully by researchers contemplating comparative endeavors.

Comparative research has also been attacked for overlooking intracultural and intranational differences. For example, women (Papanek 1978; K. Miller 1978) and minority groups are often ignored as respondents. Thus, comparative generalizations may actually be based on far less than half the population of each nation or culture. And although they may be citizens of a given nation, it is not at all clear the extent to which women and minorities share the same culture as dominant men (for a discussion and review of the concept of women's culture, see Bernard 1981, 18–24), and the extent to which what we think of as the "culture" of a given society is a construction of the dominant group (see, e.g., Foucault 1980).

In summary, comparative research in social psychology has been seen as problematic on a number of grounds: methodological soundness; researchers' ethnocentric prejudices; costs versus benefits; political and ethical concerns; and, frequently, limited generalizability even within nations or cultures. All of these considerations help explain why its use is low and/or its influence blunted. The overall result is that social psychology as a discipline is generally (though certainly not wholly) lacking in a cross-cultural perspective.

Despite the problematic aspects of comparative research, the relative lack of a comparative perspective in social psychology is increasingly viewed as a serious problem. In fact, some critics find questionable any generalizations from research that is not informed by exposure to more than one culture (Jahoda 1988; Pepitone 1986), thus faulting most extant social psychological research. This is a strong indictment of the state of the discipline. Even if one does not take that position, it is clear that the comparative approach in social psychology offers many unique advantages over noncomparative research. Many of these advantages are illustrated in the following review of actual comparative research that has made major contributions to social psychology. I review research in only one substantive area of social psychology, but one that is particularly well suited to the comparative approach: social structure and personality.

COMPARATIVE RESEARCH ON SOCIAL STRUCTURE AND PERSONALITY

Most of the comparative work in sociological social psychology is in the area of social structure and personality. While macrosocial structures and processes have not been a major concern of other subareas of social psychology (House 1977,1981; see also Kohn 1989c), the focus of social structure and personality research is on how macrosocial structures and processes affect and are affected by individual psychology and behavior. Since both culture and nation are also macrosocial phenomena, examining variations in these entities is a natural extension of work relating social structure to personality.

Historically, much of the research on social structure and personality has been comparative. From the 1920s through the 1960s a major interest in social structure and personality research was in the relationship of whole societies to holistic conceptions of personality or character "types." Comparative by nature, this work was variously labeled "society and personality," "culture and personality," or "national character" (see House 1981; Inkeles and Levinson 1969). In this body of research, explanations for personality are more cultural than structural, referring to the collective values and beliefs of entire societies. Research on national character continues, though since the 1960s it has not been the central focus of social structure and personality research. Examples of recent research on national character are the ambitious works of Hofstede (1980) and Peabody (1985), which used factor analysis to identify national cultural traits. Inkeles (1991) reviews other recent research on national character.

House (1981) notes two trends emerging since the 1960s in research on social structure and personality: a trend toward a more structural approach to explaining personality variations and a trend toward a less global approach, involving the study of components of societies and their relationship to aspects of personality. Both trends can be observed in comparative research on social structure and personality. The trend toward structural rather than cultural explanations of personality is exemplified by the convergence thesis.

The Psychological Convergence Thesis

One of the comparative research themes that emerged in the late 1950s, blossomed in the 1960s, and has recently been the subject of renewed interest is societal convergence resulting from common processes of industrialization. The basic thesis is that industrialization, more than earlier dominant modes of production, constrains the range of institutional structures societies can develop. The thesis is often extended to link converging social structures to converging attitudes, values, and behaviors of individuals in societies undergoing industrialization (see Lincoln and Kalleberg 1990, 20 for a useful discussion). Thus, two basic research questions can be distilled from this rich and often controversial body of research: (1) Does industrialization produce similarities in the basic institutional structures of societies, no matter how different the societies were initially? (2) Will the structural similarities emerging in societies create psychological convergences as well, despite initial cultural differences?

A detailed examination of the first question—essentially, the question of structural convergence—is beyond the scope of this chapter. Here we simply note that considerable structural convergence can be empirically observed in the world today, although its origins are controversial. Within the purview of this chapter is the issue of psychological convergence—that is, whether people are affected psychologically in similar ways by similar social structures, whatever their exact source, in industrialized societies. Inkeles (1960) was among the first to state this hypothesis explicitly: he proposed "that the standardized institutional environments of modern society induce standard patterns of response, despite the countervailing randomizing effects of persisting traditional patterns of culture" (p. 1). Elsewhere, Inkeles expresses the same hypothesis with more specificity: "Following the leads Marx provided when he declared that one's relationship to the mode of production shapes one's consciousness, we may expect individuals to learn to be modern by incorporating within themselves principles which are embedded in the organizational practice of the institutions in which they live and work" (Inkeles 1976, 122). This hypothesis guided Inkeles and colleagues' massive study of almost six thousand men in six industrializing nations—Argentina, Chile, India, Bangladesh, Nigeria, and Israel (Inkeles and Smith 1974). One of the central focuses of this study was to identify the psychological characteristics that the researchers saw as required by, and as developing in response to, exposure to modern institutions. A syndrome of attitudes, values, and beliefs was found to cohere empirically in the different cultures and to be related to exposure to modern institutions. This syndrome, termed *individual modernity,* consisted of the following elements (Inkeles 1969): openness to new experience; independence from traditional authority; belief in science and medicine for solving human problems; educational and occupational ambition; punctuality and orderliness; and interest in civic affairs.

In addition to Inkeles and colleagues, others studying modernization and its effects on individual social psychological functioning have developed related indexes of individual modernity and shown them to be associated with exposure to processes of societal modernization. Among them are Lerner (1958), Kahl (1968), Schnaiberg (1970), Armer and Youtz (1971), Guthrie (1977), and Yang (1981).[2]

Although overall, modernity research has found robust cross-cultural empirical relationships linking individuals' exposure to the processes of industrialization and its concomitants (e.g., the growth of urbanization, the spread of education and the mass media, and the rise in living standard), on the one hand, to distinctive, non-culture-specific psychological orientations, on the other,

research in this area has been highly controversial. The modernity thesis has been viewed as an apology for the status quo, for capitalism and/or imperialism (Wallerstein 1974, 1976), and as biased toward white, U.S., middle-class values (Portes 1973). Inkeles (1976), Form (1979), and Yang (1988) address these criticisms in detail. In a recent critique, Luke (1991), using the postmodernist framework of Foucault (1980), argues that modernity is a legitimating ideology used by power elites for facilitating social control of the masses. According to Luke, "Modernity abstractly expresses the historical, social, and cultural development of the developed in a de-historicized, de-socialized, and de-culturized social theory that guides and justifies the development of the undeveloped" (1991, 284). Other criticisms of the individual modernity concept involve its conceptualization and validity (Armer and Schnaiberg 1972, 1977; J. Cohen and Till 1977; Inkeles 1976; Inkeles and Smith 1974). One of the major validity issues is modernity's exact status as a construct independent of socioeconomic status. The various indexes of modernity are highly related to socioeconomic status but not totally explained by it, suggesting a possible need for further clarification of what is being measured (Form 1979).

Recently published work of Herbert Blumer (1990) also raises important theoretical issues relevant to modernity research. In opposition to the structural view of industrialization taken by most modernization theorists (such as Inkeles), Blumer sees industrialization as itself a product of group life and, as such, a "neutral agent," engendering a wide range of situations to which individuals make a wide range of adaptations. The consequences of industrialization are thus unpredictable and depend on the specific mechanisms that individuals or groups use to deal with changing conditions. Blumer believes the proper analytical focus of industrialization as an agent of social change should be exactly how industrialization enters group life.

Blumer's work raises profound theoretical issues concerning the nature of social structure and social life that are beyond our scope here. But his concerns also relate to the issues raised by House (1981) regarding modernity research, and social structure and personality research in general. House

(1981, 540–541) argues that to understand how a social structure, position, or system affects an individual we must address three issues: (1) We must specify the aspects or components of the social structural phenomenon that are relevant in a given situation. (2) We must specify how macrostructural processes affect the smaller structures that constitute the proximate experiences impinging on the individual. (3) We must understand the psychological processes by which social stimuli are processed and responded to. All of these concerns are addressed to some extent in modernity research. For example, Inkeles and colleagues, in many empirical analyses, break "modernization" down into components such as factory experience, education, and exposure to mass media. Furthermore, Inkeles recognizes the need to identify individuals' proximate experiences (Inkeles 1960, 1963, 1976) and theoretically posits psychological processes (reward and punishment, modeling, exemplification, and generalization) by which individuals respond to these experiences (Inkeles and Smith 1974, 140–143), although he is not fully able to test empirically for these phenomena. Thus, modernity research needs more specification of the precise linkages by which experiences with particular institutions associated with modernization are related to people's psychological orientations (see also Schooler 1990b on modernity research; Kiecolt 1988 on this need in social structure and personality research in general). I now turn to a discussion of a cross-national research program that further advances our knowledge of how components of social structure enter individuals' experience as proximate life conditions and affect their psychological functioning.

Cross-National Research on Social Structural Position, Occupational Conditions, and Psychological Functioning

In the late 1960s Melvin Kohn and Carmi Schooler launched an investigation of the critical intervening role of occupational conditions, particularly opportunities to exercise self-direction on the job, in explaining the relationship of social class and values of U.S. men (Kohn 1969; Kohn and Schooler 1969). An early cross-national replication in Italy of a portion of these findings was performed by Leonard Pearlin (1971; Pearlin and Kohn 1966). The research was expanded ten years later to include a follow-up study in the United States, including wives and selected children of the original men (Kohn and Schooler 1983) and ultimately to cross-national replications and extensions of the research in Poland (Kohn and Slomczynski 1990; J. Miller, Slomczynski, and Kohn 1985; Slomczynski, Miller, and Kohn 1981) and Japan (Kohn, Naoi et al. 1990; A. Naoi and Schooler 1985; M. Naoi and Schooler 1990; Schooler and Naoi 1988). Currently, further cross-national work is proceeding in Poland and the Ukraine (Kohn, Slomczynski et al. 1992).

This research program has contributed a great deal to our understanding of the relationship between social structure and personality (see House 1981; Spenner 1988; chapter 19 in this volume). In terms of meeting the three principles espoused by House—the components, proximity, and psychological principles—the research makes significant advances. Particularly in the later work (Kohn et al. 1990; Kohn and Slomczynski 1990), the components of social structural position are specified: job conditions are independently specified and social structural position is differentiated into social class and social stratification, an interesting and important distinction, particularly when tested cross-nationally.[3] The proximity principle—the importance of proximate conditions relating large-scale social structures to individuals' experience—is embodied in the original and primary motivating premise of the research—that job conditions, particularly opportunities to exercise self-direction in work, are a crucial explanatory link between positions in the class and stratification structures and individuals' psychological functioning. The psychological principle—the need to understand the mechanisms by which structural experiences are processed psychologically—is addressed in particular by Schooler (1984) and Kohn and Slomczynski (1990), who identify the major psychological process linking job conditions to psychological functioning as one of learning generalization. Schooler (1984) develops a more general theoretical exposition of the psychological effects of environmental complexity.

The specifically cross-national aspects of the research are important in other respects. Poland and Japan are well-chosen settings for testing the general theory developed in the United States. Both are highly industrialized nations. Poland, for which data were collected originally in 1978, represents a noncapitalist nation but one with a Western European tradition; Japan, for which data were originally collected in 1979, represents a non-Western capitalist nation. Thus, the occupational structures in both Poland and Japan are characteristic of industrialized nations, but the class and stratification systems differ because of the difference in political systems (although the former difference is much less than one might expect), and the cultural traditions are very different (see Schooler 1990a for a historical analysis of Japanese vis-à-vis European culture). These diverse elements create settings for stringent tests of the general theory relating social structural position, job conditions, and psychological functioning. The research currently being undertaken in Poland and the Ukraine will test the theory under conditions of rapid and radical social change (Kohn et al. 1992).

Overall, the findings in the United States, Poland, and Japan confirm the central elements of the theory. People more advantageously located in either the class system or the stratification system of their society are more likely to be intellectually flexible, to be self-directed in their social orientations, and to value self-direction in their children than are people who are less advantageously located. Occupational self-direction plays a crucial role in explaining these relationships, with those who do more substantively complex work, those who are less closely supervised, and those who do less routine work more likely to be located higher in the social structural hierarchy and to be more intellectually flexible and self-directed in their orientations and values. All of these findings are cross-nationally consistent.

In contrast, higher social class and more self-direction do not have cross-nationally consistent effects on affective states of distress, which include feelings of anxiety and estrangement from self and others, as indicated by indexes of anxiety, self-deprecation, lack of self-confidence, distrust of others, and believing that one's ideas differ from those of one's friends, relatives, others of one's religious faith, and society in general. In the United States, higher social class and greater occupational self-direction decrease distress, although modestly so. In Japan, as in the United States, managers and employers have relatively low distress, and occupational self-direction per se also leads to lower distress, but in Japan nonmanual workers surpass manual workers in degree of distress. The pattern in Poland is different than that in either the United States or Japan. In Poland, as in Japan, nonmanual workers have relatively high levels of distress, but the self-employed have relatively low levels and managers have markedly high levels of distress, and factory workers and nonproduction workers are less distressed than members of most other social classes. Moreover, in Poland, occupational self-direction has virtually no effect on distress.

Kohn and Slomczynski (1990, 209) see these cross-national differences as interesting and potentially important for their overall interpretation of the relationships among social structure, self-direction, and psychological functioning. Kohn et al. (1990) and Kohn and Slomczynski (1990) put forth possible explanations for the distinct patterns, but unfortunately with limited data to test them. A potentially plausible explanation is that job conditions other than self-direction have countervailing effects on distress. In Japan, for example, two job conditions positively related to occupational self-direction—working under time pressure and being held responsible for things outside one's control—are positively related to distress. In Poland, only a particular segment of managers were particularly distressed: those not members of the Polish Communist Party, and therefore subject (in 1978) to unusual uncertainties, risks, and insecurities. Other substantive explanations considered by Kohn and Slomczynski (1990) are that the psychological mechanisms that link social structure and distress are different than those that link social structure and intellectual functioning, social orientation, and values; that the processes by which people attain their positions and the meanings these positions have to them vary according to culture and historical circumstance; and that non-job conditions of life are more important for distress than for the other psychological characteristics considered. Possible evidence for the latter is that in Japan, the younger, more educated, urban workers are more distressed and also more likely to be nonmanual workers (Kohn et al. 1990). Further research would be needed to develop a definitive and comprehensive explanation for why social structural position, job conditions, and distress are related differently in different nations.

The overall evidence from Kohn, Schooler, and their colleagues' research program points to the importance, in diverse industrialized nations, of social class and stratification position as a major influence on the daily conditions under which individuals must work and the major impact of these work conditions on psychological functioning.[4] The findings are thus consistent with Marx's emphasis on the primacy of work activity as a link between the economic order and individuals' consciousness.

CONCLUSION

We may draw several broad conclusions from this review of comparative social psychology. First, based on the relative paucity of comparative research in social psychology, is that much of our research in social psychology is culture-bound— that is, bound to Western, generally American, often American dominant-group culture. Most social psychological findings are not subjected to cross-cultural verification. More crucial, though, most extant social psychological theories are derived within a Western or even more limited cultural context and contain unexamined cultural assumptions. Social psychologists are doing several things to remedy this, but they need to do more. One is to replicate our findings cross-culturally. Another is to become informed about emic research in other cultures and nations. A third is to follow the recommendations of Campbell (1964, 331) and

Faucheux to use a triangulation method: "to engage in joint projects in which a team of researchers belonging to two different cultures would study them both with two others in addition, finding within themselves, in their dialogue, through confronting their different understanding of the four cultures, further insight into the reality they are studying" (Faucheux 1976, 316).

The dawning recognition of the culture-bound limitations of many of our social psychological theories and findings has been a precipitating factor in the resurgence of interest in culture on the part of social psychologists, evidenced from this review. On a philosophical and theoretical level, the emic approach of intensively studying psychological phenomena in separate cultures is a significant, growing trend. Findings from other cultures challenge the cultural universality of some of our theories as currently formulated. Cognitive consistency (Doi 1986), self-esteem (Markus and Kitayama 1991), the "I" and the "me" as components of the self (Kumagai 1988), attribution processes (Al-Zahrani and Kaplowitz 1993; Bond 1983; Bond and Hwang 1986; Bond, Leung, and Wan 1982; Crittenden 1989, 1991; Kashima and Triandis 1986), the learned helplessness model of depression (Crittenden and Lamug 1988), and sense of distress (Kohn et al. 1990; Kohn and Slomczynski 1990) are examples of psychological constructs that appear to be different in content or operation in different cultures. Other examples are reviewed elsewhere (Bond and Hwang 1986; chapter 2 in this volume).

The emic approach, and the culturally disparate findings cited, are consistent with a view of human psychology as contextual and historically and culturally bound. This view has not been predominant in sociology as a whole or in sociological social psychology. The more common sociological approach has been etic—to view culture as context, and to search for general relationships that transcend particular circumstances. Indeed, a review of empirical work on social structure and personality shows structural effects that are independent of culture on a range of psychological phenomena. The evidence of Inkeles and others' research is that certain common psychological traits seem to accompany exposure to processes of societal modernization. These traits are consistent across specific cultures but also differentiated somewhat by social class. Kohn, Schooler, and associates find strong evidence that social structural position differentiates individuals' work conditions, which in turn impact on intellectual functioning, social orientation, and values, remarkably independently of the cultural contexts so far examined. Lincoln and Kalleberg's research shows that while the role of culture is not trivial, organizational structure has independent, additive effects in explaining employees' work commitment in Japan and the United States.

To some extent, the emic and etic approaches to comparative research differ as to what is figure and what is ground, the emic focusing on cultural diversity, the etic on structural commonality. It may be that both emic and etic approaches are necessary to merge figure and ground into a gestalt representing the fullness of reality. Yet our understanding of social psychological phenomena in different cultures and nations is not limited only by limitations in our focus of attention. The findings of cross-cultural and cross-national differences and similarities reviewed here suggest several important and unresolved questions about the relationships among particular psychological phenomena, culture, and social structure. Are certain types of psychological factors more influenced by social structure independent of culture and others more influenced by culture regardless of social structure? How do culture and social structure influence each other? Do culture and social structure interact in complex ways to influence some psychological processes? Although these questions bear on Max Weber's early concerns with the relative roles of culture and social structure in social life (Weber 1958), as yet we know relatively little that bears on these questions. The culture-structure distinction clearly needs further systematic examination.

Finally, if we are to deal more seriously with culture and nation as variables in social psychology, it should also be a priority to continue research on their dimensions. This is a difficult but important task. Specifying relevant cultural and national dimensions will help move comparative research from a descriptive to an analytic level, by demonstrating what it is about culture or nation that does or does not matter for social psychological phenomena.

NOTES

I am indebted to Bernard Farber, Alex Inkeles, K. Jill Kiecolt, Melvin Kohn, Carmi Schooler, and an anonymous reviewer for their comments on earlier drafts of this chapter and to Pete Padilla for bibliographic assistance.
1. See House (1977, 169) on Weber's comparative social psychological approach.
2. In this context the work of Inglehart (1977, 1990) is also relevant. In large-scale surveys of citizens of postindustrial Europe, Inglehart identifies increasing trends toward "postmaterialist" values—decreasing emphasis on material concerns and increasing emphasis on nonmaterial concerns, such as quality of life and self-expression. He sees this shift to be the result of the increasing affluence of postindustrial Europe.
3. Kohn et al. (1990), in their comparative analysis of social structural position and psychological functioning in the United States, Poland, and Japan, define "social classes" as "groups defined in terms of their relationship to ownership and control of the means of production, and of their control over the labor power of others" (p. 965). Their conceptualization builds on contemporary work reconceptualizing Marx's original bourgeoisie/proletariat distinction into more numerous and complex forms of ownership, control, and advantage (Gagliani 1981; Hashimoto 1986; Mach and Wesolowski 1986; Mizuno 1974; Ohashi 1971; Robinson and Kelley 1979; Steven 1983; Wright 1976, 1978, 1985). Social class is distinct from social stratification, defined as "the hierarchical ordering of society as indexed by formal education, occupational status, and job income" (Kohn et al. 1990, 965). Social stratification is thus a single continuum of positions along an ordinal scale, while social classes are distinct groups defined in relation to other social classes (Kohn and Slomczynski 1990, 31). Both social class position and social stratification position have independent psychological effects

on values, intellectual functioning, social orientation, and sense of distress in the United States, Japan, and Poland (Kohn et al. 1990), thus both are conceptually and empirically distinct and meaningful. Further, Kohn et al. (1990) find that both social class and social stratification exercise their psychological effects in large part through the opportunities for occupational self-direction they facilitate.

4. See also the review of cross-cultural studies of the social psychological concomitants of work and organizations in chapter 19.

REFERENCES

Agger, Ben. 1991. Critical theory, poststructuralism, postmodernism: Their sociological relevance. *Annual Review of Sociology* 17:105–131.

Aiken, Leona S., and Stephen G. West. 1991. *Multiple Regression: Testing and Interpreting Interactions.* Newbury Park, CA: Sage.

Al-Zahrani, Saad Said A., and Stan A. Kaplowitz. 1993. Attributional biases in individualistic and collectivistic cultures: A comparison of Americans and Saudis. *Social Psychology Quarterly* 56:223–233.

Archer, Dane. 1987. Constructing cross-national data sets: Theoretical issues and practical methods. *Comparative Social Research* 10:231–239.

Armer, Michael, and Allen Grimshaw, eds. 1973. *Comparative Social Research: Methodological Problems and Strategies.* New York: Wiley.

Armer, Michael, and Allan Schnaiberg. 1972. Measuring individual modernity: A near myth. *American Sociological Review* 37:301–316.

———. 1977. Reply to Cohen and Till. *American Sociological Review* 421:378–382.

Armer, Michael, and R. Youtz. 1971. Formal education and individual modernity in an African society. *American Journal of Sociology* 76:604–626.

Backman, Carl W. 1990. Advances in European social psychology. Paper presented at the annual meetings of the American Sociological Association, Washington, DC.

Bernard, Jessie. 1981. *The Female World.* New York: Free Press.

Berry, John W. 1969. On cross-cultural comparability. *International Journal of Psychology* 4:119–128.

———. 1980. Introduction to methodology. Pp. 1–28 in *Handbook of Cross-Cultural Psychology, 2: Methodology,* ed. H. C. Triandis and J. W. Berry. Boston: Allyn and Bacon.

Blumer, Herbert. 1990. *Industrialization as an Agent of Social Change: A Critical Analysis.* Edited and with an introduction by D. R. Maines and T. J. Morrione. New York: Aldine de Gruyter.

Bond, Michael Harris. 1983. A proposal for cross-cultural studies of attribution. Pp. 144–157 in *Attribution Theory: Social and Functional Extensions,* ed. M. Hewstone. Oxford, UK: Blackwell.

———. 1988. Introduction. Pp. 9–13 in *The Cross-Cultural Challenge to Social Psychology,* ed. M. H. Bond. Newbury Park, CA: Sage.

Bond, Michael Harris, and K. K. Hwang. 1986. The social psychology of the Chinese people. Pp. 213–266 in *The Psychology of the Chinese People,* ed. M. H. Bond. Hong Kong: Oxford University Press.

Bond, Michael Harris, Kwok Leung, and Kwok-Choi Wan. 1982. The social impact of self-effacing attribution: The Chinese case. *The Journal of Social Psychology* 118:157–166.

Brislin, Richard W., Walter J. Lonner, and Robert M. Thorndike. 1973. *Cross-Cultural Research Methods.* New York: Wiley.

Campbell, Donald T. 1964. Distinguishing differences of perception from failures of communication in cross-cultural studies. Pp. 308–336 in *Cross-Cultural Understanding: Epistemology in Anthropology,* ed. F. S. C. Northrop and H. H. Livingston. New York: Harper & Row.

Chinese Culture Connection. 1987. Chinese values and the search for culture-free dimensions of culture. *Journal of Cross-Cultural Psychology* 18:143–164.

Cohen, Ayala. 1983. Comparing regression coefficients across subsamples: A study of the statistical test. *Sociological Methods and Research* 12:77–94.

Cohen, Jere, and Amnon Till. 1977. Another look at modernity scales: Reanalysis of the convergent and discriminant validities of the Armer, Kahl, Smith and Inkeles, and Schnaiberg scales. *American Sociological Review* 42:373–378.

Cole, Michael. 1984. The world beyond our borders: What might our students need to know about it? *American Psychologist* 39:998–1105.

Crittenden, Kathleen S. 1989. Causal attribution in sociocultural context: Toward a self-presentational theory of attribution processes. *The Sociological Quarterly* 30:1–14.

——. 1991. Asian self-effacement or feminine modesty? Attributional patterns of women university students in Taiwan. *Gender and Society* 5:98–117.

Crittenden, Kathleen, and Corazon Lamug. 1988. Causal attribution and depression: A friendly refinement based on Philippine data. *Journal of Cross-Cultural Psychology* 19:216–231.

De Vos, George A., and Arthur A. Hippler. 1969. Cultural psychology: Comparative studies of human behavior. Pp. 323–417 in *The Handbook of Social Psychology,* 2nd ed., vol. 4, ed. G. Lindzey and E. Aronson. Reading, MA: Addison-Wesley.

Doi, T. 1986. *The Anatomy of the Self: The Individual Versus Society.* Translated by Mark A. Harbison. Tokyo: Kodansha.

Elder, Joseph W. 1976. Comparative cross-national methodology. *Annual Review of Sociology* 2:209–230.

Eysenck, H. J. 1986. Cross-cultural comparisons: The validity of assessment by indices of factor comparisons. *Journal of Cross-Cultural Psychology* 17:506–515.

Faucheux, Claude. 1976. Cross-cultural research in experimental social psychology. *European Journal of Social Psychology* 6:269–322.

Finifter, Bernard M. 1977. The robustness of cross-cultural findings. *Annals New York Academy of Sciences* 285:151–184.

Form, William H. 1976. *Blue-Collar Stratification: Autoworkers in Four Countries.* Princeton, NJ: Princeton University Press.

——. 1979. Comparative industrial sociology and the convergence hypothesis. *Annual Review of Sociology* 5:1–25.

Foschi, Martha. 1980. Theory, experimentation, and cross-cultural comparisons in social psychology. *Canadian Journal of Sociology* 5:91–102.

Foschi, Martha, and W. H. Hales. 1979. The theoretical role of cross-cultural comparisons in experimental social psychology. Pp. 244–254 in *Cross-Cultural Contributions to Psychology,* ed. L. H. Eckensberger, W. J. Lonner, and Y. H. Poortinga. Lisse: Swets & Zeitlinger.

Foucault, Michel. 1980. *The History of Sexuality, 1: An Introduction.* New York: Vintage.

Gabrenya, William K., Jr. 1988. Social science and social psychology: The cross-cultural link. Pp. 48–66 in *The Cross-Cultural Challenge to Social Psychology,* ed. M. H. Bond. Newbury Park, CA: Sage.

Gagliani, Giorgio. 1981. How many working classes? *American Journal of Sociology* 87:259–285.

Gerard, Harold B., and Edward S. Conolley. 1972. Conformity. Pp. 237–263 in *Experimental Social Psychology,* ed. C. G. McClintock. New York: Holt, Rinehart & Winston.

Gergen, Kenneth J. 1973. Social psychology as history. *Journal of Personality and Social Psychology* 26:309–320.

——. 1978. Experimentation in social psychology: A re-appraisal. *European Journal of Social Psychology* 8:507–527.

——. 1985. The social constructionist movement in modern psychology. *American Psychologist* 40:266–275.

Gergen, Kenneth J., and K. Davis, eds. 1985. *The Social Construction of the Person.* New York: Springer.

Guthrie, G. M. 1977. A socio-psychological analysis of modernization in the Philippines. *Journal of Cross-Cultural Psychology* 8:177–206.

Harre, R. 1981. Psychological variety. Pp. 79–103 in *Indigenous Psychologies: The Anthropology of the Self,* ed. P. Heelas and A. Lock. New York: Academic.

Hashimoto, Kenji. 1986. Gendai nihon shakai no kaikyu bunseki. (Class analysis of modern japanese society.) *Shakaigaku Hyoron* 37:175–190.

Hochschild, Arlie Russell. 1983. *The Managed Heart: Commercialization of Human Feeling.* Berkeley: University of California Press.

Hofstede, Geert. 1980. *Culture's Consequences: International Differences in Work-Related Values.* Beverly Hills: Sage.

Hogan, Robert T., and Nicholas P. Emler. 1978. The biases in contemporary social psychology. *Social Research* 45:478–534.

Horowitz, Irving Louis. 1967. *The Rise and Fall of Project Camelot.* Cambridge, MA: MIT Press.

House, James S. 1977. The three faces of social psychology. *Sociometry* 40:161–177.

——. 1981. Social structure and personality. Pp. 525–561 in *Social Psychology: Sociological Perspectives,* ed. Morris Rosenberg and Ralph H. Turner. New York: Basic Books.

Inglehart, Ronald. 1977. *The Silent Revolution: Changing Values and Political Styles Among Western Publics.* Princeton: Princeton University Press.

——. 1990. *Culture Shift in Advanced Industrial Society.* Princeton: Princeton University Press.

Inkeles, Alex. 1960. Industrial man: The relation of status to experience, perception, and value. *American Journal of Sociology* 66:1–31.

———. 1963. Sociology and psychology. Pp. 317–387 in *Psychology: The Study of a Science,* vol. 6, ed. S. Koch. New York: McGraw-Hill.

———. 1969. Making men modern: On the causes and consequences of individual change in six developing countries. *American Journal of Sociology* 75: 208–225.

———. 1976. Understanding and misunderstanding individual modernity. Pp. 103–130 in *The Uses of Controversy in Sociology,* ed. Lewis A. Coser and Otto N. Larsen. New York: Free Press.

———. 1991. National character revisited. *The Tocqueville Review* 12:83–117.

Inkeles, Alex, and Daniel Levinson. 1969. National character: The study of modal personality and sociocultural systems. Pp. 418–506 in *The Handbook of Social Psychology,* 2nd ed., vol. 4, ed. G. Lindzey and E. Aronson. Reading, MA: Addison-Wesley.

Inkeles, Alex, and David H. Smith. 1974. *Becoming Modern: Individual Change in Six Developing Countries.* Cambridge, MA: Harvard University Press.

Jaccard, James, Robert Turrisi, and Choi K. Wan. 1990. *Interaction Effects in Multiple Regression.* Newbury Park, CA: Sage.

Jahoda, Gustav. 1988. J'accuse. Pp. 86–95 in *The Cross-Cultural Challenge to Social Psychology,* ed. M. H. Bond. Newbury Park, CA: Sage.

Joreskog, Karl G., and Dag Sorbom. 1988. *LISREL 7: A Guide to the Program and Applications.* Chicago: SPSS.

———. 1989. *LISREL 7: User's Reference Guide.* Mooresville, IN: Scientific Software.

Kagitcibasi, Cigdem, and J. W. Berry. 1989. Cross-cultural psychology: Current research and trends. *Annual Review of Psychology* 40:493–531.

Kahl, Joseph A. 1968. *The Measurement of Modernism: A Study of Values in Brazil and Mexico.* Austin: University of Texas Press.

Kashima, Yoshihisa, and Harry C. Triandis. 1986. The self-serving bias as a coping strategy: A cross-cultural study. *Journal of Cross-Cultural Psychology* 17:83–97.

Kiecolt, K. Jill. 1988. Recent developments in attitudes and social structure. *Annual Review of Sociology* 14:381–403.

Kohn, Melvin L. 1969. *Class and Conformity: A Study in Values.* Homewood, IL: Dorsey Press.

———. 1989a. Cross-national research as an analytic strategy. Pp. 77–102 in *Cross-National Research in Sociology,* ed. M. L. Kohn. Newbury Park, CA: Sage.

———. 1989b. Introduction. Pp. 17–31 in *Cross-National Research in Sociology,* ed. Melvin L. Kohn. Newbury Park, CA: Sage.

———. 1989c. Social structure and personality: A quintessentially sociological approach to social psychology. *Social Forces* 68:26–33.

Kohn, Melvin L., and Carmi Schooler. 1969. Class, occupation, and orientation. *American Sociological Review* 34:659–678.

——— (with the collaboration of Joanne Miller, Karen A. Miller, Carrie Schoenbach, and Ronald Schoenberg). 1983. *Work and Personality: An Inquiry into the Impact of Social Stratification.* Norwood, NJ: Ablex.

Kohn, Melvin L., Atsushi Naoi, Carrie Schoenbach, Carmi Schooler, and Kazimierz M. Slomczynski. 1990. Position in the class structure and psychological functioning in the United States, Japan, and Poland. *American Journal of Sociology* 95: 964–1008.

Kohn, Melvin L., and Kazimierz M. Slomczynski. 1990. *Social Structure and Self-Direction: A Comparative Analysis of the United States and Poland.* Cambridge, MA: Blackwell.

Kohn, Melvin L., Kazimierz M. Slomczynski, Krystyna Janicka, Valery Khmelko, Bogdan W. Mach, Vladimir Paniotto, and Wojciech Zaborowski. 1992. Social structure and personality under conditions of radical social change: A comparative study of Poland and Ukraine. Paper presented at a plenary session of International Sociological Association's Joint Symposium on Comparative Sociology and the Sociology of Organizations, Kurashiki City, Japan.

Kroeber, Alfred L., and Clyde Kluckhohn. 1952. Culture: A critical review of concepts and definitions. *Papers of the Peabody Museum* 47:1–223.

Kuechler, Manfred. 1987. The utility of surveys for cross-national research. *Social Science Research* 16:229–244.

Kukla, Andre. 1988. Cross-cultural psychology in a post-empiricist era. Pp. 141–152 in *The Cross-Cultural Challenge to Social Psychology,* ed. M. H. Bond. Newbury Park, CA: Sage.

Kumagai, Hisa A. 1988. Ki: The "fervor of vitality" and the subjective self. *Symbolic Interaction* 11: 175–190.

Lerner, Daniel. 1958. *The Passing of Traditional Society.* Glencoe, IL: Free Press.

Leung, Kwok, and Michael H. Bond. 1989. On the empirical identification of dimensions for cross-cultural comparisons. *Journal of Cross-Cultural Psychology* 20:133–151.

Lincoln, James R., and Arne L. Kalleberg. 1990. *Culture, Control, and Commitment: A Study of Work Organization and Work Attitudes in the United States and Japan.* Cambridge, UK: Cambridge University Press.

Lonner, Walter J. 1980. The search for psychological universals. Pp. 143–204 in *Handbook of Cross-Cultural Psychology, 1: Perspectives,* ed. H. C. Triandis and W. W. Lambert. Boston: Allyn and Bacon.

Lonner, Walter J., and John W. Berry, eds. 1986. *Field Methods in Cross-Cultural Research.* Newbury Park, CA: Sage.

Luke, Timothy W. 1991. The discourse of development: A genealogy of "developing nations" and the discipline of modernity. *Current Perspectives in Social Theory* 11:71–293.

Mach, Bogdan, and Wlodzimierz Wesolowski. 1986. *Social Mobility and the Theory of Social Structure.* London: Routledge & Kegan Paul.

Markus, Hazel R., and S. Kitiyama. 1991. Culture and the self: Implications for cognition, emotion, and motivation. *Psychological Review* 98:224–253.

Messick, David M. 1988a. Coda. Pp. 286–289 in *The Cross-Cultural Challenge to Social Psychology,* ed. M. H. Bond. Newbury Park, CA: Sage.

———. 1988b. On the limitations of cross-cultural research in social psychology. Pp. 41–47 in *The Cross-Cultural Challenge to Social Psychology,* ed. M. H. Bond. Newbury Park, CA: Sage.

Milgram, Stanley. 1974. *Obedience to Authority.* New York: Harper & Row.

Miller, Joanne, Kazimierz M. Slomczynski, and Melvin L. Kohn. 1985. Continuity of learning-generalization: The effect of men's intellective process in the United States and Poland. *American Journal of Sociology* 91:593–615.

Miller, Joanne, Kazimierz M. Slomczynski, and Ronald J. Schoenberg. 1981. Assessing comparability of measurement in cross-national research: Authoritarian-conservatism in different socio-cultural settings. *Social Psychology Quarterly* 44:178–191.

Miller, Karen A. 1978. Women and modernity: A response to Papanek. *American Journal of Sociology* 83:1511–1513.

Mizuno, Ichiu. 1974. Kaikyu kaisokenkyu no kadai to hoho (The problem and method of research on class and status). *Hokkaido Rodo Kenkyu* 113:38–49.

Naoi, Atsushi, and Carmi Schooler. 1985. Occupational conditions and psychological functioning in Japan. *American Journal of Sociology* 90:729–752.

Naoi, Michiko, and Carmi Schooler. 1990. Psychological consequences of occupational conditions among Japanese wives. *Social Psychology Quarterly* 53:100–116.

Nowak, Stefan. 1989. Comparative studies and social theory. Pp. 34–56 in *Cross-National Research in Sociology,* ed. M. L. Kohn. Newbury Park, CA: Sage.

Ohashi, Ryuken. 1971. *Nihon no Kaikyu Kosei* (Japan's Class Composition). Tokyo: Iwanami Shoten.

Oyama, Nao. 1990. Some recent trends in Japanese values: Beyond the individual-collective dimension. *International Sociology* 5:445–459.

Papanek, Hanna. 1978. Comment on Gusfield's review essay on *Becoming Modern. American Journal of Sociology* 83:1507–1511.

Peabody, Dean. 1985. *National Characteristics.* Cambridge, UK: Cambridge University Press.

Pearlin, Leonard I. 1971. *Class Context and Family Relations: A Cross-National Study.* Boston: Little, Brown.

Pearlin, Leonard I., and Melvin L. Kohn. 1966. Social class, occupation, and parental values: A cross-national study. *American Sociological Review* 31: 466–479.

Pepitone, Albert. 1986. Culture and the cognitive paradigm in social psychology. *Australian Journal of Psychology* 38:245–256.

Pike, Kenneth L. 1967. *Language in Relation to a Unified Theory of the Structure of Human Behavior.* The Hague: Mouton.

Portes, Alejandro. 1973. Modernity and development: A critique. *Comparative International Development* 8:247–279.

———. 1975. Trends in international research cooperation: The Latin American case. *American Sociologist* 10:131–140.

Przeworski, Adam, and Henry Teune. 1970. *The Logic of Comparative Social Inquiry.* New York: Wiley.

Ragin, Charles. 1989. New directions in comparative research. Pp. 57–76 in *Cross-National Research in Sociology,* ed. M. L. Kohn. Newbury Park, CA: Sage.

Robinson, Robert V., and Jonathan Kelley. 1979. Class as conceived by Marx and Dahrendorf: Effects on income inequality and politics in the United States and Great Britain. *American Sociological Review* 44:38–58.

Rodrigues, A. 1982. Replication: A neglected type of research in social psychology. *Intra-American Journal of Psychology* 16:91–109.

Rokkan, Stein. 1970. Cross-cultural, cross-societal, and cross-national research. In *Main Trends of Research in the Human and the Social Sciences.* Paris: UNESCO.

Sampson, E. E. 1978. Scientific paradigms and social values: Wanted—A scientific revolution. *Journal of Personality and Social Psychology* 36: 1332–1343.

———. 1985. The decentralization of identity: Toward a revised concept of personal and social order. *American Psychologist* 40:1203–1212.

———. 1988. The debate on individualism: Indigenous psychologies of the individual and their role in personal and societal functioning. *American Psychologist* 43:15–22.

Sarapata, Adam. 1985. Researchers' habits and orientations as factors which condition international cooperation in research. *Science of Science* 5:157–182.

Scheuch, Erwin K. 1967. Society as context in cross-cultural comparisons. *Social Science Information* 6:7–23.

———. 1989. Theoretical implications of comparative survey research: Why the wheel of cross-cultural methodology keeps on being reinvented. *International Sociology* 4:147–167.

Schnaiberg, Allan. 1970. Measuring modernism: Theoretical and empirical explorations. *American Journal of Sociology* 76:399–425.

Schooler, Carmi. 1984. Psychological effects of complex environments during the life span: A review and theory. *Intelligence* 8:259–281.

———. 1990a. The individual in Japanese history: Parallels to and divergences from the European experience. *Sociological Forum* 5:569–594.

———. 1990b. Individualism and the historical and social-structural determinants of people's concerns over self-directedness and efficacy. Pp. 19–49 in *Self-Directedness: Cause and Effects Throughout the Life Course,* ed. J. Rodin, C. Schooler, and K. W. Schaie. Hillsdale, NJ: Erlbaum.

Schooler, Carmi, and Atsushi Naoi. 1988. The psychological effects of traditional and of economically peripheral job settings in Japan. *American Journal of Sociology* 94:335–355.

Schwartz, Shalom H. 1992. Universals in the content and structure of values: Theoretical advances and empirical tests in 20 countries. Pp. 1–65 in *Advances in Experimental Social Psychology,* vol. 25, ed. M. Zanna. Orlando: Academic.

———. In press. Cultural dimensions of values: Toward an understanding of national differences. In *Individualism and Collectivism: Theory and Methods,* ed. V. Kim and H. C. Triandis. Newbury Park, CA: Sage.

Seligman, M. E. P., L. Y. Abramson, A. Semmel, and C. Baeyer. 1979. Depressive attributional style. *Journal of Abnormal Psychology* 88:242–247.

Sharon, Irit, and Yehuda Amir. 1988. Cross-cultural replications: A prerequisite for the validation of social-psychological laws. Pp. 96–108 in *The Cross-Cultural Challenge to Social Psychology,* ed. M. H. Bond. Newbury Park, CA: Sage.

Sinha, D. 1983. Cross-cultural psychology: A view from the Third World. Pp. 3–17 in *Expositions in Cross-Cultural Psychology,* ed. J. B. Deregowski, S. Dziurawiec, and R. C. Annis. Lisse: Swets & Zeitlinger.

Slomczynski, Kazimierz M., Joanne Miller, and Melvin L. Kohn. 1981. Stratification, work, and values: A Polish-United States comparison. *American Sociological Review* 46:720–744.

Spenner, Kenneth I. 1988. Social stratification, work, and personality. *Annual Review of Sociology* 14: 69–97.

Steven, Rob. 1983. *Classes in Contemporary Japan.* Cambridge, UK: Cambridge University Press.

Swann, W. B., and S. J. Read. 1981a. Acquiring self-knowledge: The search for feedback that fits. *Journal of Personality and Social Psychology* 41: 1119–1128.

———. 1981b. Self verification processes: How we sustain our self-conceptions. *Journal of Experimental Social Psychology* 17:351–372.

Tedeschi, James T. 1988a. How does one describe a platypus? An outsider's questions for cross-cultural psychology. Pp. 14–28 in *The Cross-Cultural Challenge to Social Psychology,* ed. M. H. Bond. Newbury Park, CA: Sage.

———. 1988b. A second look at the platypus: A reprise. Pp. 282–285 in *The Cross-Cultural Challenge to Social Psychology,* ed. M. H. Bond. Newbury Park, CA: Sage.

Triandis, Harry C. 1982. Review of *Culture's Consequences: International Differences in Work-Related Values. Human Organization* 41:86–90.

———. 1988. Cross-cultural contributions to theory in social psychology. Pp. 122–140 in *The Cross-Cultural Challenge to Social Psychology,* ed. M. H. Bond. Newbury Park, CA: Sage.

———. 1990. Cross-cultural studies of individualism and collectivism. Pp. 41–133 in *Nebraska Symposium on Motivation 1989,* ed. J. Berman. Lincoln: University of Nebraska Press.

Triandis, Harry C., and John W. Berry, eds. 1980. *Handbook of Cross-Cultural Psychology, 2: Methodology.* Boston: Allyn and Bacon.

Trimble, Joseph E. 1988. Putting the etic to work: Applying social-psychological principles in cross-cultural settings. Pp. 109–121 in *The Cross-Cultural Challenge to Social Psychology,* ed. M. H. Bond. Newbury Park, CA: Sage.

Walker, Henry A., and Bernard P. Cohen. 1985. Scope statements: Imperatives for evaluating theory. *American Sociological Review* 50:288–301.

Wallerstein, Immanuel. 1974. The rise and future demise of the world capitalist system: Concepts for comparative analysis. *Comparative Studies in Social History* 16:287–415.

———. 1976. Modernization: Requiescat in pace. Pp. 131–135 in *The Uses of Controversy in Sociology,* ed. Lewis A. Coser and Otto N. Larsen. New York: Free Press.

Warwick, Donald P. 1980. The politics and ethics of cross-cultural research. Pp. 319–371 in *Handbook of Cross-Cultural Psychology, 1: Perspectives,* ed. H. C. Triandis and W. W. Lambert. Boston: Allyn and Bacon.

Weber, Max. [1904] 1958. *The Protestant Ethic and the Spirit of Capitalism.* New York: Scribner's.

Wright, Erik Olin. 1976. Class boundaries in advanced capitalist societies. *New Left Review* 98:3–41.

———. 1978. *Class, Crisis, and the State.* London: New Left.

———. 1985. *Classes.* London: Verso.

Yang, Kuo-Shu. 1981. Social orientation and individual modernity among Chinese students in Taiwan. *Journal of Social Psychology* 113:159–170.

———. 1988. Will societal modernization eventually eliminate cross-cultural psychological differences? Pp. 67–85 in *The Cross-Cultural Challenge to Social Psychology,* ed. M. H. Bond. Newbury Park, CA: Sage.

CHAPTER 16

Development and Socialization of Children and Adolescents

WILLIAM A. CORSARO
DONNA EDER

Psychologists and sociologists who study human development and socialization have often ignored, rejected, or coopted important theoretical and empirical developments outside their respective disciplines. Recently, however, a number of scholars have noted the diversity of positions on human development in both psychology and sociology, stressed the importance of both congruities and incongruities of psychological and sociological approaches, and called for intellectual pluralism (Featherman and Lerner 1985; Hurrelmann 1988). In the spirit of this call for pluralism, we differentiate various approaches within and across the two disciplines in terms of their emphasis on individual as opposed to collective aspects of human development. We then consider important theoretical and empirical work on development and socialization from the preschool years through adolescence and end with discussion of what we see as new directions in theory and research in this area.

PSYCHOLOGICAL THEORIES OF HUMAN DEVELOPMENT

Theories of human development in psychology are primarily concerned with intraindividual change—the individual's acquisition of skills and knowledge and general adaptation to the environment. However, psychological theories vary considerably regarding: (1) their perceptions of individuals as active or passive; (2) the importance they place on the social environment and social interaction;

and (3) their conceptions of the nature of development. Here, we briefly consider several traditional theories and then discuss more recent theoretical work in some detail.

Behaviorists (Skinner 1969) have a mechanistic view of development in which primarily passive individuals are shaped by environmental influences (both physical and social) in a probabilistic and cumulative process. Although psychoanalytic theorists (Freud 1949), like behaviorists, see individuals as basically passive, they espouse an organismic model of development in which individuals move through a series of stages marked by their emotional working out of innate sexual and aggressive drives. While cognitive developmentalists share the organismic model in that they see change as intrinsically motivated and occurring in a stage-like fashion, they differ from Freudians and behaviorists in that they have a much more active view of the developing organism. For example, cognitive developmental theorists such as Piaget (1950) argue that children interpret, organize, and use information from the environment and in the process acquire or construct adult skills and knowledge.

While contemporary behaviorists and psychoanalytic theorists share the basic models of their predecessors, they have clearly moved to a more active view of the individual and recognize the importance of social factors in human development (Bandura 1986; Bowlby 1980; Erikson 1963). A similar trend has also occurred in cognitive developmental theory. A closer review is warranted because many of these theorists have begun to consider seriously the importance of social interactive and collective processes for individual development.

Contemporary Constructivist Theories

Much recent work by constructivists seeks to extend Piagetian theory into the areas of emotional and social development. For example, Selman (1980) attempts to show how children's development of social skills and knowledge moves through a set of stages that are parallel to and affected by stages of intellectual development identified in Piaget's classic work. While some theorists call for specific refinements in Piagetian theory, such as the notion of distinct domains of development (Turiel 1983) or the synthesis of Piagetian with related theories (Youniss 1980), others argue for a more radical break from key Piagetian assumptions. Here Piaget's insistence on a stagelike model of development, his emphasis on individual "cognitive" activity as the impetus for development, and his parallelistic conception of the connection between social and intellectual development are called into question. These theorists look instead to the Soviet psychologist Vygotsky, building on his "general genetic law of cultural development" (Wertsch 1989, 18), which states that every function of the child's cultural development emerges at the interpsychological level (between people) before moving to the intrapsychological level (within the child) (Vygotsky 1978, 57).

One group of European developmental psychologists stress the importance of social context, language or discourse, and social interaction for children's cognitive and social development (Doise and Mugny 1984; Donaldson 1978; Dunn 1988). The Scottish psychologist Donaldson (1978; see also Light 1986) criticizes standard Piagetian experimental tasks and demonstrates that children's true cognitive abilities can be revealed only in situations "which make human sense to the child, i.e., when the cognitive task is set within a context which is fully intelligible to the child as a social interchange" (Light 1986, 175).

While still primarily concerned with cognitive and intellectual development as investigated by experimental methods, a group of French and Italian psychologists (Doise and Mugny 1984; Mugny and Carugati 1989) move beyond Donaldson's critique and offer a more radical revision of Piagetian theory. These theorists accept Piaget's conception of intellectual activity as coordination, but they argue that such coordination "is not only individual but to an equal extent social in nature" and that "coordinations between individuals are the source of individual coordinations," with the former preceding and producing the latter (Doise and Mugny 1984, 23). In this view cognitive development is seen as a "spiral of causality" in that "participation in social interactions ensures the formation of new, more balanced, cognitive instruments, which enable the child to participate in further, more complex, interactions, which in turn enable new cognitive formulations" (Mugny and Carugati 1989, 5). Central to this process are sociocognitive conflicts. While Piagetian theorists have long stressed the importance of conflict for creating disequilibriums and providing clues for the elaboration of new cognitive structures and skills, Doise and Mugny (1984, 160) argue that such conflicts and their resolutions are not merely cognitive but relational in that they naturally emerge in children's social interactions with adults and peers. What is crucial to cognitive development from this perspective is a social coordination of conflicting viewpoints leading to "collectively thought-out resolutions" (Mugny and Carugati 1989, 10).

While these theorists note the similarity of their views to those of Vygotsky and that such collective resolutions always occur "within a tissue of complex social relations" (Mugny and Carugati 1989, 10), their primary emphasis is on the outcomes of these collective processes for cognitive development. In contrast the British psychologist Judy Dunn (1988) focuses directly on the nature of interpersonal relations in her work on the beginnings of social understanding. The key to Dunn's "relationship" model is her emphasis on the young child's recognition of self-interests and developing sense of efficacy and control. This self-interest not only creates sociocognitive conflict favorable to further cognitive development, it also produces a tension between the child and other family members that affects both emotional and social development.

Sociocultural Theories

The work of another group of American psychologists influenced by Vygotsky can best be seen as offering a sociocultural approach to child development (Bruner 1986; Wertsch 1989). Central to the sociocultural approach are Vygotsky's concepts of "semiotically mediated activity" and the "zone of proximal development." According to Vygotsky, human activity is inherently mediational in that it is carried out with language and other cultural tools. A significant proportion of children's everyday activities take place in the zone of proximal development: *the distance between the actual developmental level as determined by independent problem solving and the level of potential development as determined through problem solving under adult guidance or in collaboration with more capable peers* (Vygotsky 1978, 86, emphasis in original). "Interactions in the zone of proximal development," argue Rogoff et al., "are the crucible of development and culture, in that they allow children to participate in activities that would be impossible for them alone, using cultural tools that themselves must be adapted to the specific activity at hand, and thus both passed along to and transformed by new generations" (1989, 211). Thus, the model of development is one in which children gradually appropriate the adult world through the communal processes of sharing and creating culture, and much of the work of sociocultural theorists has investigated these processes across cultures and the life span (Lave 1988; Rogoff 1990).

Ecological Systems and Life Span Theories

The final group of psychologists we consider here present ecological and life span views of human development. Although the views of these two groups overlap considerably, their theoretical models and research traditions have developed independently. Given the holistic and eclectic nature of the ecological and life span views, summarizing their basic tenets is no easy task. Take, for example, the definition of the ecological approach offered by its main proponent, Urie Bronfenbrenner: "The ecology of human development is the scientific study of the progressive, mutual accommodation, *throughout the life course,* between an active, growing human being, and the changing properties of the immediate settings in which the developing person lives, as this process is affected by the relations between these settings, and by the larger contexts in which the settings are embedded" (1989, 188).

There are several things to note about this definition. First is that there is a focus on "mutual accommodation" (i.e., "the set of processes through which properties of the person and environment interact to produce constancy and change" in the person over time; Bronfenbrenner 1989, 189) as opposed to "intraindividual change" (i.e., the developing organism's acquisition of more and more complex skills and knowledge). Second, although stressing change over the life course, Bronfenbrenner and associates are most interested in the effects of various levels of social context on children's development as such contexts are experienced historically in line with various types of age grading. In fact, the specification of the structural complexity of environmental contexts (e.g., distinctions among microsystems, mesosystems, exosystems, and macrosystems; see Bronfenbrenner 1979, 1989) and their effects on development has been the main concern of ecological systems theorists.

Since the mid-1970s there has been a substantial increase in research and theory related to life span developmental psychology in the United States and German-speaking countries of Western Europe (Baltes, Reese, and Lipset 1980; Brandtstädter 1984; Lerner 1984). The life span perspective "is concerned with the description, explanation, and modification (optimization) of developmental processes in the human life course from conception to death" (Baltes, Reese, and Lipset 1980, 66) and is based on a number of related assumptions and propositions. First is that development is a lifelong process and the task of life span research is "to identify the form and course of these behavioral changes as they occur at varying points in the life course, and to establish the pattern of temporal order and interrelationships" (Baltes, Reese, and Lipset 1980, 70). A second assumption, closely related to the first, is that both ontogenetic (age-related) and biocultural change are crucial to the life span perspective. These two assumptions lead life span theorists to adopt a pluralistic view of the nature and explanation of development. Rejecting irreversible, end-state models of development, life span theorists stress interindividual variability and plasticity (Lerner 1984) and argue that "developmental processes can be linear, multilinear or discontinuous" (Baltes, Reese, and Lipsitt 1980, 73). Life span theorists also reject single or primary cause theories of development, arguing that causal elements (inner biological, individual psychological, societal, cultural, etc.) are embedded at multiple levels of being and that "at any one point in time variables and processes from any and all of these variables may contribute to human functioning" (Lerner 1984, 24).

Given the pluralistic character of the life span orientation, it is not surprising that there have been attempts to develop a more general integrative framework of human development (Overton and Reese 1973). This more general "contextualist" paradigm has been contrasted with organismic and mechanistic perspectives (Lerner 1984, 24–31). The empirical utility of this highly abstract contextualist framework remains open to question, however, given its "everything is related to everything else" character.

SOCIOLOGICAL THEORIES OF SOCIALIZATION

Given psychology's movement away from a singular focus on intraindividual change as primarily a linear process from immaturity to maturity and toward more pluralistic models that stress development in context, it is becoming more difficult to differentiate psychological from sociological approaches to human development and socialization. One key difference is the use of the terms themselves. Sociologists are much more likely to use the term *socialization,* and their definitions of *socialization* "tend to emphasize the ways in which the individual learns to fit into society, and, to a lesser degree, how this process changes not only the individual but society as well" (Bush and Simmons 1981, 135). Traditionally, most sociologists have viewed the socialization process at either the macrolevel (as a societal function or a form of social control) or microlevel (the individual's acquisition of basic skills and knowledge for integration into the social structure). While a number of scholars have attempted to bridge these two levels via abstract integrative models (Habermas 1979; Parsons 1964; see Hurrelmann 1988 for a discussion of these attempts), since the mid-1980s there has been a growing dissatisfaction with the general acceptance of this bifurcation and a movement toward viewing socialization as a process of collective action and interpretive reproduction (Corsaro 1992; Featherman and Lerner 1985).

Macrolevel Approaches to Socialization

Inkeles, building on the work of Levy (1952), has argued that socialization is a functional requisite of society and that the overwhelming majority of other requisites (role differentiation and assignment, shared cognitive orientations, etc.) are directly dependent on adequate socialization (1968, 81–83). Proponents of this structural-functionalist view are chiefly concerned with how various social structural conditions of societies (e.g., age grading, Eisenstadt 1956) ensure the production of competent adults.

Other macrolevel theorists take a critical view of these socialization functions, viewing them as mechanisms of social control and the social reproduction of class inequalities (Bernstein 1981; Bourdieu and Passeron 1977; Bowles and Gintis 1976). These reproductive theories focus primarily on the nature of access to cultural resources and the differential treatment of individuals in social institutions (especially the educational system) that lead to socialization outcomes in line with the prevailing class system.

Both functionalist and reproductive theories have been criticized for their overconcentration on outcomes of socialization, deterministic views of society, and underestimation of the active and innovative capacities of social agents. In reproductive theories, as Willis argues, the "actually varied, complex, and creative field of human consciousness, culture, and capacity is reduced to the dry abstraction of structural determination" (1981, 204).

Social Structure and Personality

An intermediate level of analysis of socialization processes can be seen in work on social structure and personality (House 1981). Theoretical and empirical work in this area frequently postulates socialization as a key concept or variable for understanding the effects of society on the individual. This work often escapes the deterministic nature of more macro theories by focusing on how specific features of social structure affect interpersonal processes in various contexts of socialization (Elkin and Handel 1984; Gecas 1981). For example, there has been a great deal of work on socialization practices across cultures and across social class groups within cultures. Perhaps the best known of this work is that of Kohn (1969), who has impressively demonstrated how occupational conditions affect values (most especially those related to self-esteem and efficacy). However, Kohn's and related work has only suggested, rather than offered detailed evidence on, how these values are passed on to children through socialization practices in the family.

Another important line of inquiry in the area of social structure and personality is theoretical and empirical work on the life course (Elder 1974, 1985; Elder and Caspi 1988). From the life course perspective, "multiple influences shape the contours of human growth and development, linkages between social change and lives provide microtheories or explanations regarding the influence of social change, and people represent both the agent and consequence of their changing life paths"

(Elder and Caspi 1988, 77–78). The life course approach, thus, overcomes the static nature of cross-sectional studies and captures the complexities of socialization and personality development across generations and key historical periods.

Sociological work on the life course shares a number of basic assumptions with life span psychology (e.g., development as a lifelong process, a pluralistic view of the nature of change and development, and an interdisciplinary blend of concepts and methods). A major difference, however, relates to the basic unit of analysis. While life span theorists are primarily interested in individual change and development, life course theorists examine the trajectories and transitions of collectives or cohorts of individuals over historical periods and positions in the social structure.

In addressing this difference, Featherman and Lerner (1985) offer an interesting and promising framework for a coordinated agenda for theory and research on human development and socialization, which they refer to as developmental contextualism. Developmental contextualists view human development as a person-population process. The person-population model "represents the interactive processes that give rise to development (and aging) as residing in the evolving species gene pool, changing sociocultural institutions of a given society, and both individual and collective action" (Featherman and Lerner 1985, 662). Although the elements of the model are too complex (and, in some aspects, vague and underdeveloped) to pursue here, the model holds a great deal of promise because it avoids the reductionism of individualistic theories on the one hand and the determinism of social structural approaches on the other. A key issue is Featherman and Lerner's claim that while stressing the conditioning roles of a population's biology and sociocultural institutions, their model also "underscores the ways in which voluntaristic action can create developmental sequences" (1985, 665). Exactly how such voluntaristic action is related to the developing competencies of individuals (especially linguistic and communicative abilities) and to the nature of microcontexts of everyday life is left open to question. It is these concerns that are of most interest to the interactionist and interpretive approaches to socialization, discussed below.

Interactionist Approaches to Socialization

Interactionist approaches to socialization stem primarily from the social philosophy of G. H. Mead and symbolic interactionist theory as derived from the work of Mead and others (Mead 1934; Cooley 1922). Mead's views of the genesis of self are most central to theories of socialization. According to Mead, the individual experiences him/herself indirectly from the standpoints and responses of other members of the same social group. In this sense, the individual acquires a sense of self "by taking the attitudes of other individuals toward himself within a social environment or context of experience and behavior in which both he and they are involved" (Mead 1934, 138; see also Cottrell 1969).

It is not surprising, then, that Mead sees the genesis of self-consciousness as beginning with the child's attempts to step outside him/herself by imitating others and reaching completion when the child, through participation in games with rules, develops the ability to take on the organized social attitudes of the group to which he/she belongs. However, in Mead's stages in the genesis of self, children are acquiring more than a sense of self, they are also acquiring or "appropriating" (Vygotsky 1978) conceptions of social structure and developing a collective or group identity that is maintained throughout childhood.

Given Mead's interest in the genesis of self, it is surprising that there has been so little research in the area of childhood socialization from the symbolic interactionist perspective. While a number of symbolic interactionists have offered important insights to socialization processes in the family and peer group in the work on self and identity, self-concept, and self-esteem (Gecas 1972; Kuhn 1960; M. Rosenberg 1986a, 1986b, 1989; Stryker 1968, 1989), two theorists have offered more detailed views of socialization from a symbolic interactionist perspective: Denzin (1977), on early childhood, and Fine (1987), on preadolescence. According to Denzin, socialization "from the standpoint of sym-

bolic interactionism, represents a fluid, shifting relationship between persons attempting to fit their lines of action together into some workable, interactive relationship" (1977, 2). Socialization is, therefore, a never-ending process that is always potentially problematic and constantly negotiated. As a result, Denzin argues that interactionists have little interest in development per se and prefer "instead a naturalistic account of the growth and emergence of self-awareness and self-consciousness in childhood" (1977, 10). In pursuing this naturalistic account, Denzin explores the worlds of childhood (in a family and preschool) and the negotiated order of these worlds in the interactions among children and between children and their caretakers.

Although Denzin has undoubtedly inspired other interactionists to consider children more seriously, it is fair to say that no research tradition or theoretical innovations on childhood socialization have resulted from his work. There are at least two reasons for this. First, Denzin works hard to differentiate the interactionist perspective from developmental psychology (especially from Piagetian theory and the work on language acquisition). Although there are clear differences in the assumptions of interactionists and developmental psychologists, there are also a number of common points that can lead to fruitful integration (Featherman and Learner 1985). Second, though Denzin argues for the need to study socialization processes, he is just as interested, if not more interested, in exploring "sociological issues of a symbolic interactionist nature that might be advanced through the study of young children and their caretakers" (1977, 58).

Gary Fine has employed symbolic interactionist theory to explore friendship relations and peer culture among preadolescents. Like Denzin, Fine stresses the importance of entering and documenting the worlds and cultures of young children. In contrast to Denzin, however, Fine moves beyond studying children primarily to clarify and extend basic concepts of symbolic interactionist theory. Fine uses ethnographic data on preadolescents (1987) and adolescents (1983, 1986) to develop important conceptual ideas regarding the creation and transmission of culture in small groups (1979), while at the same time linking his ideas to research and theory on socialization and culture in anthropology, folklore, and psychology.

Interpretive Approaches to Socialization

Influenced by general theoretical developments in sociology (Cicourel 1974; Giddens 1984; Goffman 1974), anthropology (Geertz 1973; Gumperz 1982), social psychology (Moscovici 1981), and developmental psychology (Bruner 1986; Vygotsky 1987), there has recently developed an interpretive approach to socialization (Corsaro 1992; Corsaro and Rizzo 1988; Ochs 1988; Schieffelin 1990; Wentworth 1980). From the interpretive approach, socialization is a collective process that occurs in a public rather than a private realm. This approach is essentially interpretive in that the child is viewed as the discoverer of a world endowed with meaning. From this perspective, the child begins life as a social being in an already defined social network; through the growth of communication and language, children, in interaction with others, construct their social worlds. In fact, it is within these microprocesses involving children's interactions with caretakers and peers that a conception of social development as a productive-reproductive complex (Cook-Gumperz and Corsaro 1986) becomes most apparent. In everyday interactions with others, young children employ the very communicative competencies they are in the process of acquiring and at the same time learn more about the culture that they, as coparticipants, are communally producing (Corsaro and Rizzo 1988; Ochs 1988).

Children's participation in cultural routines is an essential element of the interpretive approach. Routines are recurrent and predictable activities that are basic to day-to-day social life. The habitual, taken-for-granted character of routines provides actors with the security and shared understanding of belonging to a cultural group (Giddens 1984). On the other hand, this very predictability empowers routines, providing frames within which a wide range of sociocultural knowledge can be produced, displayed, and interpreted (Goffman

1974). In this way cultural routines serve as anchors that allow us to deal with ambiguities, the unexpected, and the problematic comfortably within the friendly confines of everyday life. It is for this reason that Giddens has argued that routinization "is vital to the psychological mechanisms whereby a sense of trust or ontological security is sustained in the daily activities of social life" (1984, xxiii).

The interpretive approach views development as reproductive rather than linear. From this perspective, children enter into a social nexus and, through interaction with others, establish social understandings that become fundamental social knowledge on which they continually build. Thus, the interpretive model extends the notion of stages by viewing development as a productive-reproductive process of increasing density and reorganization of knowledge that changes with the children's developing cognitive and language abilities and with changes in their social worlds. A major change in children's worlds is their movement outside the family. By interacting with playmates in preschool settings, children produce the first in a series of peer cultures in which childhood knowledge and practices are gradually transformed into the knowledge and skills necessary to participate in the adult world.

Interpretive theorists stress that the production of peer culture is neither a matter of simple imitation nor direct appropriation of the adult world. Children creatively appropriate information from the adult world to produce their own unique peer cultures. Such appropriation is creative in that it both extends or elaborates peer culture (transforms information from the adult world to meet the concerns of the peer world) and simultaneously contributes to the reproduction of the adult culture. This process of creative appropriation can be seen as *interpretive reproduction* in line with Giddens's (1984) notion of the duality of social structure. In his theory of structuration, Giddens argues that "the structural properties of social systems are both medium and outcome of the practices they recursively organize" (1984, 25). As a result, structure is seen as both constraining and enabling. Such a view of social structure can serve as a basis for the claim that socialization is a reproductive rather than a linear process. The process is reproductive in the sense that children do not merely individually internalize the external adult culture; rather they become a part of adult culture, that is, contribute to its reproduction, through their negotiations with adults and their creative production of a series of peer cultures with other children.

HISTORICAL TRENDS IN THEORIES OF HUMAN DEVELOPMENT

This review of psychological and sociological theories of human development reveals several important historical trends. First, there has been a definite movement toward an active view of the developing organism who both is influenced by and influences others. This trend is seen in the emergence of new theoretical approaches (constructivist, life span and life course, and interpretive) and in the refinement and expansion of more traditional orientations (behaviorism, cognitive developmental, macro or reproductive, and interactionist). Second, there has been growing appreciation of the fact that development or socialization is a lifelong process. Here the recent work of life span and life course theorists goes beyond the identification of the form and function of developmental changes over the life course. These theorists challenge end-state models, stressing the importance of interindividual variability and plasticity in human development. Similarly, the interpretive view of socialization argues that collective and social processes among peers (over the life course) is essential for human development and social reproduction. Third, there is an increasing recognition of the importance of societal and sociocultural context for human development. In psychology this recognition is most evident in Bronfenbrenner's ecological approach and sociocultural theories of development based on the work of Vygotsky. In sociology there has long been an emphasis on the effects of social structure on developmental outcomes. However, more recent approaches have attempted to link macro- and microlevel processes and to argue for the importance of cross-cultural and historical factors.

Overall, the general trend in theories of human development and socialization has been one of refinement and expansion of various models. Strongly held assumptions (e.g., the crucial explanatory power of reinforcement in behaviorism, the irreversibility of stages in cognitive developmental theory, and the deterministic bias in macrolevel theories of socialization in sociology) have been challenged, theoretical gaps have been filled, and ethnocentric Western-based conceptions have been criticized and refined. While we have not seen a Kuhnian revolution in theoretical work on human development and socialization, we have seen provocative debates and important theoretical progression.

CONTEMPORARY RESEARCH ON THE DEVELOPMENT AND SOCIALIZATION OF CHILDREN AND ADOLESCENTS

In the following sections we review current research on the development and socialization of children and adolescents in a variety of social contexts. Given the enormous quantity of research in this area, our review is by no means exhaustive. First, while there is a substantial body of research on socialization in anthropology, given our goal of integrating psychological and sociological orientations we are able to consider only a few recent anthropological studies. Second, we give more attention to studies in developmental psychology that stress the importance of social structure and culture for individual development and that are based on theoretical frameworks open to interdisciplinary cooperation and integration. In reviewing work by sociologists and anthropologists we concentrate primarily on those studies that focus on both processes and outcomes, rather than research that is primarily concerned with socialization outcomes.

Early Childhood and Preadolescence

Socialization in the Family. Most studies on family socialization concentrate primarily on developmental outcomes of children's experiences in the family. For example, there is a long history of research in psychology on the effects of attachment and emotional bonding (Bowlby 1980; Kagan 1984), socialization practices and parenting styles (Peterson and Rollins 1987), family disruption (Hetherington and Arasteh 1988), and the role of media events as mediated in the family (Huesmann and Eron 1986; Singer and Singer 1986) on individual development. Sociologists who study family socialization have also investigated these topics, but they usually view them as intervening variables that are affected by social structural and cultural conditions and processes of social change (Blake 1989; Furstenberg 1990; Furstenberg and Cherlin 1990; Powell and Steelman 1990). Given the vast literature in this area and coverage of related work in chapters 17, 18, and 20, we confine our review to a brief consideration of outcome studies related to value orientations, moral development, and achievement. We then turn to a more detailed review of research on socialization processes in the family.

Outcome Studies.   Most theoretical and empirical work on socialization outcomes focuses (either directly or indirectly) on the importance of parenting styles. Psychologists have studied the effects of various combinations of control and emotional support in parenting. Although measures used in various studies are not always consistent and the findings are complex and not easily summarized (see Peterson and Rollins 1987), what Baumrind (1973) has termed an "authoritative" parenting style (where parents are affectionate, sensitive to children's needs and rights, and generous in the use of positive reinforcement but also consistently place demands on their children) leads to a number of positive outcomes for children, including high self-esteem, internalization of adult values and standards, and high achievement motivation. Finally, parenting styles and features of early adult-child interaction play an important role in theories of children's moral development. Anthropologically based theories focus on language and cultural routines in caretaker-child interaction and stress the relative nature of morals and conventions across cultures (Shweder, Mahapatra, and Miller 1987). Most developmental psychologists, on the

other hand, see caretakers either as role models who foster moral development through processes of identification and attachment (Emde, Johnson, and Easterbrooks 1987) or as moral agents who create disequilibriums that motivate children actively to construct a system of moral concepts and judgments in a general stagelike fashion (Damon 1977; Kholberg 1969; Turiel, Killen, and Helwig 1987).

Sociologists often see parenting styles as affected by social structural variables such as class, education, and race or ethnicity and thus as "intervening variables" in models of social reproduction. While reproductive theorists relate parenting styles to the inculcation of culture capital, including specific cultural knowledge, taste, and styles of speaking and self-presentation (Bernstein 1981; Bourdieu 1984), theorists such as Kohn (1969) stress the importance of social class variations in parenting styles for instilling value orientations that stress independence, creativity, and aspirations for mobility. While Kohn's work has had a great deal of influence that goes far beyond the identification of the relationship between class and conformity (e.g., Colvin and Pauly 1983 on delinquency; Parcel and Menaghan 1990 on achievement), it is fair to say that his research focuses more on the relation between the nature and complexity of work or occupation and values than on how those values are actually transmitted in the family (see Gecas 1979 and McLoyd 1990 for reviews of Kohn's work and related studies on social class, race, and socialization).

Some of the most well-known work on the relation between family socialization and children's early academic achievement has examined the importance of social class and minority status. It is well documented that parental beliefs about their children's abilities and their aspirations for their children's success are positively related to children's academic achievement in the early grades (Alexander and Entwisle 1988; Entwisle and Hayduk 1982). However, even though numerous studies have shown that African American parents (regardless of social class) value schooling highly, have high ambitions for their children, and

strongly encourage their children's academic success (Alexander and Entwisle 1988; Stevenson,
Chen, and Uttal 1990), African American children
do not perform as well academically as white children beginning in the early elementary grades.
While some researchers argue that high aspirations
are not enough and point to the lack of parental
knowledge, resources, and community support
(Alexander and Entiwisle 1988; Thompson et al.
1992), others note that cultural differences as well
as poverty play an important role in both African
American children's transition to school and their
parents' support of and involvement in their children's early education (Heath 1983, 1989; Rosier
and Corsaro, 1993).

Process Studies.   Earlier we referred to the work
of Judy Dunn (1988) as representing one of the few
attempts in developmental psychology to examine
closely the importance of interpersonal relations in
the context of family life for young children's social and emotional development. Dunn used a combination of observational and interview methods to
capture key processes in children's socioemotional
development between the ages of one and three.
Dunn found strong evidence for the rapid growth of
assertive and resistant behavior by children in their
second year in dealings with parents and siblings.
These behaviors, in turn, led to conflicts and the
display of emotions. Dunn relates these findings to
children's discovery of misbehavior (including
emotional display) as a means of gaining control
over their parents. Dunn further develops the theoretical significance of these findings by arguing
that the "urgency of self-assertion in the face of
powerful others increases along with the child's
understanding" (1988, 176). Indeed, according to
Dunn, children's self-interest drives much of their
behavior in these early years. However, Dunn argues, it is not that young children simply want their
way, it is rather that they want to be effective
members of their families. In this view "children
are motivated to understand the social rules and
relationships of their cultural world *because they
need to get things done in their family relationships*" (1988, 189).

Recently there have been a number of important cross-cultural studies of early socialization in
the family that share a definite affinity with the
work of Dunn. A central feature of this work is the
focus on children's development of communicative
competence through their involvement in everyday
cultural routines in the family with both parents
and siblings (Dunn and Kendrick 1982; Heath
1983; Miller et al. 1990; Miller and Sperry 1987;
Ochs 1988; Schieffelin 1990; Schieffelin and
Ochs 1986; Schütze, Kreppner, and Paulsen 1986;
Whiting and Edwards 1988; Zukow 1989). These
studies provide important empirical data and theoretical insights on how: (1) young children's participation in recurrent and predictable interactional
routines is essential for the acquisition of language
and culture; (2) children's taking on of various
communicative positions in a variety of social
situations contributes to their acquisition of
knowledge of status and role through language use;
and (3) children's involvement in cultural routines
is crucial to their gradual acquisition of the ability
to recognize and express feelings in context.

Socialization in the Peer Group.   In this section
we briefly review studies on the effects of peer
interaction on children's socioemotional development and then consider interactive processes and
basic themes in young children's peer cultures. The
former is the main concern of psychologists, who
primarily focus on the outcomes (both positive and
negative) of peer interaction for individual development. Sociologists and anthropologists, on the
other hand, are most often interested in peer interaction and culture in its own right. While they do
not minimize the importance of individual development, their main goal is to develop a truly
sociological and cultural view of socialization as a
collective process of interpretive reproduction (Corsaro 1992).

Outcomes of Peer Interaction.   Recently there
have been numerous studies of the effects of peer
interaction on children's emotional, cognitive, and
social development (Brendt and Ladd 1989). Overall, research has demonstrated that peer interaction

from the toddler period through adolescence has positive effects on children's development of cognitive (Doise and Mugny 1984), emotional (Furman and Buhrmester 1985; Hartup and Sancilio 1986), social cognitive (Damon 1977; Rizzo and Corsaro 1988; Shantz 1987; Youniss 1980), communicative (Corsaro 1985; Corsaro and Rizzo 1988; Goodwin 1990; Musatti and Mueller 1985), and social (Corsaro 1985; Gottman 1986; J. Parker and J. Gottman 1989; Youniss 1980) skills and knowledge.

While this work clearly demonstrates the importance of peer relations for healthy development, there is a growing literature that has documented negative outcomes for children who have consistent problems in peer interaction. These children are socially rejected (often because of their own aggressive behavior) or fail to form friendships and withdraw because of shyness or a lack of self-confidence. Most of the work in this area is by clinical and developmental psychologists who attempt to evaluate whether or not rejected or withdrawn children are "at risk" for difficulty in later life (Asher and Coie 1990; Hartup and Moore 1990; J. Parker and S. Asher 1987). Overall, the findings from research in this area are complex and open to multiple interpretations. However, J. Parker and S. Asher's (1987) review of the many (retrospective and prospective) longitudinal studies of peer relations and risk has revealed that adolescent and young adults who have dropped out of school, established juvenile or adult criminal records, or developed psychological problems often have a history of pervasive and persistent peer rejection (results for individuals with histories of being shy or withdrawn in childhood were inconclusive). Parker and Asher (1987) note that these results are often interpreted in one of two ways: (1) the existence of an underlying disturbance (whose origin is biological, environmental, or some combination of the two) leads to aggressiveness and other types of deviant behavior, which results in problems in both childhood and adulthood or (2) deviant behavior such as aggressiveness (regardless of its source) leads to low peer acceptance, which means individuals miss opportunities to develop skills and

knowledge necessary for successful movement into adulthood. Parker and Asher (1987) argue that both of these models are over simplistic and make several recommendations to improve the sophistication of theory and research in this area (also see Asher and Coie 1990).

Processes and Themes in Peer Culture. Earlier we noted that the interpretive approach to childhood socialization maintains that children creatively appropriate information from the adult world to produce their own unique peer cultures. Such appropriation is creative in that it extends or elaborates peer culture (transforms information from the adult world to meet the concerns of the peer world) and simultaneously contributes to the reproduction of the adult world (see Corsaro 1992; Corsaro and Rizzo 1988 for examples of how processes in peer culture contribute to and extend the adult culture).

Although a wide range of features of the peer culture of young children has been identified, two central themes consistently appear: children make persistent attempts to *gain control* of their lives and to *share* that control with each other. In the preschool years there is an overriding concern with social participation and with challenging and gaining control over adult authority. Once children move into elementary school such challenging of adult authority persists, but there is also a gradual movement toward social differentiation within the peer group. This differentiation is marked by negotiations and conflicts as children attempt to gain control over the attitudes and behaviors of peers.

A consistent finding in studies of young children's peer interaction is that solitary play is rare; children expend considerable time and energy in establishing and maintaining peer contacts (Corsaro 1985; Rizzo 1989). Gaining access to play groups, maintaining joint action, and making friends are demanding tasks for young children (Corsaro 1979).

Once children gain access to play groups, they discover that it is in the course of shared play that the meaning of the concepts of friend and peer arise. For example, Corsaro (1985) found that nursery school children use their developing conception of friendship to build solidarity and mutual trust. On the other hand, while friendship serves these specific integrative functions for nursery school children, Rizzo (1989) reports that first-grade children appeared to have an internalized concept of friendship that served multiple functions in peer relations. Specifically, Rizzo found that they "attempted to determine the existence of friendship by comparing the internal concept with specific features of interactions with frequent playmates, to act in accordance with this concept when with their friends, and to object when their friends failed to live up to their expectations" (1989, 105). Rizzo argues further that disputes resulting from such objections not only helped the children obtain a better understanding of what they could expect from each other as friends, but also brought about intrapersonal reflection, resulting in development of unique insight into their own actions and roles as friends.

Several studies have identified peer routines that stress communal sharing and help children gain control over fears, confusions, and curiosities from the adult world: Corsaro's (1988) identification of an "approach-avoidance routine" among American and Italian children; Goodwin's (1990) study of negotiations in children's role play; Mishler (1979) study on "trading and bargaining" of six-year-olds at lunchtime in elementary school; and Katriel's (1987) analysis of ritualized sharing among Israeli children. Katriel's study is especially interesting because it demonstrates the importance of routines and rituals in children's culture and how such routines can contribute to the reproduction of adult society.

Children's attempts to challenge adult authority and gain control over their lives is a major aspect of peer culture from the earliest years. Once children enter child-care and education settings, they quickly develop a strong group identity (Corsaro 1985) that is strengthened by challenging and even mocking teachers and other adult caretakers (Corsaro 1985, 1990; Davies 1982). In addition, children produce a wide set of innovative routines and practices that indirectly challenge and circumvent adult authority (Corsaro 1990; Davies 1982; Nasaw 1985).

While social participation and friendship are central elements of peer culture, there is a clear pattern of increased differentiation and conflict in peer relations throughout childhood. The first sign of social differentiation is increasing gender separation. Gender segregation begins in preschool (Berentzen 1984) and becomes so dramatic in elementary school that "it is meaningful to speak of separate girls' and boys' worlds" (Thorne 1986, 167). Studies of these separate worlds show that boys interact in larger groups (Lever 1976), engage in more aggressive and competitive play (Best 1983; Goodwin 1990), and frequently organize their activities and relations around organized sports (Fine 1987; Lever 1976).

Thorne, however, argues that there is a tendency to exaggerate difference in much of the research and that the studies "ignore similarities, with little theoretical effort to integrate findings of both similarity and difference" (1986, 170). Thorne (1986, 1989, 1993) offers a social contextual approach that stresses variation in cross-gender contacts or "borderwork," traveling in the world of the other sex (e.g., "tomboys"), and situations of easeful cross-gender interaction. Thorne's work and recent research by Goodwin (1990) challenge many earlier findings regarding the lack of conflict and competition in girls' interactions and the simple structure of girls' peer play.

This recent research on conflict in girls' peer interaction reflects a growing interest in the role of conflict in children's friendships and peer culture (Shantz 1987). Studies of conflict in peer culture challenge the assumption that such behavior is inherently disruptive and disorderly, demonstrating that conflicts and disputes provide children with a rich arena for the development of language, interpersonal, and social organization skills and knowledge. Although preschool children frequently quarrel over possession of play materials and entry into play groups, they are also capable of highly complex arguments and debates regarding the nature of fantasy play and claims or opinions about their social and physical worlds (Corsaro and Rizzo 1988, 1990; Eisenberg and Garvey 1981). Research on peer conflict among elementary school children clearly shows how disputes are a basic means for constructing social order, cultivating, testing and maintaining friendships, and developing and displaying social identity (Corsare and Eder, 1990; Davies 1982; Fine 1987; Goodwin 1990; Katriel 1987; Maynard 1985; Rizzo 1989).

Adolescence

Historically, the strongest influences on adolescents were the institutions of family and work. However, throughout the twentieth century the amount of schooling for youth has continued to increase. Because adolescents spend much of their school time segregated from the world of adults as well as from young people of different ages, the influence of same-age peers has expanded along with the influence of schools (Elder 1985). These changes mean that socialization processes in adolescence will involve the creation of new patterns of thinking and acting as well as reflecting those of past generations. As adolescents spend more time with same-age peers, they have more opportunities to construct new cultural beliefs and styles of interaction. However, the segregation of youth from adults also serves to diminish their impact on adults, since socializing influences operate in both directions (Elder 1985). This leaves open the opportunity for unique cohort experiences.

Increased separation from adults in the family and workplace does not mean adolescents will be exempt from influences of the larger society. Many patterns of behavior and thinking are part of our language as well as part of the institution of schooling. Since these patterns are more resistant to change, peer processes involving language or taking place in school settings are still likely to reflect the values and concerns of the larger society. Adolescents are also aware of the opportunities and constraints in the workplace, so that even if they are not part of the work force, the realities of the work force are already beginning to influence their lives. Finally, along with introducing new fads, the media often are responsible for reproducing societal values and concerns, thereby contributing to stability as well as to change in adolescent behavior.

Socialization Processes in the Family. During early adolescence, parental influence decreases relative to the influence of peers (Berndt 1979), yet throughout adolescence most children continue to report high levels of attachment to parents (Kandel and Lesser 1972; Youniss and Smollar 1985), with greater closeness reported in the early 1960s and early 1980s as compared to the 1970s (Sebald 1986). To understand better the type and extent of parental influence during adolescence, studies have attempted to identify parenting behaviors that have negative or positive consequences for adolescents as well as to examine different parenting styles.

Some studies have focused on parenting styles that put adolescents at greater risk for delinquent or deviant behavior. For example, adolescents who perceive their parents as exerting less control or being less attached to them are more likely to join delinquent or party subcultures (Hagan 1991). Failure to maintain close relationships with adolescent children also has been found to lead to greater delinquency through greater involvement with deviant peers (Marcos, Bahr, and Johnson 1986; Massey and Krohn, 1986) and greater drug use through such involvements (Kandel and Andrews 1987).

On the other hand, high parental academic expectations have been found to enhance adolescents' academic aspirations and achievements (Sewell and Hauser 1975). Academic performance has also been shown to be enhanced by parental monitoring and efforts to involve adolescents in joint decision making (Dornbusch et al. 1987). In addition, participation in joint decision making has been found to enhance self-confidence (Grotevant and Cooper 1986) and reduce delinquency (Dornbusch and Ritter 1991). Adolescents' feelings of "mattering" or "making a difference" to their parents have also been found to enhance self-esteem (Rosenberg 1985). Finally, self-confidence has been found to be strengthened by nonconflictual parental interaction, while other aspects of adolescent competence, such as intellectual commitment and dependability, were strengthened more by parents' stress on achievement, consistent discipline, and fair treatment (Clausen 1991).

Other research has attempted to examine different types of parenting styles and their relative effectiveness. In one study, the most common style of parenting as perceived by their adolescent children was democratic, used by 31 percent of fathers and 35 percent of mothers (Elder 1985). Fathers who were not democratic were more likely to be perceived as autocratic or authoritarian while mothers were more likely to be perceived as egalitarian or permissive. While social class differences were not large, lower-class parents were more likely to be perceived as being autocratic or authoritarian, especially by junior high school girls.

A democratic style of parenting led to adolescents having the best sense of parental expectations as well as considering the expectations to be "just right" (neither too high or too low). If their parents also provided explanations for their decisions, adolescents associated greater parental influence and satisfaction with their own degree of independence. Providing explanations was also important for adolescents with parents who used a more controlling style. These adolescents reported having a better sense of parental expectations, a better sense of the standards being appropriate, and greater satisfaction with their degree of independence (Elder 1985).

In a recent, in-depth study Youniss and Smollar (1985) identified differences in the ways fathers and mothers relate to their daughters and sons. The findings revealed that most father-daughter interactions are asymmetrical and tend to consist of rule making, rule enforcing, and giving advice and practical information. In contrast, daughters are more likely to confide in personal matters with their mothers and receive personal as well as practical advice. Fathers' authority and expertise were found to apply mainly to academic performance and future plans, while that of mothers relate to household rules, emotional states, and interpersonal issues. Given the greater degree of subjectivity in the latter domains, mothers engaged in more cooperative interaction styles with daughters than did fathers. While daughters report symmetrical relations (e.g., going places together, talking) with parents as most enjoyable, these activities

are relatively rare between most fathers and daughters.

In contrast, the most common type of interaction between fathers and sons involve recreational or work-related, instrumental activities, showing that sons benefit by having more shared interests with their fathers than do daughters. Sons, like daughters, are more likely to confide in their mothers. This allows mothers to develop more empathy with their children and see them more for who they are than for who they might like them to be. As a result, interactions with mothers tend to consist more of exchanges of ideas and feelings rather than simply instructional episodes designed to influence adolescents, as is the case with fathers.

Taken together, these studies provide greater understanding of the nature of parent-child interaction during adolescence. More specifically, they point to the effectiveness of a democratic parenting style for both sons and daughters as a means of having more influence as well as promoting a sense of independence in youth and enhancing closeness between parents and adolescents. Greater involvement in decision making and greater closeness have been shown to enhance academic performance and self-confidence and reduce association with deviant peers. While it is likely that adolescents' greater tendency to confide in mothers as compared to fathers in the United States, as well as the parents' influence in different domains, may contribute to the more democratic parenting on the part of mothers than fathers, it is also likely that the more authoritarian style of many American fathers inhibits such confiding on the part of youth. More research is needed to understand better the reciprocal patterns of interaction between parents and their adolescent children.

More research is needed on other socialization processes in the family. We know that the presence of siblings, particularly brothers, has negative consequences for educational achievements and college attendance (Powell and Steelman 1990). The presence of brothers also has been found to increase the likelihood of receiving punishment from parents, while having more siblings decreases the likelihood of having a less controlling and more democratic style of parenting (Elder 1985). However, little is known about other influences of siblings or processes of socialization among siblings. One of the few sociological studies of sibling relations found that solidarity between siblings is enhanced when they perceive they are being treated equitably (Handel 1986). However, Handel also found that equity among siblings is continually challenged by age differences and the tendency for some siblings to want to exercise power over others. In addition, the pressure toward loyalty often conflicts with the desire to maintain individuality. These findings suggest that socialization processes among siblings are inherently complex and require additional investigation.

Socialization in the Peer Group

Peer Relations and Concerns in Adolescence. During adolescence, best friendships are increasingly valued as a source of mutual intimacy. Many adolescents report that their best friendships are characterized by acceptance, understanding, self-disclosure, and mutual advice. Close friendships provide adolescents with an important opportunity to develop greater self-knowledge through a process of mutual reflection. Parents, especially fathers, are perceived as being less accepting and more likely to act as experts or authorities. Since these factors are likely to impede the process of mutual reflection, adolescents tend to discuss their problems, feelings, fears, and doubts with best friends rather than parents (Youniss and Smollar 1985).

The importance of mutual intimacy and openness in friendship increases during adolescence, while the importance of friendship choices based on popularity decreases (Youniss and Smollar 1985). Loyalty and commitment also become more salient in later adolescence, often replacing the importance of shared activities, especially among working-class youth (Bigelow and LaGaipa 1980; Eckert 1988; Lesko 1988). Finally, older adolescents tend to be more similar in terms of attitudes toward school, college plans, and achievement

than are younger adolescents, and their influence on these attitudes is greater (Epstein 1983; Hallinan and Williams 1990).

As compared to childhood, adolescent friendships in schools tend to be more homogeneous by race, mainly due to an increase in same-race friendship choice by whites (Shrum, Creek, and Hunter 1988). While cross-gender friendships are quite rare in middle school they become more frequent in high school, especially among adolescents in different grade levels. However, throughout high school, peer influence is greater with friends of the same gender (Hallinan and Williams 1990).

Not only is there a strong tendency toward gender segregation in friendships, there is considerable diversity in the experience and basis of friendship for girls and boys. As in early childhood, female friendship groups tend to be closely knit and egalitarian, while male friendship groups tend to be loosely knit with clear status hierarchies (Karweit and Hansell 1983). For example, Youniss and Smollar (1985) found that female friends are more likely to engage in intimate disclosure, sharing their problems, feelings, fears, and doubts with their close friends. However, while boys are less likely to engage in intimate disclosure, 40 percent of the close male friendships in their study involved a high degree of mutual intimacy. For other boys, shared activities continue to be an important basis for friendship throughout adolescence. These findings indicate that while gender and developmental differences are important in the experience of friendship, there is also considerable diversity within gender groups and age groups. (See Savin-Williams and Berndt 1990 for an excellent review of adolescent friendships.)

As friendships become more salient during adolescence, the concerns and norms of peers gain increasing importance. Traditionally adolescence has been viewed as a time of rebellion from adult norms and values. In particular, delinquent youth subcultures have been viewed as being in opposition to adult society (Cohen 1955). Others view the deviant behavior of adolescence as more reflective of the blend of conventional and deviant behavior in adult society (Hagan 1991). This has led some researchers to distinguish between subcultures that include criminal and/or violent behavior from those that focus on less severe forms of deviance, such as drinking, attending rock concerts and parties, and sexuality (Hagan 1991).

Hagan (1991) found that while weak family and school ties led to greater involvement in both subcultures, the outcomes of membership in the two subcultures were very different. Belonging to the delinquent subculture adversely affected later occupational attainments of working-class males, while having no such long-term effects on middle-class males or females. In contrast, involvement in the party subculture actually enhanced later occupational attainments of middle-class males, while offering no advantage to working-class males or females.

A number of ethnographic studies have provided a more detailed, "inside" look at the concerns and values of youth in different subcultures. Labov (1972) found that the main concerns of African American males in the street peer groups of inner-city neighborhoods were toughness, trouble, excitement, autonomy, and cleverness. Status among these males was determined primarily by courage and skill in physical fighting, experience in delinquent behavior, and skills in various verbal activities such as ritual insulting, storytelling, and joke-telling. Thus, some of the very behaviors that provide status among peers are likely to prove costly to these youth as adults.

Willis (1981) found that working-class, adolescent boys in England valued fighting skills, humor, and defiance of adult authority and rules. As they continued to seek greater control over time and space, informal peer groups became the center of their interest and excitement while at school. According to Willis (1981), this culture inadvertently prepares working-class boys better to adapt to their factory jobs, where the main interest, excitement, and opportunities for creativity are also found in informal groups rather than in the work itself.

Researchers who have focused on working-class female subcultures of resistance have found that girls, as compared to boys, tend to engage in less overt and visible acts of resistance, such as skipping school and classes, reading magazines and passing notes during class, and goofing off when the teacher is gone (Griffin 1985; Wulff 1988). Their concerns include nonconformity, excitement, pleasure, and being "grown up" (i.e., being sexually developed, having boyfriends and more adult responsibilities). Concerns with physical safety in urban neighborhoods often restrict girls' activities and increase the value of having a boyfriend. While the peer group provided opportunities for excitement and humor as it did with boys, there was less sense of a shared set of concerns and orientations across peer groups, in part because these working-class girls were headed for quite different futures, from clerical and factory work to prostitution.

Interactive Processes and Language Activities.
Ethnographers and sociolinguists have recently examined the processes by which adolescent peer cultures are created. Willis (1981), for example, found that informal group interaction and humor are essential elements for creating and maintaining a counterculture. His work demonstrates how everyday activities are critical for establishing a shared interpretation of what it means to be a working-class male.

Wulff (1988) has argued that microcultures often have considerable diversity, with individuals having different ideas, interests, and perspectives. She views culture as something that is *distributed* among people in a group, with some individuals reflecting certain meanings more strongly through their personalities than other individuals. Certain localities and events can also manifest the meanings of the subculture. Thus, a subculture is created through shared significant events, recurrent or unique experiences in certain localities, and the appearance and behaviors of certain individuals.

Another approach to understanding the creation of subcultures is to examine the language activities that provide the basis for informal group life. As in research on younger children, the concern is to identify the resources and skills needed to build the interaction. Such construction often involves adolescents incorporating their own unique contributions and modifications to aspects of adult culture. Language activities are crucial for culture production, since it is through language that shared interpretations develop. Some of the activities adolescents routinely engage in include insulting, teasing, storytelling, and gossip.

Although most research on insulting has involved African American adolescent boys (Goodwin 1990; Labov 1972), there have been recent studies of such speech events among white boys and African American and white working-class girls (Everhart 1983; Goodwin 1990). Studies of ritual insulting among boys have shown how interpreting insults as playful and responding with more clever or elaborate insults is essential for successful participation in certain male subcultures. Males who lack these skills are more likely to become targets of serious ridicule or physical attacks as a conflict escalates (Everhart 1983; Labov 1972). On the other hand, by responding playfully to insults, a sense of solidarity based on shared interpretation is developed (Everhart 1983). At the same time, since this activity is often competitive in nature, it provides boys with a way to establish and reinforce status hierarchies (Goodwin 1990; Labov 1972).

Another form of group humor that has been studied recently is playful teasing. Here again, interpreting teasing remarks as playful and responding in kind are essential skills (Eder 1991). If someone failed to respond in a playful manner when being teased, other group members might encourage him/her not to take the teasing comments seriously. On the other hand, some adolescents are able to turn a potentially serious insult into a teasing remark by responding playfully (Eder 1991). Finally, teasing is more loosely structured than ritual insulting, allowing for collaborative participation that can build solidarity among the "teasers" as well as the targets. While there is a loose structure and familiarity to teasing routines, they also allow novel responses, given their playful, humorous nature.

Storytelling is also a common activity among adolescents, taking a variety of forms, including fight stories and collaborative narratives. Since stories are based on past experiences, full partici-

pation depends on shared experiences among group members. In fact, the greater the prior shared knowledge, the more likely group members will be able to interpret the story accurately. Shuman (1986) found that the girls who had the most knowledge about a fight were entitled to tell fight stories, and only close friends were allowed to hear certain fight stories, such as those involving family disputes. Other studies have found that boys use storytelling to demonstrate cleverness and the importance of certain events (Goodwin 1990; Labov 1972). Finally, storytelling in peer culture is often collaborative (Eder 1988; Goodwin 1990), with the collaboration serving both to strengthen group ties and shared perceptions and orientations.

Although gossip is common among adolescents, it has not been adequately studied. In a study of younger adolescents, Eder and Enke (1991) found that the structure of gossip makes it difficult to challenge negative evaluations once the initial evaluation has been supported. This means that early adolescents are likely to engage in considerable negative evaluation to participate in this common activity. Through their participation they often reinforce traditional gender norms as well as negotiate new norms for gender relations. J. Parker and J. Gottman (1989) found that gossip was primarily used for group solidarity and communication of norms in early adolescence but in later adolescence provided an entry into the psychological exploration of the self. In another study of older adolescent girls, Fine (1986) found that gossip was used primarily to clarify moral concerns and values. The girls Fine studied were concerned with reaching consensus, and they minimized potential conflict by expressing counterviews in ways that allowed their views to be easily modified.

These studies suggest that some speech activities are more dominant in some subcultures than are others and that the functions of certain speech activities in a given subculture may change over time. Many of the studies show how speech activities serve to make meanings and interpretations visible to others, thus making shared meanings possible. Through detailed study of activities such as these we can better understand the role adolescents play in defining and shaping their own peer cultures.

Gender, Ethnicity, and Peer Culture. As mentioned earlier, peer groups in schools tend to be segregated by ethnicity throughout adolescence. There is also a high degree of gender segregation, particularly in early adolescence (Schofield 1982; Shrum, Cheek, and Hunter 1988). Through the development of different concerns and language activities in these highly segregated groups, adolescents receive important messages about what it means to be a member of a particular ethnic group or to be male or female. Peer cultures also provide important messages about ways to view the opposite sex as well as ways to interact with people from different ethnic groups.

In an in-depth study of a junior high school, Schofield (1982) found that racial differences in styles of interaction led to different interpretations of acts as well as certain "social identities." For example, because many whites were less familiar with challenges and insults, they interpreted these acts as being aggressive rather than playful. This led to the belief that African Americans as a group were "tough" and "aggressive." In turn, African Americans came to view whites as being "easily bullied."

Other research on early adolescents have focused primarily on gender differences. Male peer groups formed around athletics (both Little League and school-sponsored sports) place a high value on being tough—willing to be hurt and willing to hurt others (Eder and Parker 1987; Fine 1987; S. Parker 1991). They also teach boys the importance of "being cool" and in control of their feelings. This includes learning how to control anger, not to cry or mope, and to be stoic in the face of pain (Fine 1987). In contrast, girls tend to place more emphasis on their appearance and on being well-liked by other girls (Eder and Parker 1987; Eder and Sanford 1986; Simmons and Blyth 1987). This includes not acting stuck-up or snobbish. Girls also socialize each other to have greater empathy for others' feelings, including isolates and other targets of ridicule (Eder and Sanford 1986; Evans and

Eder 1989). In general, boys appear to place more emphasis on learning to control their own feelings, while girls place more emphasis on being aware of and sensitive to others' feelings.

Adolescents at this age are also beginning to learn important messages about how to view the opposite sex. For boys this includes a strong message not to let girls replace other boys as the focus of their attention, reinforcing the importance of the male peer group (Fine 1987). It also includes a focus on "sexual conquest," where girls are discussed primarily in terms of "how far they got" with them sexually (Fine 1987; S. Parker 1991). On the other hand, girls view boys primarily as targets of romantic feelings, which are being shaped by norms of heterosexuality and monogamy (Simon, Eder, and Evans 1992). In addition, some girls come to believe in the importance of "being in love continually" and are always searching for new targets for their romantic feelings (Simon, Eder, and Evans 1992).

Studies of older adolescents find that similar perceptions of the opposite gender are promoted. Working-class boys often tell stories emphasizing their sexual experiences. They view girls as sexual objects and in general see them as weak, indirect, and sexually passive (Willis 1981). The labels "slut," "whore," or "slag" continue to be used by both male and female peers to control female sexual behavior (Griffin 1985; Lees 1986; Wulff 1988). These labels are applied to any girl who is sexually promiscuous, even though such behavior is viewed as acceptable for boys. They are also used in regard to girls who have a number of boyfriends or who tend to flirt with boys, regardless of whether they engage in any sexual behavior (Lees 1986; Wulff 1988). The only way girls are able to redeem their reputation is by getting a steady boyfriend, which further promotes the importance of romance in their lives. Other studies have found that many white working-class girls develop a culture of romance as part of their resistance to middle-class academic norms (Griffin 1985; McRobbie 1978). This antischool culture places a high value on marriage, family, and fashion and beauty concerns and leads white adolescent girls to expend most of their energy on seeking a boyfriend. Asian and African American girls tend to be more critical of romance ideals and are less concerned with getting a boyfriend (Griffin 1985).

Peer cultures also have been found to promote racial segregation and inequality. In his study of white and African American adolescents, Hewitt (1986) found that the role of peer cultures differed depending on the degree of racial integration in the neighborhood. In a predominantly white neighborhood, the extensive male network discouraged cross-racial friendships, and many who previously had such friendships eventually dropped them. Boys who were attracted to the "skinhead" peer culture by its music and distinct style of dress also dropped their cross-racial friendships, and many developed more racist attitudes. However, the girls' smaller peer groups put less pressure on cross-racial friendships, and the girls themselves were less concerned about interracial dating than were boys, who viewed it as another invasion of their "territory." Because many youth placed a high value on reggae and soul music, there was some legitimacy for whites to seek out interracial contact. Those youth who did reported that their own attitudes were much less racist than those of their parents, who often disapproved of their interracial relationships. Wulff (1988) also found that the girls in her study placed more value on ethnicity and interracial contact than did their parents, and in some cases were influential in changing their parents' views.

In a more ethnically diverse neighborhood, Hewitt (1986) found that the African American youth culture and music were even more dominant. (See Willis 1990 for an excellent discussion of the importance of popular music for developing a "grounded aesthetics" among African Americans and other low-status youth.) Both African American and white youth were more aware of racism in this neighborhood, due in part to the political nature of certain African American music as well as witnessing more incidents of racism by police and other authorities. The youth culture in this particular neighborhood also strengthened African Americans' sense of ethnicity by exposing them to creole.

While African American parents discouraged this dialect at home, youth reported that it made them feel more lively and used it to express a range of emotions as well as to convey a "tough" identity.

In summary, research on peer relations has grown to include a greater understanding of the content and processes of peer group cultures. The study of speech activities in peer groups is particularly important because adolescents' eagerness to participate in peer activities leads to the development of particular speech styles as well as the transmission of many societal norms. Language also offer opportunities for self-expression and modification of these norms, as adolescents use humor to mock their culture and themselves. Finally, peer groups are important arenas for establishing identities and cultural knowledge related to gender and ethnicity. More research is needed to show how youth cultures reinforce gender and racial inequalities as well as ways in which they promote alternative and more egalitarian views of gender and ethnicity.

Socialization Processes in School Environments

The Transition to Middle and Junior High School. While most schools tend to segregate adolescents with same-age peers, thereby increasing their influence, the nature of peer processes varies depending on other structural aspects of the school setting. As students move from elementary into middle or junior high schools they are suddenly confronted with a much larger group of same-age peers, averaging five times greater in size (Simmons and Blyth 1987). This early transition into a larger social environment has been studied extensively since the 1970s. Research based on cross-sectional data indicated that early adolescents had lower self-esteem, less stable self-images, and greater self-consciousness than did younger children or older adolescents. The biggest drop in self-esteem was found to occur in seventh grade, when these adolescents entered junior high school (Simmons, Rosenberg, and Rosenberg 1973). Later research examined the possible influences of pubertal development and school environment on this drop in self-esteem (Simmons and Blyth 1987). While pubertal development was found to have varying effects on body satisfaction, it was not found to have an effect on global self-esteem or degree of self-consciousness. In contrast, entry into a junior high school environment has negative consequences for many students. Specifically, girls who entered a junior high in seventh grade were found to have much lower self-esteem compared to those who remained in an elementary school setting with kindergarten through eighth grades. Girls who entered junior high were also less likely to be leaders in extracurricular activities than were those in the kindergarten through eighth grade setting, and both boys and girls were less likely to participate in extracurricular activities in the junior high setting. Other research has found that the effects of entry into junior high school are most negative for children who fail to maintain stable friendships during this transition (Berndt 1989).

Simmons and Blyth (1987) examined the long-term consequences of attending a junior high as compared to remaining in an elementary school setting. From one perspective, which they term the "stress inoculation hypothesis," this early transition into a large school environment might better prepare students for their next transition into high school. From a developmental readiness perspective, this early transition may come too early developmentally or be so stressful that it puts these students at a disadvantage for their next transition. Their findings indicate more support for the latter perspective. Girls who attended a junior high were found to have lower self-esteem in high school than were those who remained in an elementary setting. Also, both boys and girls from junior high were less likely to participate in extracurricular activities in high school, and girls were less likely to be leaders than were those students who had not attended a junior high school. These findings show that school environments may have long-term negative consequences on students' self-images and social experiences.

An in-depth study of a middle school environment provides additional understanding as to why this type of environment may be so disadvantageous for adolescents, especially for girls (Eder 1985; Eder and Parker 1987). The large number of same-age peers along with the limited number of extracurricular activities was found to promote a unidimensional hierarchy of cliques. Since status at this age was based on "being known" by peers, students who participated in those extracurricular activities that drew large groups of spectators were much more visible than other students. In this school, as in many high schools, male athletics provided boys with both visibility and status (Coleman 1961; Cusick 1973; Eder and Parker 1987; Karweit 1983). Due to the large number of spectators at male athletic events, female cheerleaders also had increased visibility and status (Eder and Parker 1987). In addition, girls were able to gain entry into elite cliques through friendships with popular girls (Eder 1985).

This focus on social relations as an important avenue for social status for girls as compared to boys may help explain why the junior high or middle school environment has more negative consequences for girls than for boys. Earlier research showed that early adolescent girls show more concern with being well-liked and less concern with achievement than do eight- to eleven-year-old girls (F. Rosenberg and R. Simmons 1975). Early adolescent girls have also been found to have lower self-esteem and greater self-consciousness and to care more about being popular with same-sex peers than do boys at this age (Simmons and Blyth 1987). If girls rely in part on friendships to gain status with peers, while boys rely primarily on athletic achievements, it is not surprising that girls become increasingly concerned with being well-liked and less concerned with achievement when faced with the more hierarchal social environment of middle school and junior high school. Furthermore, because social status is so closely tied with friendships, girls who become popular often become the targets of negative sentiment because they are unable to or fail to respond to all the friendly overtures they receive (Eder 1985). This cycle of popularity means that even popular girls in middle school settings are likely to experience negative social interactions that could prove harmful to their self-images, given the importance of being well-liked.

Furthermore, the activity through which girls are still most likely to gain visibility and status is cheerleading. In a study of small and large middle school settings, participation in cheerleading resulted in the strongest increase in popularity of any extracurricular activity (Eder and Kinney 1988). Since cheerleading is closely tied with the importance of appearance in adolescent female culture, the salience of this activity further adds to the importance of attractiveness for adolescent girls (Eder and Parker 1987). As early as sixth grade, girls rate themselves as being less good looking and less satisfied with their appearance than boys (M. Rosenberg 1986b; Simmons and Blyth 1987). However, upon entry into junior high, girls begin to place a higher value on appearance compared to boys. The fact that the junior high school environment places so much salience on cheerleading and therefore on appearance may also contribute to the lower levels of self-esteem in girls in this setting, especially given that they already tend to view their appearance more negatively than do boys.

While girls appear to show the most negative consequences from attending junior high or middle schools, both girls and boys later complain about the extreme hierarchal nature of this environment. They report that because only a small number of students can join the elite groups, everyone else feels like "dweebs" or social failures (Kinney, 1993). This is in part because there are fewer extracurricular activities available per student at middle school than in the upper grades of elementary school or most high schools (Kinney 1993; Simmons and Blyth 1987). Also, both boys and girls show a drop in social competence upon entry into junior high, and while self-esteem was found to rebound by the end of seventh grade for these students, feelings of social competence did not (Eccles et al. 1989).

While middle and junior high school environments appear to increase social anxieties for many students, those who fail to form friendships with their peers may be most negatively affected. Students who are perceived to be unattractive, less intelligent (typically those in special education), and/or deviant in regard to gender roles often may not be accepted by their peers, who fear being associated with these perceived undesirable characteristics (Evans and Eder 1989). These students are often the targets of considerable ridicule as other students try to establish greater social distance from them or use them as outlets to relieve their own sense of social inadequacy.

Other studies indicate that the current organization of middle schools does not meet the emotional, intellectual, and interpersonal needs of early adolescents. This is evident in significant drops in students' satisfaction with school and commitment to classwork upon entering junior high school (Hirsch and Rapkin 1987) and in research that identifies other negative effects for students assigned to lower curriculum tracks (Oakes 1985). In response to these studies, a recent report on adolescent development advocated creating smaller learning communities for early adolescents by developing schools within schools (Carnegie Council 1989). This report also advocated less use of curriculum tracking and more emphasis on cooperative learning, which helps students learn and retain information, think more critically, and get along with students from diverse backgrounds.

There is research that indicates that different middle school structures can produce very different social environments, with important implications for cross-racial contact. Damico and Sparks (1986) compared two middle schools, one in which students were stratified by grade and ability level like most middle schools and one in which students were randomly assigned to learning teams that were diverse in terms of grade, ability, race, and gender. In the latter school, classroom instruction consisted of a combination of multitask, individual, and cooperative learning as compared to the use of a recitation format in the more traditional school. They found that white students in the traditionally structured school interacted less in general and in particular talked less with African American students than they did in the school with mixed teams. In the mixed-team school, whites talked to

African Americans as much as they talked to other whites and had more cross-racial friendships. The nature of talk between races was also more reciprocal in this school, whereas in the traditional school African Americans talked to whites more often than whites talked to African Americans. While this study focused primarily on the way school environments affect cross-racial interaction, it suggests that the use of different structures at the middle school level might also affect other peer processes.

High School Environments and Peer Culture. There has been considerable research on the role of extracurricular activities for the enhancement of peer status and the development of peer cultures at the high school level. Coleman's (1961) research on ten midwestern high schools showed that adolescents were much more concerned with being remembered as a star athlete or a leader in social activities than as a brilliant student. Since Coleman's study, similar findings have been reported in high schools throughout the United States (Brown 1990; Brown and Lohr 1987; Goldberg and Chandler 1989; Williams and White 1983). Cross-cultural research highlights the importance of the visibility gained through involvement in extracurricular activities. In their comparison of Danish and American youth, Kandel and Lesser (1972) found that leading crowds were less prominent in Danish high schools, which did not offer extracurricular activities. Also, Danish youth were more likely to want to be remembered as being brilliant students than were the American youth in their study. However, in a study of Australian schools, which do offer athletic activities, values promoted through football, such as aggression and toughness, were more salient than academic values, even in the upper-class schools (Kessler et al. 1985).

Other research on school environments shows that extracurricular activities provide students with resources besides visibility, such as special privileges and greater control over time and space (Eckert 1988). Typically, white middle-class students are most likely to benefit from these privileges (Eckert 1988; Lesko 1988). However, in certain urban settings, lower-class African-American boys were found to be more involved in schools than were lower-class white boys, through their greater participation in athletics (MacLeod 1987).

The role of extracurricular activities is also more complex at the high school level than at the middle school level, mainly because most high schools offer a much wider range of activities that provide students with an opportunity to demonstrate leadership or social competence. For example, in his study of a suburban high school, Larkin (1979) found three distinct elite groups based on their participation in athletics and cheerleading, in student government, and in academic activities. Thus, at the high school level, being involved in multiple activities is more likely to bring high status than participation in a single activity (Karweit 1983), and elite group members are often those who participate "in everything" (Lesko 1988).

Increased opportunities for involvement at the high school level not only change the basis and nature of status processes, they also help restore the self-esteem of adolescents who felt socially inadequate in middle school (Kinney 1993). Through involvement in even a single activity, many students gain a sense of being part of a meaningful social group and develop new social competencies. Furthermore, activities such as female athletics provide students with new cultural contexts in which they have the opportunity to integrate traditional values of female subcultures, such as cooperation and emotional support, with more competitive and achievement-oriented values (Enke 1992). In the process, adolescents not only have a chance to develop strategies that blend these two orientations, but also begin to challenge traditional forms of competition in which recognition is a scarce reward rather than a means for recognizing many types of talents and skills.

Also by high school, clearly defined subcultures of resistance are evident. In England, these subcultures have been organized largely around resistance to academic values, replacing them with values of defiance and aggression for boys and romance for girls, as discussed earlier. In American schools, these subcultures often are also responses to the elite social groups. While elite group members may define students in these groups as "apathetic" due to their failure to be more involved in school activities (Lesko 1988), the students themselves often view the elite students as being overly materialistic and too concerned with conformity and social trends (Kinney 1989). Students in these groups tend to value individualism and expressive styles of dress, and many use drugs. While these groups reject the content of elite peer cultures, they often embrace a similar process of gaining recognition through visibility—in this case through highly visible appearance and behaviors (Eckert 1988; Kinney 1989; Lesko 1988). Also, though academic values are less integrated in adolescent peer cultures in many American schools, processes such as curriculum tracking continue to influence opportunities for peer interaction as well as the nature of that interaction.

Finally, by high school awareness of some of the realities of current work situations begins to influence adolescents' choices and behaviors. For example, in her study of working-class girls, Gaskell (1986) found that many girls chose clerical tracks rather than industrial tracks because they thought manual or industrial work might be harder to obtain and provide less pleasant working conditions, due to having fewer women to interact with as well as being subject to more sexual harassment. Likewise, the awareness of the low-paying jobs available to them and other family members led to disillusionment with schooling as an avenue for social mobility among white lower-class boys and decreased their school involvement (MacLeod 1987).

In general, these studies of middle and high school environments show how they can influence the nature and salience of peer processes. More specifically, they show how American schools, in particular middle and junior high schools, tend to promote highly visible elite groups. This, in turn, intensifies status concerns for early adolescents, leading to long term detrimental effects on self-esteem, especially among girls. At the same time, evidence suggests that school environments may be modified to promote greater interracial contact. More research is needed to identify how different school environments affect this and other processes of peer interaction and socialization.

These studies also reveal the way peer status hierarchies and peer culture reflect stratification processes and values of the larger society. The social stratification processes of adolescents show that greater access to certain activities provide additional privileges, often benefitting whites, boys, and middle-class students. At the same time, the complexity of high school peer cultures, with more opportunities for participation as well as more conflict among competing values, prepares adolescents with processes for coping and maintaining self-esteem in a stratified society. Finally, schools provide some contexts, such as female athletics, in which we can see cultural change in process. More research is needed to show how school environments offer opportunities for cultural change as well as reproduce societal values.

CONCLUSION

At the start of this chapter we noted the diversity of positions on human development in both psychology and sociology and stressed the importance of considering both congruities and incongruities of psychological and sociological approaches. We feel the time is ripe for intellectual pluralism in the area of human development and that such pluralism can be built on several themes in recent theoretical and empirical work in the area.

Complete or even substantial interdisciplinary synthesis in approaches to human development and socialization is not likely, nor is it necessarily judicious. While psychologists are primarily interested in individual development, sociologists and anthropologists are primarily concerned with collective processes of productive and reproductive change. Nevertheless, we saw in our theoretical review that psychologists are increasingly recognizing the importance of collective action and social structure for individual development. On the other hand, sociologists are becoming more open to consideration of the importance of biogenetic factors as well as individual-level activity (both cognitive and behavioral) for general theories of socialization (see

Fetherman and Lerner 1985). What is important is the apparently increasing level of cross-fertilization in theory and research. Psychologists and sociologists in the area of human development and socialization are clearly reading each other's work, and there have been some attempts at broad-scale collaboration. Consider, for example, work in the areas of life span developmental psychology and sociology of the life course. There is also considerable interaction among constructivist developmental psychologists (who build on the work of Piaget and Vygotsky) and interactionist and interpretive theorists in sociology. The recent evolution of interdisciplinary scholarly associations, conferences, and training programs should contribute to these positive trends.

In addition to interdisciplinary convergence, we have seen a dramatic increase in comparative or cross-cultural research in the area of human development. These comparative studies have often challenged traditional Western theories of development and socialization and have certainly contributed to international communication and collaboration. Earlier we mentioned the international character of life span developmental psychology and the cross-cul-

tural emphasis of sociocultural approaches. There has also been a great deal of collaboration among European and American scholars in the development of interpretive approaches to socialization. Overall, the growing recognition that human development and socialization must be seen as a primarily cultural process can only be strengthened by this trend.

In sum, while we have seen important theoretical and empirical progression, there are still substantial gaps in our knowledge of childhood and adolescent development and socialization. The needed reconceptualization of socialization as a collective rather than an individualistic process has surely set us on the right path. Instead of focusing on the *autonomous child* on a lonely journey in which he/she first must learn and then use the skills and knowledge of his/her culture, this new conceptual model focuses on *children's negotiations with others* (Bruner 1986). From this perspective socialization is not something that happens to children; it is a process in which children, in interaction with others, produce their own worlds and peer cultures and eventually come to reproduce, to extend, and to join the adult world.

NOTE

William Corsaro's work is supported by grants from the Spencer and William T. Grant Foundations.

REFERENCES

Alexander, K. A., and D. R. Entwisle. 1988. Achievement in the first two years of school: Patterns and processes. *Monographs of the Society for Research in Child Development* 53(2, serial no. 218), 157 pages.

Asher, S., and J. Coie, eds. 1990. *Peer Rejection in Childhood.* New York: Cambridge University Press.

Baltes, P., H. Reese, and L. Lipsitt. 1980. Life-span developmental psychology. *Annual Review of Psychology* 31:65–110.

Bandura, A. 1986. *Social Foundations of Thought and Action: A Social Cognitive Theory.* Englewood Cliffs, NJ: Prentice Hall.

Baumrind, D. 1973. The development of instrumental competence through socialization. Pp. 3–46 in

Minnesota Symposia on Child Psychology, vol. 7, ed. A. Pick. Minneapolis: University of Minnesota Press.

Berentzen, S. 1984. *Children Constructing Their Social World* (Bergen Studies in Social Anthropology no. 36). Bergen, Norway: University of Bergen.

Berndt, T. 1979. Developmental changes in conformity to peers and parents. *Developmental Psychology* 15:606–616.

———. 1989. Obtaining support from friends in childhood and adolescence. Pp. 308–331 in *Children's Social Networks and Social Supports,* ed. D. Belle. New York: Wiley.

Berndt, T., and G. Ladd, eds. 1989. *Peer Relationships in Child Development.* New York: Wiley.

Bernstein, B. 1981. Codes, modalities, and the process of cultural reproduction: A model. *Language in Society* 10:327–363.

Best, R. 1983. *We've All Got Scars.* Bloomington: Indiana University Press.

Bigelow, B. J., and J. LaGaipa. 1980. The development of friendship values and choice. Pp. 15–44 in *Friendship and Social Relations in Children,* ed. H. C. Foot, A. J. Chapman, and J. Smith. New York: Wiley.

Blake, J. 1989. *Family Size and Achievement.* Berkeley: University of California Press.

Bourdieu, P. 1984. *Distinction: A Social Critique of the Judgement of Taste.* Cambridge, MA: Harvard University Press.

Bourdieu, P., and J. Passeron. 1977. *Reproduction in Education, Society, and Culture.* Beverly Hills: Sage.

Bowlby, J. 1980. *Attachment and Loss, 3. Loss: Sadness and Depression.* New York: Basic Books.

Bowles, S., and H. Gintis. 1976. *Schooling in Capitalist America.* New York: Basic Books.

Brandtstädter, J. 1984. Personal and social control over development: Some implications of an action perspective in life-span developmental psychology. *Life-Span Development and Behavior* 6:1–32.

Bronfenbrenner, U. 1979. *The Ecology of Human Development.* Cambridge, MA: Harvard University Press.

———. 1989. Ecological systems theory. *Annals of Child Development* 6:187–249.

Brown, B. 1990. Peer groups and peer cultures. Pp. 171–196 in *At the Threshold: The Developing Adolescent,* ed. S. Feldman and G. Elliot. Cambridge, MA: Harvard University Press.

Brown, B., and M. Lohr 1987. Peer group affiliation and adolescent self-esteem: An integration of ego-identity and symbolic interaction theories. *Journal of Personality and Social Psychology* 52:47–55.

Bruner, J. 1986. *Actual Minds, Possible Worlds.* Cambridge, MA: Harvard University Press.

Bush, D., and R. Simmons. 1981. Socialization processes over the life course. Pp. 133–164 in *Social Psychology: Sociological Perspectives,* ed. M. Rosenberg and R. Turner. New York: Basic Books.

Carnegie Council on Adolescent Development. 1989. *Turning Points: Preparing American Youth for the 21st Century.* New York: Carnegie Corporation.

Cicourel, A. 1974. *Cognitive Sociology.* New York: Free Press.

Clausen, J. 1991. Adolescent competence and the life course, or why one social psychologist needed a concept of personality. *Social Psychology Quarterly* 54:4–14.

Cohen, A. 1955. *Delinquent Boys.* New York: Free Press.

Coleman, J. 1961. *The Adolescent Society.* New York: Free Press.

Colvin, M., and J. Pauly. 1983. A critique of criminology: Toward an integrated structural-Marxist theory of delinquency production. *American Journal of Sociology* 89:513–551.

Cook-Gumperz, J., and W. Corsaro. 1986. Introduction. Pp. 1–11 in *Children's Worlds and Children's Language,* ed. J. Cook-Gumperz, W. Corsaro, and J. Streeck. Berlin: Mouton.

Cooley, C. H. 1922. *Human Nature and the Social Order.* New York: Scribner's.

Corsaro, W. 1979. "We're friends, right?": Children's use of access rituals in a nursery school. *Language in Society* 8:315–336.

———. 1985. *Friendship and Peer Culture in the Early Years.* Norwood, NJ: Ablex.

———. 1988. Routines in the peer culture of American and Italian nursery school children. *Sociology of Education* 61:1–14.

———. 1990. The underlife of the nursery school: Young children's social representations of adult rules. Pp. 11–26 in *Social Representations and the Development of Knowledge,* ed. B. Lloyd and G. Duveen. Cambridge, UK: Cambridge University Press.

———. 1992. Interpretive reproduction in children's peer cultures. *Social Psychology Quarterly* 55: 160–177.

Corsaro, W., and D. Eder. 1990. Children's peer cultures. *Annual Review of Sociology* 16:197–220.

Corsaro, W., and T. A. Rizzo. 1988. *Discussione* and friendship: Socialization processes in the peer culture of Italian nursery school children. *American Sociological Review* 53:879–894.

———. 1990. Disputes in the peer culture of American and Italian nursery school children. Pp. 21–66 in *Conflict Talk,* ed. A. D. Grimshaw. Cambridge, UK: Cambridge University Press.

Cottrell, L. 1969. Interpersonal interaction and the development of self. Pp. 543–570 in *Handbook of Socialization Theory and Research,* ed. D. Goslin. Chicago: Rand McNally.

Cusick, P. 1973. *Inside High School.* New York: Holt, Rinehart & Winston.

Damico, S., and C. Sparks. 1986. Cross-group contact opportunities: Impact on interpersonal relationships in desegregated middle schools. *Sociology of Education* 59:113–123.

Damon, W. 1977. *The Social World of the Child.* San Francisco: Jossey-Bass.

Davies, B. 1982. *Life in the Classroom and Playground: The Accounts of Primary School Children.* London: Routledge.

Denzin, N. 1977. *Childhood Socialization.* San Francisco: Jossey-Bass.

Doise, W., and G. Mugny. 1984. *The Social Development of the Intellect.* New York: Pergamon.

Donaldson, M. 1978. *Children's Minds.* New York: Norton.

Dornbusch, S., and P. Ritter. 1991. Family decision-making and authoritative parenting. Paper presented at the meetings of the Society for Research in Child Development, Seattle.

Dornbusch, S., P. Ritter, P. Leiderman, D. Roberts, and M. Fraleigh. 1987. The relation of parenting style to adolescent school performance. *Child Development* 58:1244–1257.

Dunn, J. 1988. *The Beginnings of Social Understanding.* Cambridge, MA: Harvard University Press.

Dunn, J., and C. Kendrick. 1982. *Siblings: Love, Envy and Understanding.* Cambridge, MA: Harvard University Press.

Eccles, J. S., A. Wigfield, C. Flanagan, C. Miller, A. Reuman, and D. Yee. 1989. Self-concepts, domain values, and self-esteem: Relations and changes at early adolescence. *Journal of Personality* 57:282–310.

Eckert, P. 1988. Adolescent social structure and the spread of linguistic change. *Language in Society* 17:183–208.

Eder, D. 1985. The cycle of popularity: Interpersonal relations among female adolescents. *Sociology of Education* 58:154–165.

———. 1988. Building cohesion through collaborative narration. *Social Psychology Quarterly* 51: 225–235.

———. 1991. The role of teasing in adolescent peer culture. Pp. 181–97 in *Sociological Studies of Child Development,* vol. 4, ed. S. Cahill. Greenwich, CT: JAI Press.

Eder, D., and J. Enke. 1991. The structure of gossip: Opportunities and constraints on collective expression among adolescents. *American Sociological Review* 56:495–508.

Eder, D., and D. Kinney. 1988. The effect of middle school extracurricular activities on adolescents' popu-

larity and peer status. Paper presented at the American Sociological Association Meetings, Atlanta.

Eder, D., and S. Parker. 1987. The cultural production and reproduction of gender: The effect of extracurricular activities on peer group culture. *Sociology of Education* 60:200–213.

Eder, D., and S. Sanford. 1986. The development and maintenance of interactional norms among early adolescents. Pp. 283–300 in *Sociological Studies of Child Development,* vol. 1., ed. P. A. Adler and P. Adler. Greenwich, CT: JAI Press.

Eisenberg, A., and C. Garvey 1981. Children's use of verbal strategies in resolving conflicts. *Discourse Processes* 4:149–170.

Eisenstadt, S. 1956. *From Generation to Generation.* New York: Free Press.

Elder, G. 1974. *Children of the Great Depression: Social Change in Life Experience.* Chicago: University of Chicago Press.

———. 1985. *Life Course Dynamics: Trajectories and Transitions, 1968–1980.* Ithaca, NY: Cornell University Press.

Elder, G., and A. Caspi. 1988. Human development and social change: An emerging perspective on the life course. Pp. 77–113 in *Persons in Context,* ed. N. Bolger, A. Caspi, G. Downey, and M. Moorehouse. New York: Cambridge University Press.

Elkin, F., and G. Handel. 1984. *The Child and Society: The Process of Socialization.* New York: Random House.

Emde, R., W. Johnson, and M. Easterbrooks. 1987. The do's and don'ts of early moral development: Psychoanalytic tradition and current research. Pp. 245–276 in *The Emergence of Morality in Children.* ed. J. Kagan and S. Lamb. Chicago: University of Chicago Press.

Enke, J. 1992. *Cultural Production, Reproduction, and Change Within an Athletic Context.* Ph.D. diss. Department of Sociology. Indiana University, Bloomington.

Entwisle, D. R., and L. A. Hayduk. 1982. *Early Schooling: Cognitive and Affective Outcomes.* Baltimore: Johns Hopkins University Press.

Epstein, J. 1983. Examining theories of adolescent friendships. Pp. 39–62 in *Friends in School: Patterns of Selection and Influence in Secondary Schools,* ed. J. L. Epstein and N. Karweit. New York: Academic.

Erikson, E. 1963. *Childhood and Society.* New York: Norton.

Evans, C., and D. Eder. 1989. "No exit": Processes of social isolation in the middle school. Paper presented at the American Sociological Association Meeting, San Francisco.

Everhart, R. 1983. *Reading, Writing and Resistance: Adolescence and Labor in a Junior High School.* Boston: Routledge.

Featherman, D., and R. M. Lerner. 1985. Ontogenesis and sociogenesis: Problematics for theory and research about development and socialization across the lifespan. *American Sociological Review* 50: 659–676.

Fine, G. 1979. Small groups and culture creation. *American Sociological Review* 44:733–745.

———. 1983. *Shared Fantasy.* Chicago: University of Chicago Press.

———. 1986. The social organization of adolescent gossip: The rhetoric of moral evaluation. Pp. 405–423 in *Children's Worlds and Children's Language,* ed. J. Cook-Gumperz, W. Corsaro, and J. Streeck. Berlin: Mouton.

———. 1987. *With the Boys: Little League Baseball and Preadolescent Culture.* Chicago: University of Chicago Press.

Freud, S. 1949. *Outline of Psychoanalysis.* New York: Norton.

Furman, W., and D. Buhrmester. 1985. Children's perceptions of personal relationships in their social networks. *Developmental Psychology* 21: 1016–1024.

Furstenberg, F. 1990. Divorce and the American family. *Annual Review of Sociology* 16:379–403.

Furstenberg, F., and A. Cherlin. 1990. *Divided Families.* Cambridge, MA: Harvard University Press.

Garvey, C. 1984. *Children's Talk.* Cambridge, MA: Harvard University Press.

Gaskell, J. 1986. Course enrollment in the high school: The perspective of working-class females. *Sociology of Education* 58:48–59.

Gecas, V. 1972. Parental behavior and contextual variations in adolescent self-esteem. *Sociometry* 35: 332–345.

———. 1979. The influence of social class on socialization. Pp. 365–404 in *Contemporary Theories about the Family,* vol. 1., ed. W. Burr, R. Hill, F. Nye, and I. Reiss. New York: Free Press.

———. 1981. Contexts of socialization. Pp. 165–199 in *Social Psychology: Sociological Perspectives,* ed. M. Rosenberg and R. Turner. New York: Basic Books.

Geertz, C. 1973. *The Interpretation of Cultures.* New York: Basic Books.

Giddens, A. 1984. *The Constitution of Society.* Oxford, UK: Polity.

Goffman, E. 1974. *Frame Analysis.* New York: Harper & Row.

Goldberg, A., and T. Chandler. 1989. The role of activities: The social world of high school adolescents. *Youth and Society* 21:238–255.

Goodwin, M. H. 1990. *He-Said-She-Said: Talk as Social Organization among Black Children.* Bloomington: Indiana University Press.

Gottman, J. 1986. The world of coordinated play: Same- and cross-sex friendship in young children. Pp. 139–191 in *Conversations of Friends: Speculations on Affective Development,* ed. J. Gottman and J. Parker. New York: Cambridge University Press.

Griffin, C. 1985. *Typical Girls? Young Women from School to the Job Market.* London: Routledge.

Grotevant, H., and C. Cooper. 1986. Individuation in family relationships: A perspective on individual differences in the development of identity and role-taking skill in adolescence. *Human Development* 29:82–100.

Gumperz, J. J. 1982. *Discourse Strategies.* New York: Cambridge University Press.

Habermas, J. 1979. *Communication and the Evolution of Society.* Boston: Beacon.

Hagan, J. 1991. Destiny and drift: Subcultural preferences, status attainments, and the risks and rewards of youth. *American Sociological Review* 56:567–582.

Hallinan, M., and R. Williams. 1990. Students' characteristics and the peer-influence process. *Sociology of Education* 63:122–132.

Handel, G. 1986. Beyond sibling rivalry: An empirically grounded theory of sibling relationships. Pp. 105–122 in *Sociological Studies of Child Development,* vol. 1, ed. P. A. Adler and P. Adler. Greenwich, CT: JAI Press.

Hartup, W., and S. Moore. 1990. Early peer relations: Developmental significance and prognostic implications. *Early Childhood Research Quarterly* 5: 1–17.

Hartup, W., and M. Sancilio. 1986. Children's friendships. Pp. 61–80 in *Social Behavior in Autism,* ed. E. Schopler and G. Mesibov. New York: Plenum.

Heath, S. B. 1983. *Ways with Words: Language, Life and Work in Communities and Classrooms.* New York: Cambridge University Press.

————. 1989. Oral and literate traditions among black Americans living in poverty. *American Psychologist* 44:367–373.

Hetherington, E. M., and J. Arasteh, ed. 1988. *Impact of Divorce, Single-Parenting, and Step-Parenting on Children.* Hillsdale, NJ: Erlbaum.

Hewitt, R. 1986. *White Talk Black Talk: Inter-racial Friendship and Communication Amongst Adolescents.* Cambridge, UK: Cambridge University Press.

Hirsch, B., and B. Rapkin. 1987. The transition to junior high school: A longitudinal study of self-esteem, psychological symptomatology, school life, and social support. *Child Development* 58:1235–1243.

House, J. 1981. Social structure and personality. Pp. 525–561 in *Social Psychology: Sociological Perspectives,* ed. M. Rosenberg and R. Turner. New York: Basic Books.

Huesmann, L., and L. Eron, ed. 1986. *Television and the Aggressive Child: A Cross Cultural Perspective.* Hillsdale, NJ: Erlbaum.

Hurrelmann, K. 1988. *Social Structure and Personality Development.* New York: Cambridge University Press.

Inkeles, A. 1968. Society, social structure, and child socialization. Pp. 73–129 in *Socialization and Society,* ed. J. Clausen. Boston: Little, Brown.

Kagan, J. 1984. *The Nature of the Child.* New York: Basic Books.

Kandel, D., and K. Andrews. 1987. Processes of adolescent socialization by parents and peers. *International Journal of Addictions* 22:319–342.

Kandel, D., and G. Lesser. 1972. *Youth in Two Worlds.* San Francisco: Jossey-Bass.

Karweit, N. 1983. Extracurricular activities and friendship selection. Pp. 131–140 in *Friends in School: Patterns of Selection and Influence in Secondary Schools,* ed. J. L. Epstein and N. Karweit. New York: Academic.

Karweit, N., and S. Hansell. 1983. Sex differences in adolescent relationships: Friendship and status. Pp. 115–130 in *Friends in School: Patterns of Selection and Influence in Secondary Schools,* ed. J. L. Epstein and N. Karweit. New York: Academic.

Katriel, T. 1987. "Bexibùdim!": Ritualized sharing among Israeli children. *Language in Society* 16: 305–320.

Kessler, S., D. Ashenden, R. Connell, and G. Dowsett. 1985. Gender relations in secondary schooling. *Sociology of Education* 58:34–47.

Kholberg, L. 1969. Stage and sequence: The cognitive-developmental approach to socialization. Pp. 347–480 in *Handbook of Socialization Theory and Research,* ed. D. Goslin. Chicago: Rand McNally.

Kinney, D. 1989. *Dweebs, Headbangers, and Trendies: Adolescent Identity Formation and Change within Socio-Cultural Contexts.* Ph.D. diss. Department of Sociology, Indiana University, Bloomington.

Kinney, D. 1993. From nerds to normals: The recovery of identity among adolescents from middle school to high school. *Sociology of Education* 66:21–40.

Kohn, M. 1969. *Class and Conformity: A Study in Values.* Homewood, IL: Dorsey.

Kuhn, M. 1960. Self-attitudes by age, sex, and professional training. *Sociological Quarterly* 5:5–24.

Labov, W. 1972. *Language in the Inner City: Studies in the Black English Vernacular.* Philadelphia: University of Pennsylvania Press.

Larkin, R. 1979. *Suburban Youth in Cultural Crisis.* New York: Oxford University Press.

Lave, J. 1988. *Cognition in Practice.* New York: Cambridge University Press.

Lees, S. 1986. *Losing Out: Sexuality and Adolescent Girls.* London: Hutchinson.

Lerner, R. 1984. *On the Nature of Human Plasticity.* New York: Cambridge University Press.

Lesko, N. 1988. *Symbolizing Society: Stories, Rites and Structure in Catholic High School.* Philadelphia: Falmer.

Lever, J. 1976. Sex differences in the games children play. *Social Problems* 23:478–487.

Levy, M. 1952. *The Structure of Society.* Princeton: Princeton University Press.

Light, P. 1986. Context, conservation, and conversation. Pp. 170–190 in *Children of Social Worlds: Development in a Social Context,* ed. M. Richards and P. Light. Cambridge, MA: Harvard University Press.

MacLeod, J. 1987. *Ain't No Makin' It: Leveled Aspirations in a Low-Income Neighborhood.* Boulder, CO: Westview.

Marcos, A., S. Bahr, and R. Johnson. 1986. Test of a bonding/association theory of adolescent drug use. *Social Forces* 65:135–161.

Massey, J., and M. Krohn. 1986. A longitudinal examination of an integrated social process model of deviant behavior. *Social Forces* 65:106–134.

Maynard, D. 1985. On the functions of social conflict among children. *American Sociological Review* 50: 207–223.

McLoyd, V. 1990. The impact of economic hardship on black families and children: Psychological distress, parenting, and socioemotional development. *Child Development* 61:311–346.

McRobbie, A. 1978. Working class girls and the culture of femininity. Pp. 96–108 in *Women Take Issue,* ed. Women's Studies Group: Center for Contemporary Cultural Studies. London: Hutchinson.

Mead, G. H. 1934. *Mind, Self, and Society.* Chicago: University of Chicago Press.

Miller, P., R. Potts, H. Fung, L. Hoogstra, and J. Mintz. 1990. Narrative practices and the social construction of self in childhood. *American Ethnologist* 17: 292–311.

Miller, P., and L. Sperry. 1987. The socialization of anger and aggression. *Merrill-Palmer Quarterly* 33:1–33.

Mishler, E. 1979. Won't you trade cookies with the popcorn?: The talk of trades among six-year-olds. Pp. 221–236 in *Language, Children, and Society: The Effects of Social Factors on Children's Learning to Communicate,* ed. O. Garnica and M. King. Elmsford, NY: Pergamon.

Moscovici, S. 1981. On social representations. Pp. 181–209 in *Social Cognition,* ed. J. P. Forgas. London: Academic.

Mugny, G., and F. Carugati. 1989. *Social Representations of Intelligence.* Cambridge, UK: Cambridge University Press.

Musatti, T., and E. Mueller. 1985. Expressions of representational growth in toddlers' peer communication. *Social Cognition* 3:383–399.

Nasaw, D. 1985. *Children of the City.* Garden City, NY: Anchor.

Oakes, J. 1985. *Keeping Track: How Schools Structure Inequality.* New Haven: Yale University Press.

Ochs, E. 1988. *Culture and Language Development: Language Acquisition and Language Socialization in a Samoan Village.* New York: Cambridge University Press.

Overton, W., and H. Reese. 1973. Models of development: Methodological implications. Pp. 65–86 in *Life-Span Developmental Psychology: Methodological Issues,* ed. J. Nesselroade and H. Reese. New York: Academic.

Parcel, T., and E. Menaghan. 1990. Maternal working conditions and children's verbal facility: Studying the intergenerational transmission of inequality from mothers to young children. *Social Psychology Quarterly* 53:132–47.

Parker, J., and S. Asher. 1987. Peer relations and later personal adjustment: Are low-accepted children at risk? *Psychological Bulletin* 102:357–389.

Parker, J., and J. Gottman. 1989. Social and emotional development in a relational context: Friendship interaction from early childhood to adolescence. Pp. 95–132 in *Peer Relationships in Child Development,* ed. T. Brendt and G. Ladd. New York: Wiley.

Parker, S. 1991. *Early Adolescent Male Cultures: The Importance of Organized and Informal Sport.* Ph.D. diss. Department of Sociology, Indiana University, Bloomington.

Parsons, T. 1964. *Social Structure and Personality.* New York: Free Press.

Peterson, G., and B. Rollins. 1987. Parent-child socialization. Pp. 471–507 in *Handbook of Marriage and the Family,* ed. M. Sussman and S. Steinmetz. New York: Plenum.

Piaget, J. 1950. *The Psychology of Intelligence.* London: Routledge & Kegan Paul.

Powell, B., and L. Steelman. 1990. Beyond sibship size: Sibling density, sex composition, and educational outcomes. *Social Forces* 69:181–206.

Rizzo, T. A., 1989. *Friendship Development among Children in School.* Norwood, NJ: Ablex.

Rizzo, T. A., and W. A. Corsaro. 1988. Towards a better understanding of Vygotsky's process of internalization: Its role in the development of the concept of friendship. *Developmental Review* 8:219–237.

Rogoff, B. 1990. *Apprenticeship in Thinking: Cognitive Development in Social Context.* New York: Oxford University Press.

Rogoff, B., C. Mosier, J. Mistry, and A. Göncü. 1989. Toddlers' guided participation in cultural activity. *Cultural Dynamics* 2:209–237.

Rosenberg, F., and R. Simmons. 1975. Sex differences in the self-concept in adolescence. *Sex Roles* 1:147–59.

Rosenberg, M. 1986a. *Conceiving the Self.* Malabar, FL: Krieger.

———. 1986b. Self-concept from middle childhood through adolescence. Pp. 107–36 in *Psychological Perspectives on the Self,* vol. 3, ed. J. Suls and A. Greenwald. Hillsdale, NJ: Erlbaum.

———. 1989. *Society and the Adolescent Self-Image,* rev. ed. Middletown, CT: Wesleyan University Press.

Rosier, K. B. and W. A. Corsaro. 1993. Competent parents, complex lives: Managing parenthood in poverty. *Journal of Contemporary Ethnography* 22: 171–204.

Savin-Williams, R. and T. Brendt. 1990. Friendship and peer relations. Pp. 277–307 in *At the Threshold: The Developing Adolescent,* ed. S. Shirley Feldman and G. R. Elliott. Cambridge, MA: Harvard University Press.

Schieffelin, B. 1990. *The Give and Take of Everyday Life: Language Socialization of Kaluli Children.* New York: Cambridge University Press.

Schieffelin, B., and E. Ochs, eds. 1986. *Language Socialization Across Cultures.* New York: Cambridge University Press.

Schofield, J. 1982. *Black and White in School.* New York: Praeger.

Schütze, Y., K. Kreppner, and S. Paulsen. 1986. The social construction of the sibling relationship. Pp. 129–145 in *Children's Worlds and Children's Language,* ed. J. Cook-Gumperz, W. Corsaro, and J. Streeck. Berlin: Mouton.

Sebald, H. 1986. Adolescents' shifting orientation toward parents and peers: A curvilinear trend over recent decades. *Journal of Marriage and the Family* 48:5–13.

Selman, R. 1980. *The Growth of Interpersonal Understanding.* New York: Academic.

Sewell, W., and R. Hauser. 1975. *Education, Occupation, and Earnings.* New York: Academic.

Shantz, C. 1987. Conflicts among children. *Child Development* 58:283–305.

Shrum, W., N. Cheek, and S. Hunter. 1988. Friendship in school: Gender and racial homophily. *Sociology of Education* 61:227–239.

Shuman, A. 1986. *Storytelling Rights.* Cambridge, UK: Cambridge University Press.

Shweder, R., M. Mahapatra, and J. Miller. 1987. Culture and moral development. Pp. 1–83 in *The Emergence of Morality in Children,* ed. J. Kagan and S. Lamb. Chicago: University of Chicago Press.

Simmons, R., and D. Blyth. 1987. *Moving into Adolescence: The Impact of Pubertal Change and School Context.* New York: Aldine.

Simmons, R., M. Rosenberg, and R. Rosenberg. 1973. Disturbance in the self-image at adolescence. *American Sociological Review* 39:553–568.

Simon, R., D. Eder, and C. Evans. 1992. The development of feeling norms underlying romantic love among adolescent females. *Social Psychology Quarterly.* 55:29–46.

Singer, J., and D. Singer. 1986. Family experience and television viewing as predictors of children's imagination, restlessness, and aggression. *Journal of Social Issues* 42:107–124.

Skinner, B. F. 1969. *Contingencies of Reinforcement: A Theoretical Analysis.* New York: Appleton-Century-Crofts.

Stevenson, H., C. Chen, and D. Uttal. 1990. Beliefs and achievement: A study of black, white, and Hispanic children. *Child Development* 61:508–523.

Stryker, S. 1968. Identity salience and role performance: The relevance of symbolic interaction theory for family research. *Journal of Marriage and the Family* 30:558–564.

———. 1989. Further developments in identity theory: Singularity versus multiplicity of self. Pp. 35–37 in *Theories in Progress: New Formulations,* ed. J. Berger, M. Zelditch, Jr., and B. Anderson. Newbury Park, CA: Sage.

Thompson, M., D. Entwisle, K. Alexander, and M. Sundis. 1992. The influence of family composition on children's conformity to the student role. *American Educational Research Journal* 29:405–424.

Thorne, B. 1986. Girls and boys together . . . but mostly apart: Gender arrangements in elementary school. Pp. 167–184 in *Relationships and Development,* ed. W. Hartup and Z. Rubin. Hillsdale, NJ: Erlbaum.

———. 1989. The social construction of gender in children's worlds. Pp. 139–173 in *Ethnographic Approaches to the Study of Children's Worlds,* ed. S. Berentzen, J. Trondheim, Norway: Norwegian Centre for Child Research.

———. 1993. *Gender Play: Girls and Boys in School.* Brunswick, NJ: Rutgers University Press.

Turiel, E. 1983. *The Development of Social Knowledge.* New York: Cambridge University Press.

Turiel, E., M. Killen, and C. Helwig. 1987. Morality: Its structure, functions, and vagaries. Pp. 155–243 in *The Emergence of Morality in Children,* ed. J. Kagan and S. Lamb. Chicago: University of Chicago Press.

Vygotsky, L. S. 1978. *Mind in Society.* Cambridge, MA: Harvard University Press.

———. 1987. *Thinking and Speech.* New York: Plenum.

Wentworth, M. 1980. *Context and Understanding: An Inquiry into Socialization Theory.* New York: Elsiver.

Wertsch, J. 1989. A sociocultural approach to mind. Pp. 14–33 in *Child Development Today and Tomorrow,* ed. W. Damon. San Francisco: Jossey-Bass.

Whiting, B., and C. Edwards. 1988. *Children of Different Worlds: The Formation of Social Behavior.* Cambridge, MA: Harvard University Press.

Williams, J., and K. White. 1983. Adolescent status systems for males and females at three age levels. *Adolescence* 18:381–389.

Willis, P. 1981. *Learning to Labor.* New York: Columbia University Press.

———. 1990. *Common Culture: Symbolic Work at Play in the Everyday Cultures of the Young.* Boulder, CO: Westview.

Wulff, H. 1988. *Twenty Girls: Growing Up, Ethnicity and Excitement in a South London Microculture* (Stockholm Studies in Social Anthropology, no. 21). Stockholm: University of Stockholm.

Youniss, J. 1980. *Parents and Peers in Social Development: A Sullivan-Piaget Perspective.* Chicago: University of Chicago Press.

Youniss, J., and J. Smollar. 1985. *Adolescent Relations with Mothers, Fathers and Friends.* Chicago: University of Chicago Press.

Zajonc, R., and G. Markus. 1975. Birth order and intellectual development. *Psychological Review* 82:74–88.

Zukow, P., ed. 1989. *Sibling Interaction across Cultures: Theoretical and Methodological Issues.* New York: Springer-Verlag.

CHAPTER 17

Adult Lives in a Changing Society

GLEN H. ELDER, JR.
ANGELA M. O'RAND

The study of adults and their lives has undergone profound change in the social sciences since the 1960s. Adulthood is now likely to be placed in an age-graded life course that orients study to childhood antecedents and later-life consequences for aging and old age. In their survey of the 1980s, Streib and Binstock (1990, 1) refer to the "tremendous increase in attention paid to the adult life-course (and sometimes the full life-course) context in which persons age." They conclude that "an understanding of the life course has become integral to social scientific studies of aging."

An equally important feature of this change in perspective relates adult lives to a society undergoing change. Pioneering longitudinal studies of American children born in the 1920s who grew up in times of economic depression and global war eventually followed their lives into the middle years during the 1960s and 1970s (Eichorn et al. 1981). The evolving life courses of these men and women reflect their changing historical times (Elder 1974). In addition, a demographic change toward greater longevity gave more visibility to the problems of old age, raising once again questions about prior experiences and the relation between lives and times.

These two developments are elements of a paradigm change in the social and behavioral sciences toward the greater primacy of context, temporality, and process in studies of individuals, groups, and social organizations (Featherman 1982; O'Rand and Krecker 1990). Life span developmental psychology (Baltes and Reese 1984) and life course analysis (Buchmann 1989; Elder 1975; Riley, Johnson, and Foner 1972) are part of this intellec-

tual movement. They share a general framework that addresses issues of continuity, development, and change in human lives, including assumptions about the relatedness of widely separated life transitions and life stages that determine the meaning of events and actions. As such, these orientations differ from earlier approaches to the study of human lives, such as socialization (Brim and Wheeler 1966; Bush and Simmons 1981; Dion 1985; Goslin 1969; Mortimer and Simmons 1978) and social structure and personality theories (House 1981). The field of inquiry tended to place less emphasis on the ongoing developmental consequences of the interaction between individual and context over time that produce heterogeneity in aging populations and more attention on the "internalized orientations" (e.g., values) or "situational demands" that determine individual development (Kohli 1988).

These new approaches also differ from each other in many respects, especially with regard to the historical meanings of human contexts and the role of social ties in binding lives and their pathways. Life span psychology focuses on biological and psychodynamic factors in individual development that produce pervasive and multidirectional change over the life span (Riegel 1977; Schaie and Willis 1986). Since the 1960s this area has contributed significantly to our understanding of individual agency in human development. Life course analysis, on the other hand, focuses on social processes of development, and over the same period has contributed to our growing understanding of the interaction of biography with historical social structures over time in human development. Both approaches have redirected the course of research on adult lives.

The life course represents a concept and a theoretical perspective. As a concept, it refers to age-graded life patterns embedded in social institutions and subject to historical change. The life course consists of interlocking trajectories or pathways across the life span that are marked by sequences of events and social transitions. Instead of the once prominent single-career studies, life course theory relates multiple careers or trajectories and centers on their coordination. The life course as theoretical orientation has defined a common field of inquiry by providing a framework that guides research in terms of problem identification and formulation, variable selection and rationales, and strategies of design and analysis.

We begin this chapter by discussing what is new in these contemporary views of adult lives and development. The answer takes us well beyond the observations just noted to a number of interlocking developments. Robert Merton (1968) has noted that advances in science are systemic in development and expression. Consistent with this perspective, the discovery of data archives, new methodological techniques, and the accumulation and convergence of research findings from across disciplines have influenced life course theory and redirected inquiry on adult development. In turn, the emergence of new research questions has led to the recasting of data, models, and analysis.

The second part of the chapter surveys the processes by which individual lives and developmental trajectories are constructed and reconstructed. These include selection processes by which people choose or are initiated into adult pathways under varying constraints, as well as social transition processes that alter and regulate patterns of adult development. In our discussion of these life course processes, we highlight research on adult development across diverse contexts, including family, workplace, and health. Central issues range from the stability and accentuation of personality to psychosocial adaptation and unpatterned or even disordered change.

We conclude with an emphasis on the mechanisms that connect historical change with processes of adult development. How historical factors influence specific patterns of adult lives presents itself as the final important consideration for life course research. Throughout the chapter, we keep in mind the constant interplay between changing lives and a changing society.

STUDYING ADULT LIVES: SOME CONTEMPORARY DISTINCTIONS

Contemporary distinctions in the study of adult lives and development are linked to a complex set of changes, described in terms of the life course revolution and its roots in the intellectual milieu of the 1960s. These changes include a new consciousness of lives, patterned by the contours and social discontinuities of history, that took the form of historically defined questions and a rudimentary theory of the life course (Riley, Johnson, and Foner 1972). Other changes include the mobilization of data resources well suited to the study of the life course, particularly the establishment of longitudinal studies that follow people year by year over their lives (Young, Savola, and Phelps 1991), such as the National Longitudinal Surveys of Labor Market Experience and the Michigan Panel Study of Income Dynamics (Brooks-Gunn, Phelps, and Elder 1991; Duncan and Morgan 1985). Countless smaller longitudinal studies were also established at the time.

The development of data analysis techniques kept pace with these changes through the refinement of models for the analysis of life course dynamics, from event history models to the analysis of differential rates of change and transition probabilities (Campbell and O'Rand 1988; Mayer and Tuma 1990). Procedures for collecting life record data also achieved notable advances through the development of event-history retrospective surveys (Freedman et al. 1988). The incorporation of population studies in sociology during the 1960s and 1970s contributed to many of these conceptual and technical developments, from the cohort approach (Ryder 1965) to the study of demographic events, the expansion of longitudinal studies, and multivariate techniques of data analysis. Reflecting this contribution is Featherman and Lerner's (1985) population perspective on life course development.

The increasing conceptual prominence of time, context, and process in the social sciences is expressed in these developments and in the life course framework as a whole (Elder 1985; Hagestad 1990; Kertzer and Keith 1984). Life course theory is temporal and contextual in locating people in history through birth years and in the life course through the social meanings of age-graded events and activities. The perspective also directs inquiry to processes by which life change occurs and to studies following people across time. This initiative gained momentum during the 1960s from a simple discovery that had profound repercussions for the study of adult lives and aging (Schaie 1965): the limitations of cross-sectional data for studies of life course development.

Time, History, and the Life Course

The belief that a decline in intelligence occurs with age in the later years was firmly entrenched in popular knowledge during the 1960s, though it received empirical support primarily from the cross-sectional comparison of adult samples at different ages. Such comparisons ruled out any possibility for studying life course processes over time and for unraveling the meaning of observed age differences (Baltes, Cornelius, and Nesselroade 1979; Schaie 1965, 1990). An apparent decline from one age group to another could be due to the natural course of aging and the impact of differential social change.

The older age groups belonged to cohorts with different social and cultural histories than the younger groups. For example, as better-educated and native-born people became more common in the U.S. population, younger cohorts expressed this advantage through higher performances on tests and educational attainment. The generalized image of old age decline thus was an artifact of an inappropriate research design. Questions about adult development and aging could be addressed more effectively with longitudinal data, and this conclusion added force to the rationale for more longitudinal studies.

Students of adult development also learned something from this controversy about the relation between social change and aging. Social change is always a potential explanation for age differences, in addition to biological aging. Efforts to disentangle these competing explanations thus required a comparison of two or more birth cohorts. Historical influence takes the form of a *cohort* effect when a particular type of social change, such as a drastic income decline in the Great Depression (Buchmann 1989; Elder 1974; Mayer 1986), differentiates the life patterns of successive cohorts, such as older and younger Americans born in the 1920s who grew up in the 1930s. History also takes the form of a *period* effect when the effect of a social change is relatively uniform across successive birth cohorts. Secular trends in the scheduling of marriages and first births across the twentieth century are largely an expression of massive period effects (Modell 1989). A third type of effect occurs through *maturation* or *aging*.

Attempts to partition the variance according to these effects have not advanced our understanding of social change because of the ambiguous meaning of historical effects—cohort and period. Typically, research does not address questions that specify a type of social change or the process by which it is expected to alter the life course. Instead, questions assign environmental change to an error term or compare multiple cohorts as a test of the generalization boundaries of behavioral outcomes. Even when history is substantively important, it may be operationalized as a period or cohort effect that provides no clue as to the precise nature of the influence. In addition, cohort comparisons restrict what is learned about the effects of social change by obscuring variations within successive cohorts. As studies of the Great Depression make clear (Elder 1974), families did not experience economic decline uniformly, and family hardship did not affect all subgroups of children in the same way.

Cohort Comparisons and Their Limitations

Birth cohorts represent a long-established way of relating the life course to changes in society. By locating people in historical context, the cohort analyst may be alerted to the meaning of contexts for lives. This sensitivity has much to do with the originating question. Does it focus on a particular type of change, or call for a descriptive map of the territory as a first step?

Cohort studies typically speculate about historical forces and fail to extend analysis to their actual investigation. At most we end with a plausible story that does not advance scientific understanding. It does not weigh specific forces or explicate causal processes. An example of such limitations comes from a study by Rindfuss et al. (1984) on the first birth transition among native white women in the United States. Using births from 1915 to 1939, they found a strong period effect across the cohorts. "Period factors increase[d] or decrease[d] childbearing at all ages and for all subgroups within society" (p. 368), but causal factors remained a mystery. The investigators pointed to the women's movement, rising interest rates, and soaring housing prices, but the data are inadequate to support this interpretation. Clearly, the range of potential effects under any "period" umbrella is sufficiently large to frustrate the development of conclusions about precise effects. Cohort and period effects map categories of influence that are little more than black boxes inviting speculation.

Useful information on historical influences and cohort life patterns can be obtained from the notion of historical settings as opportunity structures (Easterlin 1978). The relative size, composition, and historical niche of a birth cohort have much to do with member access to life opportunities. Thus the small birth cohorts that came of age in the 1950s were relatively advantaged on life opportunities in comparison to the larger cohorts from the baby boom who entered a troubled labor market in the 1970s. However dramatic in general outline, such contrasts remain inconclusive as to the processes involved.

Another example of this point comes from the observation that as each cohort encounters a historical event or change, it "is distinctively marked by the career stage it occupies" (Ryder 1965, 846). With a measure of the historical imprint by cohort, the next step is to demonstrate how it occurred. What is the process by which successive birth co-horts are differentially influenced by particular historical forces? To answer this question, it is important to recognize the heterogeneity of each cohort in social composition and historical experience. What are the basic subgroups in each cohort? The experiences of the middle and working classes varied markedly as to hardship during the Great Depression, as did those of men and women in the military or on the homefront during World War II. Cohort subgroups defined according to their relevance to a particular change event offer greater understanding of the life course effects of that change by cohort.

The distinctive contextual theme in contemporary studies of adult lives is coupled with an appreciation of the plasticity and agency of the individual organism (Lerner 1984). Social constraints are elements of a contextual perspective, as is the agency of the individual actor. The particular situations people select typically impose certain behavioral constraints, including barriers to leaving the field. This interplay between life contexts and agency is expressed in contemporary features of research on adult lives.

Life Transitions: Linking Life Contexts and Individual Agency

A contextual perspective on adult lives in sociology views the social environment "as a constituent force in development" (Dannefer 1984, 847) rather than a setting for the unfolding process of maturation and aging. But life contexts defined as settings for behavior still characterize much of the research on adult lives. For example, a cohort approach to adult lives is seemingly contextual, yet it identifies broad categories of potential influences that provide no clear understanding of the mechanisms which link history with individual development or change. Likewise, viewing the environment from the organism's perspective fails to extract the full implications of a changing social system for individuals. It is one thing to place people in World War II and quite another to show how mass mobilization drastically altered their options and life experiences.

Views of the environment from the behavior setting and organism are prominent in life span developmental psychology. Developmentalists are "likely to postulate a 'typical' course of ontogeny and to view non-normative and history-graded factors as modifiers, not as fundamental constituents, of development" (Hetherington and Baltes 1988, 9). Here the environment is treated as an exogenous influence whose effects serve to enable or deflect the programmed course of development, but not to generate it.

Dannefer correctly notes that the major question is whether the life span model can incorporate "the range of social processes that organize the life courses of individuals and the collective life-course patterns of cohorts" (1984, 847). Making definitional statements about the centrality of the social environment does not mean research will be designed or findings interpreted "in a way that apprehends social structure as a constitutive force in development, and that views the social environment as more than a setting that facilitates maturational unfolding."

In life course theory, this force is expressed in part through the dynamism of interdependent lives. All lives are lived interdependently, and this connectedness structures a process of self-development. Linked lives are a product of intergenerational ties and social transmission, as multigenerational studies document. Vern Bengtson's Los Angeles study (Mangen, Bengtson, and Landry 1988) of three generations is a pioneering effort along these lines.

Life span psychology generally falls short of offering this mode of analysis and interpretation, but so do models in psychology as a whole, including the ecology of human development (Bronfenbrenner 1979). Theory and research in psychology do not apprehend social structure as a constitutive force in development because the field generally views the social environment from the perspective of the individual organism.

This individual perspective and a cohort approach generally pose research questions on the adult contexts of lives that lack an informed knowledge of the workings of society, social structure, and social change relative to their human consequences. As such, they do not contribute to a theory of how social factors and systemic changes influence the adult life course. However, an individual perspective does highlight the agency of the adult and the social choices the person makes among available options.

No idea better illustrates the contemporary link between social context and the agency of the individual than the concept of *life transition,* which defines the problem as a change in states—social and psychological (Clausen 1972; Cowan and Hetherington 1991). Adults bring a history of life experiences to each transition, interpret the new circumstances in terms of this legacy, and work out adaptations that can alter their life course. When transitions disrupt habitual patterns of behavior, they provide options for new directions in life, a turning point (Elder, Gimbel, and Ivie 1991). In the adult life course, trajectories of work and family are defined by a sequence of transitions or events adults experience by choice or necessity.

All transitions involve an exit and an entry, and difficulties in leaving a social role tend to increase the risk of a troubled entry into another, as illustrated by divorce and remarriage (Furstenberg and Cherlin 1991). These two components of transitions are linked to different causal processes, as one might expect, and we are beginning to see *variation* in these processes across stages of the life course. Job loss, widowhood, and other transitions have different meanings and psychological implications from the early adult years to later life, especially when they violate normative expectations (McLanahan and Sorensen 1985; Wortman and Silver 1990). Widowhood, for example, is especially painful in young adulthood.

Transition studies of this kind have replaced life stage research as a central focus of work on adult development and aging (Hagestad 1990; Hareven 1978; Nicholson 1990). Instead of research exclusively centered on early adult status, midlife accomplishments, or economic well-being in later life, more studies are addressing the determinants and antecedents of life transitions, including transitions to adulthood (Hogan and Astone 1986; Modell 1989); transitions into and out of careers and family roles; and transitions out of the labor force in later life (Henretta and O'Rand 1983). Studies now address the connections between early and later transitions and between transitions in different generations (Burton and Bengtson 1985). We see a corresponding change in developmental studies. Stage theoretic accounts of early development, in childhood and adolescence, have declined in popularity (e.g., Piagetian theory) as interests have turned to social transitions and the mechanisms of developmental outcomes (de Ribaupierre 1989). Explication is receiving greater priority in life course studies.

Despite the empirical evidence on links between life transitions, the agency of individuals and their life choices ensures some degree of *loose coupling* between social transitions and stages. The life course is age-graded according to generalized divisions or categories, from childhood to old age, but members of a birth cohort do not move through this age structure in concert according to the social roles they occupy. Age at entry into a full-time job, completion of formal education, cohabitation and marriage, the birth of the first child—these and other events in the transition to adulthood are not experienced by all members of a birth cohort, and those who experience them do so at widely varied times in life (Modell 1989).

The choices and options in life course timing have much to do with loose coupling across transitions and statuses in the adult life course. Loose coupling reflects the agency of individuals even in constrained situations as well as their achievements in rewriting past journeys in the course of aging (Cohler 1982). The meaning of life transitions and experiences can change drastically along the pathways of aging.

Age grades and loose coupling exemplify two sides of the adult life course—its social regulation and the actor's behavior within conventional boundaries, and even outside of them. The policies and processes of social regulation depict a pattern of social order in lives as a social aggregate, while the study of individual lives and actions highlights an element of flux and disorder. Social structuring or regulation occurs informally through the network of social relationships that forms a lifelong community of significant others, from family to friends (Rossi and Rossi 1990). Structuring or regulating also occurs through societal mechanisms that "impose order and constraints on lives," (Mayer 1986, 28) including institutional careers, the cumulative effects of delayed transitions, the collective conditions associated with particular cohorts (historical circumstances, etc.), and state intervention and regulation. The growth of the state in social regulation counters the potential fragmentation of increasing institutional differentiation.

If we can speak of order in the life course—a typical sequence of life transitions—can we also speak of disorder? In an important study of the transition to adulthood, Dennis Hogan (1981) identifies a typical sequence for American men in the twentieth century that begins with an exit from school or education, continues with entry into a first full-time job, and concludes for most men with entry into marriage. A more detailed analysis of the young adult years by Rindfuss et al. (1987) obtained more than two hundred event sequences in a national sample of high school graduates from the early 1970s, an array that defied any simple overview. They point out "that understanding the nature and importance of sequence in the life course requires analyzing what the roles themselves mean and how they are causally linked" (p. 27). This requisite is the missing element in studies of event order and disorder.

Issues of life context and agency come together in explanations of adult trajectories and provide a conclusion for this introductory section on studying adult lives. Do people become more alike or more dissimilar as they move across the adult years and into old age? Can we identify groups or people who are likely to converge or diverge in line of development? Neugarten and Gutmann (1958) initially argued that men and women tend to converge in behavioral development in later life: men tend to display more feminine qualities, while women express more masculine qualities. The empirical foundation for this assertion is not persuasive today, but a perspective on behavioral convergence represents a contrast to the more compelling recent thesis of an age-related increase in the heterogeneity of individuals in birth cohorts that exceeds simple gender differences (Herzog 1989). The assertion is that men and women become more differentiated as individuals in personality and behavior as they age.

A prime explanation for increasing divergence dates back at least to the Law of Effect and its application to the behavioral consequences of individual inequality. The Law of Effect states that behavior is sustained or changed by its consequences. Competent behavior is generally rewarded by others, and Clausen (1991) shows that adolescent competence is highly predictive of adult competence in later years. One might also argue that challenging situations accentuate competencies in life course development, as does the risk of a failure experience among the less able. In the field of science, Merton (1973) has characterized the process of unequal accumulation of awards and success among talented scientists in terms of the "Matthew effect," and Dannefer (1987) applies this perspective to increasing behavioral differentiation among aging men and women.

PROCESSES IN THE CONSTRUCTION OF ADULT LIVES

These paradigmatic changes encompassed by life course perspectives on development and aging have redirected the focus of research from the invariant stages of adult life (e.g., Levinson 1986; Levinson et al. 1978) and the oversocialized view of development (criticized for its "allocation bias" by DiRenzo 1977, 286) to the ongoing processes by which lives are constructed and reconstructed from birth to death in ways only weakly correlated with age.

The complex *interplay* of time, historical and situational context, and individual agency is now the concern of research. Empirical studies since the 1960s have established the equivalent importance of these constituents of adult development and have spurred contemporary work on their connections. This effort ranges from behavioral genetics to social psychology and historical demography.

In the course of these developments, the global concept of socialization—as a primary process of development—has been eclipsed by more refined interactive conceptions of social selection, transitional contingencies, sequential effects, cumulative and interactional continuity, and accentuation. We turn now to these processes of adult development, beginning with discoveries in behavioral genetics that demonstrate the salience of individual agency for development and progressing to life course analyses that link individual agency with social contexts over time.

Selection and Transitional Processes in Development

Converging perspectives from the social and behavioral sciences after the 1960s challenged an oversocialized view of development. Phenotype-environment models of behavior in behavioral genetics led the way in changing these views at the individual level. The first was the discovery of children as active agents in their own development—as influences on their own parents (Bell 1968; Glass, Bengtson, and Dunham 1986). Studies of child-parent interactions attributed some variations in parental behavior to their children, thereby casting doubt on the assumption that parental environments accounted for all observed differences among children (Scarr 1989).

Studies of adolescent achievement, traditionally predicated on the deterministic assumption of a unidirectional parental effect, offered a similar challenge. The insertion of "family background" variables in models of child and adolescent attainment has been criticized for incorrectly attributing causal priority and for overstating the influence of small environmental variations on children (Scarr 1989). Children and adolescents actively participate in the construction of their environments through dispositional tendencies and behavioral choices (Caspi and Bem 1990; Lerner 1991).

Second, discovery among children of the often greater behavioral variation *within* than *between* families enhanced challenges to the traditional socialization model. These results prompted behavioral genetics research on the intelligence, dispositions, and social achievements of twin and adoptive children to probe the dynamics of individual-environment (or person-situation) interactions (Plomin and Thompson 1987; Scarr and Weinberg 1983). Plomin and Daniels's (1987) groundbreaking analysis of "unshared environments" established that children growing up in the same family experienced their environments differently. Clearly, environments do not have a uniform impact on the lives of individuals who occupy them, either in an immediate (instantaneous) sense or in an enduring way. Rather, development occurs as a product of individuals' engagement with their environments.

Adult development is the successive engagement of individual biography with social contexts over time (Kohli 1988). The process of engagement has cumulative and emergent interactional features. As such, successive engagement, conceptualized as a sequence or trajectory of social transitions, is more than the sum of individual attributes and the characteristics of diverse social contexts over time. It is an interactive process wherein individuals' experiences in successive contexts are uniquely conditioned by their prior histories *and* social contexts are themselves influenced as a result of this engagement. *Selection effects* and *transitional (situational) effects* interact across the life course to link biography and context, respectively. They integrate biographically accumulated individual characteristics with diverse social environments. In turn, these interactions create diverse conditions for personal continuity and change.

Fine-grained studies of social transitions illustrate the complex operation of these processes. In many cases, social transitions are at once institutionalized passages in the life courses of cohorts *and* personal experiences of individuals conditioned by their biographies and historical locations. They vary in their structuredness or degree of external regulation, duration, predictability, novelty, uncertainty, and ambiguity and in their timing and ordering. The transitions of marriage, childbirth, divorce, widowhood, unemployment, and retirement can vary in each of these ways.

These characteristics of transitions have potential consequences for development, called tran-

sitional effects. These effects are in turn contingent on the biographies of individuals. Consider the retirement experiences of recent cohorts. Retirement is experienced differently within cohorts (Dannefer 1987), within couples, and by individuals over time. Adjustment to retirement, for example, is positively associated with the early versus late timing of the transition, voluntary versus involuntary onset, and economic well-being (Palmore et al. 1985). But these transitional effects interact with such biographical characteristics or selection effects as gender, occupational background, and family history (O'Rand 1990). Individuals' prior experiences or characteristics introduce selection effects that modulate the impact of transitions. Thus, the effects of transitions are contingent on the prior histories of individuals experiencing them.

Early transitional experiences and sequences are prologues for middle and late adulthood transitions that produce heterogeneity over the life course (Hogan 1981; Hogan and Astone 1986). This development can be seen in longitudinal studies of divorce and their increasing attention to the behavioral changes coupled with it (Furstenberg and Cherlin 1991). In children as well as adults, the divorce transition appears to accentuate dispositions that were present well before the event itself. "Problem boys" after the divorce of their parents were typically engaged in problem behavior before the divorce (Cherlin et al. 1991).

Early adult transitions and experiences have consequences for subsequent transitions, even after many years have passed. They do so through behavioral consequences that set in motion cumulative effects and radiating implications for other life domains. For example, the loss of parents in childhood, whether through death or divorce, can have psychosocial costs that persist well into the middle years, diminishing feelings about self and competence (McLeod 1991). The influences of early transitions on midlife statuses are well documented in a panel study of teen mothers followed between 1966 and 1984 (Furstenberg, Brooks-Gunn, and Morgan 1987). Though early motherhood constrains subsequent attainments (educational, occupational, economic, and marital), the adolescent mothers who began with similar disadvantaged origins varied markedly in midlife economic status. Just as many had attained full-time work and middle-income status as had fallen into or remained in poverty. One source of this variation is the timing and ordering of educational, occupational, or marital events following pregnancy. The timing and ordering of early events can also influence later life events, such as retirement. Entry into full-time work early in life, even if interrupted by family responsibilities along the way, predicts higher economic status and earlier retirement among women (O'Rand and Henretta 1982).

Traditional stage (Levinson 1986) and socialization (Dion 1985) theories view transitional effects, narrowly defined, as central to development. The stages of adult life are ordered in relatively invariant, age-graded sequences with positive and negative effects that are inevitably disruptive or "stressful," thereby requiring adaptation or equilibration. Attention is generally focused on the effect of the transition, with little or no consideration for the conditioning influences of prior life experiences. This narrow transitional approach has been applied widely to the study of the mental health impact of selected life events. Scales of the stress-producing content of selected life events (e.g., Dohrenwend and Dohrenwend 1981) are presumed to be relatively invariant across life stages as stressors for different individuals.

However, recent empirical work has overturned this deterministic view (George, 1993). Social transitions carry different meanings for individuals with different histories and social resources (Kessler 1979; Lin and Ensel 1989). Socioeconomic background, for example, is a persistent selection factor in individuals' capacities to cope with life transitions. McLeod and Kessler's (1990) analyses of socioeconomic differences in the level of distress following undesirable life events replicates earlier findings but also suggests that socioeconomic background operates as a developmental factor rather than merely an index of financial resources. These authors examined five national data sets—Myers's New Haven Survey, Veroff's Survey of Modern Living, and three NIMH Community Mental Health Assessment studies—to disaggregate the effects of socioeconomic components on different stressful life events, particularly income loss, illness, separation/divorce, and death of a loved one.

Across the studies they find that lower socioeconomic effects persist in affecting vulnerability to distress across all life events. However, they conclude that these outcomes reflect more than access to financial resources; rather, they operate through "the prior socialization of resilient personality characteristics" (McLeod and Kessler 1990, 162). Education and occupation operate differently from income to influence individuals' vulnerability to different life events.

Wheaton's (1990) recent study of life transitions, role histories, and mental health also substantiates the role of selection processes and raises serious doubts that increased stress is an inevitable outcome of transition experiences. The impact of a set of events commonly ranked as highly stressful (e.g., divorce, retirement, widowhood, marriage, additional children, and job promotion) reveals that the "stressor" effect of the transition varies according to prior levels of stress. For some individuals divorce or job loss may have positive effects on well-being, if their marriage or job entailed negative experiences. As such, social transitions have no a priori status as stressors when they are embedded in individual role histories.

Similar results have been obtained in several panel studies of the impact of the "empty nest" transition on parental well-being or life satisfaction (e.g., McLanahan and Adams 1987; McLanahan and Sorensen 1985; Menaghan 1985; White and Edwards 1990). Emptying the nest was long assumed to be a stressful life event with negative effects, particularly for mothers. However, studies have shown diverse responses to the event, including increased and decreased self-satisfaction for mothers and fathers. These changes are *contingent on prior individual and family characteristics,* such as mother's employment (White and Edwards, 1990), parents' age at children's departure

(McLanahan and Sorensen 1985), and varying conditions of prior family stress (Goldscheider and Goldscheider 1988).

Other exemplary illustrations of the operation of selection and transition effects can be found in studies of divorce, its precursors, and its aftermath (Cherlin 1981). Women's responses to divorce are mediated by such contingencies as prior employment history, presence and age(s) of children, prior attitudes toward sexual behavior, self-efficacy, and other self-assessments as well as satisfaction with the marriage. Menaghan (1985) and colleagues reported on a panel study of Chicago area adults who divorced between the first and second waves of a study conducted in the early 1970s (Menaghan and Lieberman 1986). The analyses show greater depressive affect following divorce. However, this result varies according to predivorce differences in psychological well-being. The study also finds that the most adverse effects resulted from deprived life conditions produced by the divorce, such as income decline, rather than from the divorce itself.

Selection, Transition, and Accentuation

The studies summarized above examine the interaction of selection and transition effects associated with a single social transition. Longitudinal analyses demonstrate the force of social selection over time on patterns of stability and accentuation of individual characteristics across transitions. Studies of personal change (Caspi and Bem 1990) find overwhelming evidence for *ipsative stability* in the life course—persistence of individual traits across transitions. Indeed, stability coefficients tend to increase as age increases, revealing *accentuation* as a mechanism of development. Accentuation refers to an increase of emphasis or salience of prominent characteristics from the point of entry into the new situation.

The accentuation effect of interaction between personality and new situations represents a plausible mechanism for the differentiation hypothesis of aging (Elder and Caspi 1990). Countless studies have shown that situational change accentuates the

states and processes of individual dispositions and relationships (Dannefer 1987). But while the success of competence is readily understood following the Law of Effect, we have little knowledge or understanding of why maladaptive behaviors persist and even become more pronounced over the life course. As Lee Robins (1978, 611) points out, most problem children do not become problem adults.

Personal stability and accentuation over the life course are produced in complex ways by processes of social selection and social transition. Social selection, which incorporates prior transition effects, represents the accumulation of life experiences. These experiences influence patterns of choice over the life course. *Assortative processes* are a case in point. Individuals select situations (e.g., college campuses) that are compatible with prior selection-transition experiences and their developing dispositions. Such choices lead to contact with people of similar disposition, thereby reinforcing lifelong patterns. Transition experiences of this kind enhance the likelihood of continuity or accentuation.

The homophily principle in assortative marriage patterns and its long-term effects illustrate this process (Caspi and Herbener 1990; Caspi, Herbener, and Ozer 1992). Using Q-sort methods (Block 1971) to match couples' personality configurations, Caspi and colleagues find that homogamy is the basic assortative pattern. The couples did not come to resemble each other increasingly over the marriage but showed a high degree of similarity across twenty years. Net of original selection (assortative) effects, couples' shared environmental experiences (transition contexts) seem to maintain conjugal similarity over the course of the marriage.

The recently published follow-up of Newcomb's Bennington sample demonstrates similar selection and transition effects (Alwin, Cohen, and Newcomb 1991). Prior studies show that the development of political values among undergraduate women at Bennington College led to patterns of increased similarity among them over time. The Alwin et al. follow-up of these women reveals strong selection effects in assortative marriage and continuity of political values over the period following college graduation. Liberalized graduates selected liberal mates. As in the Caspi studies, assortative marriage followed homophilous patterns, which in turn reinforced or accentuated prior attitudes.

The effects of social selection on marital stability further corroborate these results. Divorce rates decline with increased marital duration. Researchers are concerned with disentangling selection and duration influences on stability. The selection argument for marital stability is that "well-matched partners will have more stable marriages" and divorce will decline with marital duration "simply because fewer incompatible couples remain at risk" (Heaton 1991, 287). Alternatively, the transitional effects argument emphasizes that the growing interdependence of couples over the duration of their marital state stabilizes the environment, thereby enhancing the prospect for permanence of the marriage.

Adult development in the workplace further illuminates the interplay of selection and transition effects. Studies of the interaction of worker characteristics such as job involvement, self-esteem, and employer identification with career stage on career attainments and other outcomes have been conducted on panel data drawn from case studies of personnel over time and from national probability samples. Among the former, the American Telephone and Telegraph Company studies of managerial lives in transition provide rich detail on selection and transition processes in the organizational career (Howard and Bray 1988). Two longitudinal studies were conducted over twenty-five years of observations—the Management Progress Study (MPS) begun in 1956 and the Management Continuity Study (MCS) begun in 1977.

The studies were designed to measure the abilities, personality traits, and work-related attitudes of young managers over the time they remained with the firm. Managers in the MPS project were studied annually during its first seven years and then followed up triannually between years ten and nineteen. Researchers examined the effects of

cultural and economic changes between the 1950s and the 1980s, the differences between the two cohorts, and managers' patterns of individual stability and change in the two panels.

Overall, their results show relatively high levels of consistency within individuals in their ability, personality, and job involvement profiles. For example, high self-esteem, ambition, and positiveness in the early period related strongly to these attitudes later, as well as to greater job ladder success and adjustment; alternatively, initial low self-esteem and ambition remained evident at later periods in the career. Managers exhibited increasing intraindividual stability and interindividual heterogeneity over twenty years of their careers.

The MPS study identified which initial (time 1) traits of managers were most predictive of subsequent success, defined by two criteria: positional advancement to the highest (general) management levels in the company and measured personal adjustment (based on the Guilford-Martin Inventory of personality characteristics). Initial characteristics predictive of both criteria were high self-esteem, high positiveness, and strong work involvement. Positional advancement was uniquely predicted by effective administrative skills, strong interpersonal skills, and high ambition, while adjustment at year twenty was specifically predicted by affability and sound mental and physical health at time 1. The primary higher-order factor subsuming these traits among others was defined as "general effectiveness" and yielded a consistency correlation of 0.40 over the twenty years.

Cohort differences between the MPS and the MCS were also striking. Older and younger managers compared in the last wave (MPS-20 and MCS) of observations demonstrated different attitudes toward themselves and their jobs. Growing up in the 1940s and 1950s was associated with stronger interests in leadership and oral communication and lower interests in nonconformity, health awareness, and compassion when compared with growing up in the 1960s and 1970s.

Similar patterns of stability were demonstrated in a national probability sample of workers (Lorence and Mortimer 1985). The researchers observed three age groups of workers sampled in the Quality of Employment Survey for 1972 to 1977, comparing the effects of "aging stability" with effects of "career stage," and reveal the social selection and transitional components of change. They found early subjective job involvement highly associated with relative job involvement later in the career.

But this selection effect varies across three career stages, labeled trial, stabilization, and maintenance. Job involvement remained relatively stable over time, but its effects were greatest during the career stabilization phase, when "job shopping" had subsided and long-term investments were made. The simultaneous consideration of selection and transition effects reveals a complex process of adult development in the workplace.

These studies clearly show that stability results from patterns of intraindividual continuity across transitions. However, episodes of discontinuity in adult lives can also produce the accentuation of cumulative individual differences. According to Elder and Caspi (1990, 218), the accentuation principle depicts the increased salience of "already prominent characteristics during social transitions in the life course" that may represent discontinuities stemming from personal or historical circumstances. Social transitions vary in the degree to which they enable individual differences to manifest themselves (Caspi and Bem 1990). Nonnormative, less socially regulated, or unexpected transitions permit greater individual heterogeneity, while more highly regulated or normative transitions permit less.

The Loose Coupling of the Life Course

The idea of loose coupling is not meant to equate life course effects with unexplained variance; rather, it takes into account the temporal processes linking life transitions in patterned ways to explain variation. As such, loose coupling orients analysis to the processes that sustain problem or achievement behaviors and even accentuate them—and the processes that generate change. Recent studies by Sampson and Laub (1990, 1993) provide compelling

evidence of the complex interaction of selection and transitional processes in the loose coupling of the life course.

They reconstructed and reanalyzed the Gluecks' (1950) landmark studies of delinquents and nondelinquents who were followed from (average) ages fourteen to thirty-two between 1940 and 1965. The Gluecks drew two samples of five hundred delinquents and five hundred nondelinquent school children in the Boston area matched case by case on age, race/ethnicity, IQ, and residential income status in 1940 and followed up (with a 92 percent success rate) at ages twenty-five and thirty-two. They gathered data on criminal, job, and family traits at each stage and compared sample characteristics using cross-sectional techniques.

Sampson and Laub reconstructed the data and applied longitudinal methods to determine the selection effects of childhood delinquency on later criminal or deviant behavior and the life course effects of subsequent adult role transitions in modifying early childhood influences. They found that early childhood delinquency predicts crime, economic dependency, divorce, and unemployment, among other behaviors, in adulthood. However, they also discovered that "adult bonds" in marriage and employment inhibit adult deviance. The stronger the adult ties to work and family among former delinquents and nondelinquents, the less crime, alcohol abuse, and general deviance.

Increased longevity and loose coupling among early and later life transitions are most evident in studies of older populations, where the selection effects of early roles and patterns of adaptation persist but only as the intervening or long-term patterns of living are considered. For example, diversity in longevity among elderly women has been found to result from differential lifelong patterns of social integration. Moen et al. (1989) conducted a thirty-year follow-up study of a panel of wives from the Elmira region of New York. They discovered that stability in lifelong patterns of multiple role encumbancy predicted women's longevity. Typically there were early and sustained patterns of participation in roles spanning the family, workplace, and voluntary domains.

Further evidence on these patterns comes from studies that used the Retirement History and New Beneficiary Surveys of the Social Security Administration to examine early life course influences on the joint behaviors of retirement-age dual-worker couples. Older couples with a less gender-segregated division of labor early in their marriage tend to retire closer in time to each other (Henretta and O'Rand 1983; O'Rand, Henretta, and Krecker 1991). Conjugal symmetry in lifetime marital roles seems to affect retirement synchronization. Specifically, joint market work during the early years of marriage tends to increase the likelihood of shared work and household experiences by couples over their marriage into retirement.

Such examinations of widely separated but linked transitions illuminate the importance of considering adulthood in the context of the total life course and its developmental sequences. Social selection processes bring earlier transitions to bear on later events. However, the meanings and consequences of earlier events can change as the life trajectory shifts in the course of development and aging.

Life course study of adulthood highlights this discontinuity by revealing heterogeneity in the sequences of persons' lives and their consequences. This heterogeneity derives from the interaction of selection and transition processes, producing adulthood patterns that tend toward increasing personal stability and interindividual heterogeneity. Cumulative and discontinuous processes, which intuitively appear to be countervailing forces in development, nevertheless serve as counterpoints over the life course, contributing to its construction and reconstruction.

Cumulative and differentiating individual life span experiences lead older populations to exhibit an ironic complement of characteristics: a relatively greater heterogeneity between individuals *and* an increased continuity within individuals, resulting from the complex selection and transition processes of "aging differently" (Maddox 1987). Interindividual heterogeneity emerges as life trajectories diverge, while intraindividual continuity

is preserved as individual characteristics become reinforced and even accentuated through processes of habituation and the selection and construction of stable environments.

The biological imperatives of aging are an essential part of this process. Changes with age in the capacity for self-regulation (homeostasis) in response to environmental stress produce discontinuities in the environment (Spence 1989). Differential rates of biological aging that occur jointly with changing environments act as underlying factors in an ongoing process of development. Their consequences are modified by individuals' enduring characteristics and the social support and economic security that mediate the effects of stress. Trajectories of decline and/or growth in cognition, personality, achievement, and other individual processes are not inevitable (Schaie and Willis 1986). Instead, multiple trajectories can and do emerge (Dannefer 1987), anchored in the life histories of individuals and constrained by the changing social order.

CHANGING TIMES AND ADULT LIVES

The individual-level dynamics of the life course that we have summarized are meaningful only as they are linked to social change. Consciousness of the interplay between lives and times represents a distinctive feature of contemporary studies. People age in different ways in response to an ever-changing world (Riley, Waring, and Foner 1988). With this in mind, an understanding of successful aging, as adaptive competence, necessarily requires knowledge of both person and society (Featherman, Smith, and Peterson 1990, 83). However, most studies of life patterns are still carried out with minimal attention to the changing world of the aging individual.

As we turn to ways of thinking about and studying adult lives in a changing society, it is well to note a restructuring of the life course and its conventional age divisions, the years of dependency, productive labor, and retirement. Since the mid-1970s, later family formation and work entry have extended the dependency years toward the age of thirty for many young people (Sweet and Bumpass 1987). This shift coincides with a decline in the median age of retirement, an increasing elimination of mandatory retirement age (Kohli 1988; Kohli et al. 1991), and a more variable set of exit pathways (Hayward, Grady, and McLaughlin 1988; Henretta 1992; O'Rand, Henretta, and Krecker 1991) than the traditional exit, with more gradual and fluctuating transitions. Recent estimates (Reimers and Honig 1989, 117) suggest that two-thirds or more of all older men will not leave the workforce at a single point in time (measured as age).

Other notable forms of change in the contemporary life course stem from or reflect the profound changes that have taken place in women's roles and lives (McLaughlin et al. 1988). These changes include the striking increase in women's paid employment since World War II at all stages of family life; a progressive weakening of the link between childbearing and marriage; a rise in the proportion of unmarried women; and the high incidence of marital instability. Developments of this kind underscore the increasing prevalence of the primary individual, apart from the family unit, and the many interconnections among lives, such as when the birth of a daughter's first child redefines her mother's status as a grandmother.

Modell's (1989) study of the transition from youth to adulthood in the United States between 1920 and 1975 illustrates both a shift toward individual choices and loose coupling. Aptly titled *Into One's Own,* Modell's historical examination of trends in the timing and sequencing of formal education, marriage, first births, first employment, divorce, and other early life course transitions across several cohorts documents the "injection of increasing volition into the youthful life course" resulting in a "weakening . . . of determinate sequences and intervals" (pp. 331, 333).

The social changes noted above express in part the changing social regulations of government and other social institutions, the influence of workplace and its complex organization, the informal controls of friends and family (Sampson and Laub, 1993), and the voluntary actions of individuals. As Mayer (1986, 167) points out, on the level of individuals, "the state legalizes, defines, and standardizes most points of entry and exit: into and out of employment, into and out of marital status, into and out of sickness and disability, into and out of formal education."

Studying Lives in Context: Matters of Perspective

Studies of lives and personality are typically based primarily on one of two perspectives—individual and social. The individual perspective assumes that any satisfactory account of an individual's developmental or aging processes begins with the person's life history, current status, and functioning. A social perspective assumes that this account requires an understanding of how the larger environment affects the person's developmental or aging processes. To assess these effects, the analysis begins with, or at least includes, evidence on the history, status, and current functioning of the larger social world, as shown in social structures, cultures, and social change.

The task of linking social forces to individual patterns of development or aging may seem to imply only a downward mode of causation, beginning with macrostructures and moving across levels to the microsocial situation. However, life course theory also assumes that people function as agents of their own life course and development. Within the social constraints and options established by a new situation, people make choices and take action in ways that shape the life course. This agentic perspective is underscored by the accumulating evidence on the role of life history and selection in shaping lives and turning points in them (Block 1971, 1981). Sampson and Laub (1993) show a pattern of cumulative misfortune in the lives of men judged ill-tempered as juvenile delinquents—unstable work, broken relationships, heavy drinking, and crime. In the language of life course, men and women bring experiences, dispositions, and knowledge to new situations, which, in turn, affect their subsequent adaptations.

A social perspective on the effects of social structures and change is unusual in developmental and life span psychology, which tend to pose questions that focus on the individual, and is uncommon even in sociology or political science. Almond and Verba's classic study (1963) of the "civic culture" in five societies focuses on attributes of the self-confident citizen who is likely to "follow politics, to discuss politics, to be a more active partisan" (pp. 206–207). The self-confident citizen not only thinks "he can participate, he thinks others ought to participate as well." Involvement in decision making in the family, school, and workplace, along with formal education, stand out as the primary developmental factors in the life histories of self-confident citizens.

But what about the historical times of these people in the United Kingdom, West Germany, Italy, Mexico, and the United States? With a wide age range of forty years or more in each of the national samples, the investigators could have indexed exposure to major historical events and trends across the twentieth century—including two world wars, a world depression, postwar affluence, and growth of the nation-state. Unfortunately, these historical forces were not specified in the research questions and so could not be studied. Almond and Verba asked about the socialization of citizen competence instead of the nature of societal change and its implications for the life course and development.

We find more attention to the social order in Inkeles and Smith's pioneering study, *Becoming Modern* (1974), but they give little attention to the historical times of institutions and men in their cross-national project. They use age data, to identify the life stage or position of working men in five societies rather than their historical locations, and consequently we never learn how the workers' lives related to the major social changes of their times. Nevertheless, Inkeles and Smith try to show how urban residence, schooling, and factory work consistently enhanced workers' modern outlook, their openness to new experience, readiness for social change, and sense of efficacy.

As points of departure, the individual and social perspectives are typically expressed in distinctive formulations of the problem or question; this is the heart of their significance. An individual perspective may lead to the identification of multiple influences, but it does not direct the investigator to assess the process by which a particular environmental influence has certain effects. The larger environment, such as war mobilization or industrial decline, is not likely to be understood in its own right from this vantage point. By comparison, a social perspective prompts questions about how particular social changes affect individuals, their life course, and aging, such as the processes by which military service leads to the development of self-efficacy and personal change.

By asking how a particular change can make a difference in health or adaptive functioning, the investigator is sensitized to the linking mechanisms. Erikson (1976) followed this option in his study of the Buffalo Creek flood, and McAdam (1988, 1989) chose this design for tracing the effects of Freedom Summer on the lives of civil rights activists. Other examples include longitudinal studies of children of the Great Depression (Elder 1974) and of World War II (Elder and Clipp 1988a) and Vietnam War veterans (Kulka et al. 1990). The life course effects of social change can also be explored in terms of social development over many decades, as in the case of educational upgrading and its consequences for intellectual development and aging (Schaie 1990).

Across these and other studies, five linking mechanisms (life stage, interdependent lives, control cycle, situational imperatives, and accentuation) provide ways of thinking about the interaction between changing times and lives. We illustrate each concept with empirical findings.

Linking Mechanisms

The first step toward understanding the effects of social change for the adult life course is to identify the life stage people occupy in the population at risk. This stage may be defined by age or age-related social roles and developmental resources. In either case, a person's life stage at a point of social change tells us something about the personal or developmental implications of the change. No study can adequately relate lives to a changing world without taking this social fact into account.

The concept of interdependent lives and social embeddedness represents another essential distinction. This concept orients analysis to the web of social ties that relate all lives to others, and thus specifies interpersonal connections to particular social changes. The functions of social support are one way to view the linking network (House, Landis, and Umberson 1988) as a source of insulation from adversity and social assurance. Freud and Burlingham (1943) follow this use in their account of parent-child relations and proximity in England during World War II. Linked lives can also bring bad news or heavy burdens and conflicts in stressful times. The personal trauma of combat is expressed in large measure by the loss of comrades (Elder and Clipp 1988b), including friends of friends.

The last three mechanisms (control cycle, situational imperatives, and accentuation) refer to the correspondence or fit between a changing environment and the life course. People accommodate their behavior to situations over time. Any change in situation produces some measure of disequilibrium, which, according to the thesis of a control cycle, sets in motion efforts to regain control and effective adaptation. The success of these efforts depends on the situation's behavioral imperatives or demands. New situations in a changing social landscape interact with the life history people bring to it to accentuate initial dispositions. Block's view (1981, 40–41) of personality and behavior patterns is consistent with this account:

> What is contended is that how experience registers, how environments are selected or modified, and how the stages of life are negotiated depends, importantly and coherently, on what the individual brings to these new encounters—the resources, the premises, the intentions, the awareness, the fears and the hopes, the forethoughts and the afterthoughts that are subsumed by what we call personality.

The Life Stage Principle. This principle assumes that the effects of social change and institutions vary in type and relative influence across the life course and thereby alert the investigator to the complexity of interactions among historical, social, psychological, and biological factors. These interactions across the dependency years have enduring consequences for the adult life course, as documented by a comparative study of two cohorts of children of the Great Depression, the Oakland Growth sample (born 1921 to 1922), and the Berkeley Guidance sample (born 1928 to 1929; Elder 1974, 1979).

The 167 men and women of the Oakland cohort were children during the prosperous 1920s, a time of unparalleled economic growth in California. Thus they entered the Great Depression after a relatively secure phase of early development. Later, they avoided the scars of joblessness after high school through wartime service. By contrast, the 214 members of the Berkeley cohort entered hard times during early childhood and experienced the pressures of adolescence in the unsettled though prosperous years of World War II. Unlike the younger Berkeley children, Oakland cohort members were old enough to minimize their vulnerability to family disruption and to play important roles in the household economy.

Not surprisingly, the enduring adverse effects of depression hardship were concentrated in the lives of the Berkeley boys, in adolescence and in the middle years. No such effects were observed among the Oakland men or among women from either cohort. In the Berkeley cohort, adolescent boys from deprived families were at much greater risk of emotional instability, passivity, and low self-esteem. However, these effects diminished to the point of insignificance by midlife, a life change so notable that it raised questions about experiences that might have redirected lives after the Great Depression.

More education, a supportive marital relationship, and a stable, rewarding job were possibilities in this regard, but war mobilization had more widespread consequences. World War II and the Korean War mobilized three of four Berkeley men into military roles. Investigation of this experience uncovered a link between depression hardship and early entry into the military and between early entry and substantial developmental gains between adolescence and the middle years (Elder 1986). This relation between personal change and early entry provides another example of the life stage principle at work.

Military entry after high school tends to precede adult commitments and thus represents a good fit between what the military offers and developmental needs. In the later years, military veterans appear to be most positive toward benefits of their active duty if they entered at an early age. The later the age at entry, the more negative the appraisal (Elder and Caspi 1990). However, the meaning of age depends on the particular field of endeavor. For example, among very late World War II entrants, physicians generally benefited most dramatically, since they had desperately needed skills (Elder, Pavalko, and Hastings 1991). Surgeons often rose quickly to command large hospitals in Europe and Southeast Asia.

Interdependent Lives. The family serves as a meeting ground for members of different cohorts through the dynamic of interdependent lives (Hagestad 1982). Diverse life histories become the interweave of family ties, softening the edges of cohort uniqueness. Exposure to war experiences provides an example. American wives of World War II veterans often had sons who faced the dilemmas and traumas of the Vietnam War. These women may regard World War II as especially important among their memories of past times, since they were adolescents during it, a uniquely formative developmental stage (Schuman and Scott 1989), but their emotional well-being in later life is likely to have more to do with the lingering wartime trauma of their Vietnam-era sons.

Linked lives broaden the range of exposure to specific social events or changes, help shape the experience itself, and determine how the change makes a difference in people's lives. McAdam's life course study (1988, 1989, 1992) of applicants to the 1964 Mississippi Freedom Summer project depicts each of these consequences. The project recruited college students to teach in freedom schools, register African-American voters, and focus attention on the denial of civil rights throughout the South. Using application materials on more than a thousand students, McAdam surveyed 212 former participants in the summer project and 118 men and women who withdrew their names from consideration. Data were available for the preproject era, the project summer itself, 1964 to 1970, and 1983 to 1984.

Activists during the last half of the 1960s were most likely to have been involved in radical organizations before Freedom Summer, to have participated in the project, and to have formed social ties with other participants. Activism during the early 1980s shows a high level of continuity with activism in the late 1960s and involvement in Freedom Summer. Activists were also less stable in work and marriage than nonactivists across this period. Analyses by gender show that organizational affiliations were more important to recruiting young women for Freedom Summer. These ties also played a critical role in sustaining their activism through a like-minded community of friends well after the project ended.

Control Cycles. Some life transitions produce a better match between person and situation, particularly when they are selected, whereas other transitions increase the disparity or lack of fit, a circumstance especially common through naturally occurring events. When social change creates a disparity between claims and resources, goals, and accomplishments, the corresponding loss of control prompts efforts to regain control. The entire process resembles a control cycle—losing control is followed by efforts to restore control over life outcomes, a process featuring reactant behavior.

Reactant feelings occur whenever one or more freedoms or expectations are eliminated or threatened. Such feelings motivate efforts to regain or preserve control. The Brehms (1981) refer to the substantial evidence for such motivation and note that "it is the threat to control (which one already had) that motivates an attempt to deal with the environment. And the attempts to deal with the environment can be characterized as attempts to regain control" (p. 375). Bandura (1986) stresses the motivating effects of setting higher goals, achieving them, and setting even higher goals. The process entails the production and reduction of discrepancies, disequilibration, and equilibration.

As people and large populations are thrust into new regimes and exposed to certain options, they generally work out adaptations that enhance their control. This is one process by which the life course is socially constructed in terms of past and present realities. Examples include the mobilization of women into the labor force of countries at war and economic adaptations worked out in times of drastic economic decline.

Situational Imperatives.   The dynamic of control cycles refers to what new situations do not offer the individual in terms of personal control. This loss of control can be thought of as a result of situational imperatives, as when a totalitarian state replaces a democratic government. Other examples are suggested by the collapse of the economy in the 1930s, which placed adults in circumstances governed by new economic realities (Elder 1974), opportunities, and constraints.

Change in the workplace provides numerous examples of a shift in the imperatives of the occupational role. The research of Kohn and Schooler (Kohn 1977; Kohn and Schooler 1983) shows how the behavioral imperatives of work shape people's thinking and actions. The most powerful imperative is occupational self-direction; the greater it is, the more workers deal with substantively complex, nonroutinized tasks that entail minimal supervision. Job conditions that favor self-direction are conducive to effective intellectual functioning and an open, flexible approach to others. Self-directed men seek control over their work, and such control reinforces a self-directed orientation.

Accentuation.   The behavioral effects of a new situation depend on what people bring to it. The accentuation effect refers to an increase in emphasis or salience of prominent characteristics from the point of entry into the new situation. This interactive dynamic is especially common in the literature on selection effects, as noted earlier.

In the Great Depression, for example, drastic economic hardship tended to make irritable and explosive men more explosive (Elder, Caspi, and Van Nguyen 1986). This behavior undermined the quality of marriages and increased the arbitrary and punitive character of parental discipline. In the same historical time, Allport et al. (1941) found some evidence of personality change among people in the Nazi revolution and concluded that it seemed to represent an accentuation of precrisis personality traits.

Life stage, interdependent lives, control cycles, situational imperatives, and accentuation refer to distinctions that have proven useful in conceptualizing linkages between social change and the life course. These connections occur through individuals, social relationships, and their interplay over time in situations with varying requirements. The dynamic occurs through families and other environments, such as friendships, work groups, and military units. From this vantage point, the intersection between historical time and lifetime is a function of changes in the life course of all family members and significant others.

CONCLUSIONS

The flourishing area of life course studies owes much to the growing recognition that any effort to make sense of adult development should consider *how lives are formed in and by a rapidly changing world.* Initially, this recognition led to a methodological solution that simply provided a way to disentangle change within lives from change within society. Cohort-sequential designs and the estimation of cohort, period, and age effects were part of this effort. In life span psychology, much of this research is based on a theoretical model that views the environment from the vantage point of the individual, rather than in terms of its own properties. While we have gained a better understanding of human agency from this perspective, its minimization of the role of social environmental influences in human development underestimates the impact of social structures and change.

Life course research emerged from the converging interests of several disciplines—social history, demography, gerontology, and sociology—to explore the roles of time and context in the processes of individual development. The availability of longitudinal data accumulated across several historical periods and social contexts made it possible to develop an approach that links environment and individual over time. This approach has now established several key empirical generalizations.

Chief among these generalizations is that heterogeneity in life course trajectories is pervasive within as well as across cohorts. The ordering, timing, and historical embeddedness of life course transitions yield diverse pathways through adulthood into old age. The construction of these pathways involves selection (or biographical) as well as transitional (or situational) factors that interact in complex ways to produce loosely coupled life stages, many of which are only weakly correlated with age.

The task of linking social change and adult lives is formidable because so little theory extends across levels. Theories are readily available on the micro- and macrolevel, but not on the connections between them. How does the upward causation process work in restructuring social environments from the aggregrate behaviors of succeeding cohorts? How does the downward causation process work in relating macroevents and environments to individual life experience?

The five linking mechanisms presented above provide a way of thinking about the connection between adult lives and a changing society. The life stage and interdependent lives principles provide the means for anchoring life transitions in historical and social (e.g., familial) time, giving them content and meaning. Adolescence, early family

formation, military service, job loss—these transitions do not carry universal meanings with and across cohorts. Rather, their meaningfulness in a life course framework is drawn from the coincidence of macroevents with socially proximate life conditions. Since these conditions coincide differentially within and across cohorts, their significance for adult lives is considerable.

The remaining three principles, relating to control cycles, situational imperatives, and accentuation processes, are directly relevant to understanding how and why individual biography and history intersect to produce diverse responses. They integrate individual agency with social imperatives and partially account for heterogeneity over time.

However, we are still faced with the question of how or whether influences persist over the life span. Under what conditions do the child's behavior patterns persist into adulthood? We have just begun to explore such questions in research that extends across adult life patterns and generations. The task of explaining how these widely separated transitions (or others similarly separated in time) are themselves linked by biography and history is before us. Studies have been more successful in linking temporally proximate events, as in the transition to adulthood or the transition to retirement.

Finally, the relationship of social structure to the construction of adult lives ultimately requires variations in social structures that transcend time and space. Historical scholarship has been building successfully over the past two decades to determine the impact of macroevents on adult lives and to trace the correlates of long-term social trends in life transitions. Comparative studies of mechanisms relating adult lives to social change across societies are only beginning to appear. The progress of theory building in life course analysis will depend on the success of this emerging endeavor.

REFERENCES

Allport, G., J. S. Bruner, and E. M. Jandorf. 1941. Personality under social catastrophe: Ninety life-histories of the Nazi Revolution. *Character and Personality* 10:1–22.

Almond, G. A., and S. Verba. 1963. *The Civic Culture: Political Attitudes and Democracy in Five Nations.* Princeton, NJ: Princeton University Press.

Alwin, D. F., R. L. Cohen, and T. M. Newcomb. 1991. *Aging, Personality, and Social Change: Attitude Persistence and Change over the Life-Span.* Madison: University of Wisconsin Press.

Baltes, P. B., S. W. Cornelius, and J. R. Nesselroade. 1979. Cohort effects in developmental psychology. Pp. 61–87 in *Longitudinal Research in the Study of Behavior and Development,* ed. J. R. Nesselroade and P. B. Baltes. New York: Academic.

Baltes, P. B., and H. W. Reese. 1984. The life-span perspective in developmental psychology. Pp. 493–531 in *Developmental Psychology: An Advanced Textbook,* ed. M. H. Bornstein and M. E. Lamb. Hillsdale, NJ: Erlbaum.

Bandura, A. 1986. *Social Foundations of Thought and Action: A Social Cognitive Theory.* Englewood Cliffs, NJ: Prentice Hall.

Bell, R. Q. 1968. A reinterpretation of the direction of effects in studies of socialization. *Psychological Review* 75:81–95.

Block, J., in collaboration with N. Haan. 1971. *Lives through Time.* Berkeley: Bancroft.

Block, J. 1981. Some enduring and consequential structures of personality. Pp. 27–43 in *Further Explorations in Personality,* ed. A. I. Rabin, A. M. Barclay, and R. A. Zucker. New York: Wiley.

Brehm, S. S., and J. W. Brehm. 1981. *Psychological Reactance: A Theory of Freedom and Control.* New York: Academic.

Brim, O. G., Jr., and S. A. Wheeler. 1966. *Socialization after Childhood: Two Essays.* New York: Wiley.

Bronfenbrenner, U. 1979. *The Ecology of Human Development: Experiments by Nature and Design.* Cambridge, MA: Harvard University Press.

Brooks-Gunn, J., E. Phelps, and G. H. Elder, Jr. 1991. Studying lives through time: Secondary data analyses in developmental psychology. *Developmental Psychology* 27:899–910

Buchmann, M. 1989. *The Script of Life in Modern Society: Entry into Adulthood in a Changing World.* Chicago: University of Chicago Press.

Burton, L. M., and V. L. Bengtson. 1985. Black grandmothers: Issues of timing and continuity of roles. Pp. 61–77 in *Grandparenthood,* ed. V. L. Bengtson and J. F. Robertson. Beverly Hills, CA: Sage.

Bush, D. M., and R. G. Simmons. 1981. Socialization processes over the life course. Pp. 133–164 in *Social psychology: Sociological Perspectives.* New York: Basic Books.

Campbell, R. T., and A. M. O'Rand. 1988. Settings and sequences: The heuristics of aging research. Pp. 58–79 in *Emergent Theories of Aging,* ed. J. E. Birren and V. L. Bengston. New York: Springer.

Caspi, A., and D. J. Bem. 1990. Personality continuity and change across the life course. Pp. 549–575 in *Handbook of Personality: Theory and Research,* ed. L. A. Pervin. New York: Guilford.

Caspi, A., and E. S. Herbener. 1990. Continuity and change: Assortative marriage and the consistency of personality in adulthood. *Journal of Personality and Social Psychology* 58:250–258.

Caspi, A., E. S. Herbener, and D. J. Ozer. 1992. Shared experience and the similarity of personalities: A longitudinal study of married couples. *Journal of Personality and Social Psychology* 62: 281–291.

Cherlin, A. 1981. *Marriage, Divorce, and Remarriage.* Cambridge, MA: Harvard University Press.

Cherlin, A. J., F. F. Furstenberg, Jr., P. L. Chase-Lansdale, K. E. Kiernan, P. K. Robins, D. R. Morrison, and J. O. Teitler. 1991. Longitudinal studies of effects of divorce on children in Great Britain and the United States. *Science* 252:1386–1389.

Clausen, J. 1972. The life course of individuals. Pp. 457–574 in *Aging and Society, 3: A Sociology of Age Stratification,* ed. M. W. Riley, M. Johnson, and A. Foner. New York: Russell Sage Foundation.

———. 1991. Early adult choices and the life course. *American Journal of Sociology* 96:805–842.

Cohler, B. J. 1982. Personal narrative and life course. Pp. 205–241 in *Life-Span Development and Behavior,* vol. 4, ed. P. B. Baltes and O. G. Brim, Jr. New York: Academic.

Cowan, P. A., and E. M. Hetherington, ed. 1991. *Family Transitions.* Hillsdale, NJ: Erlbaum.

Dannefer, D. 1984. The role of the social in life-span developmental psychology, past and future: Rejoinder to Baltes and Nesselroade. *American Sociological Review* 49:847–850.

———. 1987. Aging as intracohort differentiation: Accentuation, the Matthew effect, and the life course. *Sociological Forum* 2:211–236.

de Ribaupierre, A. ed. 1989. *Transition Mechanisms in Child Development: The Longitudinal Perspective.* Cambridge, UK: Cambridge University Press.

Dion, K. K. 1985. Socialization in adulthood. Pp. 123–147 in *Handbook of Social Psychology, 2: Special Fields and Applications,* ed. G. Lindzey and E. Aronson. New York: Random House.

DiRenzo, G. J. 1977. Socialization, personality, and social systems. *Annual Review of Sociology* 3: 261–295.

Dohrenwend, B. S., and B. P. Dohrenwend, ed. 1981. *Stressful Life Events and Their Contexts.* Monographs in Psychosocial Epidemiology, No. 2. New York: Prodist.

Duncan, G. J., and N. J. Morgan. 1985. The Panel Study of Income Dynamics. Pp. 50–71 in *Life Course Dynamics: Trajectories and Transitions, 1968–1980,* ed. G. H. Elder, Jr. Ithaca, NY: Cornell University Press.

Easterlin, R. A. 1978. What will 1984 be like? Socioeconomic implications of recent twists in age structure. *Demography* 15:397–432.

Eichorn, D. H., J. A. Clausen, N. Haan, M. P. Honzik, and P. H. Mussen, ed. 1981. *Present and Past in Middle Life.* New York: Academic.

Elder, G. H., Jr. 1974. *Children of the Great Depression: Social Change in Life Experience.* Chicago: University of Chicago Press.

———. 1975. Age differentiation and the life course. *Annual Review of Sociology* 1:165–190.

———. 1979. Historical change in life patterns and personality. Pp. 117–159 in *Life Span Development and Behavior,* vol. 2, ed. P. B. Baltes and O. G. Brim, Jr.

———. 1985. Perspectives on the life course. Pp. 23–49 in *Life Course Dynamics: Trajectories and Transitions, 1968–1980,* ed. G. H. Elder, Jr. Ithaca, NY: Cornell University Press.

———. 1986. Military times and turning points in men's lives. *Developmental Psychology* 22:233–245.

Elder, G. H., Jr., and A. Caspi. 1990. Studying lives in a changing society: Sociological and personological explorations. Pp. 201–247 in *Studying Persons and Lives,* ed. A. I. Rabin, R. A. Zucker, R. A. Emmons, and S. Frank. New York: Springer.

Elder, G. H., Jr., A. Caspi, and T. Van Nguyen. 1986. Resourceful and vulnerable children: Family influences in hard times. Pp. 167–186 in *Development as Action in Context: Problem Behavior and Normal Youth Development,* ed. R. K. Silbereisen, K. Eyferth, and G. Rudinger. Berlin: Springer.

Elder, G. H., Jr., and E. C. Clipp. 1988a. Combat experience and emotional health: Impairment and resilience in later life. *Journal of Personality* 57:311–341.

———. 1988b. Wartime losses and social bonding: Influences across 40 years in men's lives. *Psychiatry* 51:177–198.

Elder, G. H., Jr., C. Gimbel, and R. Ivie. 1991. Turning points in life: The case of military service and war. *Military Psychology* 3:215–231.

Elder, G. H., Jr., E. K. Pavalko, and T. J. Hastings. 1991. Talent, history, and the fulfillment of promise. *Psychiatry* 54:251–267.

Erikson, K. T. 1976. *Everything in Its Path: Destruction of Community in the Buffalo Creek Flood.* New York: Simon and Schuster.

Featherman, D. L. 1982. *The Life-Span Perspective in Social Science Research: The Five-Year Outlook on Science and Technology.* 1981 source materials 2. Washington, DC: National Science Foundation.

Featherman, D. L., and R. M. Lerner. 1985. Ontogenesis and sociogenesis: Problematics for theory and research about development and socialization across the life span. *American Sociological Review* 50: 659–676.

Featherman, D. L., J. Smith, and J. G. Peterson, 1990. Successful aging in post-retired society. Pp. 50–93 in *Successful Aging. Perspectives from the Behavioral Sciences,* ed. P. B. Baltes and M. M. Baltes. New York: Cambridge University Press.

Freedman, D., A. Thornton, D. Camburn, D. Alwin, and L. Young-DeMarco, 1988. The life history calendar: A technique for collecting retrospective data. *Sociological Methodology* 18:37–68.

Freud, A., and D. Burlingham. 1943. *War and Children.* New York: Medical War Books.

Furstenberg, F. F., Jr., J. Brooks-Gunn, and S. P. Morgan. 1987. *Adolescent Mothers in Later Life.* New York: Cambridge University Press.

Furstenberg, F. F., Jr., and A. J. Cherlin. 1991. *Divided Families: What Happens to Children when Parents Part.* Cambridge, MA: Harvard University Press.

George, L. K. (1993). Sociological perspectives on life transitions. *Annual Review of Sociology* 19:353–373.

Glass, J., V. L. Bengtson, and C. C. Dunham. 1986. Attitude similarity in three-generation families: Socialization, status inheritance, or reciprocal influence? *American Sociological Review* 51:685–698.

Glueck, S. 1950. *Unraveling Juvenile Delinquency.* Cambridge, MA: Harvard University Press.

Goldscheider, F., and C. Goldscheider. 1988. Family structure and conflict: Nest-leaving expectations of young adults and their parents. *Journal of Marriage and the Family* 51:87–97.

Goslin, D. A., ed. 1969. *The Handbook of Socialization Theory and Research.* Chicago: Rand McNally.

Hagestad, G. O. 1982. Parent and child: Generations in the family. Pp. 485–507 in *Review of Human Development,* ed. T. M. Field, A. Huston, H. C. Quay, L. Troll, and G. E. Finley. New York: Wiley.

————. 1990. Social perspectives on the life course. Pp. 151–168 in *The Handbook of Aging and the Social Sciences,* 3rd ed., ed. R. H. Binstock and L. K. George. San Diego: Academic.

Hareven, T. K., ed. 1978. *Transitions: The Family and the Life Course in Historical Perspective.* New York: Academic.

Hayward, M. D., W. R. Grady, and S. D. McLaughlin. 1988. Changes in the retirement process among older men in the United States: 1972–1980. *Demography* 25:371–386.

Heaton, T. B. 1991. Time-related determinants of marital dissolution. *Journal of Marriage and the Family* 53:285–295.

Henretta, J. C. 1992. Uniformity and diversity: Life course institutionalization and late-life exit. *Sociological Quarterly* 33:265–279.

Henretta, J. C., and A. M. O'Rand. 1983. Joint retirement in the dual worker family. *Social Forces* 62:504–520.

Herzog, A. R. 1989. Physical and mental health in older women: Selected research issues and data sources. Pp. 35–91 in *Health and Economic Status of Older Women: Research Issues and Data Sources,* ed. A. R. Herzog, K. Golden, and M. M. Seltzer. Amityville, NY: Baywood.

Hetherington, E. M., and P. B. Baltes. 1988. Child psychology and life-span development. Pp. 1–19 in *Child Development in Life-Span Perspective,* ed. E. M. Hetherington, R. M. Lerner, and M. Perlmutter. Hillsdale, NJ: Erlbaum.

Hogan, D. P. 1981. *Transitions and Social Change: The Early Lives of American Men.* New York: Academic.

Hogan, D. P., and N. M. Astone. 1986. The transition to adulthood. *Annual Review of Sociology* 12:109–130.

House, J. S. 1981. Social structure and personality. Pp. 525–561 in *Social Psychology: Sociological Perspectives,* ed. M. Rosenberg and R. H. Turner. New York: Basic Books.

House, J. S., K. R. Landis, and D. Umberson. 1988. Social relationships and health. *Science* 241:540–545.

Howard, A., and D. W. Bray. 1988. *Managerial Lives in Transition: Advancing Age and Changing Times.* New York: Guilford.

Inkeles, A., and D. H. Smith. 1974. *Becoming Modern: Individual Change in Six Developing Countries.* Cambridge, MA: Harvard University Press.

Kertzer, D. I., and J. Keith, ed. 1984. *Age and Anthropological Theory.* Ithaca, NY: Cornell University Press.

Kessler, R. C. 1979. A strategy for studying differential vulnerability to the psychological consequences of stress. *Journal of Health and Social Behavior* 20: 100–108.

Kohli, M. 1988. Aging as a challenge for sociological theory. *Aging and Society* 8:367–394.

Kohli, M., M. Rein, A.-M. Guillemard, and H. von Gunsteren, ed. 1991. *Time for Retirement: Comparative Studies of Early Exit from the Labor Force.* New York: Cambridge University Press.

Kohn, M. L. 1977. *Class and Conformity: A Study in Values,* 2nd ed. Chicago: University of Chicago Press.

Kohn, M. L., C. Schooler. 1983. *Work and Personality: An Inquiry into the Impact of Social Stratification.* Norwood, NJ: Ablex.

Kulka, R. A., W. E. Schlenger, J. A. Fairbank, R. L. Hough, B. K. Jordan, C. R. Marmar, and D. S. Weiss. 1990. *Trauma and the Vietnam War Generation: Report of Findings from the National Vietnam Veterans Readjustment Study.* Brunner/Mazel Psychological Stress Series, no. 18. New York: Brunner/Mazel.

Lerner, R. M. 1984. *On the Nature of Human Plasticity.* Cambridge, UK: Cambridge University Press.

————. 1991. Changing organism-context relations as the basic process of development: A developmental contextual perspective. *Developmental Psychology* 27:27–32.

Levinson, D. J. 1986. A conception of adult development. *American Psychologist* 41:3–13.

Levinson, D. J., with C. N. Darrow, E. B. Klein, M. H. Levinson, and B. McKee, 1978. *The Seasons of a Man's Life.* New York: Knopf.

Lin, N., and W. M. Ensel. 1989. Life stress and health: Stressors and resources. *American Sociological Review* 54:382–399.

Lorence, J., and J. T. Mortimer. 1985. Job involvement through the life course: A panel study of three age groups. *American Sociological Review* 50:618–638.

Maddox, G. L. 1987. Aging differently. *Gerontologist* 27:557–564.

Mangen, D. J., V. L. Bengtson, and P. H. Landry, Jr. 1988. *Measurement of Intergenerational Relations.* Newbury Park, CA: Sage.

Mayer, K. U. 1986. Structural constraints on the life course. *Human Development* 29:163–170.

Mayer, K. U., and N. B. Tuma, ed. 1990. *Event History Analysis in Life Course Research.* Madison: University of Wisconsin Press.

McAdam, D. 1988. *Freedom Summer.* New York: Oxford University Press.

———. 1989. The biographical consequences of activism. *American Sociological Review* 54:744–760.

———. 1992. Gender as a mediator of the activist experience: The case of Freedom Summer. *American Journal of Sociology* 97:1211–1240.

McLanahan, S., and J. Adams. 1987. Parenthood and psychological well-being. *Annual Review of Sociology* 13:237–257.

McLanahan, S. S., and A. B. Sorensen. 1985. Life events and psychological well-being over the life course. Pp. 217–238 in *Life Course Dynamics: Trajectories and Transitions,* ed. G. H. Elder, Jr. Ithaca, NY: Cornell University Press.

McLaughlin, S. D., B. D. Melber, J. O. G. Billy, D. M. Zimmerle, L. D. Winges, and T. R. Johnson. 1988. *The Changing Lives of American Women.* Chapel Hill: University of North Carolina Press.

McLeod, J. D. 1991. Childhood parental loss and adult depression. *Journal of Health and Social Behavior* 32:205–220.

McLeod, J. D., and R. C. Kessler. 1990. Socioeconomic status differences in vulnerability to undesirable life events. *Journal of Health and Social Behavior* 31:162–172.

Menaghan, E. G. 1985. Depressive affect and subsequent divorce. *Journal of Family Issues* 6:295–306.

Menaghan, E. G., and M. A. Lieberman. 1986. Changes in depression following divorce: A panel study. *Journal of Marriage and the Family* 48:319–328.

Merton, R. K. 1968. *Social Theory and Social Structure,* enlarged ed. New York: Free Press.

———. 1973. *The Sociology of Science: Theoretical and Empirical Investigation.* Chicago: University of Chicago Press.

Modell, J. 1989. *Into One's Own: From Youth to Adulthood in the United States 1920–1975.* Berkeley: University of California Press.

Moen, P., D. Dempster-McClain, and R. M. Williams, Jr. 1989. Social integration and longevity: An event history analysis of women's roles and resilience. *American Sociological Review* 54:635–647.

Mortimer, J. T., and R. G. Simmons. 1978. Adult socialization. *Annual Review of Sociology* 4: 421–454.

Neugarten, B. L., and D. Gutmann. 1958. *Age-Sex Roles and Personality in Middle Age: A Thematic Apperception Study.* Psychological Monographs: General and Applied 72, No. 470.

Nicholson, N. 1990. The transition cycle: Causes, outcomes, processes and forms. Pp. 83–108 in *On the Move: The Psychology of Change and Transition,* ed. S. Fisher and C. L. Cooper. New York: Wiley.

O'Rand, A. M. 1990. Stratification and the life course. Pp. 130–148 in *Handbook of Aging and the Social Sciences,* 3rd ed., ed. R. H. Binstock and L. K. George. San Diego: Academic.

O'Rand, A. M., and J. C. Henretta. 1982. Delayed career entry, industrial pension structure, and retirement in a cohort of unmarried women. *American Sociological Review* 47:365–373.

O'Rand, A. M., J. C. Henretta, and M. L. Krecker. 1991. Family pathways to retirement: Early and late life family effects on couples' work exit patterns. In *Families and Retirement: Conceptual and Methodological Issues,* ed. M. Szinovacz, D. J. Ekerdt, and B. H. Vinick. Newbury Park, CA: Sage.

O'Rand, A. M., and M. L. Krecker. 1990. Concepts of the life cycle: Their history, meanings, and uses in the social sciences. *Annual Review of Sociology* 16:241–262.

Palmore, E. B., B. M. Burchette, G. G. Fillenbaum, L. K. George, and L. M. Wallman. 1985. *Retirement: Causes and Consequences.* New York: Springer.

Plomin, R., and D. Daniels. 1987. Why are children in the same family so different from one another? *Behavioral and Brain Sciences* 10:1–59.

Plomin, R., and R. Thompson. 1987. Life-span developmental behavioral genetics. Pp. 1–31 in *Life-span development and behavior,* vol. 8, ed. P. B. Baltes, D. L. Featherman, and R. M. Lerner. Hillsdale, NJ: Erlbaum.

Reimers, C., and M. Honig. 1989. The retirement process in the United States: Mobility among full-time work, partial retirement, and full retirement. Pp. 115–131 in *Redefining the Process of Retirement: An International Perspective,* ed. W. Schmahl. Berlin: Springer.

Riegel, K. F. 1977. The dialectics of time. Pp. 3–45 in *Life-Span Developmental Psychology: Dialectical Perspectives on Experimental Research,* ed. N. Datan and H. W. Reese. New York: Academic.

Riley, M. W., M. Johnson, and A. Foner, 1972. *Aging and Society, 3: A Sociology of Age Stratification.* New York: Russell Sage Foundation.

Riley, M. W., J. Waring, and A. Foner. 1988. The sociology of age. Pp. 243–290 in *The Handbook of Sociology,* ed. N. Smelser and R. Burt. Newbury Park, CA: Sage.

Rindfuss, R. R., S. P. Morgan, and C. G. Swicegood. 1984. The transition to motherhood: The intersection of structure and temporal dimension. *American Sociological Review* 49:359–372.

Rindfuss, R. R., C. G. Swicegood, and R. A. Rosenfeld. 1987. Disorder in the life course: How common and does it matter? *American Sociological Review* 52:785–801.

Robins, L. N. 1978. Sturdy childhood predictors of adult antisocial behaviour: Replications from longitudinal studies. *Psychological Medicine* 8:611–622.

Rossi, A. S., and P. H. Rossi. 1990. *Of Human Bonding: Parent-Child Relations across the Life Course.* New York: Aldine de Gruyter.

Ryder, N. B. 1965. The cohort as a concept in the study of social change. *American Sociological Review* 30:843–861.

Sampson, R. J., and J. H. Laub. 1990. Crime and deviance over the life course: The salience of adult social bonds. *American Sociological Review* 55: 609–627.

———. 1993. *Crime in the Making: Pathways and Turning Points through Life.* Cambridge, MA: Harvard University Press.

Scarr, S. W. 1989. How genotypes and environments combine: Development and individual differences. Pp. 217–244 in *Interacting Systems in Human Development,* ed. G. Downey, A. Caspi, and N. Bolger. New York: Cambridge University Press.

Scarr, S. W., and R. A. Weinberg. 1983. The Minnesota Adoption Studies: Genetic differences and malleability. *Child Development* 54:260–267.

Schaie, K. W. 1965. A general model for the study of developmental problems. *Psychological Bulletin* 30:843–861.

———. 1990. The optimization of cognitive functioning in old age: Predictions based on cohort-sequential and longitudinal data. Pp. 94–117 in *Successful Aging: Perspectives from the Behavioral Sciences,* ed. P. B. Baltes and M. M. Baltes. New York: Cambridge University Press.

Schaie, K. W., and S. L. Willis. 1986. *Adult Development and Aging,* 2nd ed. Boston: Little, Brown.

Schuman, H., and J. Scott. 1989. Generations and collective memories. *American Sociological Review* 54:359–381.

Spence, A. P. 1989. *Biology of Human Aging.* Englewood Cliffs, NJ: Prentice Hall.

Streib, G. F., and R. H. Binstock. 1990. Aging and the social sciences: Changes in the field. Pp. 1–15 in *Handbook of Aging and the Social Sciences,* 3rd ed., ed. R. H. Binstock and L. K. George. San Diego: Academic.

Sweet, J. A., and L. L. Bumpass. 1987. *American Families and Households.* New York: Russell Sage Foundation.

Wheaton, B. 1990. Life transitions, role histories and mental health. *American Sociological Review* 55: 209–223.

White, L., and J. N. Edwards. 1990. Emptying the nest and parental well-being: An analysis of national panel data. *American Sociological Review* 55:235–242.

Wortman, C. B., and R. C. Silver. 1990. Successful mastery of bereavement and widowhood: A life-course perspective. Pp. 225–264 in *Successful Aging: Perspectives from the Behavioral Sciences,* ed. P. B. Baltes and M. M. Baltes. New York: Cambridge University Press.

Young, C. H., K. L. Savola, and E. Phelps. 1991. *Inventory of Longitudinal Studies in the Social Sciences.* Newbury Park, CA: Sage.

CHAPTER 18

Social Stratification and Mobility Processes
Interaction between Individuals and Social Structures

ALAN C. KERCKHOFF

Almost any sociological study of almost any social phenomenon routinely considers the relevance of social class or social status. If nothing else, investigators at least "control for" their subjects' positions in the stratification system while studying other social phenomena. More important, individuals' locations in the social hierarchy have a major influence on their life experiences, personal development, and behavior.

The significance of social stratification in sociological theory and research and in social life makes it especially important to seek explanations for the hierarchical distribution of individuals in society. Explanations are sought at two levels of analysis. The first considers the society as a whole and seeks to understand why there is a hierarchy at all, why some social positions are viewed as superior to others, and why there is more hierarchical differentiation in some societies than in others. This involves the study of social structures and processes in their own right and essentially ignores individual members of the society. The second approach takes the nature of the society's hierarchy as a given and seeks to understand the processes by which individuals become distributed in that hierarchy. It focuses on social processes of individual development and social mechanisms of hierarchical distribution. That is the approach taken in this discussion of the social psychology of social stratification.

The nature of the social hierarchy has been conceptualized in different ways by sociologists over the past century. For instance, Weber (1946) used three hierarchical dimensions—class, status, and party—to refer to the positions of individuals and groups in society. Class refers to the economic positions of individuals and groups, their positions in the marketplace. Status groups are communities of individuals differentiated by lifestyles reflecting shared values and by restricted social relations, such as intermarriage. Finally, party refers to the political activities of groups that share interests and seek to further them through collective action. Weber was especially interested in the interrelations among class, status, and party, such as the ways in which shared economic position facilitated joint political action. Others, such as Marx (1936), saw class as the primary structural feature of modern societies. In Marx's view, ownership of the means of production permits the ruling class to exploit the working class and to monopolize political as well as economic power.

Multiple dimensions are still recognized, but sociologists have increasingly focused on positions in the division of labor identified by occupational titles. The relative levels of occupational positions are usually measured in terms of prestige or socioeconomic status.[1] Prestige measures are based on public assessments of occupations, while socioeconomic status is measured according to the average levels of education and earnings of the individuals in those occupations. Prestige and socioeconomic status are highly correlated, although they appear to tap somewhat different aspects of occupations

(Kerckhoff et al. 1990). The distinction between those two dimensions is ignored in the discussion here, however, and the general term *status* is used to refer to the level of an occupation in the stratification hierarchy.

Any industrial society has many specialized occupations distributed across a wide range of statuses. Although the specific occupations change over time, an overall status hierarchy continues. Successive generations are born into a stratified society and, as they enter adulthood, move into occupational positions vacated (through job shifts, retirement, or death) by their predecessors. A core question is: How do we explain the fact that some individuals enter high-status positions and others enter low-status positions?

"Social mobility" refers to a change in level in the stratification hierarchy. Since each generation replaces the one before it, and in that way renews the hierarchy, the "openness" of the society becomes a significant issue. Do children tend to replace their parents in the hierarchy, or are they just as likely to occupy different levels than their parents?

Not all individuals spend their adult lives in the same occupations they first enter. Any overall difference between the stratification levels of parents and their adult children can thus result from two possible moves by the children away from their parents, one at the time they enter the labor force, the other during their work careers. The total amount of social mobility between the positions of parent and child is a combined result of both intergenerational mobility and career mobility.

Explanations for the distribution of individuals in the stratification system can emphasize either continuity across generations or social mobility. Parents attempt to position their children in the hierarchy, and high-status parents are most effective in doing so. That helps to explain the tendency for adult children to be found in about the same status levels as their parents occupied before them. (There is a correlation of about 0.40 in the United States between the status levels of fathers' and sons' occupations.) Other explanations of the distribution, though, point to the

role of the educational system as a means of social mobility.

These two explanations are not mutually exclusive, since one way parents help determine their children's adult status is to help them get a good education. A common feature of industrial societies is a strong correlation between level of education and the status of available occupations. (In the United States the correlation between level of education and occupational status is about 0.60.) Almost all high-status occupations require success in school as a prerequisite. An adequate accounting of social mobility needs to examine the relationships among origin, educational attainment, and adult position.

THE BASIC STATUS ATTAINMENT MODEL

Blau and Duncan (1967) first introduced a method of analysis that permitted us to consider simultaneously the contributions of social background and educational attainment to placement in the status hierarchy, both at labor force entry and in later adulthood. Their so-called "basic status attainment model" reflected three basic propositions: (1) the child's educational attainment is influenced by his[2] family's social status; (2) the status level of the child's first job is influenced by both his educational attainment and the family's social status; and (3) the status level of the child's later job is influenced by the status of his first job, his educational attainment, and his family's social status.

This model was an important innovation because it provided a means of including multiple sources of influence in a coherent representation of the status attainment process. One of its strengths was that it could be expanded into more complex representations of the attainment process. By representing the fundamental idea of a *process* of status attainment, it was possible to construct models that introduced intervening variables to help explain the relationships already observed. What began as a relatively simple four-stage model (origin, educational attainment, first job, later job) became a much more elaborate one with a strong social psychological emphasis.

USING SOCIAL PSYCHOLOGICAL THEORY TO EXPAND THE BASIC MODEL

Though referred to as a "social process model," the basic status attainment model raised as many questions about social processes as it answered. What do we mean when we say that father's education "influences" son's education? *How* does that occur? The processes are only implicit or assumed as a means of explanation for the observed relationships.

The most influential elaboration of the basic model, designed by William Sewell and colleagues, is referred to as "the Wisconsin model." In the basic model, educational attainment was the most important link between the social status of the student's family and his or her adult position in the stratification system. One goal of the Wisconsin research team was to explain *how* origin status affected educational attainment.

The core features of the original Wisconsin model are presented in Figure 18.1 (adapted from Sewell and Hauser 1980). It is based on social psychological theories of socialization that view educational attainment as the result of a complex set of associations among ability, ambition, and encouragement from significant others. The connection between origin and educational attainment occurs, in part, because significant others influence the aspirations of the young person, and those aspirations in turn are dynamic forces in the attainment process. The model suggests that the degree to which significant others encourage the young person varies according to the family's social status and the child's demonstrated ability. It also implies that the family and the school are the major institutional settings in which these socialization processes occur and that parents, teachers, and peers are the relevant significant others.

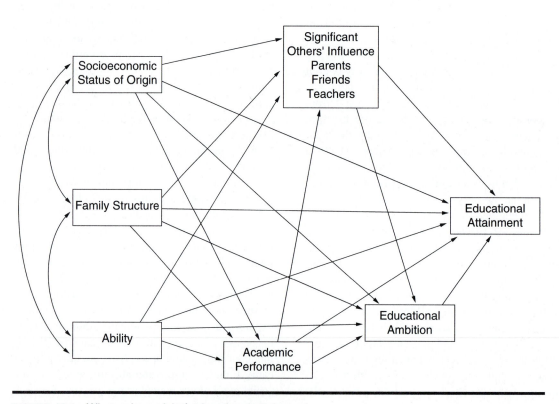

FIGURE 18.1   Wisconsin model of educational attainment.

The major social psychological variables included in the Wisconsin model are significant others' influence and ambition. These variables play a central role in most of the early attempts to develop a dynamic model of status attainment. Sewell, Haller, and Ohlendorf opined (1970, 1025) that "Perhaps the most important single finding [from research using the Wisconsin model] . . . is the critical role of significant others' influence in the status attainment process." In a later review of the model and its contributions, Archibald Haller and Alejandro Portes (1973) viewed the measures of ambition as "the strategic center of the model."

Wisconsin researchers also interpreted other elements of the model in social psychological terms. Haller and Portes (1973, 62) wrote: "The effect that family's socioeconomic status has on a person's educational and occupational attainment is due to its impact on the types of attainment-related personal influences that the person receives." Such statements reflect the theory that family processes vary with family socioeconomic status. The theory states that "inductive control" is more often used in higher-status and smaller families and that it tends to produce "socially competent behavior" in children (Rollins and Thomas 1979).

"*Inductive control*" refers to persuasive methods that seek the child's voluntary compliance. It is based on explanation and reasoning, rather than coercion. "Socially competent behavior" means a range of socially valued behaviors and characteristics, including cognitive development, internal locus of control, instrumental competence, and conformity to parental standards. These are all characteristics that are valued in school and that increase the likelihood of academic success. The Wisconsin model thus implied that family processes are one basis for explaining varying school performance and the adoption of long-range goals. Peer and teacher influences are similarly implied by the model.[3]

The Wisconsin model used the approach suggested by Blau and Duncan to develop more refined representations of the status attainment process. For each relationship in the basic model for which a theoretical interpretation was offered, intervening variables were inserted that represent core concepts in that theoretical interpretation. Since the relationship between socioeconomic status and educational attainment was thought to result from interpersonal influences on ambition that vary by socioeconomic status, measures of interpersonal influences and ambition were included in the model. If the new variables help explain the original relationship, support is provided for the theory.

Two important features of the Wisconsin model continued to influence research on status attainment for many years. First, it focused primarily on the dynamics of *educational* attainment,[4] and, second, it viewed the process as based on motivation and interpersonal influence. The theoretical stance interpreted the ultimate outcomes—the distribution of social statuses—as having been *attained* by individuals through motivated efforts that were shaped by the influence of significant others. It was an explicitly social psychological model. This was both the model's greatest strength and the basis of the sharpest critiques leveled against it, as the later discussion indicates.

The introduction of the Wisconsin model opened a floodgate of research on the status attainment process. Various investigators (Alexander and Griffin 1975; Wilson and Portes 1975) conducted analyses parallel to those of the Wisconsin team, using different data sets and slightly different variables, and summary statements appeared that indicated that the basic relationships in the Wisconsin model were quite robust (A. Haller and Portes 1973; Kerckhoff 1980; Otto and Haller 1979). The social psychological model of status attainment was a major contribution to our understanding of social mobility processes.

VARIATIONS ON A THEME

As the body of evidence grew, however, it became increasingly apparent that the power of the status attainment model was greater in some analyses than in others. The observed variations were of two kinds. Some reflected differences between categories of individuals, especially men and women and

African Americans and whites. Others reflected differences that resulted from the way social institutions are organized. The two types of variation have different theoretical implications, so it is best to consider them separately.

Studies showed that the status attainment model was more effective in explaining the attainments of white men than those of African-American men or African-American or white women (Alexander and Eckland 1974; McClendon 1976; Porter 1974; Portes and Wilson 1976; Treiman and Terrell 1975). In addition to pointing up these differences, these studies suggested some of the reasons.

The interpretations of these differences focused on two different points in the status attainment process: educational attainment and occupational attainment. Most studies find the patterns of educational attainment are much the same for white men and women. Some gender differences are attributed in part to the contingency of marriage. Not only is early marriage more common for women than men, but it appears to have a more negative effect on women's than men's educational attainments (Call and Otto 1977; Marini 1978).

Gender differences are much greater, however, when occupational attainment is considered, although fewer women are in the labor force. There are several kinds of gender differences. Women's occupational levels are less varied than men's: more men have very high- and very low-status jobs than women. Also, although both women's and men's first job levels reflect their levels of educational attainment, men experience more career mobility than women (Rosenfeld 1980; Sewell, Hauser, and Wolf 1980). Even greater differences are found in men's and women's earnings. Not only do women earn significantly less than men, their earnings are less clearly associated with either educational attainment or job status level (Marini 1989). This is in part a function of segregation of jobs by sex and in part because women less often complete college or receive meaningful on-the-job training, but even after those factors are taken into account, large earnings differences remain (England et al. 1988).

Regarding educational attainment, differences by race are more apparent than differences by gender. African Americans obtain less education than whites, and their social origins have less of an effect (Portes and Wilson 1976). The dynamics of educational attainment are different between races. African Americans' ambition levels are less affected by background (Kerckhoff and Campbell 1977b), although ambition has stronger effects on actual attainments for African Americans (Kerckhoff and Campbell 1977a). Educational attainment for African Americans seems to depend more on idiosyncratic experiences in school. Portes and Wilson (1976) refer to this pattern as indicating the position of African Americans as "outsiders," and Porter (1974) emphasizes the need for African Americans to be "sponsored" if they are to succeed in school.

Racial differences are even more apparent in the processes of occupational attainment. African Americans obtain lower-level occupations than comparably educated whites (Featherman and Hauser 1978). Racial differences in earnings are even greater than differences in occupations, so African Americans are doubly disadvantaged. African Americans have made recent gains by most measures of attainment, and the process of African-American status attainment has become more like that of whites, but significant differences remain (Farley 1984).

The differences in the status attainment process by gender and race made it clear that the process involved more than was incorporated into the general social psychological model. Even if the focus is restricted to attempting to explain educational attainment, the subgroup variations suggest that societal influences other than those represented in a general model based on ability and the socialization of ambition are involved.

INSTITUTIONAL STRUCTURE AND STATUS ATTAINMENT

The theoretical implications of these differences by race and sex needed to be spelled out and accounted for in research. Horan (1978) argued that a major problem with the status attainment model was that it was derived from a particular, though not explicitly stated, theoretical view of the stratification system and social mobility processes that was overly simplistic and essentially misleading. He stated:

> *Status attainment rests on a functionalist conception of social structure in which social positions are conceived of as levels of performance which are differentially evaluated and rewarded within a competitive market situation. . . . [T]he assumption of fully open and competitive allocation of individuals to jobs (i.e., market homogeneity) provides a source of justification for restricting attention to the individual characteristics of jobholders.* (p. 538)

The observed race and gender differences clearly cast doubt on an assumption of homogeneity. Not only are individuals unequally distributed in the labor force according to race and gender, but the processes by which they enter and change labor force positions differ.

Horan's critique was not focused on the different processes and outcomes by race and gender, however. His objection to the assumption of homogeneity was that it ignored the structured nature of the labor force. He called attention to two kinds of structural features that had largely been ignored. One was the role of power or authority in the labor force, the fact that some had greater control over the division of labor and the distribution of rewards than others (through either ownership or managerial authority). Second, he noted that the labor force is organized into firms and industrial sectors that offer different kinds of opportunities and rewards. A general status attainment model ignores these structural features of the labor force.

Horan's critique shifted the focus of much of the discussion from educational attainment to occupational attainment. His basic point, though, was that there is more involved in the status attainment process than individual characteristics and behaviors, and thus it is necessary to broaden the approach to take into account the nature of the larger societal context. The labor force is highly structured, and the locations of individuals in that structure affect their attainments, over and above any influences from their personal characteristics. Though his criticism of the implicit assumption of an "open marketplace" focused on the process of occupational attainment, it can be equally well applied to much of the research on educational attainment.

In addition to raising questions about the implicit theoretical underpinnings of the status attainment model, other critiques suggested that even the research findings using the Wisconsin model could be interpreted in ways different than from a socialization perspective. One suggestion was to use an allocation interpretation of the same findings: "Rather than differential attainment being seen as due to variations in learned motives and skills, as in a socialization model, an allocation model views attainment as due to the application of structural limitations and selection criteria" (Kerckhoff 1976, 369).

For example, the socialization interpretation of the Wisconsin model sees the association between adolescent ambition and later achievements as an indication that motivation to excel affects achievement. However, the findings may also be interpreted as an indication of the individual's recognition of probable outcomes given the societal constraints on social mobility. This is a reasonable interpretation, since the actual measure used in most studies is based on what individuals *expect* to attain, not what they *want* to attain. Reinterpreting status attainment findings in allocation terms does not alter the associations, it simply suggests different interpretations of the findings.

While Horan's critique was made in reference to the structural features of the labor force, similar structural effects can be found in educational settings. Several studies reported the effects of school context (average socioeconomic or intellectual characteristics of the student body) on individuals' attainments in the schools and interpreted those effects in terms of interpersonal and social comparison processes. Alexander and Eckland (1975) reported that the higher the average socioeconomic status of the student body, the higher a student's goals and levels of educational attainment, but the higher the average ability level of the student body, the lower the goals and levels of educational attainment. Alwin and Otto's (1977) findings suggested that those contextual effects reflected varying grading practices, parental encouragement, and friends' educational plans in these different settings.

Other research showed that the school context did not affect all students equally and, thus, differentiation within the school also needs to be taken into account. Heyns (1974) showed that curriculum or track assignments had strong independent effects on educational aspirations, beyond any effects of personal characteristics. Assignment to the college preparatory track allowed greater access to school resources, including counselors. Also, as Alexander and McDill (1976) noted, the effects of curriculum placement were at least partially due to selective association with other students. Tracking separates students into groups with relatively restricted ranges of socioeconomic and academic characteristics.

These critiques and the accumulated evidence broadened the range of investigations that could be called studies of status attainment. In particular, they led to an emphasis on the society's structural features and variations in the status attainment process in different segments of the population. Differences by race and gender, differences according to locations in the school structure, and differences according to location in the structure of the labor force had all been identified. Rather than a single status attainment process based on ability, ambition, and interpersonal influence, a much more complex picture emerged.

STATUS ATTAINMENT AND "THE NEW STRUCTURALISM"

One way researchers dealt with diversity of opportunities in the labor force was to differentiate labor force sectors according to the nature of the industries involved. Some distinguished between "core" and "peripheral" industries (according to such factors as level of capital intensity, unionization, profit margins, and market concentration) and showed that core industries provided better career opportunities and rewards (Beck, Horan, and Tolbert 1978)[5]. Individual firms also offer varied types of opportunities and rewards (Baron and Bielby 1980; Stolzenberg 1978). Larger firms often provide "internal labor markets" that facilitate mobility (Althauser and Kalleberg 1981).

Internal labor markets consist of job ladders and promotion regimes that favor those who are already part of the organization.[6] When an opening occurs in an internal labor market, those at lower levels have the chance to move up. This triggers a "vacancy chain" (Sorensen 1977), because those who move up must be replaced. Even within the same firm, however, some jobs may be "open" to all comers while others are "closed" to all but those already in the firm (Sorensen and Tuma 1981). The nature of competition for open and closed vacancies differs greatly. Thus, workers' positions in the highly structured labor force appreciably influence their opportunities.

Studies of labor force structure have focused primarily on variations in earnings by comparable individuals in different structural locations. Those in core industries or large firms generally have higher earnings, even when their jobs are comparable to those in other locations. Core industries and large firms are thought to pay more because they tend to make greater investments in worker training and are organized in ways that make jobs more interdependent (and thus labor force instability is more disruptive). Also, since internal labor markets are more common in core industries and large firms, there are greater opportunities for workers to be promoted and to obtain pay increases.

Parallel but separate analyses of the structure of educational institutions have also appeared. The two bodies of literature are rather separate, but the strong structural emphasis in the labor force analysis gave impetus to the work on educational structures. The two bodies of literature have become more relevant to each other recently, and it is reasonable to expect them to continue to influence each other.

A driving force in the increased interest in the internal structures of schools was the charge that schools' organization actively affects students' achievements.[7] In particular, grouping or tracking students based on ability has increasingly come to be seen as a means of "creating inequality" (Kerckhoff 1991). The general observation has been that grouping results in students in "high" ability groups moving ahead and those in "low" ability groups falling back in terms of academic achievement.

Research in elementary and secondary schools has shown these effects, although the kinds of studies conducted differ in the two kinds of schools. It is usual in the early grades to divide students into reading groups according to ability; students in high-level reading groups have been observed to gain and those in low-level groups to lose in comparison with students in middle-level groups or comparable students in ungrouped classrooms (Barr and Dreeben 1983; Hoffer 1991; Rowan and Miracle 1983; Weinstein 1976).

The effects of grouping in secondary schools support this conclusion that grouping affects pupil performance, though the form of grouping at this level usually differs. Group (or "track" or "stream") placement leads to differentiated pupil achievement even when an extensive set of antecedent factors and individual characteristics are taken into account (Kerckhoff 1986; Sorensen and Hallinan 1986). Those in high-level groups (or the college preparatory track) show more growth in achievement than those in other groups. In addition, grouping is associated with differences in students' educational and occupational aspirations, satisfaction with school, and self-esteem (Vanfossen, Jones, and Spade 1987).[8]

The reason most frequently given for ability grouping is that, by adjusting the level of instruction to the students' prior achievement level, it is possible to give all students lessons that will produce maximum learning in all groups (i.e., the overall "productivity" of the school will be increased; Gamoran and Mare 1989). However, if students in high-level groups gain and those in low-level groups lose—that is, if grouping actually increases achievement inequality—something else must be happening.

STRUCTURAL PLACEMENTS AND EFFECTS

There are essentially two distinct processes that need to be understood to explain the role of structural effects in status attainment. One is the process through which individuals come to be situated in one rather than another structural location. The second is the process through which individuals' attainments are altered by their locations in the social structure. Examination of either of these processes often leads us to shift our attention from overall statistical relationships to the analysis of more circumscribed social encounters and interpersonal exchanges, to the fluid and actively negotiated nature of the person-structure relationship. While comparable processes undoubtedly occur in both educational and work settings, the discussion that follows deals more fully with research on school than labor force structures, because more research has been conducted on the dynamics of the processes in schools.

Structural Placement

How do students get into hierarchical structural locations in educational institutions? The answer varies in the literature on status attainment, partly as a function of the student's age. The older the student, the greater the self-selection. College students generally choose their own courses from among a wide array of possibilities, but elementary school students are much more frequently and explicitly *placed* into classes and study groups. But even college students are not completely free to choose: admissions officers, advisors, distribution requirements, prerequisites, and class size limitations seriously circumscribe "free choice."

A persistent observation is that students from disadvantaged backgrounds are more likely to be found in low ability groups and those from advantaged backgrounds in high ability groups. The school's role in producing this outcome is interpreted in two very different ways, however. Functionalists view the schools as neutral organizations that provide "equal opportunity" for all students, although that does not necessarily mean there will be "equal results" (Coleman et al. 1966). The correlation of placement with social origin is seen as a result of the fact that higher-status families provide more stimulating home environments and more opportunities for enlightening out-of-school experiences. Children from such families enter school "ahead" of other students and are reasonably placed in advanced groups.

Conflict theorists interpret the same observations very differently. They see the school as the agent of powerful elements in the society and its structural arrangements as mechanisms by which those elements assure the success of their own children (Bowles and Gintis 1976). One way the schools do this is by being more responsive to the "cultural capital" of higher classes (Bourdieu 1973; Collins 1971). In addition, school personnel tend to be middle-class and tend to favor higher-status students.

Surveys of large samples can demonstrate only rough indications of these processes. Only studies that examine smaller, more restricted samples in greater detail can show the specific mechanisms involved. More detailed analyses of structural placements have been performed in elementary than in secondary schools. Ability grouping is widely practiced in the early grades as a means of coping with students' varied backgrounds. Usually students within a classroom are separated into small groups. Organizational constraints due to a relatively large class and a single teacher usually lead to the formation of three groups of about equal size (Hallinan and Sorensen 1983).

Many scholars argue that decisions regarding ability group placement in early elementary school are often biased against low-status students and can have strong carry-over effects throughout their schooling (Cicourel et al. 1974). Not all studies find such a bias (E. Haller and Davis 1981), however, and some have suggested that the bias varies according to teachers' social backgrounds (Alexander, Entwisle, and Thompson 1987). The relationship between the school and the students' families is another important related factor. High-status parents have more time and are better able to cope with the family-school relationship in ways that can help their children in school (Lareau 1989).

To the extent that ability grouping is practiced in successive years, each later placement decision is based on information that at least includes a record of the student's earlier placement. Entwisle and Hayduk (1988, 158) point out:

> *Not only does a high level of performance in one year facilitate a high level in the next, but . . . a "paper person" is created that follows the child from grade to grade. Cumulative records that follow children through school could support the children's high [or low] performance in the later grades by affecting subsequent teachers' expectations.*

The creation of "paper persons" produces what may be thought of as a kind of "institutional inertia" in the group assignment process. Each new teacher's expectations of the student's performance is influenced by knowledge of prior structural locations. There is thus a tendency for individuals to remain in the same level of ability group from one stage in the educational career to the next, even when their academic performance would suggest they should move up or down in the group hierarchy (Kerckhoff 1993).

In the later stages of the educational career, placements in the school structure tend to be more clearly based on prior performances and rules of access. In high school there are often course sequences, with access to advanced courses requiring success in lower-level courses. Yet students from high-status families still tend to be in the college preparatory track more often than their prior academic performance could explain (Gamoran and Mare 1989). Track placement at the secondary school level is often influenced more by counselors' advice than students' preferences (Oakes 1985), and counselors have long been recognized as important sources of influence in postsecondary curricular decisions (Clark 1960).

At the postsecondary level, entry into particular locations is both more limited and more open. It is more limited by prior achievements, especially grades and credentials, but it is more open because individuals can at least choose from among multiple alternatives, including leaving the system completely. High schools are generally more active in helping students find a suitable placement in higher education than in the labor force (Heyns 1974; Rosenbaum et al. 1990), and some high schools are more effective than others in doing so (Cookson and Persell 1985).

A major difference between educational and labor force placement is that the labor force is much more dispersed and "placement" involves more potential options for the individual. The process by which the individual moves into one of the optional locations generally varies by level of education. The higher one goes in the educational system, the more structured the job placement process becomes. College and professional school placement offices and greater specialization at the higher levels help to focus the search.

For those who do not graduate from college, however, it seems to be a haphazard process. Jobs are found through friends and relatives or through application to familiar local firms (Granovetter 1974; R. Meyer and Wise 1984; Osterman 1980). Since those with less education enter first jobs at younger ages, they generally qualify for only low-skill jobs, which are more common in small firms and the peripheral sector. Employers' distrust of very young workers also may limit their options (Hamilton 1986). Women and minorities seem to be underrepresented in large firms and core industries, but that may be largely due to the more restricted local options available to urban youth and the sex segmentation of the labor force (Baron and Bielby 1980).

The processes by which individuals become located in the educational structure and the structure of the labor force are thus quite different. The school system more fully controls the sorting process, and institutions at all levels work in a more coordinated manner, using similar principles. The process by which workers are sorted into labor force locations (firms and industries) is much less regularized, and both workers and employers have more latitude in making relevant decisions. Also, while there are clear linkages in placement processes across stages in the educational career, there is much less of an association between locations in schools and in the labor force. As noted below, this is not the case in all societies.

Structural Effects on Achievement

How does it happen that location in the structure of educational institutions has an independent effect on student achievements? Two explanations of the effects of ability grouping on achievements have been offered. One emphasizes the symbolic value of ability groups. Even in the early grades, even when euphemisms like "robins" and "bluebirds" are used to designate groups, students know where they fit in the hierarchy of ability groups (Eder 1983), and that affects their academic commitment and effort (Felmlee and Eder 1983) as well as their relations with their teachers. This is part of the "normative" effect of grouping (Dreeben and Barr 1988), part of a socially constructed set of expectations associated with group location.[9]

Students' expectations are influenced by more than the simple fact of group placement, however. Both parents and teachers understand what group placement means, and their reactions to the student's placement influence the student's own reaction. Peer definitions and responses also play a part. As Brookover et al. (1979, 6) put it: "The children take their cues from those important to them and with whom they interact, attending carefully to their expectations and definitions of appropriate behavior in the student role." It has been dramatically demonstrated that teacher expectations can affect student performance (Rosenthal and Jacobson 1968). This is part of the reason the Wisconsin model included such a strong emphasis on the role of significant others' influence in the status attainment process.

Central to the generation of academic expectations is the basic definition of *ability* in the school and the larger community. To the extent that *ability* is defined as a unidimensional and relatively unchanging quality of individuals, both teacher behavior and student response generate a uniform hierarchical differentiation in the classroom. But if ability is viewed as multidimensional (i.e., people can be more competent in one activity than another) and if grading is deemphasized, it can sharply reduce both the clarity of student ranking and the importance attributed to hierarchies (Rosenholtz and Rosenholtz 1981; Simpson 1981). To that extent, ability is socially constructed, and its affect on student achievement can vary. Of course, if ability is defined as multidimensional, it is much less likely to be used as a basis for the organization of the classroom in the first place.

The other explanation of structural effects is more direct than the normative explanation. At the elementary school level, teachers' behavior tends to vary by ability group level (Barr and Dreeben 1983; Eder 1981; Gamoran 1986). The pace of teaching is faster and the amount of material covered greater in high- than in low-ability groups. It is not clear, however, whether such observed differences should be attributed to the teachers alone or to a more complex interaction between teaching styles and student classroom behavior (Gracey 1972).

Structuring tasks in the classroom so as to differentiate between high- and low-performing students also seems to have a pervasive effect on social relations among students. Peer groups that reflect the student hierarchy tend to form, and high-performing students tend to reject the others (Bossert 1979). Peer relations thus reinforce the effects of ability grouping as reflected in curricular material and teacher behavior.

Studies at the elementary and secondary levels generally use different methods and collect different kinds of data. There is much greater use of observation and interaction analysis in elementary schools, while secondary school studies are mostly based on large-scale surveys. As a result, we know more about the dynamics of student-teacher and student-student interactions in elementary schools, but it is often difficult to judge the generalizability of the findings. Conversely, secondary school stud-

ies are a better basis for general statements, but they seldom provide the same fine-grained analysis as the elementary school studies.

Secondary school studies support the two interpretations of structural effects based on elementary school studies, however. In a study of secondary schools, Metz (1978) differentiated between two teaching styles: "incorporative" and "developmental." These teaching styles are similar to the "production" and "craftsmen" styles Gracey (1972) identified in elementary schools. The incorporative style stresses rules and discipline and regularized teaching methods, while the developmental style recognizes individual differences among students and adjusts teaching methods to them. Metz found that these styles had different effects in high and low tracks and that student cultures were very different in high and low tracks. High-track students rebelled against an incorporative approach and worked better with teachers using a developmental style. Low-track students, however, were generally alienated and neither teaching style was very effective.

Students in the low tracks have been repeatedly described as alienated and as part of a social network that either ignores or actively disrupts the academic program (Stinchcombe 1964; Willis 1977). By the time students reach secondary school, many have been repeatedly defined as academically deficient. A common response for these students is to band together in opposition to the system that has effectively rejected them. This appears to be due to long-term negative experiences, however, rather than particular kinds of teacher behavior.

Students perceive teaching styles as differing in high and low secondary school tracks (Oakes 1985). High-track teachers are more often described as enthusiastic, presenting clear task-oriented instructions, more concerned about their students, and less punitive. Given the subtle interdependence of teacher and student behaviors and attitudes, it is not clear what the causal relationship is here. But student attitudes and values do differ significantly by track location, those in high tracks reporting greater satisfaction with school, higher self-esteem, and higher educational and occupational aspirations (Vanfossen, Jones, and Spade 1987).

The most obvious source of differential academic achievement of students in secondary school tracks is the different courses they take. Students in the high or college preparatory tracks take more advanced courses (Gamoran 1987; Hotchkiss and Dorsten 1987). There is such variation of kinds and levels of courses in secondary school, however, that formal track designations are not nearly as salient as in elementary school. The courses taken, rather than a track label, thus may be a better index of the track a student is "really" in (Lucas and Gamoran 1991). Course dispersion may also help explain the disparities between official records and student self-reports of track placement (Rosenbaum 1980).

Grouping in elementary and secondary schools is so different that interpretations of its effects are bound to have different emphases. Most elementary school grouping is within classrooms. There is usually one teacher for all groups, and often the same curricular offerings are involved. Subtle differences in teaching behavior and peer group relations in high and low groups are thus of particular interest. In secondary schools, groups are more often taught by different teachers and offered different curricula. Thus, secondary school studies usually focus on differences in course work and student attitudes and motivation associated with placement in a particular group. Theoretical interpretations of the structural effects are essentially the same at the two levels, however, involving both the symbolic significance of structural locations and the actual educational processes that occur in them.

Studies of the effects of labor force structures have a different focus and emphasize different dynamics. Attainments are defined in terms of occupational level and earnings, and most analysts explain differences in those outcomes in different structural locations primarily in terms of the way firms function, rather than in terms of social psychological processes. That large firms and firms in core industries provide higher wages and greater career opportunities is explained largely in terms of

better training programs, greater investment in both training and equipment, and availability of internal labor markets.

Women and African Americans receive lower labor force returns from comparable academic achievements, in particular occupational prestige and wages (Barrett 1987; Farley 1984; Featherman and Hauser 1978; Marini 1980; Rosenfeld 1980). To some extent, these differences may result from the greater frequency with which women and African Americans work in small firms and peripheral industries, but that is certainly not the only reason.

There are thus two basic differences between studies of structural effects on achievement in schools and in the labor force. First, structural arrangements in schools are seen as purposely established to affect students' achievement levels. In contrast, labor force structures are designed to increase the firms' effectiveness. Second, explanations of the effects of structural arrangements focus on very different kinds of processes. In schools, the structures are seen as directly affecting individuals' achievements through curricula, teaching styles, social definitions, and student motives. In the labor force, differences in individual outcomes are seen as the indirect result of firm or industry organizational constraints and cost-benefit considerations.

INTERNATIONAL PERSPECTIVES

Most of the research and theoretical discussions cited above come from U.S. sources, but neither the ideas nor the processes are unique to this country. There is an extended international literature on social stratification and mobility, although studies of the processes involved are more limited.

Studies of ability grouping at the elementary school level in France (Hout and Garnier 1979), at the middle school and secondary school levels in Israel (Dar and Resh 1986), and at the secondary school level in the Netherlands (Bosker et al. 1989) show many of the same effects. Research on British students shows that these dispersive effects of ability grouping occur at all levels and that the effects are cumulative across the educational career, so that their overall effect is much greater than is suggested by studies of shorter periods (Kerckhoff 1993).

Although they do not explicitly study ability grouping in their comparative research on American, Japanese, and Chinese elementary schools, Stevenson and Lee (1990) suggest that the use of ability groups in American schools (but not in Japanese or Chinese schools) helps account for the overall poorer performance of American students. They argue that grouping reinforces a view that ability differences are innate and unchanging and thus contributes to a self-fulfilling prophesy. Grouping also gives a false sense of superiority to students in high groups and stigmatizes those in low groups, and it reduces parental involvement in the learning process.

Research in many countries shows that women are less likely to obtain postsecondary school credentials, but they are especially disadvantaged in the labor force. This is reported for Israel (Kraus and Hodge 1990) and the Netherlands (Bakker, Dronkers, and Meijnen 1989) as well as for Eastern European countries, such as Hungary (Andorka and Kolosi 1984) and Poland (Reszke 1984). This disadvantage results largely from gender segregation of occupations, especially managerial and skilled manual occupations. Ethnic differences are also reported, but the ethnic groups vary by country. In Israel, the primary difference is between those with European or American backgrounds versus those with Asian or African backgrounds (Kraus and Hodge 1990). In the Netherlands distinctions are made among various immigrant groups that show distinct mobility patterns (De-Jong 1989).

These studies point up a major difference between educational structures in Europe and the United States. Compared with the United States, most European countries more sharply differentiate among kinds of secondary education, and the kinds of education are more closely linked to kinds of occupations. This means the transition from school to work is more structured in Europe (Bynner and Roberts 1992). It is also more tightly organized in Japan (Rosenbaum et al. 1990).

Part of the strength of the European education-occupation linkage is due to a highly differentiated set of educational credentials that are occupationally relevant. Maurice et al. (1986) note that such credentials give the educational system "the capacity to structure" the distribution of workers in the labor force. European educational systems vary in the strength of that capacity, with Germany having one of the strongest, France one of the weakest, and Great Britain somewhere between. The American educational system is weaker than any of them because of the undifferentiated high school diploma instead of specific secondary school credentials. The association between educational and occupational *levels* is as strong here as anywhere, but the linkage between *kinds* of education and occupations is much weaker.

ABILITY, MOTIVATION, AND SOCIAL RELATIONS

The Wisconsin model and much of the status attainment research has highlighted the importance of ability, motivation, and interpersonal influences. Especially at the secondary school level, these core concepts are represented by measures taken from individual respondents. Ability is measured by tests, motivation by student answers to questions about their goals or expectations, and interpersonal influences by responses to questions put to students or significant others.

Two elements in educational attainment are often poorly represented by such measures. First is the social meaning of the characteristics being measured. It is not ability and motivation in some abstract, wholly intrapsychic sense that affects achievement across the educational career but rather socially visible ability and motivation. Individuals usually must demonstrate the ability to do particular academic tasks before they are given the opportunity to do so. They do that through prior achievements—by passing tests, graduating from high school, passing an entrance examination—not just by "being smart." Similarly, students must not only "want" to be in the college preparatory track or to go to college, they have to take the actions required to gain access to such opportunities.

Second, the effect of significant others will depend on whether they have this kind of information about the students. Much research on educational achievement implicitly assumes that test scores and questionnaire responses represent the kinds of knowledge educational gatekeepers and decision makers have about students and that decisions are made wholly on the basis of that knowledge. But, clearly, that is not always the case.

Official school records do not always agree with student self-reports about what track students are actually in (Rosenbaum 1980), and it is unlikely that school personnel are fully informed about students' goals. Parents can misperceive their children's goals, and children can misperceive their parents' goals for them (Kerckhoff and Huff 1974). Studies often use ability measures administered by the research team, and it is unclear whether the school personnel's information agrees with those measures. Interpretations of even official information such as grades can vary; for example, the same grade from two high schools can elicit different responses by a college admissions officer (Cookson and Persell 1985).

Equally important, information educational decision makers have about students may not be the only basis for the decisions they make and their influence on students. Teachers who form ability groups in their classrooms are constrained by the number of students in the class, space considerations, and their own views of the most suitable teaching-learning arrangements (Hallinan and Sorensen 1983). The nature of the student-placement match can vary greatly from one school to another. Garet and DeLany (1988) note that such differences seem to depend on the kinds of course requirements and the curricular alternatives offered in different schools as well as the ability composition of the student body.

The negotiated relationship between individuals and social structures during the educational career involves means-ends linkages. The status attainment process requires individuals to cope with social structures according to institutional norms and procedures. Ability involves both intelligence and knowledge about the way the institutions work. Motivation is both desire and the willingness (and ability) to do what is necessary to reach the goal. One of the reasons our large-scale analytic models have limited explanatory power is that we can measure only some elements of ability and motivation associated with various kinds and levels of attainments.

Unless we take into account the nature of institutional arrangements and actions of those besides students, we will have at best only a partial indication of the processes involved. Where any individual adult is ultimately located in the stratification system depends on his/her actions and those of many others. The self-other interactions that shape the status attainment process constitute the interface between the individual and the social structure. Those interactions reflect the personal characteristics of the individual and significant others, but they are also constrained by organizational norms and the alternatives provided by the institutions within which the interactions occur.

Until recently, our models of educational attainment have done too little to take account of institutional settings. In contrast, models of occupational attainment have emphasized the nature of the settings (firms, industrial sectors) in explaining varied outcomes but have dealt less fully with the individual workers' characteristics and the relationships between the individuals and those settings. Future work also needs to focus more fully on the individual-institution relationships and attempt to clarify the linkages between educational careers and occupational careers.

It is difficult to specify how best to do this, but at least three kinds of contributions are needed. First, we need a more careful analysis of the interface between educational and occupational institutional arrangements. That relationship is much less structured in the United States than in many other countries (Rosenbaum et al. 1990), but there may be more regularity than we have yet realized. Although there is a growing body of literature on the transition from school to work (Borman 1991; Borman and Reisman 1986; Bynner and Roberts 1992;

Coleman 1984; Mortimer, Lorence, and Kumka 1986) there is no overall conceptualization of the relationship between the two structures or the processes that organize individuals' careers through them.

Second, we need to introduce into large-scale studies conceptual refinements that will permit us to take advantage of rich, descriptive studies of processes in schools and firms. Detailed analyses of small units (classrooms, work groups) can be criticized for their lack of generalizability, and large-scale data set analyses can be criticized for their crudity. Part of the difficulty we face is distilling from the detailed studies general concepts that can be operationalized in studies based on national (or at least highly diverse) samples. Home-school relations also appear to be an important element in student achievement (Lareau 1989). We need to learn what the primary parameters of those relations are and include them in research.

Third, if we are to capture more fully the variety of individual-structure relationships in educational or work settings, we need to use more complex statistical representations of those relationships. Most research uses a simple linear additive approach to studying status attainment. When we include information about structural locations, it is usually by adding a variable (or set of variables) to regression equations. If the coefficient for the variable is significant, we conclude that location affects attainments, the coefficient indicating the average size of that effect. But structural locations may have different effects on attainments for different kinds of people—males and females, African Americans and whites, those from higher- and lower-status families, and so on. More complex statistical representations are needed to account for such interactions, and there is almost no limit to the possible number of the interactions nor to the complexity of the analyses their inclusion produces.

One promising approach to such complexities is the use of multilevel modeling techniques (Raudenbush and Willms 1991). These techniques provide separate regression equations for each unit (groups, schools, districts, firms, industries), thereby permitting estimates of systematic variations in processes across structural locations. If there is systematic variation, it is then possible to estimate the degree to which characteristics of the units (size, expenditure levels, level of unionization) can explain that variation. This is a potentially powerful tool for future research.

SUMMARY AND IMPLICATIONS

The Wisconsin model captured some of the important aspects of the dynamic process of educational attainment. Although it can legitimately be criticized, it was not so much wrong as incomplete. It focused on the characteristics of the individuals involved and on some limited aspects of their relationships with significant others. It rightly stressed the role of ability, ambition, and interpersonal influence in the attainment process, but it omitted systematic consideration of the structural characteristics of the schools and the norms of the larger society. Recent refinements of the Wisconsin model move us closer to a sensitive accounting of the structured social context within which educational attainment occurs. Similar but separate research has shown how the structure of the labor force affects individual attainments. These recent contributions help answer some of the questions raised by the earlier work, but they do not yet form a coherent model of status attainment processes.

Current models of status attainment have two basic kinds of limitation, one conceptual and the other methodological. Our conceptualization does not adequately represent the overall linkage between educational and work structures and how individuals move between them, nor does it encompass the variety of individual-structure relationships in both domains. The methodological limitations reflect continued dependence on linear additive multivariate models. We need to make better use of the results of fine-grained case studies in designing measures of varied individual-structure relationships and to use analytic techniques capable of deriving general patterns from that variety. Multilevel modeling is one promising approach to conducting such analyses.

While we can anticipate increased knowledge from these further refinements, the research conducted thus far is already sufficient to raise some important policy questions. In particular, research on ability grouping has increasingly shown how that structural feature of schools affects individual achievements, and some of those effects pose serious problems for school administrators. If being in a high-ability group serves to increase students' achievements, that looks like a positive result. But if being in a low-ability group serves to decrease students' achievements *and* we can have high-ability groups only if we also have low-ability groups, we need to question whether the low-ability group effects are too large a price to pay for the high-ability group effects. Is it possible to have the one without the other?

Close examination of school processes tells us that teachers are assigned to (or choose) the classes they teach in part on the basis of ability grouping. Most teachers seem to prefer teaching the "better" students, and the "better" teachers most often succeed in doing so (Finley 1984). Studies of teaching styles suggest that these teachers use methods that most effectively involve students in the learning process and mobilize peer relations in support of academic goals (Bossert 1979; Gracey 1972; Metz 1978). They also offer multiple and varied opportunities for students to do well, and they put less emphasis on formal grading (Rosenholtz and Rosenholtz 1981; Simpson 1981). Better teaching techniques, more active mobilization of classroom group processes, and more stimulating lesson content seem to be sources of the greater achievements of students in high-ability groups (Barr and Dreeben 1983; Eder 1981; Gamoran 1987).

This suggests that if the same kinds of advantages were offered to *all* students, school processes might operate in less divisive ways. Much of the criticism of schools emphasizes the use of social status as a basis for determining the distribution of resources, from physical facilities to good teachers to track assignments (Bowles and Gintis 1976; Kozol 1991; Oakes 1985). The evidence of uneven distribution is overwhelming, and a more equitable distribution of resources would undoubtedly reduce some of the inequalities.

There is more involved than the distribution of resources, however. The social definition of students as being "better" or "poorer" in academic potential influences all teaching and learning proc-

esses. More basic than any class bias is the school system's bias in favor of serving the needs of the more talented students. As long as schools are organized around the concept of "ability" and ability is viewed (implicitly or explicitly) as a unidimensional and relatively stable characteristic, the redistribution of resources can have only limited effects (Rosenbaum 1986).

What is needed is a combination of equitable allocation of educational resources and reduction of organizational differentiations that overtly define some students as intrinsically "better" than others. This does not mean schools should aim at turning out an undifferentiated set of "products." Schools are the "sorting machine" of society (Spring 1976); they "grade" students into different "levels." They are and will remain the primary feeders of society's stratification system. The policy issues are related to *how* the schools carry out this function, not *whether they should*. The policy issues involve the equitable distribution of resources and avoiding harmful early and persistent "talent" identification.

The organization of the labor force also affects individual achievements, but there is a major difference between the policy implications of those effects and the effects of school structures. The great majority of the labor force is employed in private firms and industries. At least in American society, such units are defined as free to follow private goals so long as harm is not done to public values. The legal responsibility of private firms to provide equal opportunities for workers' personal achievement is limited to social categories such as gender and race. It does not include providing within-firm mechanisms, such as training programs or internal labor markets. In sharp contrast, the schools are considered a public institution whose purpose is to provide the larger society with a skilled work force and an informed citizenry. Equal opportunity for personal achievement is a fundamental obligation of the schools.

The research on the effects of the schools' organizational differentiations based on ability thus raises a very basic policy problem not faced in the world of work. Yet it is also apparent that the health of the national economy depends on constant improvement in the skill level of the labor force and continued accommodations of specific skills to changing needs. To that end, it may be as much of a national obligation to ensure continued equality of opportunity for training and retraining in the labor force as in the schools.

NOTES

1. Power or authority is a third dimension used in studies of social stratification (Wright and Perrone 1977) that reflects the continuing significance of emphases in the work of theorists such as Weber and Marx. But authority is not as directly linked to occupations as such as prestige and socioeconomic status are. As important as this dimension is in the study of social stratification, it is not dealt with in this chapter. Some aspects of authority in the workplace are discussed in chapter 19.

2. Most of the early status attainment research was conducted with samples of men because of the difficulty of identifying the stratification positions of women if they were not in the labor force. Later research broadened the analysis to include women.

3. Chapter 16 offers a more in-depth discussion of the processes of social development than can be provided here.

4. The Wisconsin model included measures of occupational aspiration and educational aspiration, but the occupational aspiration measure was the only new measure added that attempted to explain occupational attainment. The two aspiration measures were taken at the same point in time (during the senior year in high school), and they were highly correlated (0.63).

5. There is little agreement about the bases of classification of labor force sectors. Beck et al. used a crude two-sector classification, while others have used much more complex classifications based on multiple dimensions and reflecting more of the complex structure of the labor force (Kaufman, Hodson, and Fligstein 1981; Zucker and Rosenstein 1981).

6. Occupations also differ in the career opportunities they offer; some provide several levels and others are undifferentiated, with most workers who enter them experiencing little career mobility (Spenner, Otto, and Call 1982; Spilerman 1977).

7. Between-school differences as well as within-school divisions are also thought to be important, and some schools are thought to be more "effective" than others. Factors that distinguish schools from each other (size, facilities, power of the principal, etc.) have been thought to be possible sources of variation in student achievements. Since the famous "Coleman report" (Coleman et al. 1966), however, a repeated finding has been that the amount of between-school variation in achievement is very small compared with within-school variation. (See Heyns 1986 for a review of this literature.) It can also be argued, however, that even small amounts of variance between schools can represent large increments or decrements in overall system productivity (Willms 1992).

8. At the same time, girls and African Americans are more likely to be in the college preparatory track, other things equal, thus making race and sex inequalities somewhat smaller than they might otherwise have been (Gamoran and Mare 1989).

9. Gamoran (1986) refers to this as an "institutional" effect. It is the normative aspect of the "charter" of ability groups calling for some groups to perform at higher levels than others (J. Meyer 1980).

REFERENCES

Alexander, Karl L., and Bruce K. Eckland. 1974. Sex differences in the educational attainment process. *American Sociological Review* 39:668–681.

———. 1975. Contextual effects in the high school attainment process. *American Sociological Review* 40:402–416.

Alexander, Karl L., Doris R. Entwisle, and Maxine S. Thompson. 1987. School performance, status relations, and the structure of sentiment: Bringing the teacher back in. *American Sociological Review* 52:665–682.

Alexander, Karl L., and Larry J. Griffin. 1975. The Wisconsin model of socioeconomic achievement: A replication. *American Journal of Sociology* 81:324–342.

Alexander, Karl L., and Edward L. McDill. 1976. Selection and allocation within schools: Some causes and consequences of curriculum placement. *American Sociological Review* 41:963–980.

Althauser, Robert P., and Arne L. Kalleberg. 1981. Firms, occupations and the structure of labor markets: A conceptual analysis and research agenda. Pp. 119–149 in *Sociological Perspectives on Labor Markets,* ed. Ivar Berg. New York: Academic.

Alwin, Duane F., and Luther B. Otto. 1977. High school context effects on aspirations. *Sociology of Education* 50:259–273.

Andorka, Rudolf, and Tamas Kolosi, ed. 1984. *Stratification and Inequality.* Budapest: Institute for Social Sciences.

Bakker, B. F. M., J. Dronkers, and G. W. Meijnen, ed. 1989. *Educational Opportunities in the Welfare State: Longitudinal Studies in Educational and Occupational Attainment in the Netherlands.* Nijmegen: Institut voor Toegepaste Sociale Wetenschappen.

Baron, James N., and William T. Bielby. 1980. Bringing the firms back in: Stratification, segmentation, and the organization of work. *American Sociological Review* 45:737–765.

Barr, Rebecca, and Robert Dreeben. 1983. *How Schools Work.* Chicago: University of Chicago Press.

Barrett, Nancy. 1987. Women and the economy. Pp. 100–149 in *The American Woman 1987–1988: A Report in Depth,* ed. Sara E. Rix. New York: Norton.

Beck, E. M., Patrick M. Horan, and Charles M. Tolbert II. 1978. Stratification in a dual economy: A sectoral model of earnings determination. *American Sociological Review* 43:704–720.

Blau, Peter M., and Otis Dudley Duncan. 1967. *The American Occupational Structure.* New York: Wiley.

Borman, Kathryn M. 1991. *The First "Real" Job: A Study of Young Workers.* Albany: State University of New York Press.

Borman, Kathryn M., and Jane Reisman, eds. 1986. *Becoming a Worker.* Norwood, NJ: Ablex.

Bosker, Roel, Rolf van der Velden, and Leun Otten. 1989. Social stratification and educational career. Pp. 99–120 in *Similar or Different?* ed. W. Jansen, J. Drokers, and K. Verrips. Amsterdam: SISWO.

Bossert, Steven. 1979. *Tasks and Social Relationships in Classrooms.* Cambridge, UK: Cambridge University Press.

Bourdieu, Pierre. 1973. Cultural reproduction and social reproduction. Pp. 71–112 in *Knowledge, Education, and Cultural Change,* ed. Richard Brown. London: Tavistock.

Bowles, Samuel, and Herbert Gintis. 1976. *Schooling in Capitalist America: Educational Reform and the Contradictions of Economic Life.* New York: Basic Books.

Brookover, Wilbur, C. Beady, P. Flood, J. Schweitzer, and J. Wisenbaker. 1979. *School Social Systems and Student Achievement.* New York: Praeger.

Bynner, John, and Ken Roberts. 1992. *Youth and Work: Transition to Employment in England and Germany.* London: Anglo-German Foundation.

Call, Vaughn R. A., and Luther B. Otto. 1977. Age at marriage as a mobility contingency: Estimates for the Nye-Berardo model. *Journal of Marriage and the Family* 39:67–79.

Cicourel, Aaron V., K. H. Jennings, S. H. M. Jennings, K. C. W. Leiter, Robert MacKay, Hugh Mehan, and D. R. Roth. 1974. *Language Use and School Performance.* New York: Academic.

Clark, Burton R. 1960. The cooling out function in higher education. *American Journal of Sociology* 65:569–576.

Coleman, James S. 1984. The transition from school to work. *Research in Social Stratification and Mobility* 3:27–59.

Coleman, James S., Ernest Q. Campbell, Carol J. Hobson, James McPartland, Alexander M. Mood, Frederick D. Weinfeld, and Robert L. York. 1966. *Equality of Educational Opportunity.* Washington, DC: U.S. Government Printing Office.

Collins, Randall. 1971. Functional and conflict theories of educational stratification. *American Sociological Review* 36:1002–1019.

Cookson, Peter W., Jr., and Caroline H. Persell. 1985. *Preparing for Power: America's Elite Boarding Schools.* New York: Basic Books.

Dar, Yehezkel, and Nura Resh. 1986. *Classroom Composition and Pupil Achievement: A Study of the Effects of Ability-Based Classes.* New York: Gordon & Breach.

DeJong, M. J. 1989. Ethnic culture, family background and educational attainment. Pp. 59–74 in *Educational Opportunities in the Welfare State,* ed. B. F. M. Bakker, J. Dronkers, and G. W. Meijnen. Nijmegen: Institut voor Toegepaste Sociale Wetenschappen.

Dreeben, Robert, and Rebecca Barr. 1988. Classroom composition and the design of instruction. *Sociology of Education* 61:129–142.

Eder, Donna. 1981. Ability grouping as a self-fulfilling prophecy: A micro-analysis of teacher-student interaction. *Sociology of Education* 54:151–162.

———. 1983. Ability grouping and students' academic self-concepts: A case study. *Elementary School Journal* 84:149–161.

England, P., G. Farkas, B. S. Kilbourne, and T. Dou. 1988. Explaining occupational sex segregation and wages: Findings from a model with fixed effects. *American Sociological Review* 53:544–558.

Entwisle, Doris R., and Leslie Alec Hayduk. 1988. Lasting effects of elementary school. *Sociology of Education* 61:147–159.

Farley, Reynolds. 1984. *Blacks and Whites: Narrowing the Gap?* Cambridge, MA: Harvard University Press.

Featherman, David L., and Robert M. Hauser. 1978. *Opportunity and Change.* New York: Academic.

Felmlee, Diane, and Donna Eder. 1983. Contextual effects in the classroom: The impact of ability groups on student attention. *Sociology of Education* 56: 77–87.

Finley, Merrilee K. 1984. Teachers and tracking in a comprehensive high school. *Sociology of Education* 57:233–243.

Gamoran, Adam. 1986. Instructional and institutional effects of ability grouping. *Sociology of Education* 59:185–198.

———. 1987. The stratification of high school learning opportunities. *Sociology of Education* 60:135–155.

Gamoran, Adam, and Robert D. Mare. 1989. Secondary school tracking and educational inequality: Compensation, reinforcement, or neutrality? *American Journal of Sociology* 94:1146–1183.

Garet, Michael S., and Brian DeLany. 1988. Students, courses and stratification. *Sociology of Education* 61:61–77.

Gracey, Harry L. 1972. *Curriculum or Craftsmanship.* Chicago: University of Chicago Press.

Granovetter, Mark. 1974. *Getting a Job.* Cambridge, MA: Harvard University Press.

Haller, Archibald O., and Alejandro Portes. 1973. Status attainment processes. *Sociology of Education* 46: 51–91.

Haller, Emil J., and Sharon A. Davis. 1981. Teacher perceptions, parental social status and grouping for reading instruction. *Sociology of Education* 54: 162–174.

Hallinan, Maureen T., and Aage B. Sorensen. 1983. The formation and stability of instructional groups. *American Sociological Review* 48:838–851.

Hamilton, S. F. 1986. Excellence and the transition from school to work. *Phi Delta Kappan* 68: 239–242.

Heyns, Barbara. 1974. Social selection and stratification within schools. *American Journal of Sociology* 79: 1434–1451.

———. 1986. Educational effects: Issues in conceptualization and measurement. Pp. 305–340 in *Handbook of Theory and Research for the Sociology of Education,* ed. John G. Richardson. New York: Greenwood.

Hoffer, Thomas. 1991. The effects of ability grouping in middle school science and math on student achievement. Paper presented at the 86th Annual Meeting of the American Sociological Association, Cincinnati.

Horan, Patrick M. 1978. Is status attainment research atheoretical? *American Sociological Review* 43: 534–541.

Hotchkiss, Lawrence, and Linda Eberst Dorsten. 1987. Curriculum effects on early post-high school outcomes. *Research in the Sociology of Education and Socialization.* 7:191–219.

Hout, Michael, and Maurice A. Garnier. 1979. Curriculum placement and educational stratification in France. *Sociology of Education* 52:146–156.

Kaufman, Robert L., Randy Hodson, and Neil Fligstein. 1981. Defrocking dualism: A new approach to defining industrial sectors. *Social Science Research* 10:1–31.

Kerckhoff, Alan C. 1976. The status attainment process: Socialization or allocation? *Social Forces* 55:368–381.

———. ed. 1980. *Longitudinal Perspectives on Educational Attainment: Research in Sociology of Education and Socialization,* vol. 1. Greenwich, CT: JAI Press.

———. 1986. Effects of ability grouping in British secondary schools. *American Sociological Review* 51: 842–858.

———. 1991. Creating inequality in the schools: A structural perspective. Pp. 153–169 in *Macro-Micro Linkages in Sociology,* ed. Joan Huber. Newbury Park, CA: Sage.

———. 1993. *Diverging Pathways: Social Structure and Career Deflections.* New York: Cambridge University Press.

Kerckhoff, Alan C., and Richard T. Campbell. 1977a. Black-white differences in the educational attainment process. *Sociology of Education* 50:15–27.

———. 1977b. Race and social status differences in the explanation of educational ambition. *Social Forces* 55:701–714.

Kerckhoff, Alan C., Richard T. Campbell, Jerry M. Trott, and Vered Kraus. 1990. The transmission of socioeconomic status and prestige in Great Britain and the United States. *Sociological Forum* 4: 155–177.

Kerckhoff, Alan C., and Judith L. Huff. 1974. Parental influence on educational goals. *Sociometry* 37: 307–327.

Kozol, Jonathan. 1991. *Savage Inequalities: Children in America's Schools.* New York: Crown.

Kraus, Vered, and Robert W. Hodge. 1990. *Promises in the Promised Land: Mobility and Inequality in Israel.* New York: Greenwood.

Lareau, Annette. 1989. *Home Advantage: Social Class and Parental Intervention in Elementary Education.* London: Falmer.

Lucas, Samuel R., and Adam Gamoran. 1991. Race and track assignment: A reconsideration with course-based indicators of track locations. Paper presented at the 86th Annual Meeting of the American Sociological Association, Cincinnati.

Marini, Margaret Mooney. 1978. The transition to adulthood: Sex differences in educational attainment and age at marriage. *American Sociological Review* 43:483–507.

———. 1980. Sex differences in the process of occupational attainment: A closer look. *Social Science Research* 9:307–361.

———. 1989. Sex differences in earnings in the United States. *Annual Review of Sociology* 15:343–380.

Marx, Karl. 1936. *Capital.* New York: Modern Library.

Maurice, Marc, Francois Sellier, and Jean-Jacques Silvestre. 1986. *The Foundations of Industrial Power: A Comparison of France and Germany.* Cambridge, MA: MIT Press.

McClendon, McKee J. 1976. The occupational status attainment process of males and females. *American Sociological Review* 41:52–64.

Metz, Mary Haywood. 1978. *Classrooms and Corridors.* Berkeley: University of California Press.

Meyer, John W. 1980. Levels of the educational system and schooling effects. Pp. 15–63 in *The Analysis of Educational Productivity, 2: Issues in Macroanalysis,* ed. Charles E. Bidwell and Douglas M. Windham. Cambridge, MA: Ballinger.

Meyer, R. H., and D. A. Wise. 1984. The transition from school to work: The experiences of blacks and whites. *Research on Labor Economics* 6: 123–176.

Mortimer, Jeylan T., Jon Lorence, and Donald S. Kumka. 1986. *Work, Family and Personality: Transition to Adulthood.* Norwood, NJ: Ablex.

Oakes, Jeannie. 1985. *Keeping Track: How Schools Structure Inequality.* New Haven: Yale University Press.

Osterman, P. 1980. *Getting Started: The Youth Labor Market.* Cambridge, MA: MIT Press.

Otto, Luther B., and Archibald O. Haller. 1979. Evidence for a social psychological view of the status attainment process: Four studies compared. *Social Forces* 57:887–914.

Porter, James N. 1974. Race, socialization and mobility in educational and early occupational attainment. *American Sociological Review* 39:303–316.

Portes, Alejandro, and Kenneth L. Wilson. 1976. Black-white differences in educational attainment. *American Sociological Review* 41:414–431

Raudenbush, Stephen W., and J. Douglas Willms, ed. 1991. *Schools, Classrooms, and Pupils: International Studies of Schooling from a Multilevel Perspective.* San Diego: Academic.

Reszke, Irena. 1984. *Social Prestige and Gender.* Warsaw: Polish Academy of Sciences Institute of Philosophy and Sociology.

Rollins, B. C., and D. L. Thomas. 1979. Parental support, power, and control techniques in the socialization of children. Pp. 317–364 in *Contemporary Theories About the Family,* vol. 1, ed. W. Burr, Reuben Hill, F. Ivan Nye and Ira L. Reiss. New York: Free Press.

Rosenbaum, James. 1980. Track misperceptions and frustrated college plans: An analysis of the effects of tracks and track perceptions in the national longitudinal survey. *Sociology of Education* 53: 74–88.

———. 1986. Institutional career structures and the social construction of ability. Pp. 139–171 in *Handbook of Theory and Research for the Sociology of Education,* ed. John Richardson. New York: Greenwood.

Rosenbaum, James, Takehiko Kariya, Rick Settersten, and Tony Maier. 1990. Market and network theories of the transition from high school to work: Their application to industrialized societies. *Annual Review of Sociology* 16:263–299.

Rosenfeld, Rachel A. 1980. Race and sex differences in career dynamics. *American Sociological Review* 45:583–609.

Rosenholtz, Susan J., and Stephen H. Rosenholtz. 1981. Classroom organization and the perception of ability. *Sociology of Education* 54:132–140.

Rosenthal, Robert, and Lenore Jacobson. 1968. *Pygmalion in the Classroom.* New York: Holt, Rinehart & Winston.

Rowan, Brian, and Andrew W. Miracle, Jr. 1983. Systems of ability grouping and the stratification of achievement in elementary schools. *Sociology of Education* 56:133–144.

Sewell, William H., Archibald O. Haller, and George W. Ohlendorf. 1970. The educational and early occupational status attainment process: Replication and revision. *American Sociological Review* 35: 1014–1027.

Sewell, William H., and Robert M. Hauser. 1980. The Wisconsin longitudinal study of social and psychological factors in aspirations and achievements. *Research in Sociology of Education and Socialization* 1:59–99.

Sewell, William H., Robert M. Hauser, and Wendy C. Wolf. 1980. Sex, schooling and occupational status. *American Journal of Sociology* 86:551–583.

Simpson, Carl. 1981. Classroom structure and the organization of ability. *Sociology of Education* 54: 120–132.

Sorensen, Aage B. 1977. The structure of inequality and the process of attainment. *American Sociological Review* 42:965–978.

Sorensen, Aage B., and Maureen T. Hallinan. 1986. Effects of ability grouping on growth in academic achievement. *American Educational Research Journal* 23:519–542.

Sorensen, Aage B., and Nancy B. Tuma. 1981. Labor market structures and job mobility. *Research in Social Stratification and Mobility* 1:67–94.

Spenner, Kenneth I., Luther B. Otto, and Vaughn R. A. Call. 1982. *Career Lines and Careers.* Lexington, MA: Lexington Books.

Spilerman, Seymour. 1977. Careers, labor market structure, and socioeconomic achievement. *American Journal of Sociology* 83:551–593.

Spring, Joel. 1976. *The Sorting Machine.* New York: David McKay.

Stevenson, Harold W., and Shin-Ying Lee. 1990. Contexts of achievement: A study of American, Chinese and Japanese children. *Monographs of the Society for Research in Child Development* 55, no. 1, 2.

Stinchcombe, Arthur L. 1964. *Rebellion in a High School.* Chicago: Quadrangle Books.

Stolzenberg, Ross M. 1978. Bringing the boss back in: Employer size, employee schooling, and socioeconomic achievement. *American Sociological Review* 43:813–828.

Treiman, Donald J., and Kermit Terrell. 1975. Sex and the process of status attainment: A comparison of working women and men. *American Sociological Review* 40:174–200.

Vanfossen, Beth, James Jones, and Joan Spade. 1987. Curriculum tracking and status maintenance. *Sociology of Education* 60:104–122.

Weber, Max. 1946. *From Max Weber: Essays in Sociology.* Edited and translated by Hans H. Gerth and C. Wright Mills. New York: Oxford University Press

Weinstein, R. S. 1976. Reading group membership in first grade: Teacher behaviors and pupil experience over time. *Journal of Educational Psychology* 68: 106–116.

Willis, Paul. 1977. *Learning to Labor: How Working Class Kids Get Working Class Jobs.* New York: Columbia University Press.

Willms, J. Douglas. 1992. *Monitoring School Performance: A Guide for Educators.* London: Falmer.

Wilson, Kenneth L., and Alejandro Portes. 1975. The educational attainment process: Results from a national sample. *American Journal of Sociology* 81: 343–363.

Wright, Erik Olin, and Luca Perrone. 1977. Marxist class categories and income inequality. *American Sociological Review* 42:32–55.

Zucker, Lynne G., and Carolyn Rosenstein. 1981. Taxonomies of institutional structure: Dual economy reconsidered. *American Sociological Review* 46: 869–884.

CHAPTER 19

Social Psychology of Work

JEYLAN T. MORTIMER
JON LORENCE

A century ago, Emile Durkheim posited that modern work is liberating, promoting the development of human beings' generalized capacities. Karl Marx (1964) argued, to the contrary, that contemporary conditions of industrial work are dehumanizing. Scholars continue to debate the psychological consequences of differentiated occupational roles, sometimes highly specialized and complex but often fragmented and simplistic. There is consensus that work, in comparison to unemployment or full-time homemaker status, is beneficial for men (Liker 1982) and women (Sorensen and Mortimer 1988). Work can provide noneconomic as well as economic benefits—providing structure to daily activities, feelings of worth and productivity, an interpersonal context for the formation of social relationships, and social identity and prestige (Jahoda 1981). It may also offer opportunities for the demonstration of competence and effectance, psychological engagement, even "optimal experience" (Csikzentmihalyi 1990) that are less available in out-of-work settings. But work may also present stressors that generate strain and, if prolonged, deterioration in both mental and physical health (Ganster and Schaubroeck 1991).

Studies of the social psychology of work have applied as well as theoretical relevance. Maintaining and enhancing productivity is of central importance to both public organizations and private firms as foreign competition mounts. Though the relationship between job satisfaction and productivity has been given considerable attention with mixed results, there are other psychological dimensions whose linkage to effort and output deserve systematic scrutiny. Vocational and industrial psychologists, managers, those concerned with issues of labor policy, and others interested in organizational functioning and effectiveness would be well informed by social psychological research. Given the amount of time adults spend working and the salience of work to personal identity, the quality of work experience is of great potential importance to the overall quality of life. Psychological orientations and mood states reflect the character of work experience and have been found to influence familial relationships. Moreover, the constraints and opportunities posed by the work role influence socioeconomic attainment as well as the status and lifestyle of the family.

The study of the effects of work on psychological functioning and overt behavior challenges those who would allege that the major determinants of personality exert their influence in childhood and adolescence, after which the person remains quite stable. Instead, the studies reviewed here demonstrate that the quality of working life has pervasive implications for adult development. Attempts to specify the circumstances in the workplace that promote mental health and well-being, on the one hand, or distress and pathology, on the other, have generated an expansive literature. However, the possibility that workers may respond differently to the conditions of their work, with such variation determined by their social backgrounds, identities, and other distinctive psychological traits, complicates the investigation and resolution of this issue.

The social psychology of work encompasses a vast body of scholarly work spanning several disciplines. We provide orientation to this literature by first introducing three broad theoretical-conceptual frameworks, corresponding to the three "faces" of social psychology (House 1977). Orientations to work are the centerpiece of this review: job satisfaction, work involvement and identity, alienation, and occupational values. We describe their determinants and consequences, inside and outside the work setting, with attention to the sustaining and growth-enhancing outcomes of job conditions, as well as their detrimental and alienating effects. A broad range of influences on work orientations are considered. This review gives particular attention to whether occupational conditions affect all workers in the same way or whether there are important differences in their effects dependent on individual characteristics. While acknowledging that factors related to social background, culture (and subculture), as well as individual psychological and other traits may affect work orientations or condition the effects of work conditions, we conclude that these are far less consequential than the actual experiences, determined by organizational and occupational structures, workers encounter in the job setting. Finally, we consider continuing debates and directions for future research and draw attention to the importance of interdisciplinary collaboration.

Given that the institution of work is a dominant structure in contemporary society and that work orientations and other presumed psychological consequences are important attributes of personality, the social structure and personality paradigm is of central importance (House 1981). Kohn, Schooler, and colleagues (1983) identified the major structural imperatives of work that have significant consequences for psychological change, with major emphasis on self-direction (i.e., the complexity of task activity), closeness of supervision, and degree of routinization. However, they recognized other relevant structural imperatives, including job pressures, extrinsic risks and rewards (e.g., responsibility for things beyond one's control), and organizational position.

For Kohn and Schooler, the psychological process presumed to mediate the effects of job on the person is "learning-generalization, . . . a straightforward translation of the lessons of the job to outside-the-job realities" (1983, 300). Joanne Miller (1988) elaborates this process by positing that self-direction is a "positive, enhancing experience . . . a fundamental reward of work and a stimulus to which the organism is attentive." She depicts learning-generalization as a "direct transfer of learning, without attention to how job experience is cognitively or emotionally interpreted." Whereas Kohn, Schooler, and colleagues provide conceptual grounding for much subsequent work, their research program has given scant attention to attitudinal dimensions such as job satisfaction and commitment (Kohn and Schooler 1973) or work identity, focusing instead on basic dimensions of "psychological functioning," such as intellectual flexibility, self-directedness of orientation, well-being, and distress.

In contrast to this first, more structural perspective, symbolic interactionists focus on the special problems faced by members of occupational groups and the interactive mechanisms through which solutions are forged (Hughes 1958). They describe the games and other distractions workers use to avert the boredom of monotonous tasks (Roy 1958), the enforcement of productivity norms, and workers' "reality maintaining" activities through "orderly talk," "restricted discourse," and other interactional strategies (J. Miller 1988). They see emergent occupational subcultures as constituting "separate worlds" whose unique character is especially evident when workers are called on to enact unusual and arduous tasks or to confront dangers and threats to well-being not present in ordinary life activities (Haas, 1977).

Vaught and Smith (1980) describe rituals enacted by coal miners, processes of "stripping and substitution" (Mortimer and Simmons 1978) that destroy old self-images and identities and make way for new ones; rites of initiation and testing that precede full acceptance; and the mechanisms through which solidarity and commitment are maintained. Their deviant, even unlawful behaviors, when gauged by conventional standards, underscore the "different world" of the miners that heightens bonding to the group and fosters a sense of safety. Here the predominant problem is life-threatening danger; the subordination of individual will is needed to ensure predictability, cooperation, and automatic compliance with shared expectations in crisis situations.

A less dramatic but more prevalent problem is the maintenance of self-respect in the face of low occupational prestige. Hospital attendants (Simpson and Simpson 1959), garbage collectors (Walsh 1982), and others accomplish this by emphasizing the important functions they perform or by developing special self-enhancing meanings and symbols. Hannah Meara (1974) notes the esteem accorded by butchers to those whose cuts and scars signify bravery and the ability to withstand the pain of recurrent injury, the pride in being able to withstand the cold freezer temperatures, and the machismo attached to the presumed protection (or exclusion) of women from these dangers. However, the structural constraints of a college campus preclude campus police officers from viewing their work positively, unlike detectives (Heinsler, Kleinman, and Stenross 1990).

Mulcahy and Faulkner (1977) examine the special problems of machine operators, who, despite severe difficulties, are prevented from collectively devising consensual definitions and collective behavioral solutions. These semiskilled operatives must pay constant attention; they are prevented from speaking by their spatial arrangements and by the deafening noise; and they face frequent machine breakdowns, which obstruct their ability to meet quotas. Emergent attitudes and modes of situational adaptation are highly individualistic—stressing the active pursuit of self-interest, technical virtuosity (in preventing breakdowns or repairing machinery), and the virtues of hard work.

Psychological social psychology offers a third perspective. Psychological social psychologists—especially those in vocational, industrial, and personnel psychology who espouse a "need satisfaction" paradigm—tend to assume that basic work orientations (e.g., vocational interests and

identity) are formed early in life, starting in childhood and crystallizing in adolescence, and are stable throughout adulthood. Such orientations are thought to have major significance for occupational decision making, work adjustment, and performance. These psychologists attach major importance to the "fit" of the worker's traits and the job, assuming that job dissatisfaction and job change will occur until there is a successful match between individual needs and job demands and rewards (Locke and Latham 1990). Psychologists have examined the consequences of work orientations for organizational functioning, such as the effects of job dissatisfaction and organizational commitment on employee turnover (Locke 1976, 1331) and performance (Locke and Latham 1990).

Assumptions about the degree to which work orientations are traitlike, stable dimensions, or situationally specific responses are major sources of divergence among the three social psychological perspectives. At one extreme are psychologists, who find evidence for genetic or physiological determination of job satisfaction, career preference, or the expression of emotion in the workplace (Arvey et al. 1989). At the other are symbolic interactionists, who contend that orientations to the job are continuously emergent and negotiated social realities, dependent on ongoing interactional processes (G. Miller 1990). Between these extremes are psychologists who emphasize environmental determinants in childhood and adolescence, particularly socialization in the family, but sometimes including adult experiences (Vondracek, Lerner, and Schulenberg 1986). Also taking an intermediate position are those in the social structure and personality camp, who see elements of psychological functioning as stable phenomena, formed initially in the family (Mortimer, Lorence, and Kumka 1986) and other pre-adult socialization contexts but nonetheless responsive later in life to key conditions of work (Kohn and Schooler 1983).

Psychological social psychologists consider the actor's expectations, values, and self-conceptions of central importance in determining behavior in the work setting (Locke and Latham 1990). According to expectancy theory (Vroom 1964), performance results from expectancy—the belief that effort will produce desired performances; instrumentality—the belief that performance will lead to rewards; and valence—the value of the rewards. The individual's self-efficacy—estimation of his/her capacity to perform in a given context—is a major determinant of expectancy. Psychological social psychologists are concerned with the interactions of individual attitudes such as these with forces in the immediate work situation. For example, Locke and Latham's (1990) "goal setting" theory posits that for goals to influence performance there must be commitment to the goals. Commitment is determined by stable personal traits (e.g., self-efficacy) and compatible values. Feedback—provided by the supervisor or coworkers or inherent in the task itself—enables one to monitor performance in relation to goals.

In this and other psychological approaches, structural, macroorganizational, and institutional factors are given little attention. However, cognitive psychology has laid out a conceptual paradigm with clear relevance to the social psychology of work (Morgan and Schwalbe 1990). Psychologists' work provides insight into the intervening psychological processes through which structural dimensions of work and social interaction may influence orientations and behavior.

PSYCHOLOGICAL DOMAINS OF INTEREST

Job Satisfaction

Job satisfaction is a "positive emotional state resulting from the appraisal of one's job or job experiences" (Locke 1976, 1300). The emphasis on job satisfaction in the social psychology of work has been criticized because of its tenuous relationship to productivity and other behaviors in the work setting (Hodson 1991). But even if job satisfaction were entirely unrelated to work behavior, it would be worthy of study as a key indicator of the quality of life. Most investigators focus on overall job satisfaction, referencing evaluation of the job as a whole, rather than facet-specific satisfactions relating to particular job aspects, such as the quality of

relationships with coworkers or income. Though much concern has been expressed about declining job satisfaction, Hamilton and Wright (1986), on the basis of several repeated national surveys (e.g, NORC, Roper, and Gallup), conclude that there is no firm evidence of this during the postwar period (to 1980). Typically, only 10 to 15 percent of respondents express any job dissatisfaction.

Work Involvement and Identity

Work involvement, often a positive correlate of job satisfaction (Mortimer and Lorence 1989), refers to the centrality or importance of work as a sphere of life activity. According to Lawler and Hall (1970), "job involvement" is "the degree to which the job situation is central to the person and his [sic] identity." Like job satisfaction, work involvement has interrelated referents (O'Reilly 1991), including the job itself (Locke 1976, 1301), the organization (Lincoln and Kalleberg, 1985), the occupation (Kohn 1969, 180) or work in general (Bielby and Bielby 1984). A person with high job involvement evaluates the job as an activity with high priority. Moreover, the job is an object of emotional investment; what happens at work has consequences for emotional well-being. However, a distinction is made between commitment to behavior (e.g, role behavior continuance or resolve to remain in the organization) and identification with the work role (Chappell 1980). Because of high levels of educational investment or other "side bets" (Becker 1960), a worker may have high commitment to remaining in an occupation or organization; however, this can be accompanied by role distance and investment in nonwork spheres. Still, it is presumed that behavioral commitment and psychological identification generally go hand in hand (Hodson and Sullivan 1985).

Work identity is sometimes considered a central component of work involvement (Lodahl and Kejner 1965) and at other times a related but conceptually distinct dimension of self—the extent to which the self-concept is defined in terms of work. Symbolic interactionists speak of hierarchies of role identities, including work, family, and others, with position dependent on the degree to which interactions and relationships with others are dependent on each role (Stryker and Statham 1985) as well as on performance evaluations (Hoelter 1983).

Work Values

Because of their presumed relevance for occupational choice and job satisfaction, work values have been the focus of considerable study (Mortimer and Lorence 1979b). There is some evidence for a tripartite structure of values (Borg 1990; Mortimer and Lorence 1979b). Intrinsic rewards derive from task activities; people-oriented rewards derive from working with people or being of service to others; and extrinsic rewards are those a worker receives for performing a job (e.g., income, advancement, security, and prestige). Other research reports a two-factor configuration, with intrinsic and extrinsic dimensions (Giorgi and Marsh 1990). But if values are defined broadly as "conceptions of the good," a much wider array of orientations come into play. For example, the "Protestant work ethic" includes beliefs that hard work builds character and that productive activity is of value in itself (Giorgi and Marsh 1990).

Worker Alienation

According to Marx's theory of alienation, humans are estranged from their natural state of being—in which work flows directly from individual purpose and social needs—by capitalist control over the tools, processes, and uses of production. Durkheim's (1951) discussion of anomie draws attention to the normlessness stemming from rapid social change. These classic ideas provide conceptual grounding for Seeman's (1983) alienation dimensions: powerlessness (absence of control over events), meaninglessness (an anomic state), social isolation (lack of social ties and supports), and self-estrangement. For the self-estranged, the self is despised, disguised (since true human feelings and capacities are not realized), and "detached," given the disjunction between activity and positive affect (i.e., work activities are not rewarding). The concept of alienated labor is often associated with machine production (Blauner 1964; Leiter 1985), but it is also pertinent to the experience of service workers (Hochschild 1983), automated industries, and clerical work (Erikson 1986).

DETERMINANTS OF WORK ORIENTATIONS

Explanations of the development of work orientations and behaviors may be grouped into two broad categories, corresponding to two general sources of influence. First are the more proximal determinants, related to distinctive organizational features and occupational conditions that structure the immediate phenomenal experience of work. Those who stress the malleability of the adult personality, including orientations and behaviors that relate directly to work, emphasize the character of opportunity, the features of the work role, and the nature of interpersonal relationships and interactions on the job as the most potent sources of work-related psychological and behavioral change. Others, in contrast, look outside the work setting to more distal sources of influence, including cultural differences within and across nations, historical cohort and age-related influences, gender, and race. Because of their association with early socialization processes and/or correspondence to core identities, they may be expected to have their most formative influence early on, in childhood and adolescence, prior to incumbency of the adult work role. As a result, they could influence both selection of and reaction to key features of the organizational and occupational context. We examine the direct influences of these contextual and individual variables on work orientations and behaviors, as well as their potential role as conditioning agents, moderating the effects of particular work conditions.

Organizational Structure and Experience

Marx linked pervasive discontent and deterioration in worker attitudes to the development of capitalist industry in the mid-nineteenth century. Contemporary class theorists point to property ownership and authority in the organization of production, with owners (who own productive property and control the labor of others) and managers (who only control others' labor) expected to manifest greater job satisfaction and other positive orientations toward work than workers, who neither own the enterprises in which their work takes place nor control the labor power of others (Kalleberg and Griffin 1980). Drawing on Weberian conceptions of the bureaucracy, some have investigated key bureaucratic features, related to size, the proliferation of formal rules, and career ladders, as sources of work orientations.

Underlying much current organizational research is the theory of "bureaucratic alienation," which assumes that large bureaucratic organizations—characterized by highly centralized, formalized, and impersonal relations and the proliferation of narrowly specialized, fragmented, and routinized tasks—foster an oppressive work environment that adversely affects employee work attitudes. To maintain commitment in such an alienating atmosphere, workers must have clearly specified career structures that reward those who fulfill formal organizational requirements. Contrary to this view is an emerging "welfare corporatist theory," which assumes that only large, formal organizations can provide the rewards and work structures that enhance job attitudes (Lincoln and Kalleberg 1990). One of the difficulties in assessing these perspectives is that so many dimensions of organizational structure are at issue: technology, firm size, rules, supervisory practices, opportunities for worker participation, career structures, and industrial sector. Only a few studies have attempted to assess simultaneously the importance of more than a limited number of these organizational dimensions.

The prevailing view that larger organizations have more impersonal and fragmented social relations, which lower job satisfaction and organizational commitment, receives mixed support. Some surveys find more negative work attitudes among employees in larger firms (e.g., Hodson 1989), others find more positive attitudes (Lincoln and Kalleberg 1990), and still others find no relationship (Mathieu and Zajac 1990). The psychological impact of size seems so slight that other organizational features related to size are likely more crucial determinants of employee attitudes. Little support exists for the hypothesis that rules and regulations have a negative effect on workers because they stifle creativity. Lincoln and Kalleberg (1990) find that formal rules and procedures do not significantly affect job satisfaction and organizational commitment of manufacturing employees. However, constantly being checked for rule violations, being closely supervised, and punitive supervisory behavior decrease both job satisfaction and organizational commitment (Hodson 1989). In addition, there is evidence that organizations permitting greater worker participation have a positive impact on job satisfaction (Neuman, Edwards, and Raju 1989), organizational commitment, employee work effort, and work unit effectiveness (Lincoln and Kalleberg 1990).

The welfare corporatist view suggests that only nationally prominent core corporations that monopolize markets can provide their workers the security and rewards necessary to enhance job attitudes. Promotional opportunities significantly raise job satisfaction and organizational commitment (Mottaz 1987), as does the presence of an internal labor market (Loscocco 1990a). Employee welfare services, more often available in monopoly firms, are also significant net determinants of workers' job satisfaction and commitment; employees in smaller independent companies report lower levels of both (Lincoln and Kalleberg 1990).

Overall, the findings tend to be more supportive of the "corporatist welfare" view of organizations than the "bureaucratic alienating" perspective. In general, we must look to the ways organizational features (e.g., size, formal rules, structures of authority) impinge on the worker, affecting career opportunities stressors, supervisor-worker relations, and the scope of employee benefits, to understand their social psychological significance.

Occupational Structure and Experience

Instead of examining broad organizational forms as sources of worker orientations, other investigators attend to the nature of work experience itself, as conditioned by key features of the work role, the nature of task, and technological conditions. Marx viewed worker alienation as stemming from capitalist industrial organization, which, in his view, stifled the expression of the worker's own will in the productive act, preventing worker control over the means as well as the uses of production. Similarly, many contemporary investigators look to the quality of work experience as the source of work orientations and behavior, either because it is believed to be of central interest in and of itself or because it is seen as the most direct, proximal influence on the worker, with potential to explain whatever psychological and behavioral variables are associated with organizational forms.

Job satisfaction is positively related to a variety of work attributes that are indicative of a "good job." Locke (1976) identifies three historical "schools" in the continuing debate about which occupational features are of greatest importance: (1) the "psychosocial economic school" of the twenties, led by Frederick Taylor, emphasizing the importance of physical working conditions and pay; (2) the "human relations school," starting in the thirties, featuring the social functions of the work group and good supervisory relations; and (3) the more contemporary "work itself (or growth) school," which gives primary attention to the interest and challenge of work. Still widely cited is the work of Frederick Herzberg and colleagues (1959), who argued that only "motivators," or intrinsic features of work (e.g., achievement, recognition, the work itself, responsibility, and advancement) generate job satisfaction. Extrinsic features, or "hygienes," relating to salary, supervision, interpersonal relations, and working conditions, produce dissatisfaction when they are deficient but were not thought to generate satisfaction (see Gurin, Veroff, and Feld 1960 for supportive evidence). Operating from a "learning-generalization" paradigm, Joanne Miller (1988) also emphasizes the psychological importance of task activity, defining the essential nature of work as the major source of gratification/deprivation. Like Herzberg, she argues that the psychological consequences of intrinsic features of work—such as its complexity,

level of autonomy, responsibility, interest, and challenge—are critical.

The importance of intrinsic features of work for job satisfaction has been confirmed in many studies (Kalleberg and Griffin 1980; Mortimer, Finch, and Maruyama 1988; Mortimer and Lorence 1989). A meta-analysis based on 101 samples found consistent positive associations between control (as indicated by autonomy and participative decision making) and job satisfaction as well as organizational commitment and involvement (Spector 1985). Psychological social psychologists (James and Jones 1980) find enhanced job satisfaction when the task is characterized by personal significance, variety, feedback, responsibility and autonomy, and identity (i.e., a whole piece of work). Considerable evidence documents the importance of autonomy and "job scope" for worker satisfaction (Stone 1976), including cross-national research in five countries that emphasized opportunities to use one's ideas and skills, to learn new things, and to set one's own work pace (Tannenbaum et al. 1974).

In Juster's (1985) study of time use, high ratings of the enjoyability of activities derived from interaction with others. When asked to indicate which job characteristics they regarded as particularly attractive or unattractive, relations with fellow employees, along with job challenge and interest, emerged as salient considerations. Consistent with this, Repetti and Cosmas (1991) report that the quality of social relationships at work is a significant determinant of employed women's job satisfaction.

When investigators compare their predictive strength, intrinsic work conditions generally are found to be of greater importance for job satisfaction than extrinsic aspects (Juster 1985; Kalleberg and Griffin 1980, 759). Still, the Herzberg thesis is not undisputed, given evidence that extrinsic concerns are significant determinants of satisfaction. However, with respect to monetary reward, there are differences in findings depending on whether actual pay or a subjective evaluation of pay is considered. Jencks et al. (1988) found that respondent ratings of the goodness of their own jobs in terms of four nonmonetary characteristics explained 23 percent of the variance in job satisfaction: the risk of job loss, on-the-job training, control over hours, and frequency of supervision. With these controlled, earnings had almost no effect. Income also is found to have no significant effect on job satisfaction when relevant work experiences and the lagged satisfaction variable is controlled, using data from the Quality of Employment Survey (QES) 1973 to 1977 panel (Mortimer, Finch, and Maruyama 1988). In Kalleberg and Griffin's (1978) study, intrinsic rewards had a stronger effect on job satisfaction than financial rewards (income) for all categories of workers except small employers.

But when the worker's subjective evaluation of extrinsic reward is measured (i.e., agreement with the statement "the pay is good," as well as evaluations of fringe benefits and job security), there is a positive effect of extrinsic reward on job satisfaction (Gruenberg 1980). Thus, it appears that subjective evaluations of pay (and other extrinsic rewards) are of greater importance for job satisfaction than actual pay. This paradox becomes more comprehensible when viewed in terms of the subjective meaning of income, which may be influenced by group processes (in accordance with the symbolic interactionist perspective). As income rises, people shift from comparisons based on the amount needed to "get along" to the amount needed to "get ahead," resulting in a U-shaped relationship between income levels and feelings of underpayment (Mirowsky 1987).

Higher-prestige occupations generally are associated with high levels of both intrinsic and extrinsic reward; not surprisingly, job satisfaction varies accordingly (Quinn, Staines, and McCullough 1974).

In comparison to the vast literature on work experience and job satisfaction, the relationships between occupational conditions and other work orientations have been given relatively little attention. However, Hodson and Sullivan (1985) find that interesting work and the utilization of skills are positively related to work commitment. Noe et al. (1990) report that "motivating" jobs (e.g., charac-

terized by autonomy and completion of whole tasks) are likewise associated with career motivation. Mortimer and Lorence (1989) found that work overload, work autonomy, and socioeconomic status were significant determinants of work involvement. Mortimer and Lorence (1979b) also showed that work values measured at the time of leaving college were accentuated over the following decade by compatible work experiences. Highly remunerative work enhanced the young worker's extrinsic values; autonomous work fostered intrinsic values; and work with high social content was linked to an increase in people-oriented values (see also Lindsay and Knox 1984). Adolescents' work values are also responsive to the intrinsic features of their jobs (Mortimer et al. 1991).

These investigations of the organizational and occupational determinants of worker orientations point to the conclusion that the broad structural features of organizations and occupations have psychological consequences only insofar as they impinge on the worker's immediate experience. Findings are inconclusive with respect to organizational size and the elaboration of formal rules, core features of bureaucracy. But if large size and formal regulation are accompanied by close and/or punitive supervision, both job satisfaction and commitment are likely to be compromised. Conversely, organizational features that enhance worker participation, promotional opportunities, and welfare services promote both psychological dimensions. Similarly, those occupational features that enhance autonomy and control, the variety, scope, and "wholeness" of the job, or the quality of interpersonal relations are likely to have more positive outcomes.

DETERMINANTS OF WORK ORIENTATIONS: CONTEXT AND BACKGROUND FACTORS

Whereas it is generally assumed that organizational/occupational structures are the central determinants of work orientations, differences dependent on social background and context (e.g., nationality, age, gender, race) have also been observed. These factors, external to the workplace, are linked to broad cultural differences, social roles, socioeconomic opportunities, and key dimensions of the quality of life. They generally begin to exert their influence via socialization processes early in childhood. For this reason, analysts have expected that these social background/contextual factors would not only have independent effects on worker attitudes and behaviors, they would also condition the effects of work experiences. As we shall see, there is some support for the first contention, that social background influences work orientations, but little for the second, more complex, moderating hypothesis. This debate bears on the more general question as to whether cultural and individual/contextual factors are of greater significance in shaping work orientations. We now consider these direct and potentially interactive influences.

Cross-National Variation

Comparative cross-national studies focus on two central questions: Are there differences in work orientations that can be attributed to cultural variation across national boundaries? Do persons, irrespective of country of origin, respond similarly to their work experiences? The impetus for cross-national research derives from Inkeles' (1960) classic study revealing that workers in different industrialized nations had similar job attitudes and beliefs. At the same time, Kerr et al. (1960) suggested that industrialization processes would result in workers from less developed nations eventually assuming the work values and attitudes held by the labor force in the industrialized West. Much ensuing research indicates the plausibility of the "convergence thesis." For example, Tannenbaum et al. (1974) found that processes determining job satisfaction are similar in the United States, Italy, Yugoslavia, and Israel. Shepard et al. (1979) reported that both Korean and American blue-collar workers are adversely affected by similar production technologies, evidencing job dissatisfaction and alienation from work. A most rigorous test of the

importance of cultural versus structural factors is Lincoln and Kalleberg's (1990) massive study of more than eight thousand American and Japanese workers from comparable industries. While noting minor differences in the effects of background traits, job tasks, and organizational characteristics, their results indicate that the determinants of job satisfaction, organizational commitment, and work values are similar. These findings suggest that social structural features of work, such as management style and organizational arrangements, rather than cultural factors, are central determinants of work attitudes and values. (See chapter 15 for a more detailed discussion.) Further support for the convergence thesis arises from evidence that workers in industrialized nations cognitively organize work values in a similar manner (Dov et al. 1991).

Nonetheless, many comparative studies of worker attitudes still find differences in levels of job satisfaction, valuation of work, and importance of job characteristics (e.g., Yankelovich, Zetterberg, and Strumpel 1985). Various surveys show that Japanese employees have the strongest work ethic and higher work centrality scores, with British and German employees at the lower end of work commitment measures. The common explanation for intersocietal differences features the diverse national and organizational cultures. For example, U.S. workers are likely to stress individual achievement while Chinese workers view good relations with coworkers and group work goals as more important than individual recognition (Farh, Dobbins, and Cheng 1991). Other research shows Chinese workers rate the contribution of work to society high but pay and material outcomes low compared to Western workers (Dov et al. 1991). The rationale is that collectivist economic and social systems engender values and attitudes different from those appropriate for a decentralized economic and social system. However, other research on a sample of scientists from the United States and the Soviet Union who immigrated to Israel show little effect of nationality and sociocultural background on work values (Toren and Griffel 1983). Whether divergent work values between Chinese and Russian workers is due to differences in levels of industrialization, political organization, or culture remains to be investigated.

Overall, these findings imply that work attitudes and values may differ in level across nations, but the way workers mentally organize work orientations and the factors impacting job attitudes and values remain similar across countries. They suggest that cross-cultural differences may be less important over time as countries assume comparable industrial structures.

Historical Cohort and Age-Related Influences

Differences in work attitudes across historical periods and by age are of continuing interest. A central concern is to determine whether age differences are attributable to historical cohort membership or to aging processes. Both cohort-related and age differences could be caused by systematic variation in work experiences and/or career patterns. Evidence bearing on the stability of work orientations by age has special relevance for the moderating hypothesis: evidence that workers are more or less responsive or vulnerable to their work conditions, depending on their age, would support a moderating effect.

Attitudinal differences among workers of different age could be attributable to historical influences specific to their particular cohorts or to changes resulting from shifts in social roles as persons grow older. Whereas a felt need for security and material success induced workers who experienced the 1930s depression and the economic hardships of World War II to make personal sacrifices that enhanced their productivity, it is said that cohorts entering the labor market since the late 1960s place greater emphasis on self-fulfillment and personal growth. Younger workers, raised in a relatively affluent era, desire jobs that provide autonomy, interesting work, and personal challenge; they emphasize leisure while devaluing work (Cherrington 1980).

Using repeated survey items that asked male members of the labor force whether they would continue working if they were rich, Hamilton and Wright (1986, 23) find little decrease in the work ethic, particularly among younger workers, during the past few decades. Similarly, Lorence (1987b) found no evidence of a declining attachment to the work role across male cohorts in the General Social Surveys from 1973 to 1985. In addition, women evidenced greater commitment to work roles outside the home; this period effect influenced women of all ages.

Nevertheless, there could be a gap between attitudes and behavior. While contemporary workers may believe work is important in itself, they may no longer be willing to make the self-sacrifices presumed to have occurred earlier. However, an examination of behavioral indicators of work commitment (absentee rates, quit rates, overtime hours, etc.) from the Department of Labor shows no systematic trends indicating declining behavioral investment in work (Hedges 1983). Thus, work appears to be of major importance to contemporary Americans, particularly when compared to the citizenry of other industrialized nations (Lipset 1990).

It should be noted that age variation does not demonstrate historical or cohort-related differences in work orientations, since it could be attributable to career stage. Young workers, faced with increasing financial needs as their families grow, stress promotional opportunities; older workers place greater emphasis on retirement and other fringe benefits, as well as interpersonal relationships at work (Wright and Hamilton 1978). Age categories may be viewed as "strata" with unequal access to occupational rewards (Riley 1985). It is reasonable to suppose that orientations reflecting subjective gratification from work would also be unequally distributed.

Job satisfaction is generally found to be higher among older workers (Mortimer, Finch, and Maruyama 1988), a pattern that has been maintained at least since 1958 (Quinn, Graham, and McCullough 1974). Age differences in job satisfaction are to be expected, given that young workers in the early stages of their careers generally have objectively poorer jobs than their more experienced elders. Kalleberg and Loscocco (1983) identify a curvilinear trend—job satisfaction increases to age forty, levels off and fluctuates until the mid-fifties, and then rises in the older age groups. They interpret this pattern in terms of life cycle and cohort effects. That is, greater satisfaction with age could result from a closer "fit" between workers and jobs as they grow older. Older workers have had longer to change jobs and to mold their work in accord with their values and needs. Values may also change over time in response to work conditions (Mortimer and Lorence 1979b). Still, cohort effects could contribute to age differences in job satisfaction (Glenn and Weaver 1985). Recent cohorts of young workers have high educational attainment relative to preceding cohorts, which could stimulate high job expectations. The baby boom cohort also faced considerable disadvantage in the job market due to its large size.

Older workers evidence a stronger work ethic than younger workers (Yankelovich, Zetterberg, and Strumpel 1985), attach greater moral importance to work (Cherrington, Condie, and England 1979), see work as a more central life interest (MOW 1987) and more crucial to their self-identity (Loscocco and Kalleberg 1988), and are more committed to their employers (Lincoln and Kalleberg 1990). While older workers are more subjectively involved with their jobs than younger workers, controlling differences in job rewards reveals no age differences in job involvement (Lorence 1987a). This pattern indicates that the greater work involvement of older workers is a reflection of age-related changes in work conditions, not cohort effects.

There is some evidence that job orientations, like other psychological characteristics, become less malleable as individuals move beyond the early adult years. According to the "aging stability hypothesis" (Sears 1981), attitudes and values become more stable with age. This increasing stability has been attributed to features of the environment as well as the person. For example, there are usually more job changes in the early adult years, which could produce shifts in work orientations. Attitude stability has also been linked to identity formation in late adolescence and early adulthood (Sears 1981); this is a period of life in which vocational identity typically crystallizes. Thereafter, the

individual may be more receptive to information and influences that are consistent with already-formed views.

Consistent with these formulations, both job satisfaction and job involvement have been found to manifest greater stability among workers older than the age of thirty than among younger workers. However, paralleling Alwin et al.'s (1991) finding of declining stability in political and social attitudes in the later years of life, Lorence and Mortimer (1985) found that the stability of work involvement declines in the forty-five- to sixty-four-year age group. They formulate a "career stage" explanation of this trend (1985, 621), as workers of this age who are on career ladders leading to the highest positions may become even more involved with their jobs, while those who have already reached the height of their careers will become less involved.

The fact that work autonomy manifests the strongest effects on both job satisfaction (Mortimer, Finch, and Maruyama 1988) and job involvement (Lorence and Mortimer 1985) in the youngest cohort of workers indicates that work attitudes are more responsive to occupational experiences shortly after individuals assume the work role (see also Nicholson 1984). Kohn (personal communication, September 20 1984), in his ten-year (1964 to 1974) longitudinal study of a national sample of male workers, also finds evidence that substantive complexity is a more powerful correlate of younger workers' job satisfaction. Finally, work stressors have been found to have different consequences depending on age (Mayes, Barton, and Ganster 1991), such that older workers manifest more strain than younger workers in response to some stressors (role conflict, skill underutilization) and less strain in response to others (having a leader who emphasized production and responsibility for others). But Kalleberg and Loscocco (1983, 82) find no significant interaction between age and occupational variables in the determination of job satisfaction.

In summary, we find little evidence for an historic decline in the work ethic, nor a basis for belief that the observed differences by age in job satisfaction are attributable to historical influences on successive cohorts. Instead, extant empirical studies point to the conclusion that age differences in work attitudes are attributable to differences in job conditions. Differences in attitudinal stability across age groups are also plausibly explained in terms of modal career patterns. That is, the early work career is typically characterized by more frequent job shifts as well as greater attitudinal instability. Though work autonomy has been found to have greater impact on job satisfaction and other work attitudes among younger workers, the moderator hypothesis, with respect to the interaction of age and other work experiences, has received relatively little systematic scrutiny. The potential power of period-related influences is evidenced by women's increasing commitment to work across historical time. Additional research is necessary before definitive conclusions can be made about cohort/historical and age differences in work orientations or about the relative effects of work conditions in different phases of life.

Gender

Prompted by the growing prominence of women in the labor force, investigators, guided by "gender" and "job" explanatory models (Feldberg and Glenn 1979), have become increasingly interested in gender differences in work orientations. That is: Do women and men have similar levels of job satisfaction and work involvement? Do they differ in terms of their work values? Do they react similarly to the structural conditions of work? The first approach (the "individualist" perspective) focuses on personal characteristics presumed to be indicative of prior socialization experiences. Women are thought to react differently to work because of their greater family and household responsibilities. In contrast, the "job" or "structural" perspective emphasizes specific facets of the job and work setting as sources of job orientations. Although the net impact of structural variables is usually larger than that of other determinants, family roles and circumstances influence both men's and women's work orientations.

Traditional gender role norms presume that men are primarily responsible for family economic well-being and should value extrinsic facets of work such as job security (Bokemeier and Lacy 1987). Women should presumably be less concerned with the extrinsic dimensions of work and emphasize features that make work more fulfilling. Indeed, when compared to men, women have been found to place greater value on good interpersonal relationships (Lincoln and Kalleberg 1990) and "convenience factors," such as hours and travel time from home to work, which make work more compatible with family responsibilities. Other research shows that women rate having a meaningful job as more important than do men (Bokemeier and Lacy 1987). However, not all surveys find gender differences congruent with traditional sex roles. Analyses of the 1973 Quality of Employment Survey show that men placed more importance on the intrinsic aspects of jobs, such as challenge and fulfillment from work, while men and women equally valued the financial dimensions of work (Kalleberg and Loscocco 1983). Bokemeier and Lacy's (1987) analyses of the General Social Surveys reveal no gender differences in preferences for jobs offering high income and promotion opportunities. More recent studies of manufacturing employees demonstrate that women evidence slightly higher extrinsic and intrinsic values than men (Lincoln and Kalleberg 1990). Women—especially those in nontraditional occupations or working because of financial necessity—apparently have begun to evaluate intrinsic and extrinsic rewards in a manner similar to men. There is evidence that family status impacts men's and women's occupational values differently (Loscocco and Kalleberg 1988). Among male manufacturing employees, being married increases the importance of pay, getting along with coworkers, and job stability, but marital status has no effect on women's occupational reward values.

Although it is commonly assumed that women consider the work role secondary to their family, examination of employed women's commitment to the work role indicates that they value working as much as men (Lorence 1987b). There is even evidence that women define working as more important for their self-identities (Bielby and Bielby, 1989). Women also evidence higher levels of subjective involvement with their jobs and greater work effort than men, after controlling job traits and background characteristics (Bielby and Bielby 1988; Lorence 1987c). Moreover, the processes affecting men's and women's subjective attachment to work roles are similar (Lorence 1987c). However, marriage and the presence of children still inhibit women from assuming or resuming a career orientation (Spenner and Rosenfeld 1990). Using data from the National Longitudinal Survey, Waite et al. (1986) found that women's career orientation fell at the onset of pregnancy and some women gave up professional career aspirations after marriage. Men's work orientations also fell after the birth of the first child. In addition, the presence of young children reduces the amount of effort women exert on their jobs, but household work decreases only men's, not women's, job effort (Bielby and Bielby 1988).

Recent meta-analyses of gender differences in *organizational* commitment report mixed findings (Mathieu and Zajac 1990), but such analyses are problematic because only bivariate correlations are examined, rather than net effects controlling other factors possibly related to gender. Many multivariate studies show that men and women are equally committed to their employers, with zero-order differences mainly due to variation in job rewards and work characteristics (Gaertner and Nollen 1989). Other research finds that women express greater subjective organizational commitment than men (Lincoln and Kalleberg 1990). Behavioral indicators of organizational attachment, such as voluntary turnover, indicate no differences between the sexes (Chelte and Tausky 1986). Few studies, however, investigate gender differences in the determinants of organizational commitment. The only significant difference that Loscocco (1990b) reports from a study of blue-collar workers is that financial rewards increase men's commitment to the employing firm at a faster rate than occurs for women. Marital status and the presence of children had little effect on organizational commitment of either

gender. However, women who observe discrimination at work are more likely to search for a new employer (Halaby and Weakliem 1989).

National and regional data indicate that women are slightly more satisfied with their jobs than men (Lincoln and Kalleberg 1990), even when controlling social background, family status, and job characteristics. Hodson (1989) speculates that women may be socialized to express less discontent with all facets of their lives, including work, and that women use other women as reference points in evaluating their status. Men and women may evaluate their jobs differently depending on the gender composition of the work setting. Hodson (1989) finds that job satisfaction is higher when women are in female-dominant occupations. Similarly, Loscocco and Spitze (1991) report that women become less satisfied with their pay as they move into gender-balanced work contexts. Alternatively, Wharton and Baron (1991) find that working in a male-dominated environment increases women's satisfaction, possibly because women in such situations view themselves as "pioneers" with opportunities to interact with male co-workers.

Some findings imply that processes affecting men's and women's job satisfaction differ. For example, men's job satisfaction is more responsive to job complexity (Hodson 1989), job autonomy, and job authority (Glenn and Weaver 1982), while discrimination has a particularly adverse effect on women's job satisfaction (Wharton and Baron 1991). Jobs with greater convenience factors increase satisfaction among female (but not male) family breadwinners (Martin and Hanson 1985). In general, job dissatisfaction among women is more likely to occur when women face conflicts between work and family or competing demands from children and spouse (Coverman 1989). In spite of these differences, the processes affecting men's and women's job satisfaction are fairly comparable (Loscocco 1990b).

In summary, whereas there is evidence that women are more satisfied and committed to work than men, the work values of men and women are converging, and there is considerable support for the contention that they react in very much the same way to their work conditions.

Race

Although race is a key variable in sociological analyses, research in the social psychology of work focusing directly on race or ethnicity is limited. Racial strife in the 1960s gave impetus to concern about whether racial differences in the work ethic could be the source of persistent black poverty. Alternatively, racial differences in work attitudes could be the consequence, not the cause, of differences in work opportunity and rewards.

Proponents of the "culture of poverty" thesis argued that African Americans have values that are incompatible with the Protestant work ethic (Andrisani 1978, 106–107). For example, analyses of NLS data revealed that whites were more likely to want to continue working than African Americans even if not financially necessary. Utilizing the 1972 to 1973 and 1977 QES, Lorence (1987a) found that even after controlling job autonomy, occupational status, and income, African-American men were slightly less committed to the general work role in 1973. However, by 1977 no racial differences in the subjective attachment to work existed. Controlling for variation in job quality among African-American and white women resulted in equal levels of work commitment in both 1973 and 1977. Additional analyses based on the General Social Surveys from the early 1970s to the mid-1980s also show no significant differences between African Americans and whites in overall subjective commitment to working (Lorence 1986). Examining subjective involvement with the respondent's particular job also indicates that African Americans are as psychologically involved with their jobs as whites (Lorence 1987c). Moreover, nonwhites are not significantly more likely to search for a new employer than whites (Halaby and Weakliem 1989). The overwhelming conclusion is that African Americans are no less committed than whites to the general work role, their specific job, and their employers. These results indicate that struc-

tural variation in the kinds of jobs held, rather than culturally divergent values, is the major source of difference in work orientations.

Similar patterns are evident from national surveys of job satisfaction. Whereas research shows that African Americans have lower job satisfaction than whites, these differences generally disappear when job rewards and other relevant variables are controlled (Coverman 1989). Moreover, Tuch and Martin's (1991) analyses of the General Social Surveys indicate that African Americans' lower level of job satisfaction is mainly due to their lower structural position in the economy, rather than to major differences in the processes that generate job satisfaction.

One aspect of the linkage between race and job satisfaction that has seldom been investigated is the racial composition of the work group. Wilson and Butler (1978, 636) speculated that minority members would experience greater dissatisfaction because "their culture and mannerisms are at odds with the majority of their workmates." Moch (1980) found that working in a same-race work group increased job satisfaction among manufacturing employees, but Dworkin et al. (1986) reported that among public school teachers being a racial token among fellow teachers did not increase work alienation. Nonetheless, white teachers who were racially different from their students experienced greater job alienation.

Much of the sociological literature implies that race may not be an important consideration in studies of the workplace. However, sociological research on racial differences in job attitudes and behavior has been limited; Hispanic, Asian, and other ethnic groups have been ignored. Organizational psychologists emphasize ethnic differences as crucial to understanding worker job attitudes and behavior. For example, a study of several hundred employees in a federal agency reveals that people of color do not share a common organizational culture; each racial group organized its experiences in a different way (O'Reilly 1991). Similarly, Cox and Nkomo (1991) find racial differences in the job attitudes of business school graduates. Thus, though we find that racial differences in job satisfaction and attachment to work are explained by variation in their structural conditions of work, social psychological research has thus far examined a rather limited domain of variables. Further studies should consider both the growing diversity of ethnic/racial groups in the work force as a result of international migration and potential variations in ethnic subcultures that extend beyond satisfaction and involvement with work.

Moderators of the Effects of Work Conditions

Given differences in work attitudes related to contextual (cross-national, historical cohort) and individual (age, gender, race) differences, the question arises as to whether these variables moderate or condition the effects of structurally induced organizational and occupational experiences. The strongest challenge to the "generalization model" is posed by psychological social psychologists, who posit that cognitive variables condition the effects of work conditions on psychological responses. Whereas Kohn and Schooler's (1983) and Herzberg et al.'s (1959) formulations posit that objective work conditions affect workers similarly, "fit" theories stress differences between workers in what is sought from a job and the significance of these differences in influencing the subjective response to work (Locke 1976). Job satisfaction is seen as a function of the fit between worker and job, of the compatibility of "external" work features and "internal" attributes the individual brings to the work situation. The latter may importantly depend on social background characteristics.

Expectancy theory emphasizes workers' selective sensitivity to job conditions, depending on their values, expectations, and needs. Of major importance is the need for self-actualization, viewed as innate or as a product of social experience (J. Miller 1988). Maslow's "hierarchy of needs" (1954) and related perspectives (e.g., Alderfer 1969) provide a theoretical framework for the "fit hypothesis." According to Maslow, workers' moti-

vations depend on their positions in the need hierarchy; thus, they will not seek self-actualization until physiological and safety requirements have been met.

Locke and Latham (1990) point out that goals affect the degree of satisfaction obtained for any given performance outcome; satisfaction will be lower for individuals with high goals. Consistently, education tends to raise expectations such that higher levels of reward are required to satisfy the more highly educated employee (Gruenberg 1980). Furthermore, highly educated workers may be particularly concerned with autonomy (Jencks, Perman, and Rainwater 1988, 1345). However, Burris (1983) finds that being overeducated for a job has limited impact on job satisfaction once the additive effects of education and educational requirements are taken into account.

Significant variations in expectations, aspirations, needs, and values among workers, related to social background and other personal characteristics, undoubtedly exist. Workers also attach varying levels of importance to work; in the language of structural symbolic interactionism, work may be high or low in the hierarchy of identities (Stryker and Statham 1985). But the crucial question for explanatory purposes is the importance of these differences for workers' reactions to their jobs. Studies of differential linkages, depending on occupational sector, between satisfaction *facets* and *overall* job satisfaction are pertinent to this issue. In a study of skilled workers and managers in electronics manufacturing, Ronen and Sadan (1984) found that extrinsic facets of satisfaction contributed to overall satisfaction more for blue-collar workers than for managers; intrinsic facets had greater predictive power for managers. Similarly, Gruenberg (1980) reports that extrinsic satisfactions are less important for skilled and professional workers, but more important for clerical, semiskilled, and unskilled workers. He finds that intrinsic satisfactions generate overall job satisfaction irrespective of occupation. In accord with a Marxian framework, he asserts there is "no evidence that workers must learn to appreciate or need intrinsic satisfaction." (p. 268) Extrinsic rewards generate satisfaction only when workers do not have access to intrinsic rewards.

Some research identifies differences in the association between work experiences and job satisfaction depending on needs (Hackman and Lawler 1971) and values (Caston and Braito 1985). Spector's (1985) meta-analysis finds that the relationship between job scope (e.g., skill variety; task identity, or the completion of an entire task; significance, or the impact of a job on others; autonomy; and feedback) and work satisfaction is greater among persons with stronger "higher-order" needs (e.g., growth, achievement, autonomy, self-actualization). However, there was no evidence that persons with "lower-order" needs respond negatively or indifferently to job scope; for them, correlations were likewise positive but of weaker magnitude. In other studies, occupational values did not modify or reverse relationships between work characteristics and job satisfaction and other work attitudes (Stone 1976).

Taken together, the findings with respect to the moderator or fit hypothesis may best be characterized as mixed. Like Mortimer (1979), Joanne Miller (1988) concludes, "It is difficult to draw general conclusions about what forms of vulnerabilities condition reactions to particular job experiences and the outcomes to which they are related." Spenner (1988, 85) likewise finds that the search for moderator variables has been inconclusive and disappointing (see also James and Jones 1980). The accumulated findings support the conclusion that individual differences in worker characteristics are not of crucial importance in moderating the effects of work on job satisfaction and dissatisfaction. There clearly are differences in job orientations related to contextual factors and individual differences. For example, as we have seen, there are cross-national differences in attitudes related to the work ethic; women consistently report greater job satisfaction than men despite their poorer work opportunities and rewards, and lower levels of self-direction. Evidence points to the conclusion that the differences in work attitudes among various social groupings (e.g., by age, gen-

der, and race) are mainly due to systematic variation in job conditions. Work features are far more important than individual attributes and interaction effects in predicting psychological outcomes (O'Brien 1986, chap. 5).

Direct assessments of whether structural conditions of work have different effects, depending on these contextual/individual differences, have for the most part yielded negative findings. The same work features generally contribute to workers' orientations in much the same way, with minor variation related to individual differences. Thus, in considering structural versus individual determinants of work orientations, the weight of evidence clearly favors an occupational/structural perspective. Moreover, the emphasis on fit tends to disregard the fact that worker values and other orientations, which could possibly condition the effects of job characteristics, are themselves responsive to work conditions.

This issue has relevance for social policy. If work attributes have similar effects on workers' subjective reactions to the job, improvements in job satisfaction will result from broad-based efforts to enrich and/or enlarge jobs and to enhance working conditions. But if the determinants of job satisfaction (and other work orientations) depend on personal characteristics, values, and frames of reference, increases in job satisfaction will depend on more specifically targeted programs.

CONSEQUENCES OF WORK ORIENTATIONS

Work orientations are of interest in themselves, but their importance is magnified by their potential consequences. Numerous studies have attempted to investigate whether workers' attitudes toward their jobs influence behaviors in the work setting—productivity, effort, turnover, and other behaviors of interest to employers. Others have assessed the implications of orientations toward work for attitudes and behaviors outside the workplace. For example, do workers compensate for a lack of interest in their jobs by participation in challenging leisure activities? Alternatively, do attitudes and behavioral propensities formed in the workplace "spill over" to nonwork activities? To what extent does work experience influence psychological functioning more generally? To these questions we now turn.

In the Work Setting

Studies of worker productivity at the Chicago Hawthorne plant of the Western Electric Company from 1924 to 1933 marked the inception of industrial sociology (I. Simpson 1989). These studies are often cited as demonstrating the influence of the work group on employee behavior, as group norms were found to increase or restrict productivity independent of individual employees' willingness to work. Although this interpretation has been criticized, recent statistical analyses of the original Hawthorne data show that each worker's output was affected by the productivity of other group members, attesting to the importance of worker interaction for the level and variability of output (Jones 1990).

Qualitative research demonstrates the work group's importance in maintaining organizational productivity. Burawoy's (1979) participant observation study showed how informal relationships in a machine shop influence worker output. Until he could show that he had mastered the ability to "make out" by producing daily quotas, Burawoy was not accepted on the shop floor. Belanger (1989) found that production line employees worked intensely during the first half of their shifts but gradually slowed down once production quotas had been met. The justification for the initial excessive (and sometimes dangerous) work effort was to allow employees the opportunity for informal socializing with fellow workers during the last few hours of the day. Similarly, an unwritten arrangement among stevedores, forepersons, and management is used to maintain productivity among dock workers (Finlay 1988). One group of stevedores will work frantically for four hours so they can rest the remainder of the day (and leave the docks). Coworkers exhort fellow workers not to fall behind in moving material because this will lead to a breakdown in output, threatening "the deal," which is mutually advantageous to all parties. Managers see it as maintaining a high level of productivity that requires little supervision.

It is often assumed that positive work orientations enhance worker productivity; organizational (and national) productivity arises from highly motivated employees who are committed to their employers (Lincoln and Kalleberg 1990). The considerable research on the relationship between job satisfaction and worker outcomes yields mixed findings. Hodson (1991) cites various studies indicating that job satisfaction has little impact on worker productivity. Industrial psychologists also find that job satisfaction is unrelated to performance ratings and absenteeism (Stepina and Perrewe 1991). Despite these negative findings, other studies indicate that satisfaction increases work performance (Petty, McGee, and Cavender 1984). Overall job satisfaction has been found to be a significant predictor of self-reported job absences (Martin and Miller 1986). Dissatisfied workers are more likely to steal from their employers and to be counterproductive through slow performance, sloppy work, or tardiness (Hollinger and Clark 1982).

The link between other work orientations and behavior is clearer. Recent reviews (Mathieu and Zajac 1990) conclude that employees with greater organizational commitment obtain higher performance ratings from their supervisors, exert greater effort, are more prompt in getting to work, and are less apt to quit their jobs. Bardo and Ross (1982) report that satisfaction with pay, trust in fellow workers, and worker commitment reduce absentee rates. Employees for whom work is a central life interest have been found to receive higher supervisor ratings on selected job behaviors (Dubin and Champoux 1974). Cross-national analyses show that work centrality scores are positively related to hours worked (MOW 1987).

Longitudinal studies based on representative samples of workers that examine the relationship between work attitudes and organizational behavior are required to understand the link between worker attitudes and outcomes better. Moreover, current quantitative research focuses only on the quantity of worker output, neglecting the "quality" of goods and services provided. However, George and Jones (1991) show how a symbolic-interactionist perspective on the expectations and desires of customers and service providers can be used to gauge the quality of services.

Outside of Work

Three general perspectives on the consequences of work orientations outside of work are the "segmentation," "compensation," and "spillover" hypotheses. They are not mutually exclusive. For example, all may operate with respect to different features of work and areas of family functioning (Rain, Lane, and Steiner 1991). According to the segmentation approach, there is little connection between attitudes and behaviors in work and nonwork spheres. The compensation thesis posits that when workers find little interest and challenge in their jobs, they seek gratification in other life spheres, investing more time and energy in nonwork domains (Strauss 1974a, 1974b). In another kind of compensation, Larson and Richards (1991) report that men in stressful jobs engage in more television viewing when at home; they interpret this as an attempt to reduce tension and to relax.

The spillover hypothesis implies that positive work orientations, such as job satisfaction, work commitment, and engagement in occupational activities, have salutary consequences for orientations and behavior in other life spheres. For example, satisfaction at work would be expected to contribute to more general satisfaction with life; in fact, the spillover hypothesis has received the greatest support in the job and life satisfaction literature (Rain, Lane, and Steiner 1991). Work satisfaction might also be expected to dampen class consciousness and political discontent. Conversely, when workers are alienated and "self-estranged," a host of problems are thought to ensue (Erikson 1986), such as substance use, depression, and prejudice. Menaghan (1991) finds evidence that low self-direction at work, overload, interpersonal problems, lack of opportunity for cooperative problem solving, job insecurities, job loss, and low

earnings have emotional repercussions, including self-esteem, control, and competence losses, uncertainty, and threat, which have negative implications for family interaction.

A kind of cognitive spillover may also occur; that is, work attitudes may lead to compatible ways of thinking in other life spheres. Karen Miller and Melvin Kohn (1983) find that workers' leisure and work activities are similar in complexity. That is, workers who have substantively complex jobs tend to engage in more intellectually demanding leisure activities. Work orientations may also affect beliefs about behaviors in nonwork spheres. Plutzer (1988) finds that among women, work commitment has a positive effect on support for feminist positions (e.g., including a belief that employed mothers can establish secure relationships with their children, approval of abortion, and liberal gender role attitudes). Similarly, Fennel et al. (1981) find evidence that work setting problems lead to a definition of drinking behavior as a tension-release mechanism.

However, Seeman (1972) raises questions about "the centrality of work and the presumed generalization of its consequences," after finding little evidence that work alienation was correlated with ethnic hostility, political disengagement, participation in civil protest, status concerns, or anomie. Seeman and Anderson (1983) also did not find that drinking problems were related to job satisfaction, intrinsically satisfying work, or substantive complexity, all factors that would diminish alienation (which they describe as a "lack of intrinsic engagement)" (p. 61). Clearly, processes of segmentation, compensation, and spillover with respect to various facets of work and nonwork activity deserve further attention.

WORK EXPERIENCE AS A DETERMINANT OF PSYCHOLOGICAL FUNCTIONING

Kohn and Schooler's continuing research pursuit began as an examination of stratification-related differences in men's childrearing values and related orientations to self and others. Opportunities to exercise occupational self-direction in work were found to be critical in understanding the relationship of social stratification and psychological functioning in a cross-sectional sample of American men (Kohn 1969; Kohn and Schooler 1969). Men whose work is substantively complex in relation to data, people, and things and characterized by variety, complex organization, and a lack of close supervision were found to have parental values emphasizing self-direction rather than conformity, more positive self-concepts, more responsible moral standards, and greater trustfulness and receptivity to change. Resurvey of the same men ten years later indicated that there is a reciprocal relationship between person and job (Kohn and Schooler 1983). That is, values, orientations, and cognitive functioning influence the exercise of occupational self-direction ten years later (some of the effects of person on job are contemporaneous rather than lagged), whereas self-direction at work fosters psychological change. Extension of the model to employed wives of these men showed that the relationships between job conditions and features of psychological functioning are essentially the same for men and women (J. Miller et al. 1979). Moreover, women have been found to respond to housework much as they do to paid work. The linkages between social stratification, self-direction, and psychological functioning have, for the most part, been replicated in other national contexts with very different cultures, social structures, and economic systems (Kohn and Schooler 1983).

The Kohn-Schooler paradigm is remarkable for its broad sweep—encompassing a wide range of "structural imperatives of the job" and dimensions of "psychological functioning"—and in its consideration of gender, age, and cross-national differences. This research charted a broad territory of scholarly work; researchers inspired by this program have conducted further investigations of particular psychological domains (e.g., self-efficacy; Mortimer and Lorence 1979a) or have extended the study of work and personality to particular subgroups (e.g., adolescents; Finch et al. 1991; Mortimer et al. 1991; Shanahan et al. 1991). Review of this large body of research is beyond the scope of this chapter; for a summary and relevant commentary, see House (1981), Spenner (1988), Kohn and Schooler (1983), Joanne Miller (1988), and chapter 15.

As we have seen, work orientations do have consequences for attitudes and behaviors, both in and outside of the workplace. Whereas studies of the effects of job satisfaction yield mixed findings, research shows that work group norms set productivity standards that do influence worker behavior. Moreover, work commitment is linked to behaviors that would enhance organizational productivity (high performance ratings, effort, low quit and absentee rates). Work satisfaction is associated with more general satisfaction with life. Work and leisure activities are similar in cognitive complexity. Finally, there is substantial evidence that work experience, particularly the degree of self-direction in the workplace, has substantial effects on psychological functioning, influencing intellectual flexibility, self-esteem, self-efficacy, and other psychological dimensions.

CONTINUING DEBATES AND DIRECTIONS FOR FUTURE RESEARCH

This review of the literature on the social psychology of work points to the conclusion that work experience may be alienating as well as sustaining and growth-enhancing. Jobs are bundles of tasks whose dimensions may sometimes work at cross-purposes to one another (e.g., be both stressful and challenging) and vary considerably depending on their organizational setting. While we conclude that organizational/occupational experiences are far more important determinants of work orientations than individual/contextual factors, much more needs to be known to assess the full implications of individual differences. Women's increasing movement into the work force and the maintenance of their labor force participation over ever-longer periods of the life course make it incumbent on researchers to continue to monitor gender differences in the etiology of work orientations and their consequences. Furthermore, there are suggestions that women's stronger presence in the workplace is transforming the manner in which work is conducted in many job settings. More needs to be known about such reciprocal impacts of the person on the environment.

As is true for sociological social psychology more generally (House and Mortimer 1990), the study of the social psychology of work, organizations, and careers would benefit from greater interdisciplinary communication (Arthur, Hall, and Lawrence 1989). Possibilities are especially ripe with respect to the social structure and personality perspective in sociology and the cognitive, expectancy, and social influence approaches in psychology. While there is reference to social comparison processes, expectancy, and equity, as we have seen, much empirical work is atheoretical in character and descriptive in scope. Few studies are explicitly guided by social psychological theory or generate alternative, theoretically based hypotheses that are then subject to empirical test (Mortimer and Lorence 1989, attempt to move in this direction).

We certainly need to know more about the key occupational conditions that influence work orientations and other individual responses, the psychological reactions themselves, and their interrelations with one another (Shore, Thornton, and Shore 1990), as well as the psychological and other mechanisms that mediate the linkages of occupational conditions and psychological responses (House 1981). To illustrate what might be gained by such interdisciplinary collaboration, two specific illustrations are offered.

First, ongoing psychological research on the situational determinants of work perceptions (see O'Reilly 1991, 440–441, for a review) addresses critical questions raised recently by Joanne Miller (1988), who points out that sociologists know little of how jobs are actually defined. She draws attention to the "social construction of a job"—common understandings of what constitute meaningful task units, including their place in the production process, and the structure of the role relationships that surround them. Such cognitive mappings of work undoubtedly begin to form prior to actual work experience and continue to develop with experience in work settings. They likely influence occu-

pational choice processes, motivations to change jobs, as well as the formation of attitudes and behavior in the work setting.

Second, psychologists are giving increasing attention to workers' emotional experiences (O'Reilly 1991), which could be further addressed in more structurally oriented studies. For example, Larson and Richards (in press) find gender differences in the nature of emotional affect in the work setting, with men much more likely to be highly attentive, alert, and immersed in their problems at work. While they attribute this response to a "male psychology of investment and instrumentality," a sociological social psychologist might examine it in terms of the particular features of typically male and female work.

Moreover, psychological social psychologists sometimes provide plausible explanations for seemingly anomalous work-attitude linkages. A case in point is Salancik and Pfeffer's (1978, 234) notion of insufficient justification: people make sense of their behavior in terms of their personal motivations, attitudes, and needs when it is not consistent with socially legitimate rewards or pressures. This could be pertinent to the frequent observation that workers report high job satisfaction even when they have objectively poor work conditions.

Researchers might heed Spenner's (1988) call for greater attention to microscopic processes (informed by psychological theories as well as by experimental and observational designs); mezzoscopic mediation—systematic variations in careers, organizational settings and practices, and the institutional mechanisms that inform work/personality linkages; and macroscopic influences presented by sociohistorical change in cultures and institutional structures. Psychological social psychologists may be willing collaborators, given O'Reilly's (1991, 449) call for greater attention to the "micro side of macro topics, such as the social psychology of top management teams, the goal-setting aspects of organizational reward systems, or the grounding of economic models in a more complex and realistic understanding of motivation."

Interdisciplinary collaboration is clearly necessary to address the key issues and debates surrounding the social psychology of work: the growth-enhancing versus alienating consequences of particular work experiences, the significance of individual and environmental features in moderating these relationships, and the special processes of work-person interaction in particular groups (defined by gender, race, age, etc.). A variety of research strategies is called for. Longitudinal designs enabling assessment of the effects of work experiences and other factors on psychological orientations over time, while controlling prior individual differences, are particularly useful. Such studies also most effectively address the question of whether work orientations have causal effects on attitudes and behaviors both inside and beyond the work setting. Panel studies of the transition from school to work, or the process of movement from one kind of job to another, would be especially illuminating. Observational studies of workers in their job contexts would be especially helpful in assessing the dynamics of the development and maintenance of orientations toward work.

NOTE

Jeylan Mortimer's research was supported by the National Institute of Mental Health (MH42843) and the National Center for Research on Vocational Education.

The authors thank Carol Krauze and Carol Zierman for careful bibliographic work and assistance in the preparation of the final manuscript.

REFERENCES

Alderfer, Clayton P. 1969. An empirical test of a new theory of human needs. *Organizational Behavior and Human Performance* 4:142–175.

Alwin, Duane F., Ronald L. Cohen, and Theodore M. Newcomb. 1991. *Aging, Personality and Social Change: Attitude Persistence and Change over the Life-Span.* Madison: University of Wisconsin Press.

Andrisani, Paul J. 1978. Work attitudes and labor market experience: Other findings. Pp. 135–174 in *Work Attitudes and Labor Market Experiences,* ed. P. J. Andrisani, E. Applebaum, R. Koppel, and R. C. Miljus. New York: Praeger.

Arthur, Michael B., Douglas T. Hall, and Barbara S. Lawrence. 1989. Generating new directions in career theory: The case for a transdisciplinary approach. Pp. 7–25 in *Handbook of Career Theory,* ed. M. B. Arthur, D. T. Hall, and B. S. Lawrence. Cambridge, UK: Cambridge University Press.

Arvey, R. D., T. J. Bouchard, Jr., N. L. Segal, and L. M. Abraham. 1989. Job satisfaction: Environmental and genetic components. *Journal of Applied Psychology* 74:187–192.

Bardo, John W., and Robert H. Ross. 1982. The satisfaction of industrial workers as predictors of production, turnover, and absenteeism. *Journal of Social Psychology* 118:29–38.

Becker, Howard S. 1960. Notes on the concept of commitment. *American Journal of Sociology* 66:32–40.

Belanger, Jacques. 1989. Job control and productivity: New evidence from Canada. *British Journal of Industrial Relations* 27:347–364.

Bielby, Denise D., and William T. Bielby. 1984. Work commitment, sex role attitudes, and women's employment. *American Sociological Review* 49:234–247.

———. 1988. She works hard for the money: Household responsibilities and the allocation of work effort. *American Journal of Sociology* 93:1031–1059.

Bielby, William T., and Denise D. Bielby. 1989. Family ties: Balancing commitment to work and family in dual earner households. *American Sociological Review* 54:776–789.

Blauner, Robert. 1964. *Alienation and Freedom: The Factory Worker and His Industry.* Chicago: University of Chicago Press.

Bokemeier, Janet L., and William B. Lacy. 1987. Job values, rewards, and work conditions as factors in job satisfaction among men and women. *Sociological Quarterly* 28:189–204.

Borg, Ingwer. 1990. Multiple facetisations of work values. *Journal of Applied Psychology* 39:401–412.

Burawoy, Michael. 1979. *Manufacturing Consent: Changes in the Labor Process under Monopoly Capitalism.* Chicago: University of Chicago Press.

Burris, Val. 1983. The social and political consequences of overeducation. *American Sociological Review* 48:454–467.

Caston, Richard J., and Rita Braito. 1985. The worker-to-job "fit" hypothesis: Further evidence. *Work and Occupations* 12:269–284.

Chappell, Neena L. 1980. Paid labor: Confirming a conceptual distinction between commitment and identification. *Sociology of Work and Occupations* 7: 81–116.

Chelte, Anthony F., and Curt Tausky. 1986. A note on organizational commitment. *Work and Occupations* 13:553–561.

Cherrington, David J. 1980. *The Work Ethic.* New York: AMACOM.

Cherrington, David J., Spencer J. Condie, and J. Lynn England. 1979. Age and work values. *Academy of Management Journal* 22:617–623.

Coverman, Shelly. 1989. Role overload, role conflict, and stress: Addressing consequences of multiple role demands. *Social Forces* 67:965–982.

Cox, Taylor H., and Stella M. Nkomo. 1991. A race and gender-group analysis of the early career experience of MBAs. *Work and Occupations* 18: 305–319.

Csikzentmihalyi, Mihaly. 1990. *Flow: The Psychology of Optimal Experience.* New York: Harper & Row.

Dov, Elizur, Ingwer Borg, Raymond Hunt, and Istvan M. Beck. 1991. The structure of work values: A cross-cultural comparison. *Journal of Organizational Behavior* 12:21–38.

Dubin, Robert, and Joseph E. Champoux. 1974. Workers' central life interest and job performance. *Work and Occupations* 1:313–326.

Durkheim, Emile. 1951. *Suicide.* New York: Free Press.

Dworkin, Anthony Gary, Janet Saltzman Chafetz, and Rosalin J. Dworkin. 1986. The effects of tokenism on work alienation among urban public school teachers. *Work and Occupations* 13:399–420.

Erikson, Kai. 1986. On work and alienation. *American Sociological Review* 51:1–8.

Farh, Jing-Lih, Gregory H. Dobbins, and Bor-Shinan Cheng. 1991. Cultural relativity in action: A comparison of self-ratings made by Chinese and U.S. workers. *Personnel Psychology* 44:129–147.

Feldberg, Roslyn L., and Evelyn N. Glenn. 1979. Male and female: Job versus gender models in the sociology of work. *Social Problems* 26:524–538.

Fennel, Mary L., Miriam B. Rodin, and Glenda K. Kantor. 1981. Problems in the work-setting, drink-ing, and reasons for drinking. *Social Forces* 60: 114–132.

Finch, Michael D., Michael J. Shanahan, Jeylan T. Mortimer, and Seongryeol Ryu. 1991. Work experience and control orientation in adolescence. *American Sociological Review* 56:597–611.

Finlay, William. 1988. *Work on the Waterfront: Worker Power and Technological Change in a West Coast Port.* Philadelphia: Temple University Press.

Gaertner, Karen N., and Stanley D. Nollen. 1989. Career experiences, perceptions of employment practices, and psychological commitments to the organization. *Human Relations* 42:975–992.

Ganster, Daniel C., and John Schaubroeck. 1991. Work stress and employee health. *Journal of Management* 17:235–271.

George, Jennifer M., and Gareth R. Jones. 1991. Towards an understanding of customer service quality. *Journal of Managerial Issues* 3:220–238.

Giorgi, L., and C. Marsh. 1990. The Protestant work ethic as a cultural phenomenon. *European Journal of Social Psychology* 20:499–517.

Glenn, Norval D., and Charles N. Weaver. 1982. Further evidence on education and job satisfaction. *Social Forces* 61:46–55.

———. 1985. Age, cohort, and reported job satisfaction in the United States. Pp. 89–109 in *Current Perspectives on Aging and the Life Cycle,* vol. 1, ed. Z. S. Blau. Greenwich, CT: JAI Press.

Gruenberg, Barry. 1980. The happy worker: An analysis of educational and occupational differences in determinants of job satisfaction. *American Journal of Sociology* 86:247–271.

Gurin, Gerald, Joseph Veroff, and Sheila Feld. 1960. *Americans View their Mental Health.* New York: Basic Books.

Haas, Jack. 1977. Learning real feelings: A study of high steel ironworkers' relations to fear and danger. *Work and Occupations* 4:147–170.

Hackman, J. Richard, and Edward E. Lawler III. 1971. Employee reactions to job characteristics. *Journal of Applied Psychology* 55:259–286.

Halaby, Charles N., and David L. Weakliem. 1989. Worker control and attachment to the firm. *American Journal of Sociology* 95:549–591.

Hamilton, Richard F., and James D. Wright. 1986. *The State of the Masses.* New York: Aldine.

Hedges, Janice Neipert. 1983. Job commitment in America: Is it waxing or waning? *Monthly Labor Review* 106:17–24.

Heinsler, Janet M., Sherryl Kleinman, and Barbara Stenross. 1990. Making work matter: Satisfied detectives and dissatisfied campus police. *Qualitative Sociology* 13:235–250.

Herzberg, Frederick, Bernard Mausner, and Barbara B. Snyderman. 1959. *The Motivation of Work,* 2nd ed. New York: Wiley.

Hochschild, Arlie Russell. 1983. *The Managed Heart: Commercialism of Human Feeling.* Berkeley: University of California Press.

Hodson, Randy. 1989. Gender differences in job satisfaction: Why aren't women more dissatisfied? *Sociological Quarterly* 30:385–399.

——— . 1991. Workplace behaviors: Good soldiers, smooth operators, and saboteurs. *Work and Occupations* 18:271–290.

Hodson, Randy, and Teresa A. Sullivan. 1985. Totem or tyrant? Monopoly, regional, and local sector effects on worker commitment. *Social Forces* 63: 716–731.

Hoelter, Jon W. 1983. The effects of role evaluation and commitment on identity salience. *Social Psychology Quarterly* 46:140–147.

Hollinger, Richard, and John Clark. 1982. Employee deviance: A response to the perceived quality of the work experience. *Work and Occupations* 9:97–114.

House, James S. 1977. The three faces of social psychology. *Sociometry* 40:161–177.

——— . 1981. Social structure and personality. Pp. 525–561 in *Social Psychology: Sociological Perspectives,* ed. M. Rosenberg and R. H. Turner. New York: Basic Books.

House, James S., and Jeylan T. Mortimer. 1990. Social structure and the individual: Emerging themes and new directions. *Social Psychology Quarterly* 53: 71–80.

Hughes, Everett C. 1958. *Men and Their Work.* New York: Free Press.

Inkeles, Alex. 1960. Industrial man: The relation of status to experience, perception, and value. *American Journal of Sociology* 66:1–31.

Jahoda, M. 1981. Work, employment, and unemployment: Values, theories and approaches in social research. *American Psychologist* 36:184–191.

James, Lawrence R., and Allan P. Jones. 1980. Perceived job characteristics and job satisfaction: An examination of reciprocal causation. *Personnel Psychology* 33:97–135.

Jencks, Christopher, Lauri Perman, and Lee Rainwater. 1988. What is a good job? A new measure of labor-market success. *American Journal of Sociology* 93:1322–1357.

Jones, Stephen R. G. 1990. Worker interdependence and output: The Hawthorne studies reevaluated. *American Sociological Review* 55:176–190.

Juster, F. Thomas. 1985. Preferences for work and leisure. Pp. 335–354 in *Time, Goods, and Well-Being,* ed. F. Thomas Juster and F. P. Stafford. Ann Arbor: Institute for Social Research.

Kalleberg, Arne L., and Larry J. Griffin. 1978. Positional sources of inequality in job satisfaction. *Sociology of Work and Occupations* 5:371–401.

——— . 1980. Class, occupation, and inequality in job rewards. *American Journal of Sociology* 85:731–768.

Kalleberg, Arne L., and Karen A. Loscocco. 1983. Aging, values, and rewards: Explaining age differences in job satisfaction. *American Sociological Review* 48:78–90.

Kerr, Clark, John T. Dunlop, Frederick Haberson, and Charles A. Myers. 1960. *Industrialism and Industrial Man.* Cambridge, MA: Harvard University Press.

Kohn, Melvin L. 1969. *Class and Conformity: A Study in Values.* Homewood, IL: Dorsey.

Kohn, Melvin L., and Carmi Schooler. 1969. Class, occupation, and orientation. *American Sociological Review* 34:659–678.

——— . 1973. Occupational experience and psychological functioning: An assessment of reciprocal effects. *American Sociological Review* 38:97–118.

Kohn, Melvin L., and Carmi Schooler, with the collaboration of Joanne Miller, Karen A. Miller, Carrie Schoenbach, and Ronald Schoenberg. 1983. *Work and Personality: An Inquiry into the Impact of Social Stratification.* Norwood, NJ: Ablex.

Larson, Reed, and Maryse Richards. in press. *Divergent Realities: The Daily Lives of Young Adolescents, Their Mothers and Fathers.* New York: Basic Books.

Lawler, Edward E., III, and Douglas T. Hall. 1970. Relationship of job characteristics to job involvement, satisfaction, and intrinsic motivation. *Journal of Applied Psychology* 54:305–312.

Leiter, Jeffrey. 1985. Work alienation in the textile industry: Reassessing Blauner. *Work and Occupations* 12:479–498.

Liker, Jeffrey K. 1982. Wage and status effects of employment on affective well-being among ex-felons. *American Sociological Review* 47:264–283.

Lincoln, James R., and Arne L. Kalleberg. 1985. Work organizations and workforce commitment: A study of plants and employees in the U.S. and Japan. *American Sociological Review* 50:738–760.

———. 1990. *Culture, Control, and Commitment: A Study of Work Organization and Work Attitudes in the United States and Japan.* Cambridge, MA: Harvard University Press.

Lindsay, Paul, and William E. Knox. 1984. Continuity and change in work values among adults: A longitudinal study. *American Journal of Sociology* 89: 918–931.

Lipset, Seymour M. 1990. The work ethic: Then and now. *The Public Interest* 98:61–69.

Locke, Edwin A. 1976. The nature and causes of job satisfaction. Pp. 1297–1394 in *Handbook of Industrial and Organizational Psychology,* ed. Marvin D. Dunnette. Chicago: Rand McNally.

Locke, Edwin A., and Gary P. Latham. 1990. Work motivation and satisfaction: Light at the end of the tunnel. *Psychological Science* 4:240–246.

Lodahl, Thomas M., and Mathilde Kejner. 1965. The definition and measurement of job involvement. *Journal of Applied Psychology* 49:24–33.

Lorence, Jon. 1986. Subjective work commitment of men and women, 1974–84. Paper presented at the annual meetings of the Southwestern Social Science Association, San Antonio.

———. 1987a. Age differences in work involvement: Analyses of three explanations. *Work and Occupations* 14:533–557.

———. 1987b. Subjective labor force commitment of U.S. men and women, 1973–1985. *Social Science Quarterly* 68:745–760.

———. 1987c. A test of "gender" and "job" models of sex differences in job involvement. *Social Forces* 66:121–142.

Lorence, Jon, and Jeylan T. Mortimer. 1985. Job involvement through the life course: A panel study of three age groups. *American Sociological Review* 50:618–638.

Loscocco, Karen. 1990a. Career structures and employee commitment. *Social Science Quarterly* 71:53–68.

———. 1990b. Reactions to blue-collar work: A comparison of women and men. *Work and Occupations* 17:152–177.

Loscocco, Karen, and Arne L. Kalleberg. 1988. Age and the meaning of work in the United States and Japan. *Social Forces* 67:337–356.

Loscocco, Karen, and Glenna Spitze. 1991. The organizational context of women's and men's pay satisfaction. *Social Science Quarterly* 72:3–19.

Martin, Jack K., and Sandra L. Hanson. 1985. Sex, family wage-earning status, and satisfaction with work. *Work and Occupations* 12:91–109.

Martin, Jack K., and George A. Miller. 1986. Job satisfaction and absenteeism: Organizational, individual, and job correlates. *Work and Occupations* 13: 33–46.

Marx, Karl. 1964. *Karl Marx: Selected Writings in Sociology and Social Philosophy.* Translated by T. B. Bottomore. New York: McGraw-Hill.

Maslow, Abraham H. 1954. *Motivation and Personality.* New York: Harper.

Mathieu, John E., and Dennis M. Zajac. 1990. A review and meta-analysis of the antecedents, correlates, and consequences of organizational commitment. *Psychological Bulletin* 108:171–199.

Mayes, Bronston T., Mary E. Barton, and Daniel C. Ganster. 1991. An exploration of the moderating effect of age on job stressor-employee strain relationships. Handbook on Job Stress (special issue). *Journal of Social Behavior and Personality* 6:289–308.

Meara, Hannah. 1974. Honor in dirty work: The case of American meat cutters and Turkish butchers. *Sociology of Work and Occupations* 1:259–283.

Menaghan, Elizabeth G. 1991. Work experiences and family interaction process: The long reach of the job? *Annual Review of Sociology* 17:419–444.

Miller, Gale. 1990. Work as reality maintaining activity: Interactional aspects of occupational and professional work. Pp. 163–183 in *Current Research on Occupations and Professions,* vol. 5, ed. Helena S. Lopata. Greenwich, CT: JAI Press.

Miller, Joanne. 1988. Jobs and work. Pp. 327–359 in *Handbook of Sociology,* ed. N. J. Smelser. Newbury Park, CA: Sage.

Miller, Joanne, Carmi Schooler, Melvin L. Kohn, and Karen A. Miller. 1979. Women and work: The psychological effects of occupational conditions. *American Journal of Sociology* 85:66–94.

Miller, Karen A., and Melvin L. Kohn. 1983. The reciprocal effects of job conditions and the intellectuality of leisure-time activities. Pp. 217–241 in *Work and Personality: An Inquiry into the Impact of Social Stratification,* ed. M. L. Kohn and C. Schooler. Norwood, NJ: Ablex.

Mirowsky, Jon. 1987. The psycho-economics of feeling underpaid: Distributive justice and the earnings of husbands and wives. *American Journal of Sociology* 92:1404–1434.

Moch, Michael. 1980. Racial differences in job satisfaction: Testing four common explanations. *Journal of Applied Psychology* 65:299–306.

Morgan, David L., and Michael L. Schwalbe. 1990. Mind and self in society: Linking social structure and social cognition. *Social Psychology Quarterly* 53:148–164.

Mortimer, Jeylan T. 1979. Changing attitudes towards work. Work in America Institute Studies in Productivity: Highlights of the Literature. Vol II. Scarsdale, NY: Work in America Institute.

Mortimer, Jeylan T., Michael D. Finch, and Geoffrey Maruyama. 1988. Work experience and job satisfaction: Variation by age and gender. Pp. 109–155 in *Work Experience and Psychological Development through the Life Span,* ed. J. T. Mortimer and K. M. Borman. Boulder: Westview.

Mortimer, Jeylan T., and Jon Lorence. 1979a. Occupational experience and the self-concept: A longitudinal study. *Social Psychology Quarterly* 42:307–323.

———. 1979b. Work experience and occupational value socialization: A longitudinal study. *American Journal of Sociology* 84:1361–1385.

———. 1989. Satisfaction and involvement: Disentangling a deceptively simple relationship. *Social Psychology Quarterly* 52:249–265.

Mortimer, Jeylan T., Jon Lorence, and Donald S. Kumka. 1986. *Work, Family, and Personality: Transition to Adulthood.* Norwood, NJ: Ablex.

Mortimer, Jeylan T., Seongryeol Ryu, Katherine Dennehy, and Chaimun Lee. 1991. Part time work and occupational value formation in adolescence. Unpublished manuscript.

Mortimer, Jeylan T., and Roberta G. Simmons. 1978. Adult socialization. *Annual Review of Sociology* 4:421–454.

Mottaz, Clifford J. 1987. An analysis of the relationship between work satisfaction and organizational commitment. *Sociological Quarterly* 28:541–558.

MOW International Research Team. 1987. *The Meaning of Work.* London: Academic.

Mulcahy, Susan DiGiacomo, and Robert R. Faulkner. 1977. Work individuation among women machine operators. *Sociology of Work and Occupations* 4: 303–326.

Neuman, George A., Jack E. Edwards, and Nambury S. Raju. 1989. Organizational development interventions: A meta-analysis of their effects on satisfaction and other attitudes. *Personnel Psychology* 42: 461–489.

Nicholson, Nigel. 1984. A theory of work role transitions. *Administrative Science Quarterly* 29:172–191.

Noe, Raymond A., Ann Wiggins Noe, and Julie A. Bachhuber. 1990. An investigation of the correlates of career motivation. *Journal of Vocational Behavior* 37:340–356.

O'Brien, Gordon E. 1986. *Psychology of Work and Unemployment.* Chichester: Wiley.

O'Reilly, Charles A., III. 1991. Organizational behavior: Where we've been, where we're going. *Annual Review of Psychology* 42:427–458.

Petty, M. M., Gail W. McGee, and Jerry W. Cavender. 1984. A meta-analysis of the relationships between individual job satisfaction and individual job performance. *Academy of Management Review* 9:712–721.

Plutzer, Eric. 1988. Work life, family life, and women's support of feminism. *American Sociological Review* 53:640–649.

Quinn, Robert P., Graham L. Staines, and Margaret R. McCullough. 1974. Job satisfaction: Is there a trend? Manpower Research Monograph no. 30. Washington, DC: Manpower Administration, U.S. Department of Labor.

Rain, Jeffrey S., Irving M. Lane, and Dirk D. Steiner. 1991. A current look at the job satisfaction/life satisfaction relationship: Review and future considerations. *Human Relations* 44:287–307.

Repetti, Rena L., and Kathryn A. Cosmas. 1991. The quality of the social environment at work and job satisfaction. *Journal of Applied Psychology* 21: 840–854.

Riley, Matilda White. 1985. Age strata in social systems. Pp. 369–411 in *Handbook of Aging and the Social Sciences,* 2nd ed., ed. Robert H. Binstock and Ethel Shanas. New York: Van Nostrand Reinhold.

Ronen, Simcha, and Simcha Sadan. 1984. Job attitudes among different occupational status groups: An economic analysis. *Work and Occupations* 11:77–98.

Roy, Donald. 1958. "Banana time": Job satisfaction and informal interaction. *Human Organization* 18:158–168.

Salancik, Gerald R., and Jeffrey Pfeffer. 1978. A social information processing approach to job attitudes and task design. *Administrative Science Quarterly* 23:224–253.

Sears, David O. 1981. Life-stage effects on attitude change, especially among the elderly. Pp. 183–204 in *Aging: Social Change,* ed. S. B. Kiesler, J. N. Morgan, and V. K. Oppenheimer. New York: Academic.

Seeman, Melvin. 1972. The symptoms of '68: Alienation in pre-crisis France. *American Sociological Review* 37:385–402.

——. 1983. Alienation motifs in contemporary theorizing: The hidden continuity of the classic themes. *Social Psychology Quarterly* 46:171–184.

Seeman, Melvin, and Carolyn S. Anderson. 1983. Alienation and alcohol: The role of work, mastery, and community in drinking behavior. *American Sociological Review* 48:60–77.

Shanahan, Michael J., Michael D. Finch, Jeylan T. Mortimer, and Seongryeol Ryu. 1991. Adolescent work experience and depressive affect. *Social Psychology Quarterly* 54:299–317.

Shepard, Jon M., Dong I. Kim, and James G. Hougland. 1979. Effects of technology in industrialized and industrializing societies. *Work and Occupations* 6:457–481.

Shore, Ted H., George C. Thornton, III, and Lynn McFarlane Shore. 1990. Distinctiveness of three work attitudes: Job involvement, organizational commitment, and career salience. *Psychological Reports* 67:851–858.

Simpson, Ida Harper. 1989. The sociology of work: Where have the workers gone? *Social Forces* 67:563–581.

Simpson, Richard L., and Ida Harper Simpson. 1959. The psychiatric attendant: Development of an occupational self-image in a low-status occupation. *American Sociological Review* 24:389–391.

Sorensen, Glorian, and Jeylan T. Mortimer. 1988. Implications of the dual roles of adult women for their health. Pp. 157–200 in *Work Experience and Psychological Development through the Life Span,* ed. J. T. Mortimer and K. M. Borman. Boulder, CO: Westview.

Spector, Paul E. 1985. Higher-order need strength as a moderator of the job scope-employee outcome relationship: A meta-analysis. *Journal of Occupational Psychology* 58:119–127.

Spenner, Kenneth I. 1988. Social stratification, work, and personality. *Annual Review of Sociology* 14:69–97.

Spenner, Kenneth I., and Rachel A. Rosenfeld. 1990. Women, work, and identities. *Social Science Research* 19:266–299.

Stepina, Lee P., and Pamela L. Perrewe. 1991. The stability of comparative referent choice and feelings of inequity: A longitudinal field study. *Journal of Organizational Behavior* 12:185–200.

Stone, Eugene F. 1976. The moderating effect of work-related values on the job scope-job satisfaction relationship. *Organizational Behavior and Human Performance* 15:147–167.

Strauss, George. 1974a. Is there a blue-collar revolt against work? Pp. 40–69 in *Work and the Quality of Life: Resource Papers for Work in America,* ed. J. O'Toole. Cambridge, MA: MIT Press.

——. 1974b. Workers: Attitudes and adjustments. Pp. 73–98 in *The Worker and the Job: Coping with Change,* ed. J. M. Rosow. Englewood Cliffs, NJ: Prentice Hall.

Stryker, Sheldon, and Anne Statham. 1985. Symbolic interactionism and role theory. Pp. 311–378 in *The Handbook of Social Psychology,* 3rd ed. vol. 1, *Theory and Method,* ed. G. Lindzey and E. Aronson. New York: Random House.

Tannenbaum, Arnold S., Bogdan Kavcic, Menachem Rosner, Mino Vianello, and George Wieser. 1974. *Hierarchy in Organizations.* San Francisco: Jossey-Bass.

Toren, Nina, and Avi Griffel. 1983. A cross-cultural examination of scientists perceived importance of work characteristics. *Social Science Research* 12:10–25.

Tuch, Steven A., and Jack K. Martin. 1991. Race in the workplace: Black/white differences in the sources of job satisfaction. *Sociological Quarterly* 32:103–116.

Vaught, Charles, and David L. Smith. 1980. Incorporation and mechanical solidarity in an underground coal mine. *Sociology of Work and Occupations* 7:159–187.

Vondracek, Fred W., Richard M. Lerner, and John E. Schulenberg. 1986. *Career Development: A Life-Span Developmental Approach.* Hillsdale, NJ: Erlbaum.

Vroom, Victor H. 1964. *Work and Motivation.* New York: Wiley.

Waite, Linda J., Gus Haggstrom, and David E. Kanouse. 1986. The effects of parenthood on the career orientation and job characteristics of young adults. *Social Forces* 65:43–73.

Walsh, Edward J. 1982. Prestige, work satisfaction, and alienation: Comparisons among garbagemen, professors, and other work groups. *Work and Occupations* 9:475–496.

Wharton, Amy S., and James N. Baron. 1991. Satisfaction? The psychological impact of gender segregation on women at work. *Sociological Quarterly* 32:365–387.

Wilson, Kenneth L., and John Sibley Butler. 1978. Race and job satisfaction in the military. *Sociological Quarterly* 19:626–638.

Wright, James D., and Richard F. Hamilton. 1978. Work satisfaction and age: Some evidence for the "job change" hypothesis. *Social Forces* 56:1140–1158.

Yankelovich, Daniel, Hans Zetterberg, and Burkhard Strumpel. 1985. *The World at Work: An International Report on Jobs, Productivity, and Human Values.* New York: Public Agenda Foundation and the Aspen Institute for Humanistic Studies.

CHAPTER 20

Social Psychology of Deviance and Law

V. LEE HAMILTON
DAVID RAUMA

In Rosenberg and Turner's (1981) volume on sociological social psychology, Gibbs's (1981) chapter on this topic was entitled "Deviance and Social Control." Our chapter concentrates instead on recent theory and research on deviance and law. Two general factors have contributed to this change in emphasis. First, as we discuss below, research on social control has increasingly come to be centered in the field of criminology, rather than coupled with social psychological investigations of deviance. Second, much social psychological research in recent decades has been devoted to the study of law or law-abiding citizens, rather than deviance per se. As we attempt to show, however, much of this research deals with such questions as personal adherence to rules and reasons for deviations from the rules. We suggest that studies of deviance and studies of law, usually carried out by different researchers using different vocabularies, might be unified under a common umbrella as "studies of normative standards and their violation."

Two broad approaches have dominated the modern study of deviance. One approach defines deviance in relatively objective or normative terms: as a violation of norms, rules, laws, or usual standards for behavior. This normative approach dominated the sociological study of deviance in the 1950s and 1960s (Liska 1987). Such a definition assumes some sort of societal consensus (or at least some authoritatively imposed standard) providing benchmarks by which to assess violation. The second approach, which began to gain strength in the 1960s, can probably be said to have dominated the field ever since. Referred to as labeling theory or societal reaction theory, this approach stresses the extent to which deviance is interactive, a result of societal reaction to a behavior rather than an intrinsic property of that behavior or its perpetrator.

Research on deviance, regardless of approach, has traditionally encompassed what Archer (1985, 744) calls "a bewildering range of acts and conditions: physical disability, homosexuality, mental retardation, alcoholism, obesity, psychosis, violence, criminality, cannibalism, and uncounted others." This chapter concentrates specifically on the nexus between deviance and law, and hence does not discuss other traditional topics, such as physical stigma (e.g., Goffman 1963) or mental illness (e.g., Rosenberg 1992; Rosenhan 1973). We hope to demonstrate how a revised and revitalized normative perspective—one that borrows elements from societal reaction theory by emphasizing the role of authority in imposing standards—has been emerging in the study of law and law violation. It is beyond the scope of this chapter, however, to attempt an extension of this analysis to such areas as stigma or mental illness.

The review that follows is organized into five sections. The first section provides a brief overview of traditional research on deviance and social control. This overview is necessarily cursory, and interested readers should consult other sources (e.g., Archer 1985; Liska 1987). The second section makes what may at first appear to be a radical turn away from the field of deviance, by presenting recent work on legal attitudes and on actions of law-abiding citizens rather than "deviants." However, this research is linked to deviance research by the thread, or issue, of norms. A recent theme of such research is the importance of norms—citizens' senses of what ought to be done—in comparison to self-interest as a determinant of rule adherence.

The third section returns explicitly to the question of norm violation but focuses on the frequently "respectable" offenders of white-collar and corporate crime; it asks about people who carry out criminal acts in organizational settings as well as people who refuse to do so. This section draws together the concerns of the first section of the chapter (deviance) and the second (adherence to law or rules). The topics of white-collar and corporate crime are of interest in their own right and have occupied a small but growing niche in sociological research.[1]

The fourth section reviews one recent theory by Braithwaite (1989) that exemplifies both the literature's new emphasis on norms and its recent attention to white-collar or corporate offenders. In a brief conclusion, we summarize what we have dubbed the new normative approach. We argue that future research by social psychologists should continue to examine the linkage between "normality" (or "conformity" or "obedience") and "deviance."

DEVIANCE AND SOCIAL CONTROL

Traditional Perspectives on Crime and Deviance

Traditional perspectives on crime and deviance have, in one fashion or another, addressed the etiology of deviant behavior. Their approaches to the question of how deviance generally arises vary from the macrolevel sociological to the social psychological. Some theorists look to social forces outside the individual as the cause of deviant behavior; others examine the processes by which such behavior is learned. Still other theorists answer the question by rejecting the notion of causality and instead look to the processes by which behaviors and individuals come to be defined as deviant. After a brief review of the initial statements of the major traditional perspectives, we examine recent developments that either attempt to integrate different perspectives or focus instead on social control issues.

Social Disorganization Theory. Robert K. Merton's (1938) strain theory is among the first examples of the social disorganization perspective. Merton characterized deviance as a violation of consensual norms resulting from macro social disorganization or strain. Strain results from a contradiction between a society's cultural values and its social organization. Specifically, Merton argues that an imbalance between cultural goals and the ability to achieve those goals results in strain and weakens the hold of rules over individuals experiencing that strain. Merton points to the United States as an example where the cultural goal of success, emphasized at the expense of culturally approved means for achieving that success, is at odds with a society whose social organization does not allow everyone to achieve that success. For Merton, economically motivated crime is a rejection of conventional means for achieving wealth.

Crime is only one deviant response to strain, but it is the response that occurs most frequently among those most disadvantaged and least able to achieve success. Strain may also be experienced by middle- and lower-middle-class individuals who aspire to higher levels of success but who are blocked from their achievement. Their response, termed deviant by Merton, often falls short of criminality. For example, they may adopt alternative lifestyles, rejecting both conventional measures of and conventional routes to success.

Merton points to cultural differences in socialization as the reason behind the concentration of deviance in the lower classes: lower-class individuals are well socialized to appreciate the cultural goals of success but, in addition to lacking access, are less well socialized in the legitimate means for achievement. Later proponents of strain theory (e.g., Cloward and Ohlin 1960; Cohen 1955) argue, for example, that inner-city youth gangs effectively represent alternative forms of social organization (sometimes referred to as subcultures) in which these youth can achieve their own forms of success through alternate means.

Travis Hirschi's (1969) control theory approaches the problem of social disorganization differently. Hirschi argues, in effect, that strain is a constant and that social controls operate to prevent norm violations generally and crime specifically. Hirschi discusses these controls in terms of the individual's internal and external relationships to conventional individuals and activities. Underlying this discussion is the notion of a rational actor who, weighing alternatives such as isolation from those individuals and activities or more formal punishments such as imprisonment as the consequences of deviant behavior, chooses whether or not to engage in deviant behavior. When these internalized controls begin to erode such that deviance is an increasingly attractive alternative, deviant behavior is a likely outcome. More specifically, Hirschi (1969) identifies four types of controls: attachment, commitment, belief, and involvement. Attachment refers to the psychological and emotional relationships with others, such as parents and friends. Commitment refers to the individual's investment in conventional goals, attitudes, and behavior; it is, in effect, a rational cost-benefit analysis of alternate lines of action. Belief measures the extent to which the individual accepts conventional belief systems. Finally, involvement refers to the actual participation of the individual in outside activities and the supervision that entails.

Differential Association Theory. Differential association theory was developed by Edwin Sutherland (1939) as a sociological alternative to biological explanations of criminal behavior. Like the social disorganization theorists, Sutherland was concerned with the etiology of criminal behavior, but from "the point of view of the person who engages in criminal behavior." The nine principles of differential association theory have been elaborated since their first statement by Sutherland (Sutherland and Cressey 1974), but among proponents they remain largely intact (Sutherland 1939, 6–7):

1. Criminal behavior is learned.
2. Criminal behavior is learned in interaction with other persons in a process of communication.

3. The principal part of the learning of criminal behavior occurs within intimate personal groups.
4. When criminal behavior is learned, the learning includes (a) techniques of committing the crime, which are sometimes very complicated, sometimes very simple; (b) the specific direction of motives, drives, rationalizations, and attitudes.
5. The specific direction of motives and drives is learned from definitions of the legal code as favorable or unfavorable.
6. A person becomes delinquent because of an excess of definitions favorable to violation of law over definitions unfavorable to violation of law.
7. Differential associations may vary in frequency, duration, priority, and intensity.
8. The process of learning criminal behavior by association with criminal and anti-criminal patterns involves all of the mechanisms that are involved in any learning.
9. While criminal behavior is an expression of general needs and values, it is not explained by those general needs and values since noncriminal behavior is an expression of the same needs and values.

Sutherland's statement of differential association clearly articulates the view that criminal behavior, and deviance more generally, is learned, normative behavior. In other words, it is like any other behavior, except that it violates some formal set of norms (e.g., the legal code). In the process of learning, the individual has replaced one set of norms with others for which the "criminal" or "deviant" behavior is acceptable (see principle 5). This perspective contrasts with social disorganization theory, which operates from the premise that crime and deviance are violations of consensual norms. In fact, Sutherland was not entirely satisfied with the idea of social disorganization. In expanding his theory to explain differences in crime rates (criminal behavior from the point of view of the community), he preferred the term *differential social or-*

ganization. Sutherland (1939, 8–9) argued that "Most communities are organized for both criminal and anti-criminal behavior and in that sense the crime rate is an expression of the differential group organization." Through the idea that different social groups may be oriented or organized differently with respect to the legal code (or other normative standards), Sutherland was able to apply his theory of individual differential association to account for how differences among social groups may produce different rates of criminal or deviant behavior.

Labeling Theory. An alternative to the traditional theories is labeling theory (or societal or social reaction theory), a perspective based on the tenet that deviant behavior is defined by the reaction of others to that behavior. Rather than address the question of etiology, labeling theory explores the ways behavior and individuals come to be called "deviant." Howard Becker, one of the earliest exponents of this approach, defines deviance in this manner:

> *I mean rather that social groups create deviance by making the rules whose infraction constitutes deviance, and by applying those rules to particular people and labeling them as outsiders. From this point of view, deviance is not a quality of the act the person commits, but rather a consequence of the application by others of rules and sanctions to an "offender." The deviant is one to whom the label has successfully been applied; deviant behavior is behavior that people so label. (Becker 1963, 9)*

The basic elements of labeling theory are displayed in Becker's statement (see also Schur 1971). Deviance is not a quality of the individual or his/her behavior; social groups create deviance through mutually agreed upon definitions of acceptable and unacceptable behavior. In contrast to the social disorganization and differential association theory, deviance as a phenomenon becomes relativistic: it may change from situation to situation, from person to person. For example, as Archer (1985) points out, the defini-

tion of deviant forms of sexual behavior has changed over the centuries, with the Victorian period standing out as one in which very specific and restrictive definitions of acceptable sexual behavior dominated.

Labeling theory in its general form leaves a number of issues unresolved. One particularly important issue is the question of etiology. Why do some individuals continue to engage in deviant behavior, knowing the reaction that behavior engenders? Edwin Lemert (1951) addresses this issue through the concepts of primary and secondary deviance. Primary deviance may occur for any of the reasons other behaviors occur; it is deviant because of the reaction to it. Furthermore, it may be the only instance of deviance committed by an individual. However, should the deviance be repeated, with the same reaction to each repetition, the individual may begin to incorporate the deviant reaction into his/her self-image. At that point, the "deviant" behavior occurs because it is deviant and consistent with the individual's new self-image. This is secondary deviance. For the most part, labeling theory focuses on secondary, rather than primary, deviance.

Conflict Theory. Conflict theory (or radical theory), is generally based on the premise that criminal behavior represents the efforts of the ruling elite to control the lower classes. This perspective shares with strain theory and differential association theory a focus on the interaction between different normative systems. Whereas differential association and differential social organization theory stress the transmission of deviant normative systems and strain theory examines the breakdown of consensual norms in the face of limited economic opportunities, a conflict perspective emphasizes the strife between normative systems and the dominance of one over the other. For example, Marxist theory posits class conflict as the source of this strife and of criminality and deviance among the lower classes (e.g., Chambliss and Seidman 1971; Quinney 1977). In this process, capitalist interests are served by the legal control of certain categories of individuals. Those most disadvantaged by capitalism are therefore kept in line by the prospect of criminal sanctions.

Vold (1979) does not identify class conflict as the source of criminality but, consistent with a Marxist viewpoint, argues that the creation of law is the result of struggles between competing interest groups. Behavior that was once acceptable may come to be defined as criminal or deviant as a result of this struggle. For example, the child-saving movement during the mid-1800s created new categories of delinquency by enforcing middle-class notions of appropriate childrearing techniques and appropriate behavior for children (Krisberg and Austin 1978).

Social Control

The labeling and radical perspectives on deviance and crime both point to the importance of legal systems in the definition of crime. Sociologists from a variety of theoretical orientations have examined the issue of how crime and deviance are created. For example, Emile Durkheim (1958, 1960) argued that deviance is present in all groups and societies as a means of defining mutual interests and goals among group or societal members. In this sense, deviance serves an important function by helping define what constitutes group membership. Durkheim also argues that levels of crime and deviance may remain relatively constant over time as a result of this functionality. If the incidence of deviance increases or decreases, changes may occur in the definition of deviant behavior to bring it back to its stable level. Kai Erikson's (1966) *Wayward Puritans* examines Durkheim's proposition with respect to Puritan communities in seventeenth-century Massachusetts, arguing that deviance served a defining role in Puritan life. Alfred Blumstein and Jacqueline Cohen (1976) have translated Durkheim's proposition into a "stability of punishment hypothesis" that, broadly conceived, states that societies and groups provide stable levels of official punishment and that definitions of crime fluctuate to maintain

that stable level. They present evidence from Sweden and the United States in support of their hypothesis. Blumstein and Cohen's provocative work has been criticized by Rauma (1981) for methodological flaws and by Berk, Rauma, et al. (1981) and Berk, Messinger, et al. (1983) for the simplicity of its approach.

Other authors have traced the development of law and the influence of the legal system on the control of deviance. William Chambliss (1964) shows that vagrancy laws emerged as a means of keeping the English labor force on feudal estates after the Black Plague decimated the English population and created a shortage of serfs to work the feudal estates. At this time, English commerce was growing and cities were emerging as a source of freedom and employment at higher wages than on the estates. The first vagrancy law made a crime of refusing work to travel to another place. This law was thus a means of guaranteeing a cheap supply of labor for the feudal lords during a time of crisis that threatened their economic and political dominance of English society. Over time, vagrancy laws changed, both in form and function, to a means of controlling criminals and undesirables.

In a different vein, Elliot Currie (1968) examines the occurrence of witchcraft in Renaissance Europe, contrasting the definition, nature, and frequency of accused witches in England and continental Europe. As a form of deviance, witchcraft represented a kind of thought crime. The "witch" was accused of making a pact with the Devil to gain power for antisocial and un-Christian ends. However, Currie found that the similarities between England and the continent ended there. In continental Europe, many accused witches were upperclass men, whereas in England they were more likely to be lower-class women. Currie traces these differences ultimately to differences between the two legal systems. Whereas England had an autonomous legal system funded by the state, European courts grew out of the Inquisition and were typically funded by the confiscated properties of convicted individuals. And, whereas England's legal system operated with the principle that accused individuals were innocent until proven guilty, the European legal system, reflecting its roots in the Inquisition, was based on the assumption that accused persons bore the burden of proving their innocence. Currie argues that the frequency of accusations of witchcraft was much less in England than on the continent, a difference that reflected the different natures of their legal systems. Currie speculates that English courts, having no vested interest in prosecuting accused witches, showed less interest in this thought crime than did their European counterparts. European courts found a source of funding in the active prosecution of accused witches and the confiscation of their properties.

At another level of analysis, sociologists have examined the processes by which individuals become deviant or are identified as deviant. Much, but not all, of this work has been done by labeling theorists and others interested in how the label of "deviant" is applied to individuals and/or groups. Becker (1963) argues that rules are created and that those who take the initiative in this "enterprise" can be referred to as "moral entrepreneurs." Rule creators and rule enforcers are of particular interest to Becker. He uses examples such as the Marijuana Tax Act and the Woman's Christian Temperance Union (WCTU) to illustrate moral entrepreneurship. As Becker outlines, the Marijuana Tax Act was passed by Congress in 1937 after an active campaign by the Federal Bureau of Narcotics to eliminate all noncommercial uses of hemp. Part of this campaign included a public relations effort to inform the public of the dangers of marijuana, particularly the loss of self-control and other "evil effects" its had on users. Similarly, the WCTU worked toward the prohibition of alcohol as a means of improving the general quality of life, particularly among the working classes.

Other researchers have investigated in greater depth the relationships between what Becker would term the "rule enforcers" and potential rule violators. For example, Aaron Cicourel (1968) examined police treatment of juveniles and found that police tended to categorize juveniles broadly as either "good" or "bad." Their subsequent treatment of these juveniles depended largely on this initial categorization. "Good" juveniles may have committed a misdeed or infraction, but these acts are not indicative of underlying immoral character. Rather, these acts stem from adverse conditions, usually at home. Official intervention (e.g., arrest, juvenile court) is not necessary. In contrast, "bad" youths must be dealt with, otherwise they will continue to get into trouble, and that trouble will likely escalate into more serious law violations. Cicourel notes that these conceptions of good and bad youth result from police theories about the causes of delinquency based on family and community disorganization.

Similarly, Piliavin and Briar (1964) found that police responded more severely to juveniles whose appearance and behavior is consistent with police stereotypes about delinquency. Such juveniles were more frequently stopped for questioning and subsequently arrested, particularly if their demeanor was in some way perceived by police as challenging to their authority. They also found that race played a large part in these stereotypes—African American juveniles were more frequently perceived as delinquent on the basis of appearance and their behavior was more frequently seen as challenging by a predominantly white police force.

Jerome Skolnick (1966) argues more generally that police reasoning with respect to crime is based on general standards of acceptable behavior. Individuals who violate these standards or whose behavior conforms to the ways in which these standards are violated are judged by police to be guilty. The task for police is then to accumulate the evidence necessary legally to find these individuals guilty. Skolnick argues that such discretion in the hands of the police is almost inevitable. Legislatures can neither foresee nor describe all possible forms of violations of law. This puts an interpretive burden on the police and other criminal justice officials. It should therefore come as no surprise that police exercise discretion in the application of law. This sentiment is echoed by Klockars (1985), who argues that the overreach of the law necessitates selective enforcement by police.

The courts similarly play a role in this interpretive process, although in this arena the identification of deviance sometimes resembles a process of negotiation. It is well known that the majority of criminal defendants who are sentenced plead guilty, typically in exchange for a reduced set of charges. Some researchers have argued that this form of settlement is a response to large caseloads by overworked court personnel (e.g., Church 1979); others argue that prosecutors and defense attorneys have chosen this mode of settlement (e.g., Schulhofer 1984; cf. Maynard 1984). Whichever is true, this mode of case settlement leaves prosecutors with tremendous discretion to drop or change the charges against criminal defendants.

David Sudnow (1965) examines how decisions about plea bargaining are made in a public defender's office. He finds that decisions about the set of charges to which the defenders' clients will plead guilty are aided by the attorneys' categorization of the components of different types of crimes. Referred to by Sudnow as "normal crimes," these categorizations impart information about the typical offender and the typical means of committing a crime that can be used to make the decision to plead guilty. For example, a defendant charged with attempted child molestation may be allowed to plead guilty to a charge of loitering near a school. Whether or not the defendant actually loitered is not important, since the attorneys know this crime typically involves loitering near a school. Therefore, the reduced charges are an acceptable alternative that will produce the desired sentence reduction.

Milton Heumann (1978) approaches the issue of decision making by examining how attorneys and judges acquire the knowledge necessary to perform their jobs. Heumann argues that legal training in and of itself is not adequate preparation for the courtroom. He goes on to document the process of socialization (or, in Heumann's terminology, adaptation) that occurs when new defense attorneys, prosecutors, and judges begin their jobs, a process that consists largely of on-the-job training accompanied by the teaching of more experienced colleagues. Interestingly, Heumann argues

for the "inevitability" of plea bargaining even when caseload pressures do not seemingly require it as a means of quick settlement. Instead, the socialization process naturally encourages cooperation among court participants and fosters the view that a reduced sentence is a reward to the defendant for pleading guilty.

Recent Developments in Criminological Theory

The traditional approaches to crime and deviance have inspired volumes of research and many findings concerning their nature and causes (Kornhauser 1978; Shoemaker 1984). However, much of this research has been inconclusive; at least partial support for any one of the major perspectives can be found in this body of work. Over time, control theory has perhaps emerged as the dominant approach to studying the etiology of crime and delinquency, largely because of its empirical support and intuitive appeal. If control theory has a competitor, it is societal reaction theory. Over the past several decades, various researchers have tried to integrate different approaches, in hopes of offsetting their limitations. As will become evident, these efforts either merge different social psychological approaches to deviance or attempt to marry macro social explanations with social psychological theories so as to produce a more general theory of deviance.

Ross Matsueda (1982) has attempted to integrate control theory with differential association theory, arguing that the process by which social controls are weakened is essentially a learning process. Since Sutherland's theory of differential association describes the learning of definitions favorable to the violation of law, it can be used to understand better how, for example, commitment and beliefs change and lead to delinquency and crime more generally. More recently, Matsueda (1992) specified a theory of the self to explain delinquent behavior. Drawing on labeling theory, particularly Lemert's concept of secondary deviance, Matsueda argues that delinquency is affected by prior delinquency and parental appraisals that affect the individual's self-appraisal. As Lemert argued, a concept of self as deviant leads to further deviant behavior.

Gottfredson and Hirschi (1990) have specified a theory of crime that draws heavily on classical criminology, which conceived of crime as a rational calculation of outcomes and consequences, while expanding on Hirschi's (1969) earlier control theory. Gottfredson and Hirschi argue that control, particularly self-control, is the predominant "cause" of crime: law-abiding individuals have greater amounts of self-control than do lawbreakers. They point to parenting techniques (e.g., supervision) as the key element in the "transmission" of self-control. By this account, class differences in parenting techniques help explain differences in crime rates between the different classes.

Sampson and Laub (1990) recently offered a different extension of control theory by combining control theory's emphasis on informal social control with insights from the life course perspective (e.g., Elder 1985); the latter stresses the importance of pathways and transitions among roles across the life span. They focus on the flow from delinquency to adult crime and on factors that may interrupt this flow. They find that both marriage and stable jobs serve to inhibit adult criminality and argue that it is the strength of social ties—and the informal social control these ties exert—that accounts for this finding.

John Hagan has offered several different integrations of theoretical perspectives on delinquency. Drawing on conflict theory, labeling theory, and a variant of control theory, Hagan and Palloni (1990) argue that the existence of criminal classes "of low social origin" may be explained by two separate but complementary processes:

> *Two quite different reproductive processes linked to the family could be involved. The first is a cultural or characterological process by which parents, through their child-raising conditions and practices, reproduce in their children the characteristics that lead to crime; the second is a structural or imputational process in which crime-control agents reproduce criminal behavior through their official treatment of the children of criminal parents. (1990, 266)*

Using longitudinal data from London, Hagan and Palloni test their perspective and find support for the central tenet that crime is produced through an intergenerational labeling process.

In another article, Hagan (1991) approaches the problem of intergenerational reproduction of crime and delinquency somewhat differently. Rather than focusing on the intergenerational aspect (i.e., child raising), Hagan examines the dynamics of how adolescents so affected become involved in delinquency and crime. Utilizing the concepts of drift (Matza 1964) and delinquent subcultures (Cohen 1955), Hagan argues that adolescents with weak ties to family and school may drift into behaviors and values (subcultural preferences) that lead to delinquency and have a negative impact on parental control, educational attainment, and later occupational attainment. Hagan tests these hypotheses with longitudinal data from Toronto and finds support for the notion that subcultural preferences during adolescence affect later occupational prestige.

From a different perspective, Katz (1988) argues that traditional approaches to explaining criminal behavior have failed because they treat variables such as social class, ethnicity, age, and so on as if they actually caused individual behavior. Katz proposes instead a phenomenological approach that uncovers the meaning of deviance for individuals who commit deviant or criminal acts. In a review of Katz's work, Turk (1991) acknowledges his documentation of limitations in criminological research and praises his efforts to develop better criminological theories. However, Turk argues that Katz has gone too far, throwing out the good as well as the bad, without offering a clearly superior alternative.

Summary

The majority of traditional approaches to deviance and crime have relied on an objectivist approach to behavior in which behavior is seen as guided by external, shared norms. These perspectives differ in the location of the processes by which such behavior is generated. Strain theory and conflict theory focus on a society's social organization, particularly the system of stratification in that society. Differential association theory and control theory focus instead on processes that more directly involve the individual. Societal reaction (labeling) theory rejects an objectivist approach, looking instead at the social reactions to behavior and the reactions of the stigmatized to their deviant labels. The latter two objectivist approaches—differential association and control theories—and labeling theory offer opportunities for the social psychological study of deviant behavior. Recent research in deviance reviewed above appears to be moving in the direction of creative fusions among these theoretical approaches. In a later section, we present Braithwaite's (1989) efforts to assess these traditional approaches and provide an alternative theory of deviance that incorporates many of their insights.

Efforts to study social control per se rely only occasionally on social psychology for insights into human behavior. However, these efforts have clearly demonstrated the importance of rule enforcers and their interpretation and application of legal rules in the creation of crime and deviance.

THE SOCIAL PSYCHOLOGY OF RULE ADHERENCE

Our focus now shifts away from the sociological and criminological study of deviance and social control toward topics more often studied by social psychologists and of a more psychological bent: moral judgment and the sense of procedural justice and injustice.[2] Conceptions of what is right, what is wrong, and what is just loom large in recent research by social psychologists, especially those with interests in the legal system. Deviance per se, or social control per se, fade out as focuses in such research. At the forefront instead are the thought processes and actions of ordinary citizens. Deviance does not disappear from this research but tends to be framed in the language of rules, rule interpretation, and rule violation. (For additional

sociological work on equity and justice, see chapter 10).

Moral Judgment and Rule Adherence

The Piagetian revolution in developmental psychology inspired both social and developmental psychologists to think about moral judgment (Piaget 1965; Piaget and Inhelder 1968). Social psychologists in sociology as well as psychology departments began to ask about the nature of the cognitive structures through which children and adults filter information about their worlds—and, inevitably, about the linkage between how they think and act regarding moral and legal rules. Theoretically, this approach challenges the implicit or explicit hedonism of learning theory views of rule adherence versus deviance; it directly attacks the arguments of learning theorists (or economists devoted to rational actor models) that people invariably seek pleasure and avoid pain and that the reason people (including children) obey is to gain rewards or avoid punishment.

Most of the cognitive developmental research has adapted or built on Kohlberg's (1969, 1984) six-stage model of moral development, which was itself based on the earlier work of Piaget. Key distinctions from the standpoint of legal reasoning and law adherence have involved the three broad levels into which Kohlberg divided his stages: the preconventional, in which reasoning stresses fear of punishment and the seeking of reward; the conventional, in which reasoning is guided by the desire to fit in and conform to the existing order; and the postconventional, in which reasoning involves consistency with general and abstract principles. (See also Levine and Tapp 1977; Tapp and Kohlberg 1977.)

This largely developmental literature on moral judgment has been linked to the traditional concern of sociological social psychologists—deviance—by the demonstration that divergent moral thought structures can accompany similar actions. The dilemma of the relation of thought to action lies at the core of the normative question: What leads people to obey rules?

For example, Haan et al. (1968) assessed the moral stage development of political protesters at the University of California at Berkeley during the time of the Free Speech Movement. In terms of Kohlberg's six stages of moral development, these authors found that both stage two (preconventional) hedonists and stage six (postconventional) principled actors were overrepresented among participants in such actions as sit-ins. Thus, deviance can follow from adherence to a "higher law" as well as from the sort of hedonistic motives that are usually assumed in research on deviance (e.g., Gottfredson and Hirschi 1990).

Recent research exploring the role of moral judgment in adherence to norms and laws attempts to combine insights from the cognitive developmental and social learning perspectives. In psychology, a social learning approach to norm adherence is most characteristically associated with such scholars as Aronfreed (1968), Bandura (1986), and Mischel (1968; Mischel and Mischel 1976). In sociology, this approach is represented in Sutherland's (1939) differential association theory and in Akers's (1978) social learning theory of deviance. The basic assumption of this school is that deviance from rules and conformity to them represent two sides of the same coin, in that each is learned through processes of reward and punishment. There is nothing particularly special about the moral domain of life, at least with regard to the processes by which we come to understand and act in that domain.

A creative field study by Cohn and White (1990) attempted to pull together the cognitive developmental and social learning approaches by examining student life in residence halls. The authors argued that the relationship between general moral or legal reasoning and specific behavior should be mediated by situational factors; they found that this relationship depended on students' attitudes toward particular rule-violating behaviors and enforcement of rules against these behaviors. In addition, students' reasoning about rules was significantly more likely to be related to their behaviors when they lived in an atmosphere that was highly participatory and self-governing than when external authority enforced the rules. Finally, the maintenance of moral-legal reasoning itself was shown to be dependent on environmental factors. Students in the participatory residence hall atmosphere maintained their initial level of reasoning over time, approved of rule-violating behavior less, and approved of rule enforcement more; the opposite was true of students in the residence hall whose enforcement pattern was nonparticipatory. Thus, it appears appropriate to view rule adherence or deviance as a joint function of relatively more stable, developmentally linked reasoning about rules or laws and potentially less stable, socially learned attitudes toward the action in question as well as the enforcement of sanctions that may ensue.

Procedural Justice

Questions of what is just are fundamental to the understanding of both law and deviance. What is meant by justice is problematic, in part because the retributive justice that is meted out in response to deviant action is but one form of justice; others may be encountered both inside and outside the legal context. Typically, researchers contrast retributive justice with at least two other variants: distributive justice, or the justice of meting out social and economic rewards; and procedural justice, or the justice of how retribution or distribution is to be carried out. Distributive justice, primarily the province of exchange and equity theorists, has a long history as a research topic in social psychology, but researchers have concentrated on such topics as fair pay for work performed and equity in romantic relationships (e.g., Emerson 1981; Walster, Walster, and Berscheid 1978). Procedural problems, however, are to be found in every justice context, including the retributive domain. One natural focus of procedural justice research has been the fairness of judicial processes and encounters with enforcers of law. It is on this arena we concentrate in discussing recent trends. (See also chapters 8 and 10.)

Modern procedural justice research began with the studies of Thibaut and Walker (1975). Procedural justice was conceived of in a manner consistent with exchange theory; the fact that people had preferences for fair procedures, even when those procedures might disadvantage them distributively, was interpreted in terms of the long-run advantages they might see in a fair procedure. More recent theorizing about procedural justice, most notably in the work of Lind and Tyler (1988), has moved away from the rational actor calculus that characterizes exchange theories. In this regard procedural justice research has parallel with the previously discussed research on the development of moral and legal reasoning, insofar as theorists have begun to demand something instead of (or more than) a hedonistic, social learning-based understanding of human action.

Lind and Tyler's (1988) comprehensive summary of the field is informed by what they term a group value theory of procedural justice. Briefly, they see procedural justice judgments as flowing from the values held by an individual's reference group and from that person's desire to belong to that group. As Lind and Earley (1992) summarize this position:

> Because people see procedures as carrying information about what the group or society values, they endorse procedures that support and embody the fundamental values of their reference group. And because people look to procedures for information about how they themselves are viewed by the group, they respond favorably to procedures that grant them full status. Thus, a procedure is viewed as fair if it is congruent with important group values or if it appears to demonstrate that the person in question is a respected, valued member of the group. (1992, 232)

Lind and Tyler (1988; Lind and Earley 1992) argue that only by moving beyond an exclusively rational actor, social exchange-based understanding of procedural justice can certain research results be explained. Among these are the finding that perceived procedural justice is enhanced when a person has a chance to express his/her views (the "voice" effect); the finding that perceived procedural justice is enhanced when people are treated respectfully, with dignity (the "dignitary process"

effect); and the fact that procedures perceived of as fair improve evaluations of outcomes and increase compliance with decisions (the "fair process" effect) (see also Folger 1977).

What specific implications, if any, does procedural justice have for legal compliance versus deviance? Recent research by Tyler (1990) has explored the role of procedural justice in citizens' perceptions of the legitimacy of legal and political authorities and in their willingness to obey the law. Tyler's panel study of a random sample of Chicago residents included detailed questions about attitudes toward law and legal authority and experiences with the law. Tyler's (1990) argument involved three levels. First, citizens' willingness to comply with law was shown to follow primarily from their own moral standards and their perceptions that the demand is legitimate, rather than from instrumental considerations such as fear of apprehension. Second, perceived legitimacy was shown to follow from normative considerations, including the citizen's perception that authorities follow fair procedures. Third, perceived procedural justice itself was shown to be derived primarily from noninstrumental factors, such as the citizen's opportunity for self-expression ("voice").

Overall, at least among ordinary citizens such as those interviewed by Tyler (1990), adherence to law is closely bound with questions of right and wrong, and answers to these questions are strongly influenced by the fairness with which authorities treat the citizenry. This work presents a serious challenge to the instrumental view of law adherence held by exchange theorists (and, more generally, social learning theorists). It instead highlights what Tyler calls normative considerations in legal compliance. Simply put, the normative view holds that people obey the law because they think it is the right thing to do.

Summary

Much of the attention social psychologists have given to the legal domain in recent decades has been focused on universal cognitive or social processes in law-abiding actors. Both the moral judgment and procedural justice fields have contributed to a re-conceptualization of human motivation, a move beyond rational actor assumptions about behavior (and beyond social learning as an undifferentiated process underlying its performance); this reconceptualization applies to deviant as well as conforming behavior. These studies can be seen as constituting a gradual integration of the study of deviance and social control with other social psychological work on rules, rule adherence, and rule breaking. They represent a return to a kind of normative theory, sharing certain underlying assumptions with earlier approaches to deviance but subsuming it under a more general theoretical umbrella.

As admitted proponents of this development, let us do a preliminary stock taking of how this "new normative" approach relates to the traditional competing theories of deviance reviewed earlier. Three basic underlying premises link the new normativism to previous approaches. First, a focus on rules requires acknowledging, with consensus theorists, that some level of societal consensus typically does exist regarding many rules and behavioral standards. As Cohn and White (1990) show, some rules of daily living are consensually held and others are not. Research generally shows substantial consensus among citizens regarding crime seriousness (e.g., Rauma 1991; Rossi et al. 1974). Second, a focus on the interpretation of rules and their administration leads to seeing deviance as a process and "deviants" as an outcome of that process, rather than a discrete category of people. Of course, this view is consistent with societal reaction theory, in that deviance is seen as a joint function of the situation and the reaction of the audience. Moral judgment research simply contributes to the picture by suggesting the importance of the actor's own interpretation of the situation as an element in this process. Third, as is more explicitly developed below, the new normativism takes as central the fact that situational definitions tend to be established by authorities. Most sociologists and most theories of deviance implicitly agree to this last point, whether they focus on consensus or conflict or labeling.

In the remainder of the chapter we argue that to promote understanding of deviance, researchers would do well to explore the interplay between deviance and authority. Nowhere is the need for such study more obvious, or more necessary, than in the arena of white-collar and corporate misdeeds. It is in this arena that otherwise ordinary people—not "deviants"—can commit extraordinary wrongs, and often for the banal reason that they are doing their jobs. By exploring paradoxical deviance, we hope to gain a better grasp of deviance as a social scientific category.

We turn next to studies of white-collar or corporate crime. Each of them is a loose concept. The category of white-collar crime, popularized by Sutherland (1949), is, at least motivationally, the more diverse of the two (Clinard and Yeager 1980; J. W. Coleman 1985; Shapiro 1990). For example, it characteristically includes such self-aggrandizing offenses as embezzlement (e.g., Cressey 1953). But the motives of embezzlers are no mystery, and we find it easy to slap on a deviant identity once the embezzler's actions come to light. It is the obedient, conforming organizational actors, those who make possible "corporate crime," whose motives need further exploration. We therefore concentrate on misdeeds in corporate hierarchies.

THE RESPECTABLE VIOLATOR

We begin this section with an overview of deviance by organizations as a whole ("corporate crime") and turn to the question of how the wrongdoing of individual actors in the corporate hierarchy, wrongdoing that makes corporate deviance possible, should be understood and how it is characteristically judged. We conclude with a discussion of the motivations and perceptions of actors who refuse to participate in corporate criminality.

Deviance by Organizations

Christopher Stone's work on corporate crime, *Where the Law Ends* (1975), addresses the fundamental problem presented by the corporation as a legal actor:

> *. . . the nuclear engineer can be charged with a bit of information, a, the architect knows b, the night watchman knows c, the research scientist task force knows d. Conceivably there will not be any single individual who has, in and of himself, such knowledge and intent as will support a charge against him individually. . . . where corporate liability is based upon imputing to the corporation the wrongs of its agents, the corporation is less subject to the law than would be a single individual doing the same thing. (Stone 1975, 52)*

Legally, the corporation is a special kind of person—a persona ficta, or fictitious person—with many of the rights but few of the responsibilities of personhood. More to the point from the standpoint of deviance, the corporation simply cannot be sanctioned in many of the ways humans traditionally are. Also relevant is that the law traditionally assumes that corporations cannot intend in the same ways humans do, and hence cannot commit certain crimes for which intention is part of the definition of the offense (including felonies such as murder). Both legal niceties and the realities of the power of corporate actors contribute to the fact that corporate misdeeds are traditionally processed legally through civil rather than criminal courts.

Thus, in most cases *corporate crime* is a misnomer in any technical sense. It is used by social scientists more to convey the notion that certain acts should be crimes than to imply that they are actually handled as such. Therefore, we generally refer to "deviance" in and by corporations. We discuss action that is perceived by the public, the media, the courts, or regulatory agencies as wrong—action that leads to harmful consequences, often of a quite serious nature.

Stone (1975) presents numerous examples of corporate offenses in which top executives or even an entire staff knowingly participated in illegal activities. We highlight incidents that in our view make a starker contrast between offenses characteristic of individuals and offenses characteristic of organizations. Deviance in a corporate context often involves something short of fully intended wrongdoing: some amalgam of mistakes, missteps, and unintended consequences (often followed by a planned, deliberate coverup). One example, discussed in the next section, is the defective gas tank of the Ford Pinto, a design problem of which the company was aware for years. The company clearly did not in any direct sense intend for customers to burn, but its policy included a deliberate weighing of the costs and benefits of correcting the gas tank design versus settling potential legal claims; it was decided that it was cheaper to settle claims than to prevent them by improving the design (Dowie 1977).

A similar pattern of initially unsought or unintended consequences and their planned coverup characterizes other defective products such as the Dalkon Shield, an intrauterine (contraceptive) device that led to painful infection, sterility, and death in numerous instances and to unwanted births and birth defects in others. The manufacturer, the A.H. Robins Company, presumably intended to make profits, not victims. At the same time, the company resisted recalling the devices for a decade after it had been asked by the Food and Drug Administration to stop selling them in the United States; it continued to sell them abroad for years and steadily resisted the flood of litigation from users (Mintz 1985). In general, it appears that a regular, if less than fully rational, way for corporate actors to deal with products gone wrong is a kind of burrowing in to "tough it out," rather than admitting initial error. This type of behavior can be seen as one instance of the more general problem of sunk costs (e.g., Staw 1976). In colloquial terms, the notion of sunk costs refers to "throwing good money after bad": continuing a course of action in which one has invested time and resources even when it has become economically irrational to do so.

Granted that corporations may plan for profits, not heists, what can we say in general about the similarities and differences between corporate and individual deviants? Public conceptions of corporate actors and corporate offenses provide one important clue to the normative status of corporate crime.

Public Views of Organizational Deviance

Experimental Studies.   Remarkably little is known about how the public views the wrongdoing of corporate as opposed to individual actors.[3] One test of the question was provided in an experiment by Hans and Ermann (1989), who presented mock jurors with a lengthy description of a civil case involving harm to employees at their workplace. The experimental manipulation consisted of whether they had been hired by "Mr. Jones" or the "Jones Corporation." The research subjects were asked to decide about the criminal negligence of the defendant (Jones/ Jones Corporation) and about recommended punishment (damage award). The results were straightforward: the corporate actor was judged more negligent than the individual actor, and substantially greater damage awards were recommended against the corporation than against "Mr. Jones." Follow-up analyses to determine why the corporation was judged more harshly suggested that the subjects applied a different, more stringent standard of care (avoidance of negligence) to the corporate actor.

Though Hans and Ermann (1989) suggest that corporations may be seen as more blameworthy than individuals for the same actions, the legal quandary in the handling of corporations has traditionally been that corporate actions that produce damage and death are not comparable to individual actions; in particular, corporate actions cannot be assumed to have the intentionality that is a legal prerequisite for many criminal charges. An ironic result is that corporate offenses may lead to much more widespread damage than offenses by individual felons without being conceived of as "criminal." A federal judge lecturing A. H. Robins's owner and top corporate officers put the contrast between ordinary criminal harm and the company's production of the Dalkon Shield succinctly:

> *If one poor young man were, by some act of his—
> without authority or consent—to inflict such dam-
> age upon one woman, he would be jailed for a good
> portion of the rest of his life. And yet your company, without warning to women, invaded their
> bodies by the millions and caused them injuries by
> the thousands. (Lord 1987, 42)*

The bulk of charges against corporations for harm to persons and property lead to civil suits rather than criminal charges, often under the strict liability rules that govern recovery for damages caused by defective products. Strict liability, as the term suggests, calls for a judgment to be made on the basis of whether a defendant caused an outcome, without regard to the defendant's state of mind; such rules are often instituted where it is impractical to prove intent or negligence. Yet a recent study by Rauma et al. (1990) shows that members of the public judging a case of this sort do use information about corporate negligence—information that would typically be used in judging individuals but is legally inappropriate in this type of case—in deciding responsibility and punishment. In their spontaneous thinking about corporate deviance, citizens appear to use the same kinds of decision rules to judge corporations and individual wrongdoers, regardless of differences called for in the law. This is one instance in which societal moral standards and legal standards may be at variance.

Content Analysis.   Another method of exploring corporate liability is to seek out cases in which corporations have been held (or at least charged as) criminal and to examine what factors seem to have contributed to their treatment as deviant. For example, to what extent do inferences of intentionality play a part?

Swigert and Farrell (1980–81) studied the treatment in the media of the Ford Pinto case from the time the Pinto's defective gas tank became news until the company was indicted in Indiana for reckless homicide in the deaths of three teenagers whose gas tank exploded (December, 1976 to September 1978). Though Ford was eventually acquitted, the Indiana case was a landmark because it was the first homicide indictment against a corporation in American history.[4] The authors' content analysis of news stories suggested two shifts in how the issue was viewed. First, news accounts increasingly focused on personal harm done to victims, rather than on impersonal accounts of the car as having a mechanical defect. Second, the company was consistently depicted as unrepentant, unwilling to take responsibility for the consequences of its defective design. The authors argued that these two trends enabled the public to see the offense in question as one like conventional criminal offenses (i.e., producing personal harm) and to see the offender as like other deviants, insofar as its lack of repentance made it appear to be "the enemy." In social psychological terms, each of these trends brings the corporate action closer to a face-to-face act with felonious intent; personalization makes the harm concrete, and lack of repentance makes it at least retroactively intentional.

In sum, the legal literature consistently presents corporate actors as difficult to bring to justice and difficult to sanction appropriately. The sketchy social scientific evidence regarding how members of the public view, or how the media depict, corporate offenders provides some insight into the problems of sanctioning these offenders. It appears that the public views the corporation as a large, powerful person who is supposed to think in the same way as individual humans—if not somewhat more carefully. Its acts can be and are evaluated according to standard criminal standards if and when they can be "brought down to size" and made to look and sound like ordinary human crimes. To the extent that they cannot be—to the extent that, for example, the type of harm lacks a clearly identifiable victim, as is often true in environmental pollution cases—the corporation may stand accused, but a criminal accusation is unlikely to stick.

Both as a practical matter of deterrence and sanctioning and as a theoretical issue, it is inevitable that the social scientist begins to ask questions about the actions of individuals within corporate hierarchies. The corporation is, after all, a collection of individual humans arrayed in a hierarchical structure. These humans do not, however, appear to see themselves or to be judged by others as autonomous controllers of their own fates and their own behaviors. Thus, the allocation of responsibility among actors in hierarchies is a key to understanding the commission of deviant acts in organizational settings. We turn next to the people within the organizational hierarchy who make corporate crime possible.

Responsibility in Organizations

With the killing of Jews I had nothing to do. I never killed a Jew, or a non-Jew, for that matter—I never killed any human being. (Adolph Eichmann, quoted in Arendt 1964, 22)

Hannah Arendt's famous discussion of the trial of Adolph Eichmann was subtitled "A Report on the Banality of Evil." The corporate offenses we have been considering, however serious, are a far cry from the eradication of millions of Jews and other unwanted citizens to which Eichmann contributed; they share with Eichmann's crimes, however, a fundamental similarity in motive. The individual offenders are respectable, law-abiding, good workers who are—or claim to be—merely doing their jobs. Offenses in corporate and other organizational hierarchies represent a natural meeting ground for the study of conformity and the study of deviance. Something about hierarchies appears to lead to a loss of the sense of responsibility for one's own actions. We seek an explanation of that loss and its implications for deviance in and by corporations. (The discussion that follows is adapted from Hamilton 1978, 1986; Hamilton and Sanders 1992b; Kelman and Hamilton 1989. See also Clinard 1983.)

Social and developmental psychologists studying the attribution of responsibility tend to view responsibility as an outgrowth of a person's deeds, particularly of the actor's intention and the act's consequences (Piaget 1965). Both legal rules themselves and recent sociological research demonstrate, however, that responsibility judgments rest on a combination of the actor's deeds and the actor's role obligations or duties (Hamilton 1978; Hamilton and Sanders 1992a, 1992b). For some roles, responsibility may be allocated solely on the basis of failing to fulfill one's obligations. Judgments of this type are referred to legally as being based on vicarious liability (one's liability for the actions of others) or strict liability (one's liability for causing an outcome, regardless of one's mental state at the time). Most situations in which strict or vicarious liability rules apply involve hierarchy in one form or another. They include actions by corporate entities, within corporate hierarchies, and in particular occupational roles to which specific expectations are attached. These latter roles can be as varied as "parent," (referring to the delinquent actions of one's children) or "bar owner" (the actions of employees who serve liquor to minors). The common element in situations of vicarious responsibility is that the person held accountable has some recognized responsibility to oversee the actions of the person who actually committed the breach of law.

Allocating responsibility to a superordinate—an authority—rather than a subordinate in a hierarchy is a tricky matter (Hamilton 1986; Kelman and Hamilton 1989). In hierarchies, unlike other settings where laws are broken, people may make things happen by causing other people to act rather than by acting on their own. This is how Eichmann could claim he had killed no Jews; he had not personally, physically done so. As philosophers of law Hart and Honoré (1959) point out, when one person causes a second to harm a third, the causal responsibility tends to be divided between the first two actors; often, in fact, the person physically closest in a chain of causation is seen as bearing the brunt of responsibility.

In hierarchies, however, responsibility based on role obligations is at issue along with responsibility based on physical production of outcomes. Typically, evidence of physical causation is clearest at the bottom of a hierarchy, closest to the concrete effect that was produced. Liability based on role is greatest at the top, but it is often the diffuse and hard-to-prove liability of one who omitted (failed to oversee others adequately) rather than committed (actually performed a misdeed). As hierarchies stretch out to include multiple ac-

tors, it becomes relatively easy to arrive at a situation in which no one is held responsible. Subordinates claim they were doing as they were told (a role-related excuse); superiors claim that what the subordinates did is not what they ordered, or even that they did not know what happened (an excuse based on lack of causal connection to the outcome).

The result is a paradoxical deviance—what Kelman and Hamilton (1989) refer to as crimes of obedience. Such wrongdoing by subordinates in hierarchies can help us to understand the fundamental dependence of deviance on the situational context. Authorities define and frame situations for subordinates; definitions of the situation, especially in organizational contexts, are not a matter of majority vote but of differential power to influence what is seen as real in that setting. Hence, in the immediate situational context, behaviors that might be considered crimes of obedience are instead defined as doing one's job. It is only outside the context as the authority has defined it that an alternative definition of the behavior as wrong, illegal, immoral, or deviant emerges.

Who can be deviant in an organizational setting (by refusing orders), thereby conforming to the rules or laws provided by some other, outside viewpoint? We turn next to this question.

Motivations for Deviance and Resistance in Organizations

Consider the following scenario from the point of view of a subordinate in a corporate hierarchy. Imagine yourself to be a laboratory technician at a pharmaceutical company, Richardson-Merrell. Your test results show that a new drug, MER/29, which is to be marketed as effective in reducing cholesterol, also produces cataracts. Your superior tells you to falsify the results, which are to be sent on to superiors in the corporate hierarchy. What do you do and why?

This scenario, which was actually part of the pattern of events that unfolded as Richardson-Merrell produced MER/29 (Stone 1975), raises two possibilities. Perhaps somehow you do not know or realize the falsification is wrong; in that case obedience is the expected behavior. If you do realize the falsification is or may be wrong, you then have to decide how to frame the situation, for you are in a dilemma in which either carrying out the directive or disobeying it might be wrong, and either behavior might be punished. How are such dilemmas resolved? Understanding obedient participation in corporate wrongdoing or resistance to it requires taking account of actors' definitions of the situation, which are, in turn, linked to their motives.

The very idea that deviance can be deterred rests on the assumption that the offender is a rational actor who chooses courses of action on the basis of reward and punishment. Yet much of the literature on organizationally based wrongdoing suggests that this model does not adequately capture the phenomenology of the subordinate who becomes involved in corporate deviance.

Authorities typically frame the situation for their subordinates, establishing for them a social definition of what they are doing and what they are supposed to be doing. Authorities attempt to reduce or eliminate the subordinate's sense of independent choice over courses of action. Motivationally speaking, the situation is transformed from the rational actor's calculus—"What's in it for me?"—to the organizational actor's calculus—"What am I supposed to do?" Whatever rationality governs the situation is the organization's rationality—its fit between goals and means—not the individual actor's.

In terms of the earlier discussion of the attribution of responsibility, subordinates who resist an authority's demands are likely to focus on the deed, in particular on the concrete and foreseeable consequences of the action. Subordinates who obey are likely to justify the action in terms of their role expectations: "just doing my job" or "following the boss's orders." This frame of reference stresses the obligations of the subordinate role over the actual deeds performed. Organizational settings encourage role-based and discourage deed-based evaluations of action on the part of subordinates. This

becomes problematic when the deeds called for are seen as illegal or immoral by outside evaluators—as was true in the case of MER/29.

Of course, individuals do vary in susceptibility to the illegitimate demands of authority and in how they judge others who succumb to those demands. Kelman and Hamilton (1989), researching on wrongdoing in military and other hierarchical contexts, reached three conclusions about individual differences. First, people have relatively stable tendencies to judge authority situations either in terms of deeds and their consequences or in terms of roles and their obligations. Those who emphasize deeds tend to assert that subordinates are responsible for their actions when they obey illegitimate commands; those who emphasize roles tend to deny this responsibility. Second, role-based responsibility denial can flow from two sources: a sense that one is being coerced by the authority and a sense that one is obligated to that authority. Third, the tendency to assert or deny responsibility and the alternative bases of denial (coercion and obligation) are distributed differently across the social structure. Those higher in occupational prestige, education, and income tend to assert that individual subordinates are responsible; those intermediate on these factors tend to deny responsibility on the basis that subordinates are obligated to obey; and those low in education, prestige, or income tend to deny responsibility on the basis that subordinates are compelled or coerced to obey. Hence those most likely to be authorities, to be in charge of their actions and those of others, tend to perceive situations as allowing for choices and therefore hold subordinates individually responsible; those most likely to be subordinates are more sensitive to the pressures that are brought to bear on subordinates in hierarchies.

Deterring corporate misdeeds, insofar as these misdeeds flow from the obedient actions of subordinates, depends on countering the authoritative framework that constricts choices and highlights obligations. Advice to employees to seek out the intervention of alternative authorities within or outside the organization may have some effectiveness, but studies on whistle-blowing suggest that those most likely to do so are in fact higher in the organizational hierarchy (e.g., Miceli and Near 1984). This is to be expected on the basis of the greater ease with which they might adopt a deed-based rather than role-based frame for understanding the situation.

In sum, actors in hierarchies judge themselves and are judged by others according to a complex calculus that includes the normative obligations of the situation and their role in it. This perspective on deviance in corporate settings is consistent with other research on the behavior of the law-abiding, reviewed above, insofar as it highlights normative factors. A simple reward-punishment or cost-benefit calculus does not adequately capture the general process of moral judgment, the importance of procedural justice, or the behavior of organizational actors asked to do something they consider wrong. We turn next to an explicitly normative theory of deviance that sheds further light on how to deter the deviant acts of those who follow the boss's orders.

NEW VIEWS OF DEVIANCE AND ITS SANCTIONING: AN EXAMPLE

> *If there is one thing that people who fail as spouses, teachers, or managers have in common, it is their inability to understand that you do not try to achieve goals by punishment until you have first tried appealing to people's better natures. (Braithwaite 1989, 130)*

Since the 1960s, labeling theory and conflict theory approaches to deviance have constituted important challenges to older views that saw norms as objectively or independently definable. The perspective on deviance in organizations outlined above shares certain features with each of these perspectives, in that it treats deviance as a contextual event embedded in a situation governed by an authority figure. In the case of organizational deviance, what is deviance and what is conformity lies in the eye of the beholder. Ultimately, however, this perspective shares with older normative theories

the notion that it is possible to specify external standards of right and wrong against which actions in organizational contexts can be evaluated.

The preceding section suggested some ways in which the domination of contexts by authorities can be counteracted. Next we return to the general problem of deviance—by individual as well as organizational actors—and ask what a normative orientation implies about the problem of deterrence and the appropriate sanction for accomplishing deterrence.

An elegant theoretical solution is found in Braithwaite's (1989) *Crime, Shame and Reintegration,* which focuses on what the author terms "predatory crime": crimes in which one person preys on another, whether the content of the act is the stuff of delinquency, street crime, or sharp business practices. Braithwaite first asks what facts a theory of predatory crime should have to explain. Reviewing a list of thirteen known conclusions about crime (e.g., it is committed disproportionately by males, by fifteen- to twenty-four-year olds, by the unmarried, and by the residentially mobile), Braithwaite argues that traditional deviance theories do rather poorly in explaining the full list. Learning theory (e.g., Sutherland's differential association) fares best but is vague and ill-specified. Labeling theory, currently a dominant perspective in the field of deviance, fares worst in Braithwaite's view. On the one hand, he grants that its proponents could argue that their goal is not to explain the facts of crime but to challenge them. On the other hand, he argues that it is clearly a weakness that labeling theorists have not even been able to establish a fundamental prediction of the theory, that more severe sanctions should lead to more secondary deviance (cf. Tittle 1980).

Braithwaite further argues that the most comprehensive explanation of the facts of predatory crime can be reached by incorporating insights from several perspectives but adding one distinction between ways in which societies sanction offenders. Specifically, he contrasts *reintegrative shaming* with *stigmatization* and argues that failure to distinguish between the two is a source of much of the confusion in the criminological literature. In reintegrative shaming, expressions of community disapproval are followed by gestures of reconciliation or reintegration; in stigmatization, in contrast, the offender is made an outcast, assigned a deviant status that cannot be shaken. The predictions of labeling theory focus on the negative effects of stigmatization. However, Braithwaite argues that effective deterrence is primarily accomplished via informal social control exerted by friends, families, and neighbors, rather than formal sanction or its threat. The driving force behind the effectiveness of informal controls, in turn, is their capacity for generating a sense of shame. Thus sanction can have either a positive or a negative impact on recidivism, depending on whether it is geared toward reintegrating the offender.

Braithwaite argues that each of the major generalizations about crime in modern industrialized nations can be seen to follow from susceptibilities and responses to shaming and whether the shaming is reintegrative or stigmatizing. Social characteristics that increase dependency and interdependency on others (hence increasing susceptibility to social pressure via reintegrative shaming) should and do relate to lowered likelihood of predatory crime. To be female or married, for example, is typically to be in a more dependent or interdependent status via significant others than to be male or unmarried. We may add that this perspective can easily incorporate the findings of Sampson and Laub (1990), discussed above, regarding the usefulness of marriage and stable jobs in deterring the delinquent from continued crime in adulthood. In Braithwaite's terminology, the potency of these informal controls is linked to the fact that one's spouse, boss, and coworkers are people with whom one is interdependent and before whom one might feel ashamed.

The major theories of criminal behavior can also be incorporated into this framework once one makes the distinction between reintegrative shaming and shaming that stigmatizes. Predictive failures of each approach can also be resolved. For example, we have noted that labeling theory asserts that the application of deviant labels generates secondary deviance. The fact that punishment obviously does not always lead to secondary deviance, but sometimes deters, can be seen as partly a function of whether the mix of punishment is tilted toward reintegrative shaming or stigmatization. Reintegrative shaming should deter; stigmatizing shaming should create a secondary deviant.

One attractive feature of this synthesis is that, unlike most theories of deviance, it explicitly incorporates offenses by organizational actors —white-collar and corporate criminals. The argument is straightforward. White-collar and corporate offenders tend to be highly integrated into the social order and hence, according to Braithwaite, susceptible to deterrence strategies that activate a sense of shame. Reintegrative shaming works for organizational actors just as it works for ordinary criminal offenders; conversely, punishments that stigmatize organizational offenders run the risk of exacerbating crime by building a deviant organizational subculture, just as is true with ordinary offenders.

In Braithwaite's view, "much thinking about corporate crime . . . adopts an overly economically rational conception of the corporation . . . it downplays the fact that the corporation is constituted of individuals with consciences" (1989, 141). His analysis complements the picture presented above of the motives and frames of reference of organizational actors by further detailing the appropriate sanctioning strategy. In both cases, the organizational actor is viewed as someone who may be trying to do the right thing—a socially malleable being, not a social renegade.

CONCLUSIONS

Research on deviance holds an important place in sociological social psychology. We first discussed major trends in research on deviance per se and the related topic of social control, indicating some of the weaknesses evident in these literatures. The remainder of the chapter concentrated on what we see as the more innovative recent trend toward subsuming the study of deviance under a larger rubric such as rule adherence and violation. Recent research on rule adherence and violation, in turn, tends to concentrate on the cognitions and behaviors of ordinary or "respectable" citizens; favored topics include such areas as moral judgment, procedural justice, and white-collar and corporate crime. The perspective of the majority of this research can be characterized as a return to a normative view of deviance in two senses: It is assumed that (1) certain acts can be defined as deviant by external standards (whether those of the larger community or those of the authorities); and (2) considerations beyond pure hedonism or a rational actor calculus govern actors' behavior.

Thinking about deviance in the 1990s, we argue, also involves thinking about obedience and rule adherence. More to the point, it requires it. At present, social psychological research on deviance appears to be alive and well, but often under labels such as the study of moral judgment or white-collar crime. We believe both theory and research in this area will profit from the interdisciplinary efforts and eclectic theoretical mixes that are beginning to emerge, some of which have been reviewed here. For example, Braithwaite's (1989) theory of predatory crime, like that of Tyler (1990), argues against a simplistic rational actor model of deviance such as that of classical economics or social learning theory.[5]

From this view of deviance flows a changed view of social control that moves beyond crime control. As Braithwaite (1989, 142) argues: "You cannot take the moral content out of social control and expect social control to work." We noted at the beginning of the chapter how the field had moved from talking about "deviance and social control" to talking about "deviance and law" in the past decade or so. Perhaps in the volume that updates this one, the chapter that replaces ours will have a title like "Deviance, Obedience, and the Social Control of Each."

NOTES

The authors are grateful to the editors and three anonymous reviewers for their helpful comments on an earlier draft. This chapter was prepared with support from NSF grant SES-9113967. The views expressed in this article are those of the authors and do not necessarily reflect the official policies or positions of their employers.

1. A search of SOCIOFILE for 1974 to 1991 showed that entries under both deviance and law actually declined over this period—both in absolute numbers and as relative percentages of all entries. However, entries for both white-collar crime and corporate crime mushroomed, albeit from a tiny original baseline.

2. Our discussion is far from all-inclusive of law-related topics studied by social psychologists; instead, it concentrates on two key areas in which normative approaches have been or have recently become central. Jury research is one important area omitted from review. Since the landmark Chicago jury project in the 1950s (Kalven and Zeisel 1965; Simon and Lynch 1989), the behaviors of juries and jurors have frequently been studied by social psychologists interested in law, group decision making, or both (Hans and Vidmar 1984; Hastie, Penrod, and Pennington 1983). Relevant topics in group decision making are covered in chapter 13.

3. Here we are contrasting particular types of offenders (corporate entities or their agents versus individuals), rather than the offenses committed. Studies of white-collar crime suggest that the public views offenses that exemplify corporate crime quite seriously and that the perceived seriousness of such offenses may be increasing (e.g., Cullen, Link, and Polzani 1982; Rossi et al. 1974).

4. This case illustrates the slippery quality of the social scientific terminology in this area. Although the company was eventually acquitted, the Pinto gas tank remains a popular example of a corporate "crime." The inconsistency is more apparent than real, however. As we have noted, social scientists use the term *corporate crime* rather loosely—not only when the actions in question are illegal, but also when they are widely considered immoral. In this vein, the Pinto case acquittal can be seen as reflecting not so much Ford's lack of culpability as the American criminal law's inadequacies in bringing corporate offenders to account (e.g., Strobel 1980; for

overviews see Hamilton and Sanders 1992b and Stone 1975).

5. We do not wish to imply that theorizing using a rational actor approach has remained static and unimproved by the challenges from normative perspectives and from other quarters (most notably psychologists studying decision making). For examples of advances in the rational actor approach, see Cook and Levi (1990) or J. S. Coleman (1990).

REFERENCES

Akers, Ronald. 1978. *Deviant Behavior.* Belmont, CA: Wadsworth.

Archer, Dane. 1985. Social deviance. Pp. 743–804 in *Handbook of Social Psychology,* ed. Gardner Lindsey and Eliot Aronson. New York: Random House.

Arendt, Hannah. 1964. *Eichmann in Jerusalem: A Report on the Banality of Evil,* rev. ed. New York: Viking.

Aronfreed, Justin. 1968. *Conduct and Conscience: The Socialization of Internalized Control Over Behavior.* New York: Academic.

Bandura, Albert. 1986. *Social Foundations of Thought and Action: A Social Cognitive Theory.* Englewood Cliffs, NJ: Prentice Hall.

Becker, Howard S. 1963. *Outsiders.* New York: Free Press.

Berk, Richard A., Sheldon L. Messinger, David Rauma, and John E. Berecochea. 1983. Prisons as self-regulating systems: A comparison of historical patterns in California for male and female offenders. *Law and Society Review* 17:547–586.

Berk, Richard A., David Rauma, Sheldon L. Messinger, and Thomas F. Cooley. 1981. A test of the stability of punishment hypothesis: The case of California, 1851–1970. *American Sociological Review* 46: 805–829.

Blumstein, Alfred, and Jacqueline Cohen. 1976. A theory of the stability of punishment. *Journal of Criminal Law and Criminology* 64:198–207.

Braithwaite, John. 1989. *Crime, Shame and Reintegration.* Cambridge, UK: Cambridge University Press.

Chambliss, William. 1964. A sociological analysis of the law of vagrancy. *Social Problems* 12:67–77.

Chambliss, William J., and Robert B. Seidman. 1971. *Law, Order, and Power.* Reading, MA: Addison-Wesley.

Church, Thomas W. 1979. In defense of bargain justice. *Law and Society Review* 13:509–525.

Cicourel, Aaron V. 1968. *The Social Organization of Juvenile Justice.* New York: Wiley.

Clinard, Marshall B., 1983. *Corporate Ethics and Crime: The Role of Middle Management.* Beverly Hills: Sage.

Clinard, Marshall B., and Peter C. Yeager. 1980. *Corporate Crime.* New York: Free Press.

Cloward, Richard A., and Lloyd Ohlin. 1960. *Delinquency and Opportunity.* New York: Free Press.

Cohen, Albert K. 1955. *Delinquent Boys.* Glencoe, IL: Free Press.

Cohn, Ellen S., and Susan O. White. 1990. *Legal Socialization: A Study of Norms and Rules.* New York: Springer-Verlag.

Coleman, James S. 1990. *Foundations of Social Theory.* Cambridge, MA: Harvard University Press.

Coleman, James W. 1985. *The Criminal Elite: The Sociology of White Collar Crime.* New York: St. Martin's.

Cook, Karen S., and Margaret Levi. 1990. *The Limits of Rationality.* Chicago: University of Chicago Press.

Cressey, Donald R. 1953. *Other People's Money: A Study in the Social Psychology of Embezzlement.* Belmont, CA: Wadsworth.

Cullen, Francis T., Bruce G. Link, and Craig W. Polzani. 1982. The seriousness of crime revisited: Have attitudes toward white-collar crime changed? *Criminology* 20:83–103.

Currie, Elliot P. 1968. Crimes without criminals: Witchcraft and its control in Renaissance Europe. *Law and Society Review* 3:7–32.

Dowie, Mark. 1977. Pinto madness. *Mother Jones.* September-October: 18–24, 28–32.

Durkheim, Emile. 1958. *The Rules of Sociological Method.* Glencoe, IL: Free Press.

———. 1960. *The Division of Labor in Society.* Glencoe, IL: Free Press.

Elder, Glen H., Jr. 1985. Perspectives on the life course. Pp. 23–49 in *Life Course Dynamics,* ed. Glen H. Elder, Jr. Ithaca, NY: Cornell University Press.

Emerson, Richard M. 1981. Social exchange theory. Pp. 30–65 in *Social Psychology: Sociological Perspectives,* ed. M. Rosenberg and R. H. Turner. New York: Basic Books.

Erikson, Kai T. 1966. *Wayward Puritans: A Study in the Sociology of Deviance.* New York: Wiley.

Folger, Robert. 1977. Distributive and procedural justice: Combined impact of "voice" and improvement on experienced inequity. *Journal of Personality and Social Psychology* 35:108–119.

Gibbs, Jack P. 1981. The sociology of deviance and social control. Pp. 483–522 in *Social Psychology: Sociological Perspectives,* ed. M. Rosenberg and R. H. Turner. New York: Basic Books.

Goffman, E. 1963. *Stigma: Notes on the Management of Spoiled Identity.* Englewood Cliffs, NJ: Prentice-Hall.

Gottfredson, Michael, and Travis Hirschi. 1990. *A General Theory of Crime.* Stanford: Stanford University Press.

Haan, Norma, M. Brewster Smith, and Jack Block. 1968. Moral reasoning of young adults: Political-social behavior, family background, and personality correlates. *Journal of Personality and Social Psychology.* 10:183–201.

Hagan, John. 1991. Destiny and drift: Subcultural preferences, status attainments, and the risks and rewards of youth. *American Sociological Review* 56: 567–582.

Hagan, John, and Alberto Palloni. 1990. The social reproduction of a criminal class in working-class London, circa 1950–1980. *American Journal of Sociology* 96:265–299.

Hamilton, V. L. 1978. Who is responsible? Toward a social psychology of responsibility attribution. *Social Psychology* 41:316–328.

———. 1986. Chains of command: Responsibility attribution in hierarchies. *Journal of Applied Social Psychology* 16:118–138.

Hamilton, V. L., and J. Sanders. 1992a. *Everyday Justice: Responsibility and the Individual in Japan and the United States.* New Haven, CT: Yale University Press.

———. 1992b. Responsibility and risk in organizational crimes of obedience. Pp. 49–90 in *Research in Organizational Behavior,* vol. 14, ed. Barry M. Staw and L. L. Cummings. Greenwich, CT: JAI Press.

Hans, Valerie P., and M. David Ermann. 1989. Responses to corporate versus individual wrongdoing. *Law and Human Behavior* 13:151–166.

Hans, Valerie P., and Neil Vidmar. 1984. *Judging the Jury.* New York: Plenum.

Hart, H. L. A., and A. M. Honoré. 1959. *Causation in the Law.* Oxford: Clarendon.

Hastie, Reid, Steven D. Penrod, and Nancy Pennington. 1983. *Inside the Jury.* Cambridge, MA: Harvard University Press.

Heumann, Milton. 1978. *Plea Bargaining.* Chicago: University of Chicago Press.

Hirschi, Travis. 1969. *Causes of Delinquency.* Los Angeles: University of California.

Kalven, Harry, and Hans Zeisel. 1966. *The American Jury.* Boston: Little, Brown.

Katz, Jack. 1988. *Seductions of Crime: Moral and Sensual Attractions in Doing Evil.* New York: Basic Books.

Kelman, Herbert C., and V. Lee Hamilton. 1989. *Crimes of Obedience.* New Haven, CT: Yale University Press.

Klockars, Carl B. 1985. *The Idea of Police.* Beverly Hills: Sage.

Kohlberg, Lawrence. 1969. Stage and development: The cognitive-developmental approach to socialization. Pp. 347–480 in *Handbook of Socialization Theory and Research,* ed. D. A. Goslin. Chicago: Rand McNally.

———. 1984. *The Psychology of Moral Development: Moral Stages and the Life Cycle. Essays on Moral Development,* vol. 2. San Francisco: Harper & Row.

Kornhauser, Ruth. 1978. *Social Sources of Delinquency.* Chicago: University of Chicago Press.

Krisberg, Barry, and James Austin. 1978. *The Children of Ishmael.* Palo Alto: Mayfield.

Lemert, Edwin. 1951. *Social Pathology.* New York: McGraw-Hill.

Levine, Felice J., and June L. Tapp. 1977. The dialectic of legal socialization in community and school. Pp. 163–182 in *Law, Justice, and the Individual in Society,* ed. F. L. Levine and J. L. Tapp. New York: Holt, Rinehart & Winston.

Lind, E. Allan, and P. Christopher Earley. 1992. Procedural justice and culture. *International Journal of Psychology* 27:227–242.

Lind, E. Allan, and Tom R. Tyler. 1988. *The Social Psychology of Procedural Justice.* New York: Plenum.

Liska, Allen E. 1987. *Perspectives on Deviance,* 2nd ed. Englewood Cliffs, NJ: Prentice Hall.

Lord, Miles W. 1987. A plea for corporate conscience. Pp. 41–46 in *Corporate Violence,* ed. S. L. Hills. Totowa, NJ: Rowman & Littlefield.

Matsueda, Ross L. 1982. Testing control theory and differential association. *American Sociological Review* 47:489–504.

———. 1992. Reflected appraisals, parental labeling, and delinquency: Specifying a symbolic interactionist theory. *American Journal of Sociology* 97: 1577–1611.

Matza, David. 1964. *Delinquency and Drift.* New York: Wiley.

Maynard, Douglas W. 1984. *Inside Plea Bargaining.* New York: Plenum.

Merton, Robert K. 1938. Social structure and anomie. *American Sociological Review* 3:672–682.

Miceli, M., and J. Near. 1984. The relationships among beliefs, organizational position, and whistle-blowing status: A discriminant analysis. *Academy of Management Journal* 27:687–705.

Mintz, Morton. 1985. *At Any Cost: Corporate Greed, Women, and the Dalkon Shield.* New York: Pantheon.

Mischel, Walter. 1968. *Personality and Assessment.* New York: Wiley.

Mischel, Walter, and Harriet N. Mischel. 1976. A cognitive social-learning approach to morality and self-regulation. Pp. 84–107 in *Moral Development and Behavior,* ed. T. Lickona. New York: Holt, Rinehart & Winston.

Piaget, Jean. 1965. *The Moral Judgment of the Child.* New York: Free Press.

Piaget, Jean, and Barbel Inhelder. 1969. *The Psychology of the Child.* New York: Basic Books.

Piliavin, Irving, and Scott Briar. 1964. Police encounters with juveniles. *American Journal of Sociology* 70: 206–214.

Quinney, Richard. 1977. *Class, State, and Crime.* New York: David McKay.

Rauma, David. 1981. Crime and punishment reconsidered: Some comments on Blumstein's stability of punishment hypothesis. *Journal of Criminal Law and Criminology* 72:1772–1798.

———. 1991. The context of normative consensus: An expansion of the Rossi/Berk consensus model, with an application to crime seriousness. *Social Science Research* 20:1–28

Rauma, David, V. Lee Hamilton, and Joseph Sanders. 1990. Strictly liable? Public judgments of corporate crime. Paper presented at the American Society of Criminology Convention, Baltimore.

Rosenberg, Morris. 1992. *The Unread Mind: Unraveling the Mystery of Madness.* New York: Lexington Books.

Rosenberg, Morris, and Ralph H. Turner, ed. 1981. *Social Psychology: Sociological Perspectives.* New York: Basic Books.

Rosenhan, David L. 1973. On being sane in insane places. *Science* 179:250–258.

Rossi, Peter H., Emily Waite, Christine E. Bose, and Richard A. Berk. 1974. The seriousness of crimes: Normative structure and individual differences. *American Sociological Review* 39:224–237.

Sampson, Robert J., and John H. Laub. 1990. Crime and deviance over the life course: The salience of adult social bonds. *American Sociological Review* 55: 609–627.

Schulhofer, Stephen J. 1984. Inside plea bargaining. *Harvard Law Review* 97:1037–1107.

Schur, Edwin M. 1971. *Labeling Deviant Behavior.* New York: Harper & Row.

Shapiro, Susan P. 1990. Collaring the crime, not the criminal: Reconsidering "white-collar crime." *American Sociological Review* 55:346–365.

Shoemaker, Donald J. 1984. *Theories of Delinquency.* New York: Oxford University Press.

Simon, Rita J., and James P. Lynch. 1989. The sociology of law: Where we have been and where we might be going. *Law and Society Review* 23: 825–847.

Skolnick, Jerome H. 1966. *Justice without Trial.* New York: Wiley.

Staw, B.M. 1976. Knee-deep in the big muddy. *Organizational Behavior and Human Performance* 16: 27–44.

Stone, Christopher D. 1975. *Where the Law Ends: The Social Control of Corporate Behavior.* New York: Harper & Row.

Strobel, Lee P. 1980. *Reckless Homicide? Ford's Pinto Trial.* South Bend, IN: And Books.

Sudnow, David. 1965. Normal crimes: Sociological features of the penal code in a public defender's office. *Social Problems* 12:255–276.

Sutherland, Edwin H. 1939. *Principles of Criminology,* 4th ed. Philadelphia: Lippincott.

———. 1949. *White Collar Crime.* New York: Dryden.

Sutherland, Edwin H., and Donald R. Cressey. 1974. *Criminology,* 9th ed. Philadelphia: Lippincott.

Swigert, Victoria L., and Ronald A. Farrell. 1980–81. Corporate homicide: Definitional processes in the creation of deviance. *Law and Society Review* 15: 161–182.

Tapp, June L., and Lawrence Kohlberg. 1977. Developing senses of law and legal justice. Pp. 89–105 in *Law, Justice, and the Individual in Society,* ed. F. J. Levine and J. L. Tapp. New York: Holt, Rinehart & Winston.

Thibaut, John, and Laurens Walker. 1975. *Procedural Justice.* Hillsdale, NJ: Erlbaum.

Tittle, Charles R. 1980. Labelling and crime: An empirical evaluation. In *The Labelling of Deviance: Evaluating a Perspective,* ed. W. R. Gove. Beverly Hills: Sage.

Turk, Austin T. 1991. Katz on magical meanness and other distractions. *Law and Social Inquiry* 16: 181–194.

Tyler, Tom R. 1990. *Why People Obey the Law.* New Haven, CT: Yale University Press.

Vold, George B. 1979. *Theoretical Criminology,* 2nd ed. New York: Oxford University Press.

Walster, Elaine, G. William Walster, and Ellen Berscheid. 1978. *Equity: Theory and Research.* Boston: Allyn and Bacon.

CHAPTER 21

Social Psychology and Health

RONALD C. KESSLER
JAMES S. HOUSE
RENEE R. ANSPACH
DAVID R. WILLIAMS

Until the early part of the twentieth century, biomedical researchers attended nearly exclusively to organic pathogens and assumed that: (1) disease is a deviation from normal biological functions; (2) diseases are generic and invariant over time and space; (3) medicine is a scientifically neutral profession uninfluenced by wider social, cultural, and political forces; and (4) each disease has a specific biological cause (Mischler 1981). This last assumption, known as the "doctrine of specific etiology," implied that a disease is best controlled by treating the culpable biological agent. The elimination of polio via vaccination during the 1950s dramatically epitomized the successful application of this model.

Despite such successes, some contemporary critics argued that disease is often a normal biological response to abnormal environmental demands rather than a biological deviation, and that health varies over time as a function of changing environmental demands (Dubos 1959). Such notions construed health as a state of adaptation between the individual and his/her environment. These ideas have deep historical roots. They inspired the public health movement of the midnineteenth century to emphasize the importance of a benign physical environment for health. In the early twentieth century, as public health advances led to a shift in the major causes of death from acute infectious diseases to chronic diseases, these ideas were broadened to emphasize the importance of not only the physical environment (e.g., clean air, water, food, and sanitation) but also the psychosocial environment (e.g., smoking, lack of exercise, and stress).

The importance of psychosocial influences on health is now a major concern of biomedical science and also a major focus of social psychological research. This convergence has led to a new perspective on health which assumes that: (1) illness has multiple determinants, both biomedical and psychosocial; (2) what is seen as a disease is not invariant over time but changes based on sociocultural and biological definitions; and (3) the medical profession is a social institution that shapes its members' views based on broad sociocultural considerations that go beyond scientific concerns.

It is impossible to encompass in a single chapter the full range of research that has evolved from this perspective; our review is necessarily selective. In the first half of the chapter, we discuss research on the psychosocial determinants of illness, and in the second half we discuss research on the psychosocial determinants of illness definition and response. In each section we present an historical overview, discuss recent developments, and propose future directions.

PSYCHOSOCIAL DETERMINANTS OF ILLNESS

Although the organism-environment adaptation perspective operates at both microscopic and macroscopic levels, the two sometimes have been estranged by disciplinary boundaries. The more microscopic perspective, characteristic of psychophysiologists and psychological social psychologists, has focused on how proximal environmental stimuli and contexts (e.g., stress and social support) affect individuals' behavior, mood, and physiology. The more macroscopic approach, characteristic of many sociologists, demographers, epidemiologists, and sociological social psychologists, has focused on the broader distribution of health and illness in populations by such characteristics as age, race, gender, and geographic location. This macroscopic approach also considers historical and contextual influences on health, providing insights not apparent from an individual perspective. The decline in smoking in the United States is a good illustration. The long-term effects of smoking intervention programs at the individual level have been modest. Yet smoking has declined markedly and steadily in the United States over the past quarter century due to broader contextual changes—restriction of smoking in public places, increases in costs, and a changing set of societal norms, attitudes, and values regarding smoking induced by political and mass media institutions working through intermediate levels of social organization. An important direction for future development would integrate the more microscopic and macroscopic traditions in an effort to illuminate how stress and adaptation are structured by broad social forces and how microsocial phenomena affect psychophysiological processes to produce observed patterns of health and illness.

Emergence of the Stress and Adaptation Perspective

During the middle of the twentieth century, physiologists Walter Cannon (1932) and Hans Selye (1956) described a syndrome of physiological responses (including adrenocortical secretions and related neuroendocrine activation, increased gastric secretions, and higher heart rate and blood pressure) to a wide range of environmental stressors or challenges, including infectious agents, heat, cold, physical pressure and restraint, and social psychological threat. Selye called this syndrome the "general adaptation syndrome" (GAS).

According to Selye, GAS originally evolved as an adaptive response to physical stressors but has become maladaptive in modern society, where many stressors are chronic and inescapable. In the face of these modern stresses, GAS can lead to what Selye called "diseases of adaptation," such as hypertension, heart disease, ulcers, and arthritis.

Although Selye's model provides a useful framework for understanding how psychosocial stresses promote physical illness, it does not explain how the subjective sense of stress itself is generated. Subsequently, social psychologists developed the framework known as the stress and adaptation model. This framework suggests that characteristics of situations and individuals combine to create perceptions of stress or threat, which ideally elicit responses that reduce stress and protect health. Failure to do so results in ill health via mechanisms such as those originally explored by Cannon and Selye or those identified by more contemporary biopsychosocial researchers. Whether situations are experienced as stressful and how persons respond to them is now seen as a function of both preexisting personal dispositions and other aspects of the situation, sometimes referred to as moderating, buffering, or vulnerability factors (see House 1981; Lazarus and Folkman 1984; McGrath 1970; for variations on this framework).

Since the mid-1970s, the stress and adaptation framework has stimulated major developments in the study of the perception of and response to potentially stressful situations in social psychology and related areas of medical sociology and health psychology. The evidence linking stress and other psychosocial factors to health is growing steadily and, although as of yet not definitive, is made quite plausible by the convergences of both laboratory studies of animals and humans and nonexperimental research on broader human populations, recently augmented by intervention studies.

The initial breakthroughs in research on psychosocial determinants of illness occurred as the psychosocial stress and adaptation perspective was just emerging. Initiated by physicians rather than social scientists, such work has been superseded by more psychosocially sophisticated and empirically accurate formulations. However, these initial research programs played a critical role in establishing that psychosocial factors are important in the etiology of morbidity and mortality and have stimulated important continuing developments in psychosocial research.

Psychosomatic Medicine

Heavily influenced by the biomedical model, one approach to studying psychosocial factors in health has been to focus on a specific disease and identify putatively distinctive psychosocial characteristics of individuals with the disease. The earliest systematic efforts of this type were made under the rubric of "psychosomatic medicine," which initially involved the extension of psychoanalytic theory and methods to problems of physical illness. Franz Alexander (1950), an early leader in this field, expounded a psychosocial doctrine of specific etiology:

> There is much evidence that just as certain pathological microorganisms have a specific affinity for certain organs, so also certain emotional conflicts possess specificities and accordingly tend to afflict certain internal organs (p. 47).

Subsequent work related personality attributes to specific illnesses. Suppressed aggression, for example, was hypothesized to cause cardiovascular disease, while dependency conflicts were implicated in an ulcer-prone personality. This tradition has continued in efforts to identify personality traits and syndromes causally associated with diseases as diverse as cancer (Levy and Heiden 1990), arthritis (Anderson 1985), diabetes (Ohwovoriole and Omololu 1986), and heart disease (Friedman 1990; Friedman and Booth-Kewley 1987).

Such research has suffered, however, from multiple methodological problems. Studies are mostly cross-sectional or retrospective, rather than prospective in design. Samples are often unrepresentative and analyses often fail to control adequately for exogenous third variables, which may spuriously produce associations between disease and personality. Thus it is difficult to interpret the associations reported in this literature in a way that rigorously evaluates the influence of personality on disease (Anderson 1985; Ohwovoriole and Omololu 1986).

The psychosomatic research has also been flawed theoretically. Generally, a given personality variable has been studied in relation to only a single disease, thus making it impossible to know whether that variable may have similar associations with other diseases. A doctrine of specific etiology has often been assumed rather than empirically demonstrated. Recent careful reviews of the literature on personality and multiple disease outcomes, in fact, demonstrate that most "personality" variables that show associations with one disease show similar associations with other diseases. For example, meta-analyses by Howard Friedman and Stephanie Booth-Kewley (1987) found that anxiety and depression are associated with coronary heart disease (CHD), asthma, arthritis, ulcers, and headaches, while a complex of variables indicating anger/hostility/aggression is associated with CHD, asthma, and arthritis, though probably not ulcers and headaches. Thus, they argue that a generally "disease-prone personality" syndrome or set of traits is more likely to exist than distinctive "arthritis-prone," "ulcer-prone," and so on personalities. We return to more contemporary research on personality below.

Type A or Coronary-Prone Behavior Pattern

Research initiated by Meyer Friedman and Ray Rosenman (1974) on what they termed the "coronary-prone behavior pattern" or "coronary-prone personality" played an even more central role in the emergence of psychosocial theory and research on the etiology and epidemiology of physical health and illness. At the same time, this research illustrates the problems posed by the doctrine of specific etiology. Friedman and Rosenman were practicing cardiologists who believed they saw characteristic patterns of behavior in many of their patients. They termed this the "type A" or coronary-prone behavior pattern, which they conceived as the result of an interaction between personality dispositions and challenging situations leading to high degrees of competitiveness, job involvement, time urgency, and hostility. Type A, assessed first via clinical interviews and later via questionnaire methods, predicted both the onset and course of coronary heart disease in several major prospective studies, leading the Review Panel on Coronary-Prone Behavior and Heart Disease of the National Heart, Lung and Blood Institute (1981) to certify the type A personality as a risk factor for coronary heart disease, in the same general class as smoking, cholesterol, and blood pressure.

Further research, however, has confused the initial understanding of type A personality and its relation to CHD. In recent studies of high-risk populations, type A has failed to predict CHD, perhaps because the controlling type A style predisposes one to adapt health-promoting behaviors widely publicized in the 1980s. Other research suggests that the effects of type A may be due to correlates (e.g., mistrust) or components (hostility and anger) (Matthews 1985). Finally, more recent research suggests that as with other putatively disease-specific personality variables or behavior patterns, type A personality is associated with a range of health problems and diseases other than CHD. As research and theory turn increasingly from seeking the psychosocial causes of CHD to understanding how psychosocial characteristics of persons and situations affect the full domains of health and illness, the type A construct may become obsolete, leaving as a legacy the certainty that psychosocial variables, including a number of key personality and situational correlates and components of type A, are significant risk factors for a range of physical and psychological disorders.

Life Events and Change

Drawing somewhat loosely on the ideas of Selye and Cannon and a variety of research indicating that major life changes could be stressful and pathogenic, Holmes and Rahe (1967) hypothesized that change, whether for better or worse, requires adaptation, and that high levels of adaptive effort could produce both physical and psychological disorder. They constructed a Social Readjustment Rating Scale, which asked individuals to indicate whether they had experienced each of forty-three life changes in the preceding year and assigned to each the average rating of the amount of adjustment involved in a model by a panel of individuals of varied social backgrounds. The summed total of adjustment units for an individual has been repeatedly found to predict the onset of a wide range of physical and psychological disorders (cf. Cockerham 1986, 76–80; Mirowsky and Ross 1989).

Further research has suggested flaws in both theory and measures propounded by Holmes and Rahe (1967). Most important, subsequent research shows that it is only more serious negative events, not change per se, that adversely affect health. Further, the life change weights of Holmes and Rahe provide little more predictive power than a simple unweighted sum of the number of serious negative events, the most serious of which (e.g., widowhood, divorce, unemployment) also have been found to have separate effects on morbidity and mortality, including cancer (Sklar and Anisman 1981), heart disease (Wells 1985), and autoimmune diseases such as rheumatoid arthritis (Solomon 1981). Although research in this area is just beginning, the available evidence suggests that life events may be more important in predicting the course of illness (e.g., speed of recovery, recurrence) than initial onset (Kessler and Wortman 1988).

A New Focus on Chronic Stress

For a time, the study of life changes and events was almost synonymous with the study of stress and health. During the 1980s, however, renewed attention was focused on chronic stress and deprivation as determinants of illness (Mirowsky and Ross 1989; Pearlin 1989). These new studies suggest that it is the more enduring stressful sequelae of such events that explain their effects on health. For example, the adverse effects of unemployment on health are partly mediated by resultant financial stresses (Kessler, Turner, and House 1987), while the relationship between widowhood and health is partly due to the effects of social isolation (Umberson, Wortman, and Kessler 1992).

This renewed attention to chronic stress draws on two long-standing epidemiologic research traditions as well as on laboratory and field experiments. The first is a tradition of research on work and health that has suggested that high levels of physical and psychological demands (e.g., workload, conflict, responsibility) can adversely affect health. Early work in this tradition compared aggregate morbidity and mortality profiles of different occupations that are comparable on all known risk factors other than job stress, yielding striking evidence that indirectly implicated job stress as a powerful determinant of ill health (Kasl 1978). A more recent approach has been to use multivariate analysis to study the effects of job conditions on worker health at the individual level of analysis. The most persuasive studies of this sort have used longitudinal data to determine the effects of job conditions on changes in health over time. Several such investigations have documented significant effects of job pressures and conflicts on mortality, coronary artery disease, peptic ulcers, diabetes, and psychological distress (e.g., House and Cottington 1986; Karasek and Theorell 1990).

A second basis of the renewed interest in chronic stress is the persistence in the United States and most other developed countries of socioeconomic, racial, ethnic, and gender differences in physical and mental health, despite substantial progress in public health and the equalization of access to medical care (Cockerham 1986; Marmot, Kogevinas, and Elston 1987). Although gaps undoubtedly remain in access to quality and preventive care, and although biological factors play some role in these aggregate differences, a growing body of research suggests that differences in exposure to chronic stress as well as other psychosocial risk factors may be central as well. For example, chronic financial stress plays a significant role in explaining socioeconomic differences in health, and socioeconomic factors are central to racial differences in health (House et al. 1992).

A major methodological problem in this research is that measures of chronic stress, which are typically based on self-reports, may be affected by acute and chronic life conditions and thereby confounded with current levels of health. Resolution of this methodological problem will require prospective studies that measure perceived levels of chronic stress at several points in time and use these reports to predict subsequent morbidity and mortality, controlling for health level at the time of the measurement of stress. In one effort of this type, House et al. (1986) found that men who reported high levels of chronic occupational stress at two points in time separated by more than two years were three times more likely to die over the succeeding decade than men who reported lower levels of job stress at either or both times, after adjustment for age, education, a variety of health indicators (e.g., blood pressure and cholesterol), and health risk (e.g., smoking) at the initial point of measurement. Similar research is needed on the effects of financial, marital, parental, and other chronic stresses.

Until such research is done, experimental studies on animals and humans will continue to provide the most powerful evidence concerning the effects of chronic stress on ill health. Several laboratory experiments and quasi-experimental studies have exposed humans to mild stress (e.g., demanding levels of workload, responsibility, or conflict with others) and have shown effects on a wide range of physiologic outcomes, including cardiovascular functioning (Manuck et al. 1989), neuroendocrine functioning (Krantz and Manuck 1984), and cellular immune response (Cohen, Tyrell, and Smith 1991). Although the stressors used are, for obvious ethical reasons, too mild to cause serious or prolonged health impairments, their effects recall the more marked manifestations of naturally occurring life crises. Animal experiments confirm data on human subjects regarding the pernicious physiological effect of stress, with recent studies documenting that long-term exposure of mice and monkeys to threatening social situations leads to impaired immune response to a variety of infections (Cohen et al. 1992).

In 1960, Jackson et al. demonstrated experimentally that people with chronic role-related stresses are more likely than others to develop upper respiratory infection when randomly exposed to a nasal spray containing viral material rather than a neutral solution. Although these studies documented effects of stress on resistance to infection through various aspects of immune function, it is unclear whether these effects are clinically significant. Further, as noted by Cohen and Williamson (1991) in a comprehensive review of this literature, the few studies that directly document that stress is associated with infectious illness fail to control for the confounding effects of differential exposure or health behaviors. A series of recent studies by Cohen et al. (1991) resolved many of these methodological problems by exposing a sample of healthy volunteers via nasal drops to either a low dose of one of five respiratory viruses or to a neutral saline solution and then quarantining the subjects for a full week after exposure to monitor and control their subsequent environmental experiences and behaviors during the period of potential infectivity. Results showed clearly that measures of negative life events, perceived stress, and negative affect assessed prior to the challenge significantly increased risk of developing a cold, controlling for a wide range of potential confounding variables (including prechallenge antibodies). Interestingly, the pathways of these effects differed across the three stress measures, with perceived stress and affectivity increasing risk of infection (i.e., the development of antibodies) and exposure to life events increasing risk of clinical symptoms once infected.

Vulnerability Factors

A consistent finding across all the areas of investigation reviewed above is that the majority of people who are exposed to all but the most extreme stressful life experiences do not develop serious health problems. Current research on stress and health tries to explain this finding and, more generally, the variation in stress reactivity. The factors that have been examined include biogenic constitution, various aspects of personality, intellectual capabilities such as cognitive flexibility and effective

problem-solving skills, interpersonal skills such as social competence and communication ability, and social resources, including financial assets and coping styles. Because full consideration of this diverse array of studies is beyond the scope of this chapter, we focus on two classes of variables that have generated intense interest over the past decade: social relationships and support and dispositional/personality variables, especially what has variously been termed "control," "efficacy," or "mastery."

Social Relationships and Support.   Current interest in the effects of social relationships and support on health was triggered by several influential papers published in the mid-1970s that reviewed diverse studies demonstrating that such things as marital status, geographic stability, and social integration are associated with both mental and physical health (Caplan 1974; Cassel 1976; Cobb 1976). A theme present in all these associations seemed to be access to social ties and supports. Here, as in the case of stress, the available evidence has come from experimental studies of animals and humans, as well as from nonexperimental studies of human populations.

The presence of a familiar member of the same species buffered the impact of experimentally induced stress on ulcers, hypertension, and neurosis in rats, mice, and goats, respectively (Cassel 1976). The presence of familiar others also reduced physiological arousal (e.g., secretion of free fatty acids) in humans in potentially stressful laboratory situations (Back and Bodgonoff 1967). Such effects may even operate across species, with affectionate petting by humans reducing the cardiovascular sequelae of stressful situations among dogs, cats, horses, and rabbits (Lynch 1979, 163–80) and even the arteriosclerotic impact of a high-fat diet on rabbits (Nerem, Levesque, and Cornhill 1980).

Nonexperimental studies of human populations have devised scales to measure social integration and support and demonstrated that these measures are associated with health. The most influential of these studies examined the effects of social relationships on subsequent mortality in prospective surveys of the general population. The first study of this sort showed that marriage, contact with family and friends, church membership, and affiliation with other social groups were all associated with reduced mortality risk over a nine-year follow-up period in a large sample of respondents living in Alameda County, California (Berkman and Syme 1979). Subsequent reports by Blazer (1982) and House, Robbins, and Metzner (1982) showed similar patterns in other longitudinal community surveys in the United States, since replicated in a number of European studies (see House, Landis, and Umberson 1988 for a review). All of these reports were based on secondary analyses and none contained a comprehensive set of social support measures. Therefore, though they provide strong evidence that social relationships increase longevity, they do not allow an estimate of the full extent of this influence or an understanding of the precise components of relationships, supportive or otherwise, that are involved.

Similar longitudinal studies have examined the association between support and onset of physical illness. The most rigorous of these have focused on coronary artery disease and are reviewed by Berkman (1985). Despite broad consistency in finding some indicator of social relationships or support associated with decreased morbidity risk, there are inconsistencies. For example, social ties are associated with disease incidence but not prevalence in some studies, while in others the only significant predictors are associated with prevalence. The effects are limited to lower-class women in one major study and appear only among men in another. The aspects of social relationships that seem to promote health vary across studies as well. Inconsistent findings of this sort further obscure the mechanisms involved in the effects of support.

While research on social relationships and physical health has focused primarily on direct effects, research on social relationships and mental health has been more concerned with stress-buffering effects. In an influential research program, for example, Brown and Harris (1978) showed that the impact of stressful life events on depression was substantially reduced among respondents who had an intimate confiding relationship with a friend or relative. While nearly 40 percent of the stressed women studied without a confidant became depressed, only 4 percent of those with a confidant did so. This paradigm has subsequently been replicated in many studies, and the general pattern of results clearly shows that access to a confidant and perceived availability of crisis support are associated with a reduced impact of stressful life events on depression and anxiety (Cohen and Wills 1985; Kessler and McLeod 1985).

Another line of investigation has used measures of social relationships and support to predict adjustment to specific life crises, such as widowhood (e.g., Umberson, Wortman, and Kessler 1992) and unemployment (e.g., Kessler, Turner, and House 1987). Almost all of these studies have been concerned with mental health outcomes, and most have found that measures of social relationships obtained shortly before or after a crisis are significant predictors of subsequent emotional adjustment. Moreover, these focused studies begin to suggest that specific kinds of supportive ties may be most helpful for particular problems. For example, Hirsch (1979) showed that low-density networks that facilitate contact with new people are particularly useful when the coping task is to obtain new information or adopt a new role. Interventions aimed at providing coping skills and support have been shown to reduce adverse health consequences of unemployment (Price, van Ryn, and Vinokur 1992) and widowhood (Raphael 1977).

Studies of specific life events or crises also provide an opportunity to examine social support processes in relation to other determinants of adjustment, such as appraisals and coping strategies, and in this way clarify the mechanisms through which support may protect against illness. Life crisis studies conducted to date have not fully realized this potential but have provided two very provocative and consistent results. One of these involves miscarried support efforts, and the other involves the distinction between perceived support and received support.

The first of the two results is based on focused examinations of exactly what supporters do and what support recipients think about these efforts. Such studies show that while support can promote adjustment to stress, well-intentioned support efforts can also have unintended negative consequences, such as making recipients feel incompetent (Coyne, Wortman, and Lehman 1988). Supportive actions can also create social costs that at times can lead to greater emotional distress than if support had not been obtained at all (Lieberman 1986). Evidence of this sort has led to a heightened interest in detailed descriptive work on the dynamics of actual support transactions, both as an aid in developing theory and as a practical guide to developing support interventions (Sandler et al. 1988).

This evidence on the mixed effects of actual support transactions has led to another important finding: while the perception that support is available is associated with good emotional adjustment to stress, there is little evidence that this association is mediated by the actual receipt of support. One possible interpretation of this finding is that the perception of support availability itself actively promotes adjustment to stress over and above any actual receipt of support. This could occur in any of several ways. The perception of support availability might lead to an appraisal of stressful situations as less threatening, thereby decreasing their psychological effects (Wethington and Kessler 1986). Alternatively, it could provide a psychological "safety net" that helps motivate self-reliant coping efforts (Rook 1990). The putative effects of perceived support on health may actually be due to some unmeasured common cause; for example, socially competent people may be more able to attract support and to manage stressful situations (Heller and Swindle 1983). Ongoing research is attempting to evaluate each of these possibilities (Cohen, Sherrod, and Clark 1986; Sarason, Pierce, and Sarason 1990).

Personality.   Although the early search for personality traits uniquely associated with particular illnesses proved fruitless, more sophisticated current research has focused on personality dispositions that can affect a broad range of health problems, either directly or as vulnerability factors. This new approach to the investigation of personality effects on health has gained momentum only in the 1980s and is therefore less well-developed than research on social relationships and support. In particular, there are few good prospective data on personality and health nor have the causal pathways linking personality to health been investigated in great detail. Only a few studies of personality and health have gone beyond main effects analyses to examine whether there are interactions between personality and stress in predicting ill health.

Most studies that have examined stress-buffering effects of personality are either studies of mental illness or laboratory studies of stress and infectious disease. The former have documented the stress-buffering effects of self-esteem, perceived control, and hardiness and the stress-exacerbating effects of neuroticism and interpersonal dependency (Pearlin et al. 1981; Cohen and Edwards 1989). The latter have shown that introversion, social skills, and negative affectivity all modify the effects of mild stress on infection (Cohen and Williamson 1991).

One of the most intriguing areas of investigation in this literature concerns a personality disposition variously termed self-efficacy, mastery, or control. Sutton and Kahn (1984) reviewed a variety of laboratory and field studies on this concept and found consistent evidence suggesting that individuals who have a greater chance to predict, understand, and control events in their lives experience less stress and fewer adverse effects of stress on their physical and mental health. In a related research program, Karasek and Theorell (1990) have shown that lack of control over one's work environment is a risk factor for cardiovascular disease and psychological distress, both directly and through a tendency to exacerbate the deleterious effects of other occupational stresses. Pearlin and colleagues (1981) have shown that a sense of mastery promotes mental health and buffers the impact of acute and chronic stress on mental health. A major program of research by Rodin (1986) and others has demonstrated that increased control over one's social environment can promote better physical and mental health, and even longer life, perhaps especially for older persons. Langer and Rodin (1976) designed an inexpensive set of structural interventions in nursing homes to create opportunities for mastery experiences. Markedly positive effects on psychological well-being, physical health, and even the longevity of nursing home residents were documented.

Finally, research on cancer and personality suggests that feelings of helplessness and hopelessness, as well as repression or denial of emotions, may both predispose people to the onset of cancer and exacerbate its course (Levy and Heiden 1990). Here animal studies yield especially dramatic results. Animals induced to become helpless through behavioral restraint and repeated exposure to stress (e.g., electric shocks) have lower rates of tumor rejection, earlier appearance of tumors, and faster tumor growth than control animals exposed to implanted tumors (e.g., Shavit et al. 1984; Visintainer, Volpicelli, and Seligman 1982). Although there are obviously no analogous experimental human studies, several prospective studies have consistently supported the hypothesis. A study of Veterans Administration patients found clear evidence of greater repression of negative affectivity on the MMPI among men who subsequently developed cancer (Dattore, Shontz, and Coyne 1980), and a prospective community study in Yugoslavia over ten years reported similar results (Grossarth-Maticek 1980). A prospective study by Greer, et al. (1985), subsequently replicated, found that helplessness/hopelessness is also associated with poor prognosis in cancer patients after controlling for objective predictors.

These epidemiologic studies provide scant information on the mechanisms involved in the effect of personality on onset and course of cancer. According to the most widely endorsed hypothesis, a sense of efficacy and control affects the immune system, which, in turn, affects host resistance to malignant transformation of cells. This hypothesis is consistent with both the broader literature on personality and immunity (Jemmott and Locke 1984) and an observed association between personality and immune competence among cancer patients (Levy et al. 1985). However, it is impossible to preclude the possibility that the association is due to an effect of illness severity on personality. Further research is needed to determine whether baseline measures of personality among cancer patients predict changes in immune function.

Another area for future research involves investigation of the structural determinants of health-related personality dispositions (Kohn et al. 1983). In one of the few studies to examine this issue, Harburg, et al. (1973) found that suppressed hostility was significantly increased in high-stress residential neighborhoods versus low-stress areas. More research of a similar sort is needed to identify the structural causes of personality and to specify the mediating effects of personality on the relationships of these structural variables to ill health. In addition, research is needed to determine whether the effects of personality on health vary depending on structural contexts. In one of the rare studies to investigate this issue, James et al. (1987) found that an active predisposition to master stress was associated with increased risk of high blood pressure among low socioeconomic status African Americans but not among either whites or higher socioeconimic status African Americans, presumably reflecting the fact that social circumstances make it unlikely that active mastery will effectively reduce stress in the face of the environmental barriers that face lower socioeconomic status African Americans. More research is needed to investigate other interactions between personality dispositions and environmental conditions.

Psychosocial Determinants of Illness: Overview

The past several decades of research and theorizing have clearly established the role of psychosocial factors in the etiology of illness. The major focus and contribution of this work has been to establish a theoretical rationale and empirical evidence for a number of psychosocial factors as consequential health risk factors: (1) major negative life events; (2) chronic stress; (3) lack of social relationships and supports; (4) lack of sense of control, efficacy, or mastery over one's work and life; and (5) high levels of hostility and/or mistrust in interpersonal relations. This research also shows that psychological distress (e.g., anxiety and depression) is both a consequence of these risk factors and itself a risk factor for physical morbidity and mortality.

Research and theoretical development are still needed. First, there is need for more prospective and longitudinal research to increase our certainty about causal relationships. Second, there is a continuing need for research to specify what aspects of the broad psychosocial risk factors are most consequential for health, and through what psychophysiological mechanisms these effects are produced. For example, we have learned that it is only major negative life events which are most deleterious for health, but we are only beginning to understand precisely what it is about those events that is deleterious and through what pathways they affect chronic and infectious disease. We know that lack of social relationships is a risk factor for mortality, arguably of a magnitude comparable to cigarette smoking, but we are only beginning to understand what it is about social relationships that is protective of health and through what mechanisms it produces such effects.

Sociological social psychologists have recently emphasized the need for theory and research to focus more on the interrelations among these various psychosocial risk factors and how they are shaped by a broader social structural context in which people are stratified along lines of race/ethnicity, gender, and socioeconomic status (Aneshensel 1992; Pearlin 1989; Williams 1990). Current research suggests that many of the persistently large differences in health by gender, race/ethnicity, and socioeconomic status can be explained by the association of these variables with the psychosocial risk factors just considered and the health-related behaviors to which we now turn (House et al. 1992; Verbrugge 1989). In quite a different vein, research

on the interplay between psychosocial and genetic factors in the etiology of health and illness is being reported just now. We return to these themes at the end of the chapter.

THE SOCIAL PSYCHOLOGY OF HEALTH BEHAVIOR AND ILLNESS BEHAVIOR

The study of health behavior and illness behavior encompasses how people perceive, define, and act toward symptoms, how they utilize medical care, how they act to promote health and produce risks, and how they adhere to medical regimens. Interest in health behavior and illness behavior grew out of a set of practical problems in medicine and public health concerning the fact that many people delay seeking medical attention, even in the face of serious and life-threatening symptoms (Leventhal, Meyer, and Nerenz 1980; Rodin 1985), while others seek medical help for complaints with no discernable organic basis (Mechanic 1992b). Furthermore, many patients refuse to do what is seemingly in their rational self-interest, continuing to smoke, drink, and overeat despite the warnings of physicians and health educators (Sackett and Haynes 1976). Finally, large numbers of patients, perhaps as many as 50 percent, fail to comply with medical advice even when this noncompliance endangers their lives (Conrad 1985; Haynes, Taylor, and Sackett 1979; Tebbi et al. 1986). These behavior patterns result in increased morbidity and mortality (Sackett and Haynes 1976), contribute to escalating medical costs (Fuchs 1974), and frustrate those who provide care (Mechanic 1992b).

These observations could not be explained using the traditional biomedical model and led health researchers to distinguish analytically between two orders of phenomena: disease—an organic and biological process; and illness—a psychological, social, and cultural process that includes symptom recognition, decision making, and utilization. It was argued that illness could not be reduced to disease (e.g., Barondess 1979; L. Eisenberg and Kleinman 1981). While early work expanded the medical model to include psychosocial factors in patient behavior, the research questions remained largely medical: understanding why patients procrastinate, take risks, or fail to follow medical advice to modify these medically inappropriate behaviors (Schneider and Conrad 1983). In this framework, medical judgments about appropriate actions were the "gold standard" against which actual patient behaviors were judged and found wanting. From a social psychological standpoint, this medical orientation excluded many important empirical issues from consideration (Mechanic 1978; Zola 1972).

Increasingly aware of these limitations, a number of social psychologists carried out patient-centered analyses of health behavior and illness behavior that moved in three broad directions: (1) away from abstract models of rational choices about health care and toward understanding the logic of lay theories and representations of illness problems; (2) away from an exclusive focus on the decision to seek medical care and toward an emphasis on patterns of health and illness behavior that do not involve physicians; and (3) away from a focus on individual characteristics as determinants of health and illness behavior toward understanding how the social environment, including the healthcare system, shapes these behaviors. Several social psychological perspectives contributed to this work. After briefly reviewing these perspectives, we examine how they are reflected in empirical research on health behavior, illness behavior, and adherence to medical regimens.

Theoretical Perspectives

Culture, Social Structure, and Patient Behavior.
Social psychologists with a cultural or social structural orientation have found that social groups differ in their responses to symptoms and patterns of care seeking and have attributed these differences to cultural orientations or structural constraints. Researchers have examined ethnic differences in the response to pain and symptoms as well as ethnic, socioeconomic, and gender differences in utilization patterns. Early research in this area often used purely correlational, cross-sectional designs that postulated reasons (often cultural) for group differences, rather than demonstrating them empirically (Cockerham 1986; Mechanic 1978). More recent work has moved toward explanatory approaches, emphasizing that the structure of social and healthcare institutions, as well as the culture of care seekers, shape health and illness behavior.

Integrative Models.   Several eclectic approaches depict illness behavior as resulting from an interplay of biological, sociocultural, and psychological factors. The best-known example of this approach is Mechanic's theory of help seeking. Basing his model on a large body of theory and research, Mechanic identifies ten cognitive, social, and psychological factors that influence the decision to seek help: (1) the visibility and salience of symptoms; (2) the extent to which symptoms are perceived as serious; (3) the extent to which they disrupt social activities; (4) the frequency and persistence of symptoms; (5) the tolerance level of those who experience symptoms; (6) available information, knowledge, and cultural assumptions; (7) basic needs that lead to denial; (8) other needs that compete with illness responses; (9) competing interpretations that can be assigned to symptoms; and (10) the available resources, physical proximity of care, and costs of taking action (Mechanic 1978). The strength of this approach is its effort to develop a comprehensive, biopsychosocial approach to care seeking. However, as Mechanic himself acknowledges, the model is physician-centered, focusing on the decision to seek conventional medical care (Schneider and Conrad 1983), though it could be broadened to include other sources of care.

Cognitive Models of Decision Making.   Social psychologists have examined the cognitive processes at work in decisions to take preventive action, to seek help, and to follow medical advice. Until recently, most psychologists employed one of a number of rational choice models that assume that people make health behavior choices on the basis of cost-benefit ratios. Perhaps the best-known rational choice theory is the health belief model. According to this model, people decide to take preventive action or follow medical advice on the basis of their subjective beliefs about the severity of the illness, their susceptibility or risk of becoming ill, and the costs, benefits, and barriers to taking action (e.g., Becker and Maiman 1975; Hochbaum 1958; Rosenstock and Kirscht 1979).

This model has been criticized for giving insufficient attention to the role of cultural values, tradition, and emotion in decision making, failing to consider cognitive and organizational limitations on information processing that lead people to simplify the decision-making process, and equating rational choices with those that conform to the standards of Western medicine (Garro 1985; Good 1985; Tversky and Kahneman 1974). In short, critics argue that this model, like other rational choice theories, provides a prescriptive, idealized view of how decisions should be made rather than an adequate description of how decisions actually are made.

More recent approaches consider the role of emotion in health decisions. Janis and Mann (1977), for example, propose that optimal decision making occurs when people engage in "vigilant information processing," which can occur only when they are aware of the risks attached to each choice, have hope of finding an alternative, and believe they have enough time to deliberate. However, because of the anxiety-provoking nature of health decisions, people often resort to one of several defective coping strategies, including unconflicted adherence to their present course of action, defensive avoidance (procrastination), or hypervigilance (panic).

Other health psychologists have focused on the role of cognitive schemas in making sense of symptoms and deciding what to do about them. People who experience bodily changes make sense of them by means of common-sense illness representations stored in memory and include attributions about the identity, causes, consequences, time course, and potential for cure (Leventhal, Zimmerman, and Gutmann 1984). Cognitive models of symptom processing depict the patient as an active processor of information and emphasize the patient's perspective. However, this approach maintains a medical orientation by emphasizing flaws in information processing, stressing the need to modify common-sense representations to bring them

into line with medical ones, and neglecting environmental and structural factors.

Phenomenological Analyses of Decision Making. Phenomenological approaches, developed in anthropology and social psychology, provide the most patient-centered perspectives on health behavior and illness behavior. These perspectives consider patterns of care outside the professional sector and attempt to discover the logic of patient decisions rather than analyzing them in terms of models the researcher formulates a priori. These models include everyday ideas about the etiology, anticipated course, and consequences of a particular illness. Explanatory model research has gone beyond cognitive approaches to explore how models of doctors and patients collide in medical encounters, how explanatory models relate to broader cultural themes, and how they assume different forms in different cultural contexts (Kleinman 1980).

Other cognitive anthropologists have developed formal models of decision making in which the researcher elicits from patients their actual considerations in making medical decisions, develops a formal model of the criteria used in health decisions, and tests the model's validity by comparing it to the actual decisions of community members (Garro 1985). Sociologists have developed a phenomenological approach to the experience of illness that examines how patients notice something is wrong, develop lay theories and explanations, decide to seek help, manage relationships with significant others and health professionals, and cope with the stigma attached to their illness. Researchers emphasize the importance of studying nonhospitalized patients and examining self-medication practices that do not involve professionals (Schneider and Conrad 1983).

Empirical Applications

Health Behavior. Health behavior refers to the actions of well people that have consequences for their future health, such as smoking, diet, exercise, and substance abuse (Mechanic 1990). A number of programs have been developed to change health behaviors. Most are based on psychological models of behavior change and, with a few notable exceptions, have generally not succeeded in effecting lasting changes in health behavior (Mechanic 1990, 1992a). In fact, a review of the long-term outcomes of many programs shows that as many as three of every four people who successfully change risk behaviors are unable to sustain these changes for as long as one year (Brownell et al. 1986).

Critics have attributed these failures to the inaccurate assumptions of some psychological models of health behaviors and have proposed new ideas about ways to modify interventions. Findings concerning the importance of cognitive representations, for example, have led to the suggestion that future interventions identify and alter participants' representations of risk, provide them with self-regulation skills, and encourage them to perceive that they can effect change (Leventhal, Zimmerman, and Gutmann 1984). Other health psychologists have called for programs that enhance perceptions of control. This recommendation is based on research showing that participants in weight reduction programs are more likely to succeed when they attribute change to their own efforts (Rodin 1985). Conversely, participants are less likely to relapse permanently when they attribute lapses to situational causes (Marlatt and Gordon 1985).

Some sociological social psychologists have also suggested that traditional interventions fail because they treat health behavior as an individual rather than a social phenomenon (Mechanic 1990; Syme and Alcalay 1982). In particular, health behaviors may have other meanings that interfere with behavior change (Mechanic 1990). Smoking, for example, can be a mark of status and a symbol of defiance in adolescent culture (Jessor, Donovan, and Costa 1990; Osgood et al. 1988; Rodin 1985). Successful interventions to modify health behaviors need to consider such symbolic meanings. This can be done by providing the individual with resources to resist interpersonal pressures. An example is Michelson's (1986) Social Skills Training Program, a wide-ranging program that teaches adolescents to evaluate health behavior options

and to resist interpersonal pressures to engage in risk behaviors. Alternately, one may attempt to change the cultural meanings of health behaviors. One of the most successful examples of this approach is the antismoking movement in the United States, a movement that changed the symbolic value of smoking in the middle class (Mechanic 1990; Syme and Alcalay 1982) and resulted in a substantial long-term reduction in smoking (Warner 1977).

The importance of facilitating social and structural conditions is not limited to symbolic meanings. It is also important to consider the functions of health behaviors in the lives of the people whose behaviors we seek to change. Alcohol and tobacco, for example, appear to be used as coping resources by many people. This raises the question of whether interventions to change the structural conditions that lead to chronic stress make more sense than interventions aimed at removing the coping resources used by people to manage chronic stress. Furthermore, if interventions do attempt to remove these coping resources there is a need to provide alternate resources. See House and Cottington (1986) and Williams (1990) for a discussion. A similar question can be raised about the logic of attempting to change individual health behavior when powerful economic interests continue to promote risk taking (McKinlay 1990; Syme and Alcalay 1982). It is noteworthy in this regard that state licensing boards permit more retail outlets for the sale of alcohol in poor and African American neighborhoods than in more affluent areas (Rabow and Watts 1982). Furthermore, more than 70 percent of billboards in the United States that advertise tobacco and alcohol are targeted to African Americans (Hacker, Collins, and Jacobson 1987). It is difficult to avoid the conclusion, based on these results, that there are systematic structural forces at work that impede individual efforts to reduce the problems of substance use among disadvantaged sectors of American society. Based on this conclusion, there is a growing belief that structural change is needed to guarantee the success of widespread health behavior change (McKinlay 1990).

Illness Behavior.   Illness behavior refers to the ways people define and respond to bodily sensations and experiences that might be seen as signs or symptoms of illness, both before seeking treatment and in response to the recommendations of healers (Mechanic 1986). Important social psychological issues in the study of illness behavior include determinants of initial symptom recognition, factors that influence how symptoms are interpreted once recognized, and social and individual variables that influence willingness to adopt the sick role. Variations in these ways of responding can have dramatic effects on the social impairment associated with illness.

Research on illness behavior shows that there are substantial individual differences in predispositions to monitor bodily sensations and that cultural and social experiences play an important part in creating these dispositions (Hansell and Mechanic 1986). For example, early research discovered that ethnic groups differ dramatically in their responses to symptoms and perceptions of pain (Sternbach and Tursky 1965; Zborowski 1952; Zola 1966). An especially intriguing result is that women generally seem more sensitive than men to bodily symptoms and are therefore more likely to recognize and seek help for health problems (Kessler 1986). This sex difference is more pronounced at the lower end of symptom severity, suggesting that women are more likely than men to monitor subtle bodily complaints. An interesting illustration comes from the work of Davis (1981), who used radiographic examination data on osteoarthritis to study self-reported knee pain and recent doctor visits for knee pain. These data documented that women with objective evidence of osteoarthritis were nearly twice as likely as comparable men to report recent doctor visits for this problem.

Research on symptom sensitivity has explored the ways cognitive schemas are used to make sense of bodily sensations and define them in illness terms. Research also has shown that most people arrive at a definition of their bodily changes as due to illness only after concerted efforts to normalize, neutralize, or minimize the significance of their symptoms, a practice that may account for common delays in seeking help (e.g., Davis 1971; Mechanic 1972; Schneider and Conrad 1983). These interpretations often involve the use of social networks. Parents, spouses, friends, and even physicians often collaborate in the normalization process (Davis 1971; Schneider and Conrad 1983).

The literature on illness representations documents many dramatic cases that illustrate this process. For example, people who are alone when they first experience a mild heart attack commonly delay calling an ambulance due to uncertainty about what has happened to them. Instead, before calling an ambulance they will call a friend or relative, describe the symptoms, and ask whether the other person thinks it was really a heart attack. This delay is associated with a dramatically increased risk of long-term cardiac damage (Alonzo 1986).

Illness behavior research also has examined how groups differ in utilization patterns. Beginning with Koos's (1954) early work on socioeconomic differences in help seeking, research has documented that the poor use health services less frequently than those more favorably situated in the social structure. Although expanded public insurance coverage has dramatically decreased socioeconomic differences in overall utilization, continuing differences in utilization patterns suggest a two-class system of health care. While higher socioeconomic groups use private physicians, the poor use a public healthcare system of outpatient clinics and hospital emergency rooms (Cockerham 1986). Early cultural explanations attributed these differences to a greater tendency of poor patients to normalize or neutralize symptoms (Koos 1954) or, alternatively, to a present-oriented culture of poverty that led poor patients to eschew prevention and delay seeking help until emergencies arose (e.g., Kosa, Antonovsky, and Zola 1969). However, more recent "systems" or "culture of medicine" explanations suggest that the highly alienating, impersonal, bureaucratic atmosphere and low quality of care in the public healthcare system leads poor patients to view medical care as a measure of the last resort (e.g., Dutton 1978; Reissman 1981).

Current research has moved away from an exclusive focus on the decision to seek medical care and toward a focus on care that extends beyond conventional medicine (e.g., Garro 1985). While early studies viewed the use of alternative practitioners as a deviant pattern of utilization confined to lower socioeconomic classes or ethnic enclaves using parochial referral networks, it has become clear based on more recent studies that many patients with chronic medical problems are turning to alternative practitioners, such as chiropractors and acupuncturists, who offer hope of symptomatic relief and more personal attention (D. Eisenberg et al. 1993; Kotarba 1983).

Although most research on illness behavior continues to study patient responses from the viewpoint of the medical establishment, a growing number of studies are questioning professional definitions of illness and giving more attention to the patient viewpoint (e.g., Roth and Conrad 1987). Whereas earlier studies invidiously contrasted lay explanations with professional ones, several contemporary researchers portray both lay and medical decisions as socially constructed. These analyses suggest that professional diagnosis and treatment decisions are influenced by the cultural assumptions of providers, the perceived characteristics of patients, and the social setting in which decisions are made (Todd 1989).

Another current trend in illness behavior research is to focus on patient self-care. This research has shown that many people diagnose and treat their own symptoms (Zola 1983). Furthermore, patients who are receiving medical treatment for chronic conditions commonly search for patterns in their symptoms, make note of antecedents to flare-ups, develop and test hypotheses, and sometimes even devise strategies thought to control symptom expression (e.g., Schneider and Conrad 1983).

Treatment Adherence. Patient failure to follow medical advice is a widespread phenomenon that reduces the effectiveness of therapy (Rodin and Salovey 1989) and may significantly increase morbidity and mortality (Sackett and Haynes 1976). Buckalew and Sallis (1986) estimated that roughly

one-third of the 750 million new prescriptions written each year in the United States and the United Kingdom are not taken at all and another one-third are taken incorrectly. Nonadherence for medication and lifestyle changes recommended to treat chronic conditions is estimated at roughly 50 percent (Haynes, Taylor, and Sackett 1979). Surprisingly, these high rates exist even for those patients with life-threatening and seriously disabling conditions. For example, Tebbi et al. (1986) found that only 50 percent of adolescent cancer patients took their prescription medications as directed, while Conrad (1985) found that only 50 percent of epileptics took their medications correctly.

Determinants of adherence include a wide variety of individual and environmental factors (DiMatteo and DiNicola 1982). As in the case of illness behavior, social and symbolic meanings of medications figure importantly in adherence. Patients view medications alternatively as an indicator of the degree of their disorder, a ticket to normality that can increase self-reliance, a symbol of dependence, or a reminder of deviance and stigma. Nonadherence is powerfully affected by these meanings. For example, some epileptic patients stop taking their medication against medical advice when they view drugs as a symbol of their dependence and wish to reassert their independence or when they view drugs as a reminder of differentness and want to escape the stigmatizing connotations (Schneider and Conrad 1983).

Illness representations also have been shown to play a prominent role in adherence. Research consistently shows that there are major discrepancies between the illness representations of patients and of healthcare providers and that these differences play an important part in adherence. Leventhal et al. (1984), for example, proposed that many patients with chronic, asymptomatic illnesses fail to follow physician advice because they use an "acute disease schema" to interpret their medical problems. That is, they believe their disease to be caused by external agents that are short-term, symptomatic, and treatable by medications that remove the symptoms and cure the disease. When their experiences in treatment clash with these perceptions, they often terminate treatment. Consistent with this perspective, Meyer, Leventhal, and Gutmann (1985) found that 90 percent of hypertensive patients believed they could "feel" their blood pressure being elevated by such symptoms as headaches and face flushing. This perception led some of the patients to adjust their medications in response to these feelings, even when the adjustments defied physician instructions. It also led some to stop taking medications when feelings of high blood pressure persisted. The persistence of an acute disease schema may also explain why patients with asymptomatic, chronic illnesses often drop out of treatment. Based on findings such as these, there is much current interest in studying the distribution of illness representations (Bishop 1987) and investigating ways to modify these common-sense representations to promote adherence (Cleary 1986).

The literature on doctor-patient interactions shows clearly that it is critical for the doctor to elicit information about patient expectations and illness representations, to confront discrepancies between these cognitions, and to explain treatment recommendations in a way congruent with the patient's theories of illness. Doctors who communicate in these ways have consistently higher rates of adherence (Whitcher-Alagna 1983). Furthermore, experimental interventions based on this perspective show that adherence can be improved by physicians changing their style of interacting with patients. Inui, Yourtee, and Williamson (1976) documented that changes in physician communication style with hypertensive patients resulting from a single two-hour training session led to a 30 percent increase in effective blood pressure control among patients experimentally assigned to the trained physicians. Similar results have been reported for a number of other cognitively-based adherence interventions (Meichenbaum and Turk 1987).

Research on doctor-patient interaction also shows that other characteristics of physician communication style—quantity of information, quality of information, and willingness to let patients ask questions—importantly affect adherence (Davis 1969; Freemon et al. 1971; Roter and Hall 1989;

Svarsted 1976). Many studies demonstrate that physicians frequently fall short on all of these dimensions. There is currently a good deal of interest in the structural determinants of these aspects of physician communication behavior aimed at understanding why many doctors interact in ways that produce the very nonadherence they find so troublesome. Some researchers argue that the logic of differential diagnosis, coupled with the demands associated with rapidly processing information in bureaucratic organizations, drastically limits what doctors can accomplish in the medical interview (Cicourel 1981). Others have suggested that as health care comes to be delivered increasingly in a colleague-dependent context of referral, physicians become oriented to the wishes of colleagues rather than the wishes of their patients. Subsequently, effective doctor-patient communication is impaired (Freidson 1970). A related observation is that providers' cultural assumptions can make them less inclined to encourage active patient participation. For example, Anspach (1993) observes that many providers have a "common-sense social psychology" that underestimates patients' competence to participate in medical decisions and overestimates the likelihood of deleterious psychological consequences that can result from participating in medical decisions. Providers' cultural assumptions also include social schemata that lead professionals to underestimate the ability of lower-class Hispanic patients to participate in certain medical decisions (Anspach 1993). In short, physicians curtail patient participation, thereby discouraging adherence, less because of conscious choice than because of organizational restraints and misguided cultural assumptions.

The Social Psychology of Health Behavior and Illness Behavior: Overview

A growing body of research shows that psychosocial factors are crucial to understanding and modifying health and illness behavior. Researchers differ as to whether they examine psychosocial processes in an effort to change patient behavior in ways that will improve health outcomes or take a patient-centered approach that examines a broader set of issues concerning lay representations of health problems and other meanings of health and illness behaviors. Researchers also focus variably on processes involved in the creation of health and illness behaviors or on the impact of macrosocial contexts on these behaviors. Unlike most other areas of social psychological research, there are many opportunities here for developing and implementing large-scale interventions that can be useful both in applying social psychological knowledge and advancing the knowledge base. A challenge for the future is to integrate research on the structural determinants of health and illness behaviors with research on the mechanisms linking meaning structures to behavioral responses and to devise methods of intervening at a more structural level than we have at present.

RETROSPECT AND PROSPECT

Theory and research on social psychology and health have developed remarkably over the past few decades, contributing to a major reorientation in the way the scientific community and society think about the nature, causes, and course of illness. The social environment and its social psychological consequences have become recognized as central to understanding and improving health.

Much of this work has focused on individual-level variables. Much remains to be clarified and learned at this level of analysis. Greater emphasis on macrosocial factors is already apparent in new lines of research on the macrosocial determinants of health and illness behaviors (Anehensel 1992; Mirowsky and Ross 1989; Pearlin 1989; Williams 1990). Such new work is beginning to document systematic structural patterns of a broad array of psychosocial determinants of health and health-related behaviors and provides important avenues for intervention (House et al. 1992). No problem is more central to our well-being than health, and in no area does social psychology have greater opportunities for advancement over the coming years.

NOTE

Work on this chapter was partially supported by grants K02 MH00507 from the National Institute of Mental Health and P01 AG05561 and R29 AG07904 from the National Institute on Aging. The authors are indebted to Karen Cook, Gary Fine, Catherine Ross, and especially David Mechanic for their constructive comments on previous drafts.

REFERENCES

Alexander, Franz. 1950. *Psychosomatic Medicine; Its Principles and Applications.* New York: Norton.

Alonzo, Angelo A. 1986. The impact of the family and lay others on care-seeking during life-threatening episodes of suspected coronary artery disease. *Social Science and Medicine* 22:1297–1311.

Anderson, Karen O. 1985. Rheumatoid arthritis: Review of psychological factors related to etiology effects and treatment. *Psychological Bulletin* 98:358–387.

Aneshensel, Carol. 1992. Social stress: Theory and research. *Annual Review of Sociology* 18:15–38.

Anspach, Renee R. 1993. *Deciding Who Lives: Fateful Choices in the Intensive-Care Nursery.* Berkeley, CA: University of California Press.

Back, Kurt W., and Morton D. Bodgonoff. 1967. Buffer conditions in experimental stress. *Behavioral Science* 12:384–390.

Barondess, Jeremiah A. 1979. Disease and illness: A crucial distinction. *American Journal of Medicine* 66:375–376.

Becker, Marshall H., and Lois A. Maiman. 1975. Sociobehavioral determinants of compliance with health and medical care recommendations. *Medical Care* 13:10–24.

Berkman, Lisa F. 1985. The relationship of social networks and social support to morbidity and mortality. Pp. 241–262 in *Social Support and Health,* ed. Sheldon Cohen and Leonard Syme. New York: Academic.

Berkman, Lisa F., and S. Leonard Syme. 1979. Social networks, host resistance, and mortality: A nine-year follow-up study of Alameda county residents. *American Journal of Epidemiology* 109:186–204.

Bishop, George D. 1987. Lay conceptions of physical symptoms. *Journal of Applied Psychology* 17: 127–146.

Blazer, Dan G. 1982. Social support and mortality in an elderly community population. *American Journal of Epidemiology* 115:685–694.

Brown, George W., and Tirril O. Harris, ed. 1978. *Social Origins of Depression: A Study of Psychiatric Disorder in Women.* New York: Free Press.

Brownell, Kelly D., G. Alan Marlatt, Edward Lichtenstein, and G. Terence Wilson. 1986. Understanding and preventing relapse. *American Psychologist* 41: 765–782.

Buckalew, L. W., and R. E. Sallis. 1986. Patient compliance with medication perception. *Journal of Clinical Psychology* 42:161–167.

Cannon, Walter B. 1932. *The Wisdom of the Body.* New York: Norton.

Caplan, Gerald, ed. 1974. *Support Systems in Community Mental Health.* New York: Behavioral Publications.

Cassel, John. 1976. Contribution of the environment to host resistance. *American Journal of Epidemiology* 104:107–223.

Cicourel, Aaron V. 1981. Notes on the integration of micro and macro levels of analysis. Pp. 1–40 in *Advances in Social Theory and Methodology: Toward an Integration of Macro- and Micro-Sociologies,* ed. K. Knorr-Cetina and A. Cicourel. London: Routeledge & Kegan Paul.

Cleary, Paul D. 1986. New directions in illness behavior research. Pp. 343–354 in *Illness Behavior: A Multidisciplinary Model,* ed. S. McHugh. New York: Plenum.

Cobb, Sidney. 1976. Social support as a moderator of life stress. *Psychosomatic Medicine* 38:300–314.

Cockerham, William C. 1986. *Medical Sociology, 3rd. ed.* Englewood Cliffs, NJ: Prentice Hall.

Cohen, Sheldon, and Jeffrey R. Edwards. 1989. Personality characteristics as moderators of the relationship between stress and disorder. Pp. 235–283 in *Advances in the Investigation of Psychological Stress,* ed. R. W. J. Neufeld. New York: Wiley.

Cohen, Sheldon, Jay R. Kaplan, Joan E. Cunnick, and Stephen B. Manuck. 1992. Chronic social stress, affiliation and cellular immune response in nonhuman primates. *Psychological Science* 3:301–304.

Cohen, Sheldon, Drury R. Sherrod, and Margaret S. Clark. 1986. Social skills and the stress-protective role of social support. *Journal of Personality and Social Psychology* 50:963–973.

Cohen, Sheldon, D. A. J. Tyrell, and A. P. Smith. 1991. Psychological stress and susceptibility to the common cold. *New England Journal of Medicine* 325: 606–612.

Cohen, Sheldon, and Gail M. Williamson. 1991. Stress and infectious disease in humans. *Psychological Bulletin* 109:5–24.

Cohen, Sheldon, and Thomas A. Wills. 1985. Stress, social support, and the buffering hypothesis. *Psychological Bulletin* 98:310–357.

Conrad, Peter. 1985. The meaning of medications: Another look at compliance. *Social Science Medicine* 20:29–37.

Coyne, James, Camille B. Wortman, and Darrin Lehman. 1988. The other side of support: Emotional over-involvement and miscarried helping. Pp. 305–330 in *Marshalling Social Support,* ed. B. H. Gottlieb. Beverly Hills: Sage.

Dattore, Patrick J., Franklin C. Shontz, and Lolafaye Coyne. 1980. Premorbid personality differentiation of cancer and noncancer groups: A test of the hypothesis of cancer proneness. *Journal of Consulting Clinical Psychology* 48:388–394.

Davis, Milton. 1969. Variations in patients' compliance with doctors' advice: An empirical analysis of patterns of communication. *American Journal of Public Health* 58:274–288.

———. 1971. Variation in patients' compliance with doctors' advice: Medical practice and doctor-patient interaction. *Psychiatry and Medicine* 2:31–54.

———. 1981. Sex differences in reporting osteoarthritic symptoms: A sociomedical approach. *Journal of Health and Social Behavior* 22:298–309.

DiMatteo, M. Robin, and D. Dante DiNicola, ed. 1982. *Achieving Patients Compliance.* Elmsford, NY: Pergamon.

Dubos, Rene. 1959. *Mirage of Health.* New York: Harper & Row.

Dutton, D. B. 1978. Explaining the use of health services by the poor: Costs, attitudes, or delivery systems? *American Sociological Review* 43:348–368.

Eisenberg, David M., Ronald C. Kessler, Cindy Foster, Frances E. Norlock, David R. Calkins, and Thomas L. Delbanco. 1993. Unconventional medicine in the United States: Prevalence, costs, and patterns of use. *New England Journal of Medicine* 328:246–252.

Eisenberg, Leon, and Arthur Kleinman. 1981. *The Relevance of Social Science for Medicine.* Boston: Reidel.

Freemon, B., Vida Negrete, Milton Davis, and Barbara Korsch. 1971. Gaps in doctor-patient communication. *Pediatric Research* 5:298–311.

Freidson, Eliot. 1970. *Profession of Medicine.* New York: Dodd-Mead.

Friedman, Howard S., ed. 1990. *Personality and Disease.* New York: Wiley.

Friedman, Howard S., and Stephanie Booth-Kewley. 1987. The disease-prone personality: A meta-analytic view of the construct. *American Psychologist* 42:539–555.

Friedman, Meyer, and Ray H. Rosenman. 1974. *Type A Behavior and Your Heart.* New York: Knopf.

Fuchs, Victor R. 1974. *Who Shall Live? Health, Economics, and Social Choice.* New York: Basic Books.

Garro, Linda. 1985. Decision-making models of treatment choice. Pp. 173–188 in *Illness Behavior: A Multidisciplinary Model,* ed. S. McHugh and T. M. Vallis. New York: Plenum.

Good, Byron J. 1985. Explanatory models and care-seeking: A critical account. Pp. 161–173 in *Illness Behavior: A Multidisciplinary Model,* ed. S. McHugh and T. M. Vallis. New York: Plenum.

Greer, Steven, Keith Pettingale, Tina Morris, and J. Haybittle. 1985. Mental attitudes to cancer: An additional prognostic factor. *Lancet* 3:750.

Grossarth-Maticek, Ronald. 1980. Social psychotherapy and course of the disease: First experiences with cancer patients. *Psychotherapy and Psychosomatics* 33:129–138.

Hacker, George A., Ronald Collins, and Michael Jacobson. 1987. *Marketing Booze to Blacks.* Washington, DC: Center for Science in the Public Interest.

Hansell, Steven, and David Mechanic. 1986. The socialization of introspection and illness behavior. Pp. 253–260 in *Illness Behavior: A Multidisciplinary Model,* ed. S. McHugh. New York: Plenum.

Harburg, Ernest, John C. Erfurt, L. Havenstein, C. Chape, W. Schull, and M. Anthony Schork. 1973. Socioecological stress, suppressed hostility, skin color, and black-white male blood pressure. *Psychosomatic Medicine* 35:276–296.

Haynes, R. Brian, D. W. Taylor, and David L. Sackett, ed. 1979. *Compliance in Health Care.* Baltimore: Johns Hopkins University Press.

Heller, Kenneth, and Ralph V. Swindle. 1983. Social networks, perceived social support, and coping with stress. Pp. 87–103 in *Preventive Psychology: Research and Practice in Community Intervention,* ed. R. D. Felner, L. A. Jason, J. Moritsugu, and S. S. Farber. New York: Pergamon.

Hirsch, Barton J. 1979. Psychological dimensions of social networks: A multimethod analysis. *American Journal of Community Psychology* 7:263–277.

Hochbaum, G. 1958. Public participation in medical screening programs: A sociopsychological study. DHEW publ. no. [PHS] 572. Washington, DC: U.S. Government Printing Office.

Holmes, Thomas H., and Richard H. Rahe. 1967. The social readjustment rating scale. *Journal of Psychosomatic Research* 11:213–218.

House, James S. 1981. *Work Stress and Social Support.* Reading, MA: Addison-Wesley.

House, James S., and Eric M. Cottington. 1986. Health and the workplace. Pp. 382–415 in *Applications of Social Science to Clinical Medicine and Health Policy,* ed. L. H. Aiken and David Mechanic. New Brunswick, NJ: Rutgers University Press.

House, James S., Ronald C. Kessler, A. Regula Herzog, Richard P. Mero, Ann M. Kinney, and Martha J. Breslow. 1992. Social stratification, age, and health. Pp. 1–32 in *Aging, Health Behaviors, and Health Outcomes,* ed. K. Warner Schaie, Dan Blazer, and James S. House. Hillsdale, NJ: Erlbaum.

House, James S., Karl R. Landis, and Debra Umberson. 1988. Social relationships and health. *Science* 241: 540–545.

House, James S., Cynthia Robbins, and Helen L. Metzner. 1982. The association of social relationships and activities with mortality: Prospective evidence from the Tecumseh Community Health Study. *American Journal of Epidemiology* 116: 123–140.

House, James S., Victor J. Strecher, Helen L. Metzner, and Cynthia A. Robbins. 1986. Occupational stress and health among men and women in the Tecumseh Community Health Study. *Journal of Health and Social Behavior* 27:62–77.

Inui, Thomas S., E. L. Yourtee, and J. W. Williamson. 1976. Improved outcomes in hypertension after physician tutorials: A controlled trial. *Annals of Internal Medicine* 84:646–651.

Jackson, G. G., H. F. Dowling, T. O. Anderson, L. Riff, J. Saporta, and M. Turck. 1960. Susceptibility and immunity to common upper respiratory viral infections: The common cold. *Annals of Internal Medicine* 53:719–738.

James, Sherman A., David S. Strogatz, S. Wing, and D. Ramsey. 1987. Socioeconomic status, John Henryism, and hypertension in blacks and whites. *American Journal of Epidemiology* 126:664–673.

Janis, Irwin L., and Leon Mann. 1977. *Decision making: A psychological analysis of conflict, choice, and commitment.* New York: Free Press.

Jemmott, John B., and Steven E. Locke. 1984. Psychosocial factors, immunologic mediation and human susceptibility to infectious disease: How much do we know? *Psychological Bulletin* 95: 78–108.

Jessor, Richard, John E. Donovan, and Frances M. Costa. 1990. Personality, perceived life chances, and adolescent health behavior. Pp. 25–41 in *Health Hazards in Adolescence,* ed. K. Hurrelmann and F. Losel. New York: Aldine de Gruyter.

Karasek, Robert A., and Thores Theorell. 1990. *Healthy Work.* New York: Basic Books.

Kasl, Stanislav V. 1978. Epidemiological contributions to the study of work stress. Pp. 3–48 in *Stress at Work,* ed. C. Cooper and R. Payne. New York: Wiley.

Kessler, Ronald C. 1986. Sex differences in the use of health services. Pp. 136–148 in *Illness Behavior: A Multidisciplinary Model,* ed. S. McHugh and Thomas M. Vallis. New York: Plenum.

Kessler, Ronald C., and Jane D. McLeod. 1985. Social support and mental health in community samples. Pp. 219–240 in *Social Support and Health,* ed. S. Cohen and L. Syme. New York: Academic.

Kessler, Ronald C., J. Blake Turner, and James S. House. 1987. Intervening processes in the relationship between unemployment and health. *Psychological Medicine* 17:949–961.

Kessler, Ronald C., and Camille Wortman. 1988. Social psychological factors in health and illness. Pp. 69–86 in *Handbook of Medical Sociology,* 4th ed., ed. H. E. Freeman and S. Levine. Englewood Cliffs: NJ: Prentice Hall.

Kleinman, Arthur. 1980. *Patients and Healers in the Context of Culture.* Berkeley: University of California Press.

Kohn, Melvin L., Carmi Schooler, Joanne Miller, Karen A. Miller, Carrie Schoenbach, and R. Schoenberg. 1983. *Work and Personality: An Inquiry into the Impact of Social Stratification.* Norwood, NJ: Ablex.

Koos, E. 1954. *The Health of Regionville.* New York: Columbia University Press.

Kosa, J., A. Antonovsky, and Irving K. Zola, ed. 1969. *Poverty and Health: A Sociological Analysis.* Cambridge, MA: Harvard University Press.

Kotarba, Joseph. 1983. *Chronic Pain: Its Social Dimensions.* Beverly Hills: Sage.

Krantz, David S., and Stephen B. Manuck. 1984. Acute psychophysiologic reactivity and risk of cardiovascular disease: A review and methodologic critique. *Psychological Bulletin* 96:435–464.

Langer, Ellen J., and Judith Rodin. 1976. The effects of choice and enhanced personal responsibility for the aged: A field experiment in an institutional setting. *Journal of Personality and Social Psychology* 34: 191–198.

Lazarus, Richard S., and Susan Folkman. 1984. *Stress, Appraisal and Coping.* New York: Springer.

Leventhal, Howard, Daniel Meyer, and David R. Nerenz. 1980. The common-sense representation on illness danger. Pp. 7–30 in *Medical Psychology,* vol. 2, ed. S. Rachman. New York: Pergamon.

Leventhal, Howard, Richard Zimmerman, and Mary Gutmann. 1984. Compliance: A self-regulation perspective. Pp. 369–436 in *Handbook of Behavioral Medicine,* ed. W. D. Gentry. New York: Guilford.

Levy, Sandra M., and Lynda A. Heiden. 1990. Personality and social factors in cancer outcome. Pp. 254–279 in *Personality and Disease,* ed. Howard S. Friedman. New York: Wiley.

Levy, Sandra M., Ronald B. Herberman, A. Maluish, Bernadene Schlien, and Marc Lippman. 1985. Prognostic risk assessment in primary breast cancer by behavioral and immunological parameters. *Health Psychology* 4:99–113.

Lieberman, Morton A. 1986. Social supports: The consequences of psychologizing—A commentary. *Journal of Consulting and Clinical Psychology* 54: 461–465.

Lynch, James J. 1979. *The Broken Heart: Medical Consequences of Loneliness.* New York: Basic Books.

Manuck, Stephen B., Alfred L. Kasprowicz, Scott M. Monroe, Kevin T. Larkin, and Jay Kaplan. 1989. Psychophysiologic reactivity as a dimension of individual differences. Pp. 365–382 in *Handbook of Research Methods in Cardiovascular Behavioral Medicine,* ed. N. Schneiderman, S. M. Weiss, and P. G. Kaufmann. New York: Plenum.

Marlatt, G. Alan, and Judith R. Gordon, ed. 1985. *Relapse Prevention: Maintenance Strategies in the*

Treatment of Addictive Behaviors. New York: Guilford.

Marmot, Michael G., M. Kogevinas, and Mary A. Elston. 1987. Social/economic status and disease. Pp. 111–135 in *Annual Review of Public Health,* vol. 8, ed. L. Breslow, J. E. Fielding, and L. B. Lave. Palo Alto, CA: Annual Reviews.

Matthews, Karen A. 1985. Assessment of type A behavior, anger, and hostility in cardiovascular disease. Pp. 153–183 in *Measuring Psychosocial Variables in Epidemiologic Studies of Cardiovascular Disease: Proceedings of a Workshop,* ed. A. M. Ostfeld and E. D. Eaker. NIH publ. no. 85–2270. Washington DC: National Institute of Health.

McGrath, Joseph. 1970. *Social and Psychological Factors in Stress.* New York: Holt, Rinehart & Winston.

McKinlay, John B. 1990. A case for refocussing upstream: The political economy of illness. Pp. 510–520 in *The Sociology of Health and Illness: Critical Perspectives,* ed. Peter Conrad and R. Kern. New York: St. Martin's.

Mechanic, David. 1972. Social psychologic factors affecting the presentation of bodily complaints. *New England Journal of Medicine* 286:1132–1139.

———. 1978. *Medical Sociology.* New York: Free Press.

———. 1986. The concept of illness behaviour: Culture, situation, and personal predisposition. *Psychological Medicine* 16:1–7.

———. 1990. Promoting health. *Society* (Jan.-Feb.): 17–22.

———. 1992a. Health and illness behavior. Pp. 795–800 in *Encyclopedia of Sociology,* ed. E. F. Borgatta and M. L. Borgatta. New York: Macmillan.

———. 1992b. Health and illness behavior and patient-practitioner relationships. *Social Science and Medicine* 34:1345–1350.

Meichenbaum, Donald, and Dennis C. Turk, ed. 1987. *Facilitating Treatment Adherence: A Practitioner's Guide.* New York: Plenum.

Meyer, Daniel, Howard Leventhal, and Mary Gutmann. 1985. Common-sense models of illness: The example of hypertension. *Health Psychology* 4:115–135.

Michelson, Larry. 1986. Cognitive-behavioral strategies in the prevention and treatment of antisocial disorders in children and adolescents. Pp. 275–310 in *Prevention of Delinquent Behavior,* ed. J. Burchard and S. Burchard. Newbury Park, CA: Sage.

Mirowsky, John, and Catherine Ross. 1989. *Social Causes of Psychological Distress.* New York: Aldine de Gruyter.

Mischler, E. G. 1981. Critical perspectives on the biomedical model. Pp. 1–23 in *Social Contexts of Health, Illness, and Patient Care,* ed. E. G. Mischler, L. Amara Singham, S. T. Hauser, R. Liem, S. D. Osherson, and N. G. Waxler. Cambridge, UK: Cambridge University Press.

Nerem, Robert M., Murina J. Levesque, and J. Frederick Cornhill. 1980. Social environment as a factor in diet-induced atherosclerosis. *Science* 208: 1475–1476.

Ohwovoriole, A. E., and C. Butler Omololu. 1986. Personality and control of diabetes mellitus. *British Journal of Medical Psychology* 59:101–104.

Osgood, D. Wayne, Lloyd D. Johnston, Patrick M. O'Malley, and Jerald G. Bachman. 1988. The generality of deviance in late adolescence and early adulthood. *American Sociological Review* 53:81–93.

Pearlin, Leonard I. 1989. The sociological study of stress. *Journal of Health and Social Behavior* 30: 241–256.

Pearlin, Leonard I., Elizabeth G. Menaghan, Morton A. Lieberman, and Joseph T. Mullan. 1981. The stress process. *Journal of Health and Social Behavior* 22: 337–356.

Price, Richard H., Michelle van Ryn, and Amiram Vinokur. 1992. Impact of a preventive job search intervention on the likelihood of depression among the unemployed. *Journal of Health and Social Behavior* 33:158–167.

Rabow, Jerome, and Ronald K. Watts. 1982. Alcohol availability, alcohol beverage sales and alcohol-related problems. *Journal of Studies on Alcohol* 43: 767–801.

Raphael, Beverley. 1977. Prevention intervention with the recently bereaved. *Archives of General Psychiatry* 34:1450–1454.

Reissman, C. K. 1981. Improving the use of health services by the poor. Pp. 541–546 in *The Sociology of Health and Illness,* ed. P. Conrad and R. Kern. New York: St. Martin's.

Review Panel on Coronary-Prone Behavior and Heart Disease. 1981. Coronary-prone behavior and coronary heart behavior and coronary heart disease: A critical review. *Circulation* 63:1199–1215.

Rodin, Judith. 1985. The application of social psychology. Pp. 805–881 in *Handbook of Social Psychol-*

ogy, ed. G. Lindzey and E Aronson. New York: Random House.

——— . 1986. Aging and health: Effects of the sense of control. *Science* 233: 1271–1276.

Rodin, Judith, and Peter Salovey. 1989. Health psychology. *Annual Review of Psychology* 40:533–579.

Rook, Karen S. 1990. Social relationships as a source of companionship: Implications for older adults' psychological well-being. Pp. 219–250 in *Social Support: An Interactional View,* ed. B. R. Sarason, Irwin G. Sarason, and Gregory R. Pierce. New York: Wiley.

Rosenstock, Irwin M., and John P. Kirscht. 1979. Why people seek health care. Pp. 161–188 in *Health Psychology: A Handbook,* ed. G. C. Stone, F. Cohen, and N. E. Adler. San Francisco: Jossey-Bass.

Roter, Debra L., and Judith A. Hall. 1989. Studies of doctor-patient interaction. *Annual Review of Public Health* 10:163–80.

Roth, Julius, and Peter Conrad, ed. 1987. *The Experience and Management of Chronic Illness.* Research in the Sociology of Health Care, vol. 6. Greenwich, CT: JAI Press.

Sackett, David L., and R. Brian Haynes, ed. 1976. *Compliance with Therapeutic Regimens.* Baltimore: Johns Hopkins University Press.

Sandler, Irwin N., J. C. Gersten, K. Reynolds, Carl A. Kallgren, and R. Ramirez. 1988. Using theory and data to plan support interventions: Design of a program for bereaved children. Pp. 53–83 in *Marshalling Social Support: Formats, Processes, and Effects,* ed. B. H. Gottlieb. Newbury Park, CA: Sage.

Sarason, Irwin G., Gregory R. Pierce, and Barbara R. Sarason. 1990. Social support and interactional processes: A triadic hypothesis. Special issue: Predicting, activating and facilitating social support. *Journal of Social and Personal Relationships* 7:495–506.

Schneider, Joseph, and Peter Conrad. 1983. *Having Epilepsy.* Philadelphia: Temple University Press.

Selye, Hans. 1956. *The Stress of Life.* New York: McGraw-Hill.

Shavit, J., J. Lewis, G. Terman, R. Gale, and J. Liebeskind. 1984. Opioid peptides mediate the suppressive effect of stress on natural killer cytotoxicity. *Science* 223:188–190.

Sklar, Lawrence S., and Hymie Anisman. 1981. Stress and cancer. *Psychological Bulletin* 89:369–406.

Solomon, George F. 1981. Emotional and personality factors in the onset and course of autoimmune disease, particularly rheumatoid arthritis. Pp. 159–182 in *Psychoneuroimmunology,* ed. R. Ader. New York: Academic.

Sternbach, R. A., and B. Tursky. 1965. Ethnic differences among housewives in psychophysical and skin potential response to electric shock. *Psychophysiology* 1:241–246.

Sutton, Robert I., and Robert L. Kahn. 1984. Prediction, understanding, and control as antidotes to organizational stress. Pp. 272–285 in *Handbook of Organizational Behavior,* ed. J. Lorsch. Cambridge, MA: Harvard University Press.

Svarsted, Bonnie. 1976. Physician-patient communication and patient conformity with medical advice. Pp. 220–238 in *The Growth of Bureaucratic Medicine,* ed. David Mechanic. New York: Wiley.

Syme, Leonard, and Rina Alcalay. 1982. Control of cigarette smoking from a social perspective. *Annual Review of Public Health* 3:179–199.

Tebbi, Cameron K., K. Michael Cummings, Michael A. Zevon, L. Smith, Mary E. Richards, and Janis C. Mallon. 1986. Compliance of pediatric and adolescent cancer patients. *Cancer* 58:1179–1184.

Todd, Alexandra. 1989. *Intimate Adversaries: Cultural Conflict between Doctors and Women Patients.* Philadelphia: University of Pennsylvania Press.

Tversky, Amos, and Daniel Kahneman. 1974. Judgment under uncertainty: Heuristics and biases. *Science* 185:1124–1131.

Umberson, Debra, Camille B. Wortman, and Ronald C. Kessler. 1992. Widowhood and depression: Explaining long-term gender differences in vulnerability. *Journal of Health and Social Behavior* 33: 10–24.

Verbrugge, Lois M. 1989. The twain meet: Empirical explanations of sex differences in health and mortality. *Journal of Health and Social Behavior* 30: 282–304.

Visintainer, Madelon A., Joseph R. Volpicelli, and Martin E. Seligman. 1982. Tumor rejection in rats after inescapable shock. *Science* 216:437–439.

Warner, Kenneth E. 1977. The effects of the anti-smoking campaign on cigarette consumption. *American Journal of Public Health* 67:645–650.

Wells, James A. 1985. Chronic life situations and life change events. Pp. 105–128 in *Measuring Psychosocial Variable in Epidemiologic Studies of Cardiovascular Disease,* ed. A. M. Ostfeld and E. A. Eaker. Washington, DC: U.S. Department of Health and Human Services.

Wethington, Elaine, and Ronald C. Kessler. 1986. Perceived support, received support, and adjustment to stressful life events. *Journal of Health and Social Behavior* 27:78–89.

Whitcher-Alagna, Sheryle. 1983. Receiving medical help: A psychosocial perspective on patient reactions. Pp. 131–161 in *New Directions in Helping,* ed. A. Nadler, J. D. Fisher, and B. M. DePaulo. New York: Academic.

Williams, David R. 1990. Socioeconomic differentials in health: A review and redirection. *Social Psychology Quarterly* 52:81–99.

Zborowski, M. 1952. Cultural components in response to pain. *Journal of Social Issues* 8:16–30.

Zola, Irving K. 1966. Culture and symptoms—An analysis of patients' presenting complaints. *American Sociological Review* 31:615–630.

———. 1972. Studying the decision to see a doctor: Review, critique and corrective. Pp. 216–236 in *Advances in Psychosomatic Medicine,* vol. 8, ed. Z. Lipowski. Basel: Karger.

———. 1983. *Socio-Medical Inquiries: Recollections, Reflections, and Reconsiderations.* Philadelphia: Temple University Press.

CHAPTER 22

Social Movements and Collective Behavior
Social Psychological Dimensions and Considerations

DAVID A. SNOW
PAMELA E. OLIVER

This chapter examines the social psychological aspects of social movements and crowd behaviors that occur in relation to them. Social movements have historically been treated as variants of collective behavior. Broadly conceived, collective behavior refers to extrainstitutional, group problem-solving behavior that encompasses an array of collective actions, ranging from protest demonstrations, to behavior in disasters, to mass or diffuse phenomena, such as fads and crazes, to social movements and even revolution.[1] Although the umbrella concept of collective behavior is still used among scholars (Curtis and Aguirre 1993; Goode 1992; Turner and Killian 1987), most research and theoretical discussion tends to focus on either social movements or more transitory and ephemeral events, such as disasters, emergency evacuations, crowd actions, and fads and crazes. Since review of both of these traditions within the space limitations would require too superficial a treatment, we focus primarily on social movements, but we do include findings about crowds and other collective behaviors as they are relevant to the themes and arguments developed throughout the chapter.[2]

As with most concepts in social science, there is ambiguity and debate about the conceptualization of social movements and crowds, with different theoretical traditions defining the terms somewhat differently. In the case of *social movements,* most conceptualizations include the following elements: change-oriented goals; some degree of organization; some degree of temporal continuity; and some extrainstitutional collective action, or at least a mixture of extrainstitutional (e.g., protesting in the streets) and institutional (e.g., political lobbying) activity. Some scholars associate these elements only with social movement organizations (SMOs), reserving the term social movement for sets of change-oriented opinions and beliefs (McCarthy and Zald 1977) or behaviors (Marwell and Oliver 1984; Oliver 1989) that transcend any particular organization. For our purposes, we can ignore these conceptual distinctions and keep in mind that social movements are marked by collective actions that occur with some degree of organization and continuity outside of institutional channels with the purpose of promoting or resisting change in the group, society, or world order of which they are a part (Benford 1992, 1880; Turner and Killian 1987, 223; J. Wilson 1973, 8; Zurcher and Snow 1981, 447).

In the case of *crowds* typically associated with collective behavior, including social movements, the following dimensions have been emphasized as central defining characteristics: (1) joint action, in the sense that some number of individuals are "engaged in one or more behaviors (e.g., orientation, locomotion, gesticulation, tactile manipulation, and/or vocalization) that can be judged common or convergent on one or more dimensions (e.g., direction, velocity, tempo, and/or substantive content)" (McPhail and Wohlstein 1983, 580–581; see also McPhail 1991); (2) close physical proximity, such that the participants can monitor each other by being visible to or within earshot of one another (Lofland 1981, 416; Snow and Paulsen 1992); (3) unconventional or extrainstitutional occurrences, in the sense that they are neither temporally nor spatially routinized but instead involve the appropriation and use of spatial areas (e.g., street, park, mall) or physical structures (e.g., office building, lunch counter, theater) for purposes other than those for which they were designed and intended (Snow and Paulsen 1992; Snow, Zurcher, and Peters 1981, 38) (4) normative regulation, in the sense that the various behaviors are coordinated rather than random and disconnected (Turner and Killian 1987); and (5) ephemerality, in the sense that they are relatively fleeting or "temporary gatherings" (McPhail 1991, 153). These defining characteristics are not peculiar to the crowds associated with social movements, but they do distinguish such crowds from more diffuse or mass collective behavior, such as fads, deviant epidemics, and mass hysteria, and from more conventional crowds that are sponsored and orchestrated by the state or community, such as sporting events, holiday parades, and electoral political rallies (Aguirre 1984). Thus, when we refer to crowds in this chapter, we have in mind those gatherings that share the above defining characteristics, such as protest marches and rallies, victory celebrations, and riots, and that are often associated with social movements as well.

The study of crowds and social movements has deep roots in both political sociology and social psychology, and a major trend in current scholarship is to integrate these traditions by focusing on the linkages between macro and micro processes (McAdam, McCarthy, and Zald 1988). In this chapter, we focus on the social psychological dimensions of crowds and social movements and give only passing attention to the ways these micro processes are linked to macro processes. More specifically, our aim is to identify the key social psychological dimensions of crowds and social movements and to elaborate how research and theorizing pertinent to these dimensions have informed our understanding of them. We begin with a brief overview of the historical association between social psychology and the study of crowds and social movements and then turn to a discussion of their key social psychological dimensions and the pertinent literature.

THE HISTORICAL LINKAGE

The association between social psychology and the study of crowd and social movement phenomena has a fairly long and intimate history, dating at least from the 1895 publication of Le Bon's *The Crowd* (1960), which strongly influenced the study of collective behavior through the 1950s (McPhail 1991; Moscovici 1985). Other early influential works by psychologists treating collective behavior and social movements as a subfield of social psychology include Freud's *Group Psychology and the Analysis of the Ego* (1921), Allport's *Social Psychology* (1924), Dollard et al.'s *Frustration and Aggression* (1939), Miller and Dollard's *Social Learning and Imitation* (1941), and Adorno et al.'s *The Authoritarian Personality* (1950). Through the 1960s, sociologists also viewed collective behavior as an important subfield of social psychology. Work rooted theoretically in symbolic interactionism was particularly important (Blumer 1939; Lang and Lang 1961; Turner and Killian 1987).[3]

However, as the protest-ridden 1960s faded into the 1970s, most social psychological perspectives on collective behavior were largely jettisoned in favor of the "resource mobilization paradigm" grounded in political sociology and the study of organizations (Gamson 1968, 1990; McCarthy and Zald 1973, 1977; Oberschall 1973; Tilly 1978). One early advocate of resource mobilization even went so far as to suggest that the social psychological collective behavior perspective was "stultifying" and constituted a "straightjacket" on the study of protest-oriented collective action (Gamson 1990, 130).

This eclipse of social psychology in the study of social movements and crowds was never thoroughgoing, however, as resource mobilization theory was firmly grounded in strands of rational decision-making theory. Early resource mobilization theorists also stressed the importance of social networks and preexisting organization as preconditions for mobilization and treated protest as goal-oriented action constrained by resources, costs, network ties, and organizational capacities. The macro forces of politics and organization were seen as creating the structures and resources that enabled people to act collectively, while the link between objective conditions and subjective perceptions or grievances was seen as unproblematic.

Resource mobilization and its rationalist assumptions were largely hegemonic in the 1970s. The tide began to turn around 1980, however. Several published articles critically assessed the contributions of resource mobilization theory and called for a reconsideration of symbolic interactionism, attribution theory and other relevant social psychological perspectives that had been tossed out indiscriminately along with such questionable notions as the "authoritarian personality" and the "conflict of generations" (Ferree and Miller 1985; Killian 1980; Turner 1981; Zurcher and Snow 1981). Social psychological processes were once again topics of discussion and research. Thus, Gamson and colleagues (1982) examined experimentally how small groups mobilized to resist unjust situations; Klandermans (1984) stressed the subjective nature of the terms in expected utility models and called for examination of the social construction processes that lead to these subjective perceptions; and Snow and colleagues (1986) drew on Goffman's framing concepts to examine and theorize the relevance of interpretive processes to movement mobilization.

By the second half of the 1980s, then, students of social movements were rediscovering the relevance of social psychological perspectives for understanding aspects of the dynamics of social movements, and thereby reestablishing the long-standing association between social psychology and the study of collective behavior. The social psychological perspectives being invoked were clearly not identical with those that had currency in

earlier times, but social psychology was once again part of the mainstream.[4]

SOCIAL PSYCHOLOGICAL DIMENSIONS OF SOCIAL MOVEMENTS AND CROWDS

The reasons for the linkage between social psychology and collective behavior phenomena are not difficult to fathom. Stated boldly, there are aspects of the empirical phenomena of crowds and social movements that are impossible to grasp or understand in the absence of social psychological and microlevel theorizing and research. This is because there are five basic social psychological dimensions or aspects of crowds and social movements: microstructural and social relational dimensions; personality dimensions and related psychological processes; socialization dimensions; cognitive dimensions; and affective dimensions. In the remainder of the chapter, we elaborate these dimensions and the research relevant to them.

Microstructural and Social Relational Dimensions

The collective decisions and actions constitutive of social movement activity, including crowd events, have long been seen as the product of dynamic interaction. However, there are two strikingly different social psychological perspectives for conceptualizing the nature of that interaction.

The older approach—variously discussed as "contagion theory" (Turner 1964; Turner and Killian 1972), "breakdown theory" (Tilly, Tilly, and Tilly 1975), and the "transformation hypothesis" (McPhail 1991)—argues that participants are highly susceptible to the influence of others either because of the anonymity provided by collective behavior gatherings or because they are socially isolated, disaffiliated individuals. In either case, conventional social constraints are not operative and participants are vulnerable to the sway of the crowd. Although this view is most commonly associated with such early writers as Tarde (1890), Le Bon (1895), and Freud (1921), it has also been featured in the writings of "deindividuation" theorists in psychological social psychology (Diener 1980; Zimbardo 1969) and of mass society theorists (Adorno et al. 1950; Kornhauser 1959). The concepts of "circular reaction" (Blumer 1939; Park and Burgess 1921) and "unilateral transfer of control" (Coleman 1990) are also consistent with this contagion-like theorizing, inasmuch as both imply the dissolution of individual decision making and interpersonal constraints in collective behavior contexts.

Standing in contrast is the perspective that emphasizes the group-based nature of behavior in crowds and social movements. The basic thesis is that all instances of crowds and social movements either are embedded in preexisting groups or networks of affiliation or grow out of emergent structures of social relation. We examine each of these patterns in turn.

Preexisting Groupings and Affiliations. By preexisting groupings and affiliations, we refer to structures of social relation that exist apart from and prior to the crowd and social movement activities in question. These preexisting structures can function both as conduits for communication and as facilitative contexts for the generation and diffusion of new ideas and actions.

Social Networks as Information Conduits and Bridges. Probably the most firmly established finding in the study of collective behavior is that preexisting social ties or network linkages function to channel the diffusion of all varieties of collective action. The evidence is overwhelming, coming from the study of religious cults and movements (Rochford 1982; Snow, Zurcher, and Ekland-Olson 1980; Stark and Bainbridge 1980), the civil rights movement (McAdam 1986; Morris 1984), the women's movement (Freeman 1973; Rosenthal et al. 1985), the Dutch peace movement (Klandermans and Oegema 1987), crowd assembling processes (McPhail and Miller 1973; Shelly, Anderson, and Mattley 1992), victory celebrations (Aveni 1977; Snow, Zurcher, and Peters 1981), looting and rioting (Berk and Aldrich 1972; Quarantelli

and Dynes 1968; Singer 1970), and even hysterical contagion (Kerckhoff, Back, and Miller 1965). All of this research underscores Knopf's (1975) conclusion regarding the relation among rumors and race riots: that "these rumors were essentially social phenomenon" and participants "neither related nor responded as isolated or independent units" (pp. 65–66).

Most such research has examined only the simple presence or absence or number of preexisting ties. More recently, however, attention has shifted from simply counting network ties to assessing their structure and multiplexity. Thus, Fernandez and McAdam (1989) found that an individual's network prominence or centrality in the University of Wisconsin's multiorganizational field predicted recruitment to Freedom Summer. Gould's (1991) examination of the role of network multiplexity in the mobilization of insurgency in the Paris Commune of 1871 revealed "that successful mobilization depended not on the sheer number of ties, but on the interplay between social ties created by insurgent organizations and preexisting social networks rooted in Parisian neighborhoods" (p. 716; see also, Gould 1993). And Marwell et al.'s (1988) computer simulation of collective actions mobilized by a single organizer showed that besides the expected simple effect of the sheer number of ties and low organizing costs, the centralization of network structures also facilitated mobilization because the person at the center could contact the critical mass of large contributors at a relatively low cost.

Such findings clearly underscore the importance of network ties, strength, density, centralization, and multiplexity in relation to mobilization processes across nearly all forms of collective behavior. It is thus tempting to conclude that little else matters in determining recruitment to crowds and social movement activities. Such a conclusion is unwarranted, however. So-called structural isolates sometimes figure significantly in the development of various forms of collective behavior (Fernandez and McAdam 1989; Kerckhoff, Back, and Miller 1965), and the relative influence of preexisting ties tends to vary with differences in the risks and costs associated with different crowd and movement activities (McAdam 1986; Wiltfang and McAdam 1991). In addition, personality, socialization, cognitive, and affective processes figure in the recruitment process and can interact with network ties in different ways in different sociocultural and historical contexts.

Facilitative Social Contexts. That some social contexts are especially facilitative of collective action has been suggested by the coinage of such concepts as "the youth ghetto" (Lofland 1968), "internal organization" and "movement halfway houses" (Morris 1981, 1984), "free spaces" (Evans and Boyte 1986) and "micromobilization contexts" (McAdam, McCarthy, and Zald 1988). Undergirding these concepts is the historical fact that movement activity clusters temporally and is contextually pocketed or generally stronger in some locales than others (Tarrow 1989a, 1989b). Focusing on the growth of the strike movement in urban Russia before the revolution, for example, Haimson (1964) found it was most heavily concentrated in the Petersburg area because of the presence and interaction of both older experienced metalworkers steeped in the revolutionary Bolshevik tradition and younger unskilled coworkers, who were subject to the political indoctrination of the old guard. The result was a more militant political context than found in other industries at the time. Petras and Zeitlin (1967) found a similar pattern in the diffusion of radical political consciousness among the peasantry in Chile in the early 1960s, where the main determinant of peasant radicalism was proximity to the highly organized and politically radical mining centers.

Differences in residential communities have also been found to affect mobilization. For example, Broadbent (1986) found that the character of environmental mobilization in Japanese communities varied with whether the "local social fabric" was communal or associational, with the former contexts mobilizing more quickly and pervasively because of greater solidarity. Portes (1971) found that lower-class urban Chileans' radicalism was predicted by how long they had lived in radical

neighborhoods. And Kriesi's (1988b) research on the Dutch peace movement revealed that support for the movement and its campaigns has varied with proximity to and integration into more leftist, locality-based neighborhoods he terms "countercultural networks." "In such localities," he notes, it is difficult to escape contact with the movement because it tends to be "integrated into everyday activities" (1988b, 69). Individuals not in these networks, by contrast, are less likely to develop "attitudes and sympathies" supporting new social movements (1988b, 73). Fernandez and McAdam (1988) found that Berkeley was such an "activist context" for Freedom Summer recruitment that network variables could not predict individuals' participation. In such contexts, the networks are so pervasive, dense, interconnected, and overlapping that the paths of diffusion cannot be easily traced: almost everyone is connected and subject to influence from multiple sources.

Such facilitative contexts thus provide fertile soil for movement mobilization, not only because of residential proximity and network density, but also because people share significant social traits, hold similar beliefs and grievances, and encounter each other during the course of their daily routines. These facilitative contexts are not a necessary condition for social movement activity, but they can certainly foster it and, as we discuss below, can ensure the transmission of movement culture from one generation to the next.

Emergent Structures of Relation. While all types of crowd and social movement activities entail some level of joint action, not all are rooted in preexisting structures of relation. Some are emergent or peculiar to the particular collective behavior episode itself. In other words, they grow out of, rather than precede, some crowd episode or social movement activity. This fact undergirds Weller and Quarantelli's (1973) contention that the social organizational basis of collective behavior is both normative and social relational and that collective behavior can therefore be predicated on either enduring or emergent norms and enduring or emergent social relations.

Evidence of the importance of emergent social relationships is particularly abundant in research on organizational and community responses to disasters (Dynes 1970; Ross 1978; Zurcher 1968). It has also been found in instances of rioting and looting associated with civil disturbances (Kerner 1969; Quarantelli and Dynes 1970) and in various social movements (Gould 1991; Killian 1984). For instance, Gould (1991) found two bases of social relation in the Paris Commune of 1871: preexisting neighborhood ties and emergent insurgent organizational ties. Importantly, both sets of ties functioned to build and maintain solidarity, thus prompting Gould to argue that "mobilization does not just depend on social ties; it also creates them" (1991, 719). Snow found this to be the case in his research on the Nichiren Shoshu Buddhist movement: commitment and solidarity were based not only on the preexisting ties that facilitated recruitment, but also on a horizontal structure of emergent peer group associations within the movement. Together, these two sets of overlapping and interlocking relationships functioned to generate "a more cohesive and highly integrated movement, and a more highly committed and mobilizable constituency" (Snow 1987, 159).

Although preestablished associations are more fundamental to the assemblage process for crowd phenomena and to the recruitment process for social movements, it seems equally clear that emergent relations are often critical for the accomplishment of specific tasks in crowd contexts and can contribute significantly to the development and maintenance of commitment and solidarity in social movements. Both preexisting and emergent relations are thus complementary rather than contradictory, fundamental to processes of mobilization, and together provide an appropriate point of departure for understanding much about the social psychology of crowds and social movements.

Group Interaction. Whether the structure of relations among collective actors is based on preexisting or emergent relations, the interacting units are typically groups rather than individuals. Thus, ana-

lysis of the dynamics of crowds and social movements should be focused in part on groups and the interaction among them.

To suggest such a focus must seem axiomatic from a sociological standpoint, yet the research and writing on crowds and social movements varies considerably in this regard. Group-level processes and dynamics have always figured more prominently in the analysis of social movements than of crowds, largely because much social movement activity is highly organized. But the group focus has moved even more center stage in the study of social movements over the past twenty years, with the ascendance of the resource mobilization perspective and its cornerstone concept of social movement organizations (SMOs) (McCarthy and Zald 1977; Zald and Ash 1966; Zald and McCarthy 1987). Correctly noting that many movements grow out of small groups, that such groups are critical to the operation of most social movements, and that they often develop their own small group cultures or "idiocultures," Fine and Stoecker (1985) have argued that the study of social movements could benefit even further by examining more closely the link between movements and small group processes.

The same argument can be made with respect to the study of crowds. Some students of crowds have long been interested in underlying group processes and dynamics, of course. The theoretical and empirical inspiration for Turner and Killian's emergent norm perspective, for example, comes largely from a series of well-known small group experiments (Asch 1952; Sherif and Harvey 1952). Still, the bulk of research and theorizing on crowd phenomena has been at the individual level of analysis, as evidenced by the broad range of research that can be subsumed under either the "convergence" and "gaming" or rational decision perspectives.

This individualistic focus notwithstanding, a number of empirical investigations of behavior in crowd contexts suggest the analytic utility of a group level focus. Based on a comparative study of 146 protest demonstrations, MacCannell argues that their natural subdivisions are *"groups,* groups of demonstrators, bystanders, press, police, and others" (1973, 1–2.) He acknowledges that "some demonstrations dissolve into individualistic behavior," but emphasizes that "no demonstration starts this way" (1973, 2).

McPhail's (1991; McPhail and Wohlstein 1983) systematic empirical examination of behaviors in crowd contexts for more than a decade also sheds light on the group nature and embeddedness of much of what transpires in those contexts. Although his research is heavily behavioral, aimed in large part at identifying, counting, and classifying the range of concrete behaviors occurring in crowd contexts, those behaviors are judged to be collective only insofar as they are "common or convergent on one or more dimensions" at the same time, and thus imply some coordinating mechanism or source.[5]

For those behaviors that fall into these two categories, it seems clear that the preponderance of them would be group-based, whether the group be preestablished or emergent. That is what MacCannell's research suggests, and it is what the field research of Snow and his colleagues shows (Snow and Anderson 1985; Snow and Paulsen 1992; Snow, Zurcher, and Peters 1981). Drawing on Wright's (1978) distinction between crowd activities (redundant behaviors common to most crowd episodes, such as assemblage, milling, and divergence) and task activities (context-specific joint activities, such as parading, picketing, and looting), they found that the course and character of a series of crowd episodes was largely a function of the interaction among four groups of actors—main task performers (e.g., demonstrators, marchers), subordinate task performers (e.g., counterdemonstrators, media), spectators or bystanders, and social control agents (e.g., police, military). In some instances the nature of the interaction was negotiated prior to the episode; in other cases it was emergent. But in all cases, the moving dynamic was group interaction.

There is mounting evidence, then, that insofar as one is interested in understanding the dynamics of crowd behavior, the focus of analysis should be at the group level. This makes good sense sociologically, but what about social psychologically? We think it makes good sense social psychologically, too—not only because it is consistent with recent research that has become increasingly more systematic, but also because a social psychology that fails to anchor itself in social context, whether it be small groups or society writ large, is one that misapprehends the locus of most social psychological states and processes.

Personality Dimensions and Related Psychological Processes

As has often been noted (Marx and Wood 1975, 388; Zurcher and Snow 1981, 449), few issues have generated as much research as differential recruitment: Why do some people rather than others devote varying degrees of time and energy to participation in crowd and social movement activities? Until recently, the dominant perspective on this issue was essentially psychological. Explicitly or implicitly located in the strand of thought that Turner (1964; Turner and Killian 1987) dubbed "convergence theory" and McPhail (1991) called the "predisposition hypothesis," the underlying assumption was that participation was primarily a function of one of three psychological factors or processes: personal deficit or pathology, personal efficacy, and/or a sense of relative deprivation.

Personality Problems and Psychological Deficit. Much of the older literature attempting to account for differential recruitment suggests a link between various psychological deficits or pathologies and participation in crowds and movements. Very generally, the basic proposition is that psychological propensities or needs render some individuals particularly susceptible to movement appeals. Some works in this tradition argue that the precipitating tensions can be relieved inasmuch as movements improve life conditions (e.g. Toch 1965); others assume that participation cannot solve the real problems producing the strain and that participation is therefore irrational or expressive (e.g., Smelser 1963).

The underlying psychological propensities and mechanisms range from those that are deep-seated and personality-based, such as the authoritarian personality (Adorno et al. 1950) and the Oedipal conflict of generations (Feuer 1969), to more sociological notions, such as status inconsistency theory, which suggests that class-based tensions are often displaced onto movement issues such as temperance, pornography, and right-wing extremism (Geschwender 1967; Gusfield 1963; Rush 1967; Zurcher and Kirkpatrick 1976). The implication of such propositions is that secure personalities or clear-thinking individuals would not be lured by the questionable appeals of social movements.[6]

Some proponents of this perspective have argued that movements are interchangeable or functional equivalents of one another inasmuch as they provide prospective participants with similar outlets or opportunities for addressing their psychological needs (Hoffer 1951; Klapp 1969). Others contend that participation is contingent on correspondence between type of personal problem or need and type of movement appeal and program (Feuer 1969; Lofland and Stark 1965). In either case, little empirical support has been forthcoming.

Personal Efficacy and Other Traits. Personality and psychological deficits have been largely abandoned as explanations of differential recruitment by scholars of crowds and movements since the 1970s because of both the lack of empirical support and the tendency for such explanations to portray participants in disparaging terms. However, if we accept the importance of movement issues and assume that people participate only in movements which make sense to them or which express their interests, there is clearly room for personality characteristics to affect the level and form of participation. One personality factor found to function in this fashion is "personal efficacy"—the belief that one has the ability to make a difference, especially when coupled with low trust in the existing power

structure (Forward and Williams 1970; Gamson 1968; Paige 1971, Seeman 1975). More broadly, Werner (1978) found, on controlling for gender and abortion attitudes, that "activists" on both sides of the abortion issue were more dominant, self-confident, energetic, and effective in using their capabilities than subjects who engaged in less activism than their attitudes would otherwise predict.

It thus appears that there is something to gain from reconsidering "personality," or at least personality variables, as a factor in movement participation, but only if it is properly placed in context. If movement participation is viewed as problem-solving or instrumental behavior, it is plausible to speculate that, when attitudes and network ties are controlled, activists will generally be found to have higher energy levels, greater sense of personal efficacy, and greater skills for the actions they are performing than nonactivists. There is scattered evidence that bears on these hypotheses (Gamson, Fireman, and Rytina 1982, 82–93; Oliver 1984) and suggests that they merit more careful research.

Relative Deprivation. Rooted in models of both psychological process and cognition, the general concept of relative deprivation organized a great deal of research in the 1960s and 1970s, including related approaches with different names (Aberle 1966; Davies 1969; Gurr 1970). These approaches are rooted in the seeming paradox that it is not the most emiserated populations that rebel, but those that seem to be improving their position or those that are among the more privileged sectors of an aggrieved group. All seek to subsume the causes of protest into an individual-level social psychological process in which what ought to be is compared with what is.

Although deprivation theory is among the most theoretically sophisticated social psychological perspectives on collective action, it has not fared particularly well when subjected to empirical examination. Indeed, one might easily conclude—in light of major empirical studies (McPhail 1971; Muller 1980; Portes 1971; Rule 1988; Snyder and Tilly 1972; Spilerman 1970) and a number of critical overviews of the concept and literature (Finkel and Rule 1986; Gurney and Tierney 1982)—that the jury is in and hypotheses linking relative deprivation to collective action are simply wrong. Such a conclusion is premature, however, for several reasons. First, few studies have directly measured a sense of relative deprivation or felt psychological tension. Instead, subjective deprivation is typically inferred from aggregate statistics of objective indicators, such as unemployment rates. The assumption of an unproblematic relation between objective conditions and subjective deprivation is not only contrary to the theory, but "the relationship between subjective evaluations of well-being and external objective conditions is itself so filtered through individual circumstances that there is little evidence of a systematic effect of macroenvironmental conditions upon overall sense of well-being" (Seeman 1981, 396).

Second, there is little reason to expect social psychological states such as deprivation to be a sufficient explanation for action. In a typical case, Klandermans and Oegema (1987) found that while 76 percent of the Dutch population endorsed a campaign against nuclear armaments, only 4 percent actually attended a large demonstration in support of the campaign. However, some sort of relative deprivation may well be a necessary condition for action. Finally, some research using direct measures of subjective deprivation have found the predicted relation to participation, as in the case of the antibusing movement in Boston and prison riots (Useem 1980, 1985; Useem and Kimball 1989). Even here, however, it is not clear whether the rather complex concept of relative deprivation can be empirically distinguished from simpler concepts such as "grievance" or the instrumentalists' "subjective interest."

In sum, there is little reason to jettison personality factors and related social psychological processes in the study of crowds and social movements. Although it is clear that much of the earlier theorizing was excessively psychological and wrongheaded, it is also likely that there are "activist types," that a sense of personal efficacy often figures in the participation equation, and that something like relative deprivation, appropriately measured

and contextualized, can affect differential recruitment and participation.

Socialization Dimensions and Processes

Broadly defined, socialization refers to two interconnected processes: the process through which individuals learn the values, norms, motives, beliefs, and roles of the groups or society with which they are associated, and a parallel process through which individuals develop and change in terms of personality and self-concept or identity (Gecas 1992). Both of these processes are apparent in social movements, yet there is a long-standing tradition of treating them as qualitatively different within movements than in the larger society. The result is that socialization is seldom used by movement scholars, and students of socialization rarely mention the occurrence of these processes within movements (e.g., Bush and Simmons 1981; Gecas 1981). We believe this tendency is misguided, since the two processes manifest themselves in at least three ways in relation to social movements: intergenerationally, in terms of childhood socialization and the transmission of activist orientations; intragenerationally, in terms of changes in worldview and identity; and intragenerationally, in terms changes over the life course.

Intergenerational Transmission of Activist Values. Past emphasis on the disjunctive aspects of collective behavior and social movements has generally led scholars to neglect the ways movement participation and activism are often continuous, rather than discontinuous, with the past. There are exceptions to this gloss, but most are based on research on student activists of the early 1960s, who tended to come from liberal to left activist families (Bengston 1970; DeMartini 1983; Flacks 1967; Westby and Braungart 1966; J. Wood and Ng 1980). Similarly, Johnston (1991) found that Catalonian nationalists' insurgent ethnic identities were formed in family conversations and church youth groups.

Anecdotal and impressionistic evidence about other movements abounds. Some ethnic, racial, and religious communities or groupings are facilitative contexts for the transmission of values and beliefs conducive to activism. Every continent in the world provides cases of ongoing ethnic, religious, and tribal conflicts that are clearly sustained across generations. In the United States, the transmission of a culture of race-consciousness and activism has been a central feature of African-American history. Prominent African-American leaders often had activist parents, such as Martin Luther King, Sr., or Earl Little, the Garveyite father of Malcolm X. High community political participation rates for educated African Americans are well established, as are the cultural norms for "race work." Many African-American churches have a long tradition of integrating religion, culture, politics, and resistance into a seamless whole (Morris 1984). And general population surveys indicate that African Americans receive more explicit political education about race and power than European Americans and are generally more supportive than European Americans of government action to produce social equality and of social movements and protest (Isaac, Mutran, and Stryker 1980). This difference seems to extend quite broadly: Kane (1992) reports that African Americans of both sexes support the women's movement and women's collective action much more than European Americans of either sex.

Cultural traditions of activism are also found among some Americans of European ancestry. Secular and religious Jews have very strong traditions of social activism and markedly more liberal attitudes than other European Americans. Quakers, Mennonites, and other groups have taught pacifism, equality, and service for generations. Even among the largely nonactivist Catholics and mainline Protestants, "social justice" and "peace" have been significant themes for generations. On the conservative side, Wood and Hughes (1984) document the relationship between "moral reform" and moral upbringing, showing that conservative moralists are reared in families, religions, and communities that socialize them into their moral worldview and thereby dispose them toward moral reform. In short, many American children have been and

are being reared with distinct moral and political ideologies that have implications for subsequent identification with and involvement in various kinds of movement activity.

Not only do preestablished communities often constitute the moral and ideological seedbeds out of which ethnic, race, religious, and political movements sometimes grow, but these communities and their movements often give rise to ongoing cultures of resistance or struggle that are transmitted across generations. In these contexts, children grow up with almost continuous exposure to a structure of grievances and beliefs that justify activism. Since there is little, if any, disjuncture between movement and community in such settings, it is difficult, if not impossible, to differentiate movement socialization from socialization more generally.

Intragenerational Changes in Value Orientation and Identity. While students of social movements may have neglected the contribution of parental values and childhood socialization to subsequent activism, no such neglect is evident with respect to changes in value orientation and identity or self-concept among movement participants. Both conversion, the process through which dramatic changes in value orientation and identity are effected, and commitment, the process through which individuals come to pursue lines of action consistent with their beliefs and identities, have been extensively studied.

Conversion and Other Personal Changes. Although research on religious conversion has been described as "a minor growth industry" (Machalek and Snow 1993, 1),[7] conceptualization and operationalization of conversion have remained somewhat elusive. Conceptualized in its most extreme form, conversion involves a radical transformation of consciousness in which a new or formerly peripheral universe of discourse comes to function as a person's primary authority. In an attempt to operationalize this conception, Snow and Machalek (1983, 1984, 173–174) have proposed four rhetorical indicators of conversion: biographical reconstruction, adoption of a master attribution scheme, suspension of analogical reasoning, and adoption of the convert role as a master status.

Since not all changes in orientation and identity that occur in social movements are as drastic as those captured by the concept of conversion, scholars have proposed other terms, such as "alternation" and "regeneration," for these milder changes (see Snow and Machalek 1984, 169–170 for a summary). Such distinctions are useful inasmuch as they signal that the change in orientation and identity frequently associated with movement participation is not unidimensional and that conversion is but one variety of personal change that occurs in social movements.

Given that the personal changes associated with movement participation can be arrayed on a continuum, ranging from the more thoroughgoing changes associated with conversion at one extreme to little, if any, change at the other, two issues beg for clarification: What is the relationship between movement type and the kinds of personal change required for participation? And, what are the causal factors that account for the change? Regarding the first issue, there are a number of works that suggest that more dramatic personal changes associated with conversion are most likely to be required under the following conditions: when movement ideology and practices are culturally idiosyncratic or discontinuous or when a movement is stridently oppositional and defined as threatening or revolutionary (McAdam 1989; Turner and Killian 1987); when a movement is more "exclusive" in terms of membership eligibility and requirements (Machalek and Snow 1993; McAdam 1989; Zald and Ash 1966); and when a movement is more "greedy" in terms of membership demands (Coser 1967; Gerlach and Hine 1970; Machalek and Snow 1993).

Regarding the issue of causation, there is an extensive and continuously expanding literature. Indeed, the bulk of the literature on conversion and related processes of personal change is concerned primarily with identification of the causal precipitants and processes. Since there are a number of recent detailed reviews of this literature (see note 7), we note only a few of the more general findings. First, while little compelling empirical support has been found for explanations of conversion that emphasize aberrant personality factors and "brainwashing" or "coercive persuasion," there is considerable support for such microstructural and social relational factors as network linkages, affective and intensive interaction, and role learning in the process through which conversion and the more milder personal changes are effected.

Second, monocausal explanations of these changes have fallen out of favor as researchers increasingly have come to realize that personal changes in orientation and identity, however dramatic, result from the combined and interactive influences of multiple factors—individual, interpersonal, and contextual.

Last, the earlier presumption that conversion to off-beat groups, religious or otherwise, required the operation of unique social and psychological processes has been derailed by the growing realization that parallel processes are often at work, whatever the context or movement. Indeed, it can be argued that the entire conversion process applies generally to most forms of intense, high-risk movement activity in the political arena and is perhaps also applicable to the process by which individuals become members of some voluntary organizations. The difference in such seemingly diverse cases resides not so much in the causal processes but in the content of the process and in the extent to which the new roles, beliefs, and identities are all-encompassing and pervasive in terms of their relevance to the various domains of life.

Commitment Processes. Commitment processes encompass the socialization processes through which individuals become bound to a group, resulting in group solidarity and mutual identification of some durability. Whereas conversion entails radical change in self and identity associated with the process of joining, commitment involves the devotion of time and energy to a cause, even in the face of adversity, and implies that one's individual needs and interests are congruent with those of the group (Kanter 1972).

Research on commitment in the collective behavior arena has focused on the processes and mechanisms contributing to the development and persistence of commitment and on variation in commitment-building capacities, requirements, mechanisms, and success across groups or movements (Gerlach and Hine 1970; Hall 1988; Hechter 1987; Hirsch 1990; Kanter 1968, 1972; McAdam 1986; Turner and Killian 1987, 337–344). Most recently, there has been increasing interest in the development of collective identity (Cohen 1985; Hunt 1991; Melucci 1985, 1988, 1989; Taylor 1989), which is clearly related to commitment. Indeed, both might be regarded as flip sides of the same coin.

Research on commitment processes and mechanisms suggests four tentative conclusions. First, commitments often evolve during the course of collective action itself. Joint action both enhances existing commitments and engenders new ones (Gamson, Fireman, and Rytina 1982; Gould 1991; Hirsch 1990; Snow 1987). Second, different commitment-building mechanisms are relevant to different dimensions of commitment (Hall 1988; Hirsch 1990; Kanter 1968, 1972). Third, movements vary not only in the commitments they require, but in their capacity to deal successfully with the problem of commitment (Hall 1988).

Finally, the development of commitment to social movements generally occurs in a context of competing commitments and in a stepwise fashion and is thus a highly contingent process. Consider these findings from a variety of contexts: there is an extraordinarily high incidence of defection from religious cults and movements (Barker 1984; Bird and Reimer 1982); only a few members of neighborhood associations are consistently active (Oliver 1984); members of unions who are dissatisfied are more likely to "exit" than exercise "voice" (Van der Veen and Klandermans 1989); and the most active members in most kinds of voluntary associations are rarely the members with the longest tenure of association (Cress and McPherson 1992). Taken together, these observations suggest that the development of strong, enduring commitment may well be the exception rather than the rule.

Intragenerational Changes over the Life Course.
A third area in which socialization processes and the study of social movements converge concerns the long-term biographical consequences of committed participation and activism. Accumulating evidence indicates that movement participation continues to have effects even long after the intense activism has ceased. This is best established for the "60s activists," who, for the most part, continued to have relatively liberal to left political beliefs, maintained involvement in political activity, were more likely to be employed in the "helping professions," and tended to marry less and have fewer children (Demerath, Morwell, and Aiken 1971; Fendrich and Lovoy 1988; Marwell, Aiken, and Demerath 1987; Marwell, Demerath, and O'Leary 1990; McAdam 1988, 1989; Whalen and Flacks 1989). Even those who were minor participants in marches and rallies show similar, though milder, differences from nonparticipants, even when predictors of participation are controlled (Sherkat and Blocker 1992).

The persistence of activist values and identities has implications for organizations as well as individuals. Yesterday's activists, for whom the "fire" continues to burn, often provide the organizational skills and ideological inspiration for new movements or keep the torch burning for the old, as Rupp and Taylor demonstrate in the case of the women's movement (1987; Taylor 1989). Thus, the socialization consequences of earlier collective action experiences can have long-term effects at both the personal and the organizational levels.

Cognitive Dimensions and Perspectives

Much of the discussion among scholars of crowds and social movements since the mid-1970s has focused on issues that are essentially cognitive: How do individuals decide to participate in a particular crowd or movement activity? What is the nature of that decision-making process? What determines the kinds of meanings that are attributed to particular activities and events? How do these meanings get constructed? We organize our discussion of such questions and issues around the "debate" between rational choice and social constructionist perspectives. These two labels point to theory groups that are themselves internally diverse, with many scholars in each group taking account of the insights from the other group. Nevertheless, we can clarify many issues by employing this dichotomy.

We believe the crucial difference between these two theory groups can be understood as the difference between treating cognitions as independent variables versus dependent variables. The "independent variable" group takes cognitions more or less as givens and attempts to predict behavior from cognitions. Variants of rational choice are currently dominant in this theory cluster, but it also includes control theory, learning theory, and relative deprivation theory. The "dependent variable" group, by contrast, seeks to explain the processes whereby the cognitions themselves are created. This group rejects the notion that cognitions can ever be treated as unproblematic givens and stresses that behavior and cognitions are interconnected in a dynamic and reflexive fashion.

Independent Variable (Rational Choice) Perspectives.
The perspectives falling into this theory group are concerned primarily with identifying either the role of different cognitions in determining behavior or the mechanisms linking cognitions and behavior. Cognitions are viewed as mediating the relationship between objective conditions and action and are assumed to bear a reasonably good fit with objective reality. Thus, these perspectives speak more often of knowledge than of belief and often explicitly treat variations or changes in cognitions as crucial determinants of behavior (Oliver and Marwell 1992).

Included in this broad grouping are tension reductionist perspectives, such as relative deprivation theory, discussed earlier; behaviorist or social learning models (Macy 1990); and rational choice or decision theory. Since the preponderance of recent work treating cognitions as independent variables has done so by explicitly or implicitly employing aspects of the latter perspective, we will concentrate on it in the remainder of this section.

Rational Decision Theories.
The central assumptions of all instrumentalist, rational choice, or subjective expected utility models are (1) that people seek to obtain benefits and minimize costs, and (2) that they cognitively process information about the likely benefits and costs of various courses of action and then make a conscious choice about their behavior (see Friedman and Hechter 1988). Thus, the central metatheoretical assumptions of these theories are that cognitions precede behaviors and choices are conscious, intentional, and rational.

Although usually assuming an unproblematic relation between objective conditions and subjective cognitions, this tradition treats subjective preferences (benefits and costs) as the operative terms. Altruism and solidarity can be subjective preferences, and models can include imperfect information. These theories often make additional assumptions to permit construction of formal models and determinate calculations, such as the assumptions that everything can be reduced to a common metric or that decisions are evaluated on an expected value criterion. These are viewed as simplifying assumptions, not empirical statements about how most people actually think.

A second crucial issue for rational choice theories of collective action is the link between individual and group interests. Mancur Olson's *The Logic of Collective Action* (1968) is the crucial watershed in thinking about this issue. Prior to this work it was widely assumed that there was a natural tendency for people with shared interests to act together to pursue those interests, that is, that there was an unproblematic congruence between individual interests and group interests. Olson argued otherwise. Drawing on standard cost-benefit microeconomics and public goods theory, he argued that rational individuals would not contribute to the provision of public or collective goods (i.e., goods that are shared by everyone whether or not they help to pay for them). There has been extensive work in the rational choice paradigm showing that Olson's claim that collective action is "irrational" is overgeneralized and misleading (Hardin 1982; Marwell and Oliver 1993; Oliver and Marwell

1988.)[8] In particular, Olson confuses the "free rider" problem, in which individuals are motivated to let others provide the good, with what Oliver and Marwell (1988) call the "efficacy problem," in which each individual cannot make a large enough difference in the collective good to justify participation. What remains is broad agreement that both the relationship between individual and group interests and mobilization around shared interests are vexing issues.

A third feature of rational choice theories also follows from Olson (1962). He argued that actors must be provided with *selective incentives*—private goods that reward contributors or coercive measures that punish nonparticipation. Although the claim that such private incentives are necessary has been rejected by subsequent theorists, Olson's work has led to a focus on individual incentives that reward participation or punish nonparticipation (see Oliver [1980] for a discussion of the difference between rewards and punishments as incentives). Olson stressed private material gain, but subsequent scholars in the rational choice tradition have extended the notion of incentives. Following James Q. Wilson (1973), most scholars recognize three broad types of incentives: material, solidary, and purposive. Material incentives are those Olson discussed and include salaries, insurance programs, and threats of physical or economic retaliation. Solidary incentives arise from social relations with other participants, such as praise, respect, and friendship shared among coparticipants or shame, contempt, and ostracism in the case of nonparticipants. Purposive incentives arise from internalized norms and values in which a person's self-esteem depends on doing the right thing. The concepts of solidary and purposive incentives have permitted rational choice theories to incorporate the influences of social networks, culture, and socialization. Thus, although the theory makes individualistic assumptions about decisions as it is employed in the study of social movements, it has come to recognize the influence of social networks, socialization, and culture on individuals.

These core features of rational choice theory—conscious intentional decisions, the importance of benefits and costs, the problematic nature of mobilization, and the importance of individual incentives for action—mesh directly with the central concerns of resource mobilization and political opportunity theories (Jenkins 1983; McAdam 1982; Tarrow 1989b; Tilly 1978; Zald and McCarthy 1987). They focus attention on resources and capacities and on a series of variables likely to promote or hinder the prospects for mobilization. Objective structural conditions are assumed to be a major determinant of subjective interests and perceived costs and capacities. Rational choice theory puts the stated "goals" of a movement or action center stage as the central explanation for participation and tends to describe participants as people concerned about a problem trying to use their available resources to address that problem.

Besides its influence on political and organizational studies in the resource mobilization paradigm, this general perspective has been employed directly in a wide variety of studies, including rebellious political behavior and violence (Muller 1980; Muller and Opp 1986; Muller, Dietz, and Finkel 1991); antiwar protest crowds and riot participation (Berk 1974; Bryan 1979); mobilization in the wake of nuclear accidents (Opp 1988; Walsh and Warland 1983); organizational dynamics in the John Birch society (Oliver and Furman 1989); and labor movement mobilization (Klandermans 1984). Specific theoretical issues addressed using this paradigm include identity incentives and collective action (Friedman and McAdam 1992); ethnic mobilization (Hechter, Friedman, and Applebaum 1982); individual thresholds for participation in collective behavior events (Granovetter 1978); the difference between rewards and punishments as incentives (Oliver 1980); the difference between collective goods that can be provided by a few large contributors and those that must be provided by many small contributors (Oliver, Marwell, and Teixeira 1985); the difference between time and money as movement resources (Oliver and Furman 1989; Oliver and Marwell 1992); and the dynamics of paid versus volunteer activism (Oliver 1983) and professional versus volunteer mobilizing technologies (Oliver and Marwell 1992).

An important trend in rational choice theory is a move away from models of individual decisions toward models of group mobilization processes. Oliver and Marwells's "critical mass theory" (Marwell and Oliver 1993; Marwell, Oliver, and Prahl 1988; Oliver and Marwell 1988; Oliver, Marwell and Teixeira 1985) provides a variety of models of organizer-centered mobilization, in which resource-constrained organizers try to maximize the total amount of resources mobilized from a heterogeneous pool of potential participants. Heckathorn (1990) discusses chains of influence, in which group members may sanction each other to enforce compliance with external demands. Macy (1990) has modified these models to replace the rational decision maker with an adaptive learner, showing that different assumptions about individuals lead to different predictions about group outcomes. In all these cases, illuminating conclusions about the differences between groups in their possibilities for collective action are obtained by making simplifying assumptions about the individuals in those groups.

Ignoring for a moment the metatheoretical presuppositions of the theory, we may consider its capacity as a predictive tool, which is often substantial. Attitude measures that can be construed as measures of a person's subjective interest in an action's goals have reasonably strong correlations with participation in many forms of collective action (Klandermans 1984; Klandermans and Oegema 1987; Oliver 1984; Opp 1988; Walsh and Warland 1983). Direct measures of solidary and purposive incentives also have the expected positive relations (Klandermans 1984; Klandermans and Oegema 1987; Opp 1988). Carden (1978) argues that activists motivated by purposive incentives require control over their actions and decentralized organizations, but generally material incentives have not been found to motivate activists. However, financial contributions from less interested members do allow for paid activism (Oliver 1983) and enable more committed members to pursue their goals (Knoke 1988).

Rational choice theorists also point to the central importance of efficacy, the perception that one's actions will make a difference in accomplishing the goals, which is the sense of hope and urgency that marks the historic moments of peak collective action (e.g., McAdam 1982). Consistent with these arguments, research generally finds that participants in movement activities are more optimistic than nonparticipants about the prospect of change and about the efficacy of their participation. In other words, they are more likely to believe change is possible and that their contribution will make a difference. This pattern was found in research on riot participants of the 1960s (Forward and Williams 1970; Paige 1971; Seeman 1975), as noted earlier, and has been a frequent finding in more recent research on social movement activity (Finkel, Muller, and Opp 1989; Klandermans 1984; McAdam 1982; Opp 1988).

However, there are two clear cases where data conflict with the theory. First, rational choice models clearly predict that costs are negatively related to action, but this prediction seems to hold only in the extreme cases of objective material constraints or severe repression. Wealthy people give more money to social causes than the poor, but they give much lower proportions of their incomes. Busy people contribute more time and energy to movement activity than those who are not busy (Oliver 1984). Most important, several studies that have measured costs subjectively found that it operated opposite to the way the theory predicts. For example, Hirsch (1990) found that participants in a campus divestment protest believed they were bearing heavy costs and making sacrifices, while nonparticipants downplayed the costs and assumed the participants were gaining intrinsic benefits. Opp (1988, 1989) found a similar pattern regarding the assessment of costs and risks associated with antinuclear protest activity. These findings can be interpreted in instrumentalist terms, but only when it is recognized that legitimacy is gained through making sacrifices for a cause and that what is seen as a cost from the outside is reinterpreted as a benefit from the vantage point of the actors themselves. But this alternative interpretation clearly raises questions about the construction of such meanings and understandings, issues that rational decision models cannot really address.

The second problem is that self-reported individual efficacy levels often seem implausible. Opp's (1989) movement participants claimed levels of individual efficacy that are so objectively impossible that it is difficult to accept their answers at face value, just as voters vastly overstate the impact their one vote has on election outcomes. Participants seem to attribute to themselves as individuals the efficacy they believe the whole movement has. Only if they are asked to distinguish very carefully their own individual contribution from that of others will they acknowledge that their contribution alone is not likely to make much difference. Instead, they appear to answer efficacy questions as if their own answer refers to the joint effect of all people like themselves. That is, they simply gloss over the individual efficacy problem in favor of a collectivist perception. Although less clearly documented for most other cases, this kind of answer or statement is often made by movement participants. At one level, this finding is consistent with rational decision models, since this transformation of the efficacy term makes action sensible and possible. But at another level, this transformation itself begs for explanation. Although Opp offers an individual cost-benefit account of why people choose to modify their perceptions of efficacy, this tendency seems to cry out for a constructionist account.

Dependent Variable (Social Constructionist) Perspectives. In response to the tendency for resource mobilization and rational choice theorists to treat preferences or values, costs and benefits, and meanings and grievances as unproblematic givens or as data points that can be plugged into an equation as independent variables, a number of scholars began to call in the first half of the 1980s for renewed attention to such cognitive and ideational factors and the processes of interpretation and symbolization (Cohen 1985; Ferree and Miller 1985; Gamson, Fireman, and Rytina 1982; Klandermans

1984; McAdam 1982; Snow et al. 1986; Turner 1983; Zurcher and Snow 1981).[9] This was not so much a new initiative as it was an attempt to rescue and resuscitate previously glossed concepts, such as ideology and grievances, and blend them with more recent strands of cognitive social psychology, such as attribution theory, symbolic interactionism broadly conceived, and the rediscovery of culture in American sociology. By the early 1990s, this initiative and the issues it raised were attracting increasing interest and being discussed under the rubric of "social constructionism." We thus use it here as an integrative cover term that is suggestive of an emerging perspective with respect to the study of crowds and social movements.

This perspective acknowledges the rationalist and resource mobilization insight that social movements constitute purposive, self-conscious attempts to produce or halt social change. But social constructionists also recognize that perceptions of grievances, costs and benefits, and possibilities for action are all socially constructed: "what is at issue is not merely the presence or absence of grievances, but the manner in which grievances are interpreted and the generation and diffusion of those interpretations" (Snow et al. 1986, 466). Thus, social constructionists are especially concerned with the processes whereby existing structures of meaning are challenged or modified and new ones are created, deployed, and diffused through processes of collective discourse and action.

A range of work clusters under the canopy of social constructionism, including Turner and Killian's (1987) continuously evolving emergent norm perspective; the framing perspective of Snow and Benford (Snow and Benford 1988, 1992; Snow et al. 1986); Klandermans's (1984, 1988) work on consensus mobilization; Gamson's (1988; Gamson and Modigliani 1989) theorizing and research on media discourse and packaging; Melucci's (1985, 1988, 1989) work on the construction and negotiation of collective identities; and a growing number of works focusing on the interface of culture, reality construction, consciousness, and contention (Benford and Hunt 1992; Fantasia 1988). Since space does not permit an overview of each of these lines of theory and research, we consider the work associated with framing processes and collective identity, the two social constructionist themes that have generated the most attention in recent years.

Framing Processes and Collective Action Frames. From a framing perspective, movement activists and organizations are not viewed merely as carriers of extant ideas and meanings, but as "signifying agents" actively engaged in the production and maintenance of meaning for constituents, antagonists, and bystanders. In addition, they are seen as being embroiled, along with the media, local governments, and the state, in "the politics of signification"—that is, the struggle to have certain meanings and understandings gain ascendance over others, or at least move up some existing hierarchy of credibility. Building on Goffman's *Frame Analysis* (1974), Snow and Benford (1992) conceptualize this signifying work with the verb *framing,* to denote the process of reality construction. This process is active, ongoing, and continuously evolving; it entails agency in the sense that what evolves is the product of joint action by movement participants in encounters with antagonists and targets; and it is contentious in the sense that it generates alternate interpretive schemes that may challenge existing frames.

Snow and Benford (1992) call the products of this activity "collective action frames," which can be defined as emergent action-oriented sets of beliefs and meaning that inspire and legitimate social movement activities and campaigns. They perform this mobilizing function by identifying a problematic condition and defining it as unjust, intolerable, and deserving of corrective action (see also Gamson, Fireman, and Rytina 1982, 14–16; Turner 1969; Turner and Killian 1987, 242–245); by attributing blame or identifying the causal agent(s) (Ferree and Miller 1985; Snow and Benford 1992); and by articulating and aligning individual orientations, interests, and life experiences with the orientation and objectives of movement organizations. Regarding the latter process, Snow and colleagues (1986) have identified four distinct alignment processes: "bridging" frame congruent or ideologically isomorphic but immobilized sentiment pools; "amplifying" existing values or beliefs; "extending" the SMO's interpretive framework to encompass interests and perspectives that are not directly relevant to its primary objectives; and "transforming" old meanings and/or generating new ones, usually through affecting conversion.

Since the initial work on frame alignment processes, the framing perspective has broadened and new research questions have been raised. First, what determines the effectiveness or mobilizing potency of movement framing efforts? Why do some proffered framings affect mobilization, while others do not? What, in other words, accounts for "frame resonance" (Snow and Benford 1988; see also Gamson 1992)? Second, to what extent and under what conditions does a collective action frame sometimes come to function as a "master frame" in relation to a cycle of protest or movement activity by coloring and constraining the orientations and activities of other movements in the cycle (Snow and Benford 1992; Tarrow 1989b)? Third, what is the link between collective action frames and the generation of incentives for action, or what Klandermans calls "action mobilization" (1984, 1988)? To what extent and how does the framing process generate "motivational frames" that function as prods to action (Benford 1993b; Snow and Benford 1988). Fourth, what are the internal and external dynamics that affect the framing process? Discussion, debate, and contention exist within movements just as between movements and their antagonists, countermovements, and targets. How do these tensions, debates, and disputes affect the framing process and/or mobilizing capacity of existing frames (Benford 1993a)? And what is the role of the media in this process, especially since one of its primary functions is framing issues and agendas (Gamson 1992; Gitlin 1980)?

During the past several years, these questions about the link between collective action frames and mobilization have generated considerable research that demonstrates the centrality of framing processes in mobilization in such diverse cases as the U.S. peace movement (Benford 1987), the IRA (White 1989), Italian protest cycles (Tarrow 1989a), protest demonstrations in West Germany (Gerhards and Rucht 1992), ideology and abeyance processes in U.S. farmers' movements (Mooney 1990), and the Catalonian nationalist movement (Johnston 1991). These empirical works and other critical assessments (Gamson 1992; Tarrow 1992) point to modifications and refinements of framing concepts while affirming their value. Transcending framing theory itself, this research demonstrates more generally that the cognitions relevant to collective action—be they preferences, values, interests or utilities, costs or benefits, punishments or rewards, self-concepts or identities, or consciousness itself—are social constructions that are dynamic and evolving entities which must be examined and explained.

Collective Identity and Collective Action. Although identity is a central concept in sociological social psychology and identities are often at stake in movement activities, emphasis on identity in the study of collective behavior has waxed and waned. It figured prominently in a number of well-known works in the 1950s and 1960s (Hoffer 1951; Keniston 1968; Klapp 1969) and then lay fallow throughout the 1970s and the early 1980s. The reason for its neglect was due largely to the tendency of earlier accounts to portray participants as suffering from spoiled identities (Hoffer 1951) or identity deficits (Klapp 1969; Kornhauser 1959) and the dominance of organizational and political perspectives in the 1970s. But despite academic neglect, there is always a very real connection between identity and movement participation. As Gamson noted recently:

> Cleansed of its assumptions about a spoiled or ersatz identity, there is a central insight that remains. Participation in social movements frequently involves enlargement of personal identity for participants and offers fulfillment and realization of self. (1992, 56)

When realization of this connection resurfaced in the late 1980s, attention shifted from individual identity deficits and quests to the construction of "collective identities." At the forefront of this line of inquiry were several European scholars associated with the "new social movements" perspective (Melucci 1985, 1988, 1989; Pizzorno 1978; Touraine 1981), with the work and voice of Melucci being most prominent.[10]

For Melucci, collective identity is inseparable from collective action and is the key to understanding its dynamics. He defines collective identity as "an interactive and shared definition produced by several interacting individuals who are concerned with the orientations of their action as well as the field of opportunities and constraints in which their action takes place" (Melucci 1989, 34). This means, according to Keane and Mier, who edited Melucci's most explicit treatment of the concept, that collective identity is "a moveable definition (that actors) have of themselves and their social world, a more or less shared and dynamic understanding of the goals of their action as well as the social field of possibilities and limits within which their action takes place" (Melucci 1989, 4). Deconstructed even further, Melucci's actors are in the "process of constructing an action system," and it is the product of this constructive process that is constitutive of collective identity (Melucci 1989, 34).

Turner (1991a) has noted that this provocative conceptualization is very similar to the Blumerian strand of symbolic interactionism and resonates with social constructionism more generally. However, it is conceptually and empirically slippery. How is it captured empirically or operationalized? How can we probe for its presence or absence? Collective identity is more than the aggregation of corresponding individual identities, but how is that difference grasped without rendering the concept tautological? Because of its empirical elusiveness, it appears that scholars who find the idea of collective identity tantalizing have opted for a conception that highlights the kinds of shared commitments and bonds of solidarity that give rise to a sense of "one-ness" or "we-ness."

Thus, Taylor and associates, in their research on collective identity in the women's movement and lesbian feminist mobilization, define collective identity as "the shared definition of a group that derives from its members' common interests and solidarity" (Taylor 1989, 771; see also Taylor and Whittier 1992). In his study of the construction of collective identity in a peace movement organization, Hunt refers to it as "the qualities and characteristics attributed to a group by members of that group" (1991, 1) and explicitly links the concept with the identity literature in social psychology (e.g., Stryker 1980; Weigert, Teitge, and Teitge 1986). These definitions make collective identity more empirically accessible, but they also make it almost indistinguishable from the concept of commitment. Perhaps that is not a problem, however, so long as Melucci's central contributions are not lost: that collective identity is not merely shared opinions but emerges out of joint action; that collective identity is both grounded in and helps to constitute the field of action; and that identities and action fields are constantly changing.

Affective Dimensions

Emotions are not peculiar to any particular domain of social life. Like other inner states, however, they are subject to differential expression contingent on differences in social circumstances, regulations, and cues. Thus, some situations are more evocative of emotion and its display than others. Clearly this is the case with collective behavior situations. Most people participate in crowd behavior and social movement activities because of problems or dilemmas they care about, and these events are often characterized by displays of emotion or at least a palpable sense of passion, anger, or solidarity. Such emotion and passion were evident in the pro-democracy demonstrations in Beijing in the Spring of 1989; in the throngs massing to celebrate the crumbling of the Berlin Wall in early November 1989; in the outpouring of shock, dismay, and anger in the wake of the Rodney King verdict in Los Angeles in May 1992; and in such ongoing conflicts as those between antiabortionists and pro-choice adherents and between environmentalists and the lumber industry. Indeed, one is hard-pressed to think of instances of collective behavior gatherings that do not evoke strong sentiments, even if their expression is restrained, as in the case of memorial gatherings for AIDS victims or the homeless.

Yet this affective dimension of collective behavior and social movements has been the least theorized and researched of all the social psychological dimensions. There are two major recent exceptions: one is Turner and Killian's (1987, 104–105) reasoned linkage of emotion and expressive tendencies in collective behavior; the other is Lofland's (1981) original taxonomy of "elementary forms of collective behavior" based on the dominance of one of three primary emotions—joy, anger, and fear. Not coincidentally, that essay was written for the initial volume of this book. Zurcher and Snow's (1981, 477–479) discussion of social movements in the same volume also called attention to the neglect of passion in relation to the ebb and flow of social movements, and hypothesized that movement viability is contingent in part on the management of the ongoing dialectic between organization and passion. But it was Lofland's chapter (1981) and other work (1985) that constituted a clarion call for greater attention to affect and emotion. Nevertheless, a decade later, the imbalance remains. McPhail's (1991) detailed and systematic discussion of the literature on crowds contains only two mentions of emotion in its index, one pointing to his review of Lofland's work and the other to Couch's (1968) critique of older stereotypes of collective behavior as emotional and irrational.

Why the obvious neglect of emotion or affect in recent studies of crowds and social movements? Probably the ultimate answer is the long-standing tradition in Western philosophy of treating reason and emotion as opposites. But the more proximate answer resides in two parallel occurrences: the ascendance of the resource mobilization and rational decision perspectives and the identification of most scholars of collective action with the

60s movements. The result was a corresponding tendency to impute heightened rationality to collective actors. This tendency notwithstanding, more and more scholars today reject the dichotomy of reason and action and would agree with Turner and Killian:

> ... the very distinctions themselves are difficult to make. Emotion and reason are not today regarded as irreconcilables. Emotion may accompany the execution of a well-reasoned plan, and the execution of an inadequately reasoned plan may be accompanied by no arousal of emotions. (1987, 13)

Moreover, emotion and cognition are often, and perhaps always, intimately linked. Emotion and emotional displays can be socially constructed and managed, as Zurcher (1982), among others, has amply demonstrated, and there is no necessary contradictory relationship between the study of emotion and rational choice perspectives. In fact, it is possible to have noninstrumentalist cost-benefit decision models for what Turner and Killian (1987, 97–105) refer to as "expressive" crowd behavior and what Rule (1988, 191, 196, pass.) calls "consummatory" actions—actions that are ends in themselves. Rule uses the example of African American rioters' expressions of anger at white businesses and white police in the 1960s. In these cases, the benefit of the action is the consummatory pleasure in the act itself, and the cost of the action is its consequences. There are also, obviously, mixed cases, in which an action is both pleasurable as an end in itself and a means to another end.

The point is that cognitive perspectives, whether rational choice or social constructionist, can inform understanding of the link between affect or emotion and crowd and social movement dynamics, and vice versa. There are, then, only ideological reasons for not pursuing this linkage more vigorously. Clearly the time has come to heed Lofland's call and move forward on this front, bearing in mind the caveat that what Turner and Killian (1987) have called the "illusion of homogeneity" applies just as readily to emotional displays as to the array of behaviors with which they are often associated.

SUMMARY

We have provided a working conceptualization of collective behavior, crowds, and social movements, discussed the historic linkage between the study of these social phenomena and social psychology, identified the five major social psychological dimensions of crowds and social movements, and synthesized and critically assessed the extensive literature relevant to these key social psychological dimensions. They include the microstructural and social relational dimension, the personality dimension and related social psychological processes, the socialization dimension, the cognitive dimension, and the affective or emotional dimension. These social psychological dimensions are relevant to all domains of social life, of course. But it is the way they operate, interact, and combine with structural and cultural factors in each domain of social life that distinguishes one domain from another.

We think our examination of the theorizing and research pertinent to these dimensions not only demonstrates how social psychology has informed understanding of issues and questions central to the study of crowds and social movements, but also indicates that the social psychology of this domain of social life is alive and well. Indeed, we would agree with the former critic of social psychological perspectives on collective action, who has done an about-face and recently asserted that "many of the major questions animating contemporary work on social movements are intrinsically social psychological" (Gamson 1992, 54–55). While others might take exception with this contention, there is little question but that a full-bodied, thoroughgoing understanding of the emergence, operation, and course and character of crowds and social movements requires consideration of the social psychological dimensions elaborated throughout this chapter.

NOTES

The authors are indebted to Rob Benford, Bill Gamson, Scott Hunt, Doug McAdam, Clark McPhail, and Ralph Turner for their useful suggestions and comments.

1. Some readers might object to the conceptualization of collective behavior as collective problem-solving activity, yet an examination of virtually any collective behavior reveals people engaging in joint action to deal with a particular problem. Even in so-called panics, where individuals are dealing with the perception of imminent danger, Johnson (1987a,1987b) finds that cooperative, coordinated behavior is typical.

2. For discussion of the range of literature on crowd phenomena and behavior in disaster situations, see Goode (1992), Turner and Killian (1987), and Dynes et al. (1987).

3. There has been a misguided tendency among resource mobilization and political opportunity theorists (e.g., McAdam 1982; McCarthy and Zald 1973; Morris 1984; Tilly 1978) to lump all pre-1965 work together as the "collective behavior tradition," ignoring important differences and distinctions among theories and thus missing important insights from past scholarship. Snow and Davis (1995) have attempted to correct this tendency in part by distinguishing among the "Harvard" strain tradition, the "Michigan" resource mobilization perspective, and the "Chicago" symbolic interactionist tradition.

4. In this same period, other scholars with more macro orientations were examining the variations and complexities of organizational forms and showing how movements' organizational forms vary cross-nationally and across time. By the late 1980s, however, most scholars had abandoned the false dichotomy of micro versus macro, social psychology versus politics and organization, and had come to see both as important. Indeed,

forging links between these aspects of movement reality is now regarded as one of the important agendas for the 1990s.

5. Drawing on the work of George Herbert Mead and William T. Powers, McPhail has developed a cybernetic model of coordination that entails individuals adjusting their behavior to bring their perceptual signals in line with a reference signal (McPhail 1991; McPhail, Powers, and Tucker 1992; McPhail and Tucker 1990).

6. Space does not permit a comprehensive listing of the various mechanisms and hypotheses associated with this perspective, much less a detailed review treating their subtleties and complexities on their own terms, but overviews can be found in Zurcher and Snow (1981, 449–454) and Turner and Killian (1987, 334–337).

7. Space does not permit a detailed review of the extensive literature on conversion; for comprehensive reviews see Machalek and Snow (1993), Robbins (1988), and Snow and Machalek (1984).

8. Most sociologists have misunderstood the logical implication of Olson's argument about the "irrationality" of collective action, which is not that collective action never occurs—clearly a false empirical claim—but that when collective action occurs it must be either because the participants are not rational actors or because they have additional individual motivations for action.

9. For corresponding but more focused critiques of rational choice perspectives on collective behavior and social movements, see Ferree (1992), Fireman and Gamson (1979), and Turner (1991b).

10. For a number of useful and overlapping discussions of this "new social movements" perspective, see Klandermans (1986), Kriesi (1988a), Rucht (1988), and Tarrow (1989b).

REFERENCES

Aberle, David. 1966. *The Peyote Religion Among the Navajo.* Chicago: Aldine.

Adorno, T., E. Frenkel-Brunswik, D. J. Levinson, and R. N. Sanford. 1950. *The Authoritarian Personality.* New York: Harper.

Aguirre, Benigno. 1984. Conventionalization of collective behavior in Cuba. *American Journal of Sociology* 90:541–566.

Allport, Floyd H. 1924. *Social Psychology.* Boston: Houghton Mifflin.

Asch, Solomon. 1952. *Social Psychology.* Englewood Cliffs, NJ: Prentice Hall.

Aveni, Adrian. 1977. The not so-lonely-crowd: Friendship groups in collective behavior. *Sociometry* 40: 96–99.

Barker, Eileen. 1984. *The Making of a Moonie: Choice or Brainwashing?* Oxford, UK: Blackwell.

Benford, Robert D. 1987. *Framing Activity, Meaning, and Social Movement Participation: The Nuclear Disarmament Movement.* Unpublished Ph.D. diss.

Department of Sociology, University of Texas, Austin.

———. 1992. Social movements. Pp. 1880–1887 in *Encyclopedia of Sociology,* vol. 4, ed. E. Borgatta and M. Borgatta. New York: Macmillan.

———. 1993a. Frame disputes within the nuclear disarmament movement. *Social Forces* 71:677–701.

———. 1993b. "You could be the hundredth monkey": Collective action frames and vocabularies of motive within the nuclear disarmament movement. *Sociological Quarterly* 34:195–216.

Benford, Robert D., and Scott A. Hunt. 1992. Dramaturgy and social movements: The social construction and communication of power. *Sociological Inquiry* 62:36–55.

Bengston, L. 1970. The generation gap: A review and typology of social psychological perspectives. *Youth and Society* 25:7–32.

Berk, Richard. 1974. A gaming approach to crowd behavior. *American Sociological Review* 39:355–373.

Berk, Richard, and Howard Aldrich. 1972. Patterns of vandalism during civil disorders as an indicator of selection of targets. *American Sociological Review* 37:533–547.

Bird, Frederick, and William Reimer. 1982. Participation rates in new religious movements and para-religious movements. *Journal for the Scientific Study of Religion* 21:1–14.

Blumer, Herbert. 1939. Collective behavior. Pp. 219–288 in *Principles of Sociology,* ed. R. E. Park. New York: Barnes & Noble.

Broadbent, Jeffrey. 1986. The ties that bind: Social fabric and the mobilization of environmental movements in Japan. *International Journal of Mass Emergencies and Disasters* 4:227–253.

Bryan, Marguerite. 1979. The social psychology of riot participation. *Research in Race and Ethnic Relations* 1:169–187.

Bush, Diane Mitsch, and Roberta G. Simmons. 1981. Socialization processes over the life course. Pp. 133–164 in *Social Psychology: Sociological Perspectives,* ed. M. Rosenberg and R. H. Turner. New York: Basic Books.

Carden, Maren L. 1978. The proliferation of a social movement. Pp. 179–196 in *Research in Social Movements, Conflict and Change,* vol. 1, ed. L. Kriesberg. Greenwich, CT: JAI Press.

Cohen, Jean L. 1985. Strategy or identity: New theoretical paradigms and contemporary social movements. *Social Research* 52:663–716.

Coleman, James S. 1990. *Foundations of Social Theory.* Cambridge, MA: Harvard University Press.

Coser, Lewis A. 1967. Greedy organizations. *Archives Europeenes de Sociologie* 8:196–215.

Couch, Carl J. 1968. Collective behavior: An examination of some stereotypes. *Social Problems* 15: 310–322.

Cress, Daniel M., and J. Miller McPherson. 1992. The paradox of persistence and participation. Unpublished manuscript.

Curtis, Russell L., Jr., and Benigno E. Aguirre, ed. 1993. *Collective Behavior and Social Movements.* Boston: Allyn and Bacon.

Davies, James C. 1969. The J-curve of rising and declining satisfaction as a cause of some great revolutions and a contained rebellion. Pp. 690–730 in *Violence in America: Historical and Comparative Perspectives,* ed. Hugh David Graham and Ted Robert Gurr. Washington, DC: U.S. Government Printing Office.

DeMartini, Joseph R. 1983. Social movement participation: Political socialization, generational consciousness and lasting effects. *Youth and Society* 15:195–233.

Demerath, N. J. III, Gerald Marwell, and Michael T. Aiken. 1971. *Dynamics of Idealism: White Activists in a Black Movement.* San Francisco: Jossey-Bass.

Diener, Edward. 1980. Deindividuation: The absence of self-awareness and self-regulation in group members. Pp. 209–244 in *Psychology of Group Influence,* ed. P. Paulus. Hillsdale, NJ: Erlbaum.

Dollard, John, Leonard Doob, Neal Miller, Herbert Mowrer, and Robert Sears. 1939. *Frustration and Aggression.* New Haven: Yale University Press.

Dynes, Russell R. 1970. *Organized Behavior in Disaster.* Lexington, MA: DC Heath.

Dynes, Russell R., Bruna DeMarchi, and Carlo Pelanda, ed. 1987. *Sociology of Disasters: Contribution of Sociology to Disaster Research.* Milan: Franco Angeli.

Evans, Sara M., and Harry C. Boyte. 1986. *Free Spaces: The Sources of Democratic Change in America.* New York: Harper & Row.

Fantasia, Rick. 1988. *Cultures of Solidarity: Consciousness, Action, and Contemporary American Workers.* Berkeley: University of California Press.

Fendrich, James, and Kenneth Lovoy. 1988. Back to the future: Adult political behavior of former student activists. *American Sociological Review* 53: 780–784.

Fernandez, Roberto and Doug McAdam. 1988. Social networks and social movements: Multiorganizational fields and recruitment to Mississippi Freedom Summer. *Sociological Forum* 3:357–382.

———. 1989. Multiorganizational fields and recruitment to social movements, Pp. 217–231 in *Organizing for Change: Social Movement Organizations in Europe and the United States,* ed. B. Klandermans. Greenwich, CT: JAI Press.

Ferree, Myra Marx. 1992. The political context of rationality: Rational choice theory and resource mobilization. Pp. 29–52 in *Frontiers in Social Movement Theory,* ed. A. Morris and C. Mueller. New Haven: Yale University Press.

Ferree, Myra Marx, and Frederick D. Miller. 1985. Mobilization and meaning: Toward an integration of social psychological and resource perspectives on social movements. *Sociological Inquiry* 55:38–61.

Feuer, Lewis S. 1969. *The Conflict of Generations.* New York: Basic Books.

Fine, Gary Alan, and Randy Stoecker. 1985. Can the circle be unbroken: Small groups and social movements. *Advances in Group Processes* 2:1–28.

Finkel, Steven E., Edward Muller, and Karl-Dieter Opp. 1989. Personal influence, collective rationality, and mass political action. *American Political Science Review* 83:885–903.

Finkel, Steven E., and James B. Rule. 1986. Relative deprivation and related psychological theories of civil violence: A critical review. Pp. 47–69 in *Social Movements, Social Conflicts, and Change,* vol. 9, ed. K. Lang and G. Lang. Greenwich, CT: JAI Press.

Fireman, Bruce, and William A. Gamson. 1979. Utilitarian logic in the resource mobilization perspective. Pp. 8–45 in *The Dynamics of Social Movements,* ed. M. Zald and J. McCarthy. Cambridge, MA: Winthrop.

Flacks, Richard. 1967. The liberated generation: an exploration of the roots of student protest. *Journal of Social Issues* 23:52–74.

Forward, J. R., and J. R. Williams. 1970. Internal-external control and black militancy. *Journal of Social Issues* 26:75–92.

Freeman, Jo. 1973. The origins of the women's liberation movement. *American Journal of Sociology* 78: 192–811.

Freud, Sigmund. 1921. *Group Psychology and Analysis of the Ego.* London: International Psychoanalytical Press.

Friedman, Debra, and Michael Hechter. 1988. The contribution of rational choice theory to macrosociological research. *Sociological Theory* 6:201–216.

Friedman, Debra, and Doug McAdam. 1992. Identity incentives and activism: Networks, choices, and the life of a social movement. Pp. 156–173 in *Frontiers in Social Movement Theory,* ed. A. Morris and C. Mueller. New Haven: Yale University Press.

Gamson, William A. 1968. *Power and Discontent.* Homewood, IL: Dorsey.

———. 1988. Political discourse and collective action. *International Social Movement Research* 1: 219–244.

———. [1975] 1990. The Strategy of Social Protest. Homewood, IL: Dorsey.

———. 1992. The social psychology of collective action. Pp. 53–76 in *Frontiers of Social Movement Theory,* ed. A. Morris and C. Mueller. New Haven: Yale University Press.

Gamson, William A., Bruce Fireman, and Steven Rytina. 1982. *Encounters with Unjust Authority.* Homewood, IL: Dorsey.

Gamson, William A., and Andre Modigliani. 1989. Media discourse and public opinion on nuclear power: A constructionist approach. *American Journal of Sociology* 95:1–37.

Gecas, Viktor. 1981. Contexts of socialization. Pp. 165–199 in *Social Psychology: Sociological Perspectives,* ed. M. Rosenberg and R. H. Turner. New York: Basic Books.

———. 1992. Socialization. Pp. 1863–1872 in *Encyclopedia of Sociology,* ed. E. Borgatta and M. Borgatta. New York: Macmillan.

Gerhards, Jurgen, and Dieter Rucht. 1992. Mesomobilization: Organizing and framing in two protest campaigns in West Germany. *American Journal of Sociology* 98:555–596.

Gerlach, Luther, and Virginia Hine. 1970. *People, Power and Change: Movements of Social Transformation.* Indianapolis: Bobbs-Merrill.

Geschwender, James A. 1967. Continuities in theories of status consistency and cognitive dissonance. *Social Forces* 46:160–171.

Gitlin, Todd. 1980. *The Whole World Is Watching.* Berkeley: University of California Press.

Goffman, Erving. 1974. *Frame Analysis.* New York: Harper.

Goode, Erich. 1992. *Collective Behavior.* New York: Harcourt Brace Jovanovich.

Gould, Roger V. 1991. Multiple networks and mobilization in the Paris commune, 1871. *American Sociological Review* 56:716–729.

———. 1993. Trade cohesion, class unity, and urban insurrection: Artisanal activisim in the Paris commune. *American Journal of Sociology* 98:721–754.

Granovetter, Mark. 1978. Threshold models of collective behavior. *American Journal of Sociology* 83:1420–1443.

Gurney, J. N., and K. T. Tierney. 1982. Relative deprivation and social movements: A critical look at twenty years of theory and research. *Sociological Quarterly* 23:33–47.

Gurr, Ted. 1970. *Why Men Rebel.* Princeton: Princeton University Press.

Gusfield, Joseph R. 1963. *Symbolic Crusade: Status Politics and the American Temperance Movement.* Urbana: University of Illinois Press.

Haimson, Leopold. 1964. The problem of social stability in urban Russia, 1905–1917, part one. *Slavic Review* 23:619–642.

Hall, John R. 1988. Social organization and pathways of commitment: Types of communal groups, rational choice theory, and the Kanter thesis. *American Sociological Review* 53:679–692.

Hardin, Russell. 1982. *Collective Action.* Baltimore: John Hopkins University Press.

Hechter, Michael. 1987. *Principles of Group Solidarity.* Berkeley: University of California Press.

Hechter, Michael, Debra Friedman, and Malka Applebaum. 1982. A theory of ethnic collective action. *Internal Migration Review* 16:412–434.

Heckathorn, Douglas. 1990. Collective sanctions and compliance norms: A formal theory of group-mediated social control. *American Sociological Review* 55:366–384.

Hirsch, Eric L. 1990. Sacrifice for the cause: Group processes, recruitment, and commitment in a student social movement. *American Sociological Review* 55:243–254.

Hoffer, Eric. 1951. *The True Believer.* New York: Harper & Row.

Hunt, Scott A. 1991. Constructing collective identity in a peace movement organization. Unpublished Ph.D. diss. Department of Sociology, University of Nebraska, Lincoln.

Isaac, Larry, Elizabeth Mutran, and Sheldon Stryker. 1980. Political protest orientations among black and white adults. *American Sociological Review* 45:191–213.

Jenkins, J. Craig. 1983. Resource mobilization theory and the study of social movements. *Annual Review of Sociology* 9:527–553.

Johnson, Norris R. 1987a. Panic and the breakdown of social order: Popular myth, social theory, empirical evidence. *Sociological Focus* 20:171–183.

———. 1987b. Panic at "The Who concert stampede": An empirical assessment. *Social Problems* 34:362–373.

Johnston, Hank. 1991. *Tales of Nationalism: Catalonia, 1939–1979.* New Brunswick, NJ: Rutgers University Press.

Kane, Emily. 1992. Race, gender, and attitudes toward gender stratification. *Social Psychology Quarterly* 55:311–320.

Kanter, Rosabeth M. 1968. Commitment and social organization: A study of commitment mechanisms in utopian communities. *American Sociological Review* 33:499–517.

———. 1972. *Commitment and Community: Communes and Utopias in Sociological Perspective.* Cambridge, MA: Harvard University Press.

Keniston, Kenneth. 1968. *Young Radicals.* New York: Harcourt, Brace & World.

Kerckhoff, Alan C., Kurt W. Back, and Norman Miller. 1965. Sociometric patterns in hysterical contagion. *Sociometry* 28:2–15.

Kerner, Otto, et al. 1969. *Report of the National Advisory Commission on Civil Disorders.* New York: Bantam Books.

Killian, Lewis M. 1980. Theory of collective behavior: The mainstream revisited. Pp. 275–289 in *Sociological Theory and Research,* ed. H. Blalock. New York: Free Press.

———. 1984. Organization, rationality and spontaneity in the civil rights movement. *American Sociological Review* 49:770–783.

Klandermans, Bert. 1984. Mobilization and participation. *American Sociological Review* 49:583–600.

———. 1986. New social movements and resource mobilization: The European and the American approach. *International Journal of Mass Emergencies and Disasters* 4:13–37.

———. 1988. The formation and mobilization of consensus. *International Social Movement Research* 1:173–196.

Klandermans, Bert, and Dirk Oegema. 1987. Potentials, networks, motivations and barriers: Steps toward participation in social movements. *American Sociological Review* 52:519–532.

Klapp, Orrin. 1969. *Collective Search for Identity.* New York: Holt, Rinehart & Winston.

Knoke, David. 1988. Incentives in collective action organizations. *American Sociological Review* 53: 311–329.

Knopf, Terry Ann. 1975. *Rumors, Race and Riots.* New Brunswick, NJ: Transaction.

Kornhauser, William. 1959. *The Politics of Mass Society.* New York: Free Press.

Kriesi, Hanspeter. 1988a. The interdependence of structure and action: Some reflections on the state of the art. *International Social Movement Research* 1: 349–368.

———. 1988b. Local mobilization for the people's social petition of the Dutch peace movement. *International Social Movement Research* 1:41–81.

Lang, Kurt, and Gladys Engel Lang. 1961. *Collective Dynamics.* New York: Crowell.

Le Bon, Gustave. [1895] 1960. *The Crowd: A Study of the Popular Mind.* New York: Viking.

Lofland, John. 1968. The youth ghetto. *Journal of Higher Education* 39:121–143.

———. 1981. Collective behavior: The elementary forms. Pp. 378–446 in *Social Psychology: Sociological Perspectives,* ed. M. Rosenberg and R. H. Turner. New York: Basic Books.

———. 1985. *Protest: Studies of Collective Behavior and Social Movements.* New Brunswick, NJ: Transaction.

Lofland, John, and Rodney Stark. 1965. Becoming a world saver: A theory of religious conversion. *American Sociological Review* 30:862–874.

MacCannell, Dean. 1973. Nonviolent action as theater. Nonviolent Action Research Project, monograph series no. 10, Haverford College Center for Nonviolent Conflict Resolution. Haverford, PA.

Machalek, Richard, and David A. Snow. 1993. Conversion to new religious movements. Pp. 53–74 in *Religion and the Social Order,* v. 38, ed. D. Bromley and J. Hadden. Greenwich, CT: JAI Press.

Macy, Michael. 1990. Learning theory and the logic of the critical mass. *American Sociological Review* 55:809–826.

Marwell, Gerald, M. T. Aiken, and N. J. Demerath III. 1987. The persistence of political attitudes among 1960's civil rights activists. *Public Opinion Quarterly* 51:383–399.

Marwell, Gerald, N. J. Demarath III, and Zena O'Leary. 1990. Trajectories of activism: 1960's civil rights workers from their 20s to their 40s. Paper presented at the Annual Meetings of American Sociological Association.

Marwell, Gerald, and Pamela Oliver. 1984. Collective action theory and social movements research. Pp. 1–27 in *Research in Social Movements, Conflicts and Change,* ed. L. Kriesberg. Greenwich, CT: JAI Press.

———. 1993. *The Critical Mass in Collective Action: A Micro-Social Theory.* New York: Cambridge University Press.

Marwell, Gerald, Pamela Oliver, and Ralph Prahl. 1988. Social networks and collective action: A theory of the critical mass, III. *American Journal of Sociology* 94:502–534. (erratum in no. 4).

Marx, Gary T., and James L. Wood. 1975. Strands of theory and research in collective behavior. *Annual Review of Sociology* 1:363–428.

McAdam, Doug. 1982. *Political Process and the Development of Black Insurgency: 1930–1970.* Chicago: University of Chicago Press.

———. 1986. Recruitment to high-risk activism: The case of Freedom Summer. *American Journal of Sociology* 92:64–90.

———. 1988. *Freedom Summer.* Oxford University Press.

———. 1989. The biographical consequences of activism. *American Sociological Review* 54:744–760.

McAdam, Doug, John McCarthy, and Mayer Zald. 1988. Social movements. Pp. 695–737 in *The Handbook of Sociology,* ed. Neil Smelser. Newbury Park, CA: Sage.

McCarthy John D., and Mayer Zald. 1973. *The Trend of Social Movements in America.* Morristown, NJ: General Learning Press.

———. 1977. Resource mobilization and social movements. *American Journal of Sociology* 82: 1212–1242.

McPhail, Clark. 1971. Civil disorder participation. *American Sociological Review* 36:1058–72.

———. 1991. *The Myth of the Madding Crowd.* New York: Aldine de Gruyter.

McPhail, Clark, and David L. Miller. 1973. The assembling process: A theoretical and empirical investigation. *American Sociological Review* 38:721–735.

McPhail, Clark, William T. Powers, and Charles W. Tucker. 1992. Simulating purposive individual and collective action. *Social Science Computer Review* 10:1–28.

McPhail, Clark, and Charles W. Tucker. 1990. Purposive collective action. *American Behavioral Scientist* 34:81–94.

McPhail, Clark, and Ronald Wohlstein. 1983. Individual and collective behavior within gatherings, demonstrations, and riots. *Annual Review of Sociology* 9:579–600.

Melucci, Alberto. 1985. The symbolic challenge of contemporary movements. *Social Research* 52:789–816.

———. 1988. Getting involved: Identity and mobilization in social movements. *International Social Movement Research* 1:329–348.

———. 1989. *Nomads of the Present: Social Movements and Individual Needs in Contemporary Society.* Edited by John Keane and Paul Mier. Philadelphia: Temple University Press.

Miller, Neal, and John Dollard. 1941. *Social Learning and Imitation.* New Haven: Yale University Press.

Mooney, Patrick H. 1990. The ideological constitution of agrarian social movements in the United States. Paper presented at the Annual Meetings of the European Society for Rural Sociology.

Morris, Aldon. 1981. Black southern sit-in movement: An analysis of internal organization. *American Sociological Review* 46:744–767.

———. 1984. *The Origins of the Civil Rights Movement: Black Communities Organizing for Change.* New York: Free Press.

Moscovici, Serge. 1985. *The Age of the Crowd.* Translated by J. C. Whitehouse. Cambridge, UK: Cambridge University Press.

Muller, Edward N., 1980. The psychology of political protest and violence. Pp. 69–99 in *Handbook of Political Conflict,* ed. T. R. Gurr. New York: Free Press.

Muller, Edward N., and Karl-Dieter Opp. 1986. Rational choice and rebellious collective action. *American Political Science Review* 80:471–487.

Muller, Edward N., Henry A. Dietz, and Steven E. Finkel. 1991. Discontent and the expected utility of rebellion: The case of Peru. *American Political Sciene Review* 85:1261–1282.

Oberschall, Anthony. 1973. *Social Conflicts and Social Movements.* Englewood Cliffs, NJ: Prentice Hall.

Oliver, Pamela E. 1980. Rewards and punishments as selective incentives for collective action: Theoretical investigations. *American Journal of Sociology* 84:1356–1375.

———. 1983. Paid and volunteer activists in neighborhood organizations. Pp. 133–170 in *Research in Social Movements, Conflict and Change,* vol. 5, ed. L. Kriesberg. Greenwich, CT: JAI Press.

———. 1984. If you don't do it, nobody else will: Active and token contributors to local collective action. *American Sociological Review* 49:601–610.

———. 1989. Bringing the crowd back in: The nonorganizational elements of social movements. Pp. 1–30 in *Research in Social Movements, Conflict and Change,* vol 11, ed. L. Kriesberg. Greenwich, CT: JAI Press.

Oliver, Pamela, and Mark Furman. 1989. Contradictions between national and local organizational strength: The case of the John Birch Society. *International Social Movement Research* 2:155–177.

Oliver, Pamela, and Gerald Marwell. 1988. The paradox of group size in collective action. *American Sociological Review* 53:1–8.

———. 1992. Mobilizing technologies for collective action. In *Frontiers in Social Movements Theory,* ed. C. Mueller and A. Morris. New Haven: Yale University Press.

Oliver, Pamela, Gerald Marwell, and Ruy Teixeira. 1985. A theory of the critical mass, I: Interdependence, group heterogeneity, and the production of collective action. *American Journal of Sociology* 91:522–556.

Olson, Mancur. 1965. *The Logic of Collective Action: Public Goods and the Theory of Groups.* Cambridge, MA: Harvard University Press.

Opp, Karl-Dieter. 1988. Grievances and participation in social movements. *American Sociological Review* 53:853–864.

———. 1989. *The Rationality of Political Protest: A Comparative Analysis of Rational Choice Theory.* In collaboration with Peter and Petra Hartmann. Boulder: Westview.

Paige, Jeffrey M. 1971. Political orientation and riot participation. *American Sociological Review* 36:810–820.

Park, Robert E., and Ernest W. Burgess. 1921. *Introduction to the Science of Sociology.* Chicago: University of Chicago Press.

Petras, James, and Maurice Zeitlin. 1967. Miners and agrarian radicalism. *American Sociological Review* 32:578–586.

Pizzorno, Alesandro. 1978. Political exchange and collective identity in industrial conflict. Pp. 277–298 in *The Resurgence of Class Conflict in Western Europe since 1968,* ed. C. Crouch and A. Pizzorno. London: Macmillan.

Portes, Alejandro. 1971. Political primitivism, differential socialization and lower-class radicalism *American Sociological Review* 36:820–835.

Quarantelli, E. L., and Russell Dynes. 1968. Looting in civil disorders: An index of social change. Pp. 131–141 in *Riots and Rebellion,* ed. L. Masotti and D. Bowen. Beverly Hills: Sage.

——— . 1970. Property norms and looting. *Phylon* 31:168–182.

Robbins, Thomas. 1988. *Cults, Converts and Charisma.* Newbury Park, CA: Sage.

Rochford, E. Burke, Jr., 1982. Recruitment strategies, ideology, and organization in the Hare Krishna movement. *Social Problems* 29:399–410.

Rosenthal, Naomi, M. Fingrutd, M. Ethier, R. Karant, and D. McDonald. 1985. Social movements in network analysis: A case of nineteenth century women's reform in New York State. *American Journal of Sociology* 90:1022–1054.

Ross, G. Alexander. 1978. Organizational innovation in disaster settings. Pp. 215–232 in *Disasters: Theory and Research,* ed. E. L. Quarantelli. Beverly Hills: Sage.

Rucht, Dieter. 1988. Themes, logics, and arenas of social movements: A structural approach. *International Social Movement Research* 1:305–328.

Rule, James B. 1988. *Theories of Civil Violence.* Berkeley: University of California Press.

Rupp, Leila J., and Verta Taylor. 1987. *Survival in the Doldrums: The American Women's Rights Movement, 1945 to the 1960s.* New York: Oxford University Press.

Rush, G. B. 1967. Status consistency and right wing extremism. *American Sociological Review* 32:86–92.

Seeman, Melvin. 1975. Alienation studies. *Annual Review of Sociology* 1:91–123.

——— . 1981. Intergroup relations. Pp. 378–410 in *Social Psychology: Sociological Perspectives,* ed. M. Rosenberg and R. Turner. New York: Basic Books.

Shelly, Robert K., Leon Anderson, and Christine Mattley. 1992. Assembly processes in a periodic gathering: Halloween in Athens, Ohio. *Sociological Focus* 25:139–150.

Sherif, Muzafer, and O. J. Harvey. 1952. A study in ego functioning: The elimination of stable anchorages in individual and group situations. *Sociometry* 15:272–305.

Sherkat, Darren E., and T. Jean Blocker. 1992. The development and trajectory of sixties activists. Paper presented at the American Sociological Association.

Singer, Benjamin D. 1970. Mass media and communication process in the Detroit Riot of 1967. *Public Opinion Quarterly* 34:236–245.

Smelser, Neil. 1963. *Theory of Collective Behavior.* New York: Free Press.

Snow, David A. 1987. Organization, ideology, and mobilization: The case of Nichiren Shoshu of America. Pp. 153–172 in *The Future of New Religious Movements,* ed. D. Bromley and P. Hammond. Macon, GA: Mercer University Press.

Snow, David A., and Leon Anderson. 1985. Field methods and conceptual advances in crowd research. Paper presented at Conference on Research Methods in Collective Behavior and Social Movements Research, Bowling Green State University.

Snow, David A., and Robert Benford. 1988. Ideology, frame resonance, and participant mobilization. *International Social Movement Research* 1:197–217.

——— . 1992. Master frames and cycles of protest. Pp. 133–155 in *Frontiers of Social Movement Theory,* ed. A. Morris and C. Mueller. New Haven: Yale University Press

Snow, David A., and Phillip Davis. 1995. The Chicago approach to collective behavior. In *The Second Chicago School of Sociology,* ed. Gary Fine. Chicago: University of Chicago Press.

Snow, David A., and Richard Machalek. 1983. The convert as a social type. Pp. 259–289 in *Sociological Theory 1983.* ed. Randall Collins. San Francisco: Jossey-Bass.

——— . 1984. The sociology of conversion. *Annual Review of Sociology* 10:167–190.

Snow, David A., and Ronelle Paulsen. 1992. Crowds and riots. Pp. 395–402 in *The Encyclopedia of Sociology,* ed. Edgar Borgatta and Maria Borgatta. New York: Macmillan.

Snow, David A., E. Burke Rochford, Jr., Steven K. Worden, and Robert D. Benford. 1986. Frame alignment processes, micromobilization and movement participation. *American Sociological Review* 51:464–481.

Snow, David, Louis A. Zurcher, Jr., and Sheldon Ekland-Olson. 1980. Social networks and social movements: A microstructural approach to differential recruitment. *American Sociological Review* 45:787–801.

Snow, David A., Louis A. Zurcher, Jr., and Robert Peters. 1981. Victory celebrations as theater: A dramaturgical approach to crowd behavior. *Symbolic Interaction* 4:21–42.

Snyder, David, and Charles Tilly. 1972. Hardship and collective violence in France, 1830–1960. *American Sociological Review* 37:520–532.

Spilerman, Seymour. 1970. The causes of racial disturbances: A comparison of alternative explanations. *American Sociological Review* 35:627–649.

Stark, R., and W. S. Bainbridge. 1980. Networks of faith: Interpersonal bonds and recruitment to cults and sects. *American Journal of Sociology* 85:1376–395.

Stryker, Sheldon. 1980. *Symbolic Interactionism: A Social Structural Version.* Menlo Park, CA: Benjamin Cummings.

Tarde, Gabriel. 1890. *The Laws of Imitation.* New York: Holt.

Tarrow, Sidney. 1989a. *Democracy and Disorder: Protest and Politics in Italy 1965–1975.* Oxford, UK: Clarendon Press.

———. 1989b. *Struggle, Politics, and Reform: Collective Action, Social Movements, and Cycles of Protest.* Ithaca NY: Center for International Studies, Cornell University.

———. 1992. Mentalities, political cultures, and collective action frames: Construction meanings through action. Pp. 174–202 in *Frontiers in Social Movement Theory,* ed. A. Morris and C. Mueller. New Haven: Yale University Press.

Taylor, Verta. 1989. Social movement continuity: The women's movement in abeyance. *American Sociological Review* 54:761–775.

Taylor, Verta, and Nancy Whittier. 1992. Collective identity in social movement communities: Lesbian feminist mobilization. Pp. 104–129 in *Frontiers in Social Movements Theory,* ed. A. Morris and C. Mueller. New Haven: Yale University Press.

Tilly, Charles. 1978. *From Mobilization to Revolution.* Reading, MA: Addison-Wesley.

Tilly, Charles, Louise Tilly, and Richard Tilly. 1975. *The Rebellious Century, 1830–1930.* Cambridge, MA: Harvard University Press.

Toch, Hans. 1965. *The Social Psychology of Social Movements.* Indianapolis: Bobbs-Merrill.

Touraine, Alain. 1981. *The Voice and the Eye: An Analysis of Social Movements.* Cambridge, UK: Cambridge University Press.

Turner, Ralph H. 1964. Collective behavior. Pp. 382–425 in *Handbook of Modern Sociology,* ed. Robert L. Faris. Chicago: Rand McNally.

———. 1969. The theme of contemporary social movements. *British Journal of Sociology* 20:390–405.

———. 1981. Collective behavior and resource mobilization as approaches to social movements: Issues and discontinuities. Pp. 1–24 in *Research in Social Movements, Conflict and Change,* ed. L. Kriesberg. Greenwich, CT: JAI Press.

———. 1983. Figure and ground in the analysis of contemporary social movements. *Symbolic Interaction* 6:175–181.

———. 1991a. Reading Melucci: The dynamics of collective identity. Paper presented at the Annual Meetings of the Pacific Sociological Association.

———. 1991b. The use and misuse of rational models in collective behavior and social psychology. *Archives of European Sociology* 32:84–108.

Turner, Ralph H., and Lewis Killian. [1957, 1972] 1987 *Collective Behavior.* Englewood Cliffs, NJ: Prentice Hall.

Useem, Bert. 1980. Solidarity model, breakdown model, and the Boston anti-busing movement. *American Sociological Review* 45:357–369.

———. 1985. Disorganization and the New Mexico prison riot of 1980. *American Sociological Review* 50:677–688.

Useem, Bert, and Peter Kimball. 1989. *States of Siege: U.S. Prison Riots 1971–1986.* New York: Oxford University Press.

Van der Veen, Gerrita, and Bert Klandermans. 1989. "Exit" behavior in social movement organizations. *International Social Movement Research* 2:179–198.

Walsh, Edward, and Rex Warland. 1983. Social movement involvement in the wake of a nuclear accident: Activists and free riders in the TMI area. *American Sociological Review* 48:764–780.

Weigert, Andrew J., J. Smith Teitge, and Dennis W. Teitge. 1986. *Society and Identity: Toward a Sociological Psychology.* London: Cambridge University Press.

Weller, Jack M., and E. L. Quarantelli. 1973. Neglected characteristics of collective behavior. *American Journal of Sociology* 79:665–685.

Werner, Paul. 1978. Personality and attitude-activism correspondence. *Journal of Personality and Social Psychology* 36:1375–1390.

Westby, David L., and Richard G. Braungart. 1966. Class and politics in the family backgrounds of student political activists. *American Sociological Review* 31:690–692.

Whalen, Jack, and Richard Flacks. 1989. *Beyond the Barricades: The Sixties Generation Grows Up.* Philadelphia: Temple University Press.

White, Robert W. 1989. From peaceful protest to guerilla war: Micromobilization of the provisional Irish Republican Army. *American Journal of Sociology* 94:1277–1302.

Wilson, James Q. 1973. *Political Organizations.* New York: Basic Books.

Wilson, John. 1973. *Introduction to Social Movements.* New York: Basic Books.

Wiltfang, Greg, and Doug McAdam. 1991. Distinguishing cost and risk in sanctuary activism. *Social Forces* 69:987–1010.

Wood, James L., and Wing-Cheung Ng. 1980. Socialization and student activism: Examination of a relationship. Pp. 21–44 in *Research in Social Movements, Conflicts and Change,* ed. L. Kriesberg. Greenwich, CT: JAI Press.

Wood, Michael, and Michael Hughes. 1984. The moral basis of moral reform. *American Sociological Review* 49:86–99.

Wright, Sam. 1978. *Crowds and Riots: A Study in Social Organization.* Beverly Hills: Sage.

Zald, Mayer N., and Roberta Ash. 1966. Social movement organizations: Growth, decay and change. *Social Forces* 44:327–341.

Zald, Mayer N., and John D. McCarthy. 1987. *Social Movements in an Organizational Society.* New Brunswick: Transaction.

Zimbardo, Phillip. 1969. Individuation, reason and order vs. deindividuation, impulse, and chaos. In *Nebraska Symposium on Motivation,* vol. 17, ed. W. J. Arnold and D. Levine. Lincoln: University of Nebraska Press.

Zurcher, Louis A. 1968. Sociological functions of ephemeral roles: A disaster work crew. *Human Organization* 27:281–297.

———. 1982. The staging of emotion: A dramaturgical analysis. *Symbolic Interaction* 5:1–19.

Zurcher, Louis A., and R. G. Kirkpatrick. 1976. *Citizens for Decency: Anti-Pornography Crusade as Status Protest.* Austin: University of Texas Press.

Zurcher, Louis A., and David A. Snow. 1981. Collective behavior: Social movements. Pp. 447–482 in *Social Psychology: Sociological Perspectives,* ed. M. Rosenberg and R. Turner. New York: Basic Books.

PART IV

Methodological Approach to Social Psychology

GARY ALAN FINE
JAMES S. HOUSE
KAREN S. COOK

INTRODUCTION: INVITATION TO METHODOLOGY

Social psychology is but speculation until we develop means of examining, expanding, and testing our thoughts. All social scientists, whether they describe themselves as empirical social scientists, social theorists, or some other way, believe ideas need to be systematically examined *in the context* of the world. To be sure, theorists are more likely to extrapolate from limited observations, but there remains a claim that any theory corresponds to the "natural world."

For too many sociologists, methodology has sometimes seemed mysterious, boring, or esoteric—a hurdle to be surmounted, rather than a summit to reach—but to understand the range of styles of research, data collection, and analysis is to be given the keys to a palace with an infinite number of rooms. Discovering how to solve a puzzle can be as rewarding as viewing the puzzle once solved. To love social psychology should properly be to learn to *do* social psychology, and it is in this bracing belief that this section is presented.

Researchers differ in some measure in the direction in which they believe theory and data should properly affect each other. Those who approach research using a "deductive" model claim that data should be employed to examine or "test" premises or "hypotheses." Explicitly stating the thesis should precede its evaluation to minimize the bias that might come from claiming that one knew all along what one eventually found. Other researchers favor an "inductive" model, in which the data "speak to" the researcher. It is by systematically examining data without preconceived notions that we can generate an understanding of the world. Insight is "grounded" in the empirical world and involves careful observation, according to an approach labeled "grounded theory." From the insights developed by the examination of empirical reality can theory be generated.

In fact, both induction and deduction are found throughout social psychological research, even when researchers are not fully aware. No hypothesis is proposed from "thin air." We develop only those hypotheses that "make sense" based on our experience ("observation") of living. Even the social psychologist most committed to deductive hypothesis testing can not avoid some inductive exposure. Even those who hope to observe with open minds have a wealth of "folk hypotheses" that influence how they make sense of what happens around them—they are subtly testing implicit hypotheses. For both inductive and deductive social scientists the evaluation of results depends on judgments of how well one's expectations have been met (deduction) and whether the formal findings make sense in light of the data as the researcher knows it (induction). While the division is both real and meaningful in styles of research, it does not create an unbridgeable chasm.

Methodological approaches can be categorized in various ways; we have selected three of the more prominent models of how to conduct research: qualitative field methods, experimental methods, and nonexperimental quantitative research. We are well aware that such important techniques as mathematical modeling, historical research, and document analysis are not covered. The authors of these chapters select methodologies and styles of research to emphasize.

In presenting these methodologies, the authors have steered away from a detailed treatment of their mechanics. This approach shows the *logic* of the methodologies, stressing the justifications and disadvantages of these techniques. The authors emphasize the *why*, rather than the *how*. As much as possible, the authors present a wide range of methodological options, rather than focusing on a single "correct" model.

The traditional approach associated with social psychology, and still dominant among psychological social psychologists, is experimentation. The experiment wrapped us in the mantle of science and made us believe we were reaching for an essential truth that is invariant over time and space. Barbara Meeker and Robert Leik, in chapter 24, specify the underlying, and occasionally ignored, logic on which the experimental model rests. They effectively demonstrate the range of models of experimentalism that have been successfully used by social psychological practitioners. By arguing that the experiment is not a given path to truth, they help the reader to gain a better sense of when and where this methodology should be selected for collecting and analyzing data.

Experimental research seeks to test or validate theoretically posited causal relationships between variables; its major strength is its ability to draw causal influences, due in most cases to experimenters' ability to manipulate or control the independent variable(s) of interest and to assign the persons or entities being studied randomly to the varying conditions or levels of the independent variable(s). As Meeker and Leik observe, even in experiments causal inferences remain inferences and can be incorrectly drawn, yet the experiment remains the strongest basis for drawing such inferences. But in many instances, for practical or ethical reasons, the phenomena of interest to social psychologists cannot be manipulated or controlled by the researcher. A major agenda of social psychologists is to understand the impact of race, gender, or socioeconomic position on individuals' life chances, behavior, thoughts, or feelings. We cannot, however, manipulate or control race or gender, and though we can to some degree alter a person's level of education, income, or occupational status, for practical and ethical reasons we cannot assign people randomly to levels of these variables. Thus, social psychologists, along with other social scientists, have played a major role in developing nonexperimental methods for observing the naturally occurring social world and formulating causal understandings of it—just as astronomers, meteorologists, and geologists have done for the physical world.

One body of techniques, reviewed by Duane Alwin in chapter 25, seeks to make and analyze quantitative observations of the social world to develop and test causal theories or models of how it operates. Nonexperimental quantitative data can come from many sources, including administrative records, systematic observation, and, most commonly, sample surveys and censuses. The associations among variables and their reliability and, to some extent, validity can be summarized via a range of statistical methods. The greatest problems are drawing causal inferences in the absence of experimental control and randomization. As Alwin demonstrates, advances in methods of statistical analysis and research design—especially the development of longitudinal design and analysis techniques—have played a major role in stimulating the development of quantitative nonexperimental social psychology on topics ranging from cognition, attitudes, emotions, or the self to the functioning of groups and networks and the relationships between individuals and macrosocial structures, institutions, and processes.

Since the emergence of experimental and quantitative nonexperimental social science in the first several decades of the twentieth century, many social scientists, especially in anthropology, sociology, and sociological social psychology, have been concerned that these methods are not adequate to understand the full nature and meaning of social life and individuals' lived experience. As Cahill, Fine, and Grant indicate in chapter 23, sociological social psychologists, particularly the Chicago school of symbolic interactionism, played a major role in the development of qualitative field methods focused on illuminating the full complexity of social action and interaction, and the ways in which it is constructed by actors giving meaning to their social worlds and selves. To some degree these methods trade off the reliability, strength of causal inference, and breadth of coverage of populations found in experimental or quantitative nonexperimental methods for greater depth and richness of observation and understanding of particular individuals and social contexts, though qualitative methods also seek to achieve causal understanding of broad or even universal social phenomena and processes.

Methodologically, as well as substantively, social psychology has become less divided and more whole recently. We and most other social psychologists now agree that no method provides a royal road to truth. Each has been and will continue to be useful in providing fuller and more adequate social psychological understanding of the social world. Since the strengths and limitations of the methods reviewed in these chapters are largely complementary, we find increasing use of multiple methods to understand important social phenomena, as illustrated in the chapters throughout this volume.

CHAPTER 23

Dimensions of Qualitative Research

SPENCER CAHILL
GARY ALAN FINE
LINDA GRANT

Only recently an orphaned stepchild, qualitative methodology has achieved some measure of sociological respectability in the past decade, recapturing some of its centrality from the first half of the twentieth century. Whether this is due to the maturation of a cohort of researchers whose views were formed in the 1960s, decreased funding during the Reagan years, changes in the gender composition of the discipline, or closer ties between social sciences and humanities, previously dominant methodological techniques such as survey research or laboratory experimentation have been joined by an array of qualitative techniques. Researchers select qualitative methodologies because they permit interpretative understanding, descriptive richness, and analytic induction and, perhaps equally significant, are often inexpensive.

This chapter concerns only some of the investigative and analytic techniques commonly subsumed under the general heading of qualitative methods, admittedly ignoring methods of sociohistorical research (Skocpol 1984) and sociological analysis of cultural products such as film (e.g., Denzin 1990). Although such research and analysis sometimes address the substantive concerns of sociological social psychology, their influence has been largely indirect and limited. Historically and currently, the influence of ethnographic or field research is more direct and far greater. This form of qualitative research, its varieties, and a few variants are the focus here.

As the name suggests, field research is conducted where everyday social life is lived. A researcher or team of researchers spends time in a social setting to gain first-hand information about what occurs there and, in most cases, about the perspectives of those who populate the setting. As Hammersley and Atkinson (1983) note, ethnography or field research is both a process and a product. The process can be flexible and typically evolves contextually in response to what the researchers see and hear. The product is a written or performed account, providing a sociological interpretation of the setting, joined by a history of the process by which the interpretation was generated. Field research usually draws on the techniques of participant observation and in-depth interviewing, often in tandem. The ethnographic account can also be informed by a review of the scholarly literature, document analysis, collection and interpretation of artifacts, responses of informants to the researcher's account, personal histories, and the researcher's reflections (Agar 1986; Denzin 1989).

Currently the health of qualitative research is robust, reflected in the success of three sociological journals—*Symbolic Interaction, Qualitative Sociology,* and *Journal of Contemporary Ethnography.* Further, although quantitative analysis is still more common than qualitative sociology in national, regional, and specialty journals, the relative number of qualitative papers published in these journals has increased since the mid-1970s (Grant and Ward 1991; Grant, Ward, and Rong 1987; Ward and Grant 1985). Formal training in qualitative methods also expanded in the 1980s. More graduate departments in sociology offered required or elective course work in qualitative and/or sociohistorical methods (*Footnotes* 1988), and the range of appropriate texts (such as the *Sage* qualitative methods monograph series) has expanded.

During the 1980s qualitative sociologists, along with their cousins in other disciplines, substantially expanded the theoretical grounding of qualitative methods (Clifford and Marcus 1986; Denzin 1989; Fetterman 1987; Patton 1990; Van Maanen 1988). In addition, an emphasis on reflexivity, sparked recently by writings of feminist researchers (Cook and Fonow 1986; Eichler 1987; Ellis 1991; Smith 1987), has encouraged scholars to include personal reactions. The illusion of the researcher as a "fly on the wall" is increasingly difficult to justify (Fine 1993).

The renaissance of qualitative sociology can be traced to several sources. First, as Fine (1990b) has noted, despite perennial predictions of demise and decline, symbolic interactionists have not disappeared but continued to produce important field research and theory, even through the period of greatest dominance of quantitative sociology. Others, like ethnomethodologists and conversation analysts, have since joined them in those efforts.

Second, the large cohort of qualitative sociologists trained at The University of Chicago in the late 1940s and 1950s reached their pinnacle of stature and influence. Though many were no longer conducting field research, they had been trained in this tradition, were sympathetic to it, taught and directed qualitative dissertations, and criticized quantitative methods.

Third, the economic organization of qualitative research nurtured this approach during the lean years for granting agencies and suspicion from policy makers. Whereas quantitative research is often capital-intensive, qualitative research is labor-intensive—a boon for graduate students, who could conduct research as competent and innovative as their seniors. A recentering of concern from political and economic issues to cultural domains also aided qualitative research. Qualitative sociologists were more accepted by cultural elites than were quantitative researchers by political elites, and this

sociopolitical reality helped make cultural and interpretive sociology seem to be "where the action is."

Fourth, the increased usage of qualitative methods may be linked to the growing feminization of sociology (Grant, Ward, and Rong 1987; Mackie 1985). Although debate exists about whether women were central to the development of qualitative sociology (cf. Deegan and Hill 1987; Lorber 1988), a review of journal articles suggests that women sociologists currently use qualitative methods more than men sociologists (Grant, Ward, and Rong 1987).

THE DEVELOPMENT OF SOCIOLOGICAL FIELD RESEARCH

In the beginning was The University of Chicago, at least as far as American sociology is concerned. It was there that the first major department of sociology in America was founded and the first periodical devoted to sociological scholarship was published (Hinkle and Hinkle 1954, 1–9). It was also there that qualitative research established roots in sociology and its distinctive brand of social psychology. W. I. Thomas and Florian Znaniecki (1918–1920) planted the seed soon after World War I with their classic *The Polish Peasant in Europe and America.*

Rather than "generate data" in the style of much contemporary research, Thomas and Znaniecki gathered information from wherever and whomever they could. They pillaged the archives of a Polish newspaper, commissioned the Polish immigrant Wladek Wisinilwski to write a lengthy autobiography, and solicited personal correspondence from members of Chicago's sizable community of Polish emigrés. There was a method to what might seem their investigative madness, growing out of the theoretical position that Thomas and Thomas (1928, 587) would later immortalize with the succinct sociological proverb about situations and their definitions. Thomas and Znaniecki were convinced that understanding social life required information about both "objective social circumstances" and the subjective interpretations of those who face those circumstances. They concluded that "personal life records, as complete as possible, constitute the perfect type of sociological material" providing insights into both. "Mass phenomena" such as official statistics or responses to questionnaires might sometimes be practically necessary, but they considered such a necessity "a defect of our present sociological method" (Thomas and Znaniecki 1918–1920, 1832–1833).

Although sympathetic with Thomas and Znaniecki's theoretical positions, some of their departmental colleagues, such as Ernest Burgess and Robert Park, were more methodologically ecumenical. Their methodological ideal was what was then known as the social survey: an extensive study involving census materials, direct observation, and interviewing in addition to collecting personal documents (Emerson 1983, 3). Park and Burgess envisioned their own and their many students' studies as contributions to such a social survey of Chicago, including life histories such as Clifford Shaw's (1926) *The Jack Roller,* analyses of official statistics, and what would later become known as ethnographies.

Recent scholarship reveals that Jane Addams and the residents of Hull House played an indirect but important part in the development of this research agenda. According to Deegan (1988, 1991), *Hull House Maps and Papers,* published in 1893, provided a blueprint for the sociological studies that came to characterize The University of Chicago during Park's tenure there. Social reformers and activists outside the academy also played crucial roles in securing financial support for those studies (Platt 1992).

Yet the methodological ecumenicalism and activist-oriented research that Park championed was being questioned. Increasingly, strident advocates of survey research, like George Lundberg (1926, 61), proclaimed that observational and biographical studies would always be "the tail of the statistical kite." In contrast, proponents of qualitative research, like Znaniecki (1934, 211ff.), likened "enumerative induction culminating in the present statistical method" to "medieval scholasticism." These positions led to a mutual hostility and resentment lasting half a century. Methodological self-

consciousness consequently spread among students of social life.

Fortunately, the young William Foote Whyte was temporarily spared from such methodological self-consciousness. In 1936, while a junior fellow at Harvard and nearly four years before enrolling in The University of Chicago, Whyte (1984, 42–51) set out to study the Italian-American slum on Boston's North End that he would immortalize as "Cornerville." After his initial attempts to establish personal contacts in the community failed, an accommodating social worker introduced Whyte to the streetwise young man readers would come to know as "Doc." Doc graciously volunteered to introduce Whyte to the people and places of Cornerville, becoming his principal informant in the community (for a discussion of this relationship, see Boelen 1992; Orlandella 1992; Whyte 1992). That was not all of Whyte's good fortune. Another junior fellow at Harvard, the social anthropologist Conard Arensberg, took an interest in Whyte's (1984, 15) study and instructed him in the methods of observation and interviewing. Taking the social anthropological example to heart, Whyte rented a room in the Cornerville home of an Italian-American family. For the next two years, he participated in the daily life and activities of the community, keeping copious notes of his observations and conversations with the residents. Whyte had anticipated the direction that the qualitative study of social life would soon take.

The Park tradition of field research at The University of Chicago was to study a community with which one already had personal contacts and experience (Hughes 1984, 547). The former hobo Nels Anderson (1923) and former probation officer Fredric Thrasher (1927), author of *The Gang,* are two examples. In contrast, many students at The University of Chicago who were attracted to sociological field research in subsequent years lacked prior knowledge of the people and places they hoped to study. For them as earlier for Whyte, gaining access to groups and settings, establishing trust and rapport, and sustaining relationships during the course of research were central concerns (Emerson 1983, 13). Like Whyte, they had the benefit of experienced anthropological advisors. Relations between sociologists and anthropologists at The University of Chicago had long been amicable, and in the late 1940s the social anthropologist Lloyd Warner became an important and influential advisor to sociology students who conducted field research.

Over time, this interdisciplinary "cluster of Chicagoans came to scrutinize their methodology more closely and to reconceptualize it around the term 'participant observation'" (Wax 1971, 40). They held seminars, solicited and privately circulated reports from sociologists and anthropologists about their experiences "in the field," and encouraged students to write about their methods. Methods of qualitative research consequently became topics as well as resources for sociological scholarship. They became the subject of entire volumes and of what has since become the obligatory methods chapter or appendix of monographs based on qualitative research.

It was also during this time that the topical scope of qualitative sociological study began to expand. From Polish peasants to corner boys, marginal, disadvantaged, and deviant groups and individuals had been qualitative sociologists' favorite subjects. Although such groups and individuals have remained popular subjects of qualitative study, sociological field researchers started to turn some of their attention to the work lives of more advantaged and respectable groups during the 1950s, thanks in large part to the influence of Everett Hughes (1958). Perhaps the most memorable of those studies was conducted by Hughes and three collaborators in the late 1950s at the University of Kansas medical school.

Starting with only a vague research design, Hughes and colleagues set out to investigate inductively "not only the collective forms of social actions that make up the medical school as an institution, but also . . . the effects on the medical student of living and working in this institution" (Becker et al. 1961, 19). They attended classes with the students, accompanied them on rounds, talked with them endlessly, and interviewed some of their instructors, keeping copious notes of what they saw

and heard. The resulting five thousand single-spaced typed pages of field notes were the empirical basis for their influential *Boys in White.* Its methodological influence was at least as great as its influence on sociological theories of professional socialization. It was instrumental in stimulating efforts to secure a place for qualitative research in the study of social life at a time when sociology was falling under the seductive spell of the technical wizardry of experimental and survey research.

Howard Becker, a prominent qualitative researcher and coauthor of *Boys in White,* argued that because field research provided "information on people acting under the very social constraints whose operation we are interested in," its findings are less likely to be artifacts of research design than are those of experimental and survey research (Becker 1970, 62). He also argued that field research involves the use of multiple sources of information and flexible procedures, allowing for more repeated and varied testing of conclusions than experimental or survey research. Yet Becker (1970, 62) was not so bold as to claim "that only field work can provide trustworthy evidence for sociological conclusions." He maintained that there was a place for qualitative research in the study of social life alongside other investigative and analytic approaches. *Boys in White* exemplifies this conciliatory strategy. It is filled with "quasi-statistical" tables reporting the numbers and relative proportions of different kinds of field note entries that support one or another conclusion. The coauthors of *Boys in White* admittedly adopted this quantitative method of analysis to allay readers' suspicions about "conclusions drawn from qualitative data" (Becker et al. 1961, 31).

Other qualitative researchers were not as given to "compromise." For instance, Barney Glaser and Anselm Strauss (1967) defended the naturalistic and qualitative study of social life as the best means for systematically generating empirically informed and informative theory. The two principle components of their *Grounded Theory* approach were the method of constant comparison and theoretical sampling. First, varied empirical information, such as observations from different settings, is repeatedly compared to develop conceptual categories and specify their properties. The emerging conceptual framework guides the collection of additional information allowing for more analytic comparisons. The purpose of this theoretical sampling is to develop and refine the emerging theory, rather than to establish the frequency or distribution of some phenomenon, as with statistical sampling. According to Glaser and Strauss (1967, 1–2), the generation of such empirically grounded theory was a needed corrective to "the overemphasis in current sociology on the verification of theory." They implied that the generation and verification of theory required different procedures. Although Glaser and Strauss made a strong case that qualitative methods were useful for generating theory, they implicitly conceded that other investigative and analytic methods are better suited for verifying theory.

These concessions to skeptics and critics were a far cry from the uncompromising case Znaniecki (1934) made some years earlier for his method of analytic induction. His method begins with the formulation of a rough definition of the phenomenon to be explained and a hypothetical explanation. A small number of cases are then examined in detail, with special attention to cases that are inconsistent with the hypothesized explanation. Either the definition of the phenomenon or the explanation is reformulated and refined in light of each. According to Znaniecki, the eventual result is a universal causal explanation of a precisely defined phenomenon. Skeptics, including Ralph Turner (1953), argued that the method of analytic induction as used in Lindesmith's (1947) *Opiate Addiction* and Cressey's (1953) *Other People's Money* yielded not causal explanations of predictive utility but definitional tautologies that stripped the phenomena of addiction and embezzlement of empirical complexity. In fact, few qualitative researchers today claim they are searching for universals, although many question the sharp distinction between theory construction and verification that Znaniecki opposed.

Qualitative researchers have also borrowed techniques and concepts from quantitative sociolo-

gists, talking about samples, generalizability, validity, and reliability. Others call for "mixed" methods, an approach often dubbed "triangulation," metaphorically drawing an analogy between land and social "surveying." They imply that "surveying" a topic from different investigative and analytic vantage points allows for comparison of results and stronger conclusions than any single method could provide. The "Robbers Cave experiment" at a camp for preadolescent boys is one of the better-known applications of this methodological strategy in sociological social psychology. In addition to observing and talking to the boys while posing as camp counselors, Muzafer Sherif and colleagues (1961) manipulated relations among the boys, subjecting them to experimental procedures, and administered sociometric questionnaires to them in investigating the dynamics of group conflict and cooperation.

The use of multiple methods and sources of information has a long tradition in sociological field research, leading back to Robert Park and The University of Chicago. Proponents of participant observation have favorably compared it to other investigative approaches on those very grounds. Howard Becker and Blanche Geer (1957) argue that participant observation avoids some of the pitfalls of interview studies because of its more varied and flexible procedures. Unlike the interviewer, the participant observer learns the subjects' native language, observes them under a variety of circumstances, and talks with them privately and in the company of others. Using examples from their study of medical students, they illustrate how comparison of these sources of information provides more opportunities to check the credibility of subjects' remarks than even a large number of lengthy interviews would provide. Becker and Geer's (1957, 28) intent was not to denigrate studies based exclusively on conversational interviews but to point out the limitations of relying on a single investigative method rather than the more varied and flexible procedures of participant observation.

Whatever the advantages of participant observation, intensive interviewing is clearly more practical when sizable groups of individuals engage in the activity of interest not in a single setting but at different times and in different places. Becker's (1963) own influential study of the process and social basis of "Becoming a Marijuana User" is based exclusively on conversational interviews rather than participant observation for exactly that reason. Apparently recognizing the practical difficulties of observing the marijuana smoking careers of a number of individuals, Becker interviewed musicians with whom he was acquainted as well as other marijuana smokers to whom he was introduced. His analysis of the resulting fifty interviews demonstrates that whatever the disadvantages of relying on conversational interviews exclusively, it is not without compensations.

The illuminating results of Becker's study of marijuana users and of many other studies based exclusively on conversational interviews suggest that Becker and Geer's invidious comparison of interview and participant observation studies is overstated. As John Lofland and Lyn Lofland (1984, 13) note, much if not most of the empirical information collected during participant observation is gathered through informal interviews, and many interview studies involve the kind of repeated and prolonged contact between investigators and subjects that is considered the hallmark of participant observation. There are also ways to compensate for investigators' lack of direct experience of subjects' everyday social lives, such as having them keep a diary or log of daily activities about which they can then be questioned (Zimmerman and Wieder 1977).

Those who have conducted qualitative sociological research have employed a variety of investigative methods and combinations of methods to arrive at an understanding of both the objective conditions and subjective interpretations of social lives. Whatever the specific investigative strategy, they are socially and often physically closer to their subjects than either experimental or survey research allows. However, the question of how close they should or can get to their subjects without losing their scholarly perspective has haunted those who have used these methods. What is the most appropriate "research role"?

A well-known typology of such research roles identifies the possibilities as complete observer, observer as participant, participant as observer, and complete participant (Gold 1958; see also Adler and Adler 1987). Generally those who engage in sociological field research adopt the role of participant as observer. Adopting that role involves informing subjects of the investigative purpose, participating in subjects' everyday social activities as much as possible, and attempting to gain acceptance as at least an honorary member of their group. At the same time, the participant observer actively resists complete identification with subjects, or "going native."

When subjects and investigators are socially similar, as in studies of professional socialization, adoption of the role of participant as observer has proven relatively unproblematic. For example, the authors of *Boys in White* and the medical students at the University of Kansas were from comparable social backgrounds, well-educated, and undoubtedly held many similar values. Thus, it is hardly surprising that the authors of that study were able to gain and maintain the students' confidence and trust. Sociological field researchers have had somewhat more difficulty gaining and maintaining the confidence and trust of other groups.

In some cases, groups accept a sociologist into their midst for their own purposes, as John Lofland (1966) learned in his study of the so-called *Doomsday Cult*. After the cult members' repeated attempts to convert Lofland failed, his access to the group ended. Then there are groups engaged in deviant and criminal activities who have good reasons not to trust outsiders, including prying students of social life. This type of research raises obvious ethical questions about potential harm to subjects, deception, covert observation, and informed consent (Punch 1986). Other groups may distrust a field researcher because of race or age, as Elliot Liebow (1967) learned when studying poor African-American men as have many who have studied children (e.g., Fine and Sandstrom 1988; Mandell 1988).

Often, subjects' distrust and hostility can be overcome through nonjudgmental acceptance and honesty, although some argue that confrontation and cunning are sometimes necessary (e.g., Douglas 1976). In either case, the goal is to become privy to subjects' guarded secrets and personal thoughts by getting as close to them as possible without becoming one of them. For those who hope to understand relations between the objective conditions and subjects' interpretations of their social lives, this is a necessary strategy.

DIVERGENT DEVELOPMENTS IN QUALITATIVE SOCIOLOGY

Field research resulting in ethnographic description has been the most common variety of qualitative sociological study, but there are other influential varieties. Perhaps most prominent are the formal analytic approach pioneered by Erving Goffman, ethnomethodology, and conversation analysis. Each differs from sociological field research in regard to theoretical inspiration, goals, and characteristic methods.

The now widespread appreciation of Goffman's many contributions to sociological social psychology and sociology more generally has not resulted in a similar appreciation of his methodological approach. Goffman studied at The University of Chicago with many of those who shaped and nurtured the tradition of sociological field research. The field research he conducted is in keeping with the spirit of that tradition of inquiry, but the impulse is quite different. Goffman's analyses of social life on the Shetland Islands (1953) and of St. Elizabeth's mental hospital (1961) are not ethnographic descriptions of those social worlds. That was not his purpose. Rather, his primary concern was to develop general theories of interactional politics and the organizational construction of persons.

Much of Goffman's work is filled with *illustrative* materials he once described as of "mixed status" (Goffman 1959, xii). Alongside his own observations and empirical examples borrowed from other students of social life are quotes from novels, newspaper stories, etiquette manuals, memoirs, and invented episodes. Such nonchalance about evidence has been the subject of much criticism, as

has Goffman's unsystematic and nonparticipatory style of observation (e.g., Schudson 1984). However, Goffman was not attempting to provide an intimate picture of the social lives and experiences of any specific group.

Goffman's analytic approach was inspired by Simmel's formalism (Goffman 1953, iv) and "the functionalism of Durkheim and Radcliffe-Brown" (Goffman 1981, 62). It was intended to identify the limited number of interactional forms behind the infinite number of social appearances: the dramaturgical techniques involved in staging the varied scenes of social life and the idiom of ritual expression that renders action and inaction socially meaningful. This goal required comparison and contrast of widely divergent empirical examples to discover common elements and the apparent consequences of their varied uses.

Goffman (1971, ix–xvii) eventually argued for a kind of interactional ethology. He suggested that students of social life could learn from the methodological example of animal ethologists, "politely" ignoring their Darwinian assumptions. His point was that we should observe human social behavior in the same close detail as ethologists observe animal behavior, and with as much control on preconception. Goffman urged students of social life to look for the unexpected behind the appearances of what they saw, heard, and read. Among other things, those who followed his methodological lead have found intimidating control of women behind seemingly innocuous public encounters (Gardner 1988) and moral education behind adults' unremarkable responses to children's public misbehavior (Cahill 1987).

The investigative and analytic goals of ethnomethodology are somewhat similar to those of Goffman, but that is where the resemblance ends. Harold Garfinkel, the "founder" of ethnomethodology, studied not at The University of Chicago but at Harvard, with Talcott Parsons. Dissatisfied with Parsons's theoretical model of social action, Garfinkel turned to Schutz's social phenomenology for inspiration. The task he assumed was to account for the socially structured scenes of daily life exclusively in terms of common-sense reasoning. Like

Goffman, Garfinkel's goal was to discover the forms of thought and interpersonal action out of which the varied features of social structure are reflexively constructed. However, the investigative and analytic methods he developed for this purpose are unlike those Goffman employed.

Rather than become familiar with a social setting, as the tradition of sociological field research and Goffman (1989) once advised, Garfinkel's general approach is to render the familiar unfamiliar. He argued that for the "seen but unnoticed" features of social life to come into view "one must be a stranger to" or "become estranged from" its life as usual character (Garfinkel 1967, 37). Perhaps Garfinkel's best-known methodological innovation is the demonstration "experiment" designed to disrupt subjects' sense of an orderly, familiar, and predictable social life. His students would act like boarders in their own homes or ask for an explanation of the standard greeting "How are you?" By creating "trouble," Garfinkel attempted to demonstrate what societal members commonly assume or do that prevents such "troubles." Similarly, the transsexual Agnes, the subject of Garfinkel's best-known case study, served as a natural demonstration "experiment." Her "passing" practices provided a perspective by incongruity that revealed the standard "recognition and production practices" implicated in the reflexive construction of gender.

Garfinkel and colleagues have not limited themselves to making trouble. Many self-identified ethnomethodologists have relied on unobtrusive observation. In contrast to more traditional field researchers, they have not been interested in subjects' interpretations of events but in the methodical *practices* they routinely employ to sustain a collective sense of social order and structure. Thus, they practice "studied detachment" to render everyday scenes of social life "strange" or to remain strangers to unfamiliar scenes. By doing so, they have identified how the assumption of a world held in common is sustained in traffic courts despite evidence to the contrary (Pollner 1974), how residents and staff of a halfway house for drug offenders strategically invoke the "convict code" to maintain orderly relations (Wieder 1974), and some of the concrete methods of scientific discovery that are never mentioned in research reports (Garfinkel, Lynch, and Livingston 1981). The goal of these studies is to discover a set of practices that could account for what is taken as "the natural facts of social life" or of one of its specialized domains. The concern is not so much to demonstrate that some particular set of practices is employed but that their employment *would* result in the observed order and structure of the social scenes or activities under study.

Influenced by ethnomethodology, a few of Goffman's students at Berkeley in the late 1960s turned their attention to talk in search of underlying forms of social life. Although Harvey Sacks initially focused on the categorization of persons in mundane conversation, he soon joined with Schegloff and Jefferson (1974) in examining the underlying form or structure of turn taking in conversation. From this effort, conversation analysis was born.

Conversation analysis is more than an analytic method. Like ethnomethodology, it is a theoretical project. Conversation analysts reason that because talk is the principal means of achieving and maintaining mutual understanding, the structure of conversation provides the very architecture of intersubjectivity (Heritage 1984, 233–292). Their preferred investigative method is electronic recording of talk, which is then transcribed in detail. The goal is to identify invariant conversational features. For example, Schegloff's (1968) study of openings of telephone conversations centers on one negative case among a large corpus of conversational openings, attempting, in the tradition of analytic induction, to develop a theoretical model of conversational opening that would explain each and every analyzed case. More recently, conversation analysts have employed the expression "preferred response," but they do not define preference in terms of statistical frequency or subjective desirability. Rather, they define preference in terms of standard conversational patterns. Preferred responses are supplied immediately, while dispreferred responses are either delayed, qualified, or prefaced with accounts or markers such as "well." For example, acceptance is the preferred response to invitations and requests, while rejection is dispreferred, indicating a kind of systematic conversational bias toward social solidarity (Heritage 1984, 265–280).

Although many conversation analysts limit their attention to the features of mundane conversation, others use what is known about the features of conversation to address other topics. They examine how interruptions are implicated in the conversational accomplishment of male dominance (West and Zimmerman 1977), the conversational accomplishment of different forms of relationship (Maynard and Zimmerman 1987), and how conversationalists reference and reproduce the distinctive features of different institutional contexts (e.g., Wilson 1991).

There is a basic similarity among conversation analysis, ethnomethodology, and Goffman's formal analytic approach despite their many differences. Their characteristic methods of inquiry and analysis differ, as do their specific focuses. Goffman focuses attention on the interaction order, ethnomethodology on common-sense reasoning and practices, and conversation analysis on mundane talk. Yet each is informed by the theoretical proposition that intersubjectivity, social order, and social structure are recurrently accomplished in the course of everyday social activities. Each attempts to answer empirically long-standing theoretical questions about the character and basis of social life. In each, theory and research are closely wedded.

The relationship between theory and sociological field research is not always as obvious. A frequent criticism of such research is that it is primarily descriptive and little more than glorified journalism. Indeed, the traditional mission of sociological field research was to collect descriptive materials from those sites to which academics might not have easy access, such as tribal societies, criminal gangs, religious cults, or youth groups. Careful depiction was critical in uncovering hidden arenas but led to the charge that field research was atheoretical, lacking generalizability.

However, many sociological field researchers have not limited themselves to description and theorizing about some particular social setting. Instead, they construct general theory based on their empirical findings and comparison of those findings to those of other field studies. Under this model, theory emerges from "data." One can enter a field setting because of its convenience and emerge with a new theoretical concept, an innovative substantive approach, or a contribution to "grand theory."

CONTEMPORARY DIRECTIONS IN QUALITATIVE SOCIOLOGY

A turn toward theory is only part of what characterizes contemporary qualitative research. Many researchers marry ethnography to other investigative and analytic methods, including field experimentation, survey research, and sociolinguistic analysis. Others combine qualitative research with cultural analysis (e.g., Becker and McCall 1990; Wolfe 1991).

Qualitative sociologists also are challenging and expanding the traditional modes of ethnographic presentation. Such challenges include the orienting of sociological work to popular as well as scholarly audiences (Hochschild 1989; Richardson 1985, 1990; Riessman 1990; Rubin 1976). Other scholars are experimenting with presentations of ethnographic work in other than written form (McCall and Becker 1990; Paget 1990).

Cross-cutting these challenges is a reexamination of issues of power and control in qualitative sociology. Reconsideration of these themes in the 1980s was sparked by qualitative feminist researchers (Cannon, Higginbotham, and Leung 1988; Eichler 1987; Krieger 1983; Stacey 1988; Warren 1988), but they have long been present in qualitative sociological research (Broadhead and Rist 1976; Rainwater and Pittman 1967). Two related ethical concerns have been prominent in recent years: appropriate relationships between researchers and those researched, and the relative power of the researcher and the subjects of research to control the production and use of the account, or representation, that results from field studies (Punch 1986).

To examine the new directions and challenges in qualitative sociological research, we first examine how researchers have attempted to combine classical field study with other forms of research. We focus on selected works, illustrative of creative approaches adopted by contemporary researchers.

Melding Methods

The Field Study Site as Research Laboratory. Traditionally, field researchers have conducted their studies at a particular research site and then moved to another site—perhaps another substantive area entirely. Few qualitative researchers in sociology, in contrast to some in anthropology (who returned to the same village year after year), were content with a single site. Once the excitement was gone, they would find a different group or setting to study. This is quite unlike the model in the natural sciences, where a researcher may spend a lifetime working on a specific set of problems.

An impressive attempt to emulate such careful examination of a specific set of issues is the research program of Donna Eder and her students at a middle school and high school in an Indiana town. Their investigations use a number of methods and address several substantive issues, but each focuses on the culture and social structure of the young Hoosiers who attend these schools. Together, these studies of adolescent peer cultures in schools and school-related extracurricular activities provide scholars with longitudinal data rare in qualitative research—information that is wide and deep, though from a single locale.

Researchers observed and informally interviewed middle school and high school students in classrooms, lunchrooms, extracurricular activities such as sports and cheerleading, and off-campus clubs and parties over several years. Observations identified naturally occurring groups of peers who interacted in and out of school. Members of these groups later were video- and audiotaped as they engaged in informal discussions on topics of their choice in a school learning center. The groups were

same-gender, paralleling patterns of social relations apparent in the middle school. This provided a useful strategy, as talk emerged as a critical component of social relations and cultural creation among adolescents, especially girls.

In papers by Eder and her team, ethnography is used to delineate the different structures of males' and females' peer groups in school settings. Girls, in particular, build cohesion and solidarity through gossip (Eder and Enke 1991), humor (Sanford and Eder 1984), collaborative problem solving (Enke 1990), and storytelling (Eder 1988).

Whereas other studies have shown that boys' discourse typically is characterized by dominance, boasting, and competitive bids to control the floor (Goodwin 1990a, 1990b; Schofield 1982), girls' discourse is used to build cohesion. Eder's analyses reveal not only gender-specific norms of interaction in students' peer groups but also some of the mechanisms by which girls take on stereotypical female roles of emotional managers and creators of links among diverse actors in a variety of social settings.

The works of Eder and her collaborators show that many phenomena attributed to personalities and developmental phases of adolescents actually have a sociological base. They also suggest that certain problems (e.g., social isolation) probably cannot be resolved by counseling individual students but may require an intervention in ongoing social relationships—relationships of which adults in school may not be aware, since they are explicitly structured to avoid adult scrutiny. These conclusions would not have been as potent if based on a single study by a lone investigator. The aggregation of empirical information collected by multiple researchers makes those conclusions more credible.

Ethnography and Sociolinguistic Analysis. The analysis of talk has always been critical to qualitative sociological research. Often it seems as if people described in ethnographies do nothing but talk. However, until recently talk has not been examined much *as talk*. This is the ethnography of speaking (Hymes 1974): discourse analysis in the field. Sociolinguistics was virtually unknown twenty years ago; today it is an active and creative area of study. A large body of research produced in the 1980s focused on the role of language in social situations and social organization. These studies reveal how social actors, even very young children (Corsaro 1988; Corsaro and Rizzo 1988), use language in a purposive manner to construct identities and manipulate social relationships. Older children are even more attuned to the niceties of language in constructing meaning (Fine 1987; Heath 1983).

Marjorie Harness Goodwin has substantially advanced sociolinguistic and conversation analysis in a long-term study of language use in the play of African-American children in West Philadelphia. Goodwin (1990a, 1990b) argues that talk is used by children to "build their ongoing social organization and the phenomenal world they inhabit." She distinguishes sociolinguistic analysis from formal linguistics by emphasizing not only the autonomous, formal system of language but the ways in which production of talk is socially contextual, a form of social action critical to human relationships and the building and maintenance of social organization. She notes that talk creates what she terms *participation frameworks,* in which an entire field of action is made relevant by forms of speech. The speaker may transform the social order of the moment by invoking different speech activities.

Studying talk adds rigor and comparability to qualitative accounts of social action. Researchers report recorded examples of talk in detail, so that other researchers might examine them for alternative interpretations. The documentation provided in sociolinguistic analysis advances qualitative sociological study and facilitates comparative research. Sociolinguistic analysis directs attention to how people perform meaningful activities in naturalistic settings.

Corsaro and Rizzo (1988), in a cross-cultural study of American and Italian nursery schools, show how forms of interaction and discourse among even very young children reflect the adult cultures in which they are immersed. For example, Italian children engage in much more overt, verbal discourse in routine interactions than do American

children, and at an earlier age. These patterns parallel adult discourse in the two societies.

Maynard (1984) uses ethnography in combination with conversation analysis to reveal how prosecuting attorneys and public defenders fashion mutually acceptable plea bargains despite disagreements and their adversarial relation. Mehan (1979) has analyzed how clashes over language use in classrooms disadvantage students whose cultural backgrounds differ from teachers'. In American schools, such students are labeled academically deficient. Riessman (1990) shows how the organization of speech—in her case into temporal or episodic presentations—varies across class and racial/ethnic status, impeding clear communication between subjects and researchers and between clients and therapists.

The combination of ethnography and sociolinguistic analysis seems especially powerful in studying hierarchical social relations. Language is the most fundamental medium of social control, and detailed study of language use can reveal the means by which dominance is routinely accomplished and maintained.

Ethnography and Field Experimentation. Although qualitative research and field experimentation might seem unlikely companions, such a methodological marriage can be powerful, as Janet Schofield (1982) has shown. Her detailed study of social relationships in a desegregated magnet school illustrates an effective use of field experimentation and structured observation in conjunction with ethnography. Schofield and a team of researchers studied responses to desegregation among students and teachers in grades six through eight. Structured observations can be distinguished from ethnographic observation in that the former involves a predetermined focus and system of data collection (McCall 1984). In structured observations, researchers decide a priori the phenomena on which they will concentrate as well as the form in which data will be recorded (e.g., checklists, coding sheets).

Ethnographic observations by Schofield and collaborators suggested how the combination of race and gender affected students' perceptions and social relationships in schools. Effects were magnified as children moved from sixth to eighth grade. By the eighth grade, gender effects on racial interaction were more salient as students began to date and became preoccupied with larger societal standards of attractiveness and appropriate dating partners. African-American boys, in particular, were perceived by white girls and their parents as more threatening as these students became more mature.

Schofield supplemented naturalistic observations with structured observations of freely chosen lunchroom seating patterns to test hypotheses about separation by race and gender derived from her ethnographic observations. Structured observations recorded seating patterns by race, gender, and grade level and supported Scofield's contention that racial separation increased with students' grade level (Schofield and Sagar 1977).

To illuminate perceptions of threat and the influence of perceived threat on students' social relationships, Schofield designed a field experiment using samples of students of varying race, gender, and grade level configurations. She provided thematic apperception cues to students evoking potentially ambiguous cross-racial themes, such as asking them to complete the paragraph that begins "Black students in this school usually . . ." Student responses varied in relation to racial and gender identities. White girls felt a heightened sense of threat that increased with grade level in comparison with other students. They were more likely to define cross-racial situations as potentially threatening, while students of other race-gender configurations interpreted them as routine and nonthreatening.

The field experiment proved an effective means to get students to talk about issues of race and of threat. The ethnographic component of the research had demonstrated that within the context of the school, race was a taboo topic. Teachers and administrators avoided explicit mention of race, a common tactic in desegregated schools in this era. Schofield suggests that the practice created interactional dilemmas (e.g., confusion on the part of teachers about how to respond to overt racist re-

marks made by students) and in the long run may have been counterproductive to successful desegregation. For example, there was no mechanism in the school for discussing or responding to the white girls' fears or their parents' concerns about their safety.

In Schofield's work, ethnography preceded other forms of data collection. Structured observations on lunchroom seating took place only after ethnographic research had verified that this would be a valid indicator of natural peer groups and friendship choices. The experimental materials were generated inductively, symbolizing recurrent and meaningful events that took place in the setting. Schofield analyzed her data using both qualitative and quantitative methods.

While Schofield's triangulation of methods is more explicit and carefully conducted than most, other qualitative researchers have used a similar strategy. For example, Whyte (1955) attempted to examine the effect of status on achievement (bowling scores) among the Cornerville boys and, as mentioned earlier, Sherif and colleagues (1961) mixed experimental manipulation and ethnographic observation in their study of group conflict and cooperation at a summer camp for boys.

Ethnography and Survey Research. Ethnography and survey research often are viewed as antithetical, proceeding from different assumptions about the nature of social life. Nevertheless, they have been successfully combined by some researchers, such as Robert Blauner (1964). His widely read account of the organization and subjective meaning of work draws on a national survey of factory workers, his own field study of a chemical plant, and a questionnaire study of workers at that plant. The survey results are used to demonstrate that various measures of worker dissatisfaction or alienation vary inversely with the degree of autonomy allowed workers in different jobs and industries, while the ethnography reveals how the organization of work can create pockets of autonomy for workers reducing their alienation.

A more recent example is Janet Lever's (1983) study of soccer in Brazil. Lever uses eclectic methods, including participant observation, intensive interviewing, reflective introspection, and extensive archival and document analysis, to probe the meaning of soccer in Brazilian society. She proposes that soccer rivalries reflect potentially explosive ethnic and class divisions in Brazilian society and that avidly followed soccer competitions provide a means to express and resolve factional disputes.

Although the core of her work is ethnographic, Lever developed a survey questionnaire to explore behaviors and perspectives of soccer fans through their "fandom." The questionnaire was administered to industrial workers representative of distinctive class and ethnic groups. Lever's prior field research had determined that the selected groups were representative of factions of Brazilian society apt to be fans of particular teams. Through the questionnaire, Lever verified that soccer was indeed a preoccupation of Brazilian males of all classes, who attended soccer matches frequently, watched soccer on television, regularly followed newspaper accounts of soccer matches, and could identify prominent soccer players more reliably than they could name prominent political and civic leaders.

Another instance of effective combination of survey research and ethnographic techniques is Wright's (1988) study of marriages affected by Alzheimer's disease. Wright interviewed thirty married couples in which one spouse had been diagnosed at an early stage of Alzheimer's and a smaller sample of control couples with no evidence of the disorder.

One component of Wright's research was a questionnaire, generated only after months of qualitative inquiry, about the division of household labor before and after the onset of Alzheimer's. The questionnaire provided detailed and specific information on the variability of the effects of Alzheimer's on the division of household labor based on the gender of the afflicted and nonafflicted spouse, chore distribution prior to the onset of illness, the couple's economic resources, and the availability of family-based and other social support. Administration of the questionnaire often provoked unan-

ticipated but valuable insights, such as Wright's discovery that some men with afflicted wives attached positive value to performing domestic chores, viewing this as repayment to wives for years in which they had provided domestic labor for their husbands. In addition, on some occasions, persons who appeared composed and alert in interviews became frustrated or confused when responding to the brief and straightforward questionnaire. Administrating the questionnaire allowed Wright to assess the progression of the disease, verifying or contradicting physicians' diagnoses and enlarging her perspective of caretakers' interactions with afflicted spouses, specifically minute-to-minute variations in mental alertness and capability. Some afflicted subjects became so upset by the questionnaire and a related problem-solving diagnostic instrument that Wright had to spend hours restoring emotional calm before terminating the interview.

Questionnaires or structured interviews are means ethnographers can use to collect information that might supplement their observations and further their analysis. Fine (1986), in his ethnographic research on mushroom collectors, sent questionnaires to members of a local mycological society, a 20 percent sample of the National Society of Mushroomers, and included a set of questions on a random household survey in Minneapolis-St. Paul. Coupled with lengthy in-depth interviews with two dozen amateur mushroomers, this permitted a clearer understanding of the contradictory views of these groups on environmentalism and nature activity. Questionnaires were a valuable supplement to three years of detailed ethnographic research.

Policy-Relevant Ethnography. During the 1970s and 1980s, ethnographies relevant to policy issues blossomed. Some studies explicitly addressed policy issues; some were conducted by evaluation researchers outside of academe, often thought of as wedded to survey methods. Often these studies contributed both to policy development around critical social issues and to sociological theory, challenging the common assumption that policy-relevant work is theoretically inconsequential.

Ray Rist's (1973, 1978) studies of all-minority and desegregated schools illuminates the bases of stratification in the daily life of schools. His works confront the belief that classrooms are autonomous settings, shielded from outside influences through norms of professional autonomy that give teachers authority for determining classroom activities. He traces the multiple means by which external culture enters classrooms, bringing in forms of racial and class stratification that teachers ostensibly wish to exclude. He also argues that peer cultures play an influential role in class life, challenging the view that teachers' attitudes are dominant. Nonacademic, class, and racial variables (dress style, language, grooming, performance of older siblings) affect evaluations of students despite the rhetoric of merit.

Linda Grant's (1984) research demonstrates how desegregation, changes in tracking systems, and other organizational change affect students differently depending on their race-gender status. African-American girls, in particular, lose when schools contain more white students. Typically the highest-ranking pupils and recipients of teacher attention in all-African-American classrooms, they lose power to white students in desegregated classes.

Metz's studies of authority relations in desegregated schools (Metz 1978) and of the contexts of three magnet schools in the same city (Metz 1986) raise important policy issues as well as substantive concerns. At the policy level, Metz pointed out that the authoritative behaviors of teachers were perceived differently across tracks enrolling different social classes. While democratic forms of instruction were well received in high tracks, low-track students and their parents perceived such teaching styles as indicating poor teacher preparation and a lack of concern. These views created crises of authority.

The writings of Michael Patton (1990) have demonstrated that even for the traditional goals of judging organizational or program effectiveness, a well-designed and carefully conducted qualitative research study can provide richer, and possibly more helpful, information to policy makers than more traditional forms of evaluation research. By perceiving the situation from the perspective of the workers or clients, one can better understand organizational effectiveness, dilemmas, and failure. There is much behind "cold numbers." Many qualitative researchers are overcoming their traditional shyness about giving advice based on their findings, spawning new models of research and new employment.

Sociological Analysis of Texts

A growing number of qualitative sociologists are turning at least some of their attention to the analysis of written texts, ranging from literary works to personal documents such as letters and diaries to graffiti. They are also analyzing both historical and contemporary materials. These textual analyses fall within the domain of qualitative sociology because of the interpretative methods employed and their scholarly goal of understanding society from the perspective of members. Increasingly, ethnographic researchers elicit production of personal documents, reviving a common strategy of the pioneers of qualitative sociological study at The University of Chicago. Lever (1978), for example, supplemented ethnographic analysis of fifth-grade children's spontaneous play activities on school playgrounds with diaries the children kept about their out-of-school play activities. Gubrium (1988) urged Alzheimer's disease-afflicted individuals and their caretakers to keep diaries of their experiences, supplementing observations of care of afflicted individuals in the home. Denzin (1987a, 1987b) uses self-reflection and personal diaries and other documents in the analysis of the process of recovery from alcoholism.

A recent example of sociological analysis of materials published for other purposes is Reinharz's (1986) interpretive account of the meaning of miscarriage in women's lives. Reinharz notes that the life history method she uses draws on Thomas and Znaniecki's methodology, relying on sympathetic introspection or "interpreting her experience as if it were my own" (Reinharz 1986, 230). Reinharz writes that her sympathetic introspection is facilitated by a somewhat similar personal experience (Reinharz 1986).

Reinharz's analysis is based on a published personal account of one woman's experience (Pitzer and Palinski 1980). The author of the account and subject of Reinharz's analysis, Chris, had one successful pregnancy but then experienced three miscarriages over a two and one-half-year period before bearing a second child. Reinharz notes that personal documents represent a form of sociological information that is not as seriously affected by reactivity as forms of data that are specifically created or generated for sociological study. Reinharz focuses her analysis on Chris's use of words and an explication of "the range of meanings behind particular words," a reference to contemporary modes of literary criticism. Chris's experience is personal, yet her actions and responses are framed by historical and macrosociological factors such as the state of medical knowledge and the organization and discourse of the medical profession. By drawing on written materials on reproduction and contraception, Reinharz demonstrates that most women, as a byproduct of realizing that they can control contraception, also come to believe that they can control conception and birth.

Reinharz's reanalysis of these materials portrays the phenomenology and emotion of this experience from women's perspective. It also illustrates the power of textual analysis to bridge links between personal experience and social structure in historical context. Further, it has implications for practice. Medical treatment surrounding miscarriage, and even counseling materials written to assist women who have this experience, seem insensitive to the emotional impact and identity transformation women experience as a result of miscarriage.

Conrad (1988) employs another type of textual analysis, linked to his ethnographic studies of medical students' socialization. He challenges the widely held stereotype that premedical students engage in cutthroat competition with classmates to obtain entry into medical school. Moving from his observational work on premedical and medical education, Conrad analyzes several examples of the recently published accounts of the medical school and residency experience written by physicians in training. The contrasts between the more global perspective of the researcher and the personal perspectives of the articulate subjects he has chosen enrich the reader's understanding of the medical school experience and blurs the boundaries between literature or journalism and sociological analysis.

Alternative Modes of Presentation

Qualitative sociologists are also stepping over the often insular boundary of traditional sociological discourse in presenting findings and analyses. Some are attempting to reach diverse audiences who might appreciate and benefit from sociological insights or whose reactions might benefit the research enterprise. Others are demonstrating that a picture can be worth, if not a thousand words, then at least two or three hundred.

For instance, Laurel Richardson (1987) ventured onto the interview and talk show circuit to disseminate her work on single women who have affairs with married men (Richardson 1985). As Richardson (1990) notes in a recent account, she welcomed opportunities to discuss her work-in-progress with general audiences because these forums provided a means to recruit diverse subjects for interviews. However, there was a price.

Richardson's work has been favorably reviewed in disciplinary journals for its theoretical contributions and for the methodological quality of its execution but has been dismissed as well because of the form of dissemination. Although such dismissals may be due in part to jealousy, writing for a popular audience involves, as Richardson recognizes, compromise, such as the qualifications one can make regarding one's "truth claims," the complexity of the analysis, and the form in which empirical evidence is presented. Some recent ethnographies, such as *The Second Shift* (Hochschild 1989), make that compromise with popular tastes at the risk of being dismissed as nonserious scholarship by professional readers who demand explicit discussions of research methods and theoretical issues. The potential gain is a wider audience for sociological ideas and greater influence over public discussion and debate.

Popularization is not the only or perhaps even the most significant of the "experiments" in which qualitative sociologists are engaging. Howard Becker, in collaboration with Michal McCall, and Marianne Paget have experimented with the presentation of qualitative sociology as performance, terming it "performance science" (Becker and McCall 1990; McCall and Becker 1990; Paget 1990). The performance of field notes is the latest in a series of innovations in the presentation of qualitative work by Becker, who has also written a widely consulted handbook on writing for social scientists. Becker and McCall believe performance of interactions studied by field researchers allows examination of these encounters from multiple perspectives. Researchers gain useful insights into the meaning of events by observing responses of diverse audiences to their recreation. Other qualitative researchers, such as Dan Rose (1990), are experimenting by incorporating poetry into their ethnographies.

The linguistic registrar is not the only area in which experimentation has occurred. Becker and several other sociologists have used photographs and other visual materials to convey to audiences more than can be transmitted in written or spoken accounts (Becker 1978, 1981). The ethnographies of Douglas Harper of hobos (1982) and a rural repairman (1987) demonstrate that understanding can be facilitated by photographs, particularly when informants contribute to the interpretation. Likewise, Naomi Bushman's photographs, in conjunction with Marcia Millman's written text, explore the social meaning of being overweight in America. In her methodological appendix, Millman (1980) discusses ways that viewing the photographs and reflecting on their messages were part of her analysis.

Anthropologists have made greater use of film and video for ethnographic purposes than have sociologists. A notable example is Barbara Myer-

hoff's film, *Number Our Days,* an outgrowth of her written ethnography of the same title (Myerhoff 1978). Her work is a sensitive, detailed ethnography of a senior citizen center in Venice, California, that serves a population of nonaffluent, elderly Jewish citizens living far from kin. In the print version of the work, Myerhoff explicitly discusses the variations in perspectives presented in the book and the film, and the justifications for the divergence. She observes that the preparation of the film was in part a response to her subjects' insistence that they receive public recognition. Many objected to the use of pseudonyms and the disguising of identifying personal life details—standard practices in sociological research (Fine 1990a). Her subjects wanted to be noticed and recognized, to leave a permanent mark of their lives before they died. The film provided such an opportunity.

Research Relations and Roles

Another area of debate among contemporary qualitative sociologists is the appropriate relationships among researcher, informants, and potential audiences. What is the ethically appropriate relationship between researcher and subjects? Should researchers practice studied detachment (if possible) or be more personally involved with their subjects and their concerns? Whose voices and perspectives should guide and inform the written account?

Relations with Subjects. Several writers argue that qualitative approaches minimize risks to informants because researchers are acutely aware of their perspectives. The long-lasting, close relationships developed during qualitative study are thought to make researchers especially sensitive to issues of exploitation and misrepresentation. This viewpoint is challenged forcefully by Judith Stacey (1988), who argues that these very relationships allow the researcher greater opportunities for emotional manipulation of research subjects and that the intimate information subjects share with researchers magnify rather than minimize ethical risks. In a 1987 presentation at the American Sociological Association meetings, Stacey discussed her difficulty in grappling with knowledge that a key subject in her account was struggling with issues of sexual orientation and finally "came out" as a lesbian to close associates and the researcher. Initially, the subject asked Stacey to withhold this information from her account. This produced an ethical dilemma for Stacey, who believed the information was essential to the account. The dilemma was resolved when the subject, without pressure, informed Stacey that she could discuss her sexual orientation in the written account. Stacey, like many researchers who have carried out both qualitative and quantitative research, found qualitative research to be more emotionally demanding.

Sociologist Lillian Rubin formed controversial relationships with research subjects in producing *Worlds of Pain* (1976), a book about working-class marriages. Like her subjects, Rubin grew up in a working-class family but had climbed into the middle class as an adult. Rubin acknowledges that issues in her personal life and her belief that sociological portrayals of working-class families were stultifying, stereotypical, and elitist motivated and guided her work. Rubin provided portions of her text to selected respondents prior to its publication, in some (but not all) instances modifying her account in light of their responses. Checking tentative interpretations with key informants is common in qualitative sociology, but sharing prepublication drafts of sociological accounts with subjects is less frequent. Rubin was aware that interviews raised painful memories and difficult personal issues for some subjects. Trained as a psychotherapist, she offered limited therapy to subjects who desired it, a controversial procedure that has drawn praise and bitter criticism (e.g. Jackall, Laslett, and Skolnick 1978; McCourt 1977).

Judith Rollins (1985) struggled with emotions, exhaustion, and ethical dilemmas in researching and writing *Between Women,* an ethnographic account of relations between domestic workers and their employers. Rollins combined archival analysis and interviewing of domestic workers and their employers with participant observation. She worked as a domestic for several employers, an experience she found to be sometimes exhausting, occasionally satisfying, and always emotionally draining. Her experience and her emotional response to it are used reflexively to enrich the accounts of her informants who worked as domestics as well as to provide insights into roles of employers. She struggled with issues of deception, as when she intentionally altered dress or language to be accepted as a "real" domestic worker in the eyes of potential employers. She ultimately made a personal decision that it was acceptable to deceive employers, denying them informed consent, but unacceptable to deceive relatively less-privileged domestic workers for research purposes.

British sociologist Ann Oakley (1981) characterizes traditional forms of qualitative interviewing as potentially exploitative of research subjects. Oakley's sensitivity to this theme was heightened in the course of her long-term qualitative study of women's experiences during pregnancy, childbirth, and the transition into motherhood. Initially attempting to maintain the stance of the "objective" researcher in interviews with pregnant women, Oakley constantly was pressed for medical information and details of her own confinements by respondents who knew she had children. She discovered that many women lacked knowledge of fundamentals of pregnancy and childbirth, as well as information on nutrition, exercise, the dangers of smoking and drug use during pregnancy, and the like. Oakley decided that to withhold such information was immoral. She answered questions where she could and urged women to confront their physicians more assertively where she could not provide answers. Oakley (1981) suggests that a more appropriate orientation for researchers and subjects is what she terms *inter-viewing,* in which both researcher and subjects mold research. Carolyn Ellis (1991) recently advocated greater use of "sociological introspection" on emotional experience to explore how emotions are felt and how they affect action. She argues that self-introspection (detailed analysis of one's own feelings) and interactive introspection (sharing one's emotional experience with subject-collaborators) can yield valuable data not attainable by other methods.

Intimate collaboration with research subjects provokes criticism from more traditional qualitative sociologists, who argue that researchers must attempt to maintain some personal distance from subjects and intervene as little as possible in their lives (e.g., Bogdan and Taylor 1975). Such critics are also suspicious of research that combines participant observation with techniques such as experimentation or survey research, because in structuring the form in which information is elicited the researcher transforms what he/she should be studying. They also question research projects in which the researcher maintains an active role in a setting and those in which the researcher develops close relationships with informants. In fact, most field researchers become actively involved in the situations they study and with their subjects. Today the very principle that field researchers should remain detached is being questioned, especially by researchers writing from a feminist or critical perspective.

Detachment versus Engagement. The debate over whether sociologists should research topics in which they have strong or little emotional investment and personal involvement is long-standing in sociology, not limited to qualitative work (Gouldner 1962; Lee 1978; Merton 1972). Often the debate is misleading, in that it is hard to find a sociologist who has no personal interest or stake in what he/she studies. The illusion is that the researcher wants "just the facts," yet most researchers want the facts about topics of personal concern to them. In field research such issues are central, since ethnographers must provide some sort of account of their interest in the phenomena to informants and to readers.

The rift between prevailing theory and sociologists' personal experience inspires revisionist analysis (Cook and Fonow 1986; Farganis 1986; Keller 1985; Smith 1987). These theorists view self-reflection and personal reactions as valuable empirical information, a still controversial position that leads to criticism that works are "polemical" if they address controversial issues of concern to the researcher. This raises anew the charge that qualitative research is nothing but advocacy or journalism and that the conclusions are nothing more than personal opinion. Whereas twenty years ago some qualitative researchers tried to emulate positivistic science with its concern with validity and reliability, today the trend is to see qualitative research as more akin to the humanities than the natural sciences.

Much of what is labeled "action research" is controversial because of its explicit partisan commitments. In this form of research, the researcher acknowledges a commitment to individuals or groups involved in a social relationship. Often the commitment is to a "have not," less powerful, or stigmatized group. The research is organized and interpreted at least partially according to the needs of the group to which the researcher has partisan ties. Some theorists, most prominently Becker (1967) and Gouldner (1962), approaching the matter differently, argue that researchers inevitably have partisan ties, acknowledged or not. Some suggest that when partisanship is unacknowledged, it serves the interests of elites, whereas others believe that qualitative researchers, like many social scientists, tend to identify with the oppressed, if not explicitly then implicitly.

Studies of families of children with cancer carried out by Mark Chesler and colleagues are qualitative forms of action research (Barbarin and Chesler 1983; Chesler and Barbarin 1987). Chesler, whose own child successfully battled leukemia, had a personal stake and emotional investment in the project, as did other members of the research team. The research was designed to address issues defined as relevant by families whose children were undergoing treatment for cancer, more than to address theoretical issues in sociology. Representatives of critical actors—afflicted children, family members, medical professionals, social workers—influenced and critiqued the work at each step. The emotional responses of participants and investigators were addressed throughout the research process and incorporated into the final product. Although the focus was on the production of "useful" information, the research also contributes to sociological theory by clarifying sources of social support and differentiating between useful and destructive forms of intended support.

Collaborative ethnography may or may not be a form of action research. It is an attempt to represent multiple perspectives. It sometimes is, and sometimes is not, linked to action research. Indeed, more traditional collaborative research was merely an attempt to gain more sources of empirical information, rather than to promote social change (Becker et al. 1961; Sherif et al. 1961; Strauss et al. 1963). For example, Cahill recruited women students as collaborators in his study of behavior in public bathrooms, for obvious investigative reasons (Cahill et al. 1985). A prominent example of collaborative ethnography is the Australian ethnographic study of schools involving researchers of varying race, gender, and ethnicity and including public school teachers as well as university-based researchers (Connell 1987; Connell et al. 1982; Kessler et al. 1985). Members of the research team vary in the degree to which they are interested in application or identified with the interests of certain groups in schools and society. The intent is not simply to ensure that the interests of all these parties are addressed by the research, but that the account incorporates the perspectives of as many diverse groups as possible. Despite a few such collaborative projects, ethnography still is largely a lone enterprise conducted and written by a single researcher.

The Voice and Voices of Qualitative Accounts.
Another problematic concern in qualitative sociology is the extent to which final accounts reflect the viewpoints and voices of subjects or merely those of their author. Feminist sociologists, in particular, have objected to the relative silence of subjects' voices in the accounts of "experts." They have attacked the voice of expertise adopted by many qualitative researchers as dishonest and intellectually misguided, leading to narrow scholarship that generalizes too facilely and makes false claims to universal truth.

Dorothy Smith (1987) argues that all sociology is written from a particular standpoint, rather than from some "objective" perspective that is ex-

ternal to any particular social position. Those who claim otherwise adopt an "abstracted mode" of thinking and writing that is part of the "apparatus of ruling" in contemporary societies. Smith argues that women and less privileged men frequently sense a deep chasm between their concrete experience and the "generalized" theories that supposedly explain their lives. Smith maintains that such chasms can be the starting point for creative, revisionist sociology that begins from the standpoint of less privileged social actors. Smith's recommended approach of treating everyday social experience as problematic fundamentally challenges mainstream sociology, whether qualitative or not. Smith details a strategy, based on research with her colleague Alison Kelly, through which social organizations, from local neighborhood groups to the global economy, can be studied from the perspective of less privileged individuals. The analysis begins with their local and particular social experience. As it moves to successively larger and more abstract levels of social organization, the experiential perspective of the subject, not the expert, is used to define the relevant questions for inquiry and the relevant empirical information.

Susan Krieger (1983) grappled with the dilemma of how much abstraction and generalization were appropriate in *The Mirror Dance,* her participant observation study of a lesbian community. Krieger found conflicting, irreconcilable visions of the community. Some participants saw it as a loose amalgamation of persons sharing intellectual concerns, while others viewed it as a tight-knit, intimate group providing emotional sustenance as well as intellectual stimulation. She reports multiple versions of the community's functions and boundaries. Krieger avoids accepting a single perspective by not revealing her judgment about the "real" community from her standpoint as the "expert." To do so would be to ignore that the community had different meanings. The divergent views of the community, and what it ought to be, revealed internal conflicts.

Blauner's (1987) discussion of the difficulties of presenting oral histories as sociology raises similar issues. Oral history is a relatively recent addition to sociological methods, and the presentation of complete and unedited oral histories is still uncommon. As a result, disciplinary standards concerning the appropriate treatment of such materials have not developed, particularly regarding how much they should be "processed." Researchers select, arrange, edit, and otherwise manipulate qualitative materials informing their accounts, yet this distorts the informants' lived reality and their ordering and interpretation of events. Refusing to place materials into traditional scholarly formats risks their dismissal as nonscholarly or nonsociological. This editing, however, distorts the coherence and meaningfulness of the account from the informant's perspective. Voice and mode of presentation are lost in translating the account into one more appealing to sociologists. By leaving such texts alone, are we abdicating our responsibility to analyze and interpret while leaving it to the reader, who will have no such qualms? Or is it our responsibility to leave analysis and interpretation to the reader?

Riessman (1990) raises a related concern in connection with her research on women's accounts of the dissolution of marriages. She found that researchers and therapists, overwhelming white and middle-class, "heard" and comprehended accounts by women of similar backgrounds who were undergoing divorce. White, middle-class subjects tended to organize accounts temporally. This narrative style coincided with how researchers analyze empirical information and construct their own accounts. Other women organized accounts thematically and episodically, a style that researchers and therapists found harder to comprehend. The closer links between the discourse of researchers and middle-class white women created temptations to take these accounts more seriously than those of the other women.

Aptheker (1989) claims that women's lives often are constructed in unrelated fragments, which she compares to quilts made of bits of different fabrics. Women talk of goals and motives differently than men, who can often exert more control over the course of their lives. Women's conversations seem to ramble more than men's and are interrupted more frequently. Further, they leap back and forth between private and public domains, which some have suggested are more separable for men than for women (DeVault 1990; Lengermann and Niebrugge-Brantley 1990). Yet sociological accounts of women's lives often attempt to "organize" these seemingly rambling conversations under topical headings, so that the form of presentation distorts how women experience and understand their own lives. Discussing one's life, like making a tapestry or quilt, can be a long and convoluted practice that may seem to lack coherence and direction. From another view, the result may be creative integration. Usual formats for presenting sociological work may distort the form of women's experience, making it seem more goal-directed, less emotional, and more linear than it actually is.

SUMMARY

This chapter was not intended as an instruction manual for conducting qualitative research. Rather, we hope to have conveyed some of the methodological diversity of qualitative sociological inquiry, analysis, and presentation. Although qualitative research has a long history in sociology, alternative methods and approaches have proliferated since the early 1970s. Obviously, each technique and strategy has strengths and weaknesses, and several raise disturbing questions about sociologists' ethical and intellectual responsibilities. Those who now engage in qualitative sociological study are condemned to grapple with such questions and to choose among an array of approaches, but this is no misfortune.

The key to successful qualitative research has long been flexibility. Investigative and analytic methods are fitted to particular topics of inquiry and theoretical goals. Qualitative researchers must also be willing to revise, sometimes radically, their methodological strategy in the course of study, as many of those mentioned in this chapter did. Conforming to one or another set of methodological rules or principles seldom leads to informative and insightful qualitative studies. Methodological flexibility and creativity often do. Those who now engage in qualitative sociological study have the good fortune of a vast array of methodological models from which to draw guidance and inspiration.

The expansion of qualitative research into most substantive areas of sociological social psychology provides a measure of the vitality and utility of this general approach. Although it shares that scholarly stage with experimental and survey research, it plays an indispensable role. Qualitative inquiry and analysis provide types of information and insights that are unavailable through other methodological means. The richness and theoretical diversity of contemporary qualitative research recommends it to the social psychologist who is more concerned with validity than reliability, with insight rather than confirmation, with induction more than deduction. The qualitative study of social life and experience is a challenging undertaking, but one that often provides considerable intellectual rewards.

NOTE

The authors are indebted to Howard Becker and Douglas Maynard for their useful comments, suggestions, and advice.

REFERENCES

Adler, Patricia, and Peter Adler. 1987. *Membership Roles in Field Research.* Newbury Park, CA: Sage.

Agar, M. 1986. *Speaking of Ethnography.* Beverly Hills: Sage.

Anderson, Nels. 1923. *The Hobo.* Chicago: University of Chicago Press.

Aptheker, B. H. 1989. *Tapestries of Life: Women's Work, Women's Consciousness, and the Meaning of Daily Experience.* Amherst: University of Massachusetts Press.

Barbarin, O., and M. Chesler. 1983. *Children with Cancer.* Maywood, IL: Eterna.

Becker, Howard. [1953] 1963. Becoming a marijuana user. Pp. 41–58 in *Outsiders.* Glencoe, IL: Free Press.

——— . 1967. History, culture and subjective experience. *Journal of Health and Social Behavior* 8: 163–176.

——— . 1970. *Sociological Work.* Chicago: Aldine.

——— . 1978. Arts and crafts. *American Journal of Sociology* 83:862–889.

——— . 1981. *Exploring Society Photographically.* Chicago: University of Chicago Press.

Becker, Howard, and Blanche Geer. 1957. Participant observation and interviewing: A comparison. *Human Organization* 16:28–32.

Becker, Howard, B. Geer, E. Hughes, and A. Strauss. 1961. *Boys in White.* Chicago: University of Chicago Press.

Becker, Howard, and M. McCall, eds. 1990. *Symbolic Interaction and Cultural Studies.* Chicago: University of Chicago Press.

Blauner, R. 1964. *Alienation and Freedom.* Chicago: University of Chicago Press.

——— . 1987. Problems of editing "first-person" sociology. *Qualitative Sociology* 10:46–64.

Boelen, W. A. Marianne. 1992. Street corner society: Cornerville revisited. *Journal of Contemporary Ethnography* 21:11–51.

Bogdan, Robert, and Steven Taylor. 1975. *Introduction to Qualitative Research Methods.* New York: Wiley.

Broadhead, R. S., and R. C. Rist. 1976. Gatekeepers and the social control of social research. *Social Problems* 23:325–336.

Cahill, Spencer. 1987 Children and civility. *Social Psychology Quarterly* 50:312–321.

Cahill, Spencer, W. Distler, C. Lachowitz, A. Meaney, R. Tarallo, and T. Willard. 1985. Meanwhile backstage: Public bathrooms and the interaction order. *Urban Life* 14:33–58.

Cannon, L., E. Higginbotham, and M. A. Leung. 1988. Race and class bias in qualitative research on women. *Gender & Society* 2:449–462.

Chesler, M. A., and O. Barbarin. 1987. *Childhood Cancer and the Family.* New York: Bruner/Mazil.

Clifford, J., and G. Marcus. 1986. *Writing Culture.* Berkeley: University of California Press.

Connell, R. W. 1987. *Gender and Power.* Stanford, CA: Stanford University Press.

Connell, R. W., D. J. Ashenden, S. Kessler, and G. W. Dowsett. 1982. *Making the Difference: Schools, Families and Social Division.* Sydney: Allen & Unwin.

Conrad, P. 1988. Learning to doctor: Reflections on recent accounts of the medical school years. *Journal of Health and Social Behavior* 29:323–332.

Cook, J., and M. M. Fonow. 1986. Knowledge and women's interest: Issues of epistemology and methodology in feminist sociological research. *Sociological Inquiry* 56:2–29.

Corsaro, William. 1988. Routines in the peer culture of Italian and American nursery school children. *Sociology of Education* 61:1–14.

Corsaro, William, and T. Rizzo. 1988. Discussion and friendship: Socialization procedures in the peer culture of American and Italian nursery school children. *American Sociological Review* 53:879–894.

Cressey, Donald. 1953. *Other People's Money.* Glencoe, IL: Free Press.

Deegan, Mary Jo. 1988. *Jane Addams and the Men of the Chicago School.* New Brunswick, NJ: Transaction.

———. 1991. *Women in Sociology: A Bio-Bibliographical Sourcebook.* New York: Greenwood.

Deegan, Mary Jo, and M. Hill, eds. 1987. *Women and Symbolic Interaction.* Boston: Allen & Unwin.

Denzin, Norman. 1987a. *The Alcoholic Self.* Beverly Hills: Sage.

———. 1987b. *The Recovering Alcoholic.* Beverly Hills: Sage.

———. 1989. *Interpretive Biography.* Newbury Park, CA: Sage.

———. 1990. On understanding emotions: The interpretative-cultural agenda. Pp. 85–116 in *Research Agendas in the Sociology of Emotions,* ed. Theodore Kemper. Albany: State University of New York Press.

DeVault, M. L. 1990. Talking and listening from women's standpoint. *Social Problems* 37:96–116.

Douglas, Jack. 1976. *Investigative Social Research.* Beverly Hills: Sage.

Eder, Donna. 1988. Building cohesion through collaborative narration. *Social Psychology Quarterly* 51:225–235.

Eder, Donna, and Janet Enke. 1991. The structure of gossip: Opportunities and constraints. *American Sociological Review* 56:494–508.

Eichler, M. 1987. *Nonsexist Research Methods.* Boston: Allen & Unwin.

Ellis, Carolyn. 1991. Sociological introspection and emotional experience. *Symbolic Interaction* 14:23–50.

Emerson, Robert. 1983. *Contemporary Field Research.* Prospect Heights, IL: Waveland.

Enke, J. 1990. Informal talk among female athletes in a high school setting. Paper presented at the American Sociological Association annual meetings, Washington, DC.

Farganis, S. 1986. Social theory and feminist theory: The need for dialogue. *Sociological Inquiry* 56:50–68.

Fetterman, D. 1987. *Ethnography: Step by Step.* Beverly Hills: Sage.

Fine, Gary Alan. 1986. Mushrooms, birds or old bottles? Mushroomers and their concerns. *McIlvainea* 7:23–30.

———. 1987. *With the Boys: Little League Baseball and Preadolescent Culture.* Chicago: University of Chicago Press.

———. 1990a. Credit and blame in ethnographic writing. *The American Sociologist* 21:76–79.

———. 1990b. Symbolic interaction in the post-Blumerian age. Pp. 117–157 in *Frontiers of Social Theory: The New Synthesis,* ed. G. Ritzer. New York: Columbia University Press.

———. 1993. Ten lies of ethnography: Moral dilemmas of field research. *Journal of Contemporary Ethnography* 22:267–294.

Fine, Gary Alan, and Kent Sandstrom. 1988. *Knowing Children: Participant Observation with Minors.* Newbury Park, CA: Sage.

Footnotes. 1988. Methods courses in U.S. sociology departments. Washington, DC: American Sociological Association.

Gardner, Carol Brooks. 1988. Access information: Public lies and private peril. *Social Problems* 35:384–397.

Garfinkel, Harold. 1967. *Studies in Ethnomethodology.* Englewood Cliffs, NJ: Prentice Hall.

Garfinkel, Harold, M. Lynch, and E. Livingston. 1981. The work of discovering science construed with materials from the optically discovered pulsar. *Philosophy of the Social Sciences* 11:131–158.

Glaser, B., and A. Strauss. 1967. *The Discovery of Grounded Theory.* Chicago: Aldine.

Goffman, Erving. 1953. *Communication Conduct in an Island Community.* Ph.D. diss. Department of Sociology, University of Chicago, Chicago.

———. 1959. *The Presentation of Self in Everyday Life.* Garden City, NY: Doubleday.

———. 1961. *Asylums.* Garden City, NY: Doubleday.

———. 1971. *Relations in Public.* New York: Basic Books.

———. 1981. Reply to Denzin and Keller. *Contemporary Sociology* 10:60–68.

———. 1989. On fieldwork. *Journal of Contemporary Ethnography* 18:123–132.

Gold, Raymond. 1958. Roles in sociological field observations. *Social Forces* 36:217–223.

Goodwin, Marjorie H. 1990a. Cooperation and competition across girls' play. Pp. 55–96 in *Gender and Discourse,* ed. A. D. Todd and S. Fishcer. Norwood, NJ: Ablex.

———. 1990b. *He Said/She Said: Talk as Social Organization among Black Children.* Bloomington: Indiana University Press.

Gouldner, A. 1962. Anti-minotaur: The myth of value-free sociology. *Social Problems* 9:199–213.

Grant, Linda. 1984. Black females' "place" in desegregated classrooms. *Sociology of Education* 57:98–111.

Grant, Linda, and K. B. Ward. 1991. Gender and publishing in sociology. *Gender & Society* 5:207–223.

Grant, Linda, K. B. Ward, and X. L. Rong. 1987. Is there an association between gender and methods in sociological research? *American Sociological Review* 52:856–862.

Gubrium, Jaber. 1988. The social preservation of the mind: The Alzheimer's disease experience. *Symbolic Interaction* 9:37–51.

Hammersley, M., and P. Atkinson. 1983. *Ethnography: Principles in Practice.* London: Tavistock.

Harper, Douglas. 1982. *Good Company.* Chicago: University of Chicago Press.

———. 1987. *Working Knowledge.* Chicago: University of Chicago Press.

Heath, S. B. 1983. *Ways with Words.* Cambridge: Cambridge University Press.

Heritage, John. 1984. *Garfinkel and Ethnomethodology.* London: Blackwell.

Hinkle, R., and G. Hinkle. 1954. *The Development of Modern Sociology.* New York: Random House.

Hochschild, A. R., with A. Machung. 1989. *The Second Shift.* New York: Viking.

Hughes, Everett. 1958. *Men and Their Work.* Glencoe, IL: Free Press.

———. [1964] 1984. Robert Park. Pp. 543–549 in *The Sociological Eye: Selected Papers.* New Brunswick, NJ: Transaction.

Hymes, Dell. 1974. *Foundations in Sociolinguistics.* Philadelphia: University of Pennsylvania Press.

Jackall, R., B. Laslett, and A. Skolnick. 1978. Symposium review of Lillian Rubin's *Worlds of Pain. Contemporary Sociology* 7:131–139.

Keller, E. F. 1985. *Reflections on Gender and Science.* New Haven: Yale University Press.

Kessler, S., D. J. Ashenden, R. W. Connell, and G. W. Dowsett. 1985. Gender relations in secondary schooling. *Sociology of Education* 58: 34–48.

Krieger, S. 1983. *The Mirror Dance.* Philadelphia: Temple University Press.

Lee, A. M. 1978. *Sociology for Whom?* New York: Oxford University Press.

Lengermann, P. M., and J. Niebrugge-Brantley. 1990. Feminist sociological theory: The near-future prospects. Pp. 316–346 in *Frontiers of Social Theory: The New Synthesis,* ed. G. Ritzer. New York: Columbia University Press.

Lever, Janet. 1978. Sex differences in the complexity of children's play and games. *American Sociological Review* 43:471–483.

———. 1983. *Soccer Madness.* Chicago: University of Chicago Press.

Liebow, Elliot. 1967. *Talley's Corner.* Boston: Little, Brown.

Lindesmith, Alfred. 1947. *Opiate Addiction.* Bloomington, IN: Principia.

Lofland, John. 1966. *Doomsday Cult.* Englewood Cliffs, NJ: Prentice Hall.

Lofland, John, and Lyn Lofland. 1984. *Analyzing Social Settings,* 2nd ed. Belmont, CA: Wadsworth.

Lorber, Judith. 1988. From the editor. *Gender & Society* 2:5–8.

Lundberg, George. 1926. Case work and statistical method. *Social Forces* 5:61–65.

Mackie, M. 1985. Female sociologists: Productivity, collegial relations, and research style examined through journal publications. *Sociology and Social Research* 69:189–207.

Mandell, Nancy. 1988. The least-adult role in studying children. *Journal of Contemporary Ethnography* 16:433–467.

Maynard, Douglas. 1984. *Inside Plea Bargaining.* New York: Plenum.

Maynard, Douglas, and D. Zimmerman. 1984. Topical talk, ritual and the social organization of relationships. *Sociological Psychology Quarterly* 47: 301–322.

McCall, G. S. 1984. Systematic field observation. *Annual Review of Sociology* 10:263–282.

McCall, M., and H. Becker. 1990. Performance science. *Social Problems* 37:117–132.

McCourt, K. 1977. Review of Lillian Rubin's *Worlds of Pain. American Journal of Sociology* 83:813–816.

Mehan, H. 1979. *Learning Lessons: Social Organization in the Classroom.* Cambridge, MA: Harvard University Press.

Merton, R. K. 1972. Insiders and outsiders. *American Journal of Sociology* 77:9–47.

Metz, Mary. 1978. *Classrooms and Corridors.* Berkeley: University of California Press.

———. 1986. *Different by Design.* New York: Routledge & Kegan Paul.

Millman, Marcia. 1980. *Such a Pretty Face.* New York: Norton.

Myerhoff, B. 1978. *Number Our Days.* New York: Dutton.

Oakley, Ann. 1981. Interviewing women: A contradiction in terms. Pp. 30–61 in *Doing Feminist Research,* ed. H. Roberts. London: Routledge.

Orlandella, Angelo Ralph. 1992. Boelen may know Holland, Boelen may know Barzini, but Boelen "doesn't know diddle about the North End!" *Journal of Contemporary Ethnography* 21:69–79.

Paget, M. 1990. Performing the text. *Journal of Contemporary Ethnography* 19:136–155.

Patton, M. Q. 1990. *Qualitative Evaluation and Research Methods,* 2nd ed. Beverly Hills: Sage.

Pitzer, H., and C. O. Palinski. 1980. *Coping with a Miscarriage.* New York: Doubleday.

Platt, Jennifer. 1992. The methods of the Chicago school sociologists. Unpublished manuscript. Brighton, UK: University of Sussex, School of Social Sciences.

Pollner, Melvin. 1974. Mundane reasoning. *Philosophy of the Social Sciences* 4:35–54.

Punch, Maurice. 1986. *The Politics and Ethics of Fieldwork.* Beverly Hills: Sage.

Rainwater, L., and D. J. Pittman. 1967. Ethical problems in studying a politically sensitive and deviant community. *Social Problems* 14.357–366.

Reinharz, S. 1986. The social psychology of miscarriage: An application of symbolic interaction theory and method. Pp. 229–249 in *Women and Symbolic Interaction,* ed. M. J. Deegan and M. Hill. New York: Allen & Unwin.

Richardson, Laurel. 1985. *The New Other Women.* New York: Free Press.

———. 1987. Disseminating research to popular audiences: The book tour. *Qualitative Sociology* 10: 164–176.

———. 1990. *Writing Strategies: Reaching Diverse Audiences.* Beverly Hills: Sage.

Riessman, C. K. 1990. Worlds of difference: Contrasting experience in marriage and narrative style. Pp. 151–176 in *Gender and Discourse,* ed. A. D. Todd and S. Fisher. Norwood, NJ: Ablex.

Rist, Ray. 1973. *Urban School: Factory for Failure.* Cambridge, MA: MIT Press.

———. 1978. *The Invisible Children: School Integration in American Society.* Cambridge, MA: Harvard University Press.

Rollins, J. 1985. *Between Women: Domestics and Their Employers.* Philadelphia: Temple University Press.

Rose, D. 1990. *Living the Ethnographic Life.* Newbury Park, CA: Sage.

Rubin, Lillian. 1976. *Worlds of Pain.* New York: Basic Books.

Sacks, H., E. Schegloff, and G. Jefferson. 1974. A simplest systematics for the organization of turn-taking for conversation. *Language* 50:696–735.

Sanford, S., and D. Eder. 1984. Adolescent humor during peer interaction. *Social Psychology Quarterly* 47:235–243.

Schegloff, E. 1968. Sequencing in conversational openings. *American Anthropologist* 70:1075–1095.

Schofield, J. W. 1982. *Black and White in School.* New York: Praeger.

Schofield, J. W., and H. A. Sagar. 1977. Peer interaction in a desegregated middle school. *Sociometry* 40: 130–138.

Schudson, Michael. 1984. Embarrassment and Goffman's idea of human nature. *Theory and Society* 13:633–648.

Shaw, Clifford. 1926. *The Jack Roller.* Chicago: University of Chicago Press.

Sherif, M., O. J. Harvey, B. J. White, W. Hood, and C. Sherif. 1961. *Intergroup Conflict and Cooperation.* Norman, OK: The University Book Exchange.

Skocpol, Theda, ed. 1984. *Vision and Method in Historical Sociology.* New York: Cambridge University Press.

Smith, Dorothy. 1987. *The Everyday World as Problematic: A Feminist Sociology.* Boston: Northeastern University Press.

Stacey, J. 1988. Can there be a feminist ethnography? *Women's Studies International Forum* 11:21–27.

Strauss, A., L. Schatzman, D. Erlich, and M. Sabshin. 1963. The hospital and its negotiated order. Pp. 147–169 in *The Hospital in Modern Society,* ed. E. Friedson. New York: Free Press.

Thomas, W. I., and D. Thomas. 1928. *The Child in America.* New York: Knopf.

Thomas, W. I., and F. Znaniecki. 1918–1920. *The Polish Peasant in Europe and America.* Chicago: University of Chicago Press.

Thrasher, Fredric. 1927. *The Gang.* Chicago: University of Chicago Press.

Turner, Ralph. 1953. The quest for universals in sociological research. *American Sociological Review* 18:604–611.

Van Maanen, John. 1988. *Tales of the Field: On Writing Ethnography.* Chicago: University of Chicago Press.

Ward, K. B., and L. Grant. 1985. The feminist critique and a decade of publishing in sociology journals. *The Sociological Quarterly* 19:139–158.

Warren, Carol. 1988. *Gender Issues in Field Research.* Beverly Hills: Sage.

Wax, Rosalie. 1971. *Doing Field Research.* Chicago: University of Chicago Press.

West, C., and D. Zimmerman. 1977. Women's place in everyday talk: Reflections on parent-child interaction. *Social Problems* 24:521–529.

Whyte, William F. [1943] 1955. *Street Corner Society.* Chicago: University of Chicago Press.

———. 1984. *Learning from the Field.* Beverly Hills: Sage.

———. 1992. In defense of *Street Corner Society. Journal of Contemporary Ethnography* 21:52–68.

Wieder, D. Lawrence. 1974. *Language and Social Reality.* The Hague: Mouten.

Wilson, Thomas P. 1991. Social structure and the sequential organization of interaction. Pp. 22–43 in *Talk and Social Structure,* ed. D. Boden and D. Zimmerman. Berkeley: University of California Press.

Wolfe, Alan, ed. 1991. *America at Century's End.* Berkeley: University of California Press.

Wright, L. K. 1988. Alzheimer's disease as developmental asychrony: A dialectical paradigm of the marital relationship of older couples. Ph.D. diss. Department of Sociology. Athens: University of Georgia.

Zimmerman, D., and D. L. Wieder. 1977. The diary: Diary-interview method. *Urban Life* 5:479–498.

Znaniecki, Florian. 1934. *The Method of Sociology.* New York: Holt, Rinehart & Winston.

CHAPTER 24

Experimentation in Sociological Social Psychology

BARBARA FOLEY MEEKER
ROBERT K. LEIK

An experiment employs the controlled creation and comparison of two or more conditions in such a way as to allow clear causal inference. Used in a program of a series of studies, experimentation can be a powerful source of information about social psychological processes. Experimentation may address theoretical questions or policy concerns. For example, in the 1978 volume of the *Annual Review of Sociology,* two articles reviewed "experimentation," with no overlap. Bonacich and Light (1978) reviewed work in several research programs that had made use of laboratory experiments, including expectation states theory, offshoots of Bales's Interaction Process Analysis studies, behavioral sociology, and prisoner's dilemma research. Riecken and Boruch (1978) gave as examples of "social experiments" the Manhattan bail bond experiment, the Kansas City Preventive Patrol Experiment, and the Health Insurance Experiment. Both types of activity are legitimately called experimentation.

CAUSALITY AND EXPERIMENTAL DESIGN

Evidence and causality

The kind of causality scientists are concerned with is what Aristotle called "efficient" cause, or the "source of motion." This is the idea that one event or circumstance creates, sets in motion, changes, or makes something else happen. This does not necessarily imply determinism: modern philosophers of science (e.g., Bunge 1979) recognize probabilistic causal processes and multiple causes for events.

If we assume that there are processes by which some events create others but these processes are not deterministic, we are faced with some problems. If causality were deterministic, one counterexample would suffice as evidence against a hypothesis of causality. However, if the processes of causality are probabilistic, a single counterexample does not provide conclusive evidence. The number of counterexamples required and under what conditions they are collected are important issues, and it is for these types of questions that experimental design crucial. The work of philosopher John Stuart Mill (1872) and the statistician Ronald A. Fisher (1960) has been important in shaping the use of experimentation to provide evidence about causality.

John Stuart Mill

In 1872, Mill, using ideas earlier introduced by Bacon (1620), listed five methods (known as "Mill's methods") for assessing whether the relationship between two phenomena is causal, as follows.

1. Method of Agreement. "If two or more instances of the phenomenon under investigation have only one circumstance in common, the circumstance in which alone all the instances agree, is the cause (or effect) of the given phenomenon." (p. 255)

2. Method of Difference. "If an instance in which the phenomenon under investigation occurs, and an instance in which it does not occur, have every circumstance in common save one, . . . the circumstance in which alone the two instances differ is the effect, or the cause, . . . of the phenomenon." (p. 254)

3. Joint Method of Agreement and Difference. "If two or more instances in which the phenomenon occurs have only one circumstance in common, while two or more instances in which it does not occur have nothing in common save the absence of the circumstance, the circumstance in which alone the two sets of instances differ, is the effect, or the cause, . . . of the phenomenon." (p. 255)

4. Method of Concomitant Variation. "Whatever phenomenon varies in any manner whenever another phenomenon varies in some particular manner, is either a cause or an effect of that phenomenon or is connected with it through some fact of causation." (p. 263)

5. Method of Residue. "Subduct from any phenomenon such part as is known by previous inductions to be the effect of certain antecedents, and the residue of the phenomenon is the effect of the remaining antecedents." (p. 260)

The method of difference is typically employed in experiments. Subjects are assigned to one of several "conditions" that are identical except for one factor, the "independent variable." If the outcome, the "dependent variable," is different for different conditions, the difference can be attributed to the causal effect of the one factor on which the conditions differ, (the independent variable). The method of concomitant variation is the basis of the logic of correlational analysis and the method of residue the basis of "statistical control" in data analysis designs such as multiple regression and analysis of covariance. The method of agreement is the basis of much case study research.

Mill's methods do not specify how to determine which of two phenomena is the cause and which the effect. In science, the criterion for establishing causality is time sequence: if event A precedes event B, then B cannot be a cause of A. For example, we would not hypothesize that level of education causes race, because people are born with racial identification and acquire education

later. However, simple time sequence does not necessarily establish causality. It can be hypothesized that race causes differences in educational level but cannot be "proved" by time sequence.

One way of establishing that one event precedes another is to create the first event and then observe the second. This is the first feature of an experiment: the deliberate manipulation of a variable at one time and observation of another variable at a later time. This is the popular meaning of experiment: we try something out and "see what happens."

If we combine the method of difference with the manipulation of events to establish a time sequence, we move closer to providing evidence for causality. This requires creating *two* sets of circumstances, which are identical except for one factor. If the results observed later are different, the difference may be attributed to the one factor. In combination with time sequence, we may say we have evidence that this factor is the cause. This is the second feature of an experiment: comparison of conditions that are identical except for one factor.

Ronald A. Fisher

Many early applications of experimental design were in the fields of agriculture and medicine. An interesting example presented by Fisher (1960) describes an experiment conducted by Charles Darwin on the relative advantages of hybrid and self-fertilized plants. Darwin grew plants from seeds, obtained by either self- or cross-fertilization, in the same pots and found that the cross-fertilized plants were larger on average. However, Darwin and even one of the most sophisticated mathematicians of the time (Galton) did not know quite how to interpret the data. Were the results sufficient to support the hypothesis that cross-fertilization is superior to self-fertilization? Or could the results be due to chance or other confounded conditions, such as soil quality, water, or temperature?

Fisher points out that with the statistical methods available to him but not to Galton, the results of Darwin's experiment can be much more precisely evaluated (he believes Darwin's hypothesis that cross-fertilized plants are larger was correct).

Two questions must be answered: (1) Are the conditions really identical except for the variable of fertilization? (2) Given a probabilistic model of causality, how much difference between kinds of plants do we need to have evidence of causality rather than chance?

Consider the first question. If, for example, we are conducting an agricultural experiment and hypothesize that variety A of corn will produce more than variety B, we grow A and B under identical circumstances—same soil, weather, cultivation, harvesting techniques, and so on—and at harvest time compare the crops yielded by A and by B. If A produces more, we attribute this to variety because there was no other difference between A and B. However, if there were any differences besides variety—for example, if A was grown on a sunny slope and B in the shade, or A in June and B in July—then we do not have conclusive evidence that variety A outproduces B.

How can a researcher be sure the conditions under which A and B are grown are identical? One way is to consider all the factors we already know affect growth and "match" the two varieties on these factors. However, even this will not solve the problem, because after we have taken into account all the factors we know, we are left with the possibility that some factor we don't know about has affected the outcome. For example, there may be some important plant nutrient as yet unknown to science, and we may have inadvertently planted all of variety A in a plot in which this nutrient is abundant and all of B in a plot in which it is absent.

A relationship between two phenomena in which they vary together but neither causes the other, both being caused by a third factor, is called a *spurious* relationship. Examples are a correlation between reading ability and foot size among children (both being caused by age), number of storks and birth rates in Europe (both being higher in rural than urban areas), or the seeds of corn variety A being available first and therefore getting the early season sun (a possible source of spurious causality in our hypothetical example). Simply matching samples does not eliminate the possibility of spurious relationships due to unknown causes.

It is at this point that the work of statisticians such as Fisher produced a solution to what seems a logically impossible question: how to equate conditions on all factors, including those of whose existence we are ignorant. The solution is randomization. If we divide the field where we plant varieties A and B into small plots and use a random device, such as tossing a coin, to decide which variety goes in each plot, then all factors both known *and unknown* on which the plots may differ will be equally likely to affect A and B. No difference between A and B can be attributed to the *systematic* operation of any other factor, since no other factor will be systematically more likely to be present in plots with A than plots with B. There may still be random or coincidental differences, but we have minimized the chance of spurious causal factors, because under random assignment the expected values of any unknown variables will be the same across all treatments. For many methodologists, a third defining characteristic of an experiment is *random assignment to conditions*. (See, however, the discussion below of ABA designs.)

Darwin and Galton's second problem was assessing the strength of their evidence. With random assignment of cases to conditions we can use statistical techniques based on the assumptions of probability to assess the seriousness of a difference between the crops produced by plots with variety A and those with variety B. In other words, randomization assures us that any *prior* differences are due to chance, which in turn allows us to calculate the probability that postexperimental differences could be explained by chance. For statistical models associated with different types of experimental designs, see Winer (1971).

EXAMPLES OF EXPERIMENTAL DESIGNS

The Medical Model: Treatment-Control Design

One source of models of experimental design comes from medicine, in which the question is: "Does drug X really help with condition Z?" The simplest experimental design that might answer this question is the classic *treatment-control* design with random assignment to treatment or control conditions. In an experimental design, the control condition is one that is identical in all respects to the treatment condition except that no treatment is administered. The control condition establishes a baseline against which to compare the effects of a treatment, keeping in mind that some patients may recover without treatment. (Note that a control *condition* in an experiment is not the same as a control *variable* in a multivariate statistical design.) A treatment-control design usually also has *before and after* measurement: the state of the subject is measured both before and after the application of treatment (or nontreatment for controls). Having both before (pretest) and after (posttest) scores enables the researcher to assess the precise effects of the treatment.

This method was adapted and popularized in social psychology by the work of Campbell and Stanley (1963; expanded in T. Cook and Campbell 1979), whose intended audience was educational researchers. As Campbell and Stanley point out, neither a "one-shot" study, in which something is simply tried, nor a study with matched groups of subjects in treatment and control conditions but without random assignment to conditions can provide conclusive evidence that one educational technique works better than another. They suggest that a variety of designs with nonrandom matched comparison groups may be useful but should be called "quasi-experiments" rather than experiments. Quasi-experimental designs produce several sources of error that render clear causal inference dubious.

Although the treatment-control model is the classic experimental design, few current experiments in nonapplied social psychological research use this model. In fact, some sociologists, such as Willer (1987), claim that the model based on Mills and Fisher is misleading for theoretically based research. Insistence on comparing a single treatment condition with a single control condition *is* often found in applied research, where the treatment is the introduction of a new program.

Even in applied research, the traditional treatment-control design has drawbacks. It tends to em-phasize single, unreplicated experiments that ignore developmental processes and the role of theory. In the medical analogy, this is like asking only whether some treatment is better than none, while ignoring the possibility that different levels of medication may have different effects and that we want to know how, as well as whether, the treatment works. More sophisticated designs provide much more information about causal processes.

Factorial Designs

Both applied and theoretical researchers are often interested in the effects of several variables, and may expect interactions between them. A *factorial* (or multifactorial) design is one in which two or more independent variables are created. A *completely crossed* factorial design is one in which all combinations of conditions of two or more variables exist, with each subject assigned randomly to a treatment that consists of a combination of conditions.

For example, imagine an experiment in which the dependent variable is rate of helpful behavior, measured by giving a subject a series of choices between an alternative that adds to another person's score (helpful) or does not (nonhelpful). We know subjects make a greater number of helpful choices when they think they are working as a group rather than as individuals and when there is no risk as opposed to some risk of lowering their own score by making a helpful choice. We suspect the underlying process includes the development of "trust," defined as an expectation that the partner will reciprocate helpful behavior (Meeker 1983). Next, we hypothesize that trust will be higher for subjects who believe their partner is similar to themselves (based on theories of interpersonal attraction) and we also wish to compare a competitive orientation with both the group and the individual orientations.

This provides a design in which there are two conditions of similarity to partner (high versus low), three conditions of orientation (work as a group, work as individuals, compete) and two conditions of risk (no risk, some risk). This is described as a 2 × 3 × 2 design—there are three independent variables with two conditions of the first, three conditions of the second, and two conditions of the third. This design has $2 \times 3 \times 2 = 12$ conditions, and if each subject experiences one condition would require 120 subjects to have ten subjects in each condition or cell. A subject in the first condition or cell would be told he/she had a very similar partner, was working as a group with that partner, and had no risk of lowering his/her own score by being helpful. A subject in the last condition or cell would be told he/she had a very dissimilar partner, was competing with that partner, and there was some risk of lowering his/her own score by being helpful. Otherwise, the instructions, setting, and task would be identical for all subjects. The same dependent variable—number of helpful choices—would be measured for every subject.

Since the dependent variable is a continuous variable, while the independent variables are categorical, the statistical design would be a three-way analysis of variance. In this hypothetical study, the theory suggests that both similarity and group orientation will increase trust and that trust will overcome the effects of risk. This means we would predict higher levels of helpfulness under similarity than dissimilarity and higher levels of helpfulness under group than individual or competitive orientation (statistically, a main effect of each of these two variables). This should be especially true under high risk (statistically, interactions between orientation and risk and between similarity and risk). By putting both orientation and similarity into the same design, we can see which has more effect and answer questions such as whether the effects of risk are overcome by either factor alone or only by both together.

The completely crossed multifactorial design is probably the most common experimental design in current use in experimental social psychology. It is often combined with a "repeated measures" design, in which some variables are "within" and some are "between" subjects. Variables for which each subject experiences only one condition (the hypothetical design above, in which each subject has only one orientation) are *between-subject* vari-

ables. *Within-subject* variables are those in which every subject experiences all conditions. If each subject spent the first half of the experiment with a similar partner and the second half with a dissimilar partner, then similarity would become a within-subject variable. Other multifactorial designs include incompletely crossed, nested, Greek square, and Latin square models (Kirk 1982; Winer 1971). Other statistical models may be used with experimental designs, including path analysis (see Alwin and Tessler 1974).

The ABA Design

The experimental design we have been describing has two or more different groups of subjects, each experiencing a different condition. It is also possible to assess the causal effect of some factor in a design in which all subjects experience all conditions in alternation. This design is used, for example, by researchers in the operant conditioning or behavioral tradition (Burgess and Bushell 1969). In part A of the experiment, a baseline level of behavior is observed for a subject under standard conditions. Part A is equivalent to a control condition. In part B, an experimental change is introduced and changes in the subject's behavior are observed until the changes level off at a new rate. Then the change is reversed so the conditions are the same as at the beginning (part A again); if the subject's behavior returns to the baseline the causal effectiveness of the experimental variable is established. For example, some behavior is identified and rewarded in part A, a different behavior is rewarded in part B, and then the reward schedule of part A is resumed.

The ability to *reverse* an effect by introducing and then removing an experimental variable is a powerful demonstration of causality. Also, in this design each subject serves as his/her own control, so the statistical variation produced by individual differences between subjects is eliminated as a source of coincidental variation. Fewer subjects are required and the information about the effects is more precise. These designs are an exception to the rule that an experiment must have random assignment to conditions; since the design demonstrates the control of the independent variable over the dependent variable by the reversal of an effect, and since each subject is his/her own control, spurious effects are eliminated without random assignment.

Field Experimentation

Field experimentation refers to using experimental methods in an existing, nonlaboratory setting. Complex organizations, such as corporations, social service agencies, or college dormitories, have been the sites for such studies, as have public settings, such as street corners and shopping malls. The purpose may be either "pure" research in a natural setting or deciding what effects a proposed change will have. The latter is typically the case in policy research. (For an introduction to policy-related field experiments, see Hausman and Wise 1985; Riecken and Boruch 1978; Rossi and Wright 1984).

The essence of good field experimentation is the same as that of laboratory work: using theory to decide what to manipulate, finding ways to accomplish the manipulation, and finding ways to assess the consequences. The advantages of field experimentation for basic research are that research can take place in a natural setting, thereby eliminating the problems of interaction of laboratory conditions with the processes under investigation, and that it may allow examination of processes impossible to create in a laboratory. For policy research, field experimentation has the advantage of demonstrating which programs work and why or why not.

An example of field experimentation is a project on the involvement of families in the Head Start program that compares two different modes of parental participation and a control group of non-Head Start families (Leik, Chalkley, and Peterson 1991). The research design was both experimental and descriptive in that it (1) created three treatment groups; (2) sampled from three racial/ethnic populations; and (3) used before and after assessments (at the beginning and end of the Head Start program year, an interval of about six months). The research was theoretically driven by a model relat-

ing child, parent, and family factors to the nature of parental participation in the program. The work took place in cooperation with the Minneapolis Head Start project known as Parents in Community Action (PICA). Approximately one hundred families were studied in 1986 to 1987 and a comparable number in 1989 to 1990.

The concerns of the project were both theoretical and to inform public policy. It has been well documented that Head Start programs have beneficial effects (Consortium for Longitudinal Studies 1983). The primary question in the Head Start Family Impact Project was not whether Head Start was beneficial, but whether involving parents in the program would have additional desirable consequences for the child, the parent, or the family. Based on theory, it was anticipated that specific types of parental participation were crucial. Thus, a special "enrichment" treatment was designed, and subject families in the Head Start sample were randomly assigned to either the regular or the enrichment treatment.

Other examples of policy-related field experiments using complex designs and based on theory include the Seattle and Denver Income Maintenance Experiments (Robins et al. 1980), designed to test formal economic models of differential incentive structures. Comparisons were between alternative program formats, not just between the program and its absence.

Survey Experiments

Some researchers have combined the advantages of survey research with experimental logic, a design called a *factorial experiment* (Rossi and Anderson 1982). One kind uses descriptions (vignettes) of hypothetical situations to which a subject/respondent is asked to react. Since vignettes can be incorporated into questionnaires, they can be administered in random sample surveys. An example is the work of Rossi and Jasso (1977) and Jasso (1978, 1980, 1990) on the contribution of different factors, such as gender, marital status, number of children, education, occupation, and income, to overall social status or social justice evaluation. All reasonable combinations of these factors were created by computer and placed into vignettes describing hypothetical individuals or couples. The vignettes were distributed to a sample of two hundred representative respondents in Baltimore, who were asked to judge the extent to which a given vignette individual or couple was underpaid or overpaid. This dependent variable, of course, is an attitude, not a behavior. The essence of experimentation (manipulation and comparison) and the benefits of a sample survey (ability to generalize results to larger populations) are combined in this study.

INTERNAL VALIDITY

As experimental designs and techniques have developed, researchers have learned important lessons about sources of error within experiments that can lead to mistaken inferences of causality. Techniques for handling many of these *issues of internal validity* have been developed.

Human Reactivity

Subject Bias.   In medical research, a problem known as the "placebo effect" arises. If in the treatment condition of a medical experiment patients know they are receiving treatment for their disease, and in the control condition they know they are not, the patients in the treatment condition may feel better because they know they are getting treatment, while the patients in the control condition may not get better because they know they are not getting treatment. In other words, any improvement in the condition of patients in the treatment condition may be due not to the treatment but to their belief in treatment. This cause is *not* eliminated by random assignment to treatment and control conditions, because it occurs *after* the assignment to conditions. In a medical experiment, then, the "control" needs to be not just a condition in which nothing happens to the subject, but one in which the subject receives a treatment that seems just like the real treatment but contains no effective ingredient (a placebo or "sugar pill"). Only if the subjects who received the real treatment get well at higher rates than those who received the placebo

treatment can the researcher conclude that the treatment, not subject reactivity to the idea of treatment, is the cause of recovery.

Subject reactivity is a problem in social psychological research also. One famous example is the Western Electric studies of worker productivity (Roethlisberger and Dickson 1939; see also Homans 1950). Here conclusions about the effects of "treatments," which were modifications in working conditions, had to be revised when the researchers realized that the subjects, the workers, knew they were being studied and responded to the fact that someone was interested in them as much as to the fact that their working conditions changed. This is called a *Hawthorne effect* (because the studies took place in the Western Electric plant in Hawthorne, Illinois). Other names for this type of effect are *demand characteristic* of the experiment, or *subject bias.*

For social psychologists, the focus in dealing with subject bias has been not on providing placebo conditions (it is often not clear what a "placebo" might be for a social psychological experiment) but on ensuring that subjects are not aware of the hypotheses of the study. It is generally agreed that under *no* circumstances should subjects be aware of the hypotheses. There is less agreement about other techniques for reducing subject bias. Concern about demand characteristics of experimental settings among some researchers has created the assumption that not only should subjects not be told the hypotheses, they should be misled as to the variables of interest—the "cover story" for an experiment should emphasize something other than the experimenter's true interest (e.g., Aronson, Brewer, and Carlsmith 1985). Other experimenters (ourselves included) feel this amount of deception is often unnecessary and undesirable.

Campbell and Stanley (1963) were concerned with an additional type of subject reactivity—reaction to measurement. This occurs in the "before-and-after" design, in which the state of the subject is measured both before and after the application of treatment (or placebo). Having both pretest and posttest scores enables the researcher to assess the precise effects of the treatment but may create a spurious effect because the subject begins to change as a result of experiencing the pretest. The solution is to have a set of control conditions in which no pretest is administered.

Experimenter Bias.   Another human involved in the experiment is the experimenter, who also may be affected by what he/she expects to happen. This is called an *experimenter bias* or *experimenter effect* and can occur at two different points in the experiment. The first point is when the supposedly standardized conditions are actually not the same in the treatment and control conditions. For example, the experimenter, because he/she expects the subjects to do better in the treatment condition, may smile more, act friendlier, or give them more time. This destroys the required feature of an experiment that two conditions be identical except for the independent variable; that is, there are now two sources of difference—the experimental independent variable and the experimenter's behavior. These are confounded, so we cannot tell which has created a difference in subject behavior. Studies on experimenter effects (e.g., Orne 1962, 1969; Rosenthal 1963, 1966) show how these effects can occur without the experimenter being aware of them.

The second point at which experimenter bias may enter is in measurement of the dependent variable; that is, expecting a certain result can influence (perhaps unconsciously) the data collected. Even the agricultural experimenter studying two varieties of corn could inadvertently fill the bin fuller, read the gauge higher, or round up instead of down for the variety he/she expected to grow more. Gould (1981) provides an instructive history of this kind of mismeasurement in physical anthropology and psychology.

The solution to problems of experimenter bias in the medical model is the *double-blind* experimental design, in which neither the subjects nor those administering the treatment and collecting the data know which condition is which. Social psychologists have developed a variety of techniques to guard against experimenter bias. The best procedure is to have the experiment run and data collected by someone who either does not know the hypotheses of the experiment or does not know which condition is being administered. Standard-

ized procedures for administering instructions to subjects (e.g., videotaped instructions), using teams of experimenters each of whom does one part of the experiment in ignorance of what has happened in other parts, and mechanized data collection are other techniques for reducing experimenter bias. Many researchers use computer systems to standardize both giving instructions and collecting data.

Manipulation Checks

Another problem recognized in experimental research is that assigning a subject to a condition does not necessarily ensure that he/she experiences the intended treatment. Subjects have sometimes not heard, understood, believed, or correctly interpreted what the experimenter intended to tell them. It is now standard procedure in experiments to include *manipulation checks*, measurements of each independent variable from the subject's perspective. For example, if the experimenter has told some subjects their partners will be attractive and other subjects their partners will be unattractive, a sociometric questionnaire is given to assess how attractive the subject thinks his/her partner is. Only if the subjects in the low attractiveness condition rate their partners lower than subjects in the high attractiveness condition can it be certain the instructions really created conditions of high and low attractiveness.

If the instructions are complex, it is important to be sure that subjects understood them. This is a problem with some game and bargaining experiments, for example. It is also important to establish whether subjects believed deceptions used in an experiment. Ethical standards for experimental research require that any deceptive statements be explained when the experiment is complete; suspicion is usually assessed during this postexperimental debriefing interview.

Differential Subject Dropout

It is not unusual in experimental studies to lose a few subjects after they have been randomly assigned to conditions, for such reasons as failure to understand or follow instructions, suspicion, breakdown of apparatus, or simply walking out. If these losses were to occur randomly, all conditions would be equally affected. However, if the dropout rates are different for different conditions, the benefits of randomization are compromised. This may happen, for example, if the instructions are more complicated or less plausible for one condition than others. It is proper procedure to report the number of subjects lost, for what reasons, whether dropout rates were different for different conditions, and whether subjects who dropped out were initially different from others. It is also important to be alert to this problem in pretests of experimental procedures and to revise the procedures if there are differential dropout rates. In interpreting experimental results, it is important to remember that every case of subject dropout may compromise the random assignment and hence causal interpretations.

Mixing Assigned and Preexisting Variables

Social psychologists are often interested in variables such as gender, personality, or race that cannot be experimentally created and randomly assigned. For example, we may want to compare the behavior of men and women in an experimental setting. Since gender is not randomly assigned, it is inappropriate to make the same kind of causal inferences about gender effects as about effects of randomly assigned variables. More appropriate approaches would include treating the study as a replication with two different subject populations, using covariate statistical designs, and developing a theory that specifies clearly what gender differences are expected and why. Procedures such as matching or blocking on an unmanipulated variable before random assignment may be used to ensure that equal numbers of subjects in different categories of the unmanipulated variable are included in each category of a manipulated variable. This does not, of course, allow the researcher to make the same kind of causal inferences about the unmanipulated variable as about the one to which subjects are randomly assigned. Issues in-

volving combining randomly assigned and preexisting variables deserve more discussion than they have received in research literature.

Ethical Standards in Experimentation

It is important that researchers, in their attempt to avoid threats to internal validity, not coerce or abuse their subjects. The American Sociological Association and the American Psychological Association publish extensive professional guidelines for ethics in research, and experiments conducted under academic sponsorship must be reviewed by an institutional review board (Human Subjects Committee). Before these standards were codified, a number of experiments were conducted that proved controversial on ethical grounds. One well-known example is the series by Milgram (1974) in which subjects were deceived into believing they were administering a dangerous electric shock to another person and that they could not discontinue their participation in the experiment. Current ethical requirements include *informed consent,* which means subjects must be aware of what they will be asked to do and of possible risks and benefits, must participate voluntarily, and must be able to withdraw during the experiment without penalty. Experimental procedures must not cause physical, emotional, or psychological harm to subjects, and data collected about subjects must be kept confidential. The permissibility of deception is a topic for debate, but certainly if deceptions are used they must be completely explained to the subjects immediately after their participation.

Examples from a Field Experiment

Although our discussion above has focused on laboratory techniques for identifying and handling problems of internal validity, these problems also occur in field settings. Some issues of internal validity can be illustrated in the Head Start field experiment described above. Although the natural setting eliminates problems of subject reactivity caused by being in a laboratory, in field experiments affected populations can recognize that something new is afoot, which can generate reactivity to the experimental process (a Hawthorne effect). Also, field experiments are subject to the intrusion of external factors that cannot be controlled by the experimenter.

Recall that this experiment had two treatment conditions (regular Head Start and enrichment) and an untreated control group. The enrichment treatment required that the parent participate in several regularly scheduled activities. The regular treatment had no such requirements. Data show that the enrichment treatment parents participated much more than the regular treatment parents (a positive manipulation check). However, a problem arose in random assignment to treatment. All of the families studied were single-parent, female-headed, poverty-level families. Some women who were randomly assigned to the enrichment treatment simply did not have time and resources to participate. These cases had to be reassigned to the regular treatment.

The problem, then, is differential subject dropout compounded by the ethical consideration of being unable to deny the regular program to subjects who could not keep up the enriched program. This means careful checks of comparability are needed before concluding that experimental factors account for any observed results. In fact, the sample of families studied in 1986 to 1987 show essentially no preexperiment difference between the three treatment groups (two Head Start treatments plus controls). For data gathered in 1989 to 1990, however, there is a significant difference in preexperiment levels of family stress between the enrichment and regular samples. Since family stress does interact with some of the variables and processes under study, the integrity of the experimental design may be compromised unless appropriate statistical adjustments (e.g., through analysis of covariance) are used.

Another set of problems emerged from the mixture of randomly assigned variables (the treatment conditions) and preexisting variables (the three racial groups), since the races had different dropout rates and show marked differences in how the child, parent, and family factors studied work together. In statistical terms, most cells of the covariance matrix for these variables interact with race. Separate models of program participation and benefit must therefore be constructed for the different racial groups, and the samples become very small for such model development. The findings are exciting at the theoretical level but frustrating from the viewpoint of formal experimental logic.

EXTERNAL VALIDITY AND EXPERIMENTATION

As we have seen, a variety of designs and procedures has been developed to deal with threats to internal validity. It is part of the conventional wisdom in research methodology that a well-conducted experiment has high internal validity and that from such an experiment conclusions about the causal effect of an independent variable can confidently be made.

Another set of problems of interpretation from experiments is called *problems of external validity* or *generalizability.* The conventional wisdom is that experiments are weak on external validity, because of the "artificiality" of experiments. This is only partly true, and the issues involved are complex.

Statistical and Theoretical Generalization

There are two distinct types of generalization: statistical and theoretical. In statistical generalization, the experimenter generalizes to a larger population from which he/she has drawn a sample; this is what is usually intended by survey researchers. In this sense, we ask whether we can use these observations to describe the existing characteristics of people or situations that were not observed. A good example is opinion polls: The question is how much error we will encounter in using the results of an interview of one thousand respondents in describing the opinions of several million. A well-designed random sample will allow us to answer this question with a known percentage of error. *This is the wrong question to ask of an experiment.* Experiments, by definition, do not study existing conditions—they create new conditions. Thus, an experiment cannot be used to generalize to the distribution of characteristics of an existing population. Although this can be described as a "weakness" or "limitation" of experiments, it is really a criticism of those who try to misuse experiments. It is not a valid criticism of a hammer that it cannot be used to sew on a button!

In theoretical generalization, we want to know how to predict or understand what may happen in future populations or populations different from those we have studied. For these questions, even a well-designed sample survey will not allow an estimate of the statistical distribution of some phenomenon.

Theoretical generalization, the question of whether and how one can apply the results of an empirical study to different situations, populations, or settings is a basic question in philosophy of science: It applies to physical and biological sciences as well as to social sciences and to surveys, case studies, and other nonexperimental methods in social psychology as well as to experiments. Theoretical generalization requires two kinds of information: (1) a general principle that has been discovered or tested in an earlier study and (2) information about how this particular principle applies to the present case. For example, if we have evidence from experimental studies that subjects conform to social norms, we can expect that people in some other setting will also conform to norms, but we need descriptive information about what the norms are in the new setting. Also (as we discuss in more detail below), some principles apply under some conditions but not others or apply differently under different conditions. The first kind of information, identification of general principles, requires that we have a theory or theoretical model; the second kind, features of a new setting, requires both a theory and accurate descriptive information about the new setting. Some critiques of generalizability of experiments are based more on the idea that there are limitations to the general principles that can be examined using experimentation, and some more on the idea that there are limitations

to finding natural settings to which a valid general principle can be applied.

Artificiality

Internal Validity.   Some concerns about *artificiality* are actually with issues of internal validity, discussed above. The question is whether such things as demand characteristics of the laboratory setting rather than the independent variables cause the subjects' responses. Other research methods have similar problems. For example, being interviewed is a highly artificial situation, and features of the interview setting, the interviewer's characteristics or behavior, or the way questions are phrased can create demand characteristics that bias the results. Likewise, a participant observer must always be alert to ways his/her presence affects the observed behavior. A study of any sort that lacks internal validity cannot provide a general theoretical principle to apply elsewhere.

A related problem, which may affect experiments more than other methods (because experiments create conditions), is that the variables created may not, in fact, represent what the experimenter thinks they do (a problem of measurement validity). This may be due to failure of manipulation but also may be due to failure to conceptualize the variables adequately, so that additional dimensions or extraneous factors are included. For example, some critics of dissonance studies claim that what the researchers thought was dissonance was really something else (e.g., Chapanis and Chapanis 1964). Experimental settings that are most like natural settings incorporate multiple dimensions and extraneous variables. Ironically, the very complexity that is necessary to mirror reality makes interpretation of results more difficult. In other words, making an experimental setting more like a natural setting may decrease internal validity.

Limited Range of Conditions.   Another concern with regard to artificiality is that experiments are conducted under a limited range of conditions, for example in laboratories, using invented tasks and highly unrealistic social arrangements and limited subject populations. This is not an argument that laboratory results apply to *no* natural settings: the results of a laboratory study may well apply to a natural setting that has the same characteristics as the experiment, but not to other natural settings. For example, a laboratory study of group decision making may apply to people interacting with strangers on an assigned task with a limited time frame (e.g., a jury) but not to interactions with intimate associates or on long-term, open-ended tasks.

Common features of laboratory experiments that may limit the range of other settings to which the principles studied apply include: (1) the subject population, which is usually a convenience sample of undergraduates from psychology or sociology classes; (2) the fact that subjects know they are being observed by a stranger; (3) the usual precaution of ensuring that subjects do not know other subjects before the experiment; (4) the fact that subjects usually have little control over what they are supposed to do and the way they are to do it; and (5) the fact that most experiments occur over a short time period.

Sears (1986) presents a useful analysis of the probable ways the typical subject population and typical laboratory setting and task reduce the generalizability of results of much laboratory experimentation. It is important to consider the *theoretical* meaning of these conditions. As Sears points out, there are theoretical and empirical literatures that suggest ways in which persons in late adolescence, specially selected for ambition and cognitive skills and isolated from their family and community settings (features of the typical undergraduate population), differ from other populations. Also, there are theoretical reasons to expect that some social processes occur differently when people are unobserved, interact with others well known to them, have a sense of control over their environment, or spend a long time.

In addition to a limited range of conditions available in a laboratory, there is always the possibility that properties of the laboratory interact with hypothesized effects such that results may be different outside the laboratory. Of course, these interactions can themselves be studied. A good example is O'Rourke's (1963) study of the same families interacting at home versus in a laboratory. Also, as noted above, not all experiments occur in laboratories, under the "artificial" conditions criticized by this perspective.

Limitations on Phenomena That Can Be Studied

Another argument against the external validity of experiments in general is that many topics of interest, such as socialization, social movements, stratification, or culture, involve conditions that cannot be randomly assigned and/or take a very long time to develop and hence cannot be studied experimentally. As Rosenberg (1968) points out, many variables studied in experiments are of the nature of "stimulus" and "response"; they are short-term, easily created in a laboratory, and easily changed. It is thus easy to manipulate conditions of different stimuli and to observe variations in subject response. On the other hand, many variables sociologists are traditionally interested in are better labeled *attributes* or *states*. A state variable is a long-lasting attribute of an individual or group, developed over a long period and not subject to manipulation and random assignment. It takes a long time for someone to develop an educational level, complete childbearing, or develop a religious belief system, and we cannot control and standardize the conditions under which these actions occur.

These are real concerns, and we must admit that there are social psychological phenomena that cannot be studied experimentally in their entirety. However, experiments may be useful in gaining knowledge about some portions of these phenomena. As Hage and Meeker (1988) point out, state variables such as educational level or social class are the result of causal processes, not the processes themselves. Thus, the intervening processes by which one state variable affects another may have some links that are amenable to experimental manipulation and observation. Likewise, the consequences of state variables may be processes that are analyzable experimentally.

In 1969, Zelditch provided an argument concerning the place of experimentation in sociology, and there are many contemporary examples of experimental research programs that address issues which are central to sociological concerns. An example is the area of social power, especially as shaped by social networks, discussed below at length. This is only part of a broader interest in interpersonal influence, leadership, and so forth. Interpersonal relationships, which anchor microsociological concerns and feed into more macro issues, both create and are affected by such factors as affect, equity, distributive justice, and interpersonal commitment. (Berger 1992 describes these and several other experimental research programs in recent sociological group process research.) Individual properties, such as identity and self-esteem, clearly develop in and impinge on existing interpersonal relationships and social structures (e.g., Backman, Secord, and Pierce 1963; Webster and Sobieszek 1974).

EXPERIMENTS AS PARTS OF RESEARCH PROGRAMS

It is our view that the question of whether, when, and how theoretical generalizations can be made from experiments is best answered by seeing individual experiments not as single, isolated studies but as parts of research programs. Following the terminology developed by the mathematician and philosopher of science Lakatos (1978) and introduced into sociology by researchers in the expectation states and status generalization tradition (Cohen 1989; Wagner and Berger 1985), we refer to a series of experiments each of which follows on the results of another as a *research program.* When the series of experiments is designed to develop a theory, it is a *theoretical research program.* (Theoretical research programs may also use nonexperimental research methods.) Within a theoretical research program, experiments are designed to advance the theory, and it is the theorist's responsibility to say how the results of the whole program relate to other settings. An individual experiment should have conditions that reflect the assumptions of the theory, rather than trying to imitate an existing reality. In fact, it is often the ability to produce conditions that are rare in natural settings that enables experimental testing of a crucial hypothesis or link in a theory.

There are a variety of generalizations that cannot be made from individual experiments but are justified from a series of related experiments conducted as part of a research program. These include information about intervening causal links and conditional causal processes. (Spurious, intervening, conditional, and other types of causal links are discussed by Hage and Meeker, 1988).

Intervening Causal Links

The steps by which one event causes another are *intervening* causal links. Formulating hypotheses and acquiring evidence for intervening causal links is at the heart of science, and experiments are well suited for this. However, a single experiment seldom demonstrates more than one link in a causal chain. An experiment is usually part of a series of studies, possibly some experimental and some not, each of which examines one possible link in a process. It is characteristic of such a series that as information about intervening processes accumulates, the experiments become more abstracted from naturally occurring settings. For example, a study of disease may proceed from examination of rates at which humans become infected, to animal studies, to studies of cells in laboratory dishes, to studies of the structure of chromosomes. It may seem a big leap from a correlation between an environmental hazard and cancer in humans to a study that shows that cells exposed to a chemical under controlled laboratory conditions develop chromosome abnormalities. However, by demonstrating a process or mechanism by which a naturally occurring condition causes cancer, knowledge of the whole phenomenon is advanced.

An example from experimental social psychology is the classic study by Sherif (1936) of the autokinetic effect. Sherif showed that the distance a light (actually stationary) is perceived as moving in a darkened room is affected by the distance others present say they see it moving. This demonstrates one of the intervening casual links between social norms and individual behavior: when a stimulus is ambiguous, what people actually perceive is influenced by what others say they perceive. Those who criticize Sherif's study on the grounds that sitting in a darkened room observing a stationary light is not a common or interesting social activity or that there are other processes involved in conformity have missed the point (see Turner 1990).

Conditional Causality

Often a causal process works one way under one set of conditions and a different way, sometimes even the opposite way, under others. The very procedures that ensure standardization and implement the method of difference may conceal processes that would work differently under other conditions (see Fisher 1960).

In the early 1970s, the psychological branch of social psychology underwent a "crisis": some experiments did not seem to replicate. An experiment conducted in proper scientific fashion, with highly standardized procedures, a homogeneous subject population, and random assignment to conditions, did not produce the same results when performed later or with a different subject population. This caused some experimental psychologists (e.g., Gergen 1973) to give up experimentation on the grounds that the processes they were studying were really historical, unique, and not representative of any general principle. It is our view that many of these disappointments about replication are due to failure to recognize the conditional nature of the causal processes we study.

One example comes from research on communication structure and efficiency of group performance (Bavelas 1948; Glanzer and Glaser 1961; Leavitt 1951; Shaw 1959; for an extensive review see Shaw 1978). To ensure a reliable and valid measure of efficiency, in the initial experiments very simple tasks were used. In this setting, results were quite consistent and easily replicated: more centralized groups were more efficient than decen-

tralized groups. However, other researchers noticed that to achieve desirable properties of control and measurement, all the studies had been run using the *same* kind of task. A subsequent series of studies using complex tasks produced the opposite results: more centralized groups were *less* efficient than decentralized groups. The solution to this apparent puzzle is that when the task is easily solved by exchange of information, having all messages go through a single person makes for faster task solution by minimizing the number of steps required. However, when the task is complex and requires much additional work, a single person becomes overloaded ("saturated") and efficiency is reduced.

Another example of an experimental research program that appeared to have found a well-replicated "effect" but in which the effect was found to reverse under other conditions is the *risky shift* phenomenon (Kogan and Wallach 1964). An initial series of studies seemed to show that groups make riskier decisions than individuals; however, a later series found an opposite, *cautious shift*. By now, both are known to be part of a more general phenomenon of group polarization (Myers and Lamm 1976; see also chapter 13).

In addition to identifying conditions under which processes work differently, theories may identify conditions under which some principles do not apply at all. Walker and Cohen (1985) and Cohen (1989) refer to these as *scope conditions*. A scope condition is a theoretically stated condition under which the assumptions of a theory are expected to hold. Outside the scope, no predictions are made so the theory cannot be tested. An example is the specification of collective orientation as a scope condition for status generalization (Berger, Conner, and Fisek 1974; Berger, Rosenholtz, and Zelditch 1980; Walker and Cohen 1985; Webster and Foschi 1988). The experiment's standardized setting must reflect the theory's scope conditions to provide a valid test.

To generalize from experimental to natural settings, we must be able to specify what conditions exist in the natural setting as well as in the experimental setting. Information about what conditions to look for is provided by a series of experiments in a theoretical research program. While a single experiment must try to standardize all features of the setting other than the independent variables, a *series* of experiments can examine a variety of conditions and should expect to find causal processes working differently under different conditions.

THEORY AND THE DESIGN OF EXPERIMENTS

A focus on the position of individual experiments in research programs and on the need for theory to guide the development of experiments has implications both for the construction of theory and for the design of experiments. As a research program matures and becomes more complex and sophisticated, it requires a type of theory that enables more than comparison of mean differences. *Theory* in this sense means a relatively formal model that is specific about its assumptions, concepts, and propositions and generates predictions about the amount of difference between conditions, the shape of the relationships between variables, or the observable ways in which processes develop over time. A scheme for analyzing relationships between theory, models, and data appears in Leik and Meeker (1975). Freese and Sell (1980) discuss the relationship between elements of a formal theory and of an experiment (see also Wagner and Berger 1985; Willer 1987).

Theory and Experimentation: A Current Example

An example of a research program using experimentation and formal theory is the current vigorous analysis of differential social power as a consequence of social structure. References in this area are numerous, but key works include those by Stolte and Emerson (1977), Willer and Anderson (1981), K. Cook and Emerson (1978), K. Cook et al. (1983, 1986), Willer (1986, 1987), Markovsky et al. (1988), and Leik (1991). This is an area driven by theory that results in formal models (both

graphic and mathematical), which are then tested in experiments derived to mirror those models.

There are two main sources of network power theory: social exchange theory (esp. Emerson 1962, 1972a, 1972b) and elementary theory (Willer, 1987; Willer and Anderson, 1981). Karen Cook et al. (1986), working from the social exchange perspective, have developed a formal model of potential network power that depends on graph theoretic principles. Markovsky et al. (1988), from the elementary theory perspective, offer a countermodel that depends on nonoverlapping chains of connectivity in the network. Each derives from formal principles, and each has been shown to have predictive power in experimental studies.

The experiments are abstract, with conditions that represent theoretical concepts such as the number of alternative bargaining partners available to a position. Factorial and repeated measures designs are used, with comparisons between different structures created in different experimental sessions or between the behaviors of occupants of positions that are structurally similar except for a key theoretical difference, such as having two rather than one bargaining partner. The experiments focus on processes: There is no simple before-after comparison; instead, exchanges run for many cycles, allowing time for differences between positions to develop. Another point worth noting is that a typical network power experiment involves no deception: physical barriers or computer controls establish network constraints, subjects bargain freely within the network constraints, the cover story is that they are there to earn money, and actual earnings in the experiment are used as indicators of relative power. The more developed models allow researchers to predict how much money occupants of different positions will earn, not just that occupants of some positions will earn more than others.

With regard to external validity, the main question for this body of work is whether the theories' scope conditions allow application of results to more complex real networks. These involve, for example, actors being able to manipulate the networks instead of just dealing within existing linkages (Leik 1991) or actors being brokers for others' dealings in the network (Marsden 1982). Broadening of scope can be achieved without loss of experimental rigor by carefully moving back and forth between the theory and the laboratory.

Computer Simulation as a Form of Experimentation

One way to develop the kind of theory needed for experimental research programs is through computer simulation. A traditional form of activity in science is a *thought experiment,* in which one thinks through what the consequences of some set of assumptions would be, possibly later comparing these with empirical observations. In sociological social psychology this is increasingly done using computer simulation. Computer simulation is not experimentation in the strictest sense, in that empirical observations are not necessarily involved (it can also be classified as a form of theory construction). In another sense, simulation is the epitome of experimentation: one can vary conditions at will and derive either precise outcomes for deterministic simulations or distributions of outcomes for stochastic simulations. Together with empirical evidence the simulation tests how accurately a theory models reality.

Leik and Tallman (1990; Tallman, Gray, and Leik 1991), for example, have developed a computer simulation linking an individual act-by-act decision model, a discrete state nonstationary Markovian process, and a four-variable continuous model into a simulation of the dynamics of dyadic relationships. The relationships may take paths leading to harmony, conflict, or dissolution; running ten simulations under one set of assumptions and ten under another provides data parallel to data from two treatment conditions of an experiment. Simulations have been used in conjunction with data from real subjects to provide a type of "control" to which to compare results from real subjects. Also, data from real subjects have been used to estimate parameters from complex simulations (e.g., Heise

1979). A third use of simulation in experiments is to have real subjects interact with simulated environments, usually without knowing that the responses they receive are not from real others.

TECHNOLOGY IN EXPERIMENTATION

Thirty years ago, a typical laboratory was equipped with one-way windows, intercoms, and possibly a series of wall panels that separated subjects in the same room but had slots for passing messages. Nowadays, a laboratory is likely also to have video recorders and computers. New technology is important to the solution of problems of both internal and external validity in experimentation.

For example, if subjects are to communicate with each other but are not face-to-face, they could write notes and pass them through slots in a wall panel. However, only simple messages can be communicated via written notes, and writing notes is time-consuming. In one example, an early study of the effects of differential exchange value of subjects on resulting patterns of stratification (Leik et al., 1975), six subjects were involved in a series of bargaining sessions, with payoffs calculated for each session. Using paper and pencil, a two-hour lab session could produce ten iterations. When a computer was installed to calculate payoffs and keep records, more than one hundred iterations could be achieved in two hours. The resulting data showed clear growth curves for the dependent variable that did not have time to develop with only ten iterations. Other examples of computer-managed experimental procedures in sociology are described by Cohen (1988) and Rainwater et al. (1988).

Other possible computer applications seem promising. Psychologists have created several very flexible computerized systems that even undergraduates can readily learn to use for designing and running experiments on simple psychological processes such as perception and memory (e.g., Henderson 1988; Schneider 1990). With the arrival of multimedia systems (computers, video, sound), even more complex experiments can be envisioned, along the lines of flight simulations. Computers could be used to allow an experiment to respond flexibly to a subject's behavior while maintaining control over interaction or to simulate environments consisting of many other persons in a multiplicity of network involvements. Such experiments could answer questions about external validity of experiments by expanding the range of conditions under which experiments can be run.

SUMMARY

Experimentation allows for the testing of causal hypotheses through creation, control, and comparison of conditions in such a way as to rule out spurious causal relationships. Experimental designs in current use include factorial, ABA, and survey experiments as well as the classic treatment-control model. Experiments can occur in a laboratory or field setting, can pursue theoretical or applied questions, and can apply to attitudes, feelings, or behaviors of individuals, groups, or organizations. Issues of internal validity concern eliminating spurious effects in an experiment, using randomization, avoiding subject and experimenter bias, doing manipulation checks, minimizing subject dropout, and avoiding inappropriate conclusions from designs that mix assigned and preexisting variables. Issues of external validity concern the generalizability of results to other settings. Recognizing that experiments are not designed to provide information about the distribution of existing phenomena, external validity is best addressed by using experimentation programmatically in a series of studies, which provides information about intervening causal links as well as the conditions under which social psychological processes occur. Computer and video technology shows promise of helping deal with questions of both internal and external validity. Finally, and most important, experimentation both depends on and contributes to developments in theory.

REFERENCES

Alwin, Duane F., and Richard C. Tessler. 1974. Causal models, unobserved variables, and experimental data. *American Journal of Sociology* 80:58–86.

Aronson, Elliot, Marilynn Brewer, and J. Merril Carlsmith. 1985. Experimentation in social psychology. Pp. 441–486 in *The Handbook of Social Psychology,* 3rd ed., vol. 1, ed. G. Lindzey and E. Aronson. New York: Random House.

Backman, Carl, Paul Secord, and Jerry R. Pierce. 1963. Resistance to change in self-concept as a function of consensus among significant others. *Sociometry* 26:102–111.

Bacon, Francis. 1620. *Novum Organum* London: J. Billium.

Bavelas, Alex. 1948. A mathematical model for group structure. *Applied Anthropology* 7:16–30.

Berger, Joseph. 1992. Expectations, theory, and group processes. *Social Psychology Quarterly* 55:3–11.

Berger, Joseph, Thomas L. Conner, and M. Hamit Fisek. 1974. *Expectation States Theory: A Theoretical Research Program.* Cambridge, MA: Winthrop.

Berger, Joseph, Susan J. Rosenholtz, and Morris Zelditch, Jr. 1980. Status organizing processes. Pp. 479–508 in *Annual Review of Sociology,* vol. 6, ed. A. Inkeles, N. J. Smelser, and R. H. Turner. Palo Alto, CA: Annual Reviews.

Bonacich, Philip, and J. Light. 1978. Laboratory experimentation in sociology. Pp. 145–170 in *Annual Review of Sociology,* vol. 4, ed. I. Inkeles, J. Coleman, and N. J. Smelser. Palo Alto, CA: Annual Reviews.

Bunge, Mario. 1979. *Causality and Modern Science,* 3rd ed. New York: Dover.

Burgess, Robert, and Don Bushell, Jr., ed. 1969. *Behavioral Sociology.* New York: Columbia University Press.

Campbell, Donald T., and Julian Stanley. 1963. *Experimental and Quasi-Experimental Designs for Research.* Chicago: Rand McNally.

Chapanis, Natalia P., and Alphonse Chapanis. 1964. Cognitive dissonance: Five years later. *Psychological Bulletin.* 61:1–22.

Cohen, Bernard P. 1988. A new experimental situation using microcomputers. Pp. 383–398 in *Status Generalization: New Theory and Research,* ed. M. Webster, Jr., and M. Foschi, Palo Alto, CA: Stanford University Press.

———. 1989. *Developing Sociological Knowledge,* 2nd ed. Chicago: Nelson-Hall.

Consortium for Longitudinal Studies. 1983. *As the Twig Is Bent.* Hillsdale, NJ: Erlbaum.

Cook, Karen S., and Richard M. Emerson. 1978. Power, equity and commitment in exchange networks. *American Sociological Review* 43:721–739.

Cook, Karen S., Mary R. Gillmore, and Toshio Yamagishi. 1983. The distribution of power in exchange networks: Theory and experimental results. *American Journal of Sociology* 89:275–305.

———. 1986. Point and line vulnerability as bases for predicting the distribution of power in exchange networks: Reply to Willer. *American Journal of Sociology* 92:445–448.

Cook, Thomas D., and Donald T. Campbell. 1979. *Quasi-Experimentation: Design and Analysis Issues for Field Settings.* Chicago: Rand McNally.

Emerson, Richard M. 1962. Power dependence relations. *American Sociological Review* 27:31–41.

———. 1972a. Exchange Theory, part II: Exchange relations and networks. Pp. 58–87 in *Sociological Theories in Progress,* vol. 2, ed. J. Berger, M. Zelditch, and B. Anderson. Boston: Houghton Mifflin.

———. 1972b. Exchange theory, part I: A psychological basis for social exchange. Pp. 38–57 in *Sociological Theories in Progress,* vol. 2, ed. J. Berger, M. Zelditch, and B. Anderson. Boston: Houghton Mifflin.

Fisher, Ronald A. [1935] 1960. *The Design of Experiments.* Edinburgh: Oliver & Boyd.

Freese, Lee, and Jane Sell. 1980. Constructing axiomatic theories in sociology. Pp. 263–368 in *Theoretical Methods in Sociology,* ed. L. Freese. Pittsburgh: University of Pittsburgh Press.

Gergen, Kenneth J. 1973. Social psychology as history. *Journal of Personality and Social Psychology* 26: 309–320.

Glanzer, Murray, and Robert Glaser. 1961. Techniques for the study of group structure and behavior, II: Empirical studies of the effects of structure in small groups. *Psychological Bulletin* 58:1–27.

Gould, Stephen J. 1981. *The Mismeasure of Man.* New York: Norton.

Hage, Jerald, and Barbara F. Meeker. 1988. *Social Causality.* Boston: Unwin Hyman.

Hausman, Jerry A., and David A. Wise, ed. 1985. *Social Experimentation.* Chicago: University of Chicago Press.

Heise, David R. 1979. *Understanding Events.* Cambridge, UK: Cambridge University Press.

Henderson, R. W. 1988. Mind Probe, Microlab, Gasp, Status, Eventlog. Milford, CT: IBM.

Homans, George C. 1950. *The Human Group.* New York: Harcourt, Brace & World.

Jasso, Guillermina. 1978. On the justice of earnings: A new specification of the justice evaluation function. *American Journal of Sociology* 83:1398–1419.

———. 1980. A new theory of distributive justice. *American Sociological Review* 45:3–32.

———. 1990. Analysis of comparison processes. Pp. 369–419 in *Sociological Methodology,* vol. 20, ed. C. C. Clogg. Cambridge, MA: Blackwell.

Kirk, Robert E. 1982. *Experimental Design: Procedures for the Behavioral Sciences.* Belmont, CA: Brooks/ Cole.

Kogan, Nathan, and Michael A. Wallach. 1964. *Risk Taking: A Study in Cognition and Personality.* New York: Holt, Rinehart & Winston.

Lakatos, Imre. 1978. *The Methodology of Scientific Research Programmes.* Cambridge, UK: Cambridge University Press.

Leavitt, Harold J. 1951. Some effects of certain communication patterns on group performance. *Journal of Abnormal and Social Psychology* 46:38–50.

Leik, Robert K. 1991. Strategic timing in network processing. Pp. 1–28 in *Advances in Group Processes,* vol. 8, ed. E. J. Lawler, B. Markovsky, C. Ridgeway, and H. A. Walker. Greenwich, CT: JAI Press.

Leik, Robert K., Mary Anne Chalkley, and Nancy J. Peterson. 1991. The impact of Head Start on family dynamics and structure. In *A Reconstruction of Family Policy,* ed. E. A. Anderson and R. Hula. New York: Greenwood.

Leik, Robert K., Sheila A. Leik, Bruce Morton, R. Brock Beardsley, and Margaret E. Hardy. 1975. The emergence and change of stratification in social exchange systems. *Social Science Research* 4: 17–40.

Leik, Robert K., and Barbara F. Meeker. 1975. *Mathematical Sociology.* Englewood Cliffs, NJ: Prentice Hall.

Leik, Robert K., and Irving Tallman. 1990. Dynamics of decision processes in social linkages. Paper presented at the Third Annual Group Processes Conference, College Park, Md. A version of this paper appears in Pp. 9–34 of *Spill og Simulering i Forskning og Undervisning, (Proceedings from the conference on games and simulations in research and education*) ed. K. Ekker and M. Stene. Steinkjer, Norway: Nord-trondelag Distriktshogskole.

Markovsky, Barry, David Willer, and Travis Patton. 1988. Power relations in exchange networks. *American Sociological Review* 53:220–236.

Marsden, Peter V. 1982. Brokerage behavior in restricted exchange networks. Pp. 201–281 in *Social Structure and Network Analysis,* ed. P. V. Marsden and N. Lin. Beverly Hills, CA: Sage.

Meeker, Barbara F. 1983. Cooperative orientation, trust, and reciprocity. *Human Relations* 37:225–243.

Milgram, Stanley. 1974. *Obedience to Authority.* New York: Harper & Row.

Mill, John S. 1872. *A System of Logic.* London: Longman.

Myers, David G., and Helmut Lamm. 1976. The group polarization phenomenon. *Psychological Bulletin* 83:602–627.

Orne, Martin. 1962. On the social psychology of the psychological experiment. *American Psychologist* 17:776–783.

———. 1969 Demand characteristics and the concept of quasi-controls. Pp. 147–179 in *Artifact in Behavioral Research,* ed. R. Rosenthal and R. L. Rosnow. New York: Academic.

O'Rourke, John F. 1963. Field and laboratory: The decision-making behavior of family groups in two experimental conditions. *Sociometry* 26:422–435.

Rainwater, Julie, Max Nelson-Kilger, and Jacqueline Cashen. 1988. Developing an open interaction experimental situation. Pp. 413–432 in *Status Generalization: New Theory and Research,* ed. M. Webster, Jr., and M. Foschi. Palo Alto, CA: Stanford University Press.

Riecken, Henry W., and Robert F. Boruch. 1978. Social experiments. Pp. 511–532 in *Annual Review of Sociology,* vol. 4, ed. R. H. Turner, J. Coleman, and R. C. Fox. Palo Alto, CA: Annual Reviews.

Robins, Philip K., R. G. Spiegelman, S. Weiner, and J. G. Bell. 1980. *A Guaranteed Annual Income: Evidence from a Social Experiment.* New York: Academic.

Roethlisberger, Fritz J., and William J. Dickson. 1939. *Management and the Worker.* Cambridge, MA: Harvard University Press.

Rosenberg, Morris. 1968. *The Logic of Survey Analysis.* New York: Basic Books.

Rosenthal, Robert. 1963. On the social psychology of the psychological experiment: The experimenter's hypothesis as unintended determinant of the experimental results. *American Scientist* 51:268–283.

———. 1966. *Experimenter Effects in Behavioral Research.* New York: Appleton-Century-Crofts.

Rossi, Peter H., and Andy B. Anderson. 1982. The factorial survey approach: An introduction. Pp. 15–67 in *Measuring Social Judgement,* ed. P. H. Rossi and S. H. Nock. Beverly Hills, CA: Sage.

Rossi, Peter H., and Guillermina Jasso. 1977. Distributive justice and earned income. *American Sociological Review* 42:639–651.

Rossi, Peter H., and James D. Wright. 1984. Evaluation research: An assessment. Pp. 331–352 in *Annual Review of Sociology,* vol. 10, ed. R. H. Turner and J. F. Short. Palo Alto, CA: Annual Reviews.

Schneider, W. 1990. Micro experimental laboratory (software). Milford, CT: IBM.

Sears, David. 1986. College sophomores in the laboratory: Influences of a narrow data base on social psychology's view of human nature. *Journal of Personality and Social Psychology* 51:515–530.

Shaw, Marvin E. 1959. Some effects of individually prominent behavior upon group effectiveness and member satisfaction. *Journal of Abnormal and Social Psychology* 59:382–286.

———. 1978. Communication networks 14 years later. Pp. 351–361 in *Group Processes,* ed. L. Berkowitz. New York: Academic.

Sherif, Muzafer. 1936. *The Psychology of Social Norms.* New York: Harper & Row.

Stolte, John, and Richard M. Emerson. 1977. Structural inequality: Position and power in network structures. Pp. 117–138 in *Behavioral Theory in Sociology,* ed. R. L. Hamblin and J. Kunkel. New Brunswick, NJ: Transaction.

Tallman, Irving, Louis N. Gray, and Robert K. Leik. 1991. Decisions, dependency and commitment: An exchange based theory of group formation. Pp. 227–257 in *Advances in Group Processes,* vol. 8, ed. E. J. Lawler, B. Markovsky, C. Ridgeway, and H. A. Walker. Greenwich, CT: JAI Press.

Turner, Ralph H. 1990. Some contributions of Muzafer Sherif to sociology. *Social Psychology Quarterly* 53:283–291.

Wagner, David G., and Joseph Berger. 1985. Do sociological theories grow? *American Journal of Sociology* 90:697–728.

Walker, Henry, and Bernard P. Cohen. 1985. Scope statements: Imperatives for evaluating theory. *American Sociological Review* 50:288–301.

Webster, Murray, and Martha Foschi, ed. 1988. *Status Generalization: New Theory and Research.* Stanford, CA: Stanford University Press.

Webster, Murray, and Barbara Sobieszek. 1974. *Sources of Self Evaluation.* New York: Wiley.

Willer, David. 1986. Vulnerability and the location of power positions. *American Journal of Sociology* 92:441–445.

———. 1987. *Theory and the Experimental Investigation of Social Structures.* New York: Gordon & Breach.

Willer, David, and Bo Anderson, ed. 1981. *Networks, Exchange and Coercion.* New York: Elsevier/Greenwood.

Winer, B. J. 1971. *Statistical Principles in Experimental Design,* 2nd ed. New York: McGraw-Hill.

Zelditch, Morris, Jr. 1969. Can you really study an army in the laboratory? Pp. 528–539 in *Complex Organizations,* ed. A. Etzioni. New York: Holt, Rinehart & Winston.

CHAPTER 25

Quantitative Methods in Social Psychology

DUANE F. ALWIN

This chapter reviews the application of quantitative methods in social psychology. This covers a range of topics and a diversity of approaches, but mainly focuses on the use of nonexperimental data for the purposes of generalizing to theoretical propositions regarding social processes and social behavior of individuals. The chapter presents the logic, strengths, and limitations of quantitative analysis of social psychological data. It is intended as a general discussion of the basic goals of quantitative social psychological research, rather than a detailed exposition of the methods. The discussion is intended to be informative to professionals and students who are not expert in these methods nor versed in statistical terminology and research jargon.

I begin with a brief discussion of the variety of methods in social psychology, then review certain "basic issues" that arise in the application of all quantitative methods—conceptualization, principles of design, measurement, and data reduction. I then review the problems of making causal inferences using quantitative data and cover six basic "building blocks" of causal analysis. This section includes a discussion of the importance of longitudinal designs for causal analysis. This is followed by a brief discussion of available multivariate statistical tools and issues surrounding their use. I conclude with a brief commentary on future developments in quantitative analysis.

METHODOLOGICAL DIVERSITY

If it can be argued that social psychology is theoretically disparate (House 1977; Liska 1977; Stry-

ker 1977), this may be even more true of the methods used. In describing this variability, it is important to distinguish first the *quantitative* versus *qualitative* axis, separating, at the one extreme, those who collect and analyze quantitative data using statistical methods and, at the other, those who use qualitative assessments or verbal accounts (e.g., ethnography, conversation analysis, content analysis, historical analysis, life history interviewing). Both qualitative and quantitative methods are vital to an understanding of society—a factor often overlooked by those in both camps—and the compatibility between the quantitative analyst of large data sets and the qualitative researcher is greater than is commonly acknowledged (e.g., Lieberson 1992; Zelditch 1962). The key is to understand which methods are most appropriate for which purposes. This chapter addresses this question by focusing on this issue with respect to quantitative methods: methods of design, analysis, and inference about quantifiable aspects of human behavior.

Diversity in quantitative analysis stems from variation in the *inferential scope* of research. Research objectives in social psychology can be divided into three broad categories of research design: (1) *experimental and quasi-experimental designs,* in which the investigator is interested in attributing changes in mean levels of specified variables (or some other parameter of interest) to an experimental manipulation, so as to arrive at a causal inference (Holland 1986); (2) *cross-sectional nonexperimental designs,* in which the investigator is interested in estimating population and subpopulation parameters (means, proportions, variances, etc.) and often in looking at relationships among variables and their properties to understand the sources of variation and covariation among variables; and (3) *longitudinal nonexperimental and historical approaches,* in which the investigator studies the occurrence of events and processes in biographical or historical time and attempts to understand their causes and consequences. These distinctions among research designs and objectives help organize the wide range of quantitative analysis techniques available to researchers: from event-history or structural equation (LISREL-type) models in the case of longitudinal designs; analysis of variance and analysis of covariance (ANOVA and ANCOVA) in the case of experimental and quasi-experimental designs; to log-linear models or regression and correlation techniques in the case of nonexperimental designs. The focus of this chapter is on quantitative methods that are mostly appropriate to the collection and analysis of nonexperimental data, although they apply equally well to experimental data (Alwin 1985; Alwin and Tessler 1974; Marwell 1992).

Another source of diversity among methods in social psychology involves whether the aims of research are *data-driven* or *theory-driven* (Hox and DeJong-Gierveld 1990). If the goal of the research is to acquire new information (e.g., about social norms or secular trends in attitudes or the behavior of social institutions) or to generate bodies of data that will aid in further exploration and discovery, then the research is said to be data-driven. If the main purpose of the research is to test one or more abstract substantive propositions, the aims are theory-driven. In the former case, the data, or analyses of them, generate hypotheses; in the latter, the hypotheses generate the data and the analyses to be carried out.

SOME BASIC ISSUES

While objectives may vary, there are certain unifying elements in all quantitative research. This section develops a framework for the basic components of quantitative research methods, whether data-driven or theory-driven and regardless of the inferential scope of the research. Paraphrasing Rosenberg (1968), there are multiple analytic approaches in social psychology, as there are in the broader terrain of social science, and for any problem there are several possible analytic routes to the basic goals of the research. This necessary flexibility in approaching quantitative analysis makes it possible to visualize the commonality of research goals amid ostensibly different strategies of analysis. Despite differences among quantitative approaches, their common goals unify them at a more abstract level of discourse.

Conceptualization

The development of concepts, the specification of relationships among concepts, and the formulation of lawlike statements linking concepts are what theory is about, but such work must be done at different levels of abstraction to link theories to research (see Merton's [1949] classic statement of this issue). Blalock (1968) described what he called the "basic dilemma" of the social scientist: that the languages of theory and research do not have any natural correspondence and "cannot be linked by any strictly logical argument." Instead, a correspondence between two concepts, one at the theoretical level and one at the operational level, "must be established by common agreement or *a priori* assumption." Research requires an array of "auxiliary" theories—specific operationalizations of more general or abstract theories—aimed at investigating and testing aspects of those more abstract theories (Blalock 1968, 23–27).

General theories transcend specific times and places and refer to the abstract level—the level of the "if, then" relationships of a functional and conditional nature; for example, if X is present, Y will follow, *or* if X changes, Y will change, if condition Z is present. By contrast, auxiliary theories are time-bound, tied to a particular set of indicators, that reflect state-of-the-art observation approaches and that make sense in a specific social setting. Thus, for any general theory, there are multiple auxiliary theories, each tied to specific research designs, populations studied, and types of measuring instruments used. But given any particular auxiliary theory and its instrumentation, it is possible to test the general theory, or some aspect of it, under a specific set of assumptions.

Description and Inference

Description is perhaps the most basic aim of all research. But in contrast to qualitative description, which is often accompanied by copious field notes involving what Geertz (1973) termed "thick" description, quantitative description is based on the assumption that numeric quantities can be used to describe important social phenomena parsimoniously. Descriptive quantitative research varies in the nature of the desired inferences and the types of design criteria used to construct those inferences. Kish (1987) codifies three major types of research objectives—representation, randomization, and realism, which in turn suggest criteria against which to evaluate research designs.

Representation is critical if the goal is to estimate characteristics of variables for specifiable populations or subpopulations. The key to this approach is probability sampling and inferences to a specific population of interest (Kish 1987). Here the methodological issues are relatively straightforward, in that the main objectives, in addition to valid and reliable measurement, are to design practical sampling techniques that will produce representative samples of these populations/subpopulations with efficient estimates of sampling variability.[1] In other instances, researchers are primarily interested in changes in variables over time and the sources of such change, using longitudinal surveys (R. Campbell 1988, 1992; G. Duncan and G. Kalton 1987). An interest in net change—the average difference in levels between times—requires repeated cross-sectional sampling, whereas an interest in gross change—the average within-individual change between times—requires repeated measurements on the same persons (see the discussion of longitudinal research designs below). From such data one can obtain descriptive informa-

tion of a variety of additional types, including univariate information, contingency table displays, correlations, regression relationships, and variance/covariance information.

Other researchers have little interest in making descriptive statistical inferences to a population of persons but wish to make strong inferences of a causal nature about the effect of X on Y, where the generalization is to a theory or a hypothesis under some set of scope conditions, not necessarily to a population of interest. Such experimental or quasi-experimental approaches require "manipulation" of variables, with random assignment of individuals (or a controlled approximation) to conditions of the treatment variable (Berk 1988; Holland 1986). Here the investigator seeks to attribute changes in mean levels of specified variables to an experimental manipulation, so as to arrive at a causal inference. Interest is primarily in ruling out the possibility that chance determined the experimental or treatment effects observed. Hence the emphasis is on randomization, on the assumption that the *only* way to draw a causal inference is under strict control of all extraneous (i.e., not experimentally manipulated) variables (Kish 1987). In this case it is extremely rare that the investigator is at the same time interested in estimating population and subpopulation parameters (means, proportions, variances, etc.) or in regression or regressionlike relationships. However, the recent rediscovery of the potential use in sample surveys of *split-ballot* experiments (e.g., Schuman and Presser 1981) and factorial designs using vignettes in surveys (e.g., Rossi and Nock 1981) are examples of a true experimental design plus an interest in estimating population parameters.

Finally, it is not always possible to use experimentation, or probability sampling. Some nonexperimental research is based on "controlled investigations," in which some type of quasi-experimental control can be introduced to approximate the statistical control achievable via randomization. Other examples of nonexperimental methods involve historical study, either of individual lives, through longitudinal research, or of populations, societies, or nations, through examination of historical records. These researches satisfy the design criterion of *contextual realism.*

According to Kish (1987), there are no perfect solutions to problems of research design, since the design of research always involves a series of compromises. Statistical designs may not always exactly link the desirable and the possible, and the issue often becomes one of trade-offs between the most desirable characteristic of designs, given a set of research objectives. Even the elegance of probability sampling from a theoretical viewpoint is compromised via imperfect lists, failed response rates, cluster sampling, interviewer error, and so on. The elegance of the true experiment with randomization is often illusory (D. Campbell and J. Stanley 1963; T. Cook and D. Campbell 1979). But most designs have some redeeming virtue, if not in their approximation to probability sampling, in their implementation of random assignment to treatments or their contextual realism. Still, this is not an excuse for poor design, as, clearly, approximations to random selection are essential for sample-based inferences to specific populations, approximations to random assignment are essential to causal inferences of the purest form, and representative time series and contextual information should be sought in drawing conclusions from nonrepresentative, nonexperimental designs. As Kish (1987, 10) indicates, each of these three kinds of research designs can be improved by supplementing them with efforts to improve their main weaknesses. For example, because a major weakness of surveys is their inability to exercise statistical control via randomization, it becomes important in survey design to gather information regarding factors that might be controlled via multivariate statistical techniques. It may then be possible to utilize such statistical controls to draw causal inferences (Berk 1988).

Measurement

Regardless of the nature of the quantitative methods used in social science (historical, experimental, quasi-experimental, or nonexperimental), *measurement* is critical. Moreover, it is important to distinguish the process of conceptualization from the processes that generate measures. In all fields of science there is a gap between the two. Thus, we must concern ourselves with measurement as a social phenomenon itself—it is the process by which the researcher ties or links certain "observable" or "indicator" variables, obtained, it is hoped, through certain specifiable and replicable operations, to unobservable concepts or hypothetical quantities.

In its most general sense, measurement represents the link between theory and the analysis of empirical data (Duncan 1984b). It is the linkage of interrelated theoretical concepts to observable variables, according to a conceptual scheme that specifies "rules of correspondence," dimensionality, and a metric or units of measurement, as well as a set of replicable operations for gathering data. Owing to this complexity, important aspects of measurement regrettably must be omitted from the present discussion for lack of space. See, for example, Rossi (1988) on modes of observation, Schuman and Presser (1981) on question wording effects, Groves (1989) on conceptualizing sources of survey error, and Alwin (1989) on estimating the reliability of survey data.

It is sometimes difficult in social psychology to distinguish concepts from indicators, because one person's concept may be another's indicator. For example, the concept of "education" might be measured as the "years of schooling completed" and the researcher might be willing to assert that by taking observations on this indicator he/she is measuring what is meant by the concept of "education." This may mean that "schooling" as a concept refers to such things as knowledge attained and skills learned and reflects similar levels of quality of teaching/learning (Alwin 1991b). Alternatively, "schooling" may be taken not as a conceptually distinct element of theory but as an indicator of another concept, for example, the concept of social status or position in the stratification system. Here, measures of a person's schooling, a rating of the prestige of the person's occupation, and the person's (or family's) income, in some combination, are sometimes conceptualized as indicators of social status or position (e.g., Kohn and Slomczynski 1990).

Data Reduction

Based on the notion that indicators only imperfectly represent concepts, quantitative researchers often build indexes or scales that better reflect the attributes or quantities they intend to measure. There is a range of techniques available for data reduction in which a composite based on several items is constructed to reflect the concept or property of interest. For example, a survey data set may contain several measures of attitudes/beliefs about abortion, (e.g., the GSS questions on abortion attitudes; Davis and Smith 1991). While much analysis of survey data proceeds on the basis of analyzing single items, it is also common to analyze the dimensions of content in such items to derive some type of composite variable on the basis of several items (Muthén 1981). In this case, the researcher is often trying to reproduce the situation where the latent variable is conceived to be continuous, and the purpose of developing a composite score is to approximate it with a more or less continuous scale based on several items.

There are many different ways to approach the development of a composite score, but most involve some form of *item analysis*. One approach is based on classical true score and factor analysis. Another is based on item response theory (IRT) analysis (Lord 1974). Often, factor analysis can be used to provide a rendering of the likely number of dimensions in the data for relatively homogeneous sets of items. Then, for sets of items linked to a particular factor, estimation of internal consistency reliability (e.g., coefficient alpha) and analysis of item-to-total correlations can often be used to improve the homogeneity of the items in the composite score (Bohrnstedt 1983). The basic goal of all such techniques is to decompose the data into discrete sets of latent variables or "factors" that are relatively independent and homogeneous in content. However, relationships among multiple factors may be conceptualized either in terms of uncorrelated (or orthogonal) sets of factors or in terms of correlated (or oblique) factors. Such analyses can be usefully supplemented with information on how to build "factor-based" scores and interpret the "psychometric" properties of the data (Borgatta 1992).

The classical true score and factor analysis approaches to item analysis and score construction are not always appropriate, especially when the investigator believes the latent variable is discrete, as in the assumptions made by latent structure models (Clogg 1981), or when the observed variables are thought to be too coarse to represent an underlying continuum. In the latter case, test psychologists and others have turned to item response theory (Lord 1974), which attempts to model the response functions linking persons and items to the latent continuous scale. These response functions are called *item-characteristic curves,* and various models attempt to describe them. One famous IRT model was proposed by the Danish statistician Rasch (1960/1980; see Andrich 1988 and O. Duncan 1984a, 1984c for a useful discussion of Rasch models applied to survey attitude data). The structure of the data one needs for IRT analysis is not uncommon, but these approaches are probably underutilized by social psychologists.

CAUSAL INFERENCES FOR QUANTITATIVE DATA

Many substantive research problems in social psychology focus on changes of individuals, groups, organizations, cohorts, and society as a whole, and vast research is oriented to identifying those elements of causal processes that stimulate change or maintain equilibrium or continuity (Alwin 1994). Indeed, the "sociological classics" were concerned with social causation. Using archival data and historical methods, the central concerns of Karl Marx, Max Weber, Emile Durkheim, and other classical European sociologists were focused on causal analysis (House 1977, 168–172). More recently, the dominant models for research into social processes have been linked either to the classical experimental paradigm or to some other model for causation aimed at assessing those factors responsible for change or lack of change. Standard among the social psychologist's bag of research tools is the regression model and related techniques (e.g., LISREL-type models), which presumably assess the extent of change expected in a predicted variable from a hypothetical unit change in a predictor variable, net of other variables.[2] Issues of change and stability, and the causes and consequences thereof, are at the heart of modern paradigms for research in social psychology and most social science, and the language for the interpretation of causal processes is a valuable tool in the analysis of social psychological theories (see Davis 1985).

CAUSAL INFERENCES IN NONEXPERIMENTAL DATA

Causal analysis techniques have been essential tools in social psychology for some time. Systematic techniques of simple two- and three-way tabular analysis were introduced for the analysis of categoric survey data by Paul Lazarsfeld (1955), and his "language of social research" has had great influence on generations of sociological social psychologists (Rosenberg 1968). Lazarsfeld was interested in elaborating bivariate relationships by categories of third (and potentially more) variables. Through this approach the analyst sought to (1) explain and remove spurious or redundant association between variables due to their determination by a common cause or correlated common causes; (2) interpret how a third variable that intervenes between two others in a causal sequence mediates or transmits the effects indirectly; or (3) identify and specify when and how the relationship between two variables may be conditioned or modified by the level of a third variable.

Lazarsfeld referred to these analytic operations using the terminology *explanation, interpretation,* and *specification.* The first two of these analytic operations are basic to the analysis of survey data, and virtually all subsequently developed multivariate approaches to data focus on providing a workable solution to these problems. The same is true of specification, although current terminology is not compatible with Lazarsfeld's use. The term

specification is now used more generally to refer to the process by which the analyst develops a causal model for purposes of analysis, estimation, and testing. Current usage reserves the term *statistical interaction* to refer to what in Lazarsfeld's tabular approach is termed *specification.* Relationships among variables analyzed by path and/or regression analysis, log-linear models, latent variable approaches, or event history models continue to be interpreted in terms of Lazarsfeld's language for social research (Alwin and Campbell 1987).

Beyond his introduction of a codification of basic analytic operations used in research, Lazarsfeld's influence has been expressed indirectly through the development of modern analytic methods for categoric data. As Otis Duncan (1982) pointed out, Lazarsfeld anticipated the subsequent development of log-linear models (Goodman 1978). The descendants of Lazarsfeld's formulation for causal analysis, however, span a much broader array of approaches, as most approaches to causal analysis in social psychology are completely compatible with his analytic scheme, including both regression and categoric data analytic approaches. Indeed, the evolution of quantitative methods in social psychology may be viewed in terms of a set of developments aimed at better accomplishing what Lazarsfeld originally set out to do (see Davis 1985).

Necessary Concepts for Causal Interpretation

A vast majority of research in social psychology involves the elucidation of relations among variables in terms of causal processes. Thus, it is valuable to review and summarize the causal modeling tools for making inferences from nonexperimental data. To clarify the question of appropriate causal inferences using nonexperimental data, I refer to Kish's (1959, 1987) very useful scheme for explicating sources of variation. In Kish's scheme, there are four classes of variables: explanatory variables, X and Y (the predictor and predictand); extraneous variables that are controlled either via randomization (R) or via statistical procedures (C); extraneous variables that are uncontrolled, which have "disturbing" influences on the dependent variable of interest (D); and extraneous variables that are uncontrolled but whose effects are randomized with respect to the explanatory variables (W). This scheme is shown in Figure 25.1. In this depiction, the dependent variable is designated as Y, the main explanatory variable as X, the controlled extraneous variables as C, the disturbing extraneous variables as D, the randomized variables as R, and the uncontrolled randomly operating variables as W. According to Kish (1987, 4–5) the efficient design places as many of the extraneous variables as possible in class C or R. The aim of randomized experiments is to place class D variables into class R. When randomization is not possible, their effects can potentially be eliminated through the use of statistical controls (class C). However, to the extent that extraneous factors are left in class D, causal inferences about sources of variation due to the explanatory variable(s) are in danger of commission of a logical fallacy, since both X and D are confounded. This places a very high premium on theoretical clarity and precise causal specification in the research design.

In this section I present several basic causal models that, regardless of the specific approach taken to data (categoric versus continuous variables), constitute basic "building blocks" of analytic investigation. The emphasis is on the logic of analysis and the nature of causal interpretations,

rather than on the available techniques for estimating the parameters of such models. For simplicity I use a path analysis framework, although my overall purpose is to generalize the logic of causal modeling, regardless of the particular technique used.[3] In Figure 25.2 are depicted six, three-variable causal models using path diagrams and path analysis notation, which are relatively exhaustive of possible "generic" causal relationships among three variables. Virtually all more complicated causal models for more than three variables are simply extensions or combinations of these models. This discussion presents neither the mathematical equations that represent these models nor the algebraic solutions for model parameters in these simple three-variable models. Rather, I summarize each of the analytic concepts captured by these six three-variable models, using the logic of directed-graphs (Davis 1985; Heise 1975), and discuss their application to substantive research issues.[4]

The Multiple-Cause Model.   Research in the social sciences often raises questions about the relative importance of variables or sets of variables in terms of their causal impact in "multiple cause" models. For example, one of the conclusions of the landmark study by Coleman et al. (1966) of school effects on student achievement was that variation in family background (variation occurring within schools) was more important than variation in fac-

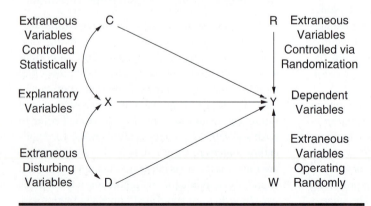

FIGURE 25.1   Kish scheme for sources of variation. *Source:* Kish, Leslie. 1987. *Statistical Design for Research.* New York: Wiley.

Model A: Multiple-Cause Model

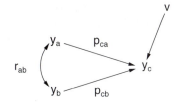

Model B: Common Cause Model

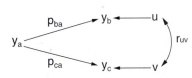

Model C: Recursive Model

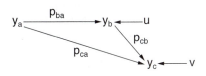

Model D: Nonrecursive Model

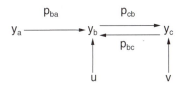

Model E: Common Factor Model

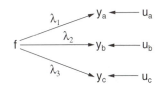

Model F: Induced-Variable Model

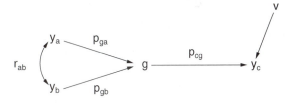

FIGURE 25.2   Six basic causal models.

tors differentiating schools from one another (between-school variation) in producing individual differences among students in achievement (see also Jencks et al. 1972). Other examples abound. The debate about the "heritability" of test scores (e.g., Jensen 1969) is essentially a debate about the relative importance of genetic inheritance versus the environment in shaping individual differences in IQ scores. And the research issues raised by status attainment and mobility research about the relative importance of ascriptive versus achieved characteristics focuses on the relative magnitudes of effects of family background versus education in the development of life chances and achievement opportunities (Sewell and Hauser 1975).

Given these interests, one causal model used in a substantial amount of research involves the examination of the relationship between two variables while controlling statistically for a third (or set of other), confounded variable(s). This embod-

ies Kish's (1987) design principle of controlling statistically for nonrandom extraneous variables (C in Figure 25.1). Thus, in contrast to the experimental design referred to in the discussion of Kish's (1987) scheme, the predictors in nonexperimental research designs are often correlated and therefore must be considered simultaneously within a multivariate framework. Estimates of various "partial coefficients," "effects," or "associations" and their relative magnitudes are evaluated while controlling for the confounding variable(s).

There are several points of view on whether it is possible or appropriate to evaluate the relative importance of variables or sets of variables by estimating coefficients in such multiple-cause models (Berk 1988). There are two fundamental problems with these models. First, causal importance need not be related to variance and the covariation among causal and caused variables (Lieberson 1985). Conditions reflecting causal impact for a particular phenomenon of interest may not vary in the populations we study, and although they may be necessary causal agents they would be assigned little causal importance if measurements of their variation were entered into the types of equations referred to here. For example, few persons would argue that the existence of schools (as we know them, or in some imagined world) is unnecessary for academic achievement. However, when differences among schools are assessed and entered into analytic models aimed at assigning relative importance of causal factors, school-to-school differences do not appear to be very important. Nevertheless, it would be a grave error in such a situation to conclude that schools as institutions do not influence achievement. Thus, from this example and others that are possible, it should be readily clear that we can assess the relative importance of variables only in the sense of the power they have to predict variation in Y, given available variation in causal factors.

A second fundamental problem in assessing the relative importance of variables is that when measured causal factors are correlated, it is difficult to distinguish relative importance (Gordon 1968). While the general practice among social scientists using these models is to infer the relative importance of variables from the relative size of partial coefficients, the relative redundancy of variables poses a serious problem in the interpretation of relative importance of variables. The higher the correlation, r_{ab}, between y_a and y_b in model A (Figure 25.2), the more severe the problem of distinguishing the relative importance of their effects. However, given a causal model relating variables in a multivariate system and the absence of very high correlations (e.g., < 0.4) among the predictor variables, it is generally possible to interpret the coefficients in these models in terms of direct causal importance (Alwin and Hauser 1975).

Common Cause Model. One of Lazarsfeld's (1955) classic research operations, known as explanation, referred to the situation in which a relationship between two variables is fully or partially "explained" by the consideration of a third causally

prior variable. This is the well-known case of *spurious correlation* (model B in Figure 25.2). This two-equation system depicts only the simplest case, where there is a single common cause, but one can generalize the example to the situation where there are multiple common causes. This type of causal model applies, for example, to the interpretation of the relationship between "authoritarianism" on the one hand and "prejudice" on the other. The well-known personalistic theory of the authoritarian personality would suggest that prejudice and intolerance are caused by authoritarianism. It can be documented that these traits tend to go together, but it is doubtful whether there is any true "causal" relationship between them, once level of schooling, a temporally prior cause of both, is controlled (Jackman 1973). The basic idea is that variables like "authoritarianism" and "prejudice" may well be highly correlated, but one must be able to rule out the existence of "spurious" causation before attempting to interpret such a relationship in causal terms.

This is probably one of the most common situations in which researchers find themselves—one in which they wish to make an inference about the causal nature of the relationship between variables but need to be able to rule out that the relationship is "genuine" and not "spurious." Obviously, if one has not taken into account all of the relevant common causes of y_b and y_c, one is hardly in a position to interpret the remaining relationship, r_{uv}, as if it were not due to potentially spurious sources. Thus, if one wishes to place more than a literal interpretation on the partial correlation, r_{uv} (i.e., the relationship between y_b and y_c controlling for y_a), it is necessary to include *all known common causes* of the two variables of interest.

A partial correlation is nothing more than the correlation of residuals where a common variable or common set of variables have been partialled out. In regression analysis terminology, residualizing the two variables on the set of common causes and calculating the correlation between the two residuals will produce the partial correlation (O. Duncan 1975a). In this case, and as depicted in model B of Figure 25.2, the influence of y_a on the relationship between y_b and y_c is literally "partialled out," and the remaining relationship, r_{uv}, is known as "the partial correlation." The correlation between u and v is equal to the partial correlation, $r_{bc.a}$, because u and v are the residuals (or disturbances) for y_b and y_c, respectively, after the linear relationship between y_a and these variables is taken into account.

Recursive Model. Model C in Figure 25.2 depicts a recursive causal model, in which y_a causes y_b and y_c directly and, via its effect on y_b, y_a affects y_c indirectly. This model has nearly the same structure as does model B. With the exception of the interpretation placed on the relationship between y_b and y_c, the two models are similar. Due to their similarities, models B and C are usefully discussed together. In model B the relationship that remains when y_a is controlled is interpreted only in correlational terms, whereas in model C, the covariance between y_b and y_c after y_a is controlled is scaled in such a way that it can be interpreted as a path coefficient, p_{cb}. Indeed, the only difference between r_{uv} and p_{cb} is in the scaling of the covariance information (Linn and Werts 1969). Using significance tests, it matters little whether one uses model B or model C for testing whether the linkage between y_b and y_c, net of y_a, is zero in the population. It can be shown that the t-statistics (or F-ratios) for the two types of coefficients are the same, as are the part correlations, and the result of the test of the null hypothesis will be same regardless of which coefficient is used, r_{uv} or p_{cb}. Of course, this holds for standardized versus unstandardized coefficients, since they are all rescalings of the same covariance information (Linn and Werts 1969). However, the two models offer a very different causal interpretation of the relationship. In model B, there is no causal relationship specified between y_b and y_c, but in model C, p_{cb} represents the causal impact of y_b on y_c, net of y_a, because y_b is known or posited to be causally and temporally prior to y_c and dependent upon y_a.

The basic issue that unites these two models is the need to specify *all* theoretically relevant and measureable prior causes of *both* y_b and y_c. This is one of the (if not *the*) central concerns for drawing causal inferences: Have spurious influences been ruled out? In these models the spurious correlation argument haunts the analyst, in that one must always entertain strong alternative explanations for one's findings/interpretations, and if there is a possibility of spurious causation, then the drawing of causal inferences is not possible. If one has omitted a variable, call it y_z, that influences both y_b and y_c, or in the case of model C influences y_c and is related to y_b, then the possible effects of y_z cannot be ruled out in the interpretation of p_{cb} or r_{uv}. Ruling out alternative explanations is, of course, basic to all science, but the analyst of nonexperimental data (either cross-sectional or longitudinal) is plagued with the problem of omitted variables that are not part of the observation design.

The recursive model, however, goes beyond the matter of addressing spurious causation. It also embodies an important concept in causal analysis—that of an *indirect effect,* via an intervening variable. In model C, y_a has two distinct types of effects on y_c, one *direct* (p_{ca}) and one *indirect* ($p_{ba}p_{cb}$), via its effect on the intervening variable, y_b, and its effect on y_c. This model embodies Lazarsfeld's notion of interpretation, in that if the direct effect of y_a on y_c (p_{ca}) is zero, the overall or total effect is said to have been interpreted by the variable(s) specified as intervening in the causal sequence (Alwin and Hauser 1975). An example of this type of model is the *social psychological model of status attainment* (or the "Wisconsin model of status attainment") introduced by William Sewell and colleagues, in which a set of relevant intervening mechanisms—level of aspirations and significant others' influence—is specified to transmit the effects of family background and adolescent intellective ability on later educationaland socioeconomic achievements (Hauser 1972; Hauser, Tsai, and Sewell 1983; Sewell and Hauser 1975).

Nonrecursive Model. Models that include "feedback loops" have come to be known as nonrecursive models.[5] Such models involve "reciprocal" influences of some pairs of variables, as shown in model D of Figure 25.2. In this model, y_a directly causes y_b (but not y_c) and y_b and y_c both directly influence one another. Perhaps the most famous example of such a nonrecursive model in social psychology is Homans's (1961) interpretation of the relationship between "propinquity" and "interpersonal attraction." Propinquity (y_a) leads to higher frequencies of interaction (y_b); the frequency of interaction, in turn, increases the probability that a mutual liking will develop between people (y_c), and the more people like one another, the more they interact (y_b). Presumably, liking may ultimately lead to increased propinquity, but Homans's model does not include that possibility. It would be difficult to estimate the parameters of such a model in the absence of longitudinal data.

Expositors of causal modeling techniques are often skeptical about the feasibility of meeting the requirements of these models. That is, the assumptions are often quite unrealistic. For example, estimating the reciprocal effects among variables requires the analyst to make specific a priori untestable assumptions about the nature of certain structural parameters. Perhaps the best discussion of nonrecursive models is Otis Duncan's (1975a), who warns against their wholesale adoption because of the nature of these required assumptions. The critical assumption required to identify these models where there are four or more variables involves the behavior of the *instrumental variables,* variables whose reduced-form effects are nonzero but structural coefficients are zero. Each pair of variables involved in reciprocal causal relationships must have an instrumental variable that does not directly affect it but strongly affects the other member of the pair (O. Duncan 1975a). One of the best examples of a situation that theoretically satisfies this type of assumption is Otis Duncan et al.'s (1968) example of peer influences. The data analyzed in that case were dyadic peer data for a student and his/her best friend. In each case the subject's parental characteristics were strongly linked to his/her own aspirations, but not to the aspirations of his/her best friend, at least not directly. Thus, each of the peer's aspiration levels has an instrument in the reduced-form model. Such types of in-

strumental variables are very difficult to find in most cases. The alternative is to separate measurements in time, identifying reciprocal effects in the overtime effects of variables on one another (O. Duncan 1970; Kessler and Greenberg 1981). However, even here these models are highly sensitive to causal specification. The estimates may be biased, for example, if there are spurious factors (see model B in Figure 25.2) that have been omitted from the model. An interesting example of an effort to disentangle "reciprocal" relationships in social psychology is Kohn and Schooler's (1973) application of nonrecursive models to the estimation of parameters describing the relationship between the substantive complexity of work and the intellectual flexibility of workers. They hypothesized that job experiences linked to opportunities and resources for the development of self-direction have a direct causal influence on a number of variables, including self-direction values, intellectual flexibility, and authoritarian attitudes. At the same time they theorized that these factors help select persons into jobs; that is, those capable of thinking flexibly and who are self-directed are much more likely to end up in jobs that are substantively complex, less routinized, and less closely supervised. Thus, there is a potentially strong selection process at work in creating the relationship between job characteristics and personal orientations. Much of their later work (Kohn, Schooler, et al. 1983; Kohn and Slomczynski 1990) has been aimed at disentangling these selection and socialization processes, but these models have not adequately included measures of family background and intellective abilities in adolescence known to be selective with respect to education and occupational attainment processes.

Latent Variable Models.   There are several approaches to data analysis in social science wherein some of the variables are thought of as "latent" or "unobservable" variables, thought to underlie other "measured" or "observed" variables (Jöreskog 1970). Such models exist for quantitative data, either categoric or continuous. Perhaps the set of models most familiar to social psychologists are factor analysis and true score models, but other latent variable models exist as well. For example, Lazarsfeld and Henry's (1968) work on latent class models for categorical data developed highly sophisticated approaches to latent variable models that share many of the same notions as factor analysis approaches, but, ironically, that work has been virtually ignored by several generations of social psychologists. Recent work (Clogg 1981, 1992; Clogg and Sawyer 1981) has partially remedied this inattention. Because of its wider applicability to data in social psychology, I focus primarily on factor analysis, but I do not intend to suggest that other approaches are not potentially valuable as well. Model E in Figure 25.2 depicts a single common factor underlying three observed variables.

As the earlier discussion of measurement suggests, probably many social psychological/sociological variables should be conceptualized as imperfectly represented by available indicators (Costner 1969). Indeed, the variables in models A to D in Figure 25.2 should probably be conceptualized as unobserved or unobservable variables. If, in reality, these models are to represent the interconnections between latent unobserved, rather than observed, variables, then one should consider the possibility of using latent variable models, where indicators are thought of as reflecting an unmeasured or unobserved latent variable. I include this type of model in this discussion because it presents a special way of thinking about relationships among variables— variables are related because they measure the same underlying latent factors.[6]

The chief purpose of factor analysis is the attainment of scientific parsimony, by positing a set of latent common factors that underlie the data. This is really a version of the common cause model (model B in Figure 25.2), in which the common causes are latent variables. The factor model was developed by Charles Spearman (1904) to be used to describe economically the correlations among observed mental test scores. Spearman's famous bifactor model of intelligence held that measures of mental abilities had two major sources, a factor common to all measures of ability that he called the g-factor (factor of general ability) and a specific component of variation (an s-factor) unique to the test. For example, a test of numerical ability may be affected in part by a general factor of intelligence, as well as by a factor specific to numerical aptitude. This model, although never the predominant psychological theory of mental tests, has persisted in our culture, in the sense that people often believe there is a general factor of intelligence underlying performance across different domains (Gould 1981). The model was extended to multiple factors by Thurstone (1931), and it is the multiple-factor model that is in wide use today.

As noted earlier, factor analysis is often used as a data reduction or item analysis technique in index construction. If one wants to measure an underlying factor thought to be important for understanding behavior or behavioral orientations, factor analysis and related techniques can be used to measure the extent to which various items/questions are good indicators of the particular factor. Factor analysis is uniquely suited to this set of problems, although there are a number of techniques, such as multidimensional scaling and smallest-space analysis, cluster analysis approaches, and grade-of-membership analysis, that can be used in this manner. Factor analysis is distinctive in its capacity to test and compare a given model specification with alternative models (Alwin and Jackson 1979; Jöreskog 1974). This is typically an exploratory exercise, however, and one must be certain the correlations analyzed among variables are representative of some population of inference.

When factor analysis is used to test statistical hypotheses about the nature of relationships among variables hypothesized to exist in some population of interest (e.g., prior hypotheses about the dimensional structure of a set of measures), it is usually referred to as *confirmatory* factor analysis. *Exploratory* factor analysis refers generally to the situation in which the researcher has no prior expectations of the number of factors or the nature of the pattern of loadings of variables on factors and is willing to let the data help determine the nature of the model, whereas the term *confirmatory* is reserved for the situation in which the investigator wishes to test hypotheses about the structure of relationships among measures under certain strong assumptions about the number of factors, the values of specific loadings, and the nature of relationships among the factors (Mulaik 1975). Finally, the factor model is often used to conceptualize relationships among multiple indicators of latent variables in a causal modeling framework in which a factor model is assumed to hold for the relationships among latent variables or factors and their indicators.

Induced-Variable Model.   Any applications of the first four of the causal models discussed above, or some combination of them, are aimed directly or indirectly at the evaluation of the relative importance of variables and/or the nature of direct and indirect causal effects. This assumes that each variable in the equation is conceptually distinct and not redundantly related to other variables in the equation. I above noted that a high degree of correlation, or redundancy, among the predictor variables makes it difficult to interpret the relative effects of these variables. The common factor model provides one solution to the problem of redundancy among measures, by essentially positing a hypothetical set of common factors to account for the redundancy. Then the "latent factor" can be incorporated into a causal model, as in model E.

Another approach to such redundancy is to estimate the combined effects of the measures/indicators by using a composite variable, wherein one simply sums several measures or forms an index in some other way (Alwin 1973b). A composite variable, y_g, might combine the effects of y_a and y_b as in the following model: $y_g = w_a y_a + w_b y_b$, where the w's are coefficients that express the weight of the component variable in forming the composite. Then one might consider the effect of the composite variable, y_g, on the set of endogenous variables (in this case a single one, y_c), rather than the independent effects of the components, as is the case in model A.

The use of such composite variables, while potentially summarizing the effects of variables in a given domain, leaves certain ambiguity in assessing which of the several variables is generating the observed effects of the composite. Another way to conceptualize the composite variable is to include it in the overall model, as in model F in Figure 25.2, so that both the composite and its components are represented in the model (Alwin and Thornton 1984). This approach represents an important solution to the problem of redundant sets of correlated exogenous variables, especially when the components of the induced variables are latent factors of the form shown in model E. In this example (model F in Figure 25.2), the composite-variable model can be phrased more generally within a causal framework as an *induced-variable model* (Alwin 1988a). The induced-variable model simply asserts that there are "multiple causes" of a particular construct. In model F, the construct g is a joint function of y_a and y_b. In this model the construct is perfectly determined by the two causal variables, thus there is no error term or disturbance on the variable represented by g. Another version of the induced-variable model allows multiple indicators of g (as well as multiple causes) and an error on the g-construct. This is called the multiple-indicator multiple-cause (MIMC) model (Figure 25.3). It essentially represents a combination of models E and F in Figure 25.2 (Hauser and Goldberger 1971; Heise 1972; Jöreskog and Goldberger 1975). Clogg (1981) discusses a similar MIMC model using categoric data and latent structure modeling.

Causal Analysis of Longitudinal Data

As indicated by the foregoing discussion, there are many issues of causation, change, and stability of potential interest to social psychologists. Longitudinal designs incorporating measurements over time (R. Campbell 1992) are increasingly viewed as vastly superior to cross-sectional studies in their ability to reveal causal influences in social processes. Because they can better pinpoint temporal order of events and experiences, such designs can better address substantive questions of importance in the analysis of causation and the sources of change. Moreover, the increasing availability of

(A)

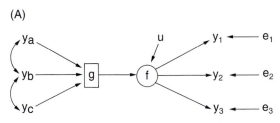

Multiple-Indicator Multiple-Cause Model

(B)

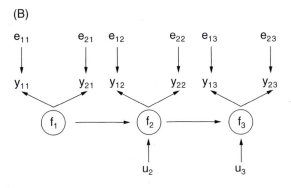

Multiple-Indicator Multiple-Time Model

(C)

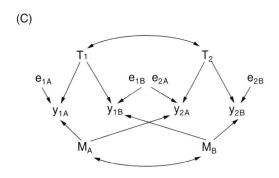

Multitrait-Multimethod Measurement Model

FIGURE 25.3 Models derived from building blocks.

longitudinal data, both in primary data collection and in the archival record, makes it possible to address many of these issues in ways that were not previously possible.

The most common types of longitudinal research designs are the following:

1. Repeated cross-section design, in which the same population(s) is measured periodically over time
2. Panel design, in which the same units of observation are measured repeatedly over time
3. Cohort-sequential design, which combines features of the repeated cross-section and panel designs, wherein a new "cohort" is measured on a periodic basis and then is measured repeatedly over time
4. Event-history design, which measures the timing and duration of events in the biographies of units of observation
5. Retrospective design, in which a cross-section (or panel) study is used to reconstruct information about earlier time

Each of these designs is uniquely suited to a different range of issues in the analysis of human and social change, and each confronts a different set of problems of implementation and inference. For example, as noted earlier, an interest in net change—the average difference in levels of variables over time—requires repeated cross-sectional sampling. An interest in gross change, the average within-individual change between times, requires repeated measurement of the same persons, or a panel design. Perhaps the most interesting feature of longitudinal designs is the promise they hold for separating the influences of aging, cohort experiences, and historical time period, on individuals (W. Mason and Fienberg 1985). In the following discussion I present examples of how these designs are used by social psychologists in ways that take time seriously, as the medium in which to formulate theories of social causation and change.

Repeated Cross-Section Design. Social change and historical influences on individuals have been of critical importance to quantitative social psychologists interested in the extent to which social change occurs because of a succession of generations or because of changes within cohorts over time (Alwin 1994). For example, Elder's (1974) study of the influences of the Great Depression on two small California birth cohorts (n = 167, born 1920 to 1921), provided a laboratory for the discussion of historical influences on aspirations and expectations for the future. Of course, because of the inherent limitations of small, single-cohort studies (Riley 1973), social change cannot be fully studied by reliance on such types of designs. Rather, one needs data on several cohorts measured over time, although not necessarily by studying the same people over time. Specifically, the repeated cross-section design, in which questions are replicated over time, as in the General Social Survey (Davis and Smith 1992) or the National Election Studies (Miller and Traugott 1989), is an important vehicle for studying social change (O. Duncan 1975b; Glenn 1987). Moreover, these designs are an extremely valuable source of data on cohort stability and change (Firebaugh 1989; Firebaugh and Davis 1988; Ryder 1965). Despite some serious problems of "cohort analyzing" data from repeated cross-sections (Glenn 1977), social psychologists have not let this stop them. The debates in the area of political social psychology regarding the influences of cohort/generational experiences versus life cycle or aging effects on "political conservatism" have made important use of such data (Alwin, Cohen, and Newcomb 1991; Converse 1976). Research using repeated cross-sections for these purposes has occurred in several domains, including racial attitudes (Firebaugh and Davis 1988) gender role attitudes (K. Mason and Lu 1988), political tolerance (Cutler and Kaufman 1975), liberal conservativism (Davis 1992), postmaterialism (Inglehart 1990), parental socialization values (Alwin 1990a), and a range of other attitudes (Alwin 1993; Glenn 1980).

Panel Designs. While the repeated cross-section design is an excellent source of information on *net change,* aggregate shifts in variables over time, measured either in the population as a whole or in subpopulations (e.g., birth cohorts), it does not provide information on *gross change*—the individual changes that "add up" to the net change component

but which are only summarized, not tracked, there. To study individual change over time, one needs a *panel design* (Lazarsfeld 1948). There are three main advantages of longitudinal panel data: (1) they allow one to disaggregate net change and distinguish persistent and transitory phenomena; (2) they allow one to disentangle ambiguities in causal relations by providing clear temporal ordering of events and transitions; and (3) they permit one to take the time dimension seriously in terms of measuring individual exposure to certain social experiences thought to be important in socialization and human development (Scott 1993). One of the premier household panel studies is the Panel Study of Income Dynamics (Hill 1992), but many other well-known panel studies of national or broadly regional scope have a much richer set of social psychological variables (e.g., Deborah Freedman et al. 1988; Sewell and Hauser 1975).

A major problem in analyzing panel data on individuals is the confounding of errors of measurement and change in the true underlying variables (Heise 1969; Wiley and Wiley 1970). One type of model that has proven useful in analyzing individual change in latent variables over time, shown in Figure 25.3, falls under the general rubric of *simplex* models (Jöreskog 1974). Such models are characterized by a series of measures of the same variables separated in time, positing a Markovian (lag-l) process to describe change and stability in the underlying latent variable. This model can be used in situations where there is a single variable measured over time (Alwin and Krosnick 1991; Brody 1986; Converse and Markus 1979; Heise 1969; Taylor 1983) or where there are multiple measures of the latent variable at each time (Alwin 1988b; Wheaton et al. 1977).[7] Such models may be estimated in a form consistent with the continuous latent variable, using LISREL-type procedures (Bollen 1989), or in a latent class formulation (Clogg 1979, 1981; Goodman 1978, 1979).

There are several recent examples of the application of simplex-type models to "synthetic cohorts" involving relatively short-term panel designs (e.g., three waves over four years), which attempt to control for historical influences and at the same time investigate differences between different age groups in the population (e.g., Alwin 1994 Alwin, Cohen, and Newcomb 1991; Alwin and Krosnick 1991; Costa and McCrae 1980; Lorence and Mortimer 1985; Mortimer, Finch, and Kumka 1982; Mortimer, Finch, and Maruyama 1988; Mortimer and Lorence 1981; Sears 1981). The basic approach is to estimate levels of stability simultaneously for several age groups, attempting to gauge the extent to which aging produces increases or decreases in stability over time. This approach can involve estimates of changes in stability in the same cohorts over time by strategically placing multiple short-term panel studies in historical time (Alwin 1994).

The Sequential Cohort Design.   One of the quasi-experimental designs suggested by Donald Campbell and Julian Stanley (1963) in their classic treatment of problems of causal inference in nonexperimental data involved what they called the "institutional cycle" design. Newcomb (Alwin, Cohen, and Newcomb 1991) used this design in his early research on attitude change at Bennington College in the 1930s. In this design a new cohort entered a particular institutional system (e.g., Bennington College) on some periodic basis, say each year, and then remained in the system for a period of time during which measurements were obtained on a particular cycle. This design was seen as having potential for reducing problems of inference, since measures are taken simultaneously on new and old cohorts.

This design can be seen quite simply as a combination of the two previous designs—the panel design and the repeated cross-sectional design. It should be seen as having great potential for removing some of the confounding of aging, period, and cohort. A form of this design was recently used in a study of drug use by American youth (O'Malley, Bachman, and Johnston 1988). O'Malley et al.'s design is based on annual surveys of nationally representative samples of high school seniors, plus annual follow-up surveys of each senior class. Several different classes of drugs, both licit and illicit, are measured. Their recent work analyzes data for

the high school classes of 1976 through 1986, covering the age range of eighteen to twenty-eight. The results of this analysis identify different interpretations of age, period, and cohort effects for each of four classes of drugs—daily cigarette use, two-week alcohol consumption, daily marijuana use, and annual cocaine use. The design is useful for these purposes.

Event History Design.   Increasingly, social psychologists interested in the life course are turning to the measurement of the timing and duration of events in the lives of individuals (e.g., Elder 1992). Event history designs are difficult to implement because of the precise measurement that is required. Measuring the timing and duration of events requires either a prospective panel design, in which event histories are obtained periodically, or a retrospective measurement design that relies on people's ability to recall this information (e.g., Deborah Freedman et al. 1988). Given such data, however, it is possible to model the underlying rate of change from one state to another (e.g., from marriage to divorce) as a dependent variable in a regression framework (Allison 1984; Teachman 1983; Tuma and Hannan 1984). Because of this, virtually all of the logical principles of causal analysis reviewed above apply to the use of these models, although most event history analysis has been formulated in terms of the multiple-cause model.

Applications of event-history models in social psychology are relatively sparse, although the diffusion of these methods into the broader discipline of sociology will presumably bring many new applications. Hallinan and Williams (1987), for example, analyze the continuation versus dissolution of friendship choices in a sample of friendship dyads formed in several elementary schools. Their focus was on the determinants, both micro- and macrolevel, of the stability of school children's interracial and same-race friendships.

Retrospective Design.   In part because of failed opportunities, lack of resources, or poor planning, researchers often find it necessary and valuable to try to get people to reconstruct their past life experiences. Among other things, social psychologists often question people concerning their social background or life history, that is, what were some of the characteristics of their family of origin (e.g., father's and mother's occupations, educational levels, native origins, marital status). Social psychologists are also sometimes interested in people's perceptions of past events and social changes (Schuman and Scott 1989; Scott and Zac 1993). In such studies there is no way to measure the veridicality of perceptions. In other cases, there is an interest is assessing the validity of retrospective reports, via inquiries into past recollections of characteristics for which data exist (Alwin, Cohen, and Newcomb 1991). In such cases it is possible to analyze the nature of the connection between past orientations and events and retrospective perceptions of them.

In quantitative social psychology, retrospective data have two major disadvantages—*differential survival* and *reliability of recall* (Scott 1993). Cross-sectional retrospective studies can, by definition, investigate only the life histories of survivors, thus any social process the remnants of which is linked to differential survivorship would be poorly represented by reliance on retrospective data (Featherman 1980). For example, a study of the determinants of marital satisfaction using retrospective data on marital histories by looking only at current intact marriages would probably be very misleading. A second problem with retrospective data is that they tend to contain considerable error. In many cases, it would be a mistake to assume that human memory can access past events and occurrences, and in general, the longer the recall period, the less reliable are retrospections (Dex 1991). In addition, several factors affect people's ability to recall the timing of past events. For example, one phenomenon known to exist in retrospective reports is *telescoping,* reporting events as happening more recently than they actually did. Also, more recent experiences may bias people's recollections about their earlier lives, making it difficult, if not impossible, to be certain about their validity (Scott and Alwin 1993).

Although retrospective data should probably not be the sole basis for information on the past,

sometimes there is little choice. And, if they are placed in the proper perspective, it is possible to learn a considerable amount from retrospective data, especially if prospective data on a particular phenomenon already exist (Alwin, Cohen, and Newcomb 1991). In this situation retrospective data can assist in understanding how people reconstruct the past, and models can be developed regarding how memories converge with or diverge from past experiences. In this sense, retrospective data can potentially assist in the interpretation of social processes.

An Example of Causal Modeling Using Longitudinal Data. I noted earlier that the basic building blocks of causal modeling—the six basic causal models given in Figure 25.2—could be combined in interesting ways to represent more complicated models. Here I present an example from the Bennington College studies (Alwin, Cohen, and Newcomb 1991). Figure 25.4 depicts a causal model aimed at understanding the process of political learning over time. This model may be viewed as one operationalization of a more general social psychological theory of attitude development over the life span (Alwin, Cohen, and Newcomb 1991). This causal diagram represents measures of attitudes on the same individuals over time, conceptualizes some of the potential sources of attitude change and stability, and registers an attempt to estimate the level of stability in latent political attitudes over biographical time. The key feature of the model is that it represents the effect of social experiences on sociopolitical attitudes. I will not reflect in great detail on this model here, as it is discussed more fully elsewhere (Alwin, Cohen, and Newcomb 1991, 212–215), but several points need to be made with respect to this as an example of *causal theory.* First, this example illustrates how one can think about concepts as unobserved, latent variables, in that it illustrates the need to think about measures and errors in measurement and to incorporate some notion of time and/or change to capture the dynamic nature of human experience. Note that the variables in boxes are directly observed (they are measures), the variables in ovals

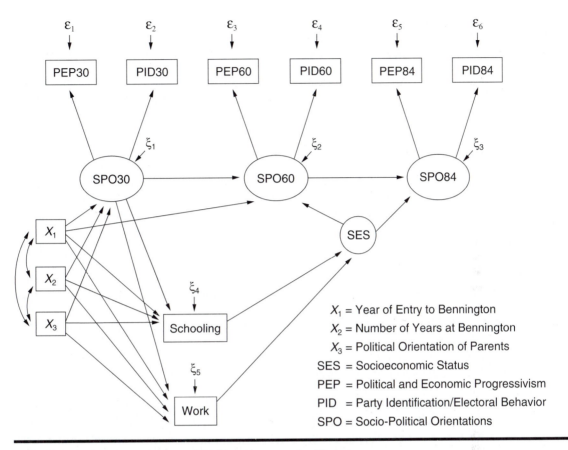

FIGURE 25.4   Causal model for political learning over the life span.
Source: Alwin, Duane F., Ronald L. Cohen, and Theodore M. Newcomb. 1991. *Political Attitudes over the Life Span: The Bennington Women after Fifty Years.* Madison: University of Wisconsin Press. Figure 9.1.

are latent, unobserved variables (in this case latent attitudes), and the variable in the circle is in an induced variable (in this case a composite of two observed variables).

This model can also help explain why researchers typically report relatively low correlations between measures of attitudes and instances of behavior assessed at different times. As latent predispositions to respond to particular stimuli in particular situations, attitudes may change, and this would reduce the over-time correlation (Alwin 1973a). According to this model, because of their nature, attitudes need to be conceptualized as latent variables, which are not necessarily directly ob-

served but may be inferred from a number of different kinds of indicators. In this model the latent attitudes (SPO—sociopolitical orientation) are reflected in two types of indicators, verbal reports of attitudes (PEP—political and economic progressivism) and reports of electoral behavior (PID—party identification). There are several exogenous sources of variation (the x's) specified as determinants of the initial attitudes, measured in the 1930s, and determinants of attitude change. What these factors do not account for is left in the disturbance or residual terms (the ξ's) and the autoregressive dependence of the latent variable on itself. Of course, the latent variable does not literally "cause itself" (Marini and Singer 1988)—the dependence represents a summary of the set of forces operating to maintain the autoregressive process as it exists. The goal of the model is to isolate empirically those factors contributing to continuity and those creating change.

If a set of stimuli, events, or structures, can be said to maintain stability of individuals, then in the presence of those stimuli, events, or structures it is reasonable to expect that both attitude and behavior measures will reflect the underlying attitude. The correlation between attitude and behavior measures will frequently not be perfect, although one can imagine circumstances when there will be a good fit between the latent population distribution of a particular attitude, say an attitude to a political candidate and the reported electoral behavior, and for most persons we would expect a high degree of consistency between attitudes and behavior (see Schwartz and Alwin 1970). In the Bennington study, the correlations between verbal attitude measures and reports of behavior ranged between 0.4 and 0.7. The lack of fit between the latent variable and the observed response may be due to motivational factors or situational constraints, reflected in the presence of a "disturbance" factor in the variation of the behavior. For example, much work has been done to investigate some of the environmental and normative influences on attitudes and on behavior (e.g., Alwin, Cohen, and Newcomb 1991; Kohn and Slomczynski 1990).

ISSUES IN QUANTITATIVE METHODS OF ANALYSIS

I have discussed the basic issues that a quantitative approach must face, including issues of conceptualization, measurement, and design. The focus has been on the logic of design and inference, rather than techniques or available analysis strategies. Here I briefly sketch researchers' main choices in approaches to data. I do this within the framework of a somewhat broad-gauged discussion of general tools and sources one can draw upon to learn about them, rather than a detailed description of available computer program packages that will perform the analyses described (but see Andrews et al. 1981).

Categoric Data versus the Use of Scales

As mentioned earlier, there are several traditions of analysis used in the social sciences, although they cluster at the ends of a continuum (or dichotomy) that involves the use of categoric data assumptions versus correlational approaches which assume underlying continuous, or at least ordered, variables. Many consider the discrete data analysis approaches to be superior, in that they make fewer assumptions about the scales that categoric data might reflect, but this does not mean categoric approaches do not make any assumptions. The nature of the underlying unobserved distribution and its linkage to categories of measurement is always a matter of assumption.

The essential difference between these traditions has to do primarily with the scaling of the dependent variable(s), as is shown in Figure 25.5, where I have cross-classified type of variable (continuous versus discrete) at the latent and observed levels. The observed dependent variable is designated as y and the latent response variable as y* in the case of continuous latent variables and Y in the case of latent classes. For present purposes the discussion assumes no measurement errors (but see below). In case a it is assumed that there is uniform correspondence between the more or less continuous variable, y*, and the observed variable; that is, $y = y*$.[8] This is the type of situation assumed in analyses based on regular product-moment correlations, such as ordinary regression analysis and ordinary factor analysis. It is very difficult, if not impossible, to obtain measures that are truly continuous, but this case is intended to represent situations in which it can be assumed there is an approximation to a one-to-one correspondence between the units of measurement and the units of the latent variable being measured. Magnitude estimation approaches to measurement attempt to solve this problem by providing subjects with a scale that is practically continuous (e.g., Dawes and Smith 1985; Saris 1988), and there is some suggestion

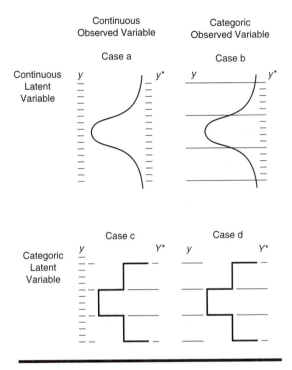

FIGURE 25.5   Types of observed and latent variables.

that response scales with greater numbers of categories may be more reliable (Alwin 1992). Other examples include, for example, units used in social exchange, such as the measurement of income in dollars or other relevant currencies (Alwin 1987). Another example of a continuous variable is the measurement of age in days, months, and years.

In case b in Figure 25.5, the nature of the latent variable, y*, is also continuous, but the observed response variable is discrete. What distinguishes case b from case a is the crudeness of measurement at the level of the observed responses. This is in the tradition of Pearson, who invented the tetrachoric correlation coefficient to estimate ρ, the population correlation among two y* variables, given the cross-tabulation of the corresponding y variables. This is also the approach taken by Jöreskog and Sörbom's PRELIS/LISREL approach (1986) and Muthén's LISCOMP approach (1988), which allow analysis of continuous latent variables from

categorical and otherwise nonnormally distributed responses.

Case c represents the situation where the latent variable of interest is categoric, say latent classes or categories, but the observed variable is represented in more or less continuous form. This is an odd type—it does not occur with great frequency. However, there are cases in which researchers collapse categories of response variables to reflect more basic divisions in the data, but typically the analyst with continuous response data will prefer to analyze the data according to the principle that y = y*, as in case a. Case d involves the more typical situation with latent categories, a one-to-one correspondence between the categories at the latent and observed levels. Such variables can be addressed by log-linear models or logistic regression techniques, as well as probit and Tobit regression methods. Where there is redundancy at the indicator level, latent class analysis, the categoric analog to factor analysis, is appropriate for identifying a more general set of Y latent classes (Clogg 1979, 1981, 1992).

Researchers who prefer taking the data (measurement categories, grouping rules, etc.) at face value and who want to stay as close to the data as possible will prefer tabular and contingency table analysis (cases c and d in Figure 25.5). Researchers who prefer less descriptive clarity and the parsimony often associated with correlational approaches are often more willing to accept untested (and often untestable) assumptions about the continuous nature of the variables that generated the measures (see O'Brien, 1979). Early approaches to tabular analysis (e.g., Davis and Jacobs 1968; Rosenberg 1968) suffered from a number of problems. Due to diminishing numbers of cases, they were often limited to three- and four-variable problems. This tended to move researchers in the direction of correlation and partial correlation statistics and related techniques (e.g., factor analysis, regression analysis). But with the introduction of log-linear models for the analysis of contingency tables and the essential ease of testing quite complicated hypotheses, the popularity of categoric data approaches has increased (O. Duncan 1982).

Lazarsfeld's (1968) approach to the analysis of relationships among variables through the analysis of cross-tabulations of data anticipated the later development and refinement of log-linear models. His early work (Lazarsfeld 1955) presented a general formula for the relationships between three dichotomous variables. His eventual parameterization of the saturated model for the three-way classification of three dichotomous variables "set the stage for the introduction of log-linear models into sociological inquiry" (O. Duncan 1982, 957). As Otis Duncan's (e.g., Duncan, Duncan, and McRae 1978) work demonstrates, the introduction of log-linear models for tabular analysis has dramatically altered the approach to categoric survey data. In sociology these developments are principally associated with the work of Leo Goodman (1979). The log-linear approach provides a unified approach to model building for categorical data, and there are few hypotheses that log-linear modeling cannot handle (O. Duncan 1982). However, the analyst frequently wishes to treat the observed response categories as if they measured the more fundamental latent variable, analyzing a set of latent Y classes, rather than the y variables (Clogg 1992). While assumptions about the underlying distribution can sometimes be tested (e.g., see Muthén and Hofacker 1988), generally the distributional properties of latent variables associated with a particular analytic technique must be assumed, because latent variables are, after all, by definition *unobserved*.

Units of Variation and Choice of Scale

Research aimed at scaling latent phenomena require some units of variation, and researchers assume that their variables have some meaningful units designating relevant theoretical quantities. As Kaplan (1964) has pointed out, the essence of measurement lies in the principle of "standardization," that is, the principle that units of variation have a constancy across time, space, and units of observation (e.g., persons). Although some such units of measure seem natural, many are arbitrary, and standardization in the sense of Kaplan is often

more an objective than a reality (see also O. Duncan 1984b, 12–36). But it seems impossible to make comparisons across units of observation if one were not reasonably sure of the standardization of units of measurement in this sense. This point applies to logistic regression models, log-linear models, and other models in which the dependent variable is limited to binary values, as well as estimation strategies that assume a continuous dependent variable. Units for measuring such effects are a matter of choice in most instances, and the choice of units for the measurement of variables used in quantitative models determines the particular interpretation of effects of variables.

One of the most common practices in the social and behavioral sciences is the "standardization" of metric (as distinct from the type of standardization referred to by Kaplan), wherein variables are scaled or normalized to have means of zero and standard deviations of one. It is sometimes argued, for example, that variables used by social scientists have no "real" units of measurement, and there is often little choice but to "standardize" variables on their "population-specific" distributions (e.g., Bielby 1986). This type of standardization is obtained by centering the variable(s) and scaling this deviation score by the reciprocal of the standard deviation(s); that is, $(y - \mu_y)/\sigma_y$. Owing to the difficulty of interpreting the magnitudes of coefficients of variables in differing units of measurement, this form of standardization is believed to allow comparison of the sizes of coefficients. By contrast, when the objective is to compare the magnitudes of coefficients for a given variable in equations specified in different populations, the general practice is to compare the regression coefficients in their original metric, rather than to rely on standardized units (e.g., Kim and Mueller 1976). Differing magnitudes of metric coefficients reflect both the units of measurement and the sizes of effects, but since the magnitudes of standardized coefficients are clearly dependent on within-population variances, which may vary significantly across populations/subpopulations, it is generally thought that the unstandardized values are more stable and therefore more appropriate. This argument can be seen as specious, since it is simply not the case that metric structural coefficients are unaffected by population or subpopulation variances. Metric coefficients are a function of both variances and covariances, and it is possibly misleading to state that they are invariant due to their independence from the distributional properties of the variables involved (Alwin 1988a; Wright 1960).

Errors of Measurement

One of the greatest impediments to the analysis of quantitative data is imperfect measurement. Without valid and reliable measures, the quantitative analysis of data hardly makes sense. I briefly review these issues here, suggesting some general approaches. The concept of *measurement validity* in its most general sense refers to the extent to which the measurement accomplishes the purpose for which it is intended. According to the *Standards for Educational and Psychological Testing* (American Psychological Association 1985), we can usefully distinguish among three types of validity in this sense—content, criterion-related, and construct validity. *Content validity* refers to the extent to which a well-specified conceptual domain has been represented by available or selected measures. This reflects a minimal requirement for social measurement in the development of auxiliary theories, since measurement content should represent theoretical content. *Criterion-related validity* refers to the predictive utility of a measure— Does it predict or correlate with other theoretically relevant factors/criteria? For example, the criterion validity of the Scholastic Aptitude Test score is typically assessed in terms of its ability to predict college grades. *Construct validity,* on the other hand, refers to the extent to which a measure assesses the theoretical or abstract concept of interest.

Despite the seeming plurality of definitions of what is meant by this concept, most discussions of validity appropriately emphasize the notion of construct validity as central to this set of concerns— Does the set of measurement procedures produce a score that reflects the underlying construct it is intended to measure (Bohrnstedt 1992)? Validity,

thus, centrally involves the question of whether the latent variables being measured, in the above examples the y* variables, or Y classes, reflect or approximate the theoretical concept of interest. However, only with a few exceptions are there direct assessments of validity, and in general this property of measurement is inferred from more indirect types of evidence. The exceptions can be cited under the heading of *record-check studies* (e.g., K. Marquis 1978), but these are very rare, and the typical content of interest to the social psychologist (e.g., latent attitudes) cannot be validated with reference to an external criterion. In seeking information that validates particular measurement procedures, the researcher normally wants to consider several types of evidence, including evidence for content validity and/or predictive validity. In other words, a variable has construct validity to the extent it produces empirical results that would be expected from the concept it purports to measure.

The issue of measurement validity and its assessment rests as much on a consensus among scientists, rooted in practical experience and a knowledge of possible measures, as it does on rigorous empirical demonstrations. In most cases, however, these issues are not addressed, in part because measures used are based on accepted practice, but also because most researchers realize that empirical validation of measures is typically beyond their reasonable grasp. I would argue that, despite these limitations, issues of validity need to be addressed as explicitly as possible. One set of standards for evaluating construct validity, which is valuable as much because it represents an orienting strategy as because it embodies a practical empirical approach, was introduced by Donald Campbell and Donald Fiske (1959). They argued that construct validation requires evidence of both *convergent* and *discriminant* validity. Convergent validity is reflected by high correlations among different approaches to measuring the same trait, whereas discriminant validity is reflected by low correlations between different traits measured by the same or similar methods. To assess these aspects of construct validity, Campbell and Fiske (1959) proposed the *multitrait-multimethod matrix* (MTMM), an organized array of correlations among multiple traits simultaneously measured by multiple methods, as shown in Figure 25.3. The design requirements of the MTMM approach are rarely met, and there are several problems with its implementation. Still, it presents a set of useful ideas for modeling correlations among multiple indicators of latent phenomena (Alwin 1974).

By explicitly considering the question of measurement validity, one acknowledges the fragility of most measurements implemented by social psychologists. But the problem is even more complicated. To this point we have assumed perfect measurement; that is, we have assumed that no errors occur in the procedures for obtaining information on a particular indicator, regardless of its validity. But in fact measurement errors are quite prevalent. Whereas validity refers to what one is measuring, the concept of measurement error concerns how well the concept is measured. Measurement error is usually defined as the difference between the recorded or observed value and the true value of the variable (Alwin 1991c). Consider the classical true score model for the relationship between an *observed score,* the *true score,* and the *measurement error:* $y = \tau + \varepsilon$, where y is the observed score, τ is the true score, and ε is measurement error. The issue of validity relates to the question of how well τ reflects the concept of interest, whereas the issue of measurement error relates to the extent of ε in the observed measure, y. In classical true score theory (Lord and Novick 1968), ε was assumed to be *random,* an assumption that is difficult to adhere to unless one also posits other sources of error.

In addition to random measurement errors, we normally consider the possibility that ε contains *constant* errors (or measurement bias) and *systematic* errors (or correlated errors). One example of such systematic errors is the phenomenon of acquiescence, in which the measurements reflect the respondent's tendency to acquiesce, or produce the socially desirable response (McClendon 1991). One theory even suggests that agreeing to some questions may reflect the respondent's need for social approval (Crowne and Marlowe 1960). An-

other example of systematic errors that creates a potential problem of correlated errors in longitudinal research is memory, or the conscious motivation to be consistent with previous responses (Moser and Kalton 1972, 353).

Reliability of measurement refers to the consistency of measurement or, more precisely, the extent to which the observed variance of survey responses can be said to be true variance rather than random error variance. The degree of reliability is an important aspect of the quality of information reported (Alwin 1991c; Marquis and Marquis 1977). Reliability is a property of both the measurement instrument—the question, in the case of survey measurement—and the population to which it is applied (Alwin 1989). In terms of the above formulation, *reliability* is defined as the ratio of the true variance to the observed variance. Frequently, systematic sources of error increase reliability. This is a major threat to the usefulness of classical true score theory about measurement reliability and an important obstacle to the interpretation of reliability estimates, since variation of factors reflecting systematic errors are presumably reliable sources of variance. The estimation of reliability is nonetheless important, since errors of measurement have significant consequences for inferences regarding substantive processes (Alwin 1989).

CONCLUSIONS

Despite considerable continuity in the theoretical issues that confront social psychologists, substantial changes have occurred in the attention given to the use of quantitative methods. The field was so underdeveloped in the early 1950s that Blumer (1956) could wage a credible attack on "variable analysis" in sociology. Even the proponents of quantitative analysis of survey data admitted there was "very little discussion of the art of analyzing material once it has been collected" (Merton and Lazarsfeld 1950, 133). Since the 1950s the situation has changed—methods of statistical analysis and available computer programs for using them are quite well-known, and in most social science departments statistical methods are now institutionalized aspects of graduate training and curriculum. The typical social sciences student today is versed in analyzing variables with SPSS-X, SAS, and BMDP, using a variety of techniques, such as factor analysis, various forms of regression, loglinear models, latent variable models, and so on.

There have been important advances in quantitative methods over the past several decades throughout the social sciences, but especially in areas where social psychology derives considerable benefit. In spite of this, recent criticisms in the wider social science literature suggest that some of the predominant applications of quantitative methods are often foolish, misguided, or even wrong (Berk 1988; David Freedman 1987, 1991; Glenn 1989; Lieberson 1985). Of course, science often proceeds via criticism and countercriticism, and debates about causal interpretations of quantitative analyses of nonexperimental data are not on the verge of dying. Applications of quantitative methods will continue to improve and will increase in rigor and importance. Qualitative methods are also increasing in scientific rigor and sophistication, with the net result that social psychology is making greater contributions than ever before.

The importance of these critiques of quantitative methods, and causal modeling in particular, is not in their shaking the foundations of methodological and statistical reasoning but in their making visible the need to grapple with necessary assumptions, issues of conceptualization, issues of measurement, implications of design flaws, and problems of causal inference generally (Blalock 1989). It no longer will do to apply quantitative methods mindlessly or to make extravagant claims from the results of quantitative analysis (see Glenn, 1989). If the influence of these and other critiques of quantitative methods is to promote greater care in their application, then their payoff will be seen in improvements in the quality of data analysis. The methodological lessons of the past several decades strongly suggest that one needs to confront quantitative analysis and causal modeling with a great deal of caution. One needs, first, to be aware of the fact that *most* concepts of interest to social

psychologists cannot be directly observed. In the above discussion I used Blalock's (1968) concept of auxiliary theory as a way of orienting the discussion to the gaps between conceptualization and measurement in social psychology. Second, theories should be replicated as often as possible to rule out sampling error, the peculiarities of measuring instruments, the limitations of field sites, and so on. Third, the testing of general theories requires alternative auxiliary theories, incorporating alternative measures, conceptually equivalent indicators, and different approaches to operationalization. Fourth, this leads to the importance of a conceptually oriented approach to operationalization and the specification of indicators and measures (Alwin 1990b). In this regard, I would emphasize the benefits that are increasingly accorded to longitudinal research designs in social psychology. Many social processes of concern to social psychologists entail events and experiences that have a temporal dimension, and research designs with a longitudinal dimension are better equipped to take the time dimension seriously (Alwin 1991a; Scott 1993).

Given the strong normative influences of the quantitative/causal modeling approach in contemporary social psychology and the extent to which these methods become a model for social science more generally, it is important that we recognize not only the shortcomings and limitations of the approach, but also the great potential for continued improvement. There is no substitute for careful theoretical analysis, and in some instances the complexity of the models used far surpasses the analyst's ability to make theoretical sense of the results. However, most current applications of methods of quantitative analysis in social psychology lead me to be confident that future applications will be even richer than in the past. There are certain fundamental issues, involving conceptualization, research design, measurement, and the logic of inference, that must always be addressed in modeling social processes and influences. I hope we will continue to strengthen the application of these methodological standards in the evaluation of the persuasiveness of quantitative results and analyses.

NOTES

The author thanks David Heise, James Davis, James House, Jacqueline Scott, Richard Campbell, Tom Carson, Laura Klem, and an anonymous reviewer for helpful comments that improved the chapter. They bear no responsibility for his use of their ideas. Jessica Sansone helped with the references.

1. I omit any further discussion of sampling here, although I consider it very important (Schuman and Kalton 1985). Rather, I focus on what other discussions of quantitative methods in social psychology omit.

2. Due to the popularity of Jöreskog and Sörbom's (1986) LISREL program for estimating structural equation models with latent variables, I refer to such models as "LISREL-type" models. One must bear in mind that LISREL is a copyrighted version of just one of several available computer programs for performing analyses of such models (see also Bentler 1989; Muthén 1988).

3. Path analysis was invented before 1920 by a geneticist, Sewell Wright (1934, 1954) as a deductive method of predicting the correlation of genetic traits among relatives of stated degree (Wright 1921), but Wright (1925) also used it inductively to model complex economic and social processes using observed correlations. Here I use

it as a general analytic device for interpreting relations among variables (O. Duncan 1966, 1975b).

4. The essential ingredients of this general scheme of three-variable causal models that are building blocks for more complicated models are probably attributable to what I learned from Robert M. Hauser.

5. The "recursive" versus "nonrecursive" designation is probably a misnomer, since *recur* means to return, and in statistical parlance *recursive* means one-way causation. *Nonrecursive* should mean nonreturning, but in the jargon of causal modeling means reciprocal causation.

6. There are several textbook discussions of factor analysis which will aid those who require further introduction to these issues. Among these, I find the texts by Mulaik (1972) and Lawley and Maxwell (1971) especially valuable.

7. See Alwin (1988b) and Rogosa (1988) for a discussion of this approach to measuring stability and change.

8. For purposes of this illustration, I have depicted the underlying distribution of y* as normal, or symmetric, although the extent of skew in the latent variable is also an important issue. Note also that I assume perfect measurement in the y variables.

REFERENCES

Allison, Paul D. 1984. *Event History Analysis.* Beverly Hills: Sage.

Alwin, Duane F. 1973a. Making inferences from attitude-behavior correlations. *Sociometry* 36: 253–278.

———. 1973b. The use of factor analysis in the construction of linear composites in social research. *Sociological Methods and Research* 2:191–214.

———. 1974. Approaches to the interpretation of relationships in the multitrait-multimethod matrix. Pp. 79–105 in *Sociological Methodology 1973–74,* ed. Herbert L. Costner. San Francisco: Jossey-Bass.

———. 1985. The analysis of experimental data using structural equation models. Pp. 82–88 in *Causal Models in Panel and Experimental Designs,* ed. Hubert M. Blalock, Jr. New York: Aldine.

———. 1987. Distributive justice and satisfaction with material well-being. *American Sociological Review* 52:83–95.

———. 1988a. Measurement and the interpretation of coefficients in structural equation models. Pp. 15–45 in *Common Problems/Proper Solutions:*

Avoiding Error in Quantitative Research, ed. J. S. Long. Beverly Hills, CA: Sage.

———. 1988b. Structural equation models in research on human development and aging. Pp. 71–170 in *Methodological Issues in Aging Research,* ed. K. Warner Schaie, Richard T. Campbell, William Meredith, and Samuel C. Rawlings. New York: Springer.

———. 1989. Problems in the estimation and interpretation of the reliability of survey data. *Quality and Quantity* 23:277–331.

———. 1990a. Cohort replacement and changes in parental socialization values. *Journal of Marriage and the Family* 52:347–360.

———. 1990b. From causal theory to causal modeling: Conceptualization and measurement in social science. Pp. 61–86 in *Operationalization and Research Strategy,* ed. J. J. Hox and J. De-Jong-Gierveld. Amsterdam: Swets & Zeitlinger.

———. 1991a. The analysis of change and stability using longitudinal research designs. Paper presented at the Workshop on Studying Stability and

Change with Longitudinal Data, annual meetings of the American Sociological Association, Cincinnati.

———. 1991b. Family of origin and cohort differences in verbal ability. *American Sociological Review* 56:625–638.

———. 1991c. Research on survey quality. *Sociological Methods and Research* 20:3–29.

———. 1992. Information transmission in the survey interview: Number of response categories and the reliability of attitude measurement. Pp. 83–118 in *Sociological Methodology 1992,* ed. Peter V. Marsden. Cambridge, MA: Blackwell.

———. 1993. Socio-political attitude development in adulthood: The role of generational and life-cycle factors. In *New Directions in Attitude Measurement,* ed. Dagmar Krebs and Peter Schmidt. Berlin: Aldine de Gruyter.

———. 1994. Aging, personality and social change: The stability of individual differences over the adult life-span. In *Life-Span Development and Behavior,* vol. 12, ed. David L. Featherman, Robert M. Lerner, and Marion Perlmutter. Hillsdale, NJ: Erlbaum.

Alwin, Duane F., and Richard T. Campbell. 1987. Continuity and change in methods of survey data analysis. *Public Opinion Quarterly* 51:S139–S155.

Alwin, Duane F., Ronald L. Cohen, and Theodore M. Newcomb. 1991. *Political Attitudes over the Life Span: The Bennington Women after Fifty Years.* Madison: University of Wisconsin Press.

Alwin, Duane F., and Robert M. Hauser. 1975. The decomposition of effects in path analysis. *American Sociological Review* 40:37–47.

Alwin, Duane F., and David J. Jackson. 1979. Measurement models for response errors in surveys: Issues and applications. Pp. 68–119 in *Sociological Methodology 1980,* ed. Karl F. Schuessler. San Francisco: Jossey-Bass.

Alwin, Duane F., and Jon A. Krosnick. 1991. Aging, cohorts, and the stability of socio-political orientations over the life-span. *American Journal of Sociology* 97:169–195.

Alwin, Duane F., and Richard C. Tessler. 1974. Causal models, unobserved variables, and experimental data. *American Journal of Sociology* 80:58–86.

Alwin, Duane F., and Arland Thornton. 1984. Family origins and the schooling process: Early vs. late influence of parental characteristics. *American Sociological Review* 49:784–802.

American Psychological Association. 1985. *Standards for Educational and Psychological Testing.* Washington, DC: American Psychological Association.

Andrews, Frank M., Laura Klem, Terrence N. Davidson, Patrick M. O'Malley, and Willard L. Rodgers. 1981. *A Guide for Selecting Statistical Techniques for Analyzing Social Science Data.* Survey Research Center, Institute for Social Research. Ann Arbor: University of Michigan.

Andrich, David. 1988. *Rasch Models for Measurement.* Beverly Hills: Sage.

Bentler, Peter M. 1989. *EQS Structural Equations Program Manual.* Los Angeles: BMDP Statistical Software, Inc., 1440 Sepulveda Boulevard, Los Angeles 90025.

Berk, Richard A. 1988. Causal inference for sociological data. Pp. 155–172 in *Handbook of Sociology,* ed. Neil J. Smelser. Beverly Hills: Sage.

Bielby, William T. 1986. Arbitrary metrics in multiple indicator models of latent variables. *Sociological Methods and Research* 15:3–23.

Blalock, Hubert M., Jr. 1968. The measurement problem: A gap between the languages of theory and research. In *Methodology in Social Research,* ed. Hubert M. Blalock and Ann B. Blalock. New York: McGraw-Hill.

———. 1989. The real and unrealized contributions of quantitative sociology. *American Sociological Review* 54:447–460.

Blumer, Herbert. 1956. Sociological analysis and the "variable." *American Sociological Review* 22: 683–690.

Bohrnstedt, George, W. 1983. Measurement. Pp. 70–121 in *Handbook of Survey Research,* ed. Peter H. Rossi, James D. Wright, and Andy B. Anderson. New York: Academic.

———. 1992. Validity. Pp. 2217–2222 in *Encyclopedia of Sociology,* ed. E. F. Borgatta and M. L. Borgatta. New York: Macmillan.

Bollen, Kenneth A. 1989. *Structural Equations with Latent Variables.* New York: Wiley.

Borgatta, Edgar F. 1992. Measurement. Pp. 1226–1236 in *Encyclopedia of Sociology,* ed. Edgar F. and Marie L. Borgatta. New York: Macmillan.

Brody, Charles J. 1986. Things are rarely black and white: Admitting gray into the converse model of attitude stability. *American Journal of Sociology* 92:657–677.

Campbell, Donald T., and Donald W. Fiske. 1959. Convergent and discriminant validation by the multitrait-multimethod matrix. *Psychological Bulletin* 56:81–105.

Campbell, Donald T., and Julian C. Stanley. 1963. Experimental and quasi-experimental designs for research on teaching. Pp. 171–246 in *Handbook of Research on Teaching,* ed. N. L. Gage. Chicago: Rand McNally.

Campbell, Richard T. 1988. Integrating conceptualization, design, and analysis in panel studies of the life course. Pp. 43–69 in *Methodological Issues in Aging Research,* ed. K. W. Schaie, R. T. Campbell, W. Meredith, and S. C. Rawlings. New York: Springer.

———. 1992. Longitudinal research. Pp. 1146–1158 in *Encyclopedia of Sociology,* ed. Edgar F. and Marie L. Borgatta. New York: Macmillan.

Clogg, Clifford C. 1979. Some latent structure models for the analysis of Likert-type data. *Social Science Research* 8:287–301.

———. 1981. New developments in latent structure analysis. Pp. 215–246 in *Factor Analysis and Measurement in Sociological Research,* ed. David J. Jackson and Edgar F. Borgatta. Beverly Hills: Sage.

———. 1992. Latent class models: Recent developments and prospects for the future. Paper presented at the International Conference on Social Science Methodology, Trento, Italy.

Clogg, Clifford C., and Darwin O. Sawyer. 1981. A comparison of alternative models for analyzing the scalability of response patterns. Pp. 240–280 in *Sociological Methodology 1981,* ed. Samuel Leinhardt. San Francisco: Jossey-Bass.

Coleman, James S., et al. 1966. *Equality of Educational Opportunity.* Washington, DC: U.S. Government Printing Office.

Cook, Thomas D., and Donald T. Campbell. 1979. *Quasi-Experimentation: Design and Analysis Issues for Field Settings.* Chicago: Rand McNally.

Converse, Philip E. 1976. *The Dynamics of Party Support: Cohort-Analyzing Party Identification.* Beverly Hills: Sage.

Converse Philip E., and Gregory B. Markus. 1979. Plus ça change . . . The New CPS Election Study Panel. *American Political Science Review* 73:32–49.

Costa, P. T., Jr., and R. R. McCrae. 1980. Still stable after all these years: Personality as a key to some issues in adulthood and old age. Pp. 65–102 in *Life-Span Development and Behavior,* vol. 3, ed. P. B. Baltes and O. G. Brim, Jr. New York: Academic.

Costner, H. L. 1969. Theory, deduction and rules of correspondence. *American Journal of Sociology* 75: 245–263.

Crowne, D. P., and D. Marlowe. 1960. A new scale of social desirability independent of psychopathology. *Journal of Consulting Psychology* 24:349–354.

Cutler, S. J., and R. L. Kaufman. 1975. Cohort changes in political attitudes: Tolerance of ideological nonconformity. *Public Opinion Quarterly* 39:63–81.

Davis, James A. 1985. *The Logic of Causal Order.* Beverly Hills: Sage.

———. 1992. Changeable weather in a cooling climate atop the liberal plateau: Conversion and replacement in forty-two general social survey items, 1972–1989. *Public Opinion Quarterly* 56:261–306.

Davis, James A., and Susan Jacobs. 1968. *International Encyclopedia of the Social Sciences.* New York: Macmillan.

Davis, James A., and Tom W. Smith. 1991. *General Social Surveys, 1972–1991: Cumulative Codebook.* Chicago: National Opinion Research Center.

———. 1992. *The NORC General Social Survey: A User's Guide.* Newbury Park, CA: Sage.

Dawes, Robyn, and Tom L. Smith. 1985. Attitude and opinion measurement. Pp. 509–566 in *Handbook of Social Psychology,* 2nd ed., vol. 1, ed. Gardner Lindzey and Eliot Aronson. New York: Random House.

Dex, Shirley. 1991. The reliability of recall data: A literature review. Working Paper no. 11, ESRC Research Centre on Micro-Social Change. Colchester: Essex.

Duncan, Greg, and Graham Kalton. 1987. Issues of design and analysis of surveys across time. *International Statistical Review* 55:97–117.

Duncan, Otis D. 1966. Path analysis: Sociological examples. *American Journal of Sociology* 72:1–16.

———. 1970. Some linear models for two-wave, two-variable panel analysis. *Psychological Bulletin* 72: 177–182.

———. 1975a. *Introduction to Structural Equation Models.* New York: Academic.

———. 1975b. Measuring social change via replication of surveys. Pp. 105–127 in *Social Indicator Models,* ed. Kenneth C. Land and Seymour Spilerman. New York: Russell Sage Foundation.

———. 1982. Statistical methods for categoric data. *American Journal of Sociology* 87:957–960.

———. 1984a. The latent trait approach in survey research: The Rasch measurement model. Pp. 210–229 in *Surveying Subjective Phenomena,* vol. 1, ed. Charles F. Turner and Elizabeth Martin. New York: Russell Sage Foundation.

———. 1984b. *Notes on Social Measurement: Historical and Critical.* New York: Russell Sage Foundation.

———. 1984c. Rasch measurement: Further examples and discussion. Pp. 367–403 in *Surveying Subjective Phenomena,* vol. 2, ed. Charles F. Turner and Elizabeth Martin. New York: Russell Sage Foundation.

Duncan, Otis D., Beverly Duncan, and James McRae. 1978. *Sex Typing and Social Roles: A Research Report.* New York: Academic.

Duncan, Otis D., Archibald O. Haller, and Alejandro Portes. 1968. Peer influence on aspirations. *American Journal of Sociology* 74:119–137.

Elder, Glen H., Jr. 1974. *Children of the Great Depression.* Chicago: University of Chicago Press.

———. 1992. Life course. Pp. 1120–1130 in *Encyclopedia of Sociology,* ed. Edgar F. and Marie L. Borgatta. New York: Macmillan.

Featherman, David L. 1980. Retrospective longitudinal research: Methodological considerations. *Journal of Economics and Business* 32:152–169.

Firebaugh, Glenn. 1989. Methods for estimating cohort replacement effects. Pp. 243–262 in *Sociological Methodology 1990,* ed. C. C. Clogg. Cambridge, MA: Blackwell.

Firebaugh, Glenn, and Kenneth E. Davis. 1988. Trends in antiblack prejudice, 1972–1984: Region and cohort effects. *American Journal of Sociology* 94: 251–272.

Freedman, David A. 1987. As others see us: A case study in path analysis. *Journal of Educational Statistics* 12:101–223.

———. 1991. Statistical models and shoe leather. *Sociological Methodology 1991.* Cambridge, MA: Blackwell.

Freedman, Deborah, Arland Thornton, Donald Camburn, Duane Alwin, and Linda Young-DeMarco. 1988. The life history calendar: A technique for collecting retrospective data. Pp. 37–68 in *Sociological Methodology* 1988, ed. Clifford C. Clogg. Washington, DC: American Sociological Association.

Geertz, Clifford. 1973. *The Interpretation of Cultures.* New York: Basic Books.

Glenn, Norval D. 1977. *Cohort Analysis.* Beverly Hills: Sage

———. 1980. Values, attitudes, and beliefs. Pp. 596–640 in *Constancy and Change in Human Development,* ed. O. G. Brim, Jr. and J. Kagan. Cambridge, MA: Harvard University Press.

———. 1987. Social trends in the U.S.: Evidence from sample surveys. *Public Opinion Quarterly* 51:S109–S126.

———. 1989. What we know, what we say we know: Discrepancies between warranted and unwarranted conclusions. Pp. 119–140 in *Crossroads of Social Science,* ed. Heinz Eulau. New York: Agathon.

Goodman, Leo A. 1978. In *Analyzing Qualitative/Categorical Data: Log-Linear Models and Latent-Structure Analysis,* ed. J. Magidson. Cambridge, MA: Abt Associates.

———. 1979. A brief guide to the causal analysis of data from surveys. *American Journal of Sociology* 84:1078–1095.

Gordon, Robert A. 1968. Issues in multiple regression. *American Journal of Sociology* 73:592–619.

Gould, S. J. 1981. *The Mismeasure of Man.* New York: Norton.

Groves, Robert M. 1989. *Survey Errors and Survey Costs.* New York: Wiley.

Hallinan, Maureen, and Richard A. Williams. 1987. The stability of students' interracial friendships. *American Sociological Review* 52:653–664.

Hauser, Robert M. 1972. Disaggregating a social psychological model of educational attainment. *Social Science Research* 1:159–188.

Hauser, Robert M., and Arthur S. Goldberger. 1971. The treatment of unobservable variables in path analysis. Pp. 81–117 in *Sociological Methodology 1971,* ed. H. L. Costner. San Francisco: Jossey-Bass.

Hauser, Robert M., S-L. Tsai, and William H. Sewell. 1983. A model of stratification with response error in social and psychological variables. *Sociology of Education* 56:20–46.

Heise, David R. 1969. Separating, reliability and stability in test-retest correlation. *American Sociological Review* 34:93–101.

———. 1972. Employing nominal variables, induced variables and block variables in path analysis. *Sociological Methods and Research* 1:147–174.

———. 1975. *Causal Analysis.* New York: Wiley.

Hill, Martha S. 1992. *The Panel Study of Income Dynamics: A User's Guide.* Newbury Park, CA: Sage.

Holland, Paul W. 1986. Statistics and causal inference. *Journal of the American Statistical Association* 81: 945–960.

Homans, George C. 1961. *Social Behavior: Its Elementary Forms.* New York: Harcourt Brace Jovanovich.

House, James S. 1977. The three faces of social psychology. *Social Psychology Quarterly* 40:161–177.

Hox, J. J., and J. DeJong-Gierveld, ed. 1990. *Operationalization and Research Strategy*. Amsterdam: Swets & Zeitlinger.

Inglehart, Ronald. 1990. *Culture Shift in Advanced Industrial Society*. Princeton, NJ: Princeton University Press.

Jackman, Mary R. 1973. Education and prejudice or education and response set? *American Sociological Review* 38:327–339.

Jencks, Christopher, et al. 1972. *Inequality: A Reassessment of the Effect of Family and Schooling in America*. New York: Basic Books.

Jensen, A. R. 1969. How much can we boost IQ and scholastic achievement? Harvard Educational Review 39:1–123.

Jöreskog, Karl. 1970. A general method for analysis of covariance structures. *Biometrika* 56:239–251.

———. 1974. Analyzing psychological data by structural analysis of covariance matrices. In *Measurement, Psychophysics, and Neural Information Processing,* ed. D. H. Kranz et al. San Francisco: Freeman.

Jöreskog, Karl, and A. S. Goldberger. 1975. Estimation of a model with multiple indicators and multiple causes of a single latent variable. *Journal of the American Statistical Association* 70:631–639.

Jöreskog, Karl G., and Dag Sörbom. 1979. *Advances in Factor Analysis and Structural Equation Models*. Cambridge, MA: Abt Associates.

———. 1986. *LISREL: Analysis of Linear Structural Relationships By the Method of Maximum-Likelihood*. User's Guide, version VI. Chicago: National Educational Resources.

———. 1988. *PRELIS: A Program for Multivariate Data Screening and Data Summarization (A Preprocessor for LISREL),* 2nd ed. Scientific Software, Inc., P. O. Box 397, Fairplay, CO 80440.

Kaplan, Abraham. 1964. *The Conduct of Inquiry*. San Francisco: Chandler.

Kessler, Ronald C., and David F. Greenberg. 1981. *Linear Panel Analysis*. New York: Academic.

Kim, Jae-On, and Charles W. Mueller, Jr. 1976. Standardized and unstandardized coefficients in causal analysis: An expository note. *Sociological Methods and Research* 4:423–438.

Kish, Leslie. 1959. Some statistical problems in research design. *American Sociological Review* 24:328–338.

———. 1987. *Statistical Design for Research*. New York: Wiley.

Kohn, Melvin L., and Carmi Schooler. 1973. Occupational experience and psychological functioning: An assessment of reciprocal effects. *American Sociological Review* 38:97–118.

Kohn, Melvin, C. Schooler, et al. 1983. *Work and Personality: An Inquiry into the Impact of Social Stratification*. Norwood, NJ: Ablex.

Kohn, Melvin L., and Kazimierz M. Slomczynski. 1990. *Social Structure and Self-Direction: A Comparative Analysis of the United States and Poland*. Cambridge, MA: Blackwell.

Lawley, D. N., and A. E. Maxwell. 1971. *Factor Analysis as a Statistical Method*. London: Butterworths.

Lazarsfeld, P. F. 1948. The use of panels in social research. Pp. 330–337 in *Continuities in the Language of Social Research,* ed. P. F. Lazarsfeld, A. K. Pasanella, and M. Rosenberg. New York: Free Press.

———. 1955. Interpretation of statistical relations as a research operation. Pp. 115–125 in *The Language of Social Research,* ed. P. F. Lazarsfeld and M. Rosenberg. Glencoe, IL: Free Press.

———. 1968. The analysis of attribute data. Pp. 419–429 in *International Encyclopedia of the Social Sciences,* vol. 15, ed. D. L. Sills. New York: Macmillan and Free Press.

Lazarsfeld, P. F., and Neil W. Henry. 1968. *Latent Structure Analysis*. Boston: Houghton Mifflin.

Lieberson, Stanley. 1985. *Making It Count: The Improvement of Social Research and Theory*. Berkeley: University of California Press.

———. 1992. Einstein, Renoir and Greeley: Evidence in sociology. *American Sociological Review* 57:1–15.

Linn, R. L., and C. E. Werts. 1969. Assumptions in making causal inferences from part correlations, and partial regression coefficients. *Psychological Bulletin* 72:307–310.

Liska, Allen E. 1977. The dissipation of sociological social psychology. *The American Sociologist* 12:2–23.

Lord, Frederic M. 1974. Individualized testing and item characteristic curve theory. In *Measurement, Psychophysics, and Neural Information Processing,* ed. D. H. Kranz et al. San Francisco: Freeman.

Lord, Frederic M., and Melvin L. Novick. 1968. *Statistical Theories of Mental Test Scores*. Reading, MA: Addison-Wesley.

Lorence, J., and J. T. Mortimer. 1985. Job involvement through the life course: A panel study of three age groups. *American Sociological Review* 50:618–638.

Marini, Margaret M., and Burton Singer. 1988. Causality in the social sciences. Pp. 347–409 in *Sociologi-*

cal Methodology 1988, ed. Clifford C. Clogg. Washington, DC: American Sociological Association.

Marquis, Kent H. 1978. *Record Check Validity of Survey Responses: A Reassessment of Bias in Reports of Hospitalization.* Santa Monica: Rand Corporation.

Marquis, M. S., and Kent H. Marquis. 1977. *Survey Measurement Design and Evaluation Using Reliability Theory.* Santa Monica: Rand Corporation.

Marwell, Gerald. 1992. Experiments. Pp. 616–620 in *Encyclopedia of Sociology,* ed. Edgar F. and Marie L. Borgatta. New York: Macmillan.

Mason, Karen O., and Yu-Hsia Lu. 1988. Attitudes toward women's familial roles: Changes in the United States, 1977–1985. *Gender and Society* 2:39–57.

Mason, William M., and Stephen E. Fienberg. 1985. *Cohort Analysis in Social Research: Beyond the Identification Problem.* New York: Springer-Verlag.

McClendon, McKee J. 1991. Acquiescence and recency response-order effects in interview surveys. *Sociological Methods and Research* 20:60–103.

Merton, Robert K. 1949. *Social Theory and Social Structure.* New York: Free Press.

Merton, Robert K., and Paul F. Lazarsfeld. 1950. *Continuities in Social Research: Studies in the Scope and Method of "The American Soldier."* Glencoe, IL: Free Press.

Miller, Warren E., and Santa A. Traugott. 1989. *American National Election Studies Data Sourcebook, 1952–1986.* Cambridge, MA: Harvard University Press.

Mortimer, J. T., M. D. Finch, and D. Kumka. 1982. Persistence and change in development: The multidimensional self-concept. Pp. 263–312 in *Life-Span Development and Behavior,* vol. 4, ed. P. B. Baltes and O. G. Brim, Jr. New York: Academic.

Mortimer, J. T., M. D. Finch, and G. Maruyama. 1988. Work experience and job satisfaction: Variation by age and gender. In *Work Experience and Psychological Development Through the Life-Span,* ed. J. T. Mortimer and K. M. Borman. Boulder, CO: Westview.

Mortimer, J. T., and J. Lorence. 1981. Self-concept stability and change from late adolescence to early adulthood. In *Research in Community and Mental Health,* vol. 2, ed. R. G. Simmons. Greenwich, CT: JAI Press.

Moser, C. A., and Graham Kalton. 1972. *Survey Methods in Social Investigation.* New York: Basic Books.

Mulaik, S. A. 1972. *The Foundations of Factor Analysis.* New York: McGraw-Hill.

———. 1975. Confirmatory factor analysis. Pp. 170–207 in *Introductory Multivariate Analysis for Educational, Psychological and Social Research,* ed. D. J. Amick and H. J. Walberg. Berkeley, CA: McCutchan.

Muthén, Bengt. 1981. Factor analysis of dichotomous variables: American attitudes toward abortion. Pp. 201–214 in *Factor Analysis and Measurement in Sociological Research,* ed. David J. Jackson and Edgar F. Borgatta. Beverly Hills: Sage.

———. 1988. *LISCOMP: Analysis of Linear Structural Equations with a Comprehensive Measurement Model: A Program for Advanced Research.* Scientific Software, P.O. Box 397, Fairplay, CO 80440.

Muthén, Bengt O., and Charles Hofacker. 1988. Testing the assumptions underlying tetrachoric correlations. *Psychometrika* 53:563–578.

O'Brien, Robert. 1979. The use of Pearson's *r* with ordinal data. *American Sociological Review* 44:851–857.

O'Malley, P. M., J. G. Bachman, and L. D. Johnston. 1988. Period, age, and cohort effects on substance use among young Americans: A decade of change, 1976–86. *American Journal of Public Health* 78:1315–1321.

Rasch, G. 1960/1980. *Probabilistic Models for Some Intelligence and Attainment Tests.* Copenhagen: Danmarks Paedogogishe Institut.

Riley, M. W. 1973. Aging and cohort succession: Interpretations and misinterpretations. *Public Opinion Quarterly* 37:35–49.

Rogosa, D. 1988. Myths about longitudinal research. Pp. 171–209 in *Methodological Issues in Aging Research,* ed. K. W. Schaie, R. T. Campbell, W. Meredith, and S. C. Rawlings. New York: Springer.

Rosenberg, Morris. 1968. *The Logic of Survey Analysis.* New York: Basic Books.

Rossi, Peter H. 1988. On sociological data. Pp. 131–154 in *Handbook of Sociology,* ed. Neil J. Smelser. Beverly Hills: Sage.

Rossi, Peter H., and Stephen L. Nock. 1981. *Measuring Social Judgements: The Factorial Survey Approach.* Beverly Hills: Sage.

Ryder, N. B. 1965. The cohort as a concept in the study of social change. *American Sociological Review* 30:843–861.

Saris, Willem E. 1988. *Variation in Response Functions: A Source of Measurement Error in Attitude*

Research. Amsterdam: Sociometric Research Foundation.

Schuman, Howard, and Graham Kalton. 1985. Survey methods. Pp. 635–697 in *Handbook of Social Psychology,* 2nd ed., vol. 1, ed. Gardner Lindzey and Eliot Aronson. New York: Random House.

Schuman, Howard, and Stanley Presser. 1981. *Questions and Answers in Attitude Surveys.* Orlando: Academic.

Schuman, Howard, and Jacqueline Scott. 1989. Generations and collective memories. *American Sociological Review* 54:359–381.

Schwartz, Michael, and Duane F. Alwin. 1971. Evaluation of social action. Pp. 609–634 in *Handbook on the Study of Social Problems,* ed. Erwin O. Smigel. Chicago: Rand McNally.

Scott, Jacqueline. 1993. Using household panels to study micro-social change. Paper presented at the British Sociological Conference on Research Imaginations, University of Essex.

Scott, Jacqueline, and Duane I. Alwin. 1993. The reliability of retrospective life history data: Implications for integrating methods. Paper presented at the annual meetings of the ASA. Miami, FL.

Scott, Jacqueline, and Lillian Zac. 1993. Collective memories in Britain and the United States. *Public Opinion Quarterly* 57:315–331.

Sears, D. O. 1981. Life-stage effects on attitude change, especially among the elderly. Pp. 183–204 in *Aging: Social Change,* ed. S. B. Kiesler, J. N. Morgan, and V. K. Oppenheimer. New York: Academic.

Sewell, William H., and Robert M. Hauser. 1975. *Education, Occupation and Earnings: Achievement in the Early Career.* New York: Academic.

Spearman, C. 1904. "General intelligence," objectively determined and measured. *American Journal of Psychology* 15:201–293.

Stryker, Sheldon. 1977. Developments in "two social psychologies": toward an appreciation of mutual relevance. *Sociometry* 40:145–160.

Taylor, Marylee C. 1983. The black-and-white model of attitude stability: A latent class examination of opinion and nonopinion in the American public. *American Journal of Sociology* 89:373–401.

Teachman, Jay D. 1983. Analyzing social processes: Life tables and proportional hazards models. *Social Science Research* 12:263–301.

Thurstone, L. L. 1931. Multiple factor analysis. *Psychological Review* 38:406–427.

Tuma, Nancy Brandon, and Michael T. Hannan. 1984. *Social Dynamics: Models and Methods.* Orlando: Academic.

Wheaton, B., B. Muthén, D. F. Alwin, and G. F. Summers. 1977. Assessing reliability and stability in panel models. Pp. 85–136 in *Sociological Methodology 1977,* ed. D. R. Heise. San Francisco: Jossey-Bass.

Wiley, D. E., and J. A. Wiley. 1970. The estimation of measurement error in panel data. *American Sociological Review* 35:112–117.

Wright, S. 1921. Systems of mating. *Genetics* 6:111–178.

———. 1925. *Corn and Hog Correlations.* U.S. Dept. of Agriculture, Bulletin no. 1300L1-60.

———. 1934. The method of path coefficients. *Annals of Mathematical Statistics* 5:161–215.

———. 1954. The interpretation of multivariate systems. Pp. 11–33 in *Statistics and Mathematics in Biology,* ed. O. Kempthorne, T. A. Bancroft, J. W. Gowen, and J. L. Lush. Ames: Iowa State College Press.

———. 1960. Path coefficients and path regressions: Alternative or complementary concepts? *Biometrics* 16:189–202.

Zelditch, Morris, Jr. 1962. Some methodological problems of field studies. *American Journal of Sociology* 67:566–576.

INDEX

Page numbers in italics cite authors in reference lists.